EDUCATION IN THE UNITED STATES
A DOCUMENTARY HISTORY

SOL COHEN is Associate Professor of Education in the Graduate School of Education at the University of California, Los Angeles. He received his Ph.D. in 1964 from Columbia University where he was a Romiett Stevens Scholar and Alumni Fellow at Teachers College. He is the author of *Progressive and Urban School Reform* (1965) and has contributed numerous articles to scholarly journals and encyclopedias. Professor Cohen has also been a Visiting Scholar at the University of London Institute of Education.

EDUCATION IN THE UNITED STATES
A DOCUMENTARY HISTORY

Edited by
SOL COHEN

UNIVERSITY OF
CALIFORNIA
LOS ANGELES

VOLUME 2

Random House New York

Reference Series Editors:

Fred L. Israel
William P. Hansen

Acknowledgments for use of material covered by
Copyright Conventions appear on pages 3395–99.

Art spots courtesy of Dover Pictorial Archives

FIRST EDITION

9 8 7 6 5 4 3 2 1

Education in the United States: A Documentary
History *is now exclusively published and distributed
by* **Greenwood Press, Inc.**
51 Riverside Avenue
Westport, Ct. 06880
ISBN 0-313-20141-2 SET
0-313-20142-0 v.1
0-313-20143-9 v.2
0-313-20144-7 v.3
0-313-20145-5 v. 4
0-313-20146-3 v.5

Designed by Marsha Picker
for computer typesetting by Volt Information Sciences, Inc.

VOLUME II
CONTENTS

BOOK TWO   The Shaping of American Education, 1789–1895

6

THE
COLLEGES

Colonial Beginnings

PETITION TO ESTABLISH A COLLEGE IN VIRGINIA (1660-1662)   From
Willing W. Hening, ed., *Statutes at Large of Virginia, 1619–1782* (Richmond, 1809–
1823), vol. II, pp. 30-31.

Bee itt enacted that there bee a petition drawn up by this grand assembly
to the king's most excellent majestie for his letters pattents to collect and gather the
charity of well disposed people in England for the erecting of colledges and
schooles in this countrye and alsoe for his majesties letters to both universities of
Oxford and Cambridge to furnish the church here with ministers for the present and
this petition to be recommended to the right honourable governor Sir William
Berkeley. (March, 1660/61).

Whereas for the advancement of learning, promoteing piety & provision of an
able & successive ministry in this country, it hath been thought fitt that a colledge
of students of the liberall arts and sciences be erected and maintayned In pursuance
whereof the right honourable his majesties governour, council of state, and
burgesses of the present grand assembly have severally subscribed severall
considerable sumes of money and quantityes of tobacco (out of their charity and
devotion) to be paid to the honourable Grand Assembly or such treasurer or
treasurers as they shall now or their successors hereafter at any time appoint upon
demand after a place is provided and built upon for that intent and purpose, It is
ordered that the commissioners of the severall county courts do att the next
followinge court in their severall countys subscribe such sumes of money &
tobaccoe towards the furthering and promoteing the said persons and necessary
worke to be paid by them or their heires, as they shall think fitt, and that they alsoe
take the subscriptions of such other persons at their said courts who shall be willing
to contribute towards the same And that after such subscriptions taken they send
orders to the vestryes of the severall parishes in their severall countys for the
subscriptions of such inhabitants and others who have not already subscribed and
that the same be returned to Francis Morrison Esquire. (March, 1660/61).

Whereas the want of able and faithful ministers in this countrey deprives us of
those great blessings and mercies that always attend upon the service of God; which
want, by reason of our great distance from our native country, cannot in probability
be always supplied from thence: Bee it enacted, that for the advance of learning,
education of youth, supply of the ministry, and promotion of piety, there be land
taken up or purchased for a college and free school: And that there be with as much

speed as may be convenient houseing erected thereon, for entertainment of students and scholars. (March, 1661/62).

VIRGINIA PETITION FOR A FREE SCHOOL AND COLLEGE (1691) From

H. R. McIlwaine, ed., *Journals of the House of Burgesses of Virginia, 1659/60-1693* (Richmond, 1931), p. 368.

To their most Excell^t Maties Wm & Mary by ye Grace of God of England, Scotland, France, Ireland, & Virg^a King & Queene Defenders of the Faith &^{c} The humble Supplication of ye Generall Assembly of Virg^a

Wee the Lt Govern^r Councill & Burgesses of this general Assembly which is the first since your Maties most Gracious & happy reigne over us being encouraged by yor Princely Zeall for Promoting Religion & vertue, and incited by ye urgent necessities of this yor Maties Dominion, where our youth is deprived of the benefitt of a liberal & vertuous Education, and many of our Parishes of that instruction & comfort which might be expected from a pious & learned ministry have unanimously Resolved as the best Remedy for those great evills, and as the most Suitable expression wee can make of our hearty concurrence with your Maties in Supporting the Protestant Religion, & the Church of *England*, humbly to Supplicate yor Maties for your Royall grant & Charter to erect & endow a free Schoole & Colledge within this yor Maties Dominion, as to the perticulars relateing to the s^d Desygne wee have given our Instructions to the Reverend Mr *James Blayre* whome wee have appointed to present this our humble Supplication, & to attend & receive your Maties Comands, thereupon, But since wee desygne that our intended free Schoole & Colledge together with learning and vertue may convey to future generations the memory of our Obligacons to your Maties which there is noe fear that wee of the present age can ever forgett, besides what is contained in the s^d Instructions wee humbly pray that the said Schoole & Colledge may transmitt to our Posterity those names which are so deare & auspicious to us, and may accordingly be called the Colledge of King *William* and Queen *Mary*, That God may make yor Maties happy in thankfull & obedient Subjects, as your Subjects are in a King & Queen that answer, their very wishes is the hearty prayers of.

VIRGINIA SOLICITS SUPPORT IN ENGLAND FOR A COLLEGE

(1691)   From Edgar W. Knight, ed., *A Documentary History of Education in the South Before 1860* (Chapel Hill, N.C., 1949), vol. I, pp. 377-80.

Instructions to Mr James Blair Comissary &c. Appointed by ye Gen^r Assembly of Virg^a for Soliciting ye Business of a Free Schoole & Colledge in England

1. That you goe directly from hence, wth this present Fleet.

2. You shall deliver to my Ld Bishop of London ye Lett^r wch you herewith receive, directed to his Lord^{sp} you shall desire his Assistance, & as to ye most Convenient Way, & manner of executing these Instructions, you shall depend on his advice & Directions.

3. You shall Use such means & Applications to deliver our humble Supplication to their Ma^{tys} as you shall think necessarie.

4. You shall endeav^r to procure from their Ma^{tys} an ample Charter for a Free Schoole & Colledge, wherein shall be taught the Lattin, Greek, & Hebrew Tongues, together wth Philosophy, Mathematicks & Divinity, & in Ord^r to this you shall make itt yor business to peruse ye best Charters in England, whereby Free Schools & Colledges have been founded, haveing Regard alwaies to ye Constitution of this Governm^t & particularly to ye Propositions presented to this Generall Assembly for a Free Schoole & Colledge, a Coppy whereof you herewth receive.

5. Pray y^t ye Free Schoole & Colledge bee erected & founded on ye South side of Yorke River, upon ye Land late of Coll Townsend deceased, now in ye possession of John Smith, & near to ye Port appointed in Yorke County.

6. Pray y^t ye s^d Colledge bee incorporated by ye Name of the Colledge of King William & Queen Mary, or if their Ma^{tys} refuse this Name, by w^t other Name they shall thinke fitt.

7. Pray y^t ye s^d Schoole & Colledge bee founded in ye Names of ye Honble Francis Nicholson Esq., Wm Cole Esq., Ralph Wormeley Esq., Wm Byrd Esq., John Lear Esq., Mr James Blair, Mr John Banister, Mr John Farnifold, Mr Stephen Fouace, Nathl Bacon Esq., John Page Esq., Tho: Milner Gent, Christopher Robinson Gent: Charles Scarbrough Gent, John Smith Gent, Benjamin Harrison Gent, Miles Cary Gent, Hen: Hartwell Gent.

8. Pray y^t ye s^d Founders may bee alsoe made Govern^{rs} of ye Lands, Possessions, Revenues, & Goods, of ye s^d Schoole & Colledge.

9. Pray y^t ye s^d Govern^{rs} before their Entry & Admittance to their respective offices, may take ye Oath of Allegiance & Supremacy to King William & Queen Mary, & their Success^{rs} Kings of Engl^d y^t they may alsoe Subscribe ye Test agst Popery, & promise by Oath to bee faithfull in ye s^d Office & Trust, & pferr Men according to their Meritts, without Fee, advantage, Favour, or Affection.

10. Pray y^t ye s^d Govern^{rs} & their Success^{rs} may have a Comon Seale for signing all Ord^{rs} & other things touching ye s^d Corporation.

11. Pray y^t ye s^d Govern^{rs} & their Success^{rs} may have power from time to tyme to Nominate & appointe to all places & Pferm^t wthin ye s^d Schoole & Colledge, & to supply ye s^d Places in Case of Vacancy by Death, Resignation, Deprivation, or otherwise.

12. And if ye s^d Govern^{rs} & their Success^{rs} doe not within Eighteen Months after such Vacancy, make such Nomination & appointment, y^t then & soe often y^e

Govern^r or Command^r in Chief for ye tyme being in this Country, shall & may by writeing under his Hand & Seale, Nominate & appointe some Learned & meet Person to supply ye s^d Place.

13. Pray y^t ye Presid^t & first Profess^r of Divinity bee ex officio of ye Number of ye Govern^{rs}.

14. Pray y^t ye s^d Govern^{rs} & their Success^{rs} may have Power and Authoritie under their Colledge Seale, to sett down & pscribe such Ord^{rs}, Rules, Statutes, & Ordinances, for ye Ord^r, Rule, & Governance of ye s^d Colledge, & of all Persons residing therein, as to ye s^d Govern^{rs} & their Success^{rs} shall seem meet & Convenient. And y^t ye s^d Ord^{rs}, Rules, Statutes, & Ordinances, soe by them made & Sett downe, shall bee established in full Strength, Force, & Virtue in Law, Provided they be not repugnant to ye Prerogative Royall, to ye Laws & Statutes of England & this Dominion, nor ye Canons & Constitutions of ye Church of England.

15. Pray y^t in case of ye Death of any of ye Govern^{rs} of ye s^d Schoole & Colledge, or ye removing of his Habitation out of this Country, ye remaineing part of them may have power to Nominate their Success^r.

16. Pray y^t ye s^d Govern^{rs} & their Success^{rs} may have Power & Authority, to demise & purchase, to sue & bee sued, to take Guifts & Legacies for ye Use of ye s^d Colledge. Notwithstanding ye Statute of Mortmaine, or any other Statute whatsoever.

17. Pray y^t ye s^d Govern^{rs} & their Success^{rs} may have Power to Elect a Chancell^r, who shall enjoy y^t Hon^r seven Yeares, & noe longer, except hee bee elected de Novo.

18. You shall endeav^r y^t ye s^d Schoole & Colledge, bee under noe other Visitation than by ye s^d Govern^{rs} & their Successours.

19. To Pvent fraudulent dealings, You shall endeav^r to have itt inserted in ye s^d Charter, y^t noe Leases shall bee granted to any y^t are Govern^{rs} of ye s^d Colledge, nor to any Psons in their Names, or for their behalfe, nor to their Success^{rs}.

20. Haveing obtained ye s^d Charter, you shall procure a good Schoolemaster, Usher & Writeing Master to bee sent into this Country; for y^e importacon & Sallary of y^e Schoolemast^r & Usher, you shall in y^e Name of y^e Assembly, promise according to y^e Propositions Psented to this Gen^{ll} Assembly, to wch we refer you, & to y^e Importacon of a fitt Man to teach Writing & Arithmetick you shall offer _____ and for his Yearly Sallary.

21. You shall use yor best endeav^{rs} to obtaine their Ma^{tys} Lyscence to aske & Collect Benevolences towards y^e s^d Schoole & Colledge, & to procure as many Subscriptions, Guifts and Benevolences thereupon as you can.

22. The Moneys, Guifts & Subscriptions soe procured, shall bee safely lodged in such Places & handes, as shall be agreed upon by ye L^d B^{sp} of London, his Exc^{ly} ye Ld Howard of Effingham Govr of Virg^a, Mr Jeffrie Jeoffries, Mr Micajah Perry, & y^r self.

23. You shall desire & endeav^r y^t all acct^s of ye s^d Money bee inspected by ye Ld Bishops of London, Salisbury & St Asaph, ye Ld Howard of Effingham, Mr Jeoffrie Jeoffryes, Mr Micajah Perry, Mr Arthur North, Mr John Cary, Mr Fra: Lee & Yo^r self.

24. And because itt is impossible soe to provide att this distance, y^t all matters relateing hereto be duely answer'd & presented, Itt is thought fitt, & you are hereby impower'd in all Cases in wch you are not already directed by these o^r Instructions, to proceed according to ye Best of yor Judgem^t and Discretion, haveing alwaies regard to ye Constitucon of this Country & Governm^t.

25. And y^t soe good a Worke may not miscarry, nor be unnecessarily delayed for want of Money, to prosecute itt.

Fr: Nicholson
William Cole Sec^{ry}
Tho Milner Speaker

By Ord^r of ye Burgesses
  Endorsed. Generall Assembly of Virginia
              Instructions to Mr James Blair
                    May 1691 Virginia

CHARTER OF WILLIAM AND MARY COLLEGE (1693) From Edgar W.
Knight, ed., *A Documentary History of Education in the South Before 1860* (Chapel Hill,
N.C., 1949), vol. I, pp. 401-05, 411-13.

WILLIAM and MARY, by the Grace of God, of England, Scotland, France
and Ireland, King and Queen, Defenders of the Faith, &c. To all to whom these our
present Letters shall come, Greeting.

Forasmuch as our well-beloved and faithful Subjects, constituting the General-
Assembly of our Colony of Virginia, have had it in their Minds, and have proposed
to themselves, to the End that the Church of Virginia may be furnished with a
Seminary of Ministers of the Gospel, and that the Youth may be piously educated in
good Letters and Manners, and that the Christian Faith may be propagated amongst
the Western Indians, to the Glory of Almighty God; to make, found, and establish a
certain Place of universal Study, or perpetual College of Divinity, Philosophy,
languages, and other good Arts and Sciences, consisting of one President, six
Masters or Professors, and an Hundred Scholars, more or less, according to the
Ability of the said College, and the Statutes of the same; to be made, encreased,
diminished, or changed there, by certain Trustees, nominated and elected by the
General-Assembly aforesaid; to wit, our faithful and well-beloved Francis Nichol-
son, our Lieutenant-Governor in our Colonies of Virginia and Maryland, William
Cole, Ralph Wormley, William Byrd, and John Lear, Esquires; James Blair, John
Farnifold, Stephen Fouace, and Samuel Gray, Clerks; Thomas Milner, Christopher
Robinson, Charles Scarborough, John Smith, Benjamin Harrison, Miles Cary, Henry
Hartwell, William Randolph, and Matthew Page, Gentlemen, or the major Part of
them, or of the longer Livers of them, on the South Side of a certain River,
commonly called York River, or elsewhere, where the General-Assembly itself shall
think more convenient, within our Colony of Virginia, to be supported and
maintained, in all Time coming.

I. And forasmuch as our well-beloved and trusty the General-Assembly of our
Colony of Virginia aforesaid, has humbly supplicated us, by our well-beloved in
Christ, James Blair, Clerk, their Agent duly constituted, That we would be pleased,
not only to grant our Royal Licence to the said . . . Gentlemen, or the major Part
of them, or of the longer Livers of them, to make, found, erect, and establish the
said College, but also to extend our Royal Bounty and Munificence, towards the
Erection and Foundation of the said College, in such Way and Manner, as to us
shall seem most expedient: We taking the Premises seriously into our Consideration, and earnestly desiring, that as far in us lies, true Philosophy, and other good

and liberal Arts and Sciences may be promoted, and that the Orthodox Christian Faith may be propagated: And being desirous, that for ever hereafter, there should be one such College, or Place of universal Study, and some certain and undoubted Way within the said College, for the Rule and Government of the same, and of the Masters or Professors, and Scholars, and all others inhabiting and residing therein, and that the said College should subsist and remain in all Time coming; of our special Grace, certain Knowledge, and mere Motion, HAVE GRANTED and given Leave, and by these Presents do grant and give Leave, for us, our Heirs and Successors, as much as in us lies, to the said . . . Gentlemen, That they or the major Part of them, or of the longer Livers of them, for promoting the Studies of true Philosophy, Languages, and other goods Arts and Sciences, and for Propagating the pure Gospel of Christ, our only Mediator, to the Praise and Honor of Almighty God, may have Power to erect, found, and establish a certain Place of universal Study, or perpetual College, for Divinity, Philosophy, Languages, and other good Arts and Sciences, consisting of One President, Six Masters or Professors, and an Hundred Scholars, more or less, Graduates and Non-Graduates . . .

*   *   *

V. And further, we Will, and for us, our Heirs, and Successors, by these Presents, do GRANT, That when the said College shall be so erected, made, founded, and established, it shall be called and denominated, for ever, the College of William and Mary, in Virginia, and that the President and Masters, or Professors, of the said College, shall be a Body politic and incorporate, in Deed and Name; and that by the Name of the President, and Masters, or Professors, of the College of William and Mary, in Virginia, they shall have perpetual Succession; and that the said President, and Masters, or Professors, shall for ever be called and denominated the President, and Masters, or Professors, of the College of William and Mary, in Virginia: And that the said President, and Masters, or Professors, and their Successors, by the Name of the President, and Masters, or Professors, of the College of William and Mary, in Virginia, shall be Persons able, capable, apt, and perpetual in Law, to take and hold Lordships, Manors, Lands, Tenements, Rents, Reversions, Rectories, Portions, Pensions, Annuities, Inheritances, Possessions, and Services, as well Spiritual as Temporal, whatsoever, and all Manner of Goods and Chattels, both of our Gift, and our Heirs and Successors, and of the Gift of the said, Francis Nicholson, William Cole, [and, as above, names of other trustees], or of the Gift of any other Person whatsoever, to the Value of Two Thousand Pounds of lawful Money of England, Yearly, and no more, to be had and held by them and their Successors for ever.

VI. And also, that the said President and Masters or Professors, by and under the Name of the President and Masters or Professors of the College of William and Mary, in Virginia, shall have Power to plead, and be impleaded, to sue, and be sued, to defend, and be defended, to answer, and be answered, in all and every Cause, Complaint, and Action real, personal, and mixed, of what Kind and Nature soever they be, in whatsoever Courts and Places of Judicature belonging to us, our Heirs and Successors or to any other Person whatsoever, before all Sorts of Justices and Judges, Ecclesiastical and Temporal, in whatsoever Kingdoms, Countries, Colonies, Dominions, or Plantations, belonging to us, or our Heirs; and to do, act, and receive, these and all other Things, in the same manner, as our other liege People, Persons able and capable in Law, within our said Colony of Virginia, or our

Kingdom of England, do, or may act, in the said Courts and Places of Judicature, and before the said Justices and Judges. . . .

TROUBLES OF WILLIAM AND MARY COLLEGE (1704)   From Mungo Ingles, "The Several Sources of the Odium and Discouragement Which the College of William and Mary in Virginia Lies Under" (1704), as quoted in *The Virginia Magazine of History and Biography*, vol. VII, pp. 391-93.

The College of William and Mary in Virginia (through an odium it has lain under ever since the charter was brought in) has not as yet arrived to any greater perfection than a grammar school. There be several sources whence this odium had its original, as (1) The prejudices of the former collectors of the penny per pound before it was given to the college, for these gentlemen, finding that the current of that money was directed from their coffers into another channel by being given to the college, began personally to entertain an odium against it, and being all of the Council and colls [colonels] of the county [country], the little people that depended on them, began to write after their copy; others (but without any reason) are angry at the place where the college is situated, which yet is absolutely the best of the whole country; but it fares with the college in this point as with towns—everyone would have one in his own county and neighbourhood, and yet the college can be but in one place; and if it had been in another place, others would have had as much to say against that. Others are enemies to it on the account of their subscriptions toward it, for his excellency (when lieutenant-governor) having issued forth a brief for subscription toward a college, to oblige and curry favour with his excellency, the principal promoter of it; others hoping and supposing it would come to nothing; and others for company's sake that they might not be thought singular or enemies to so good a work, put their hand to the brief and could never be reconciled to the college since. But a fourth source, and which has done the college most mischief than all the rest, is Mr. Blair's demanding and taking his full salary as president of this while when the college had been no more but a grammar school, by which means the master and usher and writing master had much ado (when Mr. Blair went last for England) to get any more than half salary for that year, and this is the only reason why we have had not any more of the six masters, for while the president carried away yearly 150 pounds and there remained no more money than will barely pay the master and usher and writing master, which in the above named year came very short even of that, we can never expect to have any more masters, for as no money, no swizer, so no salary, no master.

The Habits, Life, Customs, Computations, &c. of the Virginians are much the same as about London, which they esteem their Home; and for the most Part have contemptible Notions of England, and wrong Sentiments of Bristol, and the other Out-Ports, which they entertain from seeing and hearing the common Dealers, Sailors, and Servants that come from those Towns, and the Country Places in England and Scotland, whose Language and Manners are strange to them; for the Planters, and even the Native Negroes generally talk good English without Idiom or Tone, and can discourse handsomly upon most common Subjects; and conversing with Persons belonging to Trade and Navigation from London, for the most Part they are much civilized, and wear the best of Cloaths according to their Station; nay, sometimes too good for their Circumstances, being for the Generality comely handsom Persons, of good Features and fine Complexions (if they take Care) of good Manners and Address. The Climate makes them bright, and of excellent Sense, and sharp in Trade, an Ideot, or deformed Native being almost a Miracle.

Thus they have good natural Notions, and will soon learn Arts and Sciences; but are generally diverted by Business or Inclination from profound Study, and prying into the Depth of Things; being ripe for Management of their Affairs, before they have laid so good a Foundation of Learning, and had such Instructions, and acquired such Accomplishments, as might be instilled into such good natural Capacities. Nevertheless thro' their quick Apprehension, they have a Sufficiency of Knowledge, and Fluency of Tongue, tho' their Learning for the most Part be but superficial.

They are more inclinable to read Men by Business and Conversation, than to dive into Books, and are for the most Part only desirous of learning what is absolutely necessary, in the shortest and best Method.

Having this Knowledge of their Capacities and Inclination from sufficient Experience, I have composed on Purpose some short Treatises adapted with my best Judgment to a Course of Education for the Gentlemen of the Plantations; consisting in a short English Grammar; an Accidence to Christianity; an Accidence to the Mathematicks, especially to Arithmetick in all its Parts and Applications, Algebra, Geometry, Surveying of Land, and Navigation.

These are the most useful Branches of Learning for them, and such as they willingly and readily master, if taught in a plain and short Method, truly applicable to their Genius; which I have endeavoured to do, for the Use of them, and all others of their Temper and Parts.

They are not very easily persuaded to the Improvement of useful Inventions (except a few, such as Sawing Mills) neither are they great Encouragers of Manufactures, because of the Trouble and certain Expence in Attempts of this kind, with uncertain Prospect of Gain; whereas by their staple Commodity, Tobacco, they are certain to get a plentiful Provision; nay, often very great Estates.

Upon this Account they think it Folly to take off their Hands (or Negroes) and employ their Care and Time about any thing, that may make them lessen their Crop of Tobacco.

So that though they are apt to learn, yet they are fond of, and will follow their own Ways, Humours, and Notions, being not easily brought to new Projects and

Schemes; so that I question, if they would have been imposed upon by the Mississippi or South-Sea, or any other such monstrous Bubbles.

* * *

As for Education several are sent to England for it; though the Virginians being naturally of good Parts, (as I have already hinted) neither require nor admire as much Learning, as we do in Britain; yet more would be sent over, were they not afraid of the Small-Pox, which most commonly proves fatal to them.

But indeed when they come to England they are generally put to learn to Persons that know little of their Temper, who keep them drudging on in what is of least Use to them, in pedantick Methods, too tedious for their volatile Genius.

For Grammar Learning taught after the common round-about Way is not much beneficial nor delightful to them; so that they are noted to be more apt to spoil their School-Fellows than improve themselves; because they are imprisoned and have not peculiar Management proper for their Humour and Occasion.

* * *

A civil Treatment with some Liberty, if permitted with Discretion is most proper for them, and they have most Need of, and readily take polite and mathematical Learning; and in English may be conveyed to them (without going directly to Rome and Athens) all the Arts, Sciences, and learned Accomplishments of the Antients and Moderns, without the Fatigue and Expence of another Language, for which few of them have little Use or Necessity, since (without another) they may understand their own Speech; and all other Things requisite to be learn'd by them sooner and better.

Thus the Youth might as well be instructed there by proper Methods, without the Expence and Danger of coming hither; especially if they make Use of the great Advantage of the College at Williamsburgh, where they may (and many do) imbibe the Principles of all human and divine Literature, both in English and in the learned languages.

By the happy Opportunity of this College may they be advanced to religious and learned Education, according to the Discipline and Doctrine of the established Church of England; in which Respect this College may prove of singular Service, and be an advantageus and laudable Nursery and strong Bulwark against the contagious dissentions in Virginia; which is the most antient and loyal, the most plentiful and flourishing, the most extensive and beneficial Colony belonging to the Crown of Great Britain, upon which it is most directly dependant; wherein is establish'd the Church of England free from Faction and Sects, being ruled by the Laws, Customs, and Constitutions of Great Britain, which it strictly observes, only where the Circumstances and Occasion of the Country by an absolute Necessity require some small Alterations; which nevertheless must not be contrary (though different from and subservient) to the Laws of England.

THE STATUTES OF THE COLLEGE OF WILLIAM AND MARY

(1727)   From Edgar W. Knight, ed., *A Documentary History of Education in the South Before 1860* (Chapel Hill, N.C., 1949), vol. I, pp. 501-15.

The Preface

Towards the cultivating the Minds of Men, and rectifying their Manners, what a mighty Influence the Studies of good Letters, and the liberal Sciences have, appears from hence, that these Studies not only flourished of Old amongst those famous Nations the *Hebrews, Egyptians, Greeks,* and *Romans;* but in the latter Ages of the World likewise, after a great Interruption and almost Destruction of them, through the Incursions of the barbarous Nations, they are at last retrieved, and set up with Honor in all considerable Nations. Upon this there followed the Reformation of many Errors and Abuses in the Point of Religion, and the Institution of Youth to the Duties of Christian Virtues and Civility; and a due Preparation of fit Persons for all Offices in Church and State. But no where was there any greater Danger on Account of Ignorance and want of Instruction, than in the *English* Colonies of *America;* in which the first Planters had much to do, in a Country over-run with Woods and Briers, and for many Years infested with the Incursions of the barbarous *Indians,* to earn a mean Livelyhood with hard Labor. There were no Schools to be found in those Days, nor any Opportunity for good Education. Some few, and very few indeed, of the richer Sort, sent their Children to *England* to be educated. And there, after many Dangers from the Seas and Enemies, and unusual Distempers, occasioned by the Change of Country and Climate, they were often taken off by the Small-pox, and other Diseases. It was no Wonder if this occasioned a great Defect of Understanding, and all Sort of Literature, and that it was followed with a new Generation of Men, far short of their Fore-Fathers, which, if they had the good Fortune, tho' at a very indifferent Rate, to read and write, had no further Commerce with the Muses, or learned Sciences; but spent their Life ignobly at the Hoe and Spade, and other Employments of an uncultivated and unpolished Country. There remained still notwithstanding, a small Remnant of Men of better Spirit, who had either had the Benefit of better Education themselves in their Mother-Country, or at least had heard of it from others. These Men's private Conferences among themselves being communicated to greater Numbers in the like Circumstances, produced at last a Scheme of a Free-School and College, which was by them exhibited to the President and Council, in the Year *1690;* a little before the Arrival of Lieutenant-Governor *Nicholson,* which was afterwards recommended by them with Applause to the next ensuing General Assembly. This Work so luckily begun, made a very considerable Progress under his Government. For, altho' being tied up by Injunctions from my Lord *Effingham,* Chief Governor, who was then in *England,* he was not allowed to call an Assembly so soon as he would, yet that designed good Work did not sleep in the mean Time; for in that Interval of Assemblies he and the Council sent out Briefs, by which, and their own good Example, they invited and encouraged the Subscriptions of the Inhabitants. These Briefs were recommended to the Care and Management of Mr. Commissary *Blair,* a Minister, who had been one of the first Projectors of this good Work, and was a little before this made Commissary to the Bishop of *London;* with the Help of his Surrogats some of the most creditable Ministers of the Country, and brought in Subscriptions to the Value of Two Thousand Pounds Sterling. Upon this followed that famous General

Assembly of the Year *1691*. This Assembly not only approved that Scheme of a College, as well fitted to this Country, but resolved upon an humble Petition to King *William* and Queen *Mary*, for a Charter to impower certain Trustees that they named, to found such a College, and that their Majesties would likewise assist in the Funds necessary for building the Edifices, and maintaining the President and Masters. To deliver this Petition, and to negotiate this whole Affair, they made Mr. *Blair* their Agent to sollicit it at the Court of *England*. Tho' both the King and Queen were exceeding well inclined, and the good Bishops, especially Dr. *Tillotson*, Archbishop of *Canterbury*, and Dr. *Compton*, Bishop of *London*, gave all Assistance; and Mr. *Blair* followed it with Diligence and Dexterity, it was a long time before all the Difficulties, which were objected, were got over. But at last, after Two Years spent in that Service, an ample Charter was obtained, with several Gifts, both for Building and Endowment, for paying the President's and Masters Salaries; and Mr. *Blair*, by Advice of the General Assembly in *Virginia*, and the Bishops in *England*, being made President of the College, returned to see all put in Execution. In which for many Years afterwards he was involved in a great Number of Difficulties, some of which threatened the total Subversion of the Design. Especially when in the Year 1705, the Buildings and Library were destroyed by Fire; and there was no Money to repair the Loss. Yet at Length, by Patience and good Husbandry of the Revenues, and the Bounty of Queen *Anne*, the Work was finished a second Time to every one's Admiration. But to go on to another necessary Branch of this Design, which we are now about, other Obstructions being in good Measure removed, there seems to be nothing more necessary than that, according to the Advice of our most Reverend Chancellor Dr. *Wake*, Archbishop of Canterbury, some Rules and Statutes should be made for the good Government of the College, and of the President, and Masters, and Scholars, and all others, that either live in it, or are employed in the Management of its Affairs abroad, after mature Deliberation with the said Lord Archbishop, our Chancellor. But because in Progress of Time many Things will be found to be more expedient, when from small Beginnings the College shall have come to greater Perfection; and some Things too will want to be corrected and altered, as future Cases and Circumstances may require: All these Things we are very willing to leave to the Visitors and Governors, for the Time being, to be added, diminished and changed, according to the different Circumstances of the College, for promoting the Study of the learned Languages, and liberal Arts, according to the Powers granted them by the College Charter. Only that nothing may be enacted rashly, in the Heat of Disputation, no old Statute suddenly changed, or new One made; we recommend it for a Rule in these Matters, that no new Statute be enacted or prescribed, until it has been duly proposed, read and considered at Two several Meetings of the Governors of the College.

Concerning the College Senate

As to the Number, Authority, and Power of the College Senate, in chusing the Chancellor, and the President, and Masters, and in appointing and changing of Statutes, all this is sufficiently set forth in the College Charter. From whence it is evident, how much depends upon them, and how far a good Election of them conduces to the good Government of the College.

Therefore in the Election of all Visitors and Governors of the College, let such be preferred as are Persons of good Morals, and found in the Doctrine of the reformed Church of *England*; and Friends and Patrons of the College and polite

Learning; and Gentlemen in good Circumstances, such as by their Interest, if there be Occasion, can patronize and serve the College.

Let the College Senate beware, that no Differences or Parties be held up and cherished, either amongst themselves, or the President and Masters; and let them take Care that all Things be transacted quietly and moderately, without Favor or Hatred to any Person whatsoever.

Let them maintain and support the ordinary Authority of the President and Masters in the Administration of the daily Government of the College, and let them refer all common domestick Complaints to them: And not suffer themselves to be troubled, except in Matters of great Moment, where there is some Difficulty to be got over, or some Corruption or ill Practice to be reformed, or a new Statute to be made, or some other weighty Business to be transacted.

In the Election of a President or Masters, let them have a principal Regard to their Learning, Piety, Sobriety, Prudence, good Morals, Orderliness and Observance of Discipline, and that they be of a quiet and peaceable Spirit; and let them chuse such Persons into the vacant Places without Respect of Persons.

Of the Chancellor

The Chancellor is to be the *Mecoenas* or Patron of the College, such a One as by his Favor with the King, and by his Interest with all other Persons in *England,* may be enabled to help on all the College Affairs. His Advice is to be taken, especially in all such arduous and momentous Affairs, as the College shall have to do in *England.* If the College has any Petitions at any Time to the King or Queen, let them be presented by their Chancellor.

If the College wants a new President, or Professor, or Master, out of *Great-Britain,* let the College Senate rely chiefly on his Assistance, Advice, and Recommendation.

Concerning the President, and Masters, and Schools

There are three things which the Founders of this College proposed to themselves, to which all its Statutes should be directed. The First is, That the Youth of *Virginia* should be well educated to Learning and good Morals. The Second is, That the Churches of *America,* especially Virginia, should be supplied with good Ministers after the Doctrine and Government of the Church of *England;* and that the College should be a constant Seminary for this Purpose. The Third is, That the *Indians* of *America* should be instructed in the Christian Religion, and that some of the *Indian* Youth that are well-behaved and well-inclined, being first well prepared in the Divinity School, may be sent out to preach the Gospel to their Countrymen in their own Tongue, after they have duly been put in Orders of Deacons and Priests.

For carrying on these noble Designs, let there be Four Schools assigned within the College Precincts; of which, together with the Masters, or Professors, belonging to them, some Directions must be given.

The Grammar School

To this School belongs a School-Master; and if the Number of Scholars requires it, an Usher. The School-Master is One of the Six Masters, of whom, with the President, and Scholars, the College consists. But the Usher is not reckoned a Member of that Body. Let there be paid in yearly Salary to the School-Master, One Hundred and Fifty Pounds *Sterling*, and Twenty Shillings *Sterling* from each Scholar, by the Year, when there is no Usher. But if there be an Usher too in that School, let Fifteen Shillings be paid to the Master, and Five to the Usher; and for a yearly Salary, let there be paid to the Usher, Seventy-five Pounds *Sterling*. But from the poor Scholars, who are upon any charitable College Foundation, neither the Master, nor Usher, are to take any School Wages; but they are to be taught *Gratis*.

In this Grammar School let the *Latin* and *Greek* Tongues be well taught. As for Rudiments and Grammars, and Classick Authors of each Tongue, let them teach the same Books which by Law or Custom are used in the Schools of *England*. Nevertheless, we allow the School-master the Liberty, if he has any Observations on the *Latin* or *Greek* Grammars, or any of the Authors that are taught in his School, that with the Approbation of the President, he may dictate them to the Scholars. Let the Master take Special Care, that if the Author is never so well approved on other Accounts, he teach no such Part of him to his Scholars, as insinuates any thing against Religion and good Morals.

Special Care likewise must be taken of their Morals, that none of the Scholars presume to tell a Lie, or curse or swear, or talk or do any Thing obscene, or quarrel and fight, or play at Cards or Dice, or set in to Drinking, or do any Thing else that is contrary to good Manners. And that all such Faults may be so much the more easily detected, the Master shall chuse some of the most trusty Scholars for public Observators, to give him an Account of all such Transgressions, and according to the Degrees of Heinousness of the Crime, let the Discipline be used without Respect of Persons.

As to the Method of teaching, and of the Government of the School, let the Usher be obedient to the Master in every Thing, as to his Superior.

On Saturdays and the Eves of Holidays, let a sacred Lesson be prescribed out of *Castalio's* Dialogues, or *Buchanan's* Paraphrase of the Psalms, or any other good Book which the President and Master shall approve of, according to the Capacity of the Boys, of which an Account is to be taken on *Monday*, and the next Day after the Holidays.

The Master shall likewise take Care that all the Scholars learn the Church of *England* Catechism in the vulgar Tongue; and that they who are further advanced learn it likewise in *Latin*.

Before they are promoted to the Philosophy School, they who aim at the Privileges and Revenue of a Foundation Scholar, must first undergo an Examination before the President and Masters, and Ministers skilful in the learned Languages; whether they have made due Progress in their *Latin* and *Greek*. And let the same Examination be undergone concerning their Progress in the Study of Philosophy, before they are promoted to the Divinity School. And let no Blockhead or lazy Fellow in his Studies be elected.

If the Revenues of the College for the Scholars, are so well beforehand, that they are more than will serve Three Candidates in Philosophy, and as many in Divinity, then what is left let it be bestowed on Beginners in the Grammar School.

The Philosophy School

For as much as we see now daily a further Progress in Philosophy, than could be made by *Aristotle's* Logick and Physicks, which reigned so long alone in the Schools, and shut out all other; therefore we leave it to the President and Masters, by the Advice of the Chancellor, to teach what Systems of Logick, Physicks, Ethicks, and Mathematicks, they think fit in their Schools. Further we judge it requisite, that besides Disputations, the studious Youth be exercised in Declamations and Themes on various Subjects, but not any taken out of the Bible. Those we leave to the Divinity School.

In the Philosophy School we appoint Two Masters or Professors, who for their yearly Salary shall each of them receive Eighty Pounds *Sterling*, and Twenty Shillings *Sterling* a Year from each Scholar, except such poor Ones as are entertained at the College Charge, upon the Foundations; for they are to be taught *Gratis*.

One of these Masters shall teach Rhetorick, Logick, and Ethicks. The other Physicks, Metaphysicks, and Mathematicks.

And that the Youth of the College may the more chearfully apply themselves to these Studies, and endeavour to rise to the Academic Degrees, we do, according to the Form and Institution of the Two famous Universities in *England*, allot Four Years before they attain to the Degree of Bachelor, and Seven Years before they attain the Degree of Master of Arts.

The Divinity School

In this school let there be Two Professors, with a Salary of One Hundred and Fifty Pounds *Sterling* to each; they are to have nothing from the Students or Candidates of Theology.

Let one of these Professors teach the *Hebrew* Tongue, and critically expound the literal Sense of the Holy Scripture both of the Old and New Testament.

Let the other explain the common Places of Divinity, and the Controversies with Hereticks; and let them have Prelections and Disputations on those Subjects.

And let the Students of Divinity divide their Time betwixt those Two Professors.

The Indian School

There is but One Master in this School who is to teach the *Indian* Boys to read, and write, and vulgar Arithmetick. And especially he is to teach them thoroughly the Catechism and the Principles of the Christian Religion. For a yearly Salary, let him have Forty or Fifty Pounds Sterling, according to the Ability of that School, appointed by the Honorable *Robert Boyle*, or to be further appointed by other Benefactors. And in the same School the Master may be permitted to teach other Scholars from the Town, for which he is to take the usual Wages of Twenty Shillings a Year.

JOHN ELIOT REQUEST'S A COLLEGE FOR MASSACHUSETTS BAY

(**1636**)   From Franklin M. Wright, "A College First Proposed, 1633: Unpublished Letters of Apostle Eliot and William Hammond to Sir Simonds D'Ewes," in *Harvard Library Bulletin*, vol. VIII, pp. 273-74, 276.

Now for your selfe to come, I doe earnestly desire it, If God so move your heart, & not only for the common wealth sake; but also for Larnings sake, which I know you love, & will be ready to furder, & indeede we want store of such men, as will furder that, for if we norish not Larning both church & common wealth will sinke: & because I am upon this poynt I beseech you let me be bould to make one motion, for the furtheranc of Larning among us: God hath bestowed upon you a bounty full blessing; now if you should please, to imploy but one mite, of that greate welth which God hath given, to erect a schoole of larning, a colledg among us; you should doe a most glorious work, acceptable to God & man; & the commemoration of the first founder of the means of Larning, would be a perpetuating of your name & honour among us.

*   *   *

I humbly thank you for your tender care of vs, &, for your great respect to our name, in the defenc of it, against the gainsayers, I humbly thank you for putting vs in mind, of such waighty & necessary matters: for my owne part I have often spake of the wrighting a history, & some doe record the most memorable passages: but none yet have sett themselves apart for it: & for a library, & a place for the exercize of Larning, its my earnest desire & prayre, that God would stir vp the heart of some well wishers to Larning, to make an onsett in that kind, & indeed Sir I know none, every way more fitt then your selfe: I beseech you therfore consider of it, & doe that which may comfort vs: & where as a library is your first project, & then a college; I conceive vpon our experiens, that we shall most neede convenient chambers, to entertaine students at first, & a litle room I feare, will hould all our first stock of bookes, & as they increase we may inlarge the roome: but with vs in our young beginings, men want purses to make such buildings: & therfore publik exercizes of larning be not yet sett on foote, though we have many larned men, both gentlemen & ministers: but had we a place fitted, we should have our tearmes & seasons for disputations, & lectures, not only in divinity: but in other arts & sciences, & in law also: for that would be very material for the wellfaire of our common wealth: & now I will say no more, but pray that the Lord would move your heart (which yet I hope is allready moved) to be the first founder of so gloryous a worke, as this is.

DESCRIPTION OF THE FOUNDING OF HARVARD COLLEGE

(1636) From "New England's First Fruits," as quoted in Perry Miller and Thomas H. Johnson, eds., *The Puritans* (New York, 1938), pp. 701-2.

In Respect of the Colledge, and the Proceedings of Learning Therein

1. After God had carried us safe to *New-England*, and wee had builded our houses, provided necessaries for our liveli-hood, rear'd convenient places for Gods worship, and setled the Civill Government: One of the next things we longed for, and looked after was to advance Learning and perpetuate it to Posterity; dreading to leave an illiterate Ministery to the Churches, when our present Ministers shall lie in the Dust. And as wee were thinking and consulting how to effect this great Work; it pleased God to stir up the heart of one Mr. *Harvard* (a godly Gentleman, and a lover of Learning, there living amongst us) to give the one halfe of his Estate (it being in all about 1700.l.) towards the erecting of a Colledge, and all his Library: after him another gave 300.l. others after them cast in more, and the publique hand of the State added the rest: the Colledge was, by common consent, appointed to be at *Cambridge*, (a place very pleasant and accommodate) and is called (according to the name of the first founder) *Harvard Colledge.*

The Edifice is very faire and comely within and without, having in it a spacious Hall; (where they daily meet at Common Lectures) Exercises, and a large Library with some Bookes to it, the gifts of diverse of our friends their Chambers and studies also fitted for, and possessed by the Students, and all other roomes of Office necessary and convenient, with all needfull Offices thereto belonging: And by the side of the Colledge a faire *Grammar* Schoole, for the training up of young Schollars, and fitting of them for *Academicall Learning*, that still as they are judged ripe, they may be received into the Colledge of this Schoole: Master *Corlet* is the Mr., who hath very well approved himselfe for his abilities, dexterity and painfulnesse, in teaching and education of the youth under him.

Over the Colledge is master *Dunster* placed, as President, a learned conscionable and industrious man, who hath so trained up, his Pupills in the tongues and Arts, and so seasoned them with the principles of Divinity and Christianity, that we have to our great comfort, (and in truth) beyond our hopes, beheld their progresse in Learning and godlinesse also; the former of these hath appeared in their publique declamations in *Latine* and *Greeke*, and Disputations Logicall and Philosophicall, which they have beene wonted (besides their ordinary Exercises in the Colledge-Hall) in the audience of the Magistrates, Ministers, and other Schollars, for the probation of their growth in Learning upon set dayes, constantly once every moneth to make and uphold: The latter hath been manifested in sundry of them by the savoury breathings of their Spirits in their godly conversation. Insomuch that we are confident, if these early blossomes may be cherished and warmed with the influence of the friends of Learning and lovers of this pious worke, they will by the help of God, come to happy maturity in a short time.

Over the Colledge are twelve Overseers chosen by the generall Court, six of them are of the Magistrates, the other six of the Ministers, who are to promote the best good of it, and (having a power of influence into all persons in it) are to see that every one be diligent and proficient in his proper place.

FIRST RULES OF HARVARD COLLEGE (1643) From "New England's First Fruits" (1643), as quoted in Perry Miller and Thomas H. Johnson, eds., *The Puritans* (New York, 1938), pp. 702-04.

I. When any Schollar is able to understand *Tully,* or such like classical Latine Author *extempore,*and make and speake true Latine in Verse and Prose, *suo ut aiunt Marte;* And decline perfectly the Paradigm's of *Nounes* and *Verbes* in the *Greek* tongue: Let him then and not before be capable of admission into the Colledge.

2. Let every Student be plainly instructed, and earnestly pressed to consider well, the maine end of his life and studies is, *to know God and Jesus Christ which is eternall life,* Joh. 17.3. and therefore to lay *Christ* in the bottome, as the only foundation of all sound knowledge and Learning.

And seeing the Lord only giveth wisedome, Let every one seriously set himselfe by prayer in secret to seeke it of him *Prov.* 2, 3.

3. Every one shall so exercise himselfe in reading the Scriptures twice a day, that he shall be ready to give such an account of his proficiency therein, both in *Theoretticall* observations of the Language, and *Logick,* and in *Practicall* and spirituall truths, as his Tutor shall require, according to his ability; seeing *the entrance of the word giveth light, it giveth understanding to the simple,* Psalm. 119. 130.

4. That they eshewing all profanation of Gods Name, Attributes, Word, Ordinances and times of Worship, doe studie with good conscience, carefully to retaine God, and the love of his truth in their mindes, else let them know, that (notwithstanding their Learning) God may give them up *to strong delusions,* and in the end *to a reprobate minde,* 2 Thes. 2. 11, 12. Rom. 1. 28.

5. That they studiously redeeme the time; observe the generall houres appointed for all the Students, and the speciall houres for their owne *Classes:* and then diligently attend the Lectures, without any disturbance by word or gesture. And if in anything they doubt, they shall enquire, as of their fellowes, so, (in case of *Non satisfaction*) modestly of their Tutors.

6. None shall under any pretence whatsoever, frequent the company and society of such men as lead an unfit, and dissolute life.

Nor shall any without his Tutors leave, or (in his absence) the call of Parents or Guardians, goe abroad to other Townes.

7. Every Schollar shall be present in his Tutors chamber at the 7th. houre in the morning, immediately after the sound of the Bell, at his opening the Scripture and prayer, so also at the 5th. houre at night, and then give account of his owne private reading, as aforesaid in Particular the third, and constantly attend Lectures in the Hall at the houres appointed. But if any (without necessary impediment) shall absent himself from prayer or Lectures, he shall bee lyable to Admonition, if he offend above once a weeke.

8. If any Schollar shall be found to transgresse any of the Lawes of God, or the Schoole, after twice Admonition, he shall be lyable, if not *adultus,* to correction, if *adultus,* his name shall be given up to the Overseers of the Colledge, that he may bee admonished at the publick monethly Act.

THE
COLLEGES

657

HARVARD'S FIRST COMMENCEMENT (1642) From Samuel Eliot Morison, *The Founding of Harvard College* (Cambridge, Mass., 1935), pp. 436-37.

The manner of the late Commencement, Expressed in a Letter Sent over from the Governour, and Diverse of the Ministers, their Own Words These

The Students of the first Classis that have beene these foure yeeres trained up in *University-Learning* (for their ripening in the knowledge of the Tongues, and Arts) and are approved for their manner as they have kept their publick Acts in former yeares, our selves being present, at them; so have they lately kept two solemne Acts for their Commencement, when the Governour, Magistrates, and the Ministers from all parts, with all sorts of Schollars, and others in great numbers were present, and did beare their Exercises; which were Latine and Greeke Orations, and Declamations, and Hebrew Analasis, Grammaticall, Logicall & Rhetoricall of the Psalms: And their Answers and Disputations in Logicall, Ethicall, Physicall and Metaphysicall Questions; and so were found worthy of the first degree, (commonly called Batchelour) *pro more Academiarum in Anglia:* Being first presented by the President to the Magistrates and Ministers, and by him, upon their Approbation, solemnly admitted unto the same degree, and a Booke of Arts delivered into each of their hands, and power given them to read Lectures in the Hall upon any of the Arts, when they shall be thereunto called, and a liberty of studying in the Library.

All things in the Colledge are at present, like to proceed even as wee can wish, may it but please the Lord to goe on with his blessing in Christ, and stir up the hearts of his faithfull, and able Servants in our owne Native Country, and here, (as he hath graciously begun) to advance this Honourable and most hopefull worke. The beginnings whereof and progresse hitherto (generally) doe full our hearts with comfort, and raise them up to much more expectation, of the Lords Goodnesse for hereafter, for the good of posterity, and the Churches of Christ Iesus.

Boston in New-England, *September the* 26. 1642.

STATUTES OF HARVARD (c. 1646) From Samuel Eliot Morison, *The Founding of Harvard College* (Cambridge, Mass., 1935), pp. 333-37.

1. When any Scholar is able to Read Tully or such like classical Latin Author *ex tempore,* and make and speak true Latin in verse and prose *suo (ut aiunt) Marte,* and decline perfectly the paradigms of Nouns and verbs in the Greek tongue, then may he be admitted into the College, nor shall any claim admission before such qualifications.

2. Every one shall consider the main End of his life and studies, to know God and Jesus Christ which is Eternal life. John 17. 3.

3. Seeing the Lord giveth wisdom, every one shall seriously by prayer in secret, seek wisdom of Him. Prov. 2. 2, 3 etc.

4. Every one shall so exercise himself in reading the Scriptures twice a day that they be ready to give an account of their proficiency therein, both in theoretical observations of Language and Logic, and in practical and spiritual truths as their tutor shall require according to their several abilities respectively, seeing the Entrance of the word giveth light etc. Psalms 119, 130.

5. In the public Church assembly they shall carefully shun all gestures that show any contempt or neglect of God's ordinances and be ready to give an account to their tutors of their profiting and to use the helps of storing themselves with knowledge, as their tutors shall direct them. And all Sophisters and Bachelors (until themselves make common place) shall publicly repeat Sermons in the Hall whenever they are called forth.

6. They shall eschew all profanation of God's holy name, attributes, word, ordinances, and times or worship, and study with reverence and love carefully to retain God and his truth in their minds.

7. They shall honor as their parents, Magistrates, Elders, tutors and aged persons, by being silent in their presence (except they be called on to answer) not gainsaying showing all those laudable expressions of honor and reverence in their presence, that are in use as bowing before them standing uncovered or the like.

8. They shall be slow to speak, and eschew not only oaths, lies, and uncertain rumors, but likewise all idle, foolish, bitter scoffing, frothy wanton words and offensive gestures.

9. None shall pragmatically intrude or intermeddle in other men's affairs.

10. During their residence, they shall studiously redeem their time, observe the general hours appointed for all the Scholars, and the special hour for their own Lecture, and then diligently attend the Lectures without any disturbance by word or gesture: And if of any thing they doubt they shall inquire as of their fellows so in case of non-resolution modestly of their tutors.

11. None shall under any pretence whatsoever frequent the company and society of such men as lead an ungirt and dissolute life.

Neither shall any without the license of the Overseers of the College be of the Artillery or traine-Band.

Nor shall any without the license of the Overseers of the College, his tutor's leave, or in his absence the call of parents or guardians go out to another town.

12. No Scholar shall buy sell or exchange any thing to the value of six-pence without the allowance of his parents, guardians, or tutors. And whosoever is found to have sold or bought any such thing without acquainting their tutor or parents, shall forfeit the value of the commodity, or the restoring of it, according to the discretion of the President.

13. The Scholars shall never use their Mother-tongue except that in public exercises of oratory or such like, they be called to make them in English.

14. If any Scholar being in health shall be absent from prayer or Lectures, except in case of urgent necessity or by the leave of his tutor, he shall be liable to admonition (or such punishment as the President shall think meet) if he offend above once a week.

15. Every Scholar shall be called by his surname only till he be invested with his first degree; except he be fellow-commoner or a Knight's eldest son or of superior nobility.

16. No Scholars shall under any pretense of recreation or other cause whatever (unless foreshowed and allowed by the President or his tutor) be absent from his

studies or appointed exercises above an hour at morning-bever, half an hour at afternoon-bever; an hour and an half at dinner and so long at supper.

17. If any Scholar shall transgress any of the Laws of God or the House out of perverseness or apparent negligence, after twice admonition he shall be liable if not adultus to correction, if adultus his name shall be given up to the Overseers of the College that he may be publicly dealt with after the desert of his fault but in grosser offenses such gradual proceeding shall not be expected.

18. Every Scholar that on proof is found able to read the original of the Old and New Testament into the Latin tongue, and to resolve them logically withal being of honest life and conversation and at any public act hath the approbation of the Overseers, and Master of the College may be invested with his first degree.

19. Every Scholar that gives up in writing a Synopsis or summa of Logic, Natural and Moral Philosophy, Arithmetic, Geometry, and Astronomy, and is ready to defend his theses or positions, withal skilled in the originals as aforesaid and still continues honest and studious, at any public act after trial he shall be capable of the second degree of Master of Arts.

CHARTER OF HARVARD COLLEGE (1650) From The Colonial Society of Massachusetts, *Publications,* vol. XXXI, pp. 3-6.

Whereas through the good hand of God many well devoted persons have been and daily are moved and stirred up to give and bestow sundry gifts, legacies, lands, and revenues for the advancement of all good literature, arts, and sciences in Harvard College in Cambridge in the County of Middlesex, and to the maintenance of the President and Fellows, and for all accommodations of buildings and all other necessary provisions that may conduce to the education of the English and Indian youth of this country in knowledge and godliness: It is therefore ordered and enacted by this Court and the authority thereof that for the furthering of so good a work and for the purposes aforesaid from henceforth that the said college in Cambridge in Middlesex in New England shall be a corporation consisting of seven persons (to wit): a President, five Fellows, and a Treasurer or Bursar, and that Henry Dunster shall be the first president; Samuel Mather, Samuel Danford, Masters of Art; Jonathan Mitchell, Comfort Starr, and Samuel Eaton, Bachelors of Art, shall be the five fellows, and Thomas Danford to be present treasurer; all of them being inhabitants in the Bay, and shall be the first seven persons of which the said corporation shall consist. And that the said seven persons, or the greater number of them, procuring the presence of the Overseers of the college, and by their counsel and consent shall have power and are hereby authorized at any time or times to elect a new president, fellows, or treasurer, so oft[en] and from time to time as any of the said person or persons shall die or be removed; which said president and fellows for the time being shall forever hereafter in name and fact be one body politic and corporate in law, to all intents and purposes, and shall have perpetual succession; and shall be called by the name of President and Fellows of Harvard College and shall from time to time be eligible as aforesaid. And by that name they and their successors shall and may purchase and acquire to themselves, or take and receive upon free gift and donation, any lands, tenements, or hereditaments within this jurisdiction of the Massachusetts, not exceeding the value of five hundred pounds per annum and any goods and sums of money whatsoever to the use and behoof of the said president, fellows, and scholars of the said college, and also may sue and plead, or be sued and impleaded, by the name aforesaid, in all courts and places of judicature within the jurisdiction aforesaid; and that the said president, with any three of the fellows, shall have power and are hereby authorized, when they shall think fit, to make and appoint a common seal for the use of the said corporation. And the president and fellows, or the major part of them, from time to time, may meet and choose such officers and servants for the college and make such allowance to them and them also to remove, and after death or removal, to choose such others and to make from time to time such orders and by-laws, for the better ordering and carrying on the work of the college as they shall think fit, provided the said orders be allowed by the overseers. And also that the president and fellows, or major part of them, with the treasurer, shall have power to make conclusive bargains for lands and tenements to be purchased by the said corporation for valuable consideration. And for the better ordering of the government of the said college and corporation, be it enacted by the authority aforesaid: that the president and three more of the fellows shall, and may from time to time, upon due warning or notice given by the president to the rest, hold a meeting for the debating and concluding of affairs concerning the profits and revenues of any lands and disposing of their goods. Provided that all the said disposings be according to the will of the donors. And for direction in all emergent occasions, execution of all orders and by-laws, and for the procuring of a general meeting of all the overseers and society in great and difficult cases, and in cases of nonagreement; in all which cases aforesaid the conclusion shall be made by the major part, the said president having a casting voice, the overseers consenting thereunto. And that all the aforesaid transactions shall tend to and for the use and behoof of the president, fellows, scholars, and officers of the said college, and for all accommodations of buildings, books, and all other necessary provisions and furnitures as may be for the advancement and education of youth in all manner of good literature, arts, and sciences. And further be it ordered by this court and the authority thereof that all the lands, tenements or hereditaments, houses, or revenues within this jurisdiction to the aforesaid president or college appertaining, not exceeding the value of five hundred pounds per annum, shall from henceforth be freed from all civil impositions, taxes, and rates. All goods to the said corporation or to any scholars thereof appertaining shall be exempt from all manner of toll, customs, and excise whatsoever. And that the said president, fellows, and scholars, together with the servants and other necessary officers to the said president or college appertaining, not exceeding ten, viz., three to the president and seven to the college belonging, shall be exempted from all personal civil offices, military exercises or services, watchings and wardings, and such of their estates not exceeding one hundred pounds a man, shall be free from all country taxes or rates whatsoever, and none others. In Witness whereof the Court hath caused the Seal of the Colony to be hereunto affixed. Dated the One and thirtieth day of the third month called May. Anno 1650.

THO: DUDLEY
Governor

TIME AND ORDER OF STUDIES AT HARVARD IN THE SEVENTEENTH CENTURY

From Samuel Eliot Morison, *Harvard College in the Seventeenth Century* (Cambridge, Mass., 1936), vol. I, p. 140.

FIRST YEAR

	8–9 a.m.	9–10	10–11	2–3 p.m.	3–4	4–5
M.&T.	LOGIC i–iii; PHYSICS iv	study	study	Disputations	study	study
Wed.	GREEK GRAMMAR[1]	study	study	*Grammatical practice*	study	study
Thurs.	HEBREW GRAMMAR	study	study	*Hebrew Bible readings*	study	study
Fri.	RHETORIC	Declamations	study Rhetoric rest of day	HISTORY ii, iii; NATURE OF PLANTS, i, iv		
Sat.	DIVINITY CATECHETICAL	study				

SECOND YEAR

	8–9 a.m.	9–10	10–11	2–3 p.m.	3–4	4–5
M.&T.	study	ETHICS & POLITICS	study	study	Disputations	study
Wed.	study	GREEK GRAMMAR[2]	study	study	*Greek Poetry*[3]	study
Thurs.	study	ARAMAIC	study	study	*Aramaic readings*[4]	study
Fri.	RHETORIC	Declamations	study	study Rhetoric rest of day		
Sat.	DIVINITY CATECHETICAL	study				

THIRD YEAR

	8–9 a.m.	9–10	10–11	2–3 p.m.	3–4	4–5
M.&T.	study	ARITH. & GEOM. i–iii; ASTRONOMY iv		study	study	Disputations
Wed.	"Perfect their [Greek] Theory before noone"	SYRIAC		*Greek Composition*[5]	*Greek Composition*[5]	*Readings in Syriac N.T.*
Thurs.	study	study			study	
Fri.	RHETORIC	Declamations	study Rhetoric rest of day			
Sat.	DIVINITY CATECHETICAL	Commonplaces				

[1] "Etymologie and Syntax."   [2] "Prosodia and Dialects."   [3] "Practice in Poësy, Nonnus, Duport, or the like."
[4] "Ezra and Daniel."   [5] "Exercise Style, Composition, Imitation, Epitome both in Prose and Verse."

ADVICE TO A FRESHMAN AT HARVARD (1661)   From Leonard Hoar to
Josiah Flynt, March 27, 1661, as quoted in Samuel Eliot Morison, *Harvard College In The Seventeenth Century* (Cambridge, Mass., 1936), pp. 639-43.

Cosen Josiah Flint,

Your first second and 3d are before me in answer to one of mine to you the last year: the which you esteemed somewhat sharp but I thought and still doe fear that it was scarce so much as was needfull: and I am sure yourself would be of the same mind if with me you knew the unutterable misery and irreparable mischeif that follows upon the mispense of those Halcyon dayes which you do yet enjoy. The which letter, whilst you fence withall in your first by those seven or eight thin-sculd-paper-put-byes And as many empty excuses; you did but lay more open your own blame-worthinesse and augment my greif insted of giving me satisfaction.

But your two latter epistles are better Containing some acknowledgment of those grand defects, discerned in you, and those errors committed by you: together with your promises of reparation and amendment by redoubling your diligence in your studyes for the time to come. Only remember to doe what you have promised, and I thereupon have believed; that I may see some testimonyes of it in all your succeeding letters; And also hear it testyfyed by others, that shall write to me concerning you. By all things that you can either revere or desire I adjure you that you doe not aemulate those unhappy youths that reckon it a high point of their wisdom to elude the expectations of their friends for a little while; whereby they indeed not only delude, but destroy themselves for ever.

Your account of the course of your studyes, as now ordered, under the worthy Mr. Chancey, is far short of my desire; for its only of what you were then about; Wheras it should have bin a delineation of your whole method and authors, from your matriculation till commencement. Therfore I can still touch but upon a few generalls for your direction.

The first is this that you would not content yourself with the doing that only which you are tasked to; Nor to doe that, meerly as much as needs must, and is expected of you: But dayly somthing more than your task: and that task also somthing better than ordinary. Thus when the classis study only Logick or Nature you may spend some one or two spare houres in Languages Rhetorique History or Mathematiques or the like. And when they recite only the text of an author read you some other of the same subject or some commentator upon it at the same time. Also in your accustomed disputations doe not satisfy yourself only to theiv an argument but study the question before hand and if possible draw in a book on purpose a summary of the arguments and answers on all hands: unto which you may briefly subjoyn any thing choice and accurate which you have heard in the hall upon the debate of it in publick.

Nextly as you must read much that your head may be stored with notion so you must be free and much in all kinds of discourse of what you read: that your tongue may be apt to a good expression of what you doe understand. And further; of most things you must wr[ite] to; wherby you may render yourself exact in judging of what you hear or read and faithfull in remembering of what you once have known. Touching your writing take a few hints of many which I had thought to have given you. 1. let it not be in loose papers for it will prove for the most part lost labour. Secondly, nor in a fortuitous vagrant way But in distinct bookes designed for every severall purpose And the heads of all, wrote aforehand in every page with intermediate spaces left (as well as you can guesse) proportionable to the matter they are like to contain.

3. Let all those heads be in the method of the incomparable P. Ramus, as to every art which he hath wrot upon. Get his definitions and distributions into your mind and memory. Let thesse be the titles of your severall pages and repositoryes in the books aforesaid. He that is ready in these of P. Ramus, may refer all things to them And he may know where again to fetch any thing that he hath judiciously referred; for there is not one axiom of truth ever uttered, that doth not fall under some speciall rule of art.

The Genus on any page, you may (having paged your book before hand) by a figure set before it direct from what page it came: And the species thereof, one or more which, for method and understanding sake shall be set down under it, but not handled there: you may by figures after them direct to the severall pages that are made the repositoryes for the matters referrible to each of them And so need no childish confused Alphabetical indices.

Mr Alexander Richardson's Tables would be as an Ariadne's thred to you in this labyrinth. Which with other his Manuscripts in Logick Physick and Theology, by transcribing, have bin continued in your colledg ever since the foundation thereof among most that were reckoned students indeed. And if you have now lost them I know no way to recover them but of some that were of that society in former times. I suppose Mr Danforth Mr Mitchell and others have them. Mr Hancock a quondam pupil of Mr. Chaunceyes hath his Divinity. But in the utter defect of this, you may make use of the grand Mr Ramus in Grammar Rhetorique Logick (the Mathematiques must be left to your industry and memory unlesse it should be som practicall branches of it, of which you may take short notes) and then for Theology (which you may yet let alone) you have Dr Ames Medulla: Of this Theme I shall be larger: when you shall give me encouragement thereunto by attending to what I have written on the rest fore going.

4ly. As to the authors you should distill into your paper bookes in generall let them not be such as are already methodicall concise and pithy as possible: for it would be but to transcribe them: which is very tedious and uncouth. Rather keep such bookes by you for immediate perusall. But let them be such as are voluminous; intricate and more jejune: Or else those tractabuli that touch only on some smaller tendrells of any science. Especially if they be bookes that you doe only borrow, or hire to read. By this mean I have kept my library in a little compasse: (scarce yet having more bookes then my self can carry in my arms at once my paper bookes only excepted) and yet I have not quite lost any thing that did occur in my multifarious wandring readings. Were a man sure of a stable abode in a place for the whole time of his life, and had an estate also to expend; then indeed the bookes themselves in specie were the better way and only an index to be made of them all. But this was not like to be nor hath bin my condition: and it may be may not be yours. Wherefore, though it be somewhat laborious yet be not discouraged in prosecuting it. It is the surest way and most ready for use in all places and times, yielding the greatest evidences of your growth in knowledge and therefore also the greatest delight. It comprehends the other way of an index to: If for the bookes you read you keep a catalogue of their names authors scope and manner of handling and edition. And so for every severall tract you devise a certain mark, by which you may breifly quote the author from whence you had those collected notes and refer to him for more ample satisfaction in any article when as it shall be to tedious to transcribe him word for word.

5t. For bookes into which you should thus hoard your store Take at present only some quires of paper stitct together, which you may encrease or substract from, as you shall see occasion upon experience. Only let them that concern one thing be all ruld after one fashion; and let them be sewed and written so as that afterwards they may be bound into one volume, in case that you should never have time to digest them again into more handsome order. At least no further then a succinct epitome: or Synopsis.

6. One paper book more adde of the names of all philosophicall authors and divines of ordinary note: of all the severall sects in the schooles and in the Church. Of all the nations famed in the world; of all and singular the most misterious arts and sciences: And of them all write a Latine Alphabeticall Index which by figures shall direct to the severall pages in a book where you have noted or will note the characters commendations and censures which any of them doe give of other and some of the charriteristick differences by which they were known, the time of their rise their progresse subdivisions and several ends. I mean such fragments as shall occur of these things, to you by the by in your reading: and would for most part be lost, if not thus laid up. As for the full history of them werever that is found, transcribe nothing out of it, for its to laborious and endlesse: but only refer to it. Much lesse doe you doe offer to gather any thing out of the workes of authors who have written volumes to this very purpose, such as are Possewine, Sextus Senensis, Gesner, Draudius, and the like. The great use of this is to preserve these fragments that yourself shall find in your studyes, and could not be otherwise referred. Likewise, that you may know and compare their thoughts of each other especially the moderns; and that accordingly you may be directed and cautioned in the perusal of any of them. Finally that you may have of your own store those characters and lineaments by which you may presently pencill any of them at pleasure: And this not as usually upon prejudice and peradventures; but the testimonyes of some or other that you may also produce. for alway be sure in this, that you note down the author whence you excepted any thing of this nature. But this you will judg so vast as never to be accomplished, and therfore vain to be attempted, you never having heard the names of 1/10 of those things and persons that I have proposed so that you know not how so much as to begin this platform. I answer that for the progresse or compleating of this work you need not take care: Let it but grow as you studyes grow; you never need seek any thing on purpose to put into this book. And for the entrance I shall shew it easy. For if you take but one quire of paper and divide the first 2 sheets into 24 narrow columns, and every page of the rest into two: which also must be paged. Then mark the narrow columnes each with one letter of the Alphabet. And it is ready for use: for tis but to write the name of seid place or person that next occurs into your index with the figure J at it: and again that name, with what is there said of it in your first page of the quire, with the author whence you had it, and its done. And the like of the second in the second. When the index shall grow full tis but write it over again leaving larger spaces where needed. And when that quire shall grow full tis but to take up another and carry on the same columns and numbers. And when they grow to be five or 6 quires to this one index, why then, if that on any name swell to big for its column, tis but to refer it to some other column further forwards. On the contrary if any others have not nor are not like to yeild any thing much upon them, when more titles occur tis but croud those into them, referring them also, as the former, by the index and its figures. Thus I think I have made it facile and plain enough. And beleiv me you will find it beyond your estimation, both pleasant and profitable.

7. One more Quire you may take and rule each leaf into 4 columns And therin also note Alphabetically all those curious criticismes Etymologyes and derivations

that you shall meet withall in the English Latin Greek and Hebrew tongues. I still mean by the by: while you are seeking other matters. Not which you may gather out of vocabularyes and Criticks that have purposely written on such subjects. for that were but actum agere.

8. Be forward and frequent in the use of all those things which you have read, and which you have collected: judiciously molding them up with others of your own fancy and memory according to the proposed occasions. Whether it be in the penning of epistles orations Theses or Antitheses, or determinations upon a question. Analyses of any part of an author, or imitations of him, *per modum genésews*. For so much only have you profited in your studyes as you are able to doe these. And all the contemplations and collection in the world, will but only fit you for thesse: tis practise and only your own practise that will be able to perfect you.

My charg of your choyce of company I need not inculcate: nor I hope that for your constant use of the Latine tongue in all your converse together: and that in the purest phrase of Terence and Erasmus etc Musick I had almost forgot I suspect you seek it both to soon, and to much. This be assured of that if you be not excellent at it Its worth nothing at all. And if you be excellent it will take up so much of your mind and time that you will be worth little else: And when all that excellence is attained your acquest will prove little or nothing of real profit to you unlesse you intend to take upon you the trade of fidling. Howbeit hearing your mother's desires were for it for your sisters for whom tis more proper and they also have more leisure to looke after it: For them I say I have provided the Instruments desired, But I cannot now attend the sending them being hurrying away from London by this unexpected providence of your unkle Daniells sicknesse: which with some other circumst: with which its acc[ompanied] dt. nt. a ltl dist. me.[1]

My deservedly honoured friend and colleague Mr. Stoughton is coming over. he hath promised me to doe you any civill courtesy either for advice or loan of a book or the like. Therfore to him I wish you modestly to apply your self and hearken to: whom as I am sure you will find able, so I am perswaded that you will find both free and faithfull, to assist you as is meet.

I shall adde but one thing more for a conclusion: But that the crown and perfection of all the rest: which only can make your endeavours succesfull and your end blessed: And that is som thing of the dayly practice of piety and the study of the true and highest wisdome And for gods sake, and your own both present and aeternall welfares sake, let me not only entereat, but enjoyn, and obtain of you, that you doe not neglect it: No not a day. For it must be constancy, constancy, as well as labour, that compleats any such work. And if you will take me for an admonitor doe it thus. Read every morning a chapter in the old Test: and every evning one in the new: using your self alwayes as much as you can to one edition of the bible. And as you read, note lightly with your pen in the margent the severall places of remarque, with severall marks. Those I use are: for such as have any thing in them new to me, notable and evident, this sign / for those that are obscure and worthy to consult an interpreter upon: this \ For those that are seemingly contradictory to some others, this + For those that must be compared with others this > For those golden sayings that are full of the soul and power of the Gospell; worthy of highest consideration and admiration, thus ¶. And if any 3 or 4 or 10 verses together be of like import I upon the first of them set down the proper mark and double it as //\\≫.

[1.] doth not a little distress me.

ADVICE FROM THE REVEREND THOMAS SHEPHARD TO HIS SON UPON THE LATTER'S ADMISSION TO HARVARD COLLEGE

(**c. 1672**)   From *Publications of the Colonial Society of Massachusetts*, vol. XIV, pp. 192-98.

Dear Son, I think meet (partly from the advice of your renowned Grandfather to myself att my admission into the College, and partly from some other observations I have had respecting studies in that society) to leave the Remembrances and advice following with you, in this great Change of your life, rather in writing, than viva voce only; that so they may be the better considered and improved by you, and may abide upon your heart when I shall be (and that may be sooner than you are aware) taken from thee, and speak no more: requiring you frequently to read over, and seriously to ponder, and digest, as also conscientiously to putt in practice the same through the Lords assistance.

I. Remember the end of your life, which is acoming back again to God, and fellowship with God; for as your great misery is your separation, and estrangement from him, so your happiness, or last end, is your Return again to him; and because there is no coming to God but by Christs Righteousness, and no Christ to be had but by faith, and no Faith without humiliation or sense of your misery, hence therefore let all your Prayers, and tears be, that God would first humble you, that so you may fly by faith to Christ, and come by Christ to God.

II. Remember the End of this turn of your life, vizt your coming into the College, it is to fitt you for the most Glorious work, which God can call you to, vizt the Holy Ministry; that you may declare the Name of God to the Conversion and salvation of souls; for this End, your Father has sett you apart with many Tears, and hath given you up unto God, that he may accept of you; and that he would delight in you.

III. Remember therefore that God looks for and calls for much holiness from you: I had rather see you buried in your Grave, than grow light, loose, wanton, or prophane. God's secretts in the holy scriptures, which are left to instruct Ministers, are never made known to common and prophane Spirits: and therefore be sure you begin, and end every Day wherein you study with Earnest prayer to God, lamenting after the favour of God; reading some part of the Scriptures daily; and setting apart some time every Day (tho' but one Quarter of an hour) for meditation of the things of God.

IV. Remember therefore, that tho' you have spent your time in the vanity of Childhood; sports and mirth, little minding better things, yet that now, when come to this ripeness of Admission to the College, that now God and man expects you should putt away Childish things: now is the time come, wherein you are to be serious, and to learn sobriety, and wisdom in all your ways which concern God and man.

V. Remember that these are times and Days of much Light and Knowledge and that therefore you had as good be no Scholar as not excell in Knowledge and Learning. Abhorr therefore one hour of idleness as you would be ashamed of one hour of Drunkenness: Look that you loose not your precious time by falling in with Idle Companions, or by growing weary of your Studies, or by Love of any filthy lust; or by discouragement of heart that you shall never attain to any excellency of Knowledge, or by thinking too well of your self, that you have gott as much as is needfull for you, when you have gott as much as your Equals in the same year; no verily, the Spirit of God will not communicate much to you in a way of Idleness, but will curse your Soul, while this sin is nourished, which hath spoiled so many hopefull youths in their first blossoming in the College: And therefore tho' I would not have you neglect seasons of recreation a little before and after meals (and altho' I would not have you Study late in the night usually, yet look that you rise early and loose not your morning thoughts, when your mind is most fresh, and fitt for Study) but be no wicked example all the Day to any of your Fellows in spending your time Idly: And do not content yourself to do as much as your Tutor setts you about, but know that you will never excell in Learning, unless you do Somewhat else in private Hours, wherein his Care cannot reach you: and do not think that Idling away your time is no great Sin, if so be you think you can hide it from the Eyes of others: but Consider that God, who always sees you, and observes how you Spend your time, will be provoked for every hour of that precious time you now mispend, which you are like never to find the like to this in the College, all your Life after.

VI. Remember that in ordering your Studies you make them as pleasant as may be, and as fruitfull as possibly you are able, that so you may not be weary in the work God setts you about: and for this End remember these Rules, vizt

1, Single out two or three scholars most Godly, Learned and studious, and whom you can most love, and who love you best, to be helps to you in your Studies; Gett therefore into the acquaintance of some of your Equalls, to spend some time with them often in discoursing and disputing about the things you hear and read and learn; as also grow acquainted with some that are your Superiours, of whom you may often ask questions and from whom you may learn more than by your Equals only.

2, Mark every mans Disputations and Conferences, and study to gett some Good by every thing: and if your memory be not very strong, committ every notion this way gained unto Paper as soon as you gett into your Study.

3, Lett your studies be so ordered as to have variety of Studies before you, that when you are weary of one book, you may take pleasure (through this variety) in another: and for this End read some Histories often, which (they Say) make men wise, as Poets make witty; both which are pleasant things in the midst of more difficult studies.

4, Lett not your Studies be prosecuted in an immethodicall or Disorderly way; but (for the Generality) keep a fixed order of Studies Suited to your own Genius, and Circumstances of things, which in each year, att least, notwithstanding, there will be occasion of some variation of: Fix your Course, and the season for each kind of Study, and suffer no other matters, or Persons needlessly to interrupt you, or take you off therefrom.

5, Lett difficult studies have the strength and flower of your time and thoughts: and therein suffer no difficulty to pass unresolved, but either by your own labour, or by enquiry of others, or by both, master it before you pass from it; pass not cursorily or heedlessly over such things (rivet the knottyest place you meet with) 'tis not so much *multa Lectio sed sedula et attenta* that makes a scholar, as our Phrase speaks.

6, Come to your Studies with an Appetite, and weary not your body, mind, or Eyes with long poreing on your book, but break off & meditate on what you have read, and then to it again; or (if it be in fitt season) recreate your Self a little, and so to your work afresh; let your recreation be such as may stir the Body chiefly, yet not violent, and whether such or sedentry, let it be never more than may Serve to make your Spirit the more free and lively in your Studies.

7, Such books, as it is proper to read over, if they are very choice and not overlarge, read them over oftener than once: if it be not your own and that you are not like to procure it, then collect out of such book what is worthy to be noted therein: in which Collections take these Directions, (1) Write not in loose Papers, but in a fair Paperbook paged thro'out. (2) Write faithfully the words of your Author. (3) Sett down in your Paper-book the name of your Author, with the title of his book, and the page, where you find the Collection. (4) Allow a margin to your paper-book no broader than wherein you may write the letters. a. b. c. d. e. f &c. vizt att the beginning of each observable Collection, if you have more Collections than two or three in a side. (5) When you have written out such a book being marked with some distinguishing character (as 1. 2. 3. 4. &c. or α, β, π, δ, &c.) prepare another of the same dimensions as near as you can, and improve that as the former, and so onwards: which book may be (as the Merchants Journal is to his principal Ledger) preparatory for your Commonplace book, as your reason and fancy will easily Suggest how, by Short reference of any subject to be handled, found in, (suppose) the paper book, β. page 10. margine f. Suppose the subject be [Faith] you need only write in your Common place book [Faith] vide β. 10, f: if the Subject be [hope] write [hope, π 10 d.] which signifies that there is some Description of that Subject [hope] or some sentence about hope that is observable, or some story concerning that Vertue, & ye like; In the third paper book marked with [γ] and in the tenth page of that book, begun in the margin at the letter [d] [b] as you have leisure, read over your paper books, wherein you have writen your Collections at large, the frequent perusal thereof will many ways be useful to you as your Experience will in time witness.

8, Choose rather to confess your Ignorance in any matter of Learning, that you may [be] instructed by your Tutor, or another, as there may be occasion for it, than to pass from it, and so continue in your Ignorance thereof, or in any Errour about it; malo te doctum esse quam haberi.

9, Suffer not too much to be spent, and break away in visits (visiting, or being visited) let them be Such as may be a whett to you in your studies, and for your profitt in Learning some way of other, so that you be imparting to others or imparted to from them, or both, in some notion of other, upon all Such occasions.

10, Study the art of reducing all you read to practice in your orations &c: turning and improving elegantly to words and notions, and fancy of your authour to Sett of quite another subject; a delicate example whereof you have in your Chrystiados, whereof Ross is the author, causing Virgil to Evangelize: and as in your orations, so in all you do, labour for exactness, and acurateness, let not crude, lame, bungling Stuff come out of your Study: and for that end, see that you neither play nor sleep, nor idle away a moments time within your Study door, but remember your Study is your work-house only, and place of prayer.

11, So frame an order your Studies, that the one may be a furtherance to the other (the Tongues to the arts and the arts to the Tongues) and endeavour that your first years Studies may become a Clue to lead you on the more clearly, strongly, profitably, & chearfully to the Studies of the years following, making all still usefull, and subservient to Divinity, and so will your profiting in all be the more Perspicuous and methodicall.

12, Be sparing in your Diet, as to meat and drink, that so after any repast your body may be a servant to your mind, and not a Clogg and Burden.

13, Take pains in, and time for preparing in private for your recitations, declamations, disputations, and such other exercises as you are called to attend before your Tutor or others; do not hurry them off indigestly, no not under pretence of Studying some other matter first: but first (I Say in the first place) attend those (straiten not your self in time for the thorough dispatch thereof) and then afterwards you may apply yourself as aforesaid to your private and more proper Studies; In all which, mind that reading without meditation will be in a great measure unprofitable, and rawness and forgetfulness will be the Event: but meditation without reading will be barren soon; therefore read much that so you may have plenty of matter for meditation to work upon; and here I would not have you forgett a speech of your precious Grandfather to a Scholar that complained to him of a bad memory, which did discourage him from reading much in History, or other books, his answer was, [Lege! lege! aliquid haerebit] So I say to you read! read! something will stick in the mind, be diligent and good will come of it: and that Sentence in Prov. 14. 23. deserves to be written in letters of Gold upon your study-table [in all labour there is profitt &c] yet also know that reading, and meditation without prayer, will in the End be both blasted by the holy God, and therefore,

VII. Remember that not only heavenly and spiritual and Supernatural knowledge descends from God, but also all naturall, and humane learning, and abilities; and therefore pray much, not only for the one but also for the other from the Father of Lights, and mercies; and remember that prayer att Christs feet for all the learning you want, shall fetch you in more in an hour, than possibly you may gett by all the books, and helps you have otherwise in many years.

VIII. Remember to be Grave (not Childish) and amiable and loving toward all the Scholars, that you may win their hearts and Honour.

IX. Remember now to be watchful against the two great Sins of many Scholars; the first is youthful Lusts, speculative wantoness, and secret filthiness, which God sees in the Dark, and for which God hardens and blinds young mens hearts, his holy Spirit departing from such, unclean Styes. The second is malignancy and secret distaste of Holiness and the Power of Godliness, and the Professors of it, both these sins you will quickly fall into, unto your own perdition, if you be not carefull of your Company, for there are and will be such in every Scholasticall Society for the most part, as will teach you how to be filthy and how to jest, and Scorn at Godliness, and the professors thereof, whose Company I charge you to fly from as from the Devil, and abhor: and that you may be kept from these, read often that Scripture Prov. 2. 10. 11. 12, 16.

X. Remember to intreat God with Tears before you come to hear any Sermon, that thereby God would powerfully speak to your heart, and make his truth precious to you: neglect not to write after the preacher always, and write not in loose sheets but in handsome Paper-books; and be carefull to preserve and peruse the Same. And upon the Sabbath days make exceeding Conscience of Sanctification; mix not your other Studies, much less Idleness, or vain and casual discourses with the Duties of that holy Day; but remember that Command Lev. 19. 30. Ye shall keep my Sabbaths and reverence my Sanctuary, I am the Lord.

XI. Remember that whensoever you read, hear or conceive of any Divine truth, you Study to affect your heart with it and the Goodness of it. Take heed of receiving Truth into your head without the Love of it in your heart, lest God give you up to strong Delusions to believe lyes, and that in the Conclusion all your learning shall make you more fitt to deceive your Self and others. Take heed lest by seeing things with a form of Knowledge, the Lord do not bind you by that Knowledge the more, that in seeing you shall not see: If therefore God revealeth any truth to you att any time, be sure you be humbly and deeply thankfull: and when he hides any truth from you, be sure you lie down, and loath yourself, and be humble: the first degree of wisdom is to know and feel your own folly.

2 Tim. 2. 7. Consider what I say and the Lord give thee understanding in all things.

Prov. 23. 15. My Son, if thine heart be wise, my heart shall rejoice, even mine.

Pater tuus

T. SHEPARD

A PRESIDENTIAL ADDRESS BY INCREASE MATHER (c. 1687)
From Samuel E. Morison, *Harvard College in the Seventeenth Century* (Cambridge, Mass., 1936), p. 167.

It pleaseth me greatly that you, who have been initiated in the Liberal Arts, seem to savour a liberal mode of philosophizing, rather than the Peripatetic. I doubt not that the *Exercitationes* of Gassendi are familiar to you; in which he sheweth with many proofs that there are many deficiencies in Aristotle, many excesses, and many errors. It is a trite saying, *He who desireth not to be intelligible, should be negligible;* moreover there are some matters in the books of Aristotle which no mortal can comprehend. Wherefore it is alleged of Hermolaus Barbarus, that he raised a demon from hell, to explain what Aristotle meant by $\epsilon\upsilon\tau\epsilon\lambda\epsilon\chi\epsilon\iota\alpha$. A right proper interpreter of Aristotle, forsooth! How much in his writings are redolent of their author's paganism! He would have the world uncreated; he denieth a possible resurrection of the dead, he declareth the soul mortal. To Aristotle some prefer Pyrrho, father of the Sceptics; others, Zeno, father of the Stoics; many prefer Plato, father of the Academics. You who are wont to philosophize in a liberal spirit, are pledged to the words of no particular master, yet I would have you hold fast to that one truly golden saying of Aristotle: *Find a friend in Plato, a friend in Socrates* (and I say a friend in Aristotle), *but above all find a friend in* TRUTH.

OBJECTIONS OF THE CONNECTICUT ASSEMBLY TO THE LOCATION OF A COLLEGE AT NEW HAVEN (1717)
From Franklin B. Dexter, ed., *Documentary History of Yale University* (New Haven, 1916), pp. 81-82.

The Genll. Assembly of this Collony having some time given power to certain Trustees to Erect a Collegiate School in this Colony and to Determine the place of its Settlement, & having also Contributed to its yearly Maintainance & given a very Considerable Summe of Money to the building an House for Entertaining of Schollars. And whereas the Counties of N London & Hartford being more in Numbers than the rest of ye Government & paying the Greatest part of the Money given for the Subsisting the Collegiate School, & having furnished the sd. School with the greatest Number of Schollars, had reason to Expect that in apointing the place of the School Good respect should have been had to them therein. But finding it quite Otherwise, & that the Settling thereof at N Haven is attended with great Difficulty, such as cant be easily overcome, it being so very remote & the Transporting any thing by Water so uncertain, & there being so little Communication between these Counties & N Haven. & Understanding that at a Meeting of ye Major part of the Trustees at Hartford (which Major part by the Charter given to the Trustees have full power to act) did then determine that if they Could not Universally Agree to the Settlement of sd. School when they should meet at next Commencement at Saybrook, then they should refer the Nomination of the place to the Meeting of ye Genll. Assembly next October following. Those of the Trustees that Dissented from the Settling the Collegiate School at N Haven were under a Necessity in faithfullness to those Counties for whose Conveniency they were Concerned to inform the Genll. Assembly of the Same, but there being Nothing Issued: We do for or. selves declare our Dissatisfaction with the Settling of ye School at N Haven, by only an Equal part of the Trustees, & hereby Remonstrate against the same & desire that the Genll. Assembly that shall be in May next, may be moved that by an Act they may make a full Settlement thereof, & yt. it be part of the Instructions of yr. Deputies at the sd. Genll. Assembly, to offer ys. our remonstrance & Endeavour yt. the School be settled in a place, that shall be judged by them most Convenient & where it may be best subsisted & most accomodable to the greatest part of the Government.

YALE CHARTER (1745)   From Charles J. Hoadley, ed., *The Public Records of the Colony of Connecticut* (Hartford, 1876), vol. IX, pp. 113-18.

Whereas, the said trustees, partners or undertakers, in pursuance of the aforesaid grant, liberty and lycence, founded a Collegiate School at New Haven, known by the name of Yale College, which has received the favourable benefactions of many liberal and piously disposed persons, and under the blessing of Almighty God has trained up many worthy persons for the service of God in the state as well as in church: And whereas the General Court of this Colony, assembled at New Haven the tenth day of October, in the year of our Lord one thousand seven hundred and twenty-three, did explain and enlarge the aforesaid powers and priviledges granted to the aforesaid partners, trustees or undertakers, and their successors, for the purpose aforesaid, as by the respective acts, reference thereto being had, more fully and at large may appear: And whereas . . . the present trustees, partners and undertakers of the said school, and successors of those before mentioned, have petitioned that the said school with all the rights, powers, priviledges and interests thereof, may be confirmed, and that such other additional powers and priviledges may be granted as shall be necessary for the ordering and managing the said school in the most advantageous and beneficial manner, for the promoting all good literature in the present and succeeding generations: Therefore,

The Governor and Company of his Majesty's said English Colony of Connecti-cut, in General Court assembled, this ninth day of May in the year of our Lord one

thousand seven hundred and forty-five, enact, ordain and declare, and by these presents it is enacted, ordained and declared:

1. That the said Thomas Clap, Samuel Whitman, Jared Eliot, Ebenezer Williams, Jonathan Marsh, Samuel Cook, Samuel Whittelsey, Joseph Noyes, Anthony Stoddard, Benjamin Lord, and Daniel Wadsworth, shall be an incorporate society, or body corporate and politick, and shall hereafter be called and known by the name of The President and Fellows of Yale College in New Haven; and that by the same name they and their successors shall and may have perpetual succession, and shall and may be persons capable in the law to plead and be impleaded, defend and be defended, and answer and be answered unto, and also to have, take, possess, acquire, purchase or otherwise receive, lands, tenements, hereditaments, goods, chattels or other estates, and the same lands, tenements, hereditaments, goods, chattels or other estates to grant, demise, lease, use, manage or improve, for the good and benefit of the said college, according to the tenour of the donation and their discretion.

2. That all gifts, grants, bequests and donations of lands, tenements or hereditaments, of goods and chattels, heretofore made to or for the use, benefit and advantage of the Collegiate School aforesaid, whether the same be expressed to be made to the President or Rector and to the rest of the incorporate society of Yale College, or to the Trustees or Undertakers of the Collegiate School in New Haven, or to the trustees by any other name, stile or title whatsoever, whereby it may be clearly known and understood that the true intent and design of such gifts, grants, bequests and donations was to or for the use, benefit and advantage of the Collegiate School aforesaid and to be under the care and disposal of the governors thereof, shall be confirmed, and the same hereby are confirmed and shall be and remain to, and be vested in the President and Fellows of the College aforesaid and their successors, as to the true and lawful successors of the original grantees.

3. That the said President and Fellows and their successors shall and may hereafter have a common seal, to serve and use for all causes, matters and affairs of them and their successors, and the same seal to alter, break and make new, as they shall think fit.

4. That the said Thomas Clap shall be, and he is hereby established, the present President, and the said Samuel Whitman, Jared Eliot, Ebenezer Williams, Jonathan Marsh, Samuel Cook, Samuel Whittelsey, Joseph Noyes, Anthony Stoddard, Benjamin Lord, and Daniel Wadsworth, shall be, and they are hereby established, the present Fellows of the said college; and that they and their successors shall continue in their respective places during life, or until they, or either of them, shall resign or be removed or displaced, as in this act is hereafter expressed.

✳   ✳   ✳

7. That the present President and Fellows of said college and their successors, and all such tutors, professors and other officers as shall be appointed for the publick instruction and government of said college, before they undertake the execution of their respective offices and trusts, or within three months after, shall publickly in the college hall take the oaths and subscribe the declaration appointed by an act of Parliament made in the first year of King George the first, entituled An Act for the further security of his Majesty's person and government and the succession of the crown in the heirs of the late Princess Sophia, being protestants,

and for extinguishing the hopes of the pretended Prince of Wales and his open and secret abettors: that is to say, the President before the Governor, Deputy Governor, or any two of the Assistants of this Colony, for the time being, and the Fellows, tutors and other officers before the President for the time being, who is hereby impowered to administer the same; an entry of all which shall be made in the records of said college.

8. That the President and Fellows shall have the government, care and management of the said college, and all the matters and affairs thereunto belonging, and shall have power, from time to time as occasion shall require, to make, ordain and establish all such wholesome and reasonable laws, rules, and ordinances, not repugnant to the laws of England, nor the laws of this Colony, as they shall think fit and proper, for the instruction and education of the students, and ordering, governing, ruling, and managing the said college, and all matters, affairs and things thereunto belonging, and the same to repeal and alter, as they shall think fit; (which shall be laid before this Assembly as often as required, and may also be repealed or disallowed by this Assembly when they shall think proper.)

9. That the President of said college, with the consent of the Fellows, shall have power to give and confer all such honours, degrees or lycences as are usually given in colleges or universities, upon such as they shall think worthy thereof.

10. That all the lands and rateable estate belonging to the said college, not exceeding the yearly value of five hundred pounds sterling, lying in this government, and the persons, families and estates of the president and professors, lying and being in the town of New Haven, and the persons of the tutors, students, and such and so many of the servants of said college as give their constant attendance on the business of it, shall be freed and exempted from all rates, taxes, military service working at highways, and other such like duties and services.

11. And, for the special encouragement and support of said college, this Assembly do hereby grant unto the said President and Fellows and their successors, for the use of the said college, in lieu of all former grants, one hundred pounds silver money, at the rate of six shillings and eight pence per ounce, to be paid in bills of publick credit, or other currency equivalent to the said hundred pounds, (the rate or value thereof to be stated from time to time by this Assembly,) in two equal payments in October and May annually: this payment to continue during the pleasure of this Assembly.

In full testimony and confirmation of this grant and all the articles and matters therein contained, the said Governor and Company do hereby order that this act shall be signed by the Governor and Secretary, and sealed with the publick seal of the Colony, and that the same, or a duplicate or exemplification thereof, shall be a sufficient warrant to the said President and Fellows, to hold, use and exercise all the powers and priviledges therein mentioned and contained.

YALE LAWS (1745) From Franklin B. Dexter, *Biographical Sketches of the Graduates of Yale College with Annals of the College History, 1745-1763* (New York, 1896), vol. II, pp. 2-16.

Chapter I

CONCERNING ADMISSION INTO COLLEGE

1. That none may Expect to be admitted into this College unless upon Examination of the Praesident and Tutors, They shall be found able Extempore to Read, Construe and Parce Tully, Virgil and the Greek Testament: and to write True Latin Prose and to understand the Rules of Prosodia, and Common Arithmetic, and shall bring Sufficient Testamony of his Blameless and inoffensive Life.

2. That no Person shall be admitted a Freshman into this College who is more than Twenty one Years old, unless by the special allowance of ye President and Fellows or their Committee.

3. That no Person shall be admitted Undergraduate in this College until his Father, Guardian or some proper Person hath given a Sufficient Bond to the Steward of the College, to pay the Quarter Bills of the s^d Scholar allowed by the authority of College from Time to Time as long as He shall continue a Member of s^d College: which Bond The Steward Shall keep untill Such Scholar hath Taken his Second Degree, unless He Shall Receive Order from the President to Deliver it up before.

✳   ✳   ✳

Chapter II

OF A RELIGIOUS AND VIRTUOUS LIFE

1. All Scholars Shall Live Religious, Godly and Blameless Lives according to the Rules of Gods Word, diligently Reading the holy Scriptures the Fountain of Light and Truth; and constanly [*sic*] attend upon all the Duties of Religion both in Publick and Secret.

2. That the President, or in his absence One of the Tutors Shall constantly Pray in the College-Hall every morning and Evening: and Shall read a Chapter or Suitable Portion of the Holy Scriptures, unless there be Some other Theological Discourse or Religious Exercise: and Every Member of the College whether Graduates or Undergraduates, whether Residing in the College or in the Town of New-Haven Shall Seasonably Attend upon Penalty that every Undergraduate who Shall be absent (without Sufficient Excuse) Shall be Fined one Penny and for comeing Tardy after the Introductory Collect is made Shall be fin'd one half penny.

✳   ✳   ✳

5. No Student of this College Shall attend upon any Religious Meetings either Public or Private on the Sabbath or any other Day but Such as are appointed by Public Authority or Approved by the President upon Penalty of a Fine, Public Admonition, Confession or Otherwise according to the Nature or Demerit of the Offence.

THE COLLEGES

6. That if any Student Shall Prophane the Sabbath by unnecessary Business, Diversion, Walking abroad, or makeing any Indecent Noise or Disorder on the Said Day, or on the Evening before or after, or Shall be Guilty of any Rude, Profane or indecent Behaviour in the Time of Publick Worship, or at Prayer at any Time in the College Hall, He Shall be punished, Admonished or otherwise according to the Nature and Demerit of his Crime.

✻   ✻   ✻

Chapter III
CONCERNING SCHOLASTICAL EXERCISES

1. Every Student Shall diligently apply himself to his Studies in his Chamber as well as attend upon all Public Exercises appointed by the President or Tutors, and no Student Shall walk abroad, or be absent from his Chamber, Except Half an hour after Breakfast, and an hour and an half after Dinner, and from prayers at Night to Nine o' the Clock, without Leave, upon Penalty of Two Pence or more to Six pence, at the Discretion of ye President and Tutors.

2. To this End the President or Tutors Shall, by Turns, or as They conveniently can visit Student's Chambers after Nine o'Clock, to See whether They are at their Chambers, and apply themselves to their Studies.

3. That the President and Each of the Tutors Shall according to the best of their Discretion Instruct and bring forward their respective Classes in the Knowledge of the Three Learned Languages, and in the Liberal Arts and Sciences. In the first Year They Shall principally Study the Tongues & Logic, and Shall in Some measure pursue the Study of the Tongues the Two next Years. In the Second Year They Shall Recite Rhetoric, Geometry and Geography. In the Third Year Natural Philosophy, Astronomy and Other Parts of the Mathematicks. In the Fourth Year Metaphysics and Ethics. And the respective Classes Shall Recite Such Books, and in Such a manner as has been accustomed, or Such as the President upon the Consultation with the Tutors Shall think proper: but every Saturday Shall Especially be alloted to the Study of Divinity, and the Classes Shall dureing the whole Term recite the Westminster Confession of Faith received and approved by the Churches in this Colony, Wollebius, Ames Medulla, or any other System of Divinity by the Direction of the President and Fellows: and on Friday Each Undergraduate in his Order about Six at a Time Shall Declaim in the Hall in Latin, Greek, or Hebrew and in no other Language without Special Leave from the President; and Shall presently after Deliver up his Declamation to his Tutor, fairly written and Subscribed. And the two Senior Classes Shall Dispute in the Fall Twice a week; and if any Undergraduate Shall be Absent from Reciting or Disputeing without Sufficient Reason, He Shall be fined two Pence; and from Declaiming Six Pence.

Chapter IV
OF PENAL LAWS

1. If any Scholar Shall be Guilty of Blasphemy, Fornication, Robbery, Forgery, or any other such Great and Atrocious Crime he Shall be Expelled forthwith.

2. If any Scholar Shall deny the Holy Scriptures or any Part of Them to be the

Word of God: or be guilty of Heresy or any Error directly Tending to Subvert the Fundamentals of Christianity, and continuing Obstinate therein after the first and Second Admonition, He shall be Expelled.

3. If any Scholar shall be Guilty of Profane Swearing, Cursing, Vowing, any Petty or Implicit Oath, Profane or Irreverent Use of the Names, Attributes, Ordinances or Word of God; Disobedient or Contumacious or Refractory Carriage towards his Superiours, Fighting, Striking, Quarrelling, Challenging, Turbulent Words or Behaviour, Drunkenness, Uncleaness, Lacivious Words or Actions, wearing woman's Aparrel, Defrauding, Injustice, Idleness, Lying, Defamation, Tale bareing or any other Such like Immoralities, He Shall be Punished by Fine, Confession, Admonition or Expulsion, as the Nature and Circumstances of the Case may Require.

4. If any Person be Guilty of Stealing, He Shall besides the Fine Pay Trible [sic] Damage and in all other cases of Injustice Shall make full Restitution to the Party injured.

5. If any Scholar Shall break open any Other Scholars Door or Open it with a Pick-Lock or a False Key, He Shall be Fined One Shilling for the first Offence: and Two Shillings for the Second: and for the Third publickly admonished, Degraded or Expelled.

6. If any Scholar Shall Play at Cards or Dice at all: or at any Lawfull Game upon a Wager: or Shall bring any Quantity of Rum, Wine, Brandy or other Strong Liquor into College or into his Chamber where he Resides without Liberty from the President or Tutors, or Shall Go into any Tavern within Two miles of College and call for any Strong Liquor, or Spend his Time idly there unless with his Parent or Guardian, he shall for the first Offence be Fined Two Shillings and Sixpence, or be admonished: and for the Second Offence be Fined Five Shillings and be Degraded: and for the Third Offence be Expelled: and if any Scholar Shall Play at Swords, Files or Cudgels, He Shall be Fined not Exceeding One Shilling.

7. That if any Scholar Shall do any Damage to the College House, Glass, Fences, or any other Things belonging to College or Shall jump out of College Windows, or over the Board Fences, he Shall be Fined not exceeding One Shilling, and Pay all Damages to be charged in his Quarter Bill.

8. That Every Student Shall abstain from Singing, loud Talking and all other Noises in Studying Time, on Penalty of Four Pence: and if any Scholar Shall at any Time make any Rout, Disorder or Loud, Indecent Noises, Screamings or Hollowing or Shall call loud or Hollow to any other Scholar in the Presence of the President or Tutors, He Shall be fined not Exceeding Two Shillings.

9. That if any Scholar Shall associate himself with any Rude, Idle Disorderly Persons: or Shall Entertain Companions at his Chamber either in College or out after Nine o'Clock, or Shall Take any Person who is not a near Relation to Lodge with Him without Liberty from the President or a Tutor he Shall be Fined not Exceeding Two Shillings.

10. That the President or Either of the Tutors may when he See Cause Break open any College Door to Suppress any Disorder; And if any Scholar Shall refuse to Give the President or Either of the Tutors admittance into his Chamber when Demanded, or to assist in Suppressing any Disorder when required; or to come when he is Sent for, or to Give in Evidence when he is called, he Shall be Fined Two Shillings; or be punished by Admonition, Confession, Degradation or Expulsion as the Nature of the Case may Require.

11. If any Scholar Shall behave himself obstinately, refractorily or Contemtion-

ally [*sic*] toward the President or either of the Tutors, He Shall for the first Offence be punished by Fine, Admonition or Confession, or Being Deprived of the Liberty of Sending Freshman for a certain Time: For the Second Offence he Shall be Degraded or Expell'd.

12. That if any Scholar Shall write or Publish any Libel: or raise any false or Scandalous Report of the President or either of the Fellows or Tutors or the Minister of the first Church of New-Haven, or Shall directly or indirectly Say that either of Them is a Hypocrite, or Carnal or Unconverted, or use any Such reproachful or reviling Language concerning Them, He Shall for the first Offence make a Public Confession in the Hall; and for Second be Expelled.

13. If any Scholar Shall Go out of the College Yard without a Hat, Coat or Gown except at his Lawful Diversion, He Shall be Fined Three Pence: and if He Shall wear any indecent Apparrell He Shall be punished not exceeding Two Shillings.

14. If any Scholar Shall keep a Gun or Pistol, or Fire one in the College-Yard or College, or Shall Go a Gunning, Fishing or Sailing, or Shall Go more than Two Miles from College upon any Occasion whatsoever: or Shall be Present at any Court, Election, Town-Meeting, Wedding, or Meeting of young People for Diversion or any Such-like Meeting which may Occasion Mispence of precious Time without Liberty first obtain'd from the President or his Tutor, in any of the cases abovesaid he Shall be fined not exceeding Two Shillings.

15. That all the Scholars Shall behave Themselves inoffencively, blamelesly and justly toward the People in New-Haven: not unnecessarily Frequently their Houses, or Interesting Themselves into any Controversey among Them. And upon Complaint of any Wrong done by any Scholar to any of Them, or any other Scholar, the President Shall Order Them to Do Justice and make Restitution. And if any Scholar Shall refuse So to do, He Shall be publickly Admonished, and if he continue Obstinate He Shall be Expelled and his Bond put in Sale if need be.

16. That Every Freshman Shall be Obliged to Go any reasonable and proper and reasonable Errand when he is Sent by any Student in any Superior Class; and if he Shall refuse So to Do he may be punished: provided that no Graduate Shall Send a Freshman out of the College Yard, and no Undergraduate Shall Send a Freshman anywhere in Studying Time, without Liberty first had from ye President or Oone [*sic*] of the Tutors.

* * *

19. If any Scholar Shall make an assault upon the Person of ye President or either of the Tutors or Shall wound, Bruise or Strike any of Them, He Shall forthwith be Expelled.

20. That no Scholar Shall undertake to Do or Transact any Matters or Affairs of Difficulty and Importance, or which are any ways new or beside the common & approved Customs & Practises of the College, without first Consulting with the President and Obtaining his Consent.

* * *

Chapter V

OF CHAMBERS IN OR OUT OF COLLEGE

1. The President Shall from Time to Time Dispose of the Chambers and Studies in College and assign Them to particular Scholars to Live in according to his Discretion. And if any Scholar Shall not Dwell in or Shall Move out of any Chamber assigned to him, or into any other Chamber not assigned without Liberty, he Shall be Fined One Shilling, or otherwise Punished according to the Nature & Circumstances of the Offence.

*   *   *

6. That Every Scholar who Shall Live out of College in the Town of New Haven Shall obtain Liberty of the President where to Live; and Shall not remove therefrom to any other House or Place without Liberty of the President, upon Penalty of Two Shillings.

*   *   *

Chapter X

OF THE AUTHORITY OF COLLEGE

1. The Legislative Authority of college is in the President and Fellows; who have Power to make & establish all Such Laws, Rules or Orders and Directions (not repugnant to the Laws of the Civil Government) as They Shall think proper.

2. That the Executive Power of this College is principally in the President; who hath Power to Govern the College & every Student thereof whether Graduate or Undergraduate; and to Order and direct all the Affairs thereof according to Such Laws and Rules & Orders as are made by the President and Fellows & in Defect of them according to the Established Customs of the College, and where there are no Such then according to the best of his Judgment and Discretion, provided that in all Cases of Difficulty & Importance he Shall consult & advise with the Tutors: and when any extraordinary Emergency Shall happen which Shall be of great Importance & require a Speedy Determination, then the President with any Two of the Fellows Shall call a Meeting of the Corporation: or if that cannot conveniently be, then he Shall consult with as many as conveniently be got together.

3. That Each Tutor appointed by the President & Fellows Shall under the President have the Care, Inspection and Government of the College; and the Tuition of their respective Classes: and Shall have Power to punish any Undergraduate for any Breach of the College Laws not exceeding one Shilling, provided that when any matter of Difficulty fall out he shall not proceed without the Advice & Discretion of the President.

4. That no member of this College or any Person for him Shall make or Prosecute any Action, Suit or Complaint whatever against any other Member of Officer of this College for any Supposed Injury or Defect to or before Authority or Judges whatsoever besides the Authority of this College, upon Penalty, that any Scholar who Shall make Such Complaints or permit it to be made without Leave from the President or Fellows first obtain'd, Shall be forthwith Expell'd.

5. That every One who is chose President or Tutor of this College shall before he enter upon his Office, publickly, in the College-hall give his Consent to the Westminster Confession of Faith and Ecclesiastical Discipline received by the Churches of this Colony, & Established by the Laws of this Government.

The Great Awakening

JONATHAN EDWARDS ON COLLEGES AS "SCHOOLS OF THE PROPHETS" (1740) From "Some Thoughts on the Revival of Religion in New England" (1740), as quoted in *Works of President Edwards* (New York, 1856), vol. III, pp. 413-14.

And though it may be thought, that I go out of my proper sphere, to intermeddle in the affairs of the colleges, yet I will take the liberty of an Englishman (that speaks his mind freely concerning public affairs) and the liberty of a minister of Christ (who doubtless may speak his mind as freely about things that concern the kingdom of his Lord and master) to give my opinion, in some things, with respect to those societies; the original and main design of which is to train up persons, and fit them for the work of the ministry. And I would say in general, that it appears to me that care should be taken, some way or other, that those societies should be so regulated, that they should, in fact, be nurseries of piety. Otherwise, they are fundamentally ruined and undone, as to their main design, and most essential end. They ought to be so constituted, that vice and idleness should have no living there. They are intolerable in societies, whose main design is, to train up youth in Christian knowledge and eminent piety, to fit them to be pastors of the flock of the blessed Jesus. I have heretofore had some acquaintance with the affairs of a college, and experience of what belonged to its tuition and government; and I cannot but think that it is practicable enough, so to constitute such societies, that there should be no being there, without being virtuous, serious and diligent. It seems to me to be a reproach to the land, that ever it should be so with our colleges that instead of being places of the greatest advantages for true piety, one cannot send a child thither, without great danger of his being infected, as to his morals; as it has certainly sometimes been with these Societies. It is perfectly intolerable; and any thing should be done, rather than it should be so. If we pretend to have any colleges at all, under any notion of training up youth for the ministry, there should be some way found out, that should certainly prevent its being thus. To have societies for bringing persons up to be ambassadors of Jesus Christ, and to lead souls to heaven, and to have them places of so much infection, is the greatest nonsense and absurdity imaginable.

And, as thorough and effectual care should be taken that vice and idleness are not tolerated in these societies, so certainly, the design of them requires, that extraordinary means should be used in them, for training up the students in vital religion, and experimental and practical godliness; so that they should be holy societies, the very place should be as it were sacred. They should be, in the midst of the land, fountains of piety and holiness. There is a great deal of pains taken, to teach the scholars human learning; there ought to be as much, and more care, thoroughly to educate them in religion, and lead them to true and eminent holiness. If the main design of these nurseries, is to bring up persons to teach Christ, then it is of the greatest importance that there should be care and pains taken, to bring those that are there educated, to the knowledge of Christ. It has been common in our public prayers, to call these societies, *the schools of the prophets;* and if they are schools, to train up young men to be prophets, certainly there ought to be extraordinary care there taken, to train them up to be Christians.

GEORGE WHITEFIELD AT HARVARD (1740)   From George Whitefield,
Journals (London, 1960), p. 42.

Wednesday, September 24. Went this morning to see and preach at Cambridge, the chief college for training the sons of the prophets in New England. It has one president, four tutors, and about a hundred students. The college is scarce as big as one of the least colleges at Oxford; and, as far as I could gather from some who knew the state of it, not far superior to our Universities in piety. Discipline is at a low ebb. Bad books are become fashionable among the tutors and students. Tillotson and Clark are read, instead of Shepard, Stoddard, and such-like evangelical writers; and, therefore, I chose to preach from these words,—"We are not as many, who corrupt the Word of God." A great number of neighbouring ministers attended. God gave me great boldness and freedom of speech. The President of the college and minister of the parish treated me very civilly.[1] In the afternoon, I preached again, in the court, when, I believe, there were about seven thousand hearers. The Holy Spirit melted many hearts. A minister soon after wrote me word, "that one of his daughters was savingly wrought upon at that time." Lord, add daily to the Church, such as shall be saved! Paid my respects to the Lieutenant-Governor, who lives at Cambridge; and returned in the evening to Boston, and prayed with and exhorted many people who were waiting round the door for a spiritual morsel. I believe our Lord did not send them empty away. O Blessed Jesus, feed them with that Bread of Life Which cometh down from Heaven.

[1]"In my former Journal, taking things by hearsay too much, I spoke and wrote too rashly of the colleges and ministers of New England, for which, as I have already done it when at Boston last from the pulpit, I take this opportunity of asking public pardon from the press. It was rash and uncharitable and though well-meant, I fear, did hurt." (Édit. 1756.)

CRITICISM OF GEORGE WHITEFIELD BY HARVARD SCHOLARS (1744)

From *The Testimony of the President, Professors, Tutors, and Hebrew Instructor of Harvard College, against George Whitefield* (Boston, 1744), as quoted in Perry Miller and Alan E. Heimert, eds., *The Great Awakening: Documents Illustrating the Crisis . . .* (Indianapolis, 1967), pp. 341-42, 348, 351-53.

In regard of the Danger which we apprehend the People and Churches of this Land are in, on the Account of the Rev. Mr. *George Whitefield,* we have tho't ourselves oblig'd to bear our Testimony, in this Public Manner, against him and his Way of Preaching, as tending very much to the Detriment of Religion, and the entire Destruction of the Order of these Churches of Christ, which our Fathers have taken such Care and Pains to settle, as by the Platform, according to which the Discipline of the Churches of *New England* is regulated: And we do therefore hereby declare, That we look upon his going about, in an Itinerant Way, especially as he hath so much of an enthusiastic Turn, utterly inconsistent with the Peace and Order, if not the very Being of these Churches of Christ.

And now, inasmuch as by a certain Faculty he hath of raising the Passions, he hath been the Means of rousing many from their Stupidity, and setting them on thinking, whereby some may have been made really better, on which Account the People, many of them, are strongly attach'd to him (tho' it is most evident, that he hath not any superior Talent at instructing the Mind, or shewing the Force and Energy of those Arguments for a religious Life, which are directed to in the everlasting Gospel). Therefore, that the People who are thus attach'd to him, may not take up an unreasonable Prejudice against this our Testimony, we think it very proper to give some Reasons for it, which we shall offer, respecting the Man himself, and then his Way and Manner of Preaching.

First, as to the Man himself, whom we look upon as an Enthusiast, a censorious, uncharitable Person, and a Deluder of the People; which Things, if we can make out, all reasonable Men will doubtless excuse us, tho' some such, thro' a fascinating Curiosity, may still continue their Attachment to him.

First then, we charge him, with *Enthusiasm.* Now that we may speak clearly upon this Head, we mean by an *Enthusiast,* one that acts, either according to Dreams, or some sudden Impulses and Impressions upon his Mind, which he fondly imagines to be from the Spirit of God, perswading and inclining him thereby to such and such Actions, tho' he hath no Proof that such Perswasions or Impressions are from the Holy Spirit: For the perceiving a strong Impression upon our Minds, or a violent Inclination to do any Action, is a very different Thing from perceiving such Impressions to be from the Spirit of God moving upon the Heart: For our strong Faith and Belief, that such a Motion on the Mind comes from God, can never be any Proof of it; and if such Impulses and Impressions be not agreeable to our Reason, or to the Revelation of the Mind of God to us, in his Word, nothing can be more dangerous than conducting ourselves according to them; for otherwise, if we judge not of them by these Rules, they may as well be the Suggestions of the evil Spirit: And in what Condition must that People be, who stand ready to be led by a Man that conducts himself according to his Dreams, or some ridiculous and unaccountable Impulses and Impressions on his Mind? And that this is Mr. *Whitefield's* Manner, is evident both by his Life, his Journals and his Sermons: In which, the Instances of this dangerous Turn are so many, that we cannot touch on more than a very few of them. From these Pieces then it is very evident, that he us'd to govern himself by his Dreams. . . .

❋   ❋   ❋

The next Instance we shall note, is the reproachful Reflections upon the Society which is immediately under our Care. p. 55. Where are observable his Rashness and his Arrogance. His Rashness, in publishing such a disadvantageous Character of *Us*, *viz.* Because some Body had so inform'd him. Surely he ought, if he had followed our Saviour's Rule, to have had a greater Certainty of the Truth of what he publish'd of us to the whole World. But his Arrogance is more flagrant still, that such a young Man as he should take upon him to tell what Books we should allow our Pupils to read. But then he goes further still, when he says, p. 95. both of *Yale College* as well as ours, *As for the Universities, I believe it may be said, Their Light is now become Darkness, Darkness that may be felt.* What a deplorable State of Immorality and Irreligion has he hereby represented Us to be in! And as this is a most wicked and libellous Falshood (at least as to our College) as such we charge it upon him. But why doth he say thus? Why, *because this is complain'd of by the most godly Ministers.* Here we are at a Loss to think whom he means by *the most godly Ministers.* Certainly not the Rev. Gentlemen of the Town of *Boston* (with whom nevertheless he was most acquainted) for they are in the Government of the College, have assisted in making the Laws by which it is govern'd, and constantly visit us by a Committee, and themselves four Times in a Year, and make Examination how the Laws are executed. Besides, we don't know that he hath been pleas'd to allow to any one of them any such religious Character, in any one of his Journals, as should make us think he means them, but rather the reverse. Vid. p. 76 of his Journal from N. E.

But we shall finish this Head of his Censoriousness, when we have mentioned his pernicious Reflections upon the Ministers of the Churches in this Land. We say *this Land;* for it is far from a torturing of the Words, to suppose he directly means them, when he says, p. 70. *He is perswaded the generality of Preachers talk of an unknown unfelt Christ;* tho' he hath evasively said (since he came this time) that *he did not restrain the Expression to the Ministers of* N. England, *tho' he did not exclude them.* Admirably satisfactory this Explanation! But he can't come off so easily in the Reflection he makes upon our Ministers, p. 95. *Many, nay most perhaps that preach, I fear, do not experimentally know Christ—*Is it possible he should say, this is no Charge upon the Ministers of these Churches? It is true, it is not so in Form; but is it not one of the most uncharitable Things he cou'd have done, to manifest these his Fears to all the World, without Ground? Without Ground, we say; for as the greatest Part of them by far, their Conversation is as becomes the Gospel, and we may challenge him and all the World to shew the contrary.

❋   ❋   ❋

But, *lastly,* We think it our Duty to bear our strongest Testimony against that *Itinerant Way* of preaching which this Gentleman was the first promoter of among us, and still delights to continue in: For if we had nothing against the *Man*, either as an *Enthusiast*, an *uncharitable* or *delusive* Person, yet we apprehend this Itinerant Manner of preaching to be of the worst and most pernicious Tendency.

Now by an *Itinerant* Preacher, we understand One that hath no particular Charge of his own, but goes about from Country to Country, or from Town to Town, in any Country, and stands ready to Preach to any Congregation that shall call him to it; and such an one is Mr. W. for it is but trifling for him to say (as we hear he hath) That he requires in order to his preaching any where, that the Minister also should invite him to it; for he knows the Populace have such an Itch after him, that when they generally desire it, the Minister (however diverse from their's, his own Sentiments may be) will always be in the utmost Danger of his People's quarelling with, if not departing from him, shou'd he not consent to their impetuous Desires. Now as it is plain, no Man will find much Business as an *Itinerant* Preacher, who hath not something in his Manner, that is (however trifling, yea, and erroneous too, yet) very taking and agreeable to the People; so when this is the Case, as we have lately unhappily seen it, it is then in his Power to raise the People to any Degree of Warmth he pleases, whereby they stand ready to receive almost any Doctrine he is pleased to broach; as hath been the Case as to all the Itinerant Preachers who have followed Mr. W's. Example, and thrust themselves into Towns and Parishes, to the Destruction of all Peace and Order, whereby they have to the great impoverishment of the Community, taken the People from their Work and Business, to attend their Lectures and Exhortations, always fraught with Enthusiasm, and other pernicious Errors: But, *which is worse, and it is the natural Effect of these Things,* the People have been thence ready to despise their own Ministers, and their usefulness among them, in too many Places, hath been almost destroy'd.

Indeed, if there were any thing leading to this manner of·Management in the Directions and Instructions given, either by our Savior or his Apostles, we ought to be silent, and so wou'd a Man of any Modesty, if (on the other hand) there be nothing in the N. Testament leading to it. And surely Mr. W. will not have the Face to pretend he acts now as an *Evangelist,* tho' he seems to prepare for it in Journ. from *N. E.* to *Falmouth in England,* p. 12. where he says, *God seems to shew me it is my Duty to Evangelize, and not to fix in any particular Place:* For the Duty of that Officer certainly was not to go preaching of his own Head from one Church to another, where Officers were already settled, and the Gospel fully and faithfully preached. And it is without Doubt, that the Mind and Will of Christ, with respect to the Order of his Churches, and the Business of his Ministers in them, is plainly enough to be understood in the N. Testament; and yet Mr. W. has said of late, in one of his Sermons, he thinks that an Itinerant Manner of preaching may be very convenient for the furtherance of the good of the Churches, if it were under a good Regulation. Now we are apt to imagine, if such an Officer wou'd have been useful, Christ himself wou'd have appointed him; and therefore (under Favour) this is to *be wise above what is written,* and supposes either that our Lord did not know, or that he neglected to appoint all such Officers in the Ministry, as wou'd further in the best manner the Truths of the Gospel: And it is from such Wisdom as this, that all the Errors of *Popery* have come into the *Christian Church,* while the Directions of the Word of God were not strictly adhered to, but one tho't this Way or that Ceremony was very convenient and significant, and another another, till they have dress'd up the Church in such a monstrous heap of Appendages, that at this Day it can hardly be discern'd to be a Church of Christ.

And now, upon the whole, having, we think, made it evident to every one that is not prejedic'd on his Side (for such as are so, we have little hope to convince) that Mr. W. is chargeable with that *Enthusiasm, Censoriousness* and *delusive Management* that we have tax'd him with; and since also he seems resolv'd for that

Itinerant Way of preaching, which we think so destructive to the Peace of the Churches of Christ; we cannot but bear our faithful Testimony against him, as a Person very unfit to preach about as he has done heretofore, and as he has now begun to do.

And we wou'd earnestly, and with all due respect, recommend it to the Rev. Pastors of these Churches of Christ, to advise with each other in their several Associations, and consider whether it be not high Time to make a stand against the Mischiefs, which we have here suggested as coming upon the Churches.

Harvard College, Dec. 28, 1744.

CHARTER OF THE COLLEGE OF NEW JERSEY (PRINCETON UNIVERSITY (1746, 1748)[1] From Thomas Jefferson Wertenbaker, *Princeton, 1746-1896* (Princeton, N.J., 1946), pp. 396-99.

George the Second, by the Grace of God, of Great Britain, France and Ireland, King, Defender of the Faith &c. To all to Whom these Presents Shall Come, Greeting

Whereas sundry *of our loving subjects,* well disposed & publick spirited Persons, have lately by their humble Petition presented to our Trusty and well beloved [JOHN HAMILTON ESQ^r. the President of OUR COUNCIL,] *Jonathan Belcher, Esq., governor* and Commander in Chief of our Province of New Jersey in America, represented the great necessity of coming into some Method for encouraging and promoting a learned Education of Our Youth in New Jersey, and have expres'd their earnest Desire that a College may be erected in our Said Province of New Jersey *in America* for the Benefit of the *inhabitants of the* Said Province *and other,* wherein Youth may be instructed in the learned Languages, and in the Liberal Arts and Sciences. . . . And whereas by the fundamental Concessions made at the first Settlement of New Jersey by the Lord Berkley and Sir George Carteret, then Proprietors thereof, and granted under their Hands, and the Seal of the said Province, and bearing Date the Tenth Day of February [1664], *in the year of our Lord one thousand six hundred and sixty-four,* it was, among[st] other Things, conceded and [granted] *agreed,* "that no Freeman within the said Provence of New Jersey, should at any Time be molested, punished, disquieted, or Called in Question for any difference in opinion or practice in matters of Religious Concernment, who do not actually disturb the civil Peace of the Said Province, but that all and every such Person [and] *or* Persons might from Time to Time & at all Times *thereafter* freely & truly have and enjoy his and their Judgments and Consciences in Matters of Religion throughout the said Province, they behaving themselves Peaceably and quietly and not using this Liberty to Licentiousness nor to the Civil Injury or

[1]The parts of the Charter of 1746 which were omitted in the Charter of 1748 have been placed in brackets; the parts of the Charter of 1748 not included in the Charter of 1746 appear in italics.

outward Disturbance of others." As by the Said Concessions on Record in the Secretary's Office of New Jersey, at Perth Amboy, in Lib. 3 fol*io* 66 &c may appear. Wherefore *and for that* the said Petitioners have also expressed their earnest Desire that those of every Religious Denomination may have free and Equal Liberty and Advantage of Education in the Said College [notwithstanding] any different Sentiments in Religion *notwithstanding*. We being willing to grant the reasonable Requests & Prayers of all our loving Subjects, and to promote a liberal and Learned Education among them—KNOW YE, therefore that we considering the Premises, and being willing for the future that the best means of Education be established in our Province of New Jersey, for the Benefit and Advantage *of the inhabitants* of that our said Province *and others,* Do of Our special Grace, certain Knowledge and mere Motion, by these Presents, will, ordain, grant, and constitute that there be a College erected in Our Said Province of New Jersey for the Education of Youth in the Learned Languages and in the Liberal Arts and Sciences. And that the Trustees of the said College and their Successors *for* ever May, and shall be one Body Corporate & Politick, in Deed, action & Name, and shall be called, *and* named and distingui*sh*ed, by the Name of the Trustees of the College of New Jersey.—And further we have willed, given, granted, Constituted and [Ordained] *appointed,* and by this our present Charter of Our especial Grace, certain Knowledge & meer Motion. We do for Us, our Heirs and Successors [For ever] will, give, grant, constitute & ordain that there shall in the Said College from henceforth, and for ever be a Body politick Consisting of Trustees of the Said College of New Jersey, and for the more full & perfect Erection of the said Corporation and Body Politick consisting of Trustees of the College of New Jersey, we of our Especial Grace, Certain Knowledge and meer Motion, do by these Presents for Us, our Heirs & Successors, create, make, ordain, constitute, Nominate and appoint [our Trusty & well beloved WILLIAM SMITH, PETER VAN BRUGH LIVINGSTON & WILLIAM PEARTREE SMITH, of the City of New York, Gentlemen, and our trusty & well beloved JONATHAN DICKINSON, JOHN PIERSON, EBENEZER PEMBERTON & AARON BURR, Ministers of the Gospel with such others as they shall think proper to Associate until them not Exceeding the Number of twelve to be the Trustees of the Said College of New Jersey with full power and Authority to them, or any four, or greater Number of them, to nominate & appoint & associate unto them any Number of Persons, as Trustees, so that the whole Number of Trustees exceed not Twelve.] *the Governor and Commander in Chief of our said province of New Jersey, for the time being, and also our trusty and well beloved John Reading, James Hude, Andrew Johnston, Thomas Leonard, John Kinsey, Edward Shippen and William Smith, Esquires, Peter Van-Brugh Livingston, William Peartree Smith and Samuel Hazard, gentlemen, John Pierson, Ebenezer Pemberton, Joseph Lamb, Gilbert Tennent, William Tennent, Richard Treat, Samuel Blair, David Cowell, Aaron Burr, Timothy Jones, Thomas Arthur and Jacob Green, ministers of the gospel, to be Trustees of the said College of New Jersey.*

That the said Trustees do, at their first meeting, after the receipt of these presents, and before they proceed to any business take the oath appointed to be taken by an act, passed in the first year of the reign of the late King George the First, entitled, "An act for the further security of his Majesty's person and government, and the succession of the crown in the heirs of the late princess Sophia, being protestants, and for extinguishing the hopes of the pretended prince of Wales, and his open and secret abettors";, as also that they make and subscribe the declarations mentioned in an act of parliament made in the twenty-fifth year of the reign of King Charles the Second, entitled, "An act for preventing dangers which may happen from popish recusants"; and likewise take an oath for faithfully executing the office or trust reposed in them, the said oaths to be administered to them by three of his Majesty's justices of the peace, quorum unus; and when any new member or officer of this corporation is chosen, they are to take and subscribe the aforementioned oaths and declarations before their admission into their trusts or offices, the same to be administered to them in the presence of the Trustees, by such persons as they shall appoint for that service.

That no meeting of the Trustees shall be valid or legal for doing any business whatsoever, unless the clerk has duly and legally notified each and every member of the corporation of such meeting; and that before the entering of any business, the clerk shall certify such notification under his hand to the Board of Trustees.

That the said Trustees have full power and authority or any thirteen or greater number of them, to elect, nominate and appoint and associate unto them, any number of persons as Trustees upon any vacancy, so the whole number of Trustees exceed not twenty-three whereof the President of the said college for the time being, to be chosen as hereafter mentioned, to be one, and twelve of the said Trustees to be always such persons as are inhabitants of our said province of New Jersey.

PRESIDENT CLAP OF YALE DEFENDS THE SECTARIAN COLLEGE

(1754)   From Thomas Clap, *The Religious Constitution of Colleges,* (New London, Conn., 1754), pp. 5-8, 10-20.

Religious Worship, Preaching, and Instruction on the Sabbath, being one of the most important Parts, of the Education of Ministers; it is more necessary, that it should be under the Conduct, of the Authority, of the College, than any other Part of Education. The Preaching, ought to be adapted, to the superior Capacity, of those, who are to be qualified, to be *Instructors of others*; and upon all Accounts *Superior*, to that, which is ordinarily to be expected, or indeed requisite, in a common Parish.

There are many different Principles, in Religion, and Kinds of Preaching, which, when they are in any Degree faulty, cannot always be easily remedied, by Complaint, to any other Authority. And therefore, every *religious Society*, naturally chooses, as far as may be, to have, the Nomination of their own Minister. And this is much more necessary in a *College*, where the Preaching, is of such general Importan, to a whole Country; and such special Care, should be taken, that it be, upon all Accounts, of the *best Kind*. And it cannot be reasonable, nor safe, that any particular Parish, especially, that which happens to be the nearest to a College, should appoint the Minister for it. . . .

And where, as it generally happens, there are sundry Places of Worship, in the City, where a College is; if the Students should disperse to all, and every one of them, this would break up all order in the Society, and defeat the Religious Design, and Instructions of it. . . .

YALE-COLLEGE in *New-Haven*; does not come up, to the Perfection, of the Ancient Established Universities, in *Great Britain*; yet, would endeavour, to Imitate them, in most things, as far, as its present State, will admit of.

It was *Founded*, A.D. 1701. By *Ten Principal Ministers*, in the Colony of *Connecticut*; upon the Desire, of many other Ministers, and People in it; with the *License, and Approbation, of the General Assembly*. Their main Design, in that *Foundation*, was to *Educate Persons, for the Ministry of these* Churches, commonly called *Presbyterian*, or *Congregational*, according to their own *Doctrine, Discipline*, and *Mode of Worship*. . . .

The present Governors, of the College; esteem themselves, bound by *Law*, and the more *sacred Ties of Conscience, and Fidelity to their Trust, committed to them, by their Predecessors*; to pursue, and carry on, the pious Intention, and Design, of the *Founders*; and to improve, all the *College Estate*, descended to them, for that purpose.

* * *

In the mean Time, they have desired, the *President*; with some Assistance, from themselves, and others; to carry on the Work, of a Professor, of Divinity; by Preaching, in the College Hall, every Lord's Day. Being hereunto, sufficiently warranted, from, the original Nature, Design, and Practice of Colleges, and Universities; (which are, superior Societies, for Religious Purposes;) and, the several special Clauses, in the Acts, of the General Assembly; That so, the Students, may have the Advantage, of such Preaching, and Instruction, as is *best adapted, to their Capacity, State, and Design.*

The Governors, of the College, cannot, consistent, with the Trust committed, to them; give up, the ordinary, public Instruction, of the Students; especially, in Matters of Divinity; to any, but their *own Officers* and *Substitutes*. For, they can have, no sufficient Security, as such Governors, that others, who are not, of their Nomination, and under their Authority, will Teach, or Instruct, according, to the Design, of the *Founders*: and, if they should deviate from it; the Governors, could have, no Authority, to prevent it. And, upon that account, it is more necessary, that the Governors of the College, should nominate the Preacher to it, than any *other Officer*, or Instructor.

Particularly, it cannot be reasonable; that, either of the three, religious Assemblies, in *New-Haven*, should choose, a Minister, for the College; or that, the College, should be *obliged, to attend* upon such Preaching, as they, or either of them, should *choose*. They would not allow, that the College, should choose a Minister for *them*; much less, is it reasonable, that they, should choose a Minister, for the *College*; which is a religious Society, of a superior, more general, and more important Nature.

This would be, to subject the College, to a Jurisdiction out of itself; in the most important Point, of it's Institution, and Design. And no Society, or Body Politick, can be *safe*, but only, in it's having, a Principle of self-Preservation; and a Power, of Providing, every thing necessary, for it's own Subsistance, and Defence.

Indeed, as the College, receives it's Charter, and Part, of it's Support, from the *Government*; it is necessarily, *dependent* upon them; and under their Direction; and must choose, such a Minister as is agreeable to them, or otherwise, they may, withdraw their special Protection, and Support. And it cannot, reasonably, be suppos'd; that, the General Assembly, would neglect, this part, of their Superintendency; and suffer it, to be exercised, by any, particular Parish. For, by this means, it might easily happen, that the College, might be subjected, to such Preaching, as would be contrary, to the Minds, of the Generality, of the Colony; as well, as, the Design, of the *Founders*.

Some indeed, have supposed, that, the only Design of Colleges, was to teach the Arts, and Sciences; and that Religion, is no part, of a College Education: And therefore, there ought to be, no religious Worship upheld, or enjoined, by the Laws of the College; but every Student, may Worship, where, and how, he pleaseth; or, as his Parents, or Guardian, shall direct.

But, it is probable, that there is not a College, to be found upon Earth, upon such a Constitution; without any Regard, to Religion. And we know, that Religion, and the Religion of these Churches, in particular; both, as to *Doctrine*, and *Discipline*, was the main Design, of the *Founders*, of this College; (agreeable, to the minds, of the *Body, of the People*;) and, this Design, their Successors, are bound in Duty, to pursue. And indeed, Religion, is a matter, of so great Consequence, and Importance; that, the Knowledge, of the Arts, and Sciences, how excellent soever, in themselves, are comparatively, worth but little, without it. . . .

And, if Parents, have a *Right*, to order, what Worship, their Children shall attend, at College;' it would take, the Power, wholly out, of the Hands, of the Authority, of College, as to matters of Religion; and there may be, as many Kinds, of Religious Worship, at College; as there are, different Opinions, of Parents.

And, if Parents, give the *Law*; they must also, affix the *Penalty*; and indeed, *inflict it themselves*. But Parents, at a Distance, cannot, Govern, their Children, at College; neither, is it practicable, that, they should give, such, a just *System of Rules*, as the Authority, of College *can*, or *ought*, to put in Execution.

For, we may suppose, for Instance; that, there may be, an Assembly, of *Jews*, or *Arrians*, in *New Haven*; and then, the Authority, of College, may be obliged, to punish, the Students, for not attending, such a Worship, as they esteem, to be *worse than none*; and such, as they are obliged, by the Statutes, of the *Founders*, not to permit, the Students, to attend upon.

It has been said; that, *Liberty of Conscience*, ought, to be allowed to all; to Worship, as they please.

Upon which, it has been considered; that, the College acts, upon the Principles, of Liberty, of Conscience, in the *fullest Sense*; and suppose, that any Man, under the Limitations of the Law; may Found a College, or School, for such Ends, and Purposes; and upon such Conditions, and Limitations, with Respect to those, who are allow'd, the Benefit of it, *as he in his Conscience*, shall think best. And that *his* Conscience, who has the Property, of a Thing; or gives, it, upon Conditions; ought to Govern, in all Matters, relating to the Use, of that thing; and not, his Conscience, who is allowed, to take the Benefit; who, has *no Right* to it, but according to the *Will*, and Conditions of the Proprietor, or Donor. And Liberty of Conscience in, him, who is allow'd, to take the Benefit, extends no further, than to determine, whether he will accept it upon those Conditions. And to challenge the Benefit, without complying with the Conditions, would be, to rob the Proprietor, (or Feoffee in Trust,) of his Property; and Right of Disposal.

The great Design, of Founding this School, was to Educate Ministers in our *own Way*; and in Order to attain this End; the *Founders*, and *their Successors*, apprehend it to be necessary, that the Students, should ordinarily attend, upon the *same Way of Worship*: and should they give up, that Law, and Order; the College would serve Designs, and Purposes, *contrary* to that, for which it was *originally Founded*: which, in *Point of Conscience*, and Fidelity, to their Trust; *they cannot permit*. And in this Point, the College, Exercises, no kind of *Power*, or *Authority*; but only that, which Results, from the *natural Liberties*, and Privileges of all free, and *Voluntary Societies* of Men; which is to determine, *their own Design,* amongst themselves; and the Conditions, of their own Favors, and Benefits to *others.*

Yet the Governors of the College, have always freely admitted, Protestants, of all Denominations, to enjoy the Benefit, of an Education in it; they attending upon, (as they always have done,) our Way of Worship; while they are there.

It has also been said; that, all the Students, ought to attend, the Worship, of the Church of *England*; or so many of them, as shall see Cause; or, as their Parents shall order, or permit.

That, the Church of England, is the *Established Religion,* of this Colony; and that those, who do not conform to it, are *Schismaticks.*

Upon which, it has been consider'd, that the Act of Parliament, in the Common Prayer Book, for the Establishment, of the Church of *England,* is expressed limitted, to *England, and Wales, and the Town of Berwick, upon Tweed.* And it is, a well known Maxim in the Law; *that the Statutes of England, do not extend to the Plantations; unless, they are Expressly mentioned. . . .*

It has also been said; that, Governor *Yale,* and Bishop *Berkley,* who were Church Men, made large *Donations,* to this College.

Upon which, it has been consider'd that; when any Donation is given, after the Foundation is laid, the Law presumes, that it was the Intention, of the *Donors,* that their Donations, should be improved, according, to the Design, of the *Founders.* The Law presumes, that every Man, knows the Law, in that thing, wherein he Acts: And since, by Law, the Statutes of the Founders, cannot be altered, it presumes, that the Donor, had not any Design to do it. And there is not, the least Reason to suppose, that the Governor, or Bishop, intended, or Expected, that, upon their Donations, any alteration should be made, in the Laws of the College; or any Deviation, from the Design, of the Founders, towards *the Church of England or* any other way.

If it was so; it seems, as if they intended, to *Buy* the College, rather than make a *Donation,* to it. And if there was Evidence, that they made their Donations, upon that *Condition*; the College would *Resign* them back again.

And since, there is not, the least Reason to suppose that, they, expected, or desired, that, upon their Donations, any Alteration should be made, in the Laws of College; we see no Obligation to do it, in Point of *Gratitude. . . .*

Yet, we have a just Sense, of the Generosity, of those Gentlemen; and for that, and many other Reasons, are Willing to do, all that we can, to gratify, the Gentlemen, of the Church of England; consistant with the Design and Statutes, of the Founders; and particularly, have given Liberty, to those Students, who have been educated, in the Worship, of the Church of England; and are, of that Communion; to be absent, at those Times, when the Sacrament is Administered, in that Church; and upon Christmas; and, at some such other Times, as will not be, an Infraction upon, the general, and *standing Rules,* of College.

It has been further said, that there are, a Number of Church Men, in this Colony; who, in the annual public Taxes, contribute something, towards the Support, of the College.

Upon which, it has been consider'd; that, when a Community, are jointly, at some public Charge; it is equitable, that the Benefit, of each Individual, should be consulted, so far, as it is consistant, with the general Design, and Good of the whole, or the Majority. And tho' it is impossible, that such a Benefit, should be Mathematically proportioned, to each Individual; yet this College, has educated, as many Episcopal Ministers, and others, as they desired, or stood in need of; which has been a sufficient Compensation, for their Paying, about, a Half Peny Sterling, per Man; in the annual Support, of the College.

And it may still continue to be, as serviceable, to the Church of England, as it has been, if they please; for the Orders of it, remain in Substance, just the same.

It may further be consider'd, that this College, was Founded, and in a good measure, Indowed, many Years, before there were any Donations made, by Church-Men; or so much, as one Episcopal Minister, in the Colony. And if Mens contributing, something, towards the Support of the College; gives, them a Right, to order, what Worship, their Children shall attend upon, while at College; it gives the same Right, to Parents, of all other Denominations; which to admit, as was before Observ'd, would defeat the Design of the *Founders*; and destroy, the religious Order, of the College; which ought, *sacredly*, to be observed.

OPPOSITION TO A SECTARIAN COLLEGE IN NEW YORK (1753) From William Livingston et al., eds., *Weekly Essays on Sundry Important Subjects, More Particularly Adapted to the Province of New York . . .* as quoted in Herbert and Carol Schneider, eds., *Samuel Johnson, His Career and Writings* (New York, 1929), vol. IV, pp. 122-43.

[*March 22, 1753*]

There is no place where we receive a greater variety of impressions, than at colleges. Nor do any instructions sink so deep in the mind as those that are there received. . . . The students not only receive the dogmata of their teachers with an implicit faith, but are also constantly studying how to support them against every objection. The system of the college is generally taken for true, and the sole business is to defend it. Freedom of thought rarely penetrates those contracted mansions of systematical learning. But to teach the established notions, and maintain certain hypotheses, *hic Labor hoc opus est*. Every deviation from the beaten tract, is a kind of literary heresy; and if the professor be given to excommunication, can scarce escape an anathema. Hence that dogmatical turn and impatience of contradiction, so observable in the generality of academics. To this also is to be referred, those voluminous compositions, and that learned lumber of gloomy pedants, which hath so long infested and corrupted the world. In a word, all those visionary whims, idle speculations, fairy dreams, and party distinctions, which contract and imbitter the mind, and have so often turned the world topsy-turvy.

I mention not this to disparage an academical education, from which I hope I have myself received some benefit, especially after having worn off some of its rough corners, by a freer conversation with mankind. The purpose for which I urge it, is to show the narrow turn usually prevailing at colleges, and the absolute necessity of teaching nothing that will afterwards require the melancholy retro-graduation of being unlearned. . . .

At Harvard College in the Massachusetts-Bay, and at Yale College in Connecticut, the Presbyterian profession is in some sort established. It is in these colonies the commendable practice of all who can afford it, to give their sons an education at their respective seminaries of learning. While they are in the course of their education, they are sure to be instructed in the arts of maintaining the religion of the college, which is always that of their immediate instructors; and of combating the principles of all other Christians whatever. When the young gentlemen have run thro' the course of their education, they enter into the ministry, or some offices of the government, and acting in them under the influence of the doctrines espoused in the morning of life, the spirit of the college is transfused thro' the colony, and tinctures the genius and policy of the public administration, from the Governor down to the Constable. Hence the Episcopalians cannot acquire an equal strength among them, till some new regulations, in matters of religion, prevail in their colleges, which perpetually produce adversaries to the hierarchical system. Nor is it to be questioned, that the universities in North and South Britain, greatly support the different professions that are established in their respective divisions. . . .

March 29, 1753

Should our college, therefore, unhappily thro' our own bad policy, fall into the hands of any one religious sect in the province: should that sect, which is more than probable, establish its religion in the college, show favor to its votaries, and cast contempt upon others; 'tis easy to foresee, that Christians of all other denominations amongst us, instead of encouraging its prosperity, will, from the same principles, rather conspire to oppose and oppress it. Besides English and Dutch Presbyterians, which perhaps exceed all our other religious professions put together, we have Episcopalians, Anabaptists, Lutherans, Quakers, and a growing Church of Moravians, all equally zealous for their discriminating tenets. Whichsoever of these has the sole government of the college, will kindle the jealousy of the rest, not only against the persuasion so preferred, but the college itself. Nor can any thing less be expected, than a general discontent and tumult; which, affecting all ranks of people, will naturally tend to disturb the tranquility and peace of the province.

In such a state of things, we must not expect the children of any, but of that sect which prevails in the academy will ever be sent to it: for should they, the established tenets must either be implicitly received, or a perpetual religious war necessarily maintained. Instead of the liberal arts and sciences, and such attainments as would best qualify the students to be useful and ornamental to their country, party cavils and disputes about trifles, will afford topics of argumentation to their incredible disadvantage, by a fruitless consumption of time. Such gentlemen, therefore, who can afford it, will give their sons an education abroad, or at some of the neighboring academies, where equally imbibing a zeal for their own principles, and furnished with the arts of defending them, an incessant opposition to all others, on their return, will be the unavoidable consequence. . . .

It is farther to be remarked, that a public academy is, or ought to be a mere civil institution, and cannot with any tolerable propriety be monopolized by any religious sect. The design of such seminaries, hath been sufficiently shown in my last paper, to be entirely political, and calculated for the benefit of society, as a society, without any intention to teach religion, which is the province of the pulpit: tho' it must, at the same time, be confessed, that a judicious choice of our principles, chiefly depends on a free education. . . .

It has in my two last papers been shown, what an extensive and commanding influence the seat of learning will have over the whole province, by diffusing its dogmata and principles thro' every office of church and state. What use will be made of such unlimited advantages, may be easily guessed. The civil and religious principles of the trustees, will become universally established, liberty and happiness be driven without our borders, and in their room erected the banners of spiritual and temporal bondage. My readers may, perhaps, regard such reflections as the mere sallies of a roving fancy; tho', at the same time, nothing in nature can be more real. For should the trustees be prompted by ambition, to stretch their authority to unreasonable lengths, as undoubtedly they would, were they under no kind of restraint, the consequence is very evident. Their principal care would be to choose such persons to instruct our youth, as would be the fittest instruments to extend their power by positive and dogmatical precepts. Besides which, it would be their mutual interest to pursue one scheme. Their power would become formidable by being united: as on the contrary, a dissention would impede its progress. Blind obedience and servility in church and state, are the only natural means to establish unlimited sway. Doctrines of this cast would be publicly taught and inculcated. Our youth, inured to oppression from their infancy, would afterwards vigorously exert themselves in their several offices, to poison the whole community with slavish opinions, and one universal establishment become the fatal portion of this now happy and opulent province.

April 12, 1753

Instead of a charter, I would propose, that the college be founded and incorporated by Act of Assembly, and that not only because it ought to be under the inspection of the civil authority; but also, because such a constitution will be more permanent, better endowed, less liable to abuse, and more capable of answering its true end. . . .

Another reason that strongly evinces the necessity of an Act of Assembly, for the incorporation of our intended academy, is, that by this means that spirit of freedom, which I have in my former papers, shown to be necessary to the increase of learning, and its consequential advantages, may be rendered impregnable to all attacks. While the government of the college is in the hands of the people, or their guardians, its design cannot be perverted. As we all value our liberty and happiness, we shall all naturally encourage those means by which our liberty and happiness will necessarily be improved: and as we never can be supposed wilfully to barter our freedom and felicity, for slavery and misery, we shall certainly crush the growth of those principles, upon which the latter are built, by cultivating and encouraging their opposites. Our college therefore, if it be incorporated by Act of Assembly, instead of opening a door to universal bigotry and establishment in church, and tyranny and oppression in the state, will secure us in the enjoyment of our respective privileges both civil and religious. For as we are split into so great a variety of opinions and professions; had each individual his share in the government of the academy, the jealousy of all parties combating each other, would inevitably produce a perfect freedom for each particular party.

Should the college be founded upon an Act of Assembly, the Legislature would have it in their power, to inspect the conduct of its governors, to divest those of authority who abused it, and appoint in their stead, friends to the cause of learning, and the general welfare of the province. Against this, no bribes, no solicitations would be effectual: no sect or denomination plead an exemption: but as all parties are subject to their authority; so would they all feel its equal influence in this particular. Hence should the trustees pursue any steps but those that lead to public emolument, their fate would be certain, their doom inevitable. Every officer in the college being under the narrow aspect and scrutiny of the civil authority, would be continually subject to the wholesome alternative, either of performing his duty, with the utmost exactness, or giving up his post to a person of superior integrity. By this means, the prevalence of doctrines destructive of the privileges of human nature, would effectually be discouraged, principles of public virtue inculcated, and every thing promoted that bears the stamp of general utility. . . .

April 19, 1753

The Fifth Article I propose is, that no religious profession in particular be established in the college; but that both officers and scholars be at perfect liberty to attend any Protestant Church at their pleasure respectively: and that the Corporation be absolutely inhibited the making of any by-laws relating to religion, except such as compel them to attend Divine Service at some church or other, every Sabbath, as they shall be able, lest so invaluable a liberty be abused and made a cloak for licentiousness.

To this most important head, I should think proper to subjoin,

Sixthly: That the whole college be every morning and evening convened to attend public prayers, to be performed by the President, or in his absence, by either of the Fellows; and that such forms be prescribed and adhered to as all Protestants can freely join in.

ADVERTISEMENT ON THE OPENING OF KINGS COLLEGE, NEW YORK (COLUMBIA UNIVERSITY) (1754)   From *New York Mercury*, June 3, 1754.

To such parents as have now (or expect to have) children prepared to be educated in the College of New York.

I. As the gentlemen who are appointed by the Assembly to be trustees of the intended seminary or college of New York have thought fit to appoint me to take the charge of it, and have concluded to set up a course of tuition in the learned languages and in the liberal arts and sciences, they have judged it advisable that I should publish this advertisement to inform such as have children ready for a college education that it is proposed to begin tuition upon the first day of July next at the vestry room in the new schoolhouse adjoining to Trinity Church in New York, which the gentlemen of the vestry are so good as to favour them with the use of in the interim 'till a convenient place may be built.

II. The lowest qualifications they have judged requisite in order to admission into the said college are as follows, viz.: that they be able to read well and write a good legible hand, and that they be well versed in the five first rules in arithmetic, i.e., as far as division and reduction; and as to Latin and Greek, that they have a good knowledge in the grammars and be able to make grammatical Latin; and both in construing and parsing to give a good account of two or three of the first select orations of Tully and of the first books of Virgil's *Aeneid* and some of the first chapters of the Gospel of St. John in Greek. In these books, therefore, they may expect to be examined; but higher qualifications must hereafter be expected. And if there be any of the higher classes in any college or under private instruction that incline to come hither, they may expect admission to proportionably higher classes here.

III. And that people may be the better satisfied in sending their children for education to this college, it is to be understood that as to religion, there is no intention to impose on the scholars the peculiar tenets of any particular sect of Christians, but to inculcate upon their tender minds the great principles of Christianity and morality in which true Christians of each denomination are generally agreed. And as to the daily worship in the college, morning and evening, it is proposed that it should ordinarily consist of such a collection of lessons, prayers, and praises of the liturgy of the Church as are for the most part taken out of the Holy Scriptures, and such as are agreed on by the trustees to be in the best manner expressive of our common Christianity. And as to any peculiar tenets, everyone is left to judge freely for himself and to be required only to attend constantly at such places of worship on the Lord's Day as their parent or guardians shall think fit to order or permit.

IV. The chief thing that is aimed at in this college is to teach and engage the children to know God in Jesus Christ and to love and serve Him in all sobriety, godliness, and righteousness of life, with a perfect heart and a willing mind, and to train them up in all virtuous habits and all such useful knowledge as may render them creditable to their families and friends, ornaments to their country, and useful to the public weal in their generations. To which good purposes it is earnestly desired that their parents, guardians, and masters would train them up from their cradles under strict government and in all seriousness, virtue, and industry, that they may be qualified to make orderly and tractable members of this society. And above all, that in order hereunto they be very careful themselves to set them good examples of true piety and virtue in their own conduct. For as examples have a very powerful influence over young minds, and especially those of their parents, in vain are they solicitous for a good education for their children if they themselves set before them examples of impiety and profaneness or of any sort of vice whatsoever.

Vth and lastly. A serious, virtuous, and industrious course of life being first provided for, it is further the design of this college to instruct and perfect the youth in the learned languages and in the arts of reasoning exactly, of writing correctly, and speaking eloquently; and in the arts of numbering and measuring, of surveying and navigation, of geography and history, of husbandry, commerce, and government; and in the knowledge of all nature in the heavens above us, and in the air, water, and earth around us, and the various kinds of meteors, stones, mines and minerals, plants and animals, and of every thing useful for the comfort, the convenience, and elegance of life in the chief manufactures relating to any of these things. And finally, to lead them from the study of nature to the knowledge of themselves and of the God of nature and their duty to Him, themselves, and one another, and everything that can contribute to their true happiness both here and hereafter.

Thus much, gentlemen, it was thought proper to advertise you of concerning the nature and design of this college. And I pray God it may be attended with all the success you can wish for the best good of the rising generations to which, while I continue here, I shall willingly contribute my endeavours to the utmost of my power.

Gentlemen,

Your real friend and most humble servant,

Samuel Johnson

N.B. The charge of the tuition is established by the trustees to be only twenty-five shillings for each quarter.

RULES OF KINGS COLLEGE (1755)   From Herbert and Carol Schneider, eds., *Samuel Johnson, President of Kings College* (New York, 1929), pp. 225-29.

I. *Of Admissions*

First. None shall be admitted (unless by a particular act of the governors) but such as can read the first three of Tully's Select Orations and the three first books of Virgil's Aeneid into English, and the ten first chapters of St. John's Gospel in Greek, into Latin and such as are well versed in all the rules of Clark's Introduction so as to make true grammatical Latin and are expert in arithmetic so far as the rule of reduction to be examined by the president or fellows:

2ndly. Every scholar shall have a copy of these laws and his admittatur shall be signed at the end of them by the president upon his promising all due obedience to them which promise shall be expressed in writing under his hand.

II. *Of Graduation*

First. The examination of candidates for the degree of Bachelor of Arts shall be held in the college hall about six weeks before commencement by the president or fellows when any of the governors or any who have been Master of Arts in this college may be present and ask any question they think proper and such candidates as have resided four years and are then found competently versed in the sciences wherein they have been instructed shall then be admitted to expect their degree at commencement which shall be on the second Wednesday in May.

2ndly. Such as have diligently pursued their studies for three years after being admitted to their Bachelor's degree; and have been guilty of no gross immorality shall be admitted to the degree of Master of Arts.

3rdly. No candidate shall be admitted to either of these degrees without fulfilling the terms above appointed unless in case of extraordinary capacity and diligence and by a particular act of the governors of the college.

4thly. Every one that is admitted to either degree shall pay a pistole to the president.

III. Of the Public Worship

First. The president or one of the professors or fellows in his absence shall every morning and evening read the form of prayers established by the governors of the college and according to the rules and method therein prescribed.

2ndly. Every student shall constantly attend the said public service at such stated hours as the president shall appoint and those that absent themselves shall for every offense be fined twopence, and one penny for not coming in due season, unless they can allege such reasons for their absence or tardiness as shall appear sufficient to the president.

3dly. Every pupil shall constantly attend on the public worship every Lord's Day at such church or meeting as his parents or guardians order him to frequent and for every neglect shall be obliged to perform such extraordinary exercise as the president and professors or fellows shall appoint unless he hath some reasonable excuse admitted to be sufficient by the president.

4thly. Every pupil shall behave with the utmost decency at public worship, or in the hall and whoever is proved guilty of any profane or indecent behavior as talking, laughing, justling, winking, etc., he shall submit to an admonition for the first offense and to an extraordinary exercise for the second, and if obstinate, expelled.

IV. Of Moral Behavior

First. If any pupil shall be convicted of drunkenness, fornication, lying, theft, swearing, cursing, or any other scandalous immorality he shall submit to open admonition and confession of his fault or be expelled if his crime is judged to heinous for any lesser punishment and especially if he be contumacious.

2ndly. None of the pupils shall frequent houses of ill fame, or keep company with any persons of known scandalous behavior and such as may endanger either their principles or morals; and those that do so shall first be openly rebuked and if they obstinately persist in it they shall be expelled.

3rdly. None of the pupils shall fight cocks, play at cards, dice or any unlawful game upon penalty of being fined not exceeding five shillings for the first offense, and being openly admonished and confessing their fault for the second, and expulsion, if contumacious.

4thly. If any pupil shall be convicted of fighting, maiming, slandering, or grievously abusing any person he shall be fined three shillings for the first offense and if he repeats his offense he shall be further punished by fine, admonition, suspension, or expulsion according to the aggravation of his fault, especially if contumacious.

5thly. If any pupil be convicted of any dilapidations of the college or any injury done to the estates, goods or persons of any others he shall be obliged to make good all damages.

V. Of Behavior Towards Authority and Superiors

First. If any pupils be disobedient to the president, professors or fellows of the college or treat them or any others in authority with any insulting, disrespectful or contemptuous language or deportment, he shall be fined not exceeding five shillings for the first offense or submit to open admonition and confession of his fault, according to the nature of it and be expelled if he persists contumacious.

2ndly. Every pupil shall treat all his superiors and especially the authority of the college with all duty and respect by all such good manners and behavior as common decency, and good breeding require, such as rising, standing, uncovering the head, preserving a proper distance and using the most respectful language, etc., and he that behaves otherwise shall be punished at the discretion of the president and fellows or governors according to the nature and degree of his ill behavior.

VI. Of College Exercises and Due Attendance

First. The business of the first year shall be to go on and perfect their studies in the Latin and Greek classics and go over a system of rhetoric, geography and chronology and such as are designed for the pulpit shall also study the Hebrew.

2ndly. The business of the second and third years shall be after a small system of logic to study the mathematics and the mathematical and experimental philosophy in all the several branches of it, with agriculture and merchandise, together with something of the classics and criticism all the while.

3rdly. The fourth year is to be devoted to the studies of metaphysics, logic and moral philosophy, with something of criticism and the chief principles of law and government, together with history, sacred and profane.

4thly. The pupils in each of their terms shall be obliged, at such times as the president shall appoint, to make exercises in the several branches of learning suitable to their standing both in Latin and English, such as declamations and dissertations on various questions pro and con, and frequently these and syllogistical reasonings.

5thly. Whoever shall misbehave in time of exercise by talking, laughing, or justling one another, etc., shall be fined one shilling for each offense.

6thly. All the pupils shall be obliged to apply themselves with the utmost diligence to their studies and constantly attend upon all the exercises appointed by the president or their tutors or professors for their instruction.

7thly. None of the pupils shall be absent from their chambers or neglect their studies without leave obtained of the president or their respective tutors, except for morning and evening prayers and recitation and half an hour for breakfast and an hour and a half after dinner and from evening prayer till nine of the clock at night. The penalty, four pence or some exercise for each offense.

8thly. If any student shall persist in the neglect of his studies either through obstinacy or negligence and so frequently fails of making due preparation for recitation and other appointed exercises and if he refuse to submit and reform after due admonition he shall be rusticated, i. e., suspended for a time, and if he does not bring sufficient evidence of his reformation he shall be expelled.

9thly. No student shall go out of town without the president's or his tutor's leave, unless at the stated vacation upon penalty of five shillings and for repeating his fault he shall be rusticated, and if contumacious, expelled.

N.B. The stated vacations are a month after commencement, one week at

Michaelmas and a fortnight at Christmas, and Easter Week, *i.e.*, from Good Friday till the Friday following, which last being so near commencement is to be considered as only a vacation from exercises but not from the college or daily morning and evening prayers, and so does not come within the last prohibition.

All the fines shall be paid to the treasurer of the college to be laid out in books and disposed of as a reward to such of the scholars as shall excell in the course of their studies in their several classes as the president, professors and tutors or the major part of them shall direct.

COMMENCEMENT AT KINGS COLLEGE (1758)   From *New York Mercury,* June 26, 1758.

Mr. Printer, please to insert the following in your next paper. Wednesday last being the day appointed by the Governors of King's College, in this city, for the commencement, I had the pleasure of being present at the first solemnity of the kind ever celebrated here; which was, thro' the whole, conducted with much elegance and propriety. The order of the procession from the vestry room, where the college is now held, to St. George's Chapel, was as follows: The President, with his Honor the Lieutenant Governor, who, by his presence graced the solemnity, were preceded by the candidates for Bachelor's and Master's Degrees, with their heads uncovered, and were followed by the Governors of the college, the clergy of all denominations in this city, and other gentlemen of distinction of this and the neighboring provinces. After short prayers suitable to the ocassion, the Reverend Dr. Johnson, the President, from the pulpit, opened the solemnity, with a learned and elegant *Oratio Inauguralis.* The exercises of the Bachelors were introduced by a polite salutory oration, delivered by Provost, with such propriety of pronunciation, and so engaging an air, as justly gained him the admiration and applause of all present. This was followed by a metaphysical thesis, learnedly defended by Ritzema against Ver Planck and Cortlandt, with another held by Reed, and opposed by two Ogdens. The Bachelor's exercises were closed by a well composed, genteel English oration, on the advantages of a liberal education, delivered by Cortlandt, whose fine address added a beauty to the sentiment, which give universal satisfaction to that numerous assembly. After this Mr. Treadwell, in a clear and concise manner, demonstrated the revolution of the earth around the sun, both from astronomical observations, and the theory of gravity, and defended the thesis against Mr. Cutting and Mr. Wetmore, a candidate for the Degree of Master of Arts. This dispute being ended, the President descended from the pulpit, and being seated in a chair, in a solemn manner, conferred the honors of the college upon those pupils who were candidates for a Bachelor's Degree, and on several gentlemen who had received degrees in other colleges. The exercises were concluded with a Valedictory oration (in Latin) by Mr. Cutting, universally esteemed a masterly performance. The President then addressed himself in a solemn pathetic exhortation, to the Bachelors, which could not fail of answering the most valuable purposes, and leaving a lasting impression on the minds of all the pupils. The whole solemnity being finished by a short prayer, the procession returned back to the City-Arms, where an elegant entertainment was provided by the governors of the college. This important occasion drew together a numerous assembly of people of all orders, and it gave me a sincere pleasure to see the exercises performed in a manner which must reflect honor upon the college and incite every friend of his country, to promote so useful, so well regulated an institution.

HARVARD'S OPPOSITION TO A COLLEGE IN WEST MASSACHUSETTS

(1762) From Josiah Quincy, *The History of Harvard University* (Cambridge, Mass., 1840), vol. II, pp. 464-69.

"1762. 18 March. Reasons against founding a College, or Collegiate School in the County of Hampshire, humbly offered to the consideration of his Excellency Francis Bernard, Esquire, Governor of the Province of Massachusetts Bay, &c., by the Overseers of Harvard College, in New England.

"May it please your Excellency,

"(1.) We beg leave to observe, that Harvard College was originally founded by our Forefathers, with a laudable view to the general interest of learning and religion in this country; and that this is properly the College of the Government, it having been established, and all along patronized and supported, by the Legislature. For so early as the year 1642, the General Court manifested their great concern for its prosperity, and for accomplishing the important end of this institution, by constituting the Governor and Deputy Governor for the time being, all the Magistrates (or Councillors) of this jurisdiction with the teaching Elders (or Congregational Ministers) of Boston, and five other next adjoining towns, and the President of said College for the time being, the Overseers and Guardians of it. This shows the sense they had of its importance, and that they considered the common public good as closely connected with the growth and prosperity of this seminary of learning. And the charter of the College, granted afterwards in 1650, refers to the said Overseers, as being legally intrusted with the care and superintendence thereof; which charter was to all intents and purposes confirmed in and by the royal charter of William and Mary, granted to this province in the third year of their reign.

"(2.) The said Overseers have, accordingly, from first to last, superintended the affairs of the College; having taken care, while a general liberty was allowed for Christians of different denominations to send their children thither, and the rights of conscience were duly preserved, that the rules, laws, and orders of the society should be such as tended to promote substantial learning and good religious principles and morals, in conformity to the generous, pious, and extensive views of the government in its establishment, viz. the education of the "youth of this country, in knowledge and godliness;" as it is expressed in the College Charter before referred to. And the said Overseers have from time to time interested themselves in all the important concerns of the College; using their endeavours, that the true designs of this Institution might be answered, and guarding against whatever had an apparent tendency to counteract and defeat them.

"(3.) In conformity to which laudable example, as well as to the nature of the trust reposed in us by the government, we think ourselves obliged, by all lawful and honorable means, to promote the interests of said College, and to prevent, as far as in us lies, any thing which would certainly or very probably be detrimental to it. And we are humbly of opinion, that in the capacity of Overseers we not only may with the utmost propriety, but are in duty bound, as far as decency will allow, to appear in opposition to any proposal which either directly interferes with the good of the College in Cambridge, or which in our apprehension would be prejudicial to the general interest of literature and religion "in this country." Neither do we well know how to separate the real, proper interests of the College from what the government originally declared, and is known to be, the important end of its establishment.

"(4.) Your Excellency will permit us farther to say, in conformity to these sentiments, that we were not a little alarmed for the College under our care, when we first heard of a proposal for founding a College in the County of Hampshire, and of a petition preferred to the government for a charter to that end. And it touched us with a very sensible sorrow, to understand afterwards, when the said petition would not pass the General Court, that your Excellency had gratified the petitioners, by preparing a charter in his Majesty's name for the general purposes aforesaid. With the validity or legality of which charter, supposing it actually to issue, we do not now concern ourselves; being very sensible, as your Excellency intimated to us on a late occasion, that whatever our thoughts may be as to that point, it does not belong to us as Overseers of the College to declare them, or to dispute your Excellency's authority to grant charters.

"(5.) But waving this matter, as being beside our proper business in this capacity, we take the liberty to declare it as our opinion, that the founding another College in this Province, would not only be quite unnecessary, but really prejudicial to Harvard College, and to the common interest of learning and religion in the country. That establishing another College exactly, or nearly, upon *the same footing* with that at Cambridge, so as to interfere with it, or supersede the occasion for sending youth to it from other parts of the Province, would be of bad consequence in divers respects, we need not labor to prove, your Excellency at a late meeting of the Overseers having declared yourself so fully to that effect.

"(6.) We are further of opinion, with all proper deference to your Excellency, that there is no real difference betwixt a College and a Collegiate School, particularly such an one as is proposed in the County of Hampshire; and that such an institution there, agreeably to the views of the persons who lately applied to you for a charter, and according to the express tenor of the charter itself, which your Excellency had prepared to that end, would be to all intents founding, not only a real College, but a rival to that at Cambridge; one, whose interests would interfere very essentially with those of the latter, and consequently a College, which, instead of being any ways subservient or useful, would be highly detrimental to it. Although, from the concern which you have heretofore manifested for the prosperity of Harvard College, and from your late repeated declarations to that purpose, we believe it was far from your Excellency's intention to do a real prejudice thereto. But that the founding such a College, or Collegiate School, in Hampshire, (we suppose, Sir, it is quite immaterial by which name it is called,) would really be an essential detriment to Harvard College, we think evident from the following considerations.

"(7.) The known, acknowledged design of the few gentlemen, who lately made application for a charter, and who pressed that affair so warmly, was, to found such a seminary of learning as should to all intents answer the ends of a College; one, in which the education of youth in that part of the country might be completed, without their being sent to Cambridge for that purpose, which they represented as inconvenient and very expensive; this design they did not even pretend to disguise, but openly professed from the first. And there is sufficient reason to think, that they would not even have accepted, much less so importunately desired, a charter only for an inferior school; after having all the advantages of which, it should be thought necessary for their youth to come and reside at Cambridge, though but a year or two, to finish their education. This was very far from their intention, as is well known. So that the College proposed by these gentlemen was by no means one subordinate and subservient to Harvard College; but one which might serve them effectually in lieu thereof; and therefore one to be set up in competition with, if not in direct opposition to it.

"(8.) We are also humbly of opinion, that the charter, which your Excellency had prepared in order to the establishing a College in Hampshire, was in fact adapted to answer the aforesaid designs and views of those who requested it. For it constitutes them a body politic, with many great privileges; and is, in some respects, a more full and ample charter, than that of Harvard College; particularly as it allows them to hold lands or other real estate, the annual income of which shall be double to that of the lands which the other corporation is permitted to hold. The College itself is to be honored with the name of Queen's College. And whereas Harvard College has Overseers, a President, Professors, Fellows, and Tutors; it is provided, that Queen's College should have a President, Trustees, a Master, Preceptors or Tutors, expressly; and it may, in consistence with said charter, have Professors also in the various branches of science and literature. In respect of which name of this intended seminary of learning and these titles of its governors, officers, and teachers, it will be at least upon a par with Harvard College. And, to say the least, there is nothing in this charter, which discovers the intention of it to be the founding a College in any respect inferior to the other; much less preparatory and subservient to it. It is, indeed, intimated in this charter itself, that one reason for establishing a College in Hampshire is, that the people in those parts might not be subjected to the necessity, to the supposed inconvenience and greater expense, of sending their children so far as Cambridge for an education; in which respect it exactly corresponds to the known views of those in whose favor said charter was prepared, as to having a real and every way sufficient College of their own, to serve that part of the country as Harvard College used to serve the whole.

"(9.) And whereas your Excellency, since the said charter was prepared, proposed, by an additional clause, expressly to except the power of conferring degrees from the number of privileges granted thereby; we apprehend this would be very far from preventing the ill consequences of such an institution, since it would be easy, by the by-laws of the society, to make provision for giving such honorary certificates and ample testimonials, as would in a great measure defeat the intention of such a restrictive clause. But if any considerable inconvenience should be found to arise from the want of such a collegiate privilege, yet a College being once founded, we apprehend that the persons, who had influence enough to carry this most essential point, would after a while much easier find means to get that defect supplied, and their privileges extended, agreeably to their original plan. Neither can it be thought, that any thing short of this will finally satisfy them.

"(10.) These things, Sir, being duly considered,—the known professed views of the persons, who solicited for a charter, the plain tenor of *that*, prepared by your Excellency's order, and what it manifestly lays a foundation for,—we are of opinion, that if such a charter should take effect, it would actually be the erecting a College in Hampshire, as a competitor with that at Cambridge; which would operate to the disadvantage of the latter, in proportion to the number and wealth, to the reputation and influence, of those who are or shall be hereafter favorers of the former. And, with your Excellency's permission, we will now a little more particularly lay open our apprehensions with reference to the bad consequences of such an institution;—a point, as we conceive, of much the greatest importance to Harvard College, and to the interest of learning among us, that ever came under the consideration of the board of Overseers.

"(11.) One College, if well regulated and endowed, is we suppose, abundantly sufficient for this Province, considering its extent; and would be much more serviceable than two or more, whose interests interfere; as we think it evident beyond all doubt, that the interests of Harvard College, and of such an one as is proposed, would do. For though it is said, that the Collegiate Schools in England are rather subservient and useful than any ways prejudicial to the Universities there, or to the common interests of learning; we conceive, that the circumstances of the mother country and of those Universities (ancient, rich, and renowned) are so widely different from those of this country, and of our own yet young and feeble College, that there can be no good arguing from one to the other. There is no danger or possibility of those Schools ever proving rivals to, or coming into any sort of competition with, the Universities; and therefore not of their being detrimental to them. Especially when it is considered, that some of the principal of these schools, if not all of them, were, as we understand, founded expressly in subordination to, and in dependence upon, the Universities; as nurseries, out of which the brightest and most promising youths are from time to time to be selected, whose education is to be perfected at the Universities; for which it is said there are particular establishments. Whereas Queen's College, so far as appears by the charter, is to be in no respect preparatory to, or dependent upon, the College in Cambridge. Neither is the latter yet arrived to such maturity, strength, and perfection, as to be out of danger of receiving great prejudice from such a competitor or rival, as the other might prove.—We do not mean in point of real excellence in literature, of which we have no reason to be apprehensive, but in other respects. And—

"(12.) Particularly as our college, yet in its infant state, is hitherto but meanly endowed, and very poor, the unhappy consequences of which are too obvious; and we think that the founding another college would be the most probable and effectual way to prevent its being hereafter endowed in such a manner as all who desire its prosperity doubtless wish to see it. For, if such a college as is proposed were founded in Hampshire, it cannot be thought that persons living in that part of the country, who might be favorers of it, in respect of its vicinity, or on any other account, would be willing to bear a part in endowing that at Cambridge, whether in a legislative or private capacity. It may naturally be concluded that they would rather endeavour to obstruct all schemes and proposals to this end; judging very justly, that the growth and flourishing of their own college depended in some measure upon the languishing and depression of the other. At least it may be concluded, that they would represent it as a heavy, intolerable grievance to be obliged by law to do any thing towards the encouragement and support of a college, from which they expected no immediate benefit, while they had one of their own to support, on which they had their dependence, and which stood in at least equal need. And besides, if such a college were founded, it might probably receive some legacies, or private donations, which would otherwise come to the College in Cambridge. So that we conceive the latter would at least lose some friends and benefactors, if not find some positive enemies, by the establishing another college in the manner intended. And the certain consequence of such a division and opposition of interests, as we think must needs be occasioned by this means, will be the keeping low, and greatly cramping, that college, whose prosperity we so justly and sincerely desire.

CHARTER OF RHODE ISLAND COLLEGE (BROWN UNIVERSITY)

(**1764**)   From Reuben A. Guild, *Early History of Brown University, Including the Life, Times, and Correspondence of President Manning, 1756-1791* (Providence, 1897), pp. 535-42.

At the General Assembly of the Governor and Company of the English Colony of Rhode Island and Providence Plantations, in New England, in America, begun and holden by adjournment, at East Greenwich, within and for the Colony aforesaid, on the last Monday in February, in the year of our Lord One Thousand Seven Hundred and Sixty-four, and fourth of the Reign of his most sacred Majesty, George the Third, by the grace of God, King of Great Britain, and so forth.

An Act
for the
Establishment
of a
College
or
University
within this Colony.

WHEREAS institutions for liberal education are highly beneficial to society, by forming the rising generation to virtue, knowledge, and useful literature; and thus preserving in the community a succession of men duly qualified for discharging the offices of life with usefulness and reputation; they have therefore justly merited and received the attention and encouragement of every wise and well-regulated State: And whereas a public school or seminary, erected for that purpose within this Colony, to which the youth may freely resort for education in the vernacular and learned languages, and in the liberal arts and sciences, would be for the general advantage and honor of the government:

✻   ✻   ✻

And furthermore, by the authority aforesaid, it is hereby enacted, ordained and declared, that it is now, and at all times hereafter shall continue to be, the unalterable constitution of this College, or University, that the Corporation thereof shall consist of two branches, to wit: That of the Trustees, and that of the Fellowship, with distinct, separate, and respective powers: And that the number of the Trustees shall, and may be thirty-six; of which twenty-two shall forever be elected of the denomination called Baptists, or Antipedobaptists; five shall forever be elected of the denomination called Friends, or Quakers; four shall forever be elected of the denomination called Congregationalists, and five shall forever be elected of the denomination called Episcopalians: And that the succession in this branch shall be forever chosen and filled up from the respective denominations in this proportion, and according to these numbers: which are hereby fixed, and shall remain to perpetuity immutably the same.

*   *   *

And that the number of the Fellows, inclusive of the President (who shall always be a Fellow), shall and may be twelve; of which, eight shall be forever elected of the denomination called Baptists, or Antipedobaptists; and the rest indifferently of any or all denominations.

*   *   *

And furthermore, it is declared and ordained, that the succession in both branches shall at all times hereafter be filled up and supplied according to these numbers, and this established and invariable proportion from the respective denominations by the separate election of both branches of this Corporation, which shall at all times sit and act by separate and distinct powers; and in general, in order to the validity and consummation of all acts, there shall be in the exercise of their respective, separate, and distinct powers, the joint concurrence of the Trustees and Fellows, by their respective majorities, except in adjudging and conferring the academical degrees, which shall forever belong, exclusively, to the Fellowship as a learned faculty.

And furthermore, it is constituted, that the instruction and immediate government of the College shall forever be, and rest in the President and Fellows, or Fellowship.

*   *   *

And furthermore, it is hereby enacted and declared, That into this liberal and catholic Institution shall never be admitted any religious tests: But on the contrary, all the members hereof shall forever enjoy full, free, absolute, and uninterrupted liberty of conscience: And that the places of Professors, Tutors, and all other officers, the President alone excepted, shall be free and open for all denominations of Protestants: And that youth of all religious denominations shall and may be freely admitted to the equal advantages, emoluments, and honors of the College or University; and shall receive a like fair, generous, and equal treatment, during their residence therein, they conducting themselves peaceably, and conforming to the laws and statutes thereof. And that the public teaching shall, in general, respect the sciences; and that the sectarian differences of opinions shall not make any part of the public and classical instruction: Although all religious controversies may be studied freely, examined, and explained by the President, Professors, and Tutors, in a personal, separate, and distinct manner, to the youth of any or each denomination: And above all, a constant regard be paid to, and effectual care taken of the morals of the College.

And furthermore, for the honor and encouragement of literature, we constitute and declare the Fellowship aforesaid, a learned faculty; and do hereby give, grant unto, and invest them, and their successors, with full power and authority, and they are hereby authorized and empowered, by their President, and in his absence, by the senior Fellow, or one of the Fellows appointed by themselves at the anniversary Commencement, or at any other times, and at all times hereafter, to admit to, and confer any and all the learned degrees, which can or ought to be given and conferred in any of the colleges or universities in America; or any such other degrees of literary honor as they shall devise, upon any and all such candidates and persons as the President and Fellows, or Fellowship, shall judge worthy of the academical honors: Which power of conferring degrees is hereby restricted to the learned faculty, who shall or may issue diplomas, or certificates, of such degrees, or confer degrees by diplomas, and authenticate them with the public seal of the Corporation, and the hands of the President and Secretary, and of all the Professors, as witnesses, and deliver them to the graduates as honorable and perpetual testimonies.

And furthermore, for the greater encouragement of the Seminary of learning, and that the same may be amply endowed and enfranchised with the same privileges, dignities, and immunities enjoyed by the American colleges, and European universities, We do grant, enact, ordain, and declare, and it is hereby granted, enacted, ordained, and declared, That the College estate, the estates, persons, and families of the President and Professors, for the time being, lying, and being within the Colony, with the persons of the Tutors and students, during their residence at the College, shall be freed and exempted from all taxes, serving on juries, and menial services: And that the persons aforesaid shall be exempted from bearing arms, impresses, and military services, except in case of an invasion.

*　　*　　*

Signed and sealed at Newport, the twenty-fourth day of October, in the year of our
  Lord one thousand seven hundred and sixty-five, and in the fifth year of
[L. S.] His Majesty's reign, George the Third, by the grace of God, of Great Britain,
  etc. King.

SAMUEL WARD, *Governor.*

EDWARD THURSTON, JR., *Secretary.*

A SOUTH CAROLINA JEW DONATES MONEY TO RHODE ISLAND COLLEGE (1770)   From Jacob R. Marcus, ed., *Early American Jewry* (Philadelphia, 1953), vol. II, pp. 246-47.

CHARLESTOWN, 17 April, 1770.

Mess'rs Sampson & Solomon Simson,
GENTLEMEN:
    You will be so kind as to order your correspondent in Rhode Island to pay unto the Trustees of the new college the sum of five pounds York currency on my account, and to transmit me th'ir receipt in my name.

As the Rev'd Mr. Smith will inform th'm, the reason th't induces me to be a benefactor to this college is th'ir having no objection of admitting the youth of our nation without interfereing in principals of religion. If so, my donation shall exceed beyond the bounds of th'ir imagination.

I presume this college is like Merchant Taylor's School in London where I went every day for three years, as well as two of my brothers, from 9:00 to 1:00 o'clock. There was at th't time about 800 boys, sons of the principal merchants and trading people in the city. I have lived to see two Lord Mayors and seven aldermen, and many toping [excellent] merchants my school-fellows, which, I assure you, was no small service to me when I was a broker on the Royal Exchange.

I have sent yo' by the bearer two of our gazettes wherein I believe there is more news from London than at y'r place.

I sincerely wish you well, and remain, with regard, gentlemen,

Your obliged humble serv't,
Moses Lindo.

CHARTER OF DARTMOUTH COLLEGE (1769) From Elsie W. C. Parsons, *Educational Legislation and Administration of the Colonial Governments* (New York, 1899), pp. 171-74.

George the Third by the Grace of God, of Great Britain, France and Ireland, King, Defender of the Faith, etc.

To all to whom these presents shall come, greeting: Whereas it hath been represented to our trusty and well beloved John Wentworth Esq., Governor and Commander-in-chief, in and over our Province of New Hampshire, in New England in America, that the Rev. Eleazar Wheelock of Lebanon, in the colony of Connecticut, in New England aforesaid, now Doctor in Divinity, did, on or about the year of our Lord, one thousand seven hundred and fifty-four, at his own expense, on his own estate and plantation, set on foot an Indian Charity School, and for several years through the assistance of well disposed persons in America, clothed, maintained and educated a number of the children of the Indian natives, with a view to their carrying the gospel in their own language, and spreading the knowledge of the great Redeemer among their savage tribes, and hath actually employed a number of them as missionaries and schoolmasters in the wilderness for that purpose, and by the blessing of God upon the endeavors of said Wheelock, the design became reputable among the Indians, insomuch that a larger number desired the education of their children in said school, and were also disposed to receive missionaries and schoolmasters in the wilderness, more than could be supported by the charitable contributions in these American colonies. Whereupon the said Eleazar Wheelock thought it expedient that endeavor should be used to raise contributions from well disposed persons in England, for the carrying on and extending said undertaking, and for that purpose said Eleazar Wheelock requested the Rev. Nathanial Whitaker, now Doctor in Divinity, to go over to England for that purpose, and sent over with him the Rev. Sampson Occom, Indian minister, who had been educated by the said Wheelock. And to enable the said Whitaker, to the more successful performance of said work on which he was sent, said Wheelock gave him a full power of attorney, by which said Whitaker solicited those worthy, and generous contributors to the charity, viz. the right Hon. Wm. Earl of Dartmouth, the Hon. Sir Sidney Stafford Smythe, Knight, one of the barons of his Majesty's court of Exchequer, John Thornton, of Clapham, in the county of Surrey, Esq., Sam Roffey, of Lincoln's Innfields, in the county of Middlesex, Esq. Charles Hardey, of the parish of St. Mary-le-bonne, in said county, Esq. Daniel West, of Christ's Church, Spitalfields, in the county aforesaid, Esq., Samuel Savage, of the same place, gentleman; Josiah Robarts, of the parish of St. Edmund the King, Lombard Street, London, gentleman, and Robert Keen, of the parish of St. Botolph, Aldgate, London, gentleman; to receive the several sums of money which should be contributed, and to be trustees to the contributors to such charity; which they cheerfully agreed to. Whereupon, the said Whitaker did, by virtue of said power of attorney, constitute and appoint the Earl of Dartmouth, Sir Sidney Stafford Smythe, John Thornton, Samuel Roffey, Charles Hardy, and Daniel West, Esqs., and Samuel Savage, Josiah Robarts, and Robert Keen, gentleman, to be trustees of the money which had then been contributed, and which should by his means be contributed for said purpose; which trust they have accepted, as by their engrossed declaration of the same under their hands and seals, well executed fully appears, and the same hath also been ratified by a deed of trust, well executed by said Wheelock. And the said Wheelock further represents, that he has, by the power of attorney, for many weighty reasons, given full power to the said trustees, to fix upon and determine the place for said school, most subservient to the great end in view. And to enable them understandingly to give the preference, the said Wheelock has laid before the said trustees the several offers which have been generously made in the several governments in America to encourage and invite the settlement of said school among them for their own private emolument, and for the increase of learning in their respective places, as well as for the furtherance of the general design in view. And whereas a large number of the proprietors of lands in the western part of this our Province of New Hampshire, animated and excited thereto by the generous example of his Excellency their Governor, and by the liberal contributions of many noblemen and gentlemen in England, and especially by the consideration that such a situation would be as convenient as any for carrying on the great design among the Indians; and also considering that without the least impediment to the said design, the same school may be enlarged and improved to promote learning among the English, and be a means to supply a great number of churches and congregations which are likely soon to be formed in that new country, with a learned and orthodox ministry, they the said proprietors have promised large tracts of land for the uses aforesaid, provided the school shall be settled in the western part of our said Province. And they the said right Hon., Hon. and worthy trustees beforementioned, having maturely considered the reasons and arguments in favor of the several places proposed, have given the preference to the western part of our said Province, lying on Connecticut River, as a situation most convenient for said school. And the said Wheelock has further represented a necessity of a legal incorporation, in order to the safety and well-being of said seminary, and its being capable of the tenure and disposal of lands and bequests for the use of the same. And the said Wheelock has also represented, that for many weighty reasons, it will be expedient, at least in the infancy of said institution, or till it can be accommodated in that new country, and he and his friends be able to remove and settle by and round about it, that the gentlemen whom he has already nominated in his last will (which he has transmitted to the aforesaid gentlemen of the trust in England) to be trustees in America, should be of the corporation now proposed. And also as there are already large collections for said school in the hands of the aforesaid gentlemen of the trust in England, and all reason to believe from their signal wisdom, piety and zeal, to promote the Redeemer's cause (which has already procured for them the utmost confidence of the kingdom) we may expect they will appoint successors in time to come, who will be men of the same spirit, whereby great good may and will accrue many ways to the institution, and much be done by their example and influence to encourage and facilitate the whole design in view; for which reasons said Wheelock desires that the trustees aforesaid, may be vested with all that power therein which can consist with their distance from the same. Know ye therefore that we, considering the premises and being willing to encourage the laudable design of spreading Christian knowledge among the savages of our American wilderness. And also that the best means of education be established in our province of New Hampshire, for the benefit of the said province, do, of our special grace, certain knowledge and mere motion, by and with the advice of our council for said province, by these presents will, ordain, grant and constitute that there be a college erected in our said province of New Hampshire, by the name of Dartmouth College, for the education and instruction of youths of the Indian tribes in this land, in reading, writing, and all parts of learning, which shall appear necessary and expedient, for civilizing and christianizing the children of pagans, as well as in all liberal arts and sciences, and also of English youths, and any others.

JOHN WITHERSPOON ON THE COLLEGE OF NEW JERSEY

(PRINCETON) (1772)   From John Witherspoon, ''Address to the Inhabitants of Jamaica and Other West-India Islands, in Behalf of the College of New Jersey'' (1772), as quoted in *Essays upon Important Subjects* (Edinburgh, 1805), vol. III, pp. 312-18, 328-30.

I will now proceed to speak a little of the Constitution and Advantages of the College of New-Jersey in particular. . . .

The regular course of instruction is in four classes, exactly after the manner and bearing the names of the classes in the English Universities; Freshman, Sophomore, Junior and Senior. In the first year they read Latin and Greek, with the Roman and Grecian antiquities, and Rhetoric. In the second, continuing the study of the languages, they learn a compleat system of Geography, with the use of the globes, the first principles of Philosophy, and the elements of mathematical knowledge. The third, though the languages are not wholly omitted, is chiefly employed in Mathematics and Natural Philosophy. And the senior year is employed in reading the higher classics, proceeding in the Mathematics and Natural Philosophy, and going through a course of Moral Philosophy. In addition to these, the President gives lectures to the juniors and seniors, which consequently every Student hears twice over in his course, first, upon Chronology and History, and afterwards upon

Composition and Criticism. He has also taught the French language last winter, and it will continue to be taught to all who desire to learn it.

During the whole course of their studies the three younger classes, two every evening formerly, and now three, because of the increased number, pronounce an oration on a stage erected for that purpose in the hall, immediately after prayers, that they may learn by early habit presence of mind and proper pronunciation and gesture in public speaking. This excellent practice, which has been kept up almost from the first foundation of the College, has had the most admirable effects. The senior scholars every five or six weeks pronounce orations of their own composition, to which all persons of any note in the neighbourhood are invited or admitted.

The College is now furnished with all the most important helps to instruction. The Library contains a very large collection of valuable books. The lessons of Astronomy are given upon the Orrery, lately invented and constructed by David Rittenhouse, Esq; which is reckoned by the best judges the most excellent in its kind of any ever yet produced; and when what is commissioned and now upon its way is added to what the College already possesses, the appartus for Mathematics and Natural Philosophy will be equal, if not superior, to any on the continent.

As we have never yet been obliged to omit or alter it for want of scholars, there is a fixed annual Commencement on the last Wednesday of September, when, after a variety of public exercises, always attended by a vast concourse of the politest company, from the different parts of this province and the cities of New-York and Philadelphia, the students whose senior year is expiring are admitted to the degree of Batchelors of Arts; the Batchelors of three years standing, to the degree of Masters; and such other higher degrees granted as are either regularly claimed, or the Trustees think fit to bestow upon those who have distinguished themselves by their literary productions, or their appearances in public life.

On the day preceeding the Commencement last year there was (and it will be continued yearly hereafter) a public exhibition and voluntary contention for prizes, open for every member of the College. These were first, second, and third prizes, on each of the following subjects. 1. Reading the English language with propriety and grace, and being able to answer all questions on its Orthography and Grammar. 2. Reading with Latin and Greek languages in the same manner with particular attention to true quantity. 3. Speaking Latin. 4. Latin versions. 5. Pronouncing English orations. The preference was determined by ballot, and all present permitted to vote, who were graduates of this or any other College.

As to the government of the College, no correction by stripes is permitted. Such as cannot be governed by reason and the principles of honour and shame are reckoned unfit for residence in a College. The collegiate censures are, 1. Private admonition by President, Professor, or Tutor. 2. Before the Faculty. 3. Before the whole class to which the offender belongs. 4. And the last and highest, before all the Members of College assembled in the hall. And, to preserve the weight and dignity of these censures, it has been an established practice that the last or highest censure, viz. public admonition, shall never be repeated upon the same person. If it has been thought necessary to inflict it upon any one, and if this does not preserve him from falling into such gross irregularities a second time, it is understood that expulsion is immediately to follow.

Through the narrowness of the funds the government and instruction has hitherto been carried on by a President and three Tutors. At last Commencement the Trustees chose a Professor of Mathematics, and intend, as their funds are raised to have a greater number of Professorships, and carry their plan to as great perfection as possible. . . .

The circumstances to which I would entreat the attention of impartial persons are the following.

1. The College of New-Jersey is altogether independent. It hath received no favour from Government but the charter, by the particular friendship of a person now deceased. It owes nothing but to the benefactions of a public so diffusive that it cannot produce particular dependance, or operate by partial influence. From this circumstance it must be free from *two* great evils, and derive the like number of solid advantages. There is no fear of being obliged to choose Teachers upon Ministerial recommendation, or in compliance with the over-bearing weight of family interest. On the contrary the Trustees are naturally led, and in a manner forced to found their choice upon the characters of the persons and the hope of public approbation. At the same time those concerned in the instruction and government of the College are as far removed, as the state of human nature will admit, from any temptation to a fawning cringing spirit and mean servility in the hope of Court favour or promotion.

In consequence of this it may naturally be expected, and we find by experience that hitherto in fact the spirit of liberty has breathed high and strong in all the Members. I would not be understood to say that a Seminary of Learning ought to enter deeply into political contention; far less would I meanly court favour by professing myself a violent partisan in any present disputes. But surely a constitution which naturally tends to produce a spirit of liberty and independance, even though this should sometimes need to be reined in by prudence and moderation, is infinitely preferable to the dead and vapid state of one whose very existence depends upon the nod of those in power. Another great advantage arising from this is the obligation we are under to recommend ourselves, by diligence and fidelity, to the public. Having no particular prop to lean to on one side, we are obliged to stand upright and firm by leaning equally on all. We are so far from having our fund so complete as of itself to support the necessary expence, that the greater part of our annual income arises from the payments of the Scholars, which we acknowledge with gratitude have been for these several years continually increasing.

2. This leads me to observe, that it ought to be no inconsiderable recommendation of this College to those at a distance, that it has the esteem and approbation of those who are nearest it and know it best. The number of Under graduates or proper Members of College, is near four times that of any College on the continent to the southward of New-England, and probably greater than that of all the rest put together. This we are at liberty to affirm has in no degree arisen from pompous descriptions, or repeated recommendations in the public papers. We do not mean to blame the laudable attempts of others to do themselves justice. We have been often found fault with, and perhaps are to blame for neglect on this particular. It is only mentioned to give full force to the argument just now used; and the fact is certainly true. I do not remember that the name of the College of New-Jersey has been above once or twice mentioned in the news papers for three years, except in a bare recital of the acts of the annual Commencements. The present Address arises from necessity, not choice; for had not a more private application been found impracticable, the press had probably never been employed.

3. It may not be amiss to observe on this subject, that the great utility of this Seminary has been felt over an extensive country. Many of the Clergy, Episcopal and Presbyterian, in the different colonies, received their education here, whose exemplary behaviour and other merit we suffer to speak for themselves. We are also willing that the public should attend to the characters and appearance of those

Gentlemen in the Law and Medical departments, who were brought up at Nassau-Hall, and are now in the cities of New-York and Philadelphia, and in different parts of the continent or islands. Two at least of the Professors of the justly celebrated Medical School lately founded in Philadelphia, and perhaps the greatest number of their pupils received their instruction here. We are not afraid, but even wish that our claim should be decided by the conduct of those in general who have come out from us, which is one of the most conclusive arguments, for *a tree is known by its fruits.* . . .

4. The place where the College is built is most happily chosen for the health, the studies and the morals of the scholars. . . . It is upon the great post-road almost equally distant from New-York and Philadelphia, so as to be a center of intelligence, and have an easy conveyance of every thing necessary, and yet to be wholly free from the many temptations in every great city, both to the neglect of study and the practice of vice. . . . It is not in the power of those who are in great cities to keep the discipline with equal strictness, where boys have so many temptations to do evil, and can so easily and effectually conceal it after it is done. With us they live all in College under the inspection of their Masters, and the village is so small that any irregularity is immediately and certainly discovered, and therefore easily corrected.

It has sometimes happened, through rivalship or malice, that our discipline has been censured as too severe and rigorous. This reproach I always hear not with patience only but with pleasure. . . .

5. This College was founded, and hath been conducted upon the most Catholick Principles. The Charter recites as one of its grounds, "That every religious denomination may have free and equal liberty and advantage of education in the said College, any different sentiments in religion notwithstanding." Accordingly there are now, and have been from the beginning, scholars of various denominations from the most distant colonies, as well as West-India Islands; and they must necessarily confess that they never met with the least uneasiness or disrespect on this account. Our great advantage on this subject is the harmony of the Board of Trustees, and the perfect union in sentiment among all the Teachers both with the Trustees and with one another. On this account there is neither inclination or occasion to meddle with any controversy whatever. The author of this Address confesses that he was long accustomed to the order and dignity of an established church, but a church which hath no contempt or detestation of those who are differently organized. And, as he hath ever been in that church an opposer of lordly domination and sacerdotal tyranny, so he is a passionate admirer of the equal and impartial support of every religious denomination which prevails in the northern colonies, and is perfect in Pennsylvania and the Jerseys, to the unspeakable advantage of those happy and well constituted governments.

With respect to the College of New-Jersey, every question about forms of church government is so entirely excluded, that, though I have seen one set of scholars begin and finish their course, if they know nothing more of religious controversy than what they learned here, they have that Science wholly to begin. This is altogether owing to the union of sentiment mentioned above: for, if you place as Teachers in a College persons of repugnant religious principles, they must have more wisdom and self-denial than usually fall to the lot of humanity, if the whole Society is not divided into parties and marshalled under names, if the changes are not frequent, and, when they take place, as well known as any event that can happen in such a society. On the contrary there is so little occasion with us to canvass this matter at all, that, though no doubt accident must discover it as to the greatest number, yet some have left the College as to whom I am wholly uncertain at this hour to what denomination they belong. It has been and shall be our care to use every mean in our power to make them good men and good scholars; and, if this is the case, I shall hear of their future character and usefulness with unfeigned satisfaction, under every name by which a real Protestant can be distinguished.

Having already experienced the generosity of the public in many parts of the continent of America, I cannot but hope that the Gentlemen of the Islands will not refuse their assistance, according to their abilities, in order to carry this Seminary to a far greater degree of perfection than any to which it has yet arrived. The express purpose to which the benefactions now requested will be applied, is the establishment of new professorships, which will render the Institution not only more complete in itself, but less burthensome to those who have undertaken the important trust. The whole branches of Mathematics and Natural Philosophy are now taught by one Professor; and the President is obliged to teach Divinity and Moral Philosophy as well as Chronology, History, and Rhetoric, besides the superintendance and government of the whole. The short lives of the former Presidents have been by many attributed to their excessive labours, which, it is hoped, will be an argument with the humane and generous to lend their help in promoting so noble a design.

THE ESTABLISHMENT OF GEORGETOWN UNIVERSITY (1789)   From John Gilmary Shea, *Memorial of the First Centenary of Georgetown College, D.C., Comprising a History of Georgetown University* (New York, 1891), pp. 12-13.

Proposals to Establish an Academy at George Town, Patowmack River, Maryland

The object of the proposed Institution is to unite the means of communicating Science with an effectual provision for guarding and preserving the Morals of Youth. With this View, the Seminary will be superintended by those who, having had Experience in similar Institutions, know that an undivided Attention may be given to the Cultivation of Virtue and literary Improvement, and that a System of Discipline may be introduced and preserved incompatible with Indolence and Inattention in the Professor, or with incorrigible habits of Immorality in the Student.

The Benefit of this Establishment should be as general as the Attainment of its Object is desirable. It will therefore receive Pupils as soon as they have learned the first Elements of Letters, and will conduct them through the several Branches of Classical Learning to that Stage of Education from which they may proceed with Advantage to the Study of higher Sciences in the University of this or those of the neighboring States. Thus it will be calculated for every Class of Citizens;—as Reading, Writing, Arithmetic, and earlier Branches of the Mathematics, and the Grammar of our native Tongue, will be attended to no less than the learned Languages.

Agreeably to the liberal Principle of our Constitution, the Seminary will be open to Students of every religious profession. They, who, in this Respect differ from the Superintendent of the Academy, will be at Liberty to frequent the places of Worship and Instruction appointed by their Parents; but with Respect to their moral Conduct, all must be subject to general and uniform Discipline.

In the choice of Situation, Salubrity of Air, Convenience of Communication and Cheapness of Living have been principally consulted, and George Town offers these united Advantages.

The Price of Tuition will be moderate; in the Course of a few Years it will be reduced still lower, if the System formed for this Seminary be effectually carried into execution.

Such a plan of Education solicits, and, it is not presumption to add, deserves public Encouragement. The following gentlemen, and others that may be named hereafter will receive subscriptions and inform the subscribers to whom and in what proportion payments are to be made. In Maryland, the Hon. Charles Carroll of Carrollton; Henry Rozer, Notley Young, Robert Darnall, George Digges, Edmond Plowden, Esq'rs, Mr. Joseph Millard, Captain John Lancaster, Mr. Baker Brooke, Chandler Brent, Esq., Mr. Bernard O'Neill and Mr. Marsham Waring, merchants; John Darnall and Ignatius Wheeler, Esq., on the western shore; and on the eastern, Rev. Mr. Joseph Mosley, John Blake, Francis Hall, Charles Blake, William Matthews and John Tuitte, Esq'rs. In Pennsylvania, George Mead and Thomas Fitzsimmons, Esq'rs, Mr. Joseph Cauffman, Mr. Mark Wilcox and Mr. Thomas Lilly. In Virginia, Colonel Fitzgerald and George Brent, Esq'rs, and at New York, Dominick Lynch, Esq.

Subscriptions will also be received and every necessary Information given by the following Gentlemen, Directors of the Undertaking: The Rev. Messrs. John Carroll, James Pellentz, Robert Molyneux, John Ashton and Leonard Neale.

Student Life

THESES DISCUSSED BY CANDIDATES FOR THE MASTER OF ARTS DEGREE AT HARVARD (1743) From Benjamin Pierce, *A History of Harvard University* (Cambridge, Mass., 1833), pp. 111-13.

Questions methodically to be discussed by the Candidates for the Degree of Master of Arts, in Public Assembly, under the Reverend Mr. Edward Holyoke, President of Harvard College, by divine Providence, at Cambridge in New England; on the 6th of July, A.D. 1743.

I. Whether a Confession of Faith may be declared in words merely humane?
Affirmed by Thomas Prince.

II. Whether every Dissimulation be a Vice?
Deny'd by Benjamin Stevens.

III. Whether the Dissolution of Solids in corrosive Liquors be performed by Attraction?
Affirmed by Samuel Gay.

IV. Whether Private Profit ought to be the chief End of Moral Actions?
Deny'd by George Bethune.

V. Whether it be lawful to resist the Supream Magistrate, if the Common Wealth cannot otherwise be preserved?
Affirmed by Samuel Adams.

VI. Whether all Animal Motion and Sensation be performed by the Motion of the Nerves?
Affirmed by John Gibbins.

VII. Whether Civil Government ariseth out of Contract?
Affirmed by Samuel Downe.

VIII. Whether Justification be best discovered by Works attending Sanctification?
Affirmed by Samuel White.

IX. Whether the Obligation to Virtue be founded in the Abstract Relations of Things?
Affirmed by Samuel Orne.

X. Whether every Form of Divine Worship may be universally tolerated, in no manner incommoding the public good?
Affirmed by John Newman.

XI. Whether this Rule [What thou doubtest do not] may be admitted in Morality?
Affirmed by Samuel Hendley.

XII. Whether the Humane Intellect be the Measure of Divine Faith?
Deny'd by Jonathan Hoar.

XIII. Whether the Will of God be the only and adequate Rule of Moral Actions?
Affirmed by Samuel Hale.

XIV. Whether a Conscience invincibly erroneous may be blameless?
Affirmed by Nathaniel Snell.

XV. Whether the Scriptures be the perfect and only Rule of Believing and Acting?
Affirmed by Samuel Langdon.

XVI. Whether the Christian Religion may be propagated by Force and Arms?
Deny'd by James Hovey.

XVII. Whether the Law of Nations be distinct from the Law of Nature?
Affirmed by Joseph Davis.

XVIII. Whether Past and Future Sins are forgiven at the same time?
Deny'd by Amarias Frost.

XIX. Whether the Operations of the Holy Spirit in the Mind may be the improper Cause of Natural Errors?
Affirmed by Sylvanus Conant.

LIST OF FINES AT HARVARD (c. 1750)   From Josiah Quincy, *The History of Harvard University* (Cambridge. Mass., 1840), vol. II, pp. 499-500.

Absence from prayers,	£0	0	2
Tardiness at prayers,	0	0	1
Absence from Professor's public lecture,	0	0	4
Profanation of Lord's Day, not exceeding	0	3	0
Absence from public worship,	0	0	9
Ill behaviour at public worship, not exceeding	0	1	6
Going to meeting before bell-ringing,	0	0	6
Neglecting to repeat the sermon,	0	0	9
Irreverent behaviour at prayers, or public divinity lectures,	0	1	6
Absence from chambers, &c., not exceeding	0	0	6
Not declaiming, not exceeding	0	1	6
Not giving up a declamation, not exceeding	0	1	6

Absence from recitation, not exceeding	0	1	6
Neglecting analysing, not exceeding	0	3	0
Bachelors neglecting disputations, not exceeding	0	1	6
Undergraduates out of town without leave, not exceeding	0	2	6
Undergraduates tarrying out of town without leave, not exceeding *per diem,*	0	1	3
Undergraduates tarrying out of town one week without leave, not exceeding	0	10	0
Undergraduates tarrying out of town one month without leave, not exceeding	2	10	0
Lodging strangers without leave, not exceeding	0	1	6
Entertaining persons of ill character, not exceeding	0	1	6
Going out of College without proper garb, not exceeding	0	0	6
Frequenting taverns, not exceeding	0	1	6
Profane cursing, not exceeding	0	2	6
Graduates playing cards, not exceeding	0	5	0
Undergraduates playing cards, not exceeding	0	2	6
Undergraduates playing any game for money, not exceeding	0	1	6
Selling and exchanging without leave, not exceeding	0	1	6
Lying, not exceeding	0	1	6
Opening door by pick-locks, not exceeding	0	5	0
Drunkenness, not exceeding	0	1	6
Liquors prohibited under penalty, not exceeding	0	1	6
Second offence, not exceeding	0	3	0
Keeping prohibited liquors, not exceeding	0	1	6
Going upon the top of the College,	0	1	6
Cutting off the lead,	0	1	6
Concealing the transgression of the 19th Law,	0	1	6
Tumultuous noises,	0	1	6
Second offence,	0	3	0
Refusing to give evidence,	0	3	0
Rudeness at meals,	0	1	0
Butler and cook to keep utensils clean, not exceeding	0	5	0
Not lodging at their chambers, not exceeding	0	1	6
Sending freshmen in studying time,	0	0	9
Keeping guns, and going on skating,	0	1	0
Firing guns or pistols in College yard,	0	2	6
Fighting or hurting any person, not exceeding	0	1	6

HARVARD COLLEGE STUDENTS CAUGHT UP IN TURMOIL (1769)

From Andrew Eliot to Thomas Hollis, Hollis Papers, Massachusetts Historical Society (Boston, 1769), no pagination.

I shall be sorry if the Court should be at Cambridge. It hinders the Scholars in their studies. The young Gentlemen are already enough taken up with politics. They have imbibed the Spirit of the times. Their declamations and forensic disputes breathe the Spirit of Liberty. This has always been encouraged, but they have sometimes wrought themselves up to such a pitch of Enthusiasm that it has been difficult to keep them within due bounds. But their tutors are fearful of giving too great a check to a disposition which may hereafter fill the Country with Patriots and choose to leave it to age and experience to correct their ardor.

HARVARD STUDENTS PROTEST DRINKING OF INDIA TEA (1775)

From "Records of the College Faculty, March 1, 1775," *Harvard University Archives*, vol. IV, pp. 4-5.

March 1. At a Meeting of the President, Professors and Tutors

A disorder having arisen this morning in the Hall at breakfast, between some of the students, respecting the drinking of India Tea; and some of the utensils for breakfasting having been broke; and the parties having been heard—

Resolved—1. We disapprove of the conduct of both sides as imprudent.

Resolved—2. That the regulation of the Hall belongs exclusively to the Government of the College, and consequently that no students have a right to interpose with regard thereunto, and that those students who have thus interposed have conducted disorderly in this respect, and ought to make restitution for the property of their fellow students by such interposition destroyed.

Resolved—3. Since the carrying India Teas into the Hall is found to be a source of uneasiness and grief to many of the students, and as the use of it is disagreeable to the people of this Country in general; and as those who have carried Tea into the hall declare that the drinking of it in the Hall is a matter of trifling consequence with them; that they be advised not to carry it in for the future, and in this way that they, as well as the other students in all ways, discover a disposition to promote harmony, mutual affection, and confidence, so well becoming members of the same society: that so peace and happiness may be preserved within the walls of the college whatever convulsions may unhappily distract the State abroad.

DESCRIPTION OF STUDENT LIFE AT THE COLLEGE OF NEW JERSEY

(1774)   From Hunter D. Farish, ed., *The Journal and Letters of Philip Vickers Fithian, 1773-1774* (Williamsburg, Va., 1943), pp. 253-54.

Every time I reflect on that Place of retirement & Study, where I spent two years which I call the most pleasant as well as the most important Period in may past life—Always when I think upon the *Studies,* the *Discipline,* the *Companions,* the *Neighbourhood,* the *exercises, & Diversions,* it gives me a secret & real Pleasure, even the Foibles which often prevail there are pleasant on recollection; such as giving each other *names* & *characters;* Meeting & Shoving in the dark entries; knocking at Doors & going off without entering; Strewing the entries in the night with greasy Feathers; freezing the Bell; Ringing it at late Hours of the Night;—I may add that it does not seem disagreeable to think over the Mischiefs often practised by wanton Boy's—Such are writing witty pointed anonymous Papers, in *Songs, Confessions, Wills, Soliliques, Proclamations, Advertisements &c*—Picking from the neighbourhood now & then a plump fat Hen or Turkey for the private entertainment of the Club "instituted for inventing & practising several new kinds of mischief in a secret polite Manner"—Parading bad Women—Burning Curse-John—Darting Sun-Beams upon the Town-People Reconoitering Houses in the Town, & ogling Women with the Telescope—Making Squibs, & other frightful compositions with Gun-Powder, & lighting them in the Rooms of timorous Boys, & new *comers*—The various methods used in naturalizing Strangers, of incivility in the Dining-Room to make them bold; writing them sharp & threatning Letters to make them smart; leading them at first with long Lessons to make them industrious—And trying them by Jeers & Repartee in order to make them choose their Companions &c &c—

BEGINNINGS OF THE PHI BETA KAPPA SOCIETY AT WILLIAM AND MARY COLLEGE (1776-77)   From "Original Records of the Phi Beta Kappa Society," *William and Mary College Quarterly Historical Magazine,* vol. IV, pp. 215-19, 222-23.

On Thursday, the 5th of December, in the year of our Lord God one thousand seven hundred and seventy-six, and the first of the Commonwealth, a happy spirit and resolution of attaining the important ends of Society entering the minds of John Heath, Thomas Smith, Richard Booker, Armstd Smith, and John Jones, and afterwards seconded by others, prevailed, and was accordingly ratified.

And for the better establishment and sanctitude of our unanimity, a square silver medal was agreed on and instituted, engraved on the one side with S. P., the initials of the Latin S——P——, and on the other, agreeable to the former, with the Greek initials of **Φ B K** *and an index imparting a philosophical design, extended to the three stars, a part of the planetary orb, distinguished.*

In consequence of this, on Wednesday the 5th of Jan^{ry}, 1777, a session was held, in order both to adopt a mode of initiation and to provide for its better security.

And first in corporation, an oath of fidelity being considered as the strongest preservative, an initiation was accordingly resolved upon and instituted as follows:

I, A. B., do swear on the holy Evangelists of Almighty God, or otherwise, as calling the Supreme Being to attest this my oath, declaring that I will, with all my possible efforts, endeavour to prove true, just, and deeply attached to this our growing fraternity; in keeping, holding, and preserving all secrets that pertain to my duty, and for the promotion and advancement of its internal welfare.

Whereupon the oath of fidelity being thus prescribed and instituted, was afterwards severally administered to the respective gentlemen, viz.: John Heath, Thos Smith, Richard Booker, Armistead Smith, John Jones, Daniel Fitzhugh, John Stuart, Th^{ck} Fitzhugh, and John Stork, as the first essays or rudiments to an initiation. In consequence of this, we severally, freely, and jointly proceeded to the election of officers, proper and most suitable for its internal regulation.

Upon the recommendation of three members, viz.: J^{no} Heath as President, Richd Booker as Treasurer, and Thos Smith as Clerk, the society esteeming them as necessary persons for the functions of their several duties accordingly selected them.

The fraternity having gone through the business of the present session, after a recommendation of certain proper and salutary laws, to be prepared against the next ensuing meeting of March the 1st, jointly adjourned.

March 1st. Agreeable to the recommendation of our preceding session, we have severally presented the subsequent laws as proper and most conducive to the advantage of our growing fraternity:

Resolved 1st. That in every design or attempt, whether great or small, we ought to invoke the Deity, by some private sacrifice or devotion, for a fraternal prosperity.

2. That a profanation of the preceding oath of fidelity subjects the Member to the pain of the universal censures of the fraternity as well as the misery of certain expulsion.

3. That every member, after being properly initiated, shall be obliged to furnish himself with a Medal, wholly corresponding with those of the Fraternity.

4. That an orderly session of members of the Pres^{dt} downwards should be observed.

5. That in case of the incapacity or necessary absence of the President, the choice of any other member shall be left to the discretion of the Society.

6. That the non-attendance of any single member, unless by some certain obstructing inability, or cogent necessity, subjects him to the penalty of five shillings.

7. That no gentleman be initiated into the Society but Collegians, and such only who have arrived to the age of sixteen years, and from the Grammar Master upwards; and further, before his disposition be sufficiently inspected, nor then without the unanimous approbation of the Society.

8. That every member during a session behave with a becoming decency, and declare their sentiments, vicissively preventing confusion.

9. That the least appearance of intoxication or disorder of any single member by liquor, at a session, subjects him to the penalty of ten shillings.

10. That for the encouragement of any new invention of Arts and Sciences, some premium be allowed from the public treasury.

11. That six members shall be the fewest sufficient for the execution of business.

12. That each member when desirous of proposing anything to this fraternity shall rise from his seat and particularly address the President.

13. That a regular meeting of once a month, *unless* a necessity of sooner convening should *interpose,* is hereby established and ordained.

14. That the duty of Treasurer in keeping accurate estimates and accompts of all reimbursements as well as disbursements is esteemed nothing but legal and constitutional.

15. That if any dispute, attended with animosity and indignation, should arise amongst us, such a matter ought to be recognized by a session of the whole Society.

16. That the President be invested with the prerogative of convening the members of this fraternity, when he shall deem it expedient; that he have likewise the privilege of giving a decision, when there shall happen a division of voices, and the power of commanding the due attendance to be paid him while discharging the important function of his office.

17. That the duty or office of the Clerk be indispensably requisite, as well in keeping a proper roll or conscription of the fraternity, as fair and legible books in writing.

18. That four members be selected to perform at every session, two of whom in matters of argumentation and the others in apposite composition.

19. That such of the compositions as are deemed worthy by the Society shall be carefully preserved and endorsed by whom and at what time delivered.

20. That the youngest on the roll be appointed Herald for the function of convocating the members.

21. That the infringement of any of the laws enacted or to be enacted, except such as have the fines annexed, subjects the members to the discretionary punishment of the Society.

22. That no member shall be expelled without the unanimous concurrence of the Society.

23. That every person after being initiated pay into the public Treasury the sum of 6s—Dollars.[1]

24. It is also ordained that any number of members shall have full authority and Power to transact Business of any kind, when these members shall think it absolutely necessary for ye Preservation of ye Society.

25. That any Law or Laws which is, are, or may be enacted agreeable to Resolve cannot be altered or amended in less than a month after the proposed amendment, and then by a majority.

26. That if the number of members, according to Act 11th, cannot be convened, any smaller number shall have power of doing Business of any kind. But such Business, Initiation excepted, shall always be subject to be cancelled by a majority until confirmed according to Act 11th.[2]

27th. Whereas, by Resolve 19th respecting Declamation and argumentation, it is intended that those compositions only be preserved which may do honour to the Society: and, forasmuch as it is inconvenient for the whole meeting to take the merit of them into their due consideration:

Resolved that three members be appointed to judge of the Performances, and always to inform the ensuing meeting of their Determination. Provided, however,

---

[1]This word is in a different hand, and was added later. On August 22, 1778, the initiation fee was made $5. On June 27, 1779, it was raised to $10.

[2]The twenty-fifth and twenty-sixth resolutions are in a different hand, and were added July 4, 1778.

that when either of the appointed judges declaims, a temporary successor to him as judge be appointed by the meeting.[3]

March 27th. At a called meeting, Mr Isaac Hite, being recommended as a worthy member of this fraternity, was accordingly initiated. After which we jointly adjourn ourselves to the established time.

April 5th. Mr Booker having been charged at a meeting of this fraternity of a thorough infringement of three of the preceding resolves, viz.: 6th, 13th & 14th, and whereupon, being willing to receive his defence, we have postponed his examination to the next meeting. After which we jointly adjourn ourselves.

April 15th. At a call meeting, Mr Wm Short, Mr John Morison and Mr Geo. Braxton, being recommended as worthy members of this Society, were accordingly initiated. The business being finished, we adjourn ourselves.

April 19th. Mr Booker, having appeared and made his defence, was, with honour and unanimity restored to the good opinion of this Society. The business being finished, we adjourn ourselves.

May 3d. For the better distinction of the fraternity between themselves in any foreign country or place, it is resolved that a

[The rest scratched out.]

Mr Heath, having resigned the office of President, the fraternity proceeded to the appointment of a successor, and Mr T. Smith being recommended, was accordingly appointed.

In consequence of this appointment, they proceeded to the choice of a Clerk, and Mr Wm Short being recommended, was also appointed.

Ordered that an addition of the 27th Resolve be made to our Code of Laws. That Mr Hardy, Mr Hall, Mr Fitzhugh, Mr Short be appointed judges agreeable to the above resolve.

That the absentees of former meetings be exempted from Fines, & in future their excuses be examined at their next attendance without Fail.

The Business of the night being finished, an adjournment took Place.

Aug. 22nd. Resolved that the last appointment of Judges of Composition be abolished, and that three members, agreeable to Resolve 27th, be chosen by Ballot. The Society proceeded to this appointment; upon examination of the Box, the greatest Number of votes appearing in Favour of Mr Hall, Mr Short and Mr J. Stuart, they are accordingly confirmed.

Resolved, that as the Price of Initiation hitherto paid is inadequate to the Purpose, it be augmented to five Dollars.

Resolved, that in future, meetings of this Society be held regularly once a week. An adjournment.

Aug. 29th. Resolved, that three members be appointed to revise the Laws, and that an Election of them be held on the next full meeting.

That every member who desires to propose anything to this Society produce it in writing.

That every member who is absent from the Society be written to in the most pressing Terms to attend on the 5th of December in order to celebrate that glorious Day which gave Birth to this happy Union. The Society, wishing not to impose this Business altogether on the Clerk, proceeded to appoint an assistant, *Mr. Hardy,* to him for this Purpose.

Resolved, that the two members appointed to argue, agreeable to Resolve 18th,

[3]This resolve appears to have been added August 8, 1778.

shall be confined to the subject of the Compositions delivered at the same meeting; and that it be moreover strongly recommended to the other members, *as an* additional and improving *Exercise,* to give their sentiments extempore on the same subject after hearing the others.

Sep. 4. At a meeting of this Society, the President being absent, Mr Short was appointed to that Post. Mr Hall and Mr Cocke, agreeable to that last appointment, delivered their Declamations upon the advantages of an established church. Three members, agreeable to a Resolve at the last meeting, were appointed to revise the Laws, viz., Mr Stuart, Mr Hall & Mr Hardy. Mr Hall being one of the Judges, a temporary successor was appointed to inspect his performance, viz., Mr Hardy. An adjourn^t.

Sep. 11 & 18. At two meetings no Business appearing from Absence of the appointed Members. Adjournment took Place.

Oct. 10. At a meeting of this Society, resolved that a late Resolution requiring a convention of members once a week be annulled, and that in future, meetings be held as formerly, viz., once a Fortnight.

Nov. 21st. Not a sufficient number of members appearing hitherto at this meeting, it was resolved that Messrs Smith & Stuart, being the two oldest members, declaim at the next meeting, and that Messrs Fitzhugh argue on the same subject.

Resolved, that Messrs F. Fitzhugh, Morison and Cocke be appointed to make Provision for the ensuing Anniversary, that it may be celebrated with a becoming Solemnity.

Mr Archibald Stuart being recommended as a gentleman worthy an admission to this Society, was in due form introduced.

Whereas the members of this Society are willing to take under their care objects worthy of charity, Resolved, that Messrs Hardy & Cocke be appointed to look out for some Orphan likely to receive advantage from being put to a proper School, & make their report of the same to the ensuing meeting.

Resolved, that the Clerk purchase for the use of the Society two Quires of paper, & that he draw upon the Treasurer for the Price of the same. An adjournment.

Decr. 4th. At a called meeting, it appearing that the State of the Society was declining through Want of Members, Resolved, that a committee be appointed to take the same into their consideration. Resolved, that Messrs Hall, Hardy, A. Stuart, Short, & J. Stuart be appointed.

Messrs John Brown, Preeson Bowdoin, Lyttleton Eyre, & Daniel Carroll Brent, being severally recommended as gentleman worthy an admission to this Society, were accordingly initiated.

The Business of the Evening being over, the Society adjourned with an agreement to meet on to-morrow evening at the Raleigh, to celebrate the Anniversary of this fraternity.

Dec. 5th. The Society having met agreeable to appointment, after the President has resigned and delivered a valedictory on the Occasion, the Night was spent in Jollity & Mirth. M^r. J. Heath and Thos. Smith, of the former members, attended on this auspicious Day, for which they have the grateful Acknowledgements of the Society.

SUBJECTS DEBATED IN THE PHI BETA KAPPA SOCIETY AT WILLIAM AND MARY COLLEGE (1778-80)

From "Original Records of the Phi Beta Kappa Society," *William and Mary College Quarterly Historical Magazine*, vol. IV, pp. 213-40, as quoted in Edgar W. Knight, comp., *Documentary History of Education in the South Before 1860* (Chapel Hill, N.C., 1949), vol. II, pp. 258-59.

1778	
Sept. 4	The advantages of an established Church.
1779	
March 13	The Justice of African Slavery.
March 27	Whether Agriculture or Merchandise was most advantageous to a State.
April 10	Whether Brutus was justifyable in having his son executed.
April 24	The cause and origin of Society.
May 8	Whether a wise State hath any Interest nearer at heart than the education of the Youth.
June 12	Whether an Agrarian Law is consistent with the principles of a wise republic.
July 10	Whether anything is more dangerous to Civil Liberty in a free State than a standing army in time of peace.
July 24	Whether parents have a right to prevent marriage of children after entering into Contract.
August 7	Whether Commonwealths or Monarchies are most subject to Seditions and Commotions.
Nov. 27	Whether a General Assessment for the support of Religious Establishments is or is not repugnant to the principles of a Republican Government.
Dec. 4	Whether Theatrical Exhibitions are advantageous to States or the contrary.
1780	
March 4	Is a Public or a Private Education more advantageous?
April 22	Had William the Norman a right to invade England?
May 21	Whether the Execution of Charles the First was justifyable.
June 3	Whether any form of Government is more favorable to public virtue than a Commonwealth.
June 17	Whether the rape of the Sabine women are just.
July 1	Whether Religion is necessary to Government.
July 29	Whether in Civil War any person is justifyable in remaining Neuter.
August 13	Whether Duelling ought to have toleration in this or any other free State.
August 27	Whether all our affections and principles are not in some manner deducible from self love.
Sept. 12	Whether Poligamy is a dictate of Nature or not.
Sept. 23	Whether Avarice or Luxury is more beneficial to a Republic.
Oct. 6	Whether Brutus was justifyable in killing Caesar.
Oct. 22	Whether a man in extreme want is justifyable in stealing from his neighbor to relieve his present necessities.

THE HARVARD CHAPTER OF PHI BETA KAPPA (1779) From "Original
Records of the Phi Beta Kappa Society," *William and Mary College Quarterly Historical
Magazine,* vol. IV, pp. 242-44.

FORM OF A CHARTER PARTY

The Members of the Φ B K of the meeting Αλφα of William and Mary
College, Virginia, to their well and truly beloved Brother Elisha Parmeli [*sic.*]
Greeting.

Whereas it is repungnant to the liberal principles of Socieites that they should
be confined to any particular place, Men or Description of Men, and as the same
should be extended to the wise and Virtuous of every degree and of whatever
Country;

We the Members and Brothers of the Φ B K, an Institution founded on literary
principles, being willing and desirous to propagate the same, have at the instance
and petition of our good Brother Elisha Parmeli of the University of Cambridge, in
the State of Massachusetts Bay, and from the confidence we repose in the Integrity,
Discretion, and good Conduct of our said Brother, unanimously agreed and resolved
to give and delegate, and we do therefore by these our present letters of Charter
party, give and delegate by unanimous consent to you, the said Elisha Parmeli, the
following Rights, Privileges, Authority & power; that is to say

1st, That at the University of Cambridge you establish a Fraternity of the Φ B
K, to consist of not less than three persons of Honor, Probity, and good-Demeanor,
which shall be denominated the Αλφα of Massachusetts Bay. And as soon as such
number of three shall be chosen, you shall proceed to hold a Meeting, to be called
the Foundation-Meeting, & appoint your Officers according to Law.

2dly, That the form of Initiation and Oath of Secresy, shall be as well in the first,
as in every other instance, those prescribed by Law & none other.

3dly, That the governing rule of your conduct & that of the Society be to further
and promote the fundamental principles and maxims of the Φ B K, to the best of
your knowledge: and above all you are to be care full to promote friendship &
union among one another as well as to bring it forth in a communion with us here;
so far as it may be practicable & convenient.

4^{thly}, That the Code of Laws herewith transmitted, being the Laws of the
Αλφα Society, or such of them as the Society shall approve, be considered as
conclusive and binding. And except in cases where local convenience alone may
make it necessary, are not to be altered or liable to innovation.

5^{thly}, That everything suggested by you as essential to promote the generous
design of our Institution or necessary to be enacted into a Law, and all correspon-
dencies shall be through the President of each Society by means of the Table
herewith transmitted. Which table we charge you to preserve with the utmost care,
observing to be thoroughly acquainted with the use of the same, lest misunderstandings should arise in our correspondence.

6^{thly}, That you by this Charter be invested with the privileges of the Meeting
Αλφα of Virginia in granting Charters for the establishment of other Meetings any
where within the State of Massachusetts Bay, which meetings are to stand in the
same relation to you that the Junior branches of this Society stand in to the meeting
Αλφα here.

7^{thly}, That the Arcana of this Society be held inviolate.

8^{thly}, That the Members of

each of them be provided with a Medal of the same form and kind with that herewith transmitted you, without any alteration whatever, and that the token of Salutation be the same with that used here, observing to make it known as a general means of Introduction to the Members of the $\Lambda\lambda\phi\alpha$ or any of the Junior branches.

9^{thly}, That once in every year for the proper communication between the Societies, to-wit: on your Foundation day, you take a list of your Members and transmit the same as soon as possible to our President, noting your Officers & such new Members as have been initiated since the last return, with the name of their County or Place of abode.

10^{thly}, That in everything conducive to the great ends of our Institution you correspond freely & without reserve, stating fully and specially all such matters and things as you may judge worthy of our regard and attention.

11^{thly},[1] That a power be retained by this Society, to make such further and additional laws for the Government and better regulations of the

as we may judge most conducive to promote the general welfare of the whole; and that in cases considered as Constitutional, the same be declared to be within our power either for alteration or amendment.

12^{thly}, That we do hereby satisfy and confirm this charter and all the Rights, Privileges, Authority and Power incident to the same unto you the said Elisha Parmeli, the Members of the   and their successors forever, confidently relying on the prudence and discretion of you our Brother, to secure the same with our reputations and fortunes.

Witness our hands & the Seal of the Society this the fourth day of December, In the year of our Lord 1779.

WILLIAM SHORT, Junr., President,
ARCHIBALD STUART, V. President,
WILLIAM CABELL, Treasurer,
JOHN JAMES BECKLEY, Sec'ry,
THEODORICK FITZHUGH,
JOHN MORISON,
JOHN ALLEN,
JOHN NIVISON,
HARTWELL COCKE,
THOMAS HALL,
SAMUEL HARDY,
JOHN BROWN,
DANIEL C. BRENT,
THOMAS Wm BALLENDINE,
SPENCER ROANE,
WILLIAM STITH,
WILLIAM STUART,
THO^s LITTLETON SAVAGE,
JOHN PAGE.

[1][The eleventh to be void as far as it regards the Superiority of this Society over that of Cambridge.]

REPUBLICANS

Education for the New Nation

LOYALTY OATH REQUIRED OF PENNSYLVANIA TEACHERS (1777)   From James T. Mitchell and Henry Flanders, eds., *The Statutes at Large of Pennsylvania, 1682–1801* (n.p., 1903), vol. IX, pp. 111-12, 239-40.

I, ..., do swear (or affirm) that I renounce and refuse all allegiance to George the Third, King of Great Britain, his heirs and successors, and that I will be faithful and bear true allegiance to the commonwealth of Pennsylvania as a free and independent state, and that I will not at any time do or cause to be done any matter or thing that will be prejudicial or injurious to the freedom and independence thereof, as declared by Congress; and also that I will discover and make known to some one justice of the peace of the said state all treasons or traitorous conspiracies which I now know or hereafter shall know to be formed against this or any of the United States of America.

*   *   *

And be it enacted, that all trustees, provosts, rectors, professors, masters and tutors of any college or academy, and all schoolmasters and ushers . . . who shall at any time after the first day of June next, be admitted into or enter upon any of the before mentioned preferments, offices or places, or shall come into any such capacity, or shall take upon him or them any such practice, employment or business as aforesaid without having first taken and subscribed the before mentioned oath or affirmation, he or they shall be ipso facto adjudged incapable and disabled in law, to all intents and purposes whatsoever, to have, occupy or enjoy the said preferment or preferments office or offices, employment or employments or any part of them, or any matter or thing aforesaid, or any profit or advantage appertaining to them, or any of them, and every such office or place of trust shall be void and is hereby adjudged void; and any person that shall be lawfully convicted of the premises, or any of them in or upon any presentment, or indictment in any court of record in this state, shall also forfeit any sum, not exceeding five hundred pounds, which the court shall adjudge, together with costs, one-half of which said fine shall go to the use of the State, and the other half to him, her or them who shall commence and carry on such prosecution with effect.

REPUBLICANS

QUAKERS PROTEST LOYALTY OATH FOR TEACHERS (1779)   From Isaac Sharpless, *A History of Quaker Government in Pennsylvania* (Philadelphia, 1899), vol. II, pp. 184-87.

To the General Assembly of Pennsylvaia: The memorial and address of the religious Society called Quakers respectfully sheweth:

That divers laws have been lately enacted which are very injurious in their nature, oppressive in the manner of execution, and greatly affect us in our religious and civil liberties and privileges, particularly a law passed by the last Assembly entitled "A further supplement to the test laws of this State," in the operation whereof the present and succeeding generations are materially interested. We therefore apprehend it a duty owing to ourselves and our posterity to lay before you the grievances to which we are subjected by these laws.

Our predecessors on their early settlement in this part of America, being piously concerned for the posterity of the colony and the real welfare of their posterity, among other salutory institutions promoted at their own expense the establishment of schools for the instruction of their Youth in useful and necessary learning and their education in piety and virtue, the practice of which forms the most sure basis for perpetuating the enjoyment of Christian liberty and essential happiness.

By the voluntary contributions by the members of our religious Society, schools were set up in which not only their children were taught but their liberality hath been extended to poor children of other religious denominations generally, great numbers of whom have partaken thereof; and these schools have been in like manner continued and maintained for a long course of years.

Duty to Almighty God made known in the consciences of men and confirmed by the holy Scriptures is an invariable rule which should govern their judgment and actions. He is the only Lord and Sovereign of Conscience, and to him we are accountable for our conduct, as by him all men are to be finally judged. By conscience we mean the apprehension and persuasion a man has of his duty to God and the liberty of conscience we plead for is a free open profession and unmolested exercise of that duty, such a conscience as under the influence of divine grace keeps within the bounds of morality in all the affairs of human life and teacheth to live soberly righteously and godly in the world.

As a religious Society, we have ever held forth the Gospel dispensation was introduced for completing the happiness of mankind by taking away the occasion of strife contention and bloodshed and therefore we all conscientiously restrained from promoting or joining in wars and fightings: and when laws have been made to enforce our compliance contrary to the convictions of our consciences, we have thought it our duty patiently to suffer though we have often been grievously oppressed. Principle we hold in this respect requires us to be a peaceable people and through the various changes and revolutions which have occurred since our religious Society has existed, we have never been concerned in promoting or abetting any combinations insurrections or parties to endanger the public peace or by violence to oppose the authority of government apprehending it our duty quietly to admit and peaceably to demeanor ourselves under every government which Divine Providence in his unerring wisdom may permit to be placed over us; so that no government can have just occasion for entertaining fears or jealousies of disturbance or danger from us. But if any professing with us deviate from this peaceable principle into a contrary conduct and foment discords, feuds or animosities, giving just occasion of uneasiness and disquiet, we think it our duty, to declare against their proceeding.

By the same divine principle, we are restrained from complying with the injunctions and requisitions made on us of tests and declarations of fidelity to either party who are engaged in actual war lest we contradict by our conduct the profession of our faith.

It is obvious that in these days of depravity, as in former times, because of oaths the land mourns and the multiplying the use of them and such solemn engagements renders them familiar, debases the mind of the people and adds to the number of those gross evils already lamentably prevalent which have drawn down the chastisement of heaven on our guilty country.

We are not actuated by political or party motives; we are real friends to our country, who wish its prosperity and think a solicitude for the enjoyments of our equitable rights, and that invaluable privilege, Liberty of Conscience, free from coercion, cannot be justly deemed unreasonable. Many of us and other industrious inhabitants being exposed to heavy penalties and sufferings, which are abundantly encreased by the rigour of mistaken and unreasonable men under the sanction of law, whereby many are already reduced to great straits and threatened with total ruin, the effects of whose imprisonment must at length be very sensibly felt by the community at large through the decline of cultivation and the necessary employments.

We have been much abused and villified by many anonymous publications and our conduct greatly perverted and misrepresented by groundless reports and the errors of individuals charged upon us as a body in order to render us odious to the people and prepossess the minds of persons in power against us; being conscious of our innocence and "submitting our cause to the Lord who judgeth righteously" we have preferred patience in bearing the reproach to public contest, not doubting that as the minds of the people become more settled and composed, our peaceable demeanor would manifest the injustice we suffered, and being persuaded that on a cool dispassionate hearing we should be able to invalidate or remove the mistaken suggestions and reports prevailing to our prejudice.

The matters we have now freely laid before you are serious and important, which we wish you to consider wisely as men and religiously as Christians manifesting yourselves friends to true liberty and enemies to persecution, by repealing the several penal laws affecting tender consciences and restoring to us our equitable rights that the means of education and instruction of our youth which we conceive to be our reasonable and religious duty, may not be obstructed and that the oppressed may be relieved. In your consideration whereof, we sincerely desire that you may seek for and be directed by that supreme "wisdom which is pure, peaceable, gentle and easy to be entreated, full of mercy and good fruits" and are your real friends.

Signed on behalf of a meeting of the Representatives of the said people held in Philadelphia the 4th day of the 11th mo 1779.

THE SYSTEM OF PUBLIC EDUCATION IN BOSTON (1789)   From Pauline
Holmes, *A Tercentenary History of the Boston Public Latin School, 1635-1935* (Cambridge,
Mass., 1935), pp. 423-29.

THE

SYSTEM

OF

Public Education,

Adopted by the Town of Boston, 15th Octob. 1789.

I. THAT there be one School in which the rudiments of
the Latin and Greek languages shall be taught, and
scholars fully qualified for the Universities. That all candidates
for admission into this School shall be at least ten years of
age, having been previously well instructed in English Grammar;
that they shall continue in it not longer than four years, and
that they have liberty to attend the public writing Schools at
such hours as the visiting Committee shall direct.

II. That there be one writing School at the South part of the
town; one at the Centre, and one at the North part; that, in
these Schools, the children of both sexes be taught writing, and
also arithmetic in the various branches usually taught in the
Town-Schools, including Vulgar and Decimal Fractions.

III. That there be one reading School at the South part of
the Town, one at the Centre, and one at the North part; that,
in

in thefe Schools, the children of both fexes be taught to fpell, accent, and read both profe and verfe, and alfo be inftructed in Englifh Grammar and Compofition.

IV. That the children of both fexes be admitted into the reading and writing Schools at the age of feven years, having previoufly received the inftruction ufual at Women's Schools; that they be allowed to continue in the reading and writing Schools till the age of fourteen, the boys attending the year round, the girls from the 20th of April to the 20th of October following; that they attend thefe Schools alternately, at fuch times, and fubject to fuch changes, as the vifiting Committee in confultation with the Mafters fhall approve.

V. That a Committee be annually chofen by ballot, to confift of twelve, in addition to the Selectmen, whofe bufinefs it fhall be to vifit the Schools once in every quarter, and as much oftener as they fhall judge proper, with three of their number at leaft, to confult together in order to devife the beft methods for the inftruction and government of the Schools; and to communicate the refult of their deliberations to the Mafters; to determine at what hours the Schools fhall begin, and to appoint play-days; in their vifitations to enquire into the particular regulations of the Schools, both in regard to inftruction and difcipline, and give fuch advice to the Mafters as they fhall think proper; to examine the Scholars in the particular branches which they are taught; and, by all proper methods, to excite in them a laudable ambition to excel in a virtuous, amiable deportment, and in every branch of ufeful knowledge.

VOTES

VOTES of the Committee appointed to carry into Execution the System of public Education adopted by the Town of Boston, 15th October 1789.

AT a Meeting of the said Committee, held Decemb. 1, 1789,

VOTED, I. That the Latin Grammar School be divided into four Classes, and that the following Books be used in the respective Classes.

1st Class—Cheever's Accidence.
   Corderius's Colloquies—Latin and English.
   Nomenclator.
   Æsop's Fables—Latin and English.
   Ward's Latin Grammar, or Eutropius.

2d Class—Clarke's Introduction—Latin and English.
   Ward's Latin Grammar.
   Eutropius, continued.
   Selectæ è Veteri Testamento Historiæ, or,
   Castalio's Dialogues.
   The making of Latin, from Garretson's Exercises.

3d Class—Cæsar's Commentaries.
   Tully's Epistles, or Offices.
   Ovid's Metamorphoses.
   Virgil.
   Greek Grammar.
The making of Latin from King's History of the Heathen Gods.

4th Class—Virgil, continued.—Tully's Orations.
   Greek Testament.—Horace.
   Homer.—Gradus ad Parnassum.
   The making of Latin continued.

            That

That thofe Boys who attend the Latin School, be allowed to attend the Writing Schools in the following Hours, viz. The 1ft Clafs from half paft Nine o'clock, A. M. 'till Eleven, or from half paft Three P. M. as fhall be found moft convenient, and the 2d Clafs in the fame manner for the firft half of that year.

II. That the following Books be ufed in the Reading Schools. viz.—The Holy Bible.

Webfter's Spelling Book, or 1ft part of his Inftitute. The young Ladies Accidence——And Webfter's American Selection of Leffons in Reading and Speaking; or 3d part of his Grammatical Inftitute.

That the Mafters introduce the following Books when found expedient, viz.—The Children's Friend.

Morfe's Geography, abridged.

That the News Papers be introduced occafionally, at the difcretion of the Mafters.

That the upper Clafs in the Reading Schools be inftructed in Epiftolary Writing and other Compofition.

III. That an uniform method of teaching Arithmetic be ufed in the feveral Writing Schools, viz.

Numeration.
Simple Addition.
—— Subtraction.
—— Multiplication.
—— Divifion.
Compound Addition.
—— Subtraction.
—— Multiplication.
—— Divifion.
Reduction.

The

(5)

The single Rule of Three, direct.
Practice.

Tare and Tret, Interest, Fellowship, Exchange, &c. are considered as included in the above Rules.

Vulgar and Decimal Fractions.

That the Children begin to learn Arithmetic at 11 Years of Age.

That at 12 Years of Age, the Children be taught to make Pens.

IV. That the Reading Schools be divided into four Classes. —That from the third Monday in October to the third Monday in April, for one Month, viz. from the first Monday in the Month, the first and second Classes attend the Reading, and the third and fourth, the Writing Schools in the Morning.— The first and second, attend the Writing Schools, the third and fourth the Reading Schools in the Afternoon.—The Month following, the order be reversed, and so alternately during the above time.—And that from the third Monday in April to the third Monday in October, for one Month, viz. From the first Monday in the Month, all the Boys attend the Reading Schools, and all the Girls the Writing Schools in the Morning; that all the Boys attend the Writing Schools, and all the Girls the Reading Schools in the Afternoon; the Month following the order to be reversed, and thus alternately during those six Months. —That it be understood that from the third Monday in April to the first Monday in June, be considered as the first Month of the Summer Term. That from the third Monday in October to the first Monday in December, be considered as the first Month of the Winter Term.

V. That

V. That the following Hours be punctually observed in all the Schools, viz. From the third Monday in April to the third Monday in October, the Schools begin at half past 7 o'Clock, A. M. and continue 'till eleven, and begin at half past 1 o'Clock, P. M. and continue 'till five.—That from the third Monday in October to the third Monday in April, the Schools begin at half past 8 o'Clock, A. M. and continue 'till eleven, and begin at half past 1 o'Clock, P. M. and continue 'till half past four.

That in future the Schools keep 'till 11 o'Clock in the Fore-noon on Thursdays, as well as other Days.

VI. That the Masters be excused from keeping School on the following Days and Times, viz.

The Afternoon of every Thursday and Saturday throughout the year.

The Afternoon preceding Fasts and Thanksgivings.

Four half days of Artillery Training, in the Afternoon.

First Monday in April.

Six days in Election Week.

First Monday in June.

Fourth Day of July, or Anniversary of Independence.

The four last Days in Commencement Week.

Christmas Day, and

On the general Training Days.

December 7, 1789.

Voted, That the Committee be divided into seven equal parts, as Sub-Committees for the purpose of inspecting the respective Schools, and examining the scholars ; so that one Committee be assigned to each School. And the Committee was divided accordingly.

Voted,

7

Voted, That the inspecting Committees be enjoined to visit their respective Schools at least once every month, and as much oftener as they may think proper.

Voted, That the inspecting Committees make the laws of the State respecting Schools, the votes of the Town, and of this Committee, the rule of their conduct in visiting the Schools.

Voted, That the first Monday in January 1790 be the time assigned for putting into operation the new System of Education, as adopted by the Town, and regulated by this Committee.

December 14, 1789.

Voted, That it be the indispensable duty of the several School-Masters, daily to commence the duties of their office by prayer and reading a portion of the sacred Scriptures, at the hour assigned for opening the School in the morning; and close the same in the evening with prayer.

December 21, 1789.

Voted, That the Masters never expel any boy from School, but with the consent, and in the presence of the inspecting Committee.

Voted, That the Instructor of the Latin School be entitled *The Latin Grammar Master* ; the Instructors of the Reading Schools be entitled *English Grammar Masters*; the Instructors of the Writing Schools be entitled *Writing Masters*.

TIMOTHY DWIGHT ON COLLEGE-EDUCATED YOUTH IN THE POST-REVOLUTIONARY PERIOD (c. 1783)   From Timothy Dwight, *Travels in New-England and New York* (New Haven, 1821–22), vol. IV, pp. 376-77.

Youths particularly, who had been liberally educated, and who with strong passions and feeble principles, were votaries of sensuality and ambition, delighted in the prospect of unrestrained gratification, and, panting to be enrolled with men of passion and splendor, became enamored with the new doctrines.

The tenor of opinion, and even of conversation, was to a considerable extent changed at once. Striplings scarcely fledged suddenly found that the world had been enveloped in general darkness through the long succession of preceding ages, and that the light of human wisdom had just begun to dawn upon the human race.

All the science, all the information that had been acquired before the last thirty or forty years stood in their view for nothing. Experience they boldly proclaimed a plotting instructress who taught in manners, morals, and government, nothing but abecedarian lessons fitted for children only.

Religion they discovered, on the one hand, to be the vision of dotards and nursemaids, and, on the other, a system of fraud and trick, imposed by priestcraft for base purposes upon the ignorant multitude. Revelation was found to be without authority or evidence, and moral obligation a cobweb which might indeed entangle flies, but by which creatures with stronger wing nobly disdained to be confined.

The world they resolutely concluded to have been probably eternal, and matter the only existence. Man, they determined, sprang like a mushroom out of the earth like a chemical process; and the power of thinking, choice and motivity were merely the result of elective affinities. If, however, there was a God and man was a creative being, he was created only to be happy. As, therefore, animal pleasure is the only happiness, so they resolved that the enjoyment of that pleasure is the only end of his creation.

THOMAS JEFFERSON'S "BILL FOR THE MORE GENERAL DIFFUSION OF KNOWLEDGE" (1779)   From Paul L. Ford, ed., *The Works of Thomas Jefferson* (New York, 1904), vol. II, pp. 414-26.

SECTION I

Whereas it appeareth that however certain forms of government are better calculated than others to protect individuals in the free exercise of their natural rights, and are at the same time themselves better guarded against degeneracy, yet experience hath shewn, that even under the best forms, those entrusted with power have, in time, and by slow operations, perverted it into tyranny; and it is believed that the most effectual means of preventing this would be, to illuminate, as far as practicable, the minds of the people at large, and more especially to give them knowledge of those facts, which history exhibiteth, that, possessed thereby of the experience of other ages and countries, they may be enabled to know ambition under all its shapes, and prompt to exert their natural powers to defeat its purposes; And whereas it is generally true that that people will be happiest whose laws are best, and are best administered, and that laws will be wisely formed, and honestly administered, in proportion as those who form and administer them are wise and honest; whence it becomes expedient for promoting the publick happiness that those persons, whom nature hath endowed with genius and virtue, should be rendered by liberal education worthy to receive, and able to guard the sacred deposit of the rights and liberties of their fellow citizens, and that they should be called to that charge without regard to wealth, birth or other accidental condition or circumstance; but the indigence of the greater number disabling them from so educating, at their own expence, those of their children whom nature hath fitly formed and disposed to become useful instruments for the public, it is better that such should be sought for and educated at the common expence of all, than that the happiness of all should be confined to the weak or wicked:

SECTION II

Be it therefore enacted by the General Assembly, that in every county within this commonwealth, there shall be chosen annually, by the electors qualified to vote for Delegates, three of the most honest and able men of their country, to be called the Alderman of the county; and that the election of the said Aldermen shall be held at the same time and place, before the same persons, and notified and conducted in the same manner as by law is directed, for the annual election of Delegates for the county.

*   *   *

SECTION IV

The said Aldermen on the first Monday in October, if it be fair, and if not, then on the next fair day, excluding Sunday, shall meet at the courthouse of their county, and proceed to divide their said county into hundreds, bounding the same by water courses, mountains, or limits, to be run and marked, if they think necessary, by the county surveyor, and at the county expence, regulating the size of the said hundreds, according to the best of their discretion, so as that they may contain a convenient number of children to make up a school, and be of such convenient size that all the children within each hundred may daily attend the school to be established therein, and distinguishing each hundred by a particular name; which division, with the names of the several hundreds, shall be returned to the court of the county and be entered of record, and shall remain unaltered until the increase or decrease of inhabitants shall render an alteration necessary, in the opinion of any succeeding Alderman, and also in the opinion of the court of the county.

SECTION V

The electors aforesaid residing within every hundred shall meet on the third Monday in October after the first election of Aldermen, at such place, within their hundred, as the said Aldermen shall direct, notice thereof being previously given to them by such person residing within the hundred as the said Aldermen shall require who is hereby enjoined to obey such requisition, on pain of being punished by amercement and imprisonment. The electors being so assembled shall choose the most convenient place within their hundred for building a school-house. If two or more places, having a greater number of votes than any others, shall yet be equal between themselves, the Aldermen, or such of them as are not of the same hundred, on information thereof, shall decide between them. The said Aldermen shall forthwith proceed to have a school-house built at the said place, and shall see that the same shall be kept in repair, and, when necessary, that it be rebuilt; but whenever they shall think necessary that it be rebuilt, they shall give notice as before directed, to the electors of the hundred to meet at the said school-house on such a day as they shall appoint, to determine by vote, in the manner before directed, whether it shall be rebuilt at the same, or what other place in the hundred.

SECTION VI

At every of those schools shall be taught reading, writing, and common arithmetick, and the books which shall be used therein for instructing the children to read shall be such as will at the same time make them acquainted with Graecian, Roman, English, and American history. At these schools all the free children, male and female, resident within the respective hundred, shall be intitled to receive tuition gratis, for the term of three years, and as much longer, at their private expence, as their parents, guardians, or friends shall think proper.

SECTION VII

Over every ten of these schools (or such other number nearest thereto, as the number of hundreds of the county will admit, without fractional divisions) an overseer shall be appointed annually by the aldermen at their first meeting, eminent for his learning, integrity, and fidelity to the commonwealth, whose business and duty it shall be, from time to time, to appoint a teacher to each school, who shall give assurance of fidelity to the commonwealth, and to remove him as he shall see cause; to visit every school once in every half year at the least; to examine the scholars; see that any general plan of reading and instruction recommended by the visitors of William and Mary College shall be observed; and to superintend the conduct of the teacher in everything relative to his school.

SECTION VIII

Every teacher shall receive a salary of ———— by the year, which, with the expences of building and repairing the school-houses, shall be provided in such manner as other county expences are by law directed to be provided and shall also have his diet, lodging, and washing found him, to be levied in like manner, save only that such levy shall be on the inhabitants of each hundred for the board of their own teacher only.

SECTION IX

And in order that grammer schools may be rendered convenient to the youth in every part of the commonwealth, be it therefore enacted, that on the first Monday in November, after the first appointment of overseers for the hundred schools, if fair, and if not, then on the next fair day, excluding Sunday, after the hour of one in the afternoon, the said overseers appointed for the schools . . . shall fix on such place in some one of the counties in their district as shall be most proper for situating a grammer school-house, endeavoring that the situation be as central as may be to the inhabitants of the said counties, that it be furnished with good water, convenient to plentiful supplies of provision and fuel, and more than all things that it be healthy.

✳   ✳   ✳

SECTION X

The said overseers having determined the place at which the grammer school for their district shall be built, shall forthwith (unless they can otherwise agree with the proprietors of the circumjacent lands as to location and price) make application to the clerk of the county in which the said house is to be situated, who shall thereupon issue a writ, in the nature of a writ of ad quod damnum, directed to the sheriff of the said county commanding him to summon and impannel twelve fit persons to meet at the place so destined for the grammer school-house, on a certain day, to be named in the said writ, not less than five, nor more than ten, days from the date thereof; and also to give notice of the same to the proprietors and tenants of the lands to be viewed if they be found within the county, and if not, then to their agents therein if any they have. Which freeholders shall be charged by the said sheriff impartially, and to the best of their skill and judgment to view the lands round about the said place and to locate and circumscribe, by certain meets and bounds, one hundred acres thereof, having regard therein principally to the benefit and convenience of the said school, but respecting in some measure also the convenience of the said proprietors, and to value and appraise the same in so many several and distinct parcels as shall be owned or held by several and distinct owners or tenants, and according to their respective interests and estates therein. And after such location and appraisement so made, the said sheriff shall forthwith return the same under the hands and seals of the said jurors, together with the writ, to the clerk's office of the said county and the right and property of the said proprietors and tenants in the said lands so circumscribed shall be immediately devested and be transferred to the commonwealth for the use of the said grammer school, in full and absolute dominion, any want of consent or disability to consent in the said owners or tenants notwithstanding. But it shall not be lawful for the said overseers so to situate the grammer school-house, nor to the said jurors so to locate the said lands, as to include the mansion-house of the proprietor of the lands, nor the offices, curtilage, or garden, thereunto immediately belonging.

SECTION XI

The said overseers shall forthwith proceed to have a house of brick or stone, for the said grammer school, with necessary offices, built on the said lands, which grammer school-house shall contain a room for the school, a hall to dine in, four rooms for a master and usher, and ten or twelve lodging rooms for the scholars.

SECTION XII

To each of the said grammer schools shall be allowed out of the public treasury, the sum of ———— pounds, out of which shall be paid by the Treasurer, on warrant from the Auditors, to the proprietors or tenants of the lands located, the value of their several interests as fixed by the jury, and the balance thereof shall be delivered to the said overseers to defray the expense of the said buildings.

SECTION XIII

In either of these grammer schools shall be taught the Latin and Greek languages, English Grammer, geography, and the higher part of numerical arithmetick, to wit, vulgar and decimal fractions, and the extrication of the square and cube roots.

SECTION XIV

A visiter from each county constituting the district shall be appointed, by the overseers, for the county, in the month of October annually, either from their own body or from their county at large, which visiters, or the greater part of them, meeting together at the said grammer school on the first Monday in November, if fair, and if not, then on the next fair day, excluding Sunday, shall have power to choose their own Rector, who shall call and preside at future meetings, to employ from time to time a master, and if necessary, an usher, for the said school, to remove them at their will, and to settle the price of tuition to be paid by the scholars. They shall also visit the school twice in every year at the least, either together or separately at their discretion, examine the scholars, and see that any general plan of instruction recommended by the visiters, of William and Mary College shall be observed. The said masters and ushers, before they enter on the execution of their office, shall give assurance of fidelity to the commonwealth.

SECTION XV

A steward shall be employed, and removed at will by the master, on such wages as the visiters shall direct; which steward shall see to the procuring provisions, fuel, servants for cooking, waiting, house cleaning, washing, mending, and gardening on the most reasonable terms; the expence of which, together with the steward's wages, shall be divided equally among all the scholars boarding either on the public or private expence. And the part of those who are on private expence, and also the price of their tuitions due to the master or usher, shall be paid quarterly by the respective scholars, their parents, or guardians, and shall be recoverable, if withheld, together with costs, on motion in any Court of Record, ten days notice thereof being previously given to the party, and a jury impannelled to try the issue joined, or enquire of the damages. The said steward shall also, under the direction of the visiters, see that the houses be kept in repair, and necessary enclosures be made and repaired, the accounts for which, shall, from time to time, be submitted to the Auditors, and on their warrant paid by the Treasurer.

SECTION XVI

Every overseer of the hundred schools shall, in the month of September annually, after the most diligent and impartial examination and inquiry, appoint from among the boys who shall have been two years at the least at some one of the schools under his superintendance, and whose parents are too poor to give them farther education, some one of the best and most promising genius and disposition, to proceed to the grammer school of his district; which appointment shall be made in the court-house of the county and on the court day for that month if fair, and if not, then on the next fair day, excluding Sunday, in the presence of the Aldermen, or two of them at the least, assembled on the bench for that purpose, the said overseer being previously sworn by them to make such appointment, without favor or affection, according to the best of his skill and judgment, and being interrogated by the said Aldermen, either on their own motion, or on suggestions from their parents, guardians, friends, or teachers of the children, competitors for such appointment; which teachers the parents shall attend for the information of the Aldermen. On which interrogatories the said Aldermen, if they be not satisfied with the appointment proposed, shall have right to negative it; whereupon the said visiter may proceed to make a new appointment, and the said Aldermen again to interrogate and negative, and so toties quoties until an appointment be approved.

SECTION XVII

Every boy so appointed shall be authorized to proceed to the grammer school of his district, there to be educated and boarded during such time as is hereafter limited; and his quota of the expences of the house together with a compensation to the master or usher for his tuition, at the rate of twenty dollars by the year, shall be paid by the Treasurer quarterly on warrant from the Auditors.

SECTION XVIII

A visitation shall be held, for the purpose of probation, annually at the said grammer school on the last Monday in September, if fair, and if not, then on the next fair day, excluding Sunday, at which one third of the boys sent thither by appointment of the said overseers, and who shall have been there one year only, shall be discontinued as public foundationers, being those who, on the most diligent examination and enquiry, shall be thought to be the least promising genius and disposition; and of those who shall have been there two years, all shall be discontinued save one only the best in genius and disposition, who shall be at liberty to continue there four years longer on the public foundation, and shall thence forward be deemed a senior.

SECTION XIX

The visiters for the districts which, or any part of which, be southward and westward of James river, as known by that name, or by the names of Fluvanna and Jackson's river, in every other year, to wit, at the probation meetings held in the years, distinguished in the Christian computation by odd numbers, and the visiters for all the other districts at their said meetings to be held in those years, distinguished by even numbers, after diligent examination and enquiry as before directed, shall chuse one among the said seniors, of the best learning and most hopeful genius and disposition, who shall be authorized by them to proceed to William and Mary College; there to be educated, boarded, and clothed, three years; the expence of which annually shall be paid by the Treasurer on warrant from the Auditors.

THOMAS JEFFERSON'S PLAN FOR REFORMING WILLIAM AND MARY COLLEGE (1779) From "A Bill for Amending the Constitution of William and Mary, and Substituting More Certain Revenues for Its Support; Proposed by the Committee of Revisors of the Laws of Virginia, Appointed by the General Assembly in the Year, 1776" (1779), as quoted in *Sundry Documents on the Subject of a System of Public Education for the State of Virginia* (Richmond, 1817), pp. 56-60.

Sect. 2. And, whereas the experience of near an hundred years hath proved, that the said college, thus amply endowed by the public, hath not answered their expectations, and there is reason to hope, that it would become more useful, if certain articles in its constitution were altered and amended, which being fixed, as before recited, by the original charter, cannot be reformed by the said trustees, whose powers are created and circumscribed by the said charter; and the said college being erected and constituted on the requisition of the general assembly, by the chief magistrate of the state their legal fiduciary for such purposes, being founded and endowed with the lands and revenues of the public, and intended for the sole use and improvement, and no wise in nature of a private grant, the same is of right subject to the public direction, and may by them be altered and amended, until such form be devised as will render the institution publicly advantageous, in proportion as it is publicly expensive; and the late change in the form of our government, as well as the contest of arms in which we are at present engaged, calling for extraordinary abilities both in council and field, it becomes the peculiar duty of the legislature, at this time, to aid and improve that seminary, in which those who are to be the future guardians of the rights and liberties of their country may be endowed with science and virtue, to watch and preserve the sacred deposit: *Be it therefore enacted by the General Assembly,* That, instead of eighteen visitors, or governors of the said college, there shall in future be five only, who shall be appointed by joint ballot of both houses of assembly, annually, to enter on the duties of their office on the new year's day ensuing their appointment, having previously given assurance of fidelity to the commonwealth, before any justice of the peace; and to continue in office until those next appointed shall be qualified; but those who shall be first appointed, after the passing of this act, and all others appointed during the course of any year to fill up vacancies happening by death, resignation, or removal out of the commonwealth, shall enter on duty immediately on such appointment. Any four of the said visitors may proceed to business; they shall choose their own rector, at their first meeting, in every year, and shall be deemed the lawful successors of the first trustees, and invested with all the rights, powers, and capacities given to them, save only so far as the same shall be abridged by this act; nor shall they be restrained in their legislation, by the royal prerogative, or the laws of the kingdom of England, or the canons or constitution of the English church, as enjoined in the said charter. There shall be three chancellors, in like manner apointed by joint ballot of both houses, from among the judges of the high court of chancery, or of the general court, to enter on their office immediately on such appointment, and to continue therein so long as they may remain in either of the said courts; any two of whom may proceed to business: to them shall belong solely the power of removing the professors, for breach or neglect of duty, immorality, severity, contumacy, or other good cause, and the judiciary powers in all disputes which shall arise on the statutes of the college, being called on for that purpose by the rector, or by the corporation of president and professors: a copy of their sentence of deprivation being delivered to the sheriff of the county wherein the college is, he shall forthwith cause the professor deprived to be ousted of his chambers and other freehold appertaining to the said college, and the remaining professors to be re-seized thereof, in like manner and form, and subject, on failure, to the like fines by the said chancellors, as in cases of writs of *habere facias seisinam* issued from courts of record. But no person shall be capable of being both visitor and chancellor at the same time; nor shall any professor be capable of being at the same time either visitor or chancellor. Instead of the president and six professors, licensed by the said charter, and established by the former visitors, there shall be eight professors, one of whom shall also be appointed president, with an additional salary of one hundred pounds a year; before they enter on the execution of their office, they shall give assurance of fidelity to the commonwealth, before some justice of the peace.—These shall be deemed the lawful successors of the president and professors appointed under the said charter, and shall have all their rights, powers and capacities, not otherwise disposed of by this act; to them shall belong the ordinary government of the college, and administration of its revenues, taking the advice of the visitors on all matters of great concern. There shall, in like manner, be eight professorships; *to wit,* one of moral philosophy, the laws of nature and of nations, and of the fine arts; one of law and police; one of history, civil and ecclesiastical; one of mathematics; one of anatomy and medicine; one of natural philosophy and natural history; one of the ancient languages, oriental and northern; and one of modern languages. The said professors shall likewise appoint, from time to time, a missionary, of approved veracity, to the several tribes of Indians, whose business shall be to investigate their laws, customs, religions, traditions, and more particularly their languages, constructing grammars thereof, as well as may be, and copious vocabularies, and, on oath, to communicate, from time to time, to the said president and professors, the materials he collects, to be by them laid up and preserved in their library; for which trouble the said missionary shall be allowed a salary, at the discretion of the vistors, out of the revenues of the college. And forasmuch as the revenue, arising from the duties on skins and furs, and those on liquors, with which the said college was endowed, by several acts of the general assembly, is subject to great fluctuations, from circumstances unforseen, insomuch that no calculation or foresight can enable the said visitors or professors to square thereto the expenditures of the said college, which being regular and permanent should depend on stable funds: *Be it therefore enacted,* That the revenue arising from the said duties shall be henceforth transferred to the use of the public, to be applied towards supporting the contingent charges of government; and that, in lieu thereof, the said college shall be endowed with an impost of five pounds of tobacco, on every hogshead of tobacco to be exported from this commonwealth, by land, or by water, to be paid to the inspectors, if such tobacco be carried to any public ware-house, by the person receiving the said tobacco from them, and by the said inspectors accounted for, on oath, to the said president and professors, on or before the 10th day of October, in every year, with an allowance of six per centum for their trouble; and if the said tobacco be not carried to any public ware-house, then the said impost shall be paid, collected, and accounted for to the said president and professors, by the same persons, at the same times, in and under the like manner, penalties and conditions, as prescribed by the laws, which shall be in force at the time, for collecting the duties imposed on exported tobacco, towards raising supplies of money for the public exigencies.—And that this commonwealth may not be without so great an ornament, nor its youth such an help towards attaining astronomical science, as the mechanical representation, or model of the solar system, conceived and executed by the greatest of astronomers, David Ryttenhouse: *Be it further enacted,* That the visitors, first appointed under this act, and their successors, shall be authorised to engage the said David Ryttenhouse, on the part of this commonwealth, to make and erect in the said college of William and Mary, and for its use, one of the said models, to be called by the name of the Ryttenhouse: the cost and expense of making, transporting and erecting whereof shall, according to the agreement or allowance of the said visitors, be paid by the treasurer of this commonwealth, on warrant from the auditors.

APPENDIX

First.—ETHICS . . . Moral Philosophy. Law of Nations.—FINE ARTS . . . Sculpture. Painting. Gardening. Music. Architecture. Poetry. Oratory. Criticism.

Second.—LAW—Municipal . . . Common Law. Equity. Law Merchant. Law Maritime. Law Ecclesiastical.—Economical . . . Politics. Commerce.

Third.—HISTORY . . . Civil. Ecclesiastical.

Fourth.—MATHEMATICS—Pure . . . Arithmetic. Geometry.—Mixed . . . Mechanics. Optics. Acoustics. Astronomy.

Fifth.—Anatomy. Medicine.

Sixth.—NATURAL PHILOSOPHY . . . Chymistry. Statics. Hydrostatics. Pneumatics. Agriculture.—NATURAL HISTORY . . . Animals—Zoology. Vegetables—Botany. Minerals—Mineralogy.

Seventh.—ANCIENT LANGUAGES.—Oriental . . . Hebrew. Chaldee. Syriac.— Northern . . . Moeso-Gothic. Anglo Saxon. Old Icelandic.

Eighth.—MODERN LANGUAGES . . . French. Italian. German.

Missionary for Indian History, &c.

THOMAS JEFFERSON DISCUSSES HIS EDUCATIONAL PLANS FOR VIRGINIA (1782) From Thomas Jefferson, *Notes on the State of Virginia, with an Appendix* (Newark, N.J., 1801), pp. 202-3.

Query XIV

THE ADMINISTRATION OF JUSTICE AND THE DESCRIPTION OF THE LAWS?

*   *   *

Many of the laws which were in force during the monarchy being relative merely to that form of government, or inculcating principles inconsistent with republicanism, the first assembly which met after the establishment of the commonwealth appointed a committee to revise the whole code, to reduce it into proper form and volume, and report it to the assembly. This work has been executed by three gentlemen, and reported; but probably will not be taken up till a restoration of peace shall leave to the legislature leisure to go through such a work.

The plan of the revisal was this. The common law of England, by which is

REPUBLICANS

meant, that part of the English law which was anterior to the date of the oldest statutes extant, is made the basis of the work. It was thought dangerous to attempt to reduce it to a text: it was therefore left to be collected from the usual monuments of it. Necessary alterations in that, and so much of the whole body of the British statutes, and of acts of assembly, as were thought proper to be retained, were digested into 126 new acts, in which simplicity of style was aimed at, as far as was safe. The following are the most remarkable alterations proposed:

To change the rules of descent, so as that the lands of any person dying intestate shall be divisible equally among all his children, or other representatives, in equal degree.

To make slaves distributable among the next of kin, as other moveables.

To have all public expenses, whether of the general treasury, or of a parish or county, (as for the maintenance of the poor, building bridges, court-houses, &c.) supplied by assessments on the citizens, in proportion to their property.

To hire undertakers for keeping the public roads in repair, and indemnify individuals through whose lands new roads shall be opened.

To define with precision the rules whereby aliens should become citizens, and citizens make themselves aliens.

To establish religious freedom on the broadest bottom.

To emancipate all slaves born after passing the act.

✳   ✳   ✳

Another object of the revisal is, to diffuse knowledge more generally through the mass of the people. This bill proposes to lay off every county into small districts of five or six miles square, called hundreds, and in each of them to establish a school for teaching reading, writing, and arithmetic. The tutor to be supported by the hundred and every person in it entitled to send their children three years gratis, and as much longer as they please, paying for it. These schools to be under a visitor who is annually to chuse the boy, of best genius in the school, of those whose parents are too poor to give them further education, and to send him forward to one of the grammar schools, of which twenty are proposed to be erected in different parts of the country, for teaching Greek, Latin, geography, and the higher branches of numerical arithmetic. Of the boys thus sent in one year, trial is to be made at the grammar schools one or two years, and the best genius of the whole selected, and continued six years, and the residue dismissed. By this means twenty of the best geniusses will be raked from the rubbish annually, and be instructed, at the public expence, so far as the grammar schools go. At the end of six years instruction, one half are to be discontinued (from among whom the grammar schools will probably be supplied with future masters;) and the other half, who are to be chosen for the superiority of their parts and disposition, are to be sent and continued three years in the study of such sciences as they shall chuse, at William and Mary college, the plan of which is proposed to be enlarged, as will be hereafter explained, and extended to all the useful sciences. The ultimate result of the whole scheme of education would be the teaching all the children of the state reading, writing, and common arithmetic: turning out ten annually of superior genius, well taught in Greek, Latin, geography, and the higher branches of arithmetic: turning out ten others annually, of still superior parts, who, to those branches of learning, shall have added such of the sciences as their genius shall have led them to; the furnishing to the wealthier part of the people convenient schools, at which their children may be educated at their own expence.—The general objects of this law are to provide an education adapted to the years, to the capacity, and the condition of every one, and directed to their freedom and happiness. Specific details were not proper for the law. These must be the business of the visitors entrusted with its execution. The first stage of this education being the schools of the hundreds wherein the great mass of the people will receive their instruction, the principle foundations of future order will be laid here. Instead therefore of putting the Bible and Testament into the hands of the children at an age when their judgments are not sufficiently matured for religious inquiries, their memories may here be stored with the most useful facts from Grecian, Roman, European and American history. The first elements of morality too may be instilled into their minds; such as, when further developed as their judgments advance in strength, may teach them how to work out their own greatest happiness, by shewing them that it does not depend on the condition of life in which chance has placed them, but is always the result of a good conscience, good health, occupation, and freedom in all just pursuits.—Those whom either the wealth of their parents or the adoption of the state shall destine to higher degrees of learning, will go on to the grammar schools, which constitute the next stage, there to be instructed in the languages. The learning Greek and Latin, I am told, is going into disuse in Europe. I know not what their manners and occupations may call for: but it would be very ill-judged in us to follow their example in this instance. There is a certain period of life, say from eight to fifteen or sixteen years of age, when the mind like the body is not yet firm enough for laborious and close operations. If applied to such, it falls an early victim to premature exertion: exhibiting indeed at first, in these young and tender subjects, the flattering appearance of their being men while they are yet children, but ending in reducing them to be children when they should be men. The memory is then most susceptible and tenacious of impressions; and the learning of languages being chiefly a work of memory, it seems precisely fitted to the powers of this period, which is long enough too for acquiring the most useful languages ancient and modern. I do not pretend that language is science. It is only an instrument for the attainment of science. But that time is not lost which is employed in providing tools for future operation: more especially as in this case the books put into the hands of the youth for this purpose may be such as will at the same time impress their minds with useful facts and good principles. If this period be suffered to pass in idleness, the mind becomes lethargic and impotent, as would the body it inhabits if unexercised during the same time. The sympathy between body and mind during their rise, progress and decline, is too strict and obvious to endanger our being misled while we reason from one to the other.—As soon as they are of sufficient age, it is supposed they will be sent on from the grammar schools to the university, which constitutes our third and last stage, there to study those sciences which may be adapted to their views.—By that part of our plan which prescribes the selection of the youths of genius from among the classes of the poor, we hope to avail the state of those talents which nature has sown as liberally among the poor as the rich, but which perish without use, if not sought for and cultivated. But of the views of this law none is more important, none more legitimate, than that of rendering the people the safe, as they are the ultimate guardians of their own liberty. For this purpose the reading in the first stage, where *they* will receive their whole education, is proposed, as has been said, to be chiefly historical. History by apprising them of the past will enable them to judge of the future; it will avail them of the experience of other times and other nations; it will qualify them as judges of the actions and designs of men; it will enable them to know ambition under every disguise it may assume; and knowing it, to defeat its views. In every government on earth is some traces of human weakness, some germ of corruption and degeneracy, which cunning will discover, and wickedness insensibly open, cultivate and improve. Every government degenerates when trusted to the rulers of the people alone. The people themselves then are its only safe depositories. And to render them safe their minds must be improved to a certain degree. This indeed is not all that is necessary, though it be essentially necessary. An amendment of our constitution must here come in aid of the public education. The influence over government must be shared among all the people. If every individual which composes their mass participates of the ultimate authority, the government will be safe; because the corrupting the whole mass will exceed any private resources of wealth: and public ones cannot be provided but by levies on the people. In this case every man would have to pay his own price.

THOMAS JEFFERSON CALLS FOR A CRUSADE AGAINST IGNORANCE

(1786)   From Thomas Jefferson to George Wythe, August 13, 1786, as quoted in Julian P. Boyd, ed., *The Papers of Thomas Jefferson* (Princeton, N.J., 1954), vol. X, pp. 243-45.

The European papers have announced that the assembly of Virginia were occupied on the revisal of their Code of laws. This, with some other similar intelligence, has contributed much to convince the people of Europe, that what the English papers are constantly publishing of our anarchy, is false; as they are sensible that such a work is that of a people only who are in perfect tranquillity. Our act for freedom of religion is extremely applauded. The Ambassadors and ministers of the several nations of Europe resident at this court have asked of me copies of it to send to their sovereigns, and it is inserted at full length in several books now in the press; among others, in the new Encyclopedie. I think it will produce considerable good even in these countries where ignorance, superstition, poverty and oppression of body and mind in every form, are so firmly settled on the mass of the people, that their redemption from them can never be hoped. If the almighty had begotten a thousand sons, instead of one, they would not have sufficed for this task. If all the sovereigns of Europe were to set themselves to work to emancipate the minds of their subjects from their present ignorance and prejudices, and that as zealously as they now endeavor the contrary, a thousand years would not place them on that high ground on which our common people are now setting out. Ours could not have been so fairly put into the hands of their own common sense, had they not been separated from their parent stock and been kept from contamination, either from them, or the other people of the old world, by the intervention of so wide an ocean. To know the worth of this, one must see the want of it here. I think by far the most important bill in our whole code is that for the diffusion of knowledge among the people. No other sure foundation can be devised for the preservation of freedom, and happiness. If any body thinks that kings, nobles, or priests are good conservators of the public happiness, send them here. It is the best school in the universe to cure them of that folly. They will see here with their own eyes that these descriptions of men are an abandoned confederacy against the happiness of the mass of people. The omnipotence of their effect cannot be better proved than in this country particularly, where notwithstanding the finest soil upon earth, the finest climate under heaven, and a people of the most benevolent, the most gay, and amiable character of which the human form is susceptible, where such a people I say, surrounded by so many blessings from nature, are yet loaded with misery by kings, nobles and priests, and by them alone. Preach, my dear Sir, a crusade against ignorance; establish and improve the law for educating the common people. Let our countrymen know that the people alone can protect us against these evils, and that the tax which will be paid for this purpose is not more than the thousandth part of what will be paid to kings, priests and nobles who will rise up among us if we leave the people in ignorance.—The people of England, I think, are less oppressed than here. But it needs but half an eye to see, when among them, that the foundation is laid in their dispositions, for the establishment of a despotism. Nobility, wealth, and pomp are the objects of their adoration. They are by no means the free-minded people we suppose them in America. Their learned men too are few in number, and are less learned and infinitely less emancipated from prejudice than those of this country. An event too seems to be prospering, in the order of things, which will probably decide the fate of that country. It is no longer doubtful that the harbour of Cherbourg will be completed, that it will be a most excellent one, and capacious enough to hold the whole navy of France. Nothing has ever been wanting to enable this country to invade that, but a naval force conveniently stationed to protect the transports. This change of situation, must oblige the English to keep up a great standing army, and there is no king, who, with a sufficient force, is not always ready to make himself absolute.—My paper warns me it is time to recommend myself to the friendly recollection of Mrs. Wythe, of Colo. Taliaferro and his family and particularly of Mr. R. T. and to assure you of the affectionate esteem with which I am Dear Sir your friend & servt.,

TH: JEFFERSON

THOMAS JEFFERSON ON THE IMPORTANCE OF A FREE PRESS

(**1787**) From Thomas Jefferson to Edward Carrington, January 16, 1787, as quoted in Julian P. Boyd, ed., *The Papers of Thomas Jefferson* (Princeton, N.J., 1950-), vol. XII, pp. 48-49.

The tumults in America [Shays's Rebellion] I expected would have produced in Europe an unfavorable opinion of our political state. But it has not. On the contrary, the small effect of those tumults seems to have given more confidence in the firmness of our governments. The interposition of the people themselves on the side of government has had a great effect on the opinion here. I am persuaded myself that the good sense of the people will always be found to be the best army. They may be led astray for a moment, but will soon correct themselves. The people are the only censors of their governors: and even their errors will tend to keep these to the true principles of their institution. To punish these errors too severely would be to suppress the only safeguard of the public liberty. The way to prevent these irregular interpositions of the people is to give them full information of their affairs thro' the channel of the public papers, and to contrive that those papers should penetrate the whole mass of the people. The basis of our governments being the opinion of the people, the very first object should be to keep that right; and were it left to me to decide whether we should have a government without newspapers, or newspapers without a government, I should not hesitate a moment to prefer the latter. But I should mean that every man should receive those papers and be capable of reading them. I am convinced that those societies (as the Indians) which live without government enjoy in their general mass an infinitely greater degree of happiness than those who live under European governments. Among the former, public opinion is in the place of law, and restrains morals as powerfully as laws ever did any where. Among the latter, under pretence of governing they have divided their nations into two classes, wolves and sheep. I do not exaggerate. This is a true picture of Europe. Cherish therefore the spirit of our people, and keep alive their attention. Do not be too severe upon their errors, but reclaim them by enlightening them. If once they become inattentive to the public affairs, you and I, and Congress, and Assemblies, judges and governors shall all become wolves. It seems to be the law of our general nature, in spite of individual exceptions; and experience declares that man is the only animal which devours his own kind, for I can apply no milder term to the governments of Europe, and to the general prey of the rich on the poor. . . . Liberty ought to encourage Freedom of Speech. The Defence of Liberty, is a noble and heavenly Office which can only be performed where Liberty is.

THOMAS JEFFERSON ON THE NATURAL ARISTOCRACY AMONG MEN

(1813)   From letter to John Adams, October 28, 1813, as quoted in Albert E. Bergh, ed., *The Writings of Thomas Jefferson* (Washington, D.C., 1905), vol. XII, pp. 394-403.

MONTICELLO, October 28, 1813.

DEAR SIR,—According to the reservation between us, of taking up one of the subjects of our correspondence at a time, I turn to your letters of August the 16th and September the 2d.

The passage you quote from Theognis, I think has an ethical rather than a political object. The whole piece is a moral *exhortation, παραινεσις*, and this passage particularly seems to be a reproof to man, who, while with his domestic animals he is curious to improve the race, by employing always the finest male, pays no attention to the improvement of his own race, but intermarries with the vicious, the ugly, or the old, for considerations of wealth or ambition. It is in conformity with the principle adopted afterwards by the Pythagoreans, and expressed by Ocellus in another form; πεπι δε τῆς ʼεκ τῶν αλληλων ανθρων γενεσεως etc.,—ουχ ηδονης ενεκα μιξις, which, as literally as intelligibility will admit, may be thus translated: "concerning the interprocreation of men, how, and of whom it shall be, in a perfect manner, and according to the laws of modesty and sanctity, conjointly, this is what I think right. First to lay it down that we do not commix for the sake of pleasure, but of the procreation of children. For the powers, the organs and desires for coition have not been given by God to man for the sake of pleasure, but for the procreation of the race. For as it were incongruous, for a mortal born to partake of divine life, the immortality of the race being taken away, God fulfilled the purpose by making the generations uninterrupted and continuous. This, therefore, we are especially to lay down as a principle, that coition is not for the sake of pleasure." But nature, not trusting to this moral and abstract motive, seems to have provided more securely for the perpetuation of the species, by making it the effect of the *oestrum* implanted in the constitution of both sexes. And not only has the commerce of love been indulged on this unhallowed impulse, but made subservient also to wealth and ambition by marriage, without regard to the beauty, the healthiness, the understanding, or virtue of the subject from which we are to breed. The selecting the best male for a harem of well-chosen females also, which Theognis seems to recommend from the example of our sheep and asses, would doubtless improve the human, as it does the brute animal, and produce a race of veritable αριστοι. For experience proves, that the moral and physical qualities of man, whether good or evil, are transmissible in a certain degree from father to son. But I suspect that the equal rights of men will rise up against this privileged Solomon and his harem, and oblige us to continue acquiescence under the "Αμαυροσις γενεος αστον" which Theognis complains of, and to content ourselves with the accidental aristoi produced by the fortuitous concourse of breeders. For I agree with you that there is a natural aristocracy among men. The grounds of this are virtue and talents. Formerly, bodily powers gave place among the aristoi. But since the invention of gunpowder has armed the weak as well as the strong with missile death, bodily strength, like beauty, good humor, politeness and other accomplishments, has become but an auxiliary ground of distinction. There is also an artificial aristocracy, founded on wealth and birth, without either virtue or talents; for with these it would belong to the first class. The natural aristocracy I consider as the most precious gift of nature, for the instruction, the trusts, and government of society. And indeed, it would have been inconsistent in creation to have formed man for the social state, and not to have provided virtue and wisdom enough to manage the concerns of the society. May we not even say, that that form of government is the best, which provides the most effectually for a pure selection of these natural aristoi into the offices of government? The artificial aristocracy is a mischievous ingredient in government, and provision should be made to prevent its ascendency. On the question, what is the best provision, you and I differ; but we differ as rational friends, using the free exercise of our own reason, and mutually indulging its errors. You think it best to put the pseudo-aristoi into a separate chamber of legislation, where they may be hindered from doing mischief by their co-ordinate branches, and where, also, they may be a protection to wealth against the agrarian and plundering enterprises of the majority of the people. I think that to give them power in order to prevent them from doing mischief, is arming them for it, and increasing instead of remedying the evil. For if the co-ordinate branches can arrest their action, so may they that of the co-ordinates. Mischief may be done negatively as well as positively. Of this, a cabal in the Senate of the United States has furnished many proofs. Nor do I believe them necessary to protect the wealthy; because enough of these will find their way into every branch of the legislation, to protect themselves. From fifteen to twenty legislatures of our own, in action for thirty years past, have proved that no fears of an equalization of property are to be apprehended from them. I think the best remedy is exactly that provided by all our constitutions, to leave to the citizens the free election and separation of the aristoi from the pseudo-aristoi, of the wheat from the chaff. In general they will elect the really good and wise. In some instances, wealth may corrupt, and birth blind them; but not in sufficient degree to endanger the society.

It is probable that our difference of opinion may, in some measure, be produced by a difference of character in those among whom we live. From what I have seen of Massachusetts and Connecticut myself, and still more from what I have heard, and the character given of the former by yourself, (volume I, page III,) who know them so much better, there seems to be in those two States a traditionary reverence for certain families, which has rendered the offices of the government nearly hereditary in those families. I presume that from an early period of your history, members of those families happening to possess virtue and talents, have honestly exercised them for the good of the people, and by their services have endeared their names to them. In coupling Connecticut with you, I mean it politically only, not morally. For having made the Bible the common law of their land, they seem to have modeled their morality on the story of Jacob and Laban. But although this hereditary succession to office with you, may, in some degree, be founded in real family merit, yet in a much higher degree, it has proceeded from your strict alliance of Church and State. These families are canonized in the eyes of the people on common principles, "you tickle me, and I will tickle you." In Virginia we have nothing of this. Our clergy, before the revolution, having been secured against rivalship by fixed salaries, did not give themselves the trouble of acquiring influence over the people. Of wealth, there were great accumulations in particular families, handed down from generation to generation, under the English law of entails. But the only object of ambition for the wealthy was a seat in the King's Council. All their court then was paid to the crown and its creatures; and they Philipized in all collisions between the King and the people. Hence they were unpopular; and that unpopularity continues attached to their names. A Randolph, a Carter, or a Burwell must have great personal superiority over a common competitor to be elected by the people even at this day. At the first session of legislature after the Declaration of Independence, we passed a law abolishing entails. And this was followed by one abolishing the privilege of primogeniture, and dividing the lands of intestates equally among all their children, or other representatives. These laws, drawn by myself, laid the axe to the foot of pseudo-aristocracy. And had another which I prepared been adopted by the legislature, our work would have been complete. It was a bill for the more general diffusion of learning. This proposed to divide every county into wards of five or six miles square, like your townships; to establish in each ward a free school for reading, writing and common arithmetic; to provide for the annual selection of the best subjects from these schools, who might receive, at the public expense, a higher degree of education at a district school; and from these district schools to select a certain number of the most promising subjects, to be completed at an university, where all the useful sciences should be taught. Worth and genius would thus have been sought out from every condition of life, and completely prepared by education for defeating the competition of wealth and birth for public trusts. My proposition had, for a further object, to impart to these wards those portions of self-government for which they are best qualified, by confiding to them the care of their poor, their roads, police, elections, the nomination of jurors, administration of justice in small cases, elementary exercises of militia; in short, to have made them little republics, with a warden at the head of each, for all those concerns which, being under their eye, they would better manage than the larger republics of the county or State. A general call of ward meetings by their wardens on the same day through the State, would at any time produce the genuine sense of the people on any required point, and would enable the State to act in mass, as your people have so often done, and with so much effect by their town meetings. The law for religious freedom, which made a part of this system, having put down the aristocracy of the clergy, and restored to the citizen the freedom of the mind, and those of entails and descents nurturing an equality of condition among them, this on education would have raised the mass of the people to the high ground of moral respectability necessary to their own safety, and to orderly government; and would have completed the great object of qualifying them to select the veritable aristoi, for the trusts of government, to the exclusion of the pseudalists; and the same Theognis who has furnished the epigraphs of your two letters, assures us that "Ουδεμιαν πω, Κυρν', αγαθοι πολιν ωλεσαν ανδρες." [Not any state, Cyrnus, have good men yet destroyed.] Although this law has not yet been acted on but in a small and inefficient degree, it is still considered as before the legislature, with other bills of the revised code, not yet taken up, and I have great hope that some patriotic spirit will, at a favorable moment, call it up, and make it the keystone of the arch of our government.

With respect to aristocracy, we should further consider, that before the establishment of the American States, nothing was known to history but the man of the old world, crowded within limits either small or overcharged, and steeped in the vices which that situation generates. A government adapted to such men would be one thing; but a very different one, that for the man of these States. Here every one may have land to labor for himself, if he chooses; or, preferring the exercise of any other industry, may exact for it such compensation as not only to afford a comfortable subsistence, but wherewith to provide for a cessation from labor in old age. Every one, by his property, or by his satisfactory situation, is interested in the support of law and order. And such men may safely and advantageously reserve to themselves a wholesome control over their public affairs, and a degree of freedom, which, in the hands of the *canaille* of the cities of Europe, would be instantly perverted to the demolition and destruction of everything public and private. The history of the last twenty-five years of France, and of the last forty years in America, nay of its last two hundred years, proves the truth of both parts of this observation.

But even in Europe a change has sensibly taken place in the mind of man. Science had liberated the ideas of those who read and reflect, and the American example had kindled feelings of right in the people. An insurrection has consequently begun, of science, talents, and courage, against rank and birth, which have fallen into contempt. It has failed in its first effort, because the mobs of the cities, the instrument used for its accomplishment, debased by ignorance, poverty, and vice, could not be restrained to rational action. But the world will recover from the panic of this first catastrophe. Science is progressive, and talents and enterprise on the alert. Resort may be had to the people of the country, a more governable power from their principles and subordination; and rank, and birth, and tinsel-aristocracy will finally shrink into insignificance, even there. This, however, we have no right to meddle with. It suffices for us, if the moral and physical condition of our own citizens qualifies them to select the able and good for the direction of their government, with a recurrence of elections at such short periods as will enable them to displace an unfaithful servant, before the mischief he meditates may be irremediable.

I have thus stated my opinion on a point on which we differ, not with a view to controversy, for we are both too old to change opinions which are the result of a long life of inquiry and reflection; but on the suggestions of a former letter of yours, that we ought not to die before we have explained ourselves to each other. We acted in perfect harmony, through a long and perilous contest for our liberty and independence. A constitution has been acquired, which, though neither of us thinks perfect, yet both consider as competent to render our fellow citizens the happiest

REPUBLICANS

and the securest on whom the sun has ever shone. If we do not think exactly alike as to its imperfections, it matters little to our country, which, after devoting to it long lives of disinterested labor, we have delivered over to our successors in life, who will be able to take care of it and of themselves.

Of the pamphlet on aristocracy which has been sent to you, or who may be its author, I have heard nothing but through your letter. If the person you suspect, it may be known from the quaint, mystical, and hyperbolical ideas, involved in affected, new-fangled and pedantic terms which stamp his writings. Whatever it be, I hope your quiet is not to be affected at this day by the rudeness or intemperance of scribblers; but that you may continue in tranquillity to live and to rejoice in the prosperity of our country, until it shall be your own wish to take your seat among the aristoi who have gone before you. Ever and affectionately yours.

BENJAMIN RUSH PROPOSES A SYSTEM OF PUBLIC SCHOOLS FOR PENNSYLVANIA (1786)   From Benjamin Rush, *Essays, Literary, Moral, and Philosophical* (Philadelphia, 1806), pp. 1-8.

Before I proceed to the subject of this essay, I shall point out, in a few words, the influence and advantages of learning upon mankind.

I. It is friendly to religion, inasmuch as it assists in removing prejudice, superstition and enthusiasm, in promoting just notions of the Deity, and in enlarging our knowledge of his works.

II. It is favourable to liberty. Freedom can exist only in the society of knowledge. Without learning, men are incapable of knowing their rights, and where learning is confined to a few people, liberty can be neither equal nor universal.

III. It promotes just ideas of laws and government. "When the clouds of ignorance are dispelled (says the Marquis of Beccaria) by the radiance of knowledge, power trembles, but the authority of laws remains immoveable."

IV. It is friendly to manners. Learning in all countries, promotes civilization, and the pleasures of society and conversation.

V. It promotes agriculture, the great basis of national wealth and happiness. Agriculture is as much a science as hydraulics, or optics, and has been equally indebted to the experiments and researches of learned men. The highly cultivated state, and the immense profits of the farms in England, are derived wholly from the patronage which agriculture has received in that country, from learned men and learned societies.

VI. Manufactures of all kinds owe their perfection chiefly to learning—hence the nations of Europe advance in manufactures, knowledge, and commerce, only in proportion as they cultivate the arts and sciences.

For the purpose of diffusing knowledge through every part of the state, I beg leave to propose the following simple plan.

I. Let there be one university in the state, and let this be established in the capital. Let law, physic, divinity, the law of nature and nations, economy, &c. be taught in it by public lectures in the winter season; after the manner of the

European universities, and let the professors receive such salaries from the state as will enable them to deliver their lectures at a moderate price.

II. Let there be four colleges. One in Philadelphia; one at Carlisle; a third, for the benefit of our German fellow citizens, at Lancaster; and a fourth, some years hence at Pittsburg. In these colleges, let young men be instructed in mathematics and in the higher branches of science, in the same manner that they are now taught in our American colleges. After they have received a testimonial from one of these colleges, let them, if they can afford it, complete their studies by spending a season or two in attending the lectures in the university. I prefer four colleges in the state to one or two, for there is a certain size of colleges as there is of towns and armies, that is most favourable to morals and good government. Oxford and Cambridge in England are the seats of dissipation, while the more numerous, and less crouded universities and colleges in Scotland, are remarkable for the order, diligence, and decent behaviour of their students.

III. Let there be free schools established in every township, or in districts consisting of one hundred families. In these schools let children be taught to read and write the English and German languages, and the use of figures. Such of them as have parents that can afford to send them from home, and are disposed to extend their educations, may remove their children from the free school to one of the colleges.

By this plan the whole state will be tied together by one system of education. The university will in time furnish masters for the colleges, and the colleges will furnish masters for the free schools, while the free schools, in their turns, will supply the colleges and the university with scholars, students and pupils. The same systems of grammar, oratory and philosophy, will be taught in every part of the state, and the literary features of Pennsylvania will thus designate one great, and equally enlightened family.

But, how shall we bear the expense of these literary institutions?——I answer— These institutions will *lessen* our taxes. They will enlighten us in the great business of finance—they will teach us to encrease the ability of the state to support government, by encreasing the profits of agriculture, and by promoting manufactures. They will teach us all the modern improvements and advantages of inland navigation. They will defend us from hasty and expensive experiment in government, by unfolding to us the experience and folly of past ages, and thus, instead of adding to our taxes and debts, they will furnish us with the true secret of lessening and discharging both of them.

But, shall the estates of orphans, batchelors and persons who have no children, be taxed to pay for the support of schools from which they can derive no benefit? I answer in the affirmative, to the first part of the objection, and I deny the truth of the latter part of it. Every member of the community is interested in the propagation of virtue and knowledge in the state. But I will go further, and add, it will be true œconomy in individuals to support public schools. The batchelor will in time save his tax for this purpose, by being able to sleep with fewer bolts and locks to his doors—the estates of orphans will in time be benefited, by being protected from the ravages of unprincipled and idle boys, and the children of wealthy parents will be less tempted, by bad company, to extravagance. Fewer pillories and whipping posts, and smaller goals, with their usual expenses and taxes, will be necessary when our youth are properly educated, than at present; I believe it could be proved, that the expenes of confining, trying and executing criminals, amount every year, in most of the counties, to more money than would be sufficient to maintain all the schools that would be necessary in each county. The confessions of these criminals generally show us, that their vices and punishments are the fatal consequences of the want of a proper education in early life.

I submit these detached hints to the consideration of the legislature and of the citizens of Pensylvania. The plan for the free schools is taken chiefly from the plans which have long been used with success in Scotland, and in the eastern states of America, where the influence of learning, in promoting religion, morals, manners, and good government, has never been exceeded in any country.

The manner in which these schools should be supported and governed—the modes of determining the characters and qualifications of schoolmasters, and the arrangement of families in each district, so that children of the same religious sect and nation, may be educated as much as possible together, will form a proper part of a law for the establishment of schools, and therefore does not come within the limits of this plan.

BENJAMIN RUSH ON THE MODE OF EDUCATION PROPER IN A REPUBLIC (1786) From Benjamin Rush, *Essays, Literary, Moral, and Philosophical* (Philadelphia, 1806), pp. 8-13.

Of the Mode of Education Proper in a Republic

The business of education has acquired a new complexion by the independence of our country. The form of government we have assumed, has created a new class of duties to every American. It becomes us, therefore, to examine our former habits upon this subject, and in laying the foundations for nurseries of wise and good men, to adapt our modes of teaching to the peculiar form of our government.

The first remark that I shall make upon this subject is, that an education in our own, is to be preferred to an education in a foreign country. The principle of patriotism stands in need of the reinforcement of prejudice, and it is well known that our strongest prejudices in favour of our country are formed in the first one and twenty years of our lives. The policy of the Lacedemonians is well worthy of our imitation. When Antipater demanded fifty of their children as hostages for the fulfillment of a distant engagement, those wise republicans refused to comply with his demand, but readily offered him double the number of their adult citizens, whose habits and prejudices could not be shaken by residing in a foreign country. Passing by, in this place, the advantages to the community from the early attachment of youth to the laws and constitution of their country, I shall only remark, that young men who have trodden the paths of science together, or have joined in the same sports, whether of swimming, scating, fishing, or hunting, generally feel, thro' life, such ties to each other, as add greatly to the obligations of mutual benevolence.

I conceive the education of our youth in this country to be peculiarly necessary in Pennsylvania, while our citizens are composed of the natives of so many different kingdoms in Europe. Our schools of learning, by producing one general, and uniform system of education, will render the mass of the people more homogeneous, and thereby fit them more easily for uniform and peaceable government.

I proceed in the next place, to enquire, what mode of education we shall adopt so as to secure to the state all the advantages that are to be derived from the proper instruction of youth; and here I beg leave to remark, that the only foundation for a useful education in a republic is to be laid in Religion. Without this there can be no virtue, and without virtue there can be no liberty, and liberty is the object and life of all republican governments.

Such is my veneration for every religion that reveals the attributes of the Deity, or a future state of rewards and punishments, that I had rather see the opinions of Confucius or Mahomed inculcated upon our youth, than see them grow up wholly devoid of a system of religious principles. But the religion I mean to recommend in this place, is that of the New Testament.

It is foreign to my purpose to hint at the arguments which establish the truth of the Christian revelation. My only business is to declare, that all its doctrines and precepts are calculated to promote the happiness of society, and the safety and well being of civil government. A Christian cannot fail of being a republican. The history of the creation of man, and of the relation of our species to each other by birth, which is recorded in the Old Testament, is the best refutation that can be given to the divine right of kings, and the strongest argument that can be used in favor of the original and natural equality of all mankind. A Christian, I say again, cannot fail of being a republican, for every precept of the Gospel inculcates those degrees of humility, self-denial, and brotherly kindness, which are directly opposed to the pride of monarchy and the pageantry of a court. A Christian cannot fail of being useful to the republic, for his religion teacheth him, that no man "liveth to himself." And lastly, a Christian cannot fail of being wholly inoffensive, for his religion teacheth him, in all things to do to others what he would wish, in like circumstances, they should do to him.

I am aware that I dissent from one of those paradoxical opinions with which modern times abound; and that it is improper to fill the minds of youth with religious prejudices of any kind, and that they should be left to choose their own principles, after they have arrived at an age in which they are capable of judging for themselves. Could we preserve the mind in childhood and youth a perfect blank, this plan of education would have more to recommend it; but this we know to be impossible. The human mind runs as naturally into principles as it does after facts. It submits with difficulty to those restraints or partial discoveries which are imposed upon it in the infancy of reason. Hence the impatience of children to be informed upon all subjects that relate to the invisible world. But I beg leave to ask, why should we pursue a different plan of education with respect to religion, from that which we pursue in teaching the arts and sciences? Do we leave our youth to acquire systems of geography, philosophy, or politics, till they have arrived at an age in which they are capable of judging for themselves? We do not. I claim no more then for religion, than for the other sciences, and I add further, that if our youth are disposed after they are of age to think for themselves, a knowledge of one system, will be the best means of conducting them in a free enquiry into other systems of religion, just as an acquaintance with one system of philosophy is the best introduction to the study of all the other systems in the world.

Next to the duty which young men owe to their Creator, I wish to see a regard to their country, inculcated upon them. When the Duke of Sully became prime minister to Henry the IVth of France, the first thing he did, he tells us, "Was to subdue and forget his own heart." The same duty is incumbent upon every citizen of a republic. Our country includes family, friends and property, and should be preferred to them all. Let our pupil be taught that he does not belong to himself, but that he is public property. Let him be taught to love his family, but let him be taught, at the same time, that he must forsake, and even forget them, when the welfare of his country requires it. He must watch for the state, as if its liberties depended upon his vigilance alone, but he must do this in such a manner as not to defraud his creditors, or neglect his family. He must love private life, but he must decline no station, however public or responsible it may be, when called to it by the suffrages of his fellow citizens. He must love popularity, but he must despise it when set in competition with the dictates of his judgement, or the real interest of his country. He must love character, and have a due sense of injuries, but he must be taught to appeal only to the laws of the state, to defend the one, and punish the other. He must love family honour, but he must be taught that neither the rank or antiquity of his ancestors, can command respect, without personal merit. He must avoid neutrality in all questions that divide the state, but he must shun the rage, and acrimony of party spirit. He must be taught to love his fellow creatures in every part of the world, but he must cherish with a more intense and peculiar affection, the citizens of Pennsylvania and of the United States. I do not wish to see our youth educated with a single prejudice against any nation or country; but we impose a task upon human nature, repugnant alike to reason, revelation and the ordinary dimensions of the human heart, when we require him to embrace, with equal affection, the whole family of mankind. He must be taught to amass wealth, but it must be only to encrease his power of contributing to the wants and demands of the state. He must be indulged occasionally in amusements, but he must be taught that study and business should be his principal pursuits in life. Above all he must love life, and endeavour to acquire as many of its conveniences as possible by industry and economy, but he must be taught that this life "is not his own," when the safety of his country requires it. These are practicable lessons, and the history of the commonwealths of Greece and Rome show, that human nature, without the aids of Christianity, has attained these degrees of perfection.

While we inculcate these republican duties upon our pupil, we must not neglect, at the same time, to inspire him with republican principles. He must be taught that there can be no durable liberty but in a republic, and that government, like all other sciences, is of a progressive nature. The chains which have bound this science in Europe are happily unloosed in America. Here it is open to investigation and improvement. While philosophy has protected us by its discoveries from a thousand natural evils, government has unhappily followed with an unequal pace. It would be to dishonour human genius, only to name the many defects which still exist in the best systems of legislation. We daily see matter of a perishable nature rendered durable by certain chemical operations. In like manner, I conceive, that it is possible to combine power in such a way as not only to encrease the happiness, but to promote the duration of republican forms of government far beyond the terms limited for them by history, or the common opinions of mankind.

BENJAMIN RUSH'S ARGUMENT FOR FREE SCHOOLS FOR POOR CHILDREN IN PHILADELPHIA (1787)

From Benjamin Rush, "To the Citizens of Philadelphia, and of the District of Southwark and the Northern Liberties," *The Independent Gazetteer*, March 28, 1787, as quoted in Lyman H. Butterfield, ed., *Letters of Benjamin Rush* (Princeton, N.J., 1951), vol. I, pp. 412-15.

The blessings of knowledge can be extended to the poor and laboring part of the community only by the means of FREE SCHOOLS.

The remote and unconnected state of the settlements in the new counties will forbid the establishment of those schools for some years to come by a general law; but there is nothing to prevent this being set on foot immediately in the city of Philadelphia and in the old and thick-settled counties of the state.

To a people enlightened in the principles of liberty and Christianity, arguments, it is to be hoped, will be unnecessary to persuade them to adopt these necessary and useful institutions. The children of poor people form a great proportion of all communities. Their ignorance and vices when neglected are not confined to themselves; they associate with and contaminate the children of persons in the higher ranks of society. Thus they assist after they arrive at manhood in choosing the rulers who govern the whole community. They give a complexion to the morals and manners of the people. In short, where the common people are ignorant and vicious, a nation, and above all a republican nation, can never be long free and happy. It becomes us, therefore, as we love our offspring and value the freedom and prosperity of our country, immediately to provide for the education of the poor children who are so numerous in the thick-settled parts of the state.

The following plan for beginning this important business in the capital of the state is submitted to the consideration of the citizens of Philadelphia and of the districts of Southwark and the Northern Liberties.

FIRST, Let an application be made to the legislature for a law to assess 1000l. upon all estates in the city and liberties of Philadelphia, to be appropriated for the maintenance of schoolmasters, for the rent of schoolhouses, and other expenses connected with this undertaking. This mode of establishing free schools has many advantages over that of trusting them to the precarious support of charitable contributions. In Scotland and New-England the free schools are maintained by *law;* hence education and knowledge are universal in those countries. In England the free schools are supported chiefly by charity sermons; hence education and knowledge are so partially diffused through that country, and hence too the origin of the numerous executions and inventions to punish and extirpate criminals of which we daily read such melancholy accounts in the English newspapers. Charitable contributions fall unequally upon the different members of society—a tax will be more equally borne and will be so light as scarcely to be felt by anybody. The price of a bottle of wine or of a single fashionable feather will pay the tax of an ordinary freeholder for a whole year to those schools. Besides, there will be real economy in the payment of this tax; by sowing the seeds of good morals in the schools and inspiring the youth with habits of industry, the number of the poor and of course the sum of the tax paid for their maintenance will be diminished. By lessening the quantity of vice, we shall moreover lessen the expenses of jails and of the usual forms of law which conduct people to them. Above all, we shall render an acceptable service to the Divine Being in taking care of that part of our fellow creatures who appear to be the more immediate objects of his compassion and benevolence.

SECONDLY, Let the children who are sent to those schools be taught to read and write the English and (when required by their parents) the German language. Let the girls be instructed in needlework, knitting, and spinning, as well as in the branches of literature that have been mentioned. Above all, let both sexes be carefully instructed in the principles and obligations of the Christian religion. This is the most essential part of education—this will make them dutiful children, teachable scholars, and, afterwards, good apprentices, good husbands, good wives, honest mechanics, industrious farmers, peaceable sailors, and, in everything that relates to this country, good citizens. To effect this important purpose it will be necessary,

THIRDLY, That the children of parents of the same religious denominations should be educated together in order that they may be instructed with the more ease in the principles and forms of their respective churches. By these means the schools will come more immediately under the inspection of the ministers of the city, and thereby religion and learning be more intimately connected.

After the experience we have had of the advantages derived by the Friends from connecting their schools and their church together in forming the morals of their youth, nothing further need be added in favor of this part of the plan.

FOURTHLY, Let the money to be raised for the support of the schools be lodged in the hands of the city treasurer, to be appropriated in the following manner: Let a certain number of persons of each religious society be appointed trustees of the free schools of their respective churches, and let a draft signed by the president of a quorum of these trustees be a voucher to the treasurer to issue three or four pounds a year for every scholar who is educated by them. As soon as the number of scholars belonging to any religious society exceeds fifteen, let 30l. a year be allowed to them for the rent of the school room and for paper, ink, pens, books, and firewood, and 60l. a year when the number of scholars becomes so great as to require two schoolrooms. If any religious society should decline accepting of the bounty of the city, from having provided for the education of their poor by private contribution, let their proportion of it be thrown into the poor tax of the city if it should not be required for the poor children of the less wealthy societies. And,

LASTLY, Let the accounts and expenditures of the schools be open at all times to inspectors, to be appointed by the law, and published every year.

Citizens of Philadelphia, awaken at last to check the vice which taints the atmosphere of our city. The profane and indecent language which assaults our ears in every street can only be restrained by extending education to the children of poor people. The present is an era of public spirit—the Dispensary and the Humane Society will be lasting monuments of the humanity of the *present* citizens of Philadelphia. But let not the health and lives of the poor exhaust the whole stock of our benevolence. Their morals are of more consequence to society than their health or lives; and their minds must exist forever. "Blessed is he that considereth the poor, the Lord will deliver him in time of trouble. The Lord will preserve him, and keep him alive upon the earth—he will not deliver him into the will of his enemies."

NOAH WEBSTER URGES REFORM OF SPELLING (1789) From Noah Webster, "An Essay on the Necessity, Advantages, and Practicality of Reforming the Mode of Spelling and of Rendering the Orthography of Words Correspondent to Pronunciation," *Dissertations on the English Language: With Notes, Historical and Critical, to Which is Added, by Way of Appendix, an Essay on a Reformed Mode of Spelling, with Dr. Franklin's Arguments on That Subject* (Boston, 1789), pp. 391, 393-98, 405-6.

It has been observed by all writers, on the English language, that the orthography or spelling of words is very irregular; the same letters often representing different sounds, and the same sounds often expressed by different letters. For this irregularity, two principal causes may be assigned:

1. The changes to which the pronunciation of a language is liable, from the progress of science and civilization.

2. The mixture of different languages, occasioned by revolutions in England, or by a predilection of the learned, for words of foreign growth and ancient origin.

*   *   *

The question now occurs; ought the Americans to retain these faults which produce innumerable inconveniencies in the acquisition and use of the language, or ought they at once to reform these abuses, and introduce order and regularity into the orthography of the AMERICAN TONGUE?

Let us consider this subject with some attention.

Several attempts were formerly made in England to rectify the orthography of the language. But I apprehend their schemes failed to success, rather on account of their intrinsic difficulties, than on account of any necessary impracticability of a reform. It was proposed, in most of these schemes, not merely to throw out superfluous and silent letters, but to introduce a number of new characters. Any attempt on such a plan must undoubtedly prove unsuccessful. It is not to be expected that an orthography, perfectly regular and simple, such as would be formed by a "Synod of Grammarians on principles of science," will ever be substituted for that confused mode of spelling which is now established. But it is apprehended that great improvements may be made, and an orthography almost regular, or such as shall obviate most of the present difficulties which occur in learning our language, may be introduced and established with little trouble and opposition.

The principal alterations, necessary to render our orthography sufficiently regular and easy, are these:

1. The omission of all superfluous or silent letters; as *a* in *bread*. Thus *bread, head, give, breast, built, meant, realm, friend*, would be spelt, *bred, hed, giv, brest, bilt, ment, relm, frend*. Would this alteration produce any inconvenience, any embarrassment or expense? By no means. On the other hand, it would lessen the trouble of writing, and much more, of learning the language; it would reduce the true pronunciation to a certainty; and while it would assist foreigners and our own children in acquiring the language, it would render the pronunciation uniform, in different parts of the country, and almost prevent the possibility of changes.

2. A substitution of a character that has a certain definite sound, for one that is more vague and indeterminate. Thus by putting *ee* instead of *ea* or *ie*, the words

mean, near, speak, grieve, zeal, would become *meen, neer, speek, greev, zeel.* This alteration could not occasion a moments trouble; at the same time it would prevent a doubt respecting the pronunciation; whereas the *ea* and *ie* having different sounds, may give a learner much difficulty. Thus *greef* should be substituted for *grief; kee* for *key; beleev* for *believe; laf* for *laugh; dawter* for *daughter; plow* for *plough; tuf* for *tough; proov* for *prove; blud* for *blood;* and *draft* for *draught.* In this manner *ch* in Greek derivatives, should be changed into *k;* for the English *ch* has a soft sound, as in *cherish;* but *k* always a hard sound. Therefore *character, chorus, cholic, architecture,* should be written *karacter, korus, kolic, arkitecture;* and were they thus written, no person could mistake their true pronunciation.

Thus *ch* in French derivatives should be changed into *sh; machine, chaise, chevalier,* should be written *masheen, shaze, shevaleer;* and *pique, tour, oblique,* should be written *peek, toor, obleek.*

3. A trifling alteration in a character, or the addition of a point would distinguish different sounds, without the substitution of a new character. Thus a very small stroke across *th* would distinguish its two sounds. A point over a vowel, in this manner, $\dot{a}$, or $\hat{u}$, or $\bar{\imath}$, might answer all the purposes of different letters. And for the dipthong *ow,* let the two letters be united by a small stroke, or both engraven on the same piece of metal, with the left hand line of the *w* united to the *o.*

These, with a few other inconsiderable alterations, would answer every purpose, and render the orthography sufficiently correct and regular.

The advantages to be derived from these alterations are numerous, great and permanent.

1. The simplicity of the orthography would facilitate the learning of the language. It is now the work of years for children to learn to spell; and after all, the business is rarely accomplished. A few men, who are bred to some business that requires constant exercise in writing, finally learn to spell most words without hesitation; but most people remain, all their lives, imperfect masters of spelling, and liable to make mistakes, whenever they take up a pen to write a short note. Nay, many people, even of education and fashion, never attempt to write a letter, without frequently consulting a dictionary.

But with the proposed orthography, a child would learn to spell, without trouble, in a very short time, and the orthography being very regular, he would ever afterwards find it difficult to make a mistake. It would, in that case, be as difficult to spell *wrong,* as it is now to spell *right.*

Besides this advantage, foreigners would be able to acquire the pronunciation of English, which is now so difficult and embarrassing, that they are either wholly discouraged on the first attempt, or obliged, after many years labor, to rest contented with an imperfect knowledge of the subject.

2. A correct orthography would render the pronunciation of the language, as uniform as the spelling in books. A general uniformity thro the United States, would be the event of such a reformation as I am here recommending. All persons, of every rank, would speak with some degree of precision and uniformity. Such a uniformity in these states is very desireable; it would remove prejudice, and conciliate mutual affection and respect.

3. Such a reform would diminish the number of letters about one sixteenth or eighteenth. This would save a page in eighteen; and a saving of an eighteenth in the expense of books, is an advantage that should not be overlooked.

4. But a capital advantage of this reform in these states would be, that it would make a difference between the English orthography and the American. This will

startle those who have not attended to the subject; but I am confident that such an event is an object of vast political consequence. For,

The alteration, however small, would encourage the publication of books in our own country. It would render it, in some measure, necessary that all books should be printed in America. The English would never copy our orthography for their own use; and consequently the same impressions of books would not answer for both countries. The inhabitants of the present generation would read the English impressions; but posterity, being taught a different spelling, would prefer the American orthography.

Besides this, a *national language* is a band of *national union*. Every engine should be employed to render the people of this country *national;* to call their attachments home to their own country; and to inspire them with the pride of national character. However, they may boast of Independence, and the freedom of their government, yet their *opinions* are not sufficiently independent; an astonishing respect for the arts and literature of their parent country, and a blind imitation of its manners, are still prevalent among the Americans.

*   *   *

Sensible I am how much easier it is to *propose* improvements, than to *introduce* them. Every thing *new* starts the idea of difficulty; and yet it is often mere novelty that excites the appearance; for on a slight examination of the proposal, the difficulty vanishes. When we firmly *believe* a scheme to be practicable, the work is *half* accomplished. We are more frequently deterred by fear from making an attack, than repulsed in the encounter.

Habit also is opposed to changes; for it renders even our errors dear to us. Having surmounted all difficulties in childhood, we forget the labor, the fatigue, and the perplexity we suffered in the attempt, and imagin[e] the progress of our studies to have been smooth and easy. What seems intrinsically right, is so merely thro habit.

Indolence is another obstacle to improvements. The most arduous task a reformer has to execute, is to make people *think;* to rouse them from that lethargy, which, like the mantle of sleep, covers them in repose and contentment.

But America is in a situation the most favorable for great reformations; and the present time is, in a singular degree, auspicious. The minds of men in this country have been awakened. New scenes have been, for many years, presenting new occasions for exertion; unexpected distresses have called forth the powers of invention; and the application of new expedients has demanded every possible exercise of wisdom and talents. Attention is roused; the mind expanded; and the intellectual faculties invigorated. Here men are prepared to receive improvements, which would be rejected by nations, whose habits have not been shaken by similar events.

Now is the time, and *this* the country, in which we may expect success, in attempting changes favorable to language, science and government. Delay, in the plan here proposed, may be fatal; under a tranquil general government, the minds of men may again sink into indolence; a national acquiescence in error will follow; and posterity be doomed to struggle with difficulties, which time and accident will perpetually multiply.

Let us then seize the present moment, and establish a *national language,* as well as a national government. Let us remember that there is a certain respect due to the opinions of other nations. As an independent people, our reputation abroad demands that, in all things, we should be federal; be *national;* for if we do not respect *ourselves,* we may be assured that *other nations* will not respect us. In short, let it be impressed upon the mind of every American, that to neglect the means of commanding respect abroad, is treason against the character and dignity of a brave independent people.

NOAH WEBSTER ON THE NECESSITY FOR AN AMERICAN LANGUAGE

(**1789**)   From Noah Webster, "An Essay on the Necessity, Advantages, and Practicality of Reforming the Mode of Spelling . . ." *Dissertations on the English Language* . . . (Boston, 1789), pp. 17-19, 288-90, 393-98.

A regular study of language has, in all civilized countries, formed a part of a liberal education. The Greeks, Romans, Italians and French successively improved their native tongues, taught them in Academies at home, and rendered them entertaining and useful to the foreign student.

The English tongue, tho later in its progress towards perfection, has attained to a considerable degree of purity, strength and elegance, and been employed, by an active and scientific nation, to record almost all the events and discoveries of ancient and modern times.

This language is the inheritance which the Americans have received from their British parents. To cultivate and adorn it, is a task reserved for men who shall understand the connection between language and logic, and form an adequate idea of the influence which a uniformity of speech may have on national attachments.

It will be readily admitted that the pleasures of reading and conversing, the advantage of accuracy in business, the necessity of clearness and precision in communicating ideas, require us to be able to speak and write our own tongue with ease and correctness. But there are more important reasons, why the language of this country should be reduced to such fixed principles, as may give its pronunciation and construction all the certainty and uniformity which any living tongue is capable of receiving.

The United States were settled by emigrants from different parts of Europe. But their descendants mostly speak the same tongue; and the intercourse among the learned of the different States, which the revolution has begun, and an American Court will perpetuate, must gradually destroy the differences of dialect which our ancestors brought from their native countries. This approximation of dialects will be certain; but without the operation of other causes than an intercourse at Court, it will be slow and partial. The body of the people, governed by habit, will still retain their respective peculiarities of speaking; and for want of schools and proper books, fall into many inaccuracies, which, incorporating with the language of the state where they live, may imperceptibly corrupt the national language. Nothing but the establishment of schools and some uniformity in the use of books, can annihilate differences in speaking and preserve the purity of the American tongue. A sameness of pronunciation is of considerable consequence in a political view; for provincial accents are disagreeable to strangers and sometimes have an unhappy effect upon the social affections. All men have local attachments, which lead them to believe their own practice to be the least exceptionable. Pride and prejudice incline men to treat the practice of their neighbors with some degree of contempt. Thus small differences in pronunciation at first excite ridicule—a habit of laughing at the singularities of strangers is followed by disrespect—and without respect friendship is a name, and social intercourse a mere ceremony.

These remarks hold equally true, with respect to individuals, to small societies and to large communities. Small causes, such as a nick-name, or a vulgar tone in speaking, have actually created a dissocial spirit between the inhabitants of the different states, which is often discoverable in private business and public deliberations. Our political harmony is therefore concerned in a uniformity of language.

As an independent nation, our honor requires us to have a system of our own, in language as well as government. Great Britain, whose children we are, and whose language we speak, should no longer be our standard; for the taste of her writers is already corrupted, and her language on the decline. But if it were not so, she is at too great a distance to be our model, and to instruct us in the principles of our own tongue.

It must be considered further, that the English is the common root or stock from which our national language will be derived. All others will gradually waste away— and within a century and a half, North America will be peopled with a hundred millions of men, *all speaking the same language.* Place this idea in comparison with the present and possible future bounds of the language in Europe—consider the Eastern Continent as inhabited by nations, whose knowledge and intercourse are embarrassed by differences of language; then anticipate the period when the people of one quarter of the world, will be able to associate and converse together like children of the same family.[1] Compare this prospect, which is not visionary, with the state of the English language in Europe, almost confined to an Island and to a few millions of people; then let reason and reputation decide, how far America should be dependent on a transatlantic nation, for her standard and improvements in language.

Let me add, that whatever predilection the Americans may have for their native European tongues, and particularly the British descendants for the English, yet several circumstances render a future separation of the American tongue from the English, necessary and unavoidable. The vicinity of the European nations, with the uninterrupted communication in peace, and the changes of dominion in war, are gradually assimilating their respective languages. The English with others is suffering continual alterations. America, placed at a distance from those nations, will feel, in a much less degree, the influence of the assimilating causes; at the same time, numerous local causes, such as a new country, new associations of people, new combinations of ideas in arts and science, and some intercourse with tribes wholly unknown in Europe, will introduce new words into the American tongue. These causes will produce, in a course of time, a language in North America, as different from the future language of England, as the modern Dutch, Danish and Swedish are from the German, or from one another: Like remote branches of a tree springing from the same stock; or rays of light, shot from the same center, and

[1]Even supposing that a number of republics, kingdoms or empires, should within a century arise and divide this vast territory; still the subjects of all will speak the same language, and the consequence of this uniformity will be an intimacy of social intercourse hitherto unknown, and a boundless diffusion of knowledge.

diverging from each other, in proportion to their distance from the point of separation.

Whether the inhabitants of America can be brought to a perfect uniformity in the pronunciation of words, it is not easy to predict; but it is certain that no attempt of the kind has been made, and an experiment, begun and pursued on the right principles, is the only way to decide the question. Schools in Great Britain have gone far towards demolishing local dialects—commerce has also had its influence—and in America these causes, operating more generally, must have a proportional effect.

In many parts of America, people at present attempt to copy the English phrases and pronunciation—an attempt that is favored by their habits, their prepossessions and the intercourse between the two countries. This attempt has, within the period of a few years, produced a multitude of changes in these particulars, especially among the leading classes of people. These changes make a difference between the language of the higher and common ranks; and indeed between the *same* ranks in *different* states; as the rage for copying the English, does not prevail equally in every part of North America.

But besides the reasons already assigned to prove this imitation absurd, there is a difficulty attending it, which will defeat the end proposed by its advocates; which is, that the English themselves have no standard of pronunciation, nor can they ever have one on the plan they propose. The Authors, who have attempted to give us a standard, make the practice of the court and stage in London the sole criterion of propriety in speaking. An attempt to establish a standard on this foundation is both *unjust* and *idle*. It is unjust, because it is abridging the nation of its rights: The *general practice* of a nation is the rule of propriety, and this practice should at least be consulted in so important a matter, as that of making laws for speaking. While all men are upon a footing and no singularities are accounted vulgar or ridiculous, every man enjoys perfect liberty. But when a particular set of men, in exalted stations, undertake to say, "we are the standards of propriety and elegance, and if all men do not conform to our practice, they shall be accounted vulgar and ignorant," they take a very great liberty with the rules of the language and the rights of civility.

But an attempt to fix a standard on the practice of any particular class of people is highly absurd: As a friend of mine once observed, it is like fixing a light house on a floating island. It is an attempt to *fix* that which is in itself *variable;* at least it must be variable so long as it is supposed that a local practice has no standard but a *local practice;* that is, no standard but *itself*. While this doctrine is believed, it will be impossible for a nation to follow as fast as the standard changes—for if the gentlemen at court constitute a standard, they are above it themselves, and their practice must shift with their passions and their whims.

But this is not all. If the practice of a few men in the capital is to be the standard, a knowledge of this must be communicated to the whole nation. Who shall do this? An able compiler perhaps attempts to give this practice in a dictionary; but it is probable that the pronunciation, even at court, or on the stage, is not uniform. The compiler therefore must follow his particular friends and patrons; in which case he is sure to be opposed and the authority of his standard called in question; or he must give two pronunciations as the standard, which leaves the student in the same uncertainty as it found him. Both these events have actually taken place in England, with respect to the most approved standards; and of course no one is universally followed.

Besides, if language must vary, like fashions, at the caprice of a court, we must have our standard dictionaries republished, with the fashionable pronunciation, at least once in five years; otherwise a gentleman in the country will become intolerably vulgar, by not being in a situation to adopt the fashion of the day. The *new* editions of them will supersede the *old*, and we shall have our pronunciation to re-learn, with the polite alterations, which are generally corruptions.

Such are the consequences of attempting to make a local practice the *standard* of language in a *nation*. The attempt must keep the language in perpetual fluctuation, and the learner in uncertainty.

If a standard therefore cannot be fixed on local and variable custom, on what shall it be fixed? If the most eminent speakers are not to direct our practice, where shall we look for a guide? The answer is extremely easy; the *rules of the language itself*, and the *general practice of the nation*, constitute propriety in speaking. If we examine the structure of any language, we shall find a certain principle of analogy running through the whole. We shall find in English that similar combinations of letters have usually the same pronunciation; and that words, having the same terminating syllable, generally have the accent at the same distance from that termination. These principles of analogy were not the result of design—they must have been the effect of accident, or that tendency which all men feel towards uniformity. But the principles, when established, are productive of great convenience, and become an authority superior to the arbitrary decisions of any man or class of men. There is one exception only to this remark: When a deviation from analogy has become the universal practice of a nation, it then takes place of all rules and becomes the standard of propriety.

The two points therefore, which I conceive to be the basis of a standard in speaking, are these; *universal undisputed practice*, and the *principle of analogy*. *Universal practice* is generally, perhaps always, a rule of propriety; and in disputed points, where people differ in opinion and practice, *analogy* should always decide the controversy.

* * *

NOAH WEBSTER'S "FEDERAL CATECHISM" (1798) From Noah Webster, *The American Spelling Book . . .* (Boston, 1798), pp. 154-55.

A Federal Catechism (Containing a Short EXPLANATION of the CONSTITUTION of the UNITED STATES OF AMERICA, and the PRINCIPLES of GOVERNMENT) for the Use of Schools

Q. *What is a constitution of government?*

A. A constitution of government, or a political constitution, consists in certain standing rules or ordinances, agreed upon by a nation or state, determining the manner in which the supreme power shall be exercised over that nation or state, or rather how the legislative body shall be formed.

Q. *How many kinds of constitutions are there; or in how many ways may the sovereign power be exercised over a people?*

REPUBLICANS

769

A. Constitutions are commonly divided into three kinds; *monarchy, aristocracy,* and *democracy.*

Q. *Explain the sorts of government.*

A. When the sovereign power is exercised by *one* person, the constitution is a *monarchy.* When a few rich men, or nobles, have the whole supreme power in their hands, the constitution is an *aristocracy.* When the supreme power is exercised by all the citizens, in a general meeting or assembly, the constitution is a *democracy.*

Q. *What are the faults of despotic governments?*

A. In a despotic government, a whole nation is at the disposal of one person. If this person, the prince, is of a cruel or tyrannical disposition, he may abuse his subjects, take away their lives, their property, or their liberty.

Q. *What objections are there to aristocracy?*

A. In an aristocracy, where a few rich men govern, the poor may be oppressed, the nobles may make laws to suit themselves and ruin the common people. Besides, the nobles, having equal power one with another, may quarrel and throw the state into confusion; in this case there is no person of superior power to settle the dispute.

Q. *What are the defects of democracy?*

A. In democracy, where the people all meet for the purpose of making laws, there are commonly tumults and disorders. A small city may sometimes be governed in this manner; but if the citizens are numerous, their assemblies make a crowd or mob, where debates cannot be carried on with coolness and candor, nor can arguments be heard: Therefore a pure democracy is generally a very bad government. It is often the most tyrannical government on earth; for a multitude is often rash, and will not hear reason.

Q. *Is there another and better form of government than any of these?*

A. There is. A *representative republic,* in which the people freely choose deputies to make laws for them, is much the best form of government hitherto invented.

Q. *What are the peculiar advantages of representative governments?*

A. When deputies or representatives are chosen to make laws, they will commonly consult the interest of the people who choose them, and if they do not, the people can choose others in their room. Besides, the deputies coming from all parts of a state, bring together all the knowledge and information necessary to show the true interest of the whole state; at the same time, being but few in number, they can hear arguments and debate peaceably on a subject. But the great security of such a government is, that the men who make laws, are to be governed by them; so that they are not apt to do wrong willfully. When men make laws for themselves, as well as for their neighbors, they are led by their own interest to make *good* laws.

Q. *Which of the forms or kinds of government is adopted by the American States?*

A. The states are all governed by constitutions that fall under the name of representative republics. The people choose deputies to act for them in making laws; and in general, the deputies, when assembled, have as full power to make and repeal laws, as the whole body of freemen would have, if they were collected for the same purpose.

NOAH WEBSTER'S "MORAL CATECHISM" (1798)   From Noah Webster, *The American Spelling Book . . .* (Boston, 1798), pp. 145-52.

A Moral Catechism: Or Lessons for Saturday

Question. What is moral virtue?

Answer. It is an honest upright conduct in all our dealings with men.

Q. Can we always determine what is honest and just?

A. Perhaps not in every instance, but in general it is not difficult.

Q. What rules have we to direct us?

A. God's word contained in the Bible has furnished all necessary rules to direct our conduct.

Q. In what part of the Bible are these rules to be found?

A. In almost every part; but the most important duties between men are summed up in the beginning of Matthew, in Christ's Sermon on the Mount.

Of Humility

Q. What is humility?

A. A lowly temper of mind.

Q. What are the advantages of humility?

A. The advantages of humility in this life are very numerous and great. The humble man has few or no enemies. Every one loves him and is ready to do him good. If he is rich and prosperous, people do not envy him; if he is poor and unfortunate, every one pities him, and is disposed to alleviate his distresses.

Q. What is pride?

A. A lofty high minded disposition.

Q. Is pride commendable?

A. By no means. A modest self-approving opinion of our own good deeds is very right. It is natural; it is agreeable; and a spur to good actions. But we should not suffer our hearts to be blown up with pride, whatever great and good deeds we have done; for pride brings upon us the will of mankind, and displeasure of our Maker. . . .

Of Mercy

Q. What is mercy?

A. It is tenderness of heart.

Q. What are the advantages of this virtue?

A. The exercise of it tends to happify every one about us. Rulers of a merciful temper will make their *good* subjects happy; and will not torment the *bad*, with needless severity. Parents and masters will not abuse their children and servants with harsh treatment. More love, more confidence, more happiness, will subsist among men, and of course society will be happier.

REPUBLICANS

❊   ❊   ❊

Of Justice

Q. *What is justice?*
A. It is giving to every man his due.
Q. *Is it always easy to know what is just?*
A. It is generally easy; and where there is any difficulty in determining, let a man consult the golden rule—"To do to others, what he could reasonably wish they should do to him, in the same circumstances."

      *   *   *

Of Truth

Q. *What is truth?*
A. It is speaking and acting agreeable to fact.
Q. *Is it a duty to speak truth at all times?*
A. If we speak at all, we should tell the truth. It is not always necessary to tell what we know. There are many things which concern ourselves and others, which we had better not publish to the world.

      *   *   *

Of Charity and Giving Alms

Q. *What is charity?*
A. It signifies giving to the poor, or it is a favorable opinion of men and their actions.
Q. *When and how far is it our duty to give to the poor?*
A. When others really want what we can spare without material injury to ourselves, it is our duty to give them something to relieve their wants.
Q. *When persons are reduced to want by their own laziness and vices, by drunkenness, gambling and the like, is it a duty to relieve them?*
A. In general it is not. The man who gives money and provisions to a lazy vicious man, becomes a partaker of his guilt. Perhaps it may be right, to give such a man a meal of victuals to keep him from starving, and it is certainly right to feed his wife and family, and make them comfortable.

      *   *   *

Of Avarice

Q. *What is avarice?*
A. An excessive desire of gaining wealth.
Q. *Is this commendable?*
A. It is not; but one of the meanest of vices. . . .

Of Frugality and Economy

Q. *What is the distinction between frugality and avarice?*

A. Frugality is a prudent saving of property from needless waste. Avarice gathers more and spends less than is wanted.

Q. *What is economy?*

A. It is frugality in expenses—it is a prudent management of one's estate. It disposes of property for useful purposes without waste.

Q. *How far does true economy extend?*

A. To the saving of every thing which it is not necessary to spend for comfort and convenience; and the keeping one's expenses within his income or earnings.

Q. *What is wastefulness?*

A. It is the spending of money for what is not wanted. If a man drinks a dram, which is not necessary for him, or buys a cane which he does not want, he wastes his money. He injures himself, as much as if he had thrown away his money.

✳　　✳　　✳

Of Industry

Q. *What is industry?*

A. It is a diligent attention to business in our several occupations.

Q. *Is labour a curse or a blessing?*

A. Hard labor or drudgery is often a curse by making life toilsome and painful. But constant moderate labor is the greatest blessing.

Q. *Why then do people complain of it?*

A. Because they do not know the evils of *not* labouring. Labor keeps the body in health, and makes men relish all their enjoyments. "The sleep of the laboring man is sweet," so is his food. He walks cheerfully and whistling about his fields or shop, and scarcely knows pain.

The rich and indolent first lose their health for want of action—They turn pale, their bodies are enfeebled, they lose their appetite for food and sleep, they yawn out a tasteless stupid life without pleasure, and often useless to the world.

JOHN DE LA HOWE ON SCHOOLS FOR COUNTRY LIFE (1789)   From
Columbia (S.C.) Magazine, or Monthly Miscellany (April, 1789,), pp. 356-59.

Take any number of settlers, we will suppose sixty families, collected in a village, and they will be able to support a schoolmaster, and easily maintain their children at school: for twenty shillings a year, paid by each family, will make up a competent salary for the master, and the children will be cloathed and fed at home.

But if sixty families are dispersed over a large tract of country, from twenty to forty miles in extent, how shall their children receive the benefits of education? The master's salary, it is true, can be paid as in the former case; but few parents will be disposed to incur the heavy expense of sending their children from home, and boarding them at a distant school. Hence, in such a scattered settlement, general ignorance will ensue; and the people consequently degenerate into vice, irreligion and barbarism.—To remedy evils of such magnitude will be difficult; perhaps it will be thought impracticable: to attempt it, however, will be laudable; and all those who have the dearest interests of society at heart, will give the measure their support.

If by charitable donations, or by grants of the state, adequate funds could be formed, to defray the expenses of the board and tuition of such children, the evils before mentioned would be remedied: but such funds are not to be hoped for: and if they could be obtained, it might well be doubted whether that would be the best mode of educating children destined for a laborious country life. There the boys are to be the future farmers, and the girls the farmers' wives. If both could, in early life, be well instructed in the various branches of their future employments, they would make better husbands, better wives, and more useful citizens. And if the mode of communicating such instruction could at the same time enable them largely to contribute to their own support, another important advantage would be gained.— These reflections have given rise to the following PLAN OF EDUCATION for a Country Life.

1. Let three or four hundred acres of land be appropriated for the use of a school: let it consist of a meadow, tillage and wood land, in convenient proportions.

2. Let a skilful and industrious manager be provided, who shall himself be a complete farmer, and have two labourers, one acquainted with farming, the other with gardening, to assist him.

3. Let the farm be completely stocked, and all the requisite carriages and husbandry utensils provided: such tools as are designed for boys, to be made of sizes suited to their strength.

4. Let the necessary buildings be erected for a school, a boarding house, a barn and work-shop. These may be very plain and cheap, and at the same time very comfortable. The necessary furniture and tools must also be provided.

5. A school master and a schoolmistress must be chosen with much circumspection. The latter will be the housekeeper.

6. A cook will be necessary; and she should know how to dress the plain, wholesome food of the country, in the best manner.

7. The childrens' beds and bedding, cloaths and materials for cloathing must be provided by their parents.

The necessary foundations being thus laid, the school and farm may be conducted agreeably to the following regulations.

1. No boy or girl under eight years of age should be admitted.

2. Both boys and girls should be taught to read, write and cypher. The boys should also be instructed in every useful branch of husbandry and gardening, and the girls in every kind of work necessary for farmers' wives to know and practice.

3. For the purpose of working, let the boys be divided into such a number of classes as shall be judged convenient, distributing equal proportions of the larger and smaller boys to each class. Whenever the nature of the work to be done will admit of it; let equal portions of it be assigned to the several classes, in order to excite their emulation, to excel in industry and skill: and for this reason each portion of land should be cultivated, through a whole season, by the same class to which it was first allotted.—It will be obvious to direct the several boys in the same class, to perform such parts of the general labours required of it, as shall be adapted to their several capacities and strength.

4. All the boys may be taught the methods of making and rearing nurseries of the most useful kind of fruit trees, shrubs and bushes, and of improving the former by grafting and budding. Each boy should have an equal portion of land allotted to him, on which he should raise a nursery; and when he has finished his course of education, should be allowed to take home with him all the trees, shrubs and bushes he has reared and cultivated; excepting only such a proportion as shall be requisite for supplying the school-farm. In like manner he should be allowed to take home with him a collection of useful garden seeds. In this way the most valuable fruits and plants would in a few years be spread and cultivated through the whole settlement.

5. When orchards shall be grown, they may be instructed in the art of making and fermenting cyder, so as to produce a soft and pleasant liquor.

6. A small brewery may be erected on the farm, and all the boys taught to malt barley and oats; and both boys and girls may be taught the art of brewing, so far, at least, as the same might be practiced in every farmer's family.—Perhaps by extending the plan of the malthouse and brewery, they might be able to supply that wholesome and nourishing liquor, good beer, to a great part of the settlement; and thus the use of pernicious, distilled liquors be superseded. Malt, at least, might thus be furnished, and yield a small revenue towards supporting the school.

7. The management of cattle will make a necessary branch of their education; and the modern method of managing bees will well deserve their attention.

8. Tending the cattle, and providing fuel and fencing stuff, will be the principal employments of the winter. But the boys may also make the wood-work of all those utensils of husbandry which will be requisite for the ensuing session. The elder boys will be capable of handling axes, and all the other tools used in those employments.

9. The girls will be taught to sew, to knit, to spin, to cook, to make beds, to clean house, to make and mend their own cloaths, to make the boys cloaths when cut out, and to mend them—to milk cows, and to make butter and cheese.

10. That they may learn to cook and perform all other household work, they should be divided into classes, in the same manner in which the boys were classed, and assist the house keeper and cook, a week at a time, in rotation.

11. A collection of children, from eight to fourteen or fifteen years of age, thus regularly employed, on a good farm, would be nearly able to maintain themselves; and if the expences of their schooling can thus be reduced as low, or nearly as low, as when, in ordinary cases, they live at home, the great obstacle to their education will be removed.

12. The winter will be the season most favourable for the literary instruction of the children; as then they will have but few necessary avocations; perhaps no more than will occasion that degree of exercise which the preservation of their health may require. But their learning need not be wholly interrupted in the summer. Every morning the boys may spend two hours at school, and be ready to go in the field to work by eight or nine o'clock. And when they go out, the girls may enter, and also spend two hours at school. Again at one o'clock (if they dine at noon) the boys may attend the school, continuing there an hour and an half, or two hours; and the girls may succeed them, as in the forenoon, attending the school a like length of time. Thus the same master might every day teach both girls and boys; and yet, in the whole, not to be confined above seven or eight hours in a day.—An hour every evening might be allowed the children, to amuse themselves in innocent sports.

13. The employments of a country life are so congenial to the human heart, the master of this rural academy could hardly forbear to engage in them, in the intervals between school hours. He would naturally be led to read the best authors on

agriculture and rural affairs, and to get some acquaintance with botany. He would study theories, tracing useful practices back to their principles; and thus be able to communicate to the elder boys, or youth, a degree of scientific knowledge of the very important art of which, in the field, they daily learned the practice.

14. I hardly need mention, what ought to be an indispensable part of education in every literary institution. That the children at this rural academy would be taught the plainest and most important principles of religion and morality.

15. It is to be presumed that the abler farmers would continue their children at school till they should be fourteen or fifteen years old. These children of both sexes, might make further advances in learning. They might study geography, and read some instructive histories, particularly the history of the United States, and a few of the best English moral writers, in prose and verse. At the same time they might learn so much of book-keeping as would be useful in the country; and the boys might be taught geometry, practical surveying, and the principles of mechanics.

16. Perhaps some useful manufactories might be established, in which the children, both male and female, might be very serviceable.

Such an institution as that here sketched out, need not be confined to frontier settlements; tho' the first idea of it was suggested by a reflection of their situation. Rural schools, or academies, upon such a plan, would perhaps be the most useful that could be established in the country towns and counties of this and every other state in America. Numerous advantages would result from them. I will hint at a few.

1. The children would be taught the plainest and most useful principles and rules of religion and morality.

2. They would be well and uniformly educated in the most necessary learning, and in the most important arts of civil life, *husbandry* and *domestic economy.*

3. They would acquire habits of industry.

4. Their manners and behavior would be formed, and rendered mild and agreeable.

5. A few successive sets of scholars thus educated, returning to their several homes, would quite change the face of the country, in point of cultivation, and introduce a pleasing change in the knowledge, manners of the people, and abolish the invidious distinction of citizens and clowns.

SAMUEL KNOX ON A NATIONAL SYSTEM OF EDUCATION (1799) From Samuel Knox, *An Essay on the Best System of Liberal Education Adapted to the Genius of the Government of the United States* (Baltimore, 1799), Sections 2 and 3.

Section Second on the Question, Whether Public be Preferable to Private Education

Convinced of the great advantage and importance of education, in proportion as any nation or society, of which we have any knowledge from historical records, improved in the arts of civilization and refinement, so have they been forward in encouraging and patronising seminaries of learning and systems of literary instruction. The enlightened part of the ancient world were no less sensible of the great advantages of public education, than those of the same description in the modern. And though they sometimes encouraged private tuition; yet we find from the reputation of the famous academy at Athens, that public education was most approved. Many are the illustrious characters of antiquity that bear witness to the truth of this observation. Most of those, indeed, who, at any period of the world, have made a figure in literature, acquired their knowledge under the direction of some academical institution. The justly celebrated Cicero, was so conscious of the advantage to be acquired at Athens, that he sent his son there to compleat his studies; though it is probable, that, at that time, Rome was not deficient in the means of private literary instruction.

In modern times, also, we find few of those who have distinguished themselves in the higher walks of science, but have been educated on some similar plan. Indeed, the superior advantages of academical education are sufficiently obvious. As they bid fairest for being furnished with tutors or professors of the most general approved merit; and in whole abilities and character the greatest confidence may be reposed; they, thus, prevent the student from being exposed to the pedantic caprice of any tutor, whom chance, favour and necessity may have thrown in his way.

In such institutions, also, the means and apparatus for acquiring a competent knowledge of the arts and sciences, may be supposed to be more liberal and extensive, than could be expected, or indeed obtained in a domestic or private situation.

Education would diffuse its happy influence to a very contracted extent, indeed, were there no public schools or universities established by national or public encouragement.

Independent of these important considerations, emulation, which hath so powerful an influence on the human mind, especially in the season of youth, would lose its effects in promoting improvement, and the love of excellence, on any other plan than that of the academical. Indeed this consideration alone ought to be sufficiently decisive in its favour.

Love of excellence predominates in every uncorrupted youthful breast; and where this principle is under the conduct of impartial and skilful directors, it is observed to have the happiest effects in promoting that intensity of application and persevering industry, which the more abstruse and arduous departments of science necessarily require.

Granting that something resembling emulation may be excited even on a private plan of education, yet it is manifest that the great variety of abilities and genius which the university or academy exhibits must afford a much greater field for competition; as well as such public and flattering prospects of reward as are the principal incitements to a laudable emulation and love of excellence.

*   *   *

Another argument in favour of an academical education is, that such as are tutored in private are apt to form too high an opinion of their own attainments or abilities. Owing to the want of an opportunity of observing the abilities or exertions of others, it is easy to conceive that such may most probably be the consequence of that mode of instruction. It is but just to observe that to this cause we may assign that arrogance, pedantry, dogmatism and conceit that too often disgrace the scholar, who, without rivalship or competition, hath been accustomed to listen only to his own praise.

The academic school has, also, the peculiar means of affording youth an opportunity of forming such friendships and connections as often in a literary and interested view contribute eminently to their future prosperity and happiness. In that season, the youthful breast glowing with every generous, friendly and benevolent feeling is generally most attached to those who discover the same amiable qualities and disposition. Hence friendships have been formed and cemented, which no circumstance or accident, during their future lives, could intirely dissolve. The story of the two Wesminster scholars, in the civil war between Charles the first of England and the parliament is well known.

It is true that many object to public plans of education, because that from their situation in populous towns, and the various complexion of the many students who attend, opportunities are thereby given for corruption, by scenes of vice and example of debauchery.

It may with equal truth, however, be replied to this that, there are few domestic situations so private as not to admit of ground for the same objections. The first of these, as far as situation is concerned might be easily remedied—But it requires no very elaborate proof to manifest that the most dangerous temptations to vice more effectually succeed in the private and retired shades of bad example, and domestic indulgence, than in the social scene, bustling crowd or public assembly.

* * *

Section Third The Importance of Establishing a System of National Education

When we take into consideration the many great exertions, and laudable institutions which various commonwealths or nations have devised and adopted for the general benefit, in framing and maintaining wholesome laws and government, it would appear, in some degree, unaccountable that little hath yet been done in promoting some general plan of education equally suitable and salutary to the various citizens of the same state of community.

It is true that in the history of some of the most celebrate commonwealths of antiquity we find some such plans were adopted for the improvement of youth; but so circumscribed was the state of literature in those times; and such the circumstances of those commonwealths that their plans of education were rather military schools preparing them for the camp, either for self defence, or for butchering the human species, than seminaries suited to literary acquisition; the conduct of life; or the improvement of the human mind. This observation, however, extends no farther than as it applies to institutions of national education; and is by no means considered as applicable to the schools of the philosophers; or of many celebrated orators, grammarians and rhetoricians of the ancient world. If some of the states or nations of antiquity had been possessed of the means which we enjoy, since the invention of printing, of diffusing literary knowledge, it is more than probable, from what they have done, that they would have availed themselves of them in a manner superior to what we have yet accomplished.

In our own times and language, we have been favoured by ingenious men with several excellent treatises on the subject of education. The greater part of these, however, are rather speculative theories, adapted to the conduct of life and manners; than applicable to the practical diffusion of literary knowledge. What has lately been done in France excepted, I know of no plan devised by individuals, or attempted by any commonwealth in modern times, that effectually tends to the establishment of any uniform, regular system of nation education. Universities or colleges hitherto instituted by the pride or patronage of princes or other individuals, are in general too partial either in their situation or their regulations to extend the necessary advantages of literature to the more remote parts of the community for which they were intended. Immense revenues and donations have, indeed, been applied to the founding of such seminaries, while the poor, and such as most wanted literary instruction, or the means of acquiring it, have been left almost totally neglected. A few, indeed, whom wealth and leasure enabled, might drink deep of the Pierian spring, while the diffusion of its salutary streams through every department of the commonwealth has been either neglected or considered as of inferior importance.

It must be allowed that these remarks may, in some measure, apply to any plan of public education that can possibly be formed. It is not, perhaps, possible to establish any system that can render education equally convenient and equally attainable by every individual of a nation in all their various situations and circumstances.

This observation must be particularly applicable to the condition of the United States of America and the widely dispersed situations of their citizens. In undertakings, however, of the first national importance, difficulties ought not to discourage. It does not appear more impracticable to establish an uniform system of national education, than a system of legislation or civil government; provided such a system could be digested as might justly merit, and meet with general approbation.

The good effects of such a system are almost self-evident. In the present state of education however ably and successfully conducted in particular local situations, the nation is, in a great measure, incapable of judging its condition or effects. Diversity of modes of education, also, tend, not only to confound and obstruct its operation and improvement; but also give occasion to many other inconveniences and disagreeable consequences that commonly arise in the various departments of civil society; or even the polished enjoyments of social intercourse. But were any approved system of national education to be established, all these imperfections of its present state, would, in a great measure, be remedied, and at the same time accompanied with many peculiar advantages, hitherto unexperienced in the instruction and improvement of the human mind.

Great, surely, must be the difference between two communities, in the one of which, good laws are executed only in some particular situations, while in others they are almost totally neglected; and in the other are universally established with equal and impartial authority. Such, surely, must be difference between the effects of education when abandoned to the precarious uncertainty of casual, partial or local encouragement; and of that which has been established uniformly and generally by the united wisdom and exertions of a whole nation. In such a state it is elevated to no more than that importance to which it is justly intitled; and it is to be hoped that the close of the eighteenth century will be so enlightened as to see education encouraged and established, as well by this as other nations, in such a manner as to be considered next to the administration of just and wholesome laws, the first great object of national patronage and attention.

The history of human society informs us, what have been the effects of nations uniting their zealous exertions for the accomplishment of any great object to which they were directed. The happiest effects, then, might surely be expected from the united public exertions of this country in the combined cause of public virtue and literary improvement. The patronage or encouragement of the one, has certainly a very intimate connection with that of the other, more especially if it be allowed that in the same system may be comprehended the institutes of morals and the principles of civil liberty.

In a country circumstanced and situated as the United States of America, a considerable local diversity in improvement, whether with respect to morals or literature, must be the consequence of such a wide extent of territory, inhabited by citizens blending together almost all the various manners and customs of every country in Europe. Nothing, then, surely, might be supposed to have a better effect towards harmonizing the whole in these important views than an uniform system of national education.

The late much celebrated Doctor Price, in a discourse delivered before the trustees of the academy at Hackney, on the evidences of a future period of improvement in the state of mankind, earnestly urges an improvement in the state of education. He observes that it is a subject with which the world is not yet sufficiently acquainted; and believes there may remain a secret in it yet to be discovered which will contribute more than any thing to the amendment of mankind; and adds, that he who would advance one step towards making this discovery would deserve better of the world than all the learned scholars and professors who have hitherto existed.

It requires, then, little demonstration, I think, to prove, that if a justly approved plan of national education constitute not the secret alluded to by the Doctor, it is at least the most important step towards it that hath ever yet been taken. National exertions directed to this important object could not fail to have the happiest effects on society. The rays of knowledge and instruction would then be enabled to disipate every partial and intervening cloud from our literary hemisphere, and the whole community receive a more equal distribution, as well as a more effectual and salutary display of their enlightening influence. . . .

The States and Education

SEPARATION OF CHURCH AND STATE IN NORTH CAROLINA
(1776)   From Henry G. Connor and Joseph B. Cheshire, Jr., *The Constitution of North Carolina Annotated* (Raleigh, N.C., 1911), p. 63.

That all men have a natural and unalienable right to worship Almighty God according to the dictates of their own conscience.

That there shall be no establishment of any one religious church or denomination in this State, in preference to any other; neither shall any person, on any pretense whatsoever, be compelled to attend any place of worship contrary to his own faith or judgment, nor be obliged to pay for the purchase of any glebe, or the building of any house of worship, or for the maintenance of any minister or ministry, contrary to what he believes right, or has voluntarily engaged to perform; but all persons shall be at liberty to exercise their own mode of worship: Provided, that nothing herein contained shall be construed to exempt preachers of treasonable or seditious discourses, from legal trial and punishment.

THOMAS JEFFERSON ON RELIGION (1821-22)   From Albert E. Bergh, ed., *The Writings of Thomas Jefferson* (Washington, D.C., 1903–4), vol. XV, pp. 322-24, 383-85.

To Timothy Pickering, Esq.

MONTICELLO, February 27, 1821.

I have received, Sir, your favor of the 12th, and I assure you I received it with pleasure. It is true, as you say, that we have differed in political opinions; but I can say with equal truth, that I never suffered a political to become a personal difference. I have been left on this ground by some friends whom I dearly loved, but I was never the first to separate. With some others, of politics different from mine, I have continued in the warmest friendship to this day, and to all, and to yourself particularly, I have ever done moral justice.

I thank you for Mr. Channing's discourse, which you have been so kind as to forward me. It is not yet at hand, but is doubtless on its way. I had received it through another channel, and read it with high satisfaction. No one sees with greater pleasure than myself the progress of reason in its advances towards rational Christianity. When we shall have done away the incomprehensible jargon of the Trinitarian arithmetic, that three are one, and one is three; when we shall have knocked down the artificial scaffolding, reared to mask from view the simple structure of Jesus; when, in short, we shall have unlearned everything which has been taught since His day, and got back to the pure and simple doctrines He inculcated, we shall then be truly and worthily His disciples; and my opinion is that if nothing had ever been added to what flowed purely from His lips, the whole world would at this day have been Christian. I know that the case you cite, of Dr. Drake, has been a common one. The religion-builders have so distorted and deformed the doctrines of Jesus, so muffled them in mysticisms, fancies and falsehoods, have caricatured them into forms so monstrous and inconceivable, as to shock reasonable thinkers, to revolt them against the whole, and drive them rashly to pronounce its Founder an impostor. Had there never been a commentator, there never would have been an infidel. In the present advance of truth, which we both approve, I do not know that you and I may think alike on all points. As the Creator has made no two faces alike, so no two minds, and probably no two creeds. We well know that among Unitarians themselves there are strong shades of difference, as between Doctors Price and Priestley, for example. So there may be peculiarities in your creed and in mine. They are honestly formed without doubt. I do not wish to trouble the world with mine, nor to be troubled for them. These accounts are to be settled only with Him who made us; and to Him we leave it, with charity for all others, of whom, also, He is the only rightful and competent Judge. I have little doubt that the whole of our country will soon be rallied to the unity of the Creator, and, I hope, to the pure doctrines of Jesus also.

In saying to you so much, and without reserve, on a subject on which I never permit myself to go before the public, I know that I am safe against the infidelities which have so often betrayed my letters to the strictures of those for whom they were not written, and to whom I never meant to commit my peace. To yourself I wish every happiness, and will conclude, as you have done, in the same simple style of antiquity, *da operam ut valeas; hoc mibi gratius facere nibil potes.*

To Doctor Benjamin Waterhouse

MONTICELLO, June 26, 1822.

DEAR SIR,—

I have received and read with thankfulness and pleasure your denunciation of the abuses of tobacco and wine. Yet, however, sound in its principles, I expect it will be but a sermon to the wind. You will find it is as difficult to inculcate these sanative precepts on the sensualities of the present day, as to convince an Athanasian that there is but one God. I wish success to both attempts, and am happy to learn from you that the latter, at least, is making progress, and the more rapidly in proportion as our Platonizing Christians make more stir and noise about it. The doctrines of Jesus are simple, and tend all to the happiness of man.

1. That there is one only God, and He all perfect.
2. That there is a future state of rewards and punishments.
3. That to love God with all thy heart and thy neighbor as thyself, is the sum of

religion. These are the great points on which He endeavored to reform the religion of the Jews. But compare with these the demoralizing dogmas of Calvin.

1. That there are three Gods.

2. That good works, or the love of our neighbor, are nothing.

3. That faith is everything, and the more incomprehensible the proposition, the more merit in its faith.

4. That reason in religion is of unlawful use.

5. That God, from the beginning, elected certain individuals to be saved, and certain others to be damned; and that no crimes of the former can damn them; no virtues of the latter save.

Now, which of these is the true and charitable Christian? He who believes and acts on the simple doctrines of Jesus? Or the impious dogmatists, as Athanasius and Calvin? Verily I say these are the false shepherds foretold as to enter not by the door into the sheepfold, but to climb up some other way. They are mere usurpers of the Christian name, teaching a counter-religion made up of the *deliria* of crazy imaginations, as foreign from Christianity as is that of Mahomet. Their blasphemies have driven thinking men into infidelity, who have too hastily rejected the supposed Author himself, with the horrors so falsely imputed to Him. Had the doctrines of Jesus been preached always as pure as they came from his lips, the whole civilized world would now have been Christian. I rejoice that in this blessed country of free inquiry and belief, which has surrendered its creed and conscience to neither kings or priests, the genuine doctrine of one only God is reviving, and I trust that there is not a *young man* now living in the United States who will not die an Unitarian.

But much I fear, that when this great truth shall be reestablished, its votaries will fall into the fatal error of fabricating formulas of creed and confessions of faith, the engines which so soon destroyed the religion of Jesus, and made of Christendom a mere Aceldama; that they will give up morals for mysteries, and Jesus for Plato. How much wiser are the Quakers, who, agreeing in the fundamental doctrines of the Gospel, schismatize about no mysteries, and, keeping within the pale of common sense, suffer no speculative differences of opinion, any more than of feature, to impair the love of their brethren. Be this the wisdom of Unitarians, this the holy mantle which shall cover within its charitable circumference all who believe in one God, and who love their neighbor! I conclude my sermon with sincere assurances of my friendly esteem and respect.

THOMAS JEFFERSON'S "BILL FOR ESTABLISHING RELIGIOUS FREEDOM" (1779) From Paul L. Ford, ed., *The Works of Thomas Jefferson* (New York, 1904), vol. II, pp. 438-41.

SECTION I

Well aware that the opinions and belief of men depend not on their own will, but follow involuntarily the evidence proposed to their minds; that Almighty God hath created the mind free, and manifested his supreme will that free it shall remain by making it altogether insusceptible of restraint; that all attempts to influence it by temporal punishments, or burthens, or by civil incapacitations, tend only to beget habits of hypocrisy and meanness, and are a departure from the plan of the holy author of our religion, who being lord both of body and mind, yet choose not to propagate it by coercions on either, as was in his Almighty power to do, but to exalt it by its influence on reason alone; that the impious presumption of legislature and ruler, civil as well as ecclesiastical, who, being themselves but fallible and uninspired men, have assumed dominion over the faith of others, setting up their own opinions and modes of thinking as the only true and infallible, and as such endeavoring to impose them on others, hath established and maintained false religions over the greatest part of the world and through all time: That to compel a man to furnish contributions of money for the propagation of opinions which he disbelieves and abhors, is sinful and tyrannical; that even the forcing him to support this or that teacher of his own religious persuasion, is depriving him of the comfortable liberty of giving his contributions to the particular pastor whose morals he would make his pattern, and whose powers he feels most persuasive to righteousness; and is withdrawing from the ministry those temporary rewards, which proceeding from an approbation of their personal conduct, are an additional incitement to earnest and unremitting labours for the instruction of mankind; that our civil rights have no dependence on our religious opinions, any more than our opinions in physics or geometry; and therefore the proscribing any citizen as unworthy the public confidence by laying upon him an incapacity of being called to offices of trust or emolument, unless he profess or renounce this or that religious opinion, is depriving him injudiciously of those privileges and advantages to which, in common with his fellow-citizens, he has a natural right; that it tends also to corrupt the principles of that very religion it is meant to encourage, by bribing with a monopoly of worldly honours and emoluments, those who will externally profess and conform to it; that though indeed these are criminals who do not withstand such temptation, yet neither are those innocent who lay the bait in their way; that the opinions of men are not the object of civil government, nor under its jurisdiction; that to suffer the civil magistrate to intrude his powers into the field of opinion and to restrain the profession or propagation of principles on supposition of their ill tendency is a dangerous falacy, which at once destroys all religious liberty, because he being of course judge of that tendency will make his opinions the rule of judgment, and approve or condemn the sentiments of others only as they shall square with or differ from his own; that it is time enough for the rightful purposes of civil government for its officers to interfere when principles break out into overt acts against peace and good order; and finally, that truth is great and will prevail if left to herself; that she is the proper and sufficient antagonist to error, and has nothing to fear from the conflict unless by human interposition disarmed of her natural weapons, free argument and debate; errors ceasing to be dangerous when it is permitted freely to contradict them.

SECTION II

We the General Assembly of Virginia do enact that no man shall be compelled to frequent or support any religious worship, place, or ministry whatsoever, nor shall be enforced, restrained, molested, or burthened in his body or goods, or shall otherwise suffer, on account of his religious opinions or belief; but that all men shall be free to profess, and by argument to maintain, their opinions in matters of religion, and that the same shall in no wise diminish, enlarge, or affect their civil capacities.

And though we well know that this Assembly, elected by the people for their ordinary purposes of legislation only, have no power to restrain the acts of succeeding Assemblies, constituted with powers equal to our own, and that therefore to declare this act to be irrevocable would be of no effect in law; yet we are free to declare, and do declare, that the rights hereby asserted are of the natural rights of mankind, and that if any act shall be hereafter passed to repeal the present or to narrow its operations, such act will be an infringement of natural right.

VIRGINIA STATUTE FOR RELIGIOUS FREEDOM (1786) From William W. Hening, ed., *The Statutes at Large of Virginia* (Richmond, 1809-23), vol. XII, pp. 84-86.

Whereas Almighty God hath created the mind free; that all attempts to menace it by temporal punishments or burthens, or by civil incapacitations, tend only to beget habits of hypocrisy and meanness, and are a departure from the plan of the Holy author of our religion, who being Lord both of body and mind, yet chose not to propagate it by coercions on either, as was in his Almighty power to do; that the impious presumption of legislators and rulers, civil as well as ecclesiastical, who being themselves but fallible and uninspired men, have assumed dominion over the faith of others, setting up their own opinions and modes of thinking as the only true and infallible, and as such endeavouring to impose them on others, hath established and maintained false religions over the greatest part of the world, and through all time; that to compel a man to furnish contributions of money for the propagation of opinions which he disbelieves, is sinful and tyrannical; that even the forcing him to support this or that teacher of his own religious persuasion, is depriving him of the comfortable liberty of giving his contributions to the particular pastor, whose morals he would make his pattern, and whose powers he feels most persuasive to righteousness, and is withdrawing from the ministry those temporary rewards, which proceeding from an approbation of their personal conduct, are all additional incitement to earnest and unremitting labours for the instruction of mankind; that our civil rights have no dependence on our religious opinions, any more than our opinions in physics or geometry; that therefore the proscribing any citizen as unworthy the public confidence by laying upon him an incapacity of being called to offices of trust and emolument, unless he profess or renounce this or that religious opinion, is depriving him injuriously of those privileges and advantages to which in common with his fellow-citizens he has a natural right; that it tends only to corrupt the principles of that religion it is meant to encourage, by bribing with a monopoly of worldly honours and emoluments, those who will externally profess and conform to it; that though indeed these are criminal who do not withstand such temptation, yet neither are those innocent who lay the bait in their way; that to suffer the civil magistrate to intrude his powers into the field of opinion, and to restrain the profession or propagation of principles on supposition of their ill tendency, is a dangerous fallacy, which at once destroys all religious liberty, because he being of course judge of that tendency will make his opinions the rule of judgment, and approve or condemn the sentiments of others only as they shall square with or differ from his own; that it is time enough for the rightful purposes of civil government, for its officers to interfere when principles break out into overt acts against peace and good order; and finally, that truth is great and will prevail if left to herself, that she is the proper and sufficient antagonist to error, and has nothing to fear from the conflict, unless by human interposition disarmed of her natural weapons, free argument and debate, errors ceasing to be dangerous when it is permitted freely to contradict them:

II. *Be it enacted by the General Assembly,* That no man shall be compelled to frequent or support any religious worship, place, or ministry whatsoever, nor shall be enforced, restrained, molested, or burthened in his body or goods, nor shall otherwise suffer on account of his religious opinions or belief; but that all men shall be free to profess, and by argument to maintain, their opinion in matters of religion, and that the same shall in no wise diminish, enlarge, or affect their civil capacities.

III. And though we well know that this assembly elected by the people for the ordinary purposes of legislation only, have no power to restrain the acts of succeeding assemblies, constituted with powers equal to our own, and that therefore to declare this act to be irrevocable would be of no effect in law; yet we are free to declare, and do declare, that the rights hereby asserted are of the natural rights of mankind, and that if any act shall be hereafter passed to repeal the present, or to narrow its operation, such act will be an infringement of natural right.

THE ABOLITION OF SLAVERY IN RHODE ISLAND (1784)   From "An Act Authorizing the Manumission of Negroes, Mulattoes and Others, and for the Gradual Abolition of Slavery," in *Public Laws of the State of Rhode Island* (Providence, 1784), p. 7.

February, 1784

No Person or Persons, whether Negroes, Mulattoes, or others, who shall be born within the Limits of this State, on or after the First Day of March, A.D. 1784, shall be deemed or considered as Servants for Life, or Slaves; and . . . all Servitude for Life, or Slavery of Children, to be born as aforesaid, in Consequence of the Condition of their Mothers, be, and the same is hereby taken away, extinguished and for ever abolished.

And whereas Humanity requires, that Children declared free as aforesaid remain with their Mothers a convenient Time from and after their Birth; to enable therefore those who claim the Services of such Mothers to maintain and support such Children in a becoming Manner, *It is further Enacted* . . . That such Support and Maintenance be at the Expence of the respective Towns where those reside and are settled: *Provided however,* That the respective Town-Councils may bind out such Children as Apprentices, or otherwise provide for their Support and Maintenance, at any Time after they arrive to the Age of One Year, and before they arrive to their respective Ages of Twenty-one, if Males, and Eighteen, if Females.

And whereas it is the earnest Desire of this Assembly, that such Children be educated in the Principles of Morality and Religion, and instructed in Reading, Writing and Arithmetic: *Be it further Enacted . . .* That due and adequate Satisfaction be made as aforesaid for such Education and Instruction. And for ascertaining the Allowance for such Support, Maintenance, Education and Instruction, the respective Town-Councils are hereby required to adjust and settle the Accounts in this Behalf from Time to Time, as the same shall be exhibited to them: Which Settlement so made shall be final; and the respective Towns by Virtue thereof shall become liable to pay the Sums therein specified and allowed.

GEORGIA CHARTERS THE FIRST STATE UNIVERSITY (1785) From Robert and George Watkins, eds., *A Digest of the Laws of the State of Georgia . . .* (Philadelphia, 1800), pp. 299-302.

An Act for the More Full and Complete Establishment of a Public Seat of Learning in This State

As it is the distinguishing happiness of free governments, that civil order should be the result of choice, and not necessity, and the common wishes of the people become the laws of the land, their public prosperity, and even existence, very much depends upon suitably forming the minds and morals of their citizens. Where the minds of the people in general are viciously disposed and unprincipled, and their conduct disorderly, a free government will be attended with greater confusions, and with evils more horrid than the wild uncultivated state of nature: It can only be happy where the public principles and opinions are properly directed, and their manners regulated. This is an influence beyond the sketch of laws and punishments, and can be claimed only by religion and education. It should therefore be among the first objects of those who wish well to the national prosperity, to encourage and support the principles of religion and morality, and early to place the youth under the forming hand of society, that by instruction they may be moulded to the love of virtue and good order. Sending them abroad to other countries for their education will not answer these purposes, is too humiliating an acknowledgment of the ignorance or inferiority of our own, and will always be the cause of so great foreign attachments, that upon principles of policy it is not admissible.

This country, in the times of our common danger and distress, found such security in the principles and abilities which wise regulations had before established in the minds of our countrymen, that our present happiness, joined to pleasing prospects, should conspire to make us feel ourselves under the strongest obligation to form the youth, the rising hope of our land, to render the like glorious and essential services to our country.

And whereas, for the great purpose of internal education, divers allotments of land have, at different times, been made, particularly by the legislature at their sessions in July, one thousand seven hundred and eighty-three; and February, one thousand seven hundred and eighty-four all of which may be comprehended and made the basis of one general and complete establishment: THEREFORE *the* representatives of the freemen of the State of Georgia, in General assembly met, this twenty-seventh day of January, in the year of our Lord one thousand seven hundred and eighty-five, enact, ordain, and declare, and by these presents it is ENACTED, ORDAINED, AND DECLARED,

1st. The general superintendance and regulation of the literature of this State, and in particular of the public seat of learning, shall be committed and intrusted to the governor and council, the speaker of the house of assembly, and the chief justice of the State, for the time being, who shall, *ex officio*, compose one board, denominated the *Board of Visitors*, hereby vested with all the powers of visitation, to see that the intent of this institution is carried into effect, and John Houstoun, James Nathan Brownson, John Habersham, Abiel Holmes, Jenkin Davies, Hugh Lawson, William Glascock, and Benjamin Taliaferro, esquires, who shall compose another board, denominated the *Board of Trustees*. These two boards united, or a majority of each of them, shall compose the SENATUS ACADEMICUS of the University of Georgia.

2d. All statutes, laws and ordinances, for the government of the university shall be made and enacted by the two boards united or a majority of each of them, subject always to be laid before the general assembly, as often as required, and to be repealed or disallowed, as the general assembly shall think proper.

3d. Property vested in the university, shall never be sold without the joint concurrence of the two boards, and by act of the legislature; but the leasing, farming, and managing of the property of the university for its constant support, shall be the business of the board of trustees. For this purpose they are hereby constituted a body corporate and politic, by the name of *Trustees of the University of Georgia*, by which they shall have perpetual succession, and shall and may be a person in law, capable to plead, and be impleaded, defend, and be defended, answer, and be answered unto, also to have, take, possess, acquire, purchase, or otherwise receive lands, tenements, hereditaments, goods, chattels, or other estates, and the same to lease, use, manage or improve, for the good and benefit of said university, and all property given or granted to or by the government of this State for the advancement of learning in general, is hereby vested in such trustees in trust as herein described.

*　　*　　*

7th. The trustees shall have the power of filling up all vacancies of their own board, and appointing professors, tutors, secretary, treasurers, steward, or any other officers which they may think necessary, and the same to discontinue or remove, as they may think fit; but not without seven of their number, at least, concurring in such act.

8th. The trustees shall prescribe the course of public studies, appoint the salaries of the different officers, form and use a public seal, adjust and determine the expenses, and adopt such regulations, not otherwise provided for, which the good of the university may render necessary.

9th. All officers appointed to the instruction and government of the university, shall be of the christian religion; and within three months after they enter upon the execution of their trust, shall publicly take the oath of allegiance and fidelity, and the oaths of office prescribed in the statutes of the university; the president before the governor or president of council, and all other officers before the president of the university.

10th. The president, professors, tutors, students, and all officers and servants of the university whose office require their constant attendance, shall be, and they are hereby excused from military duty, and from all other such like duties and services; and all lands and other property of the university is hereby exempted from taxation.

11th. The trustees shall not exclude any person of any religious denomination whatsoever, from free and equal liberty and advantages of education, or from any of the liberties, privileges, and immunities of the university in his education, on account of his or their speculative sentiments in religion, or being of a different religious profession.

12th. The president of the university, with consent of the trustees, shall have power to give and confer all such honors, degrees and licenses as are usually conferred in colleges or universities, and shall always preside at the meeting of the trustees, and at all the public exercises of the university.

13th. The *Senatus Academicus* at their stated annual meetings shall consult and advise, not only upon the affairs of the university, but also to remedy the defects, and advance the interest of literature through the State in general. For this purpose it shall be the business of the members, previous to their meeting, to obtain an acquaintance with the State, and regulations of the schools and places of education in their respective counties, that they may be thus possessed of the whole, and have it lie before them for mutual assistance and deliberation. Upon this information they shall recommend what kind of schools and academies shall be instituted, agreeable to the constitution, in the several parts of the State, and prescribe what branches of instruction shall be taught and inculcated in each: They shall also examine and recommend the instructors to be employed in them, or appoint persons for that purpose. The president of the university, as often as the duties of his station will permit, and some of the members, at least once in a year, shall visit them, and examine into their order and performances.

14th. All public schools, instituted or to be supported by funds or public monies in this State, shall be considered as parts of members of the university, and shall be under the foregoing directions and regulations.

15th. Whatsoever public measures are necessary to be adopted for accomplishing these great and important designs, the trustees shall, from time to time, represent and lay before the general assembly.

16th. All laws and ordinances heretofore passed in any wise contrary to the true intent and meaning of the premises, are hereby repealed, and declared to be null and void.

17th. In full testimony and confirmation of this charter, ordinance and constitution, and all the articles therein contained, *The representatives of the freemen of the State of Georgia in general assembly, hereby order,* That this act shall be signed by the honorable Joseph Habersham, Esquire, speaker of the house of assembly, and sealed with the public seal of this State and the same, or the enrollment thereof in the records of this State, shall be good and effectual in law, to have and to hold the powers, privileges, and immunities, and all and singular the premises herein given, or which are meant, mentioned, or intended to be hereby given to the said *Board of Visitors,* and *Trustees,* and to their successors in office for ever.

JOSEPH HABERSHAM, *Speaker.*

SAVANNAH, January 27, 1785

REPUBLICANS

789

NEW YORK ESTABLISHES THE REGENTS OF THE UNIVERSITY OF THE STATE OF NEW YORK (1787)   From *New York Session Laws.* 1787, Chap. 82

An Act to Institute an University within this State, and for Other Purposes Therein Mentioned.

Passed the 13th of April, 1787

Whereas, By two acts of the Legislature of the State of New York, the one passed the first day of May, and the other the twenty-sixth day of November, 1784, an University is instituted within this State, in the manner and with the powers therein specified; And,

Whereas, From the representation of the Regents of the said University, it appears that there are defects in the constitution of the said University, which call for alterations and amendments; And,

Whereas, A number of acts on the same subject, amending, correcting and altering former ones, tend to render the same less intelligible and easy to be understood. Wherefore, to the end that the constitution of the said University may be properly amended, and appear entire in one law, it will be expedient to delineate and establish the same in this, and repeal all former acts relative thereto:

I. *Be it enacted, by the People of the State of New York, represented in Senate and Assembly, and it is hereby enacted by the authority of the same,* That an University be and is hereby instituted within this State, to be called and known by the name or style of The Regents of the University of the State of New York. That the said Regents shall always be twenty-one in number, of which the Governor and Lieutenant-Governor of the State for the time being shall always, in virtue of their offices, be two; . . . that all vacancies in the Regency which may happen by death, or removal, or resignation, shall from time to time be supplied by the Legislature, in the manner in which delegates to Congress are appointed. . . .

That the said University shall be and hereby is incorporated, and shall be known by the name of The Regents of the University of the State of New York, and by that name shall have perpetual succession and power to sue and be sued; to hold property, real and personal, to the amount of the annual income of forty thousand bushels of wheat; to buy and sell, and otherwise lawfully dispose of land and chattels; to make and use a common seal, and to alter the same at pleasure.

II. *And be it further enacted by the authority aforesaid,* That the said corporation shall appoint by ballot a Treasurer and Secretary, to continue in office during the pleasure of the corporation. That the Treasurer shall keep fair and true accounts of all moneys by him received and payed out; and that the Secretary shall keep a fair journal of the meetings and proceedings of the corporation, in which the yeas and nays on all questions shall be entered, if required by any one of the Regents present. And to all the books and papers of the corporation every Regent shall always have access, and be permitted to take copies of them.

III. *And be it further enacted by the authority aforesaid,* That it shall and may be lawful to and for the said Regents, and they are hereby authorized and required to visit and inspect all the Colleges, Academies and Schools which are or may be established in this State, examine into the state and system of education and discipline therein, and make a yearly report thereof to the Legislature; and also to visit every College in this State once a year by themselves or by their committees;

and yearly to report the state of the same to the Legislature; and to make such by-laws and ordinances, not inconsistent with the Constitution and Laws of the State, as they may judge most expedient for the accomplishment of the trust hereby reposed in them.

And in case the Trustees of the said Colleges, or any of them, shall leave the office of President of the College, or the Trustees of any Academy shall leave the office or place of Principal of the Academy vacant for the space of one year, it shall in all such cases be lawful for the Regents, unless a reasonable cause shall be assigned for such delay, to their satisfaction, to fill up such vacancies; and the persons by them appointed shall continue in office during the pleasure of the Regents, and shall respectively be received by the College or Academy to which they may be appointed, and shall have all the powers, and exactly the same salary, emoluments and privileges as his next immediate predecessor in office enjoyed, if any predecessor he had; if not, then such salary, as the Regents shall direct, to be paid by the Trustees, who shall, out of the funds or estate of their College or Academy, be compellable by the said President or Principal to pay the same.

IV. *And be it further enacted by the authority aforesaid,* That the said Regents shall have the right of conferring, by diplomas under their common seal . . . all such degree or degrees above or beyond those of Bachelor or Master of Arts, as are known to and usually granted by an University or College in Europe.

V. *And be it further enacted by the authority aforesaid,* That it shall and may be lawful to and for the said Regents, from time to time, to apply such part of their estate and funds in such manner as they may think most conducive to the promotion of literature and the advancement of useful knowledge within this State. *Provided, always,* That where grants shall be made to them for certain uses and purposes therein expressed and declared, the same shall not be applied, either in whole or in part, to any other uses.

* * *

VII. *And be it further enacted by the authority aforesaid,* That any citizen or citizens, or bodies corporate, within this State, being minded to found a College at any place within the same, he or they shall, in writing, make known to the Regents the place where, the plan on which, and the funds with which it is intended to found and provide for the same, and who are proposed for the first Trustees; and in case the said Regents shall approve thereof, then they shall declare their ap-probation by an instrument under their common seal, and allow a convenient time for completing the same. And if at the expiration of the said time it shall appear, to the satisfaction of the Regents, that the said plan and propositions are fully executed, then they shall, by act under their common seal, declare that the said College to be named as the founders shall signify, and with such trustees, not exceeding twenty-four, nor less than ten, as they shall name, shall forthwith become incorporated, and shall have perpetual succession, and enjoy all the corporate rights and privileges enjoyed by Columbia College, hereinafter mentioned.

VIII. *And be it further enacted by the authority aforesaid,* That the charter heretofore granted to the Governors of the College of the Province of New York, in the city of New York, in America, dated the 31st day of October, in the year of our Lord 1754, shall be, and hereby is fully and absolutely ratified and confirmed in all respects, except that the College thereby established shall be henceforth called *Columbia College;* that the style of the said corporation shall be *The Trustees of*

Columbia College in the city of New York, and that no persons shall be Trustees of the same in virtue of any offices, characters or descriptions whatever; excepting also such clauses thereof as requires the taking of oaths and subscribing the declaration therein mentioned, and which render a person ineligible to the office of President of the College on account of his religious tenets; and prescribe a form of public prayer to be used in the said College, and also excepting the clause thereof which provides that the by-laws and ordinances to be made in pursuance thereof should not be repugnant to the laws and statutes of that part of the kingdom of Great Britain called England; . . .

* * *

XII. *And whereas Academies* for the instructions of youth in the languages, and other branches of useful learning, have been erected and instituted in different parts of this State, by the free and liberal benefactions of corporations as well as individuals; and the Regents of the University having represented, that the appointment and incorporation of the trustees for each of the said Academies, with competent power to manage the funds already appropriated, and the donations which may be made to such Academies, and to superintend the morals and education of the scholars, and the conduct of the Principal, masters and teachers, would greatly conduce to their security and prosperity. *Therefore,*

Be it further enacted by the authority aforesaid, That upon the application of the founders and benefactors of any Academy, now or hereafter to be erected or established within any of the cities or counties of this State, or as many of them as shall have contributed more than one-half in value of the real and personal property and estate, collected or appropriated for the use and benefit thereof, by an instrument in writing under their hands and seals, to the Regents of the University, expressing their request, that such Academy should be incorporated, and be subject to the visitation of the Regents, nominating in such instrument the Trustees, not more than twenty-four or less than twelve, for such Academy, and specifying the name by which the said Trustees shall be called and distinguished, and whenever any such request shall be made to the said Regents, they shall in every case, if they conceive such Academy calculated for the promotion of literature, by an instrument under their common seal, signifying their approbation to the incorporation of the Trustees of such Academy, named by the founders thereof, by the name mentioned in and by their said request in writing; which said request in writing, and instrument of approbation by the said Regents, shall be recorded in the Secretary's office of the State.

* * *

XVI. *Be it further enacted by the authority aforesaid,* That the Regents of the University shall be Visitors of such Academies, and the Chancellor, Vice-Chancellor, or a Committee of the Regents, shall, as often as they see proper, visit such Academies to inquire into the state and progress of literature therein.

XVII. *And be it further enacted by the authority aforesaid,* That when any scholar who shall be educated at any of the said Academies, on due examination by the President and Professors of Columbia College, or any other College subject to the visitation of the said Regents, shall be found competent, in the judgment of the said President and Professors, to enter into the Sophomore, Junior and Senior classes of such Colleges, respectively, such scholar shall be entitled to an admission into such of the said classes for which he shall be so adjudged competent, and shall be admitted accordingly, at any one of the quarterly examinations of such respective classes.

Provided always.

XVIII. *And be it enacted by the authority aforesaid,* That to entitle the scholars of any such Academy to the privileges aforesaid, the Trustees thereof shall lay before the Regents of said University from time to time, the plan or system proposed to be adopted, for the education of the students in each of the said Academies, respectively, in order that the same may be revised and examined by the said Regents, and by them altered or amended, or approved and confirmed, as they shall judge proper.

XIX. *And be it further enacted by the authority aforesaid,* That whenever it shall appear to the said Regents, that the state of literature in any Academy is so far advanced, and the funds will admit thereof, that it may be expedient that a President be appointed for such Academy, the said Regents shall in such case signify their approbation thereof, under their common seal, which being entered of record as aforesaid, shall authorize the Trustees of such Academy to elect a President, who shall have, hold and enjoy all the powers that the President of any College recognized by this act shall or may lawfully have, hold and enjoy; and such Academy thereafter, instead of being called an Academy, shall be called and known by the same name it was called while it was an Academy, except that the word "College" shall be used in all cases instead of the word "Academy;" and be subject to the like rules, regulations, control and visitation of the Regents, as other Colleges mentioned in this act.

XX. *And be it further enacted by the authority aforesaid,* That no President or Professor shall be ineligible for or by reason of any religious tenet or tenets that he may or shall profess; or be compelled by any law or otherwise to take any test oath whatsoever; and no Professor or Tutor of any College or Academy recognized by this act shall be a Trustee of any such College or Academy, nor shall any President of any College, or Principal of any Academy, who shall be a trustee have a vote in any case relating to his own salary or emoluments; nor shall any Trustee, President, Principal, Tutor, Fellow, or other officer of any College or Academy, be a Regent of the University.

CONSTITUTIONAL PROVISION FOR SCHOOLS IN NORTH CAROLINA

(1776)   From Benjamin P. Moore, ed., *The Federal and State Constitutions, Colonial Charters, and Other Organic Laws of the United States* (Washington, D.C., 1878), vol. II, p. 1414.

Art. 41. That a school or schools shall be established by the legislature, for the convenient instruction of youth, with such salaries to the masters, paid by the public, as may enable them to instruct at low prices; and all useful learning shall be duly encouraged, and promoted, in one or more universities.

CONSTITUTIONAL PROVISION FOR SCHOOLS IN VERMONT

(1777)   From Benjamin P. Moore, ed., *The Federal and State Constitutions, Colonial Charters, and Other Organic Laws of the United States* (Washington, D.C., 1878), vol. II, p. 1865.

Sec. XL. A school or schools shall be established in every town, by the legislature, for the convenient instruction of youth, with such salaries to the masters, paid by each town; making proper use of school lands in each town, thereby to enable them to instruct youth at low prices. One grammar school in each county, and one university in this State, ought to be established by direction of the General Assembly.

Sec. XLI. Laws for the encouragement of virtue and prevention of vice and immorality, shall be made and constantly kept in force; and provision shall be made for their due execution; and all religious societies or bodies of men, that have or may be hereafter united and incorporated, for the advancement of religion and learning, or for other pious and charitable purposes, shall be encouraged and protected in the enjoyment of the privileges, immunities and estates which they, in justice ought to enjoy, under such regulations, as the General Assembly of this State shall direct.

MASSACHUSETTS SCHOOL LAW (1789)   From *Laws of the Commonwealth of Massachusetts Passed from the Year 1780 to the End of the Year 1800* (Boston, 1801), vol. I, pp. 469-73.

"An Act to Provide for the Instruction of Youth, and for the Promotion of Good Education"

Whereas the Constitution of this Commonwealth hath declared it to be the duty of the General Court, to provide for the education of youth; and whereas a general dissemination of knowledge and virtue is necessary to the prosperity of every State, and the very existence of a Commonwealth:

Section 1. Be it enacted by the Senate and House of Representatives, in General Court assembled, and by the authority of the same, That every town or district within this Commonwealth, containing *fifty* families or householders, shall be provided with a School-Master or School-Masters, of good morals, to teach children to read and write, and to instruct them in the English language, as well as in arithmetic, orthography, and decent behaviour, for such term of time as shall be equivalent to *six months* for one school in each year. And every town or district containing *one hundred* families, or householders, shall be provided with such School-Master or School-Masters, for such term of time as shall be equivalent to *twelve months* for one school in each year. And every town or district containing *one hundred and fifty* families, or householders, shall be provided with such School-Master or School-Masters, for such term of time as shall be equivalent to *six months* in each year; and shall, in addition thereto, be provided with a School-Master or School-Masters, as above described, to instruct children in the English language, for such term of time as shall be equivalent to *twelve months* for one school in each year. And every town or district containing *two hundred* families, or householders, shall be provided with a grammar School-Master, of good morals, well instructed in the Latin, Greek and English languages; and shall, in addition thereto, be provided with a School-Master or School-Masters, as above described, to instruct children in the English language, for such term of time as shall be equivalent to *twelve months* for each of said schools in each year.

And whereas by means of the dispersed situation of the inhabitants of several towns and districts in this Commonwealth, the children and youth cannot be collected in any one place for their instruction, and it has thence become expedient that the towns and districts, in the circumstances aforesaid, should be divided into separate districts for the purpose aforesaid:

Section 2. Be it therefore enacted by the authority aforesaid, That the several towns and districts in this Commonwealth, be and they are hereby authorized and empowered, in town meetings, to be called for that purpose, to determine and define the limits of school districts, within their towns and districts respectively.

And to the end that grammar School-Masters may not be prevented in their endeavours to discharge their trust in the most useful manner:

Section 3. Be it further enacted, That no youth shall be sent to such grammar schools unless they shall have learned, in some other school or in some other way, to read the English language, by spelling the same; or the Selectmen of the town where such grammar school is, shall direct the grammar School-Master to receive and instruct such youth.

Section 4. Be it further enacted by the authority aforesaid, That it shall be and it is hereby made the duty of the President, Professors and Tutors of the University at *Cambridge,* Preceptors and Teachers of Academies, and all other instructors of youth, to take diligent care, and to exert their best endeavours, to impress on the minds of children and youth, committed to their care and instruction, the principles of piety, justice, and a sacred regard to truth, love to their country, humanity, and universal benevolence, sobriety, industry and frugality, chastity, moderation and temperance, and those other virtues which are the ornament of human society, and the basis upon which the Republican Constitution is structured. And it shall be the duty of such instructors, to endeavour to lead those under their care (as their ages and capacities will admit) into a particular understanding of the tendency of the before mentioned virtues, to preserve and perfect a Republican Constitution, and to secure the blessings of liberty, as well as to promote their future happiness; and the tendency of the opposite vices to slavery and ruin.

And to the end that improper persons may not be employed in the important offices before mentioned:

Section 5. Be it further enacted by the authority aforesaid, That no person shall be employed as a School-Master as aforesaid, unless he shall have received an education at some College or University, and, before entering on the said business, shall produce satisfactory evidence thereof, or unless the person to be employed as aforesaid, shall produce a certificate from a learned minister, well skilled in the Greek and Latin languages, settled in the town or place where the school is proposed to be kept, or two other such ministers in the vicinity thereof, that they have reason to believe that he is well qualified to discharge the duties devolved upon such School-Master by this Act; and, in addition thereto, if for a grammar school, "that he is of competent skill in the Greek and Latin languages, for the said purpose." And the candidate of either of the descriptions aforesaid, shall moreover produce a certificate from a settled minister of the town, district, parish or place, to which such candidate belongs, or from the Selectmen of such town or district, or committee of such parish or place, "That to the best of his or their knowledge, he sustains a good moral character."

Provided nevertheless, This last certificate, respecting morals, shall not be deemed necessary where the candidate for such school belongs to the place where the same is proposed to be actually kept; it shall however be the duty of such Selectmen or Committee who may be authorized to hire such School-Master, specially to attend to his morals; and no settled minister shall be deemed, held, or accepted to be a School-Master, within the intent of this Act.

Section 6. And be it further enacted by the authority aforesaid, That if any town or district having the number of *fifty* families, or householders, and less than *one-hundred,* shall neglect the procuring and supporting a School-Master or School-Masters, to teach the English language as aforesaid, by the space of *six* months in one year, such deficient town or district shall incur the penalty of *Ten Pounds,* and a penalty proportionable for a less time than *six* months in a year, upon conviction thereof; and, upon having the number of *one hundred* families, or householders, and upwards, shall neglect the procuring and supporting such School-Master or School-Masters, as is herein required to be kept by such towns, for the space of one year, every such deficient town or district shall incur the penalty of *Twenty Pounds,* and a proportionable sum for a less time than a year, upon conviction of such neglect. And every town or district having *one hundred and fifty* families, or householders, which shall neglect the procuring and supporting such School-Masters and for such term of time as the schools aforesaid, are herein required to be kept by such town or district, in any one year, shall incur the penalty of *Thirty Pounds,* and a proportionable sum for a less time, upon conviction of such neglect. And every town or district having *two hundred* families, or householders, and upwards, that shall neglect the procuring and supporting such grammar School-Master, as aforesaid, for the space of one year, shall incur the penalty of *Thirty-Pounds,* and a proportionable sum for a less time than a year, upon conviction of such neglect.

Section 7. And be it further enacted by the authority aforesaid, That the penalties which may be incurred by virtue of this Act, shall be levied by warrant from the Supreme Judicial Court or Court of General Sessions of the Peace for the county to which such deficient town or district belongs, upon the inhabitants of such deficient town or district, in the same manner as other sums for the use of the county, and shall be paid into the county treasury, and the same shall be appropriated for the support of such school or schools as are prescribed by this Law in such town or towns, district or districts, in the same county, as shall have complied with this Law, and whose circumstances most require such assistance, or in such plantation or plantations in the same county, as the said Court of Sessions shall order and direct. And it shall be the duty of the Minister or Ministers of the Gospel and the Selectmen (or such other persons as shall be specially chosen by each town or district for that purpose) of the several towns or districts, to use their influence and best endeavours, that the youth of their respective towns and districts do regularly attend the schools appointed and supported as aforesaid, for their instruction; and once in every six months at least, and as much oftener as they shall determine it necessary, to visit and inspect the several schools in their respective towns and districts, and shall inquire into the regulation and discipline thereof, and the proficiency of the scholars therein, giving reasonable notice of the time of their visitation.

Section 8. Be it enacted by the authority aforesaid, That all plantations which shall be taxed to the support of Government, and all parishes and precincts, are hereby authorized and empowered, at their annual meeting in *March* or *April*, to vote and raise such sums of money upon the polls and rateable estates of their respective inhabitants for the support and maintenance of a School-Master to teach their children and youth to read, write and cypher, as they shall judge expedient, to be assessed by their Assessors in due proportion, and to be collected in like manner with the public taxes.

And whereas schools for the education of children in the most early stages of life, may be kept in towns, districts or plantations, which schools are not particularly described in this Act; and that the greatest attention may be given to the early establishing just principles in the tender minds of such children, and carefully instructing them in the first principles of reading:

Section 9. Be it enacted, That no person shall be allowed to be a Master or Mistress of such school, or to keep the same unless he or she shall obtain a certificate from the Selectmen of such town or district where the same may be kept, or the Committee appointed by such town, district or plantation, to visit their schools, as well as from a learned Minister settled therein, if such there be, that he or she is a person of sober life and conversation, and well qualified to keep such school. And it shall be the duty of such Master or Mistress, carefully to instruct the children, attending his or her school, in reading (and writing, if contracted for) and to instil into their minds a sense of piety and virtue, and to teach them decent behaviour. And if any person shall presume to keep such school without a certificate as aforesaid, he or she shall forfeit and pay the sum of *Twenty Shillings*, one moiety thereof to the informer, and the other moiety to the use of the poor of the town, district or plantation where such school may be kept.

Section 10. Be it further enacted by the authority aforesaid, That no person shall be permitted to keep, within this Commonwealth, any school described in this Act, unless, in consequence of an Act of naturalization, or otherwise, he shall be a citizen of this or some other of the United States. And if any person who is not a citizen of this or some one of the United States, shall presume to keep any such school within this State for the space of one month, he shall be subjected to pay a fine of *Twenty Pounds*, and a proportionable sum for a longer or shorter time; the one half of which fine shall be to the use of the person who shall sue for the same, and the other half thereof to the use of this Commonwealth.

CONSTITUTIONAL PROVISION FOR SCHOOLS IN PENNSYLVANIA

(**1790**)   From Benjamin P. Moore, ed., *The Federal and State Constitutions, Colonial Charters, and Other Organic Laws of the United States* (Washington, D.C., 1878), vol. II, p. 1553.

Sec. 1. The legislature shall, as soon as conveniently may be, provide, by law, for the establishment of schools throughout the State, in such manner that the poor may be taught *gratis*.

Sec. 2. The arts and sciences shall be promoted in one or more seminaries of learning.

REPUBLICANS

The National Government and Education

THOMAS JEFFERSON OPPOSES STUDYING ABROAD (1785)   From letter to John Banister, Jr., as quoted in Julian P. Boyd, ed., *The Papers of Thomas Jefferson* (Princeton, N.J., 1950-   ), vol, VIII, pp. 635-37.

Dear Sir   Paris Oct. 15, 1785.

I should sooner have answered the paragraph in your favor of Sep. 19. respecting the best seminary for the education of youth in Europe, but that it was necessary for me to make enquiries on the subject. The result of these has been to consider the competition as resting between Geneva and Rome. They are equally cheap, and probably are equal in the course of education pursued. The advantage of Geneva is that students acquire there the habits of speaking French. The advantages of Rome are the acquiring a local knowledge of a spot so classical and so celebrated; the acquiring the true pronuntiation of the Latin language; the acquiring a just taste in the fine arts, more particularly those of painting, sculpture, Architecture, and Music; a familiarity with those objects and processes of agriculture which experience has shewn best adapted to a climate like ours; and lastly the advantage of a fine climate for health. It is probable too that by being boarded in a French family the habit of speaking that language may be obtained. I do not count on any advantage to be derived in Geneva from a familiar acquaintance with the principles of it's government. The late revolution has rendered it a tyrannical aristocracy more likely to give ill than good ideas to an American. I think the balance in favor of Rome. Pisa is sometimes spoken of as a place of education. But it does not offer the 1st. and 3d. of the advantages of Rome. But why send an American youth to Europe for education? What are the objects of an useful American education? Classical knowlege, modern languages and chiefly French, Spanish, and Italian; Mathematics; Natural philosophy; Natural History; Civil History; Ethics. In Natural philosophy I mean to include Chemistry and Agriculture, and in Natural history to include Botany as well as the other branches of those departments. It is true that the habit of speaking the modern languages cannot be so well acquired in America, but every other article can be as well acquired at William and Mary College as at any place in Europe. When College education is done with and a young man is to prepare himself for public life, he must cast his eyes (for America) either on Law or Physic. For the former where can he apply so advantageously as to Mr. Wythe? For the latter he must come to Europe; the medical class of students therefore is the only one which need come to

Europe. Let us view the disadvantages of sending a youth to Europe. To enumerate them all would require a volume. I will select a few. If he goes to England he learns drinking, horse-racing and boxing. These are the peculiarities of English education. The following circumstances are common to education in that and the other countries of Europe. He acquires a fondness for European luxury and dissipation and a contempt for the simplicity of his own country; he is fascinated with the privileges of the European aristocrats, and sees with abhorrence the lovely equality which the poor enjoys with the rich in his own country: he contracts a partiality for aristocracy or monarchy; he forms foreign friendships which will never be useful to him, and loses the season of life for forming in his own country those friendships which of all others are the most faithful and permanent: he is led by the strongest of all human passions into a spirit for female intrigue destructive of his own and others happiness, or a passion for whores destructive of his health, and in both cases learns to consider fidelity to the marriage bed as an ungentlemanly practice and inconsistent with happiness: he recollects the voluptuary dress and arts of the European women and pities and despises the chaste affections and simplicity of those of his own country; he retains thro' life a fond recollection and hankering after those places which were the scenes of his first pleasures and of his first connections; he returns to his own country, a foreigner, unacquainted with the practices of domestic economy necessary to preserve him from ruin; speaking and writing his native tongue as a foreigner, and therefore unqualified to obtain those distinctions which eloquence of the pen and tongue ensures in a free country; for I would observe to you that what is called style in writing or speaking is formed very early in life while the imagination is warm, and impressions are permanent. I am of opinion that there never was an instance of a man's writing or speaking his native tongue with elegance who passed from 15. to 20. years of age out of the country where it was spoken. Thus no instance exists of a person writing two languages perfectly. That will always appear to be his native language which was most familiar to him in his youth. It appears to me then that an American coming to Europe for education loses in his knowlege, in his morals, in his health, in his habits, and in his happiness. I had entertained only doubts on this head before I came to Europe: what I see and hear since I come here proves more than I had even suspected. Cast your eye over America: who are the men of most learning, or most eloquence, most beloved by their country and most trusted and promoted by them? They are those who have been educated among them, and whose manners, morals and habits are perfectly homogeneous with those of the country.—Did you expect by so short a question to draw such a sermon on yourself? I dare say you did not. But the consequences of foreign education are alarming to me as an American. I sin therefore through zeal whenever I enter on the subject. You are sufficiently American to pardon me for it. Let me hear of your health and be assured of the esteem with which I am Dear Sir Your friend & servant,

TH: JEFFERSON

DECLARATION BY THE GEORGIA LEGISLATURE THAT YOUTHS WHO STUDY IN EUROPE SHALL BE ALIENS (1785)   From Allen D. Candler, ed., *The Colonial Records of the State of Georgia, 1732-1782* (Atlanta, 1904-16), vol, XIX, p. 378.

And be it enacted, by the authority aforesaid that if any Person or persons under the age of sixteen years shall after the passing of this Act be sent abroad without the limits of the United States and reside there three years for the purpose of receiving an education under a foreign power. Such person or persons after their return to this State shall for three Years be considered and treated as aliens in so far as not to be eligible to a Seat in the Legislature or Executive authority or to hold any office civil or military in the State for that term and so in proportion for any greater number of years as he or they shall be absent as aforesaid, but shall not be injured or disqualified in any other respect.

NOAH WEBSTER OPPOSES EUROPEAN EDUCATION FOR AMERICAN YOUTH (1788)   From *The American Magazine*, vol. I, pp. 370-73.

Before I quit this subject, I beg leave to make some remarks on a practice which appears to be attended with important consequences; I mean that of sending boys to Europe for an education, or sending to Europe for teachers. That this was right before the revolution will not be disputed; at least so far as national attachments were concerned; but the propriety of it ceased with our political relation to Great Britain.

In the first place, our honor as an independent nation is concerned in the establishment of literary institutions, adequate to all our own purposes; without sending our youth abroad, or depending on other nations for books and instructors. It is very little to the reputation of America to have it said abroad, that after the heroic achievements of the late war, this independent people are obliged to send to Europe for men and books to teach their children A B C.

But in another point of view, a foreign education is directly opposite to our political interests and ought to be discountenanced, if not prohibited.

Every person of common observation will grant, that most men prefer the manners and the government of that country where they are educated. Let ten American youths be sent, each to a different European kingdom, and live there from the age of twelve to twenty, & each will give the preference to the country where he has resided.

The period from twelve to twenty is the most important in life. The impressions made before that period are commonly effaced; those that are made during that period *always* remain for many years, and *generally* thro' life.

Ninety-nine persons of a hundred, who pass that period in England or France, will prefer the people, their manners, their laws, and their government to those of their native country. Such attachments are injurious, both to the happiness of the men, and to the political interests of their own country. As to private happiness, it is universally known how much pain a man suffers by a change of habits in living. The customs of Europe are and ought to be different from ours; but when a man has been bred in one country, his attachments to its manners make them in a great measure, necessary to his happiness; on changing his residence, he must therefore break his former habits, which is always a painful sacrifice; or the discordance between the manners of his own country and his habits, must give him incessant uneasiness; or he must introduce, into a circle of his friends, the manners in which he was educated. All these consequences may follow at the same time, and the last, which is inevitable, is a public injury. The refinement of manners in every country should keep pace exactly with the increase of its wealth—and perhaps the greatest evil American now feels is, an improvement of taste and manners which its wealth cannot support.

A foreign education is the very source of this evil—it gives young gentlemen of fortune a relish for manners and amusements which are not suited to this country; which, however, when introduced by this class of people, will always become fashionable.

But a corruption of manners is not the sole objection to a foreign education; An attachment to a *foreign* government, or rather a want of attachment to our *own*, is the natural effect of a residence abroad, during the period of youth. It is recorded of one of the Greek cities, that in a treaty with their conquerors, it was required that they should give a certain number of *male children* as hostages for the fulfilment of their engagements. The Greeks absolutely refused, on the principle that these children would imbibe the ideas and embrace the manners of foreigners, or lose their love for their own country: But they offered the same number of *old* men, without hesitation. This anecdote is full of good sense. A man should always form his habits and attachments in the country where he is to reside for life. When these habits are formed, young men may travel without danger of losing their patriotism. A boy who lives in England from twelve to twenty, will be an *Englishman* in his manners and his feelings; but let him remain at home till he is twenty, and form his attachments, he may then be several years abroad, and still be an *American*. There may be exceptions to this observation; but living examples may be mentioned, to prove the truth of the general principle here advanced, respecting the influence of habit.

It may be said that foreign universities furnish much better opportunities of improvement in the sciences than the American. This may be true, and yet will not justify the practice of sending young lads from their own country. There are some branches of science which may be studied to much greater advantage in Europe than in America, particularly chymistry. When these are to be acquired, young gentlemen ought to spare no pains to attend the best professors. It may, therefore, be useful, in some cases, for students to cross the atlantic to *complete* a course of studies; but it is not necessary for them to go early in life, nor to continue a long time. Such instances need not be frequent even now; and the necessity for them will diminish in proportion to the future advancement of literature in America.

It is, however, much questioned whether, in the ordinary course a study, a young man can enjoy greater advantages in Europe than in America. Experience inclines me to raise a doubt, whether the danger to which a youth must be exposed among the sons of dissipation abroad, will not turn the scale in favor of our American colleges. Certain it is, that four fifths of the great literary characters in America never crossed the Atlantic.

But if our universities and schools are not so good as the English or Scotch, it is the business of our rulers to improve them—not to endow them merely; for endowments alone will never make a flourishing seminary—but to furnish them with professors of the first abilities and most assiduous application, and with a complete apparatus for establishing theories by experiments. Nature has been profuse to the Americans, in genius, and in the advantages of climate and soil. If this country, therefore, should long be indebted to Europe for opportunities of acquiring any branch of science in perfection, it must be by means of a criminal neglect of its inhabitants.

The difference in the nature of the American and European governments, is another objection to a foreign education. Men form modes of reasoning or habits of thinking on political subjects, in the country where they are bred—these modes of reasoning may be founded on fact in all countries—but the same principles will not apply in all governments, because of the infinite variety of national opinions and habits. Before a man can be a good Legislator, he must be intimately acquainted with the temper of the people to be governed. No man can be thus acquainted with a people, without residing amongst them and mingling with all companies. For want of this acquaintance, a Turgot and a Price may reason most absurdly upon the constitutions of the American states; and when any person has been long accustomed to believe in the propriety or impropriety of certain maxims or regulations of government, it is very difficult to change his opinions, or to persuade him to adapt this reasoning to new and different circumstances. . . .

It is therefore of infinite importance that those who direct the councils of a nation, should be educated in that nation. Not that they should restrict their personal acquaintance to their own country, but their first ideas, attachments and habits should be acquired in the country which they are to govern and defend. When a knowledge of their own country is obtained, and an attachment to its laws and interests deeply fixed in their hearts, then young gentlemen may travel with infinite advantage and perfect safety. I wish not therefore to discourage traveling, but, if possible, to render it more useful to individuals and to the community. My meaning is, that *men* should travel, and not *boys*.

But it is time for the Americans to change their usual route, and travel thro a country which they never think of, or think beneath their notice.—I mean the United States.

While these States were a part of the British Empire, our interest, our feelings, were those of English men—our dependence led us to respect and imitate their manners—and to look up to them for our opinions. We little thought of any national interest in America—and while our commerce and government were in the hands of our parent country, and we had no common interest, we little thought of improving our acquaintance with each other or of removing prejudices, and reconciling the discordant feelings of the inhabitants of the different Provinces. But independence and union render it necessary that the citizens of different States should know each others characters and circumstances—that all jealousies should be removed—that mutual respect and confidence should succeed—and a harmony of views and interests be cultivated by a friendly intercourse. . . .

Americans, unshackle your minds, and act like independent beings. You have been children long enough, subject to the control, and subservient to the interest of a haughty parent. You have now an interest of your own to augment and defend— you have an empire to raise and support by your exertions—and a national character to establish and extend by your wisdom and virtues. To effect these great objects, it is necessary to frame a liberal plan of policy, and to build it on a broad system of education. Before this system can be formed and embraced, the Americans must *believe* and *act* from the belief, that it is dishonorable to waste life in mimicking the follies of other nations, and basking in the sunshine of foreign glory.

BENJAMIN RUSH ON THE NEED FOR A NATIONAL UNIVERSITY
(1788) From "To Friends of the Federal Government: A Plan for a Federal University," as quoted in L. H. Butterfield, ed., *Letters of Benjamin Rush* (Princeton, N.J., 1951), vol. I, pp. 491-95.

"**Y**our government cannot be executed. It is too extensive for a republic. It is contrary to the habits of the people," say the enemies of the Constitution of the United States.—However opposite to the opinions and wishes of a majority of the citizens of the United States, these declarations and predictions may be, they will certainly come to pass, unless the people are prepared for our new form of government by an education adapted to the new and peculiar situation of our country. To effect this great and necessary work, let one of the first acts of the new Congress be, to establish within the district to be allotted for them, federal university, into which the youth of the United States shall be received after they have finished their studies, and taken their degrees in the colleges of their respective states. In this University, let those branches of literature only be taught, which are calculated to prepare our youth for civil and public life. These branches should be taught by means of lectures, and the following arts and sciences should be the subjects of them.

1. The principles and forms of government, applied in a particular manner to the explanation of every part of the Constitution and laws of the United States, together with the laws of nature and nations, which last should include every thing that relates to peace, war, treaties, ambassadors, and the like.

2. History both ancient and modern, and chronology.

3. Agriculture in all its numerous and extensive branches.

4. The principles and practice of manufactures.

5. The history, principles, objects and channels of commerce.

6. Those parts of mathematics which are necessary to the division of property, to finance, and to the principles and practice of war, for there is too much reason to fear that war will continue, for some time to come, to be the unChristian mode of deciding disputes between Christian nations.

7. Those parts of natural philosophy and chemistry, which admit of an application to agriculture, manufactures, commerce and war.

8. Natural history, which includes the history of animals, vegetables and fossils. To render instruction in these branches of science easy, it will be necessary to establish a museum, as also a garden, in which not only all the shrubs, &c. but all the forest trees of the United States should be cultivated. The great Linnaeus of Upsal enlarged the commerce of Sweden, by his discoveries in natural history. He once saved the Swedish navy by finding out the time in which a worm laid its eggs, and recommending the immersion of the timber, of which the ships were built, at that season wholly under water. So great were the services this illustrious naturalist

REPUBLICANS

803

rendered his country by the application of his knowledge to agriculture, manufactures and commerce, that the present king of Sweden pronounced an eulogium upon him from his throne, soon after his death.

9. Philology which should include, besides rhetoric and criticism, lectures upon the construction and pronunciation of the English language. Instruction in this branch of literature will become the more necessary in America, as our intercourse must soon cease with the bar, the stage and the pulpits of Great Britain, from whence we received our knowledge of the pronounciation of the English language. Even modern English books should cease to be the models of style in the United States. The present is the age of simplicity in writing in America. The turgid style of Johnson—the purple glare of Gibbon, and even the studied and thick set metaphors of Junius, are all equally unnatural, and should not be admitted into our country.

✱   ✱   ✱

10. The German and French languages should be taught in this University. The many excellent books which are written in both these languages upon all subjects, more especially upon those which relate to the advancement of national improvements of all kinds, will render a knowledge of them an essential part of the education of a legislator of the United States.

11. All those athletic and manly exercises should likewise be taught in the University, which are calculated to impart health, strength, and elegance to the human body.

To render the instruction of our youth as easy and extensive as possible in several of the above mentioned branches of literature, let four young men of good education and active minds be sent abroad at the public expense, to collect and transmit to the professors of the said branches all the improvements that are daily made in Europe, in agriculture, manufactures and commerce, and in the art of war and practical government. This measure is rendered the more necessary from the distance of the United States from Europe, by which means the rays of knowledge strike the United States so partially, that they can be brought to a useful focus, only by employing suitable persons to collect and transmit them to our country. It is in this manner that the northern nations of Europe have imported so much knowledge from their southern neighbours, that the history of agriculture, manufactures, commerce, revenues and military arts of *one* of these nations will soon be alike applicable to all of them.

Besides sending four young men abroad to collect and transmit knowledge for the benefit of our country, *two* young men of suitable capacities should be employed at the public expense in exploring the vegetable, mineral and animal productions of our country, in procuring histories and samples of each of them, and in transmitting them to the professor of natural history. It is in consequence of the discoveries made by young gentlemen employed for these purposes, that Sweden, Denmark and Russia have extended their manufactures and commerce, so as to rival in both the oldest nations in Europe.

Let the Congress allow a liberal salary to the Principal of the university. Let it be his business to govern the students, and to inspire them by his conversation, and by occasional public discourses, with federal and patriotic sentiments. Let this Principal be a man of extensive education, liberal manners and dignified deportment.

Let the Professors of each of the branches that have been mentioned, have a moderate salary of 150*l.* or 200*l.* a year, and let them depend upon the number of their pupils to supply the deficiency of their maintenance from their salaries. Let each pupil pay for each course of lectures two or three guineas.

Let the degrees conferred in this university receive a new name, that shall designate the design of an education for civil and public life.

In thirty years after this university is established, let an act of Congress be passed to prevent any person being chosen or appointed into power or office, who has not taken a degree in the federal university. We require certain qualifications in lawyers, physicians and clergymen, before we commit our property, our lives or our souls to their care. We even refuse to commit the charge of a ship to a pilot, who cannot produce a certificate of his education and knowledge in his business. Why then should we commit our country, which includes liberty, property, life, wives and children, to men who cannot produce vouchers of their qualifications for the important trust? We are restrained from injuring ourselves by employing quacks in law; why should we not be restrained in like manner, by law, from employing quacks in government?

Should this plan of a federal university or one like it be adopted, then will begin the golden age of the United States. While the business of education in Europe consists in lectures upon the ruins of Palmyra and the antiquities of Herculaneum, or in disputes about Hebrew points, Greek particles, or the accent and quantity of the Roman language, the youth of America will be employed in acquiring those branches of knowledge which increase the conveniences of life, lessen human misery, improve our country, promote population, exalt the human understanding, and establish domestic, social and political happiness.

Let it not be said, "that this is not the *time* for such a literary and political establishment. Let us first restore public credit, by funding or paying our debts, let us regulate our militia, let us build a navy, and let us protect and extend our commerce. After this, we shall have leisure and money to establish a University for the purposes that have been mentioned." This is false reasoning. We shall never restore public credit, regulate our militia, build a navy, or revive our commerce, until we remove the ignorance and prejudices, and change the habits of our citizens, and this can never be done 'till we inspire them with federal principles, which can only be effected by our young men meeting and spending two or three years together in a national University, and afterwards disseminating their knowledge and principles through every country, township and village of the United States. 'Till this be done—Senators and Representatives of the United States, you will undertake to make bricks without straw. Your supposed union in Congress will be a rope of sand. The inhabitants of Massachusetts began the business of government by establishing the University of Cambridge, and the wisest Kings in Europe have always found their literary institutions the surest means of establishing their power as well as of promoting the prosperity of their people.

These hints for establishing the Constitution and happiness of the United States upon a permanent foundation, are submitted to the friends of the federal government in each of the states, by a private

CITIZEN OF PENNSYLVANIA

RESOLUTION OF THE VIRGINIA HOUSE OF DELEGATES ON A NATIONAL UNIVERSITY (1795)
From Jared Sparks, ed., *The Writings of George Washington* (Boston, 1836), vol. XI, pp. 24-25.

Dec. 1, 1795

Whereas the migration of American youth to foreign countries, for the completion of their education, exposes them to the danger of imbibing political prejudices disadvantageous to their own republican forms of government, and ought therefore to be rendered unnecessary and avoided.

1. *Resolved,* That the plan contemplated for erecting an University at the Federal City where the youth of the several states may be assembled, and their course of education finished, deserves the countenance and support of each state.

GEORGE WASHINGTON FAVORS A NATIONAL UNIVERSITY
(1795) George Washington to Robert Brooke, March 16, 1795, as quoted in Jared Sparks, ed., *The Writings of George Washington* (Boston, 1836), vol. XI, pp. 22-24.

Philadelphia, 16 March, 1795.

Sir,

Ever since the General Assembly of Virginia were pleased to submit to my disposal fifty shares in the Potomac, and one hundred in the James River Company, it has been my anxious desire to appropriate them to an object most worthy of public regard.

It is with indescribable regret, that I have seen the youth of the United States migrating to foreign countries, in order to acquire the higher branches of erudition, and to obtain a knowledge of the sciences. Although it would be injustice to many to pronounce the certainty of their imbibing maxims not congenial with republicanism, it must nevertheless be admitted, that a serious danger is encountered by sending abroad among other political systems those, who have not well learned the value of their own.

The time is therefore come, when a plan of universal education ought to be adopted in the United States. Not only do the exigencies of public and private life demand it, but, if it should ever be apprehended, that prejudice would be entertained in one part of the Union against another, an efficacious remedy will be, to assemble the youth of every part under such circumstances as will, by the freedom of intercourse and collision of sentiment, give to their minds the direction of truth, philanthropy, and mutual conciliation.

It has been represented, that a university corresponding with these ideas is contemplated to be built in the Federal City, and that it will receive considerable endowments. This position is so eligible from its centrality, so convenient to Virginia, by whose legislature the shares were granted and in which part of the

Federal District stands, and combines so many other conveniences, that I have determined to vest the Potomac shares in that university.

Presuming it to be more agreeable to the General Assembly of Virginia, that the shares in the James River Company should be reserved for a similar object in some part of that State, I intend to allot them for a seminary to be erected at such place as they shall deem most proper. I am disposed to believe, that a seminary of learning upon an enlarged plan, but yet not coming up to the full idea of a university, is an institution to be preferred for the position which is to be chosen. The students, who wish to pursue the whole range of science, may pass with advantage from the seminary to the university, and the former by a due relation may be rendered coöperative with the latter.

I cannot however dissemble my opinion, that if all the shares were conferred on a university, it would become far more important, than when they are divided; and I have been constrained from concentring them in the same place, merely by my anxiety to reconcile a particular attention to Virginia with a great good, in which she will abundantly share in common with the rest of the United States.

I must beg the favor of your Excellency to lay this letter before that honorable body, at their next session, in order that I may appropriate the James River shares to the place which they may prefer. They will at the same time again accept my acknowledgments for the opportunity, with which they have favored me, of attempting to supply so important a desideratum in the United States as a university adequate to our necessity, and a preparatory seminary. With great consideration and respect, I am, Sir &c.[1]

[1] This letter was accordingly communicated by the Governor of Virginia to the Assembly at their next session, when the following resolves were passed:

"In the House of Delegates.
1 December, 1795.

"Whereas the migration of American youth to foreign countries, for the completion of their education, exposes them to the danger of imbibing political prejudices disadvantageous to their own republican forms of government, and ought therefore to be rendered unnecessary and avoided;

"Resolved, that the plan contemplated of erecting a university in the Federal City, where the youth of the several States may be assembled, and their course of education finished, deserves the countenance and support of each State.

"And whereas, when the General Assembly presented sundry shares in the James River and Potomac Companies to George Washington, as a small token of their gratitude for the great, eminent, and unrivalled services he had rendered to this commonwealth, to the United States, and the world at large, in support of the principles of liberty and equal government, it was their wish and desire that he should appropriate them as he might think best; and whereas, the present General Assembly retain the same high sense of his virtues, wisdom, and patriotism;

"Resolved, therefore, that the appropriation by the said George Washington of the aforesaid shares in the Potomac Company to the university, intended to be erected in the Federal City, is made in a manner most worthy of public regard, and of the approbation of this commonwealth.

"Resolved, also, that he be requested to appropriate the aforesaid shares in the James River Company to a seminary at such place in the upper country, as he may deem most convenient to a majority of the inhabitants thereof."

GEORGE WASHINGTON ON THE NATIONAL UNIVERSITY (1796)   From George Washington to Alexander Hamilton, September 1, 1796, as quoted in John C. Fitzpatrick, ed., *The Writings of George Washington from the Original Manuscript Sources, 1745-1799* (Washington, D.C., 1940), vol. XXXV, pp. 198-201.

Philadelphia, September 1, 1796.

My dear Sir: About the middle of last Week I wrote to you; and that it might escape the eye of the Inquisitive (for some of my letters have lately been pried into) I took the liberty of putting it under a cover to Mr. Jay.

Since then, revolving on the Paper[1] that was enclosed therein; on the various matters it contained; and on the first expression of the advice or recommendation which was given in it, I have regretted that another subject (which in my estimation is of interesting concern to the well-being of this country) was not touched upon also: I mean Education *generally* as one of the surest means of enlightening and givg. just ways of thinkg to our Citizens, but particularly the establishment of a University; where the Youth from *all parts* of the United States might receive the polish of Erudition in the Arts, Sciences and Belle Letters; and where those who were disposed to run a political course, might not only be instructed in the theory and principles, but (this Seminary being at the Seat of the General Government) where the Legislature wd. be in Session half the year, and the Interests and politics of the Nation of course would be discussed, they would lay the surest foundation for the practical part also.

But that which would render it of the highest importance, in my opinion, is, that the Juvenal period of life, when friendships are formed, and habits established that will stick by one; the youth, or young men from different parts of the United States would be assembled together, and would by degrees discover that there was not that cause for those jealousies and prejudices which one part of the Union had imbibed against another part: of course, sentiments of more liberality in the general policy of the Country would result from it. What, but the mixing of people from different parts of the United States during the War rubbed off these impressions? A century in the ordinary intercourse, would not have accomplished what the Seven years association in Arms did: but that ceasing, prejudices are beginning to revive again, and never will be eradicated so effectually by any other means as the intimate intercourse of characters in early life, who, in all probability, will be at the head of the councils of this country in a more advanced stage of it.

[1]The Farewell Address.

**PROVISION FOR THE SUPPORT OF PUBLIC SCHOOLS IN THE LAND
ORDINANCE OF 1785** From John C. Fitzpatrick, ed., *Journals of the Continental
Congress, 1774-1789* (Washington, D.C., 1933), vol. XXVIII, p. 378.

There shall be reserved for the United States out of every township, the
four lots, being numbered 8, 11, 26, 29, and out of every fractional part of a
township, so many lots of the same numbers as shall be found thereon, for future
sale. There shall be reserved the lot No. 16, of every township, for the maintenance
of public schools, within the said township; also one third part of all gold, silver,
lead and copper mines, to be sold, or otherwise disposed of as Congress shall
hereafter direct.

THE NORTHWEST ORDINANCE AND EDUCATION (1787) From Benjamin
P. Poore, ed., *The Federal and State Constitutions, Colonial Charters, and Other Organic
Laws of the United States* (Washington, D.C., 1878), vol. I, p. 431.

ARTICLE III

Religion, morality, and knowledge being necessary to good government and
the happiness of mankind, schools and the means of education shall forever be
encouraged. The utmost good faith shall always be observed towards the Indians;
their lands and property shall never be taken from them without their consent; and
in their property, rights, and liberty they never shall be invaded or disturbed, unless
in just and lawful wars authorized by Congress; but laws founded in justice and
humanity shall, from time to time, be made, for preventing wrongs being done to
them, and for preserving peace and friendship with them.

**A JEW PETITIONS THE CONSTITUTIONAL CONVENTION FOR
EQUALITY OF RELIGIOUS RIGHTS (1787)** From Max Farrand, ed., *The Records
of the Federal Convention of 1787* (New York, 1911), vol. III, pp. 78-79.

*Letter from Jonas Phillips to the Federal Constitutional Convention,
September 7, 1787*

To His Excellency the president and the Honourable Members of the
Convention assembled:

Sires

REPUBLICANS

With leave and submission I address myself To those in Whom there is wisdom understanding and knowledge, they are the honourable personages appointed and Made overseers of a part of the terrestrial globe of the Earth, Namely the 13 united states of america in Convention Assembled, the Lord preserve them amen—

I the subscriber being one of the people called Jews of the City of Philadelphia, a people scattered & dispersed among all nations do behold with Concern that among the laws in the Constitution of Pennsylvania, there is a Clause Sect 10 to viz—I do believe in one God the Creatur and governor of the universe and Rewarder of the good & the punisher of the wicked—and I do acknowledge the Scriptures of the old & New testament to be given by divine inspiration—to swear & believe that the new testament was given by divine inspiration is absolutely against the Religious principle of a Jew, and is against his Conscience to take any such oath—By the above law a Jew is deprived of holding any publick office or place of Government which is a Contridictory [sic] to the bill of Right Sec 2 viz

That all men have a natural & unalienable Right to worship almighty God according to the dictates of their own Conscience and understanding & that no man ought or of Right can be Compelled to attend any Religious Worship or Creed or support any place of worship or Maintain any minister contrary to or against his own free will and Consent, nor can any man who acknowledges the being of a God be Justly deprived or abridged of any Civil Right as a Citizen on account of his Religious sentiments or peculiar mode of Religious Worship, and that no authority can or ought to be vested in or assumed by any power whatever that shall in any case interfere or in any manner Controul the Right of Conscience in the free Exercise of Religious Worship.—

It is well known among all the Citizens of the 13 united states that the Jews have been true and faithful whigs, & during the late Contest with England they have been foremost in aiding and assiting the states with their lifes & fortunes, they have supported the cause, have bravely fought and bled for liberty which they can not Enjoy.—

Therefore if the honourable Convention shall in their Wisdom think fit and alter the said oath & leave out the words to viz—and I do acknowledge the scripture of the new testiment to be given by divine inspiration, then the Israelites will think themself happy to live under a government where all Religious societies are on an Equal footing—I solicit this favour for myself my children & posterity, & for the benefit of all the Israelites through the 13 united states of America.

My prayers is unto the Lord. May the people of this states Rise up as a great & young lion, May they prevail against their Enemies, may the degrees of honour of his Excellency the president of the Convention George Washington, be Exhalted & Raise up. May Everyone speak of his glorious Exploits.

May God prolong his days among us in this land of Liberty—May he lead the armies against his Enemys as he has done heruntofore. May God Extend peace unto the united states—May they get up to the highest Prosperitys—May God Extend peace to them & their seed after them so long as the sun & moon Endureth—and May the almighty God of our father Abraham Isaac & Jacob indue this Noble Assembly with wisdom Judgment & unanimity in their Counsells & may they have the satisfaction to see that their present toil & labour for the wellfair of the united states may be approved of Through all the world & particular by the united states of america, is the ardent prayer of Sires

· Your most devoted obed. Servant

Jonas Phillips

Philadelphia 24th Ellul 5547 or Sepr 7th 1787.

CORRESPONDENCE BETWEEN PRESIDENT WASHINGTON AND THE NEWPORT CONGREGATION (1790) From Morris U. Schappes, ed., *A Documentary History of the Jews in the United States, 1654-1875* (New York, 1950), pp. 79-81.

From the Newport Congregation to the President of the United States, August 17, 1790

Sir,

Permit the Children of the Stock of Abraham to approach you with the most cordial affection and esteem for your person and merits—and to join with our fellow-citizens in welcoming you to New Port.

With pleasure we reflect on those days—those days of difficulty and danger, when the God of Israel, who delivered David from the peril of the sword—shielded your head in the day of battle:—and we rejoice to think that the same Spirit, who rested in the bosom of the greatly beloved Daniel, enabling him to preside over the Provinces of the Babylonish Empire, rests, and ever will rest upon you, enabling you to discharge the arduous duties of Chief Magistrate in these States.

Deprived as we have hitherto been of the invaluable rights of free citizens, we now, (with a deep sense of gratitude to the Almighty Disposer of all events) behold a Government, . . . erected by the Majesty of the People a Government which to bigotry gives no sanction, to persecution no assistance—but generously affording to All liberty of conscience, and immunities of citizenship—deeming every one, of whatever nation, tongue, or language equal parts of the great governmental machine. This so ample and extensive federal union whose basis is Philanthropy, mutual confidence, and public virtue, we cannot but acknowledge to be the work of the Great God, who ruleth in the armies of Heaven, and among the inhabitants of the Earth, doing whatsoever seemeth him good.

For all the blessings of civil and religious liberty which we enjoy under an equal and benign administration we desire to send up our thanks to the Antient of days, the great Preserver of Men—beseeching him that the Angel who conducted our forefathers through the wilderness into the promised land, may graciously conduct you through all the dangers and difficulties of this mortal life—and when like Joshua full of days, and full of honor, you are gathered to your Fathers, may you be admitted into the heavenly Paradise to partake of the water of life and the tree of immortality.

Done and signed by order of the Hebrew Congregation in New Port Rhode Island August 17th, 1790.

Moses Sexias [sic], Warden.

To the Hebrew Congregation in Newport, Rhode Island

Gentlemen,

While I receive with much satisfaction your address replete with expressions of affection and esteem; I rejoice in the opportunity of assuring you that I shall always retain a grateful remembrance of the cordial welcome I experienced in my visit to New Port from all classes of Citizens.

The reflection on the days of difficulty and danger which are past is rendered the more sweet from a consciousness that they are succeeded by days of uncommon prosperity and security. If we have wisdom to make the best use of the advantages with which we are now favored, we cannot fail, under the just administration of a good government to become a great and a happy people.

The Citizens of the United States of America have a right to applaud themselves for having given to mankind examples of an enlarged and liberal policy, a policy worthy of imitation.

All possess alike liberty of conscience and immunities of citizenship. It is now no more that toleration is spoken of, as if it was by the indulgence of one class of people, that another enjoyed the exercise of their inherent natural rights. For happily the government of the United States, which gives to bigotry no sanction, to persecution no assistance, requires only that they who live under its protection should demean themselves as good citizens, in giving it on all occasions their effectual support.

It would be inconsistent with the frankness of my character not to avow that I am pleased with your favorable opinion of my administration, and fervent wishes for my felicity.

May the children of the Stock of Abraham, who dwell in this land, continue to merit and enjoy the good will of the other inhabitants, while every one shall sit in safety under his own vine and fig-tree, and there shall be none to make him afraid.

May the Father of all mercies scatter light and not darkness in our paths and make us all in our several vocations useful here, and in his own due time and way everlastingly happy.

G Washington.

CREVECOEUR DESCRIBES THE NEW AMERICAN MAN (1782)   From Michel-Guillaume Jean de Crevecoeur, "Letter III," *Letters from an American Farmer* (Philadelphia, 1793), pp. 42-52.

I wish I could be acquainted with the feelings and thoughts which must agitate the heart and present themselves to the mind of an enlightened Englishman, when he first lands on this continent. He must greatly rejoice that he lived at a time to see this fair country discovered and settled; he must necessarily feel a share of national pride, when he views the chain of settlements which embellishes these extended shores. When he says to himself, this is the work of my countrymen, who, when convulsed by factions, afflicted by a variety of miseries and wants, restless and impatient, took refuge here. They brought along with them their national genius, to which they principally owe what liberty they enjoy, and what substance they possess. Here he sees the industry of his native country displayed in a new manner, and traces in their works the embryos of all the arts, sciences, and ingenuity which flourish in Europe. Here he beholds fair cities, substantial villages, extensive fields, an immense country filled with decent houses, good roads, orchards, meadows, and bridges, where an hundred years ago all was wild, woody, and uncultivated! What a train of pleasing ideas this fair spectacle must suggest; it is a prospect which must inspire a good citizen with the most heartfelt pleasure. The difficulty consists in the manner of viewing so extensive a scene. He is arrived on a new continent; a modern society offers itself to his contemplation, different from what he had hitherto seen. It is not composed, as in Europe, of great lords who possess everything, and of a herd of people who have nothing. Here are no aristocratical families, no courts, no kings, no bishops, no ecclesiastical dominion, no invisible power giving to a few a very visible one; no great manufacturers employing thousands, no great refinements of luxury. The rich and the poor are not so far removed from each other as they are in Europe. Some few towns excepted, we are all tillers of the earth, from Nova Scotia to West Florida. We are a people of cultivators, scattered over an immense territory, communicating with each other by means of good roads and navigable rivers, united by the silken bands of mild government, all respecting the laws, without dreading their power, because they are equitable. We are all animated with the spirit of an industry which is unfettered and unrestrained, because each person works for himself. If he travels through our rural districts he views not the hostile castle, and the haughty mansion, contrasted with the clay-built hut and miserable cabin, where cattle and men help to keep each other warm, and dwell in meanness, smoke, and indigence. A pleasing uniformity of decent competence appears throughout our habitations. The meanest of our log-houses is a dry and comfortable habitation. Lawyer or merchant are the fairest titles our towns afford; that of a farmer is the only appellation of the rural inhabitants of our country. It must take some time ere he can reconcile himself to our dictionary, which is but short in words of dignity, and names of honour. There, on a Sunday, he sees a congregation of respectable farmers and their wives, all clad in neat homespun, well mounted, or riding in their own humble waggons. There is not among them an esquire, saving the unlettered magistrate. There he sees a parson as simple as his flock, a farmer who does not riot on the labour of others. We have no princes, for whom we toil, starve, and bleed: we are the most perfect society now existing in the world. Here man is free as he ought to be; nor is this pleasing equality so transitory as many others are. Many ages will not see the shores of our great lakes replenished with inland nations, nor the unknown bounds of North America entirely peopled. Who can tell how far it extends? Who can tell the millions of men whom it will feed and contain? for no European foot has as yet travelled half the extent of this mighty continent!

The next wish of this traveller will be to know whence came all these people? they are a mixture of English, Scotch, Irish, French, Dutch, Germans, and Swedes. From this promiscuous breed, that race now called Americans have arisen. The eastern provinces must indeed be excepted, as being the unmixed descendants of Englishmen. I have heard many wish that they had been more intermixed also: for my part, I am no wisher, and think it much better as it has happened. They exhibit a most conspicuous figure in this great and variegated picture; they too enter for a great share in the pleasing perspective displayed in these thirteen provinces. I know it is fashionable to reflect on them, but I respect them for what they have done; for the accuracy and wisdom with which they have settled their territory; for the decency of their manners; for their early love of letters; their ancient college, the first in this hemisphere; for their industry; which to me who am but a farmer, is the criterion of everything. There never was a people, situated as they are, who with so ungrateful a soil have done more in so short a time. Do you think that the monarchical ingredients which are more prevalent in other governments, have purged them from all foul stains? Their histories assert the contrary.

In this great American asylum, the poor of Europe have by some means met together, and in consequence of various causes; to what purpose should they ask one another what countrymen they are? Alas, two thirds of them had no country. Can a wretch who wanders about, who works and starves, whose life is a continual scene of sore affliction or pinching penury; can that man call England or any other kingdom his country? A country that had no bread for him, whose fields procured him no harvest, who met with nothing but the frowns of the rich, the severity of the laws, with jails and punishments; who owned not a single foot of the extensive surface of this planet? No! urged by a variety of motives, here they came. Every thing has tended to regenerate them; new laws, a new mode of living, a new social system; here they are become men: in Europe they were as so many useless plants, wanting vegetative mould, and refreshing showers; they withered, and were mowed down by want, hunger, and war; but now by the power of transplantation, like all other plants they have taken root and flourished! Formerly they were not numbered in any civil lists of their country, except in those of the poor; here they rank as citizens. By what invisible power has this surprising metamorphosis been performed? By that of the laws and that of their industry. The laws, the indulgent laws, protect them as they arrive, stamping on them the symbol of adoption; they receive ample rewards for their labours; these accumulated rewards procure them lands; those lands confer on them the title of freemen, and to that title every benefit is affixed which men can possibly require. This is the great operation daily performed by our laws. From whence proceed these laws? From our government. Whence the government? it is derived from the original genius and strong desire of the people ratified and confirmed by the crown. This is the great chain which links us all, this is the picture which every province exhibits, Nova Scotia excepted. There the crown has done all; either there were no people who had genius, or it was not much attended to: the consequence is, that the province is very thinly inhabited indeed; the power of the crown in conjunction with the musketos has prevented men from settling there. Yet some parts of it flourished once, and it contained a mild harmless set of people. But for the fault of a few leaders, the whole were banished. The greatest political error the crown ever committed in America, was to cut off men from a country which wanted nothing but men!

What attachment can a poor European emigrant have for a country where he had nothing? The knowledge of the language, the love of a few kindred as poor as himself, were the only cords that tied him: his country is now that which gives him land, bread, protection, and consequence: *Ubi panis ibi patria,* is the motto of all emigrants. What then is the American, this new man? He is either an European, or the descendant of an European, hence that strange mixture of blood, which you will find in no other country. I could point out to you a family whose grandfather was an Englishman, whose wife was Dutch, whose son married a French woman, and whose present four sons have now four wives of different nations. *He* is an American, who, leaving behind him all his ancient prejudices and manners, receives new ones from the new mode of life he has embraced, the new government he obeys, and the new rank he holds. He becomes an American by being received in the broad lap of our great *Alma Mater.* Here individuals of all nations are melted into a new race of men, whose labours and posterity will one day cause great changes in the world. Americans are the western pilgrims, who are carrying along with them that great mass of arts, sciences, vigour, and industry which began long

since in the east; they will finish the great circle. The Americans were once scattered all over Europe; here they are incorporated into one of the finest systems of population which has ever appeared, and which will hereafter become distinct by the power of the different climates they inhabit. The American ought therefore to

love this country much better than that wherein either he or his forefathers were born. Here the rewards of his industry follow with equal steps the progress of his labour; his labour is founded on the basis of nature, *self-interest;* can it want a stronger allurement? Wives and children, who before in vain demanded of him a morsel of bread, now, fat and frolicsome, gladly help their father to clear those fields whence exuberant crops are to arise to feed and to clothe them all; without any part being claimed, either by a despotic prince, a rich abbot, or a mighty lord. Here religion demands but little of him; a small voluntary salary to the minister, and gratitude to God; can he refuse these? The American is a new man, who acts upon new principles; he must therefore entertain new ideas, and form new opinions. From involuntary idleness, servile dependence, penury, and useless labour, he has passed to toils of a very different nature, rewarded by ample subsistence.—This is an American.

*   *   *

There is no wonder that this country has so many charms, and presents to Europeans so many temptations to remain in it. A traveller in Europe becomes a stranger as soon as he quits his own kingdom; but it is otherwise here. We know, properly speaking, no strangers; this is every person's country; the variety of our soils, situations, climates, governments, and produce, hath something which must please everybody. No sooner does an European arrive, no matter of what condition, than his eyes are opened upon the fair prospect; he hears his language spoken, he retraces many of his own country manners, he perpetually hears the names of families and towns with which he is acquainted; he sees happiness and prosperity in all places disseminated; he meets with hospitality, kindness, and plenty everywhere; he beholds hardly any poor, he seldom hears of punishments and executions; and he wonders at the elegance of our towns, those miracles of industry and freedom. He cannot admire enough our rural districts, our convenient roads, good taverns, and our many accommodations; he involuntarily loves a country where everything is so lovely. When in England, he was a mere Englishman; here he stands on a larger portion of the globe, not less than its fourth part, and may see the productions of the north, in iron and naval stores; the provisions of Ireland, the grain of Egypt, the indigo, the rice of China. He does not find, as in Europe, a crowded society, where every place is over-stocked; he does not feel that perpetual collision of parties, that difficulty of beginning, that contention which oversets so many. There is room for everybody in America; has he any particular talent, or industry? he exerts it in order to procure a livelihood, and it succeeds. Is he a merchant? the avenues of trade are infinite; is he eminent in any respect? he will be employed and respected. Does he love a country life? pleasant farms present themselves; he may purchase what he wants, and thereby become an American farmer. Is he a labourer, sober and industrious? he need not go many miles, nor receive many informations before he will be hired, well fed at the table of his employer, and paid four or five times more than he can get in Europe. Does he want uncultivated lands? thousands of acres present themselves, which he may purchase cheap. Whatever be his talents or inclinations, if they are moderate, he may satisfy them. I do not mean that every one who comes will grow rich in a little time; no, but he may procure an easy, decent maintenance, by his industry. Instead of starving he will be fed, instead of being idle he will have employment; and these are riches enough for such men as come over here. The rich stay in Europe, it is only the middling and the poor that emigrate. Would you wish to travel in independent idleness, from north to south, you will find easy access, and the most cheerful reception at every house; society without ostentation, good cheer without pride, and every decent diversion which the country affords, with little expense. It is no wonder that the European who has lived here a few years, is desirous to remain; Europe with all its pomp, is not to be compared to this continent, for men of middle stations, or labourers.

An European, when he first arrives, seems limited in his intentions, as well as in his views; but he very suddenly alters his scale; two hundred miles formerly appeared a very great distance, it is now but a trifle; he no sooner breathes our air than he forms schemes, and embarks in designs he never would have thought of in his own country. There the plenitude of society confines many useful ideas, and often extinguishes the most laudable schemes which here ripen into maturity. Thus Europeans become Americans.

But how is this accomplished in that crowd of low, indigent people, who flock here every year from all parts of Europe? I will tell you; they no sooner arrive than they immediately feel the good effects of that plenty of provisions we possess: they fare on our best food, and they are kindly entertained; their talents, character, and peculiar industry are immediately inquired into; they find countrymen everywhere disseminated, let them come from whatever part of Europe. Let me select one as an epitome of the rest; he is hired, he goes to work, and works moderately; instead of being employed by a haughty person, he finds himself with his equal, placed at the substantial table of the farmer, or else at an inferior one as good; his wages are high, his bed is not like that bed of sorrow on which he used to lie: if he behaves with propriety, and is faithful, he is caressed, and becomes as it were a member of the family. He begins to feel the effects of a sort of resurrection; hitherto he had not lived, but simply vegetated; he now feels himself a man, because he is treated as such; the laws of his own country had overlooked him in his insignificancy; the laws of this cover him with their mantle. Judge what an alteration there must arise in the mind and thoughts of this man; he begins to forget his former servitude and dependence, his heart involuntarily swells and glows; this first swell inspires him with those new thoughts which constitute an American. What love can he entertain for a country where his existence was a burthen to him; if he is a generous good man, the love of this new adoptive parent will sink deep into his heart. He looks around, and sees many a prosperous person, who but a few years before was as poor as himself. This encourages him much, he begins to form some little scheme, the first, alas, he ever formed in his life. If he is wise he thus spends two or three years, in which time he acquires knowledge, the use of tools, the modes of working the lands, felling trees, etc. This prepares the foundation of a good name, the most useful acquisition he can make. He is encouraged, he has gained friends; he is advised and directed, he feels bold, he purchases some land; he gives all the money he has brought over, as well as what he has earned, and trusts to the God of harvests for the discharge of the rest. His good name procures him credit. He is now possessed of the deed, conveying to him and his posterity the fee simple and absolute property of two hundred acres of land, situated on such a river. What an epocha in this man's life! He is become a freeholder, from perhaps a German boor— he is now an American, a Pennsylvanian, an English subject. He is naturalised, his name is enrolled with those of the other citizens of the province. Instead of being a vagrant, he has a place of residence; he is called the inhabitant of such a county, or of such a district, and for the first time in his life counts for something; for hitherto he has been a cypher. I only repeat what I have heard many say, and no wonder their hearts should glow, and be agitated with a multitude of feelings, not easy to describe. From nothing to start into being; from a servant to the rank of a master;

from being the slave of some despotic prince, to become a free man, invested with lands, to which every municipal blessing is annexed! What a change indeed! It is in consequence of that change that he becomes an American. This great metamorphosis has a double effect, it extinguishes all his European prejudices, he forgets that mechanism of subordination, that servility of disposition which poverty had taught him; and sometimes he is apt to forget too much, often passing from one extreme to the other. If he is a good man, he forms schemes of future prosperity, he proposes to educate his children better than he has been educated himself; he thinks of future modes of conduct, feels an ardour to labour he never felt before. Pride steps in and leads him to everything that the laws do not forbid: he respects them; with a heart-felt gratitude he looks toward the east, toward that insular government from whose wisdom all his new felicity is derived, and under whose wings and protection he now lives. These reflections constitute him the good man and the good subject.

*　　*　　*

After a foreigner from any part of Europe is arrived, and become a citizen; let him devoutly listen to the voice of our great parent, which says to him, "Welcome to my shores, distressed European; bless the hour in which thou didst see my verdant fields, my fair navigable rivers, and my green mountains!—If thou wilt work, I have bread for thee; if thou wilt be honest, sober, and industrious, I have greater rewards to confer on thee—ease and independence. I will give thee fields to feed and clothe thee; a comfortable fireside to sit by, and tell thy children by what means thou hast prospered; and a decent bed to repose on. I shall endow thee beside with the immunities of a freeman. If thou wilt carefully educate thy children, teach them gratitude to God, and reverence to that government, that philanthropic government, which has collected here so many men and made them happy. I will also provide for thy progeny; and to every good man this ought to be the most holy, the most powerful, the most earnest wish he can possibly form, as well as the most consolatory prospect when he dies. Go thou and work and till; thou shalt prosper, provided thou be just, grateful, and industrious."

BOOK TWO

The Shaping of
American Education, 1790–1895

"Education, then, beyond all other devices of human origin, is the great equalizer of the conditions of men—the balance-wheel of the social machinery . . . .

The spread of education, by enlarging the cultivated class or caste, will open a wider area over which the social feelings will expand; and, if this education should be universal and complete, it would do more than all things else to obliterate factitious distinctions in society."

Horace Mann, *Seventh Annual Report to the Board of Education*

a. The structural characteristics of American education took concrete form during the 19th century. At the beginning of the century, no state could boast of having a state-wide system of public elementary schools, just as no state could lay claim to a system of public high schools or a state university. Indeed, the European two-track system of education was much in evidence. The "ladder system" so typical of modern American education, whereby elementary schools, high schools, and colleges and universities were so coordinated that a child could proceed naturally from the elementary school to the high school to the college or university did not exist. By the end of the century, most states had developed such a system.

In the early national period, schools in all regions of the country fared badly. The country was poor and debt-ridden, still overwhelmingly agricultural and indeed sparsely settled. In 1800, the population of the United States was approximately 4 million but less than 5% lived in "cities". Outside of the Northeast, the overwhelming majority of Americans lived in isolated villages and farms learning what they had to in the family, in the field, in the church.

Indeed, in the early national period, free education had become closely associated with pauperism. The Continental system of education—private schools for the well-to-do, and charity schools for the poor was much in evidence. In the constitutions of only seven of the sixteen states comprising the Union in 1800, was any mention made of education. And in those constitutions, the education provisions were limited. The Pennsylvania constitution of 1790, for example, required that "the legislature shall, as soon as conveniently may be, provide by law, for the establishment of schools throughout the state, in such manner that the poor may be taught gratis". The South, according to Allan Nevins, "was for the most part without public schools, a land where the poor man's son was likely to be untaught, and the workingman or small farmer to be ignorant if not illiterate".

The major organizations engaged in mass education were groups like the Philadelphia Society for the Free Instruction of Indigent Boys, the Benevolent Society of the City of Baltimore for the Education of the Female Poor, and the powerful Free School Society of the City of New York, founded in 1805. Although privately controlled by Protestant philanthropists, the Free School Society, which changed its name to the New York Public School Society, eventually achieved almost a complete monopoly of free elementary education and of the public money allocated for it by the city. Although the Society's monopoly was opposed by the Roman Catholic church and some Protestant groups, it endured, as we shall see, until 1842. Similar situations prevailed in other American cities. Where free elementary education was to be found, it was most often sponsored and controlled by religious and philanthropic organizations.

At the beginning of the 19th century, America possessed numerous philanthropic, and mission and tract societies, which provided Bible schools for the poor as well as Sunday schools and infant schools—all evidence of the continuing influence of English ideas even after the Revolution. The wild enthusiasm with which Englishman Joseph Lancaster's monitorial system of education initially was received in America can be explained in large part to the interest in establishing a philanthropic system of mass education. The monitorial system—a method whereby, among other innovations, one teacher taught a packaged lesson to a group of older students and these students, called monitors, in turn taught a group of younger students—it was hoped, would be efficient and cheap; it would stave off taxation for free schools. It would be the last effort to establish a charity system of mass education in the United States; Lancaster died in 1838, quite forgotten.

b. The common school, the basic unit of the American school system, emerged as a response to the conditions of American life during the period 1825–1860. Its origin is related to the play of social forces and ideas agitating the young Republic. Commerce and industry were expanding. Improvements in transportation and communication—roads, canals, and railroads—brought communities closer together, stimulating the exchange of goods and services as well as the growth of cities. In 1820 the United States boasted twelve cities of 10,000 or more; by 1860 over 100. The total percentage of the city population sharply rose from 4.9% in 1810 to about 20% in 1860. By 1860 at least thirty cities had populations of 20,000 while eight contained over 100,000; Boston had grown to 300,000; Philadelphia to 340,000. New York City, which had surpassed the one million mark, ranked as the third largest city in the world. As cities proliferated, with a corresponding increase in taxable wealth, it became more feasible to provide free tax-supported schools.

Furthermore, after the Revolution, state after state abolished property qualifications for voting and holding of public office. Political democracy and universal white male suffrage became the order of the day. In the 1820's and 30's the new states of the Old Northwest entered the Union with constitutions guaranteeing universal manhood suffrage (at least for white males) and many older states liberalized their voting requirements to enfranchise small farmers and laborers. The gradual but important shift in political power which ensued is reflected in the 1828 election when Andrew Jackson and the Democratic Party, the party of the "common man," obtained control of the national government. More public offices were made elective and more voters participated in the elections. If the mass of people were to govern, the mass of people would have to be educated. As the *Ohio State Journal* explained in 1836: "Other nations have hereditary sovereigns, and one of the most important duties of their government is to take care of the education of the heir to the throne; these children all about your streets, who cannot even speak your language, are your future sovereigns. Is it not important that they be well educated?" The connection between citizenship and education, as we have seen in Volume I, was recognized by the Revolutionary generation; virtually all of the Founding Fathers possessed deep concern for universal education as the bulwark of republican institutions. With the extension of the suffrage, the dangers of ignorance multiplied.

The emergence of the common school also owed much to the growing heterogeneity of the population. In the 1830's, 40's, and 50's came the great tide of European immigration. Between 1830 and 1860 some 4.5 million Europeans arrived in America with every country represented, but the largest number of immigrants were displaced Scandinavian tenant farmers and Irish and German peasants fleeing the potato famines. By 1860, New York, Boston, Chicago, Cincinnati and Detroit had extraordinarily large foreign born populations. This influx corresponded with a spirit of growing nationalism and patriotic sentiment—as seen in the emergence of a host of loyalty symbols like the flag, patriotic songs, and national holidays—among the home-born, home-bred, distinctively Anglo-Saxon, Protestant "Native" population. The common school would be a means of uniting the growing heterogeneous population by giving the immigrants an understanding of American ways. "Shall these adopted citizens," asked Benjamin Labaree, President of Middlebury College (Vermont), "become part of the body politic, and firm supporters of liberal institutions, or will they prove to be to our republic what the Goths and Huns were to the Roman Empire?" The answer for Labaree rested with the schoolmaster. As the forces of xenophobia and nationalism gathered strength, so did the argument that the common school offered the best hope of transforming foreign children into Americans.

The emergence of a workingman's movement also greatly influenced the development of the common school. By the second decade of the 19th century the United States was rapidly becoming an industrial as well as an urban nation. Factories sprang up over the countryside and, around them, bustling towns and cities; textile mills in Lowell, shoe factories in Brockton, pottery works in Trenton, iron mills in Richmond. An important outgrowth of this industrialism was the growth of workingman's organizations, comprised of skilled laborers who began to organize trade and craft unions in order to improve their bargaining power. It was virtually inevitable that, in the period of unrest which characterized Andrew Jackson's Administration, these organizations should develop political arms. In 1827 in Philadelphia, fifteen trade unions joined together to form the Mechanics Union of Trade Associations. The movement rapidly expanded, developing political groups called Workingman's parties, designed to agitate for legislation that would extend the rights of labor, including free public education as one of the means of improving the condition of the working class. Workingman's parties appeared in Philadelphia in 1828, in New York in 1829, and a whole flurry of them in New England during the same period. The program of these early unions and their affiliated political parties was broad, comprehensive, and progressive. Influenced by such men as Stephen Simpson, Seth Luther, and Thomas Skidmore, their programs were as much concerned with social as with economic protest.

Labor feared the consequences of the new industrialism, especially the hardening of class divisions. "We are fast approaching those extremes of wealth and extravagance on the one hand, and ignorance, poverty, and wretchedness on the other," declared the *Philadelphia Mechanics Press* in 1830, "which will eventually terminate in those unnatural and oppressive distinctions which exist in the corrupt governments of the old world." Labor leaders would not stand idly by while workers slipped downwards in economic and social status. Labor turned to public education, supported by public taxation, free to all, as a means of preserving the open society in America for their children. Education would diffuse knowledge; and knowledge was power. Some labor leaders like Robert Dale Owen and Frances Wright called for more radical measures, such as the education of all children in boarding schools—arguing that only as the same education was given to everyone in the same schools (with the same food and clothing) could true equality of educational opportunity prevail. The Workingman's parties were shortlived, but they helped spread the idea of the common school in maintaining and perfecting the ideal of social equality. It would appear then that school reformers of the 1830's and 40's appealed to a constituency already awakened by labor.

Finally, something must be said for the impact of Enlightenment philosophy. In the Age of Jackson, the Enlightenment doctrine of progress shed its glow on the common man. President-elect Jackson articulated well this doctrine: "I believe man can be elevated; can become more and more endowed with divinity; . . . . Let us go on elevating our people, perfecting our institutions, until democracy shall reach such a point of perfection that we can acclaim with truth that the voice of the people is the voice of God." The 1820's and 1830's witnessed a veritable farrago of reform and uplift movements: the abolition of slavery; more humane treatment for the insane, the criminal, the indigent; and the successful pioneering efforts to teach the deaf, the blind and the mentally deficient by Thomas Hopkins Gallaudet and Samuel Gridley Howe among others. Within this variety of movements, however, was a common faith in progress and a belief in the power of the individual to improve his lot. The common school was caught up in the enthusiasm.

    c. The fight for free schools was a hard one. Many conservatives, heavy taxpayers, farmers, and those with vested interest in church and private schools opposed the common school. Inertia too, was on their side. Yet the proponents of the common school won out. The full story, a story largely hidden in state and local records, has yet to be told. The common school was hammered out during a half-century of political activity in the legislatures of Massachusetts, Connecticut, New York, Michigan and California and other states. The movement was led by a determined group of proselytizers: in New England, Henry Barnard of Connecticut, and James Carter and Horace Mann of Massachusetts; in the West, Isaac Crary and John Pierce of Michigan, John Gage Marvin and John Swett of California, Samuel Lewis and Calvin Stowe of Ohio, Michael Frank of Wisconsin and Caleb Mills of Indiana; in the South, Charles Mercer of Virginia, Robert Breckenridge of Kentucky and Calvin Wiley of North Carolina, among others.

    The common school crusade began in the settled older regions of the East, where new social conditions were most visible and painful and spread West, frequently carried by transplanted New Englanders. Samuel Lewis, the first state superintendent of schools of Ohio, was a New Englander. So was John Pierce of Michigan as well as John Swett of California. The acknowledged leader of the common school crusade was Horace Mann. It was Mann who, perhaps better than anyone else, articulated the 19th century American faith in public education, epitomized the type of reformer active in the common school movement, and provided the program and rhetoric of common school crusaders.

    In 1837, Mann, not a teacher by profession, but a lawyer, and then president of the Massachusetts Senate, signed an act which was to shape his future. This act finally established a State Board of Education. Mann became its first secretary. Raised as a Puritan, Mann had rejected the stern Calvinist predestinarianism of his youth for the gentle, more liberal Unitarianism that attracted other New England intellectuals such as Ralph Waldo Emerson and Theodore Parker during the first half of the 19th century. As a Unitarian (and a transcendentalist, which as one historian has put it, brought emotion to Unitarianism), Mann was predisposed to visualize the education of children hopefully. His reading of George Combe's *Constitution of Man,* and his acceptance of phrenology as the true science of the human mind offered Mann confident assurance that education, if widely dispersed, could speedily effect a social reformation.

    Mann brought to his post of Secretary of the Board of Education a moral earnestness and a sense of devotion to a great cause. But the basic Enlightenment doctrine of man's perfectability also influenced his creed. On the day Mann accepted his new office he wrote: "Henceforth, so long as I hold this office I devote myself to the supremest welfare of mankind upon earth. Faith is the only sustainer. I have faith in the improvability of the race; in their accelerating improvability." Mann's twelve years in office, 1837–1848, were a crusade. Mann organized teacher's conventions and institutes, founded and edited the *Common School Journal,* studied education abroad, organized normal schools, argued with critics, persuaded the public. His *Annual Reports* were read throughout the country and occupy a commanding place in the history of American education, especially his *Seventh Annual Report*, dealing with his educational tour of Europe.

Of all the forces at work on behalf of common schools in the second quarter of the 19th century, one of the most influential were reports on education in Europe. John Griscom in 1819, Victor Cousin in 1831, Henry Barnard in 1835, and Calvin Stowe in 1837 had all published enthusiastic accounts of European education; especially on Prussian education with its state support, compulsory education, teacher-training, broadened curriculum, and modern teaching methods based on Pestalozzi. In 1843 Mann had gone to Europe to observe school practices in Prussia, France, and England. Like the others, he was especially taken by Prussia with its highly developed national school system and its highly skilled corps of well-trained and well-educated teachers. He reviewed his trip in his *Seventh Annual Report*, which would become the best-known of all his reports. Two things in particular struck Mann about the Prussian teachers—their competence, and their kindness to children; they ruled without appealing to force, fear, or pain. Mann concluded: "I do not hesitate to say that there are things abroad which we at home should do well to imitate . . . . If the Prussian schoolmaster has better methods of teaching reading, writing, grammar, geography, arithmetic, . . . surely we can copy his methods of teaching these elements without adopting his notions of passive obedience to government, or of blind obedience to the articles of a church."

Mann carefully pointed out that he meant no disparagement to American teachers, but the schoolmasters of Boston felt differently. The publication of the *Seventh* caused a furor. The heart of the issue was a quarrel over the role of authority, discipline, and corporal punishment in the classroom. This quarrel in turn was related to basic differences in beliefs about human nature; beliefs which might be called Rousseauian *vs.* Augustinian. Mann presumed the inherent goodness of children which had to be educed through love and kindness; the Boston schoolmasters presumed inborn refractoriness which had to be restrained or quelled. The schoolmasters counter-attacked. Authority, not love, must be the backbone of the teaching process. "We object," they said, " . . . to the idea that the relation of a pupil to his teacher is one 'of affection first, and then duty'. We would rather reverse the terms. . . ." But Mann held his ground: "here, then is their philosophy of school discipline. Authority, Force, Fear, Pain." For Mann "punishment should never be inflicted except in cases of extreme necessity; while the experiment of sympathy, confidence, persuasion, encouragement, should be repeated for ever and ever."

Mann was a dedicated spirit setting forth on behalf of a sacred cause. To Mann, education was a great moral undertaking. This point should be emphasized since it is so important a key to an understanding of educational thought in 19th century America. It was this, perhaps more than anything else, that gave the common school movement its crusading, evangelistic nature. The common school movement was a Cause—"I have long been accustomed to look at this great movement of education as a part of the Providence of God," explained Mann, "by which the human race is to be redeemed." Two months before he died in August, 1859, in his valedictory address at Antioch College, of which he was then president, Mann restated an injunction that had for years driven him in the cause of the common schools as well as other causes: "Be ashamed to die until you have won some victory for humanity."

d. A consensus emerged from the educational ferment of 1825–1850. The common school was to be public; not a "private" school affected with a public interest, not a "public" school supported in part by private charity, but a school controlled by publicly elected or appointed officials, financed by the public treasury. The common school was to be free, paid for by the taxpayers at large, not by tuition charged the parents. And it was to be so fine a school that no one would wish to send their children to private schools: "The common school is common," explained Bishop George W. Doane to the New Jersey legislature, "not as inferior . . ., not as the school for poor men's children, but as the light and air are common". It would teach the three R's, but also promote a non-sectarian Christian morality and a non-partisan republicanism. The common school would be public, free, of the highest quality and inculcate individual and civic virtue. With this educational creed, the American people agreed, not everywhere, not everyone, not at the same time, but gradually and with increasing conviction.

The common school movement centered in New England and was then diffused to the new states of the West and later to the South. Unfortunately we know little about the history of education in the West during this period, especially the significance of federal land-grant policy for the development of school systems on the frontier; even less about the interplay of Indian, Spanish, French, and American values in the emerging school systems. Several states in the Old Northwest did enact general school laws rather early. These states had the benefit of congressional land grants, though the proceeds derived from the sale of the land was frequently disappointing. In 1817, for example, Michigan's strange "Catholepistemiad or University of Michigania", sort of a centralized public board of education, was by law placed in charge of the entire subject of education in the state, and almost immediately enunciated a number of advanced but premature principles—of a non-sectarian, centrally controlled, tax-supported public education, extending from the lowest grade through the university level.

In 1837 Michigan created the office of Superintendent of Public Instruction, giving the office supervisory power over the schools and the management of school lands. The school law also provided for state and local taxation and the establishment of local school boards. These were the ideas of the framer of the law, John D. Pierce. In Michigan, as in many other states, public schools first emerged in the largest cities. Thus Detroit established a public school system in 1838, and made the schools free in 1842, when the city board of education was established. In Ohio, the first great strides were taken in 1837, also when the office of superintendent of common schools was created, and Samuel Lewis was chosen to fill it, though it was not until 1853 that the rate bill was abolished and the schools made free. In Indiana, the principle of free common school education was put into operation under the school law of 1853, in Illinois in 1854, and in Wisconsin a few years earlier, in 1848.

In California, the Roman Catholic Church and some Protestant churches were earnestly concerned with religious education. In contrast, the state government lagged in making adequate provision for public schools. Not until 1851 did the legislature pass a law authorizing local districts to establish public schools at their own expense, though the state was receiving the larger share of the taxes on real property. Nevertheless, in cities like San Francisco, public school systems were quickly inaugurated. The new day in education in California began in 1862 when John Swett was elected school superintendent. Swett, known as "the Horace Mann of the Pacific," secured enactments providing for a state board of education with authority to set up a curriculum and to select textbooks, a state school tax, increased county and local taxes and school libraries. Swett also established a state education journal, *The California Teacher,* inaugurated the professional preparation of teachers, and finally helped secure free schools (1867) for the state's children. It should be pointed out that in very few locales, however, East or West, were common schools in the United States free before the Civil War. To be sure, rate bills had been abolished as early as 1827 in Massachusetts and then later in Delaware and a few of the western states, but in New York, Connecticut, Rhode Island, Pennsylvania, New Jersey, and Michigan, rate bills existed until after the Civil War. New York did not attain completely free schools until 1867, Connecticut in 1868, Michigan in 1869 and New Jersey in 1871. In general, free schools became a reality only after the Civil War.

The South flagged behind the East and West. The general practice in the South was that of a decentralized and permissive district or county school system designed for poor children. Neighborhood field schools, denominational efforts, and private academies were substituted for the more universalistic practices of the North. The aristocratic attitude that it was not necessary to educate the masses, the reluctance of the people to tax themselves for educational purposes, and their marked individualism, born of isolation and rural development were among the factors responsible for this condition. Southerners saw little relation between education and life. Consequently, the view prevailed that those who could afford education could indulge themselves in securing it; and those who could not, lost little, if anything. This attitude was aptly summed up as late as 1895 by Virginia's Governor F. W. M. Holliday who said that public schools were a "luxury to be paid for like any other luxury, by the people who wish their benefits."

There was also, of course, the prevailing and hindering Southern racial ideology. During the 1830's, 40's, and 50's, the Southern states participated in the nationwide debate over the aims and instrumentalities of education. At first, there were quite a few men in Virginia and North Carolina—men like Jefferson, Philip Lindsley, and Calvin Wiley—who spoke of the need for universal, free education. By the 1850's, however, the trend was clearly away from a commitment to education as a state responsibility toward a definition of education as a private or at best a local question. Insofar as a coherent educational philosophy continued to exist in the South by the 1850's, it had become a belief that the object was not, as earlier school reformers insisted, to equip the population to guard its liberties, but rather its object was to inculcate Southern orthodoxies and to fend off criticism being directed at the region from outside.

South Carolina adopted a free school law in 1811, but it applied only to orphans and poor children. In 1810, Virginia established a "literary fund" to provide for the schooling of poor children, In 1846, Virginia enacted an education law intended to provide free education for all white children from the proceeds of the "literary fund" and a county tax. But this latter was optional and as late as 1860, accepted by only nine counties in the state. The public school system of North Carolina was, in the ante-bellum period, probably the best in the South. The North Carolina school law of 1839 established a public school system on a permissive basis. In 1853 the state superintendency was established—Calvin H. Wiley held this office until 1860. By the late 1850's about 70 per cent of the children in the state were attending school, about 90 per cent of the teachers were licensed, the average school term averaged four months, and more than $100,000 had been paid in school taxes. Although all the Southern states except South Carolina had constitutional provisions for public education by 1860, only North Carolina and Louisiana had established comprehensive school systems—systems which disappeared as the Civil

War left the South in ruin. Not until the Radicals gained political control after 1867 did state governments begin to emphasize the necessity of educating the freedmen and poor whites at the taxpayers expense. The Reconstruction period held high hopes. The federally supported Freedmen's Bureau built and operated schools; the reconstructed Southern states all accepted the principle of public support in their new constitutions; the Peabody and Slater Funds encouraged teacher education and public aid. But the burden of a dual system of education for Negroes and whites, a distinctive pattern which the Supreme Court endorsed in 1896 in *Plessy* vs. *Ferguson,* only exacerbated a problem of traditional public indifference, lack of financial resources and limited urbanization. In 1861 the number of days of schooling per person of school age in the North ranged from 49.9 to 63.5, while in the South the comparable figure was 10.6. In 1880 the average school-age child in the South received only 23.6 days of schooling, while his northern counterpart received 72 days. Not until the beginning of the 20th century would the Southern states begin to move in the direction which the rest of the country had already made considerable strides.

e. The common schools were to teach more than the three R's and facts about geography and history for Americans like Mann and his contemporaries firmly believed that schools should shape morality and character and patriotism as well as intellect. The schools were the guarantors of a healthy cohesive society; the schools would have to teach the common elements of Republicanism and the common elements of Christianity. The common elements curriculum raises the vital problem: how to build a common school system for a heterogeneous people. Thus, Mann was convinced that to make Republican government work, the schools must teach something about politics and government. But here was the problem—the danger of the classroom becoming a political battlefield to the detriment of the common school. Mann urged teachers to avoid controversy: "Those articles in the creed of Republicanism, which are accepted by all, and which form the common basis of our political faith, shall be taught to all". In the interests of harmony, exclude any subject which might endanger strife and controversy. The dictum "when in doubt leave it out" avoided partisanship and controversy, but whether it also avoided some of the most valuable things that might have been taught is another question. To criticize Mann, however, is not to argue away the problem: how to build a common school curriculum for a people of various political convictions.

The immediate challenge, however, which confronted any reformer who in 1837 might be emboldened to lead the nation forward in the cause of popular education was the religious problem—the place of religion in the common school. Protestant religious instruction had been an integral part of the elementary school curriculum throughout the entire colonial period. Following the Revolution, interest in religion declined somewhat as interest in patriotism rose. Yet, the interest in religion was still intense. Mann, with his contemporaries, believed that a community could not be moral without Christian religion and that no community will be religious without a religious education. But here was the problem. There were many religious sects: Congregational, Baptist, Episcopalian, Unitarian and Methodist. Mann was deeply religious. But he knew the common school would founder if it taught any sectarian creed. Mann's solution: Teach the common elements of Christianity as found in the Bible, without commentary on the part of the teacher. As Mann wrote in his monumental *Twelfth Annual Report:* "Our system earnestly inculcates all

Christian morals; it founds its morals in the basis of religion; it welcomes the religion of the Bible; and, in receiving the Bible, it allows it to do what it is allowed to do in no other system—*to speak for itself*."

Mann, despite his critics, never had any intention of excluding religion from the new public schools. "Non-sectarian," for Mann, did not mean non-religious, it meant non-partisan, non-denominational religion, *i.e.*, "the religion of the Bible," the Biblical truths common to all Protestant sects: "The Bible is the acknowledged expositor of Christianity, the school welcomes the Bible." in this manner, ethics, morality, and Christianity could be taught while offending none. The overwhelmingly Protestant population of Massachusetts supported Mann once he had defeated the most vigorous sectarian spokesmen, among them Frederick A. Packard of the American Sunday School Union and the Reverends Mathew Hale Smith and Edward A. Newton who considered Mann's neutralism an anti-religious position. Subsequently the Massachusetts plan spread gradually to other states.

There are, of course, several difficulties in Mann's position. What seemed "common" elements, for example, were mainly Protestant values. Mann never considered the possibility that non-Protestants and non-Christians attending the public schools would object to his kind of non-sectarian liberal Protestantism. But as Roman Catholic immigration increased in the 1830's and 1840's, Catholic spokesmen increasingly criticized what they considered to be tax-supported Protestant schools. The controversy surfaced in Philadelphia with vicious anti-Catholic "Bible riots" in May and June of 1840, but the most spectacular opposition developed in New York City. New York's school monies went to the Public School Society of New York, the non-sectarian philanthropic group mentioned earlier. Roman Catholics objected to the Protestant tone of the schools, however, and through the 1830's and 1840's waged a vehement campaign against them. Bishop John Hughes of New York stirred more controversy with his demand for monies for the support of Catholic schools. The result was a sustained, bitter and undignified brawl which abated only in 1853 with the intervention of Governor William H. Seward and the New York State Legislature, and the creation of the New York City Board of Education.

Even with the passage of the education bill, however, the public schools of New York City remained unacceptable to Bishop Hughes. Under Hughes' leadership, Catholics in New York set out to develop a comprehensive parochial school system. By mid-century, American Roman Catholic church leaders began to insist with increasing vigor that Catholic parents educate their children in Catholic parochial schools. In 1884, the Third Plenary Council of Bishops, presided over by James Cardinal Gibbons, came out strongly for the establishment of Catholic schools for Catholic children: "We urge and enjoin Catholic parents to provide their beloved children . . . an education which is truly Christian and Catholic . . ., that they therefore send them to parochial schools or other truly Catholic schools, unless in particular cases the Ordinary judges that some alternative may be permitted." To implement their injunctions, the bishops enjoined each parish priest to provide, within two years, a parochial school for the children of his parish. Further orders urged the establishment of Roman Catholic institutions of higher education for the training of teachers and other professionals. A minority of Roman Catholic spokesmen—Bishops John Lancaster Spalding and John Ireland, in particular—believed that American culture would prove extremely hospitable to Catholicism, even in public education. Thus Bishop Spalding optimistically contended that a way could be found to foster a common school education which would be both public and religious. Nevertheless, by 1900 the parochial school had become the Catholic answer to the "school problem". By 1910, close to 1.25 million children were reported as enrolled in the parish schools of the Roman Catholic Church.

Jews, and some Protestant groups like the Lutherans, who rejected the inter-denominational consensus, also were impelled to institute separate systems of parochial schools, though among Jews the parochial school answer—a Jewish education in a Jewish school, was always a minority answer, and a controversial one at that. There was some attempt to establish Jewish day schools in the 1830's-1850's, especially by German Jews in Cleveland, Cincinnati, Milwaukee and St. Louis. But the popularity of the Jewish day school reflected not so much zeal for Jewish education as the absence or poverty of public schools, or the Protestant sectarian tone of those which did exist.

The establishment in the post-Civil War years of public schools without such sectarian features as prayers, Bible and New Testament readings and moralizing sounded the death knell of the Jewish school. As Lloyd Gartner puts it, a new ideology arose in the mid-19th century which regarded the tax-supported, religious-ly neutral common school as the indispensable training ground for American citizenship. Jews enthusiastically adopted this outlook. Only here and there did Jewish voices question the view that Jewish children should be, as a matter of principle, enrolled in the new public schools. Bernard Felsenthal, a Chicago Reform rabbi, urged the need for Jewish schools to raise an American Jewish intellectual class. Such views were largely ignored. Jews were to become fully integrated citizens of the United States, differentiated only by religion; Jewish education would be the reserve of the "Sunday School," the *heder,* the *Bar Mitzvah* or Confirmation, and the *Yeshiva.* The public school became the symbol and guarantee of Jewish equality and opportunity in America.

Likewise, a number of ethnic or immigrant groups wanted their children to study their native language in school; in private school, or in bilingual public schools. Germans, for example, were especially eager to preserve their language and culture against the forces of assimilation. At first, Germans in the mid-West founded private schools to instruct children in their native language. In order to draw German children into the common schools, Ohio, in 1840, passed legislation making it the duty of the Board of Visitors of common schools to provide a number of German schools under duly qualified teachers for the instruction of such youth who desired to learn the German and English languages together. Germans, even before the Civil War, had effectively persuaded school boards in Cincinnati, Baltimore, St. Louis, Chicago, Milwaukee and New York City to introduce German into the elementary schools. In states like New Mexico and California, Hispano-Americans were also determined, though with less success, to protect themselves from assimilation into Anglo-Protestantism. For example, Mexican-Americans in Califor-nia sought schooling in both Spanish and English for their children. But the Yankees were strongly resistant. In 1855 the State Bureau of Public Instruction stipulated that all public schools must teach solely in English.

In summary, it may be said that any other position but Mann's compromise position might have meant the disintegration of the common school. Mann kept the Bible in the school, but would not permit the sects to interpret it. A general Christian influence would permeate the schools, but any specific sectarian influence would be kept out. Without some such compromise, it is doubtful if common schools could have been established, much less prosper. Mann's solution became the generally accepted Protestant position. It must be pointed out, however, that there was the closest connection between Protestantism and the schools. When the common school movement took root, the evangelical Protestant churches were a robust force in American life. Almost everywhere Protestant ministers and prominent lay churchmen were in the forefront of the common school crusade. Thus Calvin Stowe, Robert Breckenridge, and Caleb Mills were clergymen; John D. Pierce had been an agent of the American Home Missionary Society before he became superintendent of schools of Michigan. They took a proprietary interest in the institutions they helped to build. With only a little exaggeration, De Tocqueville could proclaim that in America "almost all education is entrusted to the clergy". Most of these school crusaders assumed a congruence in purpose between the common schools and the Protestant churches; indeed even among liberals like Mann, as we have seen, it was difficult to conceive of moral education without religious sanction. And reinforcing Bible reading, hymns, prayers and holiday rituals in the schools, were the pervasive Protestantism of the textbooks and the influence of Protestant teachers.

f. Mann's twelve years in office were a crusade, a successful crusade, but one which raised many important questions about the nature of school reformers, and the rhetoric and substance of school reform. Mann waged a remarkable campaign of propaganda and persuasions, by appealing to all classes and to all interests—to the hurt pride of the workingman, to the self-interest of the industrialist, to the conscience of the patriot. Universal, free, public education formed the basis of Republican government. An educated people were a more industrious and productive people. Education was the "great equalizer of the conditions of men . . . the balance wheel of the social machinery". Vice and crime would be extirpated through education. Howard Munford Jones, in a pungent characterization of Mann, points out that, in his crusade for the common school, Mann promised something to everyone.

As Mann argued, education became the penacea for every social ill and the highway to Utopia. The common school was to bring about equality in the conditions of men, ensure social harmony, advance social progress, provide a common foundation of values in which diversity could thrive. All of this became the public school ideology, its faith. Mann's messianic rhetoric aroused enthusiasts, made converts, worked wonders. The crusade for education needed, and won, support from a vast coalition of interest groups. All types of people joined the cause, often with different or conflicting motives—from the conservatives Daniel Webster and Edward Everett to the workingmen's associations. But the cause also bequeathed enormous problems. The public school has been nourished on false and inflated promises. There is an enormous chasm between the promises of schoolmen and what the schools have been able to deliver. By promising too much, there has been built into the public school system an endemic frustration, a perpetual irritation. Americans have displayed through the years a persistent and touching faith in education. Yet, one is struck by the volume of criticism of the schools. That our educational system has been such a constant disappointment is just one unfortunate consequence of making excessive claims for the redemptive powers of education. There are others. For example, by the failure on the part of the educational profession to state clearly what the school can and cannot be expected to do, by contributing to the popular myth that education is the panacea for every social and personal shortcoming, educators have greatly oversimplified social problems and obscured the relationship between schools and social problems.

The conventional wisdom is that only self-seeking and ignorant men opposed the common schools. It now becomes clear that some of the most creative minds of

19th century America entertained doubts about the efficacy of the common schools as then conceived. For example, Bronson Alcott and Henry Thoreau had taught briefly in the public school and had quit because they deeply disapproved of the authoritarian methods and the harsh discipline which was intended to make the child moral and obedient. They saw the goal of education not as inculcation and control but as self-realization and liberation; authenticity, to use more modern nomenclature. Emerson lamented in 1844: "We are students of words; we are shut up in schools, and colleges, and recitation rooms, for 10 or 15 years, and come out at last with a bag of wind, a memory of words, and do not know a thing." In the communitarian experiment at New Harmony, Indiana, established in 1825 by Robert Owen and William Maclure, Joseph Neef was brought over from Europe to introduce Pestalozzian object lessons into its schools. Bronson Alcott's Temple School assumed the objective of education was self-knowledge and self-discovery under the eyes of a loving teacher. Henry Thoreau in his "uncommon" school, Concord Academy, in the Berkshires, taught that "each man should step to his own music, however measured or far away".

Again, the conventional interpretation holds that the common school spread in response to the demands of an enlightened working class and the idealism of an elite of Eastern intellectuals. But neither the motives nor the aims of the reformers were perhaps as disinterested or as benevolent as earlier generations believed. According to Michael Katz, elaborating on a theme expounded by Merle Curti more than thirty years earlier, the common school movement represented essentially a conservative response to the rapid social changes incident to urbanization and industrialization. School reforms were advocated by an elite of wealth and position largely for their value in the fight to help solve the problems of industrial society. In alliance with them were the aspiring middle class who saw the school as an agency of social mobility for their children. Educators joined the fight for school reform to enhance their precarious professional status. The victory of school reformers was complete but, Professor Katz concludes, of mixed benefits. A common school system was established, but it was a system encrusted in a rigid bureaucracy and estranged from the immigrant and working-class community which comprised its chief clientele.

g. The common school reformers firmly established the institutional structure and ideology of public education, but what did children actually learn in the classroom? The Reverend Warren Burton, born in New Hampshire in 1800, has left an excellent account of instruction during the early 19th century in his delightful *The District School As It Was.* Reading, spelling, writing, and arithmetic constituted the principal elements in the offering. But schoolbooks offer more useful clues to the actual contents of instruction in the nineteenth century.

Textbooks taught more than the 3 R's and facts about geography and history. For most Americans believed that the school should shape character more than intelligence. The authors of American school textbooks emphatically believed that there was such a thing as a national character and that they had a duty to help form and preserve it. The lessons were distilled early in the century in Noah Webster's *Spellers* and then later in McGuffey's *Readers.* Noah Webster's "blue-backed speller" epitomized the new breed of readers. It combined speller with reader and included poetry for recitation, patriotic speeches of Revolutionary leaders and moral catechisms. In addition, it was the first text to attempt to overcome the diversity of dialects, the variety in word structure, and the chaos in spelling that existed throughout the colonies. The famous McGuffey readers, carefully graded, Protestant in tone, made their appearance in 1836 and were used by generations of students, enjoying estimated sales of 107,000,000 by 1890. The McGuffey *Readers* played an important role in American education and in American culture, and helped to shape that elusive thing we call the American character.

The stories designed specifically to build character through the development of proper moral attitudes and behavior were presented in terms of a sharp contrast between right and wrong. Reforms were astonishingly sudden, successful and permanent. The schoolbooks also reflected widely held conceptions of the child and his activities. Hard work was honored and rewarded, play discouraged. But gradually the nature of the child, his inclinations, tastes and desires became more and more dominant factors in the choice and arrangement of subject matter. Illustrations were introduced by McGuffey to make the lessons "a pleasure rather than a task".

What the men who established schools and who approved the textbooks required, and what Webster and McGuffey and the others produced were handbooks of the common morality—testament to the virtues which a half-century of experience had elevated into the culture-religion. Later in the century, the Horatio Alger books performed a similar function. Schoolbooks indoctrinated children in the familiar catalogue of moral virtues of Protestant, agrarian-commercial America: industry, thrift, practicality, temperance, honesty, plain living, piety and patriotism, while re-affirming the general belief in the superiority of American institutions and in America's unique mission in the world.

h. Thus far the ideal of the common school has been discussed entirely on the elementary school level, and for many 19th century American educators this was as far as it went. On the other hand, even before 1860, other educators pondered over another important problem almost immediately posed by the common school ideal—namely, if, how and for whom would public higher educational opportunity be made available.

The 1820's saw the formulation, first in New England, and then in other parts of the United States, of a second dimension of the common school ideal—the free public high school. In the beginning the high school was conceived simply as a continuation of the common school, a kind of upward extension of elementary education for young people who desired further education, but who couldn't afford the academy. (Another idea which received increasing voice during the pre-Civil War period was the idea of free higher education. By 1860, as we shall later see, twenty of the thirty-four states of the Union had founded state universities. Before 1860, particularly in mid-western states like Michigan, the common school system had become a ladder from the grade school to the university.)

The new era in American secondary education was inaugurated in Boston with the organization of the English High School for Boys in 1821. The objective of the Boston high school was to prepare young men not for college but for the world of business and commerce, it was intended for young men intending to become "merchants and mechanics". The school resembled the better academies, except that since Boston already maintained a Latin Grammar School to prepare boys for the university, the classical studies were omitted. That is young men, or boys really, received a three year English course. Under the prodding of some educators, like James Carter, who feared that private academies would undermine the public schools by attracting all the sons of the well-to-do, Massachusetts, in 1827, enacted legislation requiring the establishment of English high schools in towns or districts of more than 500 families; in towns or districts of 4,000 or more families the high school had to teach Latin and Greek. By 1865, the public high school movement had spread through New England, and to New York, Chicago, Philadelphia and Baltimore. The high schools, however, were to find a readier response in the post-Civil War period in the new Western states. Committed to educational democracy, already possessing state universities and a common school system, it was too inconsistent for these states to depend on private academies for the middle rung of education.

In some Northern states, including Rhode Island, Connecticut and New Jersey, the high school movement did not really get underway until after 1865, and even later in the South. Even in some Western states where the common schools were free and numerous and where the statutes provided for a state university, the status of the high school, the logical link between them, was precarious. Initially, a variety of scattered public high schools, seminaries and especially, private and semi-public academies filled the gap. In fact, during most of the 19th century, the academy dominated secondary education. In many cases, academies offered little more than the "common branches". In some academies, however, like the Phillips' Academies, students could find the best preparation for college then available.

The academy movement proved to be a powerful grass-roots movement. Henry Barnard in 1850 listed over 6,000 academies served by more than 12,000 teachers and enrolling over 250,000 students in thirty-six states and territories, and this was probably an understatement. And then there were a bewildering number of seminaries, collegiate institutions, institutes, etc. The academies taught a staggering amount of subjects. Most were small, only a few quite large. Most were co-educational. Many were boarding schools. Some were supported by public funds, many were not. The majority were impermanent, but some remain in existence to this day. Particularly in the case of Roman Catholics, the academy became an important phase of the parochial school system. Teaching orders such as the Jesuits, the Brothers of the Christian Schools, and the Sisters of Notre Dame de Namur established a number of thriving academies. While in the South the military academy particularly took root. Academies provided educational opportunities otherwise unavailable in a period when the population was widely dispersed and the tax base in most communities remained barely sufficient to support elementary schools. The academy was almost the universal form of American education above the elementary level before the Civil War; a social institution of the first importance about which we know all too little.

The academy was a popular and useful institution. But by the mid-19th century opposition to it began to develop on the grounds that it was select, exclusive and aristocratic, catering chiefly to those who could pay fees. But there were also certain social developments which greatly influenced the emergence of the public high school. For example, in the post-Civil War period an economy based on thousands of small farms and small businesses was transformed into one based on large bureaucratized organization characterized by centralized direction and administration carried out through coordinating managerial and clerical staffs. When small organizations grow large, paper orders replace verbal orders, including records of work, inventories, etc. People had to be trained to handle paper-work; prepare, type, file, process and assess them. The growth of secondary education in the United States in the post-Civil War period was, in large part, a response to the pull of the economy for a mass of white-collar workers with more than an elementary school education. Of course, the proliferation of colleges and state universities also contributed to the growth of secondary education, as did the success of the common school movement, which stimulated more and more young men and women to take advantage of a high school education.

In the post-Civil War period then a movement arose for the establishment of a system of free, public secondary schools, supported by public taxation, publicly controlled, open to all. Which is not to say that the high school did not encounter opposition. Not only the desirability and the practicality of maintaining free, tax-supported public high schools but their legality were controversial issues for a full quarter-century following the Civil War. The most important form of opposition was litigation. In New England in 1819 and again in 1846, the Supreme Court of Massachusetts ruled in favor of secondary education at public expense. But it was a series of judicial decisions in the mid-West in the 1870's, in the state courts of Illinois, Wisconsin, Kansas, Missouri, and especially Michigan, which finally laid a sound legal basis for the public high school.

The most famous and influential of these court decisions was the Kalamazoo decision, decided by the Michigan Supreme Court in 1874. The case involved the attempt in 1872 of certain citizens of Kalamazoo's School District No. 1 to prevent the school board from collecting taxes for support of high schools. (High schools had first emerged in Michigan in 1859 when school districts received legislative authority to establish them.) By 1872, practically every city in the state had a public high school, but not without some opposition. When Kalamazoo brought suit, it was very obviously a move to question the right of school authorities in general to support free high schools and to offer appropriate secondary studies in them. The complainants had no argument with the right of the state to support and maintain public elementary schools. Rather, they were arguing that secondary instruction, as it was then conceived, embraced largely the classics and foreign languages. These, they held, were by and large an accomplishment of the few rather than the many, and they should, therefore, be paid for privately.

The decision, written by Justice Thomas M. Cooley and concurred in by his three colleagues, came out squarely against the complainants. Reviewing the educational history of the Northwest Territory and of the state of Michigan, Cooley asserted that from the very beginning of statehood, Michigan had intended to furnish not only the rudiments of education, but also equal opportunity for all to proceed on to higher studies. Having specifically provided for free elementary schools, and a state university, Cooley concluded, the state would be highly inconsistent if it forced parents to secure *private* secondary instruction; the legal right of the school board to levy taxes for public high schools was clearly affirmed.

The pre-Civil War public high school was largely a terminal institution. In the wake of the Kalamazoo decision not only the useful and practical studies, but college-preparatory studies as well became the just province of the public high school. Indeed, thanks to the certifying procedures of some midwestern state universities—Michigan, Minnesota, Iowa and Wisconsin—tremendous impetus was given to the establishment of the public high school as almost exclusively a college-preparatory institution. To bring about better articulation between higher and lower schools, for example, Michigan University spearheaded the formation of the North Central Association of Colleges and Secondary Schools, one of the great regional accrediting agencies of the country. Even earlier, the University of Michigan itself in 1871 put into practice the unique concept of accrediting high schools; *i.e.*, to accredit a high school and thereafter accept without examination any of its students who presented a recommendation from the principal.

With the legal basis thus clarified by the Kalamazoo case, local school boards began to establish high schools as the demand arose. State legislatures also were encouraged to pass laws permitting local boards to establish high schools, to offer aid to those districts which did so, and, finally, actually to compel high schools to be established in certain larger and more populous districts. To be sure, such legislation came slowly. Wisconsin began to aid high schools financially in 1875; Minnesota in 1878; Maine in 1873. However, it was only during the 1890's and after that the great avalanche of high school legislation really came.

Unlike the academy, the public high school in the 19th century was mainly an urban invention. In contrast with the Latin school, which led to college, at first the high school was a projection upward of the common school, supplemented by details copied from the academy; sometimes it was simply an honorific label attached to the upper grades of the elementary school. A number of cities however supported high schools of high calibre like Woodward High School in Cincinnati. Particularly in the western cities which had no tradition of Latin grammar schools, high schools tended to base their curricula on the college-preparatory subjects. Most public high schools tended to offer at least two programs—a more practical one for terminal students and a classical one for college-preparatory students. The simple fact was that those communities which could afford a high school at all could as a rule only support one high school. Thus the *comprehensive* high school, the high school offering many parallel programs under one roof soon became the standard form of American secondary school. In noting this general pattern, however, one should not ignore the movement toward special schools serving special purposes which was increasingly evidenced in larger communities. One of the first such schools was the manual training high school developed by Professor Calvin M. Woodward at Washington University, St. Louis, in the late 1870's, to be discussed below.

By the end of the century the high school, supported and controlled by the public, had come of age. The number of public high schools mushroomed from 160 in 1870 to 800 in 1880. By 1890 there were about 200,000 children in public high schools; about 360,000 children in all secondary schools. The latter figure represented about 6.7% of the population aged fourteen–seventeen. And by the turn of the century, formal schooling was not only directly more available to more students for more years, it was obligatory as well. Massachusetts enacted a compulsory education law as early as 1852. Still, by 1873 only eight states and the District of Columbia had some form of compulsory attendance law. In 1890, compulsory attendance laws in thirty-one states and territories required children, usually from ages eight to twelve or thirteen or fourteen to attend school a certain specified number of days per year. By 1895, almost 5,000,000 children were enrolled in the public schools. While innovations like the Pestalozzian object lesson, Quincy Methods, Herbartianism, and Froebel's Kindergarten principles and practices, described below, tried to make their days in school more pleasant and profitable.

|| **a.** By mid-century then, a conception of the common school had emerged. The common school was not to be a "private" school affected with a public interest, nor a "public" school supported in part by private donations, but a school controlled by publicly appointed officials, financed from the public treasury. The common school was to be free, paid for by the taxpayers at large. The common schools would teach the three R's, and also promote a non-sectarian Christian morality, and a non-partisan Republicanism. And, ideally, the common

schools would be so excellent that no one would wish to send their children to private schools. It was time to look to teacher-training.

The educational enthusiasm of the American people was never keenly disposed to support their teachers very well. The unenviable situation of the teacher in America, as we have seen in Volume I, can be traced back to the earliest days of our history. In the colonial period securing qualified teachers was always a problem. Early American communities had intense difficulties in finding and keeping adequate schoolmasters; the opportunities for a man of learning were too great to leave many first-rate men available for the ill-compensated, low-status position then the lot of those whose lives were given to the instruction of children. Men permanently fixed in the role of schoolmaster often seem to have been of indifferent quality and extraordinarily ill-suited for the job. Although competent and dedicated teachers could be found from time to time, the misfits seemed to have been so conspicuous that they set an unflattering image of the teaching profession. The stereotype was fixed, a vicious cycle drawn. American communities found it hard to secure good teachers. They settled for what they could get. What they got was a high proportion of incompetents. Schoolboards concluded that teaching was a trade which attracted rascals and having so concluded were reluctant to pay the rascals more than they were worth. For example, in 1841 the average weekly pay of men in rural schools was $4.15; by 1861 this had increased to only $6.30. What helped American education break cut of the vicious cycle was the development of the graded primary school, the emergence of the woman teacher, and the development of the normal school.

It is difficult to fully comprehend the serious obstacles which surrounded the public school teachers of early America; the absence of training facilities, the dearth of suitable textbooks, the primitive condition of the schoolhouses, and the ungraded school. In the ungraded school, children of all ages, sizes and degrees of educational achievement were thrown into the same room to be instructed by one teacher. The school might include children from six and younger to sixteen and older. The number of pupils per teacher might range from below forty to over one-hundred, with everyone crowded together on long benches. Students often rebelled. In 1837 alone, more than ninety schools were "broken up" in Massachusetts, literally as well as figuratively, and frequently with the open support of parents. Little wonder the school often became a battleground, with the birch rod the teachers' only means of authority.

Gradually, however, in the common schools of the larger cities and towns, younger children were separated from the older children, then children divided into classes and grades depending upon age and achievement. "Grading," an emulation of German practice, was introduced into the Boston public schools in 1847 by John Philbrick; by 1860, most city schools accepted this organization. The graded school made possible a unified curriculum, centralized control, and smaller classes of more or less homogeneous groups of pupils. It also increased the need for teachers, and opened up the trade for women.

Until the 1830's, most teachers were men. The notion prevailed that women were inadequate for the disciplinary problems of the schoolroom, especially in large classes, and with older age groups. The emergence of the graded school provided a partial answer to these objections. Opponents of women teachers were still to be heard, but they could be silenced when it was pointed out that women teachers could be paid one-third to one-half as much as men. Both Horace Mann and Henry Barnard cited economy as a consideration in favor of the more general employment of women. Since it was possible to find a fair supply of admirable young girls to work at low pay, to keep them at work only so long as their personal conduct met the rigid standards of schoolboards, the acceptance of the woman teacher solved the problem of character as well as cost. By 1860, women teachers outnumbered men in some states; by 1870, it was estimated that women constituted about 60% of the nation's teachers.

b. The female school teacher helped solve the problem of character (and cost); the normal school helped solve the problem of competence. Before the 1830's there was little interest in popular education and no interest in teacher education as such. As a rule teachers in the best grammar schools received their preparation in an American college or European university. In elementary schools, the completion of the elementary course itself was a sufficient preparation for an elementary school teacher. At the beginning of the national period, the only qualifications generally required of a teacher were that he be a professed Christian, have some knowledge of the three R's, and the ability to keep order. Since almost everyone could profess Christianity or the three R's, the chief requirement for teaching was likely to be the ability (or strength) to discipline unruly children, as the hero of Edward Eggleston's novel, *The Hoosier Schoolmaster,* was to find out even as late as the post-Civil War period.

Inspired by reports of teacher training seminaries in Prussia and France, as early as the 1820's William Russell, Thomas Gallaudent, Walter R. Johnson, and James Carter stressed the need for schools for the training of teachers. Fearful that the common schools, unless competent teachers be secured, would come to be regarded as pauper schools, first Carter, and then Horace Mann began to urge the Massachusetts legislature to establish normal schools. On July 3,1839, Mann had the pleasure to preside over the opening of the first public normal school in the United States, at Lexington, Massachusetts. The school, with the Reverend Cyrus Pierce as principal, took girls at the age of sixteen and offered them a minimum one year course of study. The prerequisites were evidence of good moral character and satisfactory completion of an elementary education. The curriculum of the school comprised a review of the common branch subjects, principles and methods of teaching, the art of school government, and practice teaching. Massachusetts soon founded two more normal schools. New York, Connecticut, Michigan, Illinois and other states followed the lead of Massachusetts. By 1865, there were at least fifteen state normal schools.

The normal schools were a tremendous improvement over what had gone before, but the decision to train teachers in separate institutions was to raise critical questions for the future of the teaching profession. In effect, between 1820–1850 the decision was made that prospective teachers would be prepared in separate institutions from other professionals and would have a different type of preparation. For example, the demands put upon the student in the normal school were not high. Actually, the normal school was little more than a higher elementary school. It was only as late as 1894 that a high school diploma began to be required for admission to Massachusetts normal schools. Their narrow curriculum, at best a form of secondary education, for the most part a sort of remedial elementary education, made the normal schools objects of derision among academics. Their professional courses amounted to little more than rule of thumb and some helpful hints, as evidenced by such early books for teachers as David Page's, *Theory and Practice of Teaching,* Jacob Abbot's, *The Teacher: Or Moral Influences In the Instruction and Government of the Young,* and Samuel Hall's, *Lectures on School-Keeping.* However the normal schools were perhaps all that could have been asked for under the circumstances. There were no funds available for any more extensive establishment, and young men and women couldn't afford a longer course of preparation. Furthermore, the majority of school districts did not require and would not support teachers who had at great expense of time and money fitted for their calling. And finally there was an emergency: the schools and the students were there; they couldn't wait.

The normal school imbued low-salaried, put-upon teachers with a sense of mission, a sense of calling, a unique *esprit de corps*. But the price was paid in isolation from the larger community of scholars and from the mainstream of scholarship. It is ironic that in their haste to gain professional status for the common school teacher by establishing separate normal schools, school reformers at the same time closed the door to one of the major agencies of gaining professional status, namely, developing teacher education as a responsibility of the colleges. The effect was to hasten the development of the teacher as a technician, but not as a professional. The two problems encountered in the early normal school develop-ment—creating a profession, and determining the proper relationship between the academic and technical studies—have continued to plague teacher education.

By 1900 most states had normal schools. But many other institutions were preparing teachers for the common schools—municipal normal schools, private schools, the "teachers institute," academies, and the newly established public high schools. Even before the Civil War then, the tradition had been established that a variety of institutions would train American teachers. In 1896-7, 1,487 institutions reported that they gave courses designed for the professional training of teachers. Of these, 164 were public normal schools, 198 private normal schools, 196 colleges and universities, 507 public high schools, and 472 were private high schools or academies. The actual training varied—review of the common school subjects plus the theory and practice of teaching; special emphasis on the methods of teaching; completion of secondary and/or higher education; the integration of liberal and professional education. Nevertheless while there were almost as many variations as there were proponents, the general lines of the teacher-training programs became fairly clear during the 1890's. Most included *first*, some professionalized treatment of the academic subject matter the teacher was to teach, giving particular attention to method and to the relation between various areas of knowledge; *second*, the history and philosophy of education; *third*, the organization and administration of school systems; *fourth*, child study and development; and *fifth*, general study of teaching methods.

The post-Civil War period saw the emergence of specialized teachers colleges— Oswego (N.Y.) Normal School, Illinois State Normal University, Michigan State Normal College at Ypsilanti, and also the New York College for the Training of Teachers. In 1889 the latter was a modest school for the preparation of home economics and industrial arts teachers but under Nicholas Murray Butler, by 1892, it developed into Teachers College, becoming affiliated with Columbia University in 1898. This same period saw many state universities add "normal departments". This period also saw the formal study of education enter the college and university curriculum. In 1873 the University of Iowa established a chair of pedagogy. The University of Michigan followed Iowa's precedent in 1879, creating a chair in the Art and Science of Teaching. By the end of the century most major colleges and universities had established departments or schools of education or were offering some courses in education.

Although concern for improving the qualifications (and salaries) of teachers developed slowly, this interest was greatly increased by the organization of state teachers associations, and, finally, the establishment of the National Teachers Association in 1857, which became the National Education Association in 1870. The teachers associations also had much to do with the organization of the United States Bureau of Education in 1876. The impetus for the establishment of the Bureau was the need felt by many 19th century educators, led by Henry Barnard, for a federal agency which would be responsible for the collection and dissemination of educational statistics and information. Through the 1840's, 50's, and 60's, various educational organizations discussed the idea of a federal education department, and several petitioned Congress on its behalf. The final and successful petition was presented to Congress in 1866 by the National Teachers Association. The organic act creating an autonomous Department of Education, without cabinet status, was passed in 1867; in 1869 it became the Office of Education in the Department of Interior. The ubiquitous Barnard, who had done so much to promote Pestalozzi, Froebel, the Kindergarten, the normal school, the high school, and adult education through the pages of his *American Journal of Education*, became the first Commissioner of Education, succeeded by John Eaton in 1870.

III **a.** The tendency in America to have a great number and variety of colleges has already been referred to. These tendencies were exagerrated in the Era of the Common Man. The 1820's and 1830's were witness to a veritable college-founding mania. The American people went into the Revolution with nine colleges. They went into the Civil War with 250, of which 182 still survive. And this figure is trifling compared to the number of colleges founded in the same period which failed to survive. Many factors go into explaining the college-founding mania. The temper of the time, for example. It was the Age of Jackson. We were a busy, restless, speculating, optimistic, mobile country. America required colleges as scattered and mobile as the people themselves. The sheer continental dimensions of the United States and the difficulties of travel tended to encourage localism and regional pride, thus augmenting the number of colleges. Another element behind the seemingly reckless competition for colleges was the grassroots conviction that the average citizen was entitled to a chance at higher education and that this could be best achieved by regional and decentralized institutions of learning. With educational opportunity widely distributed, any deserving young man could go to the college of his choice in his own community.

Most important, however, was religious rivalry. After the Great Awakening of the 1730's and 1740's, religion was in temporary eclipse, overshadowed by the concerns of politics and business. But at the turn of the century the fires of religious zeal flared up again in a new series of revivals and camp meetings which swept the country from the Atlantic to the Mississippi, and set the evangelical churches off on a crusade of reform and expansion with profound effects on higher education. As the population moved West, so did the revitalized denominations. The denominations would not let religion (nor culture) die on the frontier. We can follow the churches as they moved West from the colleges they established. Presbyterians founded Alleghany College in Pennsylvania and Wabash in Indiana. Episcopalians founded Hobart in New York State, Methodists founded Randolph-Macon in Virginia; Roman Catholics founded Notre Dame in Indiana. Ohio alone, by 1850, had nineteen colleges. (In 1880 England was managing nicely with four universities for a population of 23,000,000. While Ohio, with a population of 3,000,000, boasted thirty-seven institutions of higher learning, most established by competing religious sects.)

Dissatisfaction with the sectarian nature of colleges led to state campaigns for greater public control, but the colleges resisted. The struggle for control abruptly ended in 1819 when the United States Supreme Court, heeding the eloquent appeal of Daniel Webster, upheld the right of the trustees of Dartmouth College to immunity from state legislative interference. The Dartmouth College decision guaranteed the private and denominational colleges freedom from expropriation and popular pressure. Private colleges, once chartered, would now be secure from state interference. Indirectly, the decision also helped to create a firm legal foundation for the small colleges that began to proliferate throughout the country. State legislatures retaliated, nevertheless, by reserving tax monies for the new publicly controlled state institutions of higher learning, although state universities were slow to develop in the pre-Civil War period.

Higher education in pre-Civil War America was fragmented, particularistic and decentralized. Still, unifying forces counteracted the absence of central direction—the influence of organized religion, the inherited intellectual tradition, and the collegiate way of life and the extra-curriculum. We have already stated that this was the hey-day of the religiously oriented college. This is evidenced not only by formal denominational ties, but in numerous other ways. Nine out of ten college presidents before the Civil War, for example, were clergymen. The great majority of the teaching faculty were clergymen, and most of them, presidents and faculty, would probably have agreed with Noah Webster when, at the cornerstone laying of the first building at Amherst College, he declared that one of the chief purposes of the American college was "to reclaim and evangelize the miserable children of Adam".

Perhaps more potent even than religion in impressing the colleges with a common stamp was the course of study brought over from Europe and known as the classical tradition. The curriculum of Harvard, Yale and William and Mary were transplanted to all their successors West and South, keeping pace with the building of new colleges, and marking the advance of the cultural frontier. This accounts for the astonishing sameness of American colleges, a sameness which lasted until the latter part of the nineteenth century when the land-grant college movement broke the mold. This is not to say that the status quo was maintained without a struggle. America was a rapidly growing and changing society. Increasingly, even on the Atlantic seaboard, the all-sufficiency of the inherited educational formulae was questioned. A few new colleges—Amherst, Hobart, Union and the University of Vermont—began to offer modern languages as a substitute for Latin and Greek. At the University of Virginia, thanks to Jefferson's reform efforts, students were allowed to elect from among eight different "schools," convering the subject areas of ancient languages, modern languages, mathematics, natural philosophy, natural history, medicine, moral philosophy and law. And even earlier, George Ticknor of Harvard had spoken up for change in the way of greater freedom for students in the choice of a course of study.

In the circumstances, a vigorous assertion of the merits of the old order were called for and the task fell to Yale. Any educational pronouncement from Yale was certain of wide and respectful attention. In 1828, President Jeremiah Day and his faculty drew up a sweeping polemic designed to end once and for all the growing revolt. Published as the "Yale Report on the Classics," it laid down college guide lines for the next half-century. There were two great points to be accomplished by collegiate education, Day argued, "the *discipline* and the *furniture* of the mind, expanding its powers, and storing it with knowledge. . . . ." For this, nothing was superior to the classics. The report was an able, forceful plea for the education of a Christian gentleman and scholar.

College, of course, was more than a curriculum. With its country setting, dormitories, dining commons, the paternalism and discipline and guidance of president and faculty, it became a Way of Life. Troubled as we are by our sense of educational failure, we may be too ready to imagine the old-time college as far better than it was. But the literature of the Old-Time College is a literature of bitter complaint, complaint about the neglect of mind, of body, of spirit, like that etched in the memories of countless readers of Henry Adams' *Education.* If the ante-bellum 19th century college did not totally anesthetize the minds of the undergraduates, much credit was due to the extracurriculum.

The colleges failed to make provision for contemporary issues, for fun, for exercise. The student developed his own solution in his extracurricular activities— through literary and debating societies, newspapers and periodicals, Greek-letter fraternities and sororities, and organized athletics. To anyone unfamiliar with the main developments in American higher education, the importance of students in molding and changing American higher education may come as something of a surprise. Fraternities and sororities, athletics, literature and debating societies, musical and dramatic organizations, student publications, student government—the impacts of all these parts of the extra-curriculum altered American higher education in significant ways.

b. Colleges responded very slowly to social change. In the pre-Civil War period, although a college education was a distinct advantage, a degree was not needed to become a doctor or a lawyer or a politician. Higher education remained more a luxury, less a utility than it is today. In a society so mobile, so rich, so expansive, and yet so unspecialized, opportunities beckoned to young men directly out of grammar schools or academies. Only gradually did students, parents and educators come to expect a more intimate relationship to exist between college and career, school and society.

Educational criticism quickened in the mid-19th century. In 1850 Brown's President Francis Wayland subjected the entire system of higher education to an unsparing review, questioning everything from the cost to the curriculum structure. Henry P. Tappan of Michigan University agreed with Wayland. Strongly influenced by German universities, Tappan outlined the main features of a complete system of state-supported schools, extending from the elementary grades to the summit of the educational pyramid, the university. Though Tappan met with resistance at Michigan, he had an important effect on university developments in the post-Civil War period. If the old-time college wouldn't or couldn't adjust, America would create new institutions to serve its purpose. When the changes did occur, it would be through the State University and Land-Grant College Movement. The State Universities, publicly controlled, publicly supported, free, closely aligned with, and the capstone of, the common school system, began in the mid-west as a consequence of the federal practice, beginning in 1787, of granting lands to new states to support colleges. By the Civil War, the federal government had donated 4,000,000 acres of land to fifteen states for the endowment of universities, leading to the establishment, all before the Civil War, of the State Universities of Ohio, Iowa, Indiana, Michigan, Wisconsin, Minnesota, Missouri, Utah and others. Still, the rise of the State University to a place of importance in American education did not occur until after the Civil War; only the Universities of Michigan and Wisconsin foreshadowed the great future that was before the State University. The ideal of a state university closely intertwined with the life of the people and intimately linked with government, although first expressed by Tappan at Michigan, was most nearly realized at Wisconsin. The University of Wisconsin operated, in the best sense of the word, as a service university and set an example of the potentialities for the democratic university. The rise of the State University served to democratize the college by offering practical education as well as publicly supported, publicly controlled, free higher education, and also introduced the service function into higher education. At Wisconsin University the motto: "The boundaries of the campus are the boundaries of the state," dramatized the growing devotion to service.

Federal aid supplied by the epochal Morrill Act signed by President Lincoln on July 2, 1862, encouraged the further broadening of curriculum constituency already under way. The passage of the Morrill Act, which gave federal aid to mechanical and agricultural colleges, was a recognition of the technological needs of agriculture and business. Much of the funds were used for small, struggling, ineffectual schools. But universities in Wisconsin, Minnesota, Missouri, North Carolina and Iowa were enlarged. And, the success of Cornell University was made possible partly by Morrill funds—Cornell sold land-scrip on the Morrill grants to provide an endowment. Cornell University opened in 1865 as a non-sectarian institution where intellectual life, service to the state, and vocationalism were to live happily side by side. Ezra Cornell's words, "I would found an institution where any person can find instruction in any study," which Andrew Dickson White, Cornell's first president, endorsed as "the true conception of a university," expressed the spirit of the new kind of higher education. In 1887 Congress passed the Hatch Experiment Station Act, providing for state grants to finance agricultural experiment stations in connection with Morrill Land-grant colleges. The Hatch Act was extremely significant because it brought the federal government into an important educational domain—that of research and experimentation in agriculture and conservation problems and finally demonstrated to skeptical farmers that higher education could pay off in more efficient farm management and more lucrative crops.

c. To compare the college of the 1830's and 1840's with the university of the turn of the century is to contrast two dissimilar institutions. Patterned on the German model, but reshaped by American requirements, the university grew out of the college, offering advanced degrees through the seminar, the lecture and laboratory research. While the old-time colleges believed it their duty to discipline the student's mind and required attendance at every course and every meeting of the course, the German university freed its students for individual research in whatever fields they wished. The college ideal was to graduate cultured gentlemen, conversant with broad fields of learning. The university ideal was to graduate experts, all of whom had done advanced work in some specialty. The college was a Christian, even sectarian creation; the university had no great interest in religion of any kind. The college was characterized by restrictions of many kinds—courses, curriculum, sectarianism. The university was free. "If we would maintain a university," Daniel Coit Gilman warned, "great freedom must be allowed to both teachers and scholars." Freedom implied not only religious freedom, but the elective system that would allow students to choose v hat learning they wished to pursue to mastery. It also meant freedom for the faculty to undertake research and to express in the classroom any conclusion they wished.

In 1876 Johns Hopkins, the first American university based on the German model, opened its doors. The aim, said Gilman, when he assumed its presidency, was "the encouragement of research, the promotion of young men; and the advancement of individual scholars, who by their excellence will advance the sciences they pursue . . ." Johns Hopkins adopted the lecture, the seminar, and the laboratory. American students who sought graduate education in Germany soon were channeled into our own institutions with the establishment (thanks to the largesse of new millionaires like Ezra Cornell, Cornelius Vanderbilt and John D. Rockefeller, who donated great fortunes to higher education) of Johns Hopkins in 1876, Clark in 1889, and Stanford and the University of Chicago in 1891, and the development of respectable graduate schools at Harvard, Cornell, Columbia, Princeton, Yale, and at the State Universities of Michigan and Wisconsin.

The emergence of the modern university coincided with the rise of 19th century science. The most liberating and powerful of all the scientific theories were those of Charles Darwin. The publication of Darwin's *Origin of the Species* in 1859, and the subsequent popularization of Darwin's ideas by Herbert Spencer, who was enormously influential in America, threw a bombshell into the intellectual scene. Sectarianism receded as science, long excluded from a place of prominence in the college curriculum came to the fore. "A university," said Charles W. Eliot, "cannot be built upon a sect." Secular and scientific men displaced ministers on boards of trustees and as heads of universities: Andrew Dickson White at Cornell, G. Stanley Hall at Clark, Daniel Coit Gilman at Johns Hopkins, Charles W. Eliot at Harvard, David Starr Jordan at Stanford, F. A. P. Barnard at Columbia, Arthur Hadley at Yale and Woodrow Wilson at Princeton. An awesome proliferation of knowledge produced whole new fields of study. History, sociology, anthropology, political science, economics were added to the increasing number of compartments into which the sciences were sub-divided. Trained specialists replaced the cleric teaching half-a-dozen subjects. Defenders of the classics protested in vain as their positions were pre-empted by newcomers to the scene.

The emergence of academic freedom controversies, like that involving William Graham Sumner and President Noah Porter of Yale, bespoke the new-found aggressiveness and militancy of the professors and their dedication to the advancement of knowledge. President Porter of Yale, the citadel of the old system, and President James McCosh of Princeton, defended the traditional view eloquently, and with some success, but the elective system, inaugurated by Eliot at Harvard in 1869—subsequently adopted by many colleges and universities—destroyed dependency on a single limited curriculum for all. The triple function of the 20th century American university—teaching, research, and service—was clearly apparent at the turn of the century. The ivory tower remained only as a graduation day reminiscence.

d. In the meantime various forms of adult education—the Lyceum and mechanics institutes before the Civil War, and Chautauqua, college and university extension, correspondence courses and the library movement in the late 19th century—all expanded access to education. Even women, long discriminated against in higher education, joined the throngs attending college to take advantage of the new learning.

With some exceptions to be sure, the opportunity for formal education for women scarcely existed in the late 18th century—usually little more than a genteel furnishing school education remained the normal practice. Serious advanced education eluded most women. The prevailing belief considered women mentally inferior to men and they would be quite unable to meet the standards set for men's higher education. Anyway if women did have the mental ability, there was no use for it and, in any event, women could not stand the physical strain of higher learning. But the fact of women working fourteen hours a day in the textile mills subverted the latter argument and their supposed lack of mental ability was subverted by the common school movement with its increased demand for women teachers. In the end, the work of three women helped overcome prejudice against women's higher education: Emma Willard at Troy (N.Y.) Female Seminary, (1821); Catherine Beecher at Hartford Female Seminary, (1823); and especially, Mary Lyon at Mount Holyoke Female Academy, (1837).

As early as 1819 in her now famous address to the New York State Legislature, Emma Willard had deplored the fact that female education had been left to "chance" and expressed the hope that publicly supported female seminaries "would constitute a grade of education, superior to any yet known in the history of our sex . . ." But disagreement abounded about the type of education most appropriate for the fair sex. Emma Willard emphasized religious, domestic, and "ornamental" education; Catherine Beecher stressed "physical culture". It was Mary Lyon's Mt. Holyoke with its rigorous admission policies, and three-year course in the liberal arts that became the pacesetter, although it did not achieve collegiate status until 1893. (Vassar attained this status in 1865; Wellesley, 1875; Smith, 1875; Radcliffe, 1879; and Bryn Mawr in 1885.) Still the debate, even among women, over what the girls should be taught continued throughout the 19th century—a liberal education, a domestic education, teacher-education, or a bit of all three?

In 1837, Oberlin College became the first collegiate institution to open its doors to all comers, thus inaugurating co-educational higher education. Oberlin was followed by Antioch in 1853, and Iowa University in 1856. But the real breakthrough in co-education came only after the Civil War in the new state universities—Indiana, Michigan, Wisconsin, and Cornell. Nevertheless the argument continued throughout the 19th century over not only what women should be taught but whether women should be taught in separate or co-educational institutions.

IV a. The common school reformers affirmed the belief that democracy could not exist without an educated public, that universal education was the great equalizer of the conditions of men, and they saw further benefits in the school common to all children. Indeed, the ideal of social harmony achieved by mixing children of all backgrounds was an important end in itself. For example, Horace Mann preached that the common school was designed to promote the integration of all children into the national community. And it has been widely accepted that the common school ideal triumphed by the time of the Civil War. But more careful examination of the real availability of common school education is necessary. Many children were educationally disenfranchised because of poverty, others because of race. The South in general, as we have seen, and the Negro, the American Indian, and the Oriental in particular, did not share the benefits of the common school.

By 1830, Negro slavery had been virtually abolished in the North, but not in the South. Powerful social and economic factors, the most obvious being Eli Whitney's cotton gin, made human bondage the cheapest and most productive form of labor in the South. In the ante-bellum South there had been no question of Negro education; the Negro was simply not to be educated. Legal prohibition of Negro education began in South Carolina and Georgia in the 1740's. But the most important prohibitory legislation was enacted between 1830 and 1835. It was only after Nat Turner's 1831 insurrection that most slave states passed laws prohibiting the teaching of slaves to read or write, several states even extended the prohibition to free Negroes. Most of these laws remained in force until the Civil War. Still by dint of perseverance some Negroes like Frederic Douglass secured an education. Slave narratives like those of Douglass served as an inspiration to the abolitionist cause and as impetus to the education of the Negro, though historian C. G. Woodson claims that as late as 1860 only about 10 per cent of the adult Negroes in the country North or South had acquired the rudiments of education.

As Leon F. Litwack explains in *North of Slavery; The Negro In The Free States, 1790–1860*, the Mason-Dixon Line is a convenient, but often a misleading geographical division. It has been used not only to distinguish the Old South from the new and the Confederacy from the Union, but, in an oversimplified way, to dramatize essential differences in attitudes toward the Negro—to contrast southern racism with northern benevolence and liberality. Although slavery eventually confined itself to the region below the Mason-Dixon Line, discrimination against the Negro and a firmly held belief in the superiority of the white race were not restricted to one section, but were shared by an overwhelming majority of white Americans both in the North and the South.

By 1830, whether by legislative, judicial or constitutional action, Negro slavery had been virtually abolished in the North. But freedom did not suddenly confer citizenship on the Negro; emancipation had its limitations. Until the post-Civil War era, in fact, most Northern whites maintained a careful distinction between granting Negroes a theoretical right to life, liberty and property—and real political and social equality. The Negro faced a long period of political disenfranchisement, economic discrimination and social ostracism. The Northeast (and the Northwest) may have been anti-slavery but they were not pro-Negro. De Tocqueville in 1831 wrote: "The prejudice of race appears to be stronger in the states that have abolished slavery than in those where it still exists." According to Litwack: "In virtually every phase of existence Negroes (in the North) found themselves systematically separated from whites." Indeed some historians believe that the post-Reconstruction South simply copied pre-Civil War discriminatory practices of the North.

Education was one of the foremost aspirations of the Northern Negro. "If we ever expect to see the influence of prejudice decrease and ourselves respected," a Negro national convention resolved in 1832, "it must be by the blessings of an enlightened education". This sentiment was repeated throughout the ante-bellum period. However, the Negro's quest for educational opportunities prompted strong and frequently violent protests in the North. The possibility that Negro children would be mixed with white children in the same classroom aroused even greater fears and prejudices than those which ensigned the Negro to an inferior place in the church, the theatre or the railroad car. Although some white public schools admitted Negroes, most Northern states either excluded them altogether or, as in Boston, established separate schools for them.

Before the Civil War, abolitionists had taken the schooling of the free Negro population as one of their responsibilities. But the occasional efforts they made to integrate a few Negro pupils into the public schools encountered heavy resistance. This resistance was codified by the Massachusetts Supreme Court in 1849. In that year, in the famous case of Roberts *vs.* City of Boston, won by the city, the court found no incompatability between a system of separate schools and full civil and social equality for Negroes. Rejecting the argument developed by Charles Sumner, as counsel for plaintiff, that the Massachusetts constitutional provision stating men are "born equal" necessarily means that it is beyond the power of the law to make distinctions among equal men, the court defended the "separate but equal" doctrine and established a precedent in American law. But Sumner's arguments for the losing case heralded a Massachusetts law of 1855 that prohibited school segregation in that state, the only legislative victory that black parents and children could claim before the Civil War in their struggle for equal educational rights. By 1860 most Northern states had provided for separate Negro public schools. As late as 1865, Negro children were excluded from the public schools of Indiana and were legally segregated in the public schools of Ohio, Illinois, Indiana, Michigan, Maryland and California. And if some elementary schools did admit Negro children, very few high schools did. The efforts of Negroes to establish their own college in New Haven failed when the white citizens would not allow it to be built. Within a decade after the Civil War, however, most northern states had legally proscribed separate schools.

b. As mentioned above, before the Civil War, in the South there had been no question of Negro education; the Negro was simply not to be educated. After the war, the question of what educational policy to pursue toward the freedmen became urgent. The Negro was free. What now? Was he capable of learning? If yes, what and how should he be taught? Was the Negro to attend the common schools? Was he to receive the same education as his fellow white citizens or a special education? Many Southerners were alarmed over the prospect of living among a huge mass of free, ignorant Negroes. Perhaps Negroes should therefore be instructed in reading, writing, arithmetic, and Christian religion. Many others were convinced that any intellectual elevation of the Negroes would merely make them difficult to control. Some thought the Negro had no use for education at all; others were influenced by "scientists" who told them Negroes couldn't be educated. In short, in the South, opposition to Negro education was widespread. Add to this the dire poverty and destruction in the former Confederate states, and it is clear why the South was content, by and large, to leave the responsibility of educating the Negro to the Freedmen's Bureau and charitable and religious groups.

The Bureau for Refugees, Freedmen, and Abandoned Lands, commonly known as "the Freedmen's Bureau," established by Congress in 1865, was charged with "the control of all subjects relating to refugees and freedmen". It soon found itself heavily involved in education. Under the vigorous leadership of General Oliver O. Howard, by 1870 it had established in the former Confederacy 4,250 schools, employed 9,000 teachers, and instructed around 247,000 pupils, with expenditures of almost $6,000,000. Many Negro universities and colleges like Howard, Fisk and Atlanta University were founded or substantially aided in their earliest days by the Freedmen's Bureau. General Samual Chapman Armstrong founded Hampton Institute (Virginia) to train teachers for the schools of the Freedmen's Brueau. By 1870, however, the federal government had begun transferring educational responsibilities to the newly reconstructed Southern states: in 1872 the Bureau was discontinued.

The Northern Protestant churches established numerous missionary and aid societies, and sent many teachers to the South for the care and education of freed

Negroes. The famous Port Royal (Virginia) experiment in education was inaugurated by Northern freedmen's aid societies in 1862. Under the auspices of the Protestant churches many elementary schools for Negroes were opened: schools founded under the auspices of the American Missionary Association provided nearly all the college education and most of the high school training for southern Negroes until well into the 20th century. But the African Methodist Episcopal churches also founded some colleges supported and controlled entirely by Negroes. Several philanthropic foundations were established, such as the Slater Fund, and especially the Peabody Education Fund, primarily to give aid to the education of Negroes in the South. The Peabody Fund, set up in 1867, literally breathed life into southern education.

In the early Reconstruction period (1865–67), Southern states either ignored the question of Negro education, or excluded them from public education or established separate schools. Thus in 1866 Georgia enacted laws providing for a "thoroughgoing" system of free public education for free white inhabitants between the ages of six and twenty-one. Arkansas followed suit in 1867. But under Radical Reconstruction at least one Southern state made legal provision for integrated schools. In its Constitution of 1868 Louisiana declared: "There shall be no separate schools or institutions of learning established exclusively for any race in the state . . ." There was actually a short-lived, but extremely suggestive experiment in integrated education in New Orleans in the 1870's.

The Thirteenth Amendment to the Constitution abolished slavery. The Fourteenth Amendment, ratified in 1868, after conferring citizenship on all persons born or naturalized in the United States, prohibited states from abridging the privileges and immunities of citizens or from denying equal protection of the laws: ". . . nor shall any State . . . deny to any person within its jurisdiction the equal protection of the laws," which to some Northerners seemed incompatible with separate schooling. The Civil Rights Bill of 1875, which climaxed a decade of efforts by Radical Republicans, particularly Charles Sumner, to incorporate the Negroes freedom and equal rights into the law of the land, almost contained a provision calling for "public schools open to all without distinction of race or color". But this provision was omitted in the final draft. It is interesting to note that advocates of Jim Crow in education found support in the Freedmen's Bureau, the religious agencies, and the philanthropic foundations. Thus Barnas Sears, director of the Peabody Fund, refused to contribute to the schools of states which permitted integrated education. By the 1870's, the educational provisions for Negroes in the South had become increasingly inequitous and inadequate. During the nadir of Negro rights in the United States, an ex-slave, Booker T. Washington, became chief spokesman of the Negro.

In 1895 Washington, head of Tuskegee Institute in Alabama, was invited to speak before a bi-racial audience gathered for the opening of the Atlanta Cotton States and International Exposition. His speech, later given the soubriquet, "The Atlanta Compromise," was instantly acclaimed North and South, at home and abroad.

Washington called upon the Negro to "cast down your bucket where you are". Washington went on to declare in a famous metaphor: "In all things that are purely social we can be as separate as the fingers, yet one as the hand in all things essential to mutual progress." "The agitation," he continued, "of questions of social equality is the extremest folly, . . . progress that will come to us must be the result of severe and constant struggle rather than of artificial forcing." Thwarted on every hand, his early hopes to rise through education dashed, the Southern Negro learned from

Washington a gospel of self-improvement, industrial and agricultural education, thrift, cleanliness, and acceptance of segregation. From the moment of his address till his death in 1915, Washington remained one of the most powerful men in America. The publication in 1901 of his autobiography *Up From Slavery,* raised him to the pantheon of American heroes.

The development in the post-Reconstruction period of a special "Negro education" is also largely due to the influence of Washington. Tuskegee Institute, organized in 1881 under Washington, epitomizes the education that he thought appropriate for Negroes. At Tuskegee, Washington simply applied the lessons he had learned from General Armstrong at Hampton Institute. Industrial education, as Armstrong conceived it, was as much moral as technical education—a training in industriousness, abstinence, thrift, the dignity of labor, etc., in short, the Protestant ethic. If he assimilated these values, the Negro would, like Washington himself, gradually rise "Up From Slavery". As an accommodationist, or possibilist, Washington gained the good will of some Southerners, as well as Northern philanthropists and thus attracted large-scale donations for Negro schools, raised the morale of rural Negroes, and obtained a new hearing for his race from the highest federal and state officials, while bringing down on his head the wrath of Negroes like William E. B. Du Bois for acquiescing in discrimination and inferior education.

c. C. Vann Woodward has characterized the two decades after 1877 as a time of "forgotten alternatives," a time when some real choices had to be made. One of them was over federal intervention in the field of education. With the termination of hostilities in 1865, the educational problems of the South became a matter of national concern. The needs of the region were vast; the resources to meet them inadequate. As early as 1870, Representative George F. Hoar (Republican, Massachusetts), introduced into the House a radical measure which sought to compel by federal authority the establishment of public school systems in every state. The Hoar Bill never came to a vote. Nevertheless one of the most persistent debates throughout the 1870's and 1880's revolved around the question of whether the federal government should grant public aid to education. From the first introduction of his bill in 1876 until its final defeat in 1890, the leading advocate of federal aid to education was Henry W. Blair, Republican Senator from New Hampshire. Three of Blair's bills which proposed aiding the states in proportion to the illiteracy of the states population, actually passed the Senate; in 1884, 1886 and 1888, only to be kept off the House calendar each time.

Many arguments were used against the Blair bill: that it was unconstitutional; would tend to break down the principle of the separation of church and state; would destroy local interest and initiative; would be cumbersome and unworkable; would inflame racial issues; would be expensive; and that the many federal offices created by the bill would tend to make education a "political football" to be used mainly for purposes of patronage. In general, the Republicans supported the measure while the Democrats opposed it. Gordon Lee's analysis of these extensive congressional debates on the Blair bills in his *The Struggle For Federal Aid: First Phase, 1870–1890* is thorough and exhaustive, and summarizes well the varying arguments for and against federal aid. Sectional overtones were everywhere present during the debates. If Northerners were going to grant such a large subsidy to the South, they wanted some guarantee that Negroes would benefit as much from it as whites. Senator Matthew C. Butler of South Carolina put this dilemma well when he observed that "as the Senator from Ohio (John Sherman) said . . . that he would not trust the South to disburse this money owing to our prejudice against the colored people, . . . in the same spirit . . . I would not trust him to control it." Eventually, Republicans wearied of efforts to support the southern Negro. In 1890 the Blair Bill was defeated in the Senate by a 42-36 vote. In 1884, 89% of the Senate Republicans supported it; in 1890 only 59% could be found in the ranks. But Blair never waivered from his conviction that federal aid to education was the best answer to the plight of the southern Negro and the southern states.

     d. The Declaration of Independence produced no improvement in the relations between Indians and whites. Indians were carefully excluded from the privileges of citizenship. Congress conferred citizenship on The Negro in 1866 but omitted any mention of the Indian. Indeed during the period from 1785-1871 the Indians were not considered to be American citizens and the tribes were dealt with as sovereign nations. Not until 1924 did Congress grant citizenship to all Indians. Education, however, had long been recognized as an essential part of federal policy toward the Indian.

    The earliest education program for Indians was started through the efforts of Catholic and Protestant missionaries. Up to 1817, Indian education was supported exclusively by religious groups; indeed until approximately 1860, the education of Indians was largely in the hands of missionaries. The earliest instance of governmental concern on the national level came in 1817 when the United States made a treaty with the Cherokees and requested the American Board of Commissioners for Foreign Missions to help set up a boarding school at Chickamaugah, Cherokee Nation. The Indians were to be taught religion, the three R's, and farming. In 1819 Congress finally made the federal government's cooperation with religious groups official by creating a "civilization Fund", for "civilizing" the Indians. A fund of $10,000 was to be expended anually for Indian education in the three R's and religion, and the household arts for the girls and agriculture and mechanical arts for the boys.

    The House committee which recommended the original appropriation in 1819 neatly summed up the philosophy underlying the program: "Put into the hands of their children the primer and the primer and the hoe, and they will naturally, in time, take hold of the plough . . . and they will grow up in the habits of morality and industry . . ." In effect, to civilize the Indians, the government subsidized "manual labor schools," which would set the pattern for the education of Indians for the next sixty years. In 1824 the Bureau of Indian Affairs was created within the War Department, apparently to relieve the Secretary of War's burden. The Bureau's head was officially designated in 1832 as the Commissioner of Indian Afairs. In 1849 a Board of Indian Commissioners was established by Congress in response to a general demand for a non-partisan organization to oversee the administration of Indian affairs. Staffed by distinguished reformers who served without compensation, the board had authority, however, only to audit, inspect and recommend.

    Following the War of 1812, the character of Indian-American relations changed. The United States felt less need to conciliate the Indian nations as the threat of British intervention in American affairs faded. The peremptory demands made on the Indians for more and more land reflected both the weakened positions of the tribes and the flood of settlers to the frontier. Arguments were plentiful that the Indian had to give way to progress. When arguments or bribery failed there was the threat of extermination. In 1830 President Andrew Jackson finally signed the Indian

Removal Act. Indians were to be removed from the East to territories in the West and finally to reservations, there to be prepared for eventual assimilation into American life. The Commissioner of Indian Affairs for 1851 summarized federal policy: "Indians were too wild to be of much utility; a proper program through concentration, domestication, and incorporation would ultimately force the Indians into the great body of our citizen population." The question of objective settled, only the means remained. One area of dispute centered on the question of who should be responsible for civilizing the Indian, the federal government or religious groups. Another area of dispute featured the proponents of the day school versus the advocates of the boarding school *i.e.:* on-reservation or off-reservation education. In any event, the task of the school, to civilize savages, was scarcely questioned. Little respect was shown for native Indian culture. Indian children were to discard their past—a feat to be accomplished through exclusive emphasis on the English language, the Bible, and industrial and domestic training.

At first, the government dropped the problem into the hands of the religious groups; they had a long history of seeking contact with Indians and trying to bring Indian youth into schools and converting them to Christianity. And for a long time the propriety of federal support for missionary endeavors among the Indians was not even questioned. Both the government and the missionaries regarded education and Christianization as complementary facets of any successful program for civilizing the aborigines. The initial appropriation of the Civilization Fund was regularly increased by Congress until it reached $100,000 in 1870. By the early 1880's, there were twenty or more different churches involved in the education of the Indian, all drawing sums from the government. But by then the government had decided to begin operating its own schools. Now it had to decide whether they would be on-reservation or off-reservation schools. The most promising alternative seemed to be the boarding school in which children were removed from the influence of parents and tribal ways in the hope they would adopt the outlook of the whites.

Because of mounting policy conflicts with missionary schools, the federal government made its first attempt to open a boarding school in the Yakima Indian Reservation in 1860. It was not until 1870, however, that the government finally committed itself to Indian education—Congress appropriated $200,000, most of it earmarked for government boarding schools. In 1879 the Carlisle Indian School in Pennsylvania, an extraordinary experiment and the best known of the boarding schools, opened under the direction of Army Captain Richard H. Pratt. Convinced that education would be the Indian's salvation, Pratt, influenced by Armstrong's work at Hampton Institute, secured an abandoned military reservation at Carlisle and obtained the assignment as superintendent.

Pratt believed that Indians might best be assimilated into the American community by a thorough "Americanizing" education far removed from the reservations. Carlisle, like Hampton Institute and Tuskegee, offered industrial, farm and domestic training as well as instruction in religion and the three R's. Pratt also introduced the "outing" system. Coming at the end of the Indian youth's stay at the school, this involved placing the student for a period of as much as three years with one of the rural families near Carlisle. Indian children were expected to work their way through school by taking odd jobs with white families and boarding summers with them. By 1900, 1200 students from some 79 tribes attended Carlisle.

By 1879 the government had established 147 schools; sixty-three boarding, seventy-seven day and seven industrial schools. But continuing friction among the Protestant denominations, and between Protestants and Catholics, and between the churches and the government pointed up the need for change. Soon after 1880, the Commissioner of Indian Affairs proposed a plan for Indian education to be operated exclusively by the federal government thus terminating the two systems of Indian education—one operated by the churches, the other by the federal government, both supported by federal funds. Not until 1891, however, did the government finally bring Indian education completely under federal control by eliminating funds for church schools. By this time the annual appropriation for Indian schools run by various religions approached $500,000, with the Catholic Church receiving about three-fourths of this sum. By 1899 over $2,500,000 was being expended annually on 148 boarding schools and 225 day schools with almost 20,000 Indian children in attendance.

The off-reservation boarding school was most popular in the last quarter of the 19th century. by 1900, though, the trend towards reservation day schools accelerated. Uniform textbooks and methods of instruction, together with a teacher merit system improved overall Indian education, and the strictly tribal boarding and day schools were brought into a unified federal system. While many applauded the government's decision to cease subsidizing church schools, others were pleased by the former's plans to place Indian children into the public schools as soon as possible. None of these changes, however, as William T. Hagan explains, could convert the apathy of the Indians into a thirst for the white man's knowledge

e. Separate schools were also the rule for minority children on the West coast during the 19th century. Indeed, California represents in microcosm national racial attitudes concerning minority children and the common schools. Racial prejudice was a fact of life in California since the earliest days of statehood. Peter Burnett, the first governor, urged that Negroes be excluded from California and John Bigler, the state's third chief executive, looked forward to an inevitable "war of extermination" between the Indian and white races, and urged that Chinese immigrants be excluded by Legislative act. Burnett's suggestion was, of course, not acted upon but California's few early Negroes were quickly assigned to subservient status. Bigler's predicted extermination of the Indians almost came true and prohibition of Chinese immigration finally became federal law, though not until 1882.

There is little evidence that prejudice of any significant kind affected the educational efforts of the Spaniards or Mexicans in California before 1849. On the contrary, had the Spanish and Mexican governors and Roman Catholic padres had their way, every child—whether of Indian or Spanish descent—probably would have received some education, at least a religious education in Spanish-language Roman Catholic mission or church schools. Because of a lack of competent teachers, however, and a lack of financial support, a tradition of indifference developed among the settler families. But despite this apathy, some educational gains were achieved prior to the Mexican-American War—and they benefited both white and Indian children. In fact the "American" schools that came into existence before statehood issued no prohibitions against Negro or Chinese or Indian students, although it is likely the question simply never arose. On the eve of the creation of the first public school system in California, there were a few hints of the bitter racial disputes that would later plague education in the state.

The California public school system was officially sanctioned by the framers of the State Constitution in 1849. The first state superintendent of public instruction, John Gage Marvin, favored tax money to support the predominantly Spanish-language mission schools, a position which probably cut short his career. But it was neither the Indian, nor the Spanish-speaking white—the Californio—which concerned the California politicians and schoolmen in the latter part of the 19th century, it was the Negro and the Chinese.

The first patently discriminatory school law was enacted in California in 1855 as an amendment to the educational provisions of the state constitution. The amendment provided for the collection and distribution of school funds but specified that the amounts to be apportioned would be based on a census of children in each county, but only white children would be counted. This was subsequently interpreted to mean that non-white children did not have the right to attend public schools. The California legislature in 1860 finalized this interpretation by requiring that Negroes, "Mongolians" (Chinese) and Indians be excluded from the public schools. The Superintendent of Public Instruction was authorized to withold state funds from any school which admitted these groups. Officials were permitted, however, to establish separate schools for these minority children at public expense. The California School Law of 1866 amended this permissive article to read that "the education of children of African descent, and Indian children, shall be provided for in separate schools". No mention was made of Chinese children.

Most Negro education in California began in separate schools, opened, supported, and staffed by Negroes. Such was the case in Sacramento and in San Francisco, two early centers of Negro population. None of these first Negro schools were intended to remain private or separate from local public school districts. Local committees of Negro citizens typically appealed to school officials to assume full educational responsibility, which San Francisco did in 1854, followed by Scramento two years later. Some school districts even admitted small numbers of Negro children to their "white" schools, giving rise in the 1860 law. The law of 1866 finally provided for the establishment of separate public schools for Negroes. In 1870 and again in 1874 the legislature enacted an amendment to the school law which declared: "The education of children of African descent and Indian children must be provided for in separate schools . . . If the directors or trustees fail to provide such separate schools, then such children must be admitted into the schools for white children". Until 1874 school districts with large Negro populations generally provided separate public schools, which Negroes usually felt were insufficient to their needs and inferior to white schools.

California Negroes fought for equal education opportunities for their children aided by a few whites like John Swett and Governor Newton Booth. The most important educational goal of Negroes was to assure each Negro child in the state of good public school education. This was accomplished in 1874 as a result of a Negro-initiated test of the discriminatory school law in the courts. In Ward vs. Flood (1874) the California Supreme Court forced local districts to either integrate their schools or to provide "equal" schools; most districts found it far more economical to integrate. Finally in Wysinger vs. Crookshank (1890) the California Supreme Court prohibited segregated schooling for Negro children. (But the discriminatory provision of the state school law concerning Indian children remained on the statute books long after the Indian had ceased to constitute a significant statistic in the California population. Not until 1921 did the state legislature remove the prohibition against Indians attending mixed public schools.)

By 1890 then, virtually all discriminatory school laws affecting Negroes had been abolished in California. For the Chinese, however, who soon would be barred completely from entering the United States, public education remained a problem. Not until 1885, in fact, would Chinese residents of California be guaranteed some access to the state's public schools. Indeed their plight was far more serious than that of the Negro, who was present only in comparatively small number (1,000 according to the 1850 census). The worst race violence in late 19th century California, for example, was directed at Chinese; at least twenty-two lynchings took place in Los Angeles in 1871. A special dislike seems to have been reserved for the Chinese because they were numerous, frugal, industrious, and willing to work for meager wages; the advance guard of numberless legions, a "yellow peril", that if unchecked would one day overthrow the Republic.

San Francisco excluded Chinese children from white public schools for nearly a decade after Negroes were granted admission. The state school laws of 1860 and 1866 blatantly prohibited Chinese children from attending public schools. In 1870 when the legislature repealed the discriminatory provisions of the 1866 school law, it specifically omitted any reference to "Mongolian" children, even in its provision calling for separate schools for Negro and Indian children. The School Act of 1874 likewise omitted "Mongolian" children from provisions that allowed Negro and Indian children to attend white schools if separate schools were not available. As late as 1884, the State School Superintendent refused to admit Chinese children to the public schools, basing his decision on the state constitution, which stated that public education was intended only for those who could or were to become citizens.

The Chinese, whose only educational opportunities since the 1850's had resulted from the very limited volunteer work of a handful of charitable Americans, finally obtained a surprising redress from the California courts. In 1885, in Tape *vs.* Hurley, the state appellate court ruled that a school district could not exclude Chinese from the San Francisco public schools solely on race except if they were "filthy, vicious, or diseased". Whereupon the legislature amended the School Law authorizing school districts to establish separate public schools for Chinese children. In 1887 the San Francisco Board of Education finally established a free school for Chinese children. By the turn of the century the prejudice of Californians was diverted to the Japanese, while nationally the drive for the exclusion of Orientals was being submerged in the larger movement for the restriction of all immigration.

V a. Horace Mann, Henry Barnard and the common school founders aspired to create system where they saw chaos; to have uniform textbooks and curriculum; graded classes; professional teachers; and improved school regulations and supervision. To a large degree the schoolmen succeeded in standardizing public education during the latter half of the 19th century, at least in the larger towns and cities of the Northeast and the West.

In 1874, the American educational "establishment," primarily the city and state school superintendents and college presidents, issued A *Statement of the Theory of Education In The United States*, written to explain American educational practices to Europeans, in which they incidently justified the standardization of the schools. "The commercial tone prevalent in the city," said the report, "tends to develop, in its schools, quick, alert habits and readiness to combine with others in their tasks. Military precision is required in the maneuvering of classes. Great stress is laid upon 1) punctuality, 2) regularity, 3) attention, and 4) silence, as habits necessary through life for successful combination with one's fellow man in an industrial and commercial civilization." So clear were the outlines of this new institution—the common school—that as early as 1875 the Englishman, Francis Adams, confidently described "the free school system of the United States" in his book of that name.

But success bred its own problems, often the fate of reforms when they become institutionalized. In school organization, educators endorsed simple military or industrial models. Uniformity of output and regularity of operation took precedence over functional differentiation. Thus, in practice, the schoolmen created a curriculum which was more or less identical for all children and they preferred teaching methods which promised standard results.

It took about a generation then for the purposes and practices of the common-school reform movement to settle into well-meaning orthodoxy against which a new generation of reformers and critics would fight in their turn. Throughout the latter part of the 19th century some American schoolmen utilized a series of European innovations in an attempt to loosen up the increasingly unwieldy system. For example, in the late 1850's Edward A. Sheldon brought some Pestalozzian trained teachers to the Oswego (N.Y.) public schools, of which he was superintendent, and to Oswego State Normal School, of which he was president. Sheldon subsequently adopted a form of Pestallozian object lessons in which the curriculum was minutely divided into lessons involving numbers, magnitude, form, color, weight, sounds, places, animals, plants, minerals and liquids, that attracted much enthusiasm. Teachers needed to expand their repetoire; Pestallozianism served to enrich teaching.

From about 1860 to the mid-1870's when Francis W. Parker appeared on the educational scene, Oswego methods dominated American education. Yet as more and more teachers were trained in object teaching, it rapidly took on a formalism and rigidity of its own. From the traditional notion that everything could be learned by reading a textbook, many teachers now moved to the extreme that everything could be taught by object method; the principles of Pestalozzi were obscured by a strict adherence to formula, to a crude and mechanical sequence of steps.

The criticism of mechanical education was answered in 1875 in the public schools of Quincy, Massachusetts, under newly-appointed school superintendent, Francis W. Parker, a teacher just returned from studying Rousseau, Pestalozzi, Froebel, and Herbart in Germany. Parker re-oriented the Quincy system to an activity-oriented curriculum based on the needs and interests of children. As Parker put it: "the essence . . . is the teaching of things, and not words alone." Parker introduced nature study, art, music and physical education into the Quincy curriculum. Textbooks were de-emphasized; objects were brought into the classroom, children took trips outside the classroom. Subjects were correlated around centers of interest; teachers freed to experiment with methods. In Parker's words: "The set program was first dropped, then the speller, the reader, the grammar, and the copybook. The alphabet, too, was treated with slight deference; it was not introduced to the children by name, but they were set at once to work making words and sentences. The teachers woke up, and had to depend upon lively wits for success. No longer could they comfortably hear recitations from convenient textbooks. Other books there were in plenty, and magazines and newspapers. Teachers and pupils had to learn first of all to think and observe. Then bye and bye they put these powers to work on the required subjects." From Charles Francis Adams' enthusiastic essay, *The New Departure In The Common Schools of Quincy,* came impressive testimony that Parker had succeeded and that at Quincy, teachers and pupils worked together joyously and harmoniously.

When Parker left Quincy in 1883, its public schools had become world renowned. In 1883 Parker moved on to become principal of Cook County Normal School at Chicago where he reproduced 'the humane, child-loving atmosphere" of the Quincy schools, as well as many of the essentials of object teaching. Parker's words instilled a messianic ardor among all teachers who heard them. He influenced a generation of teachers in the new view of education and of the child.

Parker's teachings are suffused with an intense religiosity; a final appeal not to Froebel or Pestalozzi or even to Rousseau, but to Christ. For example, Parker's *Talks to Teachers on Pedagogy* is permeated with religious idealism. The book constantly refers to Jesus as the source of faith and love which makes the child pre-eminent. "The child," Parker preached, "is the climax and culmination of all God's creations." And, "the spontaneous tendencies of the child are the records of inborn divinity . . . We are here my fellow teachers, for one purpose, and that purpose is to understand these tendencies and continue them in all these directions." If the child was the hearer of divinity, it was natural enough for Parker to conclude that "the centre of all movement in education is the child." It remained for G. Stanley Hall and the "child study" movement to cover child-centered education with the mantle of "science."

Child-study, like the kindergarten, discussed below, began in Europe and in part was stimulated by the kindergarten movement. Thus Froebel collected "mother plays and nursery songs." But the idea is even older than Froebel. Comenius' book on infancy revealed his interest in child traits and activities. Rousseau also urged teachers to study their pupils. Pestalozzi for a short time kept a diary of his son's development. This biographical method was followed with even greater success by the German psychologist Wilhelm Preyer.

The child-study movement attempted to replace the subjective or introspective study of adult minds to get at an understanding of child life, with a "scientific," empirical study of child life itself. G. Stanley Hall's *The Contents of Children's Minds Upon Entering School*, published in 1883, marked the beginning of the movement in the United States. Hall set out to study Boston public school children through the questionnaire method, "in order that teachers may know just what knowledge and ignorance can be assumed as a basis of teaching." The findings—almost nothing. Children were ignorant of birds, squirrels, trees, the origin of butter or milk or vegetables, at a time when the subject matter of school primers still largely consisted of country life. Hall demonstrated that there was little of which it was safe to assume of children at the outset of school life. Teachers (and parents) would have to become scientific explorers of the child's mind. *The Contents of Children's Minds* attracted enormous attention; it set off a new wave of educational enthusiasm in this country.

Hall provided encouragement and support to two rather distinct types of child study. At Clark University he established a psychological laboratory in which students were trained in expermental techniques and applies these to study of children. For Hall and many of his followers, however, the laboratory method of investigation seemed too slow or inappropriate and they turned to the questionnaire method to collect the data they wanted. With tremendous zeal, Hall enlisted the support of parents, normal school-teachers, and students by assuring them that in filling out questions they contributed valuable information to the science of childhood and to education. Popular interest was intense. In 1894, child-study was orgainzed as a department of the National Education Association. By 1895 twenty-two states had active child-study groups.

Not only did Hall believe that child-study would improve child life but it would give education what it had long lacked; a truly scientific basis, and thus help to give teachers a really professional status. For the child-study movement appeared to remove at least one obstacle to the development of a science of education—the lack of "facts"; as enormous quantities of data on every conceivable aspect of child life were collected; facts on children's vocabulary, height, weight, feelings, games, toys, hobbies, facts on creeping, walking, running, teething. Hall finally concluded that traditional methods of education ran counter to the needs and nature of the child. The school would have to adopt itself to the various stages in a child's natural development as determined by child study. In fact this should have everything to do with the way educators establish the curriculum. Educators would have to study the child and build a program around him. The school would have to be child-centered; in Hall's word, *paidocentric*. That is, underlying Hall's work was a notion more radical than the argument that subject matter might be taught more effectively if the results of child-study were used. For Hall was really saying that the content of the curriculum itself could be determined from the data of child-study. That is, the school should base its studies, its policy, not on the demands of society nor on some conception of what an educated person should be, but on the developing needs and interests of the child as revealed by child-study.

The child-study movement raised the child to a new dignity and importance. He had become a live specimen for scientific study. As such, he was accorded more freedom, and paid greater attention than ever before. No wonder a bewildered European visitor to the United States could write in 1901: "The whole of the American system (of education) centers increasingly on the child." Nevertheless, some doubters remained. William James cautioned that teachers would be making a great mistake if they believed that school programs and methods of instruction could be deduced directly from psychology. "We have of late been hearing much of the philosophy of tenderness in education," James complained in 1899. "Interest must be assiduously awakened in everything, difficulties must be smoothed away. Soft pedagogics have taken the place of the old steep and rocky path to learning." James warned student teachers that their attitude toward children, being "concrete and ethical," was necessarily opposed to the abstract and analytical approach of the psychologist. "Psychology is a science, and teaching is an art," James said; "sciences never generate arts directly out of themselves."

In the end, kindergarten doctrines were perhaps ultimately more influential than Sheldon, or Parker or Hall and the child-study movement in reforming the early grades of the elementary school. The kindergarten, the child-centered school *par excellence*, was devised by the German, Freidrich Froebel in 1837 as a special school for children of four or five. Froebel conceived the new school as a garden where children grow, an institution which would combine moral and religious instruction with directive play and group activities; a school for "the education of man." Froebel developed plays, games, and songs for children, soft cloth balls, blocks, cubes, triangles, spheres, cylinders; his "mother's songs," introduced the child to basic geometrical forms, elementary numeracy, and were intended to suggest the harmony and symmetry of life.

In spite of the efforts of Froebel and his ardent followers, the kindergarten did not make notable progress on the Continent. In the mid-1850's the kindergarten began in the United States, where it would win its greatest acceptance. It was logical that the kindergarten would be introduced to the New World by the Germans themselves. German liberals who fled the suppression of the Revolution of 1848 brought their educational ideals to America. The first kindergarten in America was founded in 1855 in Watertown, by Mrs. Carl Schurz, a former pupil of Froebel. Somewhat later Mrs. M. Kraus-Boelte introduced the kindergarten to New York City. In 1856 Henry Barnard introduced a wider audience to the kindergarten in the pages of his *American Journal of Education*. Among his readers were Elizabeth Peabody, who established the first English-speaking kindergarten in Boston in 1860, and Kate Wiggins and Emma Marwedel who brought the kingergarten to San

Francisco a few years later. In 1868, a kindergarten training school was opened in Boston by Elizabeth Peabody. One of the first graduates of this pioneer kindergarten training school was Susan Blow, who together with William Torrey Harris, the Superintendent of Schools in St. Louis, established in 1868 in that city the first public kindergarten in the United States.

While the ideal of the early kindergarten movement stressed its universality, its applicability to all children, the first kindergartens, catered to the affluent. Gradually though, the kindergarten with its emphasis on neatness and cleanliness and good manners, would receive its most important impetus as an antidote to the urban slum. Thus at the Silver Street Kindergarten in San Francisco, the first charity kindergarten on the West Coast, "street Arabs of the wildest type" were apparently transformed into exemplary children. By the turn of the century, the charitable kindergartens gave way to publicly sponsored kindergartens. By 1880, there were some 300–400 public kindergartens in the country with ten training schools for kindergarten teachers. By 1885 thousands of benevolent American teachers and parents were seriously engaged in the study of Froebel's *The Education of Man,* and *Mother and Play Songs.* They scrutinized the stages of children's growth, discussed the spiritual role of mother-child play and sought ways to cultivate the child's character through group activity. By 1915, three national organizations concerned with educating pre-schoolers had come into existence—the International Kindergarten Union, the National Kindergarten Association and the National Congress of Mothers.

   b. With the growing popularity of the kindergarten and Quincy methods, it was almost inevitable that there would be a growing concern with handwork or manual education also. The 1880's witnessed rising interest in manual training among American educators, first as technical training then as a general aspect of education. The movement was given great stimulus by the Russian Exhibit organized by Victor Della Vos, Director of the Imperial Technical School of Moscow at the Philadelphia Exposition in 1876, and provided with leadership by John C. Runkle, President of Massachusetts Institute of Technology and Calvin W. Woodward, Dean of the O'Fallon Polytechnical Institute at Washington University (St. Louis) and head of its Manual Training School.

The Russians had devised a system of carefully graded projects for the development of skills in the use of tools and materials. Basic mechanical skills and principles were taught in careful separation from the making of actual products. Runkle soon elaborated a more general theory of education based on the manual training idea. To Runkle, manual training represented the key to a new, balanced schooling that would marry the mental and the manual, and thereby prepare children more realistically for life in an industrial society. But it was Woodward, also influenced by the Russians, who effected this theory into practice at his Manual Training School, established in 1877 as the first school of its kind in the United States. The object of the Manual Training School was to provide a three-year high school program divided equally between manual and mental training. With the launching of the school, Woodward was quickly projected before the public as the protagonist of a new movement.

Like Runkle, Woodward was convinced that the manual training rationale had important implication for the reform of general education. In several decades of campaigning. Woodward insisted that the salutory effects of manual training upon the mind, hand, and character—one of his most famous slogans was the statement "Put the whole boy in school"—could be helpful to almost everyone at all levels of education; could increase technical skill, enhance the dignity of labor, and, of course, improve the mind.

The manual training movement really caught on in the eighties. Some of the movement's most avid supporters were leaders of business and industry as well as of education. One such enthusiast was Charles T. Ham of Chicago, who became a convert after visting Woodward's Manual Training School: "I made an exhaustive study of the methods of the St. Louis school, and reached the conclusion that the Philosopher's Stone in education had been discovered." Woodward's contentions did not go unchallenged, however, and during the late seventies and eighties and into the 1890's the National Education Association was an arena in which the manual training issue was hotly debated. By 1890, Woodward seemed to have the last word. Public as well as private manual training schools opened throughout the Midwest and the East; many city school systems added courses in manual training at the high school level. An 1890 survey of the United States Bureau of Education found thousands of boys and girls studying carpentry, metal and machine work, sewing, cooking and drawing in thirty-six cities representing fifteen states and the District of Columbia. And largely influenced by Swedish methods of *sloyd* (handwork, usually in wood), manual training had moved downward into the grades where it appeared as a variety of arts and crafts in the elementary school. By 1890, some educators like Felix Adler of the New York Ethical Culture Society, were contending that if the activities of the kindergarten could be joined to *sloyd* at the elementary level and manual training or homemaking in the high school, the result would be an orderly progression of manual work to parallel intellectual activities throughout the whole period of general education.

c. While many educators felt that child-centered education could contribute much to an understanding of the educational process, they were loath to give up the subjects which had traditionally comprised the school program. As William Torrey Harris, speaking for an older generation of educators, put it: "We do not begin with child-study. We begin with the great branches of human learning. Then we study the child in order to bring him from his possibility to his reality." In the circumstances, some schoolmen, sympathetic to Harris' position, but opposed to the traditional mental discipline or memoriter approach, began to look for a new approach to subject-centered education and found inspiriation once again in Germany, this time in the writings of Friedrich Herbart.

American Herbartianism was to an extraordinary degree the creation of three men, all of whom had studied the work of Herbart in Germany, at the University of Jena; and all of whom were connected with Illinois State Normal University—the McMurry brothers, Frank M. and Charles A., and Charles De Garmo. In 1893, they banded together to form the National Herbart Society for the Scientific Study of Education, later to become the National Society for the Study of Education. They brought into the rhetoric of late 19th century American education such concepts as "the doctrine of interest"; "the apperceptive mass"; "correlation and concentration" of studies; "the theory of the culture-epochs" or "the doctrine of recapitulation"; and "the five formal steps of instruction".

Herbartians emphasized the social and moral aims of education, that is, priority went to the development of character, but they believed this could be best achieved by a highly intellectualized approach to the curriculum and the learning process. Herbartians rejected the traditional organization of *separate* subjects, and called for "correlation" or "concentration"; the unification of subject matter around a central core curriculum, especially around history and geography and literature. Furthermore, to Herbartians, the mind was made up of clusters of ideas; the "apperceptive mass." Thus learning must proceed from the known to the unknown; new knowledge is always assimilated in terms of what the learner already knows, *i.e.*, the appreceptive mass. Herbartians also called on teachers to base their work on the facts of child development. Here the "culture-epochs theory" becomes significant. This is the notion that ". . . the stages of development in race and individual are essentially analogous". Thus it was important for educators, at each stage of the child's development, to choose the appropriate materials from the history of civilization which corresponded to the parallel stage in the development of the individual. Now teachers were provided with a criterion for the sequencing and selection of subject matter. The doctrine of interest was to become one of the most controversial of Herbartian doctrines. Interest had to be awakened before the students could be properly instructed: "As a pedagogical doctrine" writes one Herbartian, "interest is the immediate prerequisite of instruction. Without the live interest there can be no instruction of permanent value. It becomes, therefore, the *immediate* end of instruction." It was the teacher's responsibility to awaken and develop this interest so that new subject matter became vitally associated with the apperceptive mass.

Herbart's American followers translated his insistence upon the "association of ideas" and "interest" and the rest into a formal sequence of learning that came to be known as the "five formal steps." These comprised: 1) *preparation* — in which old ideas useful in learning the new material are called to the pupil's mind; 2) *presentation* — the actual presentation of the new material; 3) *association* — in which the new material is related to, compared with, and otherwise connected with the old; 4) *generalization* — in which rules, definitions, or general principles are drawn from the specific material studies; and 5) *application* — in which general principles are given meaning by reference to specific examples or practical situations. At a time when drill, memory-work, the recitation and highly formalized object-lessons were the principal methods of teaching, these ideas found extremely fertile soil here.

Herbartianism came on the scene when American educators, particularly in the new teachers colleges and schools of education were looking for something to teach, and when teachers were looking for a method to cope with the influx of children into the city schools. It is not surprising that in the last decades of the 19th century, Herbartian ideas came into their own, particularly among college and university professors seeking to develop a scientific approach to pedagogy. Toward the end of the century, object-teaching increasingly began to give way before Herbartian principles. More and more, teachers began to organize lessons along the five formal steps. Herbartianism provided teachers with an easily comprehended methodology of teaching, a sequence of steps that promised tangible outcomes for the teacher. Herbartians were concerned by the tendency to glorify the child as represented by the rise of the kindergarten, Qunicy methods, and the child-study movement. Herbartianism may be seen as an effort to reconcile the claims of children and the requirements of society as represented by the curriculum. Still, with their effort to psychologize the presentation of subject matter, and with their injunction to teachers to see to it that new subject matter must be presented in an interesting way, Herbartians were also contributing to the shift in emphasis from subject matter to the child.

VI a. By the end of the century, especially in cities like Boston, New York, and Chicago, centralized, rationalized school systems were in existence complete with compulsory education laws, prescribed curricula, graded classrooms, licensed teachers, a hierarchical administration, all governed by an educational bureaucracy which was winning for itself the right to establish educational norms and determine classroom content. The large city schools were becoming increasingly mechanized and structured like the large bureaucracies of industry, commerce, and the military that were arising in the latter part of the 19th century.

What this often meant in practice, Dr. Joseph Mayer Rice, a pediatrician interested in education, who had studied the new education in Germany, discovered when he visited classrooms in 36 cities during a five-month trip in 1892. In New York City, the maxim was "save the minutes." One way in which time was saved was to compel the children to stare fixedly at the blackboard or the teacher. When Rice asked the principal of one grade school whether the children were allowed to move their heads, she answered, "Why should they look behind when the teacher is in front of them?" In St. Louis, he observed recitations during which children stood on a line, perfectly motionless, their bodies erect; their knees and feet together, the tips of their shoes touching the edge of a board on the floor. Rice heard one Gradgrind ask a child, "How can you learn anything with your knees and toes out of order?" The same conditions prevailed in Chicago, Boston, Philadelphia and Cincinnati; children silent and passive, or reciting set answers in a ready-made vocabulary supplied by the textbook or untrained teacher; the works of the "great educators," Pestalozzi, Froebel, and Herbart unutilized. What Rice found to praise were the kindgergartens, nature study, art, manual-training classes, and the child-centered spirit they had fostered in the schools of Minneapolis and St. Paul, Minnesota, of Indianapolis and La Porte, Indiana, and of Parker's world-famous Cook County Normal School which had helped to set their course.

The publication of Rice's investigations, first in an influential series of articles in *The Forum*, and then as *The Public School System In The United States* (1893) created a furor. Rice, however, was more than a journalist or muckraker, he was a reformer who aimed at re-structuring and redefining American education, much as Parker and Hall and the kindergartners. In his study, Rice assumed the responsibility of pleading "justice for the child". To Rice, "the school exists for the benefit of the child and not for the benefit of boards of education, superintendents or teachers". The school had to be re-organized on new or "scientific" principles rather than old or "mechanical" principles. In the "mechanical" school poorly trained teachers stuff facts into the minds of uncomprehending children. On the other hand, the aim of the "scientific" school is to "lead the child to observe, to reason, and to acquire manual dexterity as well as to memorize facts—in a word, to develop the child naturally in all of his faculties, intellectual, moral, and physical". In these new schools the teacher will be guided in her work by "the nature of the child's mind," and by "the laws of mental development" as revealed by psychology.

b. By the spring of 1892, Rice's name had become a byword to schoolmen across the nation and the "New Education" was becoming a highly public issue. Under the circumstances, some response from the educational establishment seemed called for. The response came in two vitally important National Education Association reports—the Report of the Committee of Ten on Secondary School Studies, and the Report of the Committee of Fifteen on Elementary Education.

In the late 19th century, high schools proliferated; approximately 800 in 1870; 1200 in 1880; 2400 in 1890. The number of students rose from about 60–70,000 in

1870, to about 408,000 in 1890–94, to about 700,000 in 1900. With expansion, the hegemony of the classics came under fire from the "moderns"; English, history, modern foreign languages and the natural and social sciences, as well as from the vocational and commercial subjects. The question arose—what was to be the task of the high school? What was to be its curriculum? Who was to decide? The high schools are indigenous, local institutions, their courses determined largely by local school boards. The problem of promoting standards of secondary education that would receive nation-wide recognition was undertaken by the recognized leaders in education through the only educational organization national in scope—the National Education Association. As mentioned earlier, the NEA was organized in 1870. By 1890 it had become a prestigious organization of scholars, college presidents and college professors, headmasters of distinguished private schools and a sprinkling of public school personnel.

In 1892, to bring order out of the chaos into which the high schools seemed to be plunging, the NEA appointed an extremely prestigious Committee of Ten. The Committee was headed by Charles W. Eliot, then in his twenty-third year as president of Harvard, and the acknowledged leader of college and university reform in America. The Committee included four other college presidents, a college professor soon to be a college president, the United States Commissioner of Education, William Torrey Harris, the headmaster of a famous private secondary school, and two public high school principals. And behind the scenes, Nicholas Murray Butler, Professor of Philosophy at Columbia University (and soon to become the latter's president), and editor of the influential *Educational Review*. Wielding authority in both university and high school circles, the Committee hoped that its report would influence the high schools to standardize their programs (and influence the colleges to modify their admission requirements).

The Committee of Ten's report, largely written by Eliot, came out in 1893. It proposed the following: that high schools set up four alternative courses—classical, Latin-scientific, modern language, and English. The courses were to be differentiated in accordance with the relative emphasis on the classics—Latin, Greek, and mathematics, and the modern subjects—English, the social sciences, the natural sciences, and the modern foreign languages; German and French. But all four tracks would demand as a minimum, four years of English, four years of a foreign language, three years of history, three years of mathematics, and three years of science. The Committee of Ten made some concessions to the new subjects then, and to flexibility, but it is clear that the Committee of Ten thought of the high school as an agency for academic training. But whether it thought of the high school simply as a college-preparatory institution is not so clear. The argument is intriguing. The secondary schools of the United States, taken as a whole, the Report admits, did not exist for the purpose of preparing for college. Only an insignificant number of their graduates go to college. The high school's main function remained to prepare boys and girls "for the duties of life". How? By improving the intellectual abilities of its students through the mastery of academic subject matter.

The Report reaffirmed in classic language that the principle end of all education is the development of the mind. "The mind is chiefly developed in three ways: by cultivating the powers of discriminative observation, by strengthening the logical faculty of following an argument from point to point, and by ripening the process of comparison, that is, judgment. As studies in languages in the natural sciences are best adapted to cultivate the habits of observation; as mathematics are the traditional training of the reasoning faculties; so history and its allied branches are better adapted than any other studies to promote the invaluable mental power which we call judgment." The Committee concluded that Latin, Greek, English, modern langaguages, mathematics, science and history are best fitted "to train the pupils' powers of observation, memory expression, and reasoning". Furthermore, the program was to be the same for all, in that every subject which is taught should be taught "in the same way and to the same extent" to every pupil whether or not he is college-bound and regardless of his vocational inclinations; every child needed training in the powers of observation, memory, expression, and reasoning. It would make no difference which subjects he had chosen for his program or how long he stayed in school, the pupil would have had one, two, three or four years "of strong and effective mental training".

The influence of the Committee of Ten Report was enormous. This is not to say that no controversy developed. For example, the Report was bitterly criticized by G. Stanley Hall for not differentiating between terminal and college-bound students, and for disregarding the needs of the "incapables". Eliot responded for the Committee of Ten. Eliot rejected the distinction between fitting for life and fitting for college, claiming that all subjects fit for life. The question was how well. The Committee of Ten believed a broad liberal education fitted best. Eliot defended teaching the same subjects the same way to all pupils regardless of their destination, contending that the early classification of children into future peasants, professionals, trades-people, merchants, mechanics, though common in Europe was unacceptable in a democratic society like the United States. Finally, Eliot argued that the "incapables" formed only an insignificant proportion of the children in school. It is a curious fact, said Eliot, that we Americans habitually underestimate the capacity of our pupils at almost every stage of education. In the end, the Committee of Ten was victorious, at least temporarily. The United States Office of Education distributed 30,000 free copies. The report became the educational gospel for policy makers in the burgeoning high schools for a generation. And today it is a rallying point for those who feel our secondary schools have forgotten their central role in the training of the intellect.

c. By the turn of the century, it had been established then, that the goal of secondary education was to develop the minds of the students through the study of academic subject matter. The high schools in turn helped standardize the elementary school, as the Report of NEA's Committee of Fifteen on Elementary Education makes clear. The Report shows the fine hand of William Torrey Harris throughout. Though discipline and character development were certainly not neglected—the child was to be trained to be regular and punctual, and to restrain his desire to talk and whisper, "in these things gaining self-control day by day"; the emphasis was on linguistic training. The Committee of Fifteen asserted: "Learning to read and write should be the leading study of the pupil in his first four years of school." In fact, "inasmuch as reading is the first of the scholastic arts, the whole elementary course may be described as an extension of the process of learning the art of reading." Here, the recitation was vitally important. To paraphrase the report the pupil is assigned daily tasks. The recitation is taken up with examining and criticizing the pupil's oral statements of what he has learned. "The misunderstandings are corrected and the pupil set on the way to use more critical alertness in the preparation of his succeeding lessons . . ."

But in the end, the chief aim of the elementary school was to instill "wisdom" and character. Finally the Committee of Fifteen viewed the elementary curriculum entirely in terms of content areas. To paraphrase the Committee, the child had to be provided with the "tools of learning," language, literature, mathematics, geography, and history, with which he could appropriate the "experience of the race". The essential means for the school's work are in the shape of textbooks in which the experience of the race is stated in a clear and summary manner, so that a child may understand it. He has a teacher to direct his studies and instruct him in the proper methods of getting cut of the books the wisdom recorded therin . . . But the school also inculcates discipline, thus the elementary school creates a cultured and disciplined person—the free individual, self-controlled, self-propelled, able to use independently the tools of thought. Here was the answer to Parker and Hall and the Kindergartners and the Herbartians and the rest. The elementary school curriculum was now effectively protected against change, at least for the next decade or so.

The Committee of Ten, the Committee of Fifteen, Eliot, Harris, Butler and the rest, thought they were ushering in a new age. In retrospect they were ushering out the old. By 1910, certainly by 1915, the reports of the Committee of Ten and the Committee of Fifteen, had taken on the charm of period pieces: as a sympathetic biographer remarked of Harris'*The Psychologic Foundations of Education* (1895), "The book sealed his fate as an educational thinker". They had failed to reckon with the social forces working for change in American society in the closing decades of the 19th century. A new generation of educators and school reformers would rectify their omissions.

VII The popularization of education in the 19th century was a general, Western, and not a uniquely American phenomenon; the principal figures of the movement on both sides of the Atlantic were in constant communication. For example, George Combe, Joseph Lancaster, Herbert Spencer and Robert Owen deeply influenced American education. While the American educational experiment was itself very well known and variously interpreted by Englishmen, Frenchmen, and Germans, especially during the latter part of the century. In fact one important source of information on American education for this period are the commentaries of European observers; English, French, German. They unfold a rich store of information about the American common schools. Their writings not only have literary value but they are among the most vital records of our educational past.

Foreign visitors were impressed with the seriousness of the goals and objectives of American education, the munificence of the school buildings and school equipment, the good discipline and the effort to democratize education. In their accounts of American education, Europeans invariably called attention first to the American belief in education,amounting almost to a religious faith. Indeed, it was sometimes observed, education was all the American people really believed in. That Americans seemed willing to extend the benefits of free public education to the level of secondary education, and in some states to the university, and the widespread diffusion of educational opportunity provided for Europeans tangible evidence of this belief. While the schools most frequently described were those located in the cities of the Northeast, as the years went by visitors noted increasingly that the common schools had expanded from the Atlantic seaboard to the Pacific ocean, and were penetrating into the farthest corners of the country. In the 1870's, on a trip to America, one Englishman ventured into the "Far West", and subsequently described the "border cities" like Dubuque, Iowa: "amidst the makeshift hotel, the general store, and the dirt and dust of the prairie, was a free common school". In the early 1880's another English visitor marveled: "In Colorado, in Utah, in the southern parts of California and the wild districts of Arizona and New Mexico, in Texas and Kansas; wherever mining camps and agricultural settlements are being formed, I have seen these schools. It is truly to be said that where two or three shanties are gathered together, there is a school house in the midst of them."

Europeans offered several reasons for the American commitment to the common schools. In the first place, America depended on the common schools to bring the foreign born into the folds of democracy. In somewhat broader perspective, some maintained that education for citizenship, for *all* children, was the overriding aim of American education. There was one other element in the American faith in the common schools to which Europeans called attention, to some the "mainspring" of the American common school system; the ideal of equality of opportunity. A French visitor, Ferdinand E. Buisson, sang the praises of American education in 1879: free education in America was not limited to the primary school, but extends to the high school. America thus says to its children. "As I offer you gratuitously the benefits of a liberal education, all careers are open to you. There are no longer disinherited children among you . . . So far as social equality can be attained here below, it is attained in the American school system. There all is done that can be done to push as far and as high as possible that common instruction which obliterates the distinction between the rich and the poor." To the Englishman, Sir Michael Sadler, perhaps the most perspicacious of all European observers of American education, this was the supreme objective animating American education from the beginning: "the intense and indeed religious belief in the rightness of giving to every boy and girl in the community, as far as possible, an equal chance to make the most of his or her natural powers." This explained much, the faith in education, the widespread accessibility of schools, the provision of free high schools, and the "ladder" system of organization characteristic of the American schools. In some states, many foreigners observed, it was possible for a child to go from the Kindergarten to the University "without ever having to pay a single penny for school fees". And they were positively encouraged to do so—the text of nearly every speaker before an American school essentially pertained to the wonderful possibility of becoming president of the United States. Unlike France and Germany and England, Americans refused to believe that a child could be overeducated.

Europeans were generous in acknowledging the strength of the American ideal of the common school and the sincerity of America's effort to reach the ideal in practice. Praise for the "noble educational spirit" of the American people did not deter Europeans from criticizing American schools or otherwise commenting on certain problems in American education; certain inequities, a certain distance between the ideal and the reality. Europeans were dumbfounded by the absence in America of any strong centralized authority in educational matters. They expressed surprise that there was no national system of education, just an amazing variety of systems of local control. Thus effective supervision was not exercised over rural areas and "the more ignorant districts". Foreign visitors agreed that the nature of the work was monotonous and mechanical and "too bookish." There was too much rote memorization of facts, rules, regulations, definitions. Teachers relied too exclusively on the recitation method. There was too little attention to physical exercise and the health of the students. Europeans also observed that the American ideal of the classless common school was just that: an ideal. In practice, social distinctions did tell with marked effect in American schools. Visitors also called attention to the fact that the American ideal of equal educational opportunity was still far from being achieved in practice. The inequalities in the educational provisions in the South in general, and for the Negro in particular, came in for comment. But Europeans had no doubt that eventually the ideal must be triumphant. This was the unfinished task of American education.

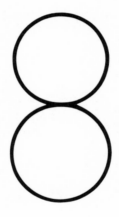

EUROPEAN INFLUENCES

The Continent

PESTALOZZI ON EDUCATION IN THE HOME (1781)   From Johann Heinrich
Pestalozzi, *Leonard and Gertrude*, Eva Channing, trans. (Boston, 1896), pp. 116–19, 129–31, 152–59.

Chapter XXII

PLANS OF REGENERATION IN BONNAL

As the Sunday approached when Arner had decreed that Hummel should be exposed to the view of the whole congregation, while the pastor held up his previous life as a warning to those present, the prisoner expressed the utmost horror of this penalty, declaring that he would rather have his punishment at the gallows repeated, than stand under the pulpit to be the laughing-stock of the town. He represented that such a ceremony could neither dispose him to thoughts of repentance, nor have a beneficial effect upon the spectators. The pastor was finally so moved by his entreaties, as well as convinced of the reasonableness of his plea, that he interceded with Arner, and induced him to remit the sentence. Accordingly, the clergyman merely took Hummel's life as a text, preaching a stirring sermon against the wickedness and corruption which had been fostered so long in their midst, and which were still rife, in almost equal measure, in the hearts of many of his listeners.

This discourse everywhere made a profound impression; the peasants could talk of nothing else on the way home, and Arner, pressing the good pastor's hand, thanked him heartily for his edifying words. He expressed, at the same time, an earnest desire to labor for the improvement of the village, and asked the clergyman if he could recommend an upright, able man from among the people, who could help him in furthering his designs. The parson mentioned at once the spinner known as Cotton Meyer, and proposed they should visit him and his sister that afternoon. They were accompanied by the Lieutenant Glülphi, one of Arner's aids in regulating the economic conditions of his government.

Cotton Meyer was sitting at his door with a child in his lap, when the three gentlemen approached, and had no suspicion that they were seeking him, until they paused before his garden gate. Then he went to meet them with so calm and dignified a bearing that Glülphi did not give him his hand, as he usually did to the peasants, and Arner addressed him less familiarly than was his wont when speaking to his dependants.

The visitors were about to seat themselves on the bench under the apple-tree; but Meyer led them into the parlor, where his sister was sitting by the table, nodding over the open Bible, as was her custom on Sunday afternoons. She started up with a cry as the door opened, and straightening her cap, closed the Bible; then, taking a sponge, she moistened it in a tin hand-basin which shone like silver, and erased the chalk figures with which her brother had covered the table, despite the remonstrance of the strangers, who feared that Meyer might have further use for his reckoning. After wiping the table carefully, she brought a large fine linen table-cloth, and laid new tin plates, with knives, forks and heavy silver spoons upon it.

"What are you doing?" inquired her guests; "we have already dined."

"I suppose so," answered Maria; "but since you have come into a peasant's house, you must take kindly to our peasant ways." Running into the kitchen, she returned with two plates of little cakes and a fine large ham, and Arner, Glülphi and the pastor seated themselves good-naturedly before the shining dishes.

When the visitors began to praise the house, the garden and the whole establishment, Maria remarked that twenty years ago they had been among the poorest in the village. "I know it," said Arner, "and I wonder at your prosperity the more, as the weavers and spinners have usually turned out the most good-for-nothing people in the country."

Meyer was forced to admit that this was true but denied that the cause lay in the industry itself. The trouble was, he said, that these poor people were not in the habit of laying up anything from their earnings, and led wretched, aimless lives. He felt sure that Arner might find many ways of winning the hearts of the people, so as to lead them into better paths, and suggested, as one expedient, that he should promise to every child, which up to its twentieth year should annually lay aside ten florins from its earnings, a field free from tithes. "But," went on Meyer, "after all, we can do very little with the people, unless the next generation is to have a very different training from that our schools furnish. The school ought really to stand in the closest connection with life of the home, instead of, as now, in strong contradiction to it."

Glülphi joined in the conversation with eagerness, and argued that a true school should develop to the fullest extent all the faculties of the child's nature. The question next arose, how such a school could be established in Bonnal. Cotton Meyer, when appealed to, rejoined: "I know a spinning-woman in the village who understands it far better than I"; and he went on to tell the others such things of Gertrude's little school and its effects upon her children, that they resolved to visit her and examine her method for themselves. They also spoke of the corruption prevailing in the village, and discussed the best method of choosing a good bailiff. Cotton Meyer showed himself through it all a man of such clear judgment and practical common sense, that his guests left him with a feeling of respect almost approaching veneration.

*　　*　　*

Chapter XXV

GERTRUDE'S METHOD OF INSTRUCTION

It was quite early in the morning when Arner, Glülphi and the pastor went to the mason's cottage. The room was not in order when they entered, for the family had just finished breakfast, and the dirty plates and spoons still lay upon the table. Gertrude was at first somewhat disconcerted, but the visitors reassured her, saying kindly: "This is as it should be; it is impossible to clear the table before breakfast is eaten!"

The children all helped wash the dishes, and then seated themselves in their customary places before their work. The gentlemen begged Gertrude to let everything go on as usual, and after the first half hour, during which she was a little embarrassed, all proceeded as if no stranger were present. First the children sang their morning hymns, and then Gertrude read a chapter of the Bible aloud, which they repeated after her while they were spinning, rehearsing the most instructive passages until they knew them by heart. In the mean time, the oldest girl had been making the children's beds in the adjoining room, and the visitors noticed through the open door that she silently repeated what the others were reciting. When this task was completed, she went into the garden and returned with vegetables for dinner, which she cleaned while repeating Bible-verses with the rest.

It was something new for the children to see three gentlemen in the room, and they often looked up from their spinning toward the corner where the strangers sat. Gertrude noticed this, and said to them: "Seems to me you look more at these gentlemen than at your yarn." But Harry answered: "No indeed! We are working hard, and you'll have finer yarn to-day than usual."

Whenever Gertrude saw that anything was amiss with the wheels or cotton, she rose from her work, and put it in order. The smallest children, who were not old enough to spin, picked over the cotton for carding, with a skill which excited the admiration of the visitors.

Although Gertrude thus exerted herself to develop very early the manual dexterity of her children, she was in no haste for them to learn to read and write. But she took pains to teach them early how to speak; for, as she said, "of what use is it for a person to be able to read and write, if he cannot speak?—since reading and writing are only an artificial sort of speech." To this end she used to make the children pronounce syllables after her in regular succession, taking them from an old A-B-C book she had. This exercise in correct and distinct articulation was, however, only a subordinate object in her whole scheme of education, which embraced a true comprehension of life itself. Yet she never adopted the tone of instructor toward her children; she did not say to them: "Child, this is your head, your nose, your hand, your finger;" or: "Where is your eye, your ear?"—but instead, she would say: "Come here, child, I will wash your little hands," "I will comb your hair," or: "I will cut your finger-nails." Her verbal instruction seemed to vanish in the spirit of her real activity, in which it always had its source. The result of her system was that each child was skilful, intelligent and active to the full extent that its age and development allowed.

The instruction she gave them in the rudiments of arithmetic was intimately connected with the realties of life. She taught them to count the number of steps from one end of the room to the other, and two of the rows of five panes each, in one of the windows, gave her an opportunity to unfold the decimal relations of numbers. She also made them count their threads while spinning, and the number of turns on the reel, when they wound the yarn into skeins. Above all, in every occupation of life she taught them an accurate and intelligent observation of common objects and the forces of nature.

All that Gertrude's children knew, they knew so thoroughly that they were able to teach it to the younger ones; and this they often begged permission to do. On this day, while the visitors were present, Jonas sat with each arm around the neck of a smaller child, and made the little ones pronounce the syllables of the A-B-C book after him; while Lizzie placed herself with her wheel between two of the others, and while all three spun, taught them the words of a hymn with the utmost patience.

When the guests took their departure, they told Gertrude they would come again on the morrow. "Why?" she returned; "You will only see the same thing over again." But Glülphi said: "That is the best praise you could possibly give yourself." Gertrude blushed at this compliment, and stood confused when the gentlemen kindly pressed her hand in taking leave.

The three could not sufficiently admire what they had seen at the mason's house, and Glülphi was so overcome by the powerful impression made upon him, that he longed to be alone and seek counsel of his own thoughts. He hastened to his room, and as he crossed the threshold, the words broke from his lips: "*I* must be schoolmaster in Bonnal!" All night visions of Gertrude's schoolroom floated through his mind, and he only fell asleep toward morning. Before his eyes were fairly open, he murmured: "I will be schoolmaster!"—and hastened to Arner to acquaint him with his resolution.

* * *

Chapter XXXI

THE ORGANIZATION OF A NEW SCHOOL

Glülphi was full of the idea of his school, and could speak of nothing else with Arner and the pastor. He used all his spare time in visiting Gertrude, in order to talk it over with her; but she seemed quite unable to explain her method in words, and usually deprecated the idea of her advice being necessary. Occasionally, however, she would let drop some significant remark which the lieutenant felt went to the root of the whole matter of education. For example, she said to him one day: "You should do for your children what their parents fail to do for them. The reading, writing and arithmetic are not, after all, what they most need; it is all well and good for them to learn something, but the really important thing is for them to *be* something,—for them to become what they are meant to be, and in becoming which they so often have no guidance or help at home."

Finally, the day arrived on which the new schoolmaster was to be formally presented to the village. Arner and the pastor led him solemnly between them to the church, which was crowded with the inhabitants of Bonnal. The good clergyman preached a sermon on the ideal function of the school in its relation to the home, and to the moral development of the community; after which Arner led Glülphi forward to the railing of the choir, and introducing him to the people, made a short but earnest plea in his behalf. The lieutenant was much affected, but mastered his emotion sufficiently to express in a few words his sense of the responsibility conferred upon him, and his hope that the parents would coöperate with him in his undertaking.

Arner was anxious to make the occasion of Glülphi's installation a festival for the school-children, so after the services at the church, he invited all the little folks to the parsonage, where, with the help of the pastor's wife, preparations had been made to receive them. It was a time-honored custom that every year, at Christmas and Easter, eggs and rolls should be distributed among the children of Bonnal. On this day, on entering the parsonage, the young people beheld even more beautifully painted eggs than they had seen at Easter; and beside each child's portion lay a bright nosegay.

The lieutenant, who knew nothing of the whole matter, was in an adjoining room, when suddenly the door was thrown open, and the children, at a sign from Theresa, struck up with one accord their prettiest song, and Glülphi found himself surrounded by the lively throng of his future charges. He was much moved, and when the song was concluded, he greeted them kindly, shaking many of them by the hand, and chatting pleasantly with them. Arner ordered some of his own wine to be brought, and the children drank the health of their new schoolmaster.

On the following morning the lieutenant began his school, and Gertrude helped him in the arrangement of it. They examined the children with regard to their previous studies, and seated those together who were equally advanced. First there were those who had not learned their letters, then those who could read separate words, and finally, those who already knew how to read. Beside reading, all were to learn writing and arithmetic, which previously had only been taught to the more wealthy, in private lessons.

At first Glülphi found it harder than he had expected; but every day, as he gained in experience, his task became easier and more delightful. A good and capable woman, named Margaret, who came to take charge of the sewing, spinning etc., proved a most valuable and conscientious helper in the work. Whenever a child's hand or wheel stopped, she would step up and restore things to their former condition. If the children's hair was in disorder, she would braid it up while they studied and worked; if there was a hole in their clothes, she would take a needle and thread, and mend it; and she showed them how to fasten their shoes and stockings properly, beside many other things they did not understand.

The new master was anxious, above all, to accustom his charges to strict order, and thus lead them to the true wisdom of life. He began school punctually on the stroke of the clock, and did not allow any one to come in late. He also laid great stress on good habits and behavior. The children were obliged to come to school clean in person and apparel, and with their hair combed. While standing, sitting, writing and working, they always were taught to keep the body erect as a candle. Glülphi's schoolroom must be clean as a church, and he would not suffer a pane of glass to be missing from the window, or a nail to be driven crooked in the floor. Still less did he allow the children to throw the smallest thing upon the floor, or to eat while they were studying; and it was even arranged that in getting up and sitting down they should not hit against each other.

Before school began, the children came up to their teacher one by one, and said: "God be with you!" He looked them over from head to foot, so that they knew by his eye if anything was wrong. If this glance was not sufficient, he spoke to them, or sent a message to their parents. A child would not infrequently come home with the word: "The schoolmaster sends greeting, and wants to know whether you have no needles and thread," or "whether water is dear," etc. At the close of school, those who had done well went up to him first, and said: "God be with you!" He held out his hand to each one, replying: "God be with you, my dear child!" Then came those who had only done partly well, and to these he merely said: "God be with you!" without giving them his hand. Finally, those who had not done well at all had to leave the room without even going to him.

The lieutenant's punishments were designed to remedy the faults for which they were inflicted. An idle scholar was made to cut fire-wood, or to carry stones for the wall which some of the older boys were constructing under the master's charge; a forgetful child was made school-messenger, and for several days was obliged to take charge of all the teacher's business in the village. Disobedience and impertinence he punished by not speaking publicly to the child in question for a number of days, talking with him only in private, after school. Wickedness and lying were punished with the rod, and any child thus chastised was not allowed to play with the others for a whole week; his name was registered in a special recordbook of offences, from which it was not erased until plain evidence of improvement was given. The schoolmaster was kind to the children while punishing them, talking with them more then than at any other time, and trying to help them correct their faults.

*　　*　　*

Chapter XXXII

A GOOD PASTOR AND SCHOOLMASTER; THE OPENING OF
A NEW ERA

In his instruction, Glülphi constantly sought to lay the foundation of that equanimity and repose which man can possess in all circumstances of life, provided the hardships of his lot have early become a second nature to him. The success of this attempt soon convinced the pastor that all verbal instruction, in so far as it aims at true human wisdom, and at the highest goal of this wisdom, true religion, ought to be subordinated to a constant training in practical domestic labor. The good man, at the same time, became aware that a single word of the lieutenant's could accomplish more than hours of his preaching. With true humility, he profited by the superior wisdom of the schoolmaster, and remodelled his method of religious instruction. He united his efforts to those of Glülphi and Margaret, striving to lead the children, without many words, to a quiet, industrious life, and thus to lay the foundations of a silent worship of God and love of humanity. To this end, he connected every word of his brief religious teachings with their actual, every-day experience, so that when he spoke of God and eternity, it seemed to them as if he were speaking of father and mother, house and home, in short, of the things with which they were most familiar. He pointed out to them in their books the few wise and pious passages which he still desired them to learn by heart, and completely ignored all questions involving doctrinal differences. He no longer allowed the children to learn any long prayers by rote, saying that this was contrary to the spirit of Christianity, and the express injunctions of their Saviour.

The lieutenant often declared that the pastor was quite unable to make a lasting impression on men, because he spoiled them by his kindness. Glülphi's own principles in regard to education were very strict, and were founded on an accurate knowledge of the world. He maintained that love was only useful in the education of men when in conjunction with fear; for they must learn to root out thorns and thistles, which they never do of their own accord, but only under compulsion, and in consequence of training.

He knew his children better in eight days than their parents did in eight years, and employed this knowledge to render deception difficult, and to keep their hearts open before his eyes. He cared for their heads as he did for their hearts, demanding that whatever entered them should be plain and clear as the silent moon in the sky. To insure this, he taught them to see and hear with accuracy, and cultivated their powers of attention. Above all, he sought to give them a thorough training in arithmetic; for he was convinced that arithmetic is the natural safeguard against error in the pursuit of truth.

PESTALOZZI ON EDUCATION ACCORDING TO NATURE (1800)   From
Johann Heinrich Pestalozzi, "How Gertrude Teaches Her Children" as quoted in Lewis Flint
Anderson, ed., *Pestalozzi* (New York, 1931), pp. 48–55, 58–61, 73.

How Gertrude Teaches Her Children

Education According to Nature

All instruction of man is then only the Art[1] of helping Nature to develop
in her own way; and this Art rests essentially on the relation and harmony between
the impressions received by the child and the exact degree of his developed powers.
It is also necessary in the impressions that are brought to the child by instruction
that there should be a sequence, so that beginning and progress should keep pace
with the beginning and progress of the powers to be developed in the child. I soon
saw that an inquiry into this sequence throughout the whole range of human
knowledge, particularly those fundamental points from which the development of
the human mind originates, must be the simple and only way ever to attain and to
keep satisfactory school and instruction books, of every grade, suitable for our
nature and our wants. I saw just as soon that in making these books the constituents
of instruction must be separated according to the degree of the growing power of
the child; and that in all matters of instruction, it is necessary to determine with the
greatest accuracy which of these constituents is fit for each age of the child, in order
on the one hand not to hold him back if he is ready; and on the other, not to load
him and confuse him with anything for which he is not quite ready.

This was clear to me. The child must be brought to a high degree of knowledge
both of things seen and of words before it is reasonable to teach him to spell or
read. I was quite convinced that at their earliest age children need psychological
training in gaining intelligent sense-impressions of all things. But since such
training, without the help of art, is not to be thought of or expected of men as they
are, the need of picture-books struck me perforce. These should precede the A-B-C
books, in order to make those ideas that men express by words clear to the children
(by means of well-chosen real objects, that either in reality, or in the form of well-
made models and drawings, can be brought before their minds).

A happy experiment confirmed my then unripe opinion in a striking way (in
spite of all the limitations of my means, and the error and one-sidedness in my
experiments). An anxious mother entrusted her hardly three-year-old child to my
private teaching. I saw him for a time every day for an hour; and for a time felt the
pulse of a method with him. I tried to teach him by letters, figures, and anything
handy; that is, I aimed at giving him clear ideas and expressions by these means. I
made him name correctly what he knew of anything—color, limbs, place, form, and
number. I was obliged to put aside that first plague of youth, the miserable letters;
he would have nothing but pictures and things.

He soon expressed himself clearly about the objects that lay within the limits of
his knowledge. He found common illustrations in the street, the garden, and the

[1]"The Art," frequently referred to hereafter, is distinguished by a capital A from art
generally; it is our "Science and Art of Education," which is here first put on a psychological
and scientific basis.

room; and soon learned to pronounce the hardest names of plants and animals, and to compare objects quite unknown to him with those known, and to produce a clear sense-impression of them in himself. Although this experiment led to byeways, and worked for the strange and distant to the disadvantage of the present, it threw a many-sided light on the means of quickening the child to his surroundings, and showing him the charm of self-activity in the extension of his powers.

But yet the experiment was not satisfactory for that which I was particularly seeking, because the boy had already three unused years behind him. I am convinced that nature brings the children even at this age to a definite consciousness of innumerable objects. It only needs that we should with psychological art unite speech with this knowledge in order to bring it to a high degree of clearness; and so enable us to connect the foundations of many-sided arts and truths with that which nature herself teaches, and also to use what nature teaches as a means of explaining all the fundamentals of art and truth that can be connected with them. Their power and their experience both are great at this age; but our unpsychological schools are essentially only artificial stifling-machines for destroying all the results of the power and experience that nature herself brings to life in them.

You know it, my friend. But for a moment picture to yourself the horror of this murder. We leave children up to their fifth year in the full enjoyment of nature; we let every impression of nature work upon them; they feel their power; they already know full well the joy of unrestrained liberty and all its charms. The free natural bent which the sensuous happy wild thing takes in his development, has in them already taken its most decided direction. And after they have enjoyed this happiness of sensuous life for five whole years, we make all nature round them vanish from before their eyes; tyrannically stop the delightful course of their unrestrained freedom; pen them up like sheep, whole flocks huddled together, in stinking rooms; pitilessly chain them for hours, days, weeks, months, years, to the contemplation of unattractive and monotonous letters, and (contrasted with their former condition) to a maddening course of life.

I cease describing; else I shall come to the picture of the greater number of schoolmasters, thousands of whom in our days merely on account of their unfitness for any means of finding a respectable livelihood have subjected themselves to the toilsomeness of this position, which they in accordance with their unfitness for anything better look upon as a way that leads little further than to keep them from starvation. How infinitely must the children suffer under these circumstances, or, at least, be spoiled!

The Search for the Laws of Human Development

The mechanism of physical (human) Nature is essentially subject to the same laws as those by which physical Nature generally unfolds her powers. According to these laws, all instruction should engraft the most essential parts of its subject of knowledge firmly into the very being of the human mind; then join on the less essential gradually but uninterruptedly to the most essential, and maintain all the parts of the subject, even to the outermost, in one living proportionate whole.

I now sought for laws to which the development of the human mind must, by its very nature, be subject. I knew they must be the same as those of physical Nature, and trusted to find in them a safe clue to a universal psychological method of instruction. "Man," said I to myself, while dreamily seeking this clue, "as you recognize in every physical ripening of the complete fruit the result of perfection in all its parts, so consider no human judgment ripe that does not appear to you to be the result of a complete sense-impression of all the parts of the object to be judged; but on the contrary, look upon every judgment that seems ripe before a complete observation (*Anschauung*) has been made as nothing but a worm-eaten and therefore apparently ripe fruit, fallen untimely from the tree."

1. Learn therefore to classify observations and complete the simple before proceeding to the complex. Try to make in every art graduated steps of knowledge, in which every new idea is only a small, almost imperceptible addition to that which has been known before, deeply impressed and not to be forgotten.

2. Again, bring all things essentially related to each other to that connection in your mind which they have in Nature. Subordinate all unessential things to the essential in your idea. Especially subordinate the impression given by the Art to that given by Nature and reality; and give to nothing a greater weight in your idea than it has in relation to your race in Nature.

3. Strengthen and make clear the impressions of important objects by bringing them nearer to you by the Art, and letting them affect you through different senses. Learn for this purpose the first law of physical mechanism, which makes the relative power of all influences of physical Nature depend on the physical nearness or distance of the object in contact with the senses. Never forget that this physical nearness or distance has an immense effect in determining your positive opinions, conduct, duties, and even virtue.

4. Regard all the effects of natural law as absolutely necessary, and recognize in this necessity the result of her power by which Nature unites together the apparently heterogeneous elements of her materials for the achievement of her end. Let the Art with which you work through instruction upon your race, and the results you aim at, be founded upon natural law, so that all your actions may be means to this principal end, although apparently heterogeneous.

5. But the richness of its charm, and the variety of its free play cause physical necessity, or natural law, to bear the impress of freedom and independence.

Let the results of your art and your instruction, while you try to found them upon natural law, by the richness of their charm and the variety of their free play bear the impression of freedom and independence.

All these laws to which the development of human nature is subject converge towards one centre. They converge towards the centre of our whole being, and we ourselves are this centre.

Friend, all that I am, all I wish, all I might be, comes out of myself. Should not my knowledge also come out of myself?

The Elements of Instruction

I long sought for a common psychological origin for all these arts of instruction, because I was convinced that only through this might it be possible to discover the *form* in which the cultivating of mankind is determined through the very laws of Nature itself. It is evident this form is founded on the general organization of the mind, by means of which our understanding binds together in imagination the impressions which are received by the senses from Nature into a whole, that is into an idea, and gradually unfolds this idea clearly.

"Every line, every measure, every word," said I to myself, "is a result of understanding that is produced by ripened sense-impressions and must be regarded as a means towards the progressive clearing up of our ideas." Again, all instruction is essentially nothing but this. Its principles must therefore be derived from the immutable first form of human mental development.

Everything depends on the exact knowledge of this prototype. I therefore once more began to keep my eye on these beginning-points from which it must be derived.

*　　*　　*

I also thought *number, form,* and *language* are, together, the elementary means of instruction, because the whole sum of the external properties of any object is comprised in its outline and its number, and is brought home to my consciousness through language.

It must then be an immutable law of the Art to start from and work within this threefold principle:

1. To teach children to look upon every object that is brought before them as a unit: that is, as separated from those with which it seems connected.
2. To teach them the form of every object: that is, its *size* and *proportions*.
3. As soon as possible to make them acquainted with all the words and names descriptive of objects known to them.

And as the instruction of children should proceed from these three elementary points, it is evident that the first efforts of the Art should be directed to the primary faculties of counting, measuring, and speaking, which lie at the basis of all accurate knowledge of objects of sense. We should cultivate them with the strictest psychological Art, endeavoring to strengthen and make them strong, and to bring them, as a means of development and culture, to the highest pitch of simplicity, consistency, and harmony.

The only difficulty which struck me in the recognition of these elementary points was the question: Why are *all* qualities of things that we know through our five senses not just as much elementary points of knowledge as number, form, and names? But I soon found that all possible objects have absolutely number, form, and names; but the other characteristics, known through our five senses, are not common to all objects. I found then such an essential and definite distinction between the number, form, and names of things and their other qualities, that I could not regard other qualities as elementary points of human knowledge. Again, I found that all other qualities can be included under these elementary points; that consequently, in instructing children, all other qualities of objects must be immediately connected with form, number, and names. I saw now that through knowing the unity, form, and name of any object, my knowledge of it becomes *precise;* by gradually learning its other qualities my knowledge of it becomes *clear;* through my consciousness of all its characteristics, my knowledge of it becomes *distinct.*

Then I found, further, that all our knowledge flows from three elementary powers:

1. From the power of making sounds, the origin of language.
2. From the *indefinite, simple sensuous-power of forming images,* out of which arises the consciousness of all forms.

3. From the *definite,* no longer merely *sensuous-power of imagination,* from which

must be derived consciousness of unity, and with it the power of calculation and arithmetic.

I thought, then, that the art of educating our race must be joined to the first and simplest results of these three primary powers—sound, form, and number; and that instruction in separate parts can never have a satisfactory effect upon our nature as a whole, if these three simple results of our primary powers are not recognized as the common starting-pointing of all instruction, determined by Nature herself. In consequence of this recognition, they must be fitted into forms which flow universally and harmoniously from the results of these three elementary powers; and which tend essentially and surely to make all instruction a steady, unbroken development of these three elementary powers, used together and considered equally important. In this way only is it possible to lead us in all three branches from vague to precise sense-impressions, from precise sense-impressions to clear images, and from clear images to distinct ideas.

Here at last I find the Art in general and essential harmony with Nature; or rather, with the prototype by which Nature makes clear to us the objects of the world in their essence and utmost simplicity. The problem is solved: *How to find a common origin of all methods and arts of instruction, and with it a form by which the development of our race might be decided through the essence of our own very nature.* The difficulties are removed of applying *mechanical laws,* which I recognize as the foundation of all human instruction, to the *form of instruction* which the experience of ages has put into the hands of mankind for the development of the race; that is, to apply them to reading, writing, arithmetic, and so on.

Sense-Impression, the Foundation of All Knowledge

Friend! When I now look back and ask myself: What have I specially done for the very being of education, I find I have fixed the highest supreme principle of instruction in the recognition of *sense-impression as the absolute foundation of all knowledge.* Apart from all *special teaching* I have sought to discover the *nature of teaching itself;* and the *prototype,* by which Nature herself has determined the instruction of our race. I find I have reduced all instruction to three elementary means; and have sought for special methods which would render the results of all instruction in these three branches absolutely certain.

Lastly, I find I have brought these three elementary means into harmony with each other; I have made instruction in all three branches in many ways harmonious not only each with itself but also with human nature; and I have brought it nearer to the course of Nature in the development of the human race.

PESTALOZZI DESCRIBES HIS WORK AT STANTZ (1807)   Letter from Johann Heinrich Pestalozzi to Heinrich Gessner, as quoted in Roger de Guimps, *Pestalozzi: His Life and Work*, J. Russell, trans. (London, 1890), pp. 149–53, 156–57, 166–71.

My friend, once more I awake from a dream; once more I see my work destroyed, and my failing strength wasted.

But, however weak and unfortunate my attempt may have been; a friend of humanity will not grudge a few moments to consider the reasons which convince me that some day a more fortunate posterity will certainly take up the thread of my hopes at the place where it is now broken.

From its very beginning I looked on the Revolution as a simple consequence of the corruption of human nature, and on the evils which it produced as a necessary means of bringing men back to a sense of the conditions which are essential to their happiness.

Although I was by no means prepared to accept all the political forms that a body of such men as the revolutionists might make for themselves, I was inclined to look upon certain points of their Constitution not only as useful measures protecting important interests, but as suggesting the principles upon which all true progress of humanity must be based.

I once more made known, therefore, as well as I could, my old wishes for the education of the people. In particular, I laid my whole scheme before Legrand (then one of the directors), who not only took a warm interest in it, but agreed with me that the Republic stood in urgent need of a reform of public education. He also agreed with me that much might be done for the regeneration of the people by giving a certain number of the poorest children an education which should be complete, but which, far from lifting them out of their proper sphere, would but attach them the more strongly to it.

I limited my desires to this one point, Legrand helping me in every possible way. He even thought my views so important that he once said to me: 'I shall not willingly give up my present post till you have begun your work.'

As I have explained my plan for the public education of the poor in the third and fourth parts of *Leonard and Gertrude*, I need not repeat it here. I submitted it to the director Stapfer, with all the enthusiasm of a man who felt that his hopes were about to be realized, and he encouraged me with an earnestness which showed how thoroughly he understood the needs of popular education. It was the same with the minister Rengger.

*　　*　　*

I opened the establishment with no other helper but a woman-servant. I had not only to teach the children, but to look after their physical needs. I preferred being alone, and, indeed, it was the only way to reach my end. No one in the world would have cared to fall in with my views for the education of children, and at that time I knew scarcely anyone capable even of understanding them. The better the education of the men who might have helped me, the less their power of understanding me and of confining themselves, even in theory, to the simple beginnings to which I sought to return. All their views as to the organization and needs of the enterprise were entirely different from mine. What they especially disagreed with was the idea that such an undertaking could be carried out without the help of any artificial means, but simply by the influence exercised on the children by Nature, and by the activity to which they were aroused by the needs of their daily life.

And yet it was precisely upon this idea that I based my chief hope of success; it was, as it were, a basis for innumerable other points of view.

Experienced teachers, then, could not help me; still less boorish, ignorant men. I had nothing to put into the hands of assistants to guide them, nor any results or apparatus by which I could make my ideas clearer to them.

Thus, whether I would or no, I had first to make my experiment alone, and collect facts to illustrate the essential features of my system before I could venture to look for outside help. Indeed, in my then position, nobody could help me. I knew that I must help myself and shaped my plans accordingly.

I wanted to prove by my experiment that if public education is to have any real value, it must imitate the methods which make the merit of domestic education; for it is my opinion that if public education does not take into consideration the circumstances of family life, and everything else that bears on a man's general education, it can only lead to an artificial and methodical dwarfing of humanity.

In any good education, the mother must be able to judge daily, nay hourly, from the child's eyes, lips, and face, of the slightest change in his soul. The power of the educator, too, must be that of a father, quickened by the general circumstances of domestic life.

Such was the foundation upon which I built. I determined that there should not be a minute in the day when my children should not be aware from my face and my lips that my heart was theirs, that their happiness was my happiness, and their pleasures my pleasures.

Man readily accepts what is good, and the child readily listens to it; but it is not for you that he wants it, master and educator, but for himself. The good to which you would lead him must not depend on your capricious humour or passion; it must be a good which is good in itself and by the nature of things, and which the child can recognize as good. He must feel the necessity of your will in things which concern his comfort before he can be expected to obey it.

Whenever he does anything gladly, anything that brings him honour, anything that helps to realize any of his great hopes, or stimulates his powers, and enables him to say with truth, *I can,* then he is exercising his will.

The will, however, cannot be stimulated by mere words; its action must depend upon those feelings and powers which are the result of general culture. Words alone cannot give us a knowledge of things; they are only useful for giving expression to what we have in our mind.

The first thing to be done was to win the confidence and affection of the children. I was sure that if I succeeded in doing that, all the rest would follow of itself. Think for a moment of the prejudices of the people, and even of the children, and you will understand the difficulties with which I had to contend.

*　　*　　*

Months passed in this way before I had the satisfaction of having my hand grasped by a single grateful parent. But the children were won over much sooner. They even wept sometimes when their parents met me or left me without a word of salutation. Several of them were perfectly happy, and used to say to their mothers: 'I am more comfortable here than at home.' At home, indeed, as they readily told me when we talked alone, they had been ill-used and beaten, and had often had neither bread to eat nor bed to lie down upon. And yet these same children would sometimes go off with their mothers the very next morning.

A good many others, however, soon saw that by staying with me they might both learn something and become something, and these never failed in their zeal and attachment. Before very long their conduct was imitated by others, though not always from the same considerations.

Those who ran away were the worst in character and the least capable. But they were not incited to go till they were free of their vermin and their rags. Several were sent to me with no other purpose than that of being taken away again as soon as they were clean and well clothed.

But after a time their better judgment overcame the defiant hostility with which they arrived. In 1799 I had nearly eighty children. Most of them were bright and intelligent, some even remarkably so.

For most of them study was something entirely new. As soon as they found that they could learn, their zeal was indefatigable, and in a few weeks children who had never before opened a book, and could hardly repeat a *Pater Noster* or an *Ave*, would study the whole day long with the keenest interest. Even after supper, when I used to say to them, 'Children, will you go to bed, or learn something?' they would generally answer, especially in the first month or two, 'Learn something.' It is true that afterwards, when they had to get up very early, it was not quite the same.

But this first eagerness did much towards starting the establishment on the right lines, and making the studies the success they ultimately were, a success, indeed, which far surpassed my expectations. And yet the difficulties in the way of introducing a well-ordered system of studies were at that time almost insurmountable.

Neither my trust nor my zeal had as yet been able to overcome either the intractability of individuals or the want of coherence in the whole experiment. The general order of the establishment, I felt, must be based upon order of a higher character. As this higher order did not yet exist, I had to attempt to create it; for without this foundation I could not hope to organize properly either the teaching or the general management of the place, nor should I have wished to do so. I wanted everything to result not from a preconceived plan, but from my relations with the children. The high principles and educating forces I was seeking, I looked for from the harmonious common life of my children, from their attention, activity, and needs. It was not, then, from any external organization that I looked for the regeneration of which they stood so much in need. If I had employed constraint, regulations and lectures, I should instead of winning and ennobling my children's hearts, have repelled them and made them bitter, and thus been farther than ever from my aim. First of all, I had to arouse in them pure, moral, and noble feelings, so that afterwards, in external things, I might be sure of their ready attention, activity, and obedience. I had, in short, to follow the high precept of Jesus Christ, 'Cleanse first that which is within, that the outside may be clean also'; and if ever the truth of this precept was made manifest, it was made manifest then.

My one aim was to make their new life in common, and their new powers, awaken a feeling of brotherhood amongst the children, and make them affectionate, just, and considerate.

I reached this end without much difficulty. Amongst these seventy wild beggar-children there soon existed such peace, friendship, and cordial relations as are rare even between actual brothers and sisters.

The principle to which I endeavoured to conform all my conduct was as follows:

Endeavour, first, to broaden your children's sympathies, and, by satisfying their daily needs, to bring love and kindness into such unceasing contact with their impressions and their activity, that these sentiments may be engrafted in their hearts; then try to give them such judgment and tact as will enable them to make a wise, sure, and abundant use of these virtues in the circle which surrounds them. In the last place, do not hesitate to touch on the difficult questions of good and evil, and the words connected with them.

*   *   *

I have now put before you my views as to the family spirit which ought to prevail in an educational establishment, and I have told you of my attempts to carry them out. I have still to explain the essential principles upon which all my teaching was based.

I knew no other order, method, or art, but that which resulted naturally from my children's conviction of my love for them, nor did I care to know any other.

Thus I subordinated the instruction of my children to a higher aim, which was to arouse and strengthen their best sentiments by the relations of every-day life as they existed between themselves and me.

I had Gedicke's reading-book, but it was of no more use to me than any other school-book; for I felt that, with all these children of such different ages, I had an admirable opportunity for carrying out my own views on early education. I was well aware, too, how impossible it would be to organize my teaching according to the ordinary system in use in the best schools.

As a general rule I attached little importance to the study of words, even when explanations of the ideas they represented were given.

I tried to connect study with manual labour, the school with the workshop, and make one thing of them. But I was the less able to do this as staff, material, and tools were all wanting. A short time only before the close of the establishment, a few children had begun to spin; and I saw clearly that, before any fusion could be effected, the two parts must be firmly established separately—study, that is, on the one hand, and labour on the other.

But in the work of the children I was already inclined to care less for the immediate gain than for the physical training which, by developing their strength and skill, was bound to supply them later with a means of livelihood. In the same way I considered that what is generally called the instruction of children should be merely an exercise of the faculties, and I felt it important to exercise the attention, observation, and memory first, so as to strengthen these faculties before calling into play the art of judging and reasoning; this, in my opinion, was the best way to avoid turning out that sort of superficial and presumptuous talker, whose false judgments are often more fatal to the happiness and progress of humanity than the ignorance of simple people of good sense.

Guided by these principles, I sought less at first to teach my children to spell, read, and write than to make use of these exercises for the purpose of giving their minds as full and as varied a development as possible.

I made them spell by heart before teaching them their A B C, and the whole class could thus spell the hardest words without knowing their letters. It will be evident to everybody how great a call this made on their attention. I followed at first the order of words in Gedicke's book, but I soon found it more useful to join the five vowels successively to the different consonants, and so form a well graduated series of syllables leading from simple to compound.

I had gone rapidly through the scraps of geography and natural history in Gedicke's book. Before knowing their letters even, they could say properly the names of the different countries. In natural history they were very quick in corroborating what I taught them by their own personal observations on plants and animals. I am quite sure that, by continuing in this way, I should soon have been able not only to give them such a general acquaintance with the subject as would have been useful in any vocation, but also to put them in a position to carry on their education themselves by means of their daily observations and experiences; and I should have been able to do all this without going outside the very restricted sphere to which they were confined by the actual circumstances of their lives. I hold it to be extremely important that men should be encouraged to learn by themselves and allowed to develop freely. It is in this way alone that the diversity of individual talent is produced and made evident.

I always made the children learn perfectly even the least important things, and I never allowed them to lose ground; a word once learnt, for instance, was never to be forgotten, and a letter once well written never to be written badly again. I was very patient with all who were weak or slow, but very severe with those who did anything less well than they had done it before.

The number and inequality of my children rendered my task easier. Just as in a family the eldest and cleverest child readily shows what he knows to his younger brothers and sisters, and feels proud and happy to be able to take his mother's place for a moment, so my children were delighted when they knew something that they could teach others. A sentiment of honour awoke in them, and they learned twice as well by making the younger ones repeat their words. In this way I soon had helpers and collaborators amongst the children themselves. When I was teaching them to spell difficult words by heart, I used to allow any child who succeeded in saying one properly to teach it to the others. These child-helpers, whom I had formed from the very outset, and who had followed my method step by step, were certainly much more useful to me than any regular schoolmasters could have been.

I myself learned with the children. Our whole system was so simple and so natural that I should have had difficulty in finding a master who would not have thought it undignified to learn and teach as I was doing.

My aim was so to simplify the means of instruction that it should be quite possible for even the most ordinary man to teach his children himself; thus schools would gradually almost cease to be necessary, so far as the first elements are concerned. Just as the mother gives her child its first material food, so is she ordained by God to give it its first spiritual food, and I consider that very great harm is done to the child by taking it away from home too soon and submitting it to artificial school methods. The time is drawing near when methods of teaching will be so simplified that each mother will be able not only to teach her children without help, but continue her own education at the same time. And this opinion is justified by my experience, for I found that some of my children developed so well as to be able to follow in my footsteps. And I am more than ever convinced that as soon as we have educational establishments combined with workshops, and conducted on a truly psychological basis, a generation will necessarily be formed which, on the one hand, will show us by experience that our present studies do not require one tenth part of the time or trouble we now give to them, and on the other, that the time and strength this instruction demands, as well as the means of acquiring it, may be made to fit in so perfectly with the conditions of domestic life, that every parent will easily be able to supply it by a member or friend of the family, a result which will daily become easier, according as the method of instruction is simplified, and the number of educated people increased.

THE EDUCATION OF THE WILD BOY OF AVEYRON (1801)   From Jean-Marc-Gaspard Itard, *The Wild Boy of Aveyron,* Translated by George and Muriel Humphrey (New York, 1962), pp. 3–4, 10–11, 14–20.

First Developments of the Young Savage of Aveyron

A child of eleven or twelve, who some years before had been seen completely naked in the Caune Woods seeking acorns and roots to eat, was met in the same place toward the end of September 1799 by three sportsmen who seized him as he was climbing into a tree to escape from their pursuit. Conducted to a neighboring hamlet and confided to the care of a widow, he broke loose at the end of a week and gained the mountains, where he wandered during the most rigorous winter weather, draped rather than covered with a tattered shirt. At night he retired to solitary places but during the day he approached the neighboring villages, where of his own accord he entered an inhabited house situated in the Canton of St. Sernin.

There he was retaken, watched and cared for during two or three days and transferred to the hospital of Saint-Afrique, then to Rodez, where he was kept for several months. During his sojourn in these different places he remained equally wild and shy, impatient and restless, continually seeking to escape. He furnished material for most interesting observations, which were collected by credible witnesses whose accounts I shall not fail to report in this essay where they can be displayed to the best advantage.[1] A minister of state with scientific interests believed that this event would throw some light upon the science of the mind. Orders were given that the child should be brought to Paris. He arrived there towards the end of September 1800 under the charge of a poor respectable old man who, obliged to part from the child shortly after, promised to come and take him again and act as a father to him should the Society ever abandon him.

The most brilliant and irrational expectations preceded the arrival of the Savage of Aveyron at Paris.[2] A number of inquisitive people looked forward with delight to witnessing the boy's astonishment at the sights of the capital. On the other hand many people otherwise commendable for their insight, forgetting that human organs

---

[1] If the expression *Savage* has been understood until now to mean a man but slightly civilized, it will be agreed that this term has never been more truly merited. I will then keep to this name by which he has always been designated until I have given an account of the motives which determined me to give him another.

[2] All that I have said and intend to say hereafter about the history of this child before his stay in Paris will be found to be guaranteed by the official reports of citizens Guiraud and Constant de Saint-Estève, government commissioners, the first near the canton of Saint-Afrique, the second near that of Saint-Sernin, and by the observations of citizens Bonaterre, professor of natural history in the Central School of the *Département de l'Aveyron* which are given in great detail in his *Notice historique sur le sauvage de l'Aveyron.*

are by so much less flexible, and imitation made by so much more difficult, in proportion as man is removed from society and from his infancy, believed that the education of this child would only be a question of some months, and that he would soon be able to give the most interesting information about his past life. In place of all this what do we see? A disgustingly dirty child affected with spasmodic movements and often convulsions who swayed back and forth ceaselessly like certain animals in the menagerie, who bit and scratched those who attended him; and who was in short, indifferent to everything and attentive to nothing.

It can easily be understood that a creature of this kind could excite only a momentary curiosity. People ran in crowds, they saw him without observing him, they passed judgment on him without knowing him, and spoke no more about him. In the midst of this general indifference the administrators of the National Institute of the Deaf and Dumb and its celebrated director never forgot that society, in taking over this unfortunate youth, had contracted towards him binding obligations that must be fulfilled. Sharing then the hopes which I founded upon a course of medical treatment, they decided that this child should be confided to my care. . . . Thus this child had lived in an absolute solitude from his seventh almost to his twelfth year, which is the age he may have been when he was taken in the Caune woods. It is then probable, and almost proved, that he had been abandoned at the age of four or five years, and that if, at this time, he already owed some ideas and some words to the beginning of an education, this would all have been effaced from his memory in consequence of his isolation.

This is what appeared to me to be the cause of his present state. It can be seen why I augured favorably from it for the success of my treatment. Indeed, considering the short time he was among people, the Wild Boy of Aveyron was much less an adolescent imbecile than a child of ten or twelve months, and a child who would have the disadvantage of anti-social habits, a stubborn inattention, organs lacking in flexibility and a sensibility accidentally dulled. From this last point of view his situation became a purely medical case, and one the treatment of which belonged to mental science, that sublime art created in England by Willis and Crichton, and newly spread in France by the success and writings of Professor Pinel.

Guided much less by the spirit of their doctrine than by their precepts, which could not be adapted to this unforeseen case, I classified under five principal aims the mental and moral education of the Wild Boy of Aveyron.

1st Aim. To interest him in social life by rendering it more pleasant to him than the one he was then leading, and above all more like the life which he had just left.

2nd Aim. To awaken his nervous sensibility by the most energetic stimulation, and occasionally by intense emotion.

3rd Aim. To extend the range of his ideas by giving him new needs and by increasing his social contacts.

4th Aim. To lead him to the use of speech by inducing the exercise of imitation through the imperious law of necessity.

5th Aim. To make him exercise the simplest mental operations upon the objects of his physical needs over a period of time afterwards inducing the application of these mental processes to the objects of instruction.

II. Second Aim. To awaken his nervous sensibility by the most energetic stimulation, and sometimes by intense emotion

Certain modern physiologists have suspected that sensitiveness is directly proportional to civilization. I do not believe that a stronger proof of this could be given than the dullness of the Wild Boy of Aveyron's sense organs. The reader may convince himself by a glance at the description that I have already given which rests on facts drawn from the most authentic source. Relative to the same subject I will add here some of my most striking observations.

Several times during the course of the winter I have seen him crossing the garden of the Deaf and Dumb, squatting half naked upon the wet ground, remaining thus exposed for hours on end to a cold and wet wind. It was not only to cold but also to intense heat that the organ of the skin and touch showed no sensitivity. When he was near the fire and the glowing embers came rolling out of the hearth it was a daily occurrence for him to seize them with his fingers and replace them without any particular haste upon the flaming fire. He has been discovered more than once in the kitchen picking out in the same way potatoes which were cooking in boiling water, and I can guarantee that he had, even at that time, a fine and velvety skin.[5]

I have often succeeded in filling the exterior cavities of his nose with snuff without making him sneeze. The inference is that between the organ of smell, which was very highly developed in other respects, and those of respiration and sight, there did not exist any of those sympathetic relations which form an integral part of our sensibility, and which in this case would have caused sneezing or the secretion of tears. Still less was the secretion of tears connected with feelings of sadness, and in spite of innumerable annoyances, in spite of the bad treatment to which his new manner of life had exposed him during the first months, I have never discovered him weeping. Of all his senses, the ear appeared the least sensitive. It was found, nevertheless, that the sound of a cracking walnut or other favorite eatable never failed to make him turn round. This observation is quite accurate: yet, nevertheless, this same organ showed itself insensible to the loudest noises and the explosion of firearms. One day I fired two pistol shots near him, the first appeared to rouse him a little, the second did not make him even turn his head.

I have collated a number of similar cases where the lack of mental attention was taken for a lack of sensibility in the organ, but found, however, that this nervous sensibility was singularly weak in most of the other sense organs as well. Consequently it became part of my plan to develop it by all possible means, and to prepare the mind for attention by preparing the senses to receive keener impressions. Of the various means I employed, the effect of heat appeared to me best to fulfill this purpose. It is admitted by physiologists[6] and political theorists[7] that the inhabitants of the South owe their exquisite sensibility, so superior to that of the northerners, entirely to the action of heat upon the skin. I employed this stimulus in all possible ways. Not only was he clothed, put to bed, and housed warmly, but every day I gave him, and at a very high temperature, a bath lasting

---

[5] "I offered him," said an observer who had seen him at Saint-Sernin, "a great number of potatoes; he was delighted to see them, took them in his hands and threw them in the fire. He withdrew them an instant after and ate them burning hot."

[6] Lacose, *Idée de l'homme, physique et moral*—Laroche, *Analyse des fonctions du système nerveux*—Fouquet, article, "Sensibilité," de *Encyclopédie par ordre alphabétique.*

[7] Montesquieu, *Esprit des lois*, Book XIV.

two or three hours during which frequent douches with the same water were administered to him on the head. I did not observe that the warmth and the frequency of the baths were followed by the debilitating effect attributed to them.

I should even have been glad if such had happened, convinced that in such a case the nervous sensibility would gain by the loss of muscular strength. But if the one effect did not follow, at least the other did not disappoint my expectations. After some time our young savage showed himself sensitive to the action of cold, made use of his hand to find out the temperature of the bath, and refused to enter when it was only lukewarm. For the same reason he soon began to appreciate the utility of clothes which until then he had only endured with much impatience. This utility once recognized, it was only a step to make him dress himself. This end was attained after some days by leaving him each morning exposed to the cold within reach of his clothes until he himself knew how to make use of them. A very similar expedient sufficed to give him at the same time habits of cleanliness and the certainty of passing the night in a cold wet bed accustomed him to get up in order to satisfy his needs. To the administration of the baths I added the use of dry frictions along the spine and even ticklings of the lumbar region. This last means was more exciting than most. I even found myself obliged to reject it, when its effects were no longer limited to producing movements of pleasure but appeared to extend further to the generative organs and to add the threat of perversion to the first stirrings of an already precocious puberty.

To these various stimulants I had to add emotional stimulants which were no less exciting. Those to which he was susceptible at this time were confined to two, joy and anger. The latter I only provoked at long intervals, for its attack was most violent and always apparently justified. I remarked sometimes that in the force of his passion his intelligence seemed to acquire a sort of extension which furnished him with some ingenious expedient in order to get himself out of trouble. Once when we wanted to make him take a bath which was as yet only lukewarm and our reiterated entreaties had made him violently angry, seeing that his governess was not convinced of the coolness of the water by the frequent tests that he made with the tips of his own fingers, he turned towards her quickly, seized her hand and plunged it into the bath.

Let me relate another act of the same nature. One day when he was in my study sitting upon a sofa I came to sit at his side and placed between us a Leyden jar lightly charged. A slight shock which he had received from it the day before had made him familiar with its effect. Seeing the uneasiness which the approach of the instrument caused him I thought he would move it further away by taking hold of the handle. He took a more prudent course which was to put his hands in the opening of his waistcoat, and to draw back some inches so that his leg would no longer touch the covering of the bottle. I drew near him a second time and again replaced it between us. Another movement on his part, another adjustment on mine. This little maneuvre continued until, driven into a corner at the end of the sofa, he found himself bounded by the wall behind, by a table in front, and at my side by the troublesome machine. It was no longer possible for him to make any movement. It was then that, seizing the moment when I advanced my arm in order to guide his,

[6]Lacose, *Idée de l'homme, physique et moral*—Laroche, *Analyse des fonctions du système nerveux*—Fouquet, article, "Sensibilité," de *Encyclopédie par ordre alphabétique.*

[7]Montesquieu, *Esprit des lois*, Book XIV.

he very adroitly lowered my wrist upon the knob of the bottle. I received the discharge.

But if sometimes in spite of the intense interest this young orphan inspired in me I took upon myself to excite his anger, I let no occasion pass of procuring happiness for him: and certainly this was neither difficult nor costly. A ray of sun reflected upon a mirror in his room and turning about on the ceiling, a glass of water let fall drop by drop from a certain height upon his finger tips while he was in the bath, and a wooden porringer containing a little milk placed at the end of his bath, which the oscillations of the water drifted, little by little, amid cries of delight, into his grasp, such simple means were nearly all that was necessary to divert and delight this child of nature almost to the point of ecstasy.

Such were, among a host of others, the stimulations, both physical and mental, with which I endeavored to develop the sensibilities of his organs. These methods produced after three months a general excitement of all the senses. His touch showed itself sensitive to the impression of hot or cold substances, smooth or rough, yielding or resistant. At that time I wore velvet breeches over which he seemed to take pleasure in passing his hand. It was with this exploratory organ that he nearly always assured himself of the degree to which his potatoes were cooked. Taking them from the pot with a spoon he would apply his fingers to them several times and decide according to their state of softness or resistance whether to eat them or throw them back again into the boiling water. When he was given a candle to light with some paper, he did not always wait until the fire had caught the wick before throwing the paper away hurriedly, although the flame was not yet near his fingers. If he was forced to push or to carry anything he would sometimes abandon it suddenly although it was neither hard nor heavy, in order to look at the ends of his fingers which were certainly neither bruised nor hurt, after which he would put his hand gently in the opening of his waistcoat. The sense of smell had also gained by this improvement. The least irritation of this organ provoked sneezing, and I judged by the fright that seized him the first time this happened, that this was a new experience to him. He immediately ran away and threw himself on his bed.

The refinement of the sense of taste was even more marked. The eating habits of this child shortly after he arrived at Paris were disgusting in the extreme. He dragged his food into the corners and kneaded it with his filthy hands.

But at the time of which I am now speaking it frequently happened he would throw away in a temper all the contents of his plate if any foreign substance fell on it: and when he had broken his walnuts under his feet, he fastidiously wiped the nuts clean.

Finally disease itself, that irrefutable and troublesome witness of the characteristic sensitiveness of civilized man, came at this point to attest the development of this principle of life.[8] Towards the first days of spring, our young savage had a violent cold in the head and some weeks later two catarrhal affections, one almost immediately succeeding the other.

Nevertheless, all his organs did not respond so quickly. Those of sight and hearing did not participate in the improvement, doubtless because these two senses, much less simple than the others, had need of a particular and longer education as may be seen by what follows.

The simultaneous improvement of the three senses, touch, taste and smell, resulting from the stimulants applied to the skin whilst these last two remained

[8]I.e., Man's sensitiveness (tr.).

unaffected is a valuable fact, worthy of being drawn to the attention of physiologists. It seems to prove, what from other sources appears probable, that the senses of touch, smell and taste are only a modification of the organ of the skin; whereas those of hearing and sight, more subjective, enclosed in a most complicated physical apparatus, are subject to other laws and ought in some measure to form a separate class.

FROEBEL'S PHILOSOPHY OF EDUCATION (1826) From Friedrich Froebel, *The Education of Man*, W. N. Hailmann, trans. (New York, 1887), pp. 8–9, 21, 27–30, 54–56, 87–89.

Groundwork of the Whole

1. In all things there lives and reigns an eternal law. To him whose mind, through disposition and faith, is filled, penetrated, and quickened with the necessity that this can not possibly be otherwise, as well as to him whose clear, calm mental vision beholds the inner in the outer and through the outer, and sees the outer proceeding with logical necessity from the essence of the inner, this law has been and is enounced with equal clearness and distinctness in nature (the external), in the spirit (the internal), and in life which unites the two. This all-controlling law is necessarily based on an all-pervading, energetic, living, self-conscious, and hence eternal Unity. This fact, as well as the Unity itself, is again vividly recognized, either through faith or through insight, with equal clearness and comprehensiveness; therefore, a quietly observant human mind, a thoughtful, clear human intellect, has never failed, and will never fail, to recognize this Unity. . . .

This Unity is God. All things have come from the Divine Unity, from God, and have

The self-active application of this knowledge in the direct development and cultivation of rational beings toward the attainment of their destiny, is *the practice of education.*

The object of education is the realization of a faithful, pure, inviolate, and hence holy life.

Knowledge and application, consciousness and realization in life, united in the service of a faithful, pure, holy life, constitute the *wisdom of life,* pure wisdom.

4. *To be wise is the highest aim of man,* is the most exalted achievement of human self-determination.

To educate one's self and others, with consciousness, freedom, and self-determination, is a twofold achievement of wisdom: it *began* with the first appearance of man upon the earth; it *was manifest* with the first appearance of full self-consciousness in man; it *begins now* to proclaim itself as a necessary, universal requirement of humanity, and to be heard and heeded as such. With this achievement man enters upon the path which alone leads to life; which surely tends to the fulfillment of the inner, and thereby also to the fulfillment of the outer, requirement of humanity; which, through a faithful, pure, holy life, attains beatitude.

5. By education, then, the divine essence of man should be unfolded, brought out, lifted into consciousness, and man himself raised into free, conscious obedience to the divine principle that lives in him, and to a free representation of this principle in his life.

Education, in instruction, should lead man to see and know the divine, spiritual, and eternal principle which animates surrounding nature, constitutes the essence of nature, and is permanently manifested in nature; and, in living reciprocity and united with training, it should express and demonstrate the fact that the same law rules both (the divine principle and nature), as it does nature and man.

Education as a whole, by means of instruction and training, should bring to man's consciousness, and render efficient in his life, the fact that man and nature proceed from God and are conditioned by him—that both have their being in God.

Education should lead and guide man to clearness concerning himself and in himself, to peace with nature, and to unity with God; hence, it should lift him to a knowledge of himself and of mankind, to a knowledge of God and of nature, and to the pure and holy life to which such knowledge leads.

✻   ✻   ✻

19. Therefore the child should, from the very time of his birth, be viewed in accordance with his nature, treated correctly, and given the free, all-sided use of his powers. By no means should the use of certain powers and members be enhanced at the expense of others, and these hindered in their development; the child should neither be partly chained, fettered, nor swathed; nor, later on, spoiled by too much assistance. The child should learn early how to find in himself the center and fulcrum of all his powers and members, to seek his support in this, and, resting therein, to move freely and be active, to grasp and hold with his own hands, to stand and walk on his own feet, to find and observe with his own eyes, to use his members symmetrically and equally. At an early period the child should learn, apply, and practice the most difficult of all arts—to hold fast the center and fulcrum of his life in spite of all digressions, disturbances, and hindrances.

✻   ✻   ✻

22. Not only in regard to the cultivation of the divine and religious elements in man, but in his entire cultivation, it is highly important that his development should proceed continuously from *one* point, and that this *continuous* progress be seen and ever guarded. Sharp limits and definite subdivisions within the continuous series of the years of development, withdrawing from attention the permanent continuity, the living connection, the inner living essence, are therefore highly pernicious, and even destructive in their influence. Thus, it is highly pernicious to consider the stages of human development—infant, child, boy or girl, youth or maiden, man or woman, old man or matron—as really distinct, and not, as life shows them, as continuous in themselves, in unbroken transitions; highly pernicious to consider the child or boy as something wholly different from the youth or man, and as something so distinct that the common foundation (*human being*) is seen but vaguely in the idea and word, and scarcely at all considered in life and for life. And yet this is the actual condition of affairs; for, if we consider common speech and life *as it actually is,* how wholly distinct do the child and the boy appear! Especially do the later stages speak of the earlier ones as something quite foreign, wholly different from

them; the boy has ceased to see in himself the child, and fails to see in the child the boy; the youth no longer sees in himself the boy and the child, nor does he see in these the youth—with affected superiority he scorns them; and, most pernicious of all, the adult man no longer finds in himself the infant, the child, the boy, the youth, the earlier stages of development, nor in these the coming adult man, but speaks of the child, the boy, and the youth as of wholly different beings, with wholly different natures and tendencies.

These definite subdivisions and sharp limitations have their origin in the want of early and continuously growing attention to the development and self-observation of his own life. It is possible only to indicate, but not to point out in their full extent, the unspeakable mischief, disturbance, and hindrance in the development and advancement of the human race, arising from these subdivisions and limitations. Suffice it to say that only rare inner force can break through the limits set up around the human being by those who influence him. Even this can be accomplished only by a violent effort that threatens to destroy, or, at least, to check and disturb, other phases of development. Therefore, there is throughout life somewhat of violence in the actions of a man who has done this at any stage of his development.

How different could this be in every respect, if parents were to view and treat the child with reference to all stages of development and age, without breaks and omissions; if, particularly, they were to consider the fact that the vigorous and complete development and cultivation of each successive stage depends on the vigorous, complete, and characteristic development of each and all preceding stages of life! Parents are especially prone to overlook and disregard this. When the human being has reached the age of boyhood, they look upon him as a boy; when he has reached the age of youth or manhood, they take him to be a youth or a man. Yet the boy has not become a boy, nor has the youth become a youth, by reaching a certain age, but only by having lived through childhood, and, further on, through boyhood, true to the requirements of his mind, his feelings, and to his body; similarly, adult man has not become an adult man by reaching a certain age, but only by faithfully satisfying the requirements of his childhood, boyhood, and youth. Parents and fathers, in other respects quite sensible and efficient, expect not only that the child should begin to show himself a boy or a youth, but, more particularly, that the boy, at least, should show himself a man, that in all his conduct he should be a man, thus jumping the stages of boyhood and youth. To see and respect *in* the child and boy the germ and promise of the coming youth and man is very different from considering and treating him as if he were already a man; very different from asking the child or boy to show himself a youth or man; to feel, to think, and to conduct himself as a youth or a man. Parents who ask this overlook and forget that they themselves became mature and efficient only in so far as they lived through the various stages in natural succession and in certain relationships which they would have their child to forego.

This disregard of the value of earlier, and particularly of the earliest, stages of development with reference to later ones, prepares for the future teacher and educator of the boy difficulties which it will be scarcely possible to overcome. In the first place, the boy so conditioned has also a notion that it is possible for him to do wholly without the instruction and training of the preceding stage of development; in the second place, he is much injured and weakened by having placed before himself, at an early period, an extraneous aim for imitation and exertion, such as preparation for a certain calling or sphere of activity. *The child, the boy, man, indeed, should know no other endeavor but to be at every stage of development wholly what this stage calls for.* Then will each successive stage spring like a new shoot from a healthy bud; and, at each successive stage, he will with the same endeavor again accomplish the requirements of this stage: for only the adequate development of man at each preceding stage can effect and bring about adequate development at each succeeding later stage.

*   *   *

30. *Play.—Play* is the highest phase of child-development—of human development at this period; for *it is self-active representation of the inner—representation of the inner from inner necessity and impulse.*

Play is the purest, most spiritual activity of man at this stage, and, at the same time, typical of human life as a whole—of the inner hidden natural life in man and all things. It gives, therefore, joy, freedom, contentment, inner and outer rest, peace with the world. It holds the sources of all that is good. A child that plays thoroughly, with self-active determination, perseveringly until physical fatigue forbids, will surely be a thorough, determined man, capable of self-sacrifice for the promotion of the welfare of himself and others. Is not the most beautiful expression of child-life at this time a playing child? A child wholly absorbed in his play?—A child that has fallen asleep while so absorbed?

As already indicated, play at this time is not trivial, it is highly serious and of deep significance. Cultivate and foster it, O mother; protect and guard it, O father! To the calm, keen vision of one who truly knows human nature, the spontaneous play of the child discloses the future inner life of the man.

The plays of childhood are the germinal leaves of all later life; for the whole man is developed and shown in these, in his tenderest dispositions, in his innermost tendencies. The whole later life of man, even to the moment when he shall leave it again, has its source in the period of childhood—be this later life pure or impure, gentle or violent, quiet or impulsive, industrious or indolent, rich or poor in deeds, passed in dull stupor or in keen creativeness, in stupid wonder or intelligent insight, producing or destroying, the bringer of harmony or discord, of war or peace. His future relations to father and mother, to the members of the family, to society and mankind, to nature and God—in accordance with the natural and individual disposition and tendencies of the child—depend chiefly upon his mode of life at this period; for the child's life in and with himself, his family, nature, and God, is as yet a unit. Thus, at this age, the child can scarcely tell which is to him dearer—the flowers, or his joy about them, or the joy he gives to the mother when he brings or shows them to her, or the vague presentiment of the dear Giver of them.

*   *   *

Let parents—more particularly fathers (for to their special care and guidance the child ripening into boyhood is confided)—let fathers contemplate what the fulfillment of their paternal duties in child-guidance yields to them; let them feel the joys it brings. It is not possible to gain from anything higher joy, higher enjoyment, than we do from the guidance of our children, from living with and for our children. It is inconceivable how we can seek and expect to find anywhere higher joy, higher enjoyment, fuller gratification of our best desires than we can find in intercourse with our children; more recreation than we can find in the family circle, where we can create joy for ourselves in so many respects.

We should be deeply impressed with the truth of these statements could we but see in his plain home-surroundings, in his happy, joyous family, the father who, from his own resources, has created what here has been but partially described. In a few words he sums up his rule of conduct: "To lead children early to think, this I consider the first and foremost object of child-training."

To give them early habits of work and industry seemed to him so natural and obvious a course as to need no statement in words. Besides, the child that has been led to think will thereby, at the same time, be led to industry, diligence—to all domestic and civic virtues.

FROEBEL'S PLAN FOR A KINDERGARTEN (1826)   From Friedrich Froebel, *Pedagogics of the Kindergarten,* Josephine Jarvis, trans. (New York, 1904), pp. 18–22, 32–33.

Plan

I. To provide plays and means of employment (consequently of culture) which satisfy the needs alike of parents and child, of age and youth, or educator and pupil; which therefore nourish and strengthen, develop and form the life of the children, as well as promote the life of the parents and adults—or at least afford them spiritual and intellectual nourishment while they employ themselves in playing with the children—indeed, we might say even while they, as experienced and intelligent parents, and observant and clear-sighted older people, merely observe the plays and spontaneous employment of these children in a thoughtful manner—that is, with spiritual and intellectual sympathy.

The spirit and character of these means of employment, and so of instruction, are therefore that—

1. They proceed from unity, and develop in all manifoldness from unity in accordance with the laws of life. They begin with the simplest, and, at each particular stage, again begin with that which is relatively the simplest; but afterward advance in reciprocally beneficial relation to one another, and according to the necessary laws contained in the nature of the things themselves, from the simplest to the most complex, from that which is as yet undeveloped to that which is fully grown, and so on in accord with natural and spiritual development—in general, with the development of life.

2. The aim of each of the means of employment, and likewise of education, is purely human instruction and cultivation—that is, such as is in itself single as well as unifying—so that through the right, judicious, and spirited use of each (even of the smallest) of these means the human being both in childhood and in maturity will be advanced, educated, and formed as an individual, and also comprehended and developed as a member of humanity—therefore as a member of his family, of his nation, and of humanity, and also as a member of Nature and of the universe—of the one-life and of the all-life.

3. The totality of the plays and means of employment, which are at the same time means of formation of character and of education, as it proceeds from a single, fundamental principle of culture observable in Nature, authenticated by history,

and proving itself to be purely human, forms a stable, coherent whole, all the parts of which reciprocally explain and mutually benefit one another. This whole, therefore, resembles a tree with its many branches.

4. Each individual thing which is attained, however small and simple, or however large and complex it may be, is therefore always a self-contained whole, and so resembles a bud, or a kernel of corn, from which manifold new developments can be called forth, which again converge into a higher unity. Wherefore he who judiciously, energetically, and carefully uses for his little charge what is attained, is himself manifoldly developed as well as harmoniously cultivated.

5. These means of employment will, in the course of their presentation, embrace the whole province of general and fundamental instruction of the faculties of perception. They also will embrace the groundwork of all future extended instruction as a whole, and are founded on the nature of man as an existent, living, and perceptive being. But, as the child at first feels and finds himself in space, and finds others occupying the space around him, these means of employment proceed from space, from the observation of space and from the knowledge which comes from that observation, going on by means of the development and training of the limbs and senses of the human being, and by means of language to comprehend Nature in its most essential directions; so that finally man, who at first could find himself only in space and by means of space, may now learn to find himself as an existent, living, feeling and thinking, understanding and intelligent, perceptive and rational being, to retain the perception of himself as such a being, and, as such, to strive to live.

6. It is quite essential to the spirit and character of these means of fostering independent action in the child that they should lead to the thoughtful observation of Nature and of life in all its parts and phenomena; but it is also essential that they should lead to the anticipation and recognition, and finally to the comprehension of the inner coherence of material things, and of the phenomena of life, and also of the oneness of the material and spiritual worlds, and the increasing similarity of their laws.

7. Thinking and discriminating parents will therefore find these plays and this playing of use and benefit in their business or calling, whether it be an inner one devoted to knowledge or an outward one devoted to work, the results of which can be seen, as even the occupying of one's self therewith in the circle of the children is invigorating and beneficial, elevating and purifying, in its retroactive effect on the life of the adult.

8. Each play, each means of employment, and each means of self-teaching will be accompanied by sufficing instructions which embrace the subject on all sides. These instructions will contain—

a. Description of the nature of play and its higher references to man and to life.

b. Statements of the relation of each individual play and means of employment to the totality, so that with each is specified what, in general, precedes it, what accompanies it, and what follows it; therefore, on what it is founded, and of what it is itself the foundation.

c. A direction sufficient to enable parents and nurses and teachers to use the play, the thing being vivified by the word, the word illustrated by drawings, and these again explained by the word and the thing itself.

d. These instructions will especially render prominent the laws of mental growth proceeding from and leading to the use of play and to its different representations; and

e. Will especially state the firmly, beautifully, and clearly formed truths of

Nature and life obviously contained therein, for the purpose of self-discovery, self-observation, and further self-development, in order to unite man more and more in and with himself, as well as with Nature and life, with the unity and fount of life.

II. In the gradual accomplishment of the whole course, such means of self-cultivation and self-instruction are to be provided as satisfy the needs and requirements of the present stage of human development, and also suffice for adults who wish to continue their own cultivation in accordance therewith. Here will be presented, in conformity with each line of culture and instruction, comprehensive summaries of all parts which belong together, and of the relatively higher unities and the highest unity of these parts. The purpose of these summaries is that the human being—as all unity is, properly speaking, invisible, and only perceptible in the innermost—may be led from the visible and external to the invisible appearance to the true being, and, thus led into himself, may also be led to God; thus man may be clearly shown to man in his nature, in his unfolding, and in his relation to totality and to unity—to Nature and to God—and so may come to man, in all the relations of life, unity and clearness, consciousness and penetration in cultivation, as well as in life and in insight, and therefore joyousness, peace, and freedom.

Since we are now deeply convinced that man, even though only unconsciously faithful to his nature and to the higher and highest demands of humanity of which he is a member, seeks to learn to comprehend and present the outer as well as the inner coherence of life in the higher and highest living unity—in spite of the actual and undeniably apparent disjointedness in life, and the generally prevailing seeking merely for that which is directly and immediately useful in the striving for information—we hope by means of this institution to answer to a need in accordance with the spirit of the age, and to provide such an education of childhood as will correspond to the deepest and most secret (even unknown to themselves) wishes and yearnings of parents and adults, as fosterers of children.

The course of plays and means of employment is to begin with that which is simplest and near; for only that which proceeds from the simplest, smallest, and near can develop from and explain by itself the manifold, great, and distant—can show the spirit of unity; and it is only the single spirit which creates the single life.

And thus we show here, for the fostering of the impulse to activity and of the creative nature of the child, first of all, the details of a whole series of boxes for the play and for the occupation of children in methodical and coherent sequences, stages, and gifts, accompanied by illustrative drawings and text.

FROEBEL ON THE SYMBOLISM OF THE BALL (1826)   From Friedrich Froebel, *Pedagogics of the Kindergarten,* Josephine Jarvis, trans. (New York, 1904), pp. 32–33.

The Ball; the First Plaything of Childhood

Even the word ball, in our significant language, is full of expression and meaning, pointing out that the ball is, as it were, an image of the all *(der B-all ist ein Bild des All);* but the ball itself has such an extraordinary charm, such a constant attraction for early childhood, as well as for later youth, that it is beyond comparison the first as well as the most important plaything of childhood especially. The child loyal to its human nature—at whatever incomplete and dim stage of observation it may be—perceives in the ball the general expression of each object as well as of itself (the child) as a self-dependent whole and unity. It is above all important for the child, as a human being destined to become and in the future to *be* conscious, to perceive that which is inclosed in itself, indeed complete (*vollendeten*), and so, as it were, the counterpart of himself and his opposite; for man seeks even as a child to develop himself as well as everything in Nature by means of that which is its opposite yet resembles it; and so the child likes to employ himself with the ball, even early in life, in order to cultivate and fashion himself, though unconsciously, through and by it, as that which is his opposite and yet resembles him. Indeed, the ball in the totality of its properties, as will be clearly shown in the course of our considerations, is in manifold respects as instructive a type for the child, as the All (the universe), with its phenomena, is for the adult.

There is yet another thing which gives to the ball not only a great charm for the children but likewise deep significance as a plaything, and so as a means of education; this is, that the child, feeling himself a whole, early seeks and must seek in conformity with his human nature and his destiny, even at the stage of unconsciousness, always to contemplate, to grasp, and to possess a whole, but never merely a part as such. He seeks to contemplate, to grasp, and to possess a whole in all things, and in each thing, or at least, by means of and with them. This can be abundantly proved in the history of the development of the individual human being as well as of whole nations, and of all humanity. Many phenomena in child-life, on the bright side of life as well as on the dark, can also be explained thereby. This whole for which the child seeks is also supplied to him by the ball.

Only we further notice in the life of the child how he—like the man in the fairy story—would like to *perceive* all *in* all, and also to make all from each. The ball is well adapted to fulfill this desire also of the child, being (as a whole inclosed in itself) the image of all in general, and also the particular image of individual things; as, for example, the apple, as well as all things which are spherical in form, and from which such manifoldness again develops, such as seed grains and the like. The ball—or, what is the same, the sphere—is actually the foundation, the germ, as it were, of all other forms which can therefore logically be developed from it in conformity with fixed simple laws . . .

Playing at Tennis.

FROEBEL'S SONGS FOR MOTHERS (1843)   From Friedrich Froebel, *Mother's Songs, Games and Stories*, Frances and Emily Lord, trans. (London, 1888), pp. 32–33.

V. A Mother who is Looking at her Growing Child

Mother sees Baby's power unfold,
And says, "This power God keep and hold!
God guide him, be he young or old."
Though in this faith she rests, if she is wise
She knows that she must do what in her lies.

My Baby's as sweet as a flower can be;
If any one doubts, let him just come and see.
His little Head's so round and bare,
So smooth and frank his Forehead there.
And with his Eyes my Child can see so far;
His Ear hears songs and knows how sweet they are.
He smells the flowers with his little Nose;
Into that little Mouth the nice soup goes.
And while he sleeps, his Cheeks get red indeed,—
What more can any little Baby need?
Baby is so fresh and bright
That he may be my delight.
His Hands he can open and shut with such ease!
You can't think how many things Baby can seize.
A little Ball he'll hold so tight—I know
He loves it, and can't bear to let it go.
His little Arms are really very strong,
Move up and down, bend short, or stretch out long.
His little legs spring up so high,
As if he'd like to reach the sky.
Baby, the strength of life in you
Is what is causing all you do.
Then let us guard this precious thing!
Strength peace and happiness will bring.
For only in a happy life you'll find
Delicious consciousness of heart and mind,
And learn to use the whole of life aright
And to enjoy your deeds with all your might.

VI. A Mother and her Child when it Stands on her Lap and Rests in her Arms

Mother, with your Child at play,
In your hearty human way,
If you feel the thing's divine,
As you cherish Darling Mine—
If you feel that there is bliss

In such simple thought as this:
"I am sun from hour to hour
To a little human flower,"—
    All is well,
    I can tell.
For wheresoe'er the sun's rays softly burn,
The inmost hearts of flowers and children turn.

Show me, Dear, your little Eyes,
They'll tell me if your Heart is wise.
Smile with those sweet rosy Lips;
Who looks at roses blessing sips;
Give me your little Mouth that is so sweet,
To kiss my blessing where the soft lips meet.
And put your tiny Hand within my own,
Hands holding hearts, and neither left alone.
Around my neck one soft weak Arm can go;
"It is so nice when Mother holds me so."
And where's your little Ear? Oh! Show me where;
Show me your little Head and fluffy Hair.
    Oh! that my Baby bright,
    Living where Love gives light,
    May bloom as lilies bloom
    When they have sun and room,
    Under home's sheltering eaves,
    And amid life's fresh leaves.
Now let your Feet stand firm on Mother's knee;
So close to her how happy you must be!
She will gladly be the Sun
Of your life, sweet little one.
But now, my Dear, you'll softly rest
On darling Mother's faithful breast;
And you and she will both feel blest.

REMINISCENCES OF FROEBEL (1849)   From Baroness Bertha Von Marenholz-Bulow, *Reminiscences of Friedrich Froebel,* Mary Mann, trans. (Boston, 1877), pp. 1–4.

In the year 1849, at the end of May, I arrived at the Baths of Liebenstein, in Thuringia, and took up my abode in the same house as in the previous year. After the usual salutations, my landlady, in answer to my inquiry as to what was happening in the place, told me that a few weeks before, a man had settled down on a small farm near the springs, who danced and played with the village children, and therefore went by the name of "the old fool." Some days after I met on my walk this so-called "old fool." A tall, spare man, with long gray hair, was leading a troop of village children between the ages of three and eight, most of

EUROPEAN
INFLUENCES

851

them barefooted and but scantily clothed, who marched two and two up a hill, where, having marshalled them for a play, he practised with them a song belonging to it. The loving patience and *abandon* with which he did this, the whole bearing of the man while the children played various games under his direction, were so moving, that tears came into my companion's eyes as well as into my own, and I said to her, "This man is called an 'old fool' by these people; perhaps he is one of those men who are ridiculed or stoned by contemporaries, and to whom future generations build monuments."

The play being ended, I approached the man with the words, "You are occupied, I see, in the education of *the people.*"

"Yes," said he, fixing kind, friendly eyes upon me, "that I am."

"It is what is most needed in our time," was my response. "Unless the people become other than they are, all the beautiful ideals of which we are now dreaming as practicable for the immediate future will not be realized."

"That is true," he replied; "but the 'other people' will not come unless we educate them. Therefore we must be busy with the children."

"But where shall the right education come from? It often seems to me that what we call education is mostly folly and sin, which confines poor human nature in the strait-jacket of conventional prejudices and unnatural laws, and crams so much into it that all originality is stifled."

"Well, perhaps I have found something that may prevent this and make a free development possible. Will you," continued the man, whose name I did not yet know, "come with me and visit my institution? We will then speak further, and understand each other better."

I was ready, and he led me across a meadow to a country-house which stood in the midst of a large yard, surrounded by outhouses. He had rented this place to educate young girls for kindergartners. In a large room, in the middle of which stood a large table, he introduced me to his scholars, and told me the different duties assigned to each in the housekeeping. Among these scholars was Henrietta Breyman, his niece. He then opened a large closet containing his play-materials, and gave some explanation of their educational aim, which at the moment gave me very little light on his method. I retain the memory of only one sentence: "Man is a *creative* being."

But the man and his whole manner made a deep impression upon me. I knew that I had to do with a true MAN, with an original, unfalsified nature. When one of his pupils called him Mr. Froebel, I remembered having once heard of a man of the name who wished to educate children by *play*, and that it had seemed to me a very perverted view, for I had only thought of *empty* play, without any serious purpose.

As Froebel accompanied me part of the way back to Liebenstein, which was about half an hour's distance from his dwelling, we spoke of the disappointment of the high expectations that had been called forth by the movements of 1848, when neither of the parties was right or in a condition to bring about the desired amelioration.

"Nothing comes without a struggle," said Froebel; "opposing forces excite it, and they find their equilibrium by degrees. Strife creates nothing by itself, it only clears the air. New seeds must be planted to germinate and grow, if we will have the tree of humanity blossom. We must, however, take care not to cut away the roots out of which all growth comes, as the destructive element of to-day is liable to do. We cannot tear the present from the past or from the future. Past, present, and future are the trinity of time. The future demands the renewing of life, which must begin in the present. In the *children* lies the seed-corn of the future!"

Thus Froebel expressed himself concerning the movements of the time, always insisting that the historical (traditional) must be respected, and that the new creation can only come forth out of the old.

"That which follows is always conditioned upon that which goes before," he would repeat. "I make that apparent to the children through my educational process." (The Second Gift of his play-materials shows this in concrete things.)

But while Froebel, with his clear comprehension, cast his eyes over the movements of the time, neither joining with the precipitate party of progress nor with the party of reaction that would hinder all progress, he was counted by those in authority among the revolutionists, and condemned with his kindergartens. He repeated again and again: "The destiny of nations lies far more in the hands of women—the mothers—than in the possessors of power, or of those innovators who for the most part do not understand themselves. We must cultivate women, who are the educators of the human race, else the new generation cannot accomplish its task." This was almost always the sum of his discourse.

JOHN GRISCOM'S REPORT ON THE AGRICULTURAL SCHOOL OF EMMANUEL DE FELLENBERG AT HOFWYL, SWITZERLAND

(1818) From *"A Year in Europe . . . ,"* as quoted in Edgar W. Knight, ed., *Reports on European Education* (New York, 1930), pp. 38–46.

After getting our passports examined, by the Austrian minister, at Berne, and taking our dinners at the table d'hote, we set off in a *voiture* provided by our landlord, for Hofwyl, two leagues from Berne, in order to visit the celebrated establishment, or *"Institut d'education,"* of Emmanuel de Fellenberg. It was a rainy day. We passed through a pretty large wood, and arrived at Hofwyl, about 4 o'clock. I was introduced to Fellenberg, by three letters; two from Paris, and one from Geneva. The visiters that resort here are so numerous, and the attention of the principal so much taken up with them, I had been advised to anticipate some difficulty in getting access to him. On presenting myself at the door, I was received by a young man, who appeared to be his clerk, and who, introducing me into the office, requested me to write my name and residence in a book which he gave me. He then announced me to Fellenberg, who politely invited me into the parlour. I produced my letters, which appeared to give him much satisfaction. He is a man of middle age, of a mild and agreeable countenance, and of polite and genteel manners. He seated me on a sofa, and entered upon an explanation of the principles of his establishment, and the particular views of education, which had induced him to engage in it. He considers society as divisible into three distinct parts; the higher, (comprehending the noble and the wealthy,) the middling, and the poor. The greatest defects of education, he supposed to exist in the two extreme classes. That, these distinctions or classes among men, would always prevail, in every civilized country, he believed to be incontrovertible; and, of course, any attempt to break down the distinction, would be fruitless. It is, therefore, of consequence that they should be each educated in a manner conformable to their situations, but both in such a way, as to develope, to the highest extent, the best faculties of their nature;

and, while it preserves the proper relation between them, it should, at the same time, encourage the feelings of kindliness and sympathy on the one part, and of respect and love on the other. This, he thought, could be affected upon no plan, so effectually, as by bringing them up side by side, so that they should have each other constantly in view, without any necessity whatever of mixing or associating. The rich, by observing the industry, the skill, and the importance of the labouring classes, would learn to entertain just sentiments respecting them, and the poor, by feeling and experiencing the kindly influence of the rich, would regard them as benefactors.

With respect to the best means of cultivating the faculties, which, in their due operation, are to promote the permanent happiness of men, he considers agriculture, as affording opportunities and advantages of the greatest importance, and next to this, the mechanic arts. Agreeably to these leading views, his establishment consists of two distinct parts; a boarding school of the sons of noblemen and gentlemen, in which no pains are spared, to provide them with teachers in every useful science; and of a house, in which boys, taken from the poorest class, are clothed and fed in a very plain, coarse, and farmer like style, and who work diligently in the fields, at employments adapted to their strength and skill. During two hours in the day, in summer, and more in winter, they are instructed in letters, and in music. They are likewise introduced into the workshops, and taught the business of a blacksmith, a carpenter, a wheelwright, a cabinet maker, a turner, a shoemaker, or a worker in brass, according as a particular talent for any of these, may manifest itself. The produce of the labour of these boys, bears no inconsiderable proportion of the expense of their maintenance and instruction.

After this brief explanation of his principles, Fellenberg introduced my companions and myself, to Count Louis de Villevielle, a gentleman from the south of France, who, reduced by the revolution, has attached himself to Fellenberg, and appears to live with him, as a sort of companion. He attends to strangers, and goes with them through the grounds, shops, &c. of the establishment. He proved to be a very sensible, well informed man, and altogether disposed to satisfy our inquiries. He conducted us to the workshops. In one of them, a new and handsome fire engine, of a large size, had just been completed in a style which would do credit to London or New York. In these shops, all the instruments of agriculture are made, and it is the constant aim of the principal, to improve upon the form and structure of them, and to invent others which experience may indicate the use of. As they make more than the farm requires, the surplus is sold to the neighbours.

In the evening the Count conducted us to the farmhouse, where the class of the poor boys are lodged, fed, and instructed. We found them at supper, on a kind of hasty-pudding, with whey and boiled potatoes. They breakfast on a piece of bread and an apple, or something as simple, and dine between eleven and twelve, on vegetable food alone. Once a week only, (on first day,) they have meat and wine. They are thus taught a lesson of simplicity, with respect to their manner of living. The furniture of the house corresponds with the dress and clothing of the boys. After supper they went up stairs to the schoolroom, to take a lesson in music. Their teacher (Vehrly) is a young man of very extraordinary qualifications. He received his early education from his father, who filled, in a distinguished manner, the office of schoolmaster for thirty years. He began at an early age to assist his parent in the discharge of his office. On coming to reside with Fellenberg, his views were further expanded, and he entered with enthusiasm into the concerns of the establishment, and willingly undertook the formation and direction of the class of the poor, in all their exercises, agricultural, literary, scientific, and moral. He lives with them, eats, sleeps, and works with them, dresses as they do, and makes himself their friend and companion, as well as their instructor. He is eminently fitted for such an occupation by his genius, his address, his temper and disposition, and above all by his religious principles. The schoolroom serves also for a shoemakers' shop, and probably accommodates, occasionally, the taylor and harness maker. The boys always take a lesson of one hour, between supper and bed. This lesson is frequently confined to music. They are taught it by principles, but they use no instrument but their vocal organs. Fellenberg lays great stress on music, as a means of bringing the mind and heart into harmony with truth, and of inspiring the mild and benevolent affections. He thinks it has been very beneficial in reclaiming many of these boys, from the vicious habits they had acquired from the low and exposed lives they had been subject to. By teaching them to sing religious songs, together with those that are simply patriotic, he says their attention is diverted from those vile ballads which are common among low bred people; and that they find, in this new entertainment, a happy substitute for the coarse and vulgar expressions to which they were addicted. The boys of this class appeared to be very healthy and contented. They are taught to pay the utmost attention to cleanliness. Their clothing in summer, is of coarse cotton, and in winter, of woollen cloth. They go barefooted, except when they work in the fields, or when the state of the weather requires them to wear shoes and stockings. They are always without any thing on their heads. Many of them, as might naturally be supposed, entered the school with the seeds of scrophulous disorders; but by the effect of a simple and wholesome diet, cleanliness, and labour, they are restored to health with scarcely any medicine. Some of them, on their entrance, were feeble and debilitated, unable to endure cold, heat, or labour; but when once they have become accustomed to the regimen of the school, they willingly encounter rain, storms, and severe cold, whenever their work calls them abroad, without shrinking from, or regarding the exposure. They are taught to mend their own clothes. In summer they rise at five, and in winter at six; and after having dressed themselves and said their prayers, they receive instruction for an hour. They then breakfast, after which they go to work until half past eleven. They have then half an hour for dinner; after which Vehrly gives them a lesson of one hour. They work out till six, and after eating their supper, receive further instruction, which concludes with prayer, and they are generally in bed between eight and nine o'clock. But this distribution of time varies according to the seasons. In winter five or six hours a day are devoted to sedentary instruction. The morning of the first day of the week, is always devoted to exercises of piety, and after dinner some hours are given to instruction in sacred history. But their lessons are by no means confined to the school room. Vehrly takes pleasure in questioning them on subjects of natural history, geography, religion, morals, or any other useful topic, while they are at work in the fields or shops; and it may readily be conceived, that with this devotion to the improvement of his pupils, occasions will perpetually present themselves, of conveying instruction in every kind of knowledge, calculated to expand the minds of children, and to cultivate their best affections.

With regard to the most effective means of eliciting the powers of the mind, and of conducting the literary exercises of young people, great credit is due to Pestalozzi, whose veteran labours, as one of the most enlightened teachers of the age, were well known and acknowledged long before the commencement of the Hofwyl Institution. His plans of communicating knowledge, are in a great measure, practised by Vehrly. Much pains are taken to impress on the minds of the pupils, a deep sense of the importance of time, and of habits of industry; and from the reports that have been published by commissioners appointed to examine the establishments, it is evident that the most favourable results have attended these endeavours. The children are so effectually redeemed from their former vicious habits, that, in their most free and noisy sports, not an expression is heard, offensive to innocence or good manners. After working 10 hours in the day, they give themselves up, when their teacher permits, to the liveliest recreation; but a word from Vehrly, is sufficient to induce them to leave their sport and to engage in some other exercise. The progress which they make in knowledge, is truly surprising, when it is considered how adverse their former habits have been to all intellectual abstraction. In a few years, or even in less time, they learn to read, write and calculate, with and without the use of pencil or pen; the elements of drawing become familiar to them; and they acquire good notions of geometry, especially in its relation to field surveying, and its application to descriptive drawing. Botany and mineralogy constitute part of their amusements. They become well acquainted with all the plants of Hofwyl, and their different qualities, both the salutary and noxious. Of the minerals also, they acquire the names and principal uses, and they make collections of all that is valuable and curious in minerals and vegetables. Some of them are very attentive to the improvement of their little cabinets. The principal, when walking with them in the fields, is often called upon to decide disputes relative to the nature of stones or vegetables. But the most admirable trait in the character of this school, is the tone of religious feeling which, it is said, pervades it. This could not be accomplished, were not Fellenberg and Vehrly, both strongly imbued with a sense of religious obligation, and unremittingly attentive to awaken those sentiments in the minds of the pupils. They have learned by heart more than 50 hymns, and many portions of sacred history. They are regularly attentive to one practice, which is a pleasing source of instruction, and at the same time serves to demonstrate the progress they have made in useful acquirements. At the close of every week, they write, in a book provided for the purpose, an account of whatever has impressed their minds with the greatest force. It may be either a moral reflection, a description of a plant, or an instrument, an account of a conversation, or an extract from some thing they have read. We saw some of these journals; they were mostly in the German language, and the greater number were written with remarkable neatness. Some of them contained drawings that evinced no inconsiderable skill, and an eye accustomed to accuracy of observation.

It will readily be conceived that a plan of instruction so admirable, and constantly directed to the best and purest affections of the mind and heart, can scarcely fail to redeem from indolence and vice, those whose habits have been the most degraded. And it has accordingly happened, that notwithstanding the boys under Vehrly's charge have been taken from the very lowest ranks, some of them the children of beggars, but one instance has occurred, of such inveterate vice, as to render it eventually necessary to abandon the culprit to his corrupt propensities, and expel him from the school.

In the religious exercises, which take place on the first day of the week, the boys of the poor school assemble with the superior class, but on no other occasion.

After seeing the evening exercise of these boys, we retired to an inn, at the village of Buchsee, about a quarter of a mile from Hofwyl. This was only a village inn, but we found in it good beds, and good attention.

HERBART ON THE SCIENCE OF EDUCATION (1806) From Johann Friedrich Herbart, *The Science of Education,* Herman M. and Emmie Felkin, trans. (Boston, 1896), pp. 106–7, 109–10, 120–21, 140–47.

Education Proper

The art of arousing a child's mind from its repose—of securing its trust and love in order to constrain and excite it at pleasure, and to plunge it into the whirl of later years before its time, would be the most hateful of all bad arts, if it had not an aim to attain, which can justify such means even in the eyes of those whose reproof is most to be feared. "You will be thankful for it some day," says the teacher to the weeping boy, and truly it is only this hope that justifies the tears wrung from him. Let him be careful that, in overweening confidence, he does not too frequently have recourse to such severe measures. Not all that is well meant is thankfully received, and there is a weak spot in the class of that teacher, who, with perverted zeal, considers that as good which his pupils only experience as evil. Hence the warning—do not educate too much; refrain from all avoidable applications of that power by which the teacher bends his pupils this way and that, dominates their dispositions, and destroys their cheerfulness. For thus, the subsequent happy recollection of childhood will also be destroyed, and that frank gratitude which is a teacher's only true thanks.

Is it then better not to educate at all? to confine ourselves to government, and limit even this to what is absolutely necessary? If every one were candid, many would agree to this. The praise already given to England would be repeated; and if once it became a question of praising, excuses would be found for the lack of government, which allows so much license to young gentlemen of position in that happy island. But let us put aside all disputes. The sole question for us is, *can we know beforehand the aims of the future man, a knowledge for which he will one day thank us, instead of having had to find and follow them by himself alone?* If so, no further foundation is needed—we *love* the children, and in them, the men; love does not love doubts any more than it cares to wait for the categorical imperative.

*   *   *

It is impossible, from the nature of the case, that unity in the aim of education can follow; simply, because everything must proceed from the single thought, namely, *that the teacher must represent the future man in the boy, consequently the aims which the pupil will as an adult place before himself in the future must be the present care of the teacher; he must prepare beforehand an inward facility for attaining them.* He ought not to stunt the activity of the future man; consequently he ought not to confine it to single points, and just as little weaken it by too much diversity. He ought to allow nothing to be lost, either in *Intension* or *Extension,* which his pupil might afterwards demand back from him. However great or little these difficulties may be, so much is clear—*since human aims are manifold, the teacher's cares must be manifold also.*

It is not however, here contended that the multiplicities of education cannot easily be classified under one or a few main formal conceptions; on the contrary, the kingdom of the pupil's future aims at once divides itself for us into the province of *merely possible aims* which he might perhaps take up at one time or other and pursue in greater or less degree as he wishes—and into the entirely distinct province of the *necessary aims* which he would never pardon himself for having neglected. In one word, the aim of education is sub-divided according to the aims of *choice*—not of the teacher, nor of the boy, but of the future man, and the aims of *morality*. These two main headings are at once clear to everyone who bears in mind the most generally recognised of the fundamental principles of ethics.

*   *   *

MANY-SIDEDNESS OF INTEREST—STRENGTH OF MORAL CHARACTER

(1) How can the teacher assume for himself beforehand the merely *possible* future aims of the pupil?

The objective of these aims as matter of mere choice has absolutely no interest for the teacher. Only the Will of the future man himself, and consequently the sum of the claims which he, in, and with, this Will, will make on himself, is the object of the teacher's *goodwill;* while the power, the initiative inclination, the activity which the future man will have wherewith to meet these claims on himself, form for the teacher matter for consideration and judgment in accordance with the idea of *perfection.* Thus it is not a certain number of separate aims that hover before us now (for these we could not beforehand thoroughly know), but chiefly the *activity* of the growing man—the totality of his inward unconditioned vitality and susceptibility. The greater this totality—*the fuller, more expanded, and harmonious*—the greater is the perfection, and the greater the promise of the realisation of our good will.

*   *   *

THE INDIVIDUALITY OF THE PUPIL AS POINT OF INCIDENCE

The teacher aims at the universal; the pupil, however, is an individual human being.

Without compounding the soul out of all kinds of forces, and without constructing the brain out of organs positively useful and able to relieve the mind of a part of its work, we must accept those experiences undisputed, and in their entirety, in harmony with which, the spirit, according to the physical form in which it is embodied, finds in its functions sundry difficulties, and their conversely relative facilities.

But however much we may be challenged to test the flexibility of such natures by experiment, and in no way out of respect for their superiority to attempt to excuse our own inertness, we see already that the purest and best presentation of humanity shows us at the same time a particular man. Yes, and we feel that the individuality *must* come to the surface, if the example of the race is not to appear insignificant by the side of the race itself, and fade away as indifferent.

*   *   *

Interest arises from interesting objects and occupations. Many-sided interest originates in the *wealth* of these. To create and develop this interest is the task of instruction, which carries on and completes the preparation begun by intercourse and experience.

In order that character may take a moral direction, individuality must be held dipped, as it were, in a fluid element, which according to circumstances either resists or favours it, but for the most part is hardly perceptible to it. This element is *discipline*, which is mainly operative on the arbitrary will (Willkür), but also partially on the judgment.

Much has already been said about discipline, when speaking of government and of instruction in the Introduction. If it is not apparent therefrom why the first place is assigned to instruction, and the second to discipline in thinking out educational measures systematically, we can only again call attention to the religion between many-sided interest and moral character in the course of this treatise. If morality has no root in many-sidedness, then certainly discipline may be properly considered independently of instruction; the teacher must then directly so grasp, so charm and so constrain the individual, that the good rises with strength, and the evil sinks and gives way. Teachers, however, must ask themselves whether a mere discipline, so abstract and compulsory, has been recognized as possible till now? If not, they have every reason to suppose that *the individuality must first be changed through widened interest, and approximate to a general form, before they can venture to think they will find it amenable to the general obligatory moral law.*

In dealing with previously neglected subjects, the teacher will have to measure that which admits of treatment, besides taking into account the individuality before him, chiefly by the subject's receptibility and fitness for a new and better circle of thought. If the estimate of this receptibility and fitness be unfavourable, it is clear that education proper must be superseded by a watchful and trustworthy government, which will have to be undertaken by the State or some other influential body.

*　　*　　*

STEPS IN INSTRUCTION

What things must take place consecutively and one through the other, and what on the contrary must do so contemporaneously, and each with its proper and original power—are questions which touch all employments and all plans in which a great number of complicated measures have to be carried out. For a beginning is always made at the same time from several sides; and much always must be prepared by what has gone before. These are as it were the two dimensions, conformably to which we have to guide our steps.

*　　*　　*

The varieties of interest then which instruction ought to cultivate, present to us only differences in things simultaneous, but not a distinct succession of steps.

On the other hand, the formal fundamental concepts developed in the beginning, are based on the antitheses between things which follow one upon another.

Concentration, above all, ought to precede reflection, but at what distance? This

EUROPEAN INFLUENCES

question remains generally undetermined. Both certainly must be kept as near as possible together, for we desire no concentrations to the detriment of personal unity, which is preserved by means of reflection. Their long and unbroken succession would create a tension, incompatible with the existence of the healthy mind in the healthy body. In order then always to maintain the mind's coherence, instruction must follow the rule of giving equal weight in every smallest possible group of its objects to concentration and reflection; that is to say, it must care equally and in regular succession for clearness of every particular, for association of the manifold, for coherent ordering of what is associated, and for a certain practice in progression through this order. Upon this depends the distinctness which must rule in all that is taught. The teacher's greatest difficulty here, perhaps, is to find real particulars—to analyze his own thoughts into their elements. Text books can in this case partly prepare the ground.

If however, instruction handles each little group of objects in this manner, many groups arise in the mind, and each one is grasped by a relative concentration until all are united in a higher reflection. But the union of the groups presupposes the perfect unity of each group. So long, therefore, as it is still possible for the last particular in the content of each group to fall apart from the rest, higher reflection cannot be thought of. But there is above this higher reflection a still higher, and so on indefinitely upwards, to the all-embracing highest, which we seek through the system of systems, but never reach. In earlier years nothing of this can be attempted; youth is always in an intermediate state between concentration and distraction. We must be contented in earlier years with not attempting to give what we call system in the higher sense, but must on the other hand so much the more create clearness in every group; we must associate the groups more sedulously and variously, and be careful that *the approach to the all-embracing reflection is made equally from all sides.*

Upon this depends the articulation of instruction. The larger members are composed of smaller, as are the lesser of the least. In each of the smallest members, four stages of instruction are to be distinguished; it must provide for Clearness, Association, Arrangement, and the Course of this order. These grades, follow one another more slowly, when those next in comprehensiveness are formed from the smallest members, and with ever-increasing spaces of time, as higher steps of reflection have to be climbed.

If we now look back on the analysis of the concept of interest, we find therein also, certain steps differentiated—Observation, Expectation, Demand and Action.

Observation depends on the relative power of a presentation to that of others which must yield to it—depends therefore partly on the intrinsic strength of the one, partly on the ease with which the remainder yield. The latter leads to the idea of a discipline of thought, which we preferred to treat of specially in the *A B C of Anschauung.* The strength of a presentation can be partly attained through the power of the sensuous impression (as, for example, through the simultaneous speaking of several children, also by the display of the same object in different ways with drawings, instruments, models, etc.), partly through the vividness of descriptions, especially if already connected presentations rest in the depths of the mind, which will unite with the one to be given. To effect this union generally, there is need of great skill and thought, which aims at anticipating future efforts by giving something to prepare the ground for them, as for instance the *A B C of Anschauung* does for mathematics, as the play of combinations does for grammar, and as narratives from antiquity do for a classical author.

Through observation the singular becomes distinct, but association, order, and progress according to order, must also be observed.

In the same way we get clearness of the expectations and association of them; in fact, systematic and methodical expectation.

Nevertheless these complications do not now claim our chief interest. We know that when the expected appears, only a new observation is produced. This is generally the case in the sphere of knowledge. Where some store of knowledge is already accumulated, it is not easy to observe anything to which expectations were not attached, yet the expectation dies out or becomes satisfied with new knowledge. If vehement desires arise therefrom, they would fall under the rule of temperance and consequently of discipline. But there is a species of observation which is not so easily satisfied or forgotten; there is a demand which is intended to be transformed into action; this is the *demand for sympathy*. Whatever rights then temperance exercises in this case, that education would nevertheless be a failure which did not leave behind resolutions to work for the good of humanity and society, as well as a certain energy of the religious postulate. Accordingly, in the cultivation of sympathy, the higher steps to which interest may pass come much into consideration. And it is quite clear that these steps correspond with those of human life. In the child a *sympathising observation* is appropriate, in the boy *expectation*, in the youth the *demand for sympathy*, that the man may *act* for it. The articulation of instruction, however, here permits again, even in the smallest subjects which belong to early years, demand (for sympathy) to be so stimulated that it would pass into action. Out of such stimulations there grows in later years, assisted at the same time by the formation of character, that powerful demand which begets actions.

Allow me briefly to define the results in few words, which can easily be understood.

Instruction must universally
> point out,
> connect,
> teach,
> philosophise.

In matters appertaining to sympathy it should be
> observing,
> continuous,
> elevating,
> active in the sphere of reality.

SEGUIN ON THE PHYSIOLOGICAL METHOD OF EDUCATION

(**1866**)   From Edouard Seguin, *Idiocy and Its Treatment By the Physiological Method* (New York, 1866), pp. 32–36.

According to this method education is the *ensemble* of the means of developing harmoniously and effectively the moral, intellectual, and physical capacities, as functions, in man and mankind.

To be physiological, education must at first follow the great natural law of action and repose, which is life itself. To adapt this law to the whole training, each function in its turn is called to activity and to rest; the activity of one favoring the repose of the other; the improvement of one reacting upon the improvement of all others; contrast being not only an instrument of relaxation, but of comprehension also.

But before entering farther into the generalities of the training, the individuality of the children is to be secured: for respect of individuality is the first test of the fitness of a teacher. At first sight all children look much alike; at the second their countless differences appear like insurmountable obstacles; but better viewed, these differences resolve themselves into groups easily understood, and not unmanageable. We find congenital or acquired anomalies of function which need to be suppressed, or to be given a better employment; deficiencies to be supplied; feebleness to be strengthened; peculiarities to be watched; eccentricities to be guarded against; propensities needing a genial object; mental aptness, or organic fitness requiring specific openings. This much, at least, and more if possible, will secure the sanctity of true originality against the violent sameness of that most considerable part of education, the general training.

The general training embraces the muscular, imitative, nervous, and reflective functions, susceptible of being called into play at any moment. All that pertains to movement, as locomotion and special motions; prehension, manipulation, and palpation, by dint of strength, or exquisite delicacy; imitation and communication from mind to mind, through languages, signs, and symbols; all that is to be treated thoroughly. Then, from imitation is derived drawing; from drawing, writing; from writing, reading; which implies the most extended use of the voice in speaking, music, etc. The senses are trained, not only each one to be perfect in itself; but, as to a certain extent other organs may be made receivers of food in lieu of the stomach and one emunctory may take the place of another, likewise the senses must be educated, so that if the use of any one be lost, another may feel and perceive for it. The same provision is to be made for the use of both sides of the body; the left being made competent to do anything for the right. But, instead of this, the present use of our senses is nearly empirical. No mechanic sees well enough at first sight all the parts of an engine; no draughtsman draws his pencil exactly where he means to; no painter can create the shades he has before him; no physician whose tact is perfect enough for the requirements of his profession: the imperfection of our sensorial and motive education always betrays, instead of executing the dictates of our will. Let our natural senses be developed as far as possible, and we are not near the limits of their capacity. Then the instruments of artificial senses are to be brought in requisition; the handling of the compass, the prism, the most philosophical of them, the microscope and others must be made familiar to all children, who shall learn how to see nature through itself, instead of through twenty-six letters of the alphabet; and shall cease to learn by rote, by trust, by faith, instead of by knowing.

True knowledge comes only in this wise. When a sense meets with a phenomenon, the mind is awakened to the reality of the latter by its elements, which mark its analogy to and difference from other phenomena, the mind receives from said analogy and difference the impression which constitutes the image to be stored, evoked, compared, combined, etc. The character of the analogies and differences presented to the mind by circumstances, and mostly by education, forms our stock of ideas; thus the same piece of muscle looked at by the butcher-boy or by the microscopist awakens images entirely different, and ideas whose associations shall differ more and more at each new combination. The comparison of simple ideas produces compound ones: ideal creations of the mind, whose existence is purely relative to that mind or to its congeners. The assemblage in the same field of comparison of a great number of ideas, primary or compound, gives rise to general ideas, as those of order, classification, configuration, etc. Ideas in their generality are abstract creations of the mind only commensurate with Immensity. As examples of generalizations may be mentioned, the progress of the knowledge of the surface of the earth, as leading to the generalization of its curves into the idea of its Globular shape: idea which sent Columbus in search of the antipodes; the idea of the quasi-infinite divisibility of matter which produced the Atomic theory; the presence of bodies everywhere, which gives plausibility to the hypothesis of Space; the suffering of the toiling masses which elevated the mind to the conception of Equality; the general harmony of the universe which dispelled the successive mythologies founded upon temporary antagonism of elements, and made room for the idea of the Unity of our nature. Thus correct sensations being the ground of correct images, images being stored as simple ideas, the contact of which produces comparisons whose abundance leads to generalizations; till the mind embraces knowingly and willingly from the simplest image to the most synthetic idea.

In previous periods the total absence of general education for the masses, and of systematic training for the perceptive, inductive, and deductive faculties in each individual, made progress a spasmodic affair, quite properly attributed to blind fate; whereas, in the future, progress resulting from the equal education of all women and men, and from the direct training of all their functions, shall appear to every mind as it really is, issuing from an intelligent and understood Providence, which leads us through a continuous series of improvements towards our religious destiny.

At this point physiological education merges into the moral training. This we cannot even sketch without going beyond the object of this introduction, which was two-fold.

1st. To trace the origin of the methodical treatment of idiots and their congeners.

2d. To present the philosophical history of the idea of training the functions, and all the faculties as functions (instead of only instructing children); from its germination to its maturation in the school for idiots, and to its actual fitness for the training of all children.

PREYER DESCRIBES THE MIND OF THE CHILD (1888)   From W. Preyer, *The Mind of the Child,* H. W. Brown, trans. (New York, 1896), vol. I, pp. ix-xv, 1–7, vol. II, pp. 3, 6–11, 208–12.

Author's Preface to the First Edition

I proposed to myself a number of years ago, the task of studying the child, both before birth and in the period immediately following, from the physiological point of view, with the object of arriving at an explanation of the origin of the separate vital processes. It was soon apparent to me that a division of the work would be advantageous to its prosecution. For life in the embryo is so essentially different a thing from life beyond it, that a separation must make it easier both for the investigator to do his work and for the reader to follow the exposition of its results. I have, therefore, discussed by itself, life before birth, the "Physiology of the Embryo." The vital phenomena of the human being in the earliest period of his independent existence in the world are, again, so complicated and so various in kind, that here too a division soon appeared expedient. I separated the physical development of the newly-born and the very young child from his mental development, and have endeavored to describe the latter in the present book; at least, I hope that, by means of personal observations carried on for several years, I have furnished facts that may serve as material for a future description.

A forerunner of the work is a lecture, "Psychogenesis" (the Genesis of Mind), given before a scientific association at Berlin on the 3d of January, 1880, and soon after made public in my book, "Naturwissenschaftliche Thatsachen and Probleme" ("Facts and Problems of Natural Science") Berlin, 1880.

This sketch has given manifold incitement to fresh observations. But great as is the number of occasional observations in regard to many children, I do not thus far know of diaries regularly kept concerning the mental development of individual children. Now precisely this chronological investigation of mental progress in the first and second years of life presents great difficulties, because it requires the daily registering of experiences that can be had only in the nursery. I have, notwithstanding, kept a complete diary from the birth of my son to the end of his third year. Occupying myself with the child at least three times a day—at morning, noon, and evening—and almost every day, with two trifling interruptions, and guarding him, as far as possible, against such training as children usually receive, I found nearly every day some fact of mental genesis to record. The substance of that diary has passed into this book.

No doubt the development of one child is rapid and that of another is slow; very great individual differences appear in children of the same parents even, but the differences are much more of time and degree than of the order in which the steps are taken, and these steps are the same in all individuals; that is the important matter. Desirable as it is to collect statistics concerning the mental development of *many* infants—the activity of their senses, their movements, especially their acquirement of speech—yet the accurate, daily repeated observation of *one* child—a child sound in health, having no brothers or sisters, and whose development was neither remarkably rapid nor remarkably slow—seemed at least quite as much to be desired. I have, however, taken notice, as far as possible, of the experiences of others in regard to other normal children in the first years of life, and have even compared many of these where opportunity offered.

But a description of the gradual appearance of brain-activity in the child, along with the most careful observation of his mental ripening, would be only a beginning. The development of mind, like the development of body, must be regarded as dating back far beyond the origin of the individual being.

If the infant brings into the world a set of organs which begin to be active only after a long time, and are absolutely useless up to that time—as, e. g., the lungs were before birth—then the question, To what causes do such organs and functions owe their existence? can have but one answer—*heredity*.

This, to be sure, explains nothing; but dim as the notion is, much is gained toward our understanding of the matter, in the fact that some functions are inherited while others are not.

What is acquired by experience is only a part. The question whether a function of the brain, on which everything depends in the development of the child's mind, is inherited, or acquired, must be answered in each individual case, if we would not go astray in the labyrinth of appearance and hypotheses.

Above all, we must be clear on this point, that the fundamental activities of the mind, which are manifested only after birth, do not originate after birth.

If they had previously no existence at all, we could not discover whence they come or at what time. The substance of a hen's egg that has been fecundated, but is frozen as hard as a stone, certainly has no sensation; but after thawing and three weeks' warming, that same substance, changed into a living chicken, has sensation.

The capacity of feeling, in case of the fulfillment of certain outward conditions, if it be not a property of the egg, must have originated during incubation from matter incapable of sentiency; that is, the material atoms must not only have arranged themselves in a different order, receiving through their union and separation different chemical properties, as actually happens; must not only have changed their physical properties—e. g., elasticity, solidity, etc., which are partly dependent on the chemical, partly independent of them—as likewise happens; but these atoms must have gained entirely new properties which were neither chemically nor physically indicated beforehand, were not to be assumed or predicated. For neither chemistry nor physics can attribute to the substances that constitute the egg other than chemical and physical properties. But if the warming, ventilation, evaporation, and liberation of carbonic acid have had their normal course during incubation, then these new mental properties present themselves, and that without the possibility of their being gained by imitation in the incubator. And these properties are similar to those of the beings that produced the egg. Hence, it must be admitted that these beings have imparted to the egg matter which contained, in addition to the known or physically and chemically discoverable properties, latent properties not chemically and physically discoverable—psychical, therefore, physiological—these being potential, so that warming, airing, etc., are necessary to their development. The same conditions are required for the development of the tissues and organs of the embryo, which likewise were not contained in the albumen, sugar, and fat, in the water and the salts of the egg; neither do their properties belong to those with which chemistry and physics are concerned, but they are like those of the generators of the egg.

Some parts of the contents of the egg, then, possess potentially properties unquestionably mental—the capacity of sensation, at least. And these parts must, at the same time, be those from which originate the cotyledons (of plants), the foundation of the embryo. As is well known, they are cellular forms with the power of independent movement, to which can not be denied, any more than to the lowest zoophytes, the capacity of discrimination. They grow and move by putting out and drawing in pseudopodia;[1] they undoubtedly appropriate nourishment, require oxygen, multiply by division, conduct themselves in general like *amoebæ*, or other simple living things. The opinion that they possess a certain crude psychical endowment, sensation of an obscure sort, can not be refuted.

Everything goes to show a continuity in the capacity of sensation. This capacity does not spring afresh each time in the human being out of material incapable of sensation, but, as a hereditary property of the parts of the egg, is differentiated in these, and by stimulus from without is brought into action—the process being hardly discernible in the embryo protected from this stimulus, but plainly visible in the new-born child.

[1]Filaments thrust out from any part of the body, serving as organs of locomotion.

The mind of the new-born child, then, does not resemble a *tabula rasa,* upon which the senses first write their impressions, so that out of these the sum-total of our mental life arises through manifold reciprocal action, but the tablet is already written upon before birth, with many illegible, nay, unrecognizable and invisible, marks, the traces of the imprint of countless sensuous impressions of long-gone generations. So blurred and indistinct are these remains, that we might, indeed, suppose the tablet to be blank, so long as we did not examine the changes it undergoes in earliest youth. But the more attentively the child is observed, the more easily legible becomes the writing, not at first to be understood, that he brings with him into the world. Then we perceive what a capital each individual has inherited from his ancestors—how much there is that is not produced by sense-impressions, and how false is the supposition that man learns to feel, to will, and to think, only through his senses. Heredity is just as important as individual activity in the genesis of mind. No man is in this matter a mere upstart, who is to achieve the development of his mind (Psyche) through his individual experience alone; rather must each one, by means of his experience, fill out and animate anew his inherited endowments, the remains of the experiences and activities of his ancestors.

It is hard to discern and to decipher the mysterious writing on the mind of the child. It is just that which constitutes a chief problem of this book.

*　　*　　*

Development of the Senses

The foundation of all mental development is the activity of the senses. We can not conceive of anything of the nature of mental genesis as taking place without that activity.

Every sense-activity is fourfold in its character: First, there is an *excitement of the nerves;* then comes *sensation;* and not until the sensation has been localized in space and referred to some point in time, do we have a *perception.* When, further, the cause of this is apprehended, then the perception becomes an *idea.*

The adult human being is a person who is responsible, who acts according to his own pleasure, and is capable of independent thought. For our understanding of his psychical states and processes, it is of great importance to know what is the condition of things as to the above stages of sense-activity, in the newly-born, and in the infant, who is not responsible, who does not act according to his pleasure, and does not think at all.

I have therefore instituted many observations concerning the gradual perfecting of the senses at the beginning of life, and I commence with a description of them. In these observations I have had especially in mind the prominent part played in the mental development of the child, at the earliest period, by the sense of sight.

Sight

The observations with regard to the development of the sense of sight during the first years relate to sensibility to light, discrimination of colors, movements of the eyelids, movements of the eyes, direction of the look, seeing of near and distant objects, and interpretation of what is seen. To these are attached some statements concerning sight in new-born animals.

1. SENSIBILITY TO LIGHT

My child's sensibility to light, when he was held toward the window in the dusk, five minutes after birth, did not seem unusually great. For he opened and shut his eyes, with alternate movement, so that the space between the lids was about five millimetres wide. Soon after, I saw in the twilight both eyes wide open. At the same time the forehead was wrinkled.

Long before the close of the first day, the child's expression, as he was held with his face toward the window, became suddenly different when I shaded his eyes with my hand. The dim light, therefore, undoubtedly made an impression, and, to judge from his physiognomy, an agreeable one; for the shaded face had a less contented look.

On the second day the eyes close quickly when a candle is brought near them; on the ninth, the head is also turned away vigorously from the flame, when the candle is brought near, immediately after the awaking of the child. The eyes are shut tight. But, on the following day, the child being in the bath, when a candle was held before him at a distance of one metre, the eyes remained wide open. The sensitiveness to light is, therefore, so much greater at the moment of waking than it is a short time afterward, that the same object causes at the one time great annoyance and at the other time pleasure.

Again, on the eleventh day, the child seemed to be much pleased by a candle burning before him at a distance of one half a metre, for he gazed at it steadily with wide-open eyes, as he did also, later, at a shining curtain-holder, when the bright object was brought into his line of vision, so that it was in the direction in which he seemed to be gazing. If I turned the child away, he became fretful and began to cry; if I turned him to the light again, then his countenance resumed the expression of satisfaction. To verify this, I held the child that same day at the same distance before a burning candle, once immediately after his waking, and again after he had been awake some time in the dark. In both cases he shut his eyes.

That he liked moderately bright daylight was apparent from the frequent turning of his head toward the window when I turned him away from it. This twisting of the head became the rule on the sixth day; on the seventh it was often repeated, and every time that the face was turned toward the window the expression of satisfaction was unmistakable.

I have repeatedly made the observation that, when the light falls upon the face of sleeping infants they suddenly close the eyes more tightly, without waking, and this from the tenth day on.

In the case of my child, I found the pupils in ordinary daylight for the most part more contracted than is the case in adults—certainly less than two millimetres in diameter; and the lessening of the space between the lids, at sight of a bright surface of snow or of a shining summer cloud, was likewise more frequent and more persistent than with adults, during the whole period of observation.

Brightly-shining objects, appearing in the field of vision, often produce, from the second month on, exclamations of delight. But other highly-colored objects also easily arouse the attention of the infant. In the tenth month he is pleased when the lamp is lighted in the evening; he laughs at the light, and reaches after the bright globe.

Of the observations of others concerning the sensibility of new-born human beings to light, the following are to be mentioned:

1. Fully-matured children just born shut the eyes quickly and convulsively when exposed to bright light. Individuals, also, among children born two months too soon, distinguish between light and darkness on the second day.

2. In the very first hours the pupil of the eye contracts in a bright light, and expands in light less bright.

3. If one eye of the new-born child is shut while the other is open, then the pupil of the latter expands.

4. Infants from two to four days old, sleeping in the dark, shut the lids tightly, and even awake with a start when the bright light of a candle comes very near their eyes.

To these statements of Prof. Kussmaul, the first of which, in particular, I can confirm, Dr. Genzmer adds that the eyes of the newly-born, when suddenly exposed to bright light, make a movement of convergence; and that sensitive infants are brought into a state of general discomfort and made to cry, by a sudden glare of light, or by a quickly-changing, dazzling light; this I can confirm. The alternate shutting and opening of the eyes, that is often to be seen in infants exposed to bright light, was seen by Genzmer even in a sleeping child two days old—a remarkable observation, which waits confirmation. On the other hand, I never saw a newborn child bear dazzling bright light quietly with open eyes. Assertions of an experience contrary to this may, perhaps, rest on the observation of children born blind.

From all the foregoing statements we conclude that, with fully-matured new-born human beings, sensibility to light is normally present either directly after birth, or a few minutes, or at most a few hours, after birth; that light and darkness are discriminated in sensation; further, that the reflex arc from the optic nerve to the *oculomotorius* already performs its function—especially is this true of the filaments that contract the pupils. Here, then, we have an inborn reflex, and that of a double sort, since both pupils contract when the light reaches one of them. Further, at the beginning, sensibility to light on awaking, or after being awhile in the dark, amounts to an aversion to light; yet a dim light is already sought, and therefore is not unpleasant. Finally, we infer that after some days ordinary daylight, or a brilliant and brightly-shining object, excites cheerfulness, the aversion to light disappears, and the head is turned oftener to the window.

2. DISCRIMINATION OF COLORS

At what age the child is capable of distinguishing colors, at least red, yellow, green, and blue, it is hard to determine. In the first days, it is certain that only the difference of light and dark is perceived, and this imperfectly; moreover (according to Flechsig), the *tractus opticus,* which in the matured child is still gray at first, does not get its nerve medulla, and with that its permanent coloring, till three or four days after birth. And even then the differentiation of simultaneous bright and dark impressions proceeds slowly.

The first object that made an impression on account of its color, upon my boy, was probably a rose-colored curtain which hung, brightly lighted by the sun but not dazzlingly bright, about a foot before the child's face. This was on the twenty-third day. The child laughed and uttered sounds of satisfaction.

As the smooth, motionless, bright-colored surface alone occupied the whole field of vision, it must have been on account either of its brightness or of its color that it was the source of pleasure. In the evening of the same day, the flame of the candle, at the distance of one metre, caused quite similar expressions of pleasure when it was placed before the eyes, which had been gazing into empty space; and so did, on the forty-second day, the sight of colored tassels in motion, but in this case the movement also was a source of pleasure.

In the eighty-fifth week, when I undertook the first systematic tests, with counters alike in form but unlike in color, no trace of discrimination in color was as yet to be discerned, although without doubt it already existed. Different as were the impressions of sound made by the words "red," "yellow," "green," "blue" (these were certainly distinguished from one another), and well as the child knew the meaning of "give," he was not able to give the counters of the right color, even when only "red" and "green" were called for. We are not to infer from this, however, an inability of the eye to distinguish one color from another, for here it is essential to consider the difficulty of associating the sound of the word "red" or "green" with the proper color-sensation, even when the sensation is present.

At this time, before the age of twenty-one months, there must have been recognition not only of the varying intensity of light (white, gray, black), but also of the quality of some colors, for the delight in striking colors was manifest. Yet in the case of little children, even after they have begun to speak, it can not be determined without searching tests what colors they distinguish and rightly name.

In order, then, to ascertain how the separate colors are related to one another in this respect, I have made several hundred color-tests with my child, beginning at the end of his second year. These I used to apply every day in the early morning, for a week; then, after an interval of a week, again almost every day, but in a different manner—as will be shown directly.

*　　*　　*

Summary of Results

Of all the facts that have been established by me through the observation of the child in the first years of his life, the *formation of concepts without language* is most opposed to the traditional doctrines, and it is just this on which I lay the greatest stress.

It has been demonstrated that the human being, at the very beginning of his life, not only distinguishes pleasure and discomfort, but may also have single distinct sensations. He behaves on the first day differently, when the appropriate sense-impressions exist, from what he does when they are lacking. The first effect of these feelings, these few sensations, is the association of their traces, left behind in the central nervous system, with inborn movements. Those traces or central impressions develop gradually the personal *memory*. These movements are the point of departure for the primitive activity of the intellect, which separates the sensations both in time and in space. When the number of the memory-images, of distinct sensations, on the one hand, on the other, of the movements that have been associated with them—e. g., "sweet" and "sucking"—has become larger, then a firmer association of sensation-and-movement-memories, i. e., of excitations of sensory and motor ganglionic cells takes place, so that excitement of the one brings with it co-excitement of the other. Sucking awakens the recollection of the sweet taste; the sweet taste of itself causes sucking. This succession is already a separation *in time* of two sensations (the sweet and the motor sensation in sucking). The separation in space requires the recollection of two sensations, each with one movement; the distinction between sucking at the left breast and sucking at the right is made after one trial. With this, the first act of the intellect is performed, the first perception made, i. e., a sensation first localized in time and space. The motor sensation of sucking has come, like the sweet taste, *after* a similar one, and it has come between two unlike relations in space that were distinguished. By means of multiplied perceptions (e. g., luminous fields not well defined, but yet defined) and multiplied movements with sensations of touch, the perception, after considerable time, acquires an object; i. e., the intellect, which already allowed nothing bright to appear without boundary-lines, and thus allowed nothing bright to appear except in space (whereas at the beginning brightness, as was the case even later with sound, had no limitation, no demarcation), begins to assign a cause for that which is perceived. Hereby perception is raised to *representation*. The often-felt, localized, sweet, warm, white wetness, which is associated with sucking, now forms an idea, and one of the earliest ideas. When, now, this idea has often arisen, the separate perceptions that have been necessary to its formation are united more and more firmly. Then, when one of these latter appears for itself, the memory-images of the others will also appear, through co-excitement of the ganglionic cells concerned; but this means simply that the *concept* is now in existence. For the concept has its origin in the union of attributes. Attributes are perceived, and the memory-images of them, that is, accordingly, memory-images of separate perceptions, are so firmly associated that, where only one appears in the midst of entirely new impressions, the concept yet emerges, because all the other images appear along with it. Language is not required for this. Up to this point, those born deaf behave exactly like infants that have all the senses, and like some animals that form concepts.

These few first ideas, namely, the individual ideas, or sense-intuitions that are generated by the first perceptions, and the simple general ideas (of a lower order), or concepts, arising out of these—the concepts of the child as yet without language, of microcephali also, of deaf-mutes, and of the higher animals—have now this peculiarity, that they have all been formed exactly in this way by the parents and the grandparents and the representatives of the successive generations (such notions as those of "food," "breast"). These concepts are not innate; because no idea can be innate, for the reason that several peripheral impressions are necessary for the formation of even a single perception. They are, however, inherited. Just as the teeth and the beard are not usually innate in man, but come and grow like those of the parents and are already implanted, piece for piece, in the new-born child, and are thus hereditary, so the first ideas of the infant, his first concepts, which arise unconsciously, without volition and without the possibility of inhibition, in every individual in the same way, must be called hereditary. Different as are the teeth from the germs of teeth in the newly-born, so different are the man's concepts, clear, sharply defined by words, from the child's ill-defined, obscure concepts, which arise quite independently of all language (of word, look, or gesture).

In this wise the old doctrine of "innate ideas" becomes clear. Ideas or thoughts are themselves either representations or combinations of representations. They thus presuppose perceptions, and can not accordingly be innate, but may some of them be inherited, those, viz., which at first, by virtue of the likeness between the brain of the child and that of the parent, and of the similarity between the external circumstances of the beginnings of life in child and parent, always rise in the same manner.

The principal thing is the innate aptitude to perceive things and to form ideas, i. e., the innate intellect. By aptitude (Anlage), however, can be understood nothing else at present than a manner of reacting, a sort of capability or excitability, impressed upon the central organs of the nervous system after repeated association of nervous excitations (through a great many generations in the same way).

The brain comes into the world provided with a great number of impressions upon it. Some of these are quite obscure, some few are distinct. Each ancestor has added his own to those previously existing. Among these impressions, finally, the useless ones must soon be obliterated by those that are useful. On the other hand, deep impressions will, like wounds, leave behind scars, which abide longer; and very frequently used paths of connection between different portions of the brain and spinal marrow and the organs of sense are easier to travel even at birth (instinctive and reflexive processes).

✻   ✻   ✻

Now, of all the higher functions of the brain, the ordering one, which compares the simple, pure sensations, the original experiences, and first sets them in an order of succession, viz., arranges them in time, then puts them side by side and one above another, and, not till later, one behind another, viz., arranges them in space— this function is one of the oldest. This ordering of the sense-impressions is *an activity of the intellect that has nothing to do with speech,* and the *capacity* for it is, as Immanuel Kant discovered, present in man "as he now is" (Kant) *before* the activity of the senses begins; but without this activity it can not assert itself.

Now, I maintain, and in doing so I take my stand upon the facts published in this book, that just as little as the intellect of the child not yet able to speak has need of words or looks or gestures, or any symbol whatever, in order to arrange in time and space the sense-impressions, so little does that intellect require those means in order to form concepts and to perform logical operations; and in this fundamental fact I see the material for bridging over the only great gulf that separates the child from the brute animal.

WUNDT'S PRINCIPLES OF PHYSIOLOGICAL PSYCHOLOGY (c. 1880)
From Wilhelm Wundt, *Principles of Physiological Psychology,* Edward Titchener, trans. (New York, 1910), vol. 1. pp. 11–16.

Physiological psychology is primarily psychology, and therefore has for its subject the manifold of conscious processes, whether as directly experienced by ourselves, or as inferred on the analogy of our own experiences from objective observation. Hence the order in which it takes up particular problems will be determined primary by psychological considerations; the phenomena of conscious-ness fall into distinct groups, according to the points of view from which they are successively regarded. At the same time, any detailed treatment of the relation between the psychical and physical aspects of vital processes presupposes a digression into anatomy and physiology such as would naturally be out of place in a purely psychological exposition. While, then, the following Chapters of this work are arranged in general upon a systematic plan, the author has not always observed the rule that the reader should be adequately prepared, at each stage of the discussion, by the contents of preceding Chapters. Its disregard has enabled him to avoid repetition; and he has acted with the less scruple, in view of the general understanding of psychology which the reading of a book like the present implies. Thus a critical review of the results of brain anatomy and brain physiology, with reference to their value for psychology, presupposes much and various psychological knowledge. Nevertheless, it is necessary, for other reasons, that the anatomical and physiological considerations should precede the properly psychological portion of the work. And similar conditions recur, now and again, even in Chapters that are pre-eminently psychological.

Combining in this way the demands of theory and the precepts of practical method, we shall in what follows (I) devote a first Part to the *bodily substrate of the mental life*. A wealth of new knowledge is here placed at our disposal by the anatomy and physiology of the central nervous system, reinforced at various points by pathology and general biology. This mass of material calls imperatively for examination from the psychological side: more especially since it has become customary for the sciences concerned in its acquisition to offer all varieties of psychological intepretation of their facts. Nay, so far have things gone, that we actually find proposals made for a complete reconstruction of psychology itself, upon an anatomical and physiological basis! But, if we are seriously to examine these conjectures and hypotheses, we must, naturally, acquaint ourselves with the present status of the sciences in question. Even here, however, our presentation of the facts will depart in some measure from the beaten path. Our aim is psychological: so that we may restrict ourselves, on the one hand, to matters of general importance, while on the other we must lay special emphasis upon whatever is significant for psychology. Thus it cannot be our task to follow brain anatomy into all the details which it has brought to light concerning the connexions of fibres within the brain,—into all those minute points whose interpretation is still altogether uncertain, and whose truth is often and again called in question. It will only be necessary for us to obtain a general view of the structure of the central organs and of such principal connexions of these with one another and with the peripheral organs as have been made out with sufficient certainty. We may then, in the light of reasonably secure principles of nerve physiology and of our psychological knowledge, proceed to discuss the probable relations of physiological structure and function to the processes of consciousness.

(2) We shall then, in a second Part, begin our work upon the problem of psychology proper, with the doctrine of the *elements of the mental life*. Psychological analysis leaves us with two such elements, of specifically different character: with *sensations*, which as the ultimate and irreducible elements of ideas we may term the objective elements of the mental life, and with *feelings*, which accompany these objective elements as their subjective complements, and are referred not to external things but to the state of consciousness itself. In this sense, therefore, we call blue, yellow, warm, cold, etc., sensations, pleasantness, unpleasantness, excitement, depression, etc., feelings. It is important that the terms be kept sharply distinct, in these assigned meanings, and not used indiscriminately, as they often are in the language of everyday life, and even in certain psychologies. It is also important that they be reserved strictly for the psychical elements, and not applied

at random both to simple and to complex contents,—a confusion that is regrettably current in physiology. Thus in what follows we shall not speak of a manifold of several tones or of a coloured extent as a 'sensation,' but as an 'idea'; and when we come to deal with the formations resulting from a combination of feelings we shall term them expressly 'complex feelings' or (if the special words that language offers us are in place) 'emotions,' 'volitions,' etc. This terminological distinction cannot, of course, tell us of itself anything whatsoever regarding the mode of origin of such complex formations from the psychical elements. It does, however, satisfy the imperative requirement that the results of psychological analysis of complex conscious contents be rendered permanent, when that analysis is completed, by fitting designations. As for these results themselves, it need hardly be said that the mental elements are never given directly as contents of consciousness in the uncompounded state. We may learn here from physiology, which has long recognised the necessity of abstracting, in its investigations of these products of analysis, from the connexions in which they occur. Sensations like red, yellow, warm, cold, etc., are considered by physiologists in this their abstract character, i.e., without regard to the connexions in which, in the concrete case, they invariably present themselves. To employ the single term 'sensation' as well for these ultimate and irreducible elements of our ideas as for the surfaces and objects that we perceive about us is a confusion of thought which works sufficient harm in physiology, and which the psychologist must once and for all put behind him.

But there is another and a still worse terminological obscurity, common both to physiology and to psychology, which has its source in the confusion of conscious processes themselves with the outcome of a later reflection upon their objective conditions. It is all too common to find sensations so named only when they are directly aroused by external sensory stimuli, while the sensations dependent upon any sort of internal condition are termed ideas, and the word idea itself is at the same time restricted to the contents known as memory images. This confusion is psychologically inexcusable. There is absolutely no reason why a sensation—blue, green, yellow, or what not—should be one thing when it is accompanied simply by an excitation in the 'visual centre' of the cortex, and another and quite a different thing when this excitation is itself set up by the operation of some external stimulus. As conscious contents, blue is and remains blue, and the idea of an object is always a thing ideated in the outside world, whether the external stimulus or the things outside of us be really present or not. It is true that the memory image is, oftentimes, weaker and more transient than the image of direct perception. But this difference is by no means constant; we may sense in dreams, or in the state of hallucination, as intensively as we sense under the operation of actual sensory stimuli. Such distinctions are, therefore, survivals from the older psychology of reflection, in which the various contents of consciousness acquired significance only as the reflective thought of the philosopher read a meaning into them. It was an accepted tenet of this psychology that ideas enjoy an immaterial existence in the mind, while sensation was regarded as something that makes its way into mind from the outside. Now all this may be right or wrong; but, whether right or wrong, it evidently has no bearing whatever upon the conscious process as such.

The attitude of physiological psychology to sensations and feelings, considered as physical elements, is, naturally, the attitude of psychology at large. At the same time, physiological psychology has to face a number of problems which do not arise for general psychology: problems that originate in the peculiar interest which attaches to the relations sustained by these ultimate elements of the mental life to the physical processes in the nervous system and its appended organs. Physiology

873

tells us, with ever-increasing conviction, that these relations, especially in the case of sensations, are absolutely uniform; and with an improved understanding of bodily expression, of affective symptomatology, we are gradually coming to see that the feelings too have their laws of correlation, no less uniform, if of an entirely different nature. But this growth of knowledge lays all the heavier charge upon psychology to determine the significance of the various psychophysical relations. A pure psychology could afford, if needs must, to pass them by, and might confine itself to a description of the elements and of their direct interrelations. A physiological psychology, on the other hand, is bound to regard this psychophysical aspect of the problems of mind as one of its most important objects of investigation.

(3) The course of our inquiry proceeds naturally from the mental elements to the complex psychical processes that take shape in consciousness from the connexion of the elements. These mental formations must be treated in order; and our third Part will be occupied with that type of complex process to which all others are referred as concomitant processes; with the *ideas* that arise from the connexion of sensations. Since physiological psychology stands committed to the experimental method, it will there pay most regard to the sense ideas aroused by external stimuli, these being most easily brought under experimental control. We may accordingly designate the contents of this section a study of the *composition of sense ideas*. Our conclusions will, however, apply equally well to ideas that are not aroused by external sensory stimuli; the two classes of ideas agree in all essential characters, and are no more to be separated than are the corresponding sensations.

The task of physiological psychology remains the same in the analysis of ideas that it was in the investigation of sensations: to act as mediator between the neighbouring sciences of physiology and psychology. At the same time, the end in view all through the doctrine of ideas is pre-eminently psychological; the specifically psychophysical problems, that are of such cardinal importance for the theory of sensation, now retire modestly into the background. Physiological psychology still takes account of the physical aspect of the sensory functions involved, but it hardly does more in this regard than it is bound to do in any psychological inquiry in which it avails itself of the experimental means placed at its disposal.

(4) The doctrine of sense ideas is followed by a fourth Part, dealing with the analysis of mental processes that, as complex products of the interconnexion of simple feelings, stand in a relation to the affective elements analogous to that sustained by ideas to the sensations of which they are compounded. It must not, of course, be understood that the two sets of formations can, in reality, be kept together separate and distinct. Sensations and feelings are, always and everywhere, complementary constituents of our mental experiences. Hence the conscious contents that are compounded of feelings can never occur except together with ideational contents, and in many cases the affective elements are as powerful to influence sensations and ideas as these are to influence the feelings. This whole group of subjective experiences, in which feelings are the determining factors, may be brought under the title of *Gemuthsbewegungen und Willenshandlungen,* Of these, *Gemuthsbewegungen* is the wider term, since it covers volitional as well as affective processes. Nevertheless, in view of the peculiar importance of the phenomena of will and of the relation which external voluntary actions bear to other organic movements,—a relation whose psychophysical implications constitute it a special problem of physiological psychology,—we retain the two words side by side in the title of our section, and limit the meaning of *Gemuthsbewegungen* on

the one hand to the *emotions,* and on the other to a class of affective processes that are frequently bound up with or pass into emotions, the *intellectual feelings.*

(5) Having thus investigated sense ideas, emotions and voluntary actions, the complex processes of the mental life, we pass in a fifth Part to the doctrine of *consciousness* and of the *interconnexion of mental processes.* The results of the two preceding sections now form the basis of an analysis of consciousness and of the connexions of conscious contents. For all these conscious connexions contain, as their proximate constituents, ideas and emotions, and consciousness itself is nothing else than a general name for the total sum of processes and their connexions. So far as our analysis of these connexions is experimental, we shall be chiefly concerned with the arbitrary modification of sense ideas and of their course in consciousness. When, on the other hand, we come to consider the interconnexions of emotions and voluntary actions, our principal dependence will be upon the results of analysis of the processes of consciousness at large.

In these five Parts, then, we confine ourselves to a purely empirical examination of the facts. (6) A sixth and final Part will treat of the *origin and principles of mental development.* Here we shall endeavor to set forth, in brief, the general conclusions that may be drawn from these facts for a comprehensive theory of the mental life and of its relation to our physical existence. So far, we have set conscious processes and the processes of the bodily life over against each other, without attempting any exact definition of either. Now at last, when our survey of their interrelations is completed, we shall be able to ascribe a definitive meaning to the terms physical and psychical. And this will help us towards a solution of the well worn problem of 'the interaction of mind and body,' a solution that shall do justice to the present status of our physiological and psychological knowledge, and shall also meet the requirements of a philosophical criticism of knowledge itself. Physiological psychology thus ends with those questions with which the philosophical psychology of an older day was wont to begin,—the questions of the nature of the mind, and the relation of consciousness to an external world; and with a characterisation of the general attitude which psychology is to take up, when it seeks to trace the laws of the mental life as manifested in history and in society.

England

MARY WOLLSTONECRAFT ON CO-EDUCATION (1792)   From *A Vindication of the Rights of Woman* (London, 1891), pp. 237–53.

I have already animadverted on the bad habits which females acquire when they are shut up together; and I think that the observation may fairly be extended to the other sex, till the natural inference is drawn which I have had in view throughout—that to improve both sexes they ought, not only in private families, but in public schools, to be educated together.

If marriage be the cement of society, mankind should all be educated after the same model, or the intercourse of the sexes will never deserve the name of fellowship, nor will women ever fulfill the peculiar duties of their sex, till they become enlightened citizens, till they become free by being enabled to earn their own subsistance, independent of men; in the same manner, I mean, to prevent misconstruction, as one man is independent of another. Nay, marriage will never be held sacred till women, by being brought up with men, are prepared to be their companions rather than their mistresses; for the mean doublings of cunning will ever render them contemptible, whilst oppression renders them timid. So convinced am I of this truth, that I will venture to predict that virtue will never prevail in society till the virtues of both sexes are founded on reason; and, till the affections common to both are allowed to gain their due strength by the discharge of mutual duties.

Were boys and girls permitted to pursue the same studies together, those graceful decencies might early be inculcated which produce modesty without those sexual distinctions that taint the mind. Lessons of politeness, and that formulary of decorum, which treads on the heels of falsehood, would be rendered useless by habitual propriety of behavior. Not indeed put on for visitors, like the courtly robe of politeness, but the sober effect of cleanliness of mind. Would not this simple elegance of sincerity be a chaste homage paid to domestic affections, far surpassing the meretricious compliments that shine with false lustre in the heartless intercourse of fashionable life?

Let an enlightened nation then try what effect reason would have to bring them back to nature, and their duty; and allowing them to share the advantages of education and government with man, see whether they will become better, as they grow wiser and become free. They cannot be injured by the experiment, for it is not in the power of man to render them more insignificant than they are at present.

To render this practicable, day schools for particular ages should be established by Government, in which boys and girls might be educated together. The school for the younger children, from five to nine years of age, ought to be absolutely free and open to all classes. A sufficient number of masters should also be chosen by a select committee in each parish, to whom any complaint of negligence, &c., might be made, if signed by six of the children's parents.

Ushers would then be unnecessary; for I believe experience will ever prove that this kind of subordinate authority is particularly injurious to the morals of youth. What, indeed, can tend to deprave the character more than outward submission and inward contempt? Yet how can boys be expected to treat an usher with respect, when the master seems to consider him in the light of a servant, and almost to countenance the ridicule which becomes the chief amusement of the boys during the play hours?

But nothing of this kind could occur in an elementary day school, where boys and girls, the rich and poor, should meet together. And to prevent any of the distinctions of vanity, they should be dressed alike, and all obliged to submit to the same discipline, or leave the school. The schoolroom ought to be surrounded by a large piece of ground, in which the children might be usefully exercised, for at this age they should not be confined to any sedentary employment for more than an hour at a time. But these relaxations might all be rendered a part of elementary education, for many things improve and amuse the senses, when introduced as a kind of show, to the principles of which, dryly laid down, children would turn a deaf ear. For instance, botany, mechanics, and astronomy; reading, writing, arithmetic, natural history, and some simple experiments in natural philosophy, might fill up the day; but these pursuits should never encroach on gymnastic plays in the open air. The elements of religion, history, the history of man, and politics, might also be taught by conversations in the Socratic form.

After the age of nine, girls and boys, intended for domestic employments, or mechanical trades, ought to be removed to other schools, and receive instruction in some measure appropriated to the destination of each individual, the two sexes being still together in the morning; but in the afternoon the girls should attend a school, where plain work, mantua-making, millinery, &c., would be their employment.

The young people of superior abilities, or fortune, might now be taught, in another school, the dead and living languages, the elements of science, and continue the study of history and politics, on a more extensive scale, which would not exclude polite literature.

Girls and boys still together? I hear some readers ask. Yes. And I should not fear any other consequence than that some early attachment might take place; which, whilst it had the best effect on the moral character of the young people, might not perfectly agree with the views of the parents, for it will be a long time, I fear, before the world will be so far enlightened that parents, only anxious to render their children virtuous, shall allow them to choose companions for life themselves. . . .

✻   ✻   ✻

I have already inveighed against the custom of confining girls to their needle, and shutting them out from all political and civil employments; for by thus narrowing their minds they are rendered unfit to fulfil the peculiar duties which nature has assigned them. . . .

Make them free, and they will quickly become wise and virtuous, as men become more so, for the improvement must be mutual, or the injustice which one-half of the human race are obliged to submit to retorting on their oppressors, the virtue of man will be worm-eaten by the insect whom he keeps under his feet.

JOSEPH LANCASTER'S MONITORIAL SYSTEM (1805) From Joseph Lancaster, *Improvements in Education, as It Respects the Industrious Classes of the Community . . .* (London, 1805), pp. 1, 31, 37–38, 40–46, 55–57, 89–90, 94, 97, 100–103.

In the year 1798, I opened a school for the instruction of poor children, in reading, writing, arithmetic, and the knowledge of the Holy Scriptures; the children were taught at the low price of fourpence per week. I knew of no modes of tuition but those usually in practice, and I had a practical knowledge of them. The number of children who attended the school at that time, varied from ninety to a hundred and twenty. Being thus engaged in the study of education, with full liberty to make what experiments I pleased, whenever I found a poor child whose parents were unable to pay for his instruction, I gave him education gratis. . . . The predominant feature in the youthful disposition is an almost irresistible propensity to action; this, if properly controlled by suitable employment, will become a valuable auxiliary to the master; but, if neglected, will be apt to degenerate into rebellion. *Active youths, when treated as cyphers, will generally show their consequence by exercising themselves in mischief.* I am convinced, by experience, that it is practicable for teachers to acquire a proper *dominion* over the minds of the youth under their care, by directing those active spirits to good purposes. This liveliness should never be repressed, but directed to useful ends; and I have ever found, the surest way to cure a *mischievous* boy was to *make him a monitor.* I never knew any thing succeed much better, if so well.

In education nothing can be more important than economy of time, even when we have a reasonable prospect of a good portion of it at our disposal; but it is most peculiarly necessary in primary schools, and in the instruction of the poor: . . . In establishing this institution, the influence a master has over his scholars, and the influence they have one over another, have been the objects of constant study and practice; it has most happily succeeded in proving, that a very large number of children may be superintended by one master; and that they can be self-educated by their own exertions, under his care.

The whole school is arranged in classes; a monitor is appointed to each, who is responsible for the cleanliness, order, and improvement of every boy in it. He is assisted by boys, either from his own or another class, to perform part of his duties for him, when the number is more than he is equal to manage himself.

The proportion of boys who teach, either in reading, writing, or arithmetic, is as one to ten. In so large a school there are duties to be performed, which simply relate to order, and have no connexion with learning; for these duties different monitors are appointed. The word monitor, in this intitution, means, any boy that has a charge either in some department of tuition or of order, and is not simply confined to those boys who teach.—The boy who takes care that the writing books are ruled, by machines made for that purpose, is the monitor of ruling. The boy who superintends the enquiries after the absentees, is called the monitor of absentees. The monitors who inspect the improvement of the classes in reading, writing, and arithmetic, are called inspecting monitors; and their offices are indeed essentially different from that of the *teaching monitors.* A boy whose business it is to give to the other monitors such books, &c. as may be wanted or appointed for the daily use of their classes, and to gather them up when done with; to see all the boys do read, and that none leave school without reading, is called the monitor-general. Another is called the monitor of slates, because he has a general charge of all the slates in the school.

*　　*　　*

On the Arrangement of the Institution, as connected with Improvements in Education

To promote emulation, and facilitate learning, the whole school is arranged into classes, and a monitor appointed to each class. A class consists of any number of boys whose proficiency is on a par: these may all be classed and taught together. If the class is small, one monitor may teach it; if large, it may still continue the same class, but with more or less assistant monitors, who, under the direction of the principal monitor, are to teach the subdivisions of the class. If only four or six boys should be found in a school, who are learning the same thing, as A, B, C, ab. &c. Addition, Subtraction, &c. I think it would be advantageous for them to pursue their studies after the manner of a class. If the number of boys studying the same lesson, in any school, should amount to six, their proficiency will be nearly doubled by being classed, and studying in conjunction. There are two descriptions of boys to be found in every school; those who are learning to read, and those who have learnt: to the last, reading is not a study, but a medium of religious or moral instruction. To the first, a progressive series of lessons, rising step by step, to that point, where children may begin to store their minds with knowledge for use in future life. This is the second object of instruction, and to which a series of reading lessons connected with those mechanical, or other pursuits in life, which they are likely to be engaged in, and with religious knowledge, is a valuable auxiliary.

*　　*　　*

FIRST CLASS

The first, or lowest class of scholars, are those who are yet unacquainted with their alphabet. This class may consist of ten, twenty, or a hundred; or any other number of children, who have not made so much progress as to know how to distinguish all their letters at first sight. If there are only ten or twenty of this description in the school, one boy can manage and teach them; if double the number, it will require two boys as teachers, and so in proportion for every additional twenty boys. The reader will observe, that, in this and in every other class, described in the succeeding plan and arrangement, the monitor has but one plain, simple object to teach, though in several ways; and the scholars the same to learn. This simplicity of system defines at once the province of each monitor in tuition. The very name of each class imports as much—and this is called the first A, B, C, class. The method of teaching is as follows: a bench is placed or fixed to the ground for the boys to sit on;

another, about a foot higher, is placed before them. On the desk before them is placed deal ledges, (a pantile lath, nailed down to the desk, would answer the same purpose,) thus:

A

B

C

The letter A, shows the entire surface of the desk, which is supported by two, three, or more legs, as usual for such desks, and according to the size. B, is a vacant space, where the boys lean their left arms, while they write or print with the right hand. The sand is placed in the space C. The double lines represent the ledges (or pantile laths) which confine the sand in its place: sand of any kind will do, but it must be dry. The boys print in the sand, with their fingers: they all print at the *command* given by their monitor. A boy who knows how to print, and distinguish some of his letters, is placed by one who knows few or none, with a view to assist him; and particularly, that he may copy the form of his letters, from *seeing* him make them. We find this copying one from another a great step towards proficiency. In teaching the boys to print the alphabet, the monitor first makes a letter on the sand, before any boy who knows nothing about it; the boy is then required to *retrace* over the same letter, which the monitor has made for him, with his fingers; and thus he is to continue employed, till he can make the letter himself, without the monitor's assistance. Then he may go on to learn another letter.

*   *   *

Another method of teaching the alphabet is, by a large sheet of pasteboard suspended by a nail on the school wall; twelve boys, from the sand class, are formed into a circle round this alphabet, standing in their numbers, 1, 2, 3, &c. to 12. These numbers are pasteboard tickets, with number 1, &c. inscribed, suspended by a string from the button of the bearer's coat, or round his neck. The best boy stands in the first place; he is also decorated with a leather ticket, gilt, and lettered *merit,* as a badge of honour. He is always the first boy questioned by the monitor, who points to a particular letter in the alphabet, "What letter is that?" If he tells readily, what letter it is, all is well, and he retains his place in the class; which he forfeits, together with his number and ticket, to the next boy who answers the question, if he cannot.

This promotes constant emulation. It employs the monitor's attention continually; he cannot look one way, while the boy is repeating his letters another; or at all neglect to attend to him, without being immediately discovered. It is not the monitor's business to teach, but to see the boys in his class or division teach each other. If a boy calls A, by the name of B, or O, he is not to say, it is not B, or O, but it is A; he is to require the next boy in succession to correct the mistakes of his senior. These two methods, of the sand and alphabet card, with their inferior arrangements detailed, are made use of daily in rotation, and serve as a mutual check and relief to each other.

The figures are taught in the same manner. Sand is a cheap substitute for books any where; but more so in those parts of the country where the soil is sandy, than in London. This method was taken in the outline from Dr. Bell, formerly of Madras;

but he did not say, in his printed account of that institution, whether wet or dry sand was used. . . .

A Method of Teaching to Spell and Read, whereby one Book will Serve instead of Six Hundred Books

It will be remembered, that the usual mode of teaching requires every boy to have a book: yet, each boy can only read or spell one lesson at a time, in that book. Now, all the other parts of the book are in wear, and liable to be *thumbed* to pieces; and, whilst the boy is learning a lesson in one part of the book, the other parts are at that time useless. Whereas, if a spelling book contains twenty or thirty different lessons, and it were possible for thirty scholars to read the thirty lessons in that book, it would be equivalent to thirty books for its utility. To effect this, it is desirable the whole of the book should be printed three times larger than the common size type, which would make it equal in size and cost to three common spelling books, value from eight-pence to a shilling each. Again, it should be printed with only one page to a leaf, which would again double the price, and make it equivalent in bulk and cost to five or six common books; its different parts should then be pasted on pasteboard, and suspended by a string, to a nail in the wall, or other convenient place: one pasteboard should contain the alphabet; others, words and syllables of from two to six letters.

*　　*　　*

When the cards are provided, as before mentioned, from twelve to twenty boys may stand in a circle round each card, and clearly distinguish the print, to read or spell, as well or better than if they had a common spelling book in each of their hands.

*　　*　　*

. . . every lesson placed on a card, will serve for twelve or twenty boys at once: and, when that twelve or twenty have repeated the whole lesson, as many times over as there are boys in the circle, they are dismissed to their spelling on the slate, and another like number of boys may study the same lesson, in succession: indeed, *two hundred boys* may all repeat their lessons from *one* card, in the space of *three hours*. If the value and importance of this plan, for saving paper and books in teaching reading and spelling, will not recommend itself, all I can say in its praise, from experience, will be of no avail. When standing in circles, to read or spell, the boys wear their numbers, tickets, pictures, &c. as described under the head, Emulation and Reward; and give place to each other, according to merit, as mentioned in the account of the two first classes.

Boy. **Book.**

In spelling by writing on the slate, the performances of the scholars are inspected, sometimes by the monitor of their class, often by an inspecting monitor, and occasionally by the master.

Printing in the sand is inspected in the same manner as in the new method of teaching arithmetic. Every boy is placed next to one who can do as well or better than himself: his business is to excel him, in which case he takes precedence of him. In reading, every reading division has the numbers, 1, 2, 3, &c. to 12, suspended from their buttons. If the boy who wears number 12, excels the boy who wears number 11, he takes his place and number; in exchange for which the other goes down to the place and number 12. Thus, the boy who is number 12, at the beginning of the lesson, may be number 1, at the conclusion of it, and *vice versa*. The boy who has number 1, has also a single leather ticket, lettered variously, as, 'Merit,'—'Merit in Reading,'—'Merit in Spelling,'—'Merit in Writing,' &c. this badge of honour he also forfeits, if he loses his place by suffering another to excel him. He has also a picture pasted on pasteboard, and suspended to his breast; this he forfeits to any boy who can excel him. Whoever is in the first place at the conclusion of the lesson, delivers the ticket and picture to a monitor appointed for that purpose. The honour of wearing the ticket and number, as marks of precedency, is all the reward attached to them; but the picture which has been worn entitles the bearer to receive another picture in exchange for it; which becomes his own. This prize is much valued by the minor boys, and regarded by all. Pictures can be made a fund of entertainment and instruction, combined with infinite variety. When a boy has a waggon, a whip-top, or ball, one thing of the kind satisfies him, till it is worn out; but he may have a continual variety of pictures, and receive fresh instruction as well as pleasure from every additional prize.

* * *

Another method of encouraging deserving youth, who distinguish themselves by their attention to study, is equally honourable but less expensive. I have established in my institution an order of merit. Every member of this order is distinguished by a silver medal, suspended from his neck by a plated chain. No boys are admitted to this order, but those who distinguish themselves by proficiency in their own studies, or in the improvement of others, and for their endeavours to check vice.

OFFENCES AND PUNISHMENTS

The chief offences committed by youth at school, arise from the liveliness of their active dispositions. Few youth do wrong for the *sake of doing so*. If precedence and pleasure be united with learning, they will soon find a delight in attending at school. Youth naturally seek whatever is pleasant to them, with avidity; and, from ample experience have I found, that they do so with learning, when innocent pleasure is associated therewith. If any misconduct should be punished by severity, vice and immorality are the chief subjects; and, I am convinced that it is not always indispensable in those cases, having known many a sensible boy reformed without, and that from practices as bad as almost any that usually occur in schools.

That children should idle away their time, or talk in school, is very improper— they cannot talk and learn at the same time. In my school talking is considered as an offence; and yet it occurs very seldom, in proportion to the number of children: whenever this happens to be the case, an appropriate punishment succeeds.

Each monitor of a class is responsible for the cleanliness, order, and quietness of those under him. He is also a lad of unimpeachable veracity—a qualification on which much depends. He should have a continual eye over every one in the class under his care, and notice when a boy is loitering away his time in talking or idleness. Having thus seen, he is bound in duty to lodge an accusation against him for *misdemeanor*. In order to do this silently, he has a number of cards, written on differently: as, 'I have seen this boy idle,'—'I have seen this boy talking,' &c. &c. This rule applies to every class, and each card has the name of the particular class written thereon: so that, by seeing a card written on as above, belonging to the first or sixth, or any other reading class, it is immediately known who is the monitor that is the accuser. This card is given to the defaulter, and he is required to present it at the head of the school—a regulation that must be complied with. On a repeated or frequent offence, after admonition has failed, the lad to whom he presents the card has liberty to put a wooden log round his neck, which serves him as a pillory, and with this he is sent to his seat. This machine may weigh from four to six pounds, some more and some less. The neck is not pinched or closely confined—it is chiefly burdensome by the manner in which it encumbers the neck, when the delinquent turns to the right or left. While it rests on his shoulders, the equilibrium is preserved; but, on the least motion one way or the other, it is lost, and the logs operate as a dead weight upon the neck. Thus, he is confined to sit in his proper position. If this is unavailing, it is common to fasten the legs of offenders together with wooden shackles: one or more, according to the offence. The *shackle* is a piece of wood about a foot, sometimes six or eight inches long, and tied to each leg. When shackled, he cannot walk but in a very slow, measured pace: being obliged to take six steps, when confined, for two when at liberty. Thus accoutred, he is ordered to walk round the school-room, till tired out—he is glad to sue for liberty, and promise *his endeavour* to behave more steadily in future. Should not this punishment have the desired effect, the left hand is tied behind the back, or wooden shackles fastened from elbow to elbow, behind the back. Sometimes the legs are tied together. Occasionally boys are put in a sack, or in a basket, suspended to the roof of the school, in the sight of all the pupils, who frequently smile at *the birds in the cage*. This punishment is one of the most terrible that can be inflicted on boys of sense and abilities. Above all, it is dreaded by the monitors: the name of it is sufficient, and therefore it is but seldom resorted to on their account. Frequent or old offenders are yoked together sometimes, by a piece of wood that fastens round all their necks: and, thus confined, they parade the school, walking backwards— being obliged to pay very great attention to their footsteps, for fear of running against any object that might cause the yoke to hurt their necks, or to keep from falling down. Four or six can be yoked together this way.

When a boy is disobedient to his parents, profane in his language, or has committed any offence against morality, or is remarkable for slovenliness, it is usualy for him to be dressed up with labels, describing his offence, and a tin or paper crown on his head. In that manner he walks round the school, two boys preceding him, and proclaiming his fault; varying the proclamation according to the different offences. When a boy comes to school with dirty face or hands, and it seems to be more the effect of habit than of accident, a girl is appointed to wash his face in the sight of the whole school. This usually creates much diversion, especially when (as previously directed) she gives his cheeks a few *gentle strokes of correction* with her hand. The same event takes place as to girls, when in habits of slothfulness.

Occasionally, such offenders against cleanliness walk round the school, preceded by a boy proclaiming her fault—and the same as to the boys. A proceeding that usually turns the *public spirit* of the whole school against the culprit.

GEORGE COMBE ON THE SCIENCE OF PHRENOLOGY (1828)   From George Combe, *Elements of Phrenology* (London, 1828), pp. 1, 6–10, 14, 17, 21, 23–25.

Introductory Observations

Phrenology treats of the faculties of the Human Mind, and of the organs by means of which they manifest themselves; but it does not enable us to predict actions.

Dr Gall, a physician of Vienna, now resident in Paris, is the founder of the system. From an early age he was given to observation, and was struck with the fact, that each of his brothers and sisters, companions in play, and schoolfellows, was distinguished from other individuals by some peculiarity of talent or disposition.

*   *   *

Being convinced by these facts, that there is a natural and constitutional diversity of talents and dispositions, he encountered in books still another obstacle to his success in determing the external signs of the mental powers. He found that, instead of faculties for languages, drawing, distinguishing places, music, and mechanical arts, corresponding to the different talents which he had observed in his schoolfellows, the metaphysicians spoke only of general powers, such as perception, conception, memory, imagination, and judgment; and when he endeavoured to discover external signs in the head, corresponding to these general faculties, or to determine the correctness of the physiological doctrines taught by the authors already mentioned, regarding the seat of the mind, he found perplexities without end, and difficulties insurmountable.

Dr Gall, therefore, abandoning every theory and preconceived opinion, gave himself up entirely to the observation of nature. Being a friend to Dr Nord, Physician to a Lunatic Asylum in Vienna, he had opportunities, of which he availed himself, of making observations on the insane. He visited prisons, and resorted to schools; he was introduced to the courts of Princes, to Colleges, and the seats of Justice; and wherever he heard of an individual distinguished in any particular way, either by remarkable endowment or deficiency, he observed and studied the development of his head. In this manner, by an almost imperceptible induction, he conceived himself warranted in believing, that particular mental powers are indicated by particular configurations of the head.

Hitherto he had resorted only to Physiognomical indications, as a means of discovering the functions of the brain. On reflection, however, he was convinced that Physiology is imperfect when separated from Anatomy. Having observed a woman of fifty-four years of age, who had been afflicted with hydrocephalus from her youth, and who, with a body a little shrunk, possessed a mind as active and intelligent as that of other individuals of her class, Dr Gall declared his conviction, that the structure of the brain must be different from what was generally conceived,—a remark which Tulpius also had made, on observing a hydrocephalic patient who manifested the mental faculties. He therefore felt the necessity of making anatomical researches into the structure of the brain.

* * *

At Vienna, in 1796, Dr Gall for the first time delivered lectures on his system.

In 1800, Dr J. G. Spurzheim began the study of Phrenology under him, having in that year assisted, for the first time, at one of his lectures. In 1804 he was associated with him in his labours; and since that period has not only added many valuable discoveries to those of Dr Gall in the anatomy and physiology of the brain, but formed the truths brought to light, by their joint observations, into a beautiful and interesting system of mental philosophy. In Britain we are chiefly indebted to his personal exertions and printed works for a knowledge of the science.

An elementary view of the result of their labours will be found in the following work.

The mind and body and intimately connected; and it is impossible for the mind to remain unaffected in certain states of the corporeal system. But the brain, and not the whole body, is the immediate organ of the mind.

* * *

The brain, then, being the organ of the mind, the next inquiry is, whether it is a single part, manifesting the whole mind equally, or an aggregate of parts, each subserving a particular mental power? All the phenomena are at variance with the former, and in harmony with the latter, or phrenological view. The brain must be a compound of parts performing distinct functions.

* * *

All authors agree that the brain gives the form to the skull. Cuvier, Monro, and many other anatomists state this.

These positions being granted, the *possibility* of Gall's discoveries becomes evident, and the question resolves itself into one of accuracy of observation, which can be determined only by actual experience.

It has been objected that the outer surface of the skull does not accurately represent the form of the inner. This objection is unfounded.

* * *

The *third* fundamental principle of phrenology is, that the power of mental manifestation is invariably in proportion, *caeteris paribus*, to the size of the cerebral organ. . . .

* * *

The principle of size being a measure of power, which is thus almost universally admitted in regard to the whole brain, is equally accurate when applied to its component parts; at least the truth of it is a fair and reasonable subject of philosophical inquiry; and, on the information obtained by observation, the phrenologists rest their whole system.

The phrenologist, therefore, compares cerebral development with the manifestations of mental power, for the purpose of discovering the functions of the brain, and the organs of the mind . . .

*　　*　　*

The following points are conceived to be established by an extensive induction of facts.

1st, The mind manifests a plurality of faculties.

2dly, The brain is the material instrument by means of which the mind acts, and is acted, upon; and it is a congeries of organs.

3dly, The brain consists of two hemispheres, separated by a strong membrane called the Falciform process of the dura mater. Each hemisphere is an aggregate of parts, and each part serves to manifest a particular mental faculty. The two hemispheres, without being absolutely symmetrical, in general correspond in form and functions; and hence there are two organs for each faculty, one situate in each hemisphere. The cerebellum in man is situate below the brain. A thick membrane, named the Tentorium, separates the two; but they are both connected with the medulla oblongata, and through it with each other.

Each organ is understood to extend from the medulla oblongata, or top of the spinal marrow, to the surface of the brain or cerebellum; and every individual possesses all the organs in a greater or less degree.

4thly, The power with which each faculty is capable of manifesting itself (other conditions being equal), bears a proportion to the size of its organs. Power and activity are distinguishable. Size appears to be essential to power, for a very energetic mind and a very small brain are never found concomitant. An error is frequently committed in supposing that absolute size, or size independent of health, constitution, and exercise, is a measure of power; but phrenologists do not hold this doctrine. Farther details will be entered into in a subsequent part of the work.

The *size* of an organ is estimated by its length and its breadth. Its length is measured by the distance from the *medulla oblongata,* or top of the spinal marrow, to the outer surface of the brain. A line drawn through the head, from the opening of one ear to that of the other, would, in the middle, pass close to, but a little before, the medulla oblongata; hence the length of an organ is measured from the line of the ear to the circumference. Its breadth is indicated by its expansion at the surface. An organ may thus be likened to an inverted cone, with its apex in the medulla, and its base at the surface of the brain; the broader the base and longer the distance betwixt it and the apex, the greater will be the size, or the quantity of matter which it will contain.

There are parts at the base of the brain, in the middle and posterior regions, the size of which cannot be discovered during life, and whose functions, in consequence, are still unknown. From analogy, and some pathological facts, they are supposed to be the organs of the sensations of hunger and thirst, heat and cold, and of some other mental affections, for which cerebral organs have not been discovered; but demonstrative evidence to this effect being wanting, this conjecture is merely stated to incite to farther investigation.

GEORGE COMBE ON EDUCATION AND THE DEVELOPMENT OF THE FACULTIES OF THE MIND (1822)

From George Combe, *Essays on Phrenology* . . . (Philadelphia, 1822), pp. 360–66, 369–71, 374–78, 383–84.

	NAMES OF THE ORGANS.	SITUATION OF THE ORGANS.	REMARKS.
1.	*Amativeness*, or physical love.	The cerebellum. At the base of the back part of the head, immediately above the middle of the neck.	Generally most developed in man and male animals; and not considerable till puberty.
2.	*Philoprogenitiveness*, or love of offspring.	The posterior part of the head, immediately above the former organ.	Most remarkable in women, and the females of other animals.
3.	*Inhabitivensss*—in animals the disposition to determine the place of dwelling—in man, love of country.	Probably seated above the centre of the preceding.	This is most conspicuous in certain animals that are fond of elevated situations.
4.	*Adhesiveness*, or disposition to form attachments.	Outward and upward on each side of the second organ.	Society results from this disposition, which is found in some of the lower animals. In man it disposes to friendship, and it is generally large in women.
5.	*Combativeness*, or disposition to quarrel and fight.	About the posterior lower angle of the parietal bone; or, in adults, about an inch and a half behind the ear.	Conspicuous in the courageous animals. In man it produces courage, and the tendency to attack.
6.	*Destructiveness*, or disposition to destroy.	On the side of the head, immediately above, and somewhat around the ear.	Very discernible in the carnivorous animals; also found in the human species. When this and the preceding organ are large, they give the tendency to rage and ferocity.
7.	*Constructiveness*, or disposition to build, &c.	At the temples, above the cheek bones; when large, it gives a kind of square appearance to that part of the face.	Remarkable in those animals which build, and in men noted for mechanical invention.
8.	*Acquisitiveness*, or disposition to obtain or acquire.	At the upper part of the temples, upward and backward a little from the preceding organ.	In excess, this leads to avarice; and when conscientiousness is small, to theft, dishonesty, &c.
9.	*Secretiveness*, or disposition to conceal.	In the middle of the side of the head, immediately above destructiveness.	Cunning, dissimulation, hypocrisy, &c. are its results, when abused or improperly directed. Legitimately employed, it enables us to suppress improper feelings.
10.	*Self-esteem*, or self-love.	The middle of the upper posterior part of the head, or top of the back part.	When not checked, it gives rein to pride, disdain and weening conceit of one's self. Most noted in men. When regulated by conscientiousness, it gives dignity and elevation to the character.
11.	*Love of Approbation*, or desire of applause.	On each side of the preceding; or the posterior upper and lateral part of the head.	Ambition and vanity are its occasional products. Most remarkable in women. Well directed, it gives the love of fame, glory and distinction.
12.	*Cautiousness*, or circumspection.	The upper posterior part of the sides of the head, or upwards and backwards, from No. 9.	Timid animals and very cautious men have it in a great degree. It produces fear when large.
13.	*Benevolence*, or kind affection.	The superior middle part of the forehead, or top of the fore part of the head.	The meek and peaceable animals have it much developed. In man it gives universal charity or philanthropy.
14.	*Veneration*, or tendency to adore.	The middle of the upper part of the head, a little before the crown.	Conceived to be proper to man, and to dispose to religion; as also to venerate any object to which it is directed.
15.	*Hope*, or inclination to expect and believe.	On each side of veneration.	In religion this sentiment produces faith; its excess occasions credulity. It paints the future fair and smiling.
16.	*Ideality*, or poetic and enthusiastic tendency.	A little above the temples, and immediately above No. 8, but extending farther back.	The opposite of cautiousness. Fancy, enthusiasm, poetical feeling, are referable to it.
17.	*Conscientiousness*, or sense of justice and duty.	On each side of the following organ.	None of the lower animals are thought to possess this sentiment. It is the moral sense of the metaphysicians.
18.	*Firmness*, or resoluteness of character, &c.	The top of the head, a little in front of self-esteem.	This serves to maintain the activity of the other faculties. It gives determination and perseverance; but in excess leads to obstinacy and infatuation.

I. ORDER. FEELINGS.

1. *Genus. Propensities.* Having the organs of

2. *Genus. Sentiments.* Having the organs of

	NAMES OF THE ORGANS.	SITUATION OF THE ORGANS.	REMARKS.
19.	*Individuality*, or faculty of knowing external objects.	The upper portion is supposed to give the fondness for history, events, &c. and is called by Spurzheim *Phenomena.* —The lower portion to give a disposition to attend to matters of fact, and is by him called *Individuality*.	These contribute to universal but superficial knowledge, and are early developed. They are conversant with facts, but do not trace their relations.
20.	*Form*, the power of considering forms.	In the internal angle of the orbit of the eye.	Form is imagined to be the first quality of bodies that is considered by the intellect.
21.	*Size*, faculty of contemplating size.	Supposed to be near the preceding.	Size the next quality considered.
22.	*Weight and Momenta*, &c.; faculty by which ideas of weight, &c. are acquired.	Conjectural; but supposed as above.	Consistency, density, and some other qualities, are supposed to be ascertained by this faculty.
23.	*Colouring*, faculty of perceiving the harmony and relation of colours.	The middle of the arch of the eyebrows.	This is not in proportion to the sense of sight. Some persons see figure and distance correctly, but cannot perceive minute shades of colour, and *vice versa.*
24.	*Locality*, faculty of contemplating places, situation, space, &c.	From above the inner angles of the eyes, towards the middle line of the forehead, or towards the lower sides of organ 19.	Gives rise to a propensity to travel, takes cognizance of space and localities, and is necessary to a landscape painter.
25.	*Order*, faculty of conceiving order, method, &c.	Betwixt the organs of colouring and number. Probable.	The notion of regularity is dependent on this faculty.
26.	*Time*, faculty of attending to the succession of events; duration.	Uncertain; but supposed to be outward and upward from 21 and 24.	Implies a succession of events. Supposed to give perception of time in music; and the feeling of duration.
27.	*Number*, faculty of calculating, &c.	About the external angle of the orbit of the eye.	Whatever concerns unity and plurality belongs to this faculty.
28.	*Tune*, faculty of perceiving melody in sounds; musical genius depends on it.	The lateral parts, or external corners of the forehead.	Much developed in singing birds and in great musicians.
29.	*Language*, faculty of acquiring and using arbitrary signs.	About the middle of the orbit, so as when considerable to give prominence to the eyes.	Not confined to oral discourse, but applies to all arbitrary signs whatever.
30.	*Comparison*, faculty of finding resemblances, using examples, &c.	The middle of the superior part of the forehead, between 19 and 13.	Does not determine the kinds of comparison. Gives a fondness for analogies, and an acuteness of discrimination.
31.	*Causality*, faculty of examining causes and relations; metaphysical genius.	The superior part of the forehead, on each side of 30.	The general relation of cause and effect is its object. This and the preceding and essential requisites in a philosophic understanding.
32.	*Wit*, faculty of the ludicrous in general; gaiety.	The upper and outward parts of the forehead, on the side of 31.	Gives the perception of the ludicrous.
33.	*Imitation*, faculty of copying or mimicking the actions, manners, &c. of others.	The superior part of the forehead, on the sides of the organ of benevolence.	Very discernible in children, actors, mimics, &c.
ADDENDA—	*Wonder*, or feeling of the marvellous.	Betwixt ideality and imitation. (Probable.)	Gives the feeling of surprise, and of pleasure from novelty. In excess, produces astonishment and a tendency to the marvellous.

Left margin labels: 2. ORDER. INTELLECT. — 1. *Genus. Knowing Faculties.* Having the organs of — 2. *Genus. Highest Faculties.* Having the organs of

Every one who has observed mankind must be convinced, that Nature has implanted certain dispositions and capacities in the mind, and that these form the basis of the character of each individual through life. The object of education is to modify these innate powers, and to regulate their manifestations, to restrain such of them as may be too energetic, or to call forth into greater activity those which may be naturally languid. Before we can hope to conduct education to advantage, we must acquire a knowledge of the innate dispositions and capacities of the mind, and learn philosophically the sphere of action of each faculty, and how far each is susceptible of being repressed or exalted. The system of Gall and Spurzheim is of great utility, as affording us such information; for it professes to treat of the innate faculties of the mind, and the modifications of which they are susceptible.

According to this system, the object of education ought to be, to regulate the manifestations of all the faculties, by the dictates of those peculiar to man; and for this purpose, to subdue the activity of the propensities common to man with the low animals, and to exalt the activity of the faculties peculiar to man, or those which produce the moral sentiments and understanding.

In treating of education, therefore, we have to consider, in the first place, On what the power of manifesting the faculties depends? In the second place, What order the faculties follow in the course of their successive development? Thirdly, What are the best means for accomplishing the modifications we may have in view? And, lastly, How far our power of modification extends.

✳ ✳ ✳

As then, the power of manifesting the faculties depends on the state of the organs, it is of importance to remark that we are able to exercise a considerable influence on the organization of the body by physical education. Parents, therefore, ought to be aware that the power of the child in future life to manifest the faculties of the mind, will often depend in a considerable degree on the mode in which his physical education is conducted. This topic is highly interesting in itself, and one on which much might be said, but being only imperfectly acquainted with the subject myself, and my object being chiefly to state principles, the observations to be now offered, are intended to excite inquiry rather than to convey ultimate information.

Too great sensibility of the nervous system is unfavourable to mental exertion, but too great muscular power is also adverse to it. The great object of parents, therefore, ought to be, to fit their children for the scenes of life in which they intend them to act. If the individual be destined to a learned profession or literary pursuits, his physical education ought to be conducted in such a way as to give him due muscular power, but not to render him too athletic. If, on the other hand, he is destined for labour, his constitution cannot be rendered too robust.

The sensibility of the nervous system will be powerfully affected by diet and exercise. Too little attention is paid to adapting the diet of children to their constitutions. The impression is too prevalent, that food to be wholesome for children must be vegetable or succulent. To many constitutions, no doubt, such kinds of food are best adapted; but where the digestive organs are weak, vegetable diet should be sparingly given, and animal food without sauce or high seasoning, more generally administered.

Exercise in the open air is favourable to all children, if not carried to excess; but if indulged to a great extent, and till too advanced a period of youth, the individual becomes in a great measure incapable of exerting the mental faculties. Exercise in the open air, and amidst new and varied objects, is unfavourable to reflection, and to those labours which require a concentration of the power of the mind. It gives a greater tendency to exert the sentiments than the reasoning faculties.

An augmentation of the tone of the muscles diminishes nervous mobility. When, therefore, weakness of mental functions, is owing to too great mobility of the organic system, exercise is beneficial, because it contributes to give stability and energy.

Repose has a contrary effect. Those who live a sedentary life, think and feel more than the active, unless their sedentary habits are carried so far as to produce diseases of the organization, and then the manifestations of the mind are less active.

*   *   *

We proceed, therefore, to the second object in our inquiry,—the order observed by the faculties in the course of their successive development. The faculties which produce the propensities and sentiments are earliest manifested in the order of nature, and therefore, a child is susceptible of moral education before he is susceptible in an equal degree of intellectual cultivation.

It is of importance to parents and teachers to attend to the fact, that the feelings and dispositions of the mind depend upon innate faculties, as well as the intellectual powers, and that the formal faculties may be cultivated as well as the latter.

*   *   *

We ought to receive as axioms in education, therefore, that the predominating dispositions manifested in childhood are innate; that their existence will be permanent; and that it is our duty only to regulate them, and not to be offended at their existence. On these principles we ought to endeavour, if possible to guide children by the law of kindness.

*   *   *

After having discovered the particular dispositions which are remarkable either for strength or deficiency in the child, our next object ought to be to cultivate them, that is, to repress the manifestations of those which are too energetic, and to increase the activity of those which are too feeble. As education is at present conducted, the feelings are not systematically cultivated at all. No system of philosophy has hitherto taught that feelings depend upon faculties; that the power of experiencing them is different in different individuals, and that that power may be increased in those in whom it is weak, by cultivating the faculties which produce them, in the same manner as the power of reasoning may be increased by cultivating the faculties of the understanding. Hence it has never formed a regular part of any plan of education to increase the power of feeling benevolence, of feeling justice, or of feeling veneration, by the special exercise of the faculties upon which those sentiments depend. Nor has any plan been laid down for cultivating the minds of individuals according to the peculiarities of their natural constitutions. Indeed, no such plan could be devised; for we have hitherto possessed no philosophic means of discovering what the peculiarities of individual constitutions are. The only cultivation which the sentiments receive, according to the present system, is from the casual influence of example. This mode of cultivation is no doubt good in itself, and, as experience shows, highly beneficial, but it is best suited to the case of individuals who are prone to virtue from innate dispositions, for we generally perceive the more intractable to be very little benefited by it.

According to this sytem, however, it is necessary to cultivate the feelings by the direct exercise of the faculties upon which they depend. Parents and guardians, therefore, ought to repress the manifestations of the lower propensities in children when they are too energetic, and to call the faculties of the higher sentiments into vigorous activity. The latter effect will be produced, as already mentioned, by the influence of example; because, by the law of social sympathy, active manifestations in one individual excite the same faculties upon which the manifestations depend into activity in the beholders. Thus, if a parent or guardian manifest the faculties of benevolence, of justice, of veneration, or of covetiveness, strongly and habitually in the presence of a child, the same faculties will, by these acts, be cultivated and excited into permanent activity in the child. This is the true account of what the metaphysicians call the Principle of Imitation in children.

*　　*　　*

As a general rule, however, for cultivating the moral powers, it may be safely laid down that, by a law of nature, the regular active manifestations of faculties in parents excite into habitual activity similar faculties in children. But this rule obtains in the faculties which are most prone to run into abuse, as well as in those of a higher order. A parent who inflicts personal chastisement often, and in a rage, or who scolds loud and long, and shows little politeness, little benevolence, and little justice towards a child, cultivates in the latter the faculties which give rise to the emotions of rage and resistance, (combativeness and destructiveness,) and outrages the higher sentiments, just as effectually, or indeed more effectually, than if he were to frame and teach a catechism recommending rage and resistance as positive duties, and decrying justice and benevolence as dangerous and prejudicial. As a general rule, whatever you wish your child to be or to do, be that, or do that to him. If you wish him to be outrageous, to be cruel, and to be quarrelsome, be outrageous, cruel and quarrelsome to him. If you wish him to be humane and polite, be humane and polite to him. If you wish him to be just and pious, be just and devout before him.

So much for the mode of cultivating the propensities and sentiments of our nature. The other faculties susceptible of education at an early period of life, are the *knowing faculties*. The functions of these faculties are to become acquainted with objects and their qualities, but not to reason. Most of these faculties may be manifested in the first stages of childhood, but the reflecting faculties, or those which trace abstract relations and consequences, cannot in general be so till a much later period in life.

The proper mode of cultivating the knowing faculties as well as the former, is by exercising them in active manifestations. If the reader will look over the list of these faculties, and their functions, already enumerated he will have no difficulty in perceiving the class of studies in which children may advantageously engage. According to the present mode of conducting education, the faculty of Language is the only one of all the knowing faculties cultivated in childhood.

* * *

The *reflecting faculties* are the last manifested in the order of time. The brain in the upper part of the forehead, which is the organ of these faculties, is not fully developed in some individuals, till the age of twenty, twenty-three or twenty-four. In others, however, the development is complete at an earlier period of life; but rarely in any one, before fourteen or fifteen.

* * *

The reflecting faculties, like all the others, will be best cultivated by that mode of exercise which makes them produce the most active manifestations. In the metaphysical systems of philosophy, ideas have been unfortunately confounded with the mind; and it has been conceived that, if we merely infuse, with sufficient assiduity, a store of moral precepts and philosophical ideas into the memory, we shall produce the highest state of cultivation in the mind. According to our system, however, all beneficial education consists in the cultivation of faculties.

* * *

This leads us to consider, as was proposed in the last place, the extent of our power to modify the manifestations of the faculties.

As this system teaches that the faculties are innate, and that each has received a determinate constitution from nature, it follows according to it that we cannot change the nature of any individual; and that all we can do is only to regulate the activity of the several faculties in their outward manifestations.

We have already discussed the best modes of increasing the activity of those faculties which we wish to cultivate; and in doing so, we have anticipated, in some degree, the discussion of the extent of our powers of modification. Great as these powers undoubtedly are, it must not be concealed that all our exertions to cultivate the moral and intellectual powers, and to restrain the propensities in their external manifestations, by example, by precept, and by active employment, may sometimes turn out unavailing; and that some individuals will prove ultimately vicious, after every endeavour, conscientiously and intelligently applied, to reclaim them. The system of Gall and Spurzheim not only admits this fact, but explains the causes of it, and affords us great assistance in applying every possible memory to the evil. Strong propensity to vice arises from great natural endowment of the faculties common to man with the lower animals, joined with a weak endowment of the faculties peculiar to man. After we have discovered, therefore, which of the lower propensities are inordinate in their activity, which we easily do by observing the actions of the individual, the next thing to be done is to discover whether the different higher faculties, such as those which give the love of approbation, the sentiment of justice, the sentiment of veneration, or of benevolence, possess considerable or moderate natural power. If they do, we must then be most sedulous in cultivating them by extraordinary efforts, so as to find in them the means of controlling the lower propensities, which are naturally too energetic. We must endeavour to increase, by all practical means, the activity and the sensibility of these higher faculties, so as, if possible, to render the pleasure resulting from their activity, equal or superior to the pleasure attending the indulgence of the others. If we can succeed in these endeavours, we gain the victory to the cause of morality by the most amiable means. If we cannot do so, we must try a remedy of another description.

ROBERT OWEN'S PLANS FOR A SCHOOL AT NEW LANARK (1813)   From Robert Owen, *A New View of Society: Essays on the Formation of Character* (London, n.d.), pp. 32–33, 39–42, 47–49.

Mr. Dale was advancing in years: he had no son to succeed him; and, finding the consequences just described to be the result of all his strenuous exertions for the improvement and happiness of his fellow-creatures, it is not surprising that he became disposed to retire from the cares of the establishment. He accordingly sold it to some English merchants and manufacturers; one of whom, under the circumstances just narrated, undertook the management of the concern, and fixed his residence in the midst of the population. This individual had been previously in the management of large establishments, employing a number of work-people, in the neighbourhood of Manchester; and, in every case, by the steady application of certain general principles, he succeeded in reforming the habits of those under his care, and who always, among their associates in similar employment, appeared conspicuous for their good conduct. With this previous success in remodeling English character, but ignorant of the local ideas, manners, and customs, of those now committed to his management, the stranger commenced his task.

*   *   *

The practice of employing children in the mills, of six, seven, and eight years of age, was discontinued, and their parents advised to allow them to acquire health and education until they were ten years old. (It may be remarked, that even this age is too early to keep them at constant employment in manufactories, from six in the morning to seven in the evening. Far better would it be for the children, their parents, and for society, that the first should not commence employment until they attain the age of twelve, when their education might be finished, and their bodies would be more competent to undergo the fatigue and exertions required of them. When parents can be trained to afford this additional time to their children without inconvenience, they will, of course, adopt the practice now recommended.)

The children were taught reading, writing, and arithmetic, during five years, that is, from five to ten, in the village school, without expense to their parents. All the modern improvements in education have been adopted, or are in process of adoption. (To avoid the inconveniences which must ever arise from the introduction of a particular creed into a school, the children are taught to read in such books as inculcate those precepts of the Christian religion, which are common to all denominations.) They may therefore be taught and well-trained before they engage in any regular employment. Another important consideration is, that all their instruction is rendered a pleasure and delight to them; they are much more anxious for the hour of school-time to arrive than to end; they therefore make a rapid progress; and it may be safely asserted, that if they shall not be trained to form such

EUROPEAN
INFLUENCES

893

characters as may be most desired, the fault will not proceed from the children; the cause will be in the want of a true knowledge of human nature in those who have the management of them and their parents.

During the period that these changes were going forward, attention was given to the domestic arrangements of the community.

Their houses were rendered more comfortable, their streets were improved, the best provisions were purchased, and sold to them at low rates, yet covering the original expense, and under such regulations as taught them how to proportion their expenditure to their income. Fuel and clothes were obtained for them in the same manner; and no advantage was attempted to be taken of them, or means used to deceive them.

In consequence, their animosity and opposition to the stranger subsided, their full confidence was obtained, and they became satisfied that no evil was intended them, they were convinced that a real desire existed to increase their happiness upon those grounds alone on which it could be permanently increased. All difficulties in the way of future improvement vanished. They were taught to be rational, and they acted rationally.

*   *   *

At the conclusion of the Second Essay, a promise was made that an account should be given of the plans which were in progress at New Lanark for the further improvement of its inhabitants; and that a practical system should be sketched, by which equal advantages might be generally introduced among the poor and working classes throughout the United Kingdom.

This account became necessary, in order to exhibit even a limited view of the principles on which the plans of the author are founded, and to recommend them generally to practice.

That which has been hitherto done for the community at New Lanark, as described in the Second Essay, has chiefly consisted in *withdrawing some of those circumstances which tended to generate, continue, or increase early bad habits; that is to say, undoing that which society had from ignorance permitted to be done.*

To effect this, however, was a far more difficult task than to train up a child from infancy in the way he should go; for that is the most easy process for the formation of character; while to unlearn and to change long acquired habits is a proceeding directly opposed to the most tenacious feelings of human nature.

Nevertheless, the proper application steadily pursued did effect beneficial changes on these habits, even beyond the most sanguine expectations of the party by whom the task was undertaken.

The principles were derived from the study of human nature itself, and they could not fail of success.

Still, however, very little, comparatively speaking, had been done for them. They had not been taught the most valuable domestic and social habits: such as the most economical method of preparing food; how to arrange their dwellings with neatness, and to keep them always clean and in order; but, what was of infinitely more importance, they had not been instructed how to train their children to form them into valuable members of the community, or to know that principles existed, which, when properly applied to practice from infancy, would ensure from man to man, without chance of failure, a just, open, sincere, and benevolent conduct.

It was in this stage of the progress of improvement, that it became necessary to form arrangements for surrounding them with circumstances which should gradually prepare the individuals to receive and firmly retain those domestic and social acquirements and habits. For this purpose a building, which may be termed the "New Institution," was erected in the centre of the establishment, with an enclosed area before it. The area is intended for a playground for the children of the villagers, from the time they can walk alone until they enter the school.

It must be evident to those who have been in the practice of observing children with attention, that much of good or evil is taught to or acquired by a child at a very early period of its life; that much of temper or disposition is correctly or incorrectly formed before he attains his second year; and that many durable impressions are made at the termination of the first twelve or even six months of his existence. The children, therefore, of the uninstructed and ill-instructed, suffer material injury in the formation of their characters during these and the subsequent years of childhood and of youth.

It was to prevent, or as much as possible to counteract, these primary evils, to which the poor and working classes are exposed when infants, that the area became part of the New Institution.

Into this playground the children are to be received as soon as they can freely walk alone; to be superintended by persons instructed to take charge of them.

As the happiness of man chiefly, if not altogether, depends on his own sentiments and habits, as well as those of the individuals around him; and as any sentiments and habits may be given to all infants, it becomes of primary importance that those alone should be given to them which can contribute to their happiness. Each child, therefore, on his entrance into the playground, is to be told in language which he can understand, that "he is never to injure his play-fellows; but that, on the contrary, hs is to contribute all in his power to make them happy." This simple precept, when comprehended in all its bearings, and the habits which will arise from its early adoption into practice, *if no counteracting principle be forced upon the young mind*, will effectually supersede all the errors which have hitherto kept the world in ignorance and misery. So simple a precept, too, will be easily taught, and as easily acquired; for the chief employment of the superintendents will be to prevent any deviation from it in practice. The older children, when they shall have experienced the endless advantages from acting on this principle, will, by their example, soon enforce the practice of it on the young strangers: and the happiness which the little groups will enjoy from this rational conduct, will ensure its speedy and general and willing adoption. The habit also which they will acquire at this early period of life by continually acting on the principle, will fix it firmly; it will become easy and familiar to them, or, as it is often termed, natural.

Thus, by merely attending to the evidence of our senses respecting human nature, and disregarding the wild, inconsistent, and absurd theories in which man has been hitherto trained in all parts of the earth, we shall accomplish with ease and certainty the supposed Herculean labour of forming a rational character in man, and that, too, chiefly before the child commences the ordinary course of education.

The character thus early formed will be as durable as it will be advantageous to the individual and to the community; for by the constitution of our nature, when once the mind fully understands that which is true, the impression of that truth cannot be erased except by mental diseases or death; while error must be relinquished at every period of life, whenever it can be made manifest to the mind in which it has been received. This part of the arrangement, therefore, will effect the following purposes:

The child will be removed, so far as is at present practicable, from the erroneous treatment of the yet untrained and untaught parents.

The parents will be relieved from the loss of time and from the care and anxiety which are now occasioned by attendance on their children from the period when they can go alone to that at which they enter the school.

The child will be placed in a situation of safety, where, with its future school-fellows and companions, it will acquire the best habits and principles, while at meal times and at night it will return to the caresses of its parents; and the affections of each are likely to be increased by the separation.

The area is also to be a place of meeting for the children from five to ten years of age, previous to and after school-hours, and to serve for a drill ground, the object of which will be hereafter explained; and a shade will be formed, under which in stormy weather the children may retire for shelter.

These are the important purposes to which a playground attached to a school may be applied.

Those who have derived a knowledge of human nature from observation, know, that man in every situation requires relaxation from his constant and regular occupations, whatever they be: and that if he shall not be provided with or permitted to enjoy innocent and uninjurious amusements, he must and will partake of those which he can obtain, to give him temporary relief from his exertions, although the means of gaining that relief should be most pernicious. For man, irrationally instructed, is ever influenced far more by immediate feelings than by remote considerations.

Those, then, who desire to give mankind the character which it would be for the happiness of all that they should possess, will not fail to make careful provision for their amusement and recreation.

The Sabbath was originally so intended. It was instituted to be a day of universal enjoyment and happiness to the human race. It is frequently made, however, from the opposite extremes of error, either a day of superstitious gloom and tyranny over the mind, or of the most destructive intemperance and licentiousness. The one of these has been the cause of the other; the latter the certain and natural consequence of the former. Relieve the human mind from useless and superstitious restraints; train it on those principles which facts, ascertained from the first knowledge of time to this day, demonstrate to be the only principles which are true; and intemperance and licentiousness will not exist; for such conduct in itself is neither the immediate nor the future interest of man; and he is ever governed by one or other of these considerations, according to the habits which have been given to him from infancy.

The Sabbath, in many parts of Scotland, is not a day of innocent and cheerful recreation to the labouring man, nor can those who are confined all the week to sedentary occupations, freely partake, without censure, of the air and exercise to which nature invites them, and which their health demands.

The errors of the times of superstition and bigotry still hold some sway, and compel those who wish to preserve a regard to their respectability in society, to an overstrained demeanour; and this demeanour sometimes degenerates into hypocrisy, and is often the cause of great inconsistency. It is destructive of every open, honest, generous, and manly feeling. It disgusts many, and drives them to the opposite extreme. It is sometimes the cause of insanity. It is founded on ignorance, and defeats its own object.

While erroneous customs prevail in any country, it would evince an ignorance of human nature in any individual to offend against them, until he has convinced the community of their error.

To counteract, in some degree, the inconvenience which arose from the misapplication of the Sabbath, it became necessary to introduce on the other days of the week some innocent amusement and recreation for those whose labours were unceasing, and in winter almost uniform. In summer, the inhabitants of the village of New Lanark have their gardens and potato grounds to cultivate; they have walks laid out to give them health and the habit of being gratified with the ever-changing scenes of nature;—for those scenes afford not only the most economical, but also the most innocent pleasures which man can enjoy; and all men may be easily trained to enjoy them.

In winter the community are deprived of these healthy occupations and amusements; they are employed ten hours and three quarters every day in the week, except Sunday, and generally every individual continues during that time at the same work: and experience has shown that the average health and spirits of the community are several degrees lower in winter than in summer; and this in part may be fairly attributed to that cause.

These considerations suggested the necessity of rooms for innocent amusements and rational recreation.

Many well-intentioned individuals, unaccustomed to witness the conduct of those among the lower orders who have been rationally treated and trained, may fancy such an assemblage will necessarily become a scene of confusion and disorder; instead of which, however, it proceeds with uniform propriety; it is highly favourable to the health, spirits, and dispositions of the individuals so engaged; and if any irregularity should arise, the cause will be solely owing to the parties who attempt to direct the proceedings being deficient in the practical knowledge of human nature.

ROBERT OWEN ON ENVIRONMENT AND THE FORMATION OF CHARACTER (1813)   From Robert Owen, *A New View of Society: Essays on the Formation of Character* (London, n.d.), pp. 14–16, 19–20, 26–29.

Essays on the Formation of Character

FIRST ESSAY

"Any general character, from the best to the worst, from the most ignorant to the most enlightened, may be given to any community, even to the world at large, by the application of proper means; which means are to a great extent at the command and under the control of those who have influence in the affairs of men."

According to the last returns under the Population Act, the poor and working classes of Great Britain and Ireland have been found to exceed fifteen millions of persons, or nearly three-fourths of the population of the British Islands.

The characters of these persons are now permitted to be very generally formed without proper guidance or direction, and, in many cases, under circumstances which directly impel them to a course of extreme vice and misery; thus rendering them the worst and most dangerous subjects in the empire; while the far greater

EUROPEAN INFLUENCES

897

part of the remainder of the community are educated upon the most mistaken principles of human nature, such, indeed, as cannot fail to produce a general conduct throughout society, totally unworthy of the character of rational beings.

The first thus unhappily situated are the poor and the uneducated profligate among the working classes, who are now trained to commit crimes, for the commission of which they are afterwards punished.

The second is the remaining mass of the population, who are now instructed to believe, or at least to acknowledge, that certain principles are unerringly true, and to act as though they were grossly false; thus filling the world with folly and inconsistency, and making society, throughout all its ramifications, a scene of insincerity and counteraction.

In this state the world has continued to the present time; its evils have been and are continually increasing; they cry aloud for efficient corrective measures, which if we longer delay, general disorder must ensue.

"But," say those who have not deeply investigated the subject, "attempts to apply remedies have been often made, yet all of them have failed. The evil is now of a magnitude not to be controlled; the torrent is already too strong to be stemmed; and we can only wait with fear or calm resignation to see it carry destruction in its course, by confounding all distinctions of right and wrong."

Such is the language now held, and such are the general feelings on this most important subject.

These, however, if longer suffered to continue, must lead to the most lamentable consequences. Rather than pursue such a course, the character of legislators would be infinitely raised, if, forgetting the petty and humiliating contentions of sects and parties, they would thoroughly investigate the subject, and endeavour to arrest and overcome these mighty evils.

The chief object of these Essays is to assist and forward investigations of such vital importance to the well-being of this country, and of society in general.

The view of the subject which is about to be given has arisen from extensive experience for upwards of twenty years, during which period its truth and importance have been proved by multiplied experiments. That the writer may not be charged with precipitation or presumption, he has had the principle and its consequences, examined, scrutinised, and fully canvassed, by some of the most learned, intelligent, and competent characters of the present day: who, on every principle of duty as well as of interest, if they had discovered error in either, would have exposed it;—but who, on the contrary, have fairly acknowledged their incontrovertible truth and practical importance.

Assured, therefore, that his principles are true, he proceeds with confidence, and courts the most ample and free discussion of the subject; courts it for the sake of humanity—for the sake of his fellow creatures—millions of whom experience sufferings which, were they to be unfolded, would compel those who govern the world to exclaim—"Can these things exist and we have no knowledge of them?" But they do exist—and even the heart-rending statements which were made known to the public during the discussions upon negro-slavery, do not exhibit more afflicting scenes than those which, in various parts of the world, daily arise from the injustice of society towards itself; from the inattention of mankind to the circumstances which incessantly surround them; and from the want of a correct knowledge of human nature in those who govern and control the affairs of men.

If these circumstances did not exist to an extent almost incredible, it would be unnecessary now to contend for a principle regarding Man, which scarcely requires more than to be fairly stated to make it self-evident.

This principle is, that *"Any general character, from the best to the worst, from the most ignorant to the most enlightened, may be given to any community, even to the world at large, by the application of proper means; which means are to a great extent at the command and under the control of those who have influence in the affairs of men."*

The principle as now stated is a broad one, and, if it should be found to be true, cannot fail to give a new character to legislative proceedings, and such a character as will be most favourable to the well-being of society.

That this principle is true to the utmost limit of the terms, is evident from the experience of all past ages, and from every existing fact.

❋　　❋　　❋

In preparing the way for the introduction of these principles, it cannot now be necessary to enter into the detail of facts to prove that children can be trained to acquire *"any language, sentiments, belief, or any bodily habits and manners, not contrary to human nature."*

❋　　❋　　❋

It will therefore be the essence of wisdom in the privileged class to co-operate sincerely and cordially with those who desire not to touch one iota of the supposed advantages which they now possess; and whose first and last wish is to increase the particular happiness of those classes, as well as the general happiness of society. A very little reflection on the part of the privileged will ensure this line of conduct; whence, without domestic revolution—without war or bloodshed—nay, without prematurely disturbing any thing which exists, the world will be prepared to receive principles which are alone calculated to build up a system of happiness, and to destroy those irritable feelings which have so long afflicted society,—solely because society has hitherto been ignorant of the true means by which the most useful and valuable character may be formed.

This ignorance being removed, experience will soon teach us how to form character, individually and generally, so as to give the greatest sum of happiness to the individual and to mankind.

These principles require only to be known in order to establish themselves; the outline of our future proceedings then becomes clear and defined, nor will they permit us henceforth to wander from the right path. They direct that the governing powers of all countries should establish rational plans for the education and general formation of the characters of their subjects. *These plans must be devised to train children from their earliest infancy in good habits of every description (which will of course prevent them from acquiring those of falsehood and deception). They must afterwards be rationally educated, and their labour be usefully directed. Such habits and education will impress them with an active and ardent desire to promote the happiness of every individual, and that without the* shadow of exception *for sect, or party, or country, or climate. They will also ensure, with the fewest possible exceptions, health, strength, and vigour of body; for the happiness of man can be erected only on the foundations of health of body and peace of mind.*

And that health of body and peace of mind may be preserved sound and entire, through youth and manhood, to old age, it becomes equally necessary that the irresistible propensities which form a part of his nature, and which now produce the endless and ever multiplying evils with which humanity is afflicted, should be so directed as to increase and not to counteract his happiness.

The knowledge however thus introduced will make it evident to the understanding, that by far the greater part of the misery with which man is encircled *may* be easily dissipated and removed; and that with mathematical precision he *may* be surrounded with those circumstances which must gradually increase his happiness.

ROBERT OWEN'S DESCRIPTION OF HIS SCHOOL AT NEW LANARK

(**c. 1833**) From *The Life of Robert Owen, by Himself* (New York, 1920), pp. 186–87, 190–95.

I had been and was making great and substantial progress with my New Lanark experiment, and it was now becoming widely known, and attracted the attention of those in advanced stations at home and abroad. I had now completed, and furnished according to my new mode of instruction by sensible signs and familiar conversation, the first institution for the formation of the infant and child character—the infants being received into it at one year old, or as soon as they could walk.

The parents at first could not understand what I was going to do with their little children at *two* years of age, but seeing the results produced they became eager to send their infants at one year old, and inquired if I could not take them yet younger.

I charged the parents, that it might not be considered a pauper school, threepence per month, or three shillings a year, for each child, and of course they paid this most willingly. The expense of this establishment of three gradations of schools was about two pounds per year for each child. But the difference between the three shillings and two pounds was amply made up by the improved character of the whole population, upon whom the school had a powerful influence for good.

The children were trained and educated without punishment or any fear of it, and were while in school by far the happiest human beings I have even seen.

The infants and young children, besides being instructed by sensible signs,—the things themselves, or models or paintings,—and by familiar conversation, were from two years and upwards daily taught dancing and singing, and the parents were encouraged to come and see their children at any of their lessons or physical exercises.

But in addition there were day schools for all under twelve years old, after which age they might, if their parents wished, enter the works, either as mechanics, manufacturers, or in any branch—for we had iron- and brass-founders, forgers, turners in wood and iron, machine makers, and builders in all branches, having continually buildings to repair and erect and machinery on a large scale to repair and renew. The annual repairs alone of the establishment cost at this period upwards of eight thousand pounds.

I also organized arrangements to supply all the wants of the population, buying every thing for money on a large scale in the first markets, and supplying them at first cost and charges. They had previously been necessitated to buy inferior articles, highly adulterated, at enormous prices, making their purchases at small grocery and grog shops, chiefly on credit; and their butcher's meat was generally little better than skin and bone. By the time the arrangements to provide for the whole circle of their wants in food, clothing, etc., etc., were completed, some of the larger families were earning two pounds per week, and the heads of these families told me that my new arrangements to supply their wants saved them in price ten shillings weekly, besides the great difference between deteriorated and the most inferior qualities and the best unadulterated articles. The grocery and grog shops speedily disappeared, and the population soon relieved themselves from the debts previously contracted to them.

All the houses in the village, with one hundred and fifty acres of land around it, formed parts of the establishment, all united, and working together as one machine, proceeding day by day with the regularity of clockwork. The order of the whole was such, that Mr. Henry Hase, the well-known cashier for so many years of the Bank of England, and who reorganized the arrangements of the bank, when on his first visit to me, after he had examined the whole with great minuteness and continually increasing interest as he advanced in his task, said—"Mr. Owen, this must be the work of some generations." How long has it been in progress to "attain this high perfection of systematic order?"

I had divided the establishment into four general departments, and had taken great pains and had given much attention to train four persons whom I placed at the head of each of these departments to understand my views respecting them and the mode of governing those placed under their immediate direction. Upon leaving the establishment when I expected to be absent for a long period, it was my practice to call these four together, and to explain fully what I wished to have done in each department during my absence. And on my return I uniformly found my wishes fulfilled, and my instructions faithfully followed.

I also adopted the same practice with the teachers in the three gradations of the schools, and with as much success as I could expect from young persons of both sexes, inexperienced in the correct knowledge of human nature, and therefore not always capable of making the due allowance for the varied natural character of each child.

I had before this period acquired the most sincere affections of all the children. I say of all—because every child above one year old was daily sent to the schools. I had also the hearts of all their parents, who were highly delighted with the improved conduct, extraordinary progress, and continually increasing happiness of their children, and with the substantial improvements by which I gradually surrounded them. But the great attraction to myself and the numerous strangers who now continually visited the establishment, was the new infant school; the progress of which from its opening I daily watched and superintended, until I could prepare the mind of the master whom I had selected for this, in my estimation, most important charge,—knowing that if the foundation were not truly laid, it would be in vain to expect a satisfactory structure.

It was in vain to look to any old teachers upon the old system of instruction by books. In the previous old schoolroom I had tried to induce the master to adopt my views; but he could not and would not attempt to adopt what he deemed to be such a fanciful "new-fangled" mode of teaching, and he was completely under the influence of the minister of the parish, who was himself also opposed to any change of system in teaching children, and who considered that the attempt to educate and teach infants was altogether a senseless and vain proceeding. I had therefore, although he was a good obstinate "dominie" of the old school, reluctantly to part with him, and I had to seek among the population for two persons who had a great love for and unlimited patience with infants, and who were thoroughly tractable and willing unreservedly to follow my instructions. The best to my mind in these respects that I could find in the population of the village, was a poor, simple-hearted weaver, named James Buchanan, who had been previously trained by his wife to perfect submission to her will, and who could gain but a scanty living by his now dying trade of weaving common plain cotton goods by hand. But he loved children strongly by nature, and his patience with them was inexhaustible. These, with his willingness to be instructed, were the qualities which I required in the master for the first rational infant school that had even been imagined by any party in any country; for it was the first practical step of a system new to the world;—and yet with all my teaching of all classes of the public, it is still little understood in principle, and not at all yet conceived in practice, although the high permanent happiness through futurity of our race depends upon the principle and practice in all their purity being correctly carried into execution by all nations and people.

Thus the simple-minded, kind-hearted James Buchanan, who at first could scarcely read, write, or spell, became the first master in a rational infant school. But infants so young, also required a female nurse, to assist the master, and one also who possessed the same natural qualifications. Such an one I found among the numerous young females employed in the cotton mills, and I was fortunate in finding for this task a young woman, about seventeen years of age, known familiarly among the villagers as "Molly Young," who of the two, in natural powers of mind, had the advantage over her new companion in an office perfectly new to both.

The first instruction which I gave them was, that they were on no account ever to beat any one of the children, or to threaten them in any manner in word or action, or to use abusive terms; but were always to speak to them with a pleasant countenance, and in a kind manner and tone of voice. That they should tell the infants and children (for they had all from one to six years old under their charge) that they must on all occasions do all they could to make their playfellows happy,— and that the older ones, from four to six years of age, should take especial care of younger ones, and should assist to teach them to make each other happy.

These instructions were readily received by James Buchanan and Molly Young, and were faithfully adhered to by them as long as they remained in their respective situations.

The children were not to be annoyed with books; but were to be taught the uses and nature or qualities of the common things around them, by familiar conversation when the children's curiosity was excited so as to induce them to ask questions respecting them.

The room for their play in bad weather was sixteen feet by twenty, and sixteen feet high.

The schoolroom for the infant instruction was of the same dimensions, and was furnished with paintings, chiefly of animals, with maps, and often supplied with natural objects from the gardens, fields, and woods,—the examination and explanation of which always excited their curiosity and created an animated conversation between the children and their instructors, now themselves acquiring new knowledge by attempting to instruct their young friends, as I always taught them to think their pupils were, and to treat them as such.

The children at four and above that age showed an early desire to understand the use of the maps of the four quarters of the world upon a large scale, which were purposely hung in the room to attract their attention. Buchanan, their master, was first taught their use, and then how to instruct the children for their amusement,— for with these infants everything was made to be amusement.

It was most encouraging and delightful to see the progress which these infants and children made in real knowledge, without the use of books. And when the best means of instruction or forming character shall be known, I doubt whether books will be ever used before children attain their tenth year. And yet without books they will have a superior character formed for them at ten, as rational beings, knowing themselves and society in principle and practice, far better than the best-informed now know these subjects at their majority, or the mass of the population of the world know them at any age.

Human nature, its capacities and powers, is yet to be learned by the world. Its faculties are unknown, unappreciated, and therefore misdirected, and wasted lamentably in all manner of ways, to the grievous injury of all our race through every succeeding generation.

When the beautiful and most wonderful organs, faculties, propensities, powers, and qualities of humanity, for the attainment of high excellence and happiness, shall be understood, and shall be rationally taught by one generation to its successor, truth will be the only language among men, and the pure spirit of enlightened charity and love will pervade the entire of the human race. And how simple is truth and real knowledge, when unmixed with the errors and prejudices of ignorance, and with a want of knowing how to apply practical measures to bring truth and knowledge into the common affairs of life! Here, with the most simple means as agents, two untaught persons, not having one idea of the office in which they were placed, or of the objects intended to be attained, accomplished, unknown to themselves, results which surprised, astonished, and confounded the most learned and wise, and the greatest men of their generation. James Buchanan and Molly Young, by being for some time daily instructed how to treat the infants and children committed to their charge within the surroundings which had been previously created and arranged for them, produced results, unconsciously to themselves, which attracted the attention of the advanced minds of the civilized world—results which puzzled the most experienced of them, to divine the power which could mould humanity into the beings they came to see.

After some short time they were unlike all children of such situated parents, and indeed unlike the children of any class of society. Those at two years of age and above had commenced dancing lessons, and those of four years of age and upwards singing lessons,—both under a good teacher. Both sexes were also drilled, and became efficient in the military exercises, being formed into divisions, led by young drummers and fifers, they became very expert and perfect in these exercises.

But to teach dancing, music, and military discipline to these infants and children, was an abomination to the Society of Friends, and I now had three partners who were Friends, and who were among the most distinguished in their society—John Walker of Arno's Grove, Joseph Foster of Bromley—both men of high, liberal, and superior minds, with the kindest dispositions,—and William Allen, a man of great pretensions in his sect, a very busy, bustling, meddling character, making great professions of friendship to me, yet underhandedly doing all in his power to undermine my views and authority in conducting the new forming of the character of the children and of the population at New Lanark. Yet such were the extraordinary good effects produced by these un-Quaker-like proceedings, that not a word was said by any of them for some years after our partnership commenced, and it was only after a lapse of some years that William Allen made objections, saying that his society did not approve of them.

Now, as I had anticipated, dancing, music, and military discipline, conducted on the principles of charity and kindness to all of humankind, were among the best and most powerful surroundings for forming a good and happy character, that could be introduced.

NEWMAN'S IDEA OF A UNIVERSITY (1852)   From John Henry Cardinal Newman, *The Idea of a University* (London, 1919), pp. ix, xiv-xx, 99–104, 106–9, 129–30.

The view taken of a University in these Discourses is the following:—That it is a place of *teaching* universal *knowledge*. This implies that its object is, on the one hand, intellectual, not moral; and, on the other, that it is the diffusion and extension of knowledge rather than the advancement. If its object were scientific and philosophical discovery, I do not see why a University should have students; if religious training, I do not see how it can be the seat of literature and science.

Such is a University in its *essence*, and independently of its relation to the Church. But, practically speaking, it cannot fulfil its object duly, such as I have described it, without the Church's assistance; or, to use the theological term, the Church is necessary for its *integrity*. Not that its main characters are changed by this incorporation: it still has the office of intellectual education; but the Church steadies it in the performance of that office.

*   *   *

Returning, then, to the consideration of the question, from which I may seem to have digressed, thus much I think I have made good,—that, whether or no a Catholic University should put before it, as its great object, to make its students "gentlemen," still to make them something or other *is* its great object, and not simply to protect the interests and advance the dominion of Science. If, then, this may be taken for granted, as I think it may, the only point which remains to be settled is, whether I have formed a probable conception of the *sort of benefit* which the Holy See has intended to confer on Catholics who speak the English tongue by recommending to the Irish Hierarchy the establishment of a University; and this I now proceed to consider.

Here, then, it is natural to ask those who are interested in the question, whether any better interpretation of the recommendation of the Holy See can be given than that which I have suggested in this Volume. Certainly it does not seem to me rash to pronounce that, whereas Protestants have great advantages of education in the Schools, Colleges, and Universities of the United Kingdom, our ecclesiastical rulers have it in purpose that Catholics should enjoy the like advantages, whatever they are, to the full. I conceive they view it as prejudicial to the interests of Religion that there should be any cultivation of mind bestowed upon Protestants which is not given to their own youth also. As they wish their schools for the poorer and middle classes to be at least on a par with those of Protestants, they contemplate the same object also as regards that higher education which is given to comparatively the few. Protestant youths, who can spare the time, continue their studies till the age of twenty-one or twenty-two; thus they employ a time of life all-important and especially favourable to mental culture. I conceive that our Prelates are impressed with the fact and its consequences, that a youth who ends his education at seventeen is no match (*caeteris paribus*) for one who ends it at twenty-two.

All classes indeed of the community are impressed with a fact so obvious as this. The consequence is, that Catholics who aspire to be on a level with Protestants in discipline and refinement of intellect have recourse to Protestant Universities to obtain what they cannot find at home. Assuming (as the Rescripts from Propaganda allow me to do) that Protestant education is inexpedient for our youth,—we see here an additional reason why those advantages, whatever they are, which Protestant communities dispense through the medium of Protestantism should be accessible to Catholics in a Catholic form.

What are these advantages? I repeat, they are in one word the culture of the intellect. Robbed, oppressed, and thrust aside, Catholics in these islands have not been in a condition for centuries to attempt the sort of education which is necessary for the man of the world, the statesman, the landholder, or the opulent gentleman. Their legitimate stations, duties, employments, have been taken from them, and the qualifications withal, social and intellectual, which are necessary both for reversing the forfeiture and for availing themselves of the reversal. The time is come when this moral disability must be removed. Our desideratum is, not the manners and habits of gentlemen;—these can be, and are, acquired in various other ways, by good society, by foreign travel, by the innate grace and dignity of the Catholic mind;—but the force, the steadiness, the comprehensiveness and the versatility of intellect, the command over our own powers, the instinctive just estimate of things as they pass before us, which sometimes indeed is a natural gift, but commonly is not gained without much effort and the exercise of years.

This is real cultivation of mind; and I do not deny that the characteristic excellences of a gentleman are included in it. Nor need we be ashamed that they should be, since the poet long ago wrote, that "Ingenuas didicisse fideliter artes Emollit mores." Certainly a liberal education does manifest itself in a courtesy, propriety, and polish of word and action, which is beautiful in itself, and acceptable to others; but it does much more. It brings the mind into form,—for the mind is like the body. Boys outgrow their shape and strength; their limbs have to be knit together, and their constitution needs tone. Mistaking animal spirits for vigour, and over-confident in their health, ignorant what they can bear and how to manage themselves, they are immoderate and extravagant; and fall into sharp sicknesses. This is an emblem of their minds; at first they have no principles laid down within them as a foundation for the intellect to build upon; they have no discriminating convictions, and no grasp of consequences. And therefore they talk at random, if they talk much, and cannot help being flippant, or what is emphatically called "*young.*" They are merely dazzled by phenomena, instead of perceiving things as they are.

It were well if none remained boys all their lives; but what is more common than the sight of grown men, talking on political or moral or religious subjects, in that offhand, idle way, which we signify by the word *unreal?* "That they simply do not know what they are talking about" is the spontaneous silent remark of any man of sense who hears them. Hence such persons have no difficulty in contradicting themselves in successive sentences, without being conscious of it. Hence others, whose defect in intellectual training is more latent, have their most unfortunate crotchets, as they are called, or hobbies, which deprive them of the influence which their estimable qualities would otherwise secure. Hence others can never look straight before them, never see the point, and have no difficulties in the most difficult subjects. Others are hopelessly obstinate and prejudiced, and, after they have been driven from their opinions, return to them the next moment without even an attempt to explain why. Others are so intemperate and intractable that there is no greater calamity for a good cause than that they should get hold of it. It is very plain from the very particulars I have mentioned that, in this delineation of intellectual infirmities, I am drawing, not from Catholics, but from the world at large; I am referring to an evil which is forced upon us in every railway carriage, in every coffee-room or *table-d'hôte*, in every mixed company, an evil, however, to which Catholics are not less exposed than the rest of mankind.

When the intellect has once been properly trained and formed to have a connected view or grasp of things, it will display its powers with more or less effect according to its particular quality and capacity in the individual. In the case of most men it makes itself felt in the good sense, sobriety of thought, reasonableness, candour, self-command, and steadiness of view, which characterize it. In some it will have developed habits of business, power of influencing others, and sagacity. In others it will elicit the talent of philosophical speculation, and lead the mind forward to eminence in this or that intellectual department. In all it will be a faculty of entering with comparative ease into any subject of thought, and of taking up with aptitude any science or profession. All this it will be and will do in a measure, even when the mental formation be made after a model but partially true; for, as far as effectiveness goes, even false views of things have more influence and inspire more respect than no views at all. Men who fancy they see what is not are more energetic, and make their way better, than those who see nothing; and so the undoubting infidel, the fanatic, the heresiarch, are able to do much, while the mere hereditary Christian, who has never realized the truths which he holds, is unable to do anything. But, if consistency of view can add so much strength even to error, what may it not be expected to furnish to the dignity, the energy, and the influence of Truth!

Some one, however, will perhaps object that I am but advocating that spurious philosophism, which shows itself in what, for want of a word, I may call "viewiness," when I speak so much of the formation, and consequent grasp, of the intellect. It may be said that the theory of University Education, which I have been delineating, if acted upon, would teach youths nothing soundly or thoroughly, and would dismiss them with nothing better than brilliant general views about all things whatever.

This indeed, if well founded, would be a most serious objection to what I have advanced in this Volume, and would demand my immediate attention, had I any reason to think that I could not remove it at once, by a simple explanation of what I consider the true *mode* of educating, were this the place to do so. But these Discourses are directed simply to the consideration of the *aims* and *principles* of Education. Suffice it, then, to say here, that I hold very strongly that the first step in intellectual training is to impress upon a boy's mind the idea of science, method, order, principle and system; of rule and exception, of richness and harmony. This is commonly and excellently done by making him begin with Grammar; nor can too great accuracy, or minuteness and subtlety of teaching be used towards him, as his faculties expand, with this simple purpose. Hence it is that critical scholarship is so important a discipline for him when he is leaving school for the University. A second science is the Mathematics: this should follow Grammar, still with the same object, viz., to give him a conception of development and arrangement from and around a common centre. Hence it is that Chronology and Geography are so necessary for him, when he reads History, which is otherwise little better than a storybook. Hence, too, Metrical Composition, when he reads Poetry; in order to stimulate his powers into action in every practicable way, and to prevent a merely passive reception of images and ideas which in that case are likely to pass out of the mind as soon as they have entered it. Let him once gain this habit of method, of starting from fixed points, of making his ground good as he goes, of distinguishing what he knows from what he does not know, and I conceive he will be gradually initiated into the largest and truest philosophical views, and will feel nothing but impatience and disgust at the random theories and imposing sophistries and dashing paradoxes, which carry away half-formed and superficial intellects.

It is a great point then to enlarge the range of studies which a University professes, even for the sake of the students; and, though they cannot pursue every subject, which is open to them, they will be the gainers by living among those and under those who represent the whole circle. This I conceive to be the advantage of a seat of universal learning, considered as a place of education. An assemblage of learned men, zealous for their own sciences, and rivals of each other, are brought, by familiar intercourse and for the sake of intellectual peace, to adjust together the claims and relations of their respective subjects of investigation. They learn to respect, to consult, to aid each other. Thus is created a pure and clear atmosphere of thought, which the student also breathes, though in his own case he only pursues a few sciences out of the multitude. He profits by an intellectual tradition, which is independent of particular teachers, which guides him in his choice of subjects, and duly interprets for him those which he chooses. He apprehends the great outlines of knowledge, the principles on which it rests, the scale of its parts, its lights and its shades, its great points and its little, as he otherwise cannot apprehend them. Hence it is that his education is called "Liberal." A habit of mind is formed which lasts through life, of which the attributes are, freedom, equitableness, calmness, moderation, and wisdom; or what in a former Discourse I have ventured to call a philosophical habit. This then I would assign as the special fruit of the education furnished at a University, as contrasted with other places of teaching or modes of teaching. This is the main purpose of a University in its treatment of its students.

And now the question is asked me, What is the use of it? and my answer will constitute the main subject of the Discourses which are to follow.

MR. GRADGRIND, TEACHER (1854)   From Charles Dickens, *Hard Times* (London, 1854), pp. 1–8.

Book The First. Sowing

Chapter I. The One Thing Needful

Now, what I want is, Facts. Teach these boys and girls nothing but Facts. Facts alone are wanted in life. Plant nothing else, and root out everything else. You can only form the minds of reasoning animals upon Facts: nothing else will ever be of any service to them. This is the principle on which I bring up my own children, and this is the principle on which I bring up these children. Stick to Facts, Sir!'

The scene was a plain, bare, monotonous vault of a schoolroom, and the speaker's square forefinger emphasized his observations by underscoring every sentence with a line on the schoolmaster's sleeve. The emphasis was helped by the speaker's square wall of a forehead, which had his eyebrows for its base, while his eyes found commodious cellarage in two dark caves, overshadowed by the wall. The emphasis was helped by the speaker's hair, which bristled on the skirts of his bald head, a plantation of firs to keep the wind from its shining surface, all covered with knobs, like the crust of a plum pie, as if the head had scarcely warehouse-room for the hard facts stored inside. The speaker's obstinate carriage, square coat, square legs, square shoulders,—nay, his very neckcloth, trained to take him by the throat with an unaccommodating grasp, like a stubborn fact, as it was,—all helped the emphasis.

'In this life, we want nothing but Facts, Sir; nothing but Facts!'

The speaker, and the schoolmaster, and the third grown person present, all backed a little, and swept with their eyes the inclined plane of little vessels then and there arranged in order, ready to have imperial gallons of facts poured into them until they were full to the brim.

Chapter II. Murdering the Innocents

Thomas Gradgrind, Sir. A man of realities. A man of facts and calculations. A man who proceeds upon the principle that two and two are four, and nothing over, and who is not to be talked into allowing for anything over. Thomas Gradgrind, Sir—peremptorily Thomas—Thomas Gradgrind. With a rule and a pair of scales, and the multiplication table always in his pocket, Sir, ready to weigh and measure any parcel of human nature, and tell you exactly what it comes to. It is a mere question of figures, a case of simple arithmetic. You might hope to get some other nonsensical belief into the head of George Gradgrind, or Augustus Gradgrind, or John Gradgrind, or Joseph Gradgrind (all supposititious, non-existent persons), but into the head of Thomas Gradgrind—no, Sir!

In such terms Mr. Gradgrind always mentally introduced himself, whether to his private circle of acquaintance, or to the public in general. In such terms, no doubt, substituting the words 'boys and girls,' for 'Sir,' Thomas Gradgrind now presented Thomas Gradgrind to the little pitchers before him, who were to be filled so full of facts.

Indeed, as he eagerly sparkled at them from the cellarage before mentioned, he seemed a kind of cannon loaded to the muzzle with facts, and prepared to blow them clean out of the regions of childhood at one discharge. He seemed a galvanizing apparatus, too, charged with a grim mechanical substitute for the tender young imaginations that were to be stormed away.

'Girl number twenty,' said Mr. Gradgrind, squarely pointing with his square forefinger, 'I don't know that girl. Who is that girl?'

'Sissy Jupe, Sir,' explained number twenty, blushing, standing up, and curtseying.

'Sissy is not a name,' said Mr. Gradgrind. 'Don't call yourself Sissy. Call yourself Cecilia.'

'It's father as calls me Sissy, Sir,' returned the young girl in a trembling voice, and with another curtsey.

'Then he has no business to do it,' said Mr. Gradgrind. 'Tell him he mustn't. Cecilia Jupe. Let me see. What is your father?'

'He belongs to the horse-riding, if you please, Sir.'

Mr. Gradgrind frowned, and waved off the objectionable calling with his hand.

'We don't want to know anything about that, here. You mustn't tell us about that, here. Your father breaks horses, don't he?'

'If you please, Sir, when they can get any to break, they do break horses in the ring, Sir.'

'You mustn't tell us about the ring, here. Very well, then. Describe your father as a horsebreaker. He doctors sick horses, I dare say?'

'Oh yes, Sir.'

'Very well, then. He is a veterinary surgeon, a farrier, and horsebreaker. Give me your definition of a horse.'

(Sissy Jupe thrown into the greatest alarm by this demand.)

'Girl number twenty unable to define a horse!' said Mr. Gradgrind, for the general behoof of all the little pitchers. 'Girl number twenty possessed of no facts, in reference to one of the commonest of animals! Some boy's definition of a horse. Bitzer, yours.'

The square finger, moving here and there, lighted suddenly on Bitzer, perhaps because he chanced to sit in the same ray of sunlight which, darting in at one of the bare windows of the intensely whitewashed room, irradiated Sissy. For, the boys and girls sat on the face of the inclined plane in two compact bodies, divided up the centre by a narrow interval; and Sissy, being at the corner of a row on the sunny side, came in for the beginning of a sunbeam, of which Bitzer, being at the corner of a row on the other side, a few rows in advance, caught the end. But whereas the girl was so dark-eyed and dark-haired, that she seemed to receive a deeper and more lustrous colour from the sun, when it shone upon her, the boy was so light-eyed and light-haired that the self-same rays appeared to draw out of him what little colour he ever possessed. His cold eyes would hardly have been eyes, but for the short ends of lashes which, by bringing them into immediate contrast with something paler than themselves, expressed their form. His short-cropped hair might have been a mere continuation of the sandy freckles on his forehead and face. His skin was so unwholesomely deficient in the natural tinge, that he looked as though, if he were cut, he would bleed white.

'Bitzer,' said Thomas Gradgrind. 'Your definition of a horse.'

'Quadruped. Graminivorous. Forty teeth, namely twenty-four grinders, four eye-teeth, and twelve incisive. Sheds coat in the spring; in marshy countries, sheds hoofs, too. Hoofs hard, but requiring to be shod with iron. Age known by marks in mouth.' Thus (and much more) Bitzer.

'Now girl number twenty,' said Mr. Gradgrind. 'You know what a horse is.'

She curtseyed again, and would have blushed deeper, if she could have blushed deeper than she had blushed all this time. Bitzer, after rapidly blinking at Thomas Gradgrind with both eyes at once, and so catching the light upon his quivering ends of lashes that they looked like the antennae of busy insects, put his knuckles to his freckled forehead, and sat down again.

The third gentleman now stepped forth. A mighty man at cutting and drying, he was; a government officer; in his way (and in most other people's too), a professed pugilist; always in training, always to be heard of at the bar of his little Public-office, ready to fight all England. To continue in fistic phraseology, he had a genius for coming up to the scratch, wherever and whatever it was, and proving himself an ugly customer. He would go in and damage any subject whatever with his right, follow up with his left, stop, exchange, counter, bore his opponent (he always fought All England) to the ropes, and fall upon him neatly. He was certain to knock the wind out of common sense, and render that unlucky adversary deaf to the call of time. And he had it in charge from high authority to bring about the great public-office Millennium, when Commissioners should reign upon earth.

'Very well,' said this gentleman, briskly smiling, and folding his arms. 'That's a horse. Now, let me ask you girls and boys, Would you paper a room with representations of horses?'

After a pause, one half of the children cried in chorus, 'Yes, Sir!' Upon which the other half, seeing in the gentleman's face that Yes was wrong, cried out in chorus, 'No, Sir!'—as the custom is, in these examinations.

'Of course, No. Why wouldn't you?'

A pause. One corpulent slow boy, with a wheezy manner of breathing, ventured the answer, Because he wouldn't paper a room at all, but would paint it.

'You *must* paper it,' said the gentleman, rather warmly.

'You must paper it,' said Thomas Gradgrind, 'whether you like it or not. Don't tell *us* you wouldn't paper it. What do you mean, boy?'

'I'll explain to you, then,' said the gentleman, after another and a dismal pause, 'why you wouldn't paper a room with representations of horses. Do you ever see horses walking up and down the sides of rooms in reality—in fact? Do you?'

'Yes, Sir!' from one half. 'No, Sir!' from the other.

'Of course, No,' said the gentleman, with an indignant look at the wrong half. 'Why, then, you are not to see anywhere, what you don't see in fact; you are not to have anywhere, what you don't have in fact. What is called Taste, is only another name for Fact.'

Thomas Gradgrind nodded his approbation.

'This is a new principle, a discovery, a great discovery,' said the gentleman. 'Now, I'll try you again. Suppose you were going to carpet a room. Would you use a carpet having a representation of flowers upon it?'

There being a general conviction by this time that 'No, Sir!' was always the right answer to this gentleman, the chorus of No was very strong. Only a few feeble stragglers said Yes: among them Sissy Jupe.

'Girl number twenty,' said the gentleman, smiling in the calm strength of knowledge.

Sissy blushed, and stood up.

'So you would carpet your room—or your husband's room, if you were a grown woman, and had a husband—with representations of flowers, would you?' said the gentleman. 'Why would you?'

'If you please, Sir, I am very fond of flowers,' returned the girl.

'And is that why you would put tables and chairs upon them, and have people walking over them with heavy boots?'

'It wouldn't hurt them, Sir. They wouldn't crush and wither, if you please, Sir. They would be the pictures of what was very pretty and pleasant, and I would fancy——'

'Ay, ay, ay! But you mustn't fancy,' cried the gentleman, quite elated by coming so happily to his point. 'That's it! You are never to fancy.'

'You are not, Cecilia Jupe,' Thomas Gradgrind solemnly repeated, 'to do anything of that kind.'

'Fact, fact, fact!' said the gentleman. And 'Fact, fact, fact!' repeated Thomas Gradgrind.

'You are to be in all things regulated and governed,' said the gentleman, 'by fact. We hope to have, before long, a board of fact, composed of commissioners of fact, who will force the people to be a people of fact, and of nothing but fact. You must discard the word Fancy altogether. You have nothing to do with it. You are not to have, in any object of use or ornament, what would be a contradiction in fact. You don't walk upon flowers in fact; you cannot be allowed to walk upon flowers in carpets. You don't find that foreign birds and butterflies come and perch upon your crockery; you cannot be permitted to paint foreign birds and butterflies upon your crockery. You never meet with quadrupeds going up and down walls; you must not have quadrupeds represented upon walls. You must see,' said the gentleman, 'for all these purposes, combinations and modifications (in primary colours) of mathematical figures which are susceptible of proof and demonstration. This is the new discovery. This is fact. This is taste.'

The girl curtseyed, and sat down. She was very young, and she looked as if she were frightened by the matter-of-fact prospect the world afforded.

'Now, if Mr. M'Choakumchild,' said the gentleman, 'will proceed to give his first lesson here, Mr. Gradgrind, I shall be happy, at your request, to observe his mode of procedure.'

Mr. Gradgrind was much obliged. 'Mr. M'Choakumchild, we only wait for you.'

So, Mr. M'Choakumchild began in his best manner. He and some one hundred and forty other schoolmasters, had been lately turned at the same time, in the same factory, on the same principles, like so many pianoforte legs. He had been put through an immense variety of paces, and had answered volumes of head-breaking questions. Orthography, etymology, syntax, and prosody, biography, astronomy, geography, and general cosmography, the sciences of compound proportion, algebra, land-surveying and levelling, vocal music, and drawing from models, were all at the ends of his ten chilled fingers. He had worked his stony way into Her Majesty's most Honourable Privy Council's Schedule B, and had taken the bloom off the higher branches of mathematics and physical science, French, German, Latin, and Greek. He knew all about the Water Sheds of all the world (whatever they are), and all the histories of all the peoples, and all the names of all the rivers and mountains, and all the productions, manners, and customs of all the countries, and all their boundaries and bearings on the two-and-thirty points of the compass. Ah, rather overdone, M'Choakumchild. If he had only learnt a little less, how infinitely better he might have taught much more!

He went to work in this preparatory lesson, not unlike Morgiana in the Forty Thieves: looking into all the vessels ranged before him, one after another, to see what they contained. Say, good M'Choakumchild. When from thy boiling store, thou shalt fill each jar brim full by-and-by, dost thou think that thou wilt always kill outright the robber Fancy lurking within—or sometimes only maim him and distort him!

JOHN STUART MILL ON EDUCATION (1859)   From John Stuart Mill, *On Liberty* (London, 1859), pp. 187–191.

I have already observed that, owing to the absence of any recognised general principles, liberty is often granted where it should be withheld, as well as withheld where it should be granted; and one of the cases in which, in the modern European world, the sentiment of liberty is the strongest, is a case where, in my

EUROPEAN
INFLUENCES

view, it is altogether misplaced. A person should be free to do as he likes in his own concerns; but he ought not to be free to do as he likes in acting for another, under the pretext that the affairs of the other are his own affairs. The State, while it respects the liberty of each in what specially regards himself, is bound to maintain a vigilant control over his exercise of any power which it allows him to possess over others. This obligation is almost entirely disregarded in the case of the family relations, a case, in its direct influence on human happiness, more important than all others taken together. The almost despotic power of husbands over wives needs not be enlarged upon here, because nothing more is needed for the complete removal of the evil, than that wives should have the same rights, and should receive the protection of law in the same manner, as all other persons; and because, on this subject, the defenders of established injustice do not avail themselves of the plea of liberty, but stand forth openly as the champions of power. It is in the case of children, that misapplied notions of liberty are a real obstacle to the fulfilment by the State of its duties. One would almost think that a man's children were supposed to be literally, and not metaphorically, a part of himself, so jealous is opinion of the smallest interference of law with his absolute and exclusive control over them; more jealous than of almost any interference with his own freedom of action; so much less do the generality of mankind value liberty than power. Consider, for example, the case of education. Is it not almost a self-evident axiom, that the State should require and compel the education, up to a certain standard, of every human being who is born its citizen? Yet who is there that is not afraid to recognise and assert this truth? Hardly any one indeed will deny that it is one of the most sacred duties of the parents (or, as law and usage now stand, the father), after summoning a human being into the world, to give to that being an education fitting him to perform his part well in life towards others and towards himself. But while this is unanimously declared to be the father's duty, scarcely anybody, in this country, will bear to hear of obliging him to perform it. Instead of his being required to make any exertion or sacrifice for securing education to the child, it is left to his choice to accept it or not when it is provided gratis! It still remains unrecognised, that to bring a child into existence without a fair prospect of being able, not only to provide food for its body, but instruction and training for its mind, is a moral crime, both against the unfortunate offspring and against society; and that if the parent does not fulfil this obligation, the State ought to see it fulfilled, at the charge, as far as possible, of the parent.

Were the duty of enforcing universal education once admitted, there would be an end to the difficulties about what the State should teach, and how it should teach, which now convert the subject into a mere battle-field for sects and parties, causing the time and labour which should have been spent in educating, to be wasted in quarrelling about education. If the government would make up its mind to *require* for every child a good education, it might save itself the trouble of *providing* one. It might leave to parents to obtain the education where and how they pleased, and content itself with helping to pay the school fees of the poorer classes of children, and defraying the entire school expenses of those who have no one else to pay for them. The objections which are urged with reason against State education, do not apply to the enforcement of education by the State, but to the State's taking upon itself to direct that education: which is a totally different thing. That the whole or any large part of the education of the people should be in State hands, I go as far as any one in deprecating. All that has been said of the importance of individuality of character, and diversity in opinions and modes of conduct, involves, as of the same unspeakable importance, diversity of education. A general

State education is a mere contrivance for moulding people to be exactly like one another: and as the mould in which it casts them is that which pleases the predominant power in the government, whether this be a monarch, a priesthood, an aristocracy, or the majority of the existing generation in proportion as it is efficient and successful, it establishes a despotism over the mind, leading by natural tendency to one over the body. An education established and controlled by the State should only exist, if it exist at all, as one among many competing experiments, carried on for the purpose of example and stimulus, to keep the others up to a certain standard of excellence. Unless, indeed, when society in general is in so backward a state that it could not or would not provide for itself any proper institutions of education, unless the government undertook the task: then, indeed, the government may, as the less of two great evils, take upon itself the business of schools and universities, as it may that of joint stock companies, when private enterprise, in a shape fitted for undertaking great works of industry, does not exist in the country. But in general, if the country contains a sufficient number of persons qualified to provide education under government auspices, the same persons would be able and willing to give an equally good education on the voluntary principle, under the assurance of remuneration afforded by a law rendering education compulsory, combined with State aid to those unable to defray the expense.

*   *   *

THE GOSPEL ACCORDING TO SAMUEL SMILES (1859)

THE GOSPEL ACCORDING TO SAMUEL SMILES (1859)   From Samuel Smiles, *Self-Help* (Boston, 1860), pp. 15–17, 67–68, 265–67, 279.

"**H**eaven helps those who help themselves," is a well-worn maxim, embodying in a small compass the results of vast human experience. The spirit of self-help is the root of all genuine growth in the individual; and, exhibited in the lives of many, it constitutes the true source of national vigor and strength. Help from without is often enfeebling in its effects, but help from within invariably invigorates. Whatever is done for *men* or classes, to a certain extent takes away the stimulus and necessity of doing for themselves; and where men are subjected to over-guidance and over-government, the inevitable tendency is to render them comparatively helpless.

Even the best institutions can give a man no active aid. Perhaps the utmost they can do is, to leave him *free* to develop himself and improve his individual condition. But in all times men have been prone to believe that their happiness and well-being were to be secured by means of institutions rather than by their own conduct. Hence the value of legislation as an agent in human advancement has always been greatly over-estimated. To constitute the millionth part of a legislature, by voting for one or two men once in three or five years, however conscientiously this duty may be performed, can exercise but little active influence upon any man's life and character. Moreover, it is every day becoming more clearly understood, thatthe function of government is negative and restrictive, rather than positive and active; being resolvable principally into protection,—protection of life, liberty and property. Hence the chief "reforms" of the last fifty years have consisted mainly in abolitions and disenactments. But there is no power of law that can make the idle man industrious, the thriftless provident, or the drunken sober, though every individual can be each and all of these if he will, by the exercise of his own free powers of action and self-denial. Indeed, all experience serves to prove that the worth and strength of a state depend far less upon the form of its institutions than upon the character of its men. For the nation is only the aggregate of individual conditions, and civilization itself is but a question of personal improvement.

National progress is the sum of individual industry, energy, and uprightness, as national decay is of individual idleness, selfishness, and vice. What we are accustomed to decry as great social evils, will, for the most part, be found to be only the outgrowth of our own perverted life; and though we may endeavour to cut them down and extirpate them by means of law, they will only spring up again with fresh luxuriance in some other form, unless the individual conditions of human life and character are radically improved. If this view be correct, then it follows that the highest patriotism and philanthropy consist, not so much in altering laws and modifying institutions, as in helping and stimulating men to elevate and improve themselves by their own free and independent action as individuals.

*   *   *

Fortune has often been blamed for her blindness; but fortune is not so blind as men are. Those who look into practical life will find that fortune is invariably on the side of the industrious, as the winds and waves are on the side of the best navigators. Success treads on the heels of every right effort; and though it is possible to overestimate success to the extent of almost deifying it, as is sometimes done, still, in any worthy pursuit, it is meritorious. Nor are the qualities necessary to insure success at all extraordinary. They may, for the most part, be summed up in these two,—common sense and perseverance. Genius may not be necessary, though even genius of the highest sort does not despise the exercise of these common qualities. The very greatest men have been among the least believers in the power of genius, and as worldly wise and persevering as successful men of the commoner sort. Some have even defined genius to be only common sense intensified. A distinguished teacher and president of a college spoke of it as the power of making efforts. John Foster held it to be the power of lighting one's own fire. Buffon said of genius,—It is patience.

*   *   *

Many popular books have been written for the purpose of communicating to the public the grand secret of making money. But there is no secret whatever about it, as the proverbs of every nation abundantly testify. "Many a little makes a meikle."— "Take care of the pennies and the pounds will take care of themselves."—"A penny saved is a penny gained."—"Diligence is the mother of good-luck."—"No pains no gains."—"No sweat no sweet."—"Sloth, the key of poverty."—"Work, and thou shalt have."—"He who will not work, neither shall he eat."—"The world is his, who has patience and industry."—"It is too late to spare when all is spent."—"Better go to bed supperless than rise in debt."—"The morning hour has gold in its mouth."— "Credit keeps the crown of the causeway." Such are specimens of the proverbial philosophy, embodying the hoarded experience of many generations, as to the best means of thriving in the world. They were current in people's mouths long before books were invented; and like other popular proverbs, they were the first codes of popular morals. Moreover they have stood the test of time, and the experience of every day still bears witness to their accuracy, force, and soundness.

CHARLES DARWIN ON THE ORIGIN OF THE SPECIES (1859)   From
Charles Darwin, *On the Origin of Species By Means of Natural Selection* (New York, 1878),
pp. XIII–XIV, 2–4.

I will here give a brief sketch of the progress of opinion on the Origin of Species. Until recently the great majority of naturalists believed that species were immutable productions, and had been separately created. This view has been ably maintained by many authors. Some few naturalists, on the other hand, have believed that species undergo modification, and that the existing forms of life are the descendants by true generation of pre-existing forms. Passing over allusions to the subject in the classical writers, the first author who in modern times has treated it in a scientific spirit was Buffon. But as his opinions fluctuated greatly at different periods, and as he does not enter on the causes or means of the transformation of species, I need not here enter on details.

Lamarck was the first man whose conclusions on the subject excited much attention. This justly-celebrated naturalist first published his views in 1801; he much enlarged them in 1809 in his 'Philosophie Zoologique,' and subsequently, in 1815, in the Introduction to his 'Hist. Nat. des Animaux sans Vertebres.' In these works he upholds the doctrine that all species, including man, are descended from other species. He first did the eminent service of arousing attention to the probability of all change in the organic, as well as in the inorganic world, being the result of law, and not of miraculous interposition. Lamarck seems to have been chiefly led to his conclusion on the gradual change of species, by the difficulty of distinguishing species and varieties, by the almost perfect gradation of forms in certain groups, and by the analogy of domestic productions. With respect to the means of modification, he attributed something to the direct action of the physical conditions of life, something to the crossing of already existing forms, and much to use and disuse, that is, to the effects of habit. To this latter agency he seems to attribute all the beautiful adaptations in nature;—such as the long neck of the giraffe for browsing on the branches of trees. But he likewise believed in a law of progressive development; and as all the forms of life thus tend to progress, in order to account for the existence at the present day of simple productions, he maintains that such forms are now spontaneously generated. . . .

*   *   *

In considering the Origin of Species, it is quite conceivable that a naturalist, reflecting on the mutual affinities of organic beings, on their embryological relations, their geographical distribution, geological succession, and other such facts, might come to the conclusion that species had not been independently

EUROPEAN
INFLUENCES

915

created, but had descended, like varieties, from other species. Nevertheless, such a conclusion, even if well founded, would be unsatisfactory, until it could be shown how the innumerable species inhabiting this world have been modified, so as to acquire that perfection of structure and coadaptation which justly excites our admiration. Naturalists continually refer to external conditions, such as climate, food, &c., as the only possible cause of variation. In one limited sense, as we shall hereafter see, this may be true; but it is preposterous to attribute to mere external conditions, the structure, for instance, of the woodpecker, with its feet, tail, beak, and tongue, so admirably adapted to catch insects under the bark of trees. In the case of the mistletoe, which draws its nourishment from certain trees, which has seeds that must be transported by certain birds, and which has flowers with separate sexes absolutely requiring the agency of certain insects to bring pollen from one flower to the other, it is equally preposterous to account for the structure of this parasite, with its relations to several distinct organic beings, by the effects of external conditions, or of habit, or of the volition of the plant itself.

It is, therefore, of the highest importance to gain a clear insight into the means of modification and coadaptation. At the commencement of my observations it seemed to me probable that a careful study of domesticated animals and of cultivated plants would offer the best chance of making out this obscure problem. Nor have I been disappointed; in this and in all other perplexing cases I have invariably found that our knowledge, imperfect though it be, of variation under domestication, afforded the best and safest clue. I may venture to express my conviction of the high value of such studies, although they have been very commonly neglected by naturalists.

From these considerations, I shall devote the first chapter of this Abstract to Variation under Domestication. We shall thus see that a large amount of hereditary modification is at least possible; and, what is equally or more important, we shall see how great is the power of man in accumulating by his Selection successive slight variations. I will then pass on to the variability of species in a state of nature; but I shall, unfortunately, be compelled to treat this subject far too briefly, as it can be treated properly only by giving long catalogues of facts. We shall, however, be enabled to discuss what circumstances are most favourable to variation. In the next chapter the Struggle for Existence amongst all organic beings throughout the world, which inevitably follows from the high geometrical ratio of their increase, will be considered. This is the doctrine of Malthus, applied to the whole animal and vegetable kingdoms. As many more individuals of each species are born than can possibly survive; and as, consequently, there is a frequently recurring struggle for existence, it follows that any being, if it vary however slightly in any manner profitable to itself, under the complex and sometimes varying conditions of life, will have a better chance of surviving, and thus be *naturally selected*. From the strong principle of inheritance, any selected variety will tend to propagate its new and modified form. . . .

Although much remains obscure, and will long remain obscure, I can entertain no doubt, after the most deliberate study and dispassionate judgment of which I am capable, that the view which most naturalists until recently entertained, and which I formerly entertained—namely, that each species has been independently created—is erroneous. I am fully convinced that species are not immutable; but that those belonging to what are called the same genera are lineal descendants of some other and generally extinct species, in the same manner as the acknowledged varieties of any one species are the descendants of that species. Furthermore, I am convinced that Natural Selection has been the most important, but not the exclusive, means of modification.

CHARLES DARWIN ON THE DESCENT OF MAN (1871) From Charles Darwin, *The Descent of Man and Selection In Relation to Sex* (New York, 1871), Volume II, pp. 368-70, 372-5, 377-8, 386-7.

The main conclusion arrived at in this work, and now held by many naturalists who are well competent to form a sound judgment, is that man is descended from some less highly-organized form. The grounds upon which this conclusion rests will never be shaken, for the close similarity between man and the lower animals in embryonic development, as well as innumerable points of structure and constitution, both of high and of the most trifling importance—the rudiments which he retains, and the abnormal reversions to which he is occasionally liable—are facts which cannot be disputed. They have long been known, but until recently they told us nothing with respect to the origin of man. Now, when viewed by the light of our knowledge of the whole organic world, their meaning is unmistakable. The great principle of evolution stands up clear and firm, when these groups of facts are considered in connection with others, such as the mutual affinities of the members of the same group, their geographical distribution in past and present times, and their geological succession. It is incredible that all these facts should speak falsely. He who is not content to look, like a savage, at the phenomena of Nature as disconnected, cannot any longer believe that man is the work of a separate act of creation. He will be forced to admit that the close resemblance of the embryo of man to that, for instance, of a dog—the construction of his skull, limbs, and whole frame, independently of the uses to which the parts may be put, on the same plan with that of other mammals—the occasional reappearance of various structures, for instance, of several distinct muscles, which man does not normally possess, but which is common to the Quadrumana—and a crowd of analogous facts—all point in the plainest manner to the conclusion that man is the codescendant with other mammals of a common progenitor.

We have seen that man incessantly presents individual differences in all parts of his body and in his mental faculties. These differences or variations seem to be induced by the same general causes, and to obey the same laws as with the lower animals. In both cases similar laws of inheritance prevail. Man tends to increase at a greater rate than his means of subsistence; consequently he is occasionally subjected to a severe struggle for existence, and natural selection will have effected whatever lies within its scope. A succession of strongly-marked variations of a similar nature are by no means requisite; slight fluctuating differences in the individual suffice for the work of natural selection. We may feel assured that the inherited effects of the long-continued use or disuse of parts will have done much in the same direction with natural selection. Modifications formerly of importance, though no longer of any special use, will be long inherited. When one part is modified, other parts will change through the principle of correlation, of which we have instances in many curious cases of correlated monstrosities. Something may be attributed to the direct and definite action of the surrounding conditions of life, such as abundant food, heat, or moisture; and lastly, many characters of slight physiological importance, some indeed of considerable importance, have been gained through sexual selection. . . .

By considering the embryological structure of man—the homologies which he presents with the lower animals—the rudiments he retains—and the reversions to which he is liable, we can partly recall in imagination the former condition of our early progenitors; and can approximately place them in their proper position in the zoological series. We thus learn that man is descended from a hairy quadruped, furnished with a tail and pointed ears, probably arboreal in its habits, and an inhabitant of the Old World. This creature, if its whole structure had been examined by a naturalist, would have been classed among the Quadrumana, as surely as would the common and still more ancient progenitor of the Old and New World monkeys. . . .

The greatest difficulty which presents itself, when we are driven to the above conclusion on the origin of man, is the high standard of intellectual power and of moral disposition which he has attained. But every one who admits the general principle of evolution, must see that the mental powers of the higher animals, which are the same in kind with those of mankind, though so different in degree, are capable of advancement. Thus the interval between the mental powers of one of the higher apes and of a fish, or between those of an ant and scale-insect, is immense. The development of these powers in animals does not offer any special difficulty; for with our domesticated animals, the mental faculties are certainly variable, and the variations are inherited. No one doubts that these faculties are of the utmost importance to animals in a state of nature. Therefore the conditions are favorable for their development through natural selection. The same conclusion may be extended to man; the intellect must have been all-important to him, even at a very remote period, enabling him to use language, to invent and make weapons, tools, traps, etc.; by which means, in combination with his social habits, he long ago became the most dominant of all living creatures. . . .

The development of the moral qualities is a more interesting and difficult problem. Their foundation lies in the social instincts, including in this term the family ties. These instincts are of a highly-complex nature, and in the case of the lower animals give special tendencies toward certain definite actions; but the more important elements for us are love, and the distinct emotion of sympathy. Animals endowed with the social instincts take pleasure in each other's company, warn each other of danger, defend and aid each other in many ways. These instincts are not extended to all the individuals of the species, but only to those of the same community. As they are highly beneficial to the species, they have in all probability been acquired through natural selection.

A moral being is one who is capable of comparing his past and future actions and motives—of approving of some and disapproving of others; and the fact that man is the one being who with certainty can be thus designated makes the greatest of all distinctions between him and the lower animals. But in our third chapter I have endeavored to show that the moral sense follows, firstly, from the enduring and always present nature of the social instincts, in which respect man agrees with the lower animals; and secondly, from his mental faculties being highly active and his impressions of past events extremely vivid, in which respects he differs from the lower animals. Owing to this condition of mind, man cannot avoid looking backward and comparing the impressions of past events and actions. He also continually looks forward. Hence after some temporary desire or passion has mastered his social instincts, he will reflect and compare the now weakened impression of such past impulses with the ever-present social instinct; and he will then feel that sense of dissatisfaction which all unsatisfied instincts leave behind them. Consequently he resolves to act differently for the future—and this is conscience. . . .

The belief in God has often been advanced as not only the greatest, but the most complete, of all the distinctions between man and the lower animals. It is, however, impossible, as we have seen, to maintain that this belief is innate or instinctive in man. On the other hand, a belief in all-pervading spiritual agencies seems to be universal; and apparently follows from a considerable advance in the reasoning powers of man, and from a still greater advance in his faculties of imagination, curiosity, and wonder. I am aware that the assumed instinctive belief in God has been used by many persons as an argument for his existence. But this is a rash argument, as we should thus be compelled to believe in the existence of many cruel and malignant spirits, possessing only a little more power than man; for the belief in them is far more general than that of a beneficent Deity. The idea of a universal and beneficent Creator of the universe does not seem to arise in the mind of man, until he has been elevated by long-continued culture.

He who believes in the advancement of man from some lowly-organized form, will naturally ask, "How does this bear on the belief in the immortality of the soul?" The barbarous races of man, as Sir J. Lubbock has shown, possess no clear belief of this kind; but arguments derived from the primeval beliefs of savages are, as we have just seen, of little or no avail. Few persons feel any anxiety from the impossibility of determining at what precise period in the development of the individual, from the first trace of the minute germinal vesicle to the child either before or after birth, man becomes an immortal being; and there is no greater cause for anxiety because the period in the gradually-ascending organic scale cannot possibly be determined.

I am aware that the conclusions arrived at in this work will be denounced by some as highly irreligious; but he who thus denounces them is bound to show why it is more irreligious to explain the origin of man as a distinct species by descent from some lower form, through the laws of variation and natural selection, than to explain the birth of the individual through the laws of ordinary reproduction. The birth both of the species and of the individual are equally parts of that grand sequence of events, which our minds refuse to accept as the result of blind chance. The understanding revolts at such a conclusion, whether or not we are able to believe that every slight variation of structure, the union of each pair in marriage, the dissemination of each seed, and other such events, have all been ordained for some special purpose. . . .

The main conclusion arrived at in this work, namely, that man is descended from some lowly-organized form, will, I regret to think, be highly distasteful to many persons. But there can hardly be a doubt that we are descended from barbarians. The astonishment which I felt on first seeing a party of Fuegians on a wild and broken shore will never be forgotten by me, for the reflection at once rushed into my mind—such were our ancestors. These men were absolutely naked and bedaubed with paint, their long hair was tangled, their mouths frothed with excitement, and their expression was wild, startled, and distrustful. They possessed hardly any arts, and, like wild animals, lived on what they could catch; they had no government, and were merciless to every one not of their own small tribe. He who has seen a savage in his native land will not feel much shame, if forced to acknowledge that the blood of some more humble creature flows in his veins. For my own part, I would as soon be descended from that heroic little monkey, who braved his dreaded enemy in order to save the life of his keeper; or from that old baboon, who, descending from the mountains, carried away in triumph his young comrade from a crowd of astonished dogs—as from a savage who delights to torture his enemies, offers up bloody sacrifices, practices infanticide without remorse, treats his wives like slaves, knows no decency, and is haunted by the grossest superstitions.

Man may be excused for feeling some pride at having risen, though not through his own exertions, to the very summit of the organic scale; and the fact of his having thus risen, instead of having been aboriginally placed there, may give him hopes for a still higher destiny in the distant future. But we are not here concerned with hopes or fears, only with the truth as far as our reason allows us to discover it. I have given the evidence to the best of my ability; and we must acknowledge, as it seems to me, that man with all his noble qualities, with sympathy which feels for the most debased, with benevolence which extends not only to other men but to the humblest living creature, with his godlike intellect which has penetrated into the movements and constitution of the solar system—with all these exalted powers—Man still bears in his bodily frame the indelible stamp of his lowly origin.

HERBERT SPENCER ON THE AIMS OF EDUCATION (1860)   From Herbert Spencer, *Education: Intellectual, Moral, and Physical* (London, 1860), pp. 12–20, 84–87.

How to live?—that is the essential question for us. Not how to live in the mere material sense only, but in the widest sense. The general problem which comprehends every special problem is—the right ruling of conduct in all directions under all circumstances. In what way to treat the body; in what way to treat the mind; in what way to manage our affairs, in what way to bring up a family; in what way to behave as a citizen; in what way to utilize all those sources of happiness which nature supplies—how to use all our faculties to the greatest advantage of ourselves and others—how to live completely? And this being the great thing needful for us to learn, is, by consequence, the great thing which education has to teach. To prepare us for complete living is the function which education has to discharge; and the only rational mode of judging of any educational course is, to judge in what degree it discharges such function.

This test, never used in its entirety, but rarely even partially used, and used then in a vague, half conscious way, has to be applied consciously, methodically, and throughout all cases. It behoves us to set before ourselves, and ever to keep clearly in view, complete living as the end to be achieved; so that in bringing up our children we may choose subjects and methods of instruction, with deliberate reference to this end. Not only ought we to cease from the mere unthinking adoption of the current fashion in education, which has no better warrant than any other fashion; but we must also rise above that rude, empirical style of judging displayed by those more intelligent people who do bestow some care in overseeing the cultivation of their children's minds. It must not suffice simply to *think* that such or such information will be useful in after life, or that this kind of knowledge is of more practical value than that; but we must seek out some process of estimating their respective values, so that as far as possible we may positively *know* which are most deserving of attention.

Doubtless the task is difficult—perhaps never to be more than approximately achieved. But, considering the vastness of the interests at stake, its difficulty is no reason for pusillanimously passing it by; but rather for devoting every energy to its mastery. And if we only proceed systematically, we may very soon get at results of no small moment.

Our first step must obviously be to classify, in the order of their importance, the leading kinds of activity which constitute human life. They may be naturally arranged into:—1. Those activities which directly minister to self-preservation; 2. Those activities which, by securing the necessaries of life, indirectly minister to self-preservation; 3. Those activities which have for their end the rearing and discipline of offspring; 4. Those activities which are involved in the maintenance of proper social and political relations; 5. Those miscellaneous activities which make up the leisure part of life, devoted to the gratification of the tastes and feelings.

That these stand in something like their true order of subordination, it needs no long consideration to show. The actions and precautions by which, from moment to moment, we secure personal safety, must clearly take precedence of all others. Could there be a man, ignorant as an infant of all surrounding objects and movements, or how to guide himself among them, he would pretty certainly lose his life the first time he went into the street: notwithstanding any amount of learning he might have on other matters. And as entire ignorance in all other directions would be less promptly fatal than entire ignorance in this direction, it must be admitted that knowledge immediately conducive to self-preservation is of primary importance.

That next after direct self-preservation comes the indirect self-preservation which consists in acquiring the means of living, none will question. That a man's industrial functions must be considered before his parental ones, is manifest from the fact, that, speaking generally, the discharge of the parental functions is made possible only by the previous discharge of the industrial ones. The power of self-maintenance necessarily preceding the power of maintaining offspring, it follows that knowledge needful for self-maintenance has stronger claims than knowledge needful for family welfare—is second in value to none save knowledge needful for immediate self-preservation.

As the family comes before the State in order of time—as the bringing up of children is possible before the State exists, or when it has ceased to be, whereas the State is rendered possible only by the bringing up of children; it follows that the duties of the parent demand closer attention than those of the citizen. Or, to use a further argument—since the goodness of a society ultimately depends on the nature of its citizens; and since the nature of its citizens is more modifiable by early training than by anything else; we must conclude that the welfare of the family underlies the welfare of society. And hence knowledge directly conducing to the first, must take precedence of knowledge directly conducing to the last.

Those various forms of pleasurable occupation which fill up the leisure left by graver occupations—the enjoyments of music, poetry, painting, &c.—manifestly imply a pre-existing society. Not only is a considerable development of them impossible without a long-established social union; but their very subject-matter consists in great part of social sentiments and sympathies. Not only does society supply the conditions to their growth; but also the ideas and sentiments they express. And, consequently, that part of human conduct which constitutes good citizenship is of more moment than that which goes out in accomplishments or exercise of the tastes; and, in education, preparation for the one must rank before preparation for the other.

Such then, we repeat, is something like the rational order of subordination:— That education which prepares for direct self-preservation; that which prepares for indirect self-preservation; that which prepares for parenthood; that which prepares for citizenship; that which prepares for the miscellaneous refinements of life. We do not mean to say that these divisions are definitely separable. We do not deny that they are intricately entangled with each other in such way that there can be no training for any that is not in some measure a training for all. Nor do we question that of each division there are portions more important than certain portions of the preceding divisions: that, for instances, a man of much skill in business but little other faculty, may fall further below the standard of complete living than one of but moderate power of acquiring money but great judgment as a parent; or that exhaustive information bearing on right social action, joined with entire want of general culture in literature and the fine arts, is less desirable than a more moderate share of the one joined with some of the other. But, after making all qualifications, there still remain these broadly-marked divisions; and it still continues substantially true that these divisions subordinate one another in the foregoing order, because the corresponding divisions of life make one another *possible* in that order.

Of course the ideal of education is—complete preparation in all these divisions. But failing this ideal, as in our phase of civilization every one must do more or less, the aim should be to maintain *a due proportion* between the degrees of preparation in each. Not exhaustive cultivation in any one, supremely important though it may be—not even an exclusive attention to the two, three, or four divisions of greatest importance; but an attention to all,—greatest where the value is greatest, less where the value is less, least where the value is least. For the average man (not to forget the cases in which pecular aptitude for some one department of knowledge rightly makes that one the bread-winning occupation)—for the average man, we say, the desideratum is, a training that approaches nearest to perfection in the things which most subserve complete living, and falls more and more below perfection in the things that have more and more remote bearings on complete living.

In regulating education by this standard, there are some general considerations that should be ever present to us. The worth of any kind of culture, as aiding complete living, may be either necessary or more or less contingent. There is knowledge of intrinsic value; knowledge of quasi-intrinsic value; and knowledge of conventional value. Such facts as that sensations of numbness and tingling commonly precede paralysis, that the resistance of water to a body moving through it varies as the square of the velocity, that chlorine is a disinfectant,—these, and the truths of Science in general, are of intrinsic value: they will bear on human conduct ten thousand years hence as they do now. The extra knowledge of our own language, which is given by an acquaintance with Latin and Greek, may be considered to have a value that is quasi-intrinsic: it must exist for us and for other races whose languages owe much to these sources; but will last only as long as our languages last. While that kind of information which, in our schools, usurps the name History—the mere tissue of names and dates and dead unmeaning events—has a conventional value only: it has not the remotest bearing upon any of our actions; and it is of use only for the avoidance of those unpleasant criticisms which current opinion passes upon its absence. Of course, as those facts which concern all mankind throughout all time must be held of greater moment than those which concern only a portion of them during a limited era, and of far greater moment than those which concern only a portion of them during the continuance of a fashion; it follows that in a rational estimate, knowledge of intrinsic worth must, other things equal, take precedence of knowledge that is of quasi-intrinsic or conventional worth.

One further preliminary. Acquirement of every kind has two values—value as *knowledge* and value as *discipline*. Besides its use for guidance in conduct, the acquisition of each order of facts has also its use as mental exercise; and its effects as a preparative for complete living have to be considered under both these heads.

These, then, are the general ideas with which we must set out in discussing a *curriculum:* —Life as divided into several kinds of activity of successively decreasing importance; the worth of each order of facts as regulating these several kinds of activity, intrinsically, quasi-intrinsically, and conventionally; and their regulative influences estimated both as knowledge and discipline.

*   *   *

Thus to the question with which we set out—What knowledge is of most worth?—the uniform reply is—Science. This is the verdict on all the counts. For direct self-preservation, or the maintenance of life and health, the all-important knowledge is—Science. For that indirect self-preservation which we call gaining a livelihood, the knowledge of greatest value is—Science. For the due discharge of parental functions, the proper guidance is to be found only in—Science. For that interpretation of national life, past and present, without which the citizen cannot rightly regulate his conduct, the indispensable key is—Science. Alike for the most perfect production and highest enjoyment of art in all its forms, the needful preparation is still—Science. And for purposes of discipline—intellectual, moral, religious—the most efficient study is, once more—Science. The question which at first seemed so perplexed, has become, in the course of our inquiry, comparatively simple. We have not to estimate the degrees of importance of different orders of human activity, and different studies as severally fitting us for them; since we find that the study of Science, in its most comprehensive meaning, is the best preparation for all these orders of activity. We have not to decide between the claims of knowledge of great though conventional value, and knowledge of less though intrinsic value; seeing that the knowledge which we find to be of most value in all other respects, is intrinsically most valuable: its worth is not dependent upon opinion, but is as fixed as is the relation of man to the surrounding world. Necessary and eternal as are its truths, all Science concerns all mankind for all time. Equally at present, and in the remotest future, must it be of incalculable importance for the regulation of their conduct, that men should understand the science of life, physical, mental, and social; and that they should understand all other science as a key to the science of life.

And yet the knowledge which is of such transcendent value is that which, in our age of boasted education, receives the least attention. While this which we call civilization could never have arisen had it not been for science; science forms scarcely an appreciable element in what men consider civilized training. Though to the progress of science we owe it, that millions find support where once there was food only for thousands; yet of these millions but a few thousands pay any respect to that which has made their existence possible. Though this increasing knowledge of the properties and relations of things has not only enabled wandering tribes to grow into populous nations, but has given to the countless members of those populous nations comforts and pleasures which their few naked ancestors never even conceived, or could have believed, yet is this kind of knowledge only now receiving a grudging recognition in our highest educational institutions. To the slowly growing acquaintance with the uniform co-existences and sequences of phenomena—to the establishment of invariable laws, we owe our emancipation from the grossest superstitions. But for science we should be still worshipping fetishes; or, with hecatombs of victims, propitiating diabolical deities. And yet this science, which, in place of the most degrading conceptions of things, has given us some insight into the grandeurs of creation, is written against in our theologies and frowned upon from our pulpits.

Paraphrasing an Eastern fable, we may say that in the family of knowledges, Science is the household drudge, who, in obscurity, hides unrecognised perfections. To her has been committed all the work; by her skill, intelligence, and devotion, have all the conveniences and gratifications been obtained; and while ceaselessly occupied ministering to the rest, she has been kept in the background, that her haughty sisters might flaunt their fripperies in the eyes of the world. The parallel holds yet further. For we are fast coming to the *dénouement*, when the positions will be changed; and while these haughty sisters sink into merited neglect, Science, proclaimed as highest alike in worth and beauty, will reign supreme.

MATTHEW ARNOLD ON CULTURE (1869)   From Matthew Arnold, *Culture and Anarchy*, J. D. Wilson, ed. (Cambridge, 1960), pp. 68–71.

So, too, Jacobinism, in its fierce hatred of the past and of those whom it makes liable for the sins of the past, cannot away with the inexhaustible indulgence proper to culture, the consideration of circumstances, the severe judgment of actions joined to the merciful judgment of persons. "The man of culture is in politics," cries Mr. Frederic Harrison, "one of the poorest mortals alive!" Mr. Frederic Harrison wants to be doing business, and he complains that the man of culture stops him with a "turn for small fault-finding, love of selfish ease, and indecision in action." Of what use is culture, he asks, except for "a critic of new books or a professor of *belles lettres?*" Why, it is of use because, in presence of the fierce exasperation which breathes, or rather, I may say, hisses, through the whole production in which Mr. Frederic Harrison asks that question, it reminds us that the perfection of human nature is sweetness and light. It is of use because, like religion,—that other effort after perfection,—it testifies that, where bitter envying and strife are, there is confusion and every evil work.

The pursuit of perfection, then, is the pursuit of sweetness and light. He who works for sweetness works in the end for light also; he who works for light works in the end for sweetness also. But he who works for sweetness and light united, works to make reason and the will of God prevail. He who works for machinery, he who works for hatred, works only for confusion. Culture looks beyond machinery, culture hates hatred; culture has one great passion, the passion for sweetness and light. It has one even yet greater!—the passion for making them *prevail*. It is not satisfied till we *all* come to a perfect man; it knows that the sweetness and light of the few must be imperfect until the raw and unkindled masses of humanity are touched with sweetness and light. If I have not shrunk from saying that we must work for sweetness and light, so neither have I shrunk from saying that we must have a broad basis, must have sweetness and light for as many as possible. Again and again I have insisted how those are the happy moments of humanity, how those are the marking epochs of a people's life, how those are the flowering times for literature and art and all the creative power of genius, when there is a *national* glow of life and thought, when the whole of society is in the fullest measure permeated by thought, sensible to beauty, intelligent and alive. Only it must be *real* thought and *real* beauty; *real* sweetness and *real* light. Plenty of people will try to give the masses, as they call them, an intellectual food prepared and adapted in the way they think proper for the actual condition of the masses. The ordinary popular literature is an example of this way of working on the masses. Plenty of people will try to indoctrinate the masses with the set of ideas and judgments constituting the creed of their own profession or party. Our religious and political organisations give an example of this way of working on the masses. I condemn neither way; but culture works differently. It does not try to reach down to the level of inferior classes; it does not try to win them for this or that sect of its own, with ready-made judgments and watchwords. It seeks to do away with classes; to make the best that has been thought and known in the world current everywhere; to make all men live in an atmosphere of sweetness and light, where they may use ideas, as it uses them itself, freely—nourished and not bound by them.

This is the *social idea;* and the men of culture are the true apostles of equality. The great men of culture are those who have had a passion for diffusing, for making prevail, for carrying from one end of society to the other, the best knowledge, the best ideas of their time; who have laboured to divest knowledge of all that was harsh, uncouth, difficult, abstract, professional, exclusive; to humanise it, to make it efficient outside the clique of the cultivated and learned, yet still remaining the *best* knowledge and thought of the time, and a true source, therefore, of sweetness and light. Such a man was Abelard in the Middle Ages, in spite of all his imperfections; and thence the boundless emotion and enthusiasm which Abelard excited. Such were Lessing and Herder in Germany, at the end of the last century; and their services to Germany were in this way inestimably precious. Generations will pass, and literary monuments will accumulate, and works far more perfect than the works of Lessing and Herder will be produced in Germany; and yet the names of these two men will fill a German with a reverence and enthusiasm such as the names of the most gifted masters will hardly awaken. And why? Because they *humanised* knowledge; because they broadened the basis of life and intelligence; because they worked powerfully to diffuse sweetness and light, to make reason and the will of God prevail. With Saint Augustine they said: "Let us not leave Thee alone to make in the secret of thy knowledge, as thou didst before the creation of the firmament, the division of light from darkness; let the children of thy spirit, placed in their firmament, make their light shine upon the earth, mark the division of night and day, and announce the revolution of the times; for the old order is passed, and the new arises; the night is spent, the day is come forth; and thou shalt crown the year with thy blessing, when thou shalt send forth labourers into thy harvest sown by other hands than theirs; when thou shalt send forth new labourers to new seed-times, whereof the harvest shall be not yet."

The Prussian Example

HENRY BARNARD ON GERMAN TEACHERS (1835) From Henry Barnard,
National Education in Europe (New York, 1854), p. 33.

The success of the school systems of Germany is universally attributed by her own educators to the above features of her school law—especially those which relate to the teacher. These provisions respecting teachers may be summed up as follows:—

1. The recognition of the true dignity and importance of the office of teacher in a system of public instruction.

2. The establishment of a sufficient number of Teachers' Seminaries, or Normal Schools, to educate, in a special course of instruction and practice, all persons who apply or propose to teach in any public primary school, with aids to self and professional improvement through life.

3. A system of examination and inspection, by which incompetent persons are prevented from obtaining situations as teachers, or are excluded and degraded from the ranks of the profession, by unworthy or criminal conduct.

4. A system of promotion, by which faithful teachers can rise in a scale of lucrative and desirable situations.

5. Permanent employment through the year, and for life, with a social position and a compensation which compare favorably with the wages paid to educated labor in other departments of business.

6. Preparatory schools, in which those who wish eventually to become teachers, may test their natural qualities and adaptation for school teaching before applying for admission to a Normal School.

7. Frequent conferences and associations for mutual improvement, by an interchange of opinion and sharing the benefit of each others' experience.

8. Exemption from military service in time of peace, and recognition, in social and civil life, as public functionaries.

9. A pecuniary allowance when sick, and provision for years of infirmity and old age, and for their families in case of death.

10. Books and periodicals, by which the obscure teacher is made partaker in all the improvements of the most experienced and distinguished members of the profession in his own and other countries.

VICTOR COUSIN REPORTS ON PUBLIC EDUCATION IN PRUSSIA

(1836)   From *Report on the State of Public Education in Prussia,* As quoted in Edgar W. Knight, ed., *Reports on European Education* (New York, 1930), pp. 123–24, 129–31, 137, 141, 167–68.

In Prussia, the minister of public instruction enjoys a rank and authority equal to those of any of his colleagues; the care of all affairs connected with the public exercise of religion falls also within his department, as in France; and as the secondary schools of medicine, and all establishments relative to public health, belong to this ministry, it bears the official denomination of Ministry of Public Instruction, of Ecclesiastical and Medical Affairs (*Ministerium des öffentlichen Unterrichts, der geistlichen-und medicinal-Angelegenheiten*).

In Prussia, as in other states, public instruction long formed a part of the business of the Minister of the Interior. It was not until 1819 that a special department of administration was consecrated to this object, with Baron von Altenstein at its head. I regard this change as of the highest importance. In the first place the service is much better performed, there being more complete unity in the central point, from which all emanates and to which all is addressed; and the authority, being more cogent, is better obeyed. In the next place, the high rank assigned to the head of public instruction marks the respect in which everything relating to that important subject is held by the government; hence science assumes her proper place in the state. Civilization, the intellectual and moral interests of society, have their appointed ministry. This ministry embraces everything relating to science, and consequently all schools, libraries, and kindred institutions,—such as botanic gardens, museums, cabinets, the lower schools of surgery and medicine, academies of music, &c. Indeed it is perfectly natural that the minister who has the faculties of medicine under his control, should also direct the inferior schools and institutions relating to that science; that the minister who presides over the faculties of letters and science, should also preside over scientific and literary academies; that the minister who is the guardian of public instruction, should be guardian of the great collections and libraries, without which instruction is impossible.

I do not attempt here to go into details. I have confined myself wholly to the endeavour to make the machinery of public instruction in Prussia intelligible to you, as a whole. To sum up all; primary instruction is parochial and departmental, and at the same time is subject to the minister of public instruction; which double character appears to me consequent on the very nature of establishments which equally require the constant superintendence of local powers, and the guidance of a superior hand, vivifying and harmonizing the whole. This double character is represented by the *Schulrath*, who has a seat in the council of the department, and is responsible, both to the ministry of the interior, and to that of public instruction.

On the other hand, all secondary instruction is under the care of the *Schulcollegium* (School-board), which forms part of the provincial consistory, and which is nominated by the minister of public instruction. All higher instruction, that of universities, has for its organ and its head the royal commissary, who acts under immediate authority of the minister. Thus nothing escapes the eye and the power of the minister, yet at the same time each of these departments of public instruction enjoys sufficient liberty of action. The universities elect their own officers. The school-board proposes and overlooks the professors of gymnasia, and takes cognisance of all the more important points of primary instruction. The *Schulrath*, with the council of regency, (or rather the council of regency, on the report of the *Schulrath*,) and in pursuance of the correspondence of the inspectors and committees, decides on the greater part of the affairs of the lower stage of instruction. The minister, without entering into the infinite details of popular instruction, is thoroughly informed as to results, and directs everything by instructions emanating from the centre, which tend to diffuse a national unity throughout the whole. He does not interfere minutely with the business of secondary instruction; but nothing is done without his sanction, and this is never given but on full and accurate reports. The same applies to universities: they govern themselves, but according to fixed laws. The professors elect their deans and their rectors, but they are themselves nominated by the minister. In short, the end of the entire organization of public instruction in Prussia is, to leave details to the local powers, and to reserve to the minister and his council the direction and general impulse given to the whole.

Duty of Parents to Send Their Children to the Primary Schools

This duty is so national, so rooted in all the legal and moral habits of the country, that it is expressed by a single word, *Schulpflichtigkeit* (school-duty, or school-obligation). It corresponds to another word, similarly formed and similarly sanctioned by public opinion, *Dienstpflichtigkeit* (service-obligation, i.e. military service). These two words are completely characteristic of Prussia: they contain the secret of its originality as a nation, of its power as a state, and the germ of its future condition. They express, in my opinion, the two bases of true civilization,—knowledge and strength. Military conscription, instead of voluntary enlistment, at first found many adversaries among us: it is now considered as a condition and a means of civilization and public order. I am convinced the time will come when popular instruction will be equally recognized as a social duty imperative on all for the sake of all.

In Prussia, the state has long imposed on all parents the strict obligation of sending their children to school, unless they are able to prove that they are giving them a competent education at home. This duty has been successfully defined and regulated with precision for the different seasons of the year (see in Neigebauer's Collection, pp. 186 and 187, the circular of Frederic the Great, dated Jan. 1, 1769); it has been subjected to a severe supervision. Lastly, in the great attempts at codification which took place in 1794, it assumed its place among the fundamental laws of the state. The two articles of the general code relating to this obligation are as follows: *Allgemeines Landrecht*, Part II. title xii.

"Art. 43. Every inhabitant who cannot, or will not, cause the needful instruction to be given to his children at home, is bound to send them to school from the age of five years.

"Art. 44. From that age no child shall omit going to school, nor absent himself from it for any length of time, unless under particular circumstances, and with the consent of the civil and ecclesiastical authorities."

CALVIN STOWE'S REPORT ON ELEMENTARY EDUCATION IN PRUSSIA

(1837)   From Calvin Stowe, *Report on Elementary Public Instruction in Europe, Made to the Thirty-sixth General Assembly of the State of Ohio,* December 19, 1837 (Boston, 1838), pp. 17–19, 27–28, 31–32, 52–53.

Internal Arrangements of the Prussian Schools

I will now ask your attention to a few facts respecting the internal management of the schools in Prussia and some other parts of Germany, which were impressed on my mind by a personal inspection of those establishments.

One of the circumstances that interested me most was the excellent order and rigid economy with which all the Prussian institutions are conducted. Particularly in large boarding schools, where hundreds, and sometimes thousands of youth are collected together, the benefits of the system are strikingly manifest. Every boy is taught to wait upon himself—to keep his person, clothing, furniture, and books, in perfect order and neatness; and no extravagance in dress, and no waste of fuel or food, or property of any kind is permitted. Each student has his own single bed, which is generally a light mattrass, laid upon a frame of slender bars of iron, because such bedsteads are not likely to be infested by insects, and each one makes his own bed and keeps it in order. In the house, there is a place for every thing and every thing must be in its place. In one closet are the shoe-brushes and blacking, in another the lamps and oil, in another the fuel. At the doors are good mats and scrapers, and every thing of the kind necessary for neatness and comfort, and every student is taught, as carefully as he is taught any other lesson, to make a proper use of all these articles at the right time, and then to leave them in good order at their proper places. Every instance of neglect is sure to receive its appropriate reprimand, and if necessary, severe punishment. I know of nothing that can benefit us more than the introduction of such oft-repeated lessons on carefulness and frugality into all our educational establishments; for the contrary habits of carelessness and wastefulness, notwithstanding all the advantages we enjoy, have already done us immense mischief. Very many of our families waste and throw away nearly as much as they use; and one third of the expenses of housekeeping might be saved by system and frugality. It is true, we have such an abundance of every thing that this enormous waste is not so sensibly felt as it would be in a more densely populated region; but it is not *always* to be so with us. The productions of our country for some years past have by no means kept pace with the increase of consumption, and many an American family during the last season has felt a hard pressure, where they never expected to feel one.

Especially should this be made a branch of female education, and studied faithfully and perseveringly by all who are to be wives and mothers, and have the care of families.

The universal success also and very beneficial results, with which the arts of drawing and designing, vocal and instrumental music, moral instruction and the Bible, have been introduced into schools, was another fact peculiarly interesting to me.

*   *   *

The whole course comprises eight years, and includes children from the ages of six till fourteen; and it is divided into four parts, of two years each. It is a first principle, that the children be well accommodated as to house and furniture. The school-room must be well constructed, the seats convenient, and the scholars made comfortable, and kept interested. The younger pupils are kept at school but four hours in the day—two in the morning and two in the evening, with a recess at the close of each hour. The older, six hours, broken by recesses as often as is necessary. Most of the schoolhouses have a bathing place, a garden and a mechanics' shop attached to them, to promote the cleanliness and health of the children, and to aid in mechanical and agricultural instruction. It will be seen by the schedule which follows, that a vast amount of instruction is given during these eight years—and, lest it should seem that so many branches must confuse the young mind, and that they must necessarily be but partially taught, I will say in the outset, that the industry, skill and energy of teachers regularly trained to their business, and depending entirely upon it; the modes of teaching; the habit of always finishing whatever is begun; the perfect method which is preserved; the entire punctuality and regularity of attendence on the part of the scholars; and other things of this kind, facilitate a rapidity and exactness of acquisition and discipline, which may well seem incredible to those who have never witnessed it.

The greatest care is taken that acquisition does not go beyond discipline; and that the taxation of mind be kept entirely and clearly within the constitutional capacity of mental and physical endurance. The studies must never weary, but always interest—the appetite for knowledge must never be cloyed, but be kept always sharp and eager. These purposes are greatly aided by the frequent interchange of topics, and by lively conversational exercises. Before the child is even permitted to learn his letters, he is under conversational instruction, frequently for six months or a year; and then a single week is sufficient to introduce him into intelligible and accurate plain reading.

Every week is systematically divided, and every hour appropriated. The scheme for the week is written on a large sheet of paper, and fixed in a prominent part of the school-room, so that every scholar knows what his business will be for every hour in the week; and the plan thus marked out is rigidly followed. As a specimen I present the following study sheet given me by Dr. Diesterweg, of Berlin, and which was the plan for his school when I visited it in September, 1836.

Through all the parts of the course there are frequent reviews and repetitions, that the impressions left on the mind may be distinct, lively and permanent. The exercises of the day are always commenced and closed with a short prayer; and the bible and hymn book are the first volumes put into the pupil's hands, and these books they always retain and keep in constant use during the whole progress of their education.

The general outline of the eight years' course is nearly as follows:

I. *First part, of two years, including children from six to eight years old—four principal branches, namely:*

1. Logical Exercises, or oral teaching in the exercise of the powers of observation and expression, including religious instruction and the singing of hymns;
2. Elements of Reading;
3. Elements of Writing;

4. Elements of Number, or Arithmetic.

II. *Second part, of two years, including children from eight to ten years old—seven principal branches, namely:*

1. Exercises in Reading;
2. Exercises in Writing;
3. Religious and Moral Instruction, in select Bible Narratives;
4. Language, or Grammar;
5. Numbers, or Arithmetic;
6. Doctrine of space and form, or Geometry;
7. Singing by note, or Elements of Music.

III. *Third part, of two years, including children from ten to twelve years old—eight principal branches:*

1. Exercises in Reading and Elocution;
2. Exercises in Ornamental Writing, preparatory to drawing;
3. Religious Instruction in the connected Bible history;
4. Language, or Grammar, with parsing;
5. Real Instruction, or knowledge of nature and the external world, including the first elements of the sciences and the arts of life—of geography and history;
6. Arithmetic, continued through fractions and the rules of proportion;
7. Geometry—doctrine of magnitudes and measures;
8. Singing, and science of vocal and instrumental music.

IV. *Fourth part, of two years, including children from twelve to fourteen years old—six principal branches, namely:*

1. Religious Instruction in the religious observation of nature; the life and discourses of Jesus Christ; the history of the Christian religion, in connection with the contemporary civil history; and the doctrines of christianity;
2. Knowledge of the world, and of mankind, including civil society, elements of law, agriculture, mechanic arts, manufactures, &c.;
3. Language, and exercises in composition;
4. Application of arithmetic and the mathematics to the business of life, including surveying and civil engineering;
5. Elements of Drawing;
6. Exercises in Singing, and the science of music.

HORACE MANN DESCRIBES TEACHER SEMINARIES IN PRUSSIA

(**1844**)   From Massachusetts Board of Education, *Seventh Annual Report of . . . The Secretary of the Board* (Boston, 1844), pp. 129–32.

Seminaries For Teachers

From the year 1820 to 1830 or 1835, it was customary, in all accounts of Prussian education, to mention the number of these Seminaries for Teachers. This item of information has now become unimportant, as there are seminaries sufficient to supply the wants of the whole country. The stated term of residence at these seminaries is three years. Lately, and in a few places, a class of preliminary institutions has sprung up,—institutions where pupils are received in order to determine whether they are fit to become candidates to be candidates. As a pupil of the seminary is liable to be set aside for incompetency, even after a three years' course of study; so the pupils of these preliminary institutions, after having gone through with a shorter course, are liable to be set aside for incompetency to become competent.

Let us look for a moment at the guards and securities which, in that country, environ this sacred calling. In the first place, the teacher's profession holds such a high rank in public estimation, that none who have failed in other employments or departments of business, are encouraged to look upon schoolkeeping as an ultimate resource. Those, too, who from any cause, despair of success in other departments of business or walks of life, have very slender prospects in looking forward to this. These considerations exclude at once all that inferior order of men, who, in some countries, constitute the main body of the teachers. Then come,—though only in some parts of Prussia,—these preliminary schools, where those who wish eventually to become teachers, go, in order to have their natural qualities and adaptation for school-keeping tested;—for it must be borne in mind that a man may have the most unexceptionable character, may be capable of mastering all the branches of study, may even be able to make most brilliant recitations from day to day; and yet, from some coldness or repulsiveness of manner, from harshness of voice, from some natural defect in his person or in one of his senses, he may be adjudged an unsuitable model or archetype for children to be conformed to, or to grow by; and hence he may be dismissed at the end of his probationary term of six months. At one of these preparatory schools, which I visited, the list of subjects at the examination,—a part of which I saw,—was divided into two classes, as follows:— 1. Readiness in Thinking, German Language, including Orthography and Composition, History, Description of the Earth, Knowledge of Nature, Thorough Bass, Calligraphy, Drawing. 2. Religion, Knowledge of the Bible, Knowledge of Nature, Mental Arithmetic, Singing, Violin Playing, and Readiness or Facility in Speaking. The examination in all the branches of the first class was conducted in writing. To test a pupil's Readiness in Thinking, for instance, several topics for composition are given out, and after the lapse of a certain number of minutes, whatever has been written must be handed in to the examiners. So questions in arithmetic are given, and the time occupied by the pupils in solving them, is a test of their quickness of thought, or power of commanding their own resources. This facility, or faculty, is considered of great importance in a teacher. In the second class of subjects the pupils were examined *orally*. Two entire days were occupied in examining a class of thirty pupils, and only twenty-one were admitted to the seminary school;—that is, only about two thirds were considered to be eligible *to become eligible*, as teachers, after three years' further study. Thus, in this first process, the chaff is winnowed out, and not a few of the lighter grains of the wheat.

It is to be understood that those who enter the seminary directly, and without this preliminary trial, have already studied, under able masters in the Common Schools, at least all the branches I have above described. The first two of the three years, they expend mainly in reviewing and expanding their elementary knowledge. The German language is studied in its relations to rhetoric and logic, and as aesthetic literature; arithmetic is carried out into algebra and mixed mathematics; geography into commerce and manufactures, and into a knowledge of the various botanical and zoological productions of the different quarters of the globe; linear drawing into perspective and machine drawing, and the drawing from models of all kinds and from objects in nature, &c. The theory and practice not only of vocal but of instrumental music occupy much time. Every pupil must play on the violin; most of them play on the organ, and some on other instruments. I recollect seeing a Normal class engaged in learning the principles of Harmony. The teacher first explained the principles on which they were to proceed. He then wrote a bar of music upon the blackboard, and called upon a pupil to write such notes for another part or accompaniment, as would make *harmony* with the first. So he would write a bar with certain intervals, and then require a pupil to write another, with such intervals, as, according to the principles of musical science, would correspond with the first. A thorough course of reading on the subject of education is undertaken, as well as a more general course. Bible history is almost committed to memory. Connected with all the seminaries for teachers are large Model or Experimental Schools. During the last part of the course much of the students' time is spent in these schools. At first they go in and look on in silence, while an accomplished teacher is instructing a class. Then they themselves commence teaching under the eye of such a teacher. At last they teach a class alone, being responsible for its proficiency, and for its condition as to order, &c., at the end of a week or other period. During the whole course, there are lectures, discussions, compositions, &c., on the theory and practice of teaching. The essential qualifications of a candidate for the office, his attainments and the spirit of devotion and of religious fidelity in which he should enter upon his work; the modes of teaching the different branches; the motive-powers to be applied to the minds of children; dissertations upon the different natural dispositions of children, and consequently the different ways of addressing them, of securing their confidence and affection, and of winning them to a love of learning and a sense of duty; and especially the sacredness of the teacher's profession,—the idea that he stands, for the time being, in the place of a parent, and therefore that a parent's responsibilities rest upon him, that the most precious hopes of society are committed to his charge and that on him depends to a great extent the temporal and perhaps the future well-being of hundreds of his fellow-creatures,—these are the conversations, the ideas, the feelings, amidst which the candidate for teaching spends his probationary years. This is the daily atmosphere he breathes. These are the sacred, elevating, invigorating influences constantly pouring in upon his soul. Hence, at the expiration of his course, he leaves the seminary to enter upon his profession, glowing with enthusiasm for the noble cause he has espoused, and strong in his resolves to perform its manifold and momentous duties.

Here then is the cause of the worth and standing of the teachers whom I had the pleasure and the honor to see. As a body of men their character is more enviable than that of either of the three, so-called, "professions." They have more benevolence and self-sacrifice than the legal or medical while they have less of sanctimoniousness and austerity, less of indisposition to enter into all the innocent amusements and joyous feelings of childhood than the clerical. They are not unmindful of what belongs to men while they are serving God; nor of the duties they owe to this world while preparing for another.

European Views on American Education

DE TOCQUEVILLE ON DEMOCRACY IN AMERICA   From Alexis de
Tocqueville, *Democracy in America*, Henry Reeve, trans. (New York, 1947), pp. 44–46,
199, 200–201, 205–6, 280–81, 283–84, 390–94.

It is not only the fortunes of men which are equal in American; even their requirements partake in some degree of the same uniformity. I do not believe that there is a country in the world where, in proportion to the population, there are so few uninstructed and at the same time so few learned individuals. Primary instruction is within the reach of everybody; superior instruction is scarcely to be obtained by any. This is not surprising; it is, in fact, the necessary consequence of what we have advanced above. Almost all the Americans are in easy circumstances, and can therefore obtain the first elements of human knowledge.

In America there are comparatively few who are rich enough to live without a profession. Every profession requires an apprenticeship, which limits the time of instruction to the early years of life. At fifteen they enter upon their calling, and thus their education ends at the age when ours begins. Whatever is done afterward is with a view to some special and lucrative object; a science is taken up as a matter of business, and the only branch of it which is attended is such as admits of an immediate practical application. In America most of the rich men were formerly poor; most of those who now enjoy leisure were absorbed in business during their youth; the consequence of which is, that when they might have had a taste for study they had no time for it, and when time is at their disposal they have no longer the inclination.

There is no class, then, in America in which the taste for intellectual pleasures is transmitted with hereditary fortune and leisure, and by which the labors of the intellect are held in honor. Accordingly, there is an equal want of the desire and the power of application to these objects.

A middle standard is fixed in America for human knowledge. All approach as near to it as they can; some as they rise, others as they descend. Of course, an immense multitude of persons are to be found who entertain the same number of ideas on religion, history, science, political economy, legislation, and government. The gifts of intellect proceed directly from God, and man cannot prevent their unequal distribution. But in consequence of the state of things which we have here represented it happens that, although the capacities of men are widely different, as the Creator has doubtless intended they should be, they are submitted to the same method of treatment.

In America the aristocratic element has always been feeble from its birth; and if at the present day it is not actually destroyed, it is at any rate so completely disabled that we can scarcely assign to it any degree of influence in the course of affairs. The democratic principle, on the contrary, has gained so much strength by time, by events, and by legislation, as to have become not only predominant but all-powerful. There is no family or corporate authority, and it is rare to find even the influence of individual character enjoying any durability.

America, then, exhibits in her social state a most extraordinary phenomenon. Men are there seen on a greater equality in point of fortune and intellect, or, in other words, more equal in their strength, than in any other country of the world, or in any age of which history has preserved the remembrance.

The political consequences of such a social condition as this are easily deductible. It is impossible to believe that equality will not eventually find its way into the political world as it does everywhere else. To conceive of men remaining forever unequal upon one single point, yet equal on all others, is impossible; they must come in the end to be equal upon all. Now I know of only two methods of establishing equality in the political world; every citizen must be put in possession of his rights, or rights must be granted to no one. For nations which are arrived at the same stage of social existence as the Anglo-Americans, it is therefore very difficult to discover a medium between the sovereignty of all and the absolute power of one man: and it would be vain to deny that the social condition which I have been describing is equally liable to each of these consequences.

There is, in fact, a manly and lawful passion for equality which excites men to wish all to be powerful and honored. This passion tends to elevate the humble to the rank of the great; but there exists also in the human heart a depraved taste for equality, which impels the weak to attempt to lower the powerful to their own level, and reduces men to prefer equality in slavery to inequality with freedom. Not that those nations whose social condition is democratic naturally despise liberty; on the contrary, they have an instinctive love of it. But liberty is not the chief and constant object of their desires; equality is their idol; they make rapid and sudden efforts to obtain liberty, and if they miss their aim resign themselves to their disappointment; but nothing can satisfy them except equality, and rather than lose it they resolve to perish.

*   *   *

There is certainly no country in the world where the tie of marriage is so much respected as in America, or where conjugal happiness is more highly or worthily appreciated. In Europe almost all the disturbances of society arise from the irregularities of domestic life. To despise the natural bonds and legitimate pleasures of home is to contract a taste for excesses, a restlessness of heart, and the evil of fluctuating desires. Agitated by the tumultuous passions which frequently disturb his dwelling, the European is galled by the obedience which the legislative powers of the State exact. But when the American retires from the turmoil of public life to the bosom of his family, he finds in it the image of order and of peace. There his pleasures are simple and natural, his joys are innocent and calm; and as he finds that an orderly life is the surest path to happiness, he accustoms himself without difficulty to moderate his opinions as well as his tastes. While the European endeavors to forget his domestic troubles by agitating society, the American derives from his own home that love of order which he afterward carries with him into public affairs.

In the United States the influence of religion is not confined to the manners, but it extends to the intelligence of the people. Among the Anglo-Americans, there are some who profess the doctrines of Christianity from a sincere belief in them, and others who do the same because they are afraid to be suspected of unbelief. Christianity, therefore, reigns without any obstacle, by universal consent; the consequence is, as I have before observed, that every principle of the moral world is fixed and determinate, although the political world is abandoned to the debates and the experiments of men. Thus the human mind is never left to wander across a boundless field; and, whatever may be its pretensions, it is checked from time to time by barriers which it cannot surmount.

*   *   *

The Americans combine the notions of Christianity and of liberty so intimately in their minds that it is impossible to make them conceive the one without the other, and with them this conviction does not spring from that barren traditionary faith which seems to vegetate in the soul rather than to live.

I have known of societies formed by the Americans to send out ministers of the Gospel into the new Western States to found schools and churches there, lest religion should be suffered to die away in those remote settlements, and the rising States be less fitted to enjoy free institutions than the people from which they emanated. I met with wealthy New Englanders who abandoned the country in which they were born in order to lay the foundations of Christianity and of freedom on the banks of the Missouri, or in the prairies of Illinois. Thus religious zeal is perpetually stimulated in the United States by the duties of patriotism. These men do not act from an exclusive consideration of the promises of a future life; eternity is only one motive of their devotion to the cause; and if you converse with these missionaries of Christian civilization, you will be surprised to find how much value they set upon the goods of this world, and that you meet with a politician where you expected to find a priest. They will tell you that 'all the American republics are collectively involved with each other; if the republics of the West were to fall into anarchy, or to be mastered by a despot, the republican institutions which now flourish upon the shores of the Atlantic Ocean would be in great peril. It is therefore our interest that the new States should be religious, in order to maintain our liberties.'

*   *   *

When I compare the Greek and Roman Republics with these American States, the manuscript libraries of the former, and their rude population, with the innumerable journals and the enlightened people of the latter; when I remember all the attempts that are made to judge the modern republics by the assistance of those of antiquity, and to infer what will happen in our time from what took place two thousand years ago, I am tempted to burn my books, in order to apply none but novel ideas to so novel a condition of society.

What I have said of New England must now, however, be applied indistinctly to the whole Union; as we advance toward the West or the South, the instruction of the people diminishes. In the States which are adjacent to the Gulf of Mexico, a certain number of individuals may be found, as in our own countries, who are devoid of the rudiments of instruction. But there is not a single district in the United States sunk in complete ignorance; and for a very simple reason: the peoples of Europe started from the darkness of a barbarous condition, to advance toward the light of civilization; their progress has been unequal; some of them have improved apace, while others have loitered in their course, and some have stopped, and are still sleeping upon the way.

Such has not been the case in the United States. The Anglo-Americans settled in a state of civilization, upon that territory which their descendants occupy; they had not to begin to learn, and it was sufficient for them not to forget. Now the children of these same Americans are the persons who, year by year, transport their dwellings into the wilds; and with their dwellings their acquired information and their esteem for knowledge. Education has taught them the utility of instruction, and has enabled them to transmit that instruction to their posterity. In the United States society has no infancy, but it is born into man's estate.

Let us transport ourselves into the midst of a democracy, not unprepared by ancient traditions and present culture to partake in the pleasures of the mind. Ranks are there intermingled and confounded; knowledge and power are both infinitely subdivided, and, if I may use the expression, scattered on every side. Here, then, is a motley multitude, whose intellectual wants are to be supplied. These new votaries of the pleasures of the mind have not all received the same education: they do not possess the same degree of culture as their fathers, nor any resemblance to them— nay, they perpetually differ from themselves, for they live in a state of incessant change of place, feelings, and fortunes. The mind of each member of the community is therefore unattached to that of his fellow citizens by tradition or by common habits; and they never have had the power, the inclination, nor the time to concert together. It is, however, from the bosom of this heterogeneous and agitated mass that authors spring; and from the same source their profits and their fame are distributed. I can understand without difficulty that, under these circumstances, I must expect to meet in the literature of such a people with but few of those strict conventional rules which are admitted by readers and by writers in aristocratic ages. If it should happen that the men of some one period were agreed upon any such rules, that would prove nothing for the following period; for among democratic nations each new generation is a new people. Among such nations, then, literature will not easily be subjected to strict rules, and it is impossible that any such rules should ever be permanent.

In democracies it is by no means the case that all the men who cultivate literature have received a literary education; and most of those who have some tinge of *belles-lettres* are either engaged in politics, or in a profession which only allows them to taste occasionally and by stealth the pleasures of the mind. These pleasures, therefore, do not constitute the principal charm of their lives; but they are considered as a transient and necessary recreation amid the serious labors of life. Such men can never acquire a sufficiently intimate knowledge of the art of literature to appreciate its more delicate beauties; and the minor shades of expression must escape them. As the time they can devote to letters is very short, they seek to make the best use of the whole of it. They prefer books which may be easily procured, quickly read, and which require no learned research to be understood. They ask for beauties, self-proffered and easily enjoyed; above all, they must have what is unexpected and new. Accustomed to the struggle, the crosses, and the monotony of practical life, they require rapid emotions, startling passages—truths of errors brilliant enough to rouse them up, and to plunge them at once, as if by violence, into the midst of a subject.

* * *

It is evident that in democratic communities the interest of individuals, as well as the security of the commonwealth, demands that the education of the greater number should be scientific, commercial, and industrial, rather than literary. Greek and Latin should not be taught in all schools; but it is important that those who by their natural disposition or their fortune are destined to cultivate letters or prepared to relish them, should find schools where a complete knowledge of ancient literature may be acquired, and where the true scholar may be formed. A few excellent universities would do more toward the attainment of this object than a vast number of bad grammar schools, where superfluous matters, badly learned, stand in the way of sound instruction in necessary studies . . .

FRANCIS LIEBER ON THE PROBLEMS OF ASSIMILATION (1835) From
Francis Lieber, *The Stranger in America* (Philadelphia, 1835), pp. 57–58, 62–64.

At my landing on the wharf in New York, I found several groups of German emigrants, just arrived from Europe. Some of them looked pretty well dressed, and showed that they had come with sufficient means to proceed immediately to the west, and to settle there; others, who looked very poor, had first to go through the ordeal of a poor emigrant, who is obliged, for want of means, to tarry in or about a large city, where he is, of course, exposed to the miseries inherent to a residence in a populous, foreign place, without any means of independence, and often becomes a prey to swindlers, with numbers of whom, as you may well imagine, they meet among their own countrymen; worthless fellows who have arrived long before them, and know all the ways of robbing these poor and helpless creatures of their last farthing. I know it from many of my acquaintances in New York, who belong to a charitable society, one of the objects of which is to assist destitute emigrants, that one of the great dangers which await the latter in that city, is, their falling into the hands of certain boarding-house keepers of their own nation (of course only *certain* of these) who strip the poor families of every thing they had the good luck to be able to bring along with them; like wolf-dogs, they are the enemies of their own species. A German emigrant generally remains in a large city only as long as he cannot help it; his great and laudable desire is always to get a farm, and to own it. The Irish are, in this respect, very different; they prefer the cities, and wherever you meet with a populous place in the United States—I do not only speak of the Atlantic cities, but also of those in the interior, such as Albany, Utica, Cincinnati, Louisville—you are sure to find a great number of poor Irish in and about it. The German, as I said, pushes on; if he has not the means to proceed immediately to the west, and must take his temporary abode in a large place, it is only in order to save, as soon as he possibly can, the requisite sum to carry him and his family to those parts of the Union where land is cheap and fertile. Here again he has not, perhaps, the means to purchase a few acres, though government sells public lands for the low price of one dollar and twenty-five cents per acre. If this is the case, he will first work for another farmer, never, however, losing sight of his main object, the having of a farm to himself. As soon as he has it, he loves it as a German trooper loves his horse; it becomes his "all in all," so that he sometimes forgets the proper mental education of his offspring. Scotch emigrants, I imagine, generally arrive here provided with sufficient means to begin farming immediately.

*　　*　　*

The Germans, as I said, form a most valuable addition to our population, when mingled with the great predominant race inhabiting the northern part of this continent. Whenever colonists settle among a different nation, in such numbers and so closely together that they may live on among themselves, without intermixture with the original inhabitants, a variety of inconveniences will necessarily arise. Living in an isolated state, the current of civilization of the country in which they live does not reach them; and they are equally cut off from that of their mother country: mental stagnation is the consequence. They remain a foreign element, an ill-joined part of the great machinery of which they still form, and needs must form, a part.

*　　*　　*

Those, therefore, who lately proposed to form a whole German state in our west, ought to weigh well their project before they set about it, if ever it should become possible to put this scheme into practice, which I seriously doubt. "Ossification," as the Germans call it, would be the unavoidable consequence. These colonists would be unable, though they might come by thousands and tens of thousands to develop for themselves German literature, German language, German law, German science, German art; every thing would remain stationary at the point where it was when they brought it over from the mother country, and within less than fifty years of our colony would degenerate into an antiquated, ill-adapted element of our great national system, with which, sooner or later, it must assimilate.

*　　*　　*

Quite a different question it is whether German emigrants ought to preserve the knowledge of German language, and German education in general among them. By all means! Have schools in which both German and English are taught. Nothing is easier than to learn from infancy two languages at once, and few things are more important than the knowledge of two languages, especially if the one besides the native idiom is the German.

FRANCIS LIEBER DESCRIBES AMERICAN WOMEN (1835) From Francis
Lieber, *The Stranger in America* (Philadelphia, 1835), pp. 78–79.

An American girl is never embarrassed; a child of ten years;—and I would hardly except a single class of the inhabitants,—receives you with a frankness and good breeding which is astonishing, and I can assure you, not unpleasing. So perfectly self-possessed are they, that blushing is decidedly of less frequent occurrence here than with you in Germany. My attention was lately drawn to a young friend of mine, a most amiable girl, who blushed; and I then thought how rarely I had seen it here. I could remember but very few girls of a large acquaintance that will now and then be seen blushing, I mean when nothing but false *embarras* is the cause. This pleasing ease and sensible frankness sometimes degenerate, as you may suppose, into unbecoming and ungraceful forwardness, as German mildness and bashfulness degenerate sometimes into shy *gaucherie*.

American ladies are possessed of much natural brightness, and converse very freely, infinitely more so than gentlemen. Altogether, boys and girls are earlier *developed* here than in Europe, partly perhaps owing to the climate, partly because they are allowed more freedom,—left more to themselves. A young man of twenty has a much more advanced position in life here than in England, and in England more so than on the continent. The Germans, it is my opinion, hold back a young man by far too much; Americans, I am equally convinced, allow their young people to leap beyond their age—each system has its inconveniences.

Good education among ladies is general. Not a few are truly superior in this respect. I think there must be numbers who are bright and fluent letter-writers, to judge from my own correspondence. I know several ladies whose attainments and natural powers would be a great ornament to society anywhere, but one of them I count among the most superior minds with whom it has ever been my good fortune to become acquainted. Yet that has nothing to do with America; such brilliant endowments are but contingencies in a nation, not the fruit of general national civilization. Would she but give proofs of her flashing mind, unfettered thought, and independent judgment, to more than her personal acquaintance! Her mind has indeed a powerful grasp. Were it not for the horror I feel at communicating letters, I would send you some of hers, and I would ask you whether they do not equal any you have ever read which have been preserved as the *stars* of memoirs.

FRANCIS GRUND'S COMPARISON OF AMERICAN AND GERMAN EDUCATION (1837) From Francis J. Grund, *The Americans, in Their Moral, Social, and Political Relations* (Boston, 1837), pp. 132–41.

There are two branches of instruction, however, which I consider to be better taught in America than even in Germany. I would refer to reading and speaking. The Americans, in general, take more care to teach a correct pronunciation to their children, than the English; and the Germans are almost wholly unmindful as to the correctness of utterance, or elegance of language. They are so much attached to the substance of thoughts, that they heed little in what form the latter are expressed, and are satisfied with teaching their pupils to understand what they are reading, or to comprehend with the eye what they are unable to express with clearness and precision. A German boy knows often more than he can express in his abstract and unmanageable language: an American says at least as much as he knows, and is seldom embarrassed except with the difficulty of the subject.

This readiness of the Americans to express with promptness and precision what they have once been able to understand, is as much owing to their system of education, as to the practical genius of the nation, and of immense advantage in the common business of life. An American is not as "manysided" as a German; but whatever he has learned he has at his fingers' ends, and he is always ready to apply it. A little, in this manner, will go a great way, and the amount of intellect and application which is thus penetrating every corner of the United States is prodigious, when compared to the seemingly slender means by which it is produced. Propose a question to a German, and he will ransack heaven and earth for an answer. He will descend to the remotest antiquity to seek for precedents; and, after having compared the histories of all nations, and the best commentaries on them in half a dozen languages, he will be so perplexed with the contradictory statements of authors, that his conscientiousness will hardly allow him to venture an opinion of his own. He will give you a most erudite *resumé* of the subject; acquaint you with all that has been said on it in Sanscrit and Arabic, and, after having made some remarks on the respective credibility of these writers, leave the conclusion to your own ingenuity. An American, with hardly one tenth of the learning, would have submitted the subject to *common sense*, and, ten chances to one, would have given you a satisfactory answer. The Germans are the best people in the world for collecting materials, but the Americans understand best how to use them. I know no better combination of character than that of German and American; and there is probably no better system of instruction than a medium between the theoretical rigor of the former, and the practical applications of the Americans.

The German system favors the development of the mind to the exclusion of almost all practical purposes; the American aims always at some application, and creates dexterity and readiness for action. One is all contemplation, the other all activity—the former is adapted to the abstract pursuits of philosophy, the latter to the practical purposes of life.

Each of these systems has its own advantages and disadvantages, and corresponds well to the genius of the respective nations among whom it is established. There is probably no better place than a school-room to judge of the character of a people, or to find an explanation of their national peculiarities. Whatever faults or weaknesses may be entailed upon them, will show themselves there without the hypocrisy of advanced age; and whatever virtue they may possess is reflected without admixture of vice and corruption. In so humble a place as a school-room may be read the commentaries on the past, and the history of the future development of a nation.

Who, upon entering an American school-room, and witnessing the continual exercises in reading and speaking, or listening to the subject of their discourses, and watching the behavior of the pupils towards each other and their teacher, could, for a moment, doubt his being amongst a congregation of young republicans? And who, on entering a German academy, would not be struck with the principle of authority and silence, which reflects the history of Germany for the last half dozen centuries. What difficulty has not an American teacher to maintain order amongst a dozen unruly little urchins; while a German rules over two hundred pupils in a class with all the ease and tranquillity of an Eastern monarch?

In an American school every thing is done from conviction; in a German, obedience is from habit and precedent. How active is not the strife for consideration and power amongst a class of young Americans; how perfectly contemplative the same collection of Germans, intent only upon their studies and the gratification of individual tastes.

The majority of the pupils of an American school will imprint their character on the institution; the personal disposition of the teacher in Germany can always be read in the behavior of his pupils. There is as little disposition on the part of American children to obey the uncontrolled will of their masters, as on the part of their fathers to submit to the mandates of kings; and it would only be necessary to conduct some doubting European politician to an American school-room, to convince him at once that there is no immediate prospect of transferring royalty to the shores of the New World.

It has been observed, that with Americans mathematics come by instinct. This is true *with regard to the applications* of the science, which in America are as well, or better understood, than in any part of Europe; but there is no taste visible for the mere abstract knowledge of it, as is the case in France and Germany.

The Americans are born analyzers, and are better able to understand a principle from its application, than to seize a truth in the abstract, nor would they think such a truth an acquisition, unless they saw its practical bearings. I have known several excellent mathematicians in Boston and Philadelphia, but their talents were all of the order I have described; and I suspect, therefore, that they are not very eminent teachers. The method of instruction must necessarily be synthetic, and implies a process of reasoning, which, as far as my experience goes, is least acceptable to American palates. In politics analysis is the only means of arriving at fair conclusions; but in the exact sciences it is less direct and secure, although it is the method of invention and the most fertile in applications. On the whole, I do not think that the Americans have a greater share of mathematical talent than Europeans; but they certainly apply it to greater advantage, and evince an acquaintance with the science in all their civil and political transactions. Mathematics with them are an active principle; not an abstract science, as in Europe.

For history, the Americans seem to have the least fondness; but they are great admirers of statistics, and have an astonishing memory of numbers. An American considers the history of his country as the beginning of a new era; and cares, therefore, less for the past, than he does for the present and the future. Statistics is nevertheless a still-standing history, and the key or index to the future fate of a nation. This truth is as well understood in America as in any other country; and accordingly, the rage for statistical tables, as a means of obtaining knowledge in a quick and easy manner, exists in the United States to a still greater degree than in England or France. I have known few persons in Europe, as well acquainted with the imports and exports, revenue and expenditure, amount of national debt, standing armies and navies, &c. of their own and foreign countries, as the great mass of Americans.

Geography is well taught from excellent text-books, some of which have been translated into several European languages. The proficiency of the pupils in this branch is highly creditable to the instructers, and surpasses in minuteness and correctness that of most scholars of the same age in Europe.

But the most surprising fact, in the whole course of American education, is the *total absence of religious instruction,* in most of the elementary schools. This is entirely left to the care of the parents, and confined, principally, to the reading of the Bible and the hearing of sermons and lectures on the Sabbath. I confess myself unable to judge of the expediency of this course, which is perhaps rendered necessary by the great number of religious sects who send children to one and the same school; but whatever its disadvantages may be, I am quite certain there is as much theoretical and practical religion in the United States as in any other country.

Before I conclude these observations on elementary instruction in America, I would mention a subject, which, as yet, seems to have escaped the attention of most travellers, though it is sufficiently interesting in itself, and explanatory of a great many peculiarities in the lives of Americans. I would allude to the precocity of children, which results from the plan of education pursued in schools and at home, and perhaps, also, from the peculiar climate of the country.

An American boy of ten or twelve years of age is as much of a young man as an European at sixteen; and when arrived at that age, he is as useful in business, and as much to be relied upon, as a German at twenty-four, or a Frenchman at fifty. Something similar to it may also be found in England; but neither climate nor education promote it to the same extent as in America. From the earliest period of his life, a young American is accustomed to rely upon himself as the principal artificer of his fortune. Whatever he learns or studies is with a view to future application; and the moment he leaves school he immerses into active life. His reputation, from the time he is able to think, is the object of his most anxious care; as it must affect his future standing in society, and increase the sphere of his usefulness.

As a school-boy, he has his opinions on politics and religion, which he defends with as much ardor as if he were a senator of the republic, or a minister of the gospel. By the time he is able to read and write, he is already forming the plan of his future independence; and I have heard boys from ten to twelve years of age enlarge on the comforts and advantages of married life, with as grave an aspect, as if they had been reciting a mathematical lesson, or discussing the merits of an essay on politics. They were calculating the prospects of domestic happiness, as a merchant would the profits of a mercantile speculation, or a banker his commission on a bill of exchange.

American children study the foibles of their parents and teachers, which they are sure to turn to their own advantage, and at the age of twenty-one are better judges of characters, and human nature in general, than many an European at the age of fifty. In girls this precocity is blended with bashfulness and modesty; but the most characteristic feature of American children, whether male or female, is, nevertheless, an early development of the understanding, and a certain untimely intelligence seldom to be found in Europe.

The Americans have a much shorter period assigned to them, for the completion of their studies than Europeans; but the quantity of knowledge acquired in that time is really prodigious, and it is a wonder if the memory can retain one fourth part of it in after life. A child from four to five years of age is already obliged to be six hours a day at school, and to study perhaps two or three more at home; and as it advances in age, the number and variety of these studies increase in a duplicate ratio. At the age of twelve, a boy will study Latin, Greek, French, Italian, Spanish, algebra, geometry, mechanics, moral philosophy, mineralogy, natural philosophy, chemistry, and Heaven knows what! and manages at least to recite his lessons to the satisfaction of his *teachers*. I have never seen an attempt at any thing similar in Europe, and am satisfied of the utter impossibility of its success, were it to be hazarded in England or Germany.

If the time devoted to an American college-course were anyways in proportion to the intensity of application on the part of the pupils, the American seminaries would be the first in the world, and its professors and students the most remarkable for application and learning. But, unfortunately, the period of a collegiate education is limited to four years, which is about one half of what ought to be allowed for the completion of the course prescribed for an American college. Not much more than the rudiments of science can be acquired in so short a period; and the American scholar, therefore, must chiefly depend on the resources of his own mind, and the assistance of libraries, to become eminent in any department of knowledge, or to compete with men of learning in Europe. A number of American students are, for this purpose, annually visiting the Universities of Europe, especially those of Germany, and many distinguished scholars in the United States are as intimately acquainted with the literature of that country, as with the literary institutions of their own.

But if the Americans do not as yet possess the higher institutions of learning, which are the ornament of the most civilized states of Europe, the elements of a classical and mathematical education are, at least, disseminated throughout their whole country, and the means of laying the foundation of scholarship in every State of the Union. They had, in 1835, not less than seventy-nine colleges, thirty-one theological seminaries, twenty-three medical, and nine law schools.

HARRIET MARTINEAU ON THE MANNERS OF AMERICAN CHILDREN

(1837)   From Harriet Martineau, *Society in America* (New York, 1837), vol. III, pp. 166–67.

The early republican consciousness of which I have spoken, and the fact of the more important place which the children occupy in a society whose numbers are small in proportion to its resources, are the two circumstances which occasion that freedom of manners in children of which so much complaint has been made by observers, and on which so much remonstrance has been wasted;—I say "wasted," because remonstrance is of no avail against a necessary fact. Till the United States cease to be republican, and their vast area is fully peopled, the children there will continue as free and easy and as important as they are. For my own part, I delight in the American children; in those who are not overlaid with religious instruction. There are instances, as there are everywhere, of spoiled, pert, and selfish children. Parents' hearts are pierced there, as elsewhere. But the independence and fearlessness of children were a perpetual charm in my eyes. To go no deeper, it is a constant amusement to see how the speculations of young minds issue, when they take their own way of thinking, and naturally say all they think. Some admirable specimens of active little minds were laid open to me at a juvenile ball at Baltimore. I could not have got at so much in a year in England. If I had at home gone in among eighty or a hundred little people, between the ages of eight and sixteen, I should have extracted little more than "Yes, ma'am," and "No, ma'am." At Baltimore, a dozen boys and girls at a time crowded round me, questioning, discussing, speculating, revealing in a way which enchanted me. In private houses, the comments slipped in at table by the children were often the most memorable, and generally the most amusing part of the conversation. Their aspirations all come out. Some of these are very striking as indicating the relative value of things in the children's minds. One affectionate little sister, of less than four years old, stimulated her brother William, (five,) by telling him that if he would be very very good, he might in time be called William Webster; and then he might get on to be as good as Jesus Christ. Three children were talking over the birth-day of the second, (ten) and how they should like to keep it. They settled that they should like of all things to have Miss Sedgwick, and Mr. Bryant, and myself, to spend the day with them. They did not venture to invite us, and had no intention of our knowing their wish.

In conversing with a truly wise parent, one day, I remarked on the change of relation which takes place when the superior children of ordinary parents become guides and protectors to those who have kept their childhood restrained under a rigid rule. We talked over the difficulties of the transition here, (by far the hardest part of filial duty,) and speculated on what the case would be after death, supposing the parties to recognize each other in a new life of progression. My friend observed that the only thing to be done is to avoid to the utmost the exercise of authority, and to make children friends from the very beginning. He and many others have done this with gladdening success. They do not lay aside their democratic principles in this relation, more than in others, because they happen to have almost unlimited power in their own hands. They watch and guard: they remove stumbling-blocks: they manifest approbation and disapprobation: they express wishes, but, at the same time, study the wishes of their little people: they leave as much as possible to natural retribution: they impose no opinions, and quarrel with none: in short they exercise the tenderest friendship without presuming upon it. What is the consequence? I had the pleasure of hearing this friend say, "There is nothing in the world so easy as managing children. You may make them anything you please." In my own mind I added, "with such hearts and minds to bring to the work as the parents of your children have."—One reason of the pleasure with which I regarded the freedom of American children was that I took it as a sign that the most tremendous suffering perhaps of human life is probably lesseded, if not obviated, there:—the misery of concealed doubts and fears, and heavy solitary troubles,—the misery which makes the early years of a shy child a fearful purgatory. Yet purgatory is not the word: for this misery purges no sins, while it originates many. I have a strong suspicion that the faults of temper so prevalent where parental authority is strong, and where children are made as insignificant as they can be made, and the excellence of temper in America, are attributable to the different management of childhood in the one article of freedom.

ON UNIFORMITY IN AMERICA (1863)   From Edward Dicey, *Six Months in the Federal States* (London, 1863), pp. 167–69.

In a moral as opposed to a material point of view, the most striking feature about American society is its uniformity. Everybody, as a rule, holds the same opinions about everything, and expresses his views, more or less, in the same language. These views are often correct, almost invariably intelligent and creditable to the holders. But still, even at the risk of hearing paradoxes defended, you cannot help wishing, at times, for a little more of originality. I believe that this monotony in the tone of American talk and opinion arises from the universal diffusion of education. Everybody is educated up to a certain point, and very few are educated above it. They have all learned the same lessons under the same teachers, and, in consequence, share the same sentiments to a degree which it is difficult for an Englishman to appreciate beforehand. This monotony is infinitely more striking in the men than in the women. Ninety-nine American lads in a hundred go through exactly the same system of training. Up to eighteen or nineteen, they are carefully, if not very deeply, grounded in all the branches of a good ordinary English education. Then they go into business, and from that time their intellectual self-culture ceases. Unless they happen to travel, they have very little time for reading anything except the newspapers. The women pursue their education even after marriage, and are in consequence better read and more intellectual in their tastes than English ladies. In the long run, however, the national tone of mind is always derived from the male sex, and therefore the prevalent tone of America is not that of a highly educated society. I do not mean to say, for one moment, that there are not hundreds and thousands of men of really first-class education in the Northern States. On the contrary, some of the most thoroughly educated men it has been my lot to meet with have been Americans. I am speaking of the mass, not of individuals. This opinion of mine, if it is correct, explains a fact which otherwise would seem discouraging: I mean the small share taken by educated men—in our sense of the word—in American politics. The truth is that if America were governed to any great extent by politicians of classical education, the country would not be fairly represented by its rulers. It is not the case that the fact of a gentleman having received a refined culture is any disqualification to him in the eyes of the constituencies. On the other hand, it is a very small recommendation. I do not deny that this is, in itself, an evil; but the true nature of the evil is not that men of education are disqualified from entering a political career in America, but that they form so small a class that they possess no political influence. Just in the same way, there is no doubt that, relatively to the period, there were more highly educated men in the Union half a century ago than there are now. The early settlers in any new country bring with them a higher degree of individual culture than they can impart to their children. In the same ratio, however, that the education of the individual decreases, the average education of the mass increases, and, on the whole, the general tone of the nation gains in consequence.

A VISIT TO THE SALEM (MASSACHUSETTS) NORMAL SCHOOL

(**1867**)   From Sophia Jex-Blake, *A Visit to Some American Schools and Colleges* (London, 1867), pp. 201–08, 211–12.

The Normal Schools in Massachusetts are four in number, two of them being devoted to the education of female teachers only, and two to that of both sexes. This fact illustrates the preponderance in number of female teachers throughout the States, though it is rare for a woman to be at the head of any of the High or Normal Schools.

Believing it better to master thoroughly the working of one Normal school than to see something of them all, I attended the one at Salem for more than a week continuously, meeting the most courteous welcome from all the teachers, and seeing more and more to interest me each day, till at length my one regret was that I could not transplant the whole affair bodily to England, that other teachers might share my pleasure in seeing any school so thoroughly well worked as this was by its excellent Head Master and a first-rate staff of most earnest lady teachers, whose actual erudition was almost overwhelming.

Indeed, the amount of sheer learning acquired by really good teachers in America has often surprised me, and it is, as I have before remarked, the more striking when, as is so often the case, it co-exists with a very imperfect knowledge of English.

Each of the teachers at Salem has her own especial class of subjects, and to each is moreover assigned more or less charge of some one of the classes.

The number of pupils at Salem is about 120, and of teachers (besides the Head Master) 8. The pupils are divided into four classes, respectively lettered A, B, C, D, of which "A" is the most advanced, and "D" the least so. At the completion of the two years of study represented by these classes, such students as desire still further instruction may enter an "Advanced Class," which, generally speaking, receives only the *crème de la crème.*

Students are not admitted to the Normal School under the age of sixteen, and spend their first term in Class D.

The studies of this class comprise grammar, including analysis and syntax, the geography of the Western Continent, history of the United States, arithmetic and algebra, with some study of chemistry and physiology. In grammar and analysis the teaching is chiefly on a system devised by a late head-master, not altogether unlike that of Morell, but not, I think, equal to his. In geography and physiology a plan is pursued which I understand to be borrowed from the Westfield Normal School. While any state or country, or any portion of the structure of the body, is described by one pupil, the whole class draws the same with chalk on black boards which surround the room. This system was entirely new to me, and seemed very efficacious in securing thorough understanding of the subject by all. Its adoption at Salem was an instance of wise and liberal variation from old custom, the teacher whose duty it was to teach the subjects above-named being a graduate of Westfield, and being allowed to teach according to her own idea.

Arithmetic and algebra are very thoroughly taught at Salem; in the several classes almost daily, and also in general *vivâ voce* examinations of the whole school, which latter take place very frequently for a few minutes at a time.

In these examinations the teacher, or sometimes a senior pupil of the advanced class, will rapidly enunciate such a question as the following, and as her voice ceases some pupil will generally be ready with the answer;—"Take two; add one; cube; take away two; square; take away one; divide by two; subtract twelve; divide by fifteen; divide by ten; square; square; square.—Miss Smith?" "Two hundred and fifty-six." "Right." And so on, just as quickly as voice can speak. Of course, splendid rapidity of calculation will follow such training, unless with a few unfortunates who may get hopelessly confused.

Class C studies arithmetic, algebra, geometry, the "geography of the Eastern Continent" (not, we will hope, excluding England), grammatical analysis, parsing, and history.

One of the plans by which history is taught struck me as curious. One pupil has specially to get up a given subject or era, and then by memory to teach it to the whole class and at the next lesson to examine them in it, the teacher in charge listening meanwhile to correct errors on either side. Such devices certainly break the monotony of study, and help to give life and spirit to the pupils. Each history class will generally include one such examination and one such lesson.

In geometry, also, there is a plan of mutual instruction. On one occasion I saw the whole of Class C divided into pairs round the great hall, which is surrounded with black boards, and then one of each pair would from memory repeat the problem in question, while the other from memory corrected errors, the figure being drawn by the scholar *pro tem.* who, having finished her recitation, forthwith became teacher in turn; and so on till the problems are all recited, the teacher in charge moving round from one to the other, criticising or approving each. Of course, such a plan would not answer with any class of students less earnest, thorough, and conscientious than the Salem girls, but with them it seemed excellent.

Class B continue the study of arithmetic and algebra, and enter on that of natural and mental philosophy, as well as of English language and literature. The lessons in both natural and mental philosophy seemed calculated to develop much thought. I noticed here, as well as elsewhere throughout the school, that when a pupil made an error, or was in doubt as to a fact, the teacher rarely, if ever, gave her the required information, but simply noted the fact of its being wanted, and passed on to other subjects for that lesson; but on the next meeting of the class made it a point to ask the said girl a question directly bearing on the subject, thus ensuring that what was not known should be *searched out.* This plan, and the success it met with, seemed to me almost the perfection of teaching, and brought into strong light the earnest and ready co-operation between teachers and scholars,—both eager to ensure the acquisition of knowledge.

Class A take some lessons in book-keeping and in perspective drawing, and devote much of their time to the study of the theory and practice of teaching and school government. They are also required to make themselves acquainted with the school laws of Massachusetts, and the constitution of the United States. Mental philosophy is further pursued into the region of logic, and also with relation to questions of the will; and physical geography, astronomy, and geology, each have some share of attention.

Those pupils who have passed successfully through these four classes, and also through written examinations, are given diplomas of proficiency, and said to be graduates of the school.

A small number of pupils remain after completing their studies in Class A, and form the Advanced Class. The subjects pursued in this division are geometry, algebra, plane and spherical trigonometry, the Latin and French languages, natural philosophy, chemistry, botany, and general history.

That Latin and French should be postponed for study in the Advanced Class seems a little curious, as both languages are usually taught at the High Schools, the standard of which should hardly be supposed to be equal to that of Normal Schools. It is, however, probable that the resolution to aim at thoroughness before all things is the true explanation of deferring these studies, as parts, at least, of the regular course.

I think, however, that the weak point in the American Normal School system is, that these schools are neither made to run parallel with the High Schools, nor to form a sequence to them; but I have heard this explained to be the consequence of the demand for "common school" (*i.e.* primary and grammar) teachers, who are not required to know all the subjects taught in the High Schools.

The Normal School certificate given at "graduation" only guarantees fitness for teaching in these lower schools. Practically, many of the pupils do enter *after* going through the High Schools, and they, of course, are able to take a much better position. The Normal School itself professes less to give instruction in *what* is to be taught, than to teach (after the knowledge has been acquired) *how* it should be imparted.

DESCRIPTION OF THE FREE-SCHOOL SYSTEM OF THE UNITED STATES (1875)   From Francis Adams, *The Free School System of the United States* (London, 1875), pp. 239-48, 252.

To sum up, it is not pretended by Americans—it never has been advanced by the section of Englishmen who are attracted by American institutions, and especially by the common school—that their system is even theoretically perfect, much less that it produces in practice the utmost measure of success. It is the habit of American educationists, ungrudgingly, and with sincere admiration, to give the palm to Germany. Nor is this a mere complimentary recognition of excellence. It is shown to be genuine by the manner in which they are accepting from Germany, not only lessons in the details of educational science, but vital principles like compulsion.

But while the German system is mature, and has probably reached, or nearly reached, the highest point of excellence, that of the United States is still in its infancy. Therefore, the most important consideration for Americans is whether they have started upon the right lines. The process of undoing, as we find in England, is sometimes more difficult and laborious than that of constructing.

That which impresses us most in regard to America is the grasp which the schools have upon the sympathy and intelligence of the people. Those of the cities are the lions of America. The intelligent foreigner, and also, as it would appear from some recent criticisms, the unintelligent foreigner who visits the States, into whatever town he goes, is taken to the schools as the first objects of interest. Amongst public questions education occupies the foremost place, and of all topics it is that upon which the American speaker is most ready and most willing to enlarge. Public intelligence has recognised the fact that the highest and best interests of the nation are indissolubly bound up with the question. Thus every American feels not only a personal but a patriotic interest in the welfare of the schools. Owing to this popular feeling their organisation possesses a spring and force and energy which are in strong contrast with the sluggish instincts of the parochial system.

This widespread popular regard which constitutes the propelling power, appears to be chiefly due to two features—government by the people, and ownership by the people. It is a vast proprietary scheme, in which every citizen has a share. While it is undoubtedly true that all do not set the same value on school rights, it is also certain that their existence immensely stimulates public interest and diffuses a sense of responsibility through the entire community.

For no reason is the principle of local government more dearly prized, than because of the control which it gives the people over the schools. They would be as ready to surrender all municipal powers and privileges as to transfer their management to a sect or to any other private organisation. This recognition of responsibility is the mainspring of the system, and the cause of its best results.

✻   ✻   ✻

That the decentralisation of the American system is excessive, and leads to inefficiency in certain cases, has already been explained. That any radical change will be made is highly improbable. The advocates of a federal law under which large powers would be vested in the National Bureau of Education, are at present in a hopeless minority. The principle of State sovereignty is too firmly rooted in the public mind, and has worked too well, to be easily shaken. Of late years, however, a disposition has been manifested to increase the powers of State Superintendents and State Boards of Education; and, in the view of Englishmen, this is a movement in the right direction. The principle of local government should be supplemented by adequate power in the Executive of the State to meet those cases in which, from public apathy or other causes, the local authorities fail to perform their duties. It is also worthy of the consideration of American educationists whether the State taxes, which now provide a very considerable portion of the school income, could not be administered by a State department under some such scheme as our English plan of "payment by results." Under such an arrangement a minimum standard might be fixed for each State, which would ensure the performance of certain definite work in a year. The danger that School Boards would limit their efforts to earning the State grant would not be great in a country where public emulation is so general. New York would still compete with Boston, and Chicago with Cincinnati, in the development of the best methods and the attainment of the highest results; and the example of all the great cities would still have its due effect upon the country towns and districts. The powers of the State Executive would then, as now, be subject to the will of the people, whose voice would determine the general policy of education. It appears to be extremely improbable that, in a country where the best intelligence circulates so commonly through all ranks of society, the schools would fall into a narrow groove, or lose the energy and independence which now characterise them. While such a scheme would incalculably benefit the backward districts, it need not, in any appreciable degree, hamper the more advanced and energetic localities.

A Ministerial department at the head of the school system in each State need not be inconsistent with the most ample exercise of local discretion; and there would be no reason to fear that in America such a department would be permitted to usurp the functions of School Boards. It is difficult to see how compulsion can be effectively carried out otherwise.

The advantages of the establishment of the National Bureau of Education cannot be over-estimated. By bringing together the results in each State educational thought and enterprise have been greatly quickened. Even with its present limited powers, the action of the Bureau is full of promise for the future.

✻   ✻   ✻

The popularity of the schools is attested by the large aggregate attendance. It is evident from the number of scholars enrolled annually, that, practically all American children, and a large percentage of the children of foreign parentage, attend school at some period. In the cities a large number attend with a great regularity, but a very considerable percentage are also very irregular in their attendance. In the country districts irregular attendance is the greatest bane of the schools. For this there is but one remedy—compulsion.

It cannot be denied that compulsion of any kind is repugnant to American ideas of government. In a country where individual freedom is a passion, to force children into school, even for their own good, appears at first sight to be an arbitrary proceeding, and opposed to popular government. Nevertheless, so strong is the determination to have efficient schools, that Americans have, to a large extent, overcome their natural repugnance to compulsory school laws, and in every State the question is being urged upon the consideration of the several Legislatures.

Indirect compulsion, in various forms, has been tried, and has failed under circumstances whcich afforded the most favourable conditions for the experiment. The co-operation of employers in Connecticut and Rhode Island, and other States to carry out the law, afforded an excellent opportunity for testing its value. The result of the experiment has proved that there is a class of parents who cannot be reached except by direct compulsion. The experience of England and the United States on this subject points to exactly the same conclusion.

The laws providing for direct compulsion which have been passed in seven or eight States are regarded as tentative. The evidence as to their operation is at present incomplete. In Michigan, it must be admitted that the result has not been satisfactory. That is owing, however, not to any strenuous opposition to the law, but to the want of proper means of administration. It only indicates the necessity of a vigorous State department to superintend the action of the local authorities.

The period of school attendance is being gradually lengthened throughout the Union. In this respect the laws are behind the spirit of the people. The school terms in many of the States are considerably longer than the periods required by law. The present compulsory laws only aim at securing from 200 to 140 attendances during the year, half of which must be consecutive. With the gradual increase of the school term, and as the idea of compulsion becomes familiar, it will no doubt be possible to increase the number of compulsory attendances.

Hitherto the work of American educationists has not, except in some of the large cities, been greatly obstructed by a "religious difficulty." The first aim of the schools has been to provide a good secular education, leaving religious instruction mainly to the Churches and the Sunday schools. The schools have generally been opened by some short religious exercise—the reading of the Bible, prayer, or singing of a hymn. A very large measure of success has attended this practice. With it the great majority of Americans are well content, and were it not for the Catholic element in the population the custom would probably continue unchallenged, at any rate for the present. As it is, however, there are indications that the peace which has hitherto so generally prevailed is about to be disturbed. The conflicts which have already taken place in New York, Cincinnati, and other cities, afford sufficient evidence that the common school will not be permitted to continue on its present basis without a contest. Either it must be abandoned, and the parochial school substituted for it, or the teaching given in it must be purely secular. Of these alternatives, there can be little doubt that the overwhelming majority of Americans would prefer the latter. The parochial or denominational system is opposed to the whole current of American feeling. The sentiment of the country must undergo the most radical change before it will be possible for it to obtain national recognition. No such revolution is probable. The Roman Catholic element consists chiefly of the Irish population. The American is not readily inoculated with Irish ideas. On the contrary, the Irishman who seeks a home in the United States becomes an American. The conversion of the Roman Catholics to the common school, as a national institution, is more likely than the conversion of Americans to a denominational system.

But it does appear probable that the common school will, in time, be made purely secular. Large numbers of schools, including all those of such cities as Cincinnati and St. Louis, are wholly secular already. And the same movement has commenced in Chicago. The idea that the secular school is godless or infidel does not exist outside the Roman Catholic communion. There is nothing horrifying to the Protestant American in teaching secular subjects at one time and place, and leaving religion to be taught at annother time and place. The fact that these secular schools do exist and find favour with the American people is noteworthy, especially when it is remembered that religious feeling is much more general, and has taken a far stronger hold upon the masses, than in this country.

It has been seen that the profession of teaching in America labours under some serious disadvantages. The want of a sufficient number of normal training schools to supply the requisite staff of trained teachers is the most marked deficiency. How to surmount this obstacle is one of the most important problems of discussion at the present time. The energy and resources of American educationists will be severely tasked in providing adequate means of training, and it must necessarily be a work of considerable time. In the interval, the deficiency of training is much less observable than in other countries, on account of the great natural aptitude of Americans, and especially of American women, for the work of teaching.

The shortness of the school term and the low rate of salaries also combine to keep the profession of the teacher below its proper level. In both these particulars considerable progress has been made within the last few years, and the improvement still continues.

As a set-off to the disadvantages which have been noted, the standing of the teachers is socially high. In this respect the contrast with England is remarkable.

The extensive employment of women as teachers has been due partly to natural causes, but more to the conviction, which experience has confirmed, that women are better qualified for the work of elementary teaching than men.

In all the discussions upon the means of supplying trained teachers, the English method of employing pupil teachers finds no support. The universal opinion is that the age when teaching may begin must be raised rather than lowered. The example of Germany in regard to this point is accepted as of higher authority than that of England.

*   *   *

The great popularity of the American system, which is manifest from the large enrolment and the amount of taxation contributed for its support, and which indeed no one disputes, is due mainly to one cause—that the schools are free. In sending a child to school no leave has to be asked, no patron has to be consulted, no charity has to be sued for or accepted. The schools belong to the people. They are proprietary schools.

EUROPEAN INFLUENCES

953

✳   ✳   ✳

The free school controversy in the States is at an end, and reformers and educationists are now united in devoting their attention to points of detail in which imperfections are admitted. That there is room for improvement no one denies, but there is nothing sluggish in action, nothing retrogressive in principle. Every movement is forward. In the ultimate accomplishment of the destiny of the Republic, the usefulness and success of its education system and its influence as a first measure in the development of national power and prosperity are unlimited.

REPORT OF THE FRENCH COMMISSION ON AMERICAN EEDUCATION   From Ferdinand E. Buisson, "Report of the French Commission on American Education," as quoted in U.S. Bureau of Education, *Circulars of Information*, no. 5 (Washington, D.C., 1879), pp. 9–16, 36–37.

The Free School System

"**A** republican government needs the whole power of education." These words of Montesquieu have, perhaps, never found a more striking application than in the subject which we are now about to consider. If there be a nation which has expected everything from this power of education, which has intimately united its national destinies with the development of its schools, which has made public instruction the supreme guarantee of its liberties, the condition of its prosperity, and the safeguard of its institutions, that nation certainly is the people of the United States.

The peculiar position assigned to the school in American social life has always been one of the first points to attract the attention of foreigners.

The great zeal for the education of the young which grows as the population increases, penetrates into the public mind more and more, and manifests itself in more and more decided ways. What may have seemed at first a transient glow of enthusiasm, a generous impulse, has in time assumed all the force of a logical conviction or rather of a positive certainty. It is no longer a movement of a few philanthropists or of a few religious societies, but it is an essential part of the public administration for which the States, the cities, and townships appropriate every year more money than any other country in the world has hitherto devoted to the education of the people. Far from limiting this generosity as much as possible to primary instruction, it goes far as to declare free for all not only primary but even secondary schools.

The laws and customs of the country are in perfect harmony in regard to this practice; public opinion approves and even insists upon these sacrifices, so evident has it become to every one that the future of the American people will be whatever its schools make it.

Among the many influences which gave the American school this unique importance, the influence of Protestant ideas was one of the first. The early settlers of New England did not recognize a more important duty or a greater privilege than that of reading the Bible. The first charter of every settlement compelled it to establish schools and compelled every family to educate its children.

As soon as democratic institutions were more fully developed, the former religious duty became gradually a political necessity. The form of the United States Government established a hundred years ago, making everything depend upon the will of the people, assumes that will to be enlightened as the only safeguard against the worst calamities.

The United States have been peopled by continuous immigration. But what does this immigration bring to the country? People of different origins, classes, and religions. The many thousands that arrive have frequently nothing in common except the desire which animates nearly all immigrants, viz, to improve their condition. No previous education has prepared them for this new political and social government which was not intended for them; for what could less resemble the Puritan colonists of New England than the heterogeneous, unstable, and ignorant mass which constitutes the greater part of the immigration? These are the elements of which a nation has to be made; without roughly assailing, too, the veneration immigrants feel for any former national or religious customs, all must be "Americanized" as fast as possible. It is necessary that within one or two generations the Irish, Germans, French, Scandinavians, Spaniards, shall not have the slightest inclination to constitute nations within the nation, but that they shall all have become Americans themselves, and be proud of being so.

What is the cause of this wonderful transformation? What instrumentality infuses American blood into the veins of these thousands of people who have hardly had time to forget Europe? Every statesman will tell you, "It is the public school;" and this single service which the school renders to the nation is considered by many Americans sufficient to justify all the expense it involves. Suppose the immigrants were left to their own inspirations, and instead of public schools should find only private institutions; everything would be different: each person would keep up his own customs or preferences; each group would constitute itself separately, preserve its own language, traditions, religious customs, its old national spirit, and its prejudices. In denominational schools the distinction between rich and poor, paying and non-paying pupils, would necessarily be perpetuated and emphasized. And without fusion of races, without a uniform language, without equality of social classes, without reciprocal toleration among the different denominations, and, above all, without an ardent love for the new country and its institutions, would the United States still be united?

That this country has become and that it remains what it is, is literally due to the public school. But in proportion as the public school grows the dangers that threaten it are increasing.

It is asserted nowadays, at least in the Northern and Eastern States, that the native American population does not increase nearly as rapidly as the population of foreign or mixed parentage. Whether the cause of this is to be sought in what General Walker describes by the words "careful avoidance of family increase," or in a physiological degeneration of the race, as some scientists assert, it is not impossible to foresee the time at which the American element, properly so called, will be in a minority; and, although this time may still be distant, the United States have an evident interest in not neglecting anything which will imbue the adopted population with the American spirit. In the absence of a sufficient number of direct descendants, the American Republic increases the number of her children by adoption, and if these are not hers by blood, she is determined that they shall be hers in spirit and in heart, and this she accomplishes by means of the public schools.

But this is not all. Not only is the race menaced, but also the public spirit, the spirit of American institutions, the very soul of the Republic. We are not of those who, overlooking the prodigious proofs of material and moral vitality which the United States have manifested, do their utmost to discover in this great body germs of decomposition or delight in predicting its approaching ruin. We do not forget that this nation has in its immense territory the greatest resources of natural wealth, in its character the most powerful impulse toward activity, in its historical traditions the most noble and lasting example of energy, labor, courage, and national honor, and political institutions the most favorable to its free development. These are the forces which are to resist the most formidable attacks. But while our faith in the destiny of the United States is unshaken, we cannot ignore the formidable problems which that country has still to solve.

*   *   *

The unanimity of effort which the cause of popular education generally evokes results from these differing and to some extent contradictory springs of action. This is the only question which no one ignores. The optimists, those who are still too proud of their country to let anything shake their confidence in the great destinies of the Union, see in the public school one of the glories of America which it is of importance to preserve in its splendor. Others, who feel anxious for the fate of the Republic, also take an interest in the school; it is the last cherished hope they will part with. And the extreme pessimists say, If the country can be saved, it will be by its schools.

If the political future of the United States depends on the efficiency of her schools, her commercial future is no less directly interested. The conditions of labor in the New World are such that success depends, as it were, on a certain degree of education. In industrial, commercial, agricultural, financial, or other occupations, the success of each will be almost in proportion to his intelligence. No one finds his career definitely marked out. If it is becoming rare in the Old World to see sons follows the profession of their fathers during several generations, in the United States it is still more exceptional. The spirit of initiative, of enterprise, of adventure, even, is the result of this entirely new civilization; there is no America without the "go ahead." Work without any other aim than a moderate salary, the humble prospect of life of toil, is not the ideal of the American. No people works more, but, also, no other people attaches a higher value to its labor than the American people. What Europeans call Yankee greed or speculation is nothing but the effect of this intelligence which accompanies their work and of the high price which they demand for their labor. "To be content with little," advice of ancient philosophy, finds no credit in the New World. Under these circumstances education has a double value: it has besides its real value a kind of surplus value, resulting from its practical and commercial usefulness. The whole political economy of the United States takes this for granted; without it, neither the farmer nor the business man would be able to calculate his chances of success; the artisan and the laborer would not endeavor to improve their work, to lessen their hardships, or to increase their profits. The wealth of the United States is incalculable precisely because intellectual wealth counts for an enormous proportion. We sometimes think that the eagerness of the Americans to support and improve schools is a kind of national pride, vanity, or show. Not at all. It is a calculation, and a sound one; enormous advances are made, but it is known that they will be returned a hundredfold.

In 1870 the United States Bureau of Education sent several thousand circulars to workmen, employers, and observers who were supposed to know the condition of the working classes. These circulars solicited information in regard to difference of skill, aptitude, or amount of work executed by persons employed which arose from a difference in their education and independent of their natural abilities; whether those who could read and write showed any greater skill, and how such skill tends to increase their wages; whether they are more economical; whether, finally, educated laborers were preferred. The answers sent to the Bureau of Education are most interesting. With one exception, all the correspondents recommend, for economical reasons, the education of the people, because, they say, intelligence increases the value of manual labor. The only exception was in the planters of the Southern States, who were almost all opposed to the education of the negroes. Some asserted that the colored people are not fit for education or civilization; others, that the negroes do not need education, and that the more they resemble beasts of burden the more easily they can be made to work.

Besides political and economical motives, there is still another, the moral motive, which must encourage the United States in their zeal for public education. If the Americans expect their public schools to prepare citizens who shall be permeated with the national spirit, it is not less necessary that the young generation be imbued with sufficient moral principles; and to accomplish this the school is the principal, often the surest, instrumentality.

From a variety of causes, family ties are far less strong in the United States than in Europe. The frequent separation of the parents which results from commercial and agricultural occupations in an immense territory; the feverish zeal of many fathers in business; the general spirit of independence; the custom of self government which the young American draws, as it were, from the air he inhales; the custom which excuses even young women from asking the permission of their parents for most of their actions, and from giving an account thereof; the laws, finally, which sanction the existing customs, frequently shorten the duration of childhood and weaken parental authority. These are some of the causes which have greatly reduced the moral influence of the family. Does the school supply this want of moral and domestic education? It is difficult to believe that it supplies it entirely, but it certainly does partially. The children of the lower classes will learn at school how to behave and will lose some of the rudeness of their manners. In school they hear the duties of respectable people authoritatively explained and receive moral directions of an elementary character for practical life; here they are trained to be members of a civilized country. This training is all the more necessary because thousands of European immigrants have in this respect everything to learn. Would it be proper for the United States to let the different denominations take care of the civilization and moral training of these ignorant masses? Certainly not; for those who need civilization most are precisely those who are without the influence of the churches; the object, moreover, of the churches is not to make citizens for the state, but converts to creeds. Not even the Sunday school has this in view; it limits its instructions to particular religious tenets held by its sect. It is thus the public day school which has to accomplish this work, and nobody calls this privilege in question.

The foregoing considerations would seem to lead to the conclusion that the American school is, more than any other public establishment, entirely in the hands of the state. This is, however, not at all the case. The Federal Government does not interfere with the schools at all; the Constitution does not even authorize it do do so. The States interfere only so far as general school legislation is concerned, and leave to the different localities liberty to organize and manage their schools as they please. If we find the American schools, especially in the Northern and Western States, in a flourishing condition, it is not that the real usefulness of the schools is appreciated by those who govern, but by those who are governed, and because the various municipalities feel themselves obliged—not by a law emanating from a central authority, but by what is a great deal stronger, the will of the people, the pressure of local interests—to establish and to support schools in conformity with the wants of the country. This gives the school system in the United States an immovable stability. The custom of leaving the care of public education to the local authorities is, however, not an isolated fact in the social organization of America.

*   *   *

We have tried to imbue ourselves with the American idea in its application to school life, to understand the organization of the free school system, to catch its spirit, to follow its development, and to note its results. We have tried to judge the American school from an American standpoint, because it is made for Americans, and not from the standpoint of Europe and France, for whom it was not intended.

We offer here a résumé of our personal observations, and not a project of reform based on those observations. The latter task belongs to others. We give the following account as simple reporters.

The American school has, as far as we have been able to ascertain, the following characteristics:

1. The primary school is essentially a national school; it is dear to the people, respected by all, established, supported, and enriched by a unanimous spirit of patriotism, which has not varied for a century; it is considered the source of public prosperity, the chief safeguard and protector of democratic institutions and of republican manners.

2. The school organization is strictly municipal.

3. The supreme control and supervision of primary instruction are intrusted to school boards which are elected and to officers sometimes elected and sometimes appointed by the board; hence result a variety of consequences: the frequent renewal of boards and superintendents; the often deplorable influence of political and local interests; the possibility of sudden changes in scholastic organization; and, finally, the necessity for the people of being informed as to the school questions which they are continually called to vote upon.

4. All degrees of primary schools are gratuitous.

5. The primary school is absolutely unsectarian.

6. Compulsory education, legalized in several States and advocated in several others, had undoubtedly aided in the development of primary instruction, but to what extent it would be difficult to say. The results thus far are not very striking. Moreover, it is impossible to establish compulsory instruction precisely where it is most needed, in the Southern States. Everywhere the most practical form in which it has appeared is the adoption of regulations for compelling truant children to attend school, and, if necessary, sending them to reform or other special schools.

7. Primary instruction, so called, in the United States, is not always limited to elementary studies, but often includes elementary, grammar, and high schools.

8. The scholastic organization (rules, courses of study, division of time, and discipline) is never left to the teacher in cities or localities of any importance, but to the educational boards and superintendents. Teachers are made to conform

rigorously to the directions they receive and to use the text books approved by the same authority. All the efforts of educational authorities are directed toward the introduction of this system in the rural schools, which, up to this time, have been left too much to themselves.

9. The training of teachers is everywhere considered as very important. State normal schools are rapidly increasing, and several large cities also have special normal schools or departments for the training of their own teachers.

10. The frequent change of the corps of teachers is unquestionably an evil, at the same time that in some respects it is compensated by the entrance of large numbers of young teachers who are energetic, instructed beyond what is necessary for teaching primary branches, and free from routine.

11. The proportion of female teachers is very large. Classes of boys of all ages are often under female teachers.

12. Coeducation is the rule in American schools. The results of this system are generally reported as excellent, both from a moral and intellectual standpoint; the only or the principal objections expressed apply to the overworking of the young girls which it involves.

13. The American schools offer a multitude of systems of organization, a large diversity of programmes, books, and methods of instruction.

14. The school-houses are comfortably and often extravagantly built and furnished.

15. Great publicity is given to the annual reports of educational officers. The interest which public opinion takes in the development of school statistics and the beautiful and simple organization of the National Bureau of Education do more for the progress and improvement of scholastic institutions than the decrees of an administrative authority with the most extensive powers could produce.

16. Private instruction is free from all inspection or control by the State.

17. Infant schools and Kindergärten generally do not yet make part of the American public school system, though the want of them is felt and is being supplied.

18. The large number of illiterates consist of foreign immigrants and of uneducated negroes in the Southern States.

GENERAL FEATURES OF AMERICAN SCHOOLS (1890)   From Joshua G. Fitch, *Notes on American Schools and Training Colleges* (London, 1890), pp. 22–25, 34–39, 49–52, 56–60.

Throughout the American Union, although each State has its own educational authority, the practical working of the school system is left to the school boards or to the committees of smaller administrative areas, such as the county or the township. Every large city, also, has its own school committee, makes from the local taxation its own appropriation of money, appoints its own officials, issues its own licenses to practise, and its own regulations and schemes of instruction. For all practical purposes the organization of public instruction in Boston or Chicago is as independent of the State authority of Massachusetts or Illinois as if the city happened to be situated in another State.

The local authorities or school boards are very differently constituted. In some cases they are nominated by the governor of the State, in others by the mayor of the city, or by the judges. In one town the body of aldermen constitutes the school committee. In other cases there is direct popular election *ad hoc*. But all the local committees, however constituted, are more or less the product of political influences, and are subject to frequent changes. One hears frequent lamentations over the personal incompetence of many of the members of such committees to serve as efficient directors of education; and over the manner in which patronage is abused and appointments of teachers are made through personal interest and favor. Especially it is urged, with some truth, that the constant changes in the composition of the boards render it difficult to pursue a continuous policy or to develop the school system on a fixed plan. There is little or no comity among the several educational authorities, scarcely any interchange of teachers, and little opportunity for comparison of experience, except by purely voluntary associations.

Notwithstanding this diversity of organization, there are certain general resemblances in the plans of instruction throughout the States. The chief features which they possess in common are the following:

The period of elementary education is from 6 to 14. The schools are divided into *primary* departments, which receive children from 6 to 10; and *grammar* departments, in which the scholars range from 10 to 14. Each division is subdivided into classes or *grades*. In schools in the great cities there are often 12 or 14 grades, some of which represent half-yearly courses of instruction; in most of the schools there are, between the ages of 6 and 14, eight yearly courses or grades; while in small ungraded schools in the country, although the scholars of advanced age are expected to show greater proficiency, a classification into two or three groups for purposes of collective instruction is recognized.

Classification by age, though not rigidly insisted on, is more common than in our schools. At the end of each period the scholars are examined for promotion, sometimes by their own teachers, more often by the school superintendent and his Inspectors, and the scholar who is not successful remains in the lower class, otherwise he is expected to be found in the class appropriate to his age. The liberty of classification enjoyed by English teachers, which enables them so often to place in the First Standard, appropriate to the eighth year, new scholars of 10 or even 11 years of age, could not, as a rule, be exercised in America, except at the risk of censure.

In the pages appended to these notes I have summarized the official requirements for the grades corresponding to the English standards, taken from several local regulations. They may be regarded as fairly typical. An English boy who goes through the course with credit up to 14 is said to have passed the Seventh Standard. An American boy who reached the same point would be said to have "graduated" in the grammar school.

Above the grammar school many States and cities provide high schools. These furnish an education adapted to scholars from 14 or 15 to 18. The admirable high schools at Boston, the English and the Latin, described with such strong appreciation in the report of the late Bishop (then Mr.) Fraser in 1866, continue to flourish and to offer a generous and stimulating course of instruction in language and history, science and mathematics. The "elective" system under which the parents are at liberty to take so much of the programme as may suit the special aptitudes and destination of their children prevails largely in the high schools as in the universities of America.

* * *

The School Buildings and Furniture

In regard to the material fabric of the schools generally, only two or three facts need to be mentioned. The teaching is conducted in separate class-rooms, but provision is nearly always made for one hall large enough to contain the whole of the pupils, and available for collective exercises, and for the annual prize giving and other ceremonials. In some instances both of these objects are fulfilled in the same apartment. At a large school in New York I saw several hundred scholars assembled for the opening exercise and singing, and immediately afterwards a number of partitions, which had been ingeniously attached to the roof, descended at a signal, and the whole of the large hall was at once transformed into a number of separate class-rooms. The schools generally are less amply furnished with playgrounds than schools of corresponding grades in England; and it seemed to me that much less use was made of them during the mid-day recess. Some of the elementary schools, especially in New York, were too crowded for health or comfort. The official regulations issued by the City Superintendent prescribe the following as the minimum of floor-space and air-space per pupil: "In the three lower classes of the primary schools, five square feet and seventy cubic feet; in the three higher grades, six square and eighty cubic feet; in the four lower grades of grammar schools, seven square feet and ninety cubic feet, and in the four higher grades, nine square feet and one hundred cubic feet per scholar." Space, however, is exceptionally valuable in the city of New York, and these minima are generally exceeded in other places. The plan of seating pupils at single separate desks is common and has many advantages; but it does not economize space well. It fills a room with desks, so that there is no space for collective movement or for causing the class to vary its position by occasional standing; and if the numbers are large the scholars are spread over so wide an area that the teacher's voice is needlessly tried.

One very useful mechanical device, which is not without an important incidental effect on the whole character of the teaching, is to be found in nearly all the best American schools. It is the continuous blackboard, or blackened surface extending all round the room, after the fashion of what house painters here call a "dado." I am frequently struck in England with the waste of power caused by the smallness of the blackboard surface accessible to the teacher. More than half of what is written or drawn in illustration of the lessons I hear at home is rubbed out directly, and before it has served its purpose, simply because room is wanted to write or draw something else. English teachers have yet to learn the proper use of a blackboard. There is much waste of time whenever anything is sketched or written upon it, and not afterwards read or referred to, and made an effective instrument of recapitulation. Unless the questions, "What have I written here?" "Why did I write it?" "What is the meaning of this diagram?" "Can you explain it to the class?" occur later in the lesson, the board should not be used at all. Nor unless the series of demonstrations, examples, or pictures remain within sight of the learner during the whole of the lesson, and for a time afterwards, is it possible for him to go back and get a clear notion of the right order of its development, or to see any continuity or wholeness in it. An American teacher generally understands this. He begins at one end of the wall behind his *estrade* and goes on to the other end; erasing nothing, but letting all the parts of his subject be illustrated in order, and referring back to them from time to time. And at the end of his lesson he sends some of the scholars to the side walls to work out in the presence of the class other problems, to reproduce a diagram, or to write an illustrative sentence. There is plenty of room on the walls for failures as well as for successes. Both are retained within sight of the pupils for a time; and in the hands of a skilful teacher the good and the bad exercises are equally instructive. The wall surface is also available for many other purposes—setting out the work to be done for home lessons; writing out the sums which have to be worked, the lists of words which have to be wrought into sentences; or giving a specimen map or diagram for imitation.

The power of rapid and effective freehand drawing is cultivated more generally, and with more success, among the best American teachers than among our own, and it gives them a great advantage. A diagram sketched out then and there to illustrate a science lesson, a map which grows under the teacher's hand as one fact after another is elicited and explained, have a far greater effect in kindling the interest of children and fixing their attention than any number of engraved or painted pictures, however good. Whatever forms part of the permanent decoration of a schoolroom is apt to be taken for granted, and practically disregarded by children. But a new drawing made *ad hoc* and associated with something which at the time is being enforced or made interesting by the teacher has a value of a far higher kind. The new regulations of our own Science and Art Department respecting the conditions of the drawing certificate for teachers emphasize strongly the importance of uncopied and free blackboard drawing. But the best of the American training colleges have for several years given special attention to this part of the teacher's qualification. I have seen the students of a normal school busily engaged during the midday recess of the juvenile practising school in dashing off with a few simple strokes outline pictures of birds and flowers, of ships or of houses, or copies of the little illustrations to be found in story books; so that when the children returned they should find something new all round the room to look at and to talk about.

Drawings and Manual Instruction

It will be seen from the tabulated statement of the requirements in the various grades how large an importance is attached to drawing in the American schools. It is, in fact, the one form of manual training on the value of which all the best educational authorities are agreed. Many misgivings are expressed even by some of the ablest of those authorities about the educational value of other kinds of *Hand-arbeit*, but none as to the importance of drawing and design. In America, as in England, discussions about "technical" and manual instruction excite great public interest. But there are two classes of persons who advocate the introduction of such training into schools; and there is a little confusion between the objects severally aimed at by these two classes. One section of educational authorities desires to train skilled handicraftsmen, and sees with alarm the increasing distaste of the American boy for manual labor. It is said with truth that by far the larger proportion of mechanical trades is in the hands of foreigners. This is not altogether surprising. The air of America is full of commercial speculation and enterprise, and of restless ambition. New royal roads to success, new ways of making rapid fortunes, are opening every day. A lad of any promise is attracted to the "store," to the railroad, or the office, and thinks that mechanical labor, if not just a little servile and undignified, is of any rate a very slow process for "getting on" in life. It is believed by many of the advocates of manual training that the best corrective for this growing evil will be the introduction of organized hand-work into the ordinary curriculum of a school; and it is hoped in this way not only to increase the tactual skill of the pupil, but also to awaken an intelligent interest in such work, and to invest it with more dignified associations. Other persons view the whole problem in a different aspect. They believe that, apart from all considerations of industry or utility, the right training of the fingers and the senses is a valuable part of general education, . . .

Elocution

The great facility possessed by the average American in the art of public speaking is not only fostered by the numerous conventions and ceremonies which form so conspicuous a feature of transatlantic life, it is largely encouraged by the discipline of the schools. Children are practised from the first in looking large numbers of other children in the face and reciting with courage and self-possession. English readers of American books, must, however, be on their guard against misunderstanding the word "recitation," which so frequently occurs in them. It does not mean, as with us, an elocutionary effort of any kind; but it simply denotes any oral lesson or catechetical exercise. Nevertheless, recitation in our sense of the word is practised in various forms. If the scholars have prepared a written exercise they are asked to read it aloud to the class. Solos are to be heard as well as choruses in the music lessons. The teacher will often write or select from a book a little dialogue, which is learned by three or four picked scholars, and recited in the hearing of the class with much dramatic action and emphasis. Connected with every school and college, from the primary school up to Harvard University, there is an annual ceremonial day, on which, in the hearing of parents and the public, the pupils who have written the best essays or who can do anything particularly well, are called on to declaim or otherwise display their powers. It is needless to say that these exhibitions are very popular, that they keep up a sense of pride and local interest in the public schools, and that they powerfully stimulate the more ambitious scholars. That they also encourage self-consciousness and the love of display, that the show compositions are often not original productions, and that there was a slight air of unreality and pretentiousness about some of the "commencement" exercises which I witnessed, must, I fear, be admitted. This drawback is fully recognized by many of the best teachers with whom I conversed on the subject, but when due precautions are taken I cannot doubt that there is a genuine advantage in these displays, both as means of enlisting popular and parental sympathy in the work of education and as an incentive to scholars to do their best.

Memory Exercise

It seemed to me that an undue proportion of what was learned was learned by heart, and that even the oral exercises which were supposed to be spontaneous were too much alike, and conformed too often to certain conventional patterns which were in constant use in the schools. What is oddly called "memorizing" is a very favorite exercise; but it is often confined to the reproduction of scraps of information or short passages from text books. Many more rules, definitions, and aphorisms are committed to memory in American than in English schools. I heard in one class the boys get up one after another and give by rote in succession a few sentences recording the names, dates, and chief performances of the eighteen presidents of the United States. In another school, the girls recited in order the names of principal inventors and discoverers, with a description of the exploits of each. Of course, all these facts are worth knowing, but the particular words in which the compiler of the textbook has embodied them have no value in themselves; and as far as they have any effect at all, learning them by rote tends to discourage any effort of thought about the subject itself. I am glad to know that in England the only purely *memoriter* exercise prescribed in the Code is the learning of good poetry, in which not only the substance is interesting, but the form is itself valuable, and has a grace and charm and therefore an educative value of its own. The practice so common in our best schools at home of learning by heart in the highest classes one hundred of the noblest lines of a play like *Julius Caesar,* and reading in connection with the whole drama some of the history of the period, is very little followed in the American schools. In many of them a great deal of what is learned by heart has no literary merit, and can therefore do little to improve the vocabulary or to refine the taste of the learner.

Lessons in Patriotism

Closely connected with this subject, another feature of American schools deserves particular mention. Special lessons are everywhere given on the American Constitution, on the rights and duties of American citizens, of the President, of Congress, of the Senate, and of the States. National anniversaries are very religiously observed. "On the school days immediately preceding the 4th of July and the 22d of February (Washington's birthday) in each year," say the regulations of the New York School Board, "the principals of all the grammar schools in the city shall assemble the pupils of their respective schools and read, or cause to be read, to them either the 'Declaration of Independence" or 'Washington's farewell address to the people of the United States,' combining therewith such other patriotic exercises as may be advisable." There can be no doubt that in this and other ways, the schools try successfully, not only to inform the children about the government under which they live, but to inspire them with a pride in their country and its institutions. An American boy thinks that in no other country would it be possible for him to enjoy real freedom, or so many civic privileges. I was talking to a class once about the meanings of some words which were written on the board as a verbal exercise, and "equality" being one of the words, I asked the boys to put it into a sentence. One after another made up a sentence about the equality of all American citizens, and when the question was further put, "Equality in what?—in height, in size, in fortune, in good looks, in wisdom, in goodness?" the negative answers were followed unanimously by the phrase, "in political rights." It was evidently the feeling of the class that such equality in political rights existed nowhere else in the world. One may be amused at this, but it is nevertheless true, on both sides of the Atlantic, that a boy is more likely hereafter to do something to make his country proud of him, if he is early taught to be proud of his country, and to have some good reason for being proud of it.

In the country places, throughout the States of the Union and the provinces of the Canadian Dominion, it is a common practice to set apart one day in April, May, or June for planting trees, shrubs, and flowers in the school precincts, and for the general ornamentation of the school premises. The authorities permit this to count as a lawful school day. During the forenoon the grounds are levelled, stones and refuse removed, holes made for the trees, a flower-bed is laid out or a part of the ground is sodded or seeded with lawn grass. While the boys are thus engaged, the girls are employed in putting in order and ornamenting the schoolroom, arranging flowers, and displaying specimens of maps, writing, and other manual work. Trees planted are associated with the name of a class or a teacher, or of some public event.

Discipline

One could not help being impressed everywhere by the excellence of the discipline, and the more so as it is said to be maintained almost uniformly without resorting to corporal punishment. Indeed, in most of the State and city regulations teachers are absolutely forbidden to inflict such punishment at all. There was no lack of evidence of high animal spirits outside the schools; but within there seemed to be little difficulty in maintaining discipline. Even at the universities, at Columbia and at Harvard, where I witnessed both the out-door sports and the academic ceremonial, I was struck by the dignity and seriousness of the students in the college itself, the absence, not merely of rowdyism, but of all unseemly shouting or unruliness.

General Character of the Schemes of Instruction

The chief feature in the schemes of instruction is the minuteness with which all the details are specified and the little room that is left for the discretion or special preferences of the teacher. In the high schools and universities the practice of prescribing "elective" subjects is very common; but here the choice is open to the parent or scholar, not to the teacher. In the schemes for primary and grammar schools, corresponding to our public elementary schools at home, there are hardly every any alternative or optional subjects. There is a fixed *menu,* and not, as in the English schedules, provision for a *diner à la carte* in the form of a list of class-subjects, or specific subject from which the teacher may choose that which he can teach best, and which is the most useful or most appreciated in his own district. Every subject is obligatory. The books to be used, the limits of work to be done in each grade or standard, are, in most cases, rigidly prescribed. I was looking at the copy-books in one school and observed that the series of exercises was graduated on a novel and rather elaborate theory, beginning with an analysis of the parts of letters. I asked the teacher whether she found the plan worked well. She replied that it worked ill and that she greatly disliked it; but, she added, "these copy-books are prescribed by the school superintendent and we must not use any other." Repeatedly I have been told, when asking some simple question closely connected with the subject at hand, that it was "beyond the grade." A class of boys of 13 was working fractions, and when I was questioning them on a fraction and suggesting that other figures similarly related would express the same fraction, I happened to use the word "proportion." The teacher stopped me at once with the remark that proportion did not come until the next grade. There is certainly less room for spontaneity or originality of plan on the part of the teacher than in our own country. It seemed to me, too, that many of the authorized time-tables cut up the day's work into too many short lessons on different subjects, and that the teaching was often scrappy and superficial, affording less room for the thorough examination of a subject than might be desired. Text-books and certain accepted formulas appeared to dominate the work of the classes too much, and, in spite of the undoubted merits of some features of the educational system, I have not the least reason to believe that American boys and girls are more soundly taught or are provided with a better intellectual outfit for the business and duties of life than English children of the same age, who are brought up in a good elementary school.

A GERMAN EDUCATOR DESCRIBES THE LATEST EDUCATIONAL REFORM MOVEMENTS IN THE UNITED STATES (1895) From Ernst Schlee, "The Latest Movements in Education in the United States," U.S. Bureau of Education, *Report of the Commissioner of Education, 1896–1897,* (Washington, D. C., 1898), vol. I, pp. 178–85.

The fundamental points which the committee of ten recognizes as fixed are (1) that the number of lessons per week be not increased, (2) that the conditions of admission to college be not increased, and (3) that the principle of unity upon which the common school rests be not disturbed. This last-mentioned point meets all demands for a differentiation or bifurcation previous to the eighth year of the course. In other words, that the pupils intending to enter college and those intending to devote themselves to business pursuits should have precisely the same elementary instruction. Yet the committee declares it impossible to prepare a suitable programme for the secondary school having a course of four years if it be built on the present course of the common school. Either instruction in foreign languages, mathematics, and natural sciences should begin in the elementary school or the secondary school should begin two years earlier, and leave only six years for the elementary school. It is claimed that elementary instruction, both with regard to matter and method, is continued too long. In all the sub or special committees the complaint was heard that the high school did not find sufficient preparatory knowledge in the pupils, and that it had to begin with all secondary branches at the same time.

Of all claims for an earlier beginning of secondary branches none was more emphatic than that for foreign languages. The valuation of modern foreign languages is naturally different in America from the European, for the American does not recognize the need of them as languages of communication. Still, knowledge of foreign languages is considered by him of great value for the training of the mind, especially for a more thorough comprehension of the mother tongue, although this is not attributed to the power of a special formative and logical training as it was formerly in relation to Latin grammar. On the other hand, the comprehension of the German language is acknowledged as a means to a recognition of German science. While the committee in its general discussion emphasized more the pedagogical gain arising from the study of foreign tongues, in the details of its plan of study it points to this more practical aim. The report does not arrive at a complete equalization of these different aims.

The committee goes farthest in its recommendations concerning modern languages, the chairman designating this as most novel and striking. They are, that German or French be introduced as a regular study in the fifth school year, tenth year of age. The report adds that Latin would offer the same advantages, but living languages seemed more suitable for grammar schools, as the upper grades of the common schools are called.

The subcommittee on Latin considers it desirable to increase the demands in that study and regrets the fact that the study of Latin is commenced at a much earlier date in England, France, and Germany as compared with America. Still the committee thinks it undesirable to make a radical change, and is satisfied with the suggestion of beginning Latin one year earlier, devoting to it five hours per week. The committee on mathematics likewise advocates earlier occupation with geometry, and so, too, the committee on natural sciences claims several years for instruction in simple natural phenomena, in botany, zoology; and again, the committee on history calls for two years of study in history, American and universal history.

The question arises whether all these proposals can be united within the limits of the common school system. Doubtless some changes might be introduced in the grammar school easily without doing violence to its character as a common school. For instance, concrete geometry may be added to mathematics; that is, the introduction to the study of geometry by means of the senses and with the aid of drawing, measuring, without formal proof. Instruction in natural sciences may also be limited to a discussion of important phenomena, animals, and plants. But the unity of the system becomes questionable when instruction in modern tongues as an optional branch is introduced; still more by the introduction of Latin, ancient history, and algebra as optional branches. These subjects should become compulsory branches during the last year's course of the elementary school. It is true ancient history does not seem as necessary for the Americans as it is for the Germans, because they have no history of the Middle Ages of their own, although their language and literature have borrowed much more from antiquity than we have. Consider the many antique proper names in America, as for instance, Athens, Sparta, Ithaca, Cincinnati, Capitol, etc. A connected history of classic antiquity is not related to the general culture of the people, and receives its value only in connection with higher education. And yet there is a proposition to teach Latin one or possibly two years in the elementary school. The subcommittee for instruction in Latin and the entire committee of ten leave this point somewhat unexplained and merely propose an earlier beginning, while at the same time offering suggestions tending to make the former nonactive.

In contradistinction, the committee of fifteen takes up Latin, with five lessons per week during the last school year of the course of the elementary school, and at the same time definitely adheres to the principle that the instruction for boys and girls should be precisely the same to the fourteenth year of age. This committee expects much from these weak beginnings in Latin, which are not continued, as it also does of algebra. Quite contrary to the sometimes excessive demand, heard in Germany also, for a definite conclusion and finish of the elementary education, the committee is of the opinion that a brief instruction in secondary subjects, like Latin and algebra, has a higher value than any elementary branch that might be substituted for them. Especially a year's instruction in Latin would place a pupil far above those who only studied English grammar, without Latin, for the beginning of any branch (discipline) lays special weight upon its fundamental ideas. During the first week of Latin lessons, the pupil is made acquainted with the remarkable phenomenon that a language can express by declensions and conjugations what his mother tongue does by means of prepositions and auxiliaries (English: to him, Latin: ei). He learns with astonishment that quite a different order of the words in syntax is to be followed, and that root words have still a concrete meaning, while the same words or their derivations in the mother tongue are abstract. These observations are mental germs, which grow and result in a better mastering of the mother tongue. Similarly the result of studying the elements of algebra are judged. For a young philosopher this might be found true, but for the majority of elementary pupils they are imaginings devoid of substance.

In this question we may see the pivotal point of the whole present educational movement in America. The weakness of secondary education is correctly recognized. The attempt ought to be made to begin earlier with foreign languages and mathematics, but any attempt to fit this plan for the entire common school, which naturally finds much opposition in America, must miscarry. Moreover, since the grammar school in the South and everywhere in rural districts closes with the sixth school year, America will have to follow the example of all other civilized countries and allow the high school and the elementary school to go side by side for a number of years. The propositions of the committee of fifteen, compared with those of the committee of ten, appear to us as a step backward. . . .

With reference to the organic connection between the high school, college, and university, the committee of ten entertains the opinion, based upon actual conditions, that the course of study should be arranged essentially for those boys and girls who do not intend to continue their studies in a higher seat of learning; that is to say, those who do not intend to enter the college, and that a preparation for higher education could only be a secondary object of the high school. But starting from the theoretic presupposition that the chief branches, if treated thoroughly, are, as regards their formative power, of equal value for admission to college, the committee considers it right that the colleges make special conditions regarding the extent and duration of school studies and require proofs as the committee on English, for instance, does by demanding that no pupil be admitted to college who can not write good English. But on the whole the committee seems to favor the suggestion that a satisfactory graduation from a four years' course be considered a suitable preparation for college or any other scientific institution. In other words, that the examination for graduation in the high school do away with an examination for admission to college; and the committee considers this profitable for the schools, colleges, and the entire country.

The subcommittees of the committee of ten express themselves in detail concerning the method of instruction. Their reports show that pedagogical theory in the United States is everywhere abreast with the present status of science, and that it is very familiar with German pedagogy and psychology from Pestalozzi to Wundt. Although the statements do not bear the character of borrowed thought, but appear to have been thought out independently, still special portions bear a very familiar face; thus, for instance, when the committee on history speaks of political economy (Volkswirtschaftslehre). There is not another question in which the persons consulted show a greater variety of opinion. Some distinguished superintendents and principals wish to have this branch taught during the last year of the high school course; some even demand daily instruction for twelve weeks, other teachers declare that there is no place for that branch in the secondary school. Under the circumstances the committee thought it wise not to recommend formal instruction in political economy, but that the most important principles be presented in connection with the history of the United States and commercial geography. The subject would therefore appear first in its most elementary features during the third year of the grammar school, and then again during the last two years of the high school. It would appear not as a special science, but as an explanation of conditions of the commonwealth and of political questions.

Observe this passage concerning the mother tongue: "Both with reference to the high school and the lower schools, the committees declare that every teacher, in whatever branch he may instruct, must consider himself responsible for the use of good English on the part of his pupils." Similar to the committee on natural science, the committee on history emphasizes the necessity of written accounts, narrations, and other compositions; and if the propositions of the nine committees become realities there would be at least one written composition daily for every pupil, which, in the interest of good English, is important.

In the face of the method of instruction in vogue in America it is particularly remarkable that all these committees consider the acquisition of mere knowledge not the aim of education, but the development of the mental powers and comprehension, exercises in observing, developing thought and expression. For this reason the various committees intend to limit the use of the text-book method and recommend its exclusion from grammar schools in studies like grammar, mathematics, and natural sciences. This method may be explained as follows: The text-book or guide is first studied, i.e., memorized by the pupil, mostly in school in so-called study lessons, and then the teacher asks for the contents of the lesson during recitations. While this reciting is going on he explains, corrects, and enlarges the matter as occasion demands. The committee of fifteen (whose report on method of instruction, written by Dr. Harris, takes its stand more on the solid ground of existing circumstances, not merely from necessity, but also from appreciation of these circumstances) gives special instruction for the treatment of this method, and recommends, for instance, the dividing each class into two divisions, so that the one study (memorize) while the other recite. The committee of ten, however, and especially its subcommittees, make oral lessons—that is, free instruction by the teacher—everywhere the principal thing. They wish that the teacher lead the child to observe and to start from observation and experience. In the interest of geography and natural sciences they recommend that one afternoon per week be utilized for excursions into the open air, and they suggest the utilization of the free Saturdays for exercise in natural-science laboratories. They further recommend more extensive equipment of the schools with the means of instruction, more drawing wherever possible, and not merely means of demonstration for the teacher, but also means for the exercise of the pupils. Special subcommittees present a methodical order of experiments, 57 for the instruction in physics and 100 for chemistry.

However, for all this teachers are necessary, and these are found in few schools. The committee of ten, and almost all its subcommittees, point to this great want and make recommendations for the preparation of suitable teachers. The committee on geography, which furnished the most extensive report, recommends a course very much in harmony with the new Herbartians (for instance, Frick), namely, to make geography a central branch and not to restrict it to a mere description of the surface of the earth, but include in it the elements of botany, zoology, astronomy, and meteorology, with all sorts of discussions concerning commerce, politics, ethnology, etc., and this commission submits a course like the one treated with us only in its first beginnings. The committee of ten designates these propositions as revolutionary, although as an ideal course which it is impossible to carry out everywhere and immediately.

We give about the same criticism to the reports concerning instruction in the sciences, including history. Some of the propositions betray that they are put forward by academic professors whose judgment is not guided by pedagogical experience; for instance, when we see that for botanical instruction in the elementary school it is proposed to furnish every pupil with at least a microscope, alcohol, glycerin, and iodine to aid his investigations of plants; or when we see the pupils of the senior high school class instructed to judge the authority of sources, especially the difference between real sources and representations at second hand; or when it is seriously recommended to allow the pupils of the same class in history to use two, three, or four parallel text-books for the purpose of accustoming them to comparison and criticism.

However, these little things do not detract from the value of the whole. The report of the committee of ten has for America the importance of an official pedagogy, scientifically progressive and professional, which will exercise an important influence upon the American school for a number of years.

And now to the committee of fifteen. For the purpose of continuing its reform propositions, the National Education Association in 1894 appointed another commission, this time of fifteen men, who should solve the same problem for the elementary school, and sketch the principles of municipal school management, and make suggestions for professional preparation of teachers.[1] To facilitate the work, this commission was divided into three sections, each of five members. Following the example of the committee of ten, they put themselves in communication with all parts of the country by submitting a number of questions to many learned men and educators, and calling for expressions of opinion.

It is not necessary to enter into the reports on the two subjects mentioned last, however important they may be for America, since they are closely connected with public institutions differing from ours. It may be remarked though that the proposals for school management intend to serve reform by making the municipal school commissions independent of political influence by means of appointment instead of election. This will increase the independence and responsibility of the school superintendent. The last question, the one concerning preparation of teachers, is perhaps the most urgent one in the United States, but its solution finds the greatest difficulties in the prevailing social conditions, which will wreck the suggestions, however logical they may be. They are, that the general education of teachers, male and female, should be four years in advance of the course of the school in which they instruct; hence that elementary teachers should have graduated from the high school, and teachers of secondary schools have passed through college; besides, that both should have pursued a partly theoretical and partly practical course of pedagogy in a normal school.

More important by far is the first of the three problems, and the report concerning it has all the more interest to us, inasmuch as it is composed by Dr. Harris, the present Commissioner of Education. We have touched upon the report in previous pages.

Its peculiar importance may be found in the fact that it has caused a commotion in the educational world of America such as has never been witnessed before. The department of school superintendence had proposed the subject, "Correlation of studies in elementary schools." This term is of doubtful meaning—at any rate, its meaning is disputed in America—more so than with us the term "concentration in instruction," a term that is used with more different interpretations by our new Herbartians (Ziller, Stoy, Kern, Dillman, Frick) than by Herbart himself, who meant it to be a connection of the entire instruction for systematic training of the soul of

[1]Their report was presented in 1895.

the pupil. In this department of superintendence, however (as is seen from the meeting of the department at Cleveland, February 19 to 21, 1895), it seemed to have been the intention to call for a report upon the different kinds of concentration and a general application of Herbartian principles to courses of study and methods of instruction. One is all the more induced to think so since not only the committee of ten, but also the subcommittees on history, geography, and natural sciences had expressed themselves quite in the sense of the new Herbartian school, and had especially suggested a combination of related branches in instruction. They had not only used the expression "association," which was plain enough, but had also used the word "correlation." We quote from page 16: "While these nine conferences desire each their own subject to be brought into the course of elementary schools, they all agree that these different subjects should be correlated and associated one with another by the programme and by actual teaching; that every subject recommended for introduction into the elementary and secondary schools should help every other, and that the teacher of each single subject should feel responsible for the advancement of the pupils in all subjects, and should distinctly contribute to this advancement." The report was expected to solve the same problem which Frick had attempted to solve in the meeting of principals of the Province of Saxony in the year 1883.

But Dr. Harris, on the whole, belongs to a conservative class of men. His scientific learning is not so much toward the natural-scientific as it is toward the historic-philologic direction. The analysis of definitions forms with him the starting point of investigation, and in the development of his course for the elementary school he does not hesitate to go back to Charlemagne's trivium and quadrivium. He can not be counted among the representatives of the grammatical specialists, since he knows how to value a correct realistic instruction and does not try to make grammar a favorite factor in the so-called formal training. Yet he stands on the philologic side of the question, and regards language as the center of instruction in elementary schools. He may have been induced to emphasize this more particularly, since in public education in America the interest in natural sciences predominates, which may be seen from the fact that the pedagogical influence of Preyer finds much applause. We may also add that Dr. Harris is a Hegelian and, particularly in psychology, an opponent of Herbart. Finally, a misunderstanding added to the agitation, for he did not use the term "correlation of studies" in the sense in which it was used in the questions submitted. In short, he did not, as was expected by a number of educators, furnish an essay concerning the proper relation of branches in the course of study. In his fine and well-weighed manner he enters upon the order in which the branches should enter the course in harmony with the development of the pupil. He then explains more particularly what Stoy designates as "statics of instruction;" that is to say, the selection and amount which would promote an all-sided harmonious development of the mental powers and interests, and how a course of study should be framed to introduce the pupil into the totality of human knowledge of the present day, and prepare him for the practical demands of the world in which he is to live.

However well this may have been thought out, there is much abstract deduction without actuality in it. The kind of correlation of studies which many had thought of he merely touches by characterizing and rejecting the artificial combination of instruction in "Gesinnungs- und Kulturstufenstoff," rejected by the American Herbartians, as is done by our modern Herbartians in Germany, and he did it in referring to Ziller's example of Robinson Crusoe. To combat the perversity of artificial concentration was wise and proper, especially the mixing up of the branches of study, which is found in Germany here and there trumped up in model lessons in which essentials are torn apart and thrown aside in order to make excursions into other fields. But Dr. Harris not only neglected to point out the correct method of association and concentration, but also failed to show the establishment of centers and unities within each branch of study by means of selection and grouping; nor did he touch upon the assistance of the various branches to one another by means of suitable reading matter and drawing; nor did he suggest a method of comprehensive relation of knowledge, but he provoked his opponents by placing his views, which are correct enough, to be sure, in direct contradistinction to the endeavors of the Herbartians. In place of concentration he advocated, especially for the beginning of instruction, the principle of analysis and isolation, so that everything individual and characteristic found in any branch of study should be clearly comprehended and become effective. While on the other side, in exaggeration of a correct idea, the study of the child's soul is made the basis of the whole science of pedagogy, Harris emphasizes sharply that it is not the psychology and the physiology of brain cells which determine the kind and extent of the branches taught, but the demands of the civilization in which the child is born, so that it be enabled to perform its duties in the family, in civil society, in state, and church. The method of instruction is to him a secondary consideration, and for external matters each science will suggest its own directions.

The consequence was that after the report was read in Cleveland February 19 to 21, 1895, the debate disclosed an almost universal and violent opposition. However, the study of educational questions, especially the Herbartian pedagogy in America, has received a stronger impetus than it would have received if the report had represented Herbart's views. According to information received from an American educator, there have never been such animated discussions in the educational world in America as at present. The United States, it is said, resembles a hotbed of pedagogical discussion, over which the gods must rejoice.

9

THE COMMON SCHOOL MOVEMENT

Schools for the Poor

PENNSYLVANIA CONSTITUTION PROVIDES FOR THE ESTABLISHMENT OF FREE SCHOOLS FOR THE POOR (1802)   From *Pennsylvania Statutes at Large from 1802–1805*, vol. XVII, pp. 81–82.

From and after the passing of this act, the guardians and overseers of the poor of the city of Philadelphia, the district of Southwark and township of the Northern Liberties, and every township and borough within this commonwealth, shall ascertain the names of all those children whose parents and guardians they shall judge to be unable to give them necessary education, and shall give notice in writing to such parents or guardians, that provision is made by law for the education of their children or the children under their care, and that they have a full and free right to subscribe, at the usual rates, and send them to any school in their neighborhood, giving notice thereof, as soon as may be, to the guardians or overseers, of the term for which they have subscribed, the number of scholars, and the rate of tuition; and in those townships where there are no guardians or overseers of the poor, the supervisors of the highways shall perform the duties herein required to be done by the guardians or overseers of the poor.

*   *   *

Every guardian, overseer of the poor, or supervisor of the highway, as the case may be, in any township or place where any such child or children shall be sent to school as aforesaid, shall enter in a book, the name or names, age and length of time such child or children shall have been so sent to school, together with the amount of schooling, school books and stationery, and shall levy and collect, in the same way and manner, and under the same regulations as poor taxes or road taxes are levied and collected, a sufficient sum of money from their respective townships, boroughs, wards, or districts, to discharge such expenses, together with the sum of five per centum for their trouble.

THE COMMON
SCHOOL
MOVEMENT

DESCRIPTION OF A SUNDAY SCHOOL FOR FACTORY CHILDREN

(1815) From George Savage White, *Memoir of Samuel Slater* (Philadelphia, 1836), pp. 107–8.

Mr. Samuel Slater, on the establishment of the old mill, introduced among the labourers therein such regulations, as his previous observations of cotton mills in Derbyshire had shown to be useful and applicable to the circumstances of an American population. Amongst these, that which every philanthropist will deem the most important, was the system of Sunday-school instruction—which had been for some time in full operation, at all the mills of Messrs. Strutt and Arkwright, when Mr. Slater left England.

These schools, the first of the kind in America, are still continued at the present day. They have been copied, and extended with the extension of the cotton manufacture through this country; and they have prompted the establishment of similar schools in our seaport towns and in foreign countries. It was from Pawtucket that they were introudced into Providence in 1815, by the young men of the latter place, one of whom, William Jenkins, had been a clerk with Mr. Slater. These institutions were at first considered as charity schools only; and the teachers paid by the young men. They were subsequently taken under the care and patronage of the different religious societies, by whom they have been made to serve the purpose of biblical instruction. In addition to these schools for Sunday instruction, the establishment and support of common day schools was promoted at all the manufactories in which Mr. Slater was interested; and in some cases, the teachers were wholly paid by himself. Regular and stated public worship, also, was liberally supported at those points where the people could be most conveniently assembled. A strict, though mild and paternal scrutiny of the conduct of the workpeople was maintained; and prudent and effectual regulations against disorderly and immoral behaviour secured the peace, harmony, and quiet, of the mill companies. The introduction of manufacturing was thus, in every place, a harbinger of moral and intellectual improvement, to the inhabitants of the vicinage, and the numerous operatives from remote and secluded parts of the country, attracted to the manufacturing villages by the employment, comforts, and conveniences which they afforded. Hundreds of families of the latter description, originally from places where the general poverty had precluded schools and public worship, brought up illiterate and without religious instruction, and disorderly and vicious in consequence of their lack of regular employment, have been transplanted to these new creations of skill and enterprise; and by the ameliorating effects of study, industry, and instruction, have been reclaimed, civilised, Christianised.

ESTABLISHMENT OF BOSTON SUNDAY SCHOOLS (1818)

From "Plan of February, 1818," as quoted in Joseph M. Wightman, *Annals of the Boston Primary School Committee* (Boston, 1855), pp. 15–16.

I. Let schools be established for the instruction of all the children from four to seven years of age, at the town's expense.

II. Let the present system of Sunday Schools go fully into operation.

III. Let three discreet, judicious, prudent, industrious, pious men be appointed in each ward, whose duty it shall be—

1st. To inquire into the state and circumstances of each poor family several times in the course of the year, and note them down, and at the same time encourage them to industry, cleanliness, and good morals; and by their advice and friendship, to assist them in contriving ways and means by which to gain a comfortable subsistence for themselves and children.

2d. To persuade them to send their children to the Public and Sunday Schools, and to go to meeting or to church themselves with their children on the Sabbath and show them what will be the result of laudable, useful, and pious practices like these.

3d. To ascertain the number of the poor in each ward, male and female, where they live, and where they were born, and to what meeting, church or parish, if any, they belong, and report their names to the minister of the parish, &c., and request him to visit and show them the use and necessity of public worship, and the advantage it will be to them; and

4th. As fast as they discover an inclination in any one to attend public worship, and having ascertained the name of the minister under whose preaching *he* or *she* inclines to sit, it shall be their duty, by the permission of the church and parish over which he presides as pastor, to furnish *him* or *her* with a seat, and direct each where to find it.

5th. That it be recommended to the Board of Overseers that no money be given to, or expended by them, arising or growing out of the public funds, grants of the town, private donations, or public charities, upon any poor person out of the Alms House, except to such as shall be pointed out and recommended by this committee as suitable persons for charity.

6th. It shall be the duty of this committee, also, to take up all vagrants and street beggars, and deliver them to the Overseers of the Poor, to be committed to the Work House or Alms House, as the case may be.

7th. It is recommended that the above committee of thirty-six gentlemen shall form a Board, called the Board of Primary Schools, for the purpose of putting into operation the above plan, except so much of it as relates to Sunday Schools.

THE PURPOSE OF INFANT SCHOOLS (1833)   From "Report of the Boston Infant School Society, 1833," as quoted in *American Annals of Education*, vol. III, pp. 296–98.

When Infant Schools were first introduced into the United States, the friends of education, everywhere, were enthusiastic in their favor. Almost without knowing what they were, they patronized them; and nearly every large town, and not a few small ones, had an Infant School. Within two years we hear comparatively little said about them. What is the difficulty? Has there been a failure? Or is there some other cause of the general silence on the subject?

1. They were, at first, misemployed. They were made the instruments of filling the mind with the words and thoughts of others. . . . The Schools were made into mere pieces of machinery for developing the intellect. . . .

2. They were in some instances perverted. Instead of being regarded as nurseries for forming the body for health, the mind for intelligence, and the whole body for happiness—and instead of being conducted simply on Bible principles, they were supposed by some to be used for sectarian purposes.

3. The purpose—we mean the legitimate purpose—of these schools is just beginning to be understood. Their friends—their real friends— have found out that a wise Providence never designed them as a grand piece of machinery for making prodigies in mere intellect, but as an aid, and for a time a substitute, for parental care. It is not an evil that the zeal of those who estimated them so differently from all this, as many have done, should tire, and their ardor wax cold. The real and intelligent friends of Infant Schools discover in this no cause of discouragement, for they perceive nothing more than might have been expected from the first.

If a few associations—and many *individuals*—whose zeal was in advance of their knowledge, or whose purpose was selfish, have remitted their exertions, and ceased to chant the praises of the Infant School *system*, we have the satisfaction of knowing that the confidence of another portion of the community in early infant education was never greater than at present. We may even go farther, and say that never were the Infant Schools of this country in a better condition than at this moment. They may, indeed, be fewer in number than formerly; though we are not sure that even this is a fact. But they are better organized—their purposes better understood—the intellect is cultivated less, in proportion, and the affections more—teachers are becoming better qualified—the methods of instructing and educating are becoming less mechanical—and the school room and its inmates, in appearance and influence, are daily assuming a stronger resemblance to the parlor and the domestic circle. The school is less frequently thronged with those visitors whose object was chiefly the gratification of an idle curiosity, or to observe and report abroad those wonderful infantile feats which would ever have done more honor to learned brutes than to beings endowed with reason.

ACTIVITIES OF THE AMERICAN SUNDAY SCHOOL UNION (1831) From
American Annals of Education, vol. I, p. 178.

A meeting was held in the city of Washington, on the 16*th* of February to consider the object proposed by the American Sunday School Union, of supplying the Valley of the Mississippi with Sunday Schools. It was very numerously attended, and conducted, apparently with great unanimity, by leading gentlemen of every political party.

The Hon. Felix Grundy, of Tennessee, was called to the chair, and Matthew St. Clair Clark, Clerk of the House of Representatives, was appointed Secretary.

The President of the United States sent an apology for not being able to attend the meeting, with his best wishes for the success of the institution. Mr. Wirt also, the late Attorney General of the United States, sent a letter assigning the reason which detained him, and enclosing a donation of fifty dollars.

A number of resolutions, approving of the project, were proposed, and accompanied with addresses by the following gentlemen of the Congress of the United States: Mr. Whittlesey and Mr. Crane of Ohio, Mr. Coleman of Kentucky, Mr. Hayne of South Carolina, Mr. Frelinghuysen of New Jersey, Mr. Wickliffe of Kentucky, and Mr. Webster of Massachusetts; and also by F. S. Key, Esq. of Georgetown, and the Rev. J. W. Danforth and Walter Lowrie, Esq. of Washington.

The most perfect harmony pervaded the meeting, which was eloquently addressed by most of the gentlemen who moved resolutions. Mr. Whittlesey spoke for some time on the benefits of Sabbath Schools in the West. Mr. Coleman went at large into the importance of Sunday School instruction in the Valley of the Mississippi, and answered objections to Sunday Schools in general. Mr. Hayne briefly advocated the truth and power of Divine Revelation, and declared the Bible to be the basis of our country's happiness and prosperity. Mr. Wickliffe bore his testimony to the excellent effects of Sunday Schools which he had witnessed. He deprecated the idea, advanced either in ignorance or malice, of a union of Church and State being the aim or the consequence of these pious exertions. On the same ground, we might object to most or all of the literary institutions of the country, as having this object. Messrs. Key, Frelinghuysen, and Webster addressed the meeting at length, in favor of this plan of benevolence.

Mr. Webster spoke of the legal provision made for the mind even by heathen legislators; but of "the far superior value and efficacy of a system of instruction founded on the Bible, that grand textbook for universal commentary."

It is highly interesting to see gentlemen so absolutely and warmly opposed to each other in political sentiments, meeting on the subject of bible education as on common ground; and cordially promoting its extension as a means of national improvement and happiness; and it shows in what light the American Sunday School Union is viewed by some of our most distinguished statesmen.

ESTABLISHMENT OF A LANCASTRIAN ACADEMY IN NORTH CAROLINA (1814)   From Editorial, *Raleigh Register,* April 1, 1814.

We congratulate our fellow-citizens on the prospect of establishing in the Preparatory School of our Academy, the highly approved mode of teaching children the first rudiments of Learning, invented by the celebrated Joseph Lancaster of London, by which one man can superintend the instruction of any number of scholars from 50 to 1000. At the monthly meeting of the trustees of the Academy on Saturday last, a favorable Report was made by a committee who had been appointed to consider this subject, from which it appeared, that when this plan shall be introduced, the children of all such parents in the city and neighborhood as are unable to pay their tuition, may be taught without additional expense, so that this institution will answer all the purposes of a free school.

The Report was unanimously concurred with, and a subscription immediately opened for effecting the object, which Mr. Glendenning generously headed with $50. Nearly $200. were subscribed by the Trustees present; and there is no doubt but a sufficient fund will be immediately raised for sending a fit person to the District of Columbia (where there is a school of this kind in operation under the direction of one of Mr. Lancaster's pupils), to receive the necessary instruction, and return hither for the purpose of undertaking the contemplated School, which it is proposed shall open with the ensuing year. Benevolent individuals who are willing to give aid to this plan for disseminating the benefits of education amongst the poorer classes of the community, are requested to place their names to the subscription paper, which is in the hands of Wm. Peace, Esq., Treasurer of the Academy.

THE PHILADELPHIA SOCIETY FOR THE ESTABLISHMENT AND SUPPORT OF CHARITY SCHOOLS PROMOTES THE LANCASTRIAN SYSTEM (1817)   From *Aurora General Advertiser,* August 21, 1817.

IN THE PRESS
And will be published in a few days,
By Benjamin Warner, No. 147 High Street
(For the Philadelphia Society
For the establishment and Support
Of Charity Schools)

A MANUAL
of the
System of Teaching
Reading, Writing, Arithmetic, and Needle-Work
In the Elementary Schools of the British
and Foreign School Society

Also

When the rapid increase of our population is compared with the means of procuring Education, it is much to be feared, that at no distant period, a large proportion of the people, in many sections of the United States, will be destitute of this important blessing, unless private benevolence or public provision should apply the remedy. The Lancastrian System, as detailed in the above Manual, presents the best mode yet discovered of spreading the benefits of Education, either in the hands of individual Tutors or School Societies: under these impressions, the Philadelphia Society believe they cannot better fulfill the purpose of their Association, than by extending the knowledge of the System, and offering the means which the Lessons afford of carrying it into complete operation.

The views of the Society, however, in their publication, are not confined to Charity Schools: every citizen is interested; because the effects of the general introduction of this System will be the same as the creation or gift of a vast capital to be expended in Education: Its economy brings it within reach of the poor man's means; and to parents in moderate circumstances it will prove a saving of money, as well as a saving of time to their children. Nor are the most wealthy above the benefits which will flow from the general introduction of this System; its morality and the peculiar and happy fitness of all its details, to the capacities and feelings of children, no less than its economy, entitle it to the approbation and support of everyone who is interested in the welfare of the rising generation.

REPORT OF THE PUBLIC-SCHOOL VISITING COMMITTEE ON A LANCASTRIAN SCHOOL IN PHILADELPHIA (1820)   From C. C. Ellis, *Lancastrian Schools in Philadelphia* (Philadelphia, 1907), p. 123.

On the morning of our appointment two of the committee visited John Ely's school, and found the room well swept and clean, the Boys were there about the appointed hour, the few who were late, by way of punishment, were to be school sweepers. After the Boys had written on their slates we examined them; many words were incorrectly spelt on several of the slates in all the classes who wrote words. They were examined in the multiplication table, and although some were able to repeat it, many were not—we then heard the first classes read and spell in Books which they had not before used; their reading was better than we had expected, and we are of the opinion their spelling was equal to any boys we have examined—The school was nearly full, and upon the whole we found more improvement than we had looked for—We privately spoke to the Teacher to endeavor to get his Monitors to perform their duties with greater care and attention.

Thomas Stewardson for himself & James Ronaldson.
Phila. 4 mo. 6, 1820.

THE COMMON
SCHOOL
MOVEMENT

981

DIFFICULTIES OF THE LANCASTRIAN SYSTEM IN PHILADELPHIA

(1826) From "Annual Report of the Controllers of the Public Schools of the First District of the State of Pennsylvania, 1826," as quoted in Ellwood P. Cubberley, *Readings in Public Education in the United States* (Boston, 1934), pp. 141–42.

The investigation has resulted in a conviction that the present arrangement and mode of conducting the Lancastrian school especially entrusted to this board [the Model School], is susceptible of great improvement. The objection to that part of its administration now confided to monitors taken from the body of the school, is of long standing, and is confirmed by the observation of almost all those engaged in its superintendence, and your committee is fully satisfied that a school of 300 pupils, which depends solely on its own classes for monitors, cannot attain to that ample and efficient usefulness of which this admirable system is capable. The tender age, intimate association, sameness of pursuits and pastimes, and perfect equality out of doors, all unite to deprive these childish tutors of that influence and authority in school which is requisite for the maintenance of discipline, and a proper attention to the routine of instruction. The teacher is thus left with an enormous school upon his hands, and often finds his labors rather augmented than diminished by the pretended assistance of these boyish adjuncts. Exceptions sometimes occur and valuable monitors are found in the classes, but their manifest superiority and brief continuance in the school furnish very strong arguments in favor of the plan presented by your teacher, viz.; that of engaging permanent monitors of an age somewhat above that of the majority of the pupils, and by proper inducements securing their continuance in the employment for a certain term. Your committee believes that this may be attained at a very moderate expense to the Board, and with decided advantage to the school. Several plans have been suggested, but the Committee prefer the following: to engage namely, four boys of about the age of fifteen, who shall enter into an agreement to remain three years and perform the duties of general monitors in the Model School during that period. As a powerful inducement and as a compensation for their services, it is proposed to offer them the advantages of an education at the High School of the Franklin Institute during this term of three years, and to furnish them with a suit of clothes or a moderate sum of money per annum. The teacher of the Model School expresses a belief, in which the Committee concurs, that two monitors of this description on duty in the school, in addition to the present class monitors, would be sufficient to secure perfect order and attention, and to maintain strict discipline, thus allowing them to attend the school of the Institute in alternate weeks. . . .

Monitors thus engaged and secured by the Board, it is believed, would contribute in an extraordinary degree to the improvement and usefulness of the school. They would hold a standing detached from and superior to the mass of the pupils,—consequently they would possess a superior degree of authority over them; the tenure of their office would depend upon their faithful discharge of its duties;— The compensation would offer a sufficient inducement for zeal and activity; their long continuance would beget perfect familiarity with the system, and whilst it enhanced the utility of the school as a seminary for Lancastrian teachers, would hold out strong encouragement to the sub-monitors of our school to accomplish themselves for their situation and thus gain admission to a higher course of education. These are some of the considerations which have led your committee to their present conclusion, and upon which they recommend it to the Board. . . .

T. Dunlap

B. W. Richards Committee

Jacob Justice

Phila., Dec. 20, 1826.

ORGANIZATION OF A FREE-SCHOOL SOCIETY FOR THE EDUCATION OF POOR CHILDREN IN NEW YORK CITY (1805) From William Oland

Bourne, *History of the Public School Society of the City of New York* (New York, 1870), pp. 3–4.

To the Representatives of the People of the State of New York, in Senate and Assembly convened:

The Memorial of the Subscribers, Citizens of New York,

Respectfully sheweth,

That, impressed with a solicitude for the general welfare of the community, they feel it their duty to address your Body on a subject which they regard as of deep concern.

Your memorialists have viewed with painful anxiety the multiplied evils which have accrued, and are daily accruing, to this city, from the neglected education of the children of the poor. They allude more particularly to that description of children who do not belong to, or are not provided for, by any religious society; and who, therefore, do not partake of the advantages arising from the different Charity Schools established by the various religious societies in this city. The condition of this class is deplorable indeed; reared up by parents who, from a variety of concurring circumstances, are become either indifferent to the best interests of their offspring, or, through intemperate lives, are rendered unable to defray the expense of their instruction, these miserable and almost friendless objects are ushered upon the stage of life, inheriting those vices which idleness and the bad example of their parents naturally produce. The consequences of this neglect of education are ignorance and vice, and all those manifold evils resulting from every species of immorality, by which public hospitals and alms-houses are filled with objects of disease and poverty, and society burthened with taxes for their support. In addition to these melancholy facts, it is to be feared that the laboring class in the community is becoming less industrious, less moral, and less careful to lay up the fruit of their earnings. What can this alarming declension have arisen from, but the existence of an error which has ever been found to produce a similar effect—a want of a *virtuous education,* especially at that early period of life when the impressions that are made generally stamp the future character?

❋   ❋   ❋

The rich having ample means of educating their offspring, it must be apparent that the laboring poor—a class of citizens so evidently useful—have a superior claim to public support.

The enlightened and excellent Government under which we live is favorable to the general diffusion of knowledge; but the blessings of such a Government can be expected to be enjoyed no longer than while its citizens continue *virtuous*, and while the majority of the people, through the advantage of a proper early education, possess sufficient knowledge to enable them to understand and pursue their best interests. This sentiment, which must meet with universal assent, was emphatically urged to his countrymen by Washington, and has been recently enforced by our present Chief Magistrate in his address on the necessity of supporting schools, and promoting useful knowledge through the State.

Trusting that the necessity of providing suitable means for the prevention of the evils they have enumerated will be apparent to your honorable Body, your memorialists respectfuly request the patronage and assistance of the Legislature in establishing a free school, or schools, in this city, for the benevolent purpose of affording education to those unfortunate children who have no other mode of obtaining it.

The personal attention to be bestowed on these children for the improvement of their morals, and to assist their parents in procuring situations for them, where industry will be inculcated and good habits formed, as well as to give them the learning requisite for the proper discharge of the duties of life, it is confidently hoped will produce the most beneficial and lasting effects.

The more effectually to accomplish so desirable an object, your memorialists have agreed to form an association under the name of "The Society for Establishing a Free School in the City of New York." They therefore respectfully solicit the Legislature to sanction their undertaking by an Act of Incorporation, and to grant them such pecuniary aid or endowment as, in your wisdom, may be deemed proper for the promotion of the benevolent object of your memorialists.

All which is respectfully submitted.

New York, 25th February, 1805.

THE FREE SCHOOL SOCIETY OF NEW YORK CITY CALLS FOR SUBSCRIBERS (1805)   From William Oland Bourne, *History of the Public School Society of the City of New York* (New York, 1870), pp. 6–8.

To the Public

ADDRESS OF THE TRUSTEES OF THE "SOCIETY FOR ESTABLISHING A FREE SCHOOL IN THE CITY OF NEW YORK, FOR THE EDUCATION OF SUCH POOR CHILDREN AS DO NOT BELONG TO, OR ARE NOT PROVIDED FOR BY, ANY RELIGIOUS SOCIETY"

While the various religious and benevolent societies in this city, with a spirit of charity and zeal which the precepts and example of the Divine Author of our religion could alone inspire, amply provide for the education of such poor children as belong to their respective associations, there still remains a large number living in total neglect of religious and moral instructions, and unacquainted with the common rudiments of learning, essentially requisite for the due management of the ordinary business of life. This neglect may be imputed either to the extreme indigence of the parents of such children, their intemperance and vice; or to a blind indifference to the best interests of their offspring. The consequences must be obvious to the most careless observer. Children thus brought up in ignorance, and amidst the contagion of bad example, are in imminent danger of ruin; and too many of them, it is to be feared, instead of being useful members of the community, will become the burden and pests of society. Early instruction and fixed habits of industry, decency, and order, are the surest safeguards of virtuous conduct; and when parents are either unable or unwilling to bestow the necessary attention on the education of their children, it becomes the duty of the public, and of individuals, who have the power, to assist them in the discharge of this important obligation. It is in vain that laws are made for the punishment of crimes, or that good men attempt to stem the torrent of irreligion and vice, if the evil is not checked at its source; and the means of prevention, by the salutary discipline of early education, seasonably applied. It is certainly in the power of the opulent and charitable, by a timely and judicious interposition of their influence and aid, if not wholly to prevent, at least to diminish, the pernicious effects resulting from the neglected education of the children of the poor.

Influenced by these considerations, and from a sense of the necessity of providing some remedy for an increasing and alarming evil, several individuals, actuated by similar motives, agree to form an association for the purpose of extending the means of education to such poor children as do not belong to, or are not provided for, by any religious society. After different meetings, numerously attended, a plan of association was framed, and a Memorial prepared and addressed to the Legislature, soliciting an Act of Incorporation, the better to enable them to carry into effect their benevolent design. Such a law the Legislature, at their last session, was pleased to pass; and at a meeting of the Society, under the Act of Incorporation, on the sixth instant, thirteen Trustees were elected for the ensuing year.

The particular plan of the school, and the rules for its discipline and management, will be made known previous to its commencement. Care will be exercised in the selection of teachers, and, besides the elements of learning usually taught in schools, strict attention will be bestowed on the morals of the children, and all suitable means be used to counteract the disadvantages resulting from the situation of their parents. It is proposed, also, to establish, on the first day of the week, a school, called a Sunday School, more particularly for such children as, from peculiar circumstances, are unable to attend on the other days of the week. In this, as in the Common School, it will be a primary object, without observing the peculiar forms of any religious Society, to inculcate the sublime truths of religion and morality contained in the Holy Scriptures.

This Society, as will appear from its name, interferes with no existing institution, since children already provided with the means of education, or attached to any other Society, will not come under its care. Humble gleaners in the wide field of benevolence, the members of this Association seek such objects only as are left by those who have gone before, or are fellow-laborers with them in the great work of charity. They, therefore, look with confidence for the encouragement and support of the affluent and charitable of every denomination of Christians; and when they consider that in no community is to be found a greater spirit of liberal and active benevolence than among the citizens of New York, they feel assured that adequate means for the prosecution of their plan will be easily obtained. In addition to the respectable list of original subscriptions, considerable funds will be requisite for the purchase or hire of a piece of ground, and the erection of a suitable building for the school, to pay the teachers, and to defray other charges incident to the establishment. To accomplish this design, and to place the Institution on a solid and respectable foundation, the Society depend on the voluntary bounty of those who may be charitably disposed to contribute their aid in the promotion of an object of great and universal concern.

De Witt Clinton, *President*

John Murray, Jr., *Vice-President.*

Leonard Bleecker, *Treasurer.*

B. D. Perkins, *Secretary.*

Gilbert Aspinwall,	Adrian Hegeman,
Thomas Eddy,	William Johnson,
Thomas Franklin,	Samuel Miller, D.D.,
Matthew Franklin,	Benjamin G. Minturn,

Henry Ten Brook.

New York, May (5th Month) 18, 1805.

DEWITT CLINTON ON THE LANCASTER SYSTEM (1809)   From DeWitt Clinton, "Address on the Opening of a New School Building," December 11, 1809, as quoted in William Oland Bourne, *History of the Public School Society of the City of New York* (New York, 1870), pp. 17–19.

A number of benevolent persons had seen, with concern, the increasing vices of the city, arising, in a great degree, from the neglected education of the poor. Great cities are, at all times, the nurseries and hot-beds of crimes. Bad men from all quarters repair to them, in order to obtain the benefit of concealment, and to enjoy in a superior degree the advantages of rapine and fraud. And the dreadful examples of vice which are presented to youth, and the alluring forms in which it is arrayed, connected with a spirit of extravagance and luxury, the never-failing attendant of great wealth and extensive business, cannot fail of augmenting the mass of moral depravity. "In London," says a distinguished writer on its police, "above twenty thousand individuals rise every morning without knowing how, or by what means, they are to be supported through the passing day, and, in many instances, even where they are to lodge on the ensuing night." There can be no doubt that hundreds are in the same situation in this city, prowling about our streets for prey, the victims of intemperance, the slaves of idleness, and ready to fall into any vice, rather than to cultivate industry and good order. How can it be expected that persons so careless of themselves, will pay any attention to their children? The mendicant parent bequeaths his squalid poverty to his offspring, and the hardened thief transmits a legacy of infamy to his unfortunate and depraved descendants. Instances have occurred of little children, arraigned at the bar of our criminal courts, who have been derelict and abandoned, without a hand to protect, or a voice to guide them through life. When interrogated as to their connections, they have replied that they were without home or without friends. In this state of turpitude and idleness, leading lives of roving mendicancy and petty depredation, they existed, a burden and a disgrace to the community.

True it is that charity schools, entitled to eminent praise, were established in this city; but they were attached to particular sects, and did not embrace children of different persuasions. Add to this that some denominations were not provided with these establishments, and that children the most in want of instruction were necessarily excluded, by the irreligion of their parents, from the benefit of education.

After a full view of the case, those persons of whom I have spoken agreed that the evil must be corrected at its source, and that education was the sovereign prescription. Under this impression they petitioned the Legislature, who, agreeably to their application, passed a law, on the 9th of April, 1805, entitled "An Act to incorporate the Society instituted in the city of New York, for the establishment of a free school for the education of poor children who do not belong to, or are not provided for by, any religious society." Thirteen trustees were elected under this act, on the first Monday of the ensuing May, with power to manage the affairs of the corporation. On convening together, they found that they had undertaken a great task and encountered an important responsibility; without funds, without teachers, without a house in which to instruct, and without a system of instruction; and that their only reliance must be on their own industry, on the liberality of the public, on the bounty of the constituted authorities, and the smiles of the Almighty Dispenser of all good.

In the year 1798, an obscure man of the name of Joseph Lancaster, possessed of an original genius and a most sagacious mind, and animated by a sublime benevolence, devoted himself to the education of the poor of Great Britain. Wherever he turned his eyes he saw the deplorable state to which they were reduced by the prevalence of ignorance and vice. He first planted his standard of charity in the city of London, where it was calculated that forty thousand children were left as destitute of instruction as the savages of the desert. And he proceeded, by degrees, to form and perfect a system which is, in education, what the neat finished machines for abridging labor and expense are in the mechanic arts.

It comprehends reading, writing, arithmetic, and the knowledge of the Holy Scriptures. It arrives at its object with the least possible trouble and at the least possible expense. Its distinguishing characters are economy, facility, and expedition, and it peculiar improvements are cheapness, activity, order, and emulation. It is impossible on this occasion to give a detailed view of the system. For this I refer you to a publication entitled "Improvements in Education, &c., by Joseph Lancaster;" and for its practical exposition I beg you to look at the operations of this seminary. Reading, in all its processes, from the alphabet upwards, is taught at the same time with writing, commencing with sand, proceeding to the slate, and from thence to the copy-book. And, to borrow a most just and striking remark, "the beauty of the system is, that nothing is trusted to the boy himself; he does not only *repeat* the lesson before a superior, but he *learns* before a superior." Solitary study does not exist in the establishment. The children are taught in companies. Constant habits of attention and vigilance are formed, and an ardent spirit of emulation kept continually alive. Instruction is performed through the instrumentality of the scholars. The school is divided into classes of ten, and a chief, denominated a monitor, is appointed over each class, who exercises a didactic and supervisional authority. The discipline of the school is enforced by shame, rather than by the infliction of pain. The punishments are varied with circumstances; and a judicious distribution of rewards, calculated to engage the infant mind in the discharge of its duty, forms the key-stone which binds together the whole edifice.

Upon this system Lancaster superintended in person a school of one thousand scholars, at an annual expense of three hundred pounds sterling. In 1806, he proposed, by establishing twenty or thirty schools in different parts of the kingdom, to educate ten thousand poor children, at four shillings per annum each. This proposition has been carried into effect, and he has succeeded in establishing twenty schools in different parts of the kingdom, all of which are under the care of teachers educated by him, few of whom are more than eighteen years old. Several of the schools have each about 300 scholars; that at Manchester has 400. His great school in Borough Road, London, flourishes very much; it has sometimes 1,100 children—seldom less than 1,000.

When I perceive that many boys in our school have been taught to read and write in two months, who did not before know the alphabet, and that even one has accomplished it in three weeks—when I view all the bearings and tendencies of this system—when I contemplate the habits of order which it forms, the spirit of emulation which it excites, the rapid improvement which it produces, the purity of morals which it inculcates—when I behold the extraordinary union of celerity in instruction and economy of expense—and when I perceive one great assembly of a thousand children, under the eye of a single teacher, marching, with unexampled rapidity and with perfect discipline, to the goal of knowledge, I confess that I recognize in Lancaster the benefactor of the human race. I consider his system as creating a new era in education, as a blessing sent down from heaven to redeem the poor and distressed of this world from the power and dominion of ignorance.

*   *   *

The trustees of this institution, after due deliberation, did not hesitate to adopt the system of Lancaster; and, in carrying it into effect, they derived essential aid from one of their body who had seen it practised in England, and who had had personal communication with its author. A teacher was also selected who has fully answered every reasonable expectation. He has generally followed the prescribed plan. Wherever he has deviated, he has improved. A more numerous, a better governed school, affording equal facilities to improvement, is not to be found in the United States.

NEWSPAPER CRITICISM OF THE LANCASTER SYSTEM IN DETROIT

(1821, 1822)   From *Detroit Gazette,* November 23, 1821; *Detroit Gazette,* February 15, 1822.

Teachers experienced in the *good old system* are much more valuable to the community than those who teach the specious and novel systems which have of late been palmed upon the world. Amongst these the famous Lancasterian system has been conspicious; it has had its artful and interested promoters, enthusiastical admirers, and wealthy patrons. But what, I will ask, can be hoped for from a system where the juvenile monitor is alone responsible for the good behavior and moral as well as scientific advancement of his little school-fellows, who are also his pupils and playfellows? Can advice, reproof, or instruction, come with proper effect from those who practice all the wild extravagancies which they affect to condemn in others? It can surely be little else than 'hide my faults and I'll hide yours,' amongst these ephemeral teachers. Can monitors, such as these, impart the knowledge of an art or science, upon the true principles of which they have scarcely ever thought? Where can *they* find fit terms to enforce or imprint on the minds of others that which is yet in embryo in their own, and of which, consequently, they can have no proper or finished idea? By this ill-concerted plan a double loss is incurred: the monitors sustain a loss, because in place of prematurely teaching others, they should be studying to improve themselves; by this means they will the more readily expedite their education; by this means alone they will acquire the mind and judgment necessary to comprehend the abstruse parts, with truth, any of the branches of education. The pupils under each monitor sustain a loss also, in consequence of the *want* of an *experienced teacher's immediate instruction,* and the confused ideas which they must naturally imbibe from the smatterings of a young Tyre placed over them by this pernicious system.

The scholars of the Lancasterian School in this place are, for want of proper discipline, more noisy and impertinent than those of any other school—and, with regard to the *accuracy* with which they are taught, the public will judge, when they are informed, that no less than *nine* questions have lately been erroneously wrought and recorded by a pupil in the Lancasterian School on one page of his registry! The questions were in the 'elementary rules,' viz. Subtraction & Multiplication. For the purpose of removing doubts, or gratifying curiosity, I have left the book of the pupil in the office of the *Detroit Gazette* for examination.

MAYOR JOSIAH QUINCY OF BOSTON PRAISES THE MONITORIAL SYSTEM (1828) From *Report of a Sub-Committee of the School Committee Recommending Various Improvements In The System of Instruction in . . . . this City* (Boston, 1828), pp. 20–21.

The advantages of the monitorial system in comparison with the old system, may briefly be thus stated. To the student it makes learning less irksome, by simplifying and facilitating his progress, it gives to instruction more interest, by alternation and variety of exercise, in which physical and intellectual action are combined; it keeps attention awake and interested, by permitting no moment of idleness or listlessness; its effects on the habits, character and intelligence of youth is highly beneficial; disposing their minds to industry, to readiness of attention, and to subordination, thereby creating in early life a love of order, preparation for business and acquaintance with the relative obligations and duties, both of pupil and instructor.

To the Master also, it renders teaching less irksome and more interesting, giving an air of sprightliness and vivacity to his duties, exciting the principles of emulation among his scholars, aiding him by the number of assistants he can thus employ, and, by relieving him from the constant necessity of direct supervision of every individual, capacitates him to concentrate his mind and efforts on points and objects of the most importance, difficulty and responsibility. To all which it may be added, though a consideration less important, yet not to be overlooked, that it is an immense saving both of time and money, in consequence of the far greater numbers which can be taught, as well by this mode, as a smaller number can be by the former.

It will be sufficient under this head, to state, that in New York three Masters, in three distinct schools, teach fifteen hundred and forty-seven boys, being an average of upwards of five hundred each. In our schools, the same number of boys would require seven schools and fifteen instructors. In New York a single female teaches a school on this principle, of four hundred. In our schools, the average number to an instructress is fifty-six. The success and progressive advancement in those schools, is asserted by men deemed competent judges, to be not less than ours. Without predicating any proposition on this statement, it is referred to as a fact, asserted by an authority deemed competent.

HORACE MANN OPPOSES LANCASTRIAN SCHOOLS (1844)   From Massachusetts Board of Education, *Seventh Annual Report of . . . the Secretary of the Board* (Boston, 1844), p. 60.

I saw many Lancastrian or Monitorial schools in England, Scotland and Ireland; and a few in France. Some mere vestiges of the plan are still to be found in the "poor schools" of Prussia; but nothing of it remains in Holland, or in many of the German States. It has been abolished in these countries by a universal public opinion. Under such an energetic and talented teacher as Mr. Crossley, of the Borough Road school, in London; or, under such men as I found several of the Edinburgh teachers to be, and especially those of the Madras College at St. Andrews, the monitorial system,—where great numbers must be taught at a small expense,—may accomplish no inconsiderable good. But at least nine-tenths of all the monitorial schools I have seen, would suggest to me the idea that the name 'monitorial' had been given them, by way of admonishing the world to avoid their adoption. One must see the difference, between the hampering, blinding, misleading instruction given by an inexperienced child, and the developing, transforming, and almost creative power of an accomplished teacher;—one must rise to some comprehension of the vast import and significance of the phrase 'to educate,'— before he can regard with a sufficiently energetic contempt that boast of Dr. Bell, "Give me twenty-four pupils to-day, and I will give you back twenty-four teachers to-morrow."

Assimilation
of the Immigrant

CONCERN FOR AMERICANIZATION OF THE IMMIGRANT IN THE WEST (1836) From *Transactions of the College of Teachers (Cincinnati), 1836,* pp. 13, 66, 67, 70, 78–80, as quoted in Allen O. Hansen, *Early Educational Leadership in the Ohio Valley* (Bloomington, Ill., 1923), pp. 21–24.

It is astonishing to witness the vast tide of immigration, yearly flowing in upon us, from all nations. The whole number of the immigrant population, coming into our country, directly, or indirectly, by way of Quebec, New York, Philadelphia, and Baltimore, can hardly be less than one hundred thousand annually. Then let anyone calculate the number of increase of blacks, let him ascertain the number added by natural increase, and compare it, and he will learn the surprising fact, that during the years 1832, 1833, and 1834, the increase by foreign immigration, was at least one-third of the whole increase . . .

I have indeed sometimes thought it was necessary that our naturalization laws should be altered and modified, so as to exclude the foreigner from the polls. But the time for this action is now past, and in fact morally, it would be of no avail. So long as they remain a distinct social race, their children will grow up to years of maturity, and come to the polls, with the same notions, prejudices, and peculiar views, which their fathers entertained. . . .

What remains, but the method proposed by this society? In my opinion there is none so effectual. Let us take their children then, and educate them in the same schools with our own, and thus *amalgamate them* with our community.

*   *   *

Your committee would here remark, that such is the flood of immigration from all quarters of the world, and so rapid is our natural progress of population, that there is not time for relaxation, if we regard the welfare of our country. The Valley, filling up at the rate of 150,000 to 200,000 a year, most importunately exhorts this body to energetic and persevering action. The most disastrous consequences would result from the ignorance and misrule of a foreign immigration, if the guardians of education and the teachers of science and morals do not act in concert, and carry through the length and breadth of the land, the most improved and able methods of imparting instruction to the rising generation.

THE COMMON
SCHOOL
MOVEMENT

*　　*　　*

By far the largest part of our immigrant population is German. There are not less than 10,000 Germans in Cincinnati and its immediate vicinity . . . They are principally from the kingdoms of Wirtemberg, Hanover, and the other Northern and Western States of Germany; some from Saxony and Bavaria; and a very few from Austria and Prussia. They all speak their native language, in its different dialects, among themselves. Not more than a fourth part of them can speak English well, and many do not understand it at all. . . . Of the 1500 immigrant children, it is believed not more than 200 of German parentage may be found in our different English schools. Let us be reminded that unless we educate our immigrants, they will be our ruin. It is no longer a mere question of benevolence, or duty, or of enlightened self-interest, but the intellectual and religious training of our foreign population has become essential to our safety; we are prompted to it by self-preservation.

*　　*　　*

It is altogether essential to our national strength and peace, if not even to our national existence, that the foreigners who settle on our soil should cease to be Europeans and become Americans; and as our national language is English, and as our literature, our manners, and our institutions are of English origin, and the whole foundation of our society English, it is necessary that they become substantially Anglo-Americans. . . . It is ungrateful as well as dangerous for the foreigners who are among us, to make for themselves interests that are different from the interests of the whole nation, and to sustain candidates for public office on the ground that they belong to their people; and partizans who tamper with feelings like these, are sowing seeds which will produce harvests of dissension and blood. . . . We must become one nation; and it must be our great endeavor to effect this object so desirable and so necessary to our American welfare.

*　　*　　*

Our population—even this very audience, is composed of representatives from almost every civilized nation. . . . Such a community is not a compound, but an unconsolidated mass; and to acquire uniformity, it must be subjected to the crucible, and the schoolmaster is the chemist who can bring fine gold out of crude and discordant materials. It is only, Sir, on the children and youth of our immigrant population, that we can act with effect. The feelings, modes of thinking and customs of the parents, are so fixed, that they can at most, be but slightly modified; and if their vernacular tongue is different from our own, they will prefer to use it still. As native Americans it is our duty to prevent the entailment of these upon our children; and the hereditary establishment among us of a distinct race of foreigners. Pennsylvania, by not attending in due time, is compelled to cherish in her bosom an exotic population.

CALVIN STOWE ON THE AMERICANIZATION OF THE IMMIGRANT

(1836)   From *Transactions of the Fifth Annual Meeting of the Western Literary Institute and College of Professional Teachers* (Cincinnati: Executive Committee, 1836), pp. 65–66, 68–71.

It is a work of the highest benevolence to receive the wandering stranger, to provide for the wants of his mind, and prepare him for usefulness, elevation, and happiness as a citizen of our own happy country. None but he who has felt it, can know all the loneliness and heart-sickness, of the poor immigrant when he first finds himself in a foreign land, surrounded by people of strange habits and an unknown tongue. How sweet in such circumstances is the voice of unexpected sympathy, especially from the lips of the intelligent teacher, inquiring after the moral welfare of himself and his children? . . .

But if neither the feelings of benevolence nor the precepts of the Bible have power to compel us to extend our fostering hand to the stranger; it would seem that an enlightened regard to our own interests might induce us to do it. A nation's strength is in the number and moral worth of its inhabitants; and the vast extent of our still uncultivated territory demands the hands of millions of cultivators. Of the fifteen hundred millions of acres in the United States, but nine hundred millions are now under cultivation, and even these are as yet imperfectly improved and might be rendered immensely more productive. On the largest calculation, our cultivated soil is to the uncultivated only as five to ten. Let us then invite cultivators who are now starving in overpeopled districts; and let us see to it, that as fast as they arrive they be made intelligent, virtuous, religious, or at least have the means of becoming so. This vast ocean of mind which is already rolling in upon us—how glorious to make it all available for good! What an empire would this be! How unspeakably superior to the glories of all the empires of the ancient world, founded in conquest and sustained by oppression! planted in blood and watered by the tears of captive millions! Empires on which the Prince of Darkness only could look with complacency! But here we would have one, that would be an object of joyful contemplation to the Almighty Prince of Peace!

Let us now be reminded, that unless we educate our immigrants, they will be our ruin. It is no longer a mere question of benevolence, of duty, or of enlightened self-interest, but the intellectual and religious training of our foreign population has become essential to our own safety; we are prompted to it by the instinct of self-preservation. The wave of immigration has begun to roll from the old world to the new, and no human power can stop it; our civil constitution affords perilous facilities for foreign naturalization, and it is probably too late to think of amending it. Perhaps it is not desirable; perhaps a wise Providence intended that we should have this spur in our sides to stimulate us to the requisite efforts in behalf of the moral welfare of the oppressed millions who are taking refuge among us. . . .

Now, we have no choice left. These people are in our midst; they are coming among us more and more: and we must labor, we must labor incessantly and perseveringly to prevent the evils, and to secure the good which may arise from their association with us.

It is not merely from the ignorant and vicious foreigner that danger is to be apprehended. To sustain an extended republic like our own, there must be a *national* feeling, a national assimilation; and nothing could be more fatal to our prospects of future national prosperity, than to have our population become a congeries of clans, congregating without coalescing, and condemned to contiguity without sympathy. The graphic imagery which the genius of oriental prophecy applied to the unwieldy and loose-jointed Roman empire, would in this case be still more fatally applicable to our own widely spread republic. . . .

It is altogether essential to our national strength and peace, if not even to our national existence, that the foreigners who settle on our soil, should cease to be Europeans and become Americans; and as our national language is English, and as our literature, our manners, and our institutions are of English origin, and the whole foundation of our society English, it is necessary that they become substantially Anglo-Americans. Let them be like grafts which become branches of the parent stock; improve its fruit, and add to its beauty and its vigor; and not like the parasitical misseltoe, which never incorporates itself with the trunk from which it derives its nourishment, but exhausts its sap, withers its foliage, despoils it of its strength, and sooner or later by destroying its support, involves itself in ruin. It is ungrateful as well as dangerous for the foreigners who are among us, to make for themselves interests that are different from the interests of the whole nation, and to sustain candidates for public office on the ground that they belong to their people; and partizans who tamper with feelings like these, are sowing seeds which will produce harvests of dissension and blood. What is their nation? and who are their people? Their nation is the American nation, and their people are the American people; or they have no business on the American soil. We must become one nation; and it must be our great endeavor to effect this object so desirable and so necessary to our national welfare.

The most effectual, and indeed the only effectual way, to produce this individuality and harmony of national feeling and character, is to bring our children into the same schools and have them educated together. The children of immigrants must be taught English and prepared for the common English schools; and the safety of the republic requires that destitute children should be sought out and made to attend the public schools. The public schools should be our best schools, and possess a character sufficiently elevated to secure the patronage of the influential and the wealthy that all the children of our republic may be educated together. This would be our strongest national aegis, the surest palladium of our country. . . .

National character is often greatly improved by the commingling of different ingredients. The peculiar excellencies of the English character, which have given it its vigor and preponderating influence, and made the English almost the universal language, and those who speak it, masters of nearly half the globe, originated in the mingling of the Norman French with the Saxon German; and that too under all the disadvantages of haughty conquest on the one hand, and hated subjection on the other. Our present circumstances are infinitely more favorable. We can unite under all the sweet influences of affection, of gratitude, and of reciprocal advantage. Let us, then, make the most of the German mind that is among us; and from the mixture produce a compound, which, like the Corinthian brass, shall be more precious than the purest gold. . . .

**THE PRESIDENT OF MIDDLEBURY COLLEGE (VT.) ON SCHOOLS AND
THE IMMIGRANT (1849)** From Benjamin Labaree, "The Education Demanded by
the Peculiar Character of our Civil Institutions," in *Lectures Delivered Before the American
Institute of Instruction . . . 1849 . . .* (Boston, 1850), pp. 34–35.

The multitude of emigrants from the old world, interfused among our
population, is rapidly changing the identity of American character. These strangers
come among us, ignorant of our institutions, and unacquainted with the modes of
thought and habits of life peculiar to a free people. Accustomed to be restrained by
the strong arm of power, and to look upon themselves as belonging to an inferior
class of the human race, they suddenly emerge from the darkness of oppression into
the light and liberty of freemen. The transition is instantaneous, and admits of no
preparation for the new life. Will not this sudden change in their political relations
produce a corresponding change in their views respecting personal rights and
duties? Would it be strange if in such circumstances, many should mistake lawless
freedom from restraint, for true and rational liberty? Shall these adopted citizens
become a part of the body politic, and firm supporters of liberal institutions, or will
they prove to our republic what the Goths and Huns were to the Roman Empire?
The answer to this question depends in a great degree upon the wisdom and fidelity
of our teachers and associated influences. They have a two-fold duty to perform in
regard to this class of our population. On the one hand they must act the part of
master-builders, and by degrees mould these unprepared and uncongenial elements
into the form and character which the peculiar nature of the edifice demands, and in
due time the youth especially may become intelligent, enterprising and liberal-
minded supporters of free institutions. On the other hand, our instructors must
prepare our native population for the suitable reception and treatment of these
strangers, must teach them to lay aside prejudices and animosities, to meet the
newcomers in the spirit of kindness and benevolence, and to enlist their sympathies
and good-will on the side of liberty, humanity and truth. If our country is to remain,
as it has been, the asylum of the oppressed, and the home of the free, a wise and
liberal policy must be pursued towards foreigners; resolute and persevering
exertions must be made to engraft them upon the republican stock, and to qualify
them for the duties of free and enlightened citizens.

**AN EDITORIAL IN "THE MASSACHUSETTS TEACHER" ON THE IRISH
IMMIGRANT (1851)** From "Immigration," *The Massachusetts Teacher*, vol. IV, pp.
289–91.

The poor, the oppressed, and, worse than all, the *ignorant* of the old
world, have found a rapid and almost a free passage to the new. So great is the
pressure upon the masses in the old countries, especially in Ireland, and so rapid and
cheap is the ocean path to a better land, that every possible inducement is held out
to the degraded and ignorant abroad to leave the land of their nativity and seek a

THE COMMON
SCHOOL
MOVEMENT

995

new home upon our shores. The constantly increasing influx of foreigners during the last ten years has been, and continues to be, a cause of serious alarm to the most intelligent of our own people. What will be the ultimate effect of this vast and unexampled immigration, is a problem which has engaged the most anxious thought of our best and wisest men. Will it, like the muddy Missouri, as it pours its waters into the clear Mississippi and contaminates the whole united mass, spread ignorance and vice, crime and disease, through our native population? or can we, by any process, not only preserve ourselves from the threatened demoralization, but improve and purify and make valuable this new element which is thus forced upon us, and which we cannot shut out if we would?

The waters of the Mississippi and Missouri when they first meet do not mingle, but run along side by side for miles—the one, sparkling and bright, in all its native purity, the other muddy and impure as it left its own valley. But the scene soon changes; the bright and the pure disappear, and the whole united mass rolls on, a great and a might river, bearing navies on its broad bosom to and from the ocean, but without the beauty and transparency of the parent stream. Its volume and power are wonderfully increased, but its purity has disappeared forever.

If such is to be our fate—if the immense aggregation made to our population by immigration, is only to increase out strength while it essentially impairs our character;—if the gradual mixture of the foreigner with the native is to tinge the latter with the ignorance, vice and crime which pervade other lands, then it had been better for us and for our children to the latest generations, that when our fathers declared these United States free and independent, they had, at the same time, established a rigid non-intercourse with the rest of the world.

But if, on the other hand, we can by any means purify this foreign people, enlighten their ignorance, and bring them up to our own level, we shall perform a work of true and perfect charity, blessing the giver and the receiver in equal measure.

AND THIS IS OUR MISSION,—a mission in which every Christian, every patriot, every philanthropist is bound to work; a mission of far greater importance to the universal welfare and improvement of the whole human race than all others save one. The task is difficult; let us be thankful that it is not an impossible one.

*   *   *

Our chief difficulty is with the Irish. The Germans, who are the next in numbers, will give us no trouble. They are more obstinate, more strongly wedded to their own notions and customs than the Irish; but they have, inherently, the redeeming qualities of industry, frugality and pride, which will save them from vice and pauperism, and they may be safely left to take care of themselves. But the poor Irish, the down-trodden, priest-ridden of centuries, come to us in another shape. So cheaply have they been held at home—so closely have they been pressed down in the social scale—that for the most part the simple virtues of industry, temperance, and frugality are unknown to them; and that wholesome pride which will induce a German, or a native American, to work hard from sun to sun for the smallest wages rather than seek or accept charitable aid, has been literally crushed out of them. We speak now of the masses. There are many and brilliant exceptions among our Irish immigrants—thousands of industrious, frugal, temperate men, who, in common with us, see and deplore the defects we have spoken of in the general character of their countrymen, and who are ready to lend a willing hand for their eradication.

To understand an evil perfectly, is a great point gained towards a remedy. In this case the principal remedial measure stands out so clearly that there is no mistaking it. With the old not much can be done; but with their children, the great remedy is EDUCATION. The rising generation must be taught as our own children are taught. We say *must be*, because in many cases this can only be accomplished by coercion. In too many instances the parents are unfit guardians of their own children. If left to their direction the young will be brought up in idle, dissolute, vagrant habits, which will make them worse members of society than their parents are; instead of filling our public schools, they will find their way into our prisons, houses of correction and almshouses. Nothing can operate effectually here but stringent legislation, thoroughly carried out by an efficient police;—the children must be gathered up and forced into school, and those who resist or impede this plan, whether parents or *priests*, must be held accountable and punished.

A second remedial measure may be found in a strict execution of the laws against intemperance; and if these laws are not sufficiently stringent they must be made more so, even if we go to the length which Maine has gone. In our large towns, where the most of our Irish population resort, a sufficient body of police should be employed to eradicate every grog hole and bring before the magistrates every drunkard. Make it impossible for these people to obtain rum—compel them to be temperate, and the battle is more than half won; for with temperance come industry and frugality.

A third remedial measure is to put an entire stop to street begging; and in order to do this effectually we must every one of us steel our hearts against all sorts of importunities. Give work if we have it to give, but give nothing else. There is no danger that any one will starve—the really needy will find their way to the proper officers who will give the proper relief, and every cent given to others than these, is a reward to idleness. Let every beggar be sent to the almshouse, and when there, if able to work, let him be made to work. If this course were adopted and thoroughly carried out, not only should we rid ourselves of street beggars, but we should decrease the number of paupers. Thousands would get their own living by labor, who now prefer begging, and even being immured in an almshouse, rather than to work for their bread.

Did our limits permit, we should be glad to go farther and deeper into this subject, for it is one of pressing weight which we must overcome, or it will conquer us and contaminate our children.

A NATIVIST INSISTS ON "AMERICA FOR THE AMERICANS" (1855) From *The Wide-Awake Gift: A Know-Nothing Token for 1855* (New York, 1855), pp. 40–43.

Is there another country under the sun, that does not belong to its own native-born people? Is there another country where the alien by birth, and often by openly boasted sympathy, is permitted to fill the most responsible offices, and preside over the most sacred trusts of the land? Is there another country that would place its secret archives and its diplomacy with foreign states, in other than native hands—with tried and trusty native hearts to back them? Is there another country that would even permit the foreigner to become a citizen, shielded by its laws and its flag, on terms such as we exact, leaving the political franchise out of sight? More than all else, is there a country, other than ours, that would acknowledge as a citizen, a patriot, a republican, or a safe man, one who stood bound by a religious oath or obligation, in political conflict with, and which he deemed temporarily higher than, the Constitution and Civil Government of that country—to which he also professes to swear fealty?

America for the Americans, we say. And why not? Didn't they plant it, and battle for it through bloody revolution—and haven't they developed it, as only Americans could, into a nation of a century and yet mightier than the oldest empire on earth? Why shouldn't they shape and rule the destinies of their own land—the land of their birth, their love, their altars, and their graves; the land red and rich with the blood and ashes, and hallowed by the memories of their fathers? Why not rule their own, particularly when the alien betrays the trust that should never have been given him, and the liberties of the land are thereby imperilled?

Lacks the American numbers, that he may not rule by the right of majority, to which is constitutionally given the political sovereignty of this land? Did he not, at the last numbering of the people, count seventeen and a half millions, native to the soil, against less than two and a half millions of actually foreign-born, and those born of foreigners coming among us for the last three-quarters of a century? Has he not tried the mixed rule, with a tolerance unexampled, until it has plagued him worse than the lice and locust plagued the Egyptian? Has he not shared the trust of office and council, until foreign-born pauperism, vice and crime, stain the whole land—until a sheltered alien fraction have become rampant in their ingratitude and insolence? Has he not suffered burdens of tax, and reproach, and shame, by his ill-bestowed division of political power?

America for Americans! That is the watchword that should ring through the length and breadth of the land, from the lips of the whole people. America for the Americans—to shape and to govern; to make great, and to keep great, strong and free, from home foes and foreign demagogues and hierarchs. In the hour of Revolutionary peril, Washington said, "Put none but Americans on guard to-night." At a later time, Jefferson wished "an ocean of fire rolled between the Old World and the New." To their children, the American people, the fathers and builders of the Republic, bequeathed it. "Eternal vigilance is the price of liberty!"—let the American be vigilant that the alien seize not his birth-right.

America for the Americans! Shelter and welcome let them give to the emigrant and the exile, and make them citizens in so far as civil privileges are concerned. But let it be looked to that paupers and criminals are no longer shipped on us by foreign states. Let it be looked to that foreign nationalities in our midst are rooted out; that foreign regiments and battalions are disarmed; that the public laws and schools of the country are printed and taught in the language of the land; that no more charters for foreign titled or foreign charactered associations—benevolent, social or other—are granted by our Legislatures; that all National and State support given to Education, have not the shadow of sectarianism about it. There is work for Americans to do. They have slept on guard—if, indeed, they have been on guard— and the enemy have grown strong and riotous in their midst.

America for the Americans! We have had enough of "Young Irelands," "Young Germanys," and "Young Italys." We have had enough of insolent alien threat to suppress our "Puritan Sabbath," and amend our Constitution. We have been a patient camel, and borne foreign burden even to the back-breaking pound. But the time is come to right the wrong; the occasion is ripe for reform in whatever we have failed. The politico-religious foe is fully discovered; he must be squarely met, and put down. We want in this free land none of this political dictation. . . . Our feeling is earnest but not bitter. The matters of which we have written are great and grave ones, and we shall not be silent until we have aided in wholly securing *America for the Americans!*

A SOLUTION TO THE GERMAN LANGUAGE QUESTION (1870) From William Steffen to John Eaton, as quoted in U.S. Bureau of Education, *Annual Report of the Commissioner of Education for 1870* (Washington, D.C., 1871), pp. 437–38.

The following communication and the article accompanying it are given to indicate the views entertained by a large class of our most intelligent citizens among the German population:

ANNAPOLIS, *November 12, 1870.*

DEAR SIR: The question concerning the education of the young has grown to be more and more interesting and important in proportion to the increasing number of German emigrants, particularly after 1848, when the percentage of men educated in normal schools and universities for the business of teaching steadily increased. Many States offer liberally, by their public schools, the means of obtaining a knowledge of the elementary branches of education; yet the system of recitations adopted by these schools differs essentially from that adopted in Germany, and the German language is in some States altogether ignored. The consequence was, that wherever a sufficient number of German families had settled elementary schools were founded by them, the settlers preferring to pay for the education of their children rather than lose all the advantages which the Germany method of school-teaching, in their opinion, offers. You will find, therefore, all over the West and North, and as far south as Baltimore, a large number of German-American schools, kept up by the people of German origin. With the growing number of educated teachers, and of children to be educated in conformity with the peculiarities of this country, grew also a desire to concert a general system of education all over the States, and to influence the public school organizations in the different sections. The Bureau of Education is most likely founded on the same principle, though it may require some time before the different States will be convinced that it is absolutely necessary to clothe the Bureau with powers similar to those of other branches of the central government. Centralization, without destroying liberty, is the spirit of the United States Constitution as well as of German institutions, and the German-Americans tried, therefore, for some time to form an organization of the teachers, being convinced that all reforms must originate in the people. It is not necessary to state, in this report, the causes which had hitherto prevented the realization of this plan; it will be sufficient to state that the exertions of Mr. E. Fellner, president, and of Mr. L. Klemm, teacher of the German-American Seminary in Detroit, were crowned with success, so that a large number of male and female teachers met in Louisville, Kentucky, on the 1st of August, and who, after three days of very harmonious and intelligent labor, constituted themselves permanently as the *'Deutsch-Amerikanischer Lehrerbund,'* (German-American Teachers' Association.) Mr. Fellner, having been elected president, stated in an address the object of the meeting, and of the proposed organization. (See *Amerikanischer Zeitung* No. 1, page 21 *et seq.*) Now, it will be well to state at once that the association does *not* intend to organize an *opposition* to the English-American system of teaching, but rather to remove the obstacles which oppose harmonious action; to bridge over the chasm which hitherto separated the two systems. The German settlers are far from wishing to be a separate people; they want to be Americans in the most extended meaning of the word. But they are convinced that every nation which becomes an element of the future homogeneous American nation should see its best qualities accepted as a contribution to the completion of the grand process of assimilation which is steadily going on in this country. The Germans can offer no better contribution to the people of the United States, besides their industry, than an improved system of education, which, when properly understood and adopted, will have a powerful influence on the intellectual and moral development of the western world, and will bring it one step nearer to its 'manifest destiny' to excel all nations in power, wealth, and happiness.

The South

**ESTABLISHMENT OF A "LITERARY FUND" FOR THE
ENCOURAGEMENT OF EDUCATION IN VIRGINIA (1810)**   From *Acts of the
General Assembly of Virginia, 1809–1810* (Richmond, 1810), p. 15.

$\mathbf{B}$e it enacted, That all escheats, confiscations, fines, penalties and forfeit-
ures, and all rights in personal property accruing to the commonwealth as derelict,
and having no rightful proprietor, be, and the same are hereby appropriated to the
encouragement of learning; and that the auditor of public accounts be, and he is
hereby required to open an account to be designated The Literary Fund. To which
he shall carry every payment hereafter made into the treasury on account of any
escheat or confiscation, which has happened or may happen, or any fine, penalty or
forfeiture which has been or may be imposed, or which may accrue: Provided
always, That his act shall not apply to militia fines.

And be it further enacted, That this act shall in no case, change the mode of
proceeding for the recovery of any of the subjects herein mentioned, but they shall
be prosecuted in the same manner as if this act had not passed.

And be it further enacted, That the fund aforesaid shall be divided and
appropriated as to the next legislature shall seem best adapted to the promotion of
literature: Provided always, That the aforesaid fund shall be appropriated to the
sole benefit of a school or schools, to be kept in each and every county within this
commonwealth, subject to such orders and regulations as the general assembly shall
hereafter direct.

This act shall be in force from the passing thereof.

**CHARLES MERCER ON THE COMMON SCHOOLS AS THE FOE OF
CLASS DISTINCTIONS (1826)**   From Charles F. Mercer, *A Discourse on Popular
Education* (Princeton, N.J., 1826), p. 76.

$\mathbf{I}$f it be one of the most salutary effects of popular instruction, to diminish
the evils arising to social order from too great a disparity of wealth, it should be so

dispensed as to place the commonwealth with regard to all her children, in the relation of a common mother.

A discrimination, therefore, in the same schools, between the children of different parents, which is calculated to implant in very early life, the feelings of humiliation and dependence in one class of society, and of superiority and pride in another, should be avoided as alike incompatible with the future harmony and happiness of both. And it is no more an answer to this objection, that time and necessity gradually overcome, among the poor, the natural indisposition to send their children to schools so organized, than that the same lenient effect of familiar habit, reconciles man to every other species of degradation, as it but too often does to guilt itself and all its consequences. It is one of the most beneficent effects of that education, which aims at the equal improvement of the understanding and the heart, to elevate the sentiments and character of every citizen of the commonwealth; and no distinction among its pupils should be retained in its first lessons, inconsistent with this benevolent and useful end.

Intellectual and moral worth constitute in America our only nobility; and this high distinction is placed by the laws, and should be brought in fact, within the reach of every citizen.

Where distinct ranks exist in society, it may be plausibly objected to the intellectual improvement of the lower classes of the community, that it will invert the public sentiment, or impose on the privileged orders the necessity of proportional exertion to protect themselves from the scorn of their inferiors. But the equality on which our institutions are founded, cannot be too intimately interwoven in the habits of thinking amoung our youth; and it is obvious that it would be greatly promoted by their continuance together, for the longest possible period, in the same schools of juvenile instruction; to sit upon the same forms; engage in the same competitions; partake of the same recreations and amusements, and pursue the same studies, in connexion with each other; under the same discipline, and in obedience to the same authority.

GEORGE FITZHUGH CALLS FOR UNIVERSAL EDUCATION (1854)   From George Fitzhugh, *Sociology for the South* (Richmond, 1854), pp. 144–48.

The abolitionists taunt us with the ignorance of our poor white citizens. This is a stigma on the South that should be wiped out. Half of the people of the South, or nearly so, are blacks. We have only to educate the other half. At the North, they educate all. Our Southern free-trade philosophy, our favorite maxim, "every man for himself," has been the cause of neglect of popular education. The civilized world differ from us and censure us. They say it is the first duty of government to provide for the education of all its citizens. Despotic Prussia compels parents to send their children to schools supported at public expense. All are educated and well educated. As our's is a government of the people, no where is education so necessary. The poor, too, ask no charity, when they demand universal education. They constitute our militia and our police. They protect men in possession of property, as in other countries; and do much more, they secure men in possession of a kind of property which they could not hold a day but for the supervision and protection of the poor. This very property has rendered the South merely agricultural, made population too sparse for neighborhood schools, prevented variety of pursuits, and thus cut the poor off as well from the means of living, as from the means of education.

Universal suffrage will soon attempt to remedy these evils. But rashness and precipitancy may occasion failure and bring about despondency. We are not yet prepared to educate all. Free schools should at once be established in all neighborhoods where a sufficient number of scholars can be collected in one school. Parents should be compelled to send their children to school. The obligation on the part of government, to educate the people, carries with it the indubitable right to employ all the means necessary to attain that end. But the duty of government does not end with educating the people. As far as is practicable, it should open to them avenues of employment in which they may use what they have learned. The system of internal improvements now carried on in the South, will directly and indirectly, quite suffice to attain this end, so far as government can aid properly in such an object. Government may do too much for the people, or it may do too little. We have committed the latter error.

The mail and the newspaper-press might be employed, as cheap and efficient agents, in teaching the masses. No family in the Union is so dull, stupid and indifferent, as not to be curious about the news of the day. Contemporaneous history is the most interesting and important part of history. That is to be had alone from newspapers. But newspapers contain on all subjects the most recent discoveries, and the most valuable information.

A large weekly newspaper might be furnished to every poor family in the State, at less than a dollar a family. If there were not a teacher within fifty miles, some member of each family would learn to read, first to get at the neighborhood news and scandals, the deaths, and marriages, and murders. Gradually they would understand and become interested in the proceedings of our government, and the news from foreign countries. The meanest newspaper in he country is worth all the libraries in Christendom. It is desirable to know what the ancients did, but it is necessary to know what our neighbors and fellow country-men are doing.

Our system of improvements, manufactures, the mechanic arts, the building up of our cities, commerce, and education should go hand in hand. We ought not to attempt too much at once. 'Tis time we were attempting something. We ought, like the Athenians, to be the best educated people in the world. When we emply all our whites in the mechanic arts, in commerce, in professions, &c., and confine the negroes to farm-work, and coarse mechanical operations, we shall be in a fair way to attain this result. The abolition movement is a harmless humbug, confined to a handful of fanatics, but the feeling of antipathy to negroes, the hatred of race, and the disposition to expel them from the country is daily increasing, North and South. Two causes are in active operation to fan and increase this hostility to the negro race. The one, the neglect to educate and provide means of employment for the poor whites in the South, who are thereby led to believe that the existence of negroes amongst us is ruin to them. The other, the theory of the Types of Mankind, which cuts off the negro from human brotherhood, and justifies the brutal and the miserly in treating him as a vicious brute. Educate all Southern whites, employ them, not as cooks, lacqueys, ploughmen, and menials, but as independent freemen should be employed and let negroes be strictly tied down to such callings as are unbecoming white men, and peace would be established between blacks and whites. The whites would find themselves elevated by the existence of negroes amongst us.

Like the Roman citizens, the Southern white man would become a noble and a privileged character, and he would then like negroes and slavery, because his high position would be due to them. Poor people can see things as well as rich people. We can't hide the facts from them. It is always better openly, honestly, and fearlessly to meet danger, than to fly from or avoid it. The last words we will utter on this subject are,—The path of safety is the path of duty! Educate the people, no matter what it may cost!

AN OPEN LETTER AGAINST COMMON SCHOOLS FOR NORTH CAROLINA (1829) From 'X,' *Raleigh Register,* November 9, 1829, as quoted in Charles L. Coon, ed., *The Beginnings of Public Education in North Carolina: A Documentary History, 1790–1840* (Raleigh, 1908), vol. I, pp. 431–33.

To the members of the approaching legislature:

What need have we of additional Roads and Canals? Have we not enough of them now? Cannot a man go from place to place, whithersoever he will without obstruction? and what more could he do, were the whole State cut up into roads and by-paths? If a person can not find his way, as things are, let him make use of his tongue and inquire. But we must forsooth have better ways of getting our produce to market. The present accommodations suited well enough our fathers, and they became rich in their use; and it is quite doubtful if, with greater facilities, we should be any better off an hundred years hence. I trust your wisdom will be, as your wisdom has been heretofore, decidedly against innovations and alterations, under the specious disguise of improvements.

You will probably be asked, Gentlemen, to render some little assistance to the University of our State. But I hope you will strenuously refuse to do this likewise. It is respectfully submitted to the wisdom above mentioned, whether our good old-field schools are not abundantly sufficient for our necessities. Our fathers and mothers jogged along uncomplainingly without colleges; and long experience proves them to be very expensive things. The University has already cost the people not a little; and the good it has accomplished thus far is extremely doubtful; if I might not rather allege it to have been productive of mischief. College learned persons give themselves great airs, are proud, and the fewer of them we have amongst us the better. I have long been of the opinion, and trust you will join me in it, that establishments of this kind are aristocratical in their nature, and evidently opposed to the plain, simple, honest matter-of-fact republicanism, which ought to flourish among us. The branches of learning cultivated in them are, for the most part, of a lofty arrogant and useless sort. Who wants Latin and Greek and abstruse mathematics in these times and in a country like this? Might we not as well patronize alchymy, astrology, heraldry and the black art? In the third place, it is possible, but not very likely I confess, thay you may be solicited to take some steps with regard to the establishment among us of common schools. Should so rediculous a measure be propounded to you, you will unquestionably, for your own interest, as well as that of your constituents, treat it with the same contemptuous neglect which it has ever met with heretofore. Common schools indeed! Money is very scarce, and the times are unusually hard. Why was such a matter never broached in better and more prosperous days? Gentlemen, it appears to me that schools are sufficiently plenty, and that the people have no desire they should be increased. Those now in operation are not all filled, and it is very doubtful if they are productive of much real benefit. Would it not redound as much to the advantage of young persons, and to the honour of the State, if they should pass their days in the cotton patch, or at the plow, or in the cornfield, instead of being mewed up in a school house, where they are earning nothing? Such an ado as is made in these times about education, surely was never heard of before. Gentlemen, I hope you do not conceive it at all necessary, that *everybody* should be able to read, write and cipher. If one is to keep a store or a school, or to be a lawyer or physician, such branches may, *perhaps,* be taught him; though I do not look upon them as by any means indispensable: but if he is to be a plain farmer, or a mechanic, they are of no manner of use, but rather a detriment. There need no arguments to make clear so self-evident a proposition. Should schools be established by law, in all parts of the State, as at the North, our taxes must be considerably increased, possibly to the amount of one per cent, and six pence on a poll; and I will ask any prudent, sane, saving man if he desires his taxes to be higher? You will doubtless be told that our State is far behind her sisters in things of this sort,—and what does this prove? Merely, that other states are before us; which is their affair and not ours. We are able to govern ourselves without reference to other members of the confederation; and thus are we perfectly independent. We shall always have reason enough to crow over them, while we have power to say, as I hope we may ever have, that our taxes are lighter than theirs.

JOSEPH CALDWELL CALLS FOR PUBLIC SCHOOLS FOR NORTH CAROLINA (1832)

JOSEPH CALDWELL CALLS FOR PUBLIC SCHOOLS FOR NORTH CAROLINA (1832) From Joseph Caldwell, "Letters on Popular Education," as quoted in Charles L. Coon, ed., *The Beginnings of Public Education in North Carolina: A Documentary History, 1790–1840* (Raleigh, 1908), vol. II, pp. 564–70.

Fellow Citizens,

My last letter was occupied in showing that inefficiency of the mode of popular education, which has been our sole dependence in North-Carolina, and the pernicious effects it produces in harassing those who look to it, in disappointing their wishes, and in planting and in propagating prejudices upon the whole subject of knowledge and education.

*   *   *

We saw that from disagreements among neighbors when schools are to be instituted, from the incompetency of teachers, their total ignorance of their profession, the profligacy, idle habits and degeneracy by which many of them are characterized, such a method of elementary instruction has left us overwhelmed in thick darkness amidst a firmament gleaming with the brightness of the most enlightened age. It is in a persevering adhesion to this system, if system it can be called, that it has become fashionable with many to decry education as a thing of no value, and as qualifying men, not for distinguished usefulness and integrity, but for dexterity in the arts of conning and selfishness. So long as we continue these methods of educating children, it threatens an invelopement in denser clouds of obscurity and prejudice. It surely behooves us to make good our escape from it without delay, from the baleful effects it has already produced, and which it will surely multiply upon us, if it cannot be replaced by something better.

Another system which in our circumstances however is beyond our reach, it is my purpose now to explain, for the single reason that it comes upon us with reiteration from year to year, with no other consequence than to occupy our time, to distract the public mind, and to dishearten us with efforts terminating in abortion. It is the method practiced in some of our sister states, especially in Connecticut, New York and others. In these states, through time, and by such resources as they could command, a vast school fund has been treasured up, to such an amount as a million and a half of dollars. By the annual interest of these funds, schools are supported for educating every child in the country. The state is divided into districts of convenient size, a school house is erected in each, and teachers are either partially or entirely maintained by appropriations from the proceeds of the school fund. In New York a district is not entitled to aid until it can report authentically that it has already provided a school-house, and is prepared to pay a certain sum towards the support of a teacher.

Let us now enter into some computation, to see whether such a plan is within our power. If it be not, it is useless to think of it. It is worse than useless, it is time mis-spent on projects which must end in baffling disappointment. To make the subject plain, let us begin with the supposition of a single school in each county of North Carolina, and that fifty dollars, only, are annually allowed from a school-fund for its support. This supposition is put not with the idea that one school is enough for a county, or fifty dollars for its maintenance, but for further calculations.

The state containing sixty-four counties, an allowance of fifty dollars to each, calls for an annual expenditure of three thousand two hundred dollars. The capital necessary to yield this interest at six per cent, is 53,333 dollars. Hence the following table is easily framed, showing the capital which must be accumulated for the maintenance of schools, from one to sixteen in each county, at fifty dollars each. Fractions are omitted, except in gaining other numbers from the preceding.

TABLE I.

For 1 school to a county, at $50 per annum a capital
must be created and kept at interest of $53.333
For 2 schools to a county, at $50 each $106.666
3 schools to a county, at $50 each 160.000
4 schools to a county, at $50 each 213.333
5 schools to a county, at $50 each 266.666
6 schools to a county, at $50 each 320.000
7 schools to a county, at $50 each 373.333
8 schools to a county, at $50 each 426.666
9 schools to a county, at $50 each 480.000
10 schools to a county, at $50 each 533.333
11 schools to a county, at $50 each 586.666
12 schools to a county, at $50 each 640.000
13 schools to a county, at $50 each 693.333
14 schools to a county, at $50 each 746.666
15 schools to a county, at $50 each 800.000
16 schools to a county, at $50 each 853.333

The counties are very different in size; and the schools assigned must vary in number, according to the circumstances. Taking thirty-two miles square for the extent of the counties one with another, and alloting a school to a space eight miles square, each county would have sixteen schools. In this case the distance which some children must go to a school is at least four miles, but they would be those only who lived at the limits of the square. For sixteen schools to a county, a fund of eight hundred and fifty-three thousand three hundred and thirty-three dollars must be vested at interest, to pay fifty dollars a year to every school. The table shows us by inspection the fund required for any less number of schools.

But it will hardly be thought that fifty dollars a year will be sufficient for the maintenance of a school. A hundred would probably be too little, but let us take that sum for exemplification. The following table is furnished upon the same basis, and we have only to double the former numbers:

TABLE II.

For 1 school to a county, at $100 per ann	$106.666
2 schools to a county, at $100 per ann	213.333
3 schools to a county, at $100 per ann	320.000
4 schools to a county, at $100 per ann	426.666
5 schools to a county, at $100 per ann	533.333
6 schools to a county, at $100 per ann	640.000
7 schools to a county, at $100 per ann	746.666
8 schools to a county, at $100 per ann	853.333
9 schools to a county, at $100 per ann	960.000
10 schools to a county, at $100 per ann	1,066.666
11 schools to a county, at $100 per ann	1,173.333
12 schools per annum, at $100 per ann	1,280.000
13 schools per annum, at $100 per ann	1,386.666
14 schools to a county, at $100 per ann	1,493.333
15 schools to a county, at $100 per ann	1,600.000
16 schools to a county, at $100 per ann	1,706.666

It is probably unnecessary to explain the use of this tabular statement. It is obvious that the fund necessary for the annual disbursement requisite for sixteen schools to a county at $100 each is one million seven hundred and six thousand six hundred and sixty-six dollars.

We can now see the extent of our enterprise, if we undertake to provide for popular education upon the plans of New York, Connecticut and some other states. If 150 dollars be allowed to each school instead of 100, the numbers of both tables must be united to exhibit the requisite funds.

But the essential question occurs, How shall the funds be created which the tables show for executing such a system? That it will be done by taxation, there is no prospect. To raise a fund of a million and a half dollars, we must be taxed to the amount of a hundred thousand dollars annually for fifteen years. Is this within the limits of probability? It is presumed that no one will announce that it is. Were we taxed at the rate of fifty thousand dollars a year, thirty years must pass away before the fund would be completed. Both the amount of the tax, and the postponement of the time, are enough singly to preclude all thought of such a measure.

Our habits are at variance with taxation for any purpose, beyond the bare necessities of governmental subsistence. Even this levy it is our anxious and ever exerted effort to reduce to the very lowest point by every device of legislation. The tax now paid by the people for the support of our state government is twenty-five thousand dollars a year. Have we any doubt whether the sum is so small as this? The Bank stock owned by the state, I am informed, amounts to seven hundred and fifty thousand dollars. The annual revenue derived from it into the treasury, at six percent is forty-five thousand dollars. If the expenses of our state government be seventy thousand, no more than twenty-five thousand are necessary beyond the interest of the stock to make up the sum, and this is not twenty cents to the poll. It is evident that I speak of bank stock in its ordinarily productive state.

Of county taxation we cannot speak with precision. In no two countries is it probably the same, and it fluctuates in each county from year to year, with the emergencies with which it is to provide. It is for those who are better informed than I am, to say whether it is likely to be more than such a sum as fifty cents to the taxable poll, upon an average through the state. Admitting this, our annual taxation in North Carolina, is at the rate of seventy-five cents to every taxable poll. If there be any mistake in these statements it is easily corrected, but it is presumed the result will not differ much from the truth. Such taxation as this, we should think, must be too small to excite discontent. But who does not know that it is habitually urged as subject of complaint, if not as oppressive. Now if while it is so inconsiderable, we have our eye ever solicitously directed upon its diminution, how shall we expect that any plan of popular education shall be accepted and carried into execution, to which additional taxation to the extent of a hundred thousand dollars a year, or fifty thousand dollars a year, or even a much smaller sum, becomes necessary for fifteen or thirty years to come?

It is now submitted to the dispassionate consideration of those who look to New York, or Connecticut, for plans of popular education, whether the proposal and discussion of them is likely to be attended with any other consequences than apprehension in the general mind that the whole subject of education is hopeless. Is it not better to drop them, and turn our eye to a different direction? There may possibly be other methods of accomplishing the object.

*   *   *

Let us not despair that one may be devised susceptible of execution by means within our power. In one assurance at least we may rest with satisfaction, that if our time may be lost in adopting this course, in cleaving to the other it certainly will.

Nor can we look with better hopes to the consent of the state to borrow the necessary funds. To loans as well as taxes for all purposes such as these, we have ever shown an invincible dislike. It is in vain to urge the authority and the example of other states. We may lament over the losses both of moral and pecuniary wealth to an incalculable amount perpetuated through every year of our existence, by what we may call our unhappy prejudices against a taxation which we should not feel, and against raising funds by loan to be attended with immense profits to the state; but to what end shall we repine, and vent our regrets in the most flowing and eloquent strains? We wish to provide a system of elementary schools. If we would busy ourselves with the least prospect of success, let us avoid placing it upon the issue of loans and taxes. While the spirit now ascendant shall continue to reign in our political atmosphere, the vessel which shall have the hardihood to venture freighted with these, may for a while buffet the surge. Her friends may with momentary exultation exclaim,

Her path is o'er the mountain wave;

but soon it shall be as a doom pronounced upon her,

Her home is in the deep.

I am yours, with the highest respect,

J. CALDWELL.

STATUTE PROVIDING FOR A STATE SUPERINTENDENT OF COMMON SCHOOLS IN NORTH CAROLINA (1852) From *Laws of the State of North Carolina* (1852), pp. 59–66.

Sec. 1. *Be it enacted by the General Assembly of the State of North Carolina, and it is hereby enacted by the authority of the same,* That there shall be appointed a Superintendent of Common Schools for the State; and said officer to be chosen by the Legislature, and to hold his office two years from the time of his election: *Provided,* That this act shall not be so construed as to prevent the Superintendent for the time being, from continuing in office until a successor is duly appointed.

Sec. 2. *Be it further enacted,* That the eighteenth section of the Act of Assembly, establishing and regulating Common Schools, printed and published under the direction of the president and directors of the Literary Fund, in the year 1849, in compliance with the act of the General Assembly, of 1848–'49, be so amended as to make it the duty of the chairman of the board of county superintendents to make their reports on or before the third Monday in November, and to send the same to the Superintendent of Common Schools for the State; and that the said chairman of county superintendents shall, in addition to the matters already required by law, to be stated in their reports, make a statement of the number of certificates issued during the year preceding the making of said report, to teachers by the committee of examination, designating in separate columns, the number of female teachers, and the number of male teachers, and giving the names of the committee of examination.

Sec. 3. *And be it further enacted,* That the Act of Assembly passed at its session of 1846–'47, chapter 106, section — be so amended as to make it the duty of the board of superintendents of Common Schools in each county in the State to appoint a committee of examination, consisting of not more than five persons, of whom the chairman of the board of county superintendents shall be one; whose duty it shall be to examine into the qualifications, both mental and moral, of all such persons, as may apply for employment as teachers in any of the common schools in their respective counties; which said committee of examination shall be convened by the chairman of the board of superintendents, at least three times during the year, at some central point in each county, of which times and places of meeting, the said committee or its chairman shall post a written notice at the door of the Court House of the county; and the said examining committee shall continue in office for one year, or until their successors are appointed; and each member, while continuing to accept and discharge the duties of his appointment on said committee, shall be exempt from road and military duties.

Sec. 4. *And be it further enacted*, That no certificate issued to a teacher, by a committee of examination, shall be good for a longer term than one year from the date thereof; and a certificate issued in any one county of the State shall not be good or valid in any other county of the State.

Sec. 5. *And be it further enacted*, That the chairman of the boards of county superintendents are authorized to refuse to pay drafts drawn upon them in favor of teachers for compensation for teaching Common Schools, unless said teachers exhibit a regular certificate of mental and moral qualifications from the majority of said examining committee, dated not more than one year from the exhibition thereof.

Sec. 6. *And be it further enacted*, That it shall be the duty of first superintendent of Common Schools for the State, appointed under the provisions of this act, to collect accurate and full information of the condition and operations of the system of free or Common Schools in each county in the State; and of the size of the school districts; to inform himself as well as possible of the causes, whether local or general, which have affected the success or impede the operations of the system in different sections; to consult with experienced teachers, when possible, and to collect statistics and information of matters materially affecting the cause of education in the State; and on or before the third Monday in November 1854, to make a report in writing to the Governor of the State, furnishing a detailed, succinct and condensed statement of the result of his inquiries in each county, of the history and prospects of the free school system in the State, with such suggestions and observations as may occur to him; which report shall be transmitted by the Governor to the Legislature of the State, that, the said body may thus be in possession of such information as will enable it to modify, if necessary revise and digest all the laws in force in regard to Common Schools, and to make such additions and alterations as may be proper to insure the greater success and efficiency of that system.

Sec. 7. *And be it further enacted*, That it shall be the duty of the Superintendent of Common Schools for the State, to superintend the operations of the system of Common Schools, and to see that the laws in relation thereto are enforced; to call on the chairman of the different boards of county superintendents who fail to make returns to him according to the provisions of this act; to see that moneys distributed for the purposes of education are not misapplied; and to see that the proper actions provided for by law, are brought against all the officers and agents of the system who are liable to the same. It shall also be the duty of said superintendent under the direction of the literary board, to look after escheated property; and to employ in each county of the State attorneys of skill in the law, to recover on behalf and in the name of the president and directors of the literary fund, all escheats in their several counties, and to see the same if they be not in money under the directions of the said Superintendent, and the president and directors of the literary fund, and pay the proceeds thereof to the treasurer of State for the use and benefit of the literary fund.

Sec. 8. *And be it further enacted*, That it shall be the duty of the Treasurer of the State to furnish an annual statement to the Superintendent of Common Schools, of the several sums disbursed from the Literary Fund to the different counties of the

State, and of the names of the persons receiving the same, for and on behalf of the said counties.

Sec. 9. *And be it further enacted,* That the Superintendent of Common Schools for the State, shall annually issue to the examining committee of each county, a circular letter of instructions and suggestions as to the qualifications of teachers. And it shall also be the duty of the said Superintendent of Common Schools for the State, to have prepared, and to send to the chairman of county superintendents, printed blanks upon which to make their returns to him, all of which said returns or reports, when received by the Superintendent of Common Schools for the State, shall be filed in the office of the State in the capital in Raleigh.

Sec. 10. *And be it further enacted,* That it shall be the duty of the Superintendent of Common Schools for the State, to arrange in convenient form and order all the laws of this State in relation to Common Schools now in force, or in force after the passage of this act, with a statement of the funds of the Literary Board, or [and] chart of forms for committee-men and examining committees, with forms of bonds; instructions to agents and officers of the system, and explanations; which work, when approved by the President and Directors of the Literary Fund shall be printed and the copies distributed by the said Superintendent of Common Schools for the State, as follows: one copy for every school committee-man, member of examining committee, member of the board of county superintendents, and five for the Clerk of the county court of each county in the State, to be sent to the chairman of the board of county superintendents, and by him distributed; and five hundred copies to be deposited in the office of the Governor of the State.

Sec. 11. *And be it further enacted,* That it shall be the duty of the Superintendent of Common Schools for the State, on or before the first Monday in December in each and every year, to make a written report to the Governor of the State, giving a detailed and condensed account of the manner in which he has performed his several duties; of the operations of the system of Common Schools, together with such suggestions and recommendations as he may deem proper; with tables showing the number of white persons, five years old, and under twenty-one, in each county in the State; the number who have attended school during the year; the length of time during which the schools have been kept open in each county; the number of school districts in each county; the number of male and female teachers licensed in each county to teach Common Schools during the year, and the average salaries of the teachers; of which reports the Governor shall cause one hundred and fifty copies to be printed in cheap pamphlet form, fifty copies for his own use, and one hundred copies for the use of the said general Superintendent; and copies of which report shall be communicated by the Governor to the Legislature, at its regular sessions.

Sec. 12. *And be it further enacted,* That the Superintendent of Common Schools for the State shall be allowed for his services, under this act, the sum of one thousand five hundred dollars per annum, to be paid out of the moneys of the Literary Fund, by the Treasurer of the State, and in the mode and at the times that other public officers of the State are paid.

Sec. 13. *And be it further enacted,* That if the Superintendent of Common Schools for the State, shall wilfully and habitually neglect his duties as specified in this act, or shall use his official position for the purpose of propagating sectarian or political party doctrines, he shall be liable to be removed by the President and Directors of the Literary Board: *Provided,* A written specification of charges, with the names and address of those preferring them, are delivered to him thirty days before his trial, and he is allowed to be heard in his defence, and to adduce evidence in his behalf; *and Provided, also,* That the said President and Directors of the Literary Fund shall unanimously agree to his removal; in which case, and in all cases of trial, a record of the proceedings and of the charges and answer, shall be made by the said President and Directors of the Literary Fund, and be subject to the inspection of the Legislature. And in case of the removal, or of the death or resignation of the general Superintendent, the President and Directors of the Literary Fund are empowered and directed to make a new appointment for the unexpired term of the late incumbent.

Sec. 14. *And be it further enacted,* That when notified, the Superintendent of Common Schools for the State shall attend the meetings of the Literary Board as long as it shall direct, and for such attendance shall be allowed the usual compensation allowed to members of the Literary Board.

Sec. 15. *And be it further enacted,* That the said Superintendent of Common Schools shall, at such times and places as he may deem proper, and as often as possible, deliver public lectures on the subject of education and endeavor to enlist the feelings of the people in the cause.

Sec. 16. *And be it further enacted,* That all moneys collected from defaulting chairmen shall be paid to the credit of the county from which collected.

CALVIN H. WILEY'S FIRST ANNUAL REPORT AS STATE SUPERINTENDENT OF COMMON SCHOOLS IN NORTH CAROLINA

(1854) From North Carolina, *Legislative Documents, Session 1854–1855,* Doc. no. 12, pp. 3–7, as quoted in Edgar W. Knight, ed., *A Documentary History of Education in the South . . .* (Chapel Hill, 1949–53), pp. 156–59.

To His Excellency, David S. Reid,
Governor of the State of North Carolina:

Sir:—The Act of Assembly providing for the appointment of a Superintendent of Common Schools, (Sec. 11,) makes it the duty of that officer to submit to the Governor of the State an annual report in writing, "giving a detailed and condensed account of the manner in which he has performed his several duties; of the operations of the system of Common Schools, together with such suggestions and recommendations as he may deem proper; with tables showing the number of white persons, five years old and under twenty-one, in each County in the State; the number who have attended school during the year; the length of time during which the schools have been kept open in each County; the number of male and female Teachers licensed in each County to teach Common Schools during the year, and the average salaries of Teachers."

It was impossible for me to make this report at the time specified by law, inasmuch as the returns received from the Chairmen of the Boards of County superintendents did not generally come in till December, and continued to arrive till the 10th of January; and when received, the examination of these returns, and the computations to be made from them, (in many, few of the columns being added up,) involve an amount of labor which cannot be performed in less than two or three weeks. The whole system is awkwardly arranged, so far as the regulations in regard to terms of office and the fiscal year are concerned; and that there may be more harmony and precision in this respect, I will if I am spared, present to the next General Assembly certain recommendations founded on my own observation and the experience of local officers of the system.

It is one of my duties, as Superintendent of Common Schools, to ascertain the condition, history and promise of the system in all parts of the State; and also to deliver lectures whenever convenient occasions offer. To discharge these two duties together and in the most satisfactory manner, I determined, at first, to go to every County seat in the State; and during much of the past year I have been traveling, giving notice some days before of my intended visit.

I desired, as a general thing, to visit first those Counties which are most remote from the centre; and those wherein natural obstructions, such as swamps and mountains, present the greatest difficulties in the way of the success of a system of District schools.

I made it a rule to deliver an address at most of the places at which I attended, whatever the size of the audience; and in these *talks,* for they were not what are termed *speeches,* my great object was to diffuse practical information, and to set the people to thinking.

From the start a great difficulty in the way has been the want of proper information; and that I might diffuse my own views as widely as possible, I have addressed to your Excellency, in letters for publication in the newspapers, the substance of a portion of my lectures. I thought I could best ascertain the condition of things in the various sections of the State by instituting enquiries on the spot, and by an actual observation of the field of operations; and I also deemed it the part of wisdom to see for myself the condition and workings of our school machinery in the several peculiar geographical divisions with respect to the cause of general education in North Carolina, with a short and correct account of the labors of the past, and of the hopes of the future, in order that the Assembly might with this addition to its own stock of information, be enabled to adopt the wisest and most efficient regulations, have been my only aims in making the accompanying Report.

To acquire even the imperfect information which I possess has lost me a good deal of labor and expense; nor would I, with the expenditure of greater sums, and with more laborious exertions, have been able in two years to have gained the little knowledge of our social and educational history and progress which I possess, but for some previous attention to these things, and to our peculiar geographical position.

Due attention to the general duties of my office—the necessity of putting myself in direct communication with all the departments of the system over which I was called to preside—my heavy correspondence, and the importance of constant attention to the operations of the schools, as they now exist, prevented me from spending much of the current year in traveling. Merely to go into all the counties and deliver lectures would do but little good, while a person so occupied could not exercise a proper supervision, and reach with statistics but a very small portion of the people. I have, however, traveled extensively; and in the collection of information have complied strictly with the spirit of the Law, while I flatter myself that I am tolerably well acquainted with the geographical, social and educational position of our State, presenting many and great diversities in all these respects. It was certainly intended that the Superintendent of Common Schools should possess this information, essential to his usefulness; and what I mean is, that I have sincerely tried fully to comply with the spirit of the Law. The first officer of the kind in this State—expected by some partial friends to do more than it was possible for mortal to do, while other honest men thought it was impossible to do any thing—seeing in the history of the past but a dim and uncertain light, and in the condition of the present a wide spread field of apparent chaos, brooded over by doubts and despondency, it was impossible for me not to err.

Wisdom in the management of complicated affairs, comes to men by experience; and knowing as the representatives of the people must well know, by what slow degrees the human race has perfected any science connected with its own progress and temporal well being, I feel no apprehensions, but that the Assembly, as your Excellency and the Library Board have done, will extend towards me a becoming charity, and make due allowances for the difficulties of my situation. Moreover, as the subject is new to our people, and not yet well understood, I would, through your Excellency, respectfully suggest to the representatives of the people, in the General Assembly, and whose high province and privilege it will be to give permanent direction to our general educational system, to make a minute and thorough examination of my official course, and of its probable results, in time; and of all my views and motives, and their policy and justice. As to the *honesty* of my intentions, I do not, of course, mean to suggest or say anything, one way or another, claiming only that I have, with an oppressive, and ever present sense of my responsibilities, most anxiously made it my study, and my prayer to God, to be enabled to do good; but it is well, and in fact, extremely proper, for the Assembly to examine carefully and rigidly the grounds and motives of my conclusions and views, and to determine their bearing and effects, that bad precedents may not be established, or good ones altered.

A SOUTH CAROLINIAN ARGUES AGAINST PUBLIC SCHOOLS

(1852)   From James Simmons, "Address delivered at the opening of the Free Schools in Charleston, June 26, 1852," *Southern Quarterly Review*, vol. VI (1852), 461, pp. 466–70.

Whenever a child is to be educated, it should be ascertained what is to be his probable destiny. We do not mean that his career is to be definitely marked out for him, that his profession is to be selected in advance; such a procedure would be unwise, if it were not impracticable. But his social position being ascertained, and the means provided for his maintenance being known, he should be educated in accordance with the condition in which he is expected to commence his career.

Every child should be taught to read, to write, and to cipher. These elements form the key to all knowlege, and should be placed within reach of all. They are as necessary to the moral and intellectual man, as food and raiment are to his body. But as the quality of the food and raiment of each man depends upon his means and his condition, so the same circumstances should determine whether the intellectual food and raiment should exceed that necessary modicum which the spirit of the age seems to require.

*   *   *

The only practicable means of improving our schools, so as to place a higher grade of education within reach of the very poor, must be found, either in a compulsory provision on the part of the State, which by directly taxing all for the support of common schools, should compel all persons of moderate fortunes to educate their children at them; or by a voluntary union of the primary schools supported by the State, with those which may be established by private enterprize. This latter plan is, we are informed, generally adopted in our upper districts. Whenever such a voluntary association of private with public means is made, we are content to rely implicitly on the wisdom which plans the arrangement. But the case is widely different when it is presented as a compulsory measure. The State has no more authority to levy a tax for a given school, than for a given church. And when men of moderate fortunes are compelled, by the operation of law, to send their children to the State school, or to none, it becomes absolute tyranny.

* * *

There is as much cant on the subject of education as on that of religion. The politician and the preacher alike call for the education of the people. Education is not only the palladium of our liberties, but the guide which is to lead us to eternal truth. We believe in neither of these dogmas. They are both repugnant to fact and to common sense. If we lived in Utopia, and our numbers were limited,—if we were not required to struggle, not only for the means of living, but for life itself,—if the circumstances of every man were such that his necessary labours were only so great as to brace his nerves and his muscles for enjoyment during his hours of relaxation,—then would universal education be, not a sweetener of life only, but a necessity. It would be essential to the perfect development of Utopian life. But our world is one of fact. Life is a sober reality. In spite of the falsehoods which constitutions proclaim to the contrary, the privileged few must govern. To the mass of mankind the character of the government is a matter of practical indifference.

* * *

Men whose lives are spent in humble toil, have little time for reflection. They are as susceptible to evil impressions as to good. Education exposes them to the danger of attacks from the demagogue, as well as to the wholesome admonitions of the patriotic. As we go northward in our country, we find every phase of political doctrine. The spirit of agrarianism is rife. In New-York the landlord has had to resort to military force to collect his rents. Throughout the whole country, from the Hudson to the Bay of Fundy, a settled determination exists to abolish slavery at the South, though it is demonstrated that Northern prosperity is dependent upon Southern slavery. Is this fanaticism? There is no doubt that the people entertain an honest conviction of the sinfulness of slavery, inspired first by the preachings of enthusiasts, and afterwards fostered by aspirants after political power, who have taken advantage of this honesty of purpose in the masses to promote their own views. The diffusion of education in New-England is likely to effect a dissolution of the Union; and no one can venture to predict, under such a result, the endless horrors which threaten the future of that imperfectly educated, but self-sufficient and misguided people.

Education effects no change in the nature of man. It is but an instrument—to the good, of good, to the bad it is only a new element of evil. There is no necessary connection between learning and freedom. In ancient times, slaves were educated for the purpose of increasing their value, and we have never heard that their value has, in modern times, been in the slightest degree diminished by the amount of their instruction. Liberty is an instinct, not a principle. There is no more freedom enjoyed in Europe now, than in the time of Alfred. The races that were free then, continue so.

CONSTITUTIONAL PROVISION FOR EDUCATION IN TEXAS (1856) From H. P. N. Gammel, ed., *The Laws of Texas, 1822–1897* (1898), vol. IV, pp. 252–53.

An Act Providing for the Support of Schools

Section 1. Be it enacted by the Legislature of the State of Texas, That the Treasurer of the State be authorized and required to transfer to the General or State account, the specie now in the Treasury, to the credit of the General School Fund account, and replace the same from the one million five hundred and seventy-five thousand dollars, United States Bonds, now standing to the credit of the State account; and it is hereby made the duty of the State Treasury, annually on the first day of July, in each year, to transfer the specie then standing to the credit of the School Fund, received from one tenth taxes to State account, and replace the same with the United States bonds from the State account, unless otherwise provided by law; that the Special School Fund of two millions dollars, created by "An act to establish a system of schools," passed January 31st, 1854, and that the General School fund, derivable from one-tenth taxes, be, and the same are blended and made one, and the interest arising from the United States Bonds, constituting said fund, and the interest arising from all monies set aside for school purposes, be, and the same is hereby appropriated to the respective counties, for the use and benefit of the children of said counties, between the age of six and eighteen years, as herein provided.

Sec. 2. It shall be the duty of the Assessor and Collector of each county in the State, during each and every year hereafter, to make out a list of all the free white population in his county, between the ages of six and eighteen years, and transmit the same under his official signature to the County Clerk of the county, and a certified copy to the Treasurer of the State, on or before the first day of July in each and every year.

Sec. 3. That it shall be the duty of the Clerk of the County Court to file and preserve in his office the list aforesaid, furnished by the Assessor and Collector. It shall be the duty of the Treasurer of the State to ascertain from the abstracts transmitted to him by the Assessor and Collector, the aggregate population between the ages of six and eighteen years. And the fund appropriated by this act shall be apportioned among the different counties in the State, according to the number of scholastic population in each county, subject to the order of the County Courts, and payable to the respective county treasurers, upon the order of the County Court, under the hand of the Chief-Justice and seal of the Court, or such amount to be placed to the credit of the Assessor and Collector of Taxes of such county, upon his payment into the Treasury of his county, the amount so appropriated to such county, and filing the receipt of the county Treasurer acknowledged by the said Treasurer before the Clerk of the County Court, and by the said Clerk, duly certified under his hand and the seal of his Court, with the Treasurer of the State.

Sec. 4. That it shall be the duty of the County Court, annually, to apportion the said School fund among the children between the ages of six and eighteen years, who may attend any school in their respective counties, in proportion to the time that each child has been taught, upon the teacher's filing with the County Clerk, an affidavit, signed and sworn to by himself, before some officer authorized to administer oaths as to the number of children taught, and the time they received instruction. And said schools are hereby declared "free public schools"; provided, that no child whose entire tuition has been paid, shall receive any money under the provision of this section.

Sec. 5. That the teacher of each school shall be required to keep a day book, and at the close of his term of teaching shall furnish the County Court with a tabular statement of the names of all the patrons and pupils of the school, the number of pupils sent by each person, and the number of days each pupil attended school, which statement shall be supported by his affidavit, made before some officer authorized to administer oaths, that the same is true and correct. And he shall further make affidavit, supported by the certificate of two responsible house-holding patrons of his school, that he has taught said school for a period of not less than three months. And upon his failure to make said report, he shall forfeit all claim for compensation for services rendered under this act.

Sec. 6. That the County Treasurer of each county shall give bond, with two or more securities, payable to the county in twice the amount of the school fund to which the county shall be entitled, so soon as the Chief-Justice shall be notified by the Treasurer of the State, of the amount to which his county is entitled, which bond shall be conditioned, that he will well and faithfully keep an account of the money to him committed, as a school fund for his county, and pay over the same, only upon the order of the Chief-Justice of the county, under his hand and the seal of the County Court. He shall keep an accurate account of all monies received and paid out by him, to register and number all orders by him paid or accepted, to be paid. He shall, between the first and tenth of the fiscal month of the Treasury of each year, renew his bond; and all suits upon such bonds shall be in the name of the county, and in other respects they shall be governed by the laws regulating the bonds of county Treasurers. If any person or patron of any school is unable to pay his tuition, and the teacher shall be satisfied of the fact, it shall be the duty of said teacher to make out a list of all such patrons together with the amount of money due from each for tuition, and forward the same under oath to the Chief-Justice of the county.

Sec. 7. The Treasurer of the State, shall be ex-officio Superintendent of schools. It shall be his duty, after the first day of the fiscal month, in each and every year, to record the abstracts of children of lawful age in different counties, apportion the monies as herein contemplated, distributing to the several counties the amount to which each is entitled, according to its scholastic population. And it shall be the duty of the Treasurer to keep a correct account of all the monies and matters appertaining to the school fund, and report to the Governor annually, at the close of the fiscal year, the condition of the school fund, distribution of monies, and such suggestions in regard to the School System as may be deemed advisable. That the fiscal scholastic year shall commence and end upon the fiscal year of the State Treasury. That the County Court of each County, after ascertaining that the patrons returned are unable to pay the tuition, shall make a return of the same to the State Treasurer, who, upon the order of the County Court, under the seal of their offices, in favor of the county, shall pay over to said County Courts their distributive shares of the interest of the School fund; and the County Courts on receiving the same, shall proceed to distribute the same, as required by this act; first providing for those children whose tuition has not been paid from inability of the patrons; provided, that orphan children, and children of widows, who have no other or greater amount of property than is exempted from forced sale, be considered indigent.

Sec. 8. That the Assessor and Collector of each county, for the year 1856 and all succeeding years, shall receive for his compensation, for discharging the duties imposed upon him by this act, twelve cents per child for two hundred children and less; eight cents per child for all less than three hundred and more than two hundred; six cents per child for less than four hundred and more than three hundred; five cents per child for all less than five hundred and more than four hundred; four cents per child for all less than a thousand and more than five hundred; three cents per child for two thousand and more than one thousand; two cents for all over two thousand. And should the Assessor and Collector refuse or fail to take and report the census of children as required by this act, he shall forfeit the whole of the compensation allowed, and be fined not less than twenty-five nor more than one hundred dollars, at the discretion of the County Court; and in case of failure from any cause whatever, of the Assessor and Collector, in making a report of the census of his respective county, to the County Clerk, on or before the first day of July, in each year, the County Court shall be authorized to appoint some suitable person to perform said labor, who shall be entitled to the same compensation as allowed to Assessors and Collectors, under this act; provided, he makes his returns by the first day of September following. Assessors and Collectors, or other persons appointed to take the census of scholastic population, shall not be entitled to compensation for their services, unless their returns are made within the time prescribed by this act.

Sec. 9. That the counties which have not heretofore received their share of the Special School Fund for either years 1854 or 1855 from failure to make returns of their scholastic population, shall be entitled to receive the same upon the following basis, to wit: Those counties that made returns for the year 1854, but none for 1855, shall be allowed an addition of five per cent to the returns of 1854, and the result be placed to the credit of such counties as their share of the fund for 1855. Those counties that made returns for 1855, but failed for the year 1854, five per cent shall be deducted from the return of 1855, and the result be placed to the credit of such counties as their share of the fund for 1854. Those counties that have failed entirely to make returns, shall upon their making due returns for some present year, be allowed a credit for the years so failing, by deducting from the number of children for the year returned, such annual per centage of increase as the aggregate returns of all the counties shown to be increase back to the year 1854. When the Assessor and Collector, or person appointed under the provisions of the previous section, shall fail to make and have on file in the Treasurer's office, by the first of the fiscal month of the Treasury, of each year, returns of the scholastic population of their respective counties, the census returns of such counties, for the previous year, shall be taken as the basis of distribution to such counties and the amount so set aside shall be paid to such counties without regard to returns that may be made to the Treasurer's office, after the date above mentioned.

Sec. 10. The Treasurer of the State shall send to each County Court and to each Assessor and Collector, a copy of this law, and require from each Court an annual report of the number of schools, the number of children, the disposition of the fund, and such other information as will give correct idea of the condition of the schools.

Sec. 11. The provisions of this act shall only extend to such children as are actually sent to schools of the State. That no school shall be entitled to the benefits of this act unless the English language is taught therein.

Sec. 12. That all laws conflicting with the provisions of this act, be, and the same are hereby thus far repealed. And that this act take effect and be in force from and after its passage.

Approved, 29th August, 1856.

The West

RESPONSIBILITIES OF THE TEACHER IN THE PUEBLO OF SAN JOSE
(**1811**)   From Frederick Hall, *The History of San Jose* (San Francisco, 1871), pp. 12–13.

I return to you, that the same may be placed in the Archives, the obligation which the inhabitants of the neighborhood have made with the infirm corporal, Rafael Villavicencio, who transmitted it to me by official letter of the 30th of last September, in which he obligated himself to teach the children of the Pueblo and vicinity, to read, write and the Doctrine; and to be paid therefore at the rate of eighteen reales per annum, by every head of a family, in grain or flour. As in this obligation of both parties, the conditions are not expressed, which I consider ought to be, I have thought proper to dictate them; that you may make it know to both parties in public, with their consent; and that it be signed by you, the Alcalde, Regidores, and the teacher, and registered in the archives.

Contract.

Firstly.—The pay of eighteen reales annually by each and every head of a family, I think is quite sufficient for the teacher; and as it is all they can give, in virtue of which, the Commissioner will be obliged to collect the same at the proper time, in order to deliver it to the teacher. The teacher, in virtue of the pay which is made to him, will also be obliged to perform his obligations with the greatest vigilance and strictness, without giving his attention to anything else but the teaching. As the hours are not expressed in which the attendance of the children ought to be at school, they will be there: six in a day: three in the morning, and three in the afternoon; in the morning from eight o'clock until eleven, and in the afternoon from two until five; it being the duty of the Commissioner to compel the fathers to make their children attend; and to see that the teacher in no instance fails.

Every Thursday and Saturday afternoons, the children will not write or read, but explanations will be given them these two afternoons, of the doctrine [faith], at which time the Commissioner will attend, and advise the teacher that he must answer for the little or much explanation which he may make.

When the teacher observes the absence of any of the scholars at the school, he will notify their fathers, who will give some satisfactory reason why they were absent on that morning or afternoon; and if they should be absent a second time, then he will notify the Commissioners, who will compel the fathers to send their children, without receiving any excuse or pretexts particularly from the mothers, because they will all be frivolous, since the children have sufficient time to do all they are required to do.

Lastly.—During the time in which the children are at school, their fathers will be exempt from being responsible to God for them, and the teacher will be the one who is thus responsible; as he will, also, in consideration of his pay, be responsible for the education and teaching of the holy dogma of the religion; and the teacher is he who must be responsible to God, the parish priest, and to their authority. It is also understood that the fathers are obliged to examine their children at home, as to the advancement which they may make, and to complain to the Commissioner when they see no advancement, in order that he may remedy the matter if necessary.

As the teacher is responsible in the Divine presence for the education and good examples of his scholars, and as he must answer to the State for the fulfilment of his obligations, he has the right to correct and punish his scholars with advice, warning, and lashes, in case of necessity; and particularly he ought to do it for any failure to learn the doctrine, for which he ought not to accept any excuse, nor to pardon any one from punishment who fails to learn it, or who does not commit to memory the lesson which may be given him.

Having made known that it should be registered as I command; God preserve you many years.

JOSÉ MA. ESTUDILLO

EDUCATIONAL PROVISION IN THE CONSTITUTION OF INDIANA (1816)
From Benjamin P. Poore, ed., *The Federal And State Constitutions Colonial Charters, And Other Organic Laws of the United States* (Washington, D.C., 1878), vol. I, p. 428

Sec. 2. It shall be the duty of the General Assembly, as soon as circumstances will permit, to provide, by law, for a general system of education, ascending in a regular gradation from township schools to a State University, wherein tuition shall be gratis, and equally open to all.

ASSEMBLY CANDIDATE ABRAHAM LINCOLN ON THE IMPORTANCE
OF EDUCATION (1832)   From Abraham Lincoln, "Communication to the People of
Sangamo County," March 9, 1832, as quoted in Roy P. Basler, ed. *The Collected Works of Abraham Lincoln* (New Brunswick, N.J., 1953), vol. I, pp. 5, 8.

March 9, 1832

FELLOW-CITIZENS; Having become a candidate for the honorable office of one of your representatives in the next General Assembly of this state, in accordance with an established custom, and the principles of true republicanism, it becomes my duty to make known to you . . . my sentiments with regard to local affairs.

Upon the subject of education, not presuming to dictate any plan or system respecting it, I can only say that I view it as the most important subject which we as a people can be engaged in. That every man may receive at least, a moderate education, and thereby be enabled to read the histories of his own and other countries, by which he may duly appreciate the value of our free institutions, appears to be an object of vital importance, even on this account alone, to say nothing of the advantages and satisfaction to be derived from being able to read the scriptures and other works, both of a religious and moral nature, for themselves. For my part, I desire to see the time when education, and by its means, morality, sobriety, enterprise, and industry, shall become much more general than at present, and should be gratified to have it in my power to contribute something to the advancement of any measure which might have a tendency to accelerate the happy period.

GOVERNOR ALBINO PEREZ CALLS FOR PUBLIC EDUCATION FOR NEW MEXICO (1836)

From Ralph Emerson Twitchell, *The Leading Facts of New Mexican History* (Cedar Rapids, Iowa, 1912), vol. II, pp. 57–59.

Ignorance, and idleness, have always been the cause of infinite evil among men in society, and to diminish them, the only remedy and the most efficacious adopted in all countries of the world, is the education of Youth. In this valuable and interesting province securing the good of the people being the principal object, the true lovers of the public weal should attend to this, and it is also the most sacred obligation of the local authorities. This important branch is in a sad state throughout the territory, and more especially in this capital, which by its very nature and elements, does not think profoundly on the means to overcome these false difficulties, which seem by their continuation, to justify the neglect. Running the streets are children who ought to be receiving the education so necessary at the fitting and proper age; youths of evil disposition, abandoned to laziness and licentiousness, practicing vices; useless aims which only serve to corrupt, like the plague, the city that tolerates and feeds them; and above all, what are the results? Robbery, immorality, poverty, desertion, and the most humiliating shame of the city, which if it were cared for by its municipal authorities, should be the enviable example of others composing a most interesting part of the Mexican Nation.

Moved by such salutary reflections, and the love I bear to the inhabitants of this soil, and by the obligation imposed upon me by my position, I issue for the relief of the Royal Municipality the following Plan of Regulation of Public Instruction.

Art. 1. There shall be in this city two schools, particularly of primary instruction, in charge of Masters who may present themselves to conduct them, and who have the proper capacity in the judgment of a commission named by the corporation, which shall examine them in reading, writing, and counting.

2. The schools of the same nature now existing, gone through by heads of families, shall be destroyed, provided always that the Masters who conduct them

have not the capacity and the approval required by the preceding article, to which end they may present themselves for examination, in opposition.

3. The Masters shall enjoy such salary or recompense as may be agreed upon with the heads of families, and shall receive pay from those known to be poor, in products of the soil, teaching gratis, orphan children, or those of the absolutely miserable, who have no livelihood or power to pay.

4. All Fathers or Guardians who have children in their care from the age of five to twelve years, are obliged to send them to one of the schools whichever best suits them, and the youths of twelve years of more [must be] in houses of artisans in the different branches of industry, that they may earn a living by honest occupation.

5. Those who fail to comply with the first part of the preceding article, by omission or neglect, shall be required by law, to pay a fine of from, one to five p. according to their means, in the first, double in the second, and triple in the third, and those who are still recalcitrant, and those who cannot pay the fine, shall be punished by law with three days arrest, doubling this punishment in the same way as the pecuniary one.

6. The Youths spoken of in the second part of the fourth article who do not consent to learn a trade, or who have no honest occupation, shall be treated as vagrant or vicious, and be tried and sentenced by the established Court and the laws governing such cases.

7. The Justices of the Wards, the wardens or deputies of the police, may arrest youths of twelve years or over, whom they find in the streets and public places engaged in betting games, at the end of eight days giving notice to one of the magistrates for the recognizance; and the children of twelve or under whom they find behaving ill, they shall take to the school that they may there suffer the same penalty of detention, advising the Master to punish them without fail.

8. Every one or two wards shall form two blocks proportionately, and designated by known names and fixed numbers.

9. To facilitate the better carrying out of this proclamation there shall be in each block a commissioner of Public Instruction, named by three justices unanimously whose duties shall be;

First. To make exact lists of the inhabitants of their blocks, with a statement of ages and occupations by which they live.

Second. To make another list of the children who shall attend the school and go to each of the two, in order to learn if they are there; an account of the youths who ought to apply themselves to a trade, in what shop and with what Masters, and of the day laborers and where, they work, so that they can certify to the correctness of all this.

Third. To announce, courteously, one, two, or three times, to the fathers of families or guardians or children, what is set forth in the clauses of the preceding articles.

Fourth. To give notice in writing, to the magistrate of the precinct of those who, having been admonished, still do not comply, so that through him or by advising the judge, the law may inflict the penalty, to which they have made themselves liable.

Fifth. To give notice, in the same manner, of all those living in idleness, who, having been admonished, do not find occupation, declaring all they can testify as to the proper or objectionable habits of the individuals.

Sixth. To give notice also, of any suspicious persons that may be in their blocks, who are spending money without knowing whether they come by it honestly, with the grounds for the suspicion.

Seventh. To visit every month, the schools to which the children go, to learn from the Masters whether they attend, and to get the information for their guidance. Similar visits shall be made to the workshops for the same purpose.

Eighth. They shall make note, in their lists, of the inhabitants who leave their blocks, to what others they go, and of those who come to live in their own.

Ninth. They shall be charged with the cleanliness of the streets and public places in their blocks, giving to the magistrate of the precinct of any neglect they notice.

Art. 10. Any person interfering with the commissioner in the discharge of his duty, shall be punished by a fine of from five to twenty-five p. without prejudice that if the fault be serious, he may be punished according to the laws relating to ordinary transgressions.

11. The duty of a commissioner of Public Instruction shall be a compulsory one, and no one can be excused from discharging it; it is obligatory for six months, without being required to continue, this term completed, until the end of the year, and the magistrates can remove him, for sufficient cause as neglect or bad management, if proven.

12. For any offense committed by the commissioner in the discharge of his duties, he shall be punished by a fine of from ten to thirty p. and deprivation of duty; and if the offence be the concealment of mischievous persons, or the toleration of them without giving notice to the Judges there shall be exacted fifty p. or two months forced labor.

13. This ordinance may be amended in whole or in part when the R. Ayuntamiento may deem proper, being convinced of its advantages or invalidity.

MICHIGAN'S SUPERINTENDENT OF SCHOOLS, JOHN PIERCE, ON THE IMPORTANCE OF COMMON SCHOOLS (1837) From Michigan Senate, "Report of the Superintendent of Public Instruction of the State of Michigan," *Senate Journal, 1837*, Doc. no. 7, as quoted in Floyd R. Dain, *Education in the Wilderness* (Lansing, Mich., 1968), pp. 229–32.

If we would preserve inviolate the sacred principles of liberty—of liberty, civil and religious—if we would perpetuate free institutions; if we would hand down to those who come after us a constitution, government and laws, based upon the essential and imperishable rights of man; if we would rear a superstructure of elements more durable than crowns and pyramids, we must dig deep and lay broad and permanent the foundations of knowledge and virtue. In an educated and virtuous community, there is safety; the rights of individuals are regarded, and property is respected and secure. Every man sits quietly under his own vine and fig tree, regaling himself with the fruits of his own industry and labor. Justice, truth, and equity are the glory of a nation, but these attributes of virtue are not to be found among an ignorant and vicious people. Generally speaking, the child uneducated in knowledge and virtue, is thoroughly educated in the school of depravity. And what is true of the individual, is true of communities. It may safely be assumed as a fundamental principle in our form of government, that knowledge is an element so essential to its existence and vigorous action, that we can have no rational hope of its perpetuation unless it is generally diffused. Unless, indeed, the corner stone of the social edifice is laid upon the intelligence and virtue of the people, it cannot stand. Without education, no people can secure themselves against the encroachments of power. Superstition and ignorance furnish the raw material of despotism; for there is nothing to prevent the tyranny of the sword, where the mind is degraded and the many unacquainted with their rights and powers.

* * *

Nothing else can secure the great mass of the people against legalized oppression; nothing else can retain them in the full possession and enjoyment of all their rights, privileges and immunities, as men—as rational beings, endowed by their common Creator with the high attributes of moral agency and freedom of choice, and the essential prerogative of self-government. How valuable soever high seminaries of learning may be, we cannot rely upon them for instructing the great body of the people, because they are to be found only in the primary schools. They ought to be the foundation of our whole system of public instruction, as they are indeed the chief support of all our free institutions. . . . It is . . . of the first importance that this foundation be laid deep and firm, not only in the constitution and laws of the country, but also in the warmest affections of our people.

* * *

However unpretending and simple in form, our government is nevertheless effective and perfect. It proceeds from the people—is supported by the people—and depends upon the people—and at the same time restrains and controls the people more effectually than the most rigid systems of despotism. But how is this political fabric to be preserved? Only by the general diffusion of knowledge. Children of every name and age must be taught the qualifications and duties of American citizens, and learn in early life the art of self-control—they must be educated. And to accomplish this object, our chief dependence must necessarily be the free school system. . . .

* * *

Let free schools be established and maintained in perpetuity, and there can be no such thing as a permanent aristocracy in our land; for the monopoly of wealth is powerless, when mind is allowed freely to come in contact with mind. It is only by erecting a barrier between the rich and the poor, which can be done only by allowing the rich a monopoly of learning as well as of wealth, that such an aristocracy can be established. But the operation of the free school system has a powerful tendency to prevent the erection of this barrier.

* * *

A faithful and honorable discharge of these duties requires a well informed mature judgment; and other qualifications of a high character, which can be obtained only by a good education. Our citizens are all electors—a high and responsible franchise—nearly all of them are liable to serve as jurors; many are necessarily incumbents of the various offices of the township, county, and state, and of the United States. . . . Since, then, by the wise provisions of our system, political power is distributed to such an extent that nearly every citizen may be called upon to share in its exercise, while he submits to its just authority; how essential that all should acquire that knowledge and those qualifications, which are requisite to the right performance of civil, judicial, and military duties. Not mere intelligence, but actual knowledge, which education alone can furnish, is required in every department of the government, in legislation, in jurisprudence, and in the daily execution of the laws.

* * *

We need wisdom, and prudence, and foresight in our councils, fixedness in purpose, integrity, and uprightness of heart in our rulers; unwavering attachment to the rights of man among all our people; but these high attributes of a noble, patriotism, these essential elements of civilization and improvement, will disappear when schools shall cease to exert an all-pervading influence through the length and breadth of our land.

* * *

Wherever the liberality and enterprise of individuals have established flourishing private institutions, they have uniformly had a pernicious influence upon the common schools. Instead of being improved and elevated by their proximity to such institutions, they have lost their character and usefulness. In those towns where private seminaries have been located and well sustained, the free schools will be found, without exception, to be in a miserable condition.

* * *

Let teachers be paid as they ought to be, let them receive such compensation as will remunerate them for their services, and sufficient numbers will be found to fit themselves for the business of teaching. And to secure their employment when fitted to teach, let the provisions of the law be such, that no township shall be entitled to any portion of the income of the public fund, which does not employ thoroughly educated teachers.

* * *

. . . the primary schools should be on the first order, the academies of the highest grade, and the universities assume and maintain a commanding position; and each and all of them be so ably conducted as to give entire satisfaction to all reasonable, unprejudiced minds. With such schools, the rising generation would be thoroughly taught, and the wants of the state adequately supplied.

OHIO SCHOOL SUPERINTENDENT SAMUEL LEWIS COMMENTS ON
THE PUBLIC SCHOOLS (1838)   From State of Ohio, *First Annual Report of the
Superintendent of Common Schools . . . 1838* (Columbus, 1838), pp. 8–10, 16–18.

As it will be impossible to give a full history of my observations, an example of the several classes must suffice. In one town a free school is taught three months in the year, by one teacher, in a district where more than one hundred children desire to attend; they rush in and crowd the school so as to destroy all hope of usefulness, the wealthy, and those in comfortable circumstances, seeing this, withdraw their children or never send them; the school thus receives the name of a school for the poor, and its usefulness is destroyed. This example is one that represents nearly all the free schools in the State, as well in the country, as in the cities and towns.

Another and much larger number of the districts, adopt a practice of which the following is an example.

The district has funds which would pay a teacher one quarter or less; but in order to keep up a school as long as possible, it is divided between two or more quarters; the teacher makes his estimate of the amount, besides public money, that must be paid by each scholar, and gets his subscription accordingly. Here none send but those who can pay the balance; of course, the children of the poor, the very intemperate and careless, with sometimes the inordinate lovers of money, are left at home. This mode, though it defeats the primary object of the law, really secures a greater aggregate amount of instruction than the other. Another class proceeds on the same plan, with the exception that the teacher is bound to take the very poor free, if they prove their total inability to pay. This is but little, if any, better than the last, since the poor woman must humble herself, and in effect take the benefit of the poor law, before she can get her children into school; and then, both she and her children must suffer, constantly, deep mortification, which frequently drives from the school some of the most promising children, who (right or wrong) are too proud to brook such humiliating conditions. It effectually banishes the children of those who love money better than learning, as well as those of the intemperate, whose sensibilities are too much vitiated to care for this subject at all. Besides, if the poor go on these terms, it invariably crowds the school to a ruinous extent; and if the teacher cannot instruct all, he will, of course, take care of his patrons first; let him be as honest as he may, he will endeavor to satisfy those that support him; and the poor, whose conscientiousness of poverty always make them jealous and watchful, detect the smallest partiality, and leave the school in disgust, or stay to scatter the seeds of discontent and insubordination. Another part of this class is, where the directors agree with the teacher at so much per month; and, after expending the school money, levy, under the statute, a tax on the scholars for the residue, sometimes admitting the poor, and sometimes rejecting all that are unable to pay the difference.

In some towns, all the teachers receive a portion of the public money at the rate of so much per scholar, which they deduct from the subscription price. In these cases, the schools are all strictly private, and no provision whatever is made for the poor. The officers in one place where this practice prevails, said that "if the schools were free, they would be so crowded as to be useless, unless they had more funds; but, by the mode they adopted, every man who sent to school, got a part of the

THE COMMON
SCHOOL
MOVEMENT

1027

public money;" if he was not able to pay the balance, he was punished by losing the whole; which is certainly a bad feature in the practice, and a gross violation of law. Another custom is not to draw the school money for several years, and then say once in two or three years, they can keep a crowded free school from three to six months. In some places public schools have not been taught this two years. These examples give the practice of all the school districts in the State; the second and third named prevail the most generally; but it is not uncommon to find all the examples adopted in different districts in the same township.

No correct idea can be given of the particular system of instruction adopted in the schools; it embraces almost every system; and in our public, as well as in our private schools, is found every variety from the very best, to those esteemed the most defective. But a small proportion of schools in the State have sufficient permanence to have adopted any specific plan, nor is it possible to produce or preserve any thing like system, until the schools have more permanence, and the art of teaching is recognized as something valuable.

In towns and large villages, the *common* schools are poorer than in the country. In the latter, neighborhoods depend more on them, and of course take a deeper interest in their control; while in the former, there is too frequently but little attention paid to these schools, by persons able to provide other means of instruction. Private schools are considered the best, and being patronized by the wealthy, create a distinction that is ruinous. I am unwilling to repeat the remarks in reference to this point, that I have often heard made; it may be sufficient to say, that in many instances, the whole tendency is to bring the schools into disrepute, if not positive disgrace.

*   *   *

Though a great majority of our citizens are enlightened and intelligent, it must be admitted, that quite a number do not regard the education of their children with sufficient interest to induce proper individual action; and unless provision for these, other than parental, be made, they will be even worse situated, in many cases, than the orphan. It is common to say of these, "They could educate their children, if they would": but visits to the houses of many people, in different counties, of whom this was said, would satisfy any man, as it has satisfied me, that if they paid for schooling, it must be taken from the already too scanty fare of an unfortunate wife and poorly provided family. In many cases, you may as well charge fifteen dollars per quarter, as fifty cents. They cannot, if they would, and too many would not, if they could, pay, as individuals, anything.

If such fathers were the only sufferers, we might be excused from labors to avert the evil; but such parents will have left the world, long before society will feel its full extent.

The children are not to blame; nor are the children of those in other circumstances, guilty of any offence that will justify their fathers in fixing upon them a great moral contagion, destroying their best interests.

The children of those several classes (and there are not a few) are practically shut out of our common schools, in nine cases out of ten, in the State. For it makes but little difference, whether we positively prohibit their attendance, or prescribe such conditions as preclude them. Nor is it a question that can influence us, whether they are correct in their views. So long as those views operate the hindrance, it is the same thing to the public. It is not by any means certain, that we should discourage a feeling of independence, in parents or children. A magnanimous friend, in doing the greatest favor, seeks how he may do it so delicately, that the favored party may not feel himself oppressed with a sense of obligation.

Though common school is a civil, rather than charitable institution, it must be admitted that a primary object is, to bring under a wholesome influence, the classes of children I have named.

Whether we regard this subject in reference to *their* interest, or that of the whole people forming the State, it is of too much importance to be passed over lightly, or justify, for a moment, the conclusion that any portion of the rising generation, on whom must devolve the government of the country, can be abandoned to accident or certain ruin. Men may discourse eloquently about family instruction, and fireside education: it is all good; better than orators have spoken, or poets sung. But we must not be misled by eloquence or poetry. The fact is, a large part of our fellow citizens, who depend on their labor for a support (and they are the majority) have no time for much of this, if they had ability. If we should rise in the morning, and before our little ones were even dressed, hurry to our work, and devote the entire day to it, returning when our fatigued bodies, without other aid, admonished us of approaching night, we should be exceptions to all general rules, if we could undertake the instruction of our sons by candle light. And the cases of three-fifths of our mothers, is still harder. Their labor begins on the first move in the house, nor ends until the last candle is out. They have, emphatically, no time to educate their daughters. Exceptions, we know, there are; persons who have risen above all these obstacles, and educated both themselves and their families. But we must stop until at least one generation shall be educated, before we can expect to make the exceptions, the general rule. We should, in providing for the people, look to their present condition as a body, and not to what they should be according to the perfection of a few characters, perhaps over-drawn, if they ever existed, except in the inventive genius of vivid imaginations.

EXAMPLE OF A RATE BILL AND A WARRANT FOR COLLECTION IN MICHIGAN (1859)

From Ellwood P. Cubberley, ed., *Readings in the History of Education* (Boston, 1920), p. 574.

Form of Rate-Bill and Warrant

Rate-Bill containing the name of each person liable for teachers' wages in District No. . . . . . ., in the township of . . . ., for the term ending on . . . . . . day of . . . ., A.D. 18 . ., and the amount for which each person not exempted from the payment thereof is so liable, with the fees of the assessor thereon.

Names of inhabitants sending to school	Whole number of days sent	Amount of school bill	Assessor's fees thereon	Amount for fuel	Whole amount to be raised
James Emerson	104	$1.04	$ .05	*	$1.09
John L. Barney	416	4.16	.21	$1.25	5.62
William Jones	313	3.13	.16	*	3.20
Peter Parley	54	.54	.03	*	.57
S. C. Goodrich	104	1.04	.05	.50	1.59
M. Barney	104	1.04	.05	*	1.09
F. Sawyer	416	4.16	.21	*	4.37

*Exemption from fuel bill because fuel was furnished to school.

Warrant

You are hereby commanded to collect from each of the persons in the annexed rate-bill named, the several sums set opposite their respective names in the last column thereof, and within sixty days after receiving this warrant, to pay over the amount so collected by you (retaining five percent for your fees) to the order of the Director of said District, countersigned by the Moderator; and in case any person named therein, shall neglect or refuse, on demand, to pay the amount set opposite his name as aforesaid, you are to collect the same by distress and sale of goods and chattels of such persons wherever found, within the county or counties in which said District is situated, having first published such sale at least ten days, by posting up notices thereof in three public places in the townships where such property shall be sold.

At the expiration of this warrant, you will make a return thereof in writing, with the rate-bill attached, to the Director; stating the amount collected on said rate-bill, the amount uncollected, and the names of the persons from whom collections have not been made.

Given under our hands this . . . . . day of . . . ., in the year of our Lord, one thousand eight hundred and . . . . . .

A. B., Director
C. D., Moderator.

THE FIRST COMPULSORY EDUCATION LAW IN ILLINOIS (1883) From
Grace Abbott, *The Child and the State* (Chicago, 1938), pp. 307–8.

Be it enacted, etc.: That every person having the control and charge of any child or children, between the ages of eight and fourteen years, shall send such child or children to a public or private school for a period of not less than twelve weeks in each school year, unless such child or children are excused from attending school by the board of education, or school directors of the city, town, or school district in which such child or children reside. Such excuse may be given by said board of education or school directors for any good cause shown why said child or children shall not be required to attend school in conformity with this act.

2. It shall be a good defense to any suit brought under this act, if the person under whose control such child or children are, can show that the mental or bodily condition of such child or children is such as to prevent its attendance at school or application to study for the period required by this act, or, that such child or children have been taught in a private school, or at home for the time specified in this act, in such branches as are ordinarily taught in primary or other schools, or have acquired the branches of learning ordinarily taught in public schools, or that no public school has been taught within two miles, by the nearest traveled road, of the residence of such child or children, within the school district in which said child or children reside, for twelve weeks during the year.

3. If any person having the control and charge of any child or children shall fail or neglect to comply with the provisions of this act, said person shall pay a fine of not less than five nor more than twenty dollars. Suit for the recovery of the fine and costs shall be brought by any director, or member of any board of education, of the district in which such person resided at the time of the committal of the offense, before any justice of the peace of said township. Jurisdiction is hereby conferred on all justices of the peace in this State for the enforcing of this act. Such fine shall be paid, when collected, to the school treasurer of said township, to be accounted for by him as other school money raised for school purposes.

4. It is hereby made the duty of school directors and members of the boards of education to prosecute offenses occurring under this act. The neglect so to prosecute by any school director, or member of any board of education, within twenty days after written notice has been served on such director, or member of such board of education, by any tax-payer residing in such district, that any person has violated this act, shall subject him or them to a fine of ten dollars, to be sued for by any tax-payer residing in the school district where the violation of this act occurred, before any justice of the peace in the township where the said school district may be located; and when such fine is collected it shall be reported by said treasurer, and accounted for as other money raised for school purposes, and become a part of the school fund of said township.

EDUCATIONAL PROVISIONS IN THE CALIFORNIA CONSTITUTION

(**1850**)   From U.S. Bureau of Education, *Annual Report of the Commissioner of Education, 1892–93* (Washington, D.C., 1893), p. 1336.

Article IX.—Education

SEC. 1. The legislature shall provide for the election, by the people, of a superintendent of public instruction, who shall hold his office for three years, and whose duties shall be prescribed by law, and who shall receive such compensation as the legislature may direct.

SEC. 2. The legislature shall encourage, by all suitable means, the promotion of intellectual, scientific, moral, and agricultural improvement. The proceeds of all land that may be granted by the United States to this State for the support of schools, which may be sold or disposed of, and the five hundred thousand acres of land granted to the new States, under an act of Congress, distributing the proceeds of the public lands among the several States of the Union, approved A.D. 1841, and all the estate of deceased persons who may have died without leaving a will, or heir, and also such per cent. as may be granted by Congress on the sale of lands in this State, shall be and remain a perpetual fund, the interest of which, together with all the rents of the unsold lands, and such other means as the legislature may provide, shall be inviolably appropriated to the support of common schools throughout the State.

SEC. 3. The legislature shall provide for a system of common schools, by which a school shall be kept up and supported in each district at least three months in every year, and any district neglecting to keep up and support such a school may be deprived of its proportion of the interest of the public fund during such neglect.

SEC. 4. The legislature shall take measures for the protection, improvement, or other disposition of such lands as have been, or may hereafter be reserved or granted by the United States or any person or persons, to the State for the use of university; and the funds accruing from the rents or sale of such lands, or from any other source for the purpose aforesaid, shall be and remain a permanent fund, the interest of which shall be applied to the support of said university, with such branches as the public convenience may demand for the promotion of literature, the arts and sciences, as may be authorized by the terms of such grant. And it shall be the duty of the legislature, as soon as may be, to provide effectual means for the improvement and permanent security of the funds of said university.

THE FIRST FREE PUBLIC SCHOOL IN SAN FRANCISCO (1850)   From John

Swett, *History of the Public School System of California* (San Francisco, 1876), p. 13.

1st. *Be it ordained by the Common Council of San Francisco,* That from and after the passage of this act, it shall be the duty of J. C. Pelton, who has been employed by the Council as a public teacher, to open a school in the Baptist Chapel.

2d. Said school shall be opened from half-past eight o'clock A. M. to twelve o'clock M., and from two o'clock P. M. until five o'clock P. M., and shall continue open from Monday until Friday at five o'clock P. M.

3d. The number of scholars shall not exceed the number of one hundred; and no scholar shall be admitted under the age of four or over the age of sixteen.

4th. All persons desirous of having their children instructed in said school shall first obtain an order from the Chairman of the Committee on Education, and all children obtaining said order shall be instructed in said school free of charge.

5th. It shall be the duty of said Pelton to report to the Council on the first of each and every month the number of scholars and the progress of said school.

H. C. MURRAY.

F. TILFORD.

PLIGHT OF PUBLIC SCHOOLS IN CALIFORNIA (1857)   From State of California, *Seventh Annual Report of the Superintendent of Schools,* as quoted in John Swett, *History of the Public School System of California* (San Francisco, 1876), p. 25.

The number of schools has increased in four years, from 53 to 367—nearly sevenfold; the number of teachers, from 50 to 486—nearly ninefold; the number of children reported by census, from 11,242 to 35,722—more than threefold; whilst the semi-annual contribution by the State has dwindled from $53,511.11 to $28,342.16, or nearly one half; and the average paid each teacher, from $955 to $58.32—that is to say, to less than one sixteenth of the average under the first apportionment.

I will not waste words on such an exhibit. If it be not convincing that the support derived from the State is altogether insufficient, and ought to be augmented, no appeal of mine could enforce it.

But this I may be permitted to say, that we have no such thing as public schools, in the full acceptation of the term—that is to say, schools at which all the children of the State may be educated, *free of expense.* That $9.72 per month, to each teacher, contributed by the State, never can maintain a public school; that the contributions by parents and guardians to keep up the schools are onerous, oftentimes unequal, and must, in time, damp their ardor in the cause of education; that our 367 schools are comparatively in their infancy, and now, above all other times, should be cherished and encouraged by the State. Lacking such fostering and encouragement, it is to be feared they will languish, and gradually lose their hold upon the popular favor. Is it not worth more than an ordinary effort to avert such a calamity?

THE COMMON
SCHOOL
MOVEMENT

JOHN SWETT ON SCHOOLS IN SOUTHERN CALIFORNIA (1865) From John Swett, "Educational Matters in the Southern Counties," *California Teacher.* vol. II, pp. 269–80.

Los Angeles and Its Schools

After a delightful trip of forty-two hours we were landed in the new and thriving town of Wilmington on the bay of San Pedro, and a three hours' stage ride over twenty-four miles of level plain, carpeted by a most luxuriant growth of clover, malva, and other grasses, brought us to the old City of Los Angeles, which lay basking in the warm sunshine at the foot of a picturesque range of mountains, in all the lazy loveliness of a semitropical climate. The city is a singular compound of adobe walls, covered by shocking bad "tiles," and brick houses, and neat white cottages, all presenting an appearance quite as "mixed" as the people who live there. Of course, we visited all the vineyards in the vicinity, tasted the old wines stored in capacious cellars, ate sweet oranges from the orange groves, and fully appreciated the delicious climate of which the Angelicans so pride themselves, believing firmly with the Icelanders, that theirs is the happiest land the sun shines on.

Were not our notes limited to educational items, we would go into statistics showing gallons of wine, baskets of oranges, bushels of corn; would speak of hides and tallow, horses and cattle, and of the undeveloped agricultural resources of the country generally. The country, like some other parts of California, is rich in "great expectations;" the people are all waiting for a good time coming to "turn up." Before the cattle all died off, none of the large land owners would sell a foot of land; and now oil expectations hold the lands at fabulous prices, so that working men of small means have no chance to get a start in farming or any thing else. The curse of "Spanish grants" rests over the whole country.

We had the opportunity of visiting all the public schools, and the pleasure of addressing a large audience of citizens and parents, on common-school topics. Los Angeles has two well-built brick schoolhouses, both furnished with school desks of a very unique and antique pattern—a model of which ought to be sent to the Patent Office—admirably adjusted to twist the spines of growing girls, and break the backs and weary the legs of the sturdier boys.

The Girls' Grammar Department is a neat, orderly, well-conducted class of forty girls, taught by Miss Hoyt. In the same building, Mrs. Foster's Primary Class of both sexes, numbering sixty scholars, seemed to be making better progress than could be expected, considering desks and numbers. The Boys' Grammar School had about thirty boys in attendance, in no wise remarkable for order, discipline, or progress. The girls' school needs a piano, a set of Willson's Charts, some calisthenic apparatus, and a small school library, and ought to have them all in a city where there are so many wealthy men as in Los Angeles.

Ther is also a small school of fifteen negro children of all the shades arising from blending all the primary colors of Spanish, American, Indian, and African parentage. They are engaged in the pursuit of knowledge under difficulties, as their little room ten by fifteen feet, has neither desks, blackboard, maps, charts, nor any kind of furniture, except a line of rough board seats without backs, around the walls.

The whole number of children in the city between four and eighteen years of age is 1,095, while the average number belonging to the public schools, last year, was one hundred and fifty-six, or fourteen per cent. of the whole. There are no private schools except the Sisters, where the attendance may be seventy-five.

San Gabriel District

The San Gabriel District, eight miles from the city, near the old mission church of the same name, has a tidy little house and an excellent school, taught by an accomplished teacher. The interest of the people in their school was manifested by a full attendance on an afternoon lecture on school matters.

L. J. Rose, the County Superintendent of the Public Schools, resides in this district and rejoices in the ownership of one of the best and most delightfully situated vineyards in the State, from the grapes of which Kohler & Frohling make their best quality of port wine. The soil of this vineyard is quite different from that in the immediate vicinity of Los Angeles, as it contains, mixed with the rich loam, a large proportion of pebbles and chalky limestone. Surrounding and in front of the house of Mr. Rose are long avenues of orange and lemon trees. Besides these are planted, in abundance, English walnuts, fig, apple, peach, pear, plum, and cherry trees. A vast strawberry bed supplies its delicious fruit in wonderful profusion during four or five months in the year. A stream of pure water, sufficient to irrigate the whole farm, flows down the gentle slope on which the vineyard and orchards are situated. His salary as County Superintendent will never make Mr. Rose rich, but we know of several schoolmasters who would not object to owning the *fac simile* of that vineyard. It is quite unnecessary to add, that a man who has exhibited so much taste, skill, and industry in the management of his home affairs, discharges his official duties correctly and impartially.

Wilmington

The new town of Wilmington—Phineas Banning's City—the seat of Drum Barracks, has suddenly sprung into existence on a barren, sandy spot on the shores of San Pedro Bay, under the magical touch of Uncle Sam's contracts. The Government storehouses are extensive and well-built, as this point is made the depot of the forts and stations in Arizona and on the Colorado. The town is supplied with water, by an extensive ditch ten or twelve miles long, from the San Gabriel Creek, principally constructed by Uncle Sam's soldiers. Wilmington has a good, well-built, well-furnished, large, and convenient school-house, and a well-taught private school, which is soon to be organized as a public school. Some thirty children are now attending; and thirty or forty more, who are too poor to pay tuition, will attend when the school is made free.

Monte District

We were disappointed in our intention to visit this noted district, famous for being located on the most fertile tract of land in the county, and notorious for its lack of American citizens, and superabundance of Dixie patriots. The district is chiefly remarkable for its school quarrels, its frequent change of teachers, its refusal to employ loyal teachers, and its inability to find any "rebs" who know enough to teach school creditably.

School Statistics of Los Angeles County

Los Angeles County contains 2,304 children, between the ages of four and eighteen years, while the average number belonging to public schools is only three hundred and sixty-two, or fifteen per cent. The total number enrolled during the year on the public school registers was seven hundred and six, and the number who attended private schools was three hundred and one. The amount of State School Fund was $4,081.56; of county school tax, $5,739. The minimum tax of two dollars per child, which the new school law requires, and which Boards of Supervisors must levy, amount in this county to twenty-six cents on one hundred dollars. The last school census returned 1,079 children, between six and eighteen years of age not attending any school whatever. The total valuation of all school property in Los Angeles County is $8,836; of apparatus and libraries, nothing. It cannot be said that Los Angeles County offers to families any superior school facilities as an inducement to settle there.

San Bernardino

This beautiful and productive valley is sixty-five miles from Los Angeles. A long ride on a cold day, through a level country, half pasturage and half desert, brought us late in the evening into the scattered village which, unlike most little California groups of houses, never has aspired to be called a city. The mountain setting of this gem of valleys is remarkably beautiful. It was early settled by the Mormons, who divided it into small farms of twenty or thirty acres each, with the water flowing in ditches around each. Its facilities for irrigation are great, and the vast quantities of corn shipped through Los Angeles to San Francisco give the best evidence of its productiveness. Many of the Mormons sold out at the time Brigham summoned the faithful home to Salt Lake; but some remained, and others have since returned, and their number is now quite numerous. They have recently experienced a revival under the organization of the New School Mormons, have erected a fine new church, and hold enthusiastic meetings in which many of the unlearned are endowed with the miraculous gift of tongues. Disavowing polygamy seems to be popular, especially in a community where men are too poor to support one wife well and to send even a small family to school. The Town of San Bernardino proper has two schools, attended by about seventy-five scholars. The school houses are not elegant, but tolerably comfortable; the desks are the roughest, meanest, rickety, broken-down looking substitutes for seats which ever disgraced a school-room, or a community pretending to be civilized. When we went to school there used to be a punishment in vogue called "sitting on nothin' "; it was preferable to San Bernardino desks. Two male teachers are employed and paid twenty-five dollars per month each out of the public funds; they probably collect about fifteen dollars a month by rate bills, and so receive a salary of forty dollars per month, or four hundred dollars a year, out of which they must board and clothe themselves.

This county has nine schools, and numbers 1,085 children of which the average number belonging to school is three hundred and two, or twenty-eight per cent. The number of children who attend private schools is only sixty-one. The whole number on the public school register is four hundred and fifteen. Last year the amount raised by county school tax was fifty-one cents per child. The law requires a minimum school tax amounting to two dollars per child, and to raise this the Supervisors this year should fix the rate at thirty cents on each one hundred dollars.

When this tax is levied and collected, it is to be hoped the Trustees will break up their old school furniture for kindlings, and order some desks, maps, black-boards, and charts for their school-rooms. The total valuation of all school property in this county is $2,180. Our stay here was necessarily so short, that we had no opportunity to lecture, or to visit the districts outside of the town.

The Route from Los Angeles to Santa Barbara—"Ile"

We took the Overland stage at Los Angeles for Santa Barbara, at four o'clock on a cold morning, and rolled away in a covered mud wagon, through the coast plain and over the hills, rapidly reducing the distance of one hundred and twenty-five miles. Four of us shivering passengers would have fared badly that day, but for the forethought of an elderly gentleman—wiser than we foolish ones—who had laid in a bountiful store of bread and beef, which he generously divided all round. No very regular provision for meals seems to be made on this line, unless the traveler can eat hay, oats, or barley, at the horse stations. At the old Mission of San Buenaventura we struck "ile," in the shape of a very Brown petroleum prospector and politician. A few miles back of this Mission, which is on the coast, are located the famous oil springs about which Professor Silliman made such glowing reports, and on which New York capitalists and speculators are building such fairy "castles in Spain." We felt strongly inclined, after hearing of all the wonders, to "lie over" one stage and locate a spring; but a sense of official duty vetoed the tempting consideration.

From San Buenaventura to Santa Barbara, the road in many places winds along on the ocean beach, and in some places is a little dangerous at high tide. We escaped the fate of Pharaoh's host, and rattled safely over a natural pavement of large rounded boulders, rather too rough for comfortable transit. In the evening we struck a "clam station," and secured several hasty plates of soup; after which we comfortably jogged along in the moonlight to Santa Barbara.

Santa Barbara

This is a fossil old town covered with "tiles," looking like some old centenarian under a shocking bad hat. The climate of Santa Barbara is delicious. Sheltered on the north and west by a high range of mountains, gently fanned by the mild ocean breezes, suffering neither extremes of heat or cold, it basks in almost perpetual warmth and sunshine. The Mission Church, a well-preserved edifice of brick and stone, has some pretensions to architectural ornament; and stands on the elevated site a mile back from the town, commanding a fine view of mountain, plain, and ocean. We rambled round the old building, its faded gardens and ruined reservoirs, at early sunrise; and again, late at night, strolled up from the town in the shadow of its whitened walls, ghostly and weird in the white moonlight. The long-treasured solemn cadences of the ocean-swell breaking on the sandy beach and the bold headland off the town, came drifting and pulsating on the air, as we sat by the side of an old crumbling sand-stone lion, or some other nondescript animal, adorning the old fountain which once ornamented the church-grounds, now dry as the ruins of Palmyra, and dreamily mused on the vanished glory of a race which had no faith in public schools. As the old bells, struck by a ghost in black, like one of Poe's "ghoals," who—

"Tolling, tolling, tolling,
In that muffled monotone,
Feel a glory in so rolling
On the human heart a stone."

As the old bell marked the "noon of night," we sauntered down to the hotel and dreamed that the old church was lighted up with coal-oil gas, and that the lion with faded face was pouring forth a rich stream of purest petroleum; that we owned an immense oil spring, and had constructed an aqueduct out of the old mission tiles, which conveyed the "ile" down to the coast into the capacious holds of a hundred clipper ships waiting in the open roadstead for a New York cargo.

The Schools of the Place

Santa Barbara Town has two public schools, one for boys and another for girls. The boys', numbering, say forty scholars, held in a comfortable brick school-house, is attended mostly by children whose mother tongue is Spanish, and who are not remarkable either for order or scholarship. The girls' school is held in a little, low, mean, unventilated adobe room, fifteen by twenty feet, which is rented at the rate of five dollars per month. Into this are crowded fifty or sixty girls. It is a libel on the town, and a disgrace to the trustees, that a school should be kept in such a place, when several large buildings could be rented at nominal rates and fitted up at little expense. Santa Barbara can boast of perhaps the very finest climate in California, and of the unexcelled thriftlessness and indolence of its native population; but not of the efficiency of its public schools.

The State Superintendent made an appointment to lecture, but as the steamer from San Francisco arrived at just a half-past seven, nobody was at the Court-house but the school ma'am and three little girls, and the meeting was adjourned *sine die*.

Montecito District

We visited this district, four miles from Santa Barbara, and found a pretty little brick school-house, neatly furnished, and in it a competent female teacher, and a quiet, orderly, and industrial school. This school has a small library, the only one, we believe, for the distance of six hundred miles south of San Francisco. This district is indebted for its neat house, maps, charts, globe, and books mainly to the efforts of one of the trustees, R. S. Williams, an "old bach," with neither chick nor child of his own to be educated. He lives a hermit life, in a pleasant little home on the seacoast—a most charming residence for some pretty school ma'am; and we hope some one, tired of teaching, may take possession of the homestead, in spite of its present occupant.

✳   ✳   ✳

School Statistics of Santa Barbara County

We were unable to visit the school of San Buenaventura; but, from the fact that the American residents there have established a private school and refuse to send their children to the public school, where the "native" children attend, we are led to suppose that its management is not the best in the world.

Santa Barbara County numbers 1,370 children, between four and eighteen years of age, of whom, last year, sixteen were returned by census as attending private schools and one hundred and seventy-one the public schools. The whole number enrolled on the school registers was one hundred and ninety-seven, and the average number belonging less than one hundred. Thus it will be seen that the average attendance of the children of the county, at both public and private schools, is only eight per cent. of the whole number. The State apportionment to the three schools of this county, last year, was $1,412; the amount raised by county tax only six hundred and sixty-three dollars. The rate of county tax levied was ten cents on one hundred dollars, equal to forty-eight cents per child—the smallest amount raised by any county in the State. The rate required by law, this year, is thirty cents on each one hundred dollars, and even this will not raise the required two dollars per child. Whether the Supervisors and Auditor will perform their duty this year, now that their attention has been called to the law, remains to be seen.

On the Road—the Gaviota Pass

At nine o'clock, on a bright, cold moonlight night we, the oil merchant, a mining agent from Arizona, and the District Judge, started in an open stage wagon for San Luis Obispo, a distance of one hundred and twenty miles. The route is one of the hardest roads known to the tribe of Jehus. We shivered all night long, counted the stars, admired the moon, stumbled on foot through the rough Gaviota Pass, but could not close our eyes for a wink of sleep, as a doze involved a tolerable certainty of being tumbled off unceremoniously in some of the sharp plunges of the rickety old wagon, which pitched about like a lumber drogher in a cross sea. At San Luis the man of oil stopped over one stage, to prospect for "indications," and we remain to hunt for schools.

San Luis Obispo

Not much can be said in commendation of the school in the dilapidated town of San Luis Obispo. The school is held in a little office, fifteen by twenty feet, in which are crowded from twenty to fifty children, as the irregular attendance may be. This model school-house contains one double-sided desk twelve feet long, with two long benches without backs. A part of the children sit on a dozen empty claret boxes turned up edgewise. This house has been rented for two or three years past, a part of the time at twenty dollars per month, and now at fifteen dollars per month—rates of rent which would be high on a business street in San Francisco. A better house could be built for two hundred and fifty dollars. Somebody evidently makes a good thing out of that house. During the past eight months it has cost the trustees twelve to seventy-five dollars for "books and stationery" supplied to the school. Either the prices of books and stationery are high, or the school consumption enormous.

School Statistics of This County

This county contains eight hundred and ninety-six children, between the ages of four and eighteen years, of whom fifty-nine, or six per cent. is the average number belonging to the public schools. The number attending private schools is twenty. The State apportionment of this county was $1,259; the amount raised by county tax, five hundred and eight dollars, or fifty-six cents per child. The Supervisors have levied this year a school tax of ten cents; it will be the duty of the Auditor to increase it to thirty cents. We trust he will comply with the first letter of the law. The total valuation of school-houses, furniture, and apparatus, including "closet boxes," used as seats, was returned last year, at two hundred dollars—a high estimate, when we consider that the only school-house owned by the county, is one at San Simeon which, we believe, is a log one.

On the Road Again—the Sulphur Springs

We started from San Luis at four o'clock in the morning, in a covered wagon, which was an agreeable change. Some thirty miles out, we reached the "Hot Sulphur Springs," on Blackburn's ranch, famous for their wonderful curative powers in cases of rheumatism, disease of the skin, and scrofulous affections. A physician from San Jose bought these springs a few years ago, built good bath-houses and a hotel—sank in the strongest kind of sulphur water some $10,000, and then surrendered the whole concern to the original owners in virtue of a mortgage. They certainly are not Pactolion springs, nor even petroleum. The present proprietor, Mr. Blackburn, is a good-hearted, jovial body, whose distinguishing trait is an intense hatred of "abolitionists" and "miscegenationists." The water of his springs is bad for Black Republicans, and the dark, colored races generally, so he says.

Down the Salinas—Old Missions on the Way

On the route we passed the ruined walls of the old Mission of Santa Margarita, and, further on, the better preserved Mission of San Miguel. A long and cold night was passed in alternate naps and walks over the rough breaks in the road. At midnight we sipped ambrosian nectar in the shape of a cup of coffee at a driver's station, and in the morning, after walking a mile up the "divide," found ourselves looking down on the town of San Juan.

Monterey County

There is a public school at San Juan, but we had no time to visit it.

Monterey County has 1,588 children between four and eighteen of which the average number belonging to ten public schools is three hundred and thirty-five. The whole number attending private schools is eighty-nine. The state apportionment last year was $2,700, and $3,524 was raised by county tax.

At San Juan we changed to a good Concord stage coach for a ride of forty miles to San José.

San José

After a ten-mile ride, we reached the Valley of San José, and then the road lay through thirty miles continuous grain fields—a most agreeable change from the rolling hills and untilled plains of the stock-raising counties. Every foot of this fertile valley seems to be sowed down to wheat and barley.

In San José a good audience assembled in the City Hall to listen to an address on public schools. The schools here are taught by competent and experienced teachers; but they labor under the great disadvantage of poor school-houses. It is not creditable to San José that she has remained so long in prosperity and wealth without a public school-house worthy of the name. The city is abundantly able to build a $25,000 house, large enough to accommodate five hundred children, and afford rooms for a High School and Grammar School. The salaries of the two male teachers in this place are so very low that out of regard to the good name of the city we forbear to mention the rates.

Santa Clara

The town has some good schools, taught by excellent teachers, but is in the same situation respecting school-houses as its neighbor, San José.

Here is located the Santa Clara College, S. J., the grounds, buildings, furniture, and apparatus of which are worth at least $300,000 or $400,000. Here is the University of the Pacific, which own a good brick house. Here is also the Methodist Female Seminary, which also own a large and convenient house. Both the public school-houses in the place are worth, at a high valuation, $2,000. The Principal of the Grammar School is a little more than half paid for his untiring labors.

School Statistics of Santa Clara County

Santa Clara County numbers 4,370 children, between the ages of four and eighteen out of which the average number belonging to the public schools is 1,348, while the whole number enrolled during the year was 2,163. The whole number reported in the last school census as attending private schools was 602. The number of school districts is forty, and the total valuation of lots, school-houses, and furniture is $19,483. The assessment roll of this county sums up $6,883,684, yet the amount per child raised by county tax for the school year ending thirty-first of August, 1863, was only one dollar and thirty-one cents. Notwithstanding the great wealth of this county in proportion to its population, few counties in the State can present so economical expenditure for public schools. This county has a superior corps of male teachers. They have a Teachers' Association, which meets in San José once a month. The association has a good teachers' library, and, to the credit of the Supervisors, it ought to be stated that they have, with commendable liberality, allowed the County Superintendent to draw the full amount allowed by law, one hundred and fifty dollars per year, for the benefit of the Teachers' Institute and Library.

Department of Public Instruction. Rules and Regulations of the Public Schools of California. Adopted by the State Board of Education, June 8, 1866, in accordance with Section 2, of the Revised School Law, and required to be enforced in all Public Schools, according to Section 42, Subdivision 2, and Section 64, of the Revised School Law.

Section 1. Teachers are required to be present at their respective school rooms, and to open them for the admission of pupils, at fifteen minutes before the time prescribed for commencing school, and to punctually observe the hours for opening and closing school.

Section 2. Unless otherwise provided by special action of Trustees or Boards of Education, the daily school session shall commence at nine o'clock A.M., and close at four o'clock, P.M., with an intermission at noon of one hour, from twelve, M., to one o'clock, P.M. There shall be allowed a recess of twenty minutes in the forenoon session, from ten-forty to eleven o'clock; and a recess of twenty-minutes in the afternoon session, from two-forty to three o'clock. When boys and girls are allowed separate recesses, fifteen minutes shall be allowed for each recess.

Section 3. In graded Primary Schools, in which the average age of the pupils is under eight years, the daily sessions shall not exceed four hours a day, exclusive of the intermission at noon, and inclusive of the recesses. If such schools are opened at nine o'clock, A.M., they shall be closed at two o'clock P.M. In ungraded schools, all children under eight years of age shall be either dismissed after a four-hour session, or allowed recesses, for play, of such length that the actual confinement in the school room shall not exceed three hours and a half.

Section 4. No pupil shall be detained in school during the intermission at noon, and a pupil, detained at any recess, shall be permitted to go out immediately thereafter. All pupils, except those detained for punishment, shall be required to pass out of the school rooms at recess, unless it would occasion an exposure of health.

Section 5. Principals shall be held responsible for the general management and discipline of the schools; and the other teachers shall follow their directions and cooperate with them, not only during the school hours, but during the time when the pupils are on the school premises, before and after school, and during recesses. Assistants shall be held responsible for the order and discipline of their own rooms under the general direction of the Principals.

Section 6. Teachers are particularly enjoined to devote their time faithfully to a vigilant and watchful care over the conduct and habits of the pupils, during the time of relaxation and play, before and after school, and during the recesses, both in the school building and on the Play Grounds.

Section 7. It is expected that teachers will exercise a general inspection over the conduct of the scholars going to, and returning from, school. They shall exert their influence to prevent all quarreling and disagreement, all rude and noisy behavior in the streets, and vulgar and profane language, all improper games, and all disrespect to citizens and strangers.

Section 8. Teachers shall prescribe such rules for the use of the yards, basements, and outbuildings connected with the school houses, as shall insure their being kept in a neat and proper condition, and shall examine them as often as may be necessary for such purpose. Teachers shall be held responsible for any want of neatness or cleanliness about their school premises.

Section 9. Teachers shall give vigilant attention to the ventilation and temperature of their school rooms. At each recess, the windows and doors shall be opened for the purpose of changing the atmosphere of the room. Teachers are cautioned against hot fires, and a high temperature.

Section 10. Teachers shall enter in the school register, in the order of their application, the names of all those applying for admission to the school, after the prescribed number of pupils has been received. Such applicants shall be admitted to seats whenever a vacancy occurs in any class for which they have been duly qualified, in order of their registration.

Section 11. Teachers are authorized to require excuses from the parents or guardians of pupils, either in person or by written note, in all cases of absence or tardiness, or of dismissal before the close of school.

Section 12. No pupil shall be allowed to retain connection with any Public School, unless furnished with books, slate, and other utensils required to be used in the class to which he belongs; *provided,* that no pupil shall be excluded for such cause unless the parent or guardian shall have been furnished by the teacher with a list of books or articles needed, and one week shall have elapsed after such notice, without the pupil's obtaining said books. Books may be furnished to indigent children by the Trustees, at the expense of the district, whenever the teacher shall have certified in writing that the pupil applying is unable to purchase such books.

Section 13. Any pupil who shall in any way cut or otherwise injure any school house, or injure any fences, trees, or outbuildings belonging to any of the school estates, or shall write any profane or obscene language, or make any obscene pictures or characters on any school premises, shall be liable to suspension, expulsion, or other punishment, according to the nature of the offense. The teacher may suspend a pupil temporarily for such offense, and shall notify the Trustees of such action. Pupils shall not be allowed to remain in any of the rooms that are provided with improved styles of furniture, except in the presence of a teacher, or of a monitor who is made specially responsible for the care of the seats and desks. All damages done to school property by any of the pupils shall be repaired at the expense of the party committing the trespass.

Section 14. All pupils who go to school without proper attention having been given to personal cleanliness, or neatness of dress, shall be sent home to be properly prepared for school, or shall be required to prepare themselves for the school room before entering. Every school room shall be provided with a wash basin, soap, and towels.

Section 15. No pupils, affected with any contagious disease, shall be allowed to remain in any of the Public Schools.

Section 16. The books used, and the studies pursued, shall be such, and such only, as may be authorized by the State Board of Education; and no teacher shall require or advise any of the pupils to purchase for use in the schools any book not contained in the list of books directed and authorized to be used in the schools.

Section 17. It shall be the duty of the teachers of the schools to read to the pupils, from time to time, so much of the school regulations as apply to them, that they may have a clear understanding of the rules by which they are governed.

Section 18. In all Primary Schools, exercises in free gymnastics, and vocal and breathing exercises shall be given at least twice a day, and for a time not less than five minutes for each exercise.

Section 19. The following supplies shall be provided by the District Clerk, under the provisions of Section 46, of the Revised School Law, on the written requisition of the teacher, viz.: clocks, brooms, dusting brushes, wash basins, water buckets, tin cups, dust pans, matches, ink, ink bottles, pens, penholders, slate pencils, crayon, chalk, hand bells, coal buckets or wood boxes, shovels, pokers, soap, towels, thermometers, door mats, scrapers and stationery.

Section 20. Trustees are authorized and recommended to employ a suitable person to sweep and take care of the school house, and to make suitable provisions for supplying the school with water.

Rules for Pupils

1. Every pupil is expected to attend school punctually and regularly; to conform to the regulations of the school, and to obey promptly all the directions of the teacher; to observe good order and propriety of deportment; to be diligent in study, respectful to teachers, and kind and obliging to schoolmates; to refrain entirely from the use of profane and vulgar language, and to be clean and neat in person and clothing.

2. Pupils are required in all cases of absence, to bring, on their return to school, an excuse in writing, from their parents or guardians, assigning good and sufficient reasons for such absence.

3. All pupils who have fallen behind their grade, by absence or irregularity of attendance, by indolence or inattention, shall be placed in the grade below, at the discretion of the teacher.

4. No pupil shall be permitted to leave school at recess, or at any other time before the regular hour for closing school, except in case of sickness, or on written request of parent or guardian.

5. Any scholar who shall be absent one week without giving notice to the teacher, shall lose all claim to his particular desk for the remainder of the term, and shall not be considered a member of the school.

6. Each scholar shall have a particular desk, and shall keep the same and the floor beneath in a neat and orderly condition.

Instructions to Teachers

1. Teachers will endeavor to make themselves acquainted with parents and guardians, in order to secure their aid and cooperation, and to better understand the temperaments, characteristics and wants of the children.

2. Teachers shall daily examine the lessons of their various classes, and make such special preparation upon them, if necessary, as not to be constantly confined to the text book, and instruct all their pupils, without partiality, in those branches of school studies which their various classes may be pursuing. In all their intercourse with their scholars, they are required to strive to impress on their minds, both by precepts and example, the great importance of continued efforts for improvement in morals, and manners, and deportment, as well as in useful learning.

3. Teachers should explain each new lesson assigned, if necessary, by familiar remarks and illustrations, that every pupil may know, before he is sent to his seat, what he is expected to do at the next recitation, and how it is to be done.

4. Teachers should only use the text book for occasional reference, and should not permit it to be taken to the recitation to be referred to by the pupils, except in

case of such exercises as absolutely require it. They should assign many questions of their own preparing, involving an application of what the pupils have learned to the business of life.

5. Teachers should endeavor to arouse and fix the attention of the whole class, and to occupy and bring into action as many of the faculties of their pupils as possible. They should never proceed with the recitation without the attention of the whole class, nor go round the class with recitation, always in the same order, or in regular rotation.

6. Teachers should at all times exhibit proper animation themselves, manifesting a lively interest in the subject taught, avoid all heavy plodding movements, all formal routine in teaching, lest the pupil be dull and drowsy, and imbibe the notion that he studies only to recite.

CALIFORNIA SECURES A MODERN PUBLIC SCHOOL SYSTEM

(**1867**) From California, *Second Biennial Report of the Superintendent of Schools*, as quoted in John Swett, *History of the Public School System of California* (San Francisco, 1867), pp. 47–49, 51–52.

The school year ending June 30, 1867, marks the transition period of California from rate-bill common schools to an American free school system.

For the first time in the history of the State, every public school was made entirely free for every child to enter.

In the smaller districts, having less than 100 children and less than $200,000 taxable property, *free* schools were maintained three months; in the larger districts, having more than 100 children and $200,000 taxable property, *free* schools were kept open *five months*.

More than 21,000 pupils attended *free* schools during the entire school year of ten months.

District 6 school, Windsor, Conn., c. 1848.

Public School No. 17, Thirteenth St., New York, N.Y., c. 1848.

Free Schools at Last

I am glad that in this, my last official report, I can say that a system of *free schools,* supported by taxation, is an accomplished fact.

When I assumed the duties of this office, five years ago, I saw clearly that it was useless to expect to improve the character of the public schools to any considerable extent without a largely increased school revenue, derived from direct taxation on property.

At the session of the Legislature in 1863, I secured a revision of the School Law, and a State school tax of five cents on the hundred dollars, which gave an additional revenue to the State Fund of $75,000 a year. A bill was also passed providing for the gradual funding of the indebtedness of the State to the School Department, then amounting to $600,000. At the next session, in 1864, an additional school revenue was secured by providing that the minimum county school tax should be equal to $2 per census child. This little clause gave an additional county school revenue of $75,000.

In 1866, by the passage of the "Revised School Law," the State school tax was raised to eight cents on the hundred dollars, and the minimum county tax was raised equal to $3 per census child, both provisions together increasing the school revenue by at least $125,000 a year. I need not say that to secure an additional school revenue of $300,000 per annum, in the face of the high county, State, and National taxation, during a period of civil war, was no holiday task.

During each successive session of the Legislature I became a persistent member of the "Third House," arguing, soliciting, meeting committees, and patiently waiting, with a determination to secure for every child in California a right guaranteed by law to an education in a system of free schools based upon the proposition that the *property* of the State ought to be taxed to educate the *children* of the State.

I saw clearly at the outset that even after the revenue was provided, the schools would be to some extent a failure, unless protected from incompetent teachers by a thorough system of State examinations and certificates, for the schools cannot rise higher than the teachers.

Professional Teachers

The second leading object of my administration has been to secure a *corps* of professional teachers, and to elevate the occupation of teaching. How far this has been accomplished, the list of professional teachers, and the graduates of the Normal School, found in this report, will show.

One third of the teachers in the State hold State diplomas and certificates, and one twelfth of the teachers are graduates of the California State Normal School.

A State Board of Education, of Examination, of Normal School Trustees; a uniform series of text-books, a course of study, rules and regulations, an educational journal—all constitute a *system* of education, in place of the irregular and unsystematized half public and half rate-bill schools of five years ago.

* * *

Average Length of Schools

The average length of time during which public schools are maintained during the year is 7.2 months. Last year, for the first time in the history of the State, *all* the schools were kept *free* to all pupils for a period of from 3 to 5 months, according to the number of children and the taxable property in the district.

It marks an epoch in the school history of the State. Had rate bills been levied as before, during the entire year, the average length of the term of tuition in the schools would doubtless have been increased.

* * *

Co-Education of the Sexes

I believe that the presence of boys and girls in the same school, far from being injurious to either sex, exerts a mutually beneficial influence. My belief is based on many years' experience in public school teaching, on an extended observation of schools, and on the opinion of the most enlightened and progressive educators.

Conclusion

Since 1863, our public schools have been quietly and peacefully revolutionized. In the grand events of national history, in the building of cities, the construction of roads, the settlement of land titles, and the excitement of life incident to a new State, the progress of schools is hardly noticed except by those who are most directly interested in them. *Then*, we had little to be proud of in our educational record; *now* California will not suffer by comparison with the most progressive educational States in the Union.

Then the annual amount of money raised for public schools was $480,000; now it is $1,287,000, or nearly three times as much.

Then, there was no direct State tax for the support of schools; now, the State tax is 8 cents on the $100, giving an annual revenue from this source alone of $120,000.

Then, the State apportionment was $130,000; *now*, it is $260,000.

Then, the amount raised by county and city school taxes was $291,000; *now*, it is nearly $600,000.

Then, the amount raised by district taxes, voted by the people, was $7000; last year the amount was $73,000, or more than ten times the amount raised in 1862.

Then, the maximum county school tax allowed by law was 25 cents, and the minimum required to be levied, *nothing at all; now*, the maximum tax is 35 cents, and the minimum tax must be equal to $3 per census child, which in many counties requires the maximum rate of 35 cents.

Then, the amount raised by rate bills of tuition was $130,000; now, it is only $79,000, showing a rapid approximation to a free school system. Three-fourths of the pupils now attend free schools during the year, and all are secured by law the right of a free school, either for three months or five months, in proportion to the size of district.

Then, the total expenditure for schools amounted to a percentage on the assessment-roll of the State, of 30 cents on each $100; *now*, it amounts to 58.1 cents on the $100.

In 1862 the amount expended per census child was $6.15; last year it was $12.61.

In 1862 the amount expended for schoolhouses was $49,000; in 1865 it was $257,000.

Then, the average length of the schools was less than six months in the year; *now*, it is seven and four-tenths months—an average length of schools which is exceeded only by Massachusetts and Nevada, of all the States in the Union.

Since then, while the number of census children has increased twenty-six per cent, the average number attending the public schools has increased more than fifty per cent.

The stronger hold which the schools have taken on public opinion, the greater skill, earnestness and enthusiasm of teachers, the consequent improvement in methods of instruction and classification, the use of better text-books, the deeper personal interest of parents, the neater and more commodious houses—all these together constitute an advancement which cannot be expressed by a contrast of statistics.

Then, we had no system of professional examinations, no educational society, no organization, and little professional pride; in fact, a man generally apologized for being forced to resort to teaching until he could find something else to do.

Examination of Teachers

Then, the "old schoolmasters" of San Francisco were examined every year by doctors, lawyers, dentists, contractors and business men, to "see if they were fit to teach the common school" they had been teaching years in succession. There was no standard of qualification, except the caprice of "accidental boards." Throughout the State, examinations were oral, and in most cases resulted in issuing to everybody who applied a certificate "to teach school one year;" *now,* a new order of things prevails. Every Board of Examination, whether State, city or county, must be composed of professional teachers exclusively; all examinations must be in writing, and in certain specified studies; and certificates are issued for life, or for a length of time proportioned to the grade of certificate issued.

California is the only State in the Union in which teachers have gained the legal right to be examined exclusively by the members of their own profession, and we have just cause to be proud of the fact. It has already done much to make the occupation of teaching respectable. It has relieved good teachers from useless annoyance and humiliation; it has increased their self-respect, stimulated their ambition, and guarded the schools against quacks and pretenders.

Our School Law is the only one in the United States which has taken broad, professional ground, by providing that the diplomas of State Normal Schools in other States shall entitle the holders to legal recognition as teachers in this State.

Strange to say, this new system of professional examinations was violently opposed four years ago, and by none so vehemently as by some common school teachers.

The world moves. Is there a single teacher here who would desire to have the old order of things re-established? But I never doubted that, once established, it would remain a part of our school system as long as schools were maintained.

It was my sanguine hope, for many years, that in this new State teaching might aspire to the dignity of a profession; that teachers might learn to combine their strength, respect themselves, command the respect of others, and honor their occupation. I have lived already to see the promise of the future. It has been and is my highest ambition to elevate the profession of teaching; for I well know that in no other way can the public schools be made the great educators of the State and the nation. If the citizens of this State desire to have good schools, they must pay professionally trained teachers high salaries.

It is only by raising the standard of attainments that the occupation can become well paid and well respected. Set the standard high, and high wages will follow; set the standard high, and good schools will be the result; set the standard high, and teachers will be content to remain in the schools.

Let all teachers who act on County, City or State Boards of Examination, discharge their duty faithfully, without reference to the pressure of friends, or the complaints of unsuccessful applicants, ever bearing in mind the duty they owe to the schools, the people, and the profession of teaching.

Professionally trained teachers, well paid for their work, will bring the schools up to their fullest measure of usefulness, and will secure from the people the most liberal support.

The East

A PETITION FROM THE MECHANICS AND MANUFACTURERS
ASSOCIATION OF PROVIDENCE FOR FREE SCHOOLS FOR RHODE
ISLAND (1799)   From Charles Carroll, *Public Education in Rhode Island* (Providence,
1918), pp. 77–78.

$\mathbf{A}$ PETITION FOR FREE SCHOOLS. To the Honorable General Assembly of
the State of Rhode Island and Providence Plantations . . .

The Memorial and Petition of the Providence Association of Mechanics and
Manufacturers respectfully presents—

That the means of education which are enjoyed in this state are very inadequate
to a purpose so highly important.

That numbers of the rising generation whom nature has liberally endowed, are
suffered to grow up in ignorance, when a common education would qualify them to
act their parts in life with advantage to the public and reputation to themselves.

That in consequence of there being no legal provision for the establishment of
school, and for want of public attention and encouragement, this so essential part of
our social duty is left to the partial patronage of individuals, whose cares do not
extend beyond the limits of their own families, while numbers in every part of the
state are deprived of a privilege which is the common right of every child to enjoy.

That when to that respect which as individuals we feel ourselves bound to
render to the representatives of the people we add our public declaration of
gratitude for the privilege we enjoy as a corporate body, we at the same time solicit
this Honorable Assembly to make legal provision for the establishment of free
schools sufficient to educate all the children in the several towns throughout the
state; with great confidence we bring this, our earnest solicitation before this
Honorable Assembly, from the interest we feel in the public welfare and from the
consideration that our society is composed of members not originally of any
particular town, but assembled mostly in our early years from almost every town in
the state.

That we feel as individuals the want of that education which we now ask to be
bestowed on those who are to succeed us in life, and which is so essential in
directing its common concerns. That we feel a still greater degree of confidence
from the consideration that while we pray this Honorable Assembly to establish free
schools, we are at the same time advocating the cause of the great majority of
children throughout the state, and in particular of those who are poor and
destitute—the son of the widow and the child of distress.

Trusting that our occupations as mechanics and manufacturers ought not to

THE COMMON
SCHOOL
MOVEMENT

1051

prevent·us from adding to these reasons an argument which cannot fail to operate on those to whom is committed the guardianship of the public welfare, and that is, liberty and security under a republican form of government depend on a general diffusion of knowledge among the people.

In confiding this petition and the reasons which have dictated it to the wisdom of the Legislature, we assure ourselves that their decision will be such as will reflect on this Honorable General Assembly the praise and the gratitude, not only of the youth of the present generation, but of thousands the date of whose existence has not commenced.

Respectfully submitted by John Howland, Joel Metcalf, William Richmond, Peter Grinnell, Richard Anthony, Grindall Reynolds, Samuel Thurber, Jr., and Nathan Foster, committee.

QUESTIONS FROM THE WORKINGMEN OF PHILADELPHIA TO A CANDIDATE FOR THE STATE LEGISLATURE REGARDING HIS VIEWS ON EDUCATION (1829)

From *New York Free Enquirer,* October 7, 1829, as quoted in John R. Commons et al., eds., *A Documentary History of American Industrial Society* (Cleveland, 1910–11), vol. V, pp. 93–94.

Sir: The Delegates of the Working Men for the city, having placed your name in the list of fourteen, (from which seven will be chosen) as a candidate for the State Legislature; they are desirous (through the medium of the undersigned committee) to obtain your views in relation to the following subjects:

First. An equal and general system of Education.

Second. The banking system, and all other exclusive monopolies, considered with regard to the good or ill effects produced upon the productive classes by their operations.

Third. Lotteries, whether a total abolishment of them is not essential to the moral as well as pecuniary interest of society. Upon the important subject of Education we wish most distinctly to understand whether you do, or do not consider it essential to the welfare of the rising generation, "That an open school and competent teachers for every child in the state, from the lowest branch of an infant school to the lecture rooms of practical science, should be established, and those who superintend them to be chosen by the people."

Our object in soliciting your views, sir, upon these several important points, is to enable us in the discharge of our duty, as delegates, to select such men for the Legislature, as are willing as well as competent, to legislate upon subjects which the Working Men of the city consider of the greatest importance, not only to themselves but the community at large. If your views should be in accordance with the interests of those we have the honor to represent, we request you to allow us to place your name on our Ticket. We are very respectfully, Sir, your obedient servants, JOHN THOMASON, THOMAS TAYLOR, WILLIAM ENGLISH, JOHN ASHTON, JR., BENJ. MIFFLIN, *Committee.*

N.B. An immediate answer is particularly requested.

ORGANIZATION BY WORKINGMEN OF AN ASSOCIATION FOR THE PROTECTION OF INDUSTRY AND FOR THE PROMOTION OF NATIONAL EDUCATION (1829) From *Working Man's Advocate*, October 31, 1829.

Reasons for the formation of the Association

Because industry is at present unprotected, oppressed, despised, and indirectly deprived of its just reward; and because there is in this republic no system of education befitting a republic; none which secures the equal maintenance, protection, and instruction of youth—of the children of the poor man as of the rich; none which is at once free from sectarian and clerical influences, and from aristocratical distinctions; none which is calculated to induce in the rising generation those habits of industry, those principles of sound morality, those feelings of brotherly love, together with those solid intellectual acquirements, which are necessary to secure to all the fair exercise of those equal political rights set forth in the institutions of the land.

Means by which the Association may attain the object

By procuring and publishing information as to the actual condition of the working class, and the actual remuneration for industry. By investigating the causes which depress industry and produce crime and suffering; and the measures which protect and favor industry, and which check oppression and vice.

By procuring information as to the state of public schools, as to the influence which rules them, and as to the value of the instruction they impart. By considering the practical means which are in the hands of the people to establish, through their representatives, a *state system of education.*

By printing and circulating tracts, calculated to give information to the people on these important subjects.

By corresponding regularly with similar societies in other towns and cities.

By promoting the gradual extension of the Association through all the states of the Union.

And, generally, by watching over the great interests of the people—a most necessary and most neglected duty; and by noting and proclaiming the influence, and opposing the success, of every measure that tends to injure or oppress them.

Character of the Association

It shall be such as to exclude no honest man. All who sign their names as members, shall be considered as having thereby expressed "THEIR INTENTION TO ASSIST IN DEFENDING THE RIGHTS AND PROMOTING THE INTERESTS OF THE PEOPLE, AND IN CARRYING THROUGH THE STATE LEGISLATURES A SYSTEM OF EQUAL REPUBLICAN EDUCATION."

Although such an Association may expect to find the true friends of equal justice and popular instruction chiefly among the industrious classes, and may therefore reasonably be distrustful of others, it will not prejudge nor exclude any man, be his class what it may.

It will not meddle with speculative opinions; neither with religion, nor with irreligion. These are matters between each man and his own conscience. He who has faith, let him have it to himself; he who is religious, let him be religious in his closet when the door is shut, but not in public—not in an Association whose object is to discuss and reform temporal concerns. Plans for this world, and hopes of another, are two distinct things, that had better be kept separate; for men may agree about the one, while they will probably quarrel about the other.

State religion and monied ascendancy have done much harm to the people in every age and in every nation. It behoves an Association, therefore, which has in view the benefit of the people, to watch the political movements of the clergy and the rich. If the clergy, forgetting that they profess to be the servants of one whose kingdom is not of this world, intermeddle with temporal matters, a popular Association ought to thwart all such mischievous and unrepublican intermeddling. If the rich, presuming on their riches, attempt to carry measures *for* themselves and *against* the laboring classes, a popular Association ought to thwart all such mischievous and unrepublican attempts. But, though it be hard for a rich man, or for a clergyman, honestly to espouse the cause of the people against monied and clerical oppression, the Association will exclude neither. Let both join it, if they see fit. Let both speak, if they will. If they speak well and advise aright, the people will be the gainers. If otherwise, the people are neither blind nor asleep; their eyes are open and their tongues are free: they can judge what is said, and they can reply to it.

The character of the Association, then, is *not exclusive and not sectarian*. It is NATIONAL.

THE WORKING MAN'S PARTY OF PHILADELPHIA CALLS FOR FREE, EQUAL EDUCATION FOR ALL (1831) From Stephen Simpson, *The Working Man's Manual, ...* (Philadelphia, 1831), pp. 119–21, 126.

Nothing is so essentially connected with the wealth of nations, and the happiness of the people, as the proper cultivation, expansion, and discipline of the popular mind. Upon this depends not only the amount of public virtue and happiness—but the aggregate of industry, ingenuity, temperance, economy, and vigour.

When we look back to the small states of GREECE, so diminutive in extent, so trivial in *physical* resources, yet so colossal in all the moral grandeur of nations; so happy in peace, so blessed with abundance, so invincible in war, so inimitable in letters, so exquisite in taste, so unparalleled in the arts, so splendid in all things—we are compelled to refer all her transcendent excellences to her mind—her *education*, her literature, her science, and her philosophy. The example of ROME, not more extended in physical limits, and not less renowned in imperishable glory—extorts the judgment to the same acknowledgment of the supremacy of intellect over matter; and the all-powerful influence of public intelligence, in forming the national character, deciding its destiny, and moulding its people. In fine, the history of the world is but a repetition of the same truth illustrated by the same renown, tracking the career of intellect in the path of glory, and showing, that kingdoms, the most insignificant in magnitude, have, by the force of knowledge, eclipsed all their gigantic rivals in wealth, resources, and fame. We might contrast England with Russia—France with China—and Greece and Rome with all!

When history glares her blaze of truth in our eyes, let us not close them to its lessons. When the intellect of Rome was quenched by a barbarian deluge, what was the condition of the world?—To what era of all those blackened by crime, and debased by ignorance, do we look back, with the greatest horror? To the DARK AGES, to the midnight of mind that overspread the world, and permitted depravity to wage an unrestricted warfare upon virtue, knowledge, science, industry, and happiness. Sufficiently admonitory, then, is the lesson of the past, to urge us to the improvement of the present, and the perfection of the future. Cast upon the stage of existence in a *new era*, let us not disgrace our destiny by failing to make our advancement conform to our opportunities.

The spirit of the age, which now points to the universal education of the people, is an unavoidable effect of that law of our nature, which ordains that means must be adapted to ends, and that causes must conform to their consequences;—that as time rolls on, and reflection lights the torch of intellect, prejudice, bigotry, and superstition, must give place to reason, and humanity maintain her rights in defiance of prejudice or interest, riches or ambition. When, as a people, we inscribed the holy precepts of justice and of truth on our declaration of independence—proclaiming that all men were created free and equal—with the same rights to the pursuit and enjoyment of happiness; we commenced the foundation, because we created the necessity of universal education, by adopting a form of government, whose existence and purity depended on the exercise of reason, and the preservation of public virtue. Where every man is an *elector*, and bound to judge and to choose those who may make laws, and administer the government;—every one ought to receive an education, commensurate to his duties, as such; and where individual opulence does not furnish the means, the public are bound to impart the blessing in the fullest measure, and to the widest extent, at the common cost of society; not, however, as a *bounty*, or a *charity*, but as a *right;* that as *all* contribute their share of labour to the expense and support of government, so *all* are equally entitled to the great benefits of popular instruction. In the same manner, that the *constitution* protects our liberties, and that the law secures our rights of person and of property, without becoming a charity to the poor; so ought *education* to be dispensed to all who desire to receive its vivifying beams, and investigating spirit. Indeed, to conceive of a *popular government* devoid of a system of *popular education,* is as difficult as to conceive of a civilized society destitute of a *system of industry.* This truth has been generally received in this country, and never, I believe, directly denied; although its force has been attempted to be evaded by the *rich* and *opposed by the aristocracy,* who have heretofore, unfortunately, been our sole *law makers,* through the odious system of *charity schools*—the bare idea of which impresses a consciousness of degradation, and leads to results the very reverse of those that ought to be produced by popular instruction. I will not, however, enlarge upon this subject, which must be familiar to all; yet all may not have remarked, that the scanty pittance of education termed *charitable,* has never realized the *equal benefits of instruction,* to which the working people have been entitled as the producers of all the wealth of society. When it is solemnly inscribed upon our constitution, that education is an essential preliminary of government, its diffusive dispensation becomes a duty and a right of the first importance and magnitude: we are bound to consider it, not as an *accidental* but as an *integral* part of government, which, when we neglect or overlook, we violate the most sacred obligations, which, as good citizens, we have sworn to discharge.

*   *   *

The influence of education on the manners, is not less important that its operation on the mind; between which there exists so close an intimacy—so powerful a sympathy. Civility, politeness, deference, and all the amiable and softer virtues, are generally found to be residents of minds refined and educated; while ignorance assumes manners of corresponding rudeness, and imperious insolence. As it is the tendency of knowledge to inspire diffidence, the more the mind imbibes, the less it presumes to trespass upon the feelings or challenge the opinions of others. Besides that, in educated people there exists a natural assimilation, the general result of which is good breeding; hence one of the most salutary consequences of popular instruction—that those who labour, and have heretofore been rude and insolent, will gradually become polite and civil: and thus remove one of the most serious difficulties that prevents the working people emerging from that debasing condition in which they are now held by the customs of intellect and power. It is to *education*, therefore, that we must mainly look for a redress of that perverted system of society, which dooms the producer to ignorance, to toil, and to penury, to moral degradation, physical want, and social barbarism.

The power of the ballot boxes will do little, without the auxiliary help of our moral and intellectual energies. How can it be a marvel, that wealth practises oppression, when it holds as its allies, all the riches of knowledge, and the exterior semblances of virtue and truth? Moving in the high orbit of science, government and laws; ordaining justice and morality after their own images, how shall we ever counteract the principles of vassalage that now prevail, unless we procure EDUCATION for our offspring, and diffuse SCIENCE among our brethren? It is through this door that we must at last enter into the temple of justice, to consecrate on the altar of reason the true rights of man. Knowledge is *power*, in respect to the procurement of equity to the great mass of the sons of labour. It is the light of intelligence that abashes despotism—it is the fire of intellect that dissolves and melts the chains that enthral seven eighths of mankind to the caprice and luxury of the other few. *"In what way shall this evil be attacked and removed?"* I have answered, by giving our children equal or superior knowledge, virtue and intelligence, to the rich—by EDUCATION to direct and qualify us for government and laws; and by concentrating our SUFFRAGE to enable us to reach that point of influence, at which we shall be able to make the laws conform to the spirit of justice, and the government congenial to the equality of human rights.

THE "PHILADELPHIA NATIONAL GAZETTE" ON COMMON SCHOOLS

(1830) From Editorials in the *Philadelphia National Gazette,* July 10, 12, August 19, 1830, as quoted in John R. Commons et al., eds., *A Documentary History of American Industrial Society* (Cleveland, 1910–11), vol. V, pp. 107–12.

We remark the following toast in one of the lists which nearly fill the papers at this season.

"Education and general information—these must indeed constitute our only true National Bulwark. May the day soon come when in point of literary acquirements the poorest peasant shall stand on a level with his more wealthy neighbours."

It is our strong inclination and our obvious interest that literary acquirements should be universal; but we should be guilty of imposture, if we professed to believe in the possibility of that consummation. Literature cannot be acquired without leisure, and wealth gives leisure. Universal opulence, or even competency, is a chimera, as man and society are constituted. There will ever be distinctions of condition, of capacity, of knowledge and ignorance, in spite of all the fond conceits which may be indulged, or the wild projects which may be tried, to the contrary. The "peasant" must labor during those hours of the day, which his wealthy neighbor can give to the abstract culture of his mind; otherwise, the earth would not yield enough for the subsistence of all: the mechanic cannot abandon the operations of his trade, for general studies; if he should, most of the conveniences of life and objects of exchange would be wanting; langour, decay, poverty, discontent would soon be visible among all classes. No government, no statesman, no philanthropist, can furnish what is incompatible with the very organization and being of civil society. Education, the most comprehensive, should be, and is, open to the whole community; but it must cost to every one, time and money; and those are means which every one cannot possess simultaneously. Doubtless, more of education and of information is attainable for all in this republic, than can be had any where else by the poor or the operatives, so called.

It is an old and sound remark, that government cannot provide for the necessities of the People; that it is they who maintain the government, and not the latter the People. Education may be among their necessities; but it is one of that description which the state or national councils cannot supply, except partially and in a limited degree. They may endow public schools for the indigent, and colleges for the most comprehensive and costly scheme of instruction. To create or sustain seminaries for the tuition of all classes—to digest and regulate systems; to adjust and manage details, to render a multitude of schools effective, is beyond their province and power. Education in general must be the work of the intelligence, need, and enterprise of individuals and associations. At present, in nearly all the most populous parts of the United States, it is attainable for nearly all the inhabitants; it is comparatively cheap, and if not the best possible, it is susceptible of improvement and likely to be advanced. Its progress and wider diffusion will depend, not upon government, but on the public spirit, information, liberality and training of the citizens themselves, who may appreciate duly the value of the object as a national good, and as a personal benefit for their children. Some of the writers about universal public instruction and discipline, seem to forget the constitution of modern society, and declaim as if our communities could receive institutions or habits like those of Sparta. The dream embraces grand Republican female academies, to make Roman matrons!

We can readily pardon the editor of the United States *Gazette* for not perceiving that the scheme of Universal Equal Education at the expense of the State, is virtually "Agrarianism." It would be a compulsory application of the means of the richer, for the direct use of the poorer classes; and so far an arbitrary division of property among them. The declared object is, to procure the opportunity of instruction for the child or children of every citizen; to elevate the standard of the education of the working classes, or equalize the standard for all classes; which would, doubtless, be to lower or narrow that which the rich may now compass. But the most sensible and reflecting possessors of property sufficient to enable them to educate their children in the most liberal and efficacious way, and upon the broadest scale, would prefer to share their means for any other purpose, or in any other mode, than such as would injuriously affect or circumscribe the proficiency of their offspring. A public meeting of "the Mechanics and other Working Men of the City and County of New York," was held in the city, on the 17th inst., and among the principles for which they have "resolved" to contend, we find the following:

"In Education—The adoption of a general system of instruction, at the expense of the State, which shall afford to children, however rich or poor, equal means to obtain useful learning. To effect this, it is believed that a system of direct taxation will not be necessary, as the surplus revenue of the State and United States Governments will, in a very few years, afford ample means—but even if it were necessary to resort to direct taxation to accomplish this all-important object, and the amount paid by the wealthy should be far greater than that paid by our less eligibly situated fellow-citizens, an equivalent to them would be found in the increased ability and usefulness of the educated citizen to serve and to promote the best interests of the State; in the increased permanency of our institutions—and in the superior protection of liberty, person and property."

Thus, a direct tax for "the equal means of obtaining useful learning" is not deemed improbable, and it is admitted that the amount which would be paid by the wealthy would be "far greater" than that paid by their "less eligibly situated fellow citizens." Here, we contend, would be the action, if not the name, of the Agrarian system. Authority—that is, the State—is to force the more eligibly situated citizens to contribute a part (which might be very considerable) of their means, for the accommodation of the rest; and this is equivalent to the idea of an actual, compulsory partition of their substance. The more thriving members of the "mechanical and other working classes" would themselves feel the evil of the direct taxation; they would find that they had toiled for the benefit of other families than their own. One of the chief excitements to industry, among those classes, is the hope of earning the means of educating their children respectably or liberally: that incentive would be removed, and the scheme of State and equal education be thus a premium for comparative idleness . . .

PLATFORM OF THE BOSTON WORKING MEN'S PARTY (1830) From

Boston Courier, August 28, 1830, as quoted in John R. Commons et al., eds., *A Documentary History of American Industrial Society* (Cleveland, 1910–11), vol. V, pp. 188–89.

1. That we are determined by all fair and honorable means, to exalt the character, and promote the cause, of those who, by their productive industry, add riches to the state, and strength to our political institutions.

2. That we exclude from our association none, who, by their honest industry, render an equivalent to society for the means of subsistence which they draw therefrom.

3. That we regard all attempts to degrade the working classes as so many blows aimed at the destruction of popular virtue—without which no human government can long subsist.

4. That we view with abhorrence every attempt to disturb the public peace by uniting with political doctrines any question of religion or antireligion.

5. That the establishment of a liberal system of education, attainable by all, should be among the first efforts of every lawgiver who desires the continuance of our national independence.

6. That provision ought to be made by law for the more extensive diffusion of knowledge, particularly in the elements of those sciences which pertain to mechanical employments, and to the politics of our common country.

7. That, as we hold to the natural and political equality of all men, we have a right to ask for laws which shall protect every good citizen from oppression, contumely and degradation.

8. That we are opposed to monopolies, under whatever guise they may be imposed on the community—whether in the shape of chartered institutions for private gain; or in that of taxes, levied, nominally for the public good, on the many for the advantage of the few.

9. That we regard the multiplication of statutes, and the mysterious phraseology in which they are ordinarily involved, as actual evils, loudly demanding correction.

10. That the people have a right to understand every law made for their government, without paying enormous fees for having them expounded by attorneys—by those perhaps who were instrumental in their construction, and in rendering them incomprehensible, even to themselves.

11. That every representative chosen to declare the sentiments of the people, is bound to obey the popular voice, and to express it, or resign his trust forthwith.

12. That we are resolved to advocate, as one of our leading objects, the entire abrogation of all laws authorizing the imprisonment of the body for debt—at least until poverty shall be rendered criminal by law.

13. That we will endeavor by all practicable means to obtain a reform in our militia system.

14. That for the purpose of securing these objects, we will adopt a system of social discipline: hereby organizing ourselves under the title of Working Men of Boston.

15. That, for the furtherance of this plan, we recommend that a general meeting of our brethren and friends in the city, be held at an early day, for the purpose of selecting two delegates from each Ward, and two from South Boston, in order to constitute a General Executive Committee.

SETH LUTHER ON THE EVILS OF CHILD LABOR (1832)   From Seth Luther,
*An Address to the Working Men of New England on the State of Education and on the
Condition of the Producing Classes in Europe and America* . . . (Boston, 1832), pp. 35–
36.

. . . Our wish is to show that education is neglected, and that as a matter of course, because if 13 hours actual labour, is required each day, it is *impossible* to attend to education among children, or improvement among adults. With regard to hours of labour in cotton mills, there is a difference here as well as in England. In Manchester 12 hours *only* is the rule, while in some other towns in England many more are required. The mills *generally* in New England, run 13 hours the year round, that is, actual labour for all hands; to which add one hour for two meals, making 14 hours actual labour—for a man, or woman, or child, must labour hard to go a quarter, and sometimes half a mile, and eat his dinner or breakfast in 30 minutes and get back to the mill. At the Eagle mills, Griswold, Connecticut, 15 hours and 10 minutes actual labour in the mill are required; at another mill in the vicinity, 14 hours of actual labour are required. It needs no argument, to prove that education *must* be, and is almost entirely neglected. Facts speak in a voice not to be misunderstood, or misinterpreted. In 8 mills all on one stream, within a distance of two miles, we have 168 persons who can neither read nor write. This is in Rhode Island. A committee of working men in Providence, report "that in Pawtucket there are at least *five hundred children,* who scarcely know what a school is. These facts, say they, are adduced to show the blighting influence of the manufacturing system as at present conducted, on the progress of education; and to add to the darkness of the picture, if blacker shades are necessary to rouse the spirit of indignation, which should glow within our breasts at such disclosures, in all the mills which the enquiries of the committee have been able to reach, books, pamphlets, and newspapers are *absolutely prohibited.* This may serve as a tolerable example for every manufacturing village in Rhode Island." In 12 of the United States, there are 57,000 persons, male and female, employed in cotton and woolen mills, and other establishments connected with them; about two-fifths of this number, or 31,044 are under 16 years of age, and 6,000 are under the age of 12 years. Of this 31,044, there are in Rhode Island *alone* 3,472 under 16 years of age. The school fund is, in that State, raised in considerable part by lottery. Now we all know, that the poor are generally the persons who support this legalized gambling; for the rich as a general rule, seldom buy tickets. This fund then, said to be raised by the rich, for the education of the poor, is actually drawn from the pockets of the *poor,* to be expended by the rich, on *their own children,* while this large number of children (3,472) are entirely, and totally deprived of all benefit of the school fund, by what is *called* the *American System.* Actually *robbed* of what is *emphatically* their own, by being *compelled* to labour in these *"principalities of the destitute"* and these *"palaces of the poor,"* for 13 hours per diem, the year round. *What must be,* the result of this state of things? "We cannot regard even in anticipation, the contamination of moral and political degradation spreading its baleful influence throughout the community, through the medium of the uneducated part of the present generation, promulgated and enhanced in the future, by the increase of posterity, without starting with horror from the scene, as from the clankings of a TYRANT's chain."

"If education and intelligence is the *only sure* FOUNDATION of public safety," and if we are convinced that there are causes in active operation sapping and mining that foundation, can any man say, "It is nothing to me?" "If the children of the poor ought to be instructed as well as the rich," ought we not to see that it is done? If it depends on education whether we "live in a peaceable, orderly community, free from excess, outrage and crime, can we say it is nothing to us?" Who knows but in the course of events his son or daughter, or sister or brother, will not be driven into a cotton mill by the hard hand of adverse fortune, and be made to suffer the evils we have described. If "without the assistance of the common people a free government cannot exist," and we find that the capability to govern depends on intelligence and learning; is it not a fearful reflection that so many thousands of children are deprived of education, and so many adults of every opportunity for mental improvement? Let us no longer be deceived. Let us not think we are free until working-men no longer trust their affairs in the hands of designing demagogues.

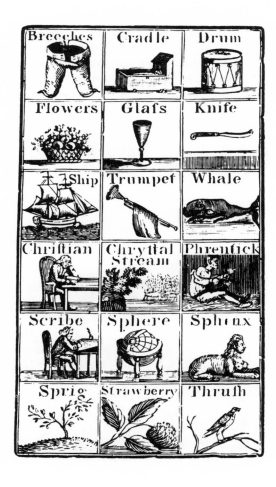

SENATOR DANIEL WEBSTER ON THE SCHOOLS AS A "WISE AND LIBERAL SYSTEM OF POLICE" (1820) From Edward Everett, ed., *Works of Daniel Webster* (Boston, 1854), vol. I, pp 41–42.

I must yet advert to another most interesting topic,—the Free Schools. In this particular, New England may be allowed to claim, I think, a merit of a preculiar character. She early adopted, and has constantly maintained the principle, that it is the undoubted right and the bounden duty of government to provide for the instruction of all youth. That which is elsewhere left to chance or to charity, we secure by law. For the purpose of public instruction, we hold every man subject to taxation in proportion to his property, and we look not to the question, whether he himself have, or have not, children to be benefited by the education for which he pays. We regard it as a wise and liberal system of police, by which property, and life, and the peace of society are secured. We seek to prevent in some measure the extension of the penal code, by inspiring a salutary and conservative principle of virtue and of knowledge in an early age. We strive to excite a feeling of respectability, and a sense of character, by enlarging the capacity and increasing the sphere of intellectual enjoyment. By general instruction, we seek, as far as possible, to purify the whole moral atmosphere; to keep good sentiments uppermost, and to turn the strong current of feeling and opinion, as well as the censures of the law and the denunciations of religion, against immorality and crime. We hope for a security beyond the law, and above the law, in the prevalence of an enlightened and well-principled moral sentiment. We hope to continue and prolong the time, when, in the villages and farm-houses of New England, there may be undisturbed sleep within unbarred doors. And knowing that our government rests directly on the public will, in order that we may preserve it we endeavor to give a safe and proper direction to that public will. We do not, indeed, expect all men to be philosophers or statesmen; but we confidently trust, and our expectation of the duration of our

system of government rests on that trust, that, by the diffusion of general knowledge and good and virtuous sentiments, the political fabric may be secure, as well against open violence and overthrow, as against the slow, but sure, undermining of licentiousness.

JAMES G. CARTER ON PUBLIC EDUCATION AS A WAY OF SECURING SOCIAL UNITY (1824) From James G. Carter, *Letters to the Honorable William Prescott . . . on the Free Schools of New England* (Boston, 1824), pp. 44–45.

In publick and large seminaries of learning, which bring together young men from different towns, states, and sections of the country, the change in habits, manners, and feelings towards each other, is astonishingly rapid. They come together with feelings and prejudices, and oftentimes with a dialect peculiar to the different places, from which they come, and each staring and wondering at the excessive *strangeness* of the other. But a very short time loosens their local prejudices, and teaches them, that all excellence is not peculiar to any one place. The whole exterior and deportment of the young man is often almost entirely transformed, in the short space of a few weeks. The change and improvement in this respect are more rapid at first, and quite as important and valuable to him, as his acquisitions in knowledge. What has a more direct tendency to improve "the manners" and deportment of the children, who attend our schools, than to observe some refinement in their instructer? Such is the personal influence of an instructer in a common school, that whether he is refined or vulgar, or whether he attends to the manners of his pupils or not, his manners will infallibly be imitated and copied by all, for the time, as a model of perfection. The different sections of our country are more free from dialects of the same language than any other in the world. What has produced this uniformity of language, so desirable on every consideration, but our public and common seminaries of learning,—the frequent and intimate commercial and literary intercourse between different parts of the country,—and the numerous points of contact between the educated and uneducated parts of the community? For the interest and happiness of the whole, and especially, the lower and uneducated classes of the community, it is certainly desirable these points of contact and intercourse should be multiplied, rather than diminished. For these reasons, the employment of instructers in our schools, who have had the advantages of some publick school or college, is an object of great consideration. Besides being the most direct and effectual means, of inculcating "decent behaviour,"—of reconciling the prejudices of different parts of the country, and different classes of the community; there is still another point of view, in which the measure is not less important. It tends more than any thing else, to lessen the distance and weaken the jealousies, which very generally subsist between the educated and uneducated. The talents and acquirements of a young man of publick education are often lost to the unlettered community for some years, while they have a delicious season of mutually hating and despising each other. These evils are in some degree obviated, when, by the kind of intercourse usually subsisting between a *publick* instructer and the *publick*, they are taught by experience their mutual worth and dependence as members of the same body politick.

THE PENNSYLVANIA LEGISLATURE ADVOCATES A GENERAL SYSTEM
OF COMMON SCHOOLS (1834)   From "Report of the Joint Committee of the Two
Houses of the Pennsylvania Legislature on the Subject of a System of General Education,"
Hazard's Register of Pennsylvania, vol. XIII, p. 97.

A radical defect in our laws upon the subject of education, is that the public aid now given, and imperfectly given, is confined *to the poor.* Aware of this, your committee have taken care to exclude the word *poor,* from the bill which will accompany this report, meaning to make the system *general;* that is to say, to form an educational association between the rich, the comparatively rich, and the destitute. Let them all fare alike in the primary schools; receive the same elementary instruction; imbibe the same republican spirit, and be animated by a feeling of perfect equality. In after life, he who is diligent at school, will take his station accordingly, whether born to wealth or not. Common schools, universally established, will multiply the chances of success, perhaps of brilliant success, among those who may forever continue ignorant. It is the duty of the State to promote and foster such establishments. That done, the career of each youth will depend upon himself. The State will have given the first impulse; good conduct and suitable application must do the rest. Among the indigent, "some flashing of a mounting genius" may be found; and among both rich and poor, in the course of nature, many no doubt will sink into mediocrity, or beneath it. Yet let them start with equal advantages, leaving no discrimination then or thereafter, but such as nature and study shall produce.

THADDEUS STEVENS' PLEA FOR FREE PUBLIC SCHOOLS FOR
PENNSYLVANIA (1835)   From "General Education—Remarks of Mr. Stevens,"
Hazard's Register of Pennsylvania, vol. XV, pp. 283–86.

Mr. Speaker,—I will briefly give you the reasons why I shall oppose the repeal of the school law. This law was passed at the last session of the legislature with unexampled unanimity, but one member of this house voting against it. It has not yet come into operation, and none of its effects have been tested by experience in Pennsylvania. The passage of such a law is enjoined by the constitution; and has been recommended by every governor since its adoption. Much to his credit, it has been warmly urged by the present executive in all his annual messages delivered at the opening of the legislature. To repeal it now, before its practical effects have been discovered, would argue that it contained some glaring and pernicious defect; and that the last legislature acted under some strong and fatal delusion, which blinded every man of them, to the interests of the commonwealth. I will attempt to show that the law is salutary, useful and important; and that consequently, the last legislature acted wisely in passing, and the present would act unwisely in repealing it.—That instead of being oppressive to the people, it will lighten their burthens, while it elevates them in the scale of human intellect.

It would seem to be humiliating to be under the necessity, in the nineteenth century, of entering into a formal argument to prove the utility, and to free governments, the absolute necessity of education. More than two thousand years ago the Deity who presided over intellectual endowments, ranked highest for dignity, chastity and virtue, among the goddesses worshipped by cultivated pagans. And I will not insult this House or our constituents by supposing any course of reasoning necessary to convince *them* of its high importance. Such necessity would be degrading to a Christian age and a free republic!

If then, education be of admitted importance to the people under all forms of governments; and of unquestioned *necessity* when they govern themselves, it follows, of cou[r]se, that its cultivation and diffusion is a matter of *public* concern; and a duty which every government owes to its people. In accordance with this principle, the ancient republics, who were most renowned for their wisdom and success, considered every child born subject to their control, as the property of the state, so far as its education was concerned; and during the proper period of instruction, they were withdrawn from the control of their parents, and placed under the guardianship of the commonwealth. There all were instructed at the same school; all were placed on perfect equality, the rich and the poor man's sons, for all were deemed children of the same common parent—of the commonwealth. Indeed, where *all* have the means of knowledge placed within their reach, and meet at common schools on equal terms, the *forms* of government seem of less importance to the happiness of the people than is generally supposed; or rather, such a people are seldom in danger of having their rights invaded by their rulers. They would not long be invaded with impunity. Prussia, whose form of government is absolute monarchy extends the blessing of free schools into every corner of the kingdom,—to the lowest and poorest of the people. With a population equal to our whole Union, she has not more than 20,000 children who do not enjoy its advantages. And the consequence is, that Prussia, although governed by an absolute monarch, enjoys more happiness and the rights of the people are better respected than in any other government in Europe.

If an elective republic is to endure for any great length of time, *every* elector must have sufficient information, not only to accumulate wealth, and take care of his pecuniary concerns, but to direct wisely the legislatures, the ambassadors, and the executive of the nation—for *some* part of all these things, *some* agency in approving or disapproving of them, falls to every freeman. If then, the permanency of our government depends upon such knowledge, it is the duty of government to see that the means of information be diffused to every citizen. This is a sufficient answer to those who deem education a private and not a public duty—who argue that they are willing to educate their *own* children, but not their *neighbor's* children.

But while but few are found ignorant and shameless enough to deny the advantages of general education, many are alarmed at its supposed burthensome operation. A little judicious reflection, or a single year's experience, would show that education, under the free school system will cost more than one one-half less, and afford better and more permanent instruction than the present disgraceful plan pursued by Pennsylvania . . .

*   *   *

The amendment which is now proposed as a substitute for the school law of last session, is, in my opinion, of a most hateful and degrading character. It is a reenactment of the pauper law of 1809. It proposes that the assessors shall take a census, and make a record of the *poor;* This shall be revised, and a new record made by the county commissioners, so that the names of those who have the misfortune to be poor men's children shall be forever preserved, as a distinct class, in the archives of the county! The teacher, too, is to keep in his school a *pauper* book, and register the names and attendance of poor scholars. Thus pointing out and recording their poverty in the midst of their companions. Sir, hereditary distinctions of rank are sufficiently odious; but that which is founded on poverty is infinitely more so. Such a law should be entitled "an act for branding and marking the poor, so that they may be known from the rich and proud."—Many complain of this tax, not so much on account of its amount, as because it is for the benefit of others and not themselves. This is a mistake. It is for *their own* benefit, inasmuch as it perpetuates the government, and ensures the due administration of the laws under which they live, and by which their lives and property are protected. Why do they not urge the same objection against all other taxes? The industrious, thrifty, rich farmer pays a heavy county tax to support criminal courts, build jails, and pay sheriffs and jail keepers, and yet probably he never has and never will have any direct personal use of either. He never gets the worth of his money by being tried for a crime before the court, allowed the privilege of the jail on conviction; or receiving an equivalent from the sheriff or his hangman officers! He cheerfully pays the tax which is necessary to support and punish convicts; but loudly complains of that which goes to prevent his fellow being from becoming criminal, and to obviate the necessity of those humiliating institutions.

This law is often objected to, because its benefits are shared by the children of the profligate spendthrift equally with those of the most industrious and economical habits. It ought to be remembered, that the benefit is bestowed, not upon the erring parents, but the innocent children. Carry out this objection and you punish children for the crimes or misfortunes of their parents. You virtually establish castes and grades founded on no merit of the particular generation, but on the demerits of their ancestors; An aristocracy of the most odious and insolent kind—the aristocracy of wealth and pride.

It is said that its advantages will be unjustly and unequally enjoyed, because the industrious, money-making man keeps his whole family *constantly* employed, and has but little time for them to spend at school; while the idle man has but little employment for his family and they will constantly attend school. I know sir, that there are some men, whose whole souls are so completely absorbed in the accumulation of wealth; and whose avarice so increases with success that they look upon their very children in no other light than as instruments of gain—that they, as well as the ox and the ass within their gates, are valuable only in proportion to their annual earnings. And according to the present system, the children of such men are reduced almost to an intellectual level with their co-laborers of the brute creation. This law will be of vast advantage to the offspring of such misers. If they are compelled to pay their taxes to support schools, their very meanness will induce them to send their children to them to get the worth of their money. Thus it will extract good out of the very penuriousness of the miser. Surely a system, which will work such wonders, ought to be as greedily sought for, and more highly prized than that coveted alchymy, which was to produce gold and silver out of the blood and entrails of vipers, lizards and other filthy vermin!

Those who would repeal this law because it is obnoxious to a portion of the people, would seem to found their justification on a desire of popularity. That is not an unworthy object, when they seek that enduring fame, which is constructed of imperishable materials.—But have these gentlemen looked back and consulted the history of their race, to learn on what foundation, and on what materials that popularity is built which outlives its possessor—which is not buried in the same grave which covers his mortal remains? Sir, I believe that kind of fame may be acquired either by deep learning, or even the love of it, by mild philanthropy, or unconquerable courage. And it seems to me, that in the present state of feeling in Pennsylvania, those who will heartily and successively support the cause of general education, can acquire, at least some portion of the honor of all these qualities combined; while those who oppose it will be remembered without pleasure, and soon pass away with the things that perish. In giving this law to posterity, you act the part of the philanthropist, by bestowing upon the poor as well as the rich the greatest earthly boon, which they are capable of receiving: you act the part of the philosopher by pointing, if you do not lead them up the hill of science: you act the part of the hero, if it be true as you say, that popular vengeance follows close upon your footsteps. Here then, if you wish true popularity, is a theatre on which you may acquire it. What renders the name of Socrates immortal, but his love of the human family, exhibited under all circumstances and in contempt of every danger? But courage, even with but little benevolence, may confer lasting renown. It is this which makes us bow with involuntary respect, at the names of Napole[o]n, of Caesar and of Richard of the Lion heart. But what earthly glory is there equal in lustre and duration to that conferred by education?—What else could have bestowed such renown upon the Philosophers, the Poets, the Statesmen, and Orators of antiquity? What else could have conferred such undisputed applause upon Aristotle, Demosthenes, and Homer; on Virgil, Horace, and Cicero? And is learning less interesting and important now than it was in centuries past, when those statesmen and orators charmed and ruled empires with their eloquence?

Sir, let it not be thought that those great men acquired a higher fame than is within the reach of the present age. Pennsylvania's sons possess as high native talents as any other nation of ancient or modern time! Many of the poorest of her children possess as bright intellectual gems, if they were as highly polished, as did the proudest scholars of Greece or Rome.—But too long—too disgracefully long, has coward, trembling, procrastinating legislation permitted them to lie buried in "dark unfathomed caves."

If you wish to acquire popularity, how often have you been admonished to build not your monuments of brass or marble, but make them of ever-living mind!—Although the period of yours, or your children's renown, cannot be as long as that of the ancients, because you start from a later period, yet it may be no less brilliant. Equal attention to the same learning; equal ardor in pursuing the same arts and liberal studies, which has rescued their names from the rust of corroding time, and handed them down to us untarnished from remote antiquity, would transmit the names of your children, and your children's children in the green undying fame down through the long vista of succeeding ages, until time shall mingle with eternity.

REV. GEORGE W. DOANE, BISHOP OF NEW JERSEY, ON PAUPER SCHOOLS (1838)   From "The State and Education," *American Journal of Education,* vol. XV, p. 5.

$\mathbf{F}$ELLOW CITIZENS:—We were appointed by the Convention of your own delegates to address you on the subject of Common Schools. We approach you with solicitude, as deeply sensible of the great importance of the interest intrusted to us; yet, as freemen speaking to freemen, with prevailing confidence.

The points which we propose for your attention, and, if we might, would press into every heart, are few, simple and practical; the necessary consequences, it seems to us, from principles which all admit. We say that *knowledge is the universal right of man:* and we need bring no clearer demonstration than that intellectual nature, capable of it, thirsting for it, expanding and aspiring with it, which is God's own argument in every living soul. We say that the assertion for himself of this inherent right, to the full measure of his abilities and opportunities, is *the universal duty of man:* and that whoever fails of it, thwarts the design of his Creator; and, in proportion as he neglects the gift of God, dwarfs and enslaves and brutifies the high capacity for truth and liberty which he inherits. And all experience, and every page of history confirm the assertion, in the close kindred, which has everywhere been proved, of ignorance and vice with wretchedness and slavery. And we say farther, that the security of this inherent right to every individual, and its extension, in the fullest measure, to the greatest number, is *the universal interest of man;* so that they who deny or abridge it to their fellows, or who encourage, or, from want of proper influence, permit them to neglect it, are undermining the foundations of government, weakening the hold of society, and preparing the way for the unsettling and dissolving of all human institutions, which must result in anarchy and ruin, and in which they who have the greatest stake must be the greatest sufferers.

✻   ✻   ✻

Omitting all considerations, then, of what has been or of what may be legislative enactments on the subject, we address you as the Sovereign People, and we say that *it is your duty and your highest interest to provide and to maintain, within the reach of every child, the means of such an education as will qualify him to discharge the duties of a citizen of the Republic;* and will enable him, by subsequent exertion, in the free exercise of the unconquerable will, to attain the highest eminence in knowledge and in power which God may place within his reach. We utterly repudiate as unworthy, not of freemen only, but of men, the narrow notion that there is to be an education for the poor, as such. Has God provided for the poor a coarser earth, a thinner air, a paler sky? Does not the glorious sun pour down his golden flood as cheerily upon the poor man's hovel as upon the rich man's palace? Have not the cotter's children as keen a sense of all the freshness, verdure, fragrance, melody, and beauty of luxuriant nature as the pale sons of kings? Or is it on the mind that God has stamped the imprint of a baser birth so that the poor man's child knows with an inborn certainty that his lot is to crawl, not climb? It is not so. God has not done it. Man can not do it. Mind is immortal. Mind is imperial. It bears no mark of high or low, of rich or poor. It heeds no bound of time or place, of rank or circumstance. It asks but freedom. It requires but light. It is heaven-born, and it aspires to heaven. Weakness does not enfeeble it. Poverty can not repress it. Difficulties do but stimulate its vigor. And the poor tallow chandler's son that sits up all the night to read the book which an apprentice lends him lest the master's eye should miss it in the morning, shall stand and treat with kings, shall add new provinces to the domain of science, shall bind the lightning with a hempen cord and bring it harmless from the skies. The Common School is *common*, not as inferior, not as the school for poor men's children, but as the light and air are common. It ought to be the best school because it is the first school; and in all good works the beginning is one-half. Who does not know the value to a community of a plentiful supply of the pure element of water? And infinitely more than this is the instruction of the common School: for it is the fountain at which the mind drinks, and is refreshed and strengthened for its career of usefulness and glory.

HENRY BARNARD ON THE NEEDS OF THE CONNECTICUT COMMON SCHOOLS (1839) From *First Annual Report of the Board of Commissioners of Common Schools in Connecticut . . . 1839,* pp. 52–54.

---

1. The first great want of our system of public schools, is a more decided, active, generous public sentiment enlisted in its support. That there is at this time a wide spread and paralizing apathy over the public mind, in relation to the whole subject—a want of proper appreciation of the immense, the inconceivable importance of good common schools to our individual, social and national well-being, is manifest, from the alarming number of children of the teachable age who are in no schools whatever, the still larger number who are in expensive private schools, the irregular attendance of those who are enrolled as pupils in the public schools, the thinly attended school meetings, both of the society and the district, and the unwillingness, not only of the public generally, but of that large class who are foremost in promoting other benevolent, patriotic and religious enterprizes, to make personal or pecuniary sacrifices to promote the increasing prosperity of common schools. The system will continue to move on in feeble and irregular action, so long as its various parts are not animated with a more vigorous principle of life. The late demonstration of increasing public interest, and the consequent activity imparted to the administration of the school system, show conclusively that the right beginning of this work of school improvement is in awakening, correcting, and elevating public sentiment in relation to it. To accomplish this, the measure recommended by the Board, the agency of the public press, the living voice, voluntary associations, seem to me as judicious and efficient, as can under present circumstances be devised. They have been found successful elsewhere. They have in some degree, it is hoped, been of service here. But all this is not enough. Public opinion will not long remain in advance of the law. Every advance, if it is of a general character, must be secured, and if proper steps are taken will very naturally be secured, by being embodied into the law.

2. A revision of our school law, with a few amendments, so as to remove obstacles in the way of improvement, seems to me indispensable. In consequence of these obstacles in the law itself, efforts to introduce a gradation of schools, to

employ two or more teachers in the same district, to build more commodious school houses, have failed, at least for the present. An amendment of the law so as to authorize districts which are prepared for it, to introduce these and other improvements, and especially the city and populous districts, cannot be objected to, because no district would be compelled to avail themselves of its provision.

To give greater efficacy to the examination of teachers, and indeed to the whole department of school superintendence, I would suggest the propriety of recommending to the Legislature, a modification of the section requiring the appointment of school visiters, so as to authorize the choice of a Board not to exceed one for a district, with power to delegate the execution of their rules and regulations to two persons who should receive a small compensation for their services. The duties are arduous, delicate, and necessary, and require both time and talent for their faithful discharge. The experience of some fifteen or twenty societies where the practice of appointing a smaller number and paying them has been adopted, is such as to satisfy me that the work will be better done all over the State, as soon as the practice is made general. The duties, too, of this class of officers should be made more specific, and a failure on their part should incur some penalty.

To secure the more general and punctual attendance of all the children enumerated, at the public schools, I think it very desirable to alter, in some respects, the present mode of sustaining them. The expense of the school, so far as those who are unable to bear it are concerned, should fall, not upon those who patronize the public school, but upon the property of the school society or town. The present mode makes it the interest of those who have property, to abandon the public school, for in so doing they avoid all the expense of supporting the schools beyond the avails of the public money. In addition to this, if the public money was distributed to the districts according to the actual attendance at the school, and not the enumeration, it would make it the *interest* of the district, and of every parent in it, to see that the attendance was general and punctual.

RECOMMENDATION BY MASSACHUSETTS GOVERNOR EDWARD EVERETT FOR A STATE BOARD OF EDUCATION (1837) From *Resolves of the General Court of Massachusetts* (1837), as quoted in Edgar W. Knight and Clifton C. Hall, eds., *Readings in American Educational History* (New York, 1951), p. 359.

The abstract of the returns of the schools throughout the Commonwealth, prepared with great judgment and care, by the Secretary of State, has been already submitted to you. I am persuaded that this document will be regarded with great interest by the Legislature. The fact that a sum of money, exceeding the whole public expenditure of the Commonwealth, is raised by taxation and voluntary contribution, for the support of schools, must be deemed, in the highest degree, honorable to our citizens.

While nothing can be farther from my purpose, than to disparage the common schools as they are, and while a deep sense of personal obligation to them will ever be cherished by me, it must yet be candidly admitted, that they are susceptible of great improvements. The school houses might, in many cases, be rendered more commodious. Provision ought to be made for affording the advantages of education, throughout the whole year, to all of a proper age to receive it. Teachers well qualified to give elementary instruction in all the branches of useful knowledge, should be employed; and small school libraries, maps, globes and requisite scientific apparatus should be furnished. I submit to the Legislature, whether the creation of a board of commissioners of schools, to serve without salary, with authority to appoint a secretary, on a reasonable compensation, to be paid from the school fund, would not be of great utility. Should the Legislature take advantage of the ample means now thrown into their hands, greatly to increase the efficiency of the school fund, I cannot but think that they would entitle themselves to the gratitude of the whole People. The wealth of Massachusetts always has been, and always will be, the minds of her children; and good schools are a treasure, a thousand fold more precious, than all the gold and silver of Mexico and Peru.

MASSACHUSETTS ESTABLISHES A BOARD OF EDUCATION (1837)   From *General Statutes of the Commonwealth of Massachusetts* (1860). pp. 210–11.

Section 1. The board of education shall consist of the governor and lieutenant-governor, and eight persons appointed by the governor with the advice and consent of the council, each to hold office eight years from the time of his appointment, one retiring each year in the order of appointment; and the governor, with the advice and consent of the council, shall fill all vacancies in the board which may occur from death, resignation, or otherwise.

Sect. 2. The board may take and hold to it and its successors, in trust for the commonwealth, any grant or device of lands, and any donation or bequest of money or other personal property, made to it for educational purposes; and shall forthwith pay over to the treasurer of the commonwealth, for safe keeping and investment, all money and other personal property so received. The treasurer shall from time to time invest all such money in the name of the commonwealth, and shall pay to the board, on the warrant of the governor, the income or principal thereof, as it shall from time to time require; but no disposition shall be made of any devise, donation, or bequest, inconsistent with the conditions or terms thereof. For the faithful management of all property so received by the treasurer he shall be responsible upon his bond to the commonwealth, as for other funds received by him in his official capacity.

Sect. 3. The board shall prescribe the form of registers to be kept in the schools, and the form of the blanks and inquiries for the returns to be made by school committees; shall annually on or before the third Wednesday of January lay before the legislature an annual report containing a printed abstract of said returns, and a detailed report of all the doings of the board, with such observations upon the condition and efficiency of the system of popular education, and such suggestions as to the most practicable means of improving and extending it, as the experience and reflection of the board dictate.

Sect. 4. The board may appoint its own secretary, who, under its direction, shall make the abstract of school returns required by section three; collect information respecting the condition and efficiency of the public schools and other means of popular education; and diffuse as widely as possible throughout the commonwealth information of the best system of studies and method of instruction for the young, that the best education which public schools can be made to impart may be secured to all children who depend upon them for instruction.

Sect. 5. The secretary shall suggest to the board and to the legislature, improvements in the present system of public schools; visit, as often as his other duties will permit, different parts of the commonwealth for the purpose of arousing and guiding public sentiment in relation to the practical interests of education; collect in his office such school-books, apparatus, maps, and charts, as can be obtained without expense to the commonwealth; receive and arrange in his office the reports and returns of the school committees; and receive, preserve, or distribute, the state documents in relation to the public school system.

Sect. 6. He shall, under the direction of the board, give sufficient notice of, and attend such meetings of teachers of public schools, members of the school committees of the several towns, and friends of education generally in any county, as may voluntarily assemble at the time and place designated by the board; and shall at such meetings devote himself to the object of collecting information of the condition of the public schools of such county, of the fulfilment of the duties of their office by members of the school committees of all the towns and cities, and of the circumstances of the several school districts in regard to teachers, pupils, books, apparatus, and methods of education, to enable him to furnish all information desired for the report of the board required in section three.

Sect. 7. He shall send the blank forms of inquiry, the school registers, the annual report of the board, and his own annual report, to the clerks of the several towns and cities as soon as may be after they are ready for distribution.

Sect. 8. He shall receive from the treasury, in quarterly payments an annual salary of two thousand dollars, and his necessary travelling expenses incurred in the performance of his official duties after they have been audited and approved by the board; and all postages and other necessary expenses arising in his office, shall be paid out of the treasury in the same manner as those of the different departments of the government.

Sect. 9. The board may appoint one or more suitable agents to visit the several towns and cities for the purpose of inquiring into the condition of the schools, conferring with teachers and committees, lecturing upon subjects connected with education, and in general of giving and receiving information upon subjects connected with education, in the same manner as the secretary might do if he were present.

Sect. 10. The incidental expenses of the board, and the expenses of the members thereof incurred in the discharge of their official duties, shall be paid out of the treasury, their accounts being first audited and allowed.

Sect. 11. The assistant librarian of the state library shall act when necessary as clerk of the board.

HORACE MANN'S THOUGHTS ON BEING CHOSEN SECRETARY OF THE MASSACHUSETTS BOARD OF EDUCATION (1837) From Mary Peabody Mann, *Life of Horace Mann* (Boston, 1865), pp. 79–81, 82–83, 86–87, 90.

June 28. This morning, received a call from Mr. Dwight on the subject of the Secretaryship; and as the meeting of the Board is appointed for to-morrow, and as he did not seem to have arrived at any certain conclusions in his own mind, I thought the time had already come when points should be stated explicitly. I therefore wrote to Mr. Dwight, saying that it would be better for the cause if the candidate who should be selected should appear to have been the first choice of the Board; that I therefore should feel it to be a duty to decline the honor of being voted for, unless it was *bonâ fide* my intention to accept; that I would accordingly regard the subject in its business aspects alone, and place the matter in a point of view not liable to be mistaken. I then stated, that, as I should have some professional business to close up, it had all along been my intention not to receive more than twenty-five hundred dollars for the first year; that as to subsequent years, if the Legislature should add any thing to the one thousand they have now appropriated as the salary of the Secretary, half of that addition should be added to the sum of twenty-five hundred until it became three thousand, but should not go beyond the latter sum; that by this it would become the interest of the Secretary so to discharge his duties as to gain the favor of the public; and that it was quite well in all cases, and with regard to all, to make their interest and their duty draw in the same direction, if possible. This was the substance of my letter; though it had the proper amount of interlardings and lubrifications. I tremble, however, at the idea of the task that possibly now lies before me. Yet I can now conscientiously say that here stands my purpose, ready to undergo the hardships and privations to which I must be subjected, and to encounter the jealousy, the misrepresentation, and the prejudice almost certain to arise; here stands my mind, ready to meet them in the spirit of a martyr. To-morrow will probably prescribe for me a course of life. Let it come! I know one thing,—if I stand by the principles of truth and duty, nothing can inflict upon me any permanent harm.

June 29. I cannot say that this day is one to which I have not looked forward with deep anxiety. The chance of being offered a station which would change the whole course of my action, and consequently of my duties, through life, was not to be regarded with indifference. The deep feeling of interest was heightened by the reflection, that, in case of my receiving the appointment of Secretary of the Board of Education, my sphere of *possible* usefulness would be indefinitely enlarged, and that my failure would forever force into contrast the noble duty and the inadequate discharge of it. The day is past. I have received the offer. The path of usefulness is opened before me. My present purpose is to enter into it. Few undertakings, according to my appreciation of it, have been greater. I know of none which may be more fruitful in beneficent results.

God grant me an annihilation of selfishness, a mind of wisdom, a heart of benevolence! How many men I shall meet who are accessible only through a single motive, or who are incased in prejudice and jealousy, and need, not to be subdued, but to be remodelled! how many who will vociferate their devotion to the public, but whose thoughts will be intent on themselves! There is but one spirit in which these impediments can be met with success: it is the spirit of self-abandonment, the spirit of martyrdom. To this, I believe, there are but few, of all those who wear the form of humanity, who will not yield. I must not irritate, I must not humble, I must not degrade any one in his own eyes. I must not present myself as a solid body to oppose an iron barrier to any. I must be a fluid sort of a man, adapting myself to tastes, opinions, habits, manners, so far as this can be done without hypocrisy or insincerity, or a compromise of principle. In all this, there must be a higher object than to win personal esteem, or favor, or worldly applause. A new fountain may now be opened. Let me strive to direct its current in such a manner, that if, when I have departed from life, I may still be permitted to witness its course, I may behold it broadening and deepening in an everlasting progression of virtue and happiness.

June 30. This morning I communicated my acceptance of the Secretaryship of the Board of Education. Afterwards I sat with the Board until they adjourned without day. I then handed to the Governor the resignation of my membership of the Board. I now stand in a new relation to them; nor to them only: I stand in a new relation to the world. Obligations to labor in the former mode are removed; but a more elevated and weighty obligation to toil supplies the place of the former. Henceforth, so long as I hold this office, I devote myself to the supremest welfare of mankind upon earth. An inconceivably greater labor is undertaken. With the highest degree of prosperity, results will manifest themselves but slowly. The harvest is far distant from the seed-time. *Faith* is the only sustainer. I have faith in the improvability of the race,—in their accelerating improvability. This effort may do, apparently, but little. But mere beginning in a good cause is never little. If we can get this vast wheel into any perceptible motion, we shall have accomplished much. And more and higher qualities than mere labor and perseverance will be requisite. Art for applying will be no less necessary than science for combining and deducing. No object ever gave scope for higher powers, or exacted a more careful, sagacious use of them. At first, it will be better to err on the side of caution than of boldness. When walking over quagmires, we should never venture long steps. However, after all the advice which all the sages who ever lived could give, there is no such security against danger, and in favor of success, as to undertake it with a right spirit,—with a self-sacrificing spirit. Men can resist the influence of talent; they will deny demonstration, if need be: but few will combat goodness for any length of time. A spirit mildly devoting itself to a good cause is a certain conqueror. Love is a universal solvent. Wilfulness will maintain itself against persecution, torture, death, but will be fused and dissipated by kindness, forbearance, sympathy. Here is a clew given by God to lead us through the labyrinth of the world.

*   *   *

BOSTON, July 2, 1837.

MY DEAR FRIEND,—How long it is since the light of your pen visited me! It really is long, and probably it seems longer than it is. In the mean time, what a change in externals has befallen me! I no longer write myself attorney, counsellor, or lawyer. My lawbooks are for sale. My office is "to let." The bar is no longer my forum. My jurisdiction is changed. I have abandoned jurisprudence, and betaken myself to the larger sphere of mind and morals. Having found the present generation composed of materials almost unmalleable, I am about transferring my efforts to the next. Men are cast-iron; but children are wax. Strength expended upon the latter may be effectual, which would make no impression upon the former.

But you will ask what is the interpretation of this oracular ambiguity. A law was passed last winter, constituting a Board of Education "consisting of the Governor and Lieut.-Governor, *ex officiis,* and eight other persons to be appointed by the Governor and Council;" which Board was authorized to appoint a Secretary, whose duty it should be "to collect information of the actual condition and efficiency of the common schools and other means of popular education, and to diffuse as widely as possible, throughout every part of the Commonwealth, information of the most approved and successful modes of instruction." I have accepted that office. If I do not succeed in it, I will lay claim at least to the benefit of the saying, that in great attempts it is glorious even to fail.

✳   ✳   ✳

BOSTON, July 16, 1837.

MY DEAR SISTER,—You will be not a little surprised to learn how great a change has come over my course of business-life since I last saw you. I have quitted the profession of the law. I hope that no necessity will ever compel me to resume it again. But why, you would ask, and for what object? I will tell you. . . . I have accepted the office of Secretary of the Board; and, as it will occupy all my time (and is sufficient to occupy me in ten places at once if that were possible), I necessarily leave my profession in order to bestow upon it my undivided attention. Could I be assured that my efforts in this new field of labor would be crowned with success, I know of no occupation that would be more agreeable to me,—more congenial to my tastes and feelings. It presents duties entirely accordant with principle. . . . Some persons think it not wise to leave my profession, which has hitherto treated me quite as well as I have deserved: others profess to think that my prospects in political life were not to be bartered for a post whose returns for effort and privation must be postponed to another generation; and that my present position in the Senate would be far preferable to being a post-rider from county to county, looking after the welfare of children who will never know whence benefits may come, and encountering the jealousy and prejudice and misrepresentation of ignorant parents. But is it not better to do good than to be commended for having done it? If no seed were ever to be sown save that which would promise the requital of a full harvest before we die, how soon would mankind revert to barbarism! If I can be the means of ascertaining what is the best construction of houses, what are the best books, what is the best arrangement of studies, what are the best modes of instruction; if I can discover by what appliance of means a non-thinking, non-reflecting, non-speaking child can most surely be trained into a noble citizen ready to contend for the right and to die for the right,—if I can only obtain and diffuse throughout this State a few good ideas on these and similar subjects, may I not flatter myself that my ministry has not been wholly in vain? . . .

✳   ✳   ✳

Nov. 3. . . . Have been engaged all the week at court in Dedham, arguing causes. The interests of a client are small, compared with the interests of the next generation. Let the next generation, then, be my client. . . .

FIRST ANNUAL REPORT OF THE MASSACHUSETTS BOARD OF
EDUCATION (1837) as quoted in *Life and Works of Horace Mann* (Boston, 1891),
vol. II, pp. 62–67.

It is not the province of the Board of Education to submit to the Legislature, in the form of specific projects of law, those measures, which they may deem advisable for the improvement of the schools and the promotion of the cause of education. That duty is respectfully left by the Board, with the wisdom of the legislature and its committees, on whom it is by usage devolved. Neither will it be expected of the Board, on the present occasion, to engage in a lengthened discussion of topics, fully treated in their Secretary's report, to which they beg leave to refer, as embodying a great amount of fact, and the result of extensive observation skilfully generalized. The Board ask permission only to submit a few remarks on some of the more important topics connected with the general subject.

1. As the comfort and progress of children at school depend, to a very considerable degree, on the proper and commodious construction of schoolhouses, the Board ask leave to invite the particular attention of the Legislature to their Secretary's remarks on this subject. As a general observation, it is no doubt too true, that the schoolhouses in most of the districts of the Commonwealth are of an imperfect construction. It is apprehended that sometimes at less expense than is now incurred, and in other cases, by a small additional expense, schoolhouses much more conducive to the health and comfort, and consequently to the happiness and progress of children, might be erected. Nor would it be necessary, in most cases, in order to introduce the desired improvements, that new buildings should be constructed. Perhaps in a majority of cases, the end might be attained to a considerable degree, by alterations and additions to the present buildings. It is the purpose of the Secretary of the Board, as early as practicable, to prepare and submit a special report on the construction of schoolhouses. When this document shall be laid before them, it will be for the Legislature to judge, whether any encouragement can, with good effect, be offered from the school-fund, with a view to induce the towns of the Commonwealth to adopt those improvements in the construction of schoolhouses, which experience and reason show to be of great practical importance in carrying on the business of education.

2. Very much of the efficiency of the best system of school education depends upon the fidelity and zeal with which the office of a school-committee-man is performed. The Board deem it unnecessary to dilate upon a subject so ably treated by their Secretary. The difficulties to be surmounted before the services of able and faithful school-committee-men can be obtained, in perhaps a majority of the towns of the Commonwealth, are confessedly great and various. They can be thoroughly overcome only by the spirit of true patriotism, generously exerting itself toward the great end of promoting the intellectual improvement of fellowmen. But it is in the power of the Legislature to remove some of the obstacles, among which not the least considerable is the pecuniary sacrifice involved in the faithful and laborious discharge of the duties of the school committee. The Board have understood, with great satisfaction, that the subject has been brought before the House of Representatives. They know of no reason why the members of school committees should not receive a reasonable compensation, as well as other municipal officers, of whom it is not usually expected that they should serve the public gratuitously. There are none

whose labors, faithfully performed, are of greater moment to the general well-being. The duties of a member of a school committee, if conscientiously discharged are onerous; and ought not to be rendered more so, by being productive of a heavy pecuniary loss, in the wholly unrequited devotion of time and labor to the public good.

3. The subject of the education of teachers has been more than once brought before the Legislature, and is of the very highest importance in connection with the improvement of our schools. That there are all degrees of skill and success on the part of teachers, is matter of too familiar observation to need repetition; and that these must depend, in no small degree, on the experience of the teacher, and in his formation under a good discipline and method of instructions in early life, may be admitted without derogating, in any measure, from the importance of natural gifts and aptitude, in fitting men for this as for the other duties of society. Nor can it be deemed unsafe to insist that, while occupations requiring a very humble degree of intellectual effort and attainment demand a long-continued training, it cannot be that the arduous and manifold duties of the instructor of youth should be as well performed without as with a specific preparation for them. In fact, it must be admitted, as the voice of reason and experience, that institutions for the formation of teachers must be established among us, before the all-important work of forming the minds of our children can be performed in the best possible manner, and with the greatest attainable success.

No one who has been the witness of the ease and effect with which instruction is imparted by one teacher, and the tedious pains-taking and unsatisfactory progress which mark the labors of another of equal ability and knowledge, and operating on materials equally good, can entertain a doubt that there is a mastery in teaching as in every other art. Nor is it less obvious that, within reasonable limits, this skill and this mastery may themselves be made the subjects of instruction, and be communicated to others.

We are not left to the deductions of reason on this subject. In those foreign countries, where the greatest attention has been paid to the work of education, schools for teachers have formed an important feature in their systems, and with the happiest result. The art of imparting instruction has been found, like every other art, to improve by cultivation in institutions established for that specific object. New importance has been attached to the calling of the instructor by public opinion, from the circumstance that his vocation has been deemed one requiring systematic preparation and culture. Whatever tends to degrade the profession of the teacher, in his own mind or that of the public, of course impairs his usefulness; and this result must follow from regarding instruction as a business which in itself requires no previous training.

The duties which devolve upon the teachers even of our Common Schools, particularly when attended by large numbers of both sexes, and of advanced years for learners (as is often the case), are various, and difficult of performance. For their faithful execution, no degree of talent and qualification is too great; and when we reflect that in the nature of things only a moderate portion of both can, in ordinary cases, be expected, for the slender compensation afforded the teacher, we gain a new view of the necessity of bringing to his duties the advantage of previous training in the best mode of discharging them.

A very considerable part of the benefit, which those who attend our schools might derive from them, is unquestionably lost for want of mere skill in the business of instruction, on the part of the teacher. This falls with especial hardship on that part of our youthful population, who are able to enjoy, but for a small portion of the year, the advantage of the schools. For them it is of peculiar importance, that, from the moment of entering the school, every hour should be employed to the greatest advantage, and every facility in imparting knowledge, and every means of awakening and guiding the mind, be put into instant operation: and where this is done, two months of schooling would be as valuable as a year passed under a teacher destitute of experience and skill. The Board cannot but express the sanguine hope, that the time is not far distant, when the resources of public or private liberality will be applied in Massachusetts for the foundation of an institution for the formation of teachers, in which the present existing defect will be amply supplied.

4. The subject of district-school libraries is deemed of very great importance by the Board. A foundation was made for the formation of such libraries, by the Act of 12th April, 1837, authorizing an expenditure by each district of thirty dollars, for this purpose, the first year, and ten each succeeding year. Such economy has been introduced into the business of printing, that even these small sums judiciously applied for a term of years will amply suffice for the desired object. To the attainment of this end, it is in the power of booksellers and publishers to render the most material aid. There is no reason to doubt, that if neat editions of books suitable for Common-School libraries were published and sold at a very moderate rate, plainly and substantially bound, and placed in cases well adapted for convenient transportation, and afterwards to serve as the permanent place of deposit, it would induce many of the districts in the Commonwealth to exercise the power of raising money for school libraries. A beginning once made, steady progress would in many cases be sure to follow. Where circumstances did not admit the establishment of a library in each district, it might very conveniently be deposited a proportionate part of the year in each district successively. But it would be highly desirable that each schoolhouse should be furnished with a case and shelves, suitable for the proper arrangement and safe-keeping of books. The want of such a provision makes it almost impossible to begin the collection of a library; and where such provision is made, the library would be nearly sure to receive a steady increase.

Although the Board are of opinion, that nothing would more promote the cause of education among us, than the introduction of libraries into our district schools, they have not deemed it advisable to recommend any measure looking to the preparation of a series of volumes, of which such a library should be composed, and their distribution, at public expense. Whatever advantages would belong to the library consisting of books expressly written for the purpose, obvious difficulties and dangers would attend such an undertaking. The Board deem it far more advisable to leave this work to the enterprise and judgment of publishers, who would, no doubt, find it for their interest to make preparations to satisfy a demand for district-school libraries in the way above indicated.

In this connection the Board would observe, that much good might unquestionably be effected by the publication of a periodical journal or paper, of which the exclusive object should be to promote the case of education, especially of Common-School education. Such a journal, conducted on the pure principles of Christian philanthropy, of rigid abstinence from party and sect, sacredly devoted to the one object of education, to collecting and diffusing information on this subject, to the discussion of the numerous important questions which belong to it, to the formation of a sound and intelligent public opinion, and the excitement of a warm and energetic public sentiment, in favor of our schools, might render incalculable service. The Board are decidedly of opinion, that a journal of this description would be the most valuable auxiliary which could be devised, to carry into execution the enlightened policy of the government, in legislating for the improvement of the schools, and they indulge a sanguine hope that its establishment will shortly be witnessed.

5. The subject of school-books is perhaps one of more immediate and pressing interest. The multiplicity of school-books, and the imperfection of many of them, is one of the greatest evils at present felt in our Common Schools. The Board know of no way, in which this evil could be more effectually remedied, than by the selection of the best of each class now in use, and a formal recommendation of them by the Board of Education. Such a recommendation would probably cause them to be generally adopted; but should this not prove effectual, and the evil be found to continue, it might hereafter be deemed expedient to require the use of the books thus recommended, as a condition of receiving a share of the benefit of the school fund.

The foregoing observations are all that now occur to the Board of Education, as proper to be made to the Legislature, in connection with the improvement of our Common Schools. They beg leave to submit an additional remark on the subject of their own sphere of operations. It is evident, from the nature of the case, that much of the efficiency and usefulness of the Board must depend on the zeal and fidelity of its Secretary, and that it is all-important to command, in this office, the services of an individual of distinguished talent and unquestioned character. No other qualifications will inspire the confidence generally of the people; and without that confidence, it is impossible that his labors or those of the Board should be crowned with success. The Board ask permission to state, that they deem themselves very fortunate in having engaged the services of a gentleman so highly qualified as their Secretary, to discharge the interesting duties of his trust; and they respectfully submit to the Legislature, the expediency of raising his compensation to an amount, which could more fairly be regarded as a satisfactory equivalent for the employment of all his time. The Board also think, that a small allowance should be made for the contingent expenses of the Secretary in the discharge of his duties, such as postage, stationery, and occasional clerk-hire. It is just, however, to add, that this proposal for an increase of salary is made wholly without suggestion on the part of the Secretary.

In conclusion, the Board would tender their acknowledgments to their fellow-citizens, who, by attending on the meetings of the county conventions, or in any other way, have afforded their co-operation in the promotion of the great cause of popular education. At most of these meetings, permanent county conventions for improvement of education have been organized. Spirited addresses have, in almost every case, emanated from the county meetings, well calculated to impart vigor and warmth to the public sentiment in reference to the cause of education. On the whole, the Board have reason to hope, that an impulse has been given to the public mind on the subject of education, from which valuable effects may be anticipated. It will be their strenuous effort, under the auspices of the Legislature, and as far as the powers vested in them extend, to encourage and augment the interest which has been excited, and they hope, as they shall acquire experience, that their labors will become more efficient. They do not flatter themselves that great and momentous reforms are to be effected at once. Where the means employed are those of calm appeal to the understanding and the heart, a gradual and steady progress is all that should be desired. The schools of Massachusetts are not every thing that we could wish, but public opinion is sound in reference to their improvement. The voice of reason will not be uttered in vain. Experience, clearly stated in its results, will command respect, and the Board entertain a confident opinion that the increased attention given to the subject will result in making our system of Common-School education fully worthy of the intelligence of the present day, and of the ancient renown of Massachusetts.

All which is respectfully submitted by

> EDWARD EVERETT,
> GEORGE HULL,
> JAMES G. CARTER,
> EDMUND DWIGHT,
> GEORGE PUTNAM,
> E. A. NEWTON,
> ROBERT RANTOUL, JUN.,
> JARED SPARKS.

Boston, February 1, 1838.

THE PROSPECTUS OF THE "COMMON SCHOOL JOURNAL" (1838)
From *Common School Journal,* vol. I, p. 1.

Prospectus

The subscribers propose to publish a Paper, to be devoted to the cause of Education. It will be called *The Common School Journal.*

The Editorial Department will be under the care of the Hon. HORACE MANN, Secretary of the Board of Education. It will be published semi-monthly, in an octavo form, of *sixteen* pages each. Twenty-four numbers will be issued each year, making an annual volume of 384 pages. The subscription price will be *One Dollar* a year.

The great object of the work will be the improvement of COMMON SCHOOLS, and other means of Popular Education. It is also intended to make it a depository of the Laws of the Commonwealth in relation to Schools, and of the Reports, Proceedings, &c., of the Massachusetts BOARD OF EDUCATION. As the documents of that Board will have a general interest, they ought to be widely diffused, and permanently preserved.

The Paper will explain, and, as far as possible, enforce upon all parents, guardians, teachers, and school officers, their respective duties towards the rising generation. It will also address to children and youth all intelligible motives to obey the laws of physical health, to cultivate "good behavior," to strengthen the intellectual faculties, and enrich them with knowledge; and to advance moral and religious sentiments into ascendency and control over animal and selfish propensities.

The Paper will be kept entirely aloof from partisanship in politics, and sectarianism in religion; vindicating, and commending to practice, only the great and fundamental truths of civil and social obligation, of moral and religious duty.

It will not be so much the object of the work to discover, as to diffuse knowledge. In this age and country, the difficulty is not so much that but few things on the subject of education are known, as it is that but few persons know them.

Many parents and teachers, not at all deficient in good sense, and abounding in good feelings and good purposes, fail only from want of information how to expand and cherish the infantile and juvenile mind; and hence they ruin children through love unguided by wisdom. It should therefore be the first effort of all friends of education to make that which is now known to any, as far as possible, known to all. The proposed Paper is designed to be the instrument of accomplishing such an object.

It is hoped that such a subscription list will be obtained as to authorize a commencement of the Paper during the current year.

TERMS.—One Dollar per annum, payable in advance; or, six copies for five dollars. Friends of education are requested to procure subscribers, and forward their lists to the publishers. *All letters must be post paid.*

MARSH, CAPEN & LYON,

133 Washington Street, Boston.

We proceed to fulfil the undertaking contained in the above Prospectus, by offering to the public the *first* number of "THE COMMON SCHOOL JOURNAL." Our numerous engagements may compel us to postpone the *second* number until the *first*, or at farthest the *middle*, of January next. After the second, the series will proceed regularly by the publication of semi-monthly numbers.

It would be easy to fill the pages of our first number with useful selections, from interesting writers, on the subject of Education. We prefer, however, to avail ourselves of this opportunity to set forth, at some length, the considerations which have induced us to incur the labor and the responsibility of preparing such a work, and to present an outline of the views which it will be our endeavor hereafter to fill up.

The title we have chosen will turn the mind of every reader to that ancient and cherished institution, the Common Schools of Massachusetts.

HORACE MANN ON GOOD SCHOOLHOUSES (1838)   From *Second Annual Report of the Secretary of the Board of Education,* as quoted in *Life and Works of Horace Mann* (Boston, 1891), vol. II, pp. 497–500.

Within the last year, also, every schoolhouse in Nantucket has been provided with a good ventilator and with new and comfortable seats. This leaves little to be desired in that town, in regard to the places where the processes of education are carried on. Competent teachers, fidelity in the committee, suitable school-books, libraries and a good apparatus, and bringing *all* the children within the beneficent influences of the school, will complete the work.

For the town school, an extensive and valuable apparatus has been provided, and also some of a less costly description for the primary schools. To accomplish these praiseworthy purposes, the town, last year, almost doubled its former appropriation.

Another highly gratifying indication of increased attention to the welfare of the schools has been given by the city of Salem. A year ago, the schoolhouses in that city were without ventilation, and many of them with such seats as excited vivid ideas of corporal punishment, and almost prompted one to ask the children for what offence they had been committed. At an expense of about two thousand dollars, the seats in all the schoolhouses, except one, have been reconstructed, and provisions for ventilation have been made. I am told, that the effect in the quiet, attention and proficiency of the pupils, was immediately manifested.

In many other places, improvements of the same kind have been made, though to a less extent and in a part only of the houses. It would be a great mistake, however, to suppose, that nothing remains to be done in this important department of the system of public instruction. The cases mentioned are the slightest exceptions, compared with the generality of the neglect. The urgent reasons for making the report on schoolhouses, the last year, still continue. In the important point of ventilation, so essential to the health, composure, and mental elasticity of the pupils, most of the houses remain without change; except, indeed, that very undesirable change which has been wrought by time and the elements;—or such change as has been effected by stripping off the external covering of the house, on some emergency for fuel. The children must continue to breathe poisonous air, and to sit upon seats, threatening structural derangement, until parents become satisfied that a little money may well be expended to secure to their offspring the blessings of sound health, a good conformation, and a strong, quick-working mind.

A highly respectable physician, who, for several years, has attended to the actual results of bad internal arrangements and bad locations for schoolhouses upon the health of the pupils, took measures, during the past summer, to ascertain with exactness the relative amount of sickness suffered by the children, in a given period of time, in two annual schools. The schools were selected on account of their proximity, being but a short distance from each other; they consisted of very nearly the same number of children, belonging to families in the same condition of life, and no *general* physical causes were known to exist, which should have distinguished them from each other, in regard to the health of the pupils. But one house was dry and well ventilated; the other damp, and so situated as to render ventilation impracticable. In the former, during a period of forty-five days, five scholars were absent, from sickness, to the amount in the whole of twenty days. In the latter, during the same period of time and for the same cause, nineteen children were absent, to an amount in the whole of one hundred and forty-five days;—that is almost four times the number of children, and more than seven times the amount of sickness; and the appearances of the children not thus detained by sickness, indicated a marked difference in their condition as to health. On such a subject, where all the causes in operation may not be known, it would be unphilosophical to draw general conclusions from a particular observation. No reason, however, can be divined, why this single result should not fairly represent the average of any given number of years. Similar results for successive years must satisfy any one, respecting the true cause of such calamities; if, indeed, any one can remain sceptical in regard to the connection between good health and pure air.

HORACE MANN COMPARES TEACHING METHODS IN MASSACHUSETTS AND GERMANY (1844)   From Massachusetts Board of Education, *Seventh Annual Report of the Secretary of the Board* (Boston, 1844), pp. 20–23, 60, 84–89, 117–18, 122–25, 128–29, 132–41.

In the course of this tour I have seen many things to deplore, and many to admire. I have visited countries where there is no National System of education at all, and countries where the minutest details of the schools are regulated by law. I have seen schools in which each word and process, in many lessons, was almost overloaded with explanation and commentary; and many schools in which 400 or 500 children were obliged to commit to memory, in the Latin language, the entire book of Psalms and other parts of the Bible—neither teachers nor children understanding a word of the language which they were prating. I have seen countries, in whose schools all forms of corporal punishment were used without stint or measure; and I have visited one nation, in whose excellent and well-ordered schools, scarcely a blow has been struck for more than a quarter of a century. On reflection, it seems to me that it would be most strange if, from all this variety of system and of no system, of sound instruction and of babbling,—of the discipline of violence and of moral means, many beneficial hints for our warning or our imitation, could not be derived; and as the subject comes clearly within the purview of my duty, "to collect and diffuse information respecting schools," I venture to submit to the Board some of the results of my observations.

On the one hand, I am certain that the evils to which our own system is exposed, or under which it now labors, exist in some foreign countries, in a far more aggravated degree than among ourselves; and if we are wise enough to learn from the experience of others, rather than await the infliction consequent upon our own errors, we may yet escape the magnitude and formidableness of those calamities under which some other communities are now suffering.

On the other hand, I do not hesitate to say, that there are many things abroad which we at home, should do well to imitate; things, some of which are here, as yet, mere matters of speculation and theory, but which, there, have long been in operation, and are now producing a harvest of rich and abundant blessings.

Among the nations of Europe, Prussia has long enjoyed the most distinguished reputation for the excellence of its schools. In reviews, in speeches, in tracts, and even in graver works devoted to the cause of education, its schools have been exhibited as models for the imitation of the rest of Christendom. For many years scarce a suspicion was breathed, that the general plan of education in that kingdom was not sound in theory and most beneficial in practice. Recently, however, grave charges have been preferred against it by high authority. The popular traveller, Laing, has devoted several chapters of his large work on Prussia, to the disparagement of its school system. An octavo volume, entitled "The Age of Great Cities," has recently appeared in England, in which that system is strongly condemned; and during the pendency of the famous "Factories' Bill" before the British House of Commons, in 1843, numerous Tracts were issued from the English press, not merely calling in question, but strongly denouncing the whole plan of education in Prussia, as being not only designed to produce, but as actually producing a spirit of blind acquiescence to arbitrary power, in things spiritual as well as temporal,—as being, in fine, a system of education, adapted to enslave and not to enfranchise the human mind. And even in some parts of the United States, the very nature and essence of whose institutions consist in the idea that the people are wise enough to distinguish between what is right and what is wrong,—even here, some have been illiberal enough to condemn, in advance, every thing that savors of the Prussian system, because that system is sustained by arbitrary power.

My opinion of these strictures will appear in the sequel. But I may here remark, that I do not believe either of the first two authors above referred to, had ever visited the schools they presumed to condemn. The English tract-writers, too, were induced to disparage the Prussian system, from a motive foreign to its merits. The "Factories' Bill" which they so vehemently assailed, proposed the establishment of schools to be placed under the control of the Church. Against this measure, the Dissenters wished to array the greatest possible opposition. As there was a large party in the kingdom, who doubted the expediency of any interference on the part of government, in respect to public education; it was seen that an argument derived from the alleged abuses of the Prussian system, could be made available to turn this class into opponents of the measure then pending in Parliament. Thus the errors of that system, unfortunately, were brought to bear, not merely against proselytising education, but against education itself.

But allowing all these charges against the Prussian system to be true, there were still two reasons why I was not deterred from examining it.

In the first place, the evils imputed to it were easily and naturally separable from the good which it was not denied to possess. If the Prussian schoolmaster has better methods of teaching reading, writing, grammar, geography, arithmetic, &c., so that, in half the time, he produces greater and better results, surely, we may copy his modes of teaching these elements, without adopting his notions of passive obedience to government, or of blind adherence to the articles of a church. By the ordinance of nature, the human faculties are substantially the same all over the world, and hence the best means for their development and growth in one place, must be substantially the best for their development and growth every where. The spirit which shall control the action of these faculties when matured, which shall train them to self-reliance or to abject submission, which shall lead them to refer all questions to the standard of reason or to that of authority,—this spirit is wholly distinct and distinguishable from the manner in which the faculties themselves should be trained; and we may avail ourselves of all improved methods in the earlier processes, without being contaminated by the abuses which may be made to follow them. The best style of teaching arithmetic or spelling has no necessary or natural connection with the doctrine of hereditary right; and an accomplished lesson in geography or grammar commits the human intellect to no particular dogma in religion.

In the second place, if Prussia can pervert the benign influences of education to the support of arbitrary power, we surely can employ them for the support and perpetuation of republican institutions. A national spirit of liberty can be cultivated more easily than a national spirit of bondage; and if it may be made one of the great prerogatives of education to perform the unnatural and unholy work of making slaves, then surely it must be one of the noblest instrumentalities for rearing a nation of freemen. If a moral power over the understandings and affections of the people may be turned to evil, may it not also be employed for good?

Besides, a generous and impartial mind does not ask whence a thing comes, but what it is. Those who, at the present day, would reject an improvement because of the place of its origin, belong to the same school of bigotry with those who inquired if any good could come out of Nazareth; and what infinite blessings would the world have lost had that party been punished by success! Throughout my whole tour, no one principle has been more frequently exemplified than this,—that wherever I have found the best institutions,—educational, reformatory, charitable, penal or otherwise,—there I have always found the greatest desire to know how similar institutions were administered among ourselves; and where I have found the worst, there I have found most of the spirit of self-complacency, and even an offensive disinclination to hear of better methods.

*   *   *

The first element of superiority in a Prussian school, and one whose influence extends throughout the whole subsequent course of instruction, consists in the proper classification of the scholars. In all places where the numbers are sufficiently large to allow it, the children are divided according to ages and attainments; and a single teacher has the charge only of a single class, or of as small a number of classes as is practicable. I have before adverted to the construction of the schoolhouses, by which, as far as possible, a room is assigned to each class. Let us suppose a teacher to have the charge of but one class, and to have talent and resources sufficient properly to engage and occupy its attention, and we suppose a perfect school. But how greatly are the teacher's duties increased, and his difficulties multiplied, if he have four, five, or half a dozen classes, under his personal inspection. While attending to the recitation of one, his mind is constantly called off, to attend to the studies and the conduct of all the others. For this, very few teachers amongst us, have the requisite capacity; and hence the idleness and the disorder that reign in so many of our schools,—excepting in cases where the debasing motive of fear puts the children in irons. All these difficulties are at once avoided by a suitable classification,—by such a classification as enables the teacher to address his instructions at the same time, to all the children who are before him, and to accompany them to the playground, at recess or intermission, without leaving any behind who might be disposed to take advantage of his absence. All this will become more and more obvious, as I proceed with a description of exercises. There is no obstacle whatever, save prescription, and that *vis inertia* of mind, which continues in the beaten track because it has not vigor enough to turn aside from it,—to the introduction, at once, of this mode of dividing and classifying scholars, in all our large towns.

In regard to this as well as other modes of teaching, I shall endeavor to describe some particular lesson that I heard. The Prussian and Saxon schools are all conducted substantially upon the same plan, and taught in the same manner. Of course, there must be those differences to which different degrees of talent and experience give rise.

In Professor Stowe's excellent report he says, "Before the child is even permitted to learn his letters, he is under conversational instruction frequently, for six months or a year; and then a single week is sufficient to introduce him into intelligent and accurate plain reading." I confess that in the numerous schools I visited, I did not find this preparatory instruction carried on for any considerable length of time, before lessons in which all the children took part were commenced.

About twenty years ago, teachers in Prussia made the important discovery that children have five senses,—together with various muscles and mental faculties,—all which, almost by a necessity of their nature, must be kept in a state of activity, and which, if not usefully, are liable to be mischievously employed. Subsequent improvements in the art of teaching, have consisted in supplying interesting and useful, instead of mischievous occupation, for these senses, muscles and faculties.

Experience has now proved that it is much easier to furnish profitable and delightful employment for all these powers, than it is to stand over them with a rod and stifle their workings, or to assume a thousand shapes of fear to guard the thousand avenues through which the salient spirits of the young play outward. Nay it is much easier to keep the eye and hand and mind at work together, than it is to employ either one of them separately from the others. A child is bound to the teacher by so many more cords, the more of his natural capacities the teacher can interest and employ.

In the case I am now to describe, I entered a classroom of sixty children, of about six years of age. The children were just taking their seats, all smiles and expectation. They had been at school but a few weeks, but long enough to have contracted a love for it. The teacher took his station before them, and after making a playful remark which excited a light titter around the room, and effectually arrested attention, he gave a signal for silence. After waiting a moment, during which every countenace was composed and every noise hushed, he made a prayer consisting of a single sentence, asking that as they had come together to learn, they might be good and diligent. He then spoke to them of the beautiful day, asked what they knew about the seasons, referred to the different kinds of fruit trees then in bearing, and questioned them upon the uses of trees in constructing houses, furniture, &c. Frequently he threw in sportive remarks which enlivened the whole school, but without ever producing the slightest symptom of disorder. During this familiar conversation which lasted about twenty minutes, there was nothing frivolous or trifling in the manner of the teacher; that manner was dignified though playful, and the little jets of laughter which he caused the children occasionally to throw out, were much more favorable to a receptive state of mind than jets of tears.

Here I must make a preliminary remark, in regard to the equipments of the scholars and the furniture of the schoolroom. Every child had a slate and pencil, and a little reading book of letters, words, and short sentences. Indeed, I never saw a Prussian or Saxon school,—above an infant school,—in which any child was unprovided with a slate and pencil. By the teacher's desk, and in front of the school, hung a blackboard. The teacher first drew a house upon the blackboard; and here the value of the art of drawing,—a power universally possessed by Prussian teachers,—became manifest. By the side of the drawing and under it, he wrote the word *house* in the German script hand, and printed it in the German letter. With a long pointing rod,—the end being painted white to make it more visible,—he ran over the form of the letters,—the children, with their slates before them and their pencils in their hands, looking at the pointing rod and tracing the forms of the letters in the air. In all our good schools, children are first taught to imitate the forms of letters on the slate before they write them on paper; here they were first imitated on the air, then on slates, and subsequently, in older classes, on paper. The next process was to copy the word "house," both in script and in print, on their slates. Then followed the formation of the sounds of the letters of which the word was composed, and the spelling of the word. Here the *names* of the letters were not given as with us, but only their powers, or the sounds which those letters have in combination. The letter *h* was first selected and set up in the reading-frame, (the same before described as part of the apparatus of all Prussian schools for young children,) and the children, instead of articulating our alphabetic *h*, (aitch,) merely gave a hard breathing,—such a sound as the letter really has in the word "house." Then the diphthong, *au*, (the German word for "house" is spelled "haus,") was taken and sounded by itself, in the same way. Then the blocks containing *h*, and *au*, were brought together, and the two sounds were combined. Lastly, the letter *s* was first sounded by itself, then added to the others, and then the whole word was spoken. Sometimes the last letter in a word was first taken and sounded,—after that the penultimate,—and so on until the word was completed. The responses of the children were sometimes individual, and sometimes simultaneous, according to a signal given by the master.

In every such school also, there are printed sheets or cards, containing the letters, diphthongs and whole words. The children are taught to sound a diphthong, and then asked in what words that sound occurs. On some of these cards there are words enough to make several short sentences, and when the pupils are a little advanced, the teacher points to several isolated words in succession, which when taken together make a familiar sentence, and thus he gives them an agreeable surprise, and a pleasant initiation into reading.

*   *   *

When the hour had expired, I do not believe there was a child in the room who knew or thought that his play-time had come. No observing person can be at a loss to understand how such a teacher can arrest and retain the attention of his scholars. It must have happened to almost every one, at some time in his life, to be present as a member of a large assembly, when some speaker, in the midst of great uproar and confusion, has arisen to address it. If, in the very commencement of his exordium, he makes what is called a happy hit which is answered by a response of laughter or applause from those who are near enough to hear it, the attention of the next circle will be aroused. If, then, the speaker makes another felicitous sally of wit or imagination, this circle too becomes the willing subject of his power; until, by a succession of flashes whether of genius or of wit, he soon brings the whole audience under his command, and sways it as the sun and moon sway the tide. This is the result of talent, of attainment, and of the successful study both of men and of things; and whoever has a sufficiency of these requisites will be able to command the attention of children, just as a powerful orator commands the attention of men. But the one no more than the other is the unbought gift of nature. They are the rewards of application and toil superadded to talent.

Now it is obvious that in the single exercise above described, there were the elements of reading, spelling, writing, grammar and drawing, interspersed with anecdotes and not a little general information; and yet there was no excessive variety, nor were any incongruous subjects forcibly brought together. There was nothing to violate the rule of 'one thing at a time.'

Compare the above method with that of calling up a class of abecedarians,—or, what is more common, a single child, and while the teacher holds a book or a card before him, and with a pointer in his hand, says, *a*, and he echoes *a*; then *b*, and he echoes *b*; and so on until the vertical row of lifeless and ill-favored characters is completed, and then of remanding him to his seat, to sit still and look at vacancy. If the child is bright, the time which passes during this lesson is the only part of the day when he does not think. Not a single faculty of the mind is occupied except that of imitating sounds; and even the number of these imitations amounts only to twenty-six. A parrot or an idiot could do the same thing. And so of the organs and members of the body. They are condemned to inactivity;—for the child who stands most like a post is most approved; nay, he is rebuked if he does not stand like a post. A head that does not turn to the right or left, an eye that lies moveless in its socket, hands hanging motionless at the side, and feet immovable as those of a statue, are the points of excellence, while the child is echoing the senseless table of a, b, c. As a general rule, six months are spent before the twenty-six letters are mastered, though the same child would learn the names of twenty-six playmates or twenty-six playthings in one or two days.

*   *   *

Again, the method I have described necessarily leads to conversation, and conversation with an intelligent teacher secures several important objects. It communicates information. It brightens ideas before only dimly apprehended. It addresses itself to the various faculties of the mind, so that no one of them ever tires or is cloyed. It teaches the child to use language, to frame sentences, to select words which convey his whole meaning, to avoid those which convey either more or less than he intends to express;—in fine, it teaches him to seek for thoughts upon a subject, and then to find appropriate language in which to clothe them. A child trained in this way will never commit those absurd and ludicrous mistakes into which uneducated men of some sense not unfrequently fall, viz. that of mismatching their words and ideas,—of hanging, as it were, the garments of a giant upon the body of a pigmy, or of forcing a pigmy's dress upon the huge limbs of a giant. Appropriate diction should clothe just ideas, as a tasteful and substantial garb fits a graceful and vigorous form.

The above described exercise occupies the eye and the hand as well as the mind. The eye is employed in tracing visible differences between different forms, and the hand in copying whatever is presented, with as little difference as possible. And who ever saw a child that was not pleased with pictures, and an attempt to imitate them? Thus, the two grand objects so strenuously insisted upon by writers, in regard to the later periods of education and the maturer processes of thought, are attained, viz. the power of recognizing analogies and dissimilarities.

I am satisfied that our greatest error in teaching children to read, lies in beginning with the alphabet;—in giving them what are called the 'Names of the Letters,' a, b, c, &c. How can a child to whom nature offers such a profusion of beautiful objects,—of sights and sounds and colors,—and in whose breast so many social feelings spring up;—how can such a child be expected to turn with delight from all these to the stiff and lifeless column of the alphabet? How can one who as yet is utterly incapable of appreciating the remote benefits, which in after-life reward the acquisition of knowledge, derive any pleasure from an exercise which presents neither beauty to his eye, nor music to his ear, nor sense to his understanding?

*   *   *

Writing and Drawing

Such excellent hand-writing as I saw in the Prussian schools, I never saw before. I can hardly express myself too strongly on this point. In Great Britain, France, or in our own country, I have never seen any schools worthy to be compared with theirs in this respect. I have before said that I found all children provided with a slate and pencil, and writing or printing letters, and beginning with the elements of drawing, either immediately or very soon after they entered school. This furnishes the greater part of the explanation of their excellent hand-writing. A part of it I think, should be referred to the peculiarity of the German script, which seems to me to be easier than our own. But after all due allowance is made for this advantage, a high degree of superiority over the schools of other countries remains to be accounted for. This superiority cannot be attributed in any degree to a better manner of holding the pen, for I never saw so great a proportion of cases in any schools where the pen was so awkwardly held. This excellence must be referred in a great degree to the universal practice of learning to draw, contemporaneously with learning to write. I believe a child will learn both to draw and to write sooner and with more ease than he will learn writing alone;—and for this reason:—the figures or objects contemplated and copied in learning to draw, are larger, more marked, more distinctive one from another, and more sharply defined with projection, angle or curve, than the letters copied in writing. In drawing there is more variety, in writing more sameness. Now the objects contemplated in drawing, *from their nature*, attract attention more readily, impress the mind more deeply, and of course will be more accurately copied than those in writing. And when the eye has been trained to observe, to distinguish, and to imitate, in the first exercise, it applies its habits with great advantage to the second.

Another reason is, that the child is taught to draw things with which he is familiar, which have some significance and give him pleasing ideas. But a child who is made to fill page after page with rows of straight marks, that look so blank and cheerless though done ever so well, has and can have no pleasing associations with his work.

*   *   *

On reviewing a period of six weeks, the greater part of which I spent in visiting schools in the North and middle of Prussia and in Saxony, (excepting of course the time occupied in going from place to place,) entering the schools to hear the first recitation in the morning, and remaining until the last was completed at night, I call to mind three things about which I cannot be mistaken. In some of my opinions and inferences, I may have erred, but of the following facts, there can be no doubt:—

1. During all this time, I never saw a teacher hearing a lesson of any kind, (excepting a reading or spelling lesson,) *with a book in his hand.*

2. I never saw a teacher *sitting,* while hearing a recitation.

3. Though I saw hundreds of schools, and thousands,—I think I may say, within bounds, tens of thousands of pupils,—*I never saw one child undergoing punishment, or arraigned for misconduct. I never saw one child in tears from having been punished, or from fear of being punished.*

During the above period, I witnessed exercises in geography, ancient and modern; in the German language,—from the explanation of the simplest words up to belles-lettres disquisitions, with rules for speaking and writing;—in arithmetic, algebra, geometry, surveying and trigonometry; in book-keeping; in civil history, ancient and modern; in natural philosophy; in botany and zoology; in mineralogy, where there were hundreds of specimens; in the endless variety of the exercises in thinking; knowledge of nature, of the world and of society; in Bible history and in Bible knowledge;—and, as I before said, in no one of these cases did I see a teacher with a book in his hand. His book,—his books,—his library, was in his head. Promptly, without pause, without hesitation, from the rich resources of his own mind, he brought forth whatever the occasion demanded. I remember calling one morning at a country school in Saxony, where every thing about the premises, and the appearance both of teacher and children, indicated very narrow pecuniary circumstances. As I entered, the teacher was just ready to commence a lesson or lecture on French history. He gave not only the events of a particular period in the history of France, but mentioned as he proceeded all the contemporary sovereigns of neighboring nations. The ordinary time for a lesson, here as elsewhere, was an hour. This was somewhat longer, for towards the close, the teacher entered upon a train of thought from which it was difficult to break off, and rose to a strain of eloquence which it was delightful to hear. The scholars were all absorbed in attention. They had paper, pen and ink before them, and took brief notes of what was said. When the lesson touched upon contemporary events in other nations,— which, as I suppose, had been the subject of previous lessons,—the pupils were questioned concerning them. A small text-book of history was used by the pupils which they studied at home.

I ought to say further, that I generally visited schools without guide, or letter of introduction,—presenting myself at the door, and asking the favor of admission. Though I had a general order from the Minister of Public Instruction, commanding all schools, gymnasia and universities in the kingdom to be opened for my inspection, yet I seldom exhibited it, or spoke of it,—at least not until I was about departing. I preferred to enter as a private individual, and uncommended visiter.

I have said that I saw no teacher sitting in his school. Aged or young, all stood. Nor did they stand apart and aloof in sullen dignity. They mingled with their pupils, passing rapidly from one side of the class to the other, animating, encouraging, sympathizing, breathing life into less active natures, assuring the timed, distributing encouragement and endearment to all. The looks of the Prussian teacher often have the expression and vivacity of an actor in a play. He gesticulates like an orator. His body assumes all the attitudes, and his face puts on all the variety of expression, which a public speaker would do, if haranguing a large assembly on a topic vital to their interests.

It may seem singular, and perhaps to some almost ludicrous, that a teacher, in expounding the first rudiments of hand-writing, in teaching the difference between a hair-stroke and a ground-stroke, or how an *l* may be turned into a *b*, or a *u* into a *w*, should be able to work himself up into an oratorical fervor, should attitudinize, and gesticulate, and stride from one end of the class to the other, and appear in every way to be as intensely engaged as an advocate when arguing an important cause to a jury;—but strange as it may seem, it is nevertheless true; and before five minutes of such a lesson had elapsed, I have seen the children wrought up to an excitement proportionally intense, hanging upon the teacher's lips, catching every word he says, and evincing great elation or depression of spirits, as they had or had not succeeded in following his instructions. So I have seen the same rhetorical vehemence on the part of the teacher, and the same interest and animation on the part of the pupils, during a lesson on the original sounds of the letters,—that is, the difference between the long and the short sound of a vowel, or the different ways of opening the mouth in sounding the consonants *b*, and *p*. This zeal of the teacher enkindles the scholars. He charges them with his own electricity to the point of explosion. Such a teacher has no idle, mischievous, whispering children around him, nor any occasion for the rod. He does not make desolation of all the active and playful impulses of childhood and call it peace; nor, to secure stillness among his scholars, does he find it necessary to ride them with the night-mare of fear. I rarely saw a teacher put questions with his lips alone. He seems so much interested in his subject, (though he might have been teaching the same lesson for the hundredth or five hundredth time,) that his whole body is in motion;—eyes, arms, limbs, all contributing to the impression he desires to make; and at the end of an hour, both he and his pupils come from the work all glowing with excitement.

Suppose a lawyer in one of our courts were to plead an important cause before a jury, but instead of standing and extemporizing, and showing by his gestures, and by the energy and ardor of his whole manner, that he felt an interest in his theme, instead of rising with his subject and coruscating with flashes of genius and wit, he should plant himself lazily down in a chair, read from some old book which scarcely a member of the panel could fully understand, and after droning away for an hour should leave them, without having distinctly impressed their minds with one fact, or led them to form one logical conclusion;—would it be any wonder if he left half of them joking with each other, or asleep;—would it be any wonder,—provided he were followed on the other side by an advocate of brilliant parts, of elegant diction and attractive manner,—by one who should pour sunshine into the darkest recesses of the case,—if he lost not only his own reputation but the cause of his client also.

These incitements and endearments of the teacher, this personal ubiquity, as it were, among all the pupils in the class, prevailed much more, as the pupils were younger. Before the older classes, the teacher's manner became calm and didactic. The habit of attention being once formed, nothing was left for subsequent years or teachers, but the easy task of maintaining it. Was there ever such a comment as this on the practice of hiring cheap teachers because the school is young, or incompetent ones because it is backward!

In Prussia and in Saxony, as well as in Scotland, the power of commanding and retaining the attention of a class is held to be a *sine qua non* in a teacher's qualifications. If he has not talent, skill, vivacity, or resources of anecdote and wit, sufficient to arouse and retain the attention of his pupils during the accustomed period of recitation, he is deemed to have mistaken his calling, and receives a significant hint to change his vocation.

Take a group of little children to a toyshop, and witness their out-bursting eagerness and delight. They need no stimulus of badges or prizes to arrest or sustain their attention; they need no quickening of their faculties by rod or ferule. To the exclusion of food and sleep, they will push their inquiries, until shape, color, quality, use, substance both external and internal, of the objects, are exhausted; and each child will want the show-man wholly to himself. But in all the boundless variety and beauty of nature's works; in that profusion and prodigality of charms with which the Creator has adorned and enriched every part of his creation; in the delights of affection; in the extatic joys of benevolence; in the absorbing interest which an unsophisticated conscience instinctively takes in all questions of right and wrong;—in all these, is there not as much to challenge and command the attention of a little child as in the curiosities of a toyshop? When as much of human art and ingenuity has been expended upon Teaching as upon Toys, there will be less difference between the cases.

The third circumstance I mentioned above was the beautiful relation of harmony and affection which subsisted between teacher and pupils. I cannot say that the extraordinary fact I have mentioned was not the result of chance or accident. Of the probability of that, others must judge. I can only say that, during all the time mentioned, I never saw a blow struck, I never heard a sharp rebuke given, I never saw a child in tears, nor arraigned at the teacher's bar for any alleged misconduct. On the contrary, the relation seemed to be one of duty first, and then affection, on the part of the teacher,—of affection first, and then duty, on the part of the scholar. The teacher's manner was better than parental, for it had a parent's tenderness and vigilance, without the foolish doatings or indulgences to which parental affection is prone. I heard no child ridiculed, sneered at, or scolded, for making a mistake. On the contrary, whenever a mistake was made, or there was a want of promptness in giving a reply, the expression of the teacher was that of grief and disappointment, as though there had been a failure, not merely to answer the question of a master, but to comply with the expectations of a friend. No child was disconcerted, disabled, or bereft of his senses, through fear. Nay, generally, at the ends of the answers, the teacher's practice is to encourage him with the exclamation, 'good,' 'right,' 'wholly right,' &c., or to check him, with his slowly and painfully articulated 'no;' and this is done with a tone of voice that marks every degree of *plus* and *minus* in the scale of approbation or regret. When a difficult question has been put to a young child, which tasks all his energies, the teacher approaches him with a mingled look of concern and encouragement; he stands before him, the light and shade of hope and fear alternately crossing his countenance; he lifts his arms and turns his body,—as a bowler who has given a wrong direction to his bowl will writhe his person to bring the ball back upon its track;—and finally, if the little wrestler with difficulty triumphs, the teacher felicitates him upon his success, perhaps seizes and shakes him by the hand, in token of congratulation; and, when the difficulty has been really formidable, and the effort triumphant, I have seen the teacher catch up the child in his arms and embrace him, as though he were not able to contain his joy. At another time, I have seen a teacher actually clap his hands with delight at a bright reply; and all this has been done so naturally and so unaffectedly as to excite no other feeling in the residue of the children than a desire, by the same means, to win the same caresses. What person worthy of being called by the name, or of sustaining the sacred relation of a parent, would not give anything, bear anything, sacrifice anything, to have his children, during eight or ten years of the period of their childhood, surrounded by circumstances, and breathed upon by sweet and humanizing influences, like these!

I mean no disparagement of our own teachers by the remark I am about to make. As a general fact, these teachers are as good as public opinion has demanded; as good as the public sentiment has been disposed to appreciate; as good as public liberality has been ready to reward; as good as the preliminary measures taken to qualify them would authorize us to expect. But it was impossible to put down the questionings of my own mind,—whether a visiter could spend six weeks in our own schools without ever hearing an angry word spoken, or seeing a blow struck, or witnessing the flow of tears.

In the Prussian schools, I observed the fair operation and full result of two practices which I have dwelt upon with great repetition and urgency at home. One is, when hearing a class recite, always to ask the question before naming the scholar who is to give the answer. The question being first asked, all the children are alert, for each one knows that he is liable to be called upon for the reply. On the contrary, if the scholar who is expected to answer is first named, and especially if the scholars are taken in succession, according to local position,—that is, in the order of their seats or stations,—then the attention of all the rest has a reprieve, until their turns shall come. In practice, this designation of the answerer before the question is propounded, operates as a temporary leave of absence, or furlough, to

all the other members of the class.

The other point referred to is that of adjusting the ease or difficulty of the questions to the capacity of the pupil. A child should never have any excuse or occasion for making a mistake; nay, at first he should be most carefully guarded from the fact, and especially from the consciousness of making a mistake. The questions should be ever so childishly simple, rather than that the answers should be erroneous. No expense of time can be too great, if it secures the habit and the desire of accuracy. Hence a false answer should be an event of the rarest occurrence,—one to be deprecated, to be looked upon with surprise and regret, and almost as an offence. Few things can have a worse effect upon a child's character than to set down a row of black marks against him, at the end of every lesson.

The value of this practice of adjusting questions to the capacities and previous attainments of the pupils, cannot be overestimated. The opposite course *necessitates* mistakes, habituates and hardens the pupils to blundering and uncertainty, disparages the value of correctness in their eyes; and,—what is a consequence as much to be lamented as any,—gives plausibility to the argument in favor of emulation as a means of bringing children back to the habit of accuracy from which they have been driven. Would the trainer of horses deserve any compensation, or have any custom, if the first draughts which he should impose upon the young animals were beyond their ability to move?

The first of the above-named practices can be adopted by every teacher, immediately, and whatever his degree of competency in other respects may be. The last improvement can only be fully effected when the teacher can dispense with all textbooks, and can teach and question from a full mind only. The case is hopeless, where a conspiracy against the spread of knowledge has been entered into between an author who complies, and a teacher who uses, a text-book, in which the questions to be put are all prepared and printed.

In former reports, I have dwelt at length upon the expediency of employing female teachers, to a greater extent, in our schools. Some of the arguments in favor of this change have been, the greater intensity of the parental instinct in the female sex, their natural love of the society of children, and the superior gentleness and forbearance of their dispositions,—all of which lead them to mildness rather than severity, to the use of hope rather than of fear as a motive of action, and to the various arts of encouragement rather than to annoyances and compulsion, in their management of the young. These views have been responded to and approved by almost all the school committee men in the State; and, within the last few years, the practice of the different districts has been rapidly conforming to this theory. I must now say that those views are calculated only for particular meridians. In those parts of Germany which I have seen, they would not be understood. No necessity for them could be perceived. There, almost all teachers, for the youngest children as well as for the oldest, are men. Two or three times, I saw a female teacher in a private school; but none in a public, unless for teaching knitting, needle work, &c. Yet in these male teachers, there was a union of gentleness and firmness that left little to be desired.

Still, in almost every German school into which I entered, I inquired whether corporal punishment were allowed or used, and I was uniformly answered in the affirmative. But it was further said, that though all teachers had liberty to use it, yet cases of its occurrence were very rare, and these cases were confined almost wholly to young scholars. Until the teacher had time to establish the relation of affection between himself and the new-comer into his school, until he had time to create that attachment which children always feel towards any one who, day after day, supplies them with novel and pleasing ideas, it was occasionally necessary to restrain and punish them. But after a short time, a love of the teacher and a love of knowledge become a substitute,—how admirable a one!—for punishment. When I asked my common question of Dr. Vogel of Leipsic, he answered, that it was still used in the schools of which he had the superintendence. "But," added he, "thank God, it is used less and less, and when we teachers become fully competent to our work, it will cease altogether."

To the above I may add, that I found all the teachers whom I visited, alive to the subject of improvement. They had libraries of the standard works on education,—works of which there are such great numbers in the German language. Every new book of any promise was eagerly sought after; and I uniformly found the educational periodicals of the day, upon the tables of the teachers. From the editor of one of these periodicals, I learned that more than thirty of this description are printed in Germany; and that the obscurest teacher in the obscurest village is usually a subscriber to one or more.

A feeling of deep humiliation overcame me, as I contrasted this state of things with that in my own country, where of all the numerous educational periodicals which have been undertaken within the last twenty years, only two, of any length of standing, still survive. All the others have failed through the indifference of teachers, and the apathy of the public. One of the remaining two,—that conducted by F. Dwight, Esq. of Albany, N. Y.—would probably have failed ere this, had not the Legislature of the State generously come to its rescue, by subscribing for twelve thousand copies,—one to be sent to each district school in that great state. The other paper, as it is well known, has never reimbursed to its editor, his actual expenses in conducting it.

HORACE MANN'S QUARREL WITH THE BOSTON SCHOOLMASTERS

(**1845**)   From Horace Mann, *Answer to the "Rejoinder" of Twenty-nine Boston Schoolmasters* (Boston, 1845), pp. 10–13.

After acquainting myself with the different school systems in the United States, and visiting schools in a large portion of the States of our Union, I went abroad. In European schools I saw many things, good, bad, and indifferent. The good I attempted to describe for imitation, and the bad for warning. Of the indifferent there is no lack of specimens in our own country. In some instances, what has been seen abroad was compared with what existed at home; but no particular teacher, or town, or class of schools, was designated for special approval or disapproval. I left the good sense of the community to make the application.

*   *   *

The Report of my tour, being prepared under the most adverse circumstances, was very far from being what I desired. Although it contains not a single assertion which I would wish to retract, yet I would have had it, in some respects more full, in others more explicit. But one thing is certain: That Report contained no special allusion to, or comparison with, any class of the Boston schools. It has had, judging from the number of copies disposed of, more than a hundred thousand readers in this country, and not one of them, that I have ever heard of, out of the city of Boston, ever surmised that it contained any attack, either open or covert, upon the Boston Masters. Nay, some of the Masters did not discern it, until their vision was aided by sharper-sighted eyes; and subsequently to their having expressed a favorable opinion. From the number of copies which have been sold, and the selections made from it by the public press, it must have been deemed to contain some useful information respecting school systems and modes of instruction and discipline . . .

It was this Report which the Boston Masters saw fit so virulently to assail. And what were its sins; or rather,—to put the question more broadly and therefore more favorably for them,—what were the supposed errors in my philosophy of instruction and discipline? On their own showing, they were four, and these only:

1. I was supposed to lean too far to the side of oral instruction, as contradistinguished from the study of textbooks.

2. I was,—mistakenly however,—supposed to approve the intense activity and excitement of some of the Scotch schools.

3. I was charged with error in advocating the method of teaching children to read, by beginning with words, instead of letters; and

4. It was numbered among my sins that I indulged the hope of seeing corporal punishment more and more disused in our schools, as its necessity might be gradually superseded, by substituting the pleasures of knowledge and high motives of action in its stead, until, at some future period (which I never attempted to fix), it might be dispensed with, except, as I was accustomed to express it, "in most extraordinary cases."

The above were proper subjects for discussion; and, in the *Common School Journal*, I had published whatever had been offered me, adverse to my own views on these points, as readily as I had published my own opinions. But, though proper subjects for discussion, they furnished no provocation for hostile attack. . . . They furnished no pretext or shadow of excuse for holding me up before the public as having been ignorant of, and indifferent to, the cause of education before my appointment as Secretary; or for attempting to array the whole State in arms against me, by the false accusation of my "great disparagement of committees, teachers, and the condition of the school system of Massachusetts"; or for assailing the Normal Schools, because I was friendly to them, or their Principals, because they were friendly to me; or for accusing me and my friends of a base collusion for most unworthy objects; or for comparing me, personally, with some of the most offensive of the English tourists who have ever visited this country; or, in fine, for the imputation of many other most dishonorable motives and actions with which the *Remarks* abound.

HORACE MANN ON THE DUTY OF THE OLD GENERATION TO THE NEW (1846) From Massachusetts Board of Education, *Tenth Annual Report . . . of the Secretary of the Board* (Boston, 1847), pp. 108–13, 124–25, 127.

It was then, amid all these privations and dangers, that the Pilgrim Fathers conceived the magnificent idea of a Free and Universal Education for the People; and, amid all their poverty, they stinted themselves to a still scantier pittance; amid all their toils, they imposed upon themselves still more burdensome labors; amid all their perils, they braved still greater dangers, that they might find the time and the means to reduce their grand conception to practice. Two divine ideas filled their great hearts,—their duty to God and to posterity. For the one, they built the church; for the other, they opened the school. Religion and Knowledge!—two attributes of the same glorious and eternal truth,—and that truth, the only one on which immortal or mortal happiness can be securely founded.

As an innovation upon all preexisting policy and usages, the establishment of Free Schools was the boldest ever promulgated, since the commencement of the Christian era. As a theory, it could have been refuted and silenced by a more formidable array of argument and experience than was ever marshalled against any other opinion of human origin. But time has ratified its soundness. Two centuries now proclaim it to be as wise as it was courageous, as beneficent as it was disinterested. It was one of those grand mental and moral experiments whose effects cannot be determined in a single generation. But now, according to the manner in which human life is computed, we are the sixth generation from its founders, and have we not reason to be grateful both to God and man for its unnumbered blessings? The sincerity of our gratitude must be tested by our efforts to perpetuate and improve what they established. The gratitude of the lips only is an unholy offering.

In surveying our vast country,—the rich savannahs of the South and the almost interminable prairies of the West,—that great valley, where, if all the nations of Europe were set down together, they could find ample subsistence,—the ejaculation involuntarily bursts forth; "WHY WERE THEY NOT COLONIZED BY MEN LIKE THE PILGRIM FATHERS!"—and as we reflect, how different would have been the fortunes of this nation, had those States,—already so numerous, and still extending, circle beyond circle,—been founded by men of high, heroic, Puritan mould;—how different in the eye of a righteous Heaven, how different in the estimation of the wise and good of all contemporary nations, how different in the fortunes of that vast procession of the generations which are yet to rise up over all those wide expanses, and to follow each other to the end of time;—as we reflect upon these things, it seems almost pious to repine at the ways of Providence; resignation becomes laborious, and we are forced to choke down our murmurings at the will of Heaven! Is it the solution of this deep mystery, that our ancestors did as much in their time, as it is ever given to one generation of men to accomplish, and have left to us and to our descendants the completion of the glorious work they began?

The alleged ground upon which the founders of our Free School system proceeded, when adopting it, did not embrace the whole argument by which it may be defended. Their insight was better than their reason. They assumed a ground, indeed, satisfactory and convincing to Protestants; but, at that time, only a small portion of Christendom was Protestant, and even now only a minority of it is so. The very ground on which our Free Schools were founded, therefore, if it were the only one, would be a reason with half of Christendom, at the present time, for their immediate abolition.

In later times, and since the achievement of American Independence, the universal and ever-repeated argument in favor of Free Schools has been, that the general intelligence which they are capable of diffusing, and which can be imparted by no other human instrumentality, is indispensable to the continuance of a republican government. This argument, it is obvious, assumes, as a postulatum, the superiority of a republican over all other forms of government; and, as a people, we religiously believe in the soundness, both of the assumption and of the argument founded upon it. But if this be all, then a sincere monarchist, a defender of arbitrary power, or a believer in the divine right of kings, would oppose Free Schools, for the identical reasons we offer in their behalf. A perfect demonstration of our doctrine,—that Free Schools are the only basis of republican institutions,—would be the perfection of reasoning to his mind, that they should be immediately exterminated.

Admitting, nay claiming for ourselves, the substantial justness and soundness of the general grounds on which our system was originally established and has since been maintained; yet it is most obvious that, unless some broader and more comprehensive principle can be found, the system of Free Schools will be repudiated by whole nations as impolitic and dangerous; and, even among ourselves, all who deny our premises will, of course, set at nought the conclusions to which they lead.

Again; the expediency of Free Schools is sometimes advocated on grounds of Political Economy. An educated people is a more industrious and productive people. Knowledge and abundance sustain to each other the relation of cause and effect. Intelligence is a primary ingredient in the Wealth of Nations. Where this does not stand at the head of the inventory, the items in a nation's valuation will be few, and the sum at the foot of the column insignificant.

The moralist, too, takes up the argument of the economist. He demonstrates that vice and crime are not only prodigals and spendthrifts of their own, but defrauders and plunderers of the means of others; that they would seize upon all the gains of honest industry, and exhaust the bounties of Heaven itself, without satiating their rapacity for new means of indulgence; and that often, in the history of the world, whole generations might have been trained to industry and virtue by the wealth which one enemy to his race has destroyed.

And yet, notwithstanding these views have been presented a thousand times, with irrefutable logic, and with a divine eloquence of truth which it would seem that nothing but combined stolidity and depravity could resist, there is not at the present time, with the exception of New England and a few small localities elsewhere, a State or a community in Christendom, which maintains a system of Free Schools for the education of its children. Even in the State of New York, with all its noble endowments, the Schools are not Free.

I believe that this amazing dereliction from duty, especially in our own country, originates more in the false notions which men entertain *respecting the nature of their right to property*, than in any thing else. In the district school meeting, in the town meeting, in legislative halls, every where, the advocates for a more generous education could carry their respective audiences with them in behalf of increased privileges for our children, were it not instinctively foreseen that increased privileges must be followed by increased taxation. Against this obstacle argument falls dead. The rich man, who has no children, declares it to be an invasion of his rights of property to exact a contribution from him to educate the children of his neighbor. The man who has reared and educated a family of children denounces it as a double tax, when he is called upon to assist in educating the children of others also; or, if he has reared his own children, without educating them, he thinks it peculiarly oppressive to be obliged to do for others, what he refrained from doing even for himself. Another, having children, but disdaining to educate them with the common mass, withdraws them from the Public School, puts them under what he calls "selecter influences," and then thinks it a grievance to be obliged to support a school which he contemns. Or if these different parties so far yield to the force of traditionary sentiment and usage, and to the public opinion around them, as to consent to do something for the cause, they soon reach the limit of expense where their admitted obligation, or their alleged charity, terminates.

It seems not relevant, therefore, in this connection, to inquire into the nature of a man's right to the property he possesses, and to satisfy ourselves respecting the question, whether any man has such an indefeasible title to his estates, or such an absolute ownership of them, as renders it unjust in the government to assess upon him his share of the expenses of educating the children of the community, up to such a point as the nature of the institutions under which he lives, and the wellbeing of society require.

I believe in the existence of a great, immutable principle of natural law, or natural ethics,—a principle antecedent to all human institutions and incapable of being abrogated by any ordinances of man,—a principle of divine origin, clearly legible in the ways of Providence as those ways are manifested in the order of nature and in the history of the race,—which proves the *absolute right* of every human being that comes into the world to an education; and which, of course, proves the correlative duty of every government to see that the means of that education are provided for all.

In regard to the application of this principle of natural law,—that is, in regard to the extent of the education to be provided for all, at the public expense,—some differences of opinion may fairly exist, under different political organizations; but under a republican government, it seems clear that the minimum of this education can never be less than such as is sufficient to qualify each citizen for the civil and social duties he will be called to discharge;—such an education as teaches the individual the great laws of bodily health; as qualifies for the fulfilment of parental duties; as is indispensable for the civil functions of a witness or a juror; as is necessary for the voter in municipal affairs; and finally, for the faithful and conscientious discharge of all those duties which devolve upon the inheritor of a portion of the sovereignty of this great republic.

The will of God, as conspicuously manifested in the order of nature, and in the relations which he has established among men, places the *right* of every child that is born into the world to such a degree of education as will enable him, and, as far as possible, will predispose him, to perform all domestic, social, civil and moral duties, upon the same clear ground of natural law and equity, as it places a child's *right,* upon his first coming into the world, to distend his lungs with a portion of the common air, or to open his eyes to the common light, or to receive that shelter, protection and nourishment which are necessary to the continuance of his bodily existence. And so far is it from being a wrong or a hardship, to demand of the possessors of property their respective shares for the prosecution of this divinely-ordained work, that they themselves are guilty of the most far-reaching injustice, who seek to resist or to evade the contribution. The complainers are the wrong-doers. The cry, "Stop thief," comes from the thief himself.

To any one who looks beyond the mere surface of things, it is obvious, that the primary and natural elements or ingredients of all property consist in the riches of the soil, in the treasures of the sea, in the light and warmth of the sun, in the fertilizing clouds and streams and dews, in the winds, and in the chemical and vegetative agencies of nature. In the majority of cases, all that we call *property*, all that makes up the valuation or inventory of a nation's capital, was prepared at the creation, and was laid up of old in the capacious store-houses of nature. For every unit that a man earns by his own toil or skill, he receives hundreds and thousands, without cost and without recompense, from the All-bountiful Giver. A proud mortal, standing in the midst of his luxuriant wheat-fields or cotton-plantations, may arrogantly call them his own; yet what barren wastes would they be, did not heaven send down upon them its dews and its rains, its warmth and its light; and sustain, for their growth and ripening, the grateful vicissitude of the seasons? It is said that from eighty to ninety per cent of the very substance of some of the great staples of agriculture are not taken from the earth but are absorbed from the air; so that these productions may more properly be called fruits of the atmosphere than of the soil. Who prepares this elemental wealth; who scatters it, like a sower, through all the regions of the atmosphere, and sends the richly-freighted winds, as His messengers, to bear to each leaf in the forest and to each blade in the cultivated field, the nourishment which their infinitely-varied needs demand? Aided by machinery, a single manufacturer performs the labor of hundreds of men. Yet what could he accomplish without the weight of the waters which God causes ceaselessly to flow; or without those gigantic forces which He has given to steam?

* * *

I bring my argument on this point, then, to a close; and I present a test of its validity, which, as it seems to me, defies denial or evasion.

In obedience to the laws of God and to the laws of all civilized communities, society is bound to protect the natural life; and the natural life cannot be protected without the appropriation and use of a portion of the property which society possesses. We prohibit infanticide under penalty of death. We practise a refinement in this particular. The life of an infant is inviolable even before he is born; and he who feloniously takes it, even before birth, is as subject to the extreme penalty of the law, as though he had struck down manhood in its vigor, or taken away a mother by violence from the sanctuary of home, where she blesses her offspring. But why preserve the natural life of a child, why preserve unborn embryos of life, if we do not intend to watch over and to protect them, and to expand their subsequent existence into usefulness and happiness? As individuals, or as an organized community, we have no natural right; we can derive no authority or countenance from reason; we can cite no attribute or purpose of the divine nature, for giving birth to any human being, and then inflicting upon that being the curse of ignorance, of poverty and of vice, with all their attendant calamities. We are brought then to this startling but inevitable alternative. The natural life of an infant should be extinguished as soon as it is born, or the means should be provided to save that life from being a curse to its possessor; and therefore every State is bound to enact a code of laws legalizing and enforcing infanticide, or a code of laws establishing Free Schools!

The three following propositions, then, describe the broad and ever-during foundation on which the Common School system of Massachusetts reposes:

The successive generations of men, taken collectively, constitute one great Commonwealth.

The property of this Commonwealth is pledged for the education of all its youth, up to such a point as will save them from poverty and vice, and prepare them for the adequate performance of their social and civil duties.

The successive holders of this property are trustees, bound to the faithful execution of their trust, by the most sacred obligations; because embezzlement and pillage from children and descendants are as criminal as the same offences when perpetrated against contemporaries.

HORACE MANN'S TWELFTH ANNUAL REPORT (1848) From Massachusetts Board of Education, *Twelfth Annual Report of . . . the Secretary of the Board* (Boston, 1849), pp. 32, 37, 42, 45, 48–49, 52–53, 58–60, 76, 84–86, 89, 93–97, 98, 116–17, 121, 124, 139–40.

The Capacities of Our Present School System to
Improve the Pecuniary Condition,
and to Elevate the Intellectual and Moral Character,
of the Commonwealth

Under the Providence of God, our means of education are the grand machinery by which the "raw material" of human nature can be worked up into inventors and discoverers, into skilled artisans and scientific farmers, into scholars and jurists, into the founders of benevolent institutions, and the great expounders of ethical and theological science. By means of early education, those embryos of talent may be quickened, which will solve the difficult problems of political and economical law; and by them, too, the genius may be kindled which will blaze forth in the Poets of Humanity. Our schools, far more than they have done, may supply the Presidents and Professors of Colleges, and Superintendents of Public Instruction, all over the land;

*   *   *

Without undervaluing any other human agency, it may be safely affirmed that the Common School, improved and energized, as it can easily be, may become the most effective and benignant of all the forces of civilization. Two reasons sustain this position. In the first place, there is a universality in its operation, which can be affirmed of no other institution whatever. If administered in the spirit of justice and conciliation, all the rising generation may be brought within the circle of its reformatory and elevating influences. And, in the second place, the materials upon which it operates are so pliant and ductile as to be susceptible of assuming a greater variety of forms than any other earthly work of the Creator. The inflexibility and ruggedness of the oak, when compared with the lithe sapling or the tender germ, are but feeble emblems to typify the docility of childhood, when contrasted with the obduracy and intractableness of man. It is these inherent advantages of the Common School, which, in our own State, have produced results so striking, from a system so imperfect, and an administration so feeble. In teaching the blind, and deaf and dumb, in kindling the latent spark of intelligence that lurks in an idiot's mind, and in the more holy work of reforming abandoned and outcast children, education has proved what it can do, by glorious experiments. These wonders it has done in its infancy, and with the lights of a limited experience; but, when its faculties shall be fully developed, when it shall be trained to wield its mighty energies for the protection of society against the giant vices which now invade and torment it;— against intemperance, avarice, war, slavery, bigotry, the woes of want and the wickedness of waste,—then, there will not be a height to which these enemies of the race can escape, which it will not scale, nor a Titan among them all, whom it will not slay.

Physical Education

In the worldly prosperity of mankind, Health and Strength are indispensable ingredients. . . .

Looking to the various disorders and disabilities, which, as every one's experience or observation shows him, do invade and prostrate the human frame, some may be slow to believe that all men, or even the majority of them, will ever be able to administer to those which fall to their share. But, in the first place, it may be remarked that a judicious course of physical training, faithfully observed through all the years of infancy, childhood, and adolescence, will avert a vast proportion of the pains and distempers, that now besiege and subdue the human system, or some of its vital organs; and hence, that one may safely be ignorant of symptoms and of remedies which he will never have occasion to recognize or to use;—as one who seeks a residence remote from wild beasts has no practical occasion to know how they are hunted;—and, in the next place, that, if every one does not know, in all cases, how it can against the wastings of ill health, and the havoc of unnecessary death; and it is bound to use equal vigilance, whether these calamities invade us from abroad, or are born of homebred ignorance and folly. And, as has been before intimated, who does not know that the aggregate suffering and loss from general and diffused causes of ill health are indefinitely greater than from the sudden irruption or outbreak of all the contagions and epidemics with which we are ever afflicted? For this greater evil, then, society is bound to provide,—not a remedy, but something better than a remedy,—a preventive. Intelligence and obedience would be an antidote, sovereign in its efficacy, and universal in its applicability.

Now it is beyond all question, that, with the rarest exceptions, every child in the Commonwealth may be indued with this intelligence; and, what is equally important, trained to conforming personal habits. Enlightened by knowledge, and impelled by the force of early and long-continued habit, he would not only see the reasonableness of adapting his regimen to his condition in the varying circumstances of life, but he would feel a personal interest in doing so, as men now feel a personal interest in procuring the gratifications of money or of power. Habit and knowledge will coincide; they will draw in the same direction; they will not be antagonists, as is now so generally the case with those adult men who acquire sound knowledge after bad habits have been enthroned,—the blind force of the latter spurning all the arguments and warnings of the former. This work may be mainly done, during the period of non-age, or before children are emancipated from parental control. Let a child wash himself all over every morning, for sixteen years, and he will as soon go without his breakfast as his bath. This is but a specimen of the effect of a long-continued observance of Nature's "Health Regulations."

Not only will a general knowledge of Human Physiology, or the Laws of Health, do much to supersede the necessity of a knowledge of Pathology, or the Laws of Disease; but the former is as much better than the latter as prevention is better than remedy;—as much better as all the comforts and securities of an unburnt dwelling are than two thirds of its value in money from the insurance office. A general diffusion of physiological knowledge will save millions annually to the State. It will gradually revolutionize many of the absurd customs and usages of society,—conforming them more and more to the rules of reason and true enjoyment, and withdrawing them more and more from the equally vicious extremes of barbarism and of artificial life. It will restrain the caprices and follies of Fashion, in regard to dress and amusement, and subordinate its ridiculous excesses to the laws of health and decency. It will reproduce the obliterated lines that once divided day and night. It will secure cleanliness and purity, more intimate and personal than any the laundress can supply. It will teach men "to eat that they may live, instead of living that they may eat." When Satan approaches in that form, in which he has hitherto been most seductive and successful,—the form of intoxicating beverages,—those who wear the talisman of this science will have an antidote against his temptations. It is a lesson of unspeakable importance, to learn that nourishment and not pleasure is the primary object of food. God, indeed, in his benevolence, has made the reception of this food not only reparative but pleasant. But to lose sight of the first object, in a brutish desire for the second, is voluntarily to alter our position in the scale of being; and, from the rank of men, to descend to the order of the beasts. Physiology would reverse the ancient fable, and transform into men the swine who now sit at epicurean tables, and drink of the Circean cup.

* * *

My general conclusion, then, under this head, is, that it is the duty of all the governing minds in society,—whether in office or out of it,—to diffuse a knowledge of these beautiful and beneficent laws of health and life, throughout the length and breadth of the State;—to popularize them; to make them, in the first place, the common acquisition of all, and, through education and custom, the common inheritance of all; so that the healthful habits naturally growing out of their observance, shall be inbred in the people; exemplified in the personal regimen of each individual; incorporated into the economy of every household; observable in all private dwellings, and in all public edifices, especially in those buildings which are erected by capitalists for the residence of their work-people, or for renting to the poorer classes; obeyed, by supplying cities with pure water; by providing public baths, public walks, and public squares; by rural cemeteries; by the drainage and sewage of populous towns, and in whatever else may promote the general salubrity of the atmosphere;—in fine, by a religious observance of all those sanitary regulations with which modern science has blessed the world.

For this thorough diffusion of sanitary intelligence, the Common School is the only agency. It is, however, an adequate agency. Let Human Physiology be introduced as an indispensable branch of study into our Public Schools; let no teacher be approved who is not master of its leading principles, and of their applications to the varying circumstances of life; let all the older classes in the schools be regularly and rigidly examined upon this study by the school committees, and a speedy change would come over our personal habits, over our domestic usages, and over the public arrangements of society. Temperance and moderation would not be such strangers at the table. Fashion, like European sovereigns, if not compelled to abdicate and fly, would be forced to compromise for the continued possession of her throne, by the surrender to her subjects of many of their natural rights. A sixth order of architecture would be invented,—the Hygienic,—which, without subtracting at all from the beauty of any other order, would add a new element of utility to them all. The "Health Regulations" of cities would be issued in a revised code,—a code that would bear the scrutiny of science. And, as the result and reward of all, a race of men and women, loftier in stature, firmer in structure, fairer in form, and better able to perform the duties and bear the burdens of life, would revisit the earth. The minikin specimens of the race, who now go on dwindling and tapering from parent to child, would reascend to manhood and womanhood. Just in proportion as the laws of health and life were discovered and obeyed, would pain, disease, insanity, and untimely death, cease from among men. Consumption would remain; but it would be consumption in the active sense.

Intellectual Education, as a Means of Removing Poverty, and Securing Abundance

* * *

Now two or three things will doubtless be admitted to be true, beyond all controversy, in regard to Massachusetts. By its industrial condition, and its business operations, it is exposed, far beyond any other state in the Union, to the fatal extremes of overgrown wealth and desperate poverty. Its population is far more dense than that of any other state. It is four or five times more dense than the average of all the other states, taken together; and density of population has always been one of the proximate causes of social inequality. According to population and territorial extent, there is far more capital in Massachusetts,—capital which is movable, and instantaneously available,—than in any other state in the Union; and probably both these qualifications respecting population and territory could be omitted without endangering the truth of the assertion. It has been recently stated, in a very respectable public journal, on the authority of a writer conversant with the subject, that, from the last of June, 1846, to the 1st of August, 1848, the amount of money invested, by the citizens of Massachusetts, "in manufacturing cities, railroads, and other improvements," is "fifty-seven millions of dollars, of which more than fifty has been paid in and expended." The dividends to be received by citizens of Massachusetts from June, 1848, to April, 1849, are estimated, by the same writer, at ten millions, and the annual increase of capital at "little short of twenty-two millions." If this be so, are we not in danger of naturalizing and domesticating among ourselves those hideous evils which are always engendered between Capital and Labor, when all the capital is in the hands of one class, and all the labor is thrown upon another?

Now, surely, nothing but Universal Education can counterwork this tendency to the domination of capital and servility of labor. If one class possesses all the wealth and the education, while the residue of society is ignorant and poor, it matters not by what name the relation between them may be called; the latter, in fact and in truth, will be the servile dependants and subjects of the former. But if education be equably diffused, it will draw property after it, by the strongest of all attractions; for such a thing never did happen, and never can happen, as that an intelligent and practical body of men should be permanently poor. Property and labor, in different classes, are essentially antagonistic; but property and labor, in the same class, are essentially fraternal. The people of Massachusetts have, in some degree, appreciated the truth, that the unexampled prosperity of the State,—its comfort, its competence, its general intelligence and virtue,—is attributable to the education, more or less perfect, which all its people have received; but are they sensible of a fact equally important?—namely, that it is to this same education that two thirds of the people are indebted for not being, to-day, the vassals of as severe a tyranny, in the form of capital, as the lower classes of Europe are bound to in the form of brute force.

Education, then, beyond all other devices of human origin, is the great equalizer of the conditions of men—the balance-wheel of the social machinery. I do not here mean that it so elevates the moral nature as to make men disdain and abhor the oppression of their fellow-men. This idea pertains to another of its attributes. But I mean that it gives each man the independence and the means, by which he can resist the selfishness of other men. It does better than to disarm the poor of their hostility towards the rich; it prevents being poor. Agrarianism is the revenge of poverty against wealth. The wanton destruction of the property of others,—the burning of hay-ricks and corn-ricks, the demolition of machinery, because it supersedes hand-labor, the sprinkling of vitriol on rich dresses,—is only agrarianism run mad. Education prevents both the revenge and the madness. On the other hand, a fellow-feeling for one's class or caste is the common instinct of hearts not wholly sunk in selfish regards for person, or for family. The spread of education, by enlarging the cultivated class or caste, will open a wider area over which the social feelings will expand; and, if this education should be universal and complete, it would do more than all things else to obliterate factitious distinctions in society.

*   *   *

Political Education

The necessity of general intelligence,—that is, of education, (for I use the terms as substantially synonymous; because general intelligence can never exist without general education, and general education will be sure to produce general intelligence,)—the necessity of general intelligence, under a republican form of government, like most other very important truths, has become a very trite one. It is so trite, indeed, as to have lost much of its force by its familiarity. Almost all the champions of education seize upon this argument, first of all; because it is so simple as to be understood by the ignorant, and so strong as to convince the sceptical. Nothing would be easier than to follow in the train of so many writers, and to demonstrate, by logic, by history, and by the nature of the case, that a republican form of government, without intelligence in the people, must be, on a vast scale, what a mad-house, without superintendent or keepers, would be, on a small one;— the despotism of a few succeeded by universal anarchy, and anarchy by despotism, with no change but from bad to worse. Want of space and time alike forbid me to attempt any full development of the merits of this theme; but yet, in the closing one of a series of reports, partaking somewhat of the nature of a summary of former arguments, an omission of this topic would suggest to the comprehensive mind the idea of incompleteness.

I have now given a hasty review of a single class of errors, those pertaining to the collection of revenue,—into which governments have fallen, through a want of intelligence;—through a want of such intelligence, it may be added, as any discreet and reflecting man would exercise in the management of his own affairs. And when will rulers be wiser than they have been? Never, until the people, to whom they are responsible, shall permit it and demand it. Never will wisdom preside in the halls of legislation and its profound utterances be recorded on the pages of the statute book, until Common Schools,—or some other agency of equal power, not yet discovered,— shall create a more far-seeing intelligence and a purer morality than has ever yet existed among communities of men. Legislators, in the execution of their high guardianship over public interests, will never secure to the State even the greatest amount of wealth, while they seek to obtain it at the price of morality. It is only when the virtue of the people is supremely cared for, that they will discover the comprehensive meaning of the Scripture, that Godliness is profitable unto all things.

However elevated the moral character of a constituency may be; however well informed in matters of general science or history, yet they must, if citizens of a Republic, understand something of the true nature and functions of the government under which they live. That any one who is to participate in the government of a country, when he becomes a man, should receive no instruction respecting the nature and functions of the government he is afterwards to administer, is a political solecism. In all nations, hardly excepting the most rude and barbarous, the future sovereign receives some training which is supposed to fit him for the exercise of the powers and duties of his anticipated station. Where, by force of law, the government devolves upon the heir, while yet in a state of legal infancy, some regency, or other substitute, is appointed, to act in his stead, until his arrival at mature age; and, in the meantime, he is subjected to such a course of study and discipline, as will tend to prepare him, according to the political theory of the time and the place, to assume the reins of authority at the appointed age. If, in England, or in the most enlightened European monarchies, it would be a proof of restored barbarism, to permit the future sovereign to grow up without any knowledge of his duties,—and who can doubt that it would be such a proof,—then, surely, it would be not less a proof of restored, or of never-removed barbarism, amongst us, to empower any individual to use the elective franchise, without preparing him for so momentous a trust. Hence, the constitution of the United States, and of our own State, should be made a study in our Public Schools. The partition of the powers of government into the three co-ordinate branches,—legislative, judicial, and executive,—with the duties appropriately devolving upon each; the mode of electing or of appointing all officers, with the reasons on which it was founded; and, especially, the duty of every citizen, in a government of laws, to appeal to the courts for redress, in all cases of alleged wrong, instead of undertaking to vindicate his own rights by his own arm; and, in a government where the people are the acknowledged sources of power, the duty of changing laws and rulers by an appeal to the ballot, and not by rebellion, should be taught to all the children until they are fully understood.

Had the obligations of the future citizen been sedulously inculcated upon all the children of this Republic, would the patriot have had to mourn over so many instances, where the voter, not being able to accomplish his purpose by voting, has proceeded to accomplish it by violence; where, agreeing with his fellow-citizens, to use the machinery of the ballot, he makes a tacit reservation, that, if that machinery does not move according to his pleasure, he will wrest or break it? If the responsibleness and value of the elective franchise were duly appreciated, the day of our State and National elections would be among the most solemn and religious days in the calendar. Men would approach them, not only with preparation and solicitude, but with the sobriety and solemnity, with which discreet and religious-minded men meet the great crises of life. No man would throw away his vote, through caprice or wantonness, any more than he would throw away his estate, or sell his family into bondage. No man would cast his vote through malice or revenge, any more than a good surgeon would amputate a limb, or a good navigator sail through perilous straits, under the same criminal passions.

But, perhaps, it will be objected, that the constitution is subject to different readings, or that the policy of different administrations has become the subject of party strife; and, therefore, if any thing of constitutional or political law is introduced into our schools, there is danger that teachers will be chosen on account of their affinities to this or that political party; or that teachers will feign affinities which they do not feel, in order that they may be chosen; and so each schoolroom will at length become a miniature political club-room, exploding with political resolves, or flaming out with political addresses, prepared, by beardless boys, in scarcely legible hand-writing, and in worse grammar.

With the most limited exercise of discretion, all apprehensions of this kind are wholly groundless. There are different readings of the constitution, it is true; and there are partisan topics which agitate the country from side to side; but the controverted points, compared with those about which there is no dispute, do not bear the proportion of one to a hundred. And what is more, no man is qualified, or can be qualified, to discuss the disputable questions, unless previously and thoroughly versed in those questions, about which there is no dispute. In the terms and principles common to all, and recognized by all, is to be found the only common medium of language and of idea, by which the parties can become intelligible to each other; and there, too, is the only common ground, whence the arguments of the disputants can be drawn.

It is obvious, on the other hand, that if the tempest of political strife were to be let loose upon our Common Schools, they would be overwhelmed with sudden ruin. Let it be once understood, that the schoolroom is a legitimate theatre for party politics, and with what violence will hostile partisans struggle to gain possession of the stage, and to play their parts upon it!

*　　*　　*

But to avoid such a catastrophe, shall all teaching, relative to the nature of our government, be banished from our schools; and shall our children be permitted to grow up in entire ignorance of the political history of their country? In the schools of a republic, shall the children be left without any distinct knowledge of the nature of a republican government; or only with such knowledge as they may pick up from angry political discussions, or from party newspapers; from caucus speeches, or Fourth of July orations,—the Apocrypha of Apocrypha?

Surely, between these extremes, there must be a medium not difficult to be found. And is not this the middle course, which all sensible and judicious men, all patriots, and all genuine republicans, must approve?—namely, that those articles in the creed of republicanism, which are accepted by all, believed in by all, and which form the common basis of our political faith, shall be taught to all. But when the teacher, in the course of his lessons or lectures on the fundamental law, arrives at a controverted text, he is either to read it without comment or remark; or, at most, he is only to say that the passage is the subject of disputation, and that the schoolroom is neither the tribunal to adjudicate, nor the forum to discuss it.

Such being the rule established by common consent, and such the practice, observed with fidelity under it, it will come to be universally understood, that political proselytism is no function of the school; but that all indoctrination into matters of controversy between hostile political parties is to be elsewhere sought for, and elsewhere imparted. Thus, may all the children of the Commonwealth receive instruction in the great essentials of political knowledge,—in those elementary ideas without which they will never be able to investigate more recondite and debatable questions;

*　　*　　*

. . . Indeed, so decisive is the effect of early training upon adult habits and character, that numbers of the most able and experienced teachers,—those who have had the best opportunities to become acquainted with the errors and the excellences of children, their waywardness and their docility,—have unanimously declared it to be their belief, that, if all the children in the community, from the age of four years to that of sixteen, could be brought within the reformatory and elevating influences of good schools, the dark host of private vices and public crimes, which now embitter domestic peace and stain the civilization of the age, might, in ninety-nine cases in every hundred, be banished from the world. When Christ taught his disciples to pray, "Thy kingdom come, thy will be done, *on earth* as it is done in heaven," did he teach them to pray for what shall never come to pass! And if this consummation is ever to be realized, is it to be by some mighty, sudden, instantaneous revolution, effected by a miracle; or is it to be produced gradually by that Providence which uses human agents as its instruments?

Were we to hear that some far-off land had been discovered, over which the tempest of war had never swept; where institutions of learning and religion were reverenced, and their ministers held in the foremost rank of honor; where falsehood, detraction, and perjury were never uttered; where neither intemperance, nor the guilty knowledge how to prepare its means, nor the guilty agents to diffuse them, were ever known; where all the obligations, growing out of the domestic relations, were sacredly kept; where office always sought the wisest and best men for incumbents, and never failed to find them; where witnesses were true, and jurors just, (for we can hardly conceive of a state of society upon earth so perfect as to exclude all differences of opinion about rights;) in fine, where all men were honest in their dealings, and exemplary in their lives,—with the exception of here and there an individual, who, from the rareness of his appearance, would be regarded almost as a monster;—were we to hear of such a realm, who, that loves peace and the happiness that comes from security and order, would not wish to escape from the turmoil and the violence, the rancor and the mean ambitions, of our present sphere, and go there to dwell and to die? And yet, it is the opinion of our most intelligent, dispassionate, and experienced teachers, that we can, in the course of two or three generations, and through the instrumentality of good teachers and good schools, superinduce, substantially, such a state of society upon the present one; and this, too, without any miracle, without any extraordinary sacrifices, or costly effort; but only by working our existing Common School system with such a degree of vigor as can easily be put forth, and at such an expense as even the poorest community can easily bear. If the leaders of society,—those whose law-giving eloquence determines what statutes shall be enacted by the Legislature, or those who speak for the common heart in self-constituted assemblies, or those who shape popular opinion through the public press, or in the private intercourse of life,—if these are not yet prepared to have faith in the reformatory power of an early and wise training for the young, the fact only shows and measures the extent of the work which teachers and educationists have yet to perform. If men decline to coöperate with us, because uninspired by our living faith, then the arguments, the labors, and the results, which will create this faith, are a preliminary step in our noble work.

❊   ❊   ❊

But, it will be said that this grand result, in Practical Morals, is a consummation of blessedness that can never be attained without Religion; and that no community will ever be religious, without a Religious Education. Both these propositions, I regard as eternal and immutable truths. Devoid of religious principles and religious affections, the race can never fall so low but that it may sink still lower; animated and sanctified by them, it can never rise so high but that it may ascend still higher. And is it not at least as presumptuous to expect that mankind will attain to the knowledge of truth, without being instructed in truth, and without that general expansion and development of faculty which will enable them to recognize and comprehend truth, in any other department of human interest, as in the department of religion? No creature of God, of whom we have any knowledge, has such a range of moral oscillation as a human being. He may despise privileges, and turn a deaf ear to warnings and instructions, such as evil spirits may never have known, and therefore be more guilty than they; or, ascending through temptation and conflict, along the radiant pathway of duty, he may reach the sublimest heights of happiness, and may there experience the joys of a contrast, such as ever-perfect beings can never feel. And can it be that our nature, in this respect, is taken out of the law that governs it in every other respect;—the law, namely, that the teachings which supply it with new views, and the training that leads it to act in conformity with those views, are ineffective and nugatory?

*　　*　　*

After years of endurance, after suffering under misconstructions of conduct, and the imputation of motives, whose edge is sharper than a knife, it was, at my suggestion, and by making use of materials which I had laboriously collected, that the Board made its Eighth Annual Report;—a document said to be the ablest argument in favor of the use of the Bible in Schools, any where to be found. This Report had my full concurrence. Since its appearance, I have always referred to it, as explanatory of the views of the Board, and as setting forth the law of a wise Commonwealth and the policy of a Christian people. Officially and unofficially, publicly and privately, in theory and in practice, my course has always been in conformity with its doctrines. And I avail myself of this, the last opportunity which I may ever have, to say, in regard to all affirmations or intimations, that I have ever attempted to exclude religious instruction from school, or to exclude the Bible from school, or to impair the force of that volume, arising out of itself, are now, and always have been, without substance or semblance of truth.

But it may still be said, and it is said, that, however sincere, or however religiously disposed, the advocates of our school system may be, still the character of the system is not to be determined by the number, nor by the sincerity of its defenders, but by its own inherent attributes; and that, if judged by these attributes, it is, in fact and in truth, an irreligious, an un-Christian, and an anti-Christian system. Having devoted the best part of my life to the promotion of this system, and believing it to be the only system which ought to prevail, or can permanently prevail, in any free country; I am not content to see it suffer, unrelieved, beneath the weight of imputations so grievous; nor is it right that any hostile system should be built up by so gross a misrepresentation of ours. That our Public Schools are not Theological Seminaries, is admitted. That they are debarred by law from inculcating the peculiar and distinctive doctrines or any one religious denomination amongst us, is claimed; and that they are also prohibited from ever teaching that what they do teach, is the whole of religion, or all that is essential to religion or to salvation, is equally certain. But our system earnestly inculcates all Christian morals; it founds its morals on the basis of religion; it welcomes the religion of the Bible; and, in receiving the Bible, it allows it to do what it is allowed to do in no other system,—*to speak for itself.* But here it stops, not because it claims to have compassed all truth; but because it disclaims to act as an umpire between hostile religious opinions.

The very terms, *Public School,* and *Common School,* bear upon their face, that they are schools which the children of the entire community may attend. Every man, not on the pauper list, is taxed for their support. But he is not taxed to support them as special religious institutions; if he were, it would satisfy, at once, the largest definition of a Religious Establishment. But he is taxed to support them, as a *preventive* means against dishonesty, against fraud, and against violence; on the same principle that he is taxed to support criminal courts as a *punitive* means against the same offences. He is taxed to support schools, on the same principle that he is taxed to support paupers; because a child without education is poorer and more wretched than a man without bread. He is taxed to support schools, on the same principle that he would be taxed to defend the nation against foreign invasion, or against rapine committed by a foreign foe; because the general prevalence of ignorance, superstition, and vice, will breed Goth and Vandal at home, more fatal to the public well-being, than any Goth or Vandal from abroad. And, finally, he is taxed to support schools, because they are the most effective means of developing and training those powers and faculties in a child, by which, when he becomes a man, he may understand what his highest interests and his highest duties are; and may be, in fact, and not in name only, a free agent. The elements of a political education are not bestowed upon any school child, for the purpose of making him vote with this or that political party, when he becomes of age; but for the purpose of enabling him to choose for himself, with which party he will vote. So the religious education which a child receives at school, is not imparted to him, for the purpose of making him join this or that denomination, when he arrives at years of discretion, for for the purpose of enabling him to judge for himself, according to the dictates of his own reason and conscience. . . . .

This topic invites far more extended exposition; but this must suffice. In bidding an official Farewell to a system, with which I have been so long connected, to which I have devoted my means, my strength, my health, twelve years of time, and, doubtless, twice that number of years from what might otherwise have been my term of life, I have felt bound to submit these brief views in its defence. In justice to my own name and memory; in justice to the Board of which I was originally a member, and from which I have always sought counsel and guidance; and in justice to thousands of the most wise, upright, and religious-minded men in Massachusetts, who have been my fellow-laborers in advancing the great cause of Popular Education, under the auspices of this system, I have felt bound to vindicate it from the aspersions cast upon it, and to show its consonance with the eternal principles of equity and justice. I have felt bound to show, that, so far from its being an irreligious, an anti-Christian, or an un-Christian system, it is a system which recognizes religious obligations in their fullest extent; that it is a system which invokes a religious spirit, and can never be fitly administered without such a spirit; that it inculcates the great commands, upon which hang all the law and the prophets; that it welcomes the Bible, and therefore welcomes all the doctrines which the Bible really contains, and that it listens to these doctrines so reverently, that, for the time being, it will not suffer any rash mortal to thrust in his interpolations of their meaning, or overlay the text with any of the "many inventions" which the heart of man has sought out. It is a system, however, which leaves open all other means of instruction,—the pulpits, the Sunday schools, the Bible classes, the catechisms, of all denominations,—to be employed according to the preferences of individual parents. It is a system which restrains itself from teaching, that what it does teach is all that needs to be taught or that should be taught; but leaves this to be decided by each man for himself, according to the light of his reason and conscience; and on his responsibility to that Great Being, who, in holding him to an account for the things done in the body, will hold him to the strictest account for the manner in which he has "trained up" his children.

*　　*　　*

Such, then, in a religious point of view, is the Massachusetts system of Common Schools. Reverently, it recognizes and affirms the sovereign rights of the Creator; sedulously and sacredly it guards the religious rights of the creature; while it seeks to remove all hindrances, and to supply all furtherances to a filial and paternal communion between man and his Maker. In a social and political sense, it is a *Free* school system. It knows no distinction of rich and poor, of bond and free, or between those who, in the imperfect light of this world, are seeking, through different avenues, to reach the gate of heaven. Without money and without price, it throws open its doors, and spreads the table of its bounty, for all the children of the State. Like the sun, it shines, not only upon the good, but upon the evil, that they may become good; and, like the rain, its blessings descend, not only upon the just, but upon the unjust, that their injustice may depart from them and be known no more.

HORACE MANN ON LEAVING THE BOARD OF EDUCATION

(1848) From Letter, May 20, 1848, as quoted in E. I. F. Williams, *Horace Mann: Educational Statesman* (New York, 1937), p. 282.

They have conferred upon me the only office I ever coveted, and have placed me in direct and active relation to the only object of ambition I have ever had,—the well-being of *all* the people, thro' the instrumentality of education. To have had an opportunity to labor in this cause, thro' such a series of years, I regard as the happiness of my life; and tho' this happiness has not been without its trials, yet I am sure that the pains of the trials will pass away, while the remembrance of the joy will survive and abide. I had long cherished the hope, that, either in a public or private capacity, I might remain in this field of labor during the residue of my life; but since the last meeting of the Board, circumstances have intervened, which will, partially and temporarily at least, divert me from this immediate work. My hands may be taken from it; but not my heart. My direct efforts may be withdrawn from it; but my interest in it can never be alienated. Among benevolent objects, it is the most benevolent; among noble pursuits, it is the noblest; among objects of ambition, I regard it as the highest.

THE "BOSTON TRANSCRIPT'S" EULOGY OF HORACE MANN ON HIS RETIREMENT FROM THE BOARD OF EDUCATION (1848) From *Boston Transcript*, December 18, 1848.

Twelve years ago, at the earnest solicitation of many true friends of their race, and far-seeing guardians of our beloved state, he was induced to relinquish honors which he held in full possession: competency, which he might have considered secure; and advancement, the path to which was wide open; for favor in prospect, which was to be earned by toil and much endurance; for pecuniary emolument, the only sure element of which was its inadequacy to meet his wants; and for advancement, not from the high point to which he had already attained, but from an humble starting place, from which to eminence not a step of the pathway had been broken.

Under such circumstances a common man would have assuredly failed; nay, he would have shrunk back, and abandoned so arduous, so humiliating, and so hopeless a task. But Mr. Mann had already accomplished many works that were sufficient guarantees for his ability, and for his readiness to sacrifice himself for the sake of others; and his earliest reports show that he did not undertake the work before he had calculated the labor and cost. He saw the limited territory and population of Massachusetts, and her daily diminution in rank and importance on this account, and he felt in its full force, the truth that nothing could save her from degradation but the superior intelligence and virtue of her citizens. The common school system, which originated with the founders of Massachusetts, and was a remarkable effort for their times, had fallen into disrepute, and had become the mere shadow of a mighty name. So far from advancing beyond its original limits, as man advanced, and science spread, and means had increased, it had come to a stand everywhere, the spirit had departed, and even the lifeless form was shrinking up through apathy and neglect. The state was improvident, the towns were indifferent, the parents were neglectful, and the teachers incompetent, and the work of awakening the state to its duty and its danger; of arousing the towns to activity, the parents to a sense of their responsibility, and the teachers to a sense of their incompetency; this and nothing short of this, was to be done, in order to meet the exigency, and avert the danger.

This task, hopeless, and thankless, and profitless as it seemed to common minds, was the task set before Mr. Mann, and those only who know the condition of the state twelve years ago, and who are aware of its present animation and substantial improvement, can form an adequate idea of the zeal, the energy, and enduring self-sacrifice, which have wrought out the reformation. To enumerate all the particulars of this remarkable work, would be to copy the twelve Annual Reports of the Secretary, each a volume, the Annual Abstracts of School Returns, each of them work enough for the year of whose labors it was a small item; the ten volumes of the Common School Journal; and the volume of Official Lectures, unmatched for their wisdom, their beauty and their power; and even then we should have but a meagre record of what the pen has done, while all that the tongue has accomplished, to conciliate the hostile, to reconcile the conflicting, to instruct the inquring, to encourage the despairing, and, as it were, to raise the dead, would remain untold.

This great work, however, has been done, and well done. There is sensation in every nerve, power in every muscle, and activity in every limb of the Commonwealth. The citizens of the districts, by their own voluntary act, have assessed themselves more than two million dollars for the erection and improvement of schoolhouses, they have doubled the amount paid to their teachers; and the quality of the teachers has risen in proportion at least to their increased remuneration; the discipline of the schools has been essentially ameliorated; the branches taught have not only been increased in number, but have been more intelligibly and thoroughly taught; the textbooks have become better adapted to practical instruction, but, what is perhaps of more importance, they have become uniform in each school, and, generally, in each entire town; the classification of pupils, and the consequent graduation of schools into primary, grammar and high schools, will form an era in the history of education; the normal schools, established and successfully conducted so far, have leavened the mass of our teachers, and taught them their duty and their claims; the school committees have become more vigilant, more earnest, more intelligent; the people have become more liberal, and disposed to claim as a right and a privilege, what before was a scandal and a burden; and finally, the government of the state has begun to feel that its strength lies in general education, and that this saving education depends upon free common schools, and can be produced by nothing else.

Such is a brief summary of the labors of Mr. Mann in his native state, but the impulse given to education has not been confined to Massachusetts. At this moment there is not, probably, a state in the Union which has not been moved, and which is not looking up to Massachusetts for direction and encouragement. The states from Maine to Texas are blessed, or to be blessed, by the example and recorded labors of Massachusetts; and while we allow something to the cooperation of many worthy minds, and many noble hearts, who does not know, who is not willing to confess, that all this is mainly the work of Horace Mann?

HORACE MANN'S VALEDICTORY ADDRESS AT ANTIOCH COLLEGE

(1859)   From Mary Peabody Mann, *Life of Horace Mann* (Boston, 1865), pp. 554–55, 573–75.

Young Ladies and Gentlemen of the Graduating Class,—

After journeying together for so many years on our passage through life, we are about to part. Another day, ay, another hour, and we separate. Would to God I could continue this journey with you through all its future course! There is no suffering of a physical nature which I could survive, that I would not gladly bear, if thereby I could be set back to your starting-point,—to the stage of life where you are now standing. When I think, after the experience of one life, what I could and would do in an amended edition of it; what I could and would do, more and better than I have done, for the cause of humanity, of temperance, and of peace; for breaking the rod of the oppressor; for the higher education of the world, and especially for the higher education of the best part of it,—woman: when I think of these things, I feel the Phœnix-spirit glowing within me; I pant, I yearn, for another warfare in behalf of right, in hostility to wrong, where, without furlough, and without going into winter-quarters, I would enlist for another fifty-years' campaign, and fight it out for the glory of God and the welfare of man. I would volunteer to join a "forlorn hope" to assault the very citadel of Satan, and carry it by storm, and bind the old heresiarch (he is the worst heresiarch who does wrong) for a thousand years; and if in that time he would not repent, of which I confess myself not without hope, then to give him his final quietus.

But alas! that cannot be; for, while the Phœnix-spirit burns within, the body becomes ashes. Not only would the sword fall from my hand; my hand would fall from the sword.

I cannot go with you. You must pursue your conquering march alone.

What, then, can I do? Can I enshrine my spirit in your hearts, so that when I fall in the ranks (as I hope to fall in the very front ranks of this contest), and when my arm shall no longer strike, and my voice no longer cheer, you may pursue the conflict, and win the victory?—the victory of righteousness under the banner of Jesus Christ. This transferrence of my enthusiasm, of the results of all my experience and study, into your young and athletic frames, is what I desire to do; what, as far as my enfeebled strength allows, I shall now attempt to do.

But, first, the new circumstances under which we assemble to-day; the new men whom I see on this stage occupying the seats of official dignity and honor; or, where the individual men are not new, the new functions they have come here to execute; in fine, the new auspices under which this commencement is held,—demand a word.

This is Antioch College still, the same as we have known and loved it heretofore; but, according to the doctrine of metempsychosis, it is by the transmigration of the old soul into a new body. The old body, with its works (that is, its scholarships and its debts, and its promises to pay without paying), is dead; and in its stead we have the resurrection of a new and glorified body,—a body without scholarships, without debts or pecuniary trespasses of any kind.

But this beneficent change has not been accomplished without a great struggle. In contests where the antagonist powers of good and evil come into collision, especially where the conflict is waged on a conspicuous arena, the respective combatants will summon their auxiliaries from above and below. We feel as if, during the last two years, our enemies had enlisted their most potent allies against us, but such as bore no tokens of coming from above. We feel as if the cause of right and truth had at last triumphed; and therefore, though ready to forget and forgive, we feel as if we have a right to congratulate ourselves, and as if it were a duty to thank Heaven for our success.

Crowding thick around you, my young friends who go forth from here to-day, I see these various classes and characters of men whom I have attempted to portray. Select which you please. Transmigrate through the forms of one class into ever-increasing nobleness and dignity, ascending to all temporal honor and renown, to end in the glories of immortality; or plunge through the other, from degradation to degradation, to a perdition that is bottomless.

I need not carry out the parallel with regard to the young ladies who are before me, and who are candidates for graduation to-day. For them, if they will have the courage to lift themselves out of the frivolities of a fashionable and a selfish life, each one, in her own sphere and in her own way, may become another Isabella, securing an outfit for another Columbus for the discovery of another hemisphere wherewith to bless mankind,—more honorable to the queenly helper than to the bold navigator. . . .

The last words I have to say to you, my young friends, are these:—

You are in the kingdom of a Divine Majesty who governs his realms according to law. By his laws, it is no more certain that fire will consume, or that water will drown, than that sin will damn. Nor is it more sure that flame will mount, or the magnetic needle point to the pole, than it is that a righteous man will ascend along a path of honor to glory and beatitude. These laws of God pervade all things, and they operate with omnipotent force. Our free agency consists merely in the choice we make to put ourselves under the action of one or another of these laws. Then the law seizes us, and sweeps us upward or downward with resistless power. If you stand on the great table-land of North America, you can launch your boat on the head waters of the Columbia, or the Mackenzie, or the St. Lawrence, or the Mississippi; but the boat, once launched, will be borne *towards* the selected one of the four points of the compass, and *from* all the others. If you place your bark in the Gulf Stream, it will bear you northward, and not southward; or though that stream is as large as three thousand Mississippis, yet you can steer your bark across it, and pass into the region of the variable or the trade winds beyond, to be borne by them.

If you seek suicide from a precipice, you have only to lose your balance over its edge, and gravitation takes care of the rest. So you have only to set your head right by knowledge, and your heart right by obedience, and forces stronger than streams or winds or gravitation will bear you up to celestial blessedness. Elijah-like, by means as visible and palpable as though they were horses of fire and chariots of fire.

Take heed to this, therefore, that the law of God is the supreme law. The judge may condemn an innocent man; but posterity will condemn the judge. The United States are mighty; but they are not almighty. How sad and how true what Kossuth said, that there had never yet been a Christian government on earth! Before there can be a Christian government, there must be Christian men and women. Be you these men and women! An unjust government is only a great bully; and though it should wield the navy in one fist and the army in the other, though it should array every gun in the armories of Springfield and Harper's Ferry into one battery, and make you their target, the righteous soul is as secure from them as is the sun at its zenith height.

While, to a certain extent, you are to live for yourselves in this life, to a greater extent you are to live for others. Great boons, such as can only be won by great labors, are to be secured; great evils are to be vanquished. Nothing to-day prevents this earth from being a paradise but error and sin. These errors, these sins, you must assail. The disabilities of poverty; the pains of disease; the enervations and folly of fashionable life; the brutishness of appetite, and the demonisms of passion; the crowded vices of cities, thicker than their inhabitants; the retinue of calamities that come through ignorance; the physical and moral havoc of war; the woes of intemperance; the wickedness of oppression, whether of the body or of the soul; the Godlessness and Christlessness of bigotry,—these are the hosts against which a war of extermination is to be waged, and you are to be the warriors. Never shrink, never retreat, because of danger: go into the strife with your epaulettes on.

At the terrible battle of Trafalgar, when Lord Nelson, on board the "Victory," the old flag-ship of Keppel and of Jervis, bore down upon the combined fleets of France and of Spain, he appeared upon the quarter-deck with his breast all blazing with gems and gold, the insignia of the "stars" and "orders" he had received. His officers, each a hero, besought him not thus to present himself a shining mark for the sharpshooters of the enemy, but to conceal or doff the tokens of his rank. "No," replied Nelson: "in honor I won them, and in honor I'll wear them!" He dashed at the French line, and grappled with the "Redoubtable" in the embrace of death. But, when the battle had raged for an hour, a musket-ball, shot from the mizzen-top of the enemy, struck his left epaulette, and, crashing down through muscle and bone and artery, lodged in his spine. He knew the blow to be fatal; but as he lay writhing in mortal agony, as the smoke of battle at intervals cleared away, and the news was brought to him that one after another of the enemy's ships—the "Redoubtable," the "Bucentaur," the "Santa Anna," the "Neptune," the "Fougueux"—had struck their colors, his death-pangs were quelled, joy illumined his face, and for four hours the energy of his will sustained his vitality; and he did not yield to death until the fleets had yielded to him.

So, in the infinitely nobler battle in which you are engaged against error and wrong, if ever repulsed or stricken down, may you always be solaced and cheered by the exulting cry of triumph over some abuse in Church or State, some vice or folly in society, some false opinion or cruelty or guilt which you have overcome! And I beseech you to treasure up in your hearts these my parting words: *Be ashamed to die until you have won some victory for humanity.*

MASSACHUSETTS COMPULSORY SCHOOL LAW OF 1852 From *Acts and Resolves Passed by the General Court of Massachusetts in the Year 1852,* pp. 170–71.

An Act Concerning the Attendance of Children at School

BE IT ENACTED BY THE SENATE AND HOUSE OF REPRESENTATIVES IN GENERAL COURT ASSEMBLED, AND BY THE AUTHORITY OF THE SAME, AS FOLLOWS:

Sect. 1. Every person who shall have any child under his control, between the ages of eight and fourteen years, shall send such child to some public school within the town or city in which he resides, during at least twelve weeks, if the public schools within such town or city shall be so long kept, in each and every year during which such child shall be under his control, six weeks of which shall be consecutive.

Sect. 2. Every person who shall violate the provisions of the first section of this act shall forfeit, to the use of such town or city, a sum not exceeding twenty dollars, to be recovered by complaint or indictment.

Sect. 3. It shall be the duty of the school committee in the several towns or cities to inquire into all cases of violation of the first section of this act, and to ascertain of the persons violating the same, the reasons, if any, for such violation, and they shall report such cases, together with such reasons, if any, to the town or city in their annual report; but they shall not report any cases such as are provided for by the fourth section of this act.

Sect. 4. If, upon inquiry by the school committee, it shall appear, or if upon the trial of any complaint or indictment under this act it shall appear, that such child has attended some school, not in the town or city in which he resides, for the time required by this act, or has been otherwise furnished with the means of education for a like period of time, or has already acquired those branches of learning which are taught in common schools, or if it shall appear that his bodily or mental condition has been such as to prevent his attendance at school, or his acquisition of learning for such a period of time, or that the person having the control of such child, is not able, by reason of poverty, to send such child to school, or to furnish him with the means of education, then such person shall be held not to have violated the provisions of this act.

Sect. 5. It shall be the duty of the treasurer of the town or city to prosecute all violations of this act. (*Approved by the Governor,* May 18, 1852.)

NEW YORK'S COMPULSORY SCHOOL LAW (1874) From *Laws of the State of New York, Passed at the Ninety-seventh Session of the Legislature* (1874), pp. 532–35.

The People of the State of New York, represented in Senate and Assembly, do enact as follows:

Section 1. All parents and those who have the care of children shall instruct them, or cause them to be instructed, in spelling, reading, writing, English grammar, geography and arithmetic. And every parent, guardian or other person having control and charge of any child between the ages of eight and fourteen years shall cause such child to attend some public or private day school at least fourteen weeks in each year, eight weeks at least of which attendance shall be consecutive, or to be instructed regularly at home at least fourteen weeks in each year in spelling, reading, writing, English grammar, geography and arithmetic, unless the physical or mental condition of the child is such as to render such attendance or instruction inexpedient or impracticable.

2. No child under the age of fourteen years shall be employed by any person to labor in any business whatever during the school hours of any school day of the school term of the public school in the school district or the city where such child is, unless such child shall have attended some public or private day-school where instruction was given by a teacher qualified to instruct in spelling, reading, writing, geography, English grammar and arithmetic, or shall have been regularly instructed at home in said branches, by some person qualified to instruct in the same, at least fourteen weeks of the fifty-two weeks next preceding any and every year in which such child shall be employed, and shall, at the time of such employment, deliver to the employer a certificate in writing, signed by the teacher, or a school trustee of the district or of a school, certifying to such attendance or instruction; and any person who shall employ any child contrary to the provisions of this section, shall, for each offense, forfeit and pay a penalty of fifty dollars to the treasurer or chief fiscal officer of the city or supervisor of the town in which such offense shall occur, and said sum or penalty, when so paid, to be added to the public school money of the school district in which the offense occurred.

3. It shall be the duty of the trustee or trustees of every school district, or public school, or union school, in every town and city, in the months of September and of

February of each year to examine into the situation of the children employed in all manufacturing establishments in such school district; and, in case any town or city is not divided into school districts, it shall, for the purposes of the examination provided for in this section, be divided by the school authorities thereof into districts, and the said trustees notified of their respective districts, on or before the first day of January of each year; and the said trustee or trustees shall ascertain whether all the provisions of this act are duly observed, and report all violations thereof to the treasurer or chief fiscal officer of said city or supervisor of said town. On such examination, the proprietor, superintendent or manager of said establishment shall, on demand, exhibit to said examining trustee, a correct list of all children between the ages of eight and fourteen years employed in said establishment with the said certificates of attendance on school, or of instruction.

4. Every parent, guardian or other person having control and charge of any child between the ages of eight and fourteen years, who has been temporarily discharged from employment in any business, in order to be afforded an opportunity to receive instruction or schooling, shall send such child to some public or private school, or shall cause such child to be regularly instructed as aforesaid at home for the period for which such child may have been so discharged, to the extent of at least fourteen weeks in all in each year, unless the physical or mental condition of the child is such as to render such an attendance or instruction inexpedient or impracticable.

5. The trustee or trustees of any school district or public school, or the president of any union school, or in case there is no such officer, then such officer as the board of education of said city or town may designate, is hereby authorized and empowered to see that sections one, two, three, four and five of this act are enforced, and to report in writing all violations thereof, to the treasurer or chief fiscal officer of his city or to the supervisor of his town; any person who shall violate any provision of sections one, three and four of this act, shall, on written notice of such violation, from one of the school officers above named, forfeit, for the first offense, and pay to the treasurer or chief fiscal officer of the city or to the supervisor of the town in which he resides, or such offense has occurred, the sum of one dollar, and after such first offense, shall, for each succeeding offense in the same year, forfeit and pay to the treasurer of said city or supervisor of said town the sum of five dollars for each and every week, not exceeding thirteen weeks in any one year during which he, after written notice from said school officer, shall have failed to comply with any of said provisions, the said penalties, when paid, to be added to the public school money of said school district in which the offense occurred.

6. In every case arising under this act where the parent, guardian, or other persons having the control of any child between the said ages of eight and fifteen years, is unable to provide such child for said fourteen weeks with the text-books required to be furnished to enable such child to attend school for said period, and shall so state in writing to the said trustee, the said trustee shall provide said text-books for said fourteen weeks at the public school for the use of such child, and the expense of the same shall be paid by the treasurer of said city or the supervisor of said town on the certificate of the said trustee, specifying the items furnished for the use of such child.

7. In case any person having the control of any child between the ages of eight and fourteen years, is unable to induce said child to attend school for the said fourteen weeks in each year and shall so state in writing to said trustee, the said child shall, from and after the date of the delivery to said trustee of said statement in writing, be deemed and dealt with as an habitual truant, and said person shall be

relieved of all penalties incurred for said year after said date, under sections one, four and five of this act, as to such child.

8. The board of education or public instruction, by whatever name it may be called in each city, and the trustees of the school districts and union school in each town by an affirmative vote of a majority of said trustees at a meeting or meetings to be called for this purpose, on ten days' notice in writing to each trustee, said notice to be given by the town clerk, are for each of their respective cities and towns hereby authorized and empowered and directed on or before the first day of January, eighteen hundred and seventy-five, to make all needful provisions, arrangements, rules and regulations concerning habitual truants and children between said ages of eight and fourteen years of age, who may be found wandering about the streets or public places of such city or town during the school hours of the school day of the term of the public school of said city or town, having no lawful occupation or business, and growing up in ignorance, and said provisions, arrangements, rules and regulations shall be such as shall, in their judgment, be most conducive to the welfare of such children, and to the good order of such city or town; and shall provide suitable places for the discipline and instruction and confinement, when necessary, of such children, and may require the aid of the police of cities and constables of towns to enforce their said rules and regulations; provided, however, that such provisions, arrangements, rules and regulations, shall not go into effect as laws for said several cities and towns, until they shall have been approved, in writing, by a justice of the supreme court for the judicial district in which said city or town is situated, and when so approved he shall file the same with the clerk of the said city or town who shall print the same and furnish ten copies thereof to each trustee of each school district or public or union school of said city or town. The said trustees shall keep one copy thereof posted in a conspicuous place in or upon each school-house in his charge during the school terms each year. In like manner, the same, in each city or town may be amended or revised annually in the month of December.

9. Justices of the peace, civil justices and police justices shall have jurisdiction, within their respective towns and cities, of all offenses and of all actions for penalties or fines described in this act, or that may be described in said provisions, arrangements, rules and regulations authorized by section eight of this act. All actions for fines and penalties under this act, shall be brought in the name of the treasurer or chief fiscal officer of the city or supervisor of the town to whom the same is payable, but shall be brought by and under the direction of the said trustee or trustees, or said officer designated by the board of education.

10. Two weeks attendance at a half time or evening school shall for all purposes of this act be counted as one week at a day school.

11. This act shall take effect on the first day of January, eighteen hundred and seventy-five.

The Religious Question
Protestants

THE NEW YORK FREE-SCHOOL SOCIETY DESCRIBES ITS VIEWS AND
MOTIVES TO THE PUBLIC (1819)   From William Oland Bourne, *History of the
Public School Society of the City of New York* (New York, 1870), pp. 36–39.

An Address

*To the Parents and Guardians of the Children belonging to the Schools under the
care of the New York Free-School Society.*

SEC. 1. The New York Free Schools, for the instruction of such children as are
the objects of a gratuitous education, have been established many years; and the
trustees have endeavored to render them useful and promotive of the moral and
literary improvement of the scholars, and they still wish to do all in their power to
advance the welfare of both children and parent.

SEC. 2. They wish to impress on your minds the importance of this establishment, that you may manifest an increasing concern for its prosperity, seeing that
much depends on your coöperation in the support of an institution which is
intended to promote not only the good of your children, but their happiness and
yours, both here and hereafter.

SEC. 3. It is of great importance that the minds of your children should be early
cultivated and moral instruction inculcated, and, that, by example as well as
precept, you should use all endeavors to preserve them in innocency.

SEC. 4. As a good education is calculated to lay the foundation of usefulness and
respectability, both in civil and religious society, it is your duty to improve every
opportunity to promote it.

SEC. 5. This institution holds out much encouragement, and you are bound by
every moral obligation to avail yourselves of the advantages which your children
may derive from a steady attendance at school, where they may acquire not only
school learning to qualify them for business, but be improved in their morals and
manners.

SEC. 6. Many of you have not been favored with the privileges your children
now enjoy—that of a gratuitous education. Every parent who is solicitous for the
welfare of his offspring, but whose circumstances may be such as not to be able to
pay the expense, is invited to come forward and place them where they may be
instructed in literature, in the paths of virtue, and in the road to happiness.

THE COMMON
SCHOOL
MOVEMENT

1119

SEC. 7. The trustees may venture to say, that this institution may be productive of great good to you, and to your children especially, if, on your part, there is a disposition to promote it. We wish your children may be furnished with a good education, and early acquire good habits. As they grow in years, they should be impressed with the importance of industry and frugality. These are virtues necessary to form useful characters.

SEC. 8. You know that many evils grow out of idleness, and many more out of the improper use of spirituous liquors; that they are ruinous and destructive to morals, and debase the human character below the lowest of all created beings; we therefore earnestly desire you may be watchful and careful in this respect, otherwise in vain may we labor to promote the welfare of your children.

SEC. 9. In domestic life there are many virtues which are requisite in order to promote the comfort and welfare of families. Temperance and economy are indispensable, but without cleanliness, your enjoyments as well as your reputation will be impaired. It is promotive of health, and ought not to be neglected. Parents can, perhaps, scarcely give a greater proof of their care for their children, than by keeping them clean and decent, especially when they are sent to school, where it is expected they will appear with their hands, faces, and heads perfectly clean, and their clothing clean and in good order. The appearance of children exhibits to every observing mind the character of the mother.

SEC. 10. Among other moral and religious duties, that of a due observance of the first day of the week, commonly called Sunday, we consider of importance to yourselves and to your children. Public worship is a duty we owe to our Creator; it is of universal obligation, and you ought to be good examples therein, encouraging your families to the due observance thereof; and believing, as we do, that the establishment of what is called Sunday schools has been a blessing to many, and may prove so to many more, we are desirous you may unite in the support of a plan so well calculated to promote the religious duties of that day, which ought to be appropriated to public worship, retirement, and other duties connected with the improvement of the mind.

SEC. 11. Seeing, next to your own souls, your children and those placed under your care are, or ought to be, the immediate objects of your constant attention and diligent concern, you ought to omit no opportunity to instruct them early in the principles of the Christian religion, in order to bring them, in their youth, to a sense of the unspeakable love and infinite wisdom and power of their Almighty Creator; for good and early impressions on tender minds often prove a lasting means of preserving them in a religious life even to old age. May you, therefore, watch over them for good, and rule over them in the fear of GOD, maintaining your authority in love; and as very much depends on the care and exemplary conduct of parents, and the judicious management of children by tutors, we cannot too strongly recommend to their serious consideration the importance of the subject, as one deeply interesting to the welfare of the rising generation, and no less connected with the best interests of civil and religious society.

SEC. 12. As the Holy Scriptures, or Bible, with which you ought all to be furnished, contain a full account of things most surely to be believed and Divine commands most faithfully to be obeyed, and are said to make wise unto salvation through faith which is in Jesus Christ (2 Tim. iii. 15), it is the duty of every Christian to be frequent and diligent in the reading of them in their families, and in privately meditating on those sacred records.

SEC. 13. The trustees of the New York Free School, however desirous they may be to promote the improvement of the scholars in school learning, to qualify and fit them for the common duties of life, cannot view with an eye of indifference the more primary object of an education calculated to form habits of virtue and industry, and to inculcate the general principles of Christianity; for in proportion, as you are established in a life of piety and virtue, you will be enabled to bring up your children in the nurture and admonition of the Lord, ever bearing in remembrance that example speaks a louder language than precept.

SEC. 14. It may not be improper to state to you, that the establishment of the New York Free School has been attended with much labor and personal exertions on the part of its friends and patrons; great expense has also accrued, and continues to be the case, where so many buildings are erected and so many teachers employed; and as all this is done in order to promote the good of your children, and to improve their condition, you cannot but feel a weight of obligation to the friends and patrons of so valuable an institution. In speaking of the teachers, it is due to them and their meritorious conduct to say, that they have manifested a zeal and concern for the welfare and improvement of the children placed under their care, and we wish they may be encouraged to persevere in the arduous service assigned them.

SEC. 15. There are divers other things which we could enumerate as connected with the subject of this address; but it cannot be expected, in a communication of this nature, we should embrace every duty or point out minutely every thing which might have a bearing on your religious and moral character; but, before we close, we think it necessary to subjoin the substance of such of the rules of the schools as may in part lay with the parents and guardians to notice and enforce. The trustees therefore call on you to see that these rules are strictly observed by your children:

1. Your children must be in school precisely at 9 o'clock in the morning and 2 o'clock in the afternoon.

2. They ought to be sent to school every day, both morning and afternoon; otherwise they may forget in one day what they learned the day before. Nothing but sickness, or some unavoidable circumstance, should induce you to keep your children at home one day. If they do not attend school regularly, the teacher is to send to you to know the reason; and if they are absent from school six days in a month without sufficient reason, or if they frequently play truant, they are liable to be expelled, and you may find it very difficult to get them into school again. The trustees therefore earnestly hope that you will not, by keeping your children at home without cause, or by suffering them to be absent, counteract their endeavors to procure for them a good education.

3. It is necessary that you should see that your children go to school with clean faces and hands, their hair combed and in good order, and their clothes as clean and whole as possible; otherwise they are liable to be punished for your neglect.

4. A morning school is intended to be kept in the summer, to begin at 6 o'clock, and close at 8 o'clock.

5. A library of interesting and useful books has been provided for the use of those children who are forward in their learning; and as they may be indulged at times to take them home for awhile, they may prove a source of pleasure and improvement to both children and parents.

6. If your children behave well, and study their lessons at home, they will be rewarded with tickets; but if they behave badly, and will not study, they must be punished.

7. In order to get a child into the Free School, it is required that application be made at the school on the second day of the week, commonly called Monday, from the hours of 4 to 5 o'clock in the afternoon.

8. No child can be admitted under six years of age.

9. The children of parents who are able to pay for schooling cannot be admitted.

10. It is expected that parents see that their children regularly attend some place of worship.

> DE WITT CLINTON, *President.*
> JOHN MURRAY, Jr., *Vice-President.*
> LEONARD BLEECKER, *Treasurer.*
> LINDLEY MURRAY, *Secretary*

PETITION OF THE NEW YORK FREE-SCHOOL SOCIETY TO THE STATE LEGISLATURE FOR FUNDS (1819) From William Oland Bourne, *History of the Public School Society of the City of New York* (New York, 1870), p. 35.

Trusting with confidence to the uniform liberality of an enlightened Legislature in diffusing the manifold blessings of education, and considering the State Government as the protecting parent, who has long nursed with parental regard this adopted child of her bounty, the New York Free-School Society, your memorialists, respectfully petition for a grant of ten thousand four hundred and sixty-five dollars, out of such funds as the wisdom of the Legislature shall designate, to enable them to complete their new improvements.

In respectfully soliciting this grant, and in congratulating the Legislature on the salutary effects of their former encouragement, your memorialists remark, that, as the city of New York rapidly increases in population, the number is multiplied of poor and suffering children, who must progress from the cradle to maturity, with no schools but those of profligacy and guilt, unless the hand of charity be extended to reclaim their steps. If we would prevent the vices and crimes of European cities from visiting our own; if we would prohibit the sanguinary penal codes of Europe from reaching our shores, we must look to early education and early habits, the fundamental springs of action and character in all communities, as the protecting resort; if we would perpetuate our civil institutions and our religious privileges, we must look to early education to guard and strengthen their foundation.

Believing those observations will be reciprocated by the public body to whom they address their memorial, they make their appeal with confidence, remembering it is to a body to whom your memorialists have never appealed in vain, when their object has been to extend the cheering light of education.

Let it be remembered, when the petition of your memorialists is considered, that nearly two thousand children will, the ensuing season, be under their care, and that it is on behalf of these, and many thousands more who will hereafter claim their charge, that your memorialists appeal to the Honorable Legislature.

PETITION OF THE NEW YORK FREE-SCHOOL SOCIETY TO THE STATE LEGISLATURE TO REORGANIZE AS THE PUBLIC SCHOOL SOCIETY OF NEW YORK (1825) From William Oland Bourne, *History of the Public School Society of the City of New York* (New York, 1870), p. 92.

Any plan that can be devised to preserve harmony and good feeling among the various religious sects, by removing all grounds for jealousy and contention, to satisfy the just complaints of our worthy laboring citizens who contribute to the common school fund, to increase, and, at the same time, to economize the means we possess of enlightening, by literary, moral, and religious instruction, our numerous youth, to break up the many inferior pay schools, to promote an independent feeling, and unite all classes of our citizens, should—and, your committee cannot doubt, would—receive the cordial approbation of the Corporation, and of our citizens generally.

On a review of the whole subject, the conclusion to which the committee have arrived is the proposition that the *Free School Society* be changed into a *Public School Society,* and that children of all classes be admitted into the schools, paying therefor such compensation as may be within their pecuniary ability; and that, for the extension and support of these public schools, the whole of the common school fund be paid annually to said Society.

A few of the advantages that would result from the adoption of a general plan of public instruction are:

1st. A more general attention would be given by our citizens to the all-important subject of education.

2d. Harmony would be preserved among religious sects.

3d. All of our citizens would contribute, and all be entitled to a share of the benefits of the fund, in the cheap and good elementary education of their children.

4th. A great increase, by the small payments from the children, of the amount expended for public instruction.

5th. A uniform system in all the elementary schools of the city, which is very important, in consequence of the frequent removals of the middle and lower classes from one part of the city to another, and which uniformity cannot be expected in the different church schools and small pay schools.

6th. Feelings of independence, which it is highly important to cultivate, would be promoted among our poor and laboring classes.

ACT INCORPORATING THE PUBLIC SCHOOL SOCIETY OF NEW YORK

(1826) From William Oland Bourne, *History of the Public School Society of the City of New York* (New York, 1870), pp. 101–2.

An Act

In Relation to the Free-School Society of New York, Passed January 28th, 1826

Whereas the trustees of said Society have presented to the Legislature a memorial requesting certain alterations in their act of incorporation, Therefore,

Be it enacted by the people of the State of New York, represented in Senate and Assembly, that the said Society shall hereafter be known by the name of the PUBLIC SCHOOL SOCIETY OF NEW YORK.

And be it further enacted, That it shall be the duty of said Society to provide, so far as their means may extend, for the education of all children in the city of New York not otherwise provided for, whether such children be or be not the proper objects of gratuitous education, and without regard to the religious sect or denomination to which such children or their parents may belong.

And be it further enacted, That it shall be lawful for the trustees to require of the pupils received into the schools under their charge a moderate compensation, adapted to the ability of the parents of such pupils, to be applied to the erection of school-houses, the payment of the teachers' salaries, and to the defraying of such other expenses as may be incident to the education of children; *Provided,* That such payment or compensation may be remitted by the trustees, in all cases in which they shall deem it proper to do so; and, *Provided, further,* That no child shall be denied the benefits of the said institution, merely on the ground of inability to pay for the same, but shall at all times be freely received and educated by the said trustees.

And be it further enacted, That nothing in this act contained shall be construed to deprive the said Society of any revenues, or of any rights to which they are now, or, if this act had not been passed, would have been by law entitled, and that the receipts of small payments from the scholars shall not preclude the trustees from drawing from the common school fund for all the chidren educated by them.

And be it further enacted, That the trustees shall have power from time to time to establish in the said city such additional schools as they may deem expedient.

And be it further enacted, That any person paying to the treasurer of said Society, for the use of said Society, the sum of ten dollars, shall become a member thereof for life.

And be it further enacted, That the annual meetings of the said Society shall hereafter be held on the second Monday in May in each year.

And be it further enacted, That the number of trustees to be chosen by the Society, at and after the next annual meeting, shall be increased to fifty, who at any legal meeting of the board may add to their number, but so as not in the whole to exceed one hundred, exclusive of the Mayor and Recorder of the city, who are hereby declared to be *ex-officio* members of the Board of Trustees.

And be it further enacted, That the stated meetings of the board shall be held quarterly, that is to say, on the first Fridays of February, May, August, and November in each year; *Provided,* That an extra stated meeting shall be held on the

Friday next following the annual meeting in each year, for the purpose of organizing the new board, and transacting any other necessary business.

And be it further enacted, That one fourth of the whole number of trustees for the time being shall constitute a quorum for the transaction of business at any legal meeting of the board.

And be it further enacted, That the said Society is hereby authorized to convey their school edifices, and other real estate, to the Mayor, Aldermen, and Commonalty of the city of New York, upon such terms and conditions, and in such forms, as shall be agreed upon between the parties, taking back from the said Corporation a perpetual lease thereof, upon condition that the same shall be exclusively and perpetually applied to the purposes of education.

> *State of New York,*
> *Secretary's Office.*

I certify the preceding to be a true copy of an original act of the Legislature of this State, on file in this office.

ALBANY, *January 28th, 1826.*

> (Signed)   ARCHIBALD CAMPBELL, *Dep. Secretary.*

MORAL AND RELIGIOUS EXERCISES IN THE SCHOOLS OF THE PUBLIC SCHOOL SOCIETY (1830)   From Samuel W. Seton, *Manual of the Public School Society,* as quoted in William Oland Bourne, *History of the Public School Society of the City of New York* (New York, 1870), pp. 643–44.

Teacher. My dear children, the intention of this school is to teach you to be good and useful in this world, that you may be happy in the world to come. What is the intention of this school?

T. We therefore first teach you "remember your Creator in the days of your youth." What do we first teach you?

T. It is our duty to teach you this, because we find it written in the Holy Bible. Why is it our duty to teach you this?

T. The Holy Bible directs us to "train you up in the way you should go." What good book directs us to train you up in the way you should go?

T. Therefore, my children, you must obey your parents.

Scholar. I must obey my parents.

T. You must obey your teachers.

S. I must obey my teachers.

T. You must never tell a lie.

S. I must never tell a lie.

T. You must never steal the smallest thing.

S. I must never steal the smallest thing.

T. You must never swear.

S. I must never swear.

T. God will not hold him guiltless that taketh His name in vain.

S. God will not hold him guiltless that taketh His name in vain.

T. God always sees you. *(Slowly, and in a soft tone.)*

S. God always sees me.

T. God hears all you say.

S. God hears all I say.

T. God knows all you do.

S. God knows all I do.

T. You should fear to offend Him, for He is most holy.

S. I should fear to offend Him, for He is most holy.

T. You should depart from evil, and learn to do well.

S. I should depart from evil, and learn to do well.

T. May all you, dear children, learn, while attending this school, to be good and useful in this world.

S. May we all, while attending this school, learn to be good and useful in this world.

T. And, with God's blessing, may you be happy in the world to come.

S. And, with God's blessing, may we be happy in the world to come.

NEW YORK GOVERNOR WILLIAM H. SEWARD ON THE COMMON SCHOOLS IN HIS ANNUAL MESSAGE TO THE STATE LEGISLATURE
(1840)   From William Oland Bourne, *History of the Public School Society of the City of New York* (New York, 1870), p. 179.

Although our system of public education is well endowed, and has been eminently successful, there is yet occasion for the benevolent and enlightened action of the Legislature. The advantages of education ought to be secured to many, especially in our large cities, whom orphanage, the depravity of parents, or some form of accident or misfortune seems to have doomed to hopeless poverty and ignorance. Their intellects are as susceptible of expansion, of improvement, of refinement, of elevation, and of direction, as those minds which, through the favor of Providence, are permitted to develop themselves under the influence of better fortunes. They inherit the common lot to struggle against temptations, necessities, and vices; they are to assume the same domestic, social, and political relations, and they are born to the same ultimate destiny.

The children of foreigners, found in great numbers in our populous cities and towns, are in the vicinity of our public works, are too often deprived of the advantages of our system of public education, in consequence of prejudices arising from difference of language or religion. It ought never to be forgotten that the public welfare is as deeply concerned in their education as in that of our own children. I do not hesitate, therefore, to recommend the establishment of schools, in which they may be instructed by teachers speaking the same language with themselves, and professing the same faith. There would be no inequality in such a measure, since it happens from the force of circumstances, if not from choice, that the responsibilities of education are in most instances confided by us to native citizens; and occasions seldom offer for a trial of our magnanimity by committing that trust to persons differing from ourselves in language or religion.

Since we have opened our country, and all its fulness, to the oppressed of every nation, we should evince wisdom equal to such generosity, by qualifying their children for the high responsibilities of citizenship.

ADDRESS BY BISHOP JOHN HUGHES TO NEW YORK CITY CATHOLICS ON THE SCHOOL QUESTION (1840) From William Oland Bourne, *History of the Public School Society of the City of New York* (New York, 1870), pp. 187–88.

Whereas, The wisdom and liberality of the Legislature of this State did provide, at the public expense, for the education of the poor children of the State, without injury or detriment to the civil and religious rights vested in their parents or guardians by the laws of nature and of the land; and, *whereas,* the administration of that system, as now conducted, is such that the parents or guardians of Catholic children cannot allow them to frequent such schools without doing violence to these rights of conscience which the Constitution secures equal and inviolable to all citizens, viz.: They cannot allow their children to be brought up under a system with proposes to shut the door against Christianity, under the pretext of excluding sectarianism, and which yet has not the merit of being true to its bad promise;

And, *whereas,* Catholics who are the least wealthy, and most in need of the education intended by the bounty of the State, are those cut off from the benefit of funds to which they are obliged to contribute, and constrained either to contribute new funds for the purposes of education among themselves, or else to see their children brought up under a system of free-thinking and practical irreligion, or else to see them left in that ignorance which they dread, and which it was the benevolent and wise intention of the Legislature to remove; therefore,

1. *Resolved,* That the operation of the common school system, as the same is now administered, is a violation of our civil and religious rights.

2. *Resolved,* That we should not be worthy of our proud distinction as Americans and American citizens, if we did not resist such invasion by every lawful means in our power.

3. *Resolved,* That in seeking the redress of our grievances, we have confidence in our rulers, more especially, as by granting that redress they will but carry out the principles of the Constitution, which secures equal civil and religious rights to all.

4. *Resolved,* That a committee of eight be appointed to prepare and report an address to the Catholic community and the public at large, on the injustice which is done to the Catholics, in their civil and religious right, by the present operation of the common school system.

5. *Resolved,* That a committee of three he appointed to prepare a report on the public moneys which have been expended by the bounty of this State for education, both in colleges and in common schools, to which Catholics have contributed their proportion of taxes, like other citizens, but from which they have never received any benefit.

PETITION OF NEW YORK CATHOLICS FOR A SHARE OF THE
COMMON-SCHOOL FUND (1840) From L. Kehoe, ed., *Complete Works of the Most Rev. John Hughes* (New York, 1866), vol. I, pp. 102–7.

Petition

To the Honorable the Board of Aldermen of the City of New York:

The petition of the Catholics of New York RESPECTFULLY REPRESENTS:

That your petitioners yield to no class in their performance of, and disposition to perform, all the duties of citizens. They bear, and are willing to bear their portion of every common burden; and feel themselves entitled to a participation in every common benefit.

This participation, they regret to say, has been denied them for years back, in reference to common school education in the city of New York, except on conditions with which their conscience, and, as they believe, their duty to God, did not, and does not, leave them at liberty to comply.

The rights of conscience in this country are held by both the Constitution and universal consent, to be sacred and inviolable. No stronger evidence of this need be adduced than the fact, that one class of citizens are exempted from the duty or obligation of defending their country against any invading foe, out of delicacy and deference to the rights of conscience which forbids them to take up arms for any purpose.

Your petitioners only claim the benefit of this principle, in regard to the public education of their children. They regard the public education, which the State has provided as a common benefit, in which they are most desirous, and feel that they are entitled, to participate; and therefore they pray your honorable body that they may be permitted to do so, without violating thier conscience.

*   *   *

But your petitioners do not ask that this prayer be granted, without assigning their reasons for preferring it.

In ordinary cases, men are not required to assign the motives of conscientious scruples in matters of this kind. But your petitioners are aware that a large, wealthy, and concentrated influence is directed against their claim by the corporation called the Public School Society. And that this influence, acting on a public opinion already but too much predisposed to judge unfavorably of the claims of your petitioners, requires to be met by facts which justify them in thus appealing to your honorable body, and which may, at the same time, convey a more correct impression to the public mind. Your petitioners adopt this course the more willingly, because the justice and impartiality which distinguish the decisions of public men in this country, inspire them with the confidence that your honorable body will maintain, in their regard, the principle of the rights of conscience, if it can be done without violating the rights of others; and on no other condition is the claim solicited.

It is not deemed necessary to trouble your honorable body with a detail of the circumstances by which the monopoly of the public education of children in the city of New York, and of the funds provided for that purpose, at the expense of the

State, have passed into the hands of a private corporation, styled, in its act of charter, "The Public School Society of the City of New York." It is composed of men of different sects or denominations. But that denomination of Friends, which is believed to have the controlling influence, both by its numbers and otherwise, holds as a *sectarian principle*, that any formal or official teaching of religion is, at best, unprofitable. And your petitioners have discovered that such of *their* children as have attended the public schools are generally, and at an early age, imbued with the same principle—that they become untractable, disobedient, and even contemptuous toward their parents—unwilling to learn any thing of religion—as if they had become illuminated, and could receive all the knowledge of religion necessary for them by instinct or inspiration. Your petitioners do not pretend to assign the cause of this change in their children; they only attest the fact as resulting from their attendance at the public schools of the Public School Society.

This Society, however, is composed of gentlemen of various sects, including even one or two Catholics. But they profess to exclude all sectarianism from their schools. If they do not exclude sectarianism, they are avowedly no more entitled to the school funds than your petitioners, or any other denomination of professing Christians. If they do as they profess, exclude sectarianism, than your petitioners contend that they exclude Christianity, and leave to the advantage of infidelity the tendencies which are given to the minds of youth by the influence of this feature and pretension of their system. If they could accomplish what they profess, other denominations would join your petitioners in remonstrating against their schools. But they do not accomplish it. Your petitioners will show your honorable body that they do admit what Catholics call sectarianism (although others may call it only religion), in a great variety of ways.

In their twenty-second report, as far back as the year 1827, they tell us, p. 14, that they "are aware of the importance of early religious instruction," and that none but what is "exclusively general and scriptural in its character, should be introduced into the schools under their charge." Here, then, is their own testimony that they did introduce and authorize "religious instruction" in their schools. And that they solved, with the utmost composure, the difficult question on which the sects disagree by determining what kind of "religious instruction" is "exclusively general and scriptural in its character."

Neither could they impart this "early religious instruction" themselves. They must have left it to their teachers; and these, armed with official influence, could impress those "early religious instructions" on the susceptible minds of the children, with the authority of dictators.

The Public School Society, in their report for the year 1832, p. 10, describe the effects of these "early religious instructions," without, perhaps, intending to do so, but yet precisely as your petitioners have witnessed it in such of their children as attended those schools. "The age at which children are usually sent to school affords a much better opportunity to mould their minds to peculiar and exclusive forms of faith, than any subsequent period of life." In p. 11 of the same report, they protest against the injustice of supporting "religion in any shape" by public money—as if the early religious instruction, which they themselves authorized in their schools five years before, was not "religion in some shape," and was not supported by public taxation. They tell us again, in more guarded language, "The trustees are deeply impressed with the importance of imbuing the youthful mind with religious impressions; and they have endeavored to attain this object, as far as the nature of the institution will admit." Report of 1837, p. 7.

In their thirty-third annual report, they tell us that "they would not be understood as regarding religious impressions in early youth as unimportant. On the contrary, they desire to do all which may with propriety be done to give a right direction to the minds of the children entrusted to their care. Their schools are uniformly opened with the reading of the Scriptures, and the class-books are such as recognize and enforce the great and generally acknowledged principles of Christianity." Page 7.

In their thirty-fourth annual report, for the year 1839, they pay a high compliment to a deceased teacher for the "moral and religious influence exerted by her over the three hundred girls daily attending her school," and tell us that "it could not but have a lasting effect on many of their susceptible minds." Page 7. And yet in all these "early religious instructions—religious impressions, and religious influence," essentially anti-Catholic—your petitioners are to see nothing sectarian. But if, in giving the education which the State requires, they were to bring the same influences to bear on the "susceptible minds of their *own* children, in favor, and not against their *own* religion, then this Society contends that it would be sectarian!"

Your petitioners regret there is no means of ascertaining to what extent the teachers in the schools of the Society carried out the views of their principals, on the importance of conveying "early religious instructions" to the susceptible minds of the children. But they believe it is in their power to prove that, in some instances, the Scriptures have been explained, as well as read, to the pupils.

Even the reading of the Scriptures in those schools, your petitioners cannot regard otherwise than as sectarian; because Protestants would certainly consider as such the intention of the Catholic Scriptures, which are different from theirs: and the Catholics have the same ground to objection when the Protestant version is made use of. Your petitioners have to state further, as grounds of their conscientious objections to those schools, that many of the selections in their elementary reading-lessons contain matter prejudicial to the Catholic name and character. The term "popery" is repeatedly found in them. This term is known and employed as one of insult and contempt toward the Catholic religion, and it passes into the minds of children with the feelings of which it is the outward expression. Both the historical and religious portions of the reading-lessons are selected from Protestant writers, whose prejudices against the Catholic religion tender them unworthy of confidence in the mind of your petitioners, at least so far as their own children are concerned.

The Public School Society have heretofore denied that their books contained any thing reasonably objectionable to Catholics. Proofs of the contrary could be multiplied, but it is unnecessary, as they have recently retracted their denial, and discovered, after fifteen years' enjoyment of their monopoly, that their books do contain objectionable passages. But they allege that they have proffered repeatedly to make such corrections as the Catholic clergy might require. Your petitioners conceive that such a proposal could not be carried into effect by the Public School Society, without giving just grounds for exceptions to other denominations. Neither can they see with what consistency that Society can insist, as it has done, on the perpetuation of its monopoly, when the trustees thus avow their incompetency to present unexceptionable books, without the aid of the Catholic or any other clergy. They allege, indeed, that with the best intentions they have been unable to ascertain the passages which might be offensive to Catholics. With their intentions, your petitioners cannot enter into any question. Nevertheless, they submit to your honorable body that this Society is eminently incompetent for the superintendence of public education, if they could not see that the following passage was unfit for the public schools, and especially unfit to be placed in the hands of Catholic children.

They will quote the passage as one instance, taken from "Putnam's Sequel," p. 296.

> Huss, John, a zealous reformer from popery, who lived in Bohemia toward the close of the fourteenth, and the beginning of the fifteenth centuries. He was bold and persevering; but at length, trusting to the *deceitful Catholics*, he was by them brought to trial, condemned as heretic, and burnt at the stake.

The Public School Society may be excused for not knowing the historical inaccuracies of this passage; but surely assistance of the Catholic clergy could not have been necessary to an understanding of the word "deceitful," as applied to all who profess the religion of your petitioners.

For these reasons, and others of the same kind, your petitioners cannot in conscience, and conscientously with their sense of duty to God and to their offspring, intrust the Public School Society with the office of giving "a right direction to the minds of their children." And yet this Society claims that office, and claims for the discharge of it the common school funds to which your petitioners, in common with other citizens, are contributors. In so far as they are contributors, they are not only deprived of any benefit in return, but their money is employed to the damage and detriment of their religion, on the minds of their own children, and of the rising generation of the community at large. The contest is between the *guaranteed* rights, civil and religious, of the citizen on the one hand, and the pretensions of the Public School Society on the other; and whilst it has been silently going on for years, your petitioners would call the attention of your honorable body to its consequences on the class for whom the benefits of public education are most essential—the children of the poor.

This class (your petitioners speak only so far as relates to their own denomination), after a brief experience of the schools of the Public School Society, naturally and deservedly withdraw all confidence from it. Hence the establishment by your petitioners of schools for the education of the poor.

The expense necessary for this was a second taxation, required not by the laws of the land, but the no less imperious demands of their conscience.

They were reduced to the alternative of seeing their children growing up in entire ignorance, or else taxing themselves anew for private schools, whilst the funds provided for education, and contributed in part by themselves, were given over to the Public School Society, and by them employed as has been stated above.

Now your petitioners respectfully submit, that without this confidence, no body of men can discharge the duties of education as intended by the State and required by the people. The Public School Society are, and have been at all times, conscious that they had not the confidence of the poor. In their twenty-eighth report, they appeal to the ladies of New York to create or procure it by the "persuasive eloquence of female kindness," p. 5; and from this they pass on to the next page, to the more efficient eloquence of coercion under penalties and privations, to be visited on all persons, "whether emigrant or otherwise," who, being in the circumstances of poverty referred to, should not send their children to some "public or other daily school."

In their twenty-seventh report, pp. 15 and 16, they plead for the doctrine, and recommend it to public favor, by the circumstance that it will affect but "few natives." But why should it be necessary at all, if they possessed that confidence of the poor, without which they need never hope to succeed? So well are they convinced of this, that no longer ago than last year, they gave up all hope of inspiring it, and loudly called for coercion by *"the strong arm of the civil power"* to supply its deficiency.

∗   ∗   ∗

Your petitioners, therefore, pray that your honorable body will be pleased to designate as among the schools entitled to participate in the common school fund, upon complying with the requirements of the law and the ordinances of the Corporation of the city, or for such other relief as to your honorable body, shall seem meet—St. Patrick's school, St. Peter's school, St. Mary's school, St. Joseph's school, St. James' school, St. Nicholas' school, Transfiguration Church school, and St. John's school.

And your petitioners further request, in the event of your honorable body's determining to hear your petitioners on the subject of their petition that such time may be appointed as may be most agreeable to your honor able body; and that a full session of your honorable board be convened for that purpose.

And your petitioners, &c.

THOMAS O'CONNOR, *Chairman.*

GREGORY DILLON,
ANDREW CARRIGAN,   *Vice-Chairmen,*
PETER DUFFY,

Of a general meeting of the Catholics of the city of New York, convened in the school-room of St. James' Church, 21st of September, 1840.

B. O'CONNOR, J. KELLY, J. McLAUGHLIN, *Secretaries.*

THE PUBLIC SCHOOL SOCIETY'S OPPOSITION TO THE PETITION OF NEW YORK CITY CATHOLICS (1840)   From William Oland Bourne, *History of the Public School Society of the City of New York* (New York, 1870), pp. 180–81.

To the Common Council:

The undersigned, in their associate capacity as Trustees of the Public School Society, and in their individual character as citizens, hereby respectfully but urgently remonstrate against the granting of a request presented by the trustees of the Catholic schools for a participation in the common school moneys.

Your remonstrants are opposed to this proposition, as being unconstitutional and inexpedient.

Unconstitutional—because in our State charter, and in our statute-book, the common school fund is appropriated to and for the benefit and support of *common* schools only and exclusively; and we deem it self-evident that no school can be so called, unless opened to all classes and descriptions of citizens, and conducted on a system to which none can reasonably object. Such is not the case with the Catholic schools. The peculiar sectarian tenets of that faith are part, and by them thought to be an essential part of the course of instruction; and hence all unbelievers in Catholic doctrines are unwilling, and may with good reason object, to send their children to such schools.

Unconstitutional—because it is utterly at variance with the letter and spirit of our chartered rights, and with the genius of our political institutions, that the community should be taxed to support an establishment in which sectarian dogmas are inculcated, whether that establishment be a school or a church.

Inexpedient—because the public schools, open to all without discrimination, and so conducted that no reasonable objection can be made by any to sending their children to them, are now in a very flourishing and satisfactory condition, and are annually increasing in numbers and usefulness; and which schools would, by the admission of church schools to participate in the school fund, be crippled, and probably destroyed.

Inexpedient—because the question was fully examined by the Common Council in 1822, and all the church schools, including the Catholic, which has previously drawn from the school fund, were cut off; and the great principle of non-sectarianism adopted as the basis for subsequent appropriations from this fund.

Inexpedient—because, by the concentration of the fund in one channel, a much greater amount of good is produced, than could be the case were it divided and subdivided among many; for in the public schools the same expense for teachers, &c., would be incurred in a school of 100 or 150, as in one of double the number.

Induced by these leading positions, which they consider fully tenable, and by others which brevity induces the omission of, your remonstrants urgently protest against the admission of the Catholic, or any other sectarian school, to a participation in the public moneys. And of such great importance do they consider the subject, that, unless the Common Council are prepared, on a mere statement of these objections, to deny the application, your remonstrants respectfully request that they may be heard, in defence of their positions, before a joint meeting of your two boards.

Our Executive Committee will prepare and present a remonstrance more in detail.

REMONSTRANCE OF THE METHODIST EPISCOPAL CHURCH

(1840)   From William Oland Bourne, *History of the Public School Society of the City of New York* (New York, 1870), pp. 199–201.

To the Honorable the Common Council of the City of New York:

The undersigned committee, appointed by the pastors of the Methodist Episcopal Church in this city, on the part of said pastors and churches, do MOST RESPECTFULLY REPRESENT:

That they have heard with surprise and alarm that the Roman Catholics have renewed their application to the Common Council for an appropriation from the common school fund, for the support of the schools under their own direction, in which they teach, and propose still to teach, their own sectarian dogmas, not only to their own children, but to such Protestant children as they may find means to get into these schools.

Your memorialists had hoped that the clear, cogent, and unanswerable arguments by which the former application for this purpose was resisted, would have saved the Common Council from further importunity.

It was clearly shown, that the Council could not legally make any sectarian appropriation of the public funds; and it was as clearly shown that it would be utterly destructive of the whole scheme of public school instruction to do so, even if it could be legally done. But it seems that neither the Constitution of the State nor the public welfare are to be regarded, when they stand in the way of Roman Catholic sectarianism and exclusiveness.

It must be manifest to the Common Council, that, if the Roman Catholic claims are granted, all the other Christian denominations will urge their claims for a similar appropriation, and that the money raised for education by a general tax will be solely applied to the purposes of proselytism, through the medium of sectarian schools. But if this were done, would it be the price of peace? or would it not throw the apple of discord into the whole Christian community, should we agree in the division of the spoils? Would each sect be satisfied with the portion allotted to it? We venture to say that the sturdy claimants who now beset the Council would not be satisfied with much less than the lion's share; and we are sure that there are other Protestant denominations beside ourselves who would not patiently submit to the exaction. But, when all the Christian sects shall be satisfied with their individual share of the public fund, what is to become of those children whose parents belong to none of these sects, and who cannot conscientiously allow them to be educated in the peculiar dogmas of any one of them? The different committees who, on a former occasion, approached your honorable body, have shown that, to provide schools for these only, would require little less than is now expended; and it requires little arithmetic to show that, when the religious sects have taken all, nothing will remain for those who have not yet been able to decide which of the Christian denominations to prefer. It must be plain to every impartial observer, that the applicants are opposed to the whole system of public school instruction; and it will be found that the uncharitable exclusiveness of their creed must ever be opposed to all public instruction which is not under the direction of their own priesthood. They may be conscientious in all this; but, though it be no new claim on their part, we cannot yet allow to guide and control the consciences of all the rest of the community. We are sorry that the reading of the Bible in the public schools, without note or commentary, is offensive to them; but we cannot allow the Holy Scriptures to be accompanied with *their* notes and commentaries, and to be put into the hands of the children who may hereafter be the rulers and legislators of our beloved country; because, among other bad things taught in these commentaries, is to be found the lawfulness of murdering heretics, and the unqualified submission, in all matters of conscience, to the Roman Catholic Church.

But if the principle on which this application is based should be admitted, it must be carried far beyond the present purpose.

If all are to be released from taxation when they cannot conscientiously derive any benefit from the disbursement of the money collected, what will be done for the Society of Friends, and other sects who are opposed to war under all circumstances? Many of these, besides the tax paid on all foreign goods thus consumed, pay direct duties at the Custom House, which go to the payment of the army and to purchase the munitions of war. And even when the Government finds it necessary to lay direct war taxes, these conscientious sects are compelled to pay their proportion, on the ground that the public defence requires it. So, it is believed, the public interest requires the education of the whole rising generation; because it would be unsafe to commit the public liberty, and the perpetuation of our republican institutions, to those whose ignorance of their nature and value would render them careless of their preservation, or the easy dupes of artful innovators; and hence every citizen is required to contribute in proportion to his means to the public purpose of universal education.

The Roman Catholics complain that books have been introduced into the public schools which are injurious to them as a body. It is allowed, however, that the passages in these books to which such reference is made are chiefly, if not entirely, historical; and we put it to the candor of the Common Council to say, whether any history of Europe for the last ten centuries could be written which could either omit to mention the Roman Catholic Church, or mention it without recording historical facts unfavorable to that Church? We assert, that if all the historical facts in which the Church of Rome has taken a prominent part could be taken from writers of her own communion only, the incidents might be made more objectionable to the complainants than any book to which they now object.

History itself, then, must be falsified for their accommodation; and yet they complain that the system of education adopted in the public schools does not teach the sinfulness of lying! They complain that no religion is taught in these schools, and declare that any, even the worst form of Christianity, would be better than none: and yet they object to the reading of the Holy Scriptures, which are the only foundation of true religion. Is it not plain, then, that they will not be satisfied with anything short of the total abandonment of public school instruction, or the appropriation of such portion of the public fund as they may claim to their own sectarian purposes.

But this is not all. They have been complaisantly offered the censorship of the books to be used in the public schools. The committee to whom has been confided the management of these schools in this city offered to allow the Roman Catholic bishop to expurgate from these books any thing offensive to him.

But the offer was not accepted;—perhaps for the same reason that he declined to decide on the admissibility of a book of extracts from the Bible, which had been sanctioned by certain bishops in Ireland. An appeal, it seems, had gone to the pope on the subject, and nothing could be said or done in the matter until His Holiness had decided. The Common Council of New York will therefore find that, when they shall have conceded to the Roman Catholics of this city the selection of books for the use of the public schools, that these books must undergo the censorship of a foreign potentate. We hope the time is far distant when the citizens of this country will allow any foreign power to dictate to them in matters relating to either general or municipal law.

We cannot conclude this memorial without noticing one other ground on which the Roman Catholics, in their late appeal to their fellow-citizens, urged their sectarian claims, and excused their conscientious objections to the public schools. Their creed is dear to them, it seems, because some of their ancestors have been martyrs to their faith. This was an unfortunate allusion. Did not the Roman Catholics know that they addressed many of their fellow-citizens who could not recur to the memories of their own ancestors without being reminded of the revocation of the Edict of Nantes, the massacre of St. Bartholomew's day, the fires of Smithfield, or the crusade against the Waldenses? We would willingly cover these scenes with the mantle of charity, and hope that our Roman Catholic fellow-citizens will, in future, avoid whatever has a tendency to revive the painful remembrance.

Your memorialists had hoped that the intolerance and exclusiveness which had characterized the Roman Catholic Church in Europe had been greatly softened under ·the benign influences of our civil institutions. The pertinacity with which their sectarian interests are now urged has dissipated the illusion. We were content with their having excluded us, *ex cathedra,* from all claim to heaven, for we were sure they did not possess the keys, notwithstanding their confident pretension; nor did we complain that they would not allow us any participation in the benefits of purgatory, for it is a place they have made for themselves, and of which they may claim the exclusive property; but we do protest against any appropriation of the public school fund for their exclusive benefit, or for any other purposes whatever.

Assured that the Common Council will do what it is right to do in the premises, we are, gentlemen, with great respect,

Your most obedient servants,

N. BANGS,

THOMAS E. BOND,

GEORGE PECK.

REJECTION OF THE CATHOLICS' PETITION BY THE SPECIAL COMMITTEE ON SCHOOLS OF THE NEW YORK CITY BOARD OF ALDERMEN (1840)   From William Oland Bourne, *History of the Public School Society of the City of New York* (New York, 1870), pp. 322–23.

Your committee deem it proper to remark, in vindication of the School Society, that they were only one of the numerous remonstrants against the prayer of the petitioners. Their views were represented in the late discussion before the board only by their legal advisers, Messrs. Sedgewick and Ketchum. The other gentlemen who participated in the discussion represented other bodies which are not in any manner connected with them. Sentiments were uttered by some of them which the School Society do not entertain, and for which they are not justly accountable. This explanation is deemed proper, in consequence of a remark in the above proposition of the petitioners which appears to be founded on an erroneous impression. The unwillingness of the petitioners to agree to any terms which did not recognize the distinctive character of their schools as Catholic schools, or which would exclude sectarian supervision from them entirely, was the obstacle to a compromise, which could not be overcome. However much we may lament the consequences, we are not disposed to question the right of our Catholic fellow-citizens to keep their children separated from intercourse with other children; but we do not believe the Common Council would be justified in *facilitating* such an object. They have an unquestionable right to pursue such a course, if the dictates of conscience demand it of them; and they have a just claim to be sustained by the Common Council in the exercise of that right; but they cannot justly claim public *aid* to carry out such intentions, unless they can show that the public good would be promoted by it, and that such public aid can be extended to them without trespassing upon the conscientious rights of others. But if any religious society or sect should be allowed the exclusive right to select the books, appoint or nominate the teachers, or introduce sectarian peculiarities of any kind into a public school, the exercise of such a right, in any one particular, would very clearly constitute such school a sectarian school, and its support at the public expense would, in the opinion of the committee, be a trespass upon the conscientious rights of every taxpayer who disapproved of the religion inculcated by the sect to which such school might be attached; because they would be paying taxes for the support of a religion which they disapproved. Your committee are, therefore, fully of the opinion that the granting of the prayer of the petitioners, or conforming to the terms of the proposals submitted by the committee who represented them, would render the school system liable to the charge of violating the rights of conscience—a charge which would be fatal to the system, because it would invalidate its just claim to public patronage.

The proposition of the committee who represent the Public School Society appears to us to have been conceived in a liberal spirit. Your committee think it goes as far as a due regard to the true objects of the institution would warrant, and seems to open an avenue which we would fain hope may yet lead to a satisfactory arrangement. Both propositions exhibit more liberality, probably, than either party had before given the other credit for; and we hope that result may prove to be an important step toward the accomplishment of an object which every patriot must desire with intense anxiety. Your committee respectfully ask to be discharged from the further consideration of the subject.

WILLIAM CHAMBERLAIN,
ROBERT JONES,
JOSIAH RICH.

REV. JOHN POWER, VICAR-GENERAL OF THE DIOCESE OF NEW YORK, ON THE "SECTARIAN" SCHOOLS OF THE PUBLIC SCHOOL SOCIETY (1840)   From Letter to the Editor, New York Freeman's Journal, as quoted in William Oland Bourne, History of the Public School Society of the City of New York (New York, 1870), pp. 329–30.

You, Mr. Editor, will agree with me, that the object of public instruction is to fit man for society. It is also an axiom, that man has various duties to fulfil, both of a public and private nature, toward the community. He has also, as a rational and accountable being, duties to perform toward his Maker. Now, without religion, what security have we that those duties will be punctually discharged? What guarantee have we that man will be honest in the dark, and without a witness? We have no pledge, sir, that the claims of society will be answered; and I therefore assert that a purely intellectual education will not fit a man for society. On this principle, sir, I am decidedly opposed to the education which is now given in our "public schools." It is not based, as in a Christian community it ought to be, on the Christian religion. Its tendency is to make deists.

There are, it is true, beautiful lessons in the class-books on the providence of God, the immortality of the soul, man's accountability, &c.; but these lessons do not constitute Christianity. We learn them from the light of reason alone, while the positive ordinances of the Christian religion are learned from revelation; and, as there is not the slightest allusion to these ordinances, we say that pure deism alone is taught in these schools.

My second exception is founded on the sectarian character of the public schools. The Holy Scriptures are read every day, with the restriction that no specific tenets are to be inculcated. Here, sir, we find the great demarcating principle between the Catholic Church and the sectaries introduced *silently*. The Catholic Church tells her children that they must be taught their religion by AUTHORITY. The sects say, Read the Bible, judge for yourselves. The Bible is read in the public schools, the children are allowed to judge for themselves. The Protestant principle is therefore acted upon, silently inculcated, and the schools are sectarian. It may be said that the Bible is introduced for the mere purpose of teaching its morality. But recollect, sir, that the morality of the Bible is founded on the law of nature, and is a clearer evolution or expression of that law; and as the motive for introducing the Bible into the schools is the inculcation of its morality only, a severe logic forces me to say, that the holy Book is made ancillary to pure deism.

There are libraries connected with our public schools, and it is notorious, that books which to Catholics must be exceptionable, as containing the most malevolent and foul attacks on their religion, were placed in the way of Catholic children, no doubt for the very laudable purpose of teaching them to abhor and despise that monster called popery.

How, then, sir, can we think of sending, under these circumstances, our children to those schools, in which every artifice is resorted to in order to seduce them from their religion?

One word to parents, before I close this hasty communication. If it be of acknowledged moment that parents should engage in those duties which concern the temporal welfare of their children, should not the most animated zeal be indulged in fixing and giving life to every moral and religious principle? In moral and religious acquirements consist the chief dignity and happiness of man. Deprive him these, and you leave him ignorant of the true grounds of rectitude and honor, and dry up the purest sources of human joy; you degrade him in the creation, and render him an improper object for the future reward of his Maker. Many parents, sir, by their inattention to this part of their duty, are the cause of ruin to those whom they professedly love, and, instead of being their best friends, become their worst enemies.

The objections to our claims for a due portion of the school fund are, I think, urged in bad faith. It is said that the State cannot lend itself to the support of sectarian principles. But recollect, sir, that this objection is urged by those whose conduct is truly sectarian, as far as regards the management of the public schools. This, I think, I have abundantly proved.

When the common school fund was created, it was not considered unconstitutional to extend it to the charity schools in connection with the incorporated religious societies in this city; and, if I am not much mistaken, the philanthropic and enlightened statesman with whom the measure originated, thought that the best application of the fund lay in giving it to those who would make a proper use of it, by giving that instruction which alone can save man from the tyranny of his passions, and make him a good member of society.

Would it not, Mr. Editor, be a libel on the memory of the founders of our glorious Constitution, to pervert that instrument to such an extent as to think that they, in disclaiming a *civil* preference for any form of Christianity, thereby intended that the public education of the country should not be founded on religion? In this respect I apprehend they did not depart from the rule of all wise legislators, and never contemplated that our charity schools should not participate in the fund set apart for public education, because the catechisms of the different religious societies of which this republic is composed would be taught in them.

I, sir, would be the last man to wish that the State would spend its means in supporting sectarianism; and the principle that induces me to make this avowal, bids me also to express my conviction that, unless public instruction be connected with religious instruction, there is no guarantee for the permanence of our civil institutions. I would, then, most respectfully say to our rulers, Let mental cultivation be general, but let it have religion for its basis. This will be the surest foundation not only for your internal improvement, but for the increase of your general prosperity. This will be the means by which your rank and consideration are to be raised into competition with the foremost of polished nations.

I am, sir, with great respect, your very humble servant,
JOHN POWER, *Vicar-General of the Diocese of New York.*
NEW YORK, *July 9, 1840.*

REQUEST BY THE BOOK COMMITTEE OF THE NEW YORK CITY COMMON COUNCIL FOR EXPURGATION OF PASSAGES OFFENSIVE TO CATHOLICS (1840) From William Oland Bourne, *History of the Public School Society of the City of New York* (New York, 1870), p. 477.

New York Reader.—Page 205, erase last paragraph.

English Reader.—Page 51, strike out paragraph, "the Queen's bigoted zeal," &c., to "eternal welfare." Page 152, erase, "the most credulous monk in a Portuguese convent."

Sequel, Murray's.—The whole article, "Life of Luther." Pages 84 and 85, paste up "Execution of Cranmer." Page 279, erase, "and anon in penance, planning sins anew."

Putnam's Sequel.—Erase the article, "John Huss."

Maltebrun's Geography.—Page 111, erase first five lines. Page 123, erase last paragraph, chapter 134. Page 140, erase five lines from the top, "and there is no doubt the lower classes of Ireland are so." Page 145, erase, "inflict the most horrible tortures." Page 148, erase, "Italy to be submitted to the Catholic bishop." Page 155, erase, "from their religion," down to "ceremonies."

Hale's History of the United States.—Page 11, erase, "from the persecution of the Catholics," section 22.

Scripture Lessons.—Erase, in the title-page, the words, "without note or comment."

BISHOP JOHN HUGHES' CALL FOR A CATHOLIC SCHOOL TICKET

(1840) From *New York Freeman's Journal,* October 23, 1840.

With political controversies and party questions I have nothing whatever to do. . . . It is impossible for me to say any thing personally of those whose names have been recommended to be placed on the list of candidates, and I would not for one moment urge that they should be placed there, had I not been assured, on the most positive evidence, and which I could not doubt, that they are friendly to an alteration in the present system of public education. . . . I will now request the Secretary to read the names placed on the ticket. Of that ticket I have approved. It presents the names of the only friends we could find already before the public, and those whom, not being so prominently before the public, we have found for ourselves.

(The Secretary then read the following list):

SENATORS.

Thomas O'Connor,   J. G. Gottsberger.

ASSEMBLY.

Tighe Davey,	David R. Floyd Jones,
Daniel C. Pentz,	Solomon Townsend,
George Weir,	John L. O'Sullivan,
Paul Grout,	Auguste Davezac,
Conrad Swackhamer,	William McMurray,
William B. Maclay,	Michael Walsh,

Timothy Daly.

*   *   *

You have now, gentlemen, heard the names of men who are willing to risk themselves in support of your cause. Put these names out of view, and you cannot, in the lists of our political candidates, find that of one solitary public man who is not understood to be pledged against us. What, then, is your course? You now, for the first time, find yourselves in the position to vote at least for yourselves. You have often voted for others, and they did not vote for you; but now you are determined to uphold, with your own votes, your own rights. (Thunders of applause, which lasted several minutes.) Will you, then, stand by the rights of your offspring, who have for so long a period, and from generation to generation, suffered under the operation of this injurious system? (Renewed cheering.) Will you adhere to the nomination made? (Loud cries of "We will! we will!" and vociferous applause.) Will you be united? (Tremendous cheering—the whole immense assembly rising *en masse,* waving of hats, handkerchiefs, and every possible demonstration of applause.) Will you let all men see that you are worthy sons of that nation to which you belong? (Cries of "Never fear—we will!" "We will, till death!" and terrific cheering.) Will you prove yourselves worthy of friends? (Tremendous cheering.) Will none of you flinch? (The scene that followed this emphatic query is indescribable, and exceeded all the enthusiastic and almost frenzied displays of passionate feeling we have sometimes witnessed at Irish meetings. The cheering, the shouting, the stamping of feet, waving of hats and handkerchiefs, beggared all powers of description.) Very well, then; the tickets will be prepared and distributed amongst you, and, on the day of election, go, like freemen, with dignity and calmness, entertaining due respect for your fellow-citizens and their opinions, and deposit your votes. I ask, then, once for all, and with the answer let the meeting close, Will this meeting pledge its honor, as the representative of that oppressed portion of the community for whom I have so often pleaded, here as well as elsewhere—will it pledge its honor that it will stand by these candidates, whose names have been read, and that no man composing this vast audience will ever vote for any one pledged to oppose our just claims and incontrovertible rights? (Terrific cheering and thunders of applause, which continued for several minutes, amid which Bishop Hughes resumed his seat.)

GOVERNOR WILLIAM H. SEWARD ON A NEW ORGANIZATION FOR THE PUBLIC SCHOOLS OF NEW YORK CITY (1842) From "Message to the New York State Legislature, 1842," as quoted in State of New York, *Messages from the Governors*, Charles Lincoln, ed. (Albany, 1909), vol. III, pp. 947–51.

In our general system of common schools, trustees chosen by taxpaying citizens, levy taxes, build school houses, employ and pay teachers, and govern schools which are subject to visitation by similarly elected inspectors, who certify the qualifications of teachers; and all schools thus constituted participate in just proportion in the public moneys, which are conveyed to them by commissioners also elected by the people. Such schools are found distributed in average spaces of two and a half square miles throughout the inhabited portions of the State, and yet neither popular discontent, nor political strife, nor sectarian discord, has ever disturbed their peaceful instructions or impaired their eminent usefulness. In the public school system of the city, one hundred persons are trustees and inspectors, and by continued consent of the common council, are the dispensers of an annual average sum of $35,000, received from the Common School Fund of the State, and a sum equal to $95,000, derived from an undiscriminating tax upon the real and personal estates of the city. They built school houses chiefly with public funds, they appoint and remove teachers, fix their compensation, and prescribe the moral, intellectual and religious instruction which one-eighth of the rising generation of the State shall be required to receive. Their powers, more effective and far reaching than are exercised by the municipality of the city, are not derived from the community whose children are educated and whose property is taxed, nor even from the State, which is so great an almoner, and whose welfare is so deeply concerned, but from an incorporated and perpetual association which grants upon pecuniary subscription the privileges even of life membership and yet holds in fee simple the public school edifices, values at eight hundred thousand dollars. Lest there might be too much responsibility, even to the association, that body can elect only one half of the trustees, and those thus selected appoint their fifty associates.

The philanthropy and patriotism of the present managers of the public schools, and their efficiency in imparting instruction, are cheerfully and gratefully admitted. Nor is it necessary to maintain that agents thus selected will become unfaithful, or that a system that so jealously excludes popular interference must necessarily be unequal in its operation. It is only insisted that the institution, after a fair and sufficient trial, has failed to gain that broad confidence reposed in the general system of the State, and indispensable to every scheme of universal education. No plan for that purpose can be defended, except on the ground that public instruction is one of the responsibilities of the Government. It is, therefore, a manifest legislative duty to correct errors and defects in whatever system is established. In the present case, the failure amounts virtually to an exclusion of all the children thus withheld. I cannot overcome my regret that every suggestion of amendment encounters so much opposition from those who defend the public school system of the metropolis, as to show that, in their judgment, it can admit of no modification, either from tenderness to the consciences or regard to the civil rights of those aggrieved, or even for the reclamation of those for whose culture the State has no munificently provided; as if society must conform itself to the public schools, instead of the public schools adapting themselves to the exigencies of society. The late eminent Superintendent, after exposing the greatness of this public misfortune, and tracing it to the discrepancy between the local and general systems, suggested a remedy, which, although it is not urged to the exclusion of any other, seems to deserve dispassionate consideration. I submit, therefore, with entire willingness, to approve whatever adequate remedy you may propose, the expediency of restoring to the people of the city of New York—what I am sure the people of no other part of the State would, upon any consideration, relinquish—the education of their children. For this purpose, it is only necessary to vest the control of the common schools in a board, to be composed of commissioners elected by the people; which board shall apportion the school moneys among all the schools, including those now existing, which shall be organized and conducted in conformity to its general regulations and the laws of the State, in the proportion of the number of pupils instructed. It is not left doubtful that the restoration to the common schools of the city of this simple and equal feature of the common schools of the State would remove every complaint, and bring into the seminaries the offspring of want and misfortune, presented by a grand jury, on a recent occasion, as neglected children of both sexes, who are found in hordes upon the wharves and in corners of the streets, surrounded by evil associations, disturbing the public peace, committing petty depredations, and going from bad to worse, until their course terminates in high crimes and infamy.

This proposition to gather the young from the streets and wharves into the nurseries which the State, solicitous for her security against ignorance, has prepared for them, has sometimes been treated as a device to appropriate the school fund to the endowment of seminaries for teaching languages and faiths, thus to perpetuate the prejudices it seeks to remove; sometimes as a scheme for dividing that precious fund among a hundred jarring sects, and thus increasing the religious animosities it strives to heal; sometimes as a plan to subvert the prevailing religion, and introduce one repugnant to the consciences of our fellow-citizens, while, in truth, it simply proposes, by enlightening equally the minds of all, to enable them to detect error wherever it may exist, and to reduce uncongenial masses into one intelligent, virtuous, harmonious, and happy people. Being now relieved from all such misconceptions, it presents the questions whether it is wiser and more humane to educate the offspring of the poor, than to leave them to grow up in ignorance and vice; whether juvenile vice is more easily eradicated by the Court of Sessions than by common schools; whether parents have a right to be heard concerning the instruction and instructors of their children, and taxpayers in relation to the expenditure of public funds; whether, in a republican government, it is necessary to interpose an independent corporation between the people and the schoolmaster; and whether it is wise and just to disfranchise an entire community of all control over public education, rather than suffer a part to be represented in proportion to its numbers and contributions. Since such considerations are now involved, what has hitherto been discussed as a question of benevolence and of universal education, has become one of equal civil rights, religious tolerance, and liberty of conscience. We could bear with us, in our retirement from public service, no recollection more worthy of being cherished through life, than that of having met such a question in the generous and confiding spirit of our institutions, and decided it upon the immutable principles on which they are based.

AN ACT ESTABLISHING A BOARD OF EDUCATION FOR NEW YORK CITY (1842) From William Oland Bourne, *History of the Public School Society of the City of New York* (New York, 1870), pp. 521–25.

An Act

To Extend to the City and County of New York the Provisions of the General Act in Relation to Common Schools

The people of the State of New York, represented in Senate and Assembly, do enact as follows:

Sec. 1. There shall be elected in each of the wards of the city and county of New York, two commissioners, two inspectors, and five trustees of common schools, who shall be elected by ballot, at a special election to be held on the first Monday of June in each year, by the persons qualified to vote for charter officers in the said wards, and to be conducted in the same manner, by the same inspectors, at the same ward districts, and subject to the same laws, rules, and regulations as now govern the charter elections in said city.

The commissioners of common schools so elected shall constitute a Board of Education for the city of New York, a majority of whom shall constitute a quorum; they shall elect one of their number president of said board, who shall preside at the meetings thereof, which shall be held at least as often as once in three months; and they may appoint a clerk, whose compensation shall be fixed and paid by the supervisors of said city and county.

The commissioners so elected in each ward shall be the commissioners of schools thereof, with the like powers and duties of commissioners of common schools in the several towns in this State, except as hereinafter provided.

The said inspectors of common schools so elected in the several wards shall have the like powers and be subject to the same duties with the inspectors of common schools of the several towns of this State, except as hereinafter provided.

The trustees of common schools so elected in their respective wards shall be the trustees of the school districts which may be formed and organized therein, with the like powers and duties as the trustees of school districts in the several towns in this State, except as hereinafter provided.

Sec. 2. All such provisions of the third, fourth, fifth, and sixth articles of Title Two, chapter fifteen, part first, of the Revised Statutes, and of the several acts amending and in addition to, and relating to the same, not inconsistent with the provisions in this act contained, shall be, and the same are hereby, declared applicable to the city and county of New York.

Sec. 3. For all the purposes of this act, each of the several wards into which the said city and county of New York now is, or may be hereafter, divided, shall be considered as a separate town, and liable to all the duties imposed; and entitled to all the powers, privileges, immunities, and advantages granted by the said third, fourth, fifth, and sixth articles of Title Two, chapter fifteen, part first, of the Revised Statutes, to the several towns in this State, so far as the same are consistent with this act.

Sec. 4. The forty-fourth section of the act entitled "An Act to Amend the Second Title of the Fifteenth Chapter of the First Part of the Revised Statutes, Relating to Common Schools," passed May 26, 1841, is hereby repealed; and all the other sections of the said act not inconsistent with the provisions of this act are hereby declared applicable to the city and county of New York.

Sec. 5. No compensation shall be allowed to the commissioners, inspectors, or trustees of common schools for any services performed by them; but the commissioners and inspectors shall receive their actual and reasonable expenses while attending to the duties of their office, to be audited and allowed by the supervisors of said city and county.

Sec. 6. The said commissioners of common schools of each ward are hereby authorized to appoint a club, whose compensation shall be settled and paid by the Board of Supervisors.

Sec. 7. Whenever the trustees elected in any ward shall certify in writing to the commissioners and inspectors of common schools thereof, that it is necessary to organize one or more schools in said ward, in addition to the schools mentioned in the thirteenth section of this act, it shall be the duty of said commissioners and inspectors to meet together and examine into the facts and circumstances of the case; and if they shall be satisfied of such necessity, they shall certify the same under their hands, to the said Board of Education, and shall then proceed to organize one or more school districts therein, and shall procure a school-house, and all things necessary to organize a school in such district, the expense of which shall be levied and raised pursuant to the provisions of section nine of this act; and the title to all lands purchased by virtue of this act, with the buildings thereon, shall be vested in the city and county of New York.

Sec. 8. Whenever the clerk of the city and county of New York shall receive notice from the Superintendent of Common Schools of the amount of moneys apportioned to the city and county of New York, for the support and encouragement of common schools therein, he shall immediately lay the same before the supervisors of the city and county aforesaid.

Sec. 9. The said supervisors shall annually raise and collect by tax, upon the inhabitants of said city and county, a sum of money equal to the sum specified in such notice, at the same time and in the same manner as the contingent charges of the said city and county are levied and collected; also, a sum of money equal to one twentieth of one per cent. of the value of real and personal property in the said city, liable to be assessed therein, to be applied exclusively to the purposes of common schools in said city; and such farther sum as may be necessary for the support and benefit of common schools in said city and county to be raised, levied, and collected in like manner, and which shall be in lieu of all taxes and assessments, to the support of common schools for said city and county.

Sec. 10. The said supervisors shall, on or before the first day of May in every year, direct that a sum of money equal to the amount last received by the chamberlain of said city and county, from the common school fund, be deposited by him, together with the sum so received from the school fund, in one of the incorporated banks of the said city and county (each bank to be designated by the said supervisors), to the credit of the commissioners of common schools in each of the said several wards, in the proportion to which they shall respectively be entitled, and subject only to the drafts of the said commissioners respectively; who shall pay the amount apportioned to the several schools enumerated in the thirteenth section of this act, to the treasurer of the societies or schools entitled thereto, or to some person duly authorized by the trustees of such societies or schools to receive the same.

Sec. 11. So much of the seventh article of Title Second, chapter fifteen, part first, of the Revised Statutes, and the several acts amending and in addition to, and relating to the said article, as is specially applicable to the city and county of New York, and all other acts, and all provisions therein providing for, or directing, or concerning the disbursing or appropriation of the funds created for or applicable to common school education in the city and county of New York, and all and every provision for raising any fund, or for the imposition of any tax therefor, so far as the same are inconsistent with this act, are hereby repealed.

Sec. 12. All children between the ages of four and sixteen, residing in said city and county, shall be entitled to attend any of the common schools therein; and the parents, guardians, or other persons having the custody of care of such children not be liable to any tax, assessment, or imposition for the tuition of any such children, other than is hereinbefore provided.

Sec. 13. The schools of the Public School Society, the New York Orphan Asylum School, the Roman Catholic Orphan Asylum School, the schools of the two Half-Orphan Asylums, the school of the Mechanics' School Society, the Harlem School, the Yorkville Public School, the Manhattanville Free School, the Hamilton Free School, the Institution for the Blind, the school connected with the Almshouse of the said city, and the school of the association for the benefit of Colored Orphans, shall be subject to the general jurisdiction of the said commissioners of the respective wards in which any of the said schools now are, or hereafter may be, located, subject to the direction of the Board of Education, but under the immediate government and management of their respective trustees, managers, and directors, in the same manner and to the same extent as herein provided in respect to the district schools herein first before mentioned in said city and county; and, so far as relates to the distribution of the common school moneys, each of the said schools shall be district schools of the said city.

Sec. 14. No school above mentioned, or which shall be organized under this act, in which any religious sectarian doctrine or tenet shall be taught, inculcated, or practised, shall receive any portion of the school moneys to be distributed by this act, as hereinafter provided; and it shall be the duty of the trustees, inspectors, and commissioners of schools in each ward, and of the deputy Superintendent of Schools, from time to time, and as frequently as need be, to examine and ascertain and report to the said Board of Education whether any religious sectarian doctrine or tenet shall have been taught, inculcated, or practised in any of the schools in their respective wards; and it shall be the duty of the commissioners of schools in the several wards to transmit to the Board of Education all reports made to them by the trustees and inspectors of their respective wards. The Board of Education, and any member thereof, may at any time visit and examine any school subject to the provisions of this act, and individual commissioners shall report to the board the result of their examinations.

Sec. 15. It shall be the duty of the said Board of Education to apply for the use of the several districts such moneys as shall be raised to erect, purchase, or lease school-houses, or to procure the sites therefor; and also to apportion among the several schools and districts provided for by this act, the school money to be paid over to the commissioners of schools in each ward, by virtue of the tenth section of this act, and shall file with the chamberlain of said city and county, on or before the fifteenth day of April in each year, a copy of such apportionment, and stating the amount thereof to be paid to the commissioners of each ward; which apportionment shall be made among the said several schools and districts according to the average number of children over four and under sixteen years of age, who shall have actually attended such school the preceding year. But no such school shall be entitled to a portion of such moneys that has not been kept open at least nine months in the year, or in which any religious sectarian doctrine or tenet shall have been taught, inculcated, or practised, or which shall refuse to permit the visits and examinations provided for by this act.

Sec. 16. The commissioners of schools of the respective wards, when they have received from the chamberlain of said city and county the money apportioned to the several schools and districts in their several wards, shall apply the same to the use of the schools and districts in their several wards, according to the apportionment thereof so made by the said Board of Education.

Sec. 17. The said commissioners of each ward shall, within fifteen days after their election, execute and deliver to the supervisors aforesaid a bond, with such sureties as said supervisors shall approve, in the penalty of double the amount of public money appropriated to the use of the common schools of their respective wards, conditional for the faithful performance of the duties of their office, and the proper application of all moneys coming in their hands for common school purposes; such bond shall be filed by the said supervisors in the office of the County Clerk.

Sec. 18. This act shall take effect immediately.

PETITION OF BISHOP FRANCIS PATRICK KENRICK OF PHILADELPHIA FOR USE OF CATHOLIC BIBLE FOR CATHOLIC CHILDREN IN THE PUBLIC SCHOOLS (1842) From Hugh J. Nolan, *The Most Reverend Francis Patrick Kenrick, Third Bishop of Philadelphia, 1830–1851* (Philadelphia, 1948), pp. 293–95.

To the Board of Comptrollers of Public Schools in the city and county of Philadelphia.

Gentlemen: Sympathy for a respectable lady who has been deprived for many months past of her only means of support for the following the dictates of her conscience, and a solemn sense of duty to the Catholic community, whose religious interests are entrusted to my guardianship, prompt me to submit respectfully to your consideration the conscientious objections of Catholics to the actual regulations of the Public Schools.

Among them I am informed one is that the teachers shall read and cause to be read, The Bible; by which is understood the version published by command of King James. To this regulation we are forced to object, inasmuch as Catholic children are thus led to view as authoritative a version which is rejected by the Church. It is not expected that I should state in detail the reasons of this rejection. I shall only say that several books of Divine Scripture are wanting in that version and that the meaning of the original text is not faithfully expressed. It is not incumbent on us to prove either position, since we do not ask you to adopt the Catholic version for general use; but we feel warranted in claiming that our conscientious scruples to recognize or use the other, be respected. In Baltimore the Directors of the Public Schools have thought it their duty to provide Catholic children with the Catholic version. Is it too much for us to expect the same measure of justice?

The consciences of Catholics are also embarrassed by the mode of opening and closing the School exercises which, I understand, is by the singing of some hymn, or by prayer. It is not consistent with the laws and discipline of the Catholic Church for her members to unite in religious exercises with those who are not of her communion. We offer up prayers and supplications to God for all men; we embrace all in the sincerity of Christian affection; but we confine the marks of religious brotherhood to those who are of the household of the faith. Under the influence of this conscientious scruple, we ask that the Catholic children be not required to join in the singing of hynms or other religious exercises.

I have been assured that several of the books used in the public schools, and still more those contained in the libraries attached to them, contain misrepresentations of our tenets and statements to our prejudice, equally groundless and injurious. It is but just to expect that the books used in the schools shall contain no offensive matter, and that books decidedly hostile to our faith shall not under any pretext by placed in the hands of Catholic children.

The School law which provides that "the religious predilections of the parents shall be respected," was evidently framed in the spirit of our Constitution, which holds the rights of conscience to be inviolable. Public education should be conducted on principles which will afford its advantages to all classes of the community, without detriment to their conscientious convictions. Religious liberty must be especially guarded in children, who, of themselves, are unable to guard against the wiles and assaults of others. I appeal then, Gentlemen, with confidence to your justice that the regulations of the Schools may be modified so as to give to Catholic pupils and teachers, equal rights, without wounding tender consciences.

For my interposition in this matter, besides the responsibility of my station, I have specially to plead the assurance I have received from a respectable source, that some desire had been expressed to know distinctly from me, what modifications Catholics desire in the School system. It was also suggested that an appeal of this kind would receive every just consideration from the Board; and would anticipate effectually the danger of public excitement on a point on which the Community is justly sensitive, the sacred rights of conscience.

With great respect, I remain, gentlemen,

Your obedient servant,
Francis Patrick, Bp. Phila.

DESCRIPTION OF RELIGIOUS CONFLICT OVER THE PUBLIC SCHOOLS IN PHILADELPHIA (1844)   From Editorial, *Pennsylvanian,* May 13, 1844.

Sunday in Philadelphia—soldiers marching and counter-marching in the streets, not for display or peaceful purposes, but prepared for actual battle—marines under arms—sailors of the United States Navy, with cutlasses, pistols, boarding pikes, and all the appliances of war, ready for deadly use upon the instant—the echoes awakened by the hoofs of the cavalry, and around the closed churches 'which still remain' are seen waving plumes and flashing bayonets. Such is a Sunday in the nineteenth century in the city of Philadelphia. Religious toleration enforced—by loaded muskets, drawn sabres, and at the cannon's mouth—charity secured through dread of 'grape and cannister.'

THE RELIGIOUS CLAUSE IN THE MASSACHUSETTS SCHOOL LAW OF 1827   From State of Massachusetts, *General Laws of 1826,* chap. 143, enacted March 10, 1827.

SECT. 7. *Be it further enacted,* That the school committee of each town, shall direct and determine the class books to be used in the respective classes, in all the several schools kept by said town; and the scholars sent to such schools shall be supplied by their parents, masters or guardians, with the books prescribed for their classes; . . . *Provided nevertheless,* that in cases where children are already supplied with books, which shall not be considered by the committee as being extremely faulty, in comparision with others, which might be obtained and which may be possessed in such numbers as to admit of the proper and convenient classification of the school, then, and in that case, the committee shall not direct the purchase of new books, without first obtaining the consent of the parents, masters, or guardians of a majority of the children so already provided for, under the term of two years from the passing of this act, unless such books become so worn, as to be unfit for use: *Provided also,* that said committee shall never direct any school books to be purchased or used, in any of the schools under their superintendence, which are calculated to favour any particular religious sect or tenet.

ESTABLISHMENT OF RELIGIOUS FREEDOM IN MASSACHUSETTS

(**1833**)   From Constitution of Massachusetts, as quoted in *The General Laws of the Commonwealth of Massachusetts* (1921), vol. I, p. xc.

Art. XI. Instead of the Third Article of the Bill of Rights, the Following Modification and Amendment Thereof Is Substituted

"**A**s the public worshop of GOD and instructions in piety, religion and morality, promote the happiness and prosperity of a people and the security of a republican government;—therefore, the several religious societies of this commonwealth, whether corporate or unincorporate, at any meeting legally warned and holden for that purpose, shall ever have the right to elect their pastors or religious teachers, to contract with them for their support, to raise money for erecting and repairing houses for public worship, for the maintenance of religious instruction, and for the payment of necessary expenses: and all persons belonging to any religious society shall be taken and held to be members, until they shall file with the clerk of such society, a written notice, declaring the dissolution of their membership and thenceforth shall not be liable for any grant or contract which may be thereafter made, or entered into by such society:—and all religious sects and denominations, demeaning themselves peaceably, and as good citizens of the commonwealth, shall be equally under the protection of the law; and no subordination of any one sect or denomination to another shall ever be established by law."

CONTROVERSY BETWEEN HORACE MANN, THE EDITOR OF THE "CHRISTIAN WITNESS," AND EDWARD A. NEWTON OVER THE PLACE OF RELIGION IN THE COMMON SCHOOLS (1844)

From Edward A. Newton, "Christian Education," as quoted in *Christian Witness and Church Advocate*, February 23, 1844; Horace Mann, Letter to the Editor "Our Common Schools," *Boston Courier*, May 29, 1844, as quoted in *The Common School Controversy . . .* (Boston, 1844), pp. 24, 31–32.

Mr. Editor: I beg to draw the attention of your readers to the following beautiful sketch of a part of the speech of Mr. Webster, in the celebrated "Girard case," now under discussion in the Supreme Court of the United States at Washington, published in the Daily Advertiser, of this city. Every Christian heart will respond with delight to the sentiments there expressed; they are truth, and righteousness, and well would it be for our country, if they were universally adopted and acted upon. This was the principle upon which education in Massachusetts was originally established by our Pilgrim fathers, and we cherish the recollection of it with the profoundest thankfulness.

But what are we doing now? Can any one tell wherein the system of Mr. Girard, and the present system of our "Board of Education," or rather of its Secretary, differs; or where the *essential* line of agreement, varies? I abstain from pressing the

THE COMMON
SCHOOL
MOVEMENT

1149

subject further at present, desiring only at this time to draw the attention of Christians of all denominations, holding Orthodox creeds, to the grave question, with the hope that they will examine for themselves. There is scarcely a subject that so much requires, perhaps *demands*, more thoughtful investigation.

Mr. Webster commenced his argument before the Supreme Court this morning, February 10, in the great Girard case, occupying the time of the court from its opening, 11 A. M. till about 3 P. M., when it adjourned. He conclusively proved that the system of education directed to be pursued at the Institution, by Mr. Girard, professed to be based upon principles of morality, but which were separated entirely from religion. He, also, showed that it was not in the power of man to separate them, demonstrating them to be inseparable—as co-existing, or not at all; and that, without religion, there could be no such thing existing as genuine charity.

The religious sectarianism of which it was the aim of Mr. G. to divest the contemplated institution, was admirably shown up. He proved that by the manner in which he proposed to accomplish it, he was attempting only the lopping off the branches of sectarianism, while he laid the axe at the root of Christianity itself. He traced the principles of Girard's grand moral system of instruction to Paine's "Age of Reason," and Volney's "Views of Religion." He exposed the inevitable tendency of those principles, and showed it to be the undermining of the fabric of Christianity. Whatever might have been Girard's view of religion and morality, he proved that he did not adapt the means to the end he had proposed—that end being a high morality—for he closed the door against morals as well as religion. He, likewise, proved that there could have been no principle of Christianity whatever to have influenced the mind of Mr. Girard in establishing the institution; as, in my estimation, he showed that he lived as he died, without the influence of religion; therefore, the grand principle was wanting, and there could be no *charity*.

To the Editor of the Courier:

After a respite of six weeks, the editor of the "Christian Witness and Church Advocate" has again returned to the charge against the Board of Education and myself. As I have presented one dispassionate communication to that editor, in reply to his injurious attacks, and have been repulsed, I entertain no hope that he would now permit *my* defence to follow *his* accusations. It is therefore that I ask again the favor of being heard through your columns.

The article in the "Witness," to which I wish to draw attention, is signed with the initials E. A. N.; and its writer now avows himself the author of the original article on the subject. As it has long been known that that article was written by Edward A. Newton. Esq., of Pittsfield, and as the present one bears the initials E. A. N., it would be affectation any longer to treat the communications as anonymous. I trust, therefore, it will be deemed no discourtesy in me if, in order to avoid circumlocution, I speak of the author by name. Besides, it is always more agreeable to see one's antagonist and to look in his eye, than to be confronted by a blank mask, or a shadow. I only regret that Mr. Newton had not taken the more open course of avowing himself, in the first instance, instead of waiting till he was discovered.

It is to some extraordinary statements and views in Mr. Newton's last communication that I wish to draw attention. Though personally, and, as I think most unjustly implicated in Mr. Newton's allegations, I feel no disposition to make an acrimonious reply. The cause at stake, either as he views it, or as I view it,

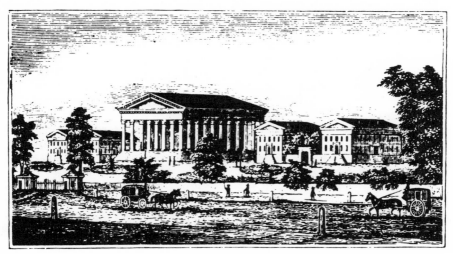

Girard College (work in progress 1835: Thomas Walter, architect), Philadelphia, Penn.

should lift us infinitely above the region of personalities, and should make truth our only object and aim.

In Mr. Newton's original article, Mr. Girard (the founder of the Girard College) is charged with having "laid the axe at the root of Christianity itself"; with having derived his principles of instruction from "Paine's 'Age of Reason' and Volney's 'Views of religion' "; with having "undermined Christianity," and with having been "influenced by no principle of Christianity whatever"; and in view of these charges, Mr. Newton said, "Can any one tell wherein the system of Mr. Girard, and the present system of our Board of Education, or rather of its Secretary, differs; or where the *essential* line of agreement varies?"

The first point now made by Mr. Newton, is, that this was interrogative merely; put only by way of inquiry; that he "guarded his language carefully," &c. He says he did not mean to accuse the Rev. Dr. Humphrey, President of Amherst College, Mr. Sears, President of the Newton Theological Seminary, the Rev. Dr. Robbins, and the other members of the Board, with being disciples of "Volney or Paine, and their like,—those enemies both to God and man."

Let me put a case. Suppose a merchant goes on 'Change and says publickly, "You know that Mr. A. is a knave, a swindler and a thief. Can any one tell wherein Mr. B's character 'differs' from that of Mr. A?"

* * *

You ask, "Does any one believe that the Puritan Fathers, of whom we so highly boast, would have submitted to this?"—that is, to exemption from sectarian teaching in our schools, and to equal religious privileges for all. Pardon my presumption, sir, if it is such, but I feel an inward and resistless prompting, as it were, commanding me, in the name of every lover of God and man, to answer you, that they would.

Did they now live, with the more clearly-defined notions of religious liberty and of human rights, which have been evolved by two centuries of experience and investigation; did they live in our times, when certainly more than one third part of the people of this Commonwealth have become dissenters from their faith, I should consider it the foulest of all dishonors I could cast upon their name, to say they would not have yielded the law of force and the rigors of compulsion, to the demands of justice and the spirit of the age. They would have obeyed the divine injunctions of the venerable Robinson, when, as if moved by a double spirit of inspiration, he poured his last farewell into their souls in the following words:

"If God reveal anything to you by any other instrument of his, be as ready to receive it as ever you were to receive any truth by my ministry; for I am verily persuaded, I am very confident, that the Lord has more truth yet to breathe forth out of his holy word. For my part I cannot sufficiently bewail the condition of the reformed churches, who are come to a period in religion, and will go, at present, no farther than the instruments of their reformation. The Lutherans cannot be drawn to go beyond what Luther saw; whatever part of his will our good God has revealed to Calvin, they will rather die than embrace it. And the Calvinists, you see, stick fast where they were left by that great man of God, who yet saw not all things. This is a misery much to be lamented, for though they were burning and shining lights in their times, yet they penetrated not into the whole counsel of God,—but *were they now living, would be as willing to embrace further light*, as that which they first received. I beseech you remember, it is an article of your church covenant, 'That you be ready to receive whatever truth shall be made known to you from the written word of God.' "

Yes, Mr. Newton! even among them, were they now here, you would stand alone in your advocacy of intolerance!

You complain that the schools are no longer as they once were, when the "Assembly's Catechism" was taught "daily or weekly" in them. The law, or the interpretation of the law, which forbids this, you call an "excrescence" upon our original Common School system. Would you also be rid of the corresponding "excrescence" upon our political system? Time was, when no one but a church member, a communicant had a right to vote; and were he ex-communicated from the church, he lost his political franchise also. The changes in regard to political and religious rights, have gone on hand in hand. From the early days of the Colony, the statute book is full of laws providing for the enlargement of both political and religious privileges. The Constitution itself has been twice altered to adapt it to the resistless current of public opinion. And what is remarkable is, that the point of liberty and equality, in regard to both subjects, was reached almost at the same identical time. Now, not only may every man vote who will comply with certain conditions applicable to all, but he has a claim for damages against the officers who would defeat his wishes. So in regard to religion. Every man is perfectly free to adopt whatever views he pleases, both for himself and his children, and when he lifts his own eye to Heaven, or points his children's thitherward, and a bigot's hand is thrust out to intercept their vision, he has a right to smite it to the earth.

The inference which I draw from all this is, not that we should restore the ancient laws either political or religious, for that is impossible, even were it desirable; but that we should exert ourselves to the highest tension of the last fibre of our strength, to do what we can, through our Common Schools, for the improvement of the habits, for the enlightening of the intellect, for the cultivation of the affections, for enkindling love of God and man on the altar of every heart, and for a sacred adhesion to that principle of Jesus,—now so openly disavowed and practically denied,—to do to others as we would that they should do to us.

I am sorry to introduce myself in this connection, but charged as I have been with sinister motives in favor of my own religious views, and with conspiring with the Board of Education, to accomplish unlawful objects by clandestine means, I must take the liberty to add that, intimate as I have been with every member of the Board, and with opportunities to know all their plans and designs, I do not believe there has been but one member of that body who would avail himself of his official influence, for the unlawful extension of his own doctrines. That member, as I have before stated, left the Board because, by a vote otherwise unanimous, they adopted the plan of a School Library, from which the "great controverted topics of the day," in religion and politics, were to be excluded. Had I the slightest reason to suppose that it was the design or the desire of the Board to make use of me for such a person, I would retain my office no longer than would be necessary to write my resignation. Although I have a faith or belief on this subject, which I think I could die to sustain, yet while others hold that faith to be erroneous, I do not desire—I would not permit, that it should be compulsorily introduced into the schools. The same conscience that compels me to decide for myself, and to stand by that decision, forbids my deciding for others.

In writing this long and I fear tedious letter, on the questions, what constitutes religious freedom in regard to public education, and what course the Board of Education has taken respecting it, I began by disclaiming, with Mr. Newton, all desire to be personal. In following the line of fact and accuracy, I have been obliged to deviate far from his path; but in closing, I will adopt his words, saying with him, in regard to the great points of difference between us, "Let the public decide."

Very truly and sincerely yours, &c.
HORACE MANN.

Boston, May 24, 1844.

CRITICISM OF THE PUBLIC SCHOOLS OF MASSACHUSETTS BY REV. MATHEW HALE SMITH, A BOSTON CLERGYMAN (1847) From Mathew Hale Smith, *The Ark of God on a New Cart* (Boston, 1847), pp. 11–12.

An effort has been made, and that too with some success, to do three things with our common schools. 1. To get out of them the Bible and all religious instruction. 2. To abolish the use of the rod, and all correction, but a little talk. 3. To make common schools a counterpoise to religious instruction at home and in Sabbath schools. The Board of Education in Massachusetts has aided in this work in two ways. 1. By allowing an individual, under the sanction of its authority, to disseminate through the land crude and destructive principles, principles believed to be at war with the Bible and with the best interests of the young for time and eternity. 2. By a library which excludes books as sectarian that inculcate truths, which *nine-tenths of professed Christians of all names believe,* while it accepts others that inculcate the most deadly heresy—even universal salvation. We ask not that religion shall be sustained by law; but we do ask that impiety and irreligion shall not be supported by the state. When religious and intellectual culture are divorcéd, is it strange that we have a harvest of crime? When, under the sanction of the highest powers, punishments are ridiculed as well as denounced, is it strange that the arm of parental authority is weakened, and the master finds his law without a penalty? Is it strange that our juvenile courtesy, is of that Doric sort which expresses itself in "Yes and No," "I will and I won't"? Is it strange that we have such a harvest of rebellion and crime? One of the reformers of this day said in a lecture in New York, that he had no hope of the clergy, none of the church; but his hope was in the lyceum and the common school. Before the lyceum last winter, in this city, a course of atheistical lectures were given. We see what is to be done with the schools, and what the hope is. Soon Christians will have to consider the question, whether a mere intellectual education with no moral basis is worth the having? Already the question has been before the Presbyterian church of the United States, whether the time has not come when they must establish schools of their own, in which moral training will be blended with intellectual, and the Bible be allowed in schools.

From causes such as I have named, has this harvest of crime sprung up. And while we boast of our common schools as the glory of our land, let us beware that they do not become our shame. Even now, in our best schools in this city, insubordination and licentiousness abound. They are developed in the circulation of obscene French prints in school, and in the efforts of girls in school to corrupt their associates.

HORACE MANN ANSWERS THE REV. MATHEW HALE SMITH

(1847) From *Sequel to the So Called Correspondence Between the Rev. M. H. Smith and Horace Mann, Surreptitiously Published by Mr. Smith; Containing a Letter from Mr. Mann, Suppressed by Mr. Smith, with the Reply Therein Promised* (Boston, 1847), p. 46.

I leave you for a moment, Mr. Smith, in order to address a few considerations to those who think that *doctrinal* religion should be taught in our schools; and who would empower each town or school district to determine the *kind* of doctrine to be taught. It is easy to see that the experiment would not stop with having half a dozen conflicting creeds taught by authority of law, in the different schools of the same town or vicinity. Majorities will change in the same place. Ony sect may have the ascendency, to-day; another, tomorrow. This year, there will be three Persons in the Godhead; next year, but One; and the third year, the Trinity will be restored, to hold its precarious sovereignty, until it shall be again dethroned by the worms of the dust it has made. This year, the everlasting fires of hell will burn, to terrify the impenitent; next year, and without any repentance, its eternal flames will be extinguished,—to be rekindled forever, or to be quenched forever, as it may be decided at annual town meetings. This year, under Congregational rule, the Rev. Mr. So and So, and the Rev. Dr. So and So, will be on the committee; but next year, these Reverends and Reverend Doctors will be plain Misters,—never having had apostolical consecration from the Bishop. This year, the ordinance of baptism is inefficacious without immersion; next year one drop of water will be as good as forty fathoms. Children attending the district school will be taught one way; going from the district school to the town high school, they will be taught another way. In controversies involving such momentous interests, the fiercest party spirit will rage, and all the contemplations of heaven be poisoned by the passions of earth. Will not town lines and school district lines be altered, to restore an unsuccessful, or to defeat a successful party? Will not fiery zealots move from place to place, to turn the theological scale, as, it is said, is sometimes now done, to turn a political one? And will not the godless make a merchandise of religion by being bribed to do the same thing? Can aught be conceived more deplorable, more fatal to the interests of the young than this? Such strifes and persecutions on the question of total depravity, as to make all men depraved at any rate; and such contests about the nature and the number of Persons in the Godhead in heaven, as to make little children atheists upon earth.

If the question, "What theology shall be taught in school?" is to be decided by districts or towns, then all the prudential and the superintending school committees must be chosen with express reference to their faith; the creed of every candidate for teaching must be investigated; and when litigations arise,—and such a system will breed them in swarms,—an ecclesiastical tribunal,—some Star Chamber, or High Commission Court, must be created to decide them. If the Governor is to have power to appoint the Judges of this Spiritual Tribunal, he also must be chosen with reference to the appointments he will make, and so too must the Legislators who are to define their power, and to give them the Purse and Sword of the State, to execute their authority. . . . The establishment of the true faith will not stop with the schoolroom. Its grasping jurisdiction will extend over all schools, over all private faith and public worship; until at last, after all our centuries of struggle and of suffering, it will come back to the inquisition, the fagot and the rack!

PETITION OF DETROIT CATHOLICS FOR SCHOOL FUNDS (1853) From Michigan Board of Public Instruction, *Report of the Superintendent of Public Instruction* (1853). pp. 190–91.

We, the undersigned, citizens of Michigan, respectfully represent to your Honorable Body, that we have labored, and are still laboring under grievances to which neither Justice nor Patriotism require longer submission on our part, without an effort for their removal.

We, your petitioners, wish to represent to your Honorable Body, that notwithstanding the Constitution guarantees liberty of conscience to every citizen of the State, yet our Public School laws compel us to violate our conscience, or deprive us unjustly of our share of the Public School Funds, and also impose on us taxes for the support of schools, which, as a matter of conscience, we cannot allow our children to attend.

To convince your Honorable Body of the magnitude of these grievances, we have but to refer you to the fact, that in the cities of Monroe and Detroit alone, there are educated at the expense of their parents, and charitable contributions, some 2500 of our children. Your petitioners might bear longer their present grievances, hoping that our fellow-citizens would soon discover the injustice done to us by the present School laws, and that the love of public justice for which they are distinguished, would prompt them to protest against laws which are self-evidently a violation of liberty of conscience, a liberty which is equally dear to every American citizen; but, as the new Constitution requires that free schools be established in every district in our State, and as the present Legislature will be called upon to act upon the subject, your petitioners consider that their duty to themselves, their duty to their children, and their duty to their country, the liberties of which they are morally and religiously bound to defend, as well as their duty to their God, require that they apprise your Honorable Body of the oppressive nature of our present School laws, the injustice of which is equalled only by the laws of England, which compel the people of all denominations to support a church, the doctrines of which they do not believe.

Your petitioners would not wish to be understood as being opposed to education; on the contrary they are prepared to bear every reasonable burden your Honorable Body are willing to impose on them, to promote the cause of education, providing that our schools be free indeed. But they do not consider schools free when the law imposes on parents the necessity of giving their children such an education as their conscience cannot approve of. But that your Honorable Body may not be ignorant of what they understand by free schools, your petitioners wish to say that in their opinions, schools can be free only, when the business of school teaching be placed on the same legal footing as the other learned professions, when all may teach who will, their success depending, as in other cases, on their fitness for their profession, and the satisfaction that they may render to the public; that in all cases the parent be left free to choose the teacher to whom he will entrust the education of his child, as he is left to choose his physician, his lawyer, etc.; that each person teaching any public school in the State should be entitled to draw from the public school fund, such sums as the law might provide for every child so taught by the month, quarter, or otherwise, on producing such evidence as the law might require in such cases. Schools established on such principles are what your petitioners understand by free schools.

Your petitioners, therefore, respectfully urge that the public school system, for our State, be based on these broad democratic principles of equal liberty to all, allowing freedom of conscience to the child, who also has a conscience, as well as to the instructor and parent. And your petitioners will ever pray.

MICHIGAN BISHOP SAMUEL A. McCOSKRY'S OPPOSITION TO THE CATHOLIC PETITION (1853)   From Michigan Board of Public Instruction, *Report of the Superintendent of Public Instruction* (1853), p. 205.

The undersigned is the Bishop of the Protestant Episcopal Church in the Diocese of Michigan: He has learned from the public newspapers, and from petitions about to be presented to your honorable bodies, that an application is to be made for a division of the school fund of this State, so that "in all cases the parent be left free to choose the teacher to whom he will entrust the education of his child." Such application (if granted) he considers as giving the right not only to parents, but to every religious body, to select teachers who will teach the peculiarities of the religious views of opinions they may hold. It will place the school fund of this State in the hands of religious bodies or sects, and entrust to them the education of the children of the State; for the right, if given to one, will be claimed by each and all. Whatever opinion the writer may entertain in reference to the system and effects of the common-school education, he begs leave to say, that he has no wish or desire to interfere with, or in any way alter, or abridge the system which has been the pride of the State, and which has furnished to so many thousands of her children the means of obtaining a high secular education; nor does he wish that the fund so generously granted to the people of the State, and so carefully guarded by her Legislature, and so highly prized by her citizens, should be used for the promotion of sectarian strife and bitterness.

It is one of the distinguishing features of our free institutions, and one which lies at the foundation of happiness and freedom of the people, that neither religous tests nor religious preferences form any part of our legislation. All religious bodies are placed on precisely the same footing, and whatever may be the exclusive claims of each and all, they can be settled only by an appeal to a higher and different authority than State legislatures. But if your honorable bodies see fit to overturn and destroy that system which has been heretofore so carefully guarded, and which has introduced into every occupation and profession, some of the most distinguished men of the State, and which has brought to the door of the poor man the means of educating his children; and if the Priests and Clergymen of every religious body are to take the place of the common-school teacher, and the State is to assume the duty, through them, of extending and building up religious differences, and of fomenting strife and contention, then, the undersigned (most reluctantly) would claim to have a share in this work. If then such a change is to be made in our common-school law, so as to allow parents to choose teachers for their children, the undersigned would respectfully ask for his proportion of the common-school fund, so that the people entrusted to his spiritual oversight may employ such teachers as will fully carry out their religious preferences. He would freely and frankly state to your honorable bodies that the amount thus granted, shall be carefully used in teaching the principles and doctrines of the Protestant Episcopal Church, and that the services of as many clergymen and laymen of the Church will be secured and used, so that no other principles and doctrines shall find any place in the different schools.

The Religious Question
Catholics

PASTORAL LETTER OF BISHOP JOHN CARROLL (1792) From Peter Guilday, ed., *The National Pastorals of the American Hierarchy, 1792–1919* (Washington, D.C., 1923), pp. 2–5

John, by Divine permission and with the approbation of the Holy See, Bishop of Baltimore: To my dearly beloved Brethren, the members of the Catholic Church in this Diocess, Health and Blessing, Grace to you and peace from God our Father, and from the Lord Jesus Christ

The great extent of my diocess and the necessity of ordering many things concerning its government at the beginning of my episcopacy, have not yet permitted me, my dear brethren, to enjoy the consolation, for which I most earnestly pray, of seeing you all, and of leaving with you, according to the nature of my duty, some words of exhortation, by which you may be strengthened in faith, and encouraged in the exercises of a Christian life. Esteeming myself as a debtor to all, and knowing the rigorous account which I must render for your souls, to the Shepherd of Shepherds, our Lord and Savior Jesus Christ, I shall have cause to tremble, while I leave anything undone, by which religion and true piety may be promoted, and the means of salvation multiplied for you.

In compliance with the obligation, resulting from the relation in which I stand to you, my endeavours have been turned towards obtaining and applying, for the preservation and extension of faith and for the sanctification of souls, means calculated to produce lasting effects, not only on the present, but on future generations. I thought that Almighty God would make the ministers of His sanctuary, and myself particularly, accountable to Him, if we did not avail ourselves of the liberty enjoyed under our equitable government and just laws, to attempt establishments, in which you, dear brethren, may find permanent resources, suited to your greatest exigencies.

Knowing, therefore, that the principles instilled in the course of a Christian education, are generally preserved through life, and that *a young man according to his way, even when he is old, he will not depart from it* (Proverbs 21:6), I have considered the virtuous and Christian instruction of youth as a principal object of pastoral solicitude. Now who can contribute so much to lighten this burthen, which weighs so heavy on the shoulders of the pastors of souls and who can have so great an interest and special duty in the forming of youthful minds to habits of virtue and religion, as their parents themselves? Especially while their children retain their native docility, and their hearts are uncorrupted by vice.

How many motives of reason and religion require, that parents should be unwearied in their endeavours, to inspire in them the love and fear of God; docility and submission to His doctrines, and a careful attention to fulfil His commandments? Fathers—bring up your children *in the discipline and correction of the Lord* (Ephesians 6:4). If all, to whom God has given sons and daughters, were assiduous in the discharge of this important obligation, a foundation would be laid for, and great progress made in, the work of establishing a prevailing purity of manners. The same habits of obedience to the will of God; the same principles of a reverential love and fear of Him; and of continual respect for his Holy Name; the same practices of morning and evening prayer; and of the frequentation of the sacraments; the same dread of cursing and swearing; of fraud and duplicity; of lewdness and drunkenness; the same respectful and dutiful behavior to their fathers and mothers; in a word, the remembrance and influence of the parental counsels and examples received in their youth, would continue with them during life.

And if ever the frailty of nature, or worldly seduction, should cause them to offend God, they would be brought back again to His service and to true repentance by the efficacy of the religious instruction received in their early age. Wherefore, fathers and mothers, be mindful of the words of the Apostles, and bring up your children in the discipline and correction of the Lord. In doing this, you not only render an acceptable service to God, and acquit yourselves of a most important duty, but you labour for the preservation and increase of true religion, for the benefit of our common country, whose welfare depends on the morals of its citizens, and for your own happiness here as well as hereafter; since you may be assured of finding, in those sons and daughters whom you shall train up to virtue and piety, by your instructions and examples, support and consolation in sickness and old age. They will remember with gratitude, and repay with religious duty, your solicitude for them in their infancy and youth.

These being the advantages of a religious education, I was solicitous for the attainment of a blessing so desirable to that precious portion of my flock, the growing generation. A school has been instituted at George-Town, which will continue to be under the superintendence and government of some of my reverend brethren, that is, of men devoted by principle and profession to instruct all, who resort to them, in useful learning, and those of our own religion, in its principles and duties. I earnestly wish, dear brethren, that as many of you, as are able, would send your sons to this school of letters and virtue. I know and lament, that the expense will be too great for many families, and that their children must be deprived of the immediate benefit of this institution; but, indirectly, they will receive it; at least, it may be reasonably expected, that some after being educated at George-Town, and having returned into their own neighbourhood, will become, in their turn, the instructors of the youths who cannot be sent from home; and, by pursuing the same system of uniting much attention to religion with a solicitude for other improvements, the general result will be a great increase of piety, the necessary consequence of a careful instruction in the principles of faith, and Christian morality. . . .

ACCOUNT OF THE OPENING OF THE UNIVERSITY OF NOTRE DAME

(**1847**)   From John Tracy Ellis, ed., *Documents of American Catholic History* (Milwaukee, 1956), pp. 298–301.

University of Notre-Dame-du-Lac,
St. Joseph County, Indiana
Under the Direction of the Priests of
the Holy Cross

This Institution commenced under the auspices of the Rt. Rev'd Bishop of Vincennes who presented to the priests of the Holy cross, the beautiful and elegant site upon which the buildings are erected, is now in full operation. Notre-Dame-du-Lac is at a distance of 1 mile from South Bend, the County seat; 80 miles from Chicago, Illinois; 180 from Detroit, Mich. with which there is direct communication by railroad, and 60 from Fort Wayne, Ia.

The edifice is of brick, four and a half story [*sic*] high and not inferior in point of style or structure to any of the colleges of the United States, and is situated upon a commanding eminence on the verge of two picturesque and commodious Lakes, which, with the river St. Joseph and the surrounding country, present a most magnificent prospect. The rooms are spacious, well ventilated and furnished, with every thing conducive to regularity and comfort.

The Infirmary is intrusted to Sisters similar in their Institute to the Sisters of Charity; their well known kindness and skill are a sufficient guarantee, that the invalids will be attended to with all the diligence and care, which devotion and affection can suggest.

The disciplinary government is mild, yet sufficiently energetic, to preserve that good order, so essential to the well-being of the Institution. The morals and general deportment of the pupils are watched over with the greatest assiduity and solicitude; their personal comfort receives the most paternal attention, and no pains are spared to prepare them for fulfilling their respective duties in society. In their daily recreations, they are always accompanied by a member of the Institution; all books in their possession are subject to the inspection of the Prefect of Studies; and none are allowed circulation without his approval. Corporal punishments will never be inflicted, but more conciliatory and effective means of correction are judiciously used; should a pupil prove refractory, and incorrigible, he will be dismissed.

The faculty is formed of the priests of the Holy Cross: a member is annually sent to Europe to complete whatever contingent circumstances may require. In the reception of pupils no distinction of creed is made, and the parents of those, not professing the Catholic faith, may rest assured that there will be no interference with their religious tenets; they are required only to attend to the religious exercises with decorum, this being in conformity with the rules of all the catholic colleges in the United States.

TERMS

Board, washing and medical attendance, with the English Course, embracing all the branches of a practical education; Orthography, Reading, Writing, Arithmetic, Grammar and Composition, to which particular attention is paid; Geography, Ancient and Modern History; the most approved methods of Book-keeping,

Surveying, Mensuration, Mathematics, Astronomy, the use of the Globes, Rhetoric, Vocal Music, &c. Free admittance to the Museum, lessons of natation and
Equestrian exercises &c. ....$100 per ann.
Half Boarders,... 40 per ann.
Day scholars in the above course .... 20 per ann.
The same in the preparatory School, ... 16 per ann.
 The classical course of Latin, and Greek an additional sum of..... 20 per ann.
The French, German languages are taught at an extra charge of..... 12 per ann.
Instrumental Music and Drawing   20 per ann.
Piano   40 per ann.

 Class books, Stationary [*sic*], and Medicines furnished at the usual rates.

 The payments must be made semi-annually in advance; from this rule there can be no deviation whatever, as the charges are based upon the lowest estimate, the object of the Institution being to increase the facilities of instruction, without any view to pecuniary reward.

 The distribution of Premiums takes place on the 1st Tuesday of August, and the commencement of the scholastic year is irrevocably fixed on the 1st Friday of October.

 The Institution being in possession of all the powers and privileges of a University: degrees will be conferred after the public examination.

 No boarder will be received for a shorter term than half a year, and no deduction made for absence, except in case of sickness or dismission.

 Examinations take place at the end of each Quarter, and reports are forwarded semi-annually to parents, informing them of the progress, health, &c., of their children. Public examinations, before the distribution of premiums, will take place in the last week of July in every year.

DIRECTIONS FOR PARENTS

Each pupil must be provided with bed and bedding, (if furnished by the Institution, they form an extra charge,) six shirts, six pair of stockings, six pocket handkerchiefs, six towels (all of which must be marked,) a knife and fork, a table and tea spoon, a hat and cap, two suits of clothes, an over-coat, a pair of shoes and a pair of boots for winter; three suits of clothing and two pair of shoes for summer. No advances will be made by the Institution for clothing or other expenses.

 The pupils will not be allowed to have money in their possession; their pocket money must be deposited in the Treasurer's hands, in order to guard against abuses, and to enable the Institution to apply the money as an incentive to virtue and industry. When parents wish to have their children sent home, they must give timely notice, settle all accounts, and supply means to defray their traveling expenses.

 Visitors cannot be permitted to interrupt the pupils during the hours of study. The mid-day recreation commences at half past 12 and ends at half past one o'clock. This is the most appropriate time for the visits of parents and friends.

 All letters to pupils or members of the Institution must be post paid.

              Rev. E. SORIN, *President*

Notre Dame du Lac, St. Joseph
County, Indiana, January 1st, 1847.
References to the Rt. Rev. Bishop of Vincennes and to the Rt. Rev.
Bishop of Detroit Rev. Mr. Benoit, Fort-Wayne, Ia. [*sic*].

THE FIRST PLENARY COUNCIL ON THE SUBJECT OF CATHOLIC
SCHOOLS (1852) From Peter Guilday, ed., *The National Pastorals of the American Hierarchy, 1792–1919* (Washington, D.C., 1923), pp. 189–90.

No portion of our charge fills us with greater solicitude than that which our Divine Master, by word and example, has taught us to regard with more than ordinary sentiments of affection—the younger members of our flock. If our youth grow up in ignorance of their religious duties or unpractised in their consoling fulfilment; if, instead of the words of eternal life, which find so full and sweet an echo in the heart of innocence, the principles of error, unbelief or indifferentism, are imparted to them; if the natural repugnance, even in the happiest period of life, to bend under the yoke of discipline, be increased by the example of those whose relation to them gives them influence or authority,—what are we to expect but the disappointment of all hopes which cause the Church to rejoice in the multiplication of her children! We therefore address you brethren, in the language of affectionate warning and solemn exhortation. Guard carefully those little ones of Christ; "suffer them to approach Him, and prevent them not, for of such is the kingdom of heaven." To you, Christian parents, God has committed these His children, whom he permits you to regard as yours; and your natural affection towards whom must ever be subordinate to the will of Him "from whom all paternity in heaven and on earth is named." Remember that if for them you are the representatives of God, the source of their existence, you are to be for them depositaries of His authority, teachers of His law, and models by imitating which they may be perfect, even as their Father in heaven is perfect. You are to watch over the purity of their faith and morals with jealous vigilance, and to instil into their young hearts principles of virtue and perfection. What shall be the anguish of the parent's heart,—what terrible expectation of judgment that will fill his soul, should his children perish through his criminal neglect, or his obstinate refusal to be guided in the discharge of his paternal duties, by the authority of God's Church. To avert this evil give your children a Christian education, that is an education based on religious principles, accompanied by religious practices and always subordinate to religious influence. Be not led astray by the false and delusive theories wh[i]ch are so prevalent, and which leave youth without religion, and, consequently, without anything to control the passions, promote the real happiness of the individual, and make society find in the increase of its members, a source of security and prosperity. Listen not to those who would persuade you that religion can be separated from secular instruction. If your children, while they advance in human sciences, are not taught the science of the saints, their minds will be filled with every error, their hearts will be receptacles of every vice, and that very learning which they have acquired, in itself so good and so necessary, deprived of all that could shed on it the light of heaven, will be an additional means of destroying the happiness of the child, embittering still more the chalice of parental disappointment, and weakening the foundations of social order. Listen to our voice, which tells us to walk in the ancient paths; to bring up your children as you yourselves were brought up by your pious parents; to make religion the foundation of the happiness you wish to secure for those whom you love so tenderly, and the promotion of whose interests is the motive of all your efforts, the solace which sustains you in all your fatigues and privations. Encourage the establishment and support of Catholic schools; make every sacrifice which may be necessary for this object; spare our hearts the pain of beholding the youth whom, after the example of our Master, we so much love, involved in all the evils of an uncatholic education, evils too multiplied and too obvious to require that we should do more than raise our voices in solemn protest against the system from which they spring. In urging on you the discharge of this duty, we are acting on the suggestion of the Sovereign Pontiff, who in an encyclical letter, dated 21 November, 1851, calls on all the Bishops of the Catholic world, to provide for the religious education of youth. We are following the example of the Irish Hierarchy, who are courageously opposing the introduction of a system based on the principle which we condemn, and who are now endeavoring to unite religious with secular instruction of the highest order, by the institution of a Catholic University,—an undertaking in the success of which we necessarily feel a deep interest, and which, as having been suggested by the Sovereign Pontiff, powerfully appeals to the sympathies of the whole Catholic world.

INSTRUCTION OF THE CONGREGATION OF PROPAGANDA DE FIDE CONCERNING AMERICAN PUBLIC SCHOOLS (1875)   From "Instruction of the Congregation of Propaganda de Fide Concerning Catholic Children Attending American Public Schools, November 24, 1875," as quoted in John Tracy Ellis, ed., *Documents of American Catholic History* (Milwaukee, Wis., 1956), pp. 417–20.

The Sacred Congregation of Propaganda has been many times assured that for the Catholic children of the United States of America evils of the gravest kind are likely to result from the so-called public schools.

The sad intelligence moved the Propaganda to propose to the illustrious prelates of that country a series of questions, with the object of ascertaining, first, why the faithful permit their children to attend non-catholic schools, and secondly, what may be the best means of keeping the young away from schools of this description. The answers, as drawn up by the several prelates, were submitted, owing to the nature of the subject, to the Supreme Congregation of the Holy Office. The decision reached by their Eminences, Wednesday, June 30, 1875, they saw fit to embody in the following *Instruction*, which the Holy Father graciously confirmed on Wednesday, November 24, of the same year.

1. The first point to come under consideration was the system of education itself, quite peculiar to those schools. Now, that system seemed to the S. Congregation most dangerous and very much opposed to Catholicity. For the children in those schools, the very principles of which exclude all religious instruction, can neither learn the rudiments of the faith nor be taught the precepts of the Church; hence, they will lack that knowledge, of all else, necessary to man without which there is no leading a Christian life. For children are sent to these schools from their earliest years, almost from their cradle; at which age, it is admitted, the seeds sown of virtue or of vice take fast root. To allow this tender age to pass without religion is surely a great evil.

2. Again, these schools being under no control of the Church, the teachers are selected from every sect indiscriminately; and this, while no proper precaution is

THE COMMON SCHOOL MOVEMENT

1163

taken to prevent them injuring the children, so that there is nothing to stop them from infusing into the young minds the seeds of error and vice. Then evil results are certainly to be dreaded from the fact that in these schools, or at least in very many of them, children of both sexes must be in the same class and class-room and must sit side by side at the same desk. Every circumstance mentioned goes to show that the children are fearfully exposed to the danger of losing their faith and that their morals are not properly safeguarded.

3. Unless this danger of perversion can be rendered remote, instead of proximate, such schools cannot in conscience be used. This is the dictate of natural as well as of divine law. It was enunciated in unmistakable terms by the Sovereign Pontiff, in a letter addressed to a former Archbishop of Freiburg, July 14, 1864. He thus writes: "There can be no hesitation, wherever the purpose is afoot or carried out of shutting out the Church from all authority over the schools, there the children will be sadly exposed to loss of their faith. Consequently the Church should, in such circumstances, not only put forth every effort and spare no pains to get for the children the necessary Christian training and education, but would be further compelled to remind the faithful and publicly declare that schools hostile to Catholicity cannot in conscience be attended." These words only express a general principle of natural and divine law and are consequently of universal application wherever that most dangerous system of training youth has been unhappily introduced.

4. It only remains, then, for the prelates to use every means in their power to keep the flocks committed to their care from all contact with the public schools. All are agreed that there is nothing so needful to this end as the establishment of Catholic schools in every place,—and schools no whit inferior to the public ones. Every effort, then must be directed towards starting Catholic schools where they are not, and, where they are, towards enlarging them and providing them with better accommodations and equipment until they have nothing to suffer, as regards teachers or equipment, by comparison with the public schools. And to carry out so holy and necessary a work, the aid of religious brotherhoods and of sisterhoods will be found advantageous where the bishop sees fit to introduce them. In order that the faithful may the more freely contribute the necessary expenses, the bishops themselves should not fail to impress on them, at every suitable occasion, whether by pastoral letter, sermon or private conversation, that as bishops they would be recreant to their duty if they failed to do their very utmost to provide Catholic schools. This point should be especially brought to the attention of the more wealthy and influential Catholics and members of the legislature.

5. In that country there is no law to prevent Catholics having their own schools and instructing and educating their youth in every branch of knowledge. It is therefore in the power of Catholics themselves to avert, with God's help, the dangers with which Catholicity is threatened from the public school system. Not to have religion and piety banished from the school-room is a matter of the very highest interest, not only to certain individuals and families, but to the entire country,—a country now so prosperous and of which the Church has had reason to conceive such high hopes.

6. However, the S. Congregation is now aware that circumstances may be sometimes such as to permit parents conscientiously to send their children to the public schools. Of course, they cannot do so without having sufficient cause. Whether there be a sufficient cause in any particular case is to be left to the conscience and judgment of the bishop. Generally speaking, such cause will exist when there is no Catholic school in the place, or the one that is there cannot be

considered suitable to the condition and circumstances in life of the pupils. But even in these cases, before the children can conscientiously attend the public school, the danger, greater or less, of perversion, which is inseparable from the system, must be rendered remote by proper precaution and safeguards. The first thing to see to, then, is whether the danger of perversion, as regards the school in question, is such as cannot possibly be rendered remote; as, for instance, whether the teaching there is such, or the doings of a nature so repugnant to Catholic belief and morals, that ear cannot be given to the one, nor part taken in the other without grievous sin. It is self-evident that danger of this character must be shunned at whatever cost, even life itself.

7. Further, before a child can be conscientiously placed at a public school, provision must be made for giving it the necessary Christian training and instruction, at least out of school hours. Hence parish priests and missionaries in the United States should take seriously to heart the earnest admonitions of the Council of Baltimore, and spare no labor to give children thorough catechetical instructions, dwelling particularly on those truths of faith and morals which are called most in question by Protestants and unbelievers: children beset with so many dangers they should guard with tireless vigilance, induce them to frequent the sacraments, excite in them devotion to the Blessed Virgin and on all occasions animate them to hold firmly by their religion. The parents or guardians must look carefully after those children. They must .examine them in their lessons, or if not able themselves, get others to do it. They must see what books they use and, if the books contain passages likely to injure the child's mind, explain the matter. They must keep them from freedom and familiarity with those of the other school children whose company might be dangerous to their faith or morals, and absolutely away from the corrupt.

8. Parents who neglect to give this necessary Christian training and instruction to their children, or who permit them to go to schools in which the ruin of their souls is inevitable, or finally, who send them to the public school without sufficient cause and without taking the necessary precautions to render the danger of perversion remote, and do so while there is a good and well-equipped Catholic school in the place, or the parents have the means to send them elsewhere to be educated,—that such parents, if obstinate, cannot be absolved, is evident from the moral teaching of the Church.

PRESIDENT GRANT OPPOSES PUBLIC FUNDS FOR RELIGIOUS SCHOOLS (1875) From *Congressional Record*, 44th Congress, 1st Session (Washington, D.C., 1876), vol. IV, p. 175.

As we are now about to enter upon our second centennial—commencing our manhood as a nation—it is well to look back upon the past and study what will be best to preserve and advance our future greatness. From the fall of Adam for his transgression to the present day, no nation has ever been free from threatened danger to its prosperity and happiness. We should look to the dangers threatening us, and remedy them so far as lies in our power. We are a republic whereof one

THE COMMON
SCHOOL
MOVEMENT

1165

man is as good as another before the law. Under such a form of government it is of the greatest importance that all should be possessed of education and intelligence enough to cast a vote with the right understanding of its meaning. A large association of ignorant men cannot, for any considerable period, oppose a successful resistance to tyranny and oppression from the educated few, but will inevitably sink into acquiescence to the will of intelligence, whether directed by the demagogue or by priestcraft. Hence the education of the masses becomes of the first necessity for the preservation of our institutions. They are worth preserving, because they have secured the greatest good to the greatest proportion of the population of any form of government yet devised. All other forms of government approach it just in proportion to the general diffusion of education and independence of thought and action. As the primary step, therefore, to our advancement in all that has marked our progress in the past century, I suggest for your earnest consideration—and most earnestly recommend it—that a constitutional amendment be submitted to the Legislatures of the several States for ratification making it the duty of the several States to establish and forever maintain free public schools adequate to the education of all the children in the rudimentary branches within their respective limits, irrespective of sex, color, birthplace, or religions; forbidding the teaching in said schools of religious, atheistic, or pagan tenets; and prohibiting the granting of any school funds, or school taxes, or any part thereof, either by the legislative, municipal, or other authority, for the benefit or in aid, directly or indirectly, of any religious sect or denomination, or in aid for the benefit of any other object of any nature or kind whatever.

SELECTIONS ON EDUCATION FROM THE PRONOUNCEMENTS OF THE THIRD PLENARY COUNCIL OF BALTIMORE (1884)   From Frederick E. Ellis, trans., "Parochial and Public Schools: A Point of View," *Educational Forum,* vol. XIV, pp. 25–30, 32–35.

On the Catholic Education of Youth

Of Catholic Schools, Particularly Parish Schools

I. OF THEIR GREAT NECESSITY

194. . . . For many years, men deeply imbued with a worldly spirit, have left no stone unturned to deprive the Church of the task of teaching Catholic youth, a responsibility which she, herself, received from Christ (Matthew XXVIII: 19; Mark X: 14), and they deliver it into the hands of civil society or entrust it to the power of the secular government. Nor is this a strange thing. For inasmuch as the most evil spirit of indifferentism, naturalism and materialism has invaded the minds of many persons, they cannot conceive that the end and happiness of man can be sought or found except in this temporal life and the material world. The philosophy of education which aims to elevate man and to direct him towards the future life and eternal blessedness seems to some foolish and useless, and to others pernicious,

something to be necessarily abolished. However, the chief mission of the Church on earth is to lead individuals, reborn in Christ through baptism, from their earliest perception of truth and justice to a supernatural destiny. It is a natural right and a divine imperative that parents provide a Christian education for their children. Hence the Church cannot allow Catholic parents in any manner to provide a merely secular education for them, one, indeed, which can scarcely supply the necessary means for the recognition and attainment of their final end.

195. Among those who vigorously advocate a merely secular education there are many, to be sure, who wish no harm to religion nor would they endanger young people. Nevertheless it follows from the very nature of the matter, and indeed sad experience confirms it, that merely secular education has gradually degenerated until it has become irreligious, impious and harmful to the faith and morals of adolescents. If according to the words of Christ: "No man can serve two masters, for either one is hated and the other loved; or one is supported and the other is despised," (Matthew VI: 24) and if according to the oracle of divine Wisdom, "Whosoever is not for me is against me," (Luke XI: 23) and finally if Christ teaches that the spirit of the world fills its followers with an impeccable hatred of those who are moved by the Spirit of God, it can scarcely be otherwise than that youth imbued with a secular spirit from childhood gradually become not only blinded lovers of the world, but for that reason also haters of Christ and adversaries of the Church. We are taught by the clear testimony of our enemies as well as of the faithful that the number of those who were instructed by a secular education is great; their defection from the Church gives us ample cause for grief but brings joy to our enemies.

196. Therefore, not only out of paternal affection, but also by whatever authority we are invested, we urge and enjoin Catholic parents to provide their beloved children—given to them by God, reborn in Christ through baptism and destined for heaven—an education which is truly Christian and Catholic. Further, that they defend them throughout infancy and childhood from the perils of a purely secular education and place them in safe-keeping; that they therefore send them to parochial schools or other truly Catholic schools, unless in particular cases the Ordinary judges that some alternative may be permitted.

✳   ✳   ✳

198. Although the necessity and obligation of teaching Catholic youth in Catholic schools is apparent, it may sometimes happen "that Catholic parents knowingly send their children to public schools"—as even the above instruction indicates. They should not do this unless they have sufficient cause for their actions, and whether or not there is sufficient cause in any given case will be left to the conscience and judgement of the Ordinaries. Further, the situation will arise when either there is no Catholic school nearby, or the school available is not of such quality as to teach young people properly or to meet their needs adequately. In order that they may, in conscience, attend public schools, the dangers of perversion must be separated from the operation and adminstration of the schools by suitable remedies and cautions.

When, therefore, with sufficient cause and with the approval of the Ordinaries, parents wish to send their children to public schools—providing caution is taken against contingent dangers—we strictly warn that no one whether a bishop or a presbyter dare keep these parents from the sacraments either by pretended threats or by overt actions. The Pope has forbidden such action through the pronouncements of the Holy Office. This should be understood all the more in the case of children. In consequence, let pastors of souls, while they warn the faithful entrusted in their care of the dangers of these schools, be particularly careful, lest motivated by immoderate zeal, they seem to violate either by word or by deed the wisest counsel and precepts of the Holy See.

199. Having deliberated these matters thoroughly, we state and decree:

I. That wherever at least one church exists, within two years from the promulgation of this Council, parochial schools are to be established and maintained forever, unless the bishop decides that a delay should be granted because of grave difficulties.

II. That any priest who, during this time either impedes the construction or maintenance of a school through his negligence, or does not take care of these matters after repeated warning from the bishop, will merit removal from his church.

III. That any mission or parish which neglects to assist its priest in the construction or maintenance of a school so that because of such negligence it is impossible to have a school, should be reproved by the bishop, and in the most efficatious and prudent manner be induced to provide the necessary support.

IV. That all Catholic parents ought to be compelled to send their children to parochial schools, unless either at home or in other Catholic schools they attend sufficiently and specifically to the Christian education of their children. With sufficient cause, approved by the bishop, and with proper cautions and remedies, they may send them to other schools. However, the definition of what constitutes a Catholic school is to be left to the judgement of the Ordinary.

2. OF THE WAYS AND MEANS BY WHICH PAROCHIAL SCHOOLS MAY BEST BE ESTABLISHED

200. If on the one hand we overly burden the consciences of priests, of the faithful and especially of Catholic parents by the decrees given above in the name of the Lord, on the other hand, this is truly our duty and we feel it in our innermost being, and confess frankly that to the extent of our ability we shall see to it that Catholic parents find for their children not just any kind of school, but good and effective ones not at all inferior to the public schools, as advised by the instructions of the Holy Congregation. Therefore we propose and order certain means the provisions of which will enable parochial schools to be improved to the degree of usefulness and perfection demanded and deserved by the honor of the Church, and the eternal and temporal salvation of children, and finally by the generous devotion of parents exercising their full rights. These means, however, require especially that priests, the laity and the schoolmasters know their duties towards their schools and discharge them faithfully.

201. First of all, in regard to that which pertains to priests, we state that the candidates for Sacred Theology already in the seminaries be taught continuously that one of the chief duties of priests, particularly in our times, is the Christian education of youth. . . .

❊   ❊   ❊

202. We exhort and order that the laity be instructed in these matters both by the bishop and by the priests so that they become accustomed to regarding the

parochial schools as a necessary part of their parishes without which the future existence of the parish itself is endangered. Let them be taught plainly and firmly that a school is least of all a certain work of supererogation chosen by the priest either to demonstrate his great zeal or joyfully to while away the time. On the contrary, the Church imposes this responsibility upon the priest as a duty and an obligation, to be executed religiously, but not without the help of the laity. With no less enthusiasm and prudence must the erroneous opinion be erased in the minds of those members of the laity who think that the care of the schools belongs only to that part of the parish which is used directly and actually for children. Demonstrate by these same obvious arguments that the fruits and blessings which are derived from the faith and morals as they are maintained in parochial schools redounds to the benefit of the entire community. Through the means proposed here, it will come about that the laity of a parish will prize no other place more nor serve it better than the parochial school—the conservatory of faith and morals, and the seminary for youth, indeed, a joy and solace to all.

Let the laity supply adequate and generous support for the schools. Thus with united strength they will enthusiastically see that parishes are always furnished the supplies and running expenses for their schools. The faithful will also be reminded "either by pastoral letters, sermons, or by private conversation that they will gravely fail in their responsibility unless they can provide to the best of their ability and to the extent of their resources for the expenses of Catholic schools. They must be warned about this as many of them surpass others in wealth and in their authority among people." (Instruction of the Holy Congregation) Let parents, therefore, pay promptly and willingly the monthly stipend ordinarily charged for each child. Let not other members of the parish refuse to produce and to increase the financial return to the church necessary to the support of the schools. Let all, whether parents, heads of families, or young people who have their own incomes be enrolled in the societies which are especially recommended in each parish having been previously introduced to the parishes and blessed by the Supreme Pontiff himself. Through these societies the faithful may aid the schools with small but regular contributions, so that the schools will be, if not altogether, at least in part, free schools. With funds generously provided by all the faithful for this sacred cause, care should be taken to see that the external appearance of the schools as well as their interior appointments be improved, and that the number of teachers be increased. Further, see to it that the pupils are grouped in classes of small numbers so that each class may readily be distinguished from another and classified according to grade. All these things will work splendidly to the degree that our schools shall be raised to a higher state of perfection. Let there be granted to the laity certain rights and privileges accurately defined by the diocesan statutes pertaining to schools, and provide strict ecclesiastical regulations in regard to the appointment and dismissal of teachers as well as in regard to their discipline and the direction of their teaching.

✢　　✢　　✢

Of the Higher Catholic Schools

208. Since the number of Catholic youth who aspire to higher education because of sufficient funds or because of ability, or who have finished parochial

schools in an outstanding manner, it pleases us to add a few words in regard to higher Catholic schools. Some Catholic boys turn their minds and eyes to the sacred ministry; others propose to strive for a so-called liberal profession. For those who wish to enter the sacred ministry, there is already sufficient and ample provision in Catholic academies and colleges and seminaries; as for the rest, there ought to be available several better and safer ways of achieving their objectives. Would that already (and we certainly hope that it will come about) it might be possible that young Catholics from Catholic elementary schools could enter higher Catholic schools and arrive at their desired goals through them. It happens too frequently that pure and pious boys from Christian families and from under the roof of a Catholic school, in non-Catholic colleges are inflated by science and return to their homes deprived of faith and Christian morals.

209. We therefore warn and in the name of the Lord we implore our faithful to hasten with united strength that happy state of affairs in which there will be Catholic academies, colleges and universities so numerous and so excellent that every single Catholic youth who wishes it, either because his parents propose it, or because he himself chooses it, can attend Catholic schools.

210. In order that this may come about as soon as possible, we exhort parents in the name of the Lord to send their children who have finished in parochial schools and for whom they wish to provide a higher education, to higher Catholic schools already in existence. If Catholic schools lack any special course of studies for them to follow, and parents wish to send their children to non-Catholic schools for this reason, we strongly urge them to remove as far as possible from their children the dangers to their faith and morals, being always mindful of the words of the Lord: "What shall it profit a man if he gain the whole world but lose his soul?" (Matth. XVI: 26.)

211. We ask those of our faithful who are enriched with worldly wealth, by the mercy of God and in behalf of the Catholic name, to open their purses for the increase of Catholic colleges, to this great end chiefly that ways and means be provided poorer children who by their genius, their nature and morals always hold before themselves the standard of future good, usefulness, and even perhaps, excellence. With the greatest joy we have discovered in several dioceses noble and generous Catholic men who because of their works of Catholic charity merit the thanks of studious youth, the applause of all good Catholic men and the approbation of the Supreme Pontiff, as well as the benediction of God, the Best and Greatest. Oh, that the wealthy men in all dioceses would imitate their noble example to the extent that in the future it will not be necessary, as it ought not to have been in the past without a sense of shame, to warn Catholic men that they might learn what their responsibilities in this matter may be from those who are outside the Church or even from the very enemies of the Church.

The Holy Congregation for the Propagation of the Faith has frequently been informed that young Catholics in the United States of America are threatened by the greatest danger from the public schools, as they are called. This sad message means that the Holy Congregation has appraised certain questions which have been proposed to the large number of bishops of this jurisdiction; questions which pertain in part to why the faithful permit their children to attend non-Catholic schools, and partly to the means by which young people may be more easily kept from these schools. These matters were carefully discussed on the 30th of June 1875 by the Supreme Congregation of the Inquisition, and it was judged that they be resolved through the following instruction which the Most Holy Father saw fit to approve and to confirm on the 24th of November of the same year.

The very philosophy of education underlying the instruction of youth in these schools ought to be discussed first of all. It is seen by the Holy Congregation to be fraught with danger and contrary to Catholic principles. Since the philosophy of these schools excludes all religious teaching, the students neither learn well the rudiments of faith nor are taught according to the precepts of the Church. For this reason they lack the knowledge which is extremely necessary for man, and without which he cannot live as a Christian. Indeed, in schools of this type children are educated from their earliest childhood, an age which, as is well known, holds tenaciously either to the seeds of virtue or vice. If, during such a plastic age, children grow up without religion it is truly a deplorable state-of-affairs. Inasmuch as these schools are separated from the authority of the Church and their teachers are drawn indiscriminantly from every sect, and since no precaution is taken by any regulation to keep the children from harm, there is free scope to infuse errors and vices into tender minds. Likewise, certain corruptive influences stem from this fact, namely, that in these schools, or at least in most of them, youth of both sexes are ordered to sit together—males next to females on the same bench. All of which means that young people are wretchedly exposed to harm in regard to their faith and their morals are greatly endangered.

Thus, unless this danger of perversion is removed from their proximity, the public schools cannot be attended with a clear conscience by Catholics. Both divine and natural law proclaim this.

BISHOP JOHN LANCASTER SPALDING ON STATE AND CHURCH AND EDUCATION (1882)   From *Lectures and Discourses* (New York, 1882), pp. 124–26.

The toleration which exists so widely at present throughout the civilized world is the result of the interaction of many causes. The Christian doctrines concerning the worth of the soul, the inviolability of conscience, the brotherhood of all men, the distinction between Church and state, the duty of charity and justice even to the slave, created, little by little, a social condition in which the spirit of a true and wise tolerance was naturally developed; and this spirit would have

THE COMMON
SCHOOL
MOVEMENT

1171

continued to grow and diffuse itself with the progress of learning and the refinement of manners, even had the harmony and unity of the Christian religion not been broken by the heresies and schisms of the sixteenth century. The multitude of religions, however, together with the infidelity and indifference which were the inevitable results of this crisis in European history, have in conjunction with industry and commerce and the more frequent and rapid intercourse made possible by mechanical inventions, greatly accelerated and otherwise modified the movement of the modern nations towards larger liberty and toleration. As to the form of civil government the Church is indifferent, and leaves the people to shape their political constitutions upon monarchical, aristocratic, or democratic principles, according to their customs and preferences.

Whatever the form of govenment may be, there are interests which concern alike the Church and the state, and which neither, consequently, should be asked to abandon. The question of education at once suggests itself as the most important of these common interests, and the one concerning which conflict of authority has in our day most frequently arisen.

Whoever educates necessarily influences, whether for good or evil, man's whole being. In thought we separate the intellect from the conscience and the soul from the body, but in the living man they are always united, and to develop the one without at the same time acting upon the other is not possible; and hence a school system which professes to eliminate religious and moral truth from the process of education, and to impart secular knowledge alone, commits itself to an impossible task. The thoughts, opinions, sentiments, the morals, laws, and history, of a people are all interpenetrated by and blended with their religious beliefs; and the attempt to eliminate religion from knowledge, sentiment from morality, or the past history of a people from its present life is as absurd as would be the effort to abstract from the character of the man the agencies and influences that wrought upon him in childhood and in youth. As the child is father of the man, so is faith the mother of knowledge; and the deepest and highest form of faith is religious faith. Hence when the state organizes a system of education from which the teaching of religious doctrines is excluded, it fatally, though possibly unconsciously and negatively, commits itself to an irreligious and infidel propagandism; since to ignore religious doctrines while striving to develop the intellectual and moral faculties must result in the gradual extinction of faith, as the disuse of an organ or a faculty super-induces atrophy and gradual disappearance. The plea that the Church is the proper place for religious instruction is not to the point; for, if religion is true or valuable, it must, like the air of heaven, envelop and interpenetrate the whole life of man; and hence to exclude it from the daily, systematic efforts to awaken in the child quicker perception and fuller consciousness is equivalent to a denial of its truth and efficacy; and the practical tendency of such a school system will inevitably lie in the direction of its logical bearing.

Religion, which is the bond between the Creator and the creature, founds, both in idea and in fact, the first society. The first association of human beings, however, both in idea and in fact, is the family, whose essential constitution looks not merely to the propagation of the race, but above all, to its education; since without the family the race might be propagated, while it is not conceivable that without it, it could, in any proper sense, be educated. Hence parents are the natural educators, and any system which tends to weaken their control over their children or interferes with the free exercise of their natural rights is radically vicious. It is therefore the duty of both Church and state to cooperate with the family in the work of education, since when the spirit of the school is in conflict with the spirit which prevails in the child's home, the result must necessarily be an incomplete and inharmonious type of manhood. A state which professes to tolerate different forms of religion contradicts its own principles and becomes intolerant whenever it compels its citizens to support a uniform system of schools. Such a system, if it ignores or excludes all religious instruction, does violence to the consciences of all sincere and thoughtful believers; and if it teaches the tenets of some one creed, it wrongs those of a different faith. Nor is it possible to escape from the difficulty by accepting the beliefs which are common to all. As a matter of fact, in the modern state no such common beliefs exist, since there are sects of atheists, materialists, and pantheists in all countries in which the bond of Christian unity has been broken. But, even if this were not so, beliefs which are common to a multitude of sects are not held in common, but as parts of integral systems which are distinct and unlike, and to separate them from the organism to which they belong is to mutilate them and thereby to deprive them of their true meaning and efficacy.

The state, therefore, which tolerates different forms of religion is thereby debarred from the right to establish a uniform school system; and yet it is unreasonable to ask the state to do nothing to promote and spread education, since, after religion, education is the chief agent of civilization, and, in the absence of governmental aid and supervision, many parents, and ministers of religion even, will either altogether neglect this most important work or at best perform it in an inefficient and careless manner. In a free state, then, where religious tolerance is a fundamental principle of law, the government, in fostering education, is bound to respect scrupulously the rights of the family and liberty of conscience; and this it cannot do, if the schools are supported by taxation, except by instituting what is known as the denominational system of education. The practical difficulties to be overcome are not insuperable; and since there is question here of a fundamental principle of free government, the obstacles to its practical acceptance and enforcement should but serve to inspire just and enlightened statesmen with a more determined will to remove them. If, however, the state should establish a school system from which religion is excluded, it becomes the imperative duty of Catholics to found schools to which they can, with a safe conscience, send their children; and if, instead of doing this, they remain passive, with a sort of vague hope that somehow or other a change for the better will be brought about, they have denied the faith, according to the doctrine of St. Paul: "But if any man have not care of his own, and especially those of his house, he hath denied the faith."

BISHOP SPALDING AT THE LAYING OF THE CORNERSTONE OF THE CATHOLIC UNIVERSITY OF AMERICA (1888) From John Lancaster Spalding, "University Education," *Education and the Higher Life* (Chicago, 1891), pp. 197–203.

Certainly a true university will be the home both of ancient wisdom and of new learning; it will teach the best that is known, and encourage research; it will stimulate thought, refine taste, and awaken the love of excellence; it will be at once a scientific institute, a school of culture, and a training ground for the business of life; it will educate the minds that give direction to the age; it will be a nursery of ideas, a centre of influence. The good we do men is quickly lost, the truth we leave them remains forever; and therefore the aim of the best education is to enable students to see what is true, and to inspire them with the love of all truth. Professional knowledge brings most profit to the individual; but philosophy and literature, science and art, elevate and refine the spirit of the whole people, and hence the university will make culture its first aim, and its scope will widen as the thoughts and attainments of men are enlarged and multiplied. Here if anywhere shall be found teachers whose one passion is the love of truth, which is the love of God and of man; who look on all things with a serene eye; who bring to every question a calm, unbiassed mind; who, where the light of the intellect fails, walk by faith and accept the omen of hope; who understand that to be distrustful of science is to lack culture, to doubt the good of progress is to lack knowledge, and to question the necessity of religion is to want wisdom; who know that in a God-made and God-governed world it must lie in the nature of things that reason and virtue should tend to prevail, in spite of the fact that in every age the majority of men think foolishly and act unwisely. How divine is not man's apprehensive endowment! When we see beauty fade, the singer lose her charm, the performer his skill, we feel no commiseration; but when we behold a noble mind falling to decay, we are saddened, for we cannot believe that the godlike and immortal faculty should be subject to death's power. It is a reflection of the light that never yet was seen on sea or land; it is the magician who shapes and colors the universe, as a drop of water mirrors the boundless sky. Is not this the first word the Eternal speaks?—"Let there be light." And does not the blessed Savior come talking of life, of light, of truth, of joy, and peace? Have not the Christian nations moved forward following after liberty and knowledge? Is not our religion the worship of God in spirit and in truth? Is not its motive Love, divine and human, and is not knowledge Love's guide and minister?

The future prevails over the present, the unseen over what touches the senses only in high and cultivated natures; and it is held to be the supreme triumph of God over souls when the young, to whom the earth seems to be heaven revealed and made palpable, turn from all the beauty and contagious joy to seek, to serve, to love Him who is the infinite and only real good. Yet this is what we ask of the lovers of intellectual excellence, who work without hope of temporal reward and without the strength of heart which is found in obeying the Divine Will; for mental improvement is seldom urged as a religious duty, although it is plain that to seek to know truth is to seek to know God, in whom and through whom and by whom all things are, and whose infinite nature and most awful power may best be seen by the largest and most enlightened mind. Mind is Heaven's pioneer making way for faith, hope and love, for higher aims and nobler life; and to doubt its worth and excellence is to deny the reasonableness of religion, since belief, if not wholly blind, must rest on knowledge. The best culture serves spiritual and moral ends. Its aim and purpose is to make reason prevail over sense and appetite; to raise man not only to a perception of the harmonies of truth, but also to the love of whatever is good and fair. Not in a darkened mind does the white ray of heavenly light break into prismatic glory; not through the mists of ignorance is the sweet countenance of the divine Savior best discerned. If some have pursued a sublime art frivolously; have soiled a fair mind by ignoble life,—this leaves the good of the intellect untouched. Some who have made strongest profession of religion, who have held high and the highest places in the Church, have been unworthy, but we do not thence infer that the tendency of religion is to make men so. They who praise the bliss and worth of ignorance are sophists. Stupidity is more to be dreaded than malignity; for ignorance, and not malice, is the most fruitful cause of human misery. Let knowledge grow, let truth prevail. Since God is God, the universe is good, and the more we know of its laws, the plainer will the right way become. The investigator and the thinker, the man of culture and the man of genius, cannot free themselves from bias and limitation; but the work they do will help me and all men.

Indifference or opposition to the intellectual life is but a survival of the general anti-educational prejudices of former ages. It is also a kind of envy, prompting us to find fault with whatever excellence is a reproach to our unworthiness. The disinterested love of truth is a rare virtue, most difficult to acquire and most difficult to preserve. If knowledge bring power and wealth, if it give fame and pleasure, it is dear to us; but how many are able to love it for its own sake? Do not nearly all men strive to convince themselves of the truth of those opinions which they are interested in holding? What is true, good, or fair is rarely at once admitted to be so; but what is practically useful men quickly accept, because they live chiefly in the world of external things, and care little for the spiritual realms of truth and beauty. The ignorant do not even believe that knowledge gives power and pleasure, and the educated, except the chosen few, value it only for the power and pleasure it gives. As the disinterested love of truth is rare, so is perfect sincerity. Indeed, insincerity is here the radical vice. Good faith is essential to faith; and a sophistical mind is as immoral and irreligious as a depraved heart. Let a man be true, seek and speak truth, and all good things are possible; but when he persuades himself that a lie may be useful and ought to be propagated, he becomes the enemy of his own soul and the foe of all that makes life high and godlike.

Now, to be able to desire to see things as they are, whatever their relations to ourselves may be, and to speak of them simply as they appear to us, is one result of the best training of the intellect, which in the world of thought and opinion gives us that sweet indifference which is the rule of saints when they submit the conduct of their lives wholly to divine guidance. Why should he whose mind is strong, and rests on God, be disturbed? It is with opinion as with life. We cannot tell what moment truth will overthrow the one and death the other; but thought cannot change the nature of things. The clouds dissolve, but the eternal heavens remain. Over the bloodiest battlefields they bend calm and serene, and trees drink the sunlight and flowers exhale perfume. The moonbeam kisses the crater's lip. Over buried cities the yellow harvest waves, and all the catastrophes of endless time are present to God, who dwells in infinite peace. He sees the universe and is not troubled, and shall not we who are akin to him learn to look upon our little meteorite without losing repose of mind and heart? Were it not a sweeter piety to trust that he who made all things will know how to make all things right; and therefore not to grow anxious lest some investigator should find him at fault or thwart his plans? As living bodies are immersed in an invisible substance which feeds the flame of life, so souls breathe and think and love in the atmosphere of God, and the higher their thought and love the more do they partake of the divine nature. Many things, in this age of transition, are passing away; but true thoughts and pure love are immortal, and whatever opinions as to other things a man may hold, all know that to be human is to be intelligent and moral, and therefore religious. A hundred years hence our present machinery may seem to be as rude as the implements of the middle age look to us, and our political and social organization may appear barbarous—so rapid has the movement of life become. But we do not envy those who shall then be living, partly it may be because we can have but dim visions of the greater blessings they shall enjoy, but chiefly because we feel that after all the true worth of life lies in nothing of this kind, but in knowing and doing, in believing and loving; and that it would not be easier to live for truth and righteousness were electricity applied to aerial navigation and all the heavens filled with argosies of magic sail. It is not possible to love sincerely the best thoughts, as it is not possible to love God when our aim is something external, or when we believe that what is mechanical merely has power to regenerate and exalt mankind.

ARCHBISHOP JOHN IRELAND ON PUBLIC SCHOOLS (1890)   From "State Schools and Parish Schools—Is Union Between Them Impossible?" National Education Association *Journal of Addresses and Proceedings* (St. Paul, Minn., 1890), pp. 179–85.

I will beg leave to make at once my profession of faith. I declare most unbounded loyalty to the constitution of my country. I desire no favors. I claim no rights that are not in consonance with its letter and its spirit. The rights which the constitution allows I do claim, and in doing so I am but a truer and more loyal American. In what I may say to this distinguished audience, the principles of our common American citizenship shall inspire my words. I beg that you listen to me and discuss my arguments in the light of those principles.

I am the friend and the advocate of the state school. In the circumstances of the present time I uphold the parish school. I do sincerely wish that the need of it did not exist. I would have all schools for the children of the people state schools.

The accusation has gone abroad that Catholics are bent on destroying the state school. Never was there an accusation more unfounded. I will summarize the articles of my school creed; they follow all the lines upon which the state school is built.

The right of the state school to exist, I consider, is a matter beyond the stage of discussion. I most fully concede it. To the child must be imparted instruction in no mean degree, that the man may earn for himself an honest competence, and acquit himself of the duties which society exacts from him for its own prosperity and life. This proposition, true in any country of modern times, is peculiarly true in America. The imparting of this instruction is primarily the function of the child's parent. The family is prior to the state. The appointment of Providence is that under the care and direction of the parent, the child shall grow both in body and in mind. The state intervenes whenever the family cannot or will not do the work that is needed. The state's place in the function of instruction is loco parentis. As things are, tens of thousands of children will not be instructed if parents remain solely in charge of the duty. The state must come forward as an agent of instruction; else ignorance will prevail. Indeed, in the absence of state action, there never was that universal instruction which we have so nearly attained and which we deem necessary. In the absence of state action I believe universal instruction would never, in any country, have been possible.

State action in favor of instruction implies free schools in which knowledge is conditioned in the asking; in no other manner can we bring instruction within the reach of all children. Free schools! Blest indeed is the nation whose vales and hillsides they adorn, and blest the generations upon whose souls are poured their treasure! No tax is more legitimate than that which is levied for the dispelling of mental darkness, and the building-up within a nation's bosom of intelligent manhood and womanhood. The question may not be raised: how much good accrues to the individual tax-payer; the general welfare is richly served, and this suffices. It is scarcely necessary to add that the money paid in school tax is the money of the state, and is to be disbursed solely by the officials of the state, and solely for the specific purposes in view of which it was collected.

I unreservedly favor state laws making instruction compulsory. Instruction is so much needed by each citizen for his own sake and for that of society that the father who neglects to provide for his child's instruction sins against the child and against society, and it behooves the state to punish him. Of course, first principles must not be forgotten, and since instruction is primarily the function of the parent, the state entering into action loco parentis, the parent enjoys the right to educate his child in the manner suitable to himself; provided always that the education given in this manner suffices for the ulterior duties of the child toward himself and society. Compulsory education implies attendance in schools maintained and controlled by the state only when there is no attendance in other schools known to be competant to impart instruction in the required degree. The compulsory laws recently enacted in certain States of the Union are, to my judging, objectionable in a few of their incidental clauses. These, I am confident, will readily be altered in approaching legislative sessions. With the body of the laws, and their general intent in the direction of hastening among us universal instruction, I am in most hearty accord.

It were idle for me to praise the work of the state school of America in the imparting of secular instruction. We all confess its value. It is our pride and our glory. The republic of the United States has solemnly affirmed its resolve that within its borders no clouds of ignorance shall settle upon the minds of the children of its people. To reach this result its generosity knows no limit. The free school of America—withered be the hand raised in sign of its destruction!

Can I be suspected of enmity to the state schools because I fain would widen the expanse of its wings until all the children of the people find shelter beneath their cover, because I tell of defects which for very love of the state school I seek to remedy?

I turn to the parish school. It exists. I repeat my regret that there is the necessity for its existence. In behalf of the state school I call upon my fellow-Americans to aid in the removal of this necessity.

Catholics are foremost in establishing parish schools. Seven hundred and fifty thousand children, it is estimated, are educated in their parish schools. A lack of material means prevents them from housing their full number of children. Lutherans exhibit great zeal in favor of parish schools. Many Episcopalians, and some in different other Protestant denominations, commend and organize parish schools. The different denominational colleges of the country are practically parish schools for the children of the richer classes. The spirit of the parish school, if not the school itself, is widespread among American Protestants, and is made manifest by their determined opposition to the exclusion of Scripture-reading and other devotional exercises from the school-room.

There is dissatisfaction with the state school, as at present organized. The state school, it is said, tends to the elimination of religion from the minds and hearts of the youth of the country.

This is my grievance against the state school of to-day. Believe me, my Protestant fellow-citizens, that I am absolutely sincere, when I now declare that I am speaking for the weal of Protestantism as well as for that of Catholicism. I am a

Catholic, of course, to the tiniest fiber of my heart, unflinching and uncompromising in my faith. But God forbid that I desire to see in America the ground which Protestantism occupies exposed to the chilling and devastating blast of unbelief. Let me be your ally in stemming the swelling tide of irreligion, the death-knell of Christian life and of Christian civilization, the fatal foe of souls and of country. This is what we have to fear—the materialism which sees not beyond the universe a living, personal God, or the agnosticism which reduces him to an indescribable perhaps. The evil is abroad, scorning salvation through the teaching and graces of Christ Jesus, sneering at the Biblical page, warring upon the sacredness of the Christian Sabbath and the music of its church-bells, telling of Heaven and of the hopes of immortal souls. Let us be on our guard. In our jealousies lest Protestants gain some advantage over Catholics, or Catholics over Protestants, we play into the hands of unbelievers and secularists. We have given over to them the school, the nursery of thought. Are we not securing to them the mastery of the future?

The state school is non-religious. It ignores religion. There is and there can be no positive religious teaching where the principle of non-sectarianism rules. What follows? The school deals with immature, childish minds, upon which silent facts and examples make deepest impression. The school claims nearly all the time remaining to pupils outside of rest and recreation; to the school they will perforce amid the struggles of later life look back for inspiration. It treats of land and sea, but not of Heaven; it speaks of statesmen and warriors, but is silent on God and Christ; it tells how to attain success in this world, but says nothing as to the world beyond the grave. The pupil sees and listens; the conclusion is inevitable, that religion is of minor importance. Religious indifference will be his creed; his manhood will be, as his childhood in the school, estranged from God and the positive influences of religion. The brief and hurried lessons of the family fireside and the Sunday school will not avail. At best, the time is too short for that most difficult of lessons, religion. The child is tired from the exacting drill of the schoolroom, and will not relish an extra task, of the necessity of which the teacher, in whom he confides most trustingly, has said nothing. The great mass of children receive no fireside lessons, and attend no Sunday school, and the great mass of the children of America are growing up without religion. Away with theories and dreams: let us read the facts. In ten thousand homes of the land the father hastens to his work in the early dawn before his children have risen from their slumbers, and in the evening an exhausted frame bids him seek at once repose, with scarcely time allowed to kiss his little ones. The mother toils from morning to night, that they may eat and be clothed; it is mockery to ask her to be their teacher. What may you expect from the Sunday school? An hour in the week to learn religion is as nothing, and only the small number will be present during that hour. The churches are open and teachers are at hand, but the non-religious school has claimed the attention and the hard work of the child during five days of the week; he is unwilling to submit to the drudgery of a further hour's work on Sunday. Accidentally, and unintentionally, it may be, but, in fact, most certainly, the state school crowds out the work of the church, and takes from it the opportunities to secure a hearing. The state need not teach religion; but for the sake of its people, and for its own sake, it should permit and facilitate the action of the church. It hinders and prevents this action. The children of the masses are learning no religion. The religion of thousands, who are supposed to be religious, is the merest veneering of mind and heart. Its doctrines are vaguest and most chaotic notions as to what God is, and what our relations to Him are. Very often it is mere sentimentality, and its precepts are the decorous rulings of natural culture and natural policy. This is not the religion that built up in the past our Christian civilization, and that will maintain it in the future. This is not the religion that will subjugate passion and repress vice. It is not the religion that will guard the family and save society.

Let that state look to itself. The mind which it polishes is a two-edged sword—an instrument for good or an instrument for evil. It were fatal to polish it without the assurance that in all likelihood it shall be an instrument for good.

* * *

I come to the chief difficulty in the premises. The American people at large are Christians; but they are divided among themselves. Yes, they are divided. Not to speak of other differences, there is a radical and vital one between Protestantismsm of all forms and Catholicism. I am not arguing. I am relating facts. Well-meaning and well-deserving men have proposed as a remedy in this instance, that there be taught in connection with the schools a common Christianity. This will not do. Catholics in fidelity to their principles cannot accept a common Christianity. What comes to them not bearing on its face the stamp of Catholicity, is Protestant in form and in implication, even if it be Catholic in substance. This being the settled fact, American Catholics will not, of course, inflict Catholicism upon non-Catholic or Protestant children, and with similar fair-mindedness American Protestants will not inflect Protestantism upon Catholic children. Some compromise becomes necessary. Is it not ten thousand times better that we make the compromise rather than allow secularism to triumph and own the country?

I turn to all Americans—secularists as well as Christian believers—and I address them in the name of American citizenship. We are a practical people, and when we find facts before us, whether we like or dislike them, we deal with them with an eye to the general good. Dissatisfaction does exist with the state school because of its exclusion of religion. The dissatisfaction will exist so long as no change is made. It is founded on conscience.

Is not the fact of this dissatisfaction sufficient that Americans set to work earnestly and with a good will to remove its cause? The welfare of the country demands peace and harmony among citizens. Let us put an end to the constant murmurings and bitter recriminations with which our school war fills the air. Since we are proud of our state school and prize its advantages, let us make an effort that all the children of the people enjoy those advantages. If there be a public institution, as the state school, supported by all the people, avowedly for the benefit of all the people, let it be such that all may use it. Be there no taxation without representation in the enjoyment of the benefits thereof. Let us most studiously avoid raising barriers to the use of those benefits, and, in a most special manner, such barriers that the opposition to them comes in the name of conscience.

I invoke the spirit of American liberty and American institutions. Our views, perhaps, differ diametrically from those of others of our fellow-citizens; we may deem their views utterly wrong. Still, is not the duty of Americans that of peace and concession, so that others be as undisturbed in their conscience as we are in ours? Does it matter that we happen to be in the majority? Brute numerical force may be legal; it is not justice, it is not the spirit of America. Minorities have rights, and as speedily as it is possible with the public weal should the majority recognize them. It is no honor to America that ten millions or more be compelled by law to pay taxes for the support of schools to which their conscience forbids access, and to be furthermore, in order to be conscientious, compelled by their zeal for the instruction of their children, to build school-houses of their own, and pay their own teachers. It is no honor for the remaining fifty millions to profit for themselves of the taxes paid by the ten millions. The cry that the state schools are open to them if they silence their consciences, is not a defense that will hold before the bar of justice. The aspect of the case is the more serious when we consider that those ten millions are largely among the poorer classes of the population, and that they are sincerely and loyally desirous to obtain the benefits of the state school, if only the obstacles be removed.

It is no honor to the American republic that she be more than any other nation foremost in efforts to divorce religion from the schools. No country goes in this direction so far as ours. We have entered upon a terrible experiment; the very life of our civilization and of our country is at stake. I know not how to account for this condition of things, passing strange in America. Neither the genius of our country nor its history gives countenance to it. The American people are naturally reverent and religious. Their laws and public observances breathe forth the perfume of religion. The American school, as it first reared its long walls amid the villages of New England, was religious through and through. The present favor to a non-religious school is, I verily believe, the thoughtlessness of a moment, and it will not last.

I solve the difficulty by submitting it to the calm judgment of the country. No question is insoluble to Americans which truth and justice press home to them. Other countries, whose civilization we do not despise, have found a solution. I instance but England and Prussia. We are not inferior to them in practical legislation and the spirit of peaceful compromise. Suggestions of mine must be necessarily crude in form, and local and temporary in application. I will, however, speak them. I would permeate the regular state school with the religion of the majority of the children of the land, be it as Protestant as Protestantism can be, and I would, as they do in England, pay for the secular instruction given in denominational schools according to results; that is, each pupil passing the examination before state officials, and in full accordance with the state program, would secure to his school the cost of the tuition of a pupil in the state school. This is not paying for the religious instruction given to the pupil, but for the secular instruction demanded by the state, and given to the pupil as thoroughly as he could have received it in the state school.

Another plan: I would do as Protestants and Catholics in Poughkeepsie and other places in our own country have agreed to do to the greatest satisfaction of all citizens and the great advancement of educational interests. In Poughkeepsie the city school board rents the buildings formerly used as parish schools, and from the hour of 9 a.m. to that of 3 p.m. the school is in every particular a state school—teachers engaged and paid by the board, teachers and pupils examined, state books used, the door always open to superintendent and members of the board. There is simply the tacit understanding that so long as the teachers in those schools, Catholic in faith, pass their examinations and do their work as cleverly and as loyally as other teachers under the control of the board, teachers of another faith shall not be put in their places. Nor are they allowed to teach positive religion during school hours. This is done outside the hours for which the buildings are leased to the board. The state, it is plain, pays not one cent for the religious instruction of the pupils. In the other schools Protestant devotional exercises take place in fullest freedom before the usual school hour.

Do not tell me of difficulties of detail in the working out of either of my schemes. There are difficulties; but will not the result be fullest compensation for the struggle to overcome them? Other schemes, more perfect in conception and easier of application, will perhaps be presented in time; meanwhile, let us do as best we know.

Allow me one word as a Catholic. I have sought to place on the precise line where it belongs, the objection of Catholics to the state school. Is it fair, is it honest, to raise the cry that Catholics are opposed to education, to free schools, to the American school system? I do lose my patience when adversaries seek to place us in this false position, so contrary to all our convictions and resolves. In presence of this vast and distinguished assembly, to have addressed which is an honor I shall never forget, I protest with all the energy of my soul against the charge that the schools of the nation have their enemies among Catholics. Not one stone of the wondrous edifice which Americans have built up in their devotion to education, will Catholics remove or permit to be removed. They would fain add to the splendor and majesty by putting side by side religion and the school, neither interfering with the work of the other, each one borrowing from the other aid and dignity. Do the schools of America fear contact with religion? The Catholics demand the Christian state school. In so doing they prove themselves the truest friends of the school and the state.

The Religious Question
Jews

THE BOARD OF TRUSTEES OF SHEARITH ISRAEL CONGREGATION ON THE PURPOSE OF JEWISH EDUCATION (1804) From *Publications of the American Jewish Historical Society*, vol. XXVII, pp. 82–83.

In order to make your Children truly Virtuous, You must rear them in the strict principles of our Holy religion, and this cannot be efficiently done without they understand what they are saying when addressing the deity. It is thus that religion becomes the soother of all our sorrows and the source of all our real joys, and which will prevade our thoughts in order to answer the design of God in our Creation.

Education, generally speaking, is the first thing which ought to be pursued in life, in order to constitute us rational, how much then is to be expected from having in addition thereto, a compleat and full knowledge of the Hebrew Language, being that in which all our prayers are read. Yet notwithstanding this, it is with regret that it is perceived, few, very few indeed, are concern'd about it.

An Opinion has been express'd by many of our Congregation that Children are incapable of profiting by Instruction 'till their reason is matured. This is conceived to be erroneous in the extreme, for there are instances of children having preferr'd the good to the evil without knowing why they did. They are directed by the Eye to follow the examples before them, hence the necessity of an early and Scrupulous Education—We are admonish'd "to train up a child in the way he should go and when he is old he will not depart from it." And this maxim generally holds good. Let us wisely begin early to plant those seeds from which we wish to reap fruit, let us root up the Weeds and Prune off what might hinder the growth. But these things must be done at a proper time, for if the season be suffer'd to Slip away, much, if not all may be lost.

A Statement will be laid before the Congregation of the Monies received and expended for the Institution, and of the Number of pay and free Scholars that have been admitted. 21st April 1804.

By order of the Board of Trustees
AARON LEVY   I. B. KURSHEEDT   NAPHTALI PHILLIPS

A JEW AT HARVARD (1815)   From Joseph L. Blau and Salo W. Baron, eds., *The Jews of the United States, 1790–1840: A Documentary History* (New York, 1963), vol. II, pp. 457–58.

Nathan Nathans to His Guardian

Brighton, May 21st, 1815.

Wm Meredith Esqr.

Dear Sir. There is one thing that I neglected mentioning in my last letter. I would wish to know wether it is your wish for Doctor Allen to prepare me, for the Cambridge Collegge or the University at Philada as I think there will be some difficulty about my religion at Cambridge, as I understand they are very strict; I think that it will be much better for me, to be prepared for the University at Philada as it will be much more agreeable to myself & family. & I therefore hope it will meet your approbation. Give my best respects to Mr. Gratz, & be pleased to write me soon as school will commence the 29 this month.

I remain Dear Sir, Your affectionate ward,   NATHAN NATHANS.

Report of Nathan Nathans's Tutor

New Hope, Decr. 14, 1815

Wm. Meredith Esqr.

Dear Sir, Agreeably to your request I drop you a few lines relative to the young gentleman whom you have placed under my care. It affords me real pleasure that I am able to give you so good an account of him. He has behaved with the strictest propriety in every respect. In his conduct he is respectful, & in his application to his studies, he is assiduous. I found him defective in his acquaintance with his Latin Grammar, owing I suppose to his having been permitted to translate Latin without sufficient previous acquaintance with it: but this defect I hope will ere long be remedied. I had feared lest there might be some difficulty on account of the peculiarities of his religious sentiment, & the regulations of my School relative to the observance of the Christian Sabbath; but I am happy to say there is none. He is permitted to observe his own Sabbath; & of his own accord, without any requisition from me he has reularly attended with the other young gentlemen under my care at the Church in which I preach, on our Sabbath. The moral & religious instruction which the young gentlemen who are with me receive on the Sabbath has a very beneficial influence on their conduct & their attention to their studies thro the week & I therefore consider it a matter of great importance strictly to attend to it. I hope to visit the City between Christmas and the New Year, & will then do myself the pleasure of calling on you: at present I shall only add that I am much pleased with young Mr. Nathans & I hope that his future conduct may prove as correct as is his present. Be pleased to present my respects to Mrs. Meredith & your family.

With sincere esteem & respect I remain Your Obdt. Servt.

SAML. B. HOW.

A PROPOSAL FOR A MODERN JEWISH SCHOOL (1830)   From D. L. M. Peixotto, *Anniversary Discourse* (New York, 1830), pp. 32–36.

The first [proposal] is the formation of a school on principles similar to those of Pestalozzi. Let a few acres of ground be purchased at a convenient distance from the city, a plain neat tenement erected thereon, and here let a number of pupils be educated in the various branches of useful knowledge, and in the practical arts and sciences. It is not necessary that all the pupils be infants or mere boys. Those more advanced might likewise be admitted, and from all who possessed the means, some compensation should be required towards defraying the expenses of the establishment. Nor should the rich disdain to mingle with the poor. It is the beauty and perfection of the plan of Pestalozzi, that all children, of whatever rank, are educated on equal terms, and brought up to a simultaneous knowledge of morality and learning. And here I trust I shall be pardoned if I step out of my path to recommend generally to all our brethren, both those who are members of our society and those who are not, the study of the practical sciences of life. There is no individual, whatever the pursuit in which he may be engaged, who will not gain fast accessions to his means of happiness and usefulness, by extending the boundaries of his general knowledge. The means of accomplishing this important object are within every man's grasp. The "Society for the Diffusion of Useful Knowledge" publish comprehensive but concise treatises on all the sciences, in numbers which can be had for the trifling sum of twelve and a half cents each. The introductory essay on the advantages and pleasures of science, from the master pen of Brougham, should be universally perused.

In the school to be erected, I would direct that one of the first objects to be taught the pupil should be a knowledge of the Hebrew language. An acquaintance with the language of our forefathers and of our sacred laws, is the only guarantee we have for the preservation of our faith and our duty, and for the sacred bonds of a common descent.

Than a school such as I now propose, I know of no more effectual means to ensure the progressive and permanent advancement of our people. An eloquent writer of this country, illustrating the advantages of public schools, thus forcibly and beautifully expresses himself:

"If a stranger should enquire of me," says this philanthropist, "the principal cause and source of the greatness of my country, would I bid him look on the ocean widely loaded with our merchandise, and proudly ranged by our navy? or on the lands where it is girdled with roads and burthened with the produce of industry and ingenuity? Would I bid him look on these things, as the spring of our prosperity? Indeed I would not. Nor would I show him our colleges and literary institutions, for he can see nobler ones elsewhere. I would pass all these by, and would lead him out by some winding highway among the hills and woods, and when the cultivated spots grew small and infrequent, and the houses became few and scattered, and a state of primitive nature seemed to be immediately before us, I would stop in some sequestered spot, and directed by a steady hum, like that of bees, I would point to him a lowly building, hardly better than a shed, but full of blooming, happy children, collected together from the remote and unseen farmhouses, conning over their various tasks, or reading with a voice of reverential monotony, a portion of the word of God; and I would bid him note, that even here in the midst of poverty and sterility, was a specimen of the thousand nurseries in which all our children are taught of the Lord and formed, some to legislate for the land, and all to understand its constitution and laws, to maintain their unspotted birthright, and contribute to the great aggregate of the intelligence, the morality, the power, and the peace of this mighty commonwealth."

How, it may be asked, are we to procure a teacher? And this leads me to the second means which I would suggest.

2. Let this Society unite with the different congregations and societies of our people to contribute a mutual fund towards educating, in the most liberal manner, a youth of promise and character; let his heart be imbued with the great principles of our holy religion, and when he has attained to proper years, he may enter on the discharge of the duties of teacher of his brethren. With this duty should be blended that of expositor of the scriptures, and moral instructor to the congregation which support him; a duty which, in this country, has been hitherto only performed at intervals, and never by individuals expressly educated for its arduous and delicate discharge. That the members of our congregations would derive benefit from the adoption of this plan; and that the rising generation more especially, who are now threatened with a total want of religious and moral instruction, require an office of this kind to be instituted, must be self-evident to every one acquainted with the actual condition of our people, and anxious for its improvement.

JUDGE MORDECAI NOAH'S CALL FOR A HEBREW COLLEGE (1843)
From Mordecai M. Noah, "Call for a Hebrew College," *Occident,* vol. I, pp. 301–07.

Mr. Editor—For several years past my friends have urged me to organize and propose a plan for the establishment of a Hebrew College in the United States, pressing the necessity of such an institution as specially desirable to the Jewish population, and referring to the literary establishments of other religious denominations throughout the Union, as an incentive for us to make a similar experiment.

Hitherto my occupations have prevented that attention to the subject which its importance demanded. Having now leisure to reflect upon a plan which may finally be successful in carrying out the wishes of our friends, I avail myself with pleasure of your kind permission to publish the details in your periodical, which, having an extensive circulation, will reach those who are particularly interested in the successful issue of the project.

The great increase of the Jewish population in our country, and the facilities and advantages which our free institutions hold forth to our co-religionaries throughout the world, the success they [the Jews here] have already met with, and their general spirit of enterprize, warrant the belief that in a few years the Jews will constitute a large portion of the freemen of this Union. It becomes therefore necessary to consider what steps are required to improve their condition, and enable them to assume and maintain a proper rank among their fellow-citizens, and, consequently, to secure for themselves and their posterity that consideration and respect which a sound education and a high moral bearing cannot fail to achieve.

Independently of emigration, it is also proper to know that the native-born

Jewish population is rapidly on the increase, and it remains for us to ascertain what can now be done to elevate their character as a separate and distinct people, and place them on the road to honour and preferment, in common with their fellow-citizens of other religious denominations. With this object in view, it is desirable to establish a *Hebrew College,* where children of the Jewish persuasion can obtain a classical education, and, at the same time, be properly instructed in the Hebrew language where they can live in conformity to our laws, and acquire a liberal knowledge of the principles of their religion.

The difficulty of obtaining the necessary funds for the endowment of a college, for the purchase of a library and philosophical apparatus, for the salary and maintenance of professors, would present almost insurmountable obstacles to this experiment, situated as we are, having no government to appeal to, no nation taking an immediate interest in our welfare. Individual enterprize, therefore, is the only mode by which this desirable object can be accomplished. Someone must embark his own means and enlist his own energies in carrying out this important project, provided parents, who have the inclination and ability to pay for the education and support of their sons, will second this enterprize by committing their children to the care of such a person, and thus laying the foundation of an institution, which may hereafter be carried out on a broader and more extended scale.

I have long lamented the necessity of sending Jewish children to Christian boarding schools, not from any illiberal feelings towards schools of that denomination, but on account of the manifest injury to them in a religious point of view. Jewish parents who have a sincere attachment and regard for our holy and venerable faith are naturally desirous that their children should be educated as Jews. However liberal they may justly feel towards all religious denominations, however anxious they may be to see their children grow up with enlarged views and tolerant feelings towards other sects: still they wish them to be Jews, to understand their religion, to be able to explain its principles and defend its divine origin.

It is difficult to attain this desirable object in Christian colleges and boarding schools. The Jewish scholars [students] are compelled to live in daily violation of the Mosaic institutions, to neglect the Sabbath, and attend church on Sunday, in conformity with the regulations of the school. The consequences are that our sons, having finished their education, return to the bosom of their families, well instructed, it is true, but retaining only the name of Jews, unacquainted with the principles of their religion, perfectly indifferent to its obligations, and, probably, with prejudices against it, the result of other and early impressions, and if compelled by the urgency of business enterprize to go abroad [to leave home], forgetting in a short time that they were born to Jewish parents, and marrying in[to] other denominations and communities.

The successful establishment of a Hebrew College may, and I think will, remedy these evils, and relieve parents from a responsibility which at all times is peculiarly painful. In such an institution, under proper government [guidance], sons of Jewish parents can acquire a classical education, all the accomplishments taught in other schools, all the exercise necessary for the promotion of health and comfort, while devoting a reasonable portion of their time in acquiring a thorough and grammatical knowledge of the Hebrew language, going through their daily prayers, attending worship on the Sabbath, and becoming practically acquainted with the ceremonies and obligations of our holy religion, a religion which only can be properly estimated by those who have enjoyed the benefits of a liberal education.

In proposing to establish this institution several eligible positions [localities] have presented themselves, each holding out certain peculiar advantages. The college should not be in the immediate vicinity of the city, as students might be induced by its amusements and attractions to spend more time in it than would be beneficial either to their health or morals, nor should it be so remote as to exclude early intelligence of what is going on in the commercial metropolis. I should prefer Newport, Rhode Island, from its healthy position, from there being a synagogue at that place liberally endowed [by Abraham and Judah Touro], and from its having formerly possessed a congregation distinguished for great wealth and respectability. The difficulty might be in finding at Newport suitable buildings ready for immediate occupation.

In the vicinity of this city [of New York], we have Flushing, a place of great celebrity for education, and New Brighton. On the North River [the Hudson], we have the advantage of water prospect, and its atmospheric influence, combined with pure mountain air. Poughkeepsie, Mount Pleasant, and Tarrytown, very pleasant villages, each present great advantages of location, in their daily communication with the city, in their already established literary institutions, and each having spacious buildings which could be procured forthwith. This point, however, would be reserved for future deliberation.

Our object and intentions should be to secure for this institution a reputation which will bear comparison with any college throughout the Union, by the employment of competent classical teachers in every department, by guaranteeing a thorough scholarship in every branch of study, by a high moral and intellectual training, a love of truth and justice, a veneration for religion, an honourable, high-minded feeling, a self-respect, and all those just, generous, and amiable feelings calculated to establish the character of an honourable, well-bred man.

The classical department should embrace a course of study of Latin, Greek, and Hebrew, ancient history and mathematics; the English department, one of grammar, arithmetic, geography, penmanship, history, moral philosophy, elocution, composition, and bookkeeping, together with French and drawing, each branch applicable to the age and capacity of the pupil, advancing each by degrees, until attaining every department, and dividing the hours of study and recreation, so as to ensure a steady progress, while not neglecting that exercise so conducive to health.

The principal, scholars, and teachers should constitute one family, eating together, and sleeping under the same roof. The Hebrew professor should at the same time be the hazan [minister] and shochet [ritual slaughterer], read daily prayers, also on the Sabbath and holidays in the synagogue, which should be in the college, and it would be the duty of the principal occasionally to deliver an English discourse on religious and moral obligations. There should be two vacations: one of two weeks during the Passover, and one of four weeks during the fall holidays.

Such, sir, are the mere outlines of a plan to establish a Hebrew Seminary, which is every way feasible of execution, requiring only the cordial and prompt co-operation of our friends to carry it into effect. If a person possessing the entire confidence of the Jewish population can be found, with adequate means to carry out this enterprize, and lay the foundation of an institution which hereafter may do honour to our religion, I will most cheerfully assist in carrying the plan into successful execution. But such is my confidence in the successful issue of the project, that if no proper person can be found to embark in the enterprize, I am willing to commence it at my cost and risk, and thus give an earnest of my sincerity in carrying out this interesting experiment.

I believe that parents may rely upon my declaration that the treatment of pupils will be paternal and liberal, the management firm and kind, and the moral and physical training sedulously regarded. The entire expense of each scholar, including boarding, lodging, tuition in every branch of education, with the exception of music and drawing, will be two hundred and fifty dollars per annum; no children admitted under six years of age.

I invite my friends to communicate freely with me, to interchange opinions, and to take an interest in carrying out this useful and important project. If a reasonable number of students shall offer from different parts of the Union, and the West India Islands, to commence with, I think I can say that all the preparations will be completed for their reception by the first day of November next.

New York, August 18th, 1843.   M. M. NOAH

ISIDOR BUSH URGES JEWISH PARENTS IN ST. LOUIS TO SEND THEIR CHILDREN TO PUBLIC SCHOOLS (1855) From *The Occident,* vol. XIII (May 1855), pp. 85–89.

The income of the St. Louis public schools during the year 1854, amounted to $87,088.55, and is increasing every year. The value of its real estate in St. Louis far exceeds one million of dollars! Religious, or rather Christian instruction has been kept out of its system by its wise founders, and I have some reason to believe that this has been done partly, with regard to our confession. One of the directors of the present school-board is an Israelite (Mr. Adoph Levi). He, and every good republican, whatever his individual religious views may be, will watch, that no sectarian influence shall ever be permitted to control it. And *why* should we refuse to participate in the blessings of this grand institution, towards whose support we contribute our mite, and to the benefits of which we are fully entitled?

Thus we have arrived at the second question; and I do not hesitate to declare that, after mature reflection and due consideration of all its bearings, I am utterly opposed to all sectional or sectarian schools, nor would I change my opinion if our means were as ample as they are deficient. I have but lately written an article about this subject for one of our Jewish periodicals, in which I have endeavored to show the evils of the system. I have there given my views of the most feasible plan by which a good religious instruction might be given to our children, without retarding their progress in other knowledge, and by which this boon might be extended to a much larger number. But in order to avoid the error of some authors and lecturers who always copy and quote themselves, I prefer on this occasion to present to your consideration the arguments of those gentlemen who are the champions of the opposite view, of the warm friends of sectional schools, as far as their arguments have come to my knowledge through the press and private conversation.

Some urge as their main argument, the desire to *separate* "the seed of Abraham that dwell among the Gentiles, that their faith might never lose aught of its purity." Others in their fanaticism, deem it necessary "to make the children susceptible for the sufferings of their religion." On the other hand they say, "the Jewish child soon observes, when mixing with others, that even in America his *religion* is ridiculed and heartily despised by the great majority around him. This may operate to make him anxious to conceal his being a Jew from those with whom he associates, and act as much like them as possible, in order not be to noticed for his *religious singularity.*" If this should have happened but once, it would be proof strong enough for the cause they advocate, that is: "to establish Jewish schools, where they could escape sneers and ridicule; where their keeping the Sabbaths and festivals of the Lord will not expose them to being deprived of their equal right to progress with their class;" that, "when our children attend Gentile schools[1] there are constantly intimations held out, which are at least unpleasant to them, still which they have to submit to, if they wish not to incur the ill-will of their teachers."

My own experience of the working of public schools convinces me that this charge is unfounded. It is doing injustice to the pure heart of all children, no matter of what persuasion, to accuse them of hatred, hatred for the sake of religion. They know no such feeling; at least not toward their school-fellows and playmates. And woe to the teacher of a public school, who would dare to ridicule or sneer at a child, or to show it any ill-will for the sake of its religion. On Sabbaths, public schools are not kept open; and for those very few festivals that may happen to fall on some other day of the week, it requires but one word from the parents to excuse their children, without preventing them from progressing with their class. A *"religious singularity,"* necessarily obvious in their appearance, and which children might be anxious to conceal, is a thing entirely unknown and unintelligible to us; unless it refers to the PECULIARITY of a singing brogue, a slovenly dress, *et id omne genus.* If these be "singularities," nothing could be more desirable than that our children should learn to quit them in their early youth.

But granting even, for argument's sake, that this charge is partly true, and not quite unfounded, would this separation be the proper way to cure the evil? Would the descendants of our Christian fellow-citizens be more liberal than their ancestors, or would they not rather be strengthened in their lamentable prejudice? On the other hand, let me ask you, which class of our children are in a better condition to meet and overcome the spectre of Intolerance: those whom we have thus excluded from all intercourse with the children of others, who, when they leave the Jewish school are wholly unprepared to meet "the spectre," or those who already learnt to know it, and under our guidance have been taught how to repel such indignity in this country of civil and religious freedom?

Another objection raised against the public schools, is, that it *might* be demanded of our children to read the Bible in some Christian version, or even the books called the gospels, &c. But this is as futile an argument as the rest; for in most of the States this question has been fully discussed and finally decided against the admission of any Bible or religious instruction whatsoever.

Having thus refuted the standing arguments for sectarian schools, I cannot think of any object to be attained by them, to which full justice could not be done be establishing good Sabbath, Sunday, and evening schools for religious and Hebrew instruction only. Procure Sabbath lectures adapted to the mind and understanding of our children; let there be two-hour lessons on each Sabbath and Sunday in Mosaic religion and Hebrew reading; let this work be done by some respectable members of our congregations, both ladies and gentlemen; let these lessons be made more attractive by gifts to the diligent scholars, and let them be super-intended by some competent man, as for instance, our Rev. Dr. Illowy. Finally, establish an evening

[1]If this denomination is intended for public schools, it is as unjust and improper as the accusation itself; if for Catholic, or other sectarian schools, the whole would be idle talk, as no sensible Israelite has ever advocated, or ever will be in favor of sending our children there.—I. B.

school for those who wish to attain a more thorough knowledge of the Hebrew and the Holy Bible in its original language—and you have furnished the means which we proposed, and which we believe will not only answer to the just demands for religious instruction, but will bestow this blessing upon a much larger number of our children than has been, or could ever be accomplished by our sectarian day-school.

But let us see what our honorable opponents may have to say against this plan. They admit that such schools are very good; and Mr. Leeser, himself, informs us in his above-mentioned address, that "a lady whom we all esteem and on whose head may the Almighty shower many blessings for the good she has accomplished," has established in Philadelphia a Hebrew Sunday-school, which exists now near fourteen years, and still continues to accomplish much good; but he ventures to say that "its honored founder will be the first to acknowledge that it has never been universally resorted to, and that, moreover, the amount of instruction imparted has been far from adequate." I venture to say, and hazard little in saying it, that the same has been the case with your day-school, and that this highly estimable lady will coincide with me in asserting that her institution would have been more successful than your association-school, if to it had been applied but one half of the means, the zeal, &c, that were heaped upon the latter. It is farther objected, that "the Sabbath and Sunday-school are insufficient to counteract the ignorance of parental instructors in the merest elements of a religious life; to supply the defective conversation of the family circle; the little influence a father or mother can have, where both are not earnest in the service of the Lord." And, again I ask only, can the day-school be sufficient to counteract these influences of home; can it remove from the child's observing eyes the contradictions between faith and practice, where it exists in their families? *This* evil might be remedied perhaps by boarding-schools, where children are entirely separated from their parents;—but even there, conflicts of that kind could not be fully obviated.

I cheerfully praise the eloquent style of Mr. Leeser's address; but I cannot find one argument in it which would shake my full confidence in the efficiency and preferability of the system we propose to you; on the contrary, I find a great contradiction in it; for while at the one hand he is the champion of every-day sectarian schools, he on the other hand admits "that if but a small portion of the time devoted to learning French and music were bestowed by your children in learning the Scriptures in the original language, there would be none among them who could not take up his Hebrew Bible and enjoy the blessings of the word of God. Then also would that gross ignorance which does not practise religion because it does not know it, not be found among us"; and in short everything would be well enough!

But alas! a certain zeal to imitate the institutions of our brethren in Europe (where I admit such institutions to be very praiseworthy, nay, most necessary, because of many peculiar circumstances widely different from ours in this country), a certain ambition to emulate the institutions of other congregations in these United States, without carefully examining how they operate; sometimes even a kind of propensity to ape Christian institutions, established by priestcraft, make us blind—blind to the most evident contradictions and deaf to the voice of common sense.

My friendly hearers, if this were not a matter of such high importance, so dear to my heart, I would have preferred to withdraw in silence from this school-committee; but I would deem it treacherous to the holy cause of religious education if I would do so.

It is my firm conviction, that a Jewish school, embracing all branches of instruction, could not exist for one year in St. Louis, and would at the same time be prejudicial, in many respects, to our children, that it would be resorted to but by a very small number, and would thus leave by far the greater number of our sons and daughters without all religious instruction. And I believe, on the other hand, that by devoting our zeal, means and energy to an exclusively religious school, in the way we have proposed, sending our children at the same time to our public schools for the acquirement of other branches of learning, the result would exceed our most sanguine expectations:—that thus our children will become good pious Israelites, and worthy American citizens, our pleasure in life, our support and pride in the eve of our days.

Say you will try it, and let us join hand in hand.

MEMOIR OF THE HEBREW SUNDAY SCHOOL IN PHILADELPHIA

(c. 1850)   From Rosa Mordecai, "Memoir of Rebecca Gratz and the Hebrew Sunday School of Philadelphia," *Publications of the American Jewish Historical Society*, vol. XLII (1953), pp. 397–400.

My first distinct impression of going to the Hebrew Sunday school was some years after it was organized by my great-aunt, Miss Rebecca Gratz, and while she was still its moving spirit (some time, I think, in the early fifties). The room which the school then occupied was on Zane Street (now Filbert Street) above Seventh Street, over the Phoenix Hose Company. This was prior to the days of the paid fire department. Before mounting the stairs, I would linger, as many of the girls and all the boys did, to admire the beautifully-kept machines, with the gentlemanly loungers, who never wearied of answering our questions. The sons of our most "worthy and respected" citizens ran after the Phoenix in those days. But I catch a glimpse of Miss Gratz approaching, and we all scatter as she says: "Time for school, children!"

The room in which we assembled was a large one with four long windows at the end. Between the centre windows was a raised platform with a smaller one upon which stood a table and a chair. On the table was a much worn Bible containing both the Old and the New Testaments (Rev. Isaac Leeser's valuable edition of the Hebrew Bible had not then been published), a hand-bell, Watt's Hymns, and a penny contribution box "for the poor of Jerusalem."

Here Miss Gratz presided. A stately commanding figure, always neatly dressed in plain black, with thin white collar and cuffs, close-fitting bonnet over her curled front, which time never touched with grey; giving her, even in her most advanced years, a youthful appearance. Her eyes would pierce every part of the hall and often detect mischief which escaped the notice of the teachers.

The only punishment I can recall was for the delinquent to be marched through the school and seated upon the little platform, before mentioned, under the table. Sometimes this stand would be full, and I was rather disposed to envy those children who had no lessons to say. But, her duties over, Miss Gratz would call them by name to stand before her for reproof, which, apparently mild, was so soul-stirring that even the most hardened sinner would quail before it. She was extremely particular to instill neatness and cleanliness. A soiled dress, crooked collar, or sticky hands never escaped her penetrating glance, and the reproof or remedy was instantaneous.

The benches held about ten children each. They were painted bright yellow, with an arm at each end; on the board across the back were beautiful medallions of mills, streams, farmhouses, etc., etc.

The instruction must have been principally oral in those primitive days. Miss Gratz always began school with the prayer, opening with "Come ye children, hearken unto me, and I will teach you the fear of the Lord." This was followed by a prayer of her own composition, which she read verse by verse, and the whole school repeated after her. Then she read a chapter of the Bible, in a clear and distinct voice, without any elocution, and this could be heard and understood all over the room. The closing exercises were equally simple: a Hebrew hymn sung by the children, then one of Watts's simple verses, whose rhythm the smallest child could easily catch as all repeated: "Send me the voice that Samuel heard," etc., etc.

Many old scholars can still recall the question: "Who formed you, child, and made you live?" and the answer: "God did my life and spirit give"—the first lines of that admirable Pyke's *Catechism*, which long held its place in the Sunday school, and was, I believe, the first book printed for it. The Scripture lessons were taught from a little illustrated work published by the Christian Sunday School Union. Many a long summer's day have I spent, pasting pieces of paper over answers unsuitable for Jewish children . . .

Pyke's *Catechism* was freely distributed, and instead of being taught, parrot-fashion, by the teacher, the tiny green books went home to many Jewish households, with a penalty of five cents attached if injured or lost; and this fee was strictly exacted by the young librarian, who was a great disciplinarian. Books were not very often allowed by him to be taken home, but were read, after the lessons were recited by the scholars, or aloud by the teacher, if it so happened that all her class studied in the same book, or the same lesson. Generally, however, owing to private reasons, kinship or popularity, a class would be composed of eight or ten boys and girls of different ages and ability, and consequently these were taught out of several books, or even different parts of the same book.

The annual examination was held about Purim time. Why at that time, I never could find out, as the work of the class had to be immediately recommenced, unless it was a sort of anniversary, as the school was first opened March 4th, which, by a curious coincidence, was Miss Gratz's birthday. . . . The classes were arranged in a semicircle, according to the part of the book they studied, the pupils returning to their seats when the limit of their lessons had been reached. One teacher stood in the centre, giving the questions, or, if the classes were numerous, walked gradually around the circle. Thus every child was really examined, and each book recited in whole or in part.

The monotony was varied by monologues and dialogues; then came the distribution of prizes, which were called out by Mr. Hart, giving the name of the teacher with the three best scholars. The first prize was always a Bible; or, rather, a Bible and two books were given to each class. These books were most carefully selected by Miss Gratz herself, and handed by her to each child with a kind, encouraging word, often with a written line on the flyleaf. As the happy children went out orderly by class, through the back door, each was given an orange and a pretzel.

Simple days of our youth, where are you now?

Of all the inflexible demands which his religion and his duty make on each Israelite, the first and foremost is to give his child a good education; to equip it for the journey through life and give it the means to find its way. The American schools, of which we are about to speak, certainly guarantee this in part; but it is much to be regretted that, because they exclude all religion and confessions of faith—not with an unwise purpose—I must say with the deepest regret that the study of the Holy Scriptures, particularly, is much neglected among the daughters of Israel.

Jewish boys after a fashion—for that is the established way—are instructed in their religion, as is also the case with the sons and daughters of Christians. The Jewish boys attend some Hebrew school or other, or are instructed privately; but in this respect, what does the situation look like for the daughters of Israel? What a great difference! How sad is the provision for the religious instruction of these Jewish housewives and mothers of the future! How little do they learn of their duties towards God and man! What do they know of what our faith requires and of the commandments that they must obey as daughters of Israel! Should not those who are to perform the holiest religious duties be thoroughly prepared for such performance? These duties are indeed many and noble and it is with regret and astonishment that one learns that half of the American Jewesses are at present unable to undertake and fulfil worthily the place in life for which they are intended; nevertheless, it is unfortunately all too true. And why? The reason for this lies in their neglected education.

To throw more light on this statement and confirm the truth of it, let us describe the upbringing that the American Jewish women of today receive, and then let us proceed to show how the evil may, and should be remedied.

The mother of a little girl, a good-hearted, rather well-to-do woman, let us say, will try to impress on the young spirit of her child as much good instruction as ever she can. This private care lasts until the child is five. Then the child, it is obvious, must be sent to a public school or, what is more respectable, to a so-called "institute." Accepted by the "institute," the child begins the usual course of studies, makes the acquaintance of girls of other religions and has friends among them, and may well, without any objection or even realization of its significance, kneel during morning prayers which are arranged for those of other faiths, before classes begin. After school, she studies her lessons for the next day or, like all children, plays. Upon going to bed or arising in the morning, she may very likely recite for her mother some Hebrew or English prayers; but as for Judaism, the child experiences nothing and knows nothing.

In this manner the girl continues to be brought up until she is fifteen, except for the unimportant difference that in time she leaves the institute to attend a high-school or college. On her fifteenth birthday a new life begins; the longed-for day arrived at last; Papa and Mamma have promised her that on this day she shall be free and shall leave school, and she "graduates," to her great joy. What useful knowledge has she gained during this time? Extremely little in fact. She has spent ten years of her precious life among all kinds of books, and, with all that, she has not advanced in the least; the time is lost, indeed, forever. What she has learned is of no use to her and of no profit. She does not know how to sew, has no knowledge of household affairs, and still less of higher things. Ask her who has created her, who clothes her, who gives her her daily bread; and she may have the correct answer—perhaps, but it is more likely that she will say: "That was not in my book."

Her good parents have increased their wealth during these ten years and have taken the commendable resolution that their daughter should not forget all that she has learnt. Accordingly, they provide her—to complete her education—with a music-teacher, a singing-teacher, a drawing-teacher, and a governess to continue the practice of French; the latter also teaches her how to sew, knit and the like; and, to give it all a final touch, they assign a teacher to give her Hebrew lessons. He must make her acquainted with the alphabet of a language in which, as a child, she should have lisped the name of God. She will find this last teacher, as is only to be expected, a bore. She will find Hebrew too dull and also too difficult; she will weep over her lessons so that her yielding parents, who will be touched by her tears and moved to pity, will give the teacher notice—he whom they should have engaged first and dismissed last. But they took the opposite course, out of their own lack of true religious feeling, and so they engaged him last and, again, dismissed him first.

Since, in this manner, the girl has come to the end of her religious upbringing, she continues to recite in English the few prayers which she has learnt from her mother. Should she, quite by accident, attend synagogue, she takes a book in the same language. Her other teachers soon share the same fate as her former Hebrew teacher. Because of the parties, balls, soirées, and so on, which have now become the important questions of the day for her, and at which she remains until the last, the girl becomes full of whims, her mind is distracted. She listens to the chatter of young men and all thought of study and the desire for it is gone. The young lady—she will no longer permit herself to be called a girl—believes that her upbringing is now completed in every respect, considers herself qualified to take her place in the world, able to make a man happy and to become a Jewish mother. I must remark that, unfortunately, this can serve as an example for a thousand cases that occur in this land with only slight variations.

REFORM RABBI BERNARD FELSENTHAL OF CHICAGO ON JEWISH DAY SCHOOLS (1865) From *Judisches Schulwesen in America* (Chicago, 1866), pp. 10–13, as quoted in Lloyd P. Gartner, ed., *Jewish Education in the United States* (New York, 1969), pp. 83–84.

But will Jewish schools not cause a dividing wall to be erected between Jewish and non-Jewish children? We see how the reactionary parties in Europe maintain sectarian schools. . . . And in free America shall we speak of sectarian schools? Send your children to the non-sectarian schools of the country, and if you wish to provide for their religious education, take care to have special Sabbath schools!

We would be entirely against specifically Jewish schools, if the body of Jewish knowledge which we consider desirable for our children could easily be acquired in Sabbath schools. But there is too large an amount of subject matter to master. The vast majority of Israelites here are of German stock, and nearly every Israelite father wants and requires—rightly so—that children in school be taught not only English but also basic German and, secondarily, Hebrew. However, if the boys and girls are to be so advanced that at the close of their school years they have fully mastered two languages, English and German, and the third, Hebrew, understand well enough so that the Hebrew portions of our liturgy do not seem alien, and the easier books of the Bible are practically comprehensible in their original tongue, then we must establish for them such institutions in which this goal is attainable.

In a Sabbath school where the Jewish children assemble once weekly, this given goal cannot be reached, especially when, as is the case in the American cities on account of the Jews having settled en masse, these Sabbath schools are overcrowded and pedagogic personnel and facilities do not exist in adequate quantity. One must review daily the subject matter of Jewish education, if it is to be paralleled by deeper teaching. Sabbath schools are [only] a command of necessity. Yes, Jewish day schools! Or many more day schools, in which the pupils will also have the opportunity to acquire for themselves the desirable Jewish learning.

If not also absolutely necessary, it is to the highest degree desirable that our growing youth acquire a full grasp of Jewish teachings concerning faith and practice; familiarity with the main facts of Biblical and post-Biblical history; somewhat advanced knowledge of the Hebrew language, in which the Bible and in large measure the rich post-Biblical writings are composed.

A REPORT ON JEWISH EDUCATION (1870)   From J. J. Noah, "Hebrew Education," in U.S. Bureau of Education, *Annual Report of the Commissioner of Education for the Year 1870* (Washington, D.C., 1871), pp. 364–68.

It is safe to assert that, although the Israelites are of all nationalities, and scattered promiscuously over the face of the world, they are the only people who can be fairly classed as universally educated. There may be a few who cannot read or write, but this number is insignificant. Indeed, it is asserted by those who claim to know, that no Israelite can be found who cannot read or write, if not in their modern or domiciliary language, certainly in the Hebrew. If there are any thus in default, they may be found principally in London, or in other large cities of Great Britain, where, from degraded associations, they have been outcast from the society of their own people.

*   *   *

One of the most praiseworthy results of Hebrew education is the fact that it teaches and begets education. They keenly appreciate the idea of Plato, that "education consists in giving to the body and the soul all the perfection of which they are susceptible." Therefore a poor Israelite will sacrifice everything he possesses in order that his children may be educated. In European countries, where it was not possible to promote Jewish schools, the Israelites, whenever it was permitted, contributed freely to the schools of other sects, to the end that they might enjoy the benefit of educating their youth therein, even at the expense of their religious conscience.

In the United States, however, it is worthy of remark that, as we have progressed in education, liberal laws, and unrestricted liberty, the progress and reforms of the Israelites have been commensurately achieved. It was reserved for this republic first to unveil the obscurity and hermetic character of Jewish education. It has not been compelled here to secrecy, as in mediaeval and even modern times it existed in Europe, and therefore has been thrown open for public examination.

The American Israelite undoubtedly rejoices in our system of free schools, and watches with anxiety and hope the progress of American education. He is grateful for the blessings of free government, and therefore is in accord with the wisdom of Aristotle, who asserts that "the most effective way of preserving a state is to bring up the citizens in the spirit of the Government; to fashion, and, as it were, to cast them in the mould of the Constitution."

It is Hebrew education to insist that inasmuch as the promoting of wise and liberal government is the true aim of education, so the government, in return, should foster and conserve it as the most important end to be attained, and as contributing the greatest happiness to the masses. It therefore follows that prominent educational reformers among the American Jews do not consider it any longer absolutely essential to the well-being of their race that they should educate their children exclusively according to the old Hebraic customs. They feel that they are citizens of this Republic, entitled to enjoy all of its blessings, to share in its advantages and to contribute to its well-being. They believe that education should be common and universal, but leaving religious instruction to the care of the different denominations. They rejoice in the existence of civil and religious liberty, in the separation of church and state, and in the enactment of recent laws which proclaim the obliteration of all distinctions of race and condition, all being equal in citizenship and receiving equal application of the laws. This is their present education.

It is not astonishing that the public has but little correct information regarding the Jews, for it is only recently that the prejudice entertained against them appears to have given way. It is not generally known that in all American synagogues prayers are specially offered for the President and Congress, the governors of States, and all local officers, soliciting the Throne of Divine Grace to preserve and protect all our rulers, and to endow them with wisdom and mercy to all people, and particularly toward the children of Israel, who have stood in such sore need of the blessings of wise and humane government.

* * *

Education, to Israelites, in the Hebrew language, now is purely secondary, and is only taught for the purpose of enabling them to participate in the various religious ceremonies which are given in Hebrew. Modern American reforms, introduced in synagogue worship, do away with the exclusiveness of the Hebrew, and sermons, or lectures are now commonly preached in the English and German languages. Some reformers insist that all the services should be conducted in English, or German, so that all the congregation should understand; for it is true that the percentage of Hebrews attending synagogue, and employing the Hebraic understandingly, is very small. In other words, it is evident that the Hebrew language is fast losing its importance among the Jews, it being no longer necessary to employ it hermetically, although the orthodox Israelites cling with great pertinacity to the old habits and customs, and refuse to be separated from the ancient landmarks. It is but a question of time, however, with orthodox Judaism—it must give way to the reformatory spirit of the age.

The Talmud is no longer taught in Jewish schools as an exclusive study. It is referred to and interwoven with other school exercises, but is not a specialty. The Israelites do not, as heretofore, compel their children to an exclusive study of Hebrew, and of Hebrew law, at the age of five and six years; but they impart to them a general knowledge of Hebrew, so that they may read it fluently, even if they understand it but imperfectly, to the end that when they become *Bar-mitzvah*, or thirteen years of age, (the Oriental age of manhood, when parental authority is considered to cease,) they may read their portion of the *Torah*, or the law of Moses, in the synagogue, as the first witness and exhibit of their entry into the mystic rite of manhood. The Hebrew has been heretofore wrongfully classified among the dead languages. It has never expired, but has constantly had life. When it is considered, however, that the Hebrew youth are no longer compelled to master it, or to use it as a language of conversation, it is fast going into decadence, and, like the Latin, will only serve the purposes of a language of religious ceremony.

It is not uncommon, however, in Germany and Poland to use the written Hebrew for the purposes of record and correspondence, and letters in the German vernacular are even now frequently written and spelled in Hebraic characters. This is a custom, however, which has obtained among the Hebrews by reason of their peculiar civic condition, being inhabitants, but deprived of civil rights. Fearful of their letters miscarrying, and the consequent exposure of family secrets, they have adopted the use of the Hebraic to avoid the probable consequences of accident.

But the important question arises as to how the Hebrews, notwithstanding their exile, their persecutions, the constant destruction of their schools of learning and of science, their deprivations of civil rights, their compulsory nomadic habits, their merging into all the nationalities of Europe, Asia, Africa, and America, have preserved their advanced literary culture, their morals, their education in all the arts and sciences, and their individuality from the date of their delivery from Egyptian bondage to the present hour? It must be because of the superiority of their education, mental, moral, and physical; of the love, reverence, and respect which they entertain toward their teachers, and for the further reason that the influences of the home circle have ever been maintained as paramount. The children are obedient to their parents, who neglect no opportunity to instruct and guide them, and between the old and young there exists a perfect accord; the elders to teach, the youth to listen and learn, and this has been pursued from generation to generation, and from father to son, from the days of the prophets to this era of advanced civilization.

* * *

No one but a Jew can commensurately appreciate the intense happiness of the Hebrew people in this country. Free America is the modern Moses who has delivered them from European bondage, perhaps far worse than the Egyptian. They have not been made to drink the bitter waters of Marah in this land; they have not thirsted in the wilderness of Shur, nor hankered after the flesh-pots. They have sped to this hospitable province, this modern "Elim," where there are more than "twelve wells of water, and three score and ten palm trees," and *they are wanderers no more.*

Although the names of Hebrew scholars are legion, it may not be amiss to indicate a few, such as Josephus, the ablest and truest of all ancient historians, Maimonides who lived in the twelfth century, and as a law writer and philosopher surpassed all contemporaries, Jehuda Hallevi, the rival of King Solomon as a poet, the noted traveler, Benjamin, of Tudela, and Immanuel, the Italian poet and imitator of Dante. In the eighteenth century the two greatest writers of the age on philosophy were Spinoza and Moses Mendelssohn, and Wessely, Euchel, Lowe, and Friedländer are foremost in the ranks of German poets. In later days may be mentioned the names of Disraeli, Cremieux, Montefiore, Börne, Auerbach, Heinrich Heine, Jules Janin, Grace Aguilar, and Fould, and in the United States, Messrs. Noah, Raphael, Wise, Lilienthal, Leeser, Einhorn, and Isaacs, all noticed by modern encyclopedists. To enumerate the Hebrew Talmudists, divines, poets, philosophers, philologists, historians, publicists, linguists, mathematicians, astronomers, physiologists, ichthyologists, and orators of ancient and modern days, would occupy too much space in this necessarily limited "paper." Politics, law, medicine, the fine arts and the drama have many representatives, and in music Meyerbeer, Halezy, Herz, and Gottschalk have become as immortal as has Rachel in tragedy. In finance and commerce, special mention is absolutely unnecessary, for in these essentials they lead the world.

It is a historical fact that, notwithstanding the federal Constitution, the State of North Carolina once forbade the election of any Jew to office. An eminent Hebrew patriot by the name of Henry was, despite this law, elected to the State Senate. He was, however, denied his seat, but was allowed the privilege of addressing the House on the main question. The speech he made on that occasion was at once eloquent and reproachful, creating such an impression upon the minds of the people of North Carolina, that public sentiment demanded and procured a repeal of the disgraceful prohibition.

In America, as well as latterly in Europe, the Israelites have been honored with, and creditably filled, the highest official stations. They have held seats in the French Chamber, the British Parliament, and in the Senate and House of Representatives; have been governors of States and Territories, attorneys general, sat upon the "woolsack," and in fact hold and have held prominent public positions in common with other eminent and praiseworthy citizens.

Although the Hebrews are not naturally politicians, they carefully note and give countenance to every species of legislation, every doctrine of political economy, and every public act calculated to extend liberty and to diffuse education. Nothing in this regard escapes them. The Hebrews throughout Europe and America purchased our bonds liberally, and aided in their negotiation, thus manifesting their confidence in American securities. It is believed that they hold fully one-fifth of our outstanding indebtedness in Europe and America.

It is not possible to give any extended statistics appertaining exclusively to Hebrew schools, for since the recent emancipation of the Jews from their previous civil disabilities, their education has been gradually merged into the general community system. In many eminent universities, in Germany, France, and Great Britain, professorships are now given to Hebrews in the various chairs of science and learning, and at Göttingen no less than nine of these preferments are filled by Jews. Jewish students consequently now largely derive educational advantages in common with others. In Rome, however, the Hebrews still labor under great educational and personal disadvantages, which they are endeavoring to have relieved by appealing to the liberality of the new Italian government. A petition was presented in 1860 to a proposed congress of European powers for the settlement of international questions, in which the Jews in Rome asked the consideration of an amelioration of their condition in that city. The address of grievances sets forth that no Jew in Rome can be an artist, nor be a pupil in a school of art, nor frequent a public gallery for practice; nor could any college, medical school, law university, or other scientific institution receive Jewish students. None of their people can follow any other mechanical trade but cobbling shoes, and they are not permitted to sing or play on any instrument in public. They are confined to the *Ghetto,* or Jews' quarter, on the low ground of the Tiber, admitted to be the most unhealthy and wretched portion of the city.

In the United States exclusively Jewish schools are not looked upon with great favor, nor to be as much desired as formerly. This is explained by the fact that the American Hebrews are extremely proud of their citizenship; and although they are anxious to advocate and inculcate, in our common schools and other institutions of learning, the superiority of their education in many essentials, they are unwilling to retard or in any manner complicate the progress of free education. They are satisfied at being permitted the unrestricted use of our common-school system, particularly as religious instruction is now being confined to the different denominations, and the school-room made free to all shades of religious sentiment.

Although the Hebrews still worship on Saturday, or the seventh day, they entertain reverence and respect for Sunday, and are loth to violate the Sabbath of the Christian. For many years, in several of our large cities, Jewish congregations have regularly maintained Sunday-schools, and Hebrew children may be seen regularly wending their way to the Sunday-school exercises of their synagogues. In Philadelphia the Portuguese congregation, formerly presided over by the late Rev. Mr. Leeser, has maintained a Sunday-school for the past thirty years or more.

In the new "Temple Immanuel," one of the grandest edifices in New York city, on the Fifth avenue, a thoroughly organized Sunday-school is maintained. Each class has a separate room set apart for its use, and competent teachers are employed and liberally paid for their services. Order is maintained in the most thorough manner and no confusion or noise is permitted. The assembly of scholars is had in the main hall, and one of the scholars recites a prayer, the congregation remaining standing until the "Amen" is given; after which, to the music of a measured march, the classes separate and retire, each to its appropriate apartment. About two hours are employed in religious instruction, when, returning to the assembly room, a prayer is offered and they are dismissed, retiring in the most perfect order.

The Hebrew Sabbath or Sunday schools are founded solely to impart religious instruction to Israelitish children. The scholastic year begins after the feast of the Tabernacles, (*Succoth,*) the commencement of the Jewish New Year, in the latter part of September or first of October, and continues until the last Sunday in June; and it is usually requisite that children should have attended some other school for a year prior to admission. Pupils are required to enrol their names in advance; and a programme of studies for the scholastic year is presented for inspection and adoption by the board of trustees. Corporal punishment is interdicted, and punishment is only in the mildest form, at worst, resulting in suspension, and, in extreme cases, in dismission. Records of punishment and absence are carefully kept, and a public examination and distribution of prizes annually celebrated. Every effort is made to conduce happiness and to attract, rather than repel, the pupils to the school.

J. J. NOAH.

SURVEY OF JEWISH EDUCATION IN SOME LARGE AMERICAN CITIES

(1870)   From U.S. Bureau of Education, *Annual Report of the Commissioner of Education for 1870* (Washington, D.C., 1871), pp. 368–70.

Philadelphia

The Rev. George Jacobs, of Philadelphia, writes:

In the city of Philadelphia there are seven Jewish synagogues. The benevolent associations number eleven lodges of the order of "B'nae Brith," ("Sons of the Covenant,") numbering 1,025 members, and with funds on hand to the amount of $38,850 39. There are also seven lodges of the "Free Sons of Israel," numbering 800, and with a fund of $10,000. The United Hebrew Charities, consolidated from five separate benevolent organizations, received, from September 1869 to February 1870, $14,773 22, most of which was distributed in relieving 682 persons. The Ladies' Hebrew Benevolent Society, organized in 1819, receives and disburses about $1,100 per annum. The Jewish Foster Home numbers some 28 inmates. In addition to these is the Jewish hospital, open to all patients, which has cared for 91 patients during the year, at an expense of nearly $8,000.

Of distinctive Jewish schools there are three, with 10 male and 3 female teachers, and with 454 pupils, 264 male and 190 female.

The Maimonides College, recently established, and in which, in addition to the usual classical and modern studies, the higher branches of the Hebrew are taught, numbers 6 professors. The Hebrew Sunday-school, founded in 1838 by Miss Rebecca Gratz, was the first Hebrew Sunday-school in the United States. It numbers 115 boys and 110 girls, and 5 male and 18 female teachers. The majority of Jewish children attend the State public schools in the city. Very few, if any, Jewish children fail to attend some school.

Boston, Massachusetts

There are three Hebrew benevolent associations exclusively for the assistance of the poor, and seven for the relief of the sick and the care of widows and orphans. There are five Jewish schools where some 300 children receive religious instruction. It is estimated that some 500 Hebrew boys and girls attend the public high and normal schools.

Baltimore, Maryland

Rev. S. Deutsch says that in Baltimore, as elsewhere, a large majority of the Jewish children attend the public schools of the city.

There is one exclusively Jewish private school of 150 pupils, and also a German private school where Hebrew and religious instruction are given if desired. There are two Sunday-schools, with a total attendance of 260 pupils. There are three Jewish charitable associations.

St. Louis, Missouri

Rev. Dr. Sonneschein has furnished the following information:

There are four Jewish charitable associations: two for the assistance of the poor, one for the support of widows and orphans, and one for the interment of the poor. A Jewish hospital is in progress.

There are no Jewish private schools. It is estimated that 1,120 Jewish children attend the public schools, 630 male and 490 female. There are three Jewish Sabbath-schools, with an aggregate attendance of 398: 215 male and 183 female.

✻   ✻   ✻

Chicago, Illinois

The Rev. B. Felsenthal, of Chicago, writes that Chicago has an estimated Jewish population of 10,000. He estimates that 90 per cent. of the Jewish children attend the public schools, and remarks that "it is safe to assert that every Jewish child receives at least a good elementary education, the care for the proper education of the children being an old and firmly-rooted trait of the Jewish character." There is one private school in the city, taught by Rev. L. Adler, where instruction is given in Hebrew. About 100 children are in attendance. For instruction in Hebrew parents generally rely on the Jewish Sabbath-schools and on private tuition.

There are six Hebrew congregations, each of which has a Sabbath-school. In all these the rudiments of Hebrew are taught. From 500 to 600 children attend these Sabbath-schools.

There are five lodges of the order of B'nae Brith (Sons of the Covenant,) and seven other benevolent societies. A Jewish hospital is supported, where poor sick persons of all beliefs, are received. The Hebrew Orphan Asylum, at Cleveland, receives considerable contributions from Chicago. (The Jews of the Eastern States have their orphan asylum in New York, those of the South in New Orleans, and those of the Pacific States in San Francisco.) Besides the Chicago congregations, there are in Illinois four others—two in Quincy, one in Springfield, and one in Peoria.

Rev. Isaac M. Wise, of Cincinnati, furnishes the following information:

In reply to your official note of the 28th ultimo, I have the honor to state:

1. There are no Jewish elementary schools in this city. The last *Talmid Yeladim* institute was dissolved three years ago.

2. There are three Hebrew schools for religious instruction attached to three congregations, viz:

a. Benai Yeshurun congregation, superintendent, Isaac M. Wise; four teachers; 110 pupils; two sessions weekly, Saturday and Sunday; objects, Hebrew, Jewish religion and history.

b. Benai Israel congregation, superintendent, Max Lilienthal; three teachers; 150 pupils; sessions and objects as above.

c. Ahabash Achim congregation, M. Goldemmer, teacher and superintendent; sixty pupils; sessions and objects as above.

Besides, the above named three rabbi teach, each, annually a confirmation or graduating class of twenty to forty pupils.

It is our settled opinion here that the education of the young is the business of the State, and the religious instruction, to which we add the Hebrew, is the duty of religious bodies. Neither ought to interfere with the other. The secular branches belong to the public schools, religion to the Sabbath schools, exclusively. Therefore I cannot give you any particular statistics as to Hebrew children in the various schools.

RULES FOR THE SABBATH SCHOOL OF CONGREGATION SHAARE EMETH IN ST. LOUIS (1870)   From U.S. Bureau of Education, *Annual Report of the Commissioner of Education for 1870* (Washington, D.C., 1871), p. 279.

I. The Sabbath-school is founded solely to impart religious instruction to Israelitish children belonging to above congregation.

II. The scholastic year begins on the first Sunday after the feast of the Tabernacles and closes on the last Sunday in June.

III. Such children only who have attended some other school at least one year can be admitted to the Sabbath-school.

IV. Names of pupils must be enrolled fourteen days prior to commencement of the scholastic year.

V. The teachers shall, during the aforesaid fourteen days, draught a programme and a course of studies for the ensuing scholastic year, and hand the same, for adoption, to the school board.

VI. Pupils desirous of attending the school during the scholastic year can be admitted only after having first obtained the consent of the school board.

VII. The school board will hold regular monthly meetings during the scholastic year on the Sunday after the 15th day of each month.

VIII. The acting superintendent of the school shall preside at the meetings of the school board.

IX. At the regular meetings of the school board the teachers shall attend to act in an advisory capacity; they shall not, however, be entitled to vote upon any question.

X. The superintendent is entitled to vote only when a tie occurs.

XI. Whenever two members of the school board shall desire, or the superintendent deems it necessary to call a special meeting of the school board, the members thereof shall be convened.

XII. It shall be the duty of every member of the school board to attend the Sabbath-school during hours of instruction at least twice each month.

XIII. Corporal punishment is strictly prohibited.

XIV. Punishment in the third, or mildest, degree shall be, 'Removal of the pupil from his bench during the hours of instruction;' in the second degree, 'Removal of the pupil from the school room to that of the superintendent during same time;' in the first degree, 'Suspension of the pupil from school for two weeks.'

XV. The consent of the superintendent must first be obtained ere the pupil can be dismissed from the school.

XVI. Pupils punished with the first, or highest, punishment three times, can be dismissed from the school entirely, provided a resolution to that effect has been passed by the school board.

XVII. Every teacher shall keep a correct record of punishments meted out to pupils, for monthly communication with the parents.

XVIII. Each absence of the pupil from school must be accounted for by a written excuse from the parents.

XIX. Every teacher shall keep a correct list of the attending pupils and report the absentees to the school board.

XX. The superintendent only shall have the right to interrupt the regular school exercises by asking questions or imparting information.

XXI. A public examination and distribution of prizes shall take place at the close of the scholastic year.

(Adopted at the meeting of the trustees of the congregation held May 8, 1870.)

Educational Alternatives

BRONSON ALCOTT ON INFANT EDUCATION (1830)   From Bronson Alcott, *Observations on the Principles and Methods of Infant Instruction* (Boston, 1830), pp. 4–13.

The early influences operating upon infancy, embrace a variety of subjects, principles, and methods. Early education, involving the expansion, direction, and perfecting of the faculties of infant nature, is a subject wide and intricate. All the elements of this nature are embraced as its objects; in its principles and methods a discipline is required, adapted to the order in which these faculties appear, to their relative importance as aids in life, and to their gradual and harmonious developement by a wise selection of exercises and means. The animal nature, the affections, the conscience, and the intellect, present their united claims for distinct and systematic attention. The whole being of the child asks for expansion and guidance. In the constitution of his nature, shall we, therefore, find the principles of infant cultivation.

If we observe the habits of infancy in a physiological point of view, its active propensities cannot fail to meet our notice. The child is essentially an active being. His chief enjoyment consists in the free and natural exercise of his material frame. The quickening instinct of his nature urges him to the exertion of all its functions and to seek in this, every means for their varied and happy activity. A reverential respect for the author of so benevolent a law of its animal economy, will suggest a faithful obedience to its requisitions. The claims of animal nature in infancy, are primary and paramount to all others; and it is not till these are anticipated and relieved by unrestrained movement, that the intellect can be successfully addressed. By encouraging the free and natural activity of the body, the functions on which intellectual energy and happiness depend, are invigorated and most effectually prepared for the lessons of instruction. Play is the appointed dispensation of childhood; and a beneficent wisdom consists in turning this to its designed purpose. When the force of animal impulse has expended itself by free and natural recreation, and left the physical system in a state of tranquillity, the mind imbibes the influence, and forgetting the scenes and activities of its previous joys, yields itself to the loftier claims of its nature, and asks the sympathy and guidance of instruction; and it is by creating, and applying these states of the animal and intellectual nature, for the advancement of the child, that successful results are chiefly produced in early instruction.

The primary want of infancy is enjoyment. In seeking to supply this want from the variety of surrounding objects, the child often fails of his purpose, from the want of reflection and experience. His mind thus becomes saddened by disappointment, his temper impaired, his reason sophisticated and weakened. He needs the hand of friendly guidance and aid. The means employed by the infant system, should guide him to the true and lasting sources of enjoyment. Respecting all the laws of his animal economy, they should associate pleasure with the action of all his faculties, investing all his instructions with an interest, a certainty, and a love, which future experience shall not diminish, nor maturer reason disapprove. By yielding a more intelligent homage to the active propensities of infancy, furnishing a greater proportion, and a more intellectual kind of recreation, than is permitted by other forms of discipline, the infant system diffuses over the young mind the benign and improving influences of happiness, and thus imparts intellectual and moral life to the infant spirit.

The provision which is thus made for the exercise of the animal functions, extends its influence beyond their development, to the affectionate nature of the child. Associating with minds like his own in the common purposes of amusement and happiness, his affections find free and spontaneous action to multiply and elevate the joys of his existence, to connect him in ties of sympathy and love with his infant friends, and thus to unseal within him the fountains of future felicity. By multiplying and purifying the sensations of his nature, an experienced wisdom is acquired by the child, which, under more restrained and unsocial influences, it would be impossible to impart. A play-room thus becomes an important aid both to intellectual improvement and happiness. An attentive instructor will see in its amusements the true results of his labors; for it is in the freedom of these, that infant character is most clearly revealed. As in the theatre of adult life, we learn the true characters of men by friendly intercommunication, and frequent collision of purposes and interests; so in the amusements of the play-room, the arena of infant activity and impulse, will a wise instructer obtain a just knowledge of infant character. Instruction, unless connected with active duty, and expressed in character, can be at best but a doubtful good. For the improvement of the animal and the affectionate nature, the play-room thus becomes an indispensable appendage to the Infant School. In its unpremeditated sports, and under careful superintendence, without restraint or interdiction, except in cases of obvious wrong, the child is happily employed, and most effectually prepared for the more formal lessons of the school-room.

In the general culture resulting from the play-room, it would be as unwise as impracticable to attempt systematic exercises, or descend into positive detail. It is in the school-room that the faculties of infancy are to be separately addressed, and that systematic attention becomes a necessary requisite. And in proceeding to more systematic labors, the intelligent teacher will seek, as before, his chief guidance in the principles pervading the intellectual and moral constitution of the child. By these will he shape out his system, and on these will he raise the fabric of infant character.

The affections will claim his first attention. On the cultivation and direction of these, much of infant happiness depends. A beneficent wisdom will not fail to discern in their early strength and prominence, the obvious intentions of nature, and yield a religious obedience to her unerring requisitions. Affectionate and familiar conversation is the chief avenue to the infant mind. This will invariably reach its recesses, and reflect its influences, in corresponding tones and emotions. This is the powerful spring which puts the young heart in action, and unfolds all its faculties in the sweetest harmony and perfection. What only is felt by the teacher can become effectual in its purpose, or happy in its influence upon the taught; for all truly efficient results must come from the heart.

In an institution so purely moral in its purpose as the Infant School, much depends upon the character of the teacher. Moral results can come only from moral means; and of these the teachers agency is the chief. In him the infant mind should find the object of its imitation and its love. To a pure and affectionate heart, an unsophisticated conscience, and elevated principles of action, the teacher should unite an amiableness of temper, a simplicity of manner, and a devotion to his work, which shall associate with it his happiness and his duty. His mind should be well disciplined by various experience; beautified and adorned by the cultivation of its moral attributes, and purified and elevated by the faith and hopes of Christianity. To these should be added, as an indispensable requisite, a familiar acquaintance with the infant mind, and a deep reverence for its author. He should possess the power of reaching the infant understanding in the simplest and happiest forms; of investing truth in the loveliest attributes, associating liberty and delight with all the means of its pursuit. Free from prejudices and partialities, he should impart instructions from the pure fountains of truth and love alone. Taking a benevolent view of the works of nature and the ways of Providence, his piety should diffuse itself through all his teachings, and with a silent, quickening power, draw wisdom and improvement from every event. Of mere learning he may have little or much; an intelligent philanthropy, a desire to be useful, are more important requisites, and without which his other attainments will be of little avail. Of patience and self-control he should be a thorough and constant disciple.

Intimately connected with the cultivation of the affections, is the diviner nature of the child; the conscience. This fundamental principle of all virtue early reveals itself as a subject of attention and culture. To train and elevate this by frequent appeals to the unerring laws of reason, rectitude, and benevolence, is an all-important work. It is on this portion of infant nature, that the purest influences should fall, and from which the noblest results should be anticipated. Conscientiousness is the parent of all the noblest virtues, and forms the primary attribute of a pure and lofty character. It is by its wise and happy cultivation that the infant mind finds within, the sources of self-dependence, and self-control, and by its divine suggestions is led to the knowledge and worship of its author, and to the divine truths of the christian revelation. An unrelaxing attention should, therefore, be given to all instruction that affects motive, since it is this which lays the permanent foundations of character, and constitutes the true glory of the soul.

The union of these influences, operation upon the animal, the affectionate, and the spiritual nature, like the quickening and expanding airs of spring upon the material world, reaches the intellectual portion of the child, and prepares the way for direct intellectual culture. Every mental faculty should be effectually addressed, and be made to operate in the independent acquisition of knowledge. Formal precepts, abstract reasonings, and unintelligible instructions, should here find no place; but interesting incidents, familiar descriptions, approaching as nearly as possible to the circumstances and relations of life, should embody no inconsiderable portion of the lessons of infancy. All that connects the child with the pure, the good, and the happy around him, should be impressed deeply in his mind. From the opened volume of nature, always perused with delight by childhood; from the varied records of life and experience, and from the deeper foundations of the mind, and of revelation, illustrations of truth and love may be drawn to expand the infant soul, to elevate and enrich it with knowledge and piety, for the coming years of its existence. Truth alone, in its divine unity and beauty, should be presented. All lessons should reach the mind in an intelligible and visible form. In this way alone can they find a response in the heart, operate in conscience, and impart energy and life to knowledge and duty.

The work of the infant teacher, simple and attainable as it may seem, involves, however, in its methods and details, resources of the purest and happiest character; imposes responsibilities of the deepest kind. But these considerations will never deter the true friend of infancy, from the prosecution of his work. In the simple desire to bless, in the consciousness that of all others, his are labors of usefulness and love, dwells both the principle and the means, that shall lead him in time to reward and success. Patience and experience will become his sure and confiding friends. Acquainted with the constitution of the infant mind, and knowing that immediate and apparent results are not to come from his labors, his anxiety will not prematurely hasten their approach. The mind, he knows, is not to be perfected in a day; nor is truth to reach it, and stamp its permanent impression; nor character attain its symmetry, and reveal its strength and perfection, at once. These are the slow product of time and labor: they are the united results of nature and art: they come from providence and instruction. It is the imperceptible and gentle influence of the dews of heaven that gradually expands the opening flower into all its beauty, fragrance and perfection; and so must it be with the opening mind of infancy. And much early labor will consist in shielding this from noxious influences, ere habit, and conscience, and principle have reached their full strength and activity. A religious reverence for the infant mind as the image of its author, will not wantonly pervert its powers by premature temptation, dim its joys by the regrets of disappointment, nor corrode its nature by the restraints of distrust and fear. Infant happiness should be but another name for infant progress; nature, and providence, and instruction, cooperating in their influences to elevate and to bless the infant spirit.

The methods by which the principles and purposes of early culture are applied in the exercise of the school-room, are of the most simple and unpretending character. They preserve all the primary habits of infancy, as expressed in the nursery, and under the observation and affection of a judicious and devoted mother at home. Instruction drawn from common circumstances and objects, assumes all the freedom and simplicity of domestic conversation; and so far as consistent with common order and discipline, follows the unpremeditated thoughts and feelings of every child. The teachers comes as much in direct contact with each as he can; avoiding all general instructions, except for the purpose of mental relaxation, or of improving the faculties of sympathy, and imitation. Much systematic instruction is repulsive to the habits and feelings of infancy. Order and system, when carried into minute detail, often become to the child, but other names for restraint and unhappiness, and whatever associates these with the operations of the mind, or the impulses of duty, claims no place among early influences. The more direct, therefore, and individual the methods of instruction become in their influence, the more efficient and happy will be their results. The growth and energy of the mind depend upon the freedom and happiness of its movements, and the restraints imposed by system for its action with others, cannot essentially conduce to its benefit. Instruction should refer to the circumstances of coming life and duty. In these, general movements are seldom required. It is through individual channels that the purest and most efficient influences reach the mind, and from this, connect themselves, in the same way, with duty and improvement.

There is no attainment of the teacher more difficult to possess, and at the same time more indispensable, than the power of making himself understood; of conversing intelligibly with children. The range of the infant mind is comparatively confined; all its operations are within a narrow circle. With the fleeting and varied impressions made by the objects within this circle upon its perception power, through the medium of the senses, it is the work of the instructer to become acquainted, and to give the image of permanence and truth, by the terms of language. And he is besides this to bring up from the fountains of love and thought, the more refined and evanescent objects within, and give them their true expression and beauty. The language of the teacher, and all his methods of intellectual communion, to be intelligent, must, therefore, descend to the scanty vocabulary of infant thought, drawn from the circle of its observation and experience. It must find a response and an interpreter within, or to the infant ear, he utters instructions in an unknown tongue, and converses only with himself. From whatever source the lessons of the infant school are drawn, the truths they contain should be invested in the simplest and purest forms of language, and associated with nature and happiness. Early impressions, whether true or false, derive their chief power over the mind, and exert their influence upon life and happiness, through association; and this is the result of education. How important is it therefore in infant instruction, that the distinctions between truth and error, should be religiously preserved, and correctly associated with intelligence and duty. Of this associating power, language is the chief instrument to be used; the connecting link between material and intellectual nature; the channel through which thought and feeling, truth and love, are to pass between the teacher and the child. Let him be careful of perverting this power. Let him be sure that he well understands what he presents to their minds; and that they understand what he presents: for in all misapprehension on the part of either, there is perversion, there is error; and who shall answer for the conseqence! There is no principle in infant instruction, in yielding obedience to which, the responsibility and the success of the teacher, are more involved than in this.

BRONSON ALCOTT ON THE TRUE TEACHER (1836)   From Bronson Alcott,
The Doctrine and Discipline of Human Culture (Boston, 1836), pp. 18–21, 24–25.

To fulfil its end, Instruction must be an Inspiration. The true Teacher, like Jesus, must inspire in order to unfold. He must know that instruction is something more than mere impression on the understanding. He must feel it to be a kindling influence; that, in himself alone, is the quickening, informing energy; that the life and growth of his charge preëxist in him. He is to hallow and refine as he tempts forth the soul. He is to inform the understanding, by chastening the appetites, allaying the passions, softening the affections, vivifying the imagination, illuminating the reason, giving pliancy and force to the will; for a true understanding is the issue of these powers, working freely and in harmony with the Genius of the soul, conformed to the law of Duty. He is to put all the springs of Being in motion. And to do this, he must be the personation and exampler of what he would unfold in his charge. Wisdom, Truth, Holiness, must have preëxistence in him, or they will not appear in his pupils. These influence alone in the concrete. They must be made flesh and blood in him, to reappear to the senses, and reproduce their like.—And thus shall his Genius subordinate all to its own force. Thus shall all be constrained to yield to its influence; and this too, without violating any Law, spiritual, intellectual, corporeal—but in obedience to the highest Agency, co-working with God. Under the melting force of his Genius, thus employed, Mind shall become fluid, and he shall mould it into Types of Heavenly Beauty. His agency is that of mind leaping to meet mind; not of force acting on opposing force. The Soul is touched by the live coal of his lips. A kindling influence goes forth to inspire; making the mind think; the heart feel; the pulse throb with his own. He arouses every faculty. He awakens the Godlike. He images the fair and full features of a Man. And thus doth he drive at will the drowsy Brute, that the Eternal hath yoked to the chariot of Life, to urge man across the Finite!

To work worthily in the ministry of Instruction, requires not only the highest Gifts, but that these should be refined in Holiness. This is the condition of spiritual and intellectual clearness. This alone unfolds Genius, and puts Nature and Life to their fit uses. "If any man will know of the Doctrine, let him do the will of my Father," said Jesus; and he, who does not yield this obedience, shall never shine forth in the true and fully glory of his nature.

Yet this truth seems to have been lost sight of in our measures of Human Culture. We incumber the body by the gluts of the appetites; dim the senses by self-indulgence; abuse nature and life in all manner of ways, and yet dream of unfolding Genius amidst all these diverse agencies and influences. We train Children amidst all these evils. We surround them by temptations, which stagger their feeble virtue, and they fall too easily into the snare which we have spread. Concupiscence defiles their functions; blunts the edge of their faculties; obstructs the passages of the soul to the outward, and blocks it up. The human body, the soul's implement for acting on Nature, in the ministry of life, is thus depraved; and the soul falls an easy prey to the Tempter. Self-Indulgence too soon rings the knell of the spiritual life, as the omen of its interment in the flesh. It wastes the corporeal functions; mars the Divine Image in the human form; estranges the affections; paralyzes the will; clouds the intellect; dims the fire of genius; seals conscience, and corrupts the whole being. Lusts entrench themselves in the Soul; unclean spirits and demons nestle therein. Self-subjection, self-sacrifice, self-renewal are not made its habitual exercises, and it becomes the vassal of the Body. The Idea of Spirit dies out of the Consciousness; and Man is shorn of his glories. Nature grows over him. He mistakes Images for Ideas, and thus becomes an Idolater. He deserts the Sanctuary of the Indwelling Spirit, and worships at the throne of the Outward.

✳   ✳   ✳

Yet, dimmed as is the Divine Image in Man, it reflects not the full and fair Image of the Godhead. We seek it alone in Jesus in its fulness; yet sigh to behold it with our corporeal senses. And this privilege God ever vouchsafes to the pure and undefiled in heart; for he ever sends it upon the earth in the form of the Child. Herein have we a Type of the Divinity. Herein is our Nature yet despoiled of none of its glory. In flesh and blood he reveals his Presence to our senses, and pleads with us to worship and revere.

Yet few there are who apprehend the significance of the Divine Type. Childhood is yet a problem that we have scarce studied. It has been and still is a mystery to us. Its pure and simple nature; its faith and its hope, are all unknown to us. It stands friendless and alone, pleading in vain for sympathy and aid. And, though wronged and slighted, it still retains its trustingness; still does it cling to the Adult for renovation and light.—But thus shall it not be always. It shall be apprehended. It shall not be a mystery and made to offend. "Light is springing up, and the day-spring from on high is again visiting us." And, as in times sacred to our associations, the Star led the Wise Men to the Infant Jesus, to present their reverent gifts, and was, at once, both the herald and the pledge of the advent of the Son of God on the earth; even so is the hour approaching, and it lingers not on its errand, when the Wise and the Gifted, shall again surround the cradles of the New Born Babe, and there proffer, as did the Magi, their gifts of reverence and of love to the Holiness that hath visited the earth, and shines forth with a celestial glory around their heads;—and these, pondering well, as did Mary, the Divine Significance, shall steal from it the Art—so long lost in our Consciousness—of unfolding its powers into the fulness of the God.

ELIZABETH PEABODY DESCRIBES BRONSON ALCOTT'S TEMPLE SCHOOL (1834) From Elizabeth Peabody, *The Record of Mr. Alcott's School, Exemplifying the General Principles and Methods of Moral Culture* (Boston, 1874), pp. 13–15, 17–19.

Mr. Alcott reopened his school in Boston, after four years' interval, September, 1834, at the Masonic Temple.

Conceiving that the objects which meet the senses every day for years must necessarily mold the mind, he chose a spacious room, and ornamented it, not with such furniture as only an upholsterer can appreciate, but with such forms as would address and cultivate the imagination and heart.

In the four corners of the room, therefore, he placed, upon pedestals, busts of Socrates, Shakspeare, Milton, and Scott; and on a table, before the large Gothic window by which the room is lighted, the Image of Silence, "with his finger up, as though he said, Beware." Opposite this window was his own desk, whose front is the arc of a circle. On this he placed a small figure of a child aspiring. Behind was a very large bookcase, with closets below, a black tablet above, and two shelves filled with books. A fine cast of Christ in basso-relievo, fixed into this bookcase, is made to appear to the scholars just over the teacher's head. The bookcase itself is surmounted with a bust of Plato.

On the northern side of the room, opposite the door, was the table of the assistant, with a small figure of Atlas bending under the weight of the world. On a small bookcase behind the assistant's chair were placed figures of a child reading and a child drawing. Some old pictures, one of Harding's portraits, and several maps were hung on the walls.

The desks for the scholars, with conveniences for placing all their books in sight, and with black tablets hung over them, which swing forward when they wish to use them, are placed against the wall round the room, that when in their seats for study no scholar need look at another. On the right hand of Mr. Alcott is a sofa for the accommodation of visitors, and a small table with a pitcher and bowl. Great advantages arise from this room, every part of which speaks the thoughts of Genius. It is a silent reproach upon rudeness.

About twenty children came the first day. They were all under ten years of age, excepting two or three girls. I became his assistant, to teach Latin to such as might desire to learn.

Mr. Alcott sat behind his desk, and the children were placed in chairs in a large arc around him; the chairs so far apart that they could not easily touch each other. He then asked each one separately what idea he or she had of the purpose of coming to school. To learn, was the first answer. To learn what? By pursuing this question, all the common exercises of the school were brought up by the children themselves; and various subjects of arts, science, and philosophy. Still Mr. Alcott intimated that this was not all; and at last some one said, "To behave well;" and in pursuing this expression into its meanings, they at last agreed that they came to learn to feel rightly, to think rightly, and to act rightly. A boy of seven years old suggested that the most important of these three was right action.

Simple as all this seems, it would hardly be believed what an evident exercise it was to the children, to be led of themselves to form and express these conceptions and few steps of reasoning. Every face was eager and interested. From right actions, the conversation naturally led into the means of bringing them out. And the necessity of feeling in earnest, of thinking clearly, and of school discipline, was talked over. School discipline was very carefully considered; both Mr. Alcott's duty, and the children's duties, also various means of producing attention, self-control, perseverance, faithfulness. Among these means, correction was mentioned; and, after a consideration of its nature and issues, they all agreed that it was necessary, and that they preferred Mr. Alcott should correct them rather than leave them in their faults, and that it was his duty to do so. Various punishments were mentioned, and hurting the body was admitted to be necessary and desirable whenever words were found insufficient to command the memory of conscience.

*　　*　　*

When children are committed to his charge very young, the first discipline to which he puts them is of the eye, by making them familiar with pictures. The art of Drawing has well been called the art of learning to see; and perhaps no person ever began to learn to draw, without astonishment at finding how imperfectly he had always been seeing. He finds that the most common forms are not only very falsely defined on his sense, but a vast deal that is before the eyes is entirely overlooked.

*　　*　　*

It is from considerations of this kind that Mr. Alcott very early presents to children pictured forms of things; and he selects them in the confidence that the general character of these forms will do much toward setting the direction of the current of activity, especially if we attend to and favor those primal sympathies with which Nature seems to wed different minds to different portions of the universe. But the practice of the eye in looking at forms, and that of the hand in imitating them, should be simultaneous. Mr. Alcott thinks the slate and pencil, or the chalk and blackboard, can hardly be given too early. The latter is even better than the former; for children should have free scope, as we find that their first shapings are usually gigantic. And is it not best that they should be so? Miniature, when it appears first in the order of development, seems to be always the effect of checked spirit or some artificial influence.

With such education of the eye, as a preliminary, reading and writing are begun simultaneously; and the former will be very much facilitated, and the latter come to perfection, in a much shorter time than by the usual mode. By copying print, which does not require such a sweep of hand as the script character, a clear image of each letter is gradually fixed in the mind; and while the graceful curves of the script are not attained till afterwards, yet they are attained quite as early as by the common method of beginning with them; and the clearness and distinctness of print is retained in the script, which, from being left to form itself so freely, becomes also characteristic of each individual's particular mind.

BRONSON ALCOTT, SUPERINTENDENT OF SCHOOLS AT CONCORD, MASS., DESCRIBES THE NORTH PRIMARY SCHOOL (1860) From *Reports of the Selectmen And Other Officers of The Town of Concord From March 7, 1859, to March 5, 1860, . . ., Also, The Report of the School Committee For The Year Ending April 1, 1860* (Concord, 1860), pp. 14–15.

This is a pleasant school and select. The children are comely; mostly bright, and well behaved. Their knowledge of the rudiments is commendable considering their ages, some of them being scarcely four, and none, I judge, much over ten years or so. They number over forty in all, and their attendance has been generally steady and punctual. The youngest of them print their spelling and other lessons on their slates; the older ones write handsomely some of them in their copy-books with the pen. All practice more or less on the black-board. (Please look in sometime, and see how delicately they use the pencil.) The mistress has happy expedients for interesting them in the proprieties of behavior, the pleasures of study. They sing prettily. Some of them take kindly to speaking. They are thoughtful too, and prompt at their recitations. I think them under good training; and forward for children admitted so lately into the mysteries of letters, and of their faculties. They are a happy group, and a benefit to see: a credit to themselves and to the families they come from. If a drawing master, I should be tempted to take some pretty portraits I could name.

Miss Hosmer is mistress of the art of persuasion. She takes a sisterly interest and comfort in her charge. She makes them pains-taking, mannerly; holding them fast and softly to her wishes by invisible threads,—the sunny countenance, sound sense, the kind regards. It is personal presence, the sway of manners, the power of a mechanism working unseen, for the benefit of giver and receiver.

Everything is favorable to a good school in this attractive neighborhood. It is the chairman's own: the children live near their school room, and are of interesting ages. It would be surprising if under all these advantages, the school were not attractive and successful.

The school appeared well at the examination, which was chiefly conducted by the teacher; Messrs. Keyes, Dr. Reynolds, and the Superintendent, assisting a little. Mr. Bull was present, and a few of the parents.

I regret to find so few calls noted in the register. I think I may commend such as being very delightful in themselves, besides very good for confession and repentance.

*   *   *

The school houses are ornaments of New England. Great improvements have been made upon the former ones, and there was need of it. Ours are all new. They might have been better placed. But the rooms are convenient generally and comfortable; ample in all cases, save the one now occupied by the Intermediate school. Most of them have a time-piece. Maps of the hemispheres and of the several countries, and of Concord town, adorn the walls.

Good desks, easy seats, and one to every child, small as he may be. Then to these advantages and facilities for study are added the blackboard, and a slate and pencil to the least. The under classes in the outer districts and the primaries, should have Philbrick's tablets. They are designed to occupy and interest them during the intervals coming between the lessons and out-door pastimes, while they please also and beguile them into some acquaintance with the rudiments; and spare the penalties and pains incident upon having nothing given them to do. I consider them as a necessary part of the child's outfit; as a gift and a pleasure he has waited for long and will approve.

His tasks shall seem irksome to him at best, and tedious with every attraction we can lend; by agreeable apartments, kind manners, lively illustration, sallies apt, pictures, conversation, the illusions of fable; by consulting his taste, his aptitudes for study and methods of work. As fas as in us lies we should cast around him every allurement to learning and the virtues, varying his studies with pleasures at home and out of doors. Let us catch his fancy and his heart by every lure. We cannot commence too soon, since "those who have the office of education should do most in their first years, for they can do more with half the power. And as some farmers believe their fields prove the most fertile which are sown during a mist, so do we reap more abundantly from what is sown during the first thick mist that crowned the morning of our childhood."

BRONSON ALCOTT ON METHODS OF TEACHING (c. 1860) From O. B.
Frothingham, *Transcendentalism in New England* (New York, 1880), pp. 275–81.

The school is the primary interest of the community. Every parent naturally desires a better education for his children than he received himself, and spends liberally of his substance for this pleasure; wisely hoping to make up his deficiencies in that way, and to complement himself in their better attainments; esteeming these the richest estate he can leave, and the fairest ornaments of his family name.

Especially have I wished to introduce the young to the study of their minds, the love of thinking; often giving examples of lessons in analysis and classification of their faculties. I think I may say that these exercises have given much pleasure, and have been found profitable alike to the teacher and the children. In most instances, I have closed my visits by reading some interesting story or parable. These have never failed of gaining attention, and in most cases, prompt responses. I consider these readings and colloquies as among the most profitable and instructive of the superintendent's labors.

The graceful exercise of singing has been introduced into some of the schools. It should prevail in all of them. It softens the manners, cultivates the voice, and purifies the taste of the children. It promotes harmony and good feelings. The old masters thought much of it as a discipline. "Let us sing" has the welcome sound of "Let us play,"—and is perhaps the child's prettiest translation of "Let us pray,"— admitting him soonest to the intimacy he seeks.

Conversations on words, paraphrases and translations of sentences, are the natural methods of opening the study of language. A child should never be suffered to lose sight of the prime fact that he is studying the realities of nature and of the mind through the picture books of language. Any teaching falling short of this is hollow and a wrong done to the mind.

For composition, let a boy keep his diary, write his letters, try his hand at defining from a dictionary and paraphrasing, and he will find ways of expressing himself simply as boys and men did before grammars were invented.

Teaching is a personal influence for the most part, and operating as a spirit unsuspected at the moment. I have wished to divine the secret source of success attained by any, and do justice to this; it seemed most becoming to regard any blemishes as of secondary account in the light of the acknowledged deserts. We require of each what she has to give, no more. Does the teacher awaken thought, strengthen the mind, kindle the affections, call the conscience, the common sense into lively and controlling activity, so promoting the love of study, the practice of the virtues; habits that shall accompany the children outwards into life? The memory is thus best cared for the end of study answered; the debt of teacher to parents, of parents to teacher discharged, and so the State's bounty best bestowed.

A little gymnasticon, a system of gestures for the body might be organized skilfully and become part of the daily exercises in our schools. Graceful steps, pretty musical airs, in accompaniment of songs—suiting the sentiment to the motions, the emotions, ideas of the child—would be conducive to health of body and mind alike. We shall adopt dancing presently as a natural training for the manners and morals of the young.

Conversation is the mind's mouth-piece, its best spokesman; the leader elect and prompter in teaching; practised daily, it should be added to the list of school studies; an art in itself, let it be used as such, and ranked as an accomplishment second to none that nature or culture can give. Certainly the best we can do is to teach ourselves and children how to talk. Let conversation displace much that passes current under the name of recitation; mostly sound and parrotry, a repeating by rote not by heart, unmeaning sounds from the memory and no more. "Take my mind a moment," says the teacher, "and see how things look through that prism," and the pupil sees prospects never seen before or surmised by him in that lively perspective.

*   *   *

Perhaps we are correcting the old affection for flogging at some risk of spoiling the boys of this generation. Girls have always known how to cover with shame any insult of that sort, but the power of persuasion comes slow as a promptitude to supersede its necessity. Who deals with a child, deals with a piece of divinity obeying laws as innate as those he transgresses and which he must treat tenderly, lest he put spiritual interests in jeopardy. Punishment must be just, else it cannot be accepted as good, and least of all by the wicked and weak.

The accomplished teacher combines in himself the art of teaching and of ruling; power over the intellect and the will, inspiration and persuasiveness. And this implies a double consciousness in its possessor that carries forward the teaching and ruling together; noting what transpires in motive as in act; the gift that in seeing controls. It is the sway of presence and of mien; a conversion of the will to his wishes, without which other gifts are of little avail.

Be sure the liveliest dispensations, the holiest, are his (the unruly boy's)—his as cordially as ours, and sought for as kindly. We must meet him where he is. Best to follow his bent if bent beautifully; else bending him gently, not fractiously, lest we snap or stiffen a stubbornness too stiff already. Gentleness now; the fair eye, the conquering glances straight and sure; the strong hand, if you must, till he fall penitent at the feet of Persuasion; the stroke of grace before the smiting of the birch; for only so is the conquest complete, and the victory the Lord's. If she is good enough she may strike strong and frequent, till thanks come for it; but who is she, much less he, that dares do it more than once, nor repents in sorrow and shame for the strokes given? Only 'the shining ones' may do it for good.

It is difficult to reach the sources of ignorance and consequent crime in a community like ours, calling itself free, and boasting of its right to do what it will. But freedom is a social not less than an individual concern, and the end of the State is to protect it. The first object of a free people is the preservation of their liberties. It becomes, then, their first duty to assume the training of all the children in the principles of right knowledge and virtue, as the only safeguard of their liberties. We cannot afford to wait at such hazards. The simplest humanities are also the least costly, and the nearest home. We should begin there. The State is stabbed at the hearthside and here liberty and honor are first sold. It is injured by family neglect, and should protect itself in securing its children's virtue against their parents' vices; for, by so doing, can it alone redeem its pledges to humanity and its citizens' liberties. A virtuous education is the greatest alms it can bestow on any of its children.

FRANCES WRIGHT CALLS FOR PUBLIC BOARDING SCHOOLS
(**1819**)   From *The Free Inquirer* (New York), December 12, 1829.

Having now traced with you what knowledge is in matter and in mind; what virtue is in human conduct, where its rules are to be sought, and how they may be found; tested, by the standard thus supplied, the ruling topic of discussion and instruction throughout this country; shown that, while this topic subtracts from the wealth of the country twenty millions per annum, and from the hearts and minds of the people social fellowship and common sense, it has in nature no real existence—is not knowledge, but only imagination—is not fact, but only theory; and, having shown, moreover, that theory can supply no subject matter of instruction; that the teaching of opinions is as erroneous in principle as it is dangerous in practice; that the duty of the instructor is simply to enrich the mind with knowledge, to awaken the eye, and the ear, and the touch, to the perception of things, the judgment to their comparison and arrangement, and to leave the free, unbiased mind to draw its own conclusions from the evidence thus collected,—I shall now present a few observations on the necessity of commencing, and gradually perfecting a radical reform in your existing outlays of time and money—on and in churches, theological colleges, privileged and exclusive seminaries of all descriptions, religious Sabbath schools, and all their aids and adjuncts of Bibles, tracts, missionaries, priests and preachers, multiplied and multiplying throughout the land, until they promise to absorb more capital than did the temple of Solomon, and to devour more of the first fruits of industry than did the tribe of Levi in the plenitude of its power;—on the necessity I say, of substituting for your present cumbrous, expensive, useless, or rather pernicious, system of partial, opinionative, and dogmatical instruction, one at once national, rational, and republican; one which shall take for its study our own world and our own nature; for its object the improvement of man; and for its means, the practical development of truth, the removal of temptations to evil, and the gradual equalization of human condition, human duties, and human enjoyments, by the equal diffusion of knowledge without distinction of class or sect—both of which distinctions are inconsistent with republican institutions as they are with reason and with common sense, with virtue and with happiness.

Time is it in this land to commence this reform. Time is it to check the ambition of an organized clergy, the demoralizing effects of a false system of law; to heal the strife fomented by sectarian religion and legal disputes; to bring down the pride of ideal wealth, and to raise honest industry to honor. Time is it to search out the misery in the land, and to heal it at the source. Time is it to remember the poor and the afflicted, ay! and the vicious and the depraved. Time is it to perceive that every sorrow which corrodes the human heart, every vice which diseases the body and the mind, every crime which startles the ear and sends back the blood affrighted to the heart—is the product of one evil, the foul growth from one root, the distorted progeny of one corrupt parent—IGNORANCE.

Time is it to perceive this truth; to proclaim it on the housetop, in the market place, in city and forest, throughout the land; to acknowledge it in the depths of our hearts, and to apply all our energies to the adoption of those salutary measures which this salutary truth spontaneously suggests. Time is it, I say, to turn our churches into halls of science, our schools of faith into schools of knowledge, our privileged colleges into state institutions for all the youth of the land. Time it is to arrest our speculations respecting unseen words and inconceivable mysteries, and to address our enquiries to the improvement of our human condition, and our efforts to the practical illustration of those beautiful principles of liberty and equality enshrined in the political institutions, and, first and chief, in the national declaration of independence.

And by whom and how, are these changes to be effected? By whom! And do a free people ask the question? By themselves. By themselves—*the people.* . . .

Hitherto, my friends, in government as in every branch of morals, we have but too much mistaken words for truths and forms for principles. To render men free, it sufficeth not to proclaim their liberty; to make them equal, it sufficeth not to call them so. True, the 4th of July '76 commenced a new era for our race. True, the sun of promise then rose upon the world. But let us not mistake for the fulness of light what was but its harbinger. Let us not conceive that man in signing the declaration of his rights secured their possession; that having framed the theory he had not, and hath not still, the practice to seek.

Your fathers, indeed, on the day from which dates your existence as a nation, opened the gates of the temple of human liberty. But think not they entered, nor that you have entered, the sanctuary. They passed not, nor have you passed, even the threshold.

Who speaks of liberty while the human mind is in chains? Who of equality while the thousands are in squalid wretchedness, the millions harrassed with health-destroying labor, the few afflicted with health-destroying idleness, and all tormented by health-destroying solicitude? Look abroad on the misery which is gaining on the land! Mark the strife, and the discord, and the jealousies, the shock of interests and opinions, the hatreds of sect, the estrangements of class, the pride of wealth, the debasement of poverty, the helplessness of youth unprotected, of age uncomforted, of industry unrewarded, of ignorance unenlightened, of vice unreclaimed, of misery unpitied, of sickness, hunger, and nakedness unsatisfied, unalleviated, and unheeded. Go! mark all the wrongs and the wretchedness with which the eye and the ear and the heart are familiar, and then echo in triumph and celebrate in jubilee the insulting declaration—*all men are free and equal!* . . .

The noble example of New England has been imitated by other states, until all not possessed of common schools blush for the popular remissness. But, after all, how can *common schools,* under their best form, and in fullest supply, effect even the purpose which they have in view?

The object proposed by common schools (if I rightly understand it) is to impart to the whole population those means for the acquirement of knowledge which are in common use: reading and writing. To these are added arithmetic, and, occasionally perhaps, some imperfect lessons in the simpler sciences. But, I would ask, supposing these institutions should even be made to embrace all the branches of intellectual knowledge, and, thus, science offered gratis to all the children of the land, how are the children of the very class, for whom we suppose the schools instituted, to be supplied with the food and raiment, or instructed in the trade necessary to their future subsistence, while they are following these studies? How are they, I ask, to be fed and clothed, when, as all facts show, the labor of the parents is often insufficient for their own sustenance, and, almost universally, inadequate to the provision of the family without the united efforts of all its members? In your manufacturing districts you have children worked for twelve hours a day; and, in the rapid and certain progress of the existing system, you will soon have them, as in England, *worked to death*, and yet unable, through the period of their miserable existence, to earn a pittance sufficient to satisfy the cravings of hunger. At this present time, what leisure or what spirit, think you, have the children of the miserable widows of Philadelphia, realizing, according to the most favorable estimate of your city and county committee, sixteen dollars per annum, for food and clothing—what leisure or what spirit may their children find for visiting a school, although the same should be open to them from sunrise to sunset? Or what leisure have usually the children of your most thriving mechanics, after their strength is sufficiently developed to spin, sew, weave, or wield a tool? It seems to me, my friends, that to build school houses nowadays is something like building churches. When you have them, you need some measure to ensure their being occupied.

But, as our time is short, and myself somewhat fatigued by continued exertions, I must hasten to the rapid development of the system of instruction and protection which has occurred to me as capable, and alone capable, of opening the door to universal reform.

In lieu of all common schools, high schools, colleges, seminaries, houses of refuge, or any other juvenile institution, instructional or protective, I would suggest that the state legislatures be directed (after laying off the whole in townships or hundreds) to organize, at suitable distances, and in convenient and healthy situations, establishments for the general reception of all the children resident within the said school district. These establishments to be devoted, severally, to children between a certain age. Say, the first to infants between two and four, or two and six, according to the density of the population, and such other local circumstances as might render a greater or less number of establishments necessary or practicable. The next to receive children from four to eight, or six to twelve years. The next from twelve to sixteen, or to an older age if found desirable. Each establishment to be furnished with instructors in every branch of knowledge, intellectual and operative, with all the apparatus, land, and conveniences necessary for the best development of all knowledge; the same, whether operative or intellectual, being always calculated to the age and strength of the pupils.

To obviate, in the commencement, every evil result possible from the first mixture of a young population, so variously raised in error or neglect, a due separation should be made in each establishment; by which means those entering with bad habits would be kept apart from the others until corrected. How rapidly reform may be effected on the plastic disposition of childhood, has been sufficiently proved in your houses of refuge, more especially when such establishments have been under *liberal* superintendence, as was formerly the case in New York. Under their orthodox directors, those asylums of youth have been converted into jails.

It will be understood that, in the proposed establishments, the children would pass from one to the other in regular succession, and that the parents, who would necessarily be resident in their close neighborhood, could visit the children at suitable hours, but, in no case, interfere with or interrupt the rules of the institution.

In the older establishments, the well directed and well protected labor of the pupil would, in time, suffice for, and, then, exceed, their own support; when the surplus might be devoted to the maintenance of the infant establishments.

In the beginning, and until all debt was cleared off, and so long as the same should be found favorable to the promotion of these best palladiums of a nation's happiness, a double tax might be at once expedient and politic.

First, a moderate tax per head for every child, to be laid upon its parents conjointly or divided between them, due attention being always paid to the varying strength of the two sexes, and to the undue depreciation which now rests on female labor. The more effectually to correct the latter injustice, as well as to consult the convenience of the industrious classes generally, this parental tax might be rendered payable either in money, or in labor, produce, or domestic manufactures, and should be continued for each child until the age when juvenile labor should be found, on the average, equivalent to the educational expenses, which, I have reason to believe, would be at twelve years.

This first tax on parents to embrace equally the whole population; as, however moderate, it would inculcate a certain forethought in all the human family; more especially where it is most wanted—in young persons, who, before they assumed the responsibility of parents, would estimate their fitness to meet it.

The second tax to be on property, increasing in percentage with the wealth of the individual. In this manner I conceive the rich would contribute, according to their riches, to the relief of the poor, and to the support of the state, by raising up its best bulwark—an enlightened and united generation.

Preparatory to, or connected with, such measures, a registry should be opened by the state, with offices through all the townships, where, on the birth of every child, or within a certain time appointed, the same should be entered, together with the names of its parents. When two years old, the parental tax should be payable, and the juvenile institution open for the child's reception; from which time forward it would be under the protective care and guardianship of the state, while it need never be removed from the daily, weekly, or frequent inspection of the parents.

Orphans, of course, would find here an open asylum. If possessed of property, a contribution would be paid from its revenue to the common educational fund; if unprovided, they would be sustained out of the same.

In these nurseries of a free nation, no inequality must be allowed to enter. Fed at a common board; clothed in a common garb, uniting neatness with simplicity and convenience; raised in the exercise of common duties, in the acquirement of the same knowledge and practice of the same industry, varied only according to individual taste and capabilities; in the exercise of the same virtues; in the enjoyment of the same pleasures; in the study of the same nature; in pursuit of the same object—their own and each other's happiness—say! would not such a race, when arrived at manhood, and womanhood work out the reform of society—perfect the free institutions of America?

ROBERT DALE OWEN CALLS FOR PUBLIC BOARDING SCHOOLS
(**1830**)   From *The Working Man's Advocate*, vol. I, p. 4.

If state schools are to be, as now in New England, common day schools only, we do not perceive how either of these requisitions are to be fulfilled. In republican schools, there must be no temptation to the growth of aristocratical prejudices. The pupils must learn to consider themselves as fellow citizens, as equals. Respect ought to be paid, and will always be paid, to virtue and to talent; but it ought not to be paid to riches, or withheld from poverty. Yet, if the children from these state schools are to go every evening, the one to his wealthy parent's soft carpeted drawing room, and the other to its poor father's or widowed mother's comfortless cabin, will they return the next day as friends and equals? He knows little of human nature who thinks they will.

*   *   *

We conceive, then, that state schools, to be republican, efficient, and acceptable to all, must receive the children, not for six hours a day, but altogether; must feed them, clothe them, lodge them; must direct not their studies only, but their occupations and amusements; must care for them until their education is completed, and then only abandon them to the world, as useful, intelligent, virtuous citizens.

THE COMMON
SCHOOL
MOVEMENT

1219

We have yet to learn, that the world can go on without two classes, one to ride and the other to be ridden; one to roll in the luxuries of life, and the other to struggle with its hardships. We have yet to learn how to amalgamate these classes; to make of men, not fractions of human beings, sometimes mere producing machines, sometimes mere consuming drones, but integral republicans, at once the creators and the employers of riches, at once masters and servants, governors and governed.

How can this most desirable and most republican amalgamation take place? By uniting theory to practice, which have been too long kept separate. By combining mechanical and agricultural with literary and scientific instruction. By making every scholar a workman, and every workman a scholar. By associating cultivation and utility, the productive arts and the abstract sciences.

The system of Public Education, then, which we consider capable, and only capable, of regenerating this nation, and of establishing practical virtue and republican equality among us, is one which provides for all children at all times; receiving them at the earliest age their parents chose to entrust them to the national care, feeding, clothing, and educating them, until the age of majority.

We propose that all the children so adopted should receive the same food; should be dressed in the same simple clothing; should experience the same kind treatment; should be taught (until their professional education commences) the same branches; in a word, that nothing savoring of inequality, nothing reminding them of the pride of riches or the contempt of poverty, should be suffered to enter these republican safeguards of a young nation of equals. We propose that the destitute widow's child or the orphan boy should share the public care equally with the heir to a princely estate; so that all may become, not in word but in deed and in feeling, free and equal.

THOREAU ON READING (1854)   From Henry David Thoreau, *Walden, or Life in the Woods* (Boston, 1893), pp. 156–60, 171–73.

With a little more deliberation in the choice of their pursuits, all men would perhaps become essentially students and observers, for certainly their nature and destiny are interesting to all alike. In accumulating property for ourselves or our posterity, in founding a family or a state, or acquiring fame even, we are mortal; but in dealing with truth we are immortal, and need fear no change nor accident. The oldest Egyptian or Hindoo philosopher raised a corner of the veil from the statue of the divinity; and still the trembling robe remains raised, and I gaze upon as fresh a glory as he did, since it was I in him that was then so bold, and it is he in me that now reviews the vision. No dust has settled on that robe; no time has elapsed since that divinity was revealed. That time which we really improve, or which is improvable, is neither past, present, nor future.

My residence was more favorable, not only to thought, but to serious reading, than a university; and though I was beyond the range of the ordinary circulating library, I had more than ever come within the influence of those books which circulate round the world, whose sentences were first written on bark, and are now merely copied from time to time on to linen paper. Says the poet Mir Camar Uddin Mast, "Being seated, to run through the region of the spiritual world; I have had this advantage in books. To be intoxicated by a single glass of wine; I have experienced this pleasure when I have drunk the liquor of the esoteric doctrines." I kept Homer's Iliad on my table through the summer, though I looked at his page only now and then. Incessant labor with my hands, at first, for I had my house to finish and my beans to hoe at the same time, made more study impossible. Yet I sustained myself by the prospect of such reading in future. I read one or two shallow books of travel in the intervals of my work, till that employment made me ashamed of myself, and I asked where it was then that *I* lived.

The student may read Homer or Æschylus in the Greek without danger of dissipation or luxuriousness, for it implies that he in some measure emulate their heroes, and consecrate morning hours to their pages. The heroic books, even if printed in the character of our mother tongue, will always be in a language dead to degenerate times; and we must laboriously seek the meaning of each word and line, conjecturing a larger sense than common use permits out of what wisdom and valor and generosity we have. The modern cheap and fertile press, with all its translations, has done little to bring us nearer to the heroic writers of antiquity. They seem as solitary, and the letter in which they are printed as rare and curious, as ever. It is worth the expense of youthful days and costly hours, if you learn only some words of an ancient language, which are raised out of the trivialness of the street, to be perpetual suggestions and provocations. It is not in vain that the farmer remembers and repeats the few Latin words which he has heard. Men sometimes speak as if the study of the classics would at length make way for more modern and practical studies; but the adventurous student will always study classics, in whatever language they may be written and however ancient they may be. For what are the classics but the noblest recorded thoughts of man? They are the only oracles which are not decayed, and there are such answers to the most modern inquiry in them as Delphi and Dodona never gave. We might as well omit to study Nature because she is old. To read well, that is, to read true books in a true spirit, is a noble exercise, and one that will task the reader more than any exercise which the customs of the day esteem. It requires a training such as the athletes underwent, the steady intention almost of the whole life to this object. Books must be read as deliberately and reservedly as they were written. It is not enough even to be able to speak the language of that nation by which they are written, for there is a memorable interval between the spoken and the written language, the language heard and the language read. The one is commonly transitory, a sound, a tongue, a dialect merely, almost brutish, and we learn it unconsciously, like the brutes, of our mothers. The other is the maturity and experience of that; if that is our mother tongue, this is our father tongue, a reserved and select expression, too significant to be heard by the ear, which we must be born again in order to speak. The crowds of men who merely *spoke* the Greek and Latin tongues in the Middle Ages were not entitled by the accident of birth to *read* the works of genius written in those languages; for these were not written in that Greek or Latin which they knew, but in the select language of literature. They had not learned the nobler dialects of Greece and Rome, but the very materials on which they were written were waste paper to them, and they prized instead a cheap contemporary literature. But when the several nations of Europe had acquired distinct though rude written languages of their own, sufficient for the purposes of their rising literatures, then first learning revived, and scholars were enabled to discern from that remoteness the treasures of antiquity. What the Roman and Grecian multitude could not *hear,* after the lapse of ages a few scholars *read,* and a few scholars only are still reading it.

However much we may admire the orator's occasional bursts of eloquence, the noblest written words are commonly as far behind or above the fleeting spoken language as the firmament with its stars is behind the clouds. *There* are the stars, and they who can may read them. The astronomers forever comment on and observe them. They are not exhalations like our daily colloquies and vaporous breath. What is called eloquence in the forum is commonly found to be rhetoric in the study. The orator yields to the inspiration of a transient occasion, and speaks to the mob before him, to those who can *hear* him; but the writer, whose more equable life is his occasion, and who would be distracted by the event and the crowd which inspire the orator, speaks to the intellect and heart of mankind, to all in any age who can *understand* him.

No wonder that Alexander carred the Iliad with him on his expeditions in a precious casket. A written word is the choicest of relics. It is something at once more intimate with us and more universal than any other work of art. It is the work of art nearest to life itself. It may be translated into every language, and not only be read but actually breathed from all human lips;—not be represented on canvas or in marble only, but be carved out of the breath of life itself. The symbol of an ancient man's thought becomes a modern man's speech. Two thousand summers have imparted to the monuments of Grecian literature, as to her marbles, only a maturer golden and autumnal tint, for they have carried their own serene and celestial atmosphere into all lands to protect them against the corrosion of time. Books are the treasured wealth of the world and the fit inheritance of generations and nations. Books, the oldest and the best, stand naturally and rightfully on the shelves of every cottage. They have no cause of their own to plead, but while they enlighten and sustain the reader his common sense will not refuse them. Their authors are a natural and irresistible aristocracy in every society, and, more than kings or emperors, exert an influence on mankind. When the illiterate and perhaps scornful trader has earned by enterprise and industry his coveted leisure and independence, and is admitted to the circles of wealth and fashion, he turns inevitably at last to those still higher but yet inaccessible circles of intellect and genius, and is sensible only of the imperfection of his culture and the vanity and insufficiency of all his riches, and further proves his good sense by the pains which he takes to secure for his children that intellectual culture whose want he so keenly feels; and thus it is that he becomes the founder of a family.

Those who have not learned to read the ancient classics in the language in which they were written must have a very imperfect knowledge of the history of the human race; for it is remarkable that no transcript of them has ever been made into any modern tongue, unless our civilization itself may be regarded as such a transcript. Homer has never yet been printed in English, nor Æschylus, nor Virgil even,—works as refined, as solidly done, and as beautiful almost as the morning itself; for later writers, say what we will of their genius, have rarely, if ever, equalled the elaborate beauty and finish and the lifelong and heroic literary labors of the ancients. They only talk of forgetting them who never knew them. It will be soon enough to forget them when we have the learning and the genius which will enable us to attend to and appreciate them. That age will be rich indeed when those relics which we call Classics, and the still older and more than classic but even less known Scriptures of the nations, shall have still further accumulated, when the Vaticans shall be filled with Vedas and Zendavestas and Bibles, with Homers and Dantes and Shakespeares, and all the centuries to come shall have successively deposited their trophies in the forum of the world. By such a pile we may hope to scale heaven at last.

*   *   *

The best books are not read even by those who are called good readers. What does our Concord culture amount to? There is in this town, with a very few exceptions, no taste for the best or for very good books even in English literature, whose words all can read and spell. Even the college-bred and so-called liberally educated men here and elsewhere have really little or no acquaintance with the English classics; and as for the recorded wisdom of mankind, the ancient classics and Bibles, which are accessible to all who will know of them, there are the feeblest efforts anywhere made to become acquainted with them. I know a woodchopper, of middle age, who takes a French paper, not for news as he says, for he is above that, but to "keep himself in practice," he being a Canadian by birth; and when I ask him what he considers the best thing he can do in this world, he says, beside this, to keep up and add to his English. This is about as much as the college-bred generally do or aspire to do, and they take an English paper for the purpose. One who has just come from reading perhaps one of the best English books will find how many with whom he can converse about it? Or suppose he comes from reading a Greek or Latin classic in the original, whose praises are familiar even to the so-called illiterate; he will find nobody at all to speak to, but must keep silence about it. Indeed, there is hardly the professor in our colleges, who, if he has mastered the difficulties of the language, has proportionally mastered the difficulties of the wit and poetry of a Greek poet, and has any sympathy to impart to the alert and heroic reader; and as for the sacred Scriptures, or Bibles of mankind, who in this town can tell me even their titles? Most men do not know that any nation but the Hebrews have had a scripture. A man, any man, will go considerably out of his way to pick up a silver dollar; but here are golden words, which the wisest men of antiquity have uttered, and whose worth the wise of every succeeding age have assured us of;—and yet we learn to read only as far as Easy Reading, the primers and classbooks, and when we leave school, the "Little Reading," and story-books, which are for boys and beginners; and our reading, our conversation and thinking, are all on a very low level, worthy only of pygmies and manikins.

I aspire to be acquainted with wiser men than this our Concord soil has produced, whose names are hardly known here. Or shall I hear the name of Plato and never read his book? As if Plato were my townsman and I never saw him,—my next neighbor and I never heard him speak or attended to the wisdom of his words. But how actually is it? His Dialogues, which contain what was immortal in him, lie on the next shelf, and yet I never read them. We are underbred and low-lived and illiterate; and in this respect I confess I do not make any very broad distinction between the illiterateness of my townsman who cannot read at all and the illiterateness of him who has learned to read only what is for children and feeble intellects. We should be as good as the worthies of antiquity, but partly by first

THE COMMON SCHOOL MOVEMENT

knowing how good they were. We are a race of tit-men, and soar but little higher in our intellectual flights than the columns of the daily paper.

*　　*　　*

We boast that we belong to the Nineteenth Century and are making the most rapid strides of any nation. But consider how little this village does for its own culture. I do not wish to flatter my townsmen, nor to be flattered by them, for that will not advance either of us. We need to be provoked,—goaded like oxen, as we are, into a trot. We have a comparatively decent system of common schools, schools for infants only; but excepting the half-starved Lyceum in the winter, and latterly the puny beginning of a library suggested by the State, no school for ourselves. We spend more on almost any article of bodily aliment or ailment than on our mental aliment. It is time that we had uncommon schools, that we did not leave off our education when we begin to be men and women. It is time that villages were universities, and their elder inhabitants the fellows of universities, with leisure—if they are, indeed, so well off—to pursue liberal studies the rest of their lives. Shall the world be confined to one Paris or one Oxford forever? Cannot students be boarded here and get a liberal education under the skies of Concord? Can we not hire some Abélard to lecture to us? Alas! what with foddering the cattle and tending the store, we are kept from school too long, and our education is sadly neglected. In this country, the village should in some respects take the place of the nobleman of Europe. It should be the patron of the fine arts. It is rich enough. It wants only the magnanimity and refinement. It can spend money enough on such things as farmers and traders value, but it is thought Utopian to propose spending money for things which more intelligent men know to be of far more worth. This town has spent seventeen thousand dollars on a town-house, thank fortune or politics, but probably it will not spend so much on living wit, the true meat to put into that shell, in a hundred years. The one hundred and twenty-five dollars annually subscribed for a Lyceum in the winter is better spent than any other equal sum raised in the town. If we live in the Nineteenth Century, why should we not enjoy the advantages which the Nineteenth Century offers? Why should our life be in any respect provincial? If we will read newspapers, why not skip the gossip of Boston and take the best newspaper in the world at once?—not be sucking the pap of "neutral family" papers, or browsing "Olive-Branches" here in New England. Let the reports of all the learned societies come to us, and we will see if they know anything. Why should we leave it to Harper & Brothers and Redding & Co. to select our reading? As the nobleman of cultivated taste surrounds himself with whatever conduces to his culture,—genius—learning—wit—books—paintings—statuary—music—philosophical instruments, and the like; so let the village do,—not stop short at a pedagogue, a parson, a sexton, a parish library, and three select-men, because our Pilgrim forefathers got through a cold winter once on a bleak rock with these. To act collectively is according to the spirit of our institutions; and I am confident that, as our circumstances are more flourishing, our means are greater than the nobleman's. New England can hire all the wise men in the world to come and teach her, and board them round the while, and not be provincial at all. That is the *uncommon* school we want. Instead of noblemen, let us have noble villages of men. If it is necessary, omit one bridge over the river, go round a little there, and throw one arch at least over the darker gulf of ignorance which surrounds us.

RALPH WALDO EMERSON CALLS FOR A DECLARATION OF INDEPENDENCE FOR THE AMERICAN SCHOLAR (1837)

From "The American Scholar," *Nature, Addresses and Lectures* (Boston, 1876), pp. 81–87, 94–96, 100–106, 113–15.

Mr. President and Gentlemen:

I greet you on the recommencement of our literary year. Our anniversary is one of hope, and, perhaps, not enough of labor. We do not meet for games of strength or skill, for the recitation of histories, tragedies, and odes, like the ancient Greeks; for parliaments of love and poesy, like the Troubadours; nor for the advancement of science, like our contemporaries in the British and European capitals. Thus far, our holiday has been simply a friendly sign of the survival of the love of letters amongst a people too busy to give to letters any more. As such it is precious as the sign of an indestructible instinct. Perhaps the time is already come when it ought to be, and will be, something else; when the sluggard intellect of this continent will look from under its iron lids and fill the postponed expectation of the world with something better than the exertions of mechanical skill. Our day of dependence, our long apprenticeship to the learning of other lands, draws to a close. The millions that around us are rushing into life, cannot always be fed on the sere remains of foreign harvests. Events, actions arise, that must be sung, that will sing themselves. Who can doubt that poetry will review and lead in a new age, as the star in the constellation Harp, which now flames in our Zenith, astronomers announce, shall one day be the polestar for a thousand years?

In this hope I accept the topic which not only usage but the nature of our association seem to prescribe to this day—the American Scholar. Year by year we come hither to read one more chapter of his biography. Let us inquire what light new days and events have thrown on his character and his hopes.

It is one of those fables which out of an unknown antiquity convey an unlooked-for wisdom, that the gods, in the beginning, divided Man into men, that he might be more helpful to himself; just as the hand was divided into fingers, the better to answer its end.

The old fable covers a doctrine ever new and sublime; that there is One Man—present to all particular man only partially, or through one faculty; and that you must take the whole society to find the whole man. Man is not a farmer, or a professor, or an engineer, but he is all. Man is priest, and scholar, and statesman, and producer, and soldier. In the *divided* or social state these functions are parceled out to individuals, each of whom aims to do his stint of the joint work, whilst each other performs his. The fable implies that the individual, to possess himself, must sometimes return from his own labor to embrace all the other laborers. But, unfortunately, this original unit, this fountain of power, has been so distributed to multitudes, has been so minutely subdivided and peddled out, that it is spilled into drops, and cannot be gathered. The state of society is one in which the members have suffered amputation from the trunk, and strut about so many walking monsters—a good finger, a neck, a stomach, an elbow, but never a man.

Man is thus metamorphosed into a thing, into many things. The planter, who is Man sent out into the field to gather food, is seldom cheered by any idea of the true dignity of his ministry. He sees his bushel and his cart, and nothing beyond, and sinks into the farmer, instead of Man on the farm. The tradesman scarcely ever gives an ideal worth to his work, but is ridden by the routine of his craft, and the soul is subject to dollars. The priest becomes a form; the attorney a statute-book; the mechanic a machine; the sailor a rope of the ship.

In this distribution of functions the scholar is the delegated intellect. In the right state he is *Man Thinking*. In the degenerate state, when the victim of society, he tends to become a mere thinker, or still worse, the parrot of other men's thinking.

In this view of him, as Man Thinking, the theory of his office is contained. Him Nature solicits with all her placid, all her monitory pictures; him the past instructs; him the future invites. Is not indeed every man a student, and do not all things exist for the student's behoof? And, finally, is not the true scholar the only true master? But the old oracle said, "All things have two handles: beware of the wrong one." In life, too often, the scholar errs with mankind and forfeits his privilege. Let us see him in his school, and consider him in reference to the main influences he receives.

I. The first in time and the first in importance of the influences upon the mind is that of nature. Every day, the sun; and, after sunset, Night and her stars. Ever the winds blow; ever the grass grows. Every day, men and women, conversing, beholding and beholden. The scholar is he of all men whom this spectacle most engages. He must settle its value in his mind. What is nature to him? There is never a beginning, there is never an end, to the inexplicable continuity of this web of God, but always circular power returning into itself. Therein it resembles his own spirit, whose beginning, whose ending, he never can find—so entire, so boundless. Far too as her splendors shine, system on system shooting like rays, upward, downward, without center, without circumference—in the mass and in the particle, Nature hastens to render account of herself to the mind. Classification begins. To the young mind every thing is individual, stands by itself. By and by, it finds how to join two things and see in them one nature; then three, they three thousand; and so, tyrannied over by its own unifying instinct, it goes on tying things together, diminishing anomalies, discovering roots running underground whereby contrary and remote things cohere and flower out from one stem. It presently learns that since the dawn of history there has been a constant accumulation and classifying of facts. But what is classification but the perceiving that these objects are not chaotic, and are not foreign, but have a law which is also a law of the human mind? The astronomer discovers that geometry, a pure abstraction of the human mind, is the measure of planetary motion. The chemist finds proportions and intelligible method throughout matter; and science is nothing but the finding of analogy, identity, in the most remote parts. The ambitious soul sits down before each refractory fact; one after another reduces all strange constitutions, all new powers, to their class and their law, and goes on forever to animate the last fiber of organization, the outskirts of nature, by insight.

Thus to him, to this schoolboy under the bending dome of day, is suggested that he and it proceed from one root; one is leaf and one is flower; relation, sympathy, stirring in every vein. And what is that root? Is not that the soul of his soul? A thought too bold; a dream too wild. Yet when this spiritual light shall have revealed the law of more earthly natures—when he has learned to worship the soul, and to see that the natural philosophy that now is, is only the first groupings of its gigantic hand, he shall look forward to an ever expanding knowledge as to a becoming creator. He shall see that nature is the opposite of the soul, answering to it part for part. One is seal and one is print. Its beauty is the beauty of his own mind. Its laws are the laws of his own mind. Nature then becomes to him the measure of his attainments. So much of nature as he is ignorant of, so much of his own mind does he not yet possess. And, in fine, the ancient precept, "Know thyself," and the modern precept, "Study nature," become at last one maxim.

II. The next great influence into the spirit of the scholar is the mind of the Past—in whatever form, whether of literature, of art, of institutions, that mind is inscribed. Books are the best type of the influence of the past, and perhaps we shall get at the truth—learn the amount of this influence more conveniently—by considering their value alone.

The theory of books is noble. The scholar of the first age received into him the world around; brooded thereon; gave it the new arrangement of his own mind, and uttered it again. It came into his life; it went out from him truth. It came to him short-lived actions; it went out from him immortal thoughts. It came to him business; it went from him poetry. It was dead fact; now, it is quick thought. It can stand, it can go. It now endures, it now flies, it now inspires. Precisely in proportion to the depth of mind from which it issued, so high does it soar, so long does it sing.

✳ ✳ ✳

III. There goes in the world a notion that the scholar should be a recluse, a valetudinarian—as unfit for any handiwork or public labor as a penknife for an axe. The so-called "practical men" sneer at speculative men, as if, because they speculate or *see*, they could do nothing. I have heard it said that the clergy—who are always, more universally than any other class, the scholars of their day—are addressed as women; that the rough, spontaneous conversation of men they do not hear, but only a mincing and diluted speech. They are often virtually disfranchised; and indeed there are advocates for their celibacy. As far as this is true of the studious classes, it is not just and wise. Action is with the scholar subordinate, but it is essential. Without it he is not yet man. Without it thought can never ripen into truth. Whilst the world hangs before the eye as a cloud of beauty, we cannot even see its beauty. Inaction is cowardice, but there can be no scholar without the heroic mind. The preamble of thought, the transition through which it passes from the unconscious to the conscious is action. Only so much do I know, as I have lived. Instantly we know whose words are loaded with life, and whose not.

The world—this shadow of the soul, or *other me*—lies wide around. Its attractions are the keys which unlock my thoughts and make me acquainted with myself. I run eagerly into this resounding tumult. I grasp the hands of those next me, and take my place in the ring to suffer and to work, taught by an instinct that so shall the dumb abyss be vocal with speech. I pierce its order; I dissipate its fear; I dispose of it within the circuit of my expanding life. So much only of life as I know by experience, so much of the wilderness have I vanquished and planted, or so far have I extended my being, my dominion. I do not see how any man can afford, for the sake of his nerves and his nap, to spare any action in which he can partake. It is pearls and rubies to his discourse. Drudgery, calamity, exasperation, want, are instructors in eloquence and wisdom. The true scholar grudges every opportunity of action past by, as a loss of power. It is the raw material out of which the intellect molds her splendid products. A strange process, too, this by which experience is converted into thought, as a mulberry leaf is converted into satin. The manufacture goes forward at all hours.

✳ ✳ ✳

I have now spoken of the education of the scholar by nature, by books, and by action. It remains to say somewhat of his duties.

They are such as become Man Thinking. They may all be comprised in self-trust. The office of the scholar is to cheer, to raise, and to guide men by showing them facts amidst appearances. He plies the slow, unhonored, and unpaid task of observation. Flamsteed and Herschel, in their glazed observatories, may catalogue the stars with the praise of all men, and the results being splendid and useful, honor is sure. But he, in his private observatory, cataloguing obscure and nebulous stars of the human mind, which as yet no man has thought of as such—watching days and months sometimes for a few facts; correcting still his old records;—must relinquish display and immediate fame. In the long period of his preparation he must betray often an ignorance and shiftlessness in popular arts, incurring the disdain of the able who shoulder him aside. Long he must stammer in his speech; often forgo the living for the dead. Worse yet, he must accept—how often!—poverty and solitude. For the ease and pleasure of treading the old road, accepting the fashions, the education, the religion of society, he takes the cross of making his own, and, of course, the self-accusation, the faint heart, the frequent uncertainty and loss of time, which are the nettles and tangling vines in the way of the self-relying and self-directed; and the state of virtual hostility in which he seems to stand to society, and especially to educated society. For all this loss and scorn, what offset? He is to find consolation in exercising the highest function of human nature. He is one who raises himself from private considerations and breathes and lives on public and illustrious thoughts. He is the world's eye. He is the world's heart. He is to resist the vulgar prosperity that retrogrades ever to barbarism, by preserving and communicating heroic sentiments, noble biographies, melodious verse, and the conclusions of history. Whatsoever oracles the human heart, in all emergencies, in all solemn hours, has uttered as its commentary on the world of actions—these he shall receive and impart. And whatsoever new verdict Reason from her inviolable seat pronounces on the passing men and events of today—this he shall hear and promulgate.

*   *   *

Another sign of our times, also marked by an analogous political movement, is the new importance given to the single person. Everything that tends to insulate the individual—to surround him with barriers of natural respect, so that each man shall feel the world is his, and man shall treat with man as a sovereign state with a sovereign state—tends to true union as well as greatness. "I learned," said the melancholy Pestalozzi, "that no man in God's wide earth is either willing or able to help any other man." Help must come from the bosom alone. The scholar is that man who must take up into himself all the ability of the time, all the contributions of the past, all the hopes of the future. He must be an university of knowledges. If there be one lesson more than another which should pierce his ear, it is, The world is nothing, the man is all; in yourself is the law of all nature, and you know not yet how a globule of sap ascends; in yourself slumbers the whole of Reason; it is for you to know all; it is for you to dare all. Mr. President and Gentlemen, this confidence in the unsearched might of man belongs by all motives, by all prophecy, by all preparation, to the American Scholar. We have listened too long to the courtly

muses of Europe. The spirit of the American freeman is already suspected to be timid, imitative, tame. Public and private avarice make the air we breathe thick and fat. The scholar is decent, indolent, complaisant. See already the tragic consequence. The mind of this country, taught to aim at low objects, eats upon itself. There is no work for any but the decorous and the complaisant. Young men of the fairest promise, who begin life upon our shores, inflated by the mountain winds, shined upon by all the stars of God, find the earth below not in unison with these, but are hindered from action by the disgust which the principles on which business is managed inspire, and turn drudges, or die of disgust, some of them suicides. What is the remedy? They did not yet see, and thousands of young men as hopeful now crowding to the barriers for the career do not yet see, that if the single man plant himself indomitably on his instincts, and there abide, the huge world will come round to him. Patience—patience; with the shades of all the good and great for company; and for solace and perspective of your own infinite life; and for work the study and the communication of principles, the making those instincts prevalent, the conversion of the world. Is it not the chief disgrace in the world, not to be an unit;—not to be reckoned one character;—not to yield that peculiar fruit which each man was created to bear, but to be reckoned in the gross, in the hundred, or the thousand, of the party, the section, to which we belong; and our opinion predicted geographically as the north, or the south? Not so, brothers and friends—please God, ours shall not be so. We will walk on our own feet; we will work with our own hands; we will speak our own minds. The study of letters shall be no longer a name for pity, for doubt, and for sensual indulgence. The dread of man and the love of man shall be a wall of defense and a wreath of joy around all. A nation of men will for the first time exist, because each believes himself inspired by the Divine Soul which also inspires all men.

RALPH WALDO EMERSON, "SELF-RELIANCE" (1841)   From Bliss Perry, ed.,
Selections from the Prose Works of Ralph Waldo Emerson (Boston, 1926), pp. 96–98, 99,
103, 105, 114–17.

I read the other day some verses written by an eminent painter which were original and not conventional. The soul always hears an admonition in such lines, let the subject be what it may. The sentiment they instil is of more value than any thought they may contain. To believe your own thought, to believe that what is true for you in your private heart is true for all men,—that is genius. Speak your latent conviction, and it shall be the universal sense; for the inmost in due time becomes the outmost, and our first thought is rendered back to us by the trumpets of the Last Judgment. Familiar as the voice of the mind is to each, the highest merit we ascribe to Moses, Plato and Milton is that they set at naught books and traditions, and spoke not what men, but what they thought. A man should learn to detect and watch that gleam of light which flashes across his mind from within, more than the lustre of the firmament of bards and sages. Yet he dismisses without notice his thought, because it is his. In every work of genius we recognize our own rejected thoughts; they come back to us with a certain alienated majesty. Great works of art have no more affecting lesson for us than this. They teach us to abide by our spontaneous impression with good-humored inflexibility then most when the whole cry of voices is on the other side. Else to-morrow a stranger will say with masterly good sense precisely what we have thought and felt all the time, and we shall be forced to take with shame our own opinion from another.

There is a time in every man's education when he arrives at the conviction that envy is ignorance; that imitation is suicide; that he must take himself for better for worse as his portion; that though the wide universe is full of good, no kernel of nourishing corn can come to him but through his toil bestowed on that plot of ground which is given to him to till. The power which resides in him is new in nature, and none but he knows what that is which he can do, nor does he know until he has tried. Not for nothing one face, one character, one fact, makes much impression on him, and another none. This sculpture in the memory is not without preëstablished harmony. The eye was placed where one ray should fall, that it might testify of that particular ray. We but half express ourselves, and are ashamed of that divine idea which each of us represents. It may be safely trusted as proportionate and of good issues, so it be faithfully imparted, but God will not have his work made manifest by cowards. A man is relieved and gay when he has put his heart into his work and done his best; but what he has said or done otherwise shall give him no peace. It is a deliverance which does not deliver. In the attempt his genius deserts him; no muse befriends; no invention, no hope.

Trust thyself: every heart vibrates to that iron string. Accept the place the divine providence has found for you, the society of your contemporaries, the connection of events. Great men have always done so, and confided themselves childlike to the genius of their age, betraying their perception that the absolutely trustworthy was seated at their heart, working through their hands, predominating in all their being. And we are now men, and must accept in the highest mind the same transcendent destiny; and not minors and invalids in a protected corner, not cowards fleeing before a revolution, but guides, redeemers and benefactors, obeying the Almighty effort and advancing on Chaos and the Dark.

What pretty oracles nature yields us on this text in the face and behavior of children, babes, and even brutes! That divided and rebel mind, that distrust of a sentiment because our arithmetic has computed the strength and means opposed to our purpose, these have not. Their mind being whole, their eye is as yet unconquered, and when we look in their faces we are disconcerted. Infancy conforms to nobody; all conform to it; so that one babe commonly makes four or five out of the adults who prattle and play to it. So God has armed youth and puberty and manhood no less with its own piquancy and charm, and made it enviable and gracious and its claims not to be put by, if it will stand by itself. Do not think the youth has no force, because he cannot speak to you and me. Hark! in the next room his voice is sufficiently clear and emphatic. It seems he knows how to speak to his contemporaries. Bashful or bold then, he will know how to make us seniors very unnecessary.

The nonchalance of boys who are sure of a dinner, and would disdain as much as a lord to do or say aught to conciliate one, is the healthy attitude of human nature. . . .

. . . Society everywhere is in conspiracy against the manhood of every one of its members. Society is a joint-stock company, in which the members agree, for the better securing of his bread to each shareholder, to surrender the liberty and culture of the eater. The virtue in most request is conformity. Self-reliance is its aversion. It loves not realities and creators, but names and customs.

Whoso would be a man, must be a nonconformist. He who would gather immortal palms must not be hindered by the name of goodness, but must explore if it be goodness. Nothing is at last sacred but the integrity of your own mind. Absolve you to yourself, and you shall have the suffrage of the world. I remember an answer which when quite young I was prompted to make to a valued adviser who was wont to importune me with the dear old doctrines of the church. On my saying, "What have I to do with the sacredness of traditions, if I live wholly from within?" my friend suggested,—"But these impulses may be from below, not from above." I replied, "They do not seem to me to be such; but if I am the Devil's child, I will live then from the Devil." No law can be sacred to me but that of my nature. Good and bad are but names very readily transferable to that or this; the only right is what is after my constitution; the only wrong what is against it. A man is to carry himself in the presence of all opposition as if everything were titular and ephemeral but he. I am ashamed to think how easily we capitulate to badges and names, to large societies and dead institutions. Every decent and well-spoken individual affects and sways me more than is right. I ought to go upright and vital, and speak the rude truth in all ways.

*   *   *

The other terror that scares us from self-trust is our consistency; a reverence for our past act or word because the eyes of others have no other data for computing our orbit than our past acts, and we are loth to disappoint them.

But why should you keep your head over your shoulder? Why drag about this corpse of your memory, lest you contradict somewhat you have stated in this or that public place? Suppose you should contradict yourself, what then? It seems to be a rule of wisdom never to rely on your memory alone, scarcely, even in acts of pure memory, but to bring the past for judgment into the thousand-eyed present, and live ever in a new day. In your metaphysics you have denied personality to the Deity, yet when the devout motions of the soul come, yield to them heart and life, though they should clothe God with shape and color. Leave your theory, as Joseph his coat in the hand of the harlot, and flee.

A foolish consistency is the hobgoblin of little minds, adored by little statesmen and philosophers and divines. With consistency a great soul has simply nothing to do. He may as well concern himself with his shadow on the wall. Speak what you think now in hard words and to-morrow speak what to-morrow thinks in hard words again, though it contradict everything you said to-day.—"Ah, so you shall be sure to be misunderstood."—Is it so bad then to be misunderstood? Pythagoras was misunderstood, and Socrates, and Jesus, and Luther, and Copernicus, and Galileo, and Newton, and every pure and wise spirit that ever took flesh. To be great is to be misunderstood.

RALPH WALDO EMERSON ON EDUCATION (1876)   From "Education,"
Lectures and Biographical Sketches (Boston, 1884), vol. X, pp. 130–36.

It is ominous, a presumption of crime, that this word Education has so cold, so hopeless a sound. A treatise on education, a convention for education, a lecture, a system, affects us with slight paralysis and a certain yawning of the jaws. We are not encouraged when the law touches it with its fingers. Education should be as broad as man. Whatever elements are in him that should foster and demonstrate. If he be dexterous, his tuition should make it appear; if he be capable of dividing men by the trenchant sword of his thought, education should unsheathe and sharpen it; if he is one to cement society by his all-reconciling affinities, oh! hasten their action! If he is jovial, if he is mercurial, if he is great-hearted, a cunning artificer, a strong commander, a potent ally, ingenious, useful, elegant, witty, prophet, diviner,—society has need of all these. The imagination must be addressed. Why always coast on the surface and never open the interior of nature, not by science, which is surface still, but by poetry? Is not the Vast an element of the mind? Yet what teaching, what book of this day appeals to the Vast?

Our culture has truckled to the times,—to the senses. It is not manworthy. If the vast and the spiritual are omitted, so are the practical and the moral. It does not make us brave or free. We teach boys to be such men as we are. We do not teach them to aspire to be all they can. We do not give them a training as if we believed in their noble nature. We scarce educate their bodies. We do not train the eye and the hand. We exercise their understandings to the apprehension and comparison of some facts, to a skill in numbers, in words; we aim to make accountants, attorneys, engineers; but not to make able, earnest, greathearted men. The great object of Education should be commensurate with the object of life. It should be a moral one; to teach self-trust: to inspire the youthful man with an interest in himself; with a curiosity touching his own nature; to acquaint him with the resources of his mind, and to teach him that there is all his strength, and to inflame him with a piety towards the Grand Mind in which he lives. Thus would education conspire with the Divine Providence. A man is a little thing whilst he works by and for himself, but, when he gives voice to the rules of love and justice, is godlike, his word is current in all countries; and all men, though his enemies, are made his friends and obey it as their own.

In affirming that the moral nature of man is the predominant element and should therefore be mainly consulted in the arrangements of a school, I am very far from wishing that it should swallow up all the other instincts and faculties of man. It should be enthroned in his mind, but if it monopolize the man he is not yet sound, he does not yet know his wealth. He is in danger of becoming merely devout, and wearisome through the monotony of his thought. It is not less necessary that the intellectual and the active faculties should be nourished and matured. Let us apply to this subject the light of the same torch by which we have looked at all the phenomena of the time; the infinitude, namely, of every man. Everything teaches that.

One fact constitutes all my satisfaction, inspires all my trust, viz., this perpetual youth, which, as long as there is any good in us, we cannot get rid of. It is very certain that the coming age and the departing age seldom understand each other. The old man thinks the young man has no distinct purpose, for he could never get anything intelligible and earnest out of him. Perhaps the young man does not think it worth his while to explain himself to so hard and inapprehensive a confessor. Let him be led up with a long-sighted forbearance, and let not the sallies of his petulance or folly be checked with disgust or indignation or despair.

I call our system a system of despair, and I find all the correction, all the revolution that is needed and that the best spirits of this age promise, in one word, in Hope. Nature, when she sends a new mind into the world, fills it beforehand with a desire for that which she wishes it to know and do. Let us wait and see what is this new creation, of what new organ the great Spirit had need when it incarnated this new Will. A new Adam in the garden, he is to name all the beasts in the field, all the gods in the sky. And jealous provision seems to have been made in his constitution that you shall not invade and contaminate him with the worn weeds of your language and opinions. The charm of life is this variety of genius, these contrasts and flavors by which Heaven has modulated the identity of truth, and there is a perpetual hankering to violate this individuality, to warp his ways of thinking and behavior to resemble or reflect your thinking and behavior. A low self-love in the parent desires that his child should repeat his character and fortune; an expectation which the child, if justice is done him, will nobly disappoint. By working on the theory that this resemblance exists, we shall do what in us lies to defeat his proper promise and produce the ordinary and mediocre. I suffer whenever I see that common sight of a parent or senior imposing his opinion and way of thinking and being on a young soul to which they are totally unfit. Cannot we let people be themselves, and enjoy life in their own way? You are trying to make that man another *you*. One's enough.

Or we sacrifice the genius of the pupil, the unknown possibilities of his nature, to a neat and safe uniformity, as the Turks white-wash the costly mosaics of ancient art which the Greeks left on their temple walls. Rather let us have men whose manhood is only the continuation of their boyhood, natural characters still; such are able and fertile for heroic action; and not that sad spectacle with which we are too familiar, educated eyes in uneducated bodies.

I like boys, the masters of the playground and of the street,—boys, who have the same liberal ticket of admission to all shops, factories, armories, town-meetings, caucuses, mobs, target-shootings, as flies have; quite unsuspected, coming in as naturally as the janitor,—known to have no money in their pockets, and themselves not suspecting the value of this poverty; putting nobody on his guard, but seeing the inside of the show,—hearing all the asides. There are no secrets from them, they know everything that befalls in the fire-company, the merits of every engine and of every man at the brakes, how to work it, and are swift to try their hand at every part; so too the merits of every locomotive on the rails, and will coax the engineer to let them ride with him and pull the handles when it goes to the engine-house. They are there only for fun, and not knowing that they are at school, in the courthouse, or the cattle-show, quite as much and more than they were, an hour ago, in the arithmetic class.

They know truth from counterfeit as quick as the chemist does. They detect weakness in your eye and behavior a week before you open your mouth, and have given you the benefit of their opinion quick as a wink. They make no mistakes, have no pedantry, but entire belief on experience. Their elections at base-ball or cricket are founded on merit, and are right. They don't pass for swimmers until they can swim, nor for stroke-oar until they can row: and I desire to be saved from their contempt. If I can pass with them, I can manage well enough with their fathers.

Everybody delights in the energy with which boys deal and talk with each other; the mixture of fun and earnest, reproach and coaxing, love and wrath, with which the game is played;—the good-natured yet defiant independence of a leading boy's behavior in the school-yard. How we envy in later life the happy youths to whom their boisterous games and rough exercise furnish the precise element which frames and sets off their school and college tasks, and teaches them, when least they think it, the use and meaning of these. In their fun and extreme freak they hit on the topmost sense of Horace. The young giant, brown from his hunting-tramp, tells his story well, interlarded with lucky allusions to Homer, to Virgil, to college-songs, to Walter Scott; and Jove and Achilles, partridge and trout, opera and binomial theorem, Caesar in Gaul, Sherman in Savannah, and hazing in Holworthy, dance through the narrative in merry confusion, yet the logic is good. If he can turn his books to such picturesque account in his fishing and hunting, it is easy to see how his reading and experience, as he has more of both, will interpenetrate each other. And every one desires that this pure vigor of action and wealth of narrative, cheered with so much humor and street rhetoric, should be carried into the habit of the young man, purged of its uproar and rudeness, but with all its vivacity entire. His hunting and campings-out have given him an indispensable base: I wish to add a taste for good company through his impatience of bad. That stormy genius of his needs a little direction to games, charades, verses of society, song, and a correspondence year by year with his wisest and best friends. Friendship is an order of nobility; from its revelations we come more worthily into nature. Society he must have or he is poor indeed; he gladly enters a school which forbids conceit, affectation, emphasis and dulness, and requires of each only the flower of his nature and experience; requires good-will, beauty, wit, and select information; teaches by practice the law of conversation, namely, to hear as well as to speak.

Meantime, if circumstances do not permit the high social advantages, solitude has also its lessons. The obscure youth learns there the practice instead of the literature of his virtues; and, because of the disturbing effect of passion and sense, which by a multitude of trifles impede the mind's eye from the quiet search of that fine horizon-line which truth keeps,—the way to knowledge and power has ever been an escape from too much engagement with affairs and possessions; a way, not through plenty and superfluity, but by denial and renunciation, into solitude and privation; and, the more is taken away, the more real and inevitable wealth of being is made known to us. The solitary knows the essence of the thought, the scholar in society only its fair face. There is no want of example of great men, great benefactors, who have been monks and hermits in habit. The bias of mind is sometimes irresistible in that direction. The man is, as it were, born deaf and dumb, and dedicated to a narrow and lonely life. Let him study the art of solitude, yield as gracefully as he can to his destiny. Why cannot he get the good of his doom, and if it is from eternity a settled fact that he and society shall be nothing to each other, why need he blush so, and make wry faces to keep up a freshman's seat in the fine world? Heaven often protects valuable souls charged with great secrets, great ideas, by long shutting them up with their own thoughts. And the most genial and amiable of men must alternate society with solitude, and learn its severe lessons.

There comes the period of the imagination to each, a later youth; the power of beauty, the power of books, of poetry. Culture makes his books realities to him, their characters more brilliant, more effective on his mind, than his actual mates. Do not spare to put novels into the hands of young people as an occasional holiday and experiment; but, above all, good poetry in all kinds, epic, tragedy, lyric. If we can touch the imagination, we serve them, they will never forget it. Let him read "Tom Brown at Rugby," read "Tom Brown at Oxford,"—better yet, read "Hodson's Life"—Hodson who took prisoner the king of Delhi. They teach the same truth,—a trust, against all appearances, against all privations, in your own worth, and not in tricks, plotting, or patronage.

I believe that our own experience instructs us that the secret of Education lies in respecting the pupil. It is not for you to choose what he shall know, what he shall do. It is chosen and foreordained, and he only holds the key to his own secret. By your tampering and thwarting and too much governing he may be hindered from his end and kept out of his own. Respect the child. Wait and see the new product of Nature. Nature loves analogies, but not repetitions. Respect the child. Be not too much his parent. Trespass not on his solitude.

But I hear the outcry which replies to this suggestion:—Would you verily throw up the reins of public and private discipline; would you leave the young child to the mad career of his own passions and whimsies, and call this anarchy a respect for the child's nature? I answer,—Respect the child, respect him to the end, but also respect yourself. Be the companion of his thought, the friend of his friendship, the lover of his virtue,—but no kinsman of his sin. Let him find you so true to yourself that you are the irreconcilable hater of his vice and the imperturbable slighter of his trifling.

The two points in a boy's training are, to keep his *naturel* and train off all but that:—to keep his *naturel*, but stop off his uproar, fooling and horse-play;—keep his nature and arm it with knowledge in the very direction in which it points. Here are the two capital facts, Genius and Drill. The first is the inspiration in the well-born healthy child, the new perception he has of nature. Somewhat he sees in forms or hears in music or apprehends in mathematics, or believes practicable in mechanics or possible in political society, which no one else sees or hears or believes. This is the perpetual romance of new life, the invasion of God into the old dead world, when he sends into quiet houses a young soul with a thought which is not met, looking for something which is not there, but which ought to be there: the thought is dim but it is sure, and he casts about restless for means and masters to verify it; he makes wild attempts to explain himself and invoke the aid and consent of the bystanders. Baffled for want of language and methods to convey his meaning, not yet clear to himself, he conceives that though not in this house or town, yet in some other house or town is the wise master who can put him in possession of the rules and instruments to execute his will. Happy this child with a bias, with a thought which entrances him, leads him, now into deserts now into cities, the fool of an idea. Let him follow it in good and in evil report, in good or bad company; it will justify itself; it will lead him at last into the illustrious society of the lovers of truth.

The High School

THE "ENGLISH" COURSE, PHILLIPS EXETER ACADEMY, NEW
HAMPSHIRE (1818)   From Laurence M. Crosbie, *The Phillips Exeter Academy: A
History* (Exeter, N.H., 1924), p. 292.

English Department

Candidates for admission into this department must be at least twelve years of age, well instructed in reading and spelling, familiarly acquainted with Arithmetick through Simple Proportion with the exception of Fractions, with Murray's English Grammar through Syntax, and must be able to parse simple English sentences.

The following is the course of Instruction and Study in the English Department, which, with special exceptions, will comprise three years.

First Year

English Grammar, including exercises in parsing and analysing, in the correction of bad English, Punctuation, and Prosody; Arithmetick, Geography and Colburn's Algebra.

Second Year

English Grammar continued, Geometry, Plane Trigonometry, and its application to Heights and Distances, Mensuration of Superfices and Solids, Elements of Ancient History, Logick, Rhetorick, English composition and Exercises of the Forensick, kind.

Third Year

Surveying, Navigation, Elements of Chemistry and Natural Philosophy, with experiments, Elements of Modern History, particularly of the United States, Astronomy, Moral and Political Philosophy, with English Composition, Forensicks, and Declamation continued.

A course of Theological Instruction is given to the several classes, and likewise

Instruction in Sacred Musick. Writing is daily taught in both departments by an *approved master.*

Those, who shall have spent at least one year in the department of languages, and have made good improvement, may enter upon the course of English education without the examination prescribed for mere English scholars. Students qualified to enter College, may be allowed the privilege of completing, if able, the course of English education in two years. The same privilege may be extended to others, whose superior improvement shall appear on examination, to authorize such advancement.

At the close of each Term the several classes of both departments are critically examined in all the studies of that Term; Those students, who are found to excel, are advanced or otherwise distinguished; but those, who prove materially deficient, are prohibited from proceeding with their class, until deficiencies are made up.

To those students, who honourably complete their Academical course, testimonials are publickly presented by the Principal at the annual Exhibition.

THE COLLEGE PREPARATORY COURSE, PHILLIPS EXETER ACADEMY, NEW HAMPSHIRE (1818) From Laurence M. Crosbie, *The Phillips Exeter Academy: A History* (Exeter, N.H., 1924), p. 291.

Course of Preparation for College

First Year

Adams's Latin Grammar, Jacobs's Latin Reader, Viri Romani, Caesar's Commentaries, Latin Prosody, Virgil's Bucolics, Geography and Arithmetick.

Second Year

Arithmetick, Exercises in reading and making Latin continued, Cicero's Select Orations, Buttmann's Greek Grammar, Jacobs's Greek Reader, Danzel's Collectanea Graeca Minora, Greek Testament, Sallust, Virgil's Aeneid, English Grammar and Declamation.

Third Year

The same Latin and Greek authors in revision, English Grammar and Declamation continued, Virgil's Georgics, Algebra, exercises in Latin and English translations and compositions.

Advanced Class

Horatius Flaccus, Titus Livius, Excerpta Latina, Parts of Terence's Comedies, Collectanea Majora, Homer's Iliad,—or such Latin and Greek authors as may best comport with the student's future destination; Algebra, Geometry, Adams's Roman Antiquities and Elements of Ancient History.

THE COLLEGE PREPARATORY COURSE, PHILLIPS EXETER ACADEMY, NEW HAMPSHIRE (1873–74) From Laurence M. Crosbie, *The Phillips Exeter Academy: A History* (Exeter, N.H., 1924), pp. 294–95.

Preparatory Class

Latin: Allen and Greenough's Grammar, Leighton's Latin Lessons, Caesar, books I–IV, Nepos, 1,000 lines, Prosody, Latin composition. Mathematics: Arithmetic to percentage. Ancient History: Smith's Smaller History of Rome. Ancient Geography.

Junior Class

Latin: 3,000 lines of Ovid, Cicero, four Catilinarian orations, Manilian Law, Ligarius. Greek: Goodwin's Grammar, Leighton's Lessons, Anabasis, Book I. Mathematics: Arithmetic finished, Greenleaf's Elementary Algebra. Ancient History: Smith's Smaller History of Greece.

Middle Class

Latin: Virgil, Books I–VI, Caesar, Nepos, Ovid, reviewed. Greek: Anabasis, Books II–V, Homer, Iliad, Books I–II. Mathematics: Algebra, Todhunter's or Hamblin Smith's two Books of Chauvenet's Geometry. Ancient History: Smith's Smaller History of Greece. English: Grammar and Composition. Ancient Geography, reviewed.

Senior Class

Latin: Cicero, De Senectute, Virgil, Bucolics. Greek: Herodotus, Book VII, Homer, Iliad, Book III. Mathematics: Chauvenet's Geometry, Books III–V, Peirce's Elements and Tables of Logarithms. French: Otto's Grammar, Bocher's Reader. Histoire Grecque. English: Shakespere, Scott and Goldsmith. Modern and Physical Geography, Guyot's Physics.

JAMES CARTER ON THE ACADEMIES' INFLUENCE ON PUBLIC
SCHOOLS (1826)   From James G. Carter, *Essays on Popular Education* (Boston, 1826), pp. 27–32.

The academies were unknown in Massachusetts before the revolution. The oldest of these institutions is Phillips' Academy at Andover, the date of whose charter is 1780. Before this time, all public schools, it should seem, were also free. The number of these seminaries or high schools did not much increase for many years after the close of the revolutionary war. But, during a short period, about ten or fifteen years since, they were multiplied to a very great extent. The people of Massachusetts, always desirous of following the policy of the pilgrims of Plymouth in regard to schools, seemed for a time absurdly to suppose, that they had but to get an academy incorporated and established in their neighborhood, and that their children would be educated without farther trouble. But in this too sanguine expectation, they have been most of them somewhat disappointed. An act of incorporation has not been found, on experiment, to be quite so efficacious as was, at first, anticipated. And many of these institutions, which, in the imagination of their projectors, rose at once almost to the dignity of colleges, are now found in a very inefficient, indeed, in a most wretched condition.

The legislature of the State, then willing and anxious to encourage "learning and good morals" among the people,—a duty, which the constitution solemnly enjoins upon them,—by all means in their power, granted as many acts of incorporation as were petitioned for; and to many of these corporations, in token of their good will, they appropriated townships of land in the interiour and northerly part of Maine, which then formed a part of Massachusetts. Some of these townships of land, by the way, it is to be feared may be found on the wrong side of the boundary line to be drawn between Maine and the British Provinces. So far as this policy evinced a desire to encourage the diffusion of knowledge, it should receive the commendation, which good intentions always deserve; but, for all practical purposes for perhaps fifty years from the date of these charters and appropriations, the legislature might about as well have assigned to the petitioners for them a tract of the Moon.

When these hungry corporate beings had been created by the legislature, and their first cries for sustenance had been soothed by the unsavoury dish of eastern lands, they were then abandoned to the charity of their friends; or, if they proved cold, to a lingering death by starvation. The eastern lands, which constituted the patrimony of the State, were in most cases utterly unavailable. The benevolence of friends was, generally, exhausted in accumulating the means to erect suitable buildings. And the corporation were left to rely upon their own sagacity for procuring other resources to put their institution in operation. The more essential, indeed, almost the only essential part of a good academy, viz: a good instructer, was left unprovided for. The only expedient which remained, was, to support the teacher by a tax upon the scholars. It seemed but reasonable that those, who enjoyed the exclusive benefit of the institution, should pay for their own instruction. But this condition, though perhaps but a small sum was required of each pupil in order to produce an adequate salary for an instructer, removed the advantages of the academies, at once, beyond the reach of a large proportion of the inhabitants. The appropriations of the State, therefore, for the support of these schools, if they benefitted any body in particular, surely benefitted not the poor, but the rich and middling classes of the community. At least, these enjoyed the chief advantage of them, the direct rays of the State's favour; while the poor could feel only a dim reflection of them.

That the academies, at least, those of them which have been put and sustained in a tolerably respectable condition, have been a great accommodation to a few of our inhabitants, cannot be doubted. And how few are those, who have received any advantages from them, may be easily estimated by comparing the small number of children instructed in them, with the whole number in the Commonwealth. Still these are, or may be, useful institutions. I have certainly no desire to lessen the high repute, in which they seem to be held. On the contrary, I wish they were in higher estimation than they really are. And, what is more, I wish they were more worthy of that estimation. But they should be appreciated for the character which they possess, and never for that which they do not possess. And they are not establishments for the instruction of the poor. Neither can they be relied upon as efficient means for the education of the mass or even a majority of the people; because as has been before intimated, their conditions exclude nineteen twentieths of the whole population of the State from a participation of their advantages. If they are sustained, therefore, it must be upon some other ground. What that ground is, it is not my purpose now to inquire. But what has been their influence upon the free or town schools?

One influence, which they undoubtedly have had, has been to prepare young instructers *some* better than they could be prepared in the town schools themselves. This is a good influence. And if the same object could not be attained much better by other means, it would deserve great consideration in estimating the utility, which we are to expect from those establishments for the future. But the preparation of instructers for the free schools, never formed a part of the original design of the academies. They were intended to afford instruction in other and higher branches of education, than those usually taught in the free schools; and not merely to give better instruction in the same branches. Much less did it come within the wide scope of their purposes to give instruction in the science of teaching generally. So that the little good derived from them in this respect is only incidental.

The preparation of instructers for free schools is a subject of such moment to this community, that it will hardly be thought expedient, on reflection, to trust it to chance or to incidents. Experience and observation have convinced those, who have attended to the subject, that adequate instructers for the free schools are not prepared by these incidental means. In order to be efficient and effectual in attaining that desirable object, means must be applied directly to it. But of the education of instructers, more by and by. I wish merely now to say, and I trust I have shown, that the academies cannot be relied upon for accomplishing that object, so as in any good degree to meet the demands and answer the reasonable expectations of the community.

But the academies have had another influence upon the public town schools, which has much impaired their usefulness, and, if not soon checked, it will ultimately destroy them. This influence, operating for a series of years, has led, already, to the abandonment of a part of the free school system, and to a depreciation in the character and prospects of the remaining part. And it is working, not slowly, the destruction of the vital principle of the institution, more valuable to us than any other, for the preservation of enlightened freedom. The pernicious influence, to which I allude, will be better understood, by taking an example of its operation on a small scale; and then extending the same principle of examination to the whole State, or to New England.

Take any ten contiguous towns in the interiour of this Commonwealth, and suppose an academy to be placed in the centre of them. An academy, as I have before observed, commonly means a corporation, with a township of land in Maine, given them by the State, and a pretty convenient house, built generally by the patriotic subscriptions of those who expect to use it; the instructer being supported, chiefly or altogether, by a separate tax on the scholars. In each of these ten towns, select the six individuals, who have families to educate, who set the highest value on early education, and who are able to defray the expenses of the best which can be had, either in a private school among themselves, or at the academy, which, by the supposition, is in their neighbourhood. Now of what immediate consequence can it be to the six families of each town, or to the sixty families of the ten towns, whether there be such a thing as a free school in the Commonwealth or not! They have a general interest in them, to be sure, because they have themselves been there instructed, and the early associations of childhood and youth are strong; and they have a sort of speculative belief, if it be not rather an innate sentiment, that free schools make a free people. But how are their own particular, personal, and immediate interests affected? Without any libel upon good nature, these are the main springs to human actions. These are the motives, which find their way soonest to the human heart, and influence most powerfully and steadily the opinions of men, and the conduct founded upon and resulting from them.

As soon as difficulties and disagreements, in regard to the free schools, arise, as they necessarily must, upon various topics; such as, the amount of money to be raised, the distribution of it among the several districts, the manner of appropriation, whether it be to the "summer schools" or to the "winter schools," to pay the instructer from this family or from that family, of higher qualifications or of lower qualifications, of this or that political or religious creed, or a thousand other questions which are constantly occurring; disgusted with any course which may be adopted, they will, immediately, abandon the free schools, and provide for the education of their children in their own way. They may organize a private school, for their own convenience, upon such principles as they most approve. Or, they may send their scholars, at an expense trifling to them, to the academy in their neighbourhood. Well, what if they do? The free schools remain, all taxes are paid, cheerfully, for their support, and the number of scholars is lessened. What is the evil of their sending their children somewhere else to be educated? We should, at first, suppose that it would be an advantage; inasmuch as the amount of money to be expended would be left the same, and the number of pupils to receive the benefit of it would be considerably diminished.

But the evils of this course, and the general policy of the State government, which has led to it, are very serious ones. When the six individuals of any country town, who are, by the supposition, first in point of wealth and interest in the subject, and who will generally be also first in point of intelligence and influence in town affairs, withdraw their children from the common schools; there are, at the same time, withdrawn a portion of intelligence from their direction and heartfelt interest from their support. This intelligence is needed, to manage the delicate and important concerns of the schools. And this heartfelt interest is needed, to lead the way to improvements, to stimulate and encourage larger and larger appropriations, and to ensure vigilance in their expenditure. Patriotism and philanthropy are dull motives to exertions for the improvement of common schools compared with parental affection. And this quickening power has gone off to the academies or somewhere else with the children, who are the objects of it.

The Sub-Committee to whom was referred the resolutions offered to the School Committee at a Meeting on the 17th June proposing to establish an English Classical School in the Town of Boston, having taken the subject of those resolutions into consideration, and devoted to it that attention which its importance demanded, Respectfully ask leave to Report.—

Though the present system of education, and the munificence with which it is supported are highly beneficial and honorable to the Town, Yet in the Opinion of the Committee it is susceptible of a greater degree of perfection and usefulness without Materially Augmenting the Weight of the public burdens.—Till recently our system Occupied a middle Station: it neither commenced with the rudiments of education, nor extended to the higher branches of knowledge.—This system was supported by the town at a very great expense, and to be admitted to its advantages, certain preliminary qualifications were required at individual cost which had the effect of excluding many children of the poor and unfortunate classes of the community from the benefits of a public education. The Town saw & felt this inconsistency in the plan and have removed the defect, by providing Schools, in which the children of the poor can be fitted for admission into the public seminaries.

The present system, in the Opinion of the Committee requires, still further amendment.—the studies that are pursued at the English Grammar Schools, are merely elementary, and more time than is necessary is devoted to their acquisition. A Scholar is admitted at seven, and is dismissed at fourteen Years of Age; thus seven years are expended in the acquisition of a degree of knowledge, which with ordinary diligence and common capacity, may be easily & perfectly acquired in five. If, then, a Boy remain the usual term, a large portion of the time will have been idly, or uselessly expended, as he may have learned all that he has been taught long before its expiration. This loss of time Occurs at that interesting and critical period of life, when the habits and inclinations are forming by which the future character will be fixed & determined.

This evil therefore should be removed, by enlarging the present system, not merely that the time now lost may be saved, but that those early habits of industry and application may be acquired, which are so essential in leading to a future life of Virtue and usefulness.

Nor are these the only existing evils. The mode of education now adopted and the branches of knowledge that are taught at our English Grammar Schools, are not sufficiently extensive, nor otherwise calculated to bring the powers of the mind into operation, nor to qualify a youth to fill usefully and respectably many of those Stations, both public and private in which he may be placed.—A parent who wishes to give a child an education that shall fit him for Active life, and shall serve as a foundation for eminence in his profession, whether Mercantile or Mechanical, is under the necessity of giving him a different education from any which our public Schools can now furnish.—Hence many children are separated from their parents, and sent to private academies in this vicinity, to acquire that instruction which cannot be obtained at the public seminaries.—Thus many parents who contribute largely to the Support of these institutions, are subjected to heavy expense, for the same object in other Towns.

The Committee for these and many other weighty considerations that might be offered; and in Order to render the present system of public education more nearly perfect, are of Opinion that an additional school is required.—They, therefore, recommend the founding of a seminary to be called the English classical School, and submit the following as a general outline of a plan for its organization and of the course of studies to be pursued.—

1st. That the term of time for pursuing the course of studies proposed be three Years.—

2ndly. That the School be divided into three Classes, and one Year be assigned to the study of each Class.—

3dly. That the age of admission be not less than twelve Years.

4thly. That, the School be for Boys exclusively.

5thly. That Candidates for admission be proposed on a given day annually, but scholars with suitable qualifications may be admitted at any intermediate time to an advanced standing.

6thly. That Candidates for admission shall be subject to a strict examination, in such manner as the School Committee may direct, to Ascertain their qualifications according to these Rules.—

7thly. That it be required of every candidate to qualify him for admission, that he be well acquainted with reading, writing, English Grammar in all its branches, & Arithmetic as far as simple proportion.—

8thly. That it be required of the Masters & Ushers, as a necessary qualification, that they shall have been regularly educated at some University.

The Studies of the first Class to be as follows.—

Composition;
Reading from the most approved Authors;—Exercises in criticism, comprising critical analyses of the language, grammar and stile of the best English Authors, their errors and beauties; Declamation; Geography; Arithmetic, continued; Algebra.

The Studies of the Second Class.—

Composition; Reading:
Exercises in Criticism; Declamation; Algebra: Continued
Ancient & Modern history & chronology; Logic; Geometry;
Plane Trigonometry, and its application to mensuration of heights and distances;
Navigation; Surveying;
Mensuration of Superficies and Solids;
Forensic discussions.

The Studies of the third Class.—

Composition; Exercises in Criticism; Declamation; Mathematics; Continued
Logic; History, particularly that of the United States
Natural Philosophy, including Astronomy; Moral & Political Philosophy

To conduct a seminary of this description, the Committee are of Opinion, that one principal Master, one submaster and two Ushers, will be required;

The Principal at a Salary of . . . . $1500 Pr. Ann
Sub Master . . . . $1200 ”
Two Ushers, one at $700, one at $600 . . . . $1300 ”

$4000

This sum in the opinion of the Committee, with other annual expenses of Schools, will be adequate to the support of such an institution. No additional building will be required; as those which are now built, and authorized by the Town to be built will be sufficient.

The Committee therefore recommend, that an annual Appropriation of this sum, be obtained from the Town, and that a further sum be raised either by private subscription, or from public Munificence, to furnish the School, with the necessary instruments and philosophical Apparatus.—The Committee are further of Opinion, that the expense which would be incurred, by the establishment, of such an institution, would be fully justified by its great and manifold advantages.—No money can be better expended, than that which is appropriated to the support of public Schools.—If anything will preserve tranquility and order in a community, perpetuate the blessing of society and free government and promote the happiness and prosperity of a people, it must be the general diffusion of knowledge.—These Salutary effects the Committee conceive would flow from the institution of this seminary.—Its establishment, they think would raise the literary and scientific character of the Town, would incite our Youth to a laudable ambition of distinguishing themselves in the pursuit and acquisition of knowledge, and would give strength and stability to the civil and religious institutions of our Country.

All of which is respectfully submitted by Order of the Committee.

S. A. WELLS, *Chairman*

Boston Octr 26, 1820

BOSTON OBTAINS A PUBLIC HIGH SCHOOL (1821) From "Report of the Boston School Committee," as quoted in Elmer E. Brown, *The Making of Our Middle Schools* (New York, 1903), pp. 298–301.

Though the present system of public education, and the munificence with which it is supported, are highly beneficial and honorable to the Town; yet in the opinion of the Committee, it is susceptible of a greater degree of perfection and usefulness, without materially augmenting the weight of the public burdens. Till recently, our system occupied a middle station: it neither commenced with the rudiments of Education, nor extended to the higher branches of knowledge. This system was supported by the Town at a very great expense, and to be admitted to its advantages, certain preliminary qualifications were required at individual cost, which have the effect of excluding many children of the poor and unfortunate classes of the community from the benefits of a public education. The Town saw and felt this inconsistency in the plan, and have removed the defect by providing Schools in which the children of the poor can be fitted for admission into the public seminaries.

The present system, in the opinion of the Committee, requires still farther amendment. The studies that are pursued at the English grammar schools are merely elementary, and more time than is necessary is devoted to their acquisition. A scholar is admitted at seven, and is dismissed at fourteen years of age; thus, seven years are expended in the acquisition of a degree of knowledge, which with ordinary diligence and a common capacity, may be easily and perfectly acquired in five. If then, a boy remain the usual term, a large portion of the time will have been idly or uselessly expended, as he may have learned all that he may have been taught long before its expiration. This loss of time occurs at that interesting and critical period of life, when the habits and inclinations are forming by which the future character will be fixed and determined. This evil, therefore, should be removed, by enlarging the present system, not merely that the time now lost may be saved, but that those early habits of industry and application may be acquired, which are so essential in leading to a future life of virtue and usefulness.

Nor are these the only existing evils. The mode of education now adopted, and the branches of knowledge that are taught at our English grammar schools, are not sufficiently extensive nor otherwise calculated to bring the powers of the mind into operation nor to qualify a youth to fill usefully and respectably many of those stations, both public and private, in which he may be placed. A parent who wishes to give a child an education that shall fit him for active life, and shall serve as a foundation for eminence in his profession, whether Mercantile or Mechanical, is under the necessity of giving him a different education from any which our public schools can now furnish. Hence, many children are separated from their parents and sent to private academies in this vicinity, to acquire that instruction which cannot be obtained at the public seminaries. Thus, many parents, who contribute largely to the support of these institutions, are subjected to heavy expense for the same object, in other towns.

The Committee, for these and many other weighty considerations that might be offered, and in order to render the present system of public education more nearly perfect, are of the opinion that an additional School is required. They therefore, recommend the founding of a seminary which shall be called the English Classical School, and submit the following as a general outline of a plan for its organization and of the course of studies to be pursued.

1st. That the term of time for pursuing the course of studies proposed, be three years.

2ndly. That the School be divided into three classes, and one year be assigned to the studies of each class.

3rdly. That the age of admission be not less than twelve years.

4thly. That the School be for Boys exclusively.

5thly. That candidates for admission be proposed on a given day annually; but scholars with suitable qualifications may be admitted at any intermediate time to an advanced standing.

6thly. That candidates for admission shall be subject to a strict examination, in such manner as the School Committee may direct, to ascertain their qualifications according to these rules.

7thly. That it be required of every candidate, to qualify him for admission, that he be well acquainted with reading, writing, English grammar in all its branches, and arithmetic as far as simple proportion.

8thly. That it be required of the Masters and Ushers, as a necessary qualification, that they shall have been regularly educated at some University.

The Studies of the First Class to be as follows:

Composition.
Reading from the most approved authors.
Exercises in Criticism; comprising critical analyses of the language, grammar, and style of the best English authors, their errors & beauties.
Declamation.
Geography.
Arithmetic continued.

The Studies of the Second Class

Composition.
Exercises in Criticism.
Reading.   [*continued*]
Declamation.
Algebra.
Ancient and Modern History and Chronology.
Logic.
Geometry.
Plane Trigonometry; and its application to mensuration of Heights and Distances
Navigation.
Surveying.
Mensuration of Superficies & Solids.
Forensic Discussions.

The Studies of the Third Class

Composition;
Exercises in Criticism;
Declamation;
Mathematics;   continued
Logic;
History; particularly that of the United States;
Natural Philosophy, including Astronomy;
Moral and Political Philosophy.

ADVERTISEMENT FOR A HIGH SCHOOL FOR GIRLS IN BOSTON

(1825)   From *Columbian Sentinel,* November 5, 1825.

Monitorial High School for Girls

Public notice is hereby given that, on Tuesday, 15th November next, the School Committee will meet for the appointment of a Master for the High School for Girls, about to be established in this city; The school is to be conducted upon the system of *monitorial* or *mutual instruction;*—and it is expected that the master will be prepared to teach, on this system, so far as it shall be found practicable, Reading, Spelling, Writing, words and sentences from dictation, English Grammar, with exercises in the same, Composition, Modern and Ancient Geography, Intellectual and Written Arithmetic, Rhetoric, General History, History of the United States, of England, Rome and Greece, Bookkeeping by Single Entry, Elements of Geometry, Demonstrative Geometry, Algebra, the Latin and French Languages, Natural Philosophy, Chemistry, Botany, Logic, Astronomy, the use of Globes, Projection of Maps, Principles of Perspective, Moral Philosophy, and the Evidences of Christianity.

Application for this appointment will be received by the subscriber, at any time previous to the day above mentioned.

By order of the Committee,

JOHN PIERPONT, *Sec'ry.*

REGULATIONS OF A BOSTON HIGH SCHOOL FOR GIRLS (1827)   From

Boston School Committee, *Regulations of the High School for Girls* (Boston, 1827), pp. 4–11.

No scholar shall be admitted into the school until she shall have attained the age of *fourteen years,* nor after she shall have attained the age of *sixteen,* or shall remain in the school longer than one year. An exception is made in favor of the present scholars, who, having been originally admitted for three years, are permitted to remain until the next annual exhibition.

The requisitions for admission into the school, shall be every thing taught in the public Grammar and Writing schools.

Candidates for admission shall be examined in Reading, Writing, Modern Geography, and Colburn's First Lessons in Arithmetic, and they shall be able to parse fluently any English composition in prose or verse.[1]

The school shall be opened on the second Monday of December annually.

[1]It is desired that young ladies bring with them a specimen of their writing, when they offer themselves for examination. And teachers, whose pupils may make application for admission into the High School, are respectfully requested to furnish them with testimonials, certifying that they have been through the course of studies required.

Candidates for admission shall be examined on the Friday and Saturday preceding the first Monday of that month.

From the first Monday in April to the first Monday in October, the school shall be begun at 8 A. M.—and from the first Monday in October to the first Monday in April, at 9 A. M.—and it shall be kept to 2 P. M. through the year.

The holy-days and vacations allowed to the school, are, days of Fast and Thanksgiving; Christmas day; the first Monday in June; the fourth of July; the days of general trainings; Election week; Commencement week; the remainder of the week after the annual exhibition of the public schools for boys in August; and the time between the last Thursday in November and the second Monday in December.

The *course of studies* originally prescribed, was calculated to occupy *three years;* and it has not yet been revised to adapt it to the altered circumstances of the school.

The annual public exhibition of the school shall be on the day after the public exhibition of the girls in the several Grammar and Writing schools of the city, to wit, on the last Thursday in November, in the forenoon.

The direction which follows, is from the general Regulations of the School Committee. "All the masters shall be required to keep bills or books, which shall be furnished at the public expense, and shall remain the property of the schools, in which they shall record the names, ages, places of residence, absences and tardinesses of their pupils, and such other particulars of their conduct, application, improvement, promotion and general character, as shall enable the Committees at their visitations (on all of which it shall be the duty of the masters to exhibit the same to them) to form an adequate idea of the state of the schools; and it shall be the duty of the instructers frequently to remind their pupils of the important consequences, which may result to them individually from these perpetual records."

To these *official regulations* of the School Committee, I have thought it might be well to subjoin, for the information of the parents and friends of my pupils, a few of the leading principles, upon which the school is governed and instructed; without intending, however, to go minutely into the details of the system, at the present time.

The High School for Girls is conducted on the general plan of monitorial or mutual instruction; but no prescribed system has been followed. Indeed, I can no more conceive of a set of rules and forms and a routine of exercises, of universal application in the business of education, than of a sovereign specific, for the curing of all the diseases that "flesh is heir to," in the practice of medicine. Such arrangements have been made, as seemed best adapted to the peculiar circumstances of the school; and they are, in most respects, unlike those of any other institution. In forming the system, I have made free use of whatever information on the subject I could find in books, as well as of the suggestions of my own experience in teaching. The school was regarded, as its commencement, as an experiment; and it is not for me to speak of the result. But this I may be permitted to say, that no pupils of mine have ever manifested a more generous spirit in their deportment, or made a greater proficiency in their studies, than those now under my care, notwithstanding their number is so large for a single instructer.

It is not pretended that the explanations and illustrations of monitors, are always as thorough and happy as they might be; but this evil may be remedied by a judicious use of *oral instructions,* and by frequent and regular reviews to the master. Upon the whole, if the monitorial system possesses some defects,—and what system is perfect in every respect?—they are more than counterbalanced by its commanding and salutary influence upon character, in a moral and intellectual point of view,—by its tendency to inspire decision and energy and thought, and to promote habits of industry, a cheerful spirit and a correct deportment. Here its advantages are great and peculiar. In bearing this testimony in favor of monitorial instruction,—against which I formerly felt some prejudices, in spite of myself, although I theoretically understood, as I thought, its various advantages and defects,—I make no account of the common argument of economy. The system of education is to be preferred which is *best*, not that which is *cheapest*. Neither am I influenced by motives of personal ease; for my cares, confinement and labors, are vastly greater than they have ever been in any other school. Independently of all such considerations, I estimate the new method with reference to its merits alone,—its *practical* influence upon mind, manners and character. If it did not enable a master to teach a single additional scholar, I should still regard it as a great and invaluable improvement in conducting the business of education.

Our desks are arranged in ten rows or *sections*, of twelve seats each, and numbered from 1 to 120,—No. 1, being the *lowest* desk in point of honor. The school is reorganised once a quarter, when every scholar is required to leave her desk in good order, or it is repaired at her expense. The young ladies are usually addressed by the numbers of their seats, and not by their names; and this is *always* the case, when they are noted as being out of order. The delinquent thus escapes the mortification of being exposed to the school; for these numbers are so placed, that they cannot be seen by the scholars in their seats.

Good order is regarded as indispensable, and as much silence is preserved in the school, as the nature of its varied and numerous operations will admit; but no severe and unncessary restraints are imposed. The scholars are allowed to consult their own convenience, in preparing for their exercises; and an idler is seldom seen. They are also permitted to study their own happiness in their own way, provided they neither disturb the general order, nor encroach upon the rights of their neighbors,—to do any thing, *openly and without disguise*, not inconsistent with a lady-like deportment; and it is seldom any one so far forgets the respect she owes to her own character, as to be guilty of disorderly and improper conduct. Of all offences, an attempt at concealment and a manifestation of disingenuousness, even in an innocent matter, would receive the most marked and severe censure.

The health and comfort of the scholars, are carefully regarded. They are not often confined to the same position, either in their seats or on the floor, for a longer period than twenty or thirty minutes; and their evolutions are so directed as to unite exercise and order. By the present construction of the rooms, only half of the school can conveniently recite together: this is to be regretted, as much time might be saved daily, by a different arrangement.

No medals or pecuniary rewards are given; and no means are used for promoting punctuality and exciting emulation, but such as are congenial to the legitimate objects of a school. If such means are sufficient to produce the desired effect, it would seem worse than useless to appeal to mercenary motives; and that they are so, is abundantly proved by the regular attendance of the scholars, and by the fact, that longer lessons and extra-exercises are requested almost daily,—shorter lessons, very seldom, and without good reasons, never. Their exercises are all *voluntary*, as far as practicable; and they are assigned, in a great measure, by those who are to perform them. However, if a lesson has been badly recited, the scholars are not consulted by their teacher in assigning the next; but if none of the members of a section have failed, they have a right to demand as long a lesson as they please, for the next exercise of the same kind.

The government of the school is vested in a set of books, in which is recorded an accurate and minute account of every scholar's performances, deportment, absence and tardiness; and at the end of each quarter, she is advanced to a higher, or degraded to a lower, section or seat, as this record shall appear in her favor or against her. The whole business is regulated by fixed principles, that are well understood; and every individual is, literally speaking, the artificer of her own rank, which is affected by every exercise she performs, and by every error she commits, either in recitation or conduct. Every thing depends upon numerical calculation; and, were it expedient, the school might be classed by the scholars themselves.

A *Credit* is given to every member of the school, for each regular recitation, which is performed in a correct and satisfactory manner.

A *Check* is given to such as fail in their lessons. Thus, in every recitation, each pupil receives either a check or a credit.

Merits are awarded for correct and orderly deportment, for excellence in the unusual exercises of school, and for voluntary labors.

The marks which indicate violations of order and improper conduct, for the want of a better name, are called *Misdemeanors*. For the more common instances of misconduct, only one is given, but for the higher offences, such as disrespect to a teacher or monitor, the number would be graduated by the circumstances of the case.

Forfeits are incurred by neglecting to attend to required exercises, at the proper time, and in a proper manner, by making appeals without sufficient grounds, and by slight irregularities of conduct.

In making the quarterly records of the school, by which the rank of the scholars is determined, every check cancels one credit, or two merits, and every misdemeanor, five merits. These principles were discussed and settled by a large committee of the scholars themselves. The forfeits are not entered upon the records, but kept on the bills until the are redeemed by an equal number of merits.

Various classes of agents are employed in the government, instruction and general administration of the affairs of the school, to each of which are assigned specific duties.

The *Head Monitor* holds the highest and most responsible situation. She has the general superintendence of the school, and, in the absence of the Principal, she supplies his place. The *Monitor of Attendance,* and the *Monitor of Dictation,* in addition to their own proper duties, act as assistants to the head monitor. Their authority extends over the whole school, and they are selected to fill their respective places, as marks of distinguished and general merit. They occupy an elevated desk, which commands a view of the other scholars.

The *Monitors of Sections,* as such, are not employed in the instruction of the school; but their duties are nevertheless important. Each one has the superintendence of the section next below her; in which if she observe any disorder, it is her duty to report it to the head monitor, without delay. I would here remark, that spies and informers, receive no encouragement in the school. All complaints, to be regarded, must be made in an official form, and by those whose *duty* it is to make them. These monitors also keep class-bills of their respective sections, in which they record the results of their recitations, and report them to the head monitor, weekly, to be entered in her Journal. In selecting the monitors of sections and their *Assistants,* who perform the duties of the monitors, in their absence, I pay no regard to scholarship, unless it is connected with ingenuousness, an observance of order and an amiable and lady-like deportment; as a reward for which high qualifications, if I should not rather say cardinal virtues, these appointments are exclusively reserved.

The *Examiners* pass through their respective sections, every morning, to attend to such voluntary exercises as may be offered; and, under certain limitations, to award the merits they may deserve. They keep the bills of merits and forfeits, as do the monitors, those of credits and checks; and, like them, they make weekly reports to the head monitor.

In selecting the *Teachers*, particular attention is paid to their attainments in the several branches, in which they are to give instruction, and their *aptness* for the business. In those studies, however, which require little more in the teacher, than to *hear a recitation*, the reverse of this rule is sometimes adopted, by a selection of such as will be the most benefited by reviewing what they have already learned. No teacher, ordinarily, hears the same section in two branches; and no one is required to hear another class, while her own is reciting. The scholars are encouraged to detect the errors of their teachers and of each other: this secures their undivided attention to the exercise before them, makes the teacher careful in the discharge of her duty, and brings to her assistance all the knowledge of her pupils. An account of the recitation is entered on a slate, provided for the purpose, and read to the class, that the errors, if any, may be corrected at the time. It is then transferred to the bill of the proper monitor. The teachers are held responsible for the order of their respective classes, from the time they have their seats till they return to them again.

The *Messengers* are the highest scholars in their several sections. Through them are made all communications to and from the Principal, while their classes are reciting; and by their agency much disorder and delay are prevented. To illustrate the nature of their duties, suppose a scholar does not give a prompt and satisfactory answer to a question proposed; her teacher says 'check!' Should she think the question not an important one, or that her answer was sufficiently accurate,—as they are encouraged in the use of their own words, instead of these of their books,—her reply is 'appeal!' The messenger then brings the case before the instructer for his consideration, stating all the circumstances, except the name of the individual. This is done in writing, when it can be with convenience. The check is continued or removed, according to the decision given.

As there is but one instructer, it seemed necessary that provision should be made for the school to go on without his being present. So far as order is concerned, this has been effectually done, by vesting the government in books of record; and the past head monitors are constituted a *Board of Appeal*, whenever the master is detained from school, by sickness or any other casualty.

The only penalty for absence, is, that scholars obtain neither credit nor merit marks; and for the plain reason, that they do nothing to earn them. Excuses for absence are not now required; and yet the attendance is highly gratifying, even in the most inclement weather.

From this account,—too brief I fear to be distinct, although much longer than was contemplated,—the operations of the school may appear complicated and confused. But nothing could be farther from the truth. All understand their duties, because they are precisely defined; and the parts are so adjusted, that there is no jarring, or crossing each other.

It may be supposed, too, that the business of the records must be cumbrous and unwieldy, and occupy a large share of the time both of the master and many of the scholars; and yet a stranger might spend days in the room and know nothing of the matter, unless it were pointed out to him. The work is so distributed and arranged, that no one has much to do, in this department, except the head monitor, who requires an hour, perhaps, on Saturday, to make up her journal for the week. The system is so compact, that a single quire of paper will serve as a waste-book for the whole school, in which all the facts are entered in detail, for almost three years; and in the permanent Record, which is kept by the master, four lines give the whole history of a scholar's progress, even to the minutest facts, for a year.

It may be asked, what security we have that these various agents perform their respective duties, with fidelity and impartiality? It might be sufficient to answer, the same security which we have that any person will perform his duty, in any situation; for I am yet to learn that the young, with their glowing and generous feelings, are less ingenuous, less liable to be governed by sentiments of justice and principles of integrity, and less tenderly alive to all the sweet influences of truth and honor and honesty, than they whose judgements may be more mature, but who have been longer hackneyed in the crooked ways of the world. Let the moral sense be properly cultivated,—let scholars learn to respect themselves, by seeing that they are respected by others,—let a prudent and generous confidence reposed in their integrity, prompt them to an exact and faithful discharge of their duties, and there is little to be apprehended on the side of injustice, or from the abuse of power.

But all the means, which circumstances allow, are used to prevent even 'the appearance of evil.' Every award, either of merit or censure, must be made *openly,* and in the presence of all interested, that if any error is committed, or injustice done, it may be at once corrected. An *appeal* from the decision of a monitor or teacher, may at all times be made to the Principal, for which a uniform and easy course is prescribed. Indeed, appeals have been made to the desk, and not unfrequently with success, against decisions of the master himself, when acting in the capacity of a monitor or teacher. In a word, such is the system of checks established, to detect all violations of the rules of the school and to secure equity and good order, that no individual *can* suffer injustice to be done to herself, or partiality to be shown to another, but through her own negligence or fault.

To be sure that the teachers do their duty faithfully, I regularly review the scholars in all their studies. The books of the school are divided into proper and convenient *stages;* and a section cannot go forward to a new stage, before they have passed a thorough and critical examination in the last. In this way, I eventually attend to all the studies of the school in person. The salutary influence of these reviews, both upon the teachers and their pupils, will be readily conceived. The pupils, on their part, are anxious to go on *fast,* that the lower sections may not pass by them; and the teachers are as anxious that they should go on *well,* that they may not incur the mortification which must result from an unsatisfactory review.

E. BAILEY.

MASSACHUSETTS SCHOOL LAW CALLS FOR THE ESTABLISHMENT OF PUBLIC HIGH SCHOOLS (1827) From Edgar W. Knight and Clifton L. Hall, eds., *Readings in American Educational History* (New York, 1951), p. 247.

B*e it enacted,* That each town or district within this Commonwealth, containing fifty families, or householders, shall be provided with a teacher or teachers, of good morals, to instruct children in orthography, reading, writing, English grammar, geography, arithmetic, and good behavior, for such term of time as shall be equivalent to six months for one school in each year; and every town or district containing one hundred families or householders, shall be provided with such teacher or teachers, for such term of time as shall be equivalent to eighteen months, for one school in each year. In every city, town, or district, containing five hundred families, or householders shall be provided with such teacher or teachers for such term of time as shall be equivalent to twenty-four months, shall also be provided with a master of good morals, competent to instruct, in addition to the branches of learning aforesaid, in the history of the United States, bookkeeping by single entry, geometry, surveying, algebra; and shall employ such master to instruct a school in such city, town, or district, for the benefit of all the inhabitants thereof, at least ten months in each year, exclusive of vacations, in such convenient places, or alternately at such places in such city, town, or district, as said inhabitants, at their meeting in March, or April, annually, shall determine; and in every city, or town, and district, containing four thousand inhabitants, such master shall be competent in addition to all the foregoing branches, to instruct the Latin and Greek languages, history, rhetoric, and logic.

THE BOSTON SCHOOL COMMITTEE MAKES UP AN EXAMINATION FOR THE GRAMMAR SCHOOLS (1845) From "Report of the Sub-Committee On Grammar Schools of the School Committee of the City of Boston" as quoted in Otis W. Caldwell and Stuart A Courtis, *Then And Now In Education, 1845–1923 (New York,* 1924), pp. 275–81.

Worcester's History

Question 1.   What is History?
Question 2.   What are some of the uses of History?
Question 3.   Enumerate some of the sources of History.
Question 4.   What nations are among the first mentioned in History?
Question 5.   For what were the Egyptians distinguished?
Question 6.   For what were the Phoenicians distinguished?
Question 7.   Who was the founder of Babylon, and about what period did he live?
Question 8.   Who was the founder of the Persian empire?
Question 9.   Who were some of the most distinguished orators and poets of Greece?
Question 10. Who was the founder of Rome?
Question 11. What was the character of the early government of Rome?
Question 12. Can you mention the names of the Roman Emperors?
Question 13. Can you give any account of the feudal system?
Question 14. What were the purposes of the Crusades?
Question 15. In what century was the great French Revolution, and who were some of the characters who figured in it?
Question 16. What nation ruled Britain at the commencement of the Christian Era?
Question 17. Who were the Saxons, and how came they to invade Britain?

Question 18.   What do you understand by the Norman Conquest?
Question 19.   What was the period of the Commonwealth in England, and who was the most distinguished character in it?
Question 20.   About what period did the first colonists come to New England, and what were the supposed motives for their leaving the mother country?
Question 21.   How long did they continue subject to the mother country, and what were some of the assigned reasons for throwing off her government?
Question 22.   When did the war of the American Revolution commence, and who were the allies of the Americans?
Question 23.   When was the great Federal Constitution formed, during or after the war of the Revolution, and how many States accepted it at its formation?
Question 24.   About what period was the embargo laid by President Jefferson, and non-intercourse substituted for it?
Question 25.   About what period did the last war between Great Britain and the United States commence, and what were the causes assigned by the Americans for its declaration?
Question 26.   What do you understand by an embargo?
Question 27.   How many more members are there now, in the Senate of the United States than there were at its first adoption?
Question 28.   What was the result of the invasion of Canada by the Americans in the last war?
Question 29.   What is Chronology?
Question 30.   What are the eras the most used in Chronology?

Arithmetic

1—How many is 1/2 of 1/3 of 9 hours and 18 minutes?

2—What part of 100 acres is 63 acres, 2 roods, and 7 rods?

3—What is the quotient of one ten thousandth, divided by ten thousand? Express the answer in decimal and vulgar fractions.

4—A stationer sold quills at 10s 6d per thousand, by which he cleared 1/3 of the price—but the quills growing scarce, he raised the price to 12s per thousand. What per cent would he clear by the latter price?

5—Suppose A owes me $100 due at the end of 3 months, and $100 due at the end of 9 months, and he agrees to give me a note for $200 payable at such a time that its present worth shall be the same as the sum of the present value of the two first mentioned notes. How long after date must this note be made payable?

6—A man has a square piece of ground which contains one quarter of one acre and a quarter, on which are trees, which will make wood enough to form a pile around on the inside of the bounds of the land 3 feet high and 4 feet wide. How many cords of wood are there?

7—A sold goods for $1,500, to be paid for one half in 6 months, and one half in 9 months. What is the present worth of the goods, interest being at 7 per cent?

8—A merchant in New York where interest is 7 per cent gives his note, dated at Boston, where interest is 6 per cent for $5,000, payable at the Merchants' Bank, Boston, on demand. Thirty days after the date of the note demand is made. A year after demand $200 are paid on the note. What sum remains due at the end of two years from the date of the note?

9—What is the square root of 5/9 of 4/5 of 4/7 of 7/9?

10—The City of Boston has 120,000 inhabitants, half males, and its property liable to taxation is one hundred millions. It levies a poll tax of 2/3 of a dollar each on one half of its male population. It taxes income to the amount of $50,000, and its whole tax is $770,000. What should a man pay whose taxable property amounts to $190,000?

Geography

Question 1. Name the principal lakes in North America.

Question 2. Name the principal rivers in North America.

Question 3. Name the rivers running eastward into the Mississippi.

Question 4. Name the rivers running westward into the Mississippi.

Question 5. Name the states which lie upon each bank of the Mississippi, and their capitals.

Question 6. Do the waters of Lake Erie run into Lake Ontario, or the waters of Ontario into Erie?

Question 7. Which is most elevated above the level of the sea, Lake Superior or Lake Huron?

Question 8. Write down the boundaries of Lake Erie.

Question 9. Quebec is (according to your maps) 4°40′ north from Boston; Ithaca in New York, is 5°30′ west from Boston. Which place is farthest from Boston?

Question 10. What is the general course of the rivers in North and South Carolina?

Question 11. What is the general course of the rivers in Kentucky and Tennessee?

Question 12. What is the cause of the rivers in these four contiguous states running in opposite directions?

Question 13. Which is most accessible in its interior parts, to ships and to commerce, Europe or Africa?

Question 14. Name the empires of Europe.

Question 15. Name the kingdoms of Europe.

Question 16. Name the republics of Europe.

Question 17. What is the nearest route from England to India,—by Cape of Good Hope, or by the Red Sea?

Question 18. What do you understand by the line of perpetual snow?

Question 19. On which range of mountains is the line of perpetual snow most elevated above the oceans, on the Rocky Mountains of North America, or on the Cordilleras of Mexico?

Question 20. The city of Mexico is in 20° of N. latitude; the city of New Orleans is in 30° of N. latitude. Which has the warmest climate?

Question 21. Name the rivers, gulfs, oceans, seas and straits, through which a vessel must pass in going from Pittsburg in Pennsylvania, to Vienna in Austria.

Question 22. On which bank of the Ohio is Cincinnati, on the right or left?

Question 23. What are the principal natural and artificial productions of New England?

Question 24. Over what continents and islands does the line of the equator pass?

Question 25.   What parts of the globe have the longest days?

Question 26.   If a merchant in Moscow dines at 3 o'clock, P.M., and a merchant in Boston at 2 o'clock, which dines first?

Question 27.   Name the countries which lie around the Mediterranean Sea.

Question 28.   What countries lie around the Black Sea?

Question 29.   What rivers flow into the Black Sea?

Question 30.   Name the principal ports of Russia on the Black Sea, on the White Sea, and on the Gulf of Finland.

Question 31.   Draw an outline map of Italy.

Words to be Defined

1. Monotony	15. Aërial
2. Convocation	16. Sphinx
3. Bifurcation	17. Rosemary
4. Panegyric	18. Thanatopsis
5. Vicegerent	19. Monody
6. Esplanade	20. Anthology
7. Preternatural	21. Pother
8. Forum	22. Misnomer
9. Evanescence	23. Zoönomia
10. Importunate	24. Maniacal
11. Infatuated	25. Hallucination
12. Kirk	26. Machiavelli
13. Connoisseur	27. Madrigals
14. Dormant	28. Hades

There are two or three of these words, as Thanatopsis, Zoönomia, etc., which, being in the reading lessons, the scholars would meet with, and not being in the Dictionary, they would not be likely to understand unless the masters taught them their meaning. They are, therefore, a better test than words which may be found in the dictionary, of the endeavours of the masters to secure on the part of the children, an understanding of what they read. It is so obvious, as hardly to need the authority of the best instructors and of all good writers on Education, that the habit of reading without understanding and without knowing whether one understands or not, is easily formed and confirmed, and is most injurious; while the pupil who never passes a word without knowing whether he understands it, and inquiring into its meaning if he does not, has acquired a habit of mind, which will be almost sufficient, of itself, to insure constant improvement. The difference amongst our Schools, in this respect, is very great. Thus, in the Bowdoin School, taught by Mr. Andrews, thirty-seven girls out of forty-three defined "Thanatopsis" correctly; and in some other Schools, not one.

Grammar

1. Parse the following sentence, and write a full account of each word:— Withhold not good from them to whom it is due.

2. Parse the following:—The wages of sin is death.

3. Write a short sentence, containing an active transitive verb, and an objective case.

4. A sentence containing a neuter verb, a relative pronoun, and an adjective in the comparative degree.

5. A sentence, with the verb to comfort, in the passive voice, potential mode, perfect tense, 2nd person plural.
6. In what cases do we use a instead of an?
7. What is the difference between an active and a neuter verb?
8. The difference between ordinal and numeral adjectives?
9. What is an allegory?
10. Punctuate the following sentences; correct all the errors you may find in them; and write them out grammatically if you think them to be ungrammatical:
   Your brother was there and said to my sister and i i am tired and must go and lay down to rest me and when he was laying down we tried to lie a vail over his face.
11. I shall come to see you this afternoon unless it rains.
12. Vain man thou presumest too much neither the lion nor the tiger will bow their necks to thee.
13. To be or not to be that is the question.
14. The property of such rules are doubtful.

Natural Philosophy

1. What is the difference between Natural History and Natural Philosophy?
2. What is the difference between Zoölogy and Geology?
3. Define the attraction of gravitation, attraction of cohesion, and chemical attraction or affinity?
4. What do you understand by the centre of gravity of a body?
5. Define momentum.
6. What is the reason that when a coach in motion is suddenly stopped, the passengers are thrown forward?
7. What is the rate of velocity of falling bodies?
8. How much farther will a body fall in ten seconds than in five?
9. What is the reason that you can cut a piece of pasteboard or hard substance, more easily by holding it close up to the rivet of a pair of scissors, than by holding it near the ends of the blades?
10. Why is it that when you skip a stone over the surface of water it does not sink the first time it strikes the water, since it is heavier than the water?
11. Which could you stop most easily, a railroad car weighing a ton going at the rate of 10 miles an hour, or a car weighing 100 tons, creeping along at the rate of 1/4 of a mile an hour?
12. Explain the hydrostatic press.
13. What is specific gravity?
14. How high can you raise water in a common pump, with a single box?
15. How high can you raise quicksilver by the same contrivance?
16. In building a cistern should it be made stronger at the top or at the bottom? Why?
17. If a grindstone should be suddenly split in pieces, while whirling rapidly around, would the fragments fall directly to the ground, or not? Explain the principle.
18. Is a stage coach with baggage upon the top, more liable to be overset than the same coach with the baggage hung under the axletree? Is so, why?
19. In a small boat which is in danger of being overset, should the passengers stand up, or lie down in the bottom? Why?

20. Which occupies the most space, a pound of water when liquid, or when in the state of ice?

Astronomy

Question 1.   What is the radius of a circle?
Question 2.   What is the arc of a circle?
Question 3.   How many degrees are there in the quarter of a circle?
Question 4.   Which circle contains the greater number of degrees, the equator or arctic circle?
Question 5.   What do you understand by the terms zenith and nadir?
Question 6.   What is the horizon?
Question 7.   What is the axis of the horizon?
Question 8.   What is a vertical circle?
Question 9.   What is the altitude of a heavenly body?
Question 10.   What is the azimuth of a heavenly body?
Question 11.   Has the earth the greatest velocity in the rotation upon its axis, or the revolution around the sun?
Question 12.   In the diurnal revolution of the earth, who are moved with greatest velocity, the inhabitants of Mexico or of Boston?
Question 13.   What difference will there be in the velocity with which the inhabitants of the above named cities are moved in the annual revolution of the earth around the sun?
Question 14.   Suppose one man is on the top of a mountain, another at its foot, and a third in a deep cavern,—all on the same parallel of latitude,—which will pass through the greatest space in one revolution of the earth upon its axis?
Question 15.   Which moves with the least velocity?
Question 16.   At what angle is the axis of the earth inclined to the plane of its orbit?
Question 17.   Suppose the angle of the earth were perpendicular to the plane of its orbit, what effect would it have upon the order of the seasons?
Question 18.   Explain the causes of the change of seasons.
Question 19.   How many times does the moon revolve around the earth in one year?
Question 20.   How often does the moon revolve upon her axis?
Question 21.   Why is it that we see only one side of the moon?
Question 22.   What causes an eclipse of the moon?
Question 23.   What causes an eclipse of the sun?
Question 24.   How many primary planets are there in our solar system?
Question 25.   How many secondary planets?
Question 26.   How many satellites has Jupiter?
Question 27.   How many satellites has the earth?
Question 28.   Which way does the earth move around the sun, from east to west, or from west to east?
Question 29.   What is the principal cause of the tides?
Question 30.   What do you understand by neap tides?
Question 31.   What do you understand by the transit of a planet?

HENRY BARNARD'S ARGUMENT FOR PUBLIC HIGH SCHOOLS

(1848)   From *American Journal of Education,* vol. III, pp. 185–89.

By a Public or Common High School, is intended a public or common school for the older and more advanced scholars of the community in which the same is located, in a course of instruction adapted to their age, and intellectual and moral wants, and, to some extent, to their future pursuits in life. It is common or public in the same sense in which the district school, or any lower grade of school established and supported under a general law and for the public benefit, is common or public. It is open to all the children of the community to which the school belongs, under such regulations as to age, attainments, &c., as the good of the institution may require, or the community may adopt. A Public High School is not necessarily a free school. It may be supported by a fund, a public tax, or an assessment or rate of tuition per scholar, or by a combination of all, or any two of these modes. Much less is it a public or common school in the sense of being cheap, inferior, ordinary. To be truly a public school, a High School must embrace in its course of instruction studies which can be more profitably pursued there than in public schools of a lower grade, or which gather their pupils from a more circumscribed territory, and as profitably as in any private school of the same pretensions. It must make a good education common in the highest and best sense of the word common—common because it is good enough for the best, and cheap enough for the poorest family in the community. It would be a mockery of the idea of such a school, to call it a Public High School, if the course of instruction pursued in it is not higher and better than can be got in public schools of a lower grade, or if it does not meet the wants of the wealthiest and best educated families, or, if the course of instruction is liberal and thorough, and at the same time the worthy and talented child of a poor family is shut out from its privileges by a high rate of tuition. The school, to be common practically, must be both cheap and good. To be cheap, its support must be provided for wholly or mainly out of a fund, or by public tax. And to justify the imposition of a public tax, the advantages of such a school must accrue to the whole community. It must be shown to be a common benefit, a common interest, which cannot be secured so well, or at all, except through the medium of taxation. What, then, are the advantages which may reasonably be anticipated from the establishment of a Public High School, properly organized, instructed, and supervised?

First. Every thing which is now done in the several district schools, and schools of lower grade, can be better done, and in a shorter time, because the teachers will be relieved from the necessity of devoting the time and attention now required by few of the older and more advanced pupils, and can bestow all their time and attention upon the preparatory studies and younger children. These studies will be taught in methods suited to the age and attainments of the pupils. A right beginning can thus be made in the lower schools, in giving a thorough practical knowledge of elementary principles, and in the formation of correct mental and moral habits, which are indispensable to all sound education. All this will be done under the additional stimulus of being early and thoroughly fitted for the High School.

Second. A High School will give completeness to the system of public instruction which may be in operation. It will make suitable provision for the older

THE COMMON SCHOOL MOVEMENT

and more advanced pupils of both sexes, and will admit of the methods of instruction and discipline which cannot be profitably introduced into the schools below. The lower grade of schools—those which are established for young children,—require a large use of oral and simultaneous methods, and a frequent change of place and position on the part of the pupils. The higher branches, especially all mathematical subjects, require patient application and habits of abstraction on the part of the older pupils, which can with difficulty, if at all, be attained by many pupils amid a multiplicity of distracting exercises, movements, and sounds. The recitations of this class of pupils, to be profitable and satisfactory, must be conducted in a manner which requires time, discussion, and explanation, and the undivided attention both of pupils and teacher. The course of instruction provided in the High School will be equal in extent and value to that which may be given in any private school, academy, or female seminary in the place, and which is now virtually denied to the great mass of the children by the burdensome charge of tuition.

As has been already implied, the advantages of a High School should not be confined to the male sex. The great influence of the female sex, as daughters, sisters, wives, mothers, companions, and teachers, in determining the manners, morals, and intelligence of the whole community, leaves no room to question the necessity of providing for the girls the best means of intellectual and moral culture. The course of instruction should embrace the first principles of natural and mechanical philosophy, by which inventive genius and practical skill in the useful arts can be fostered; such studies as navigation, book-keeping, surveying, botany, chemistry, and kindred studies, which are directly connected with success in the varied departments of domestic and inland trade, with foreign commerce, with gardening, agriculture, the manufacturing and domestic arts; such studies as astronomy, physiology, the history of our own state and nation, the principles of our state and national constitutions, political economy, and moral science; in fine, such a course of study as is now given in more than fifty towns and cities in New England, and which shall prepare every young man, whose parents may desire it, for business, or for college, and give to every young woman a well disciplined mind, high moral aims, refined tastes, gentle and graceful manners, practical views of her own duties, and those resources of health, thought, conversation, and occupation, which bless alike the highest and lowest station in life. When such a course is provided and carried out, the true idea of the High School will be realized.

Third. It will equalize the opportunities of a good education, and exert a happy, social influence throughout the whole community from which it gathers its scholars. From the want of a public school of this character, the children of such families as rely exclusively on the district school are isolated, and are condemned to an inferior education, both in quality and quantity; they are cut off from the stimulus and sympathy which the mingling of children of the same age from different parts of the same community would impart. The benefits, direct and indirect, which will result to the country districts, or poor families who live in the outskirts of the city, from the establishment of a school of this class, cannot easily be overestimated. The number of young men and young women who will receive a thorough education, qualifying them for business, and to be teachers, will increase from year to year; and the number who will press up to the front ranks of scholarship in the school bearing away the palm of excellence by the vigor of sound minds in sound bodies, of minds and bodies made vigorous by long walks and muscular labor in the open air, will be greater in proportion to their number than from the city districts. It will do both classes good, the children of the city, and the children of the country districts, to measure themselves intellectually in the same fields of study, and to subject the peculiarities of their respective manners, the roughness and awkwardness sometimes characteristic of the one, and the artificiality and flippancy of the other, to the harmonizing influence of reciprocal action and reaction. The isolation and estrangement which now divide and subdivide the community into country and city clans, which, if not hostile, are strangers to each other, will give place to the frequent intercourse and esteem of individual and family friendship, commenced in the school-room, and on the play-ground of the school. The school will thus become a bond of union, a channel of sympathy, a spring-head of healthy influence, and stimulus to the whole community.

Fourth. The privileges of a good school will be brought within the reach of all classes of the community, and will actually be enjoyed by children of the same age from familities of the most diverse circumstances as to wealth, education, and occupation. Side by side in the same recitations, heart and hand in the same sports, pressing up together to the same high attainments in knowledge and character, will be found the children of the rich and poor, the more and the less favored in outward circumstances, without knowing or caring to know how far their families are separated by the arbitrary distinctions which divide and distract society. With nearly equal opportunities of education in childhood and youth, the prizes of life, its best fields of usefulness, and sources of happiness will be open to all, whatever may have been their accidents of birth and fortune. From many obscure and humble homes in the city and in the country, will be called forth and trained inventive talent, productive skill, intellectual taste, and Godlike benevolence, which will add to the general wealth, multiply workshops, increase the value of farms, and carry forward every moral and religious enterprise which aims to bless, purify, and elevate society.

Fifth. The influence of the annual or semi-annual examination of candidates for admission into the High School, will operate as a powerful and abiding stimulus to exertion throughout all the lower schools. The privileges of the High School will be held forth as the reward of exertion in the lower grade of schools; and promotion to it, based on the result of an impartial examination, will form an unobjectional standard by which the relative standing of the different schools can be ascertained, and will also indicate the studies and departments of education to which the teachers in particular schools should devote special attention. This influence upon the lower schools, upon scholars and teachers, upon those who reach, and those who do not reach the High School, will be worth more than all it costs, independent of the advantages received by its pupils.

Sixth. While the expenses of public or common schools will necessarily be increased by the establishment of a school of this class, in addition to those already supported, the aggregate expenditures for education, including public and private schools, will be diminished. Private schools of the same relative standing will be discontinued for want of patronage, while those of a higher grade, if really called for by the educational wants of the community, will be improved. A healthy competition will necessarily exist between the public and private schools of the highest grade, and the school or schools which do not come up to the highest mark, must go down in public estimation. Other things being equal, viz., school-houses, teachers, classification, and the means and appliances of instruction, the public school is always better than the private. From the uniform experience of those places where a High School has been established, it may be safely stated, that there will be an annual saving in the expenses of education to any community, equal to one half the amount paid for tuition in private schools, and, with this savings of expense, there will be a better state of education.

Seventh. The successful establishment of a High School, by improving the whole system of common schools, and interesting a larger number of families in the prosperity of the schools, will create a better public sentiment on the subject than has heretofore existed, and the schools will be regarded as the common property, the common glory, the common security of the whole community. The wealthy will feel that the small additional tax required to establish and sustain this school, if not saved to them in the diminished tuition for the education of their own children in private schools, at home and abroad, is returned to them a hundred fold in the enterprse which it will quicken, in the increased value given to property, and in the number of families which will resort to the place where it is located, as a desirable residence, because of the facilities enjoyed for a good education. The poor will feel that, whatever may betide them, their children are born to an inheritance more valuable than lands or shops, in the free access to institutions where as good an education can be had as money can buy at home or abroad. The stranger will be invited to visit not only the institutions which public or individual benevolence has provided for the poor, the orphan, the deaf mute, and the criminal, but schools where the children and youth of the community are trained to inventive and creative habits of mind, to a practical knowledge of the fundamental principles of business, to sound moral habits, refined tastes, and respectful manners. And in what balance, it has well been asked in reference to the cost of good public schools, as compared with these advantages, shall we weigh the value of cultivated, intelligent, energetic, polished, and virtuous citizens? How much would a community be justified in paying for a physician who should discover or practice some mode of treatment through which many lives should be preserved? How much for a judge, who, in the able administration of the laws, should secure many fortunes, or rights more precious than fortunes, that might else be lost? How much for a minister of religion who should be the instrument of saving hundreds from vice and crime, and persuading them to the exertion of their best powers for the common good? How much for the ingenious inventor, who, proceeding from the first principles of science onward, should produce some improvement that should enlarge all the comforts of society, not to say a steam-engine or a magnetic telegraph? How much for the patriotic statesman, who, in difficult times, becomes the savior of his country? How much for the well-instructed and enterprising merchant who should suggest and commence the branches of business that should bring in a vast accession of wealth and strength? One such person as any of these might repay what a High School would cost for centuries. Whether, in the course of centuries, every High School would produce one such person, it would be useless to prophesy. But it is certain that it would produce many intelligent citizens, intelligent men of business, intelligent servants of the state, intelligent teachers, intelligent wives and daughters, who, in their several spheres, would repay to any community much more than they and all their associates had received. The very taxes of a town, in twenty years, will be lessened by the existence of a school which will continually have sent forth those who were so educated as to become not burdens but benefactors.

These results have been realized wherever a Public High School has been opened under circumstances favorable to the success of a private school of the same grade,—wherever a good school-house, good regulations, (for admission, attendance, studies, and books,) good teachers, and good supervision have been provided.

REGULATIONS OF THE PRESBYTERIAN PAROCHIAL SCHOOLS IN PRINCETON, NEW JERSEY (1848)
From Lewis J. Sherrill, *Presbyterian Parochial Schools, 1846-1870* (New Haven, 1932), pp. 210-12.

Regulations Adopted by Session of the First Presbyterian Church of Princeton, New Jersey, June 20, 1848, for the Conduct of Their Parochial Schools

I. Of the Teachers

1. It shall be deemed an indispensable qualification for a parochial school teacher that he or she be a member of this church.

2. The teachers of the parochial schools shall be elected from year to year, by the Session, in the month of January, and their term of office shall extend from the first day of April, each year, to the first day of April in the next year.

3. It is to be sought by every teacher, as one leading object of his labours, to imbue the mind and fill the memories of his pupils with divine truth.

II. Oversight of Session

1. The Session shall appoint one Elder for every month, who with the Pastor shall be a visiting committee; to visit and inspect the condition of the school, during the month.

2. Twice in the year, Examinations shall take place, upon days appointed by the Session, at which Examinations, the Session shall feel it to be the duty of every member to be present, unless providentially hindered.

3. Each parochial teacher shall keep a daily record of the proficiency of the scholars in the various branches of study; and as to their punctuality and regularity; and shall, after each semi-annual examination, make a condensed report thereof to the Session.

III. Studies and Books

1. Each pupil, able to read, shall posses a Bible, a Shorter Catechism, and a Hymn Book of the kind used in the church.

2. All other books to be used, shall be such as the Session shall approve, and the teachers are to introduce no class books, unless approved by the Session.

3. The Bible shall be daily read aloud in all the parochial schools, by the pupils, as a class exercise, with questions on a short portion; i.e., as a Bible recitation. It shall also be read in short portions by the teachers at the opening of the school in the morning.

4. The school shall be opened every morning with a brief prayer; and closed with singing.

5. The Shorter Catechism shall be memorized and recited by every pupil, at the rate of at least four questions per week. Those pupils, however, in the school for smallest children, whom the teacher may judge to be not sufficiently advanced to learn the Shorter Catechism may learn the Child's Catechism, published by the Presby^n B'd of Publication.

6. As far as practicable, every pupil shall be taught the science and practice of vocal music, and the school shall be called to engage in singing at least twice each day.

7. Not less than once, in a fortnight, the pupils shall be required to memorize a hymn from the Book in use in the church, and oftener at the discretion of the teacher.

IV. Pecuniary Arrangements

1. A committee shall, every January, be appointed by Session to take all necessary measures for securing whatever aid may be derived from the public school monies, or from the funds in the hands of the Board of Education. This committee shall be empowered to use some of these funds in supplying the free scholars with books; and shall report to the Session what repairs of the School-building may be necessary.

2. The rate of tuition shall —— [sic] dollars per quarter for smallest children (to be called School No. 1); —— [sic] dollars per quarter in the school for larger boys (to be called No. 2); and —— [sic] dollars per quarter in the school for larger girls (to be called No. 3).

3. The Session shall have power to exclude from the schools, any pupil whose character may be seem [sic] to them to demand such exclusion; and the teacher shall expel or exclude no pupil without a previous consultation of the Session.

4. The remuneration of the Teachers shall consist of the tuition-money, at the rates above fixed, together with the free use of the schoolroom (if the school be taught in the Session house) and such monies as may be apportioned by the Session to the schools from funds derived from the Superintendent of Common Schools, and from the Board of Education: provided that the Session shall have the privilege of sending to the schools, free of all tuition such a number of indigent scholars as, charged at the above rate of tuition, would amount to the sum derived by the exemption from room-rent, and from the monies mentioned.

The Committee, in addition to the above regulations, would recommend the following resolutions:

First, Resolved, That the Session are determined always to keep it in view as one of the most important results to be hoped for, that the parochial schools may be instrumental in bringing forward suitable young persons of the congregation, some to become ministers of the Gospel, and others to become teachers, and they will therefore, when pupils may be found in whom shall be united good natural talents, aptitude and faithful assiduity in learning, with hopeful piety—do all in their power as a Session, to help such pupils in the acquisition of a suitable education for those stations in which they may seem fitted to be useful.

ADVERTISEMENT FOR A PAROCHIAL SCHOOL IN LOUISVILLE

(**1849**)   From Presbyterian Herald, Jan. 11, 1849, as quoted in Lewis J. Sherrill, *Presbyterian Schools, 1846–1870* (New Haven, 1932) p. 213.

Parochial School

The Session of the Fourth Presbyterian Church would inform the church and congregation and the public generally, that they have opened a Male Parochial School, two doors above Fontaine's Mill, on Market Street. They have secured the services of MR. JAMES GRAY, who is an experienced and competent teacher. A committee of Session visits it monthly, and the Pastor once or twice weekly, to catechize and see that every interest is duly attended to. It is designed to carry it on strictly on the parochial plan, mingling the truths of the Bible with each day's tuition. All the pupils will be treated alike in regard to each department of instruction. The price for tuition, for pupils learning to read and spell, $15 for the year; for those studying Geography, Grammar and Arithmetic, $20; for those in Philosophy, Algebra, &c, $25.

M. D. WILLIAMS
ROBERT STEELE
W. J. DINWIDDIE   *Session*
W. S. BEATTY
M. FONTAINE
I. F. STONE

Louisville, January 11, 1849.

THE COURSE OF STUDY AT THE PUBLIC HIGH SCHOOL OF CHICAGO

(**1856**)   From *American Journal of Education,* vol. III, pp. 530–31.

The most eventful event in the history of public schools for the year 1856 is the organization of a High School for both sexes, and embracing three distinct departments—Classical, English High, and Normal. . . . The number and character of the girls admitted affords abundant evident of the wisdom of our Common Council in making the same provision for them as for the other sex. . . .

The building erected for the Public High School, in 1856, is 88 feet long by 52 feet, with central projections 5 by 25 feet. The first and second stories are each 14 feet, and the third 17 feet in the clear, with a basement 7 feet high. There are ten classrooms 23 by 35 feet, and a hall in the third story 48 × 48 feet. The outer walls are built of stone, and the partitions throughout of brick. The whole cost of the building and furniture was about $50,000, exclusive of the lot, which is 200 feet square, and is estimated at $20,000.

The number of pupils enrolled in the High School at the present time is 151. Of these, 50 belong to the Classical Department, 79 to the English Course, and 22 to the Normal Department. The building has accommodations for about 320 pupils.

The following course of study and instruction has been adopted by the Board of Inspectors:

FIRST YEAR.

First Session.

English Grammar, *Brown or Pinneo,* completed.
English History, *Goodrich or Markham,* completed.
Algebra, *Ray's, to Section* 172.
Five lessons in each of the above weekly.

Second Session.

Latin Lessons, *Weld's,* to Part Second.
Physical Geography, *Fitch,* completed.
Latin Grammar, *Andrews' and Stoddard's.*
Algebra, Ray's, to Section 305.
Five lessons each week in Latin and Algebra.
Three lessons in Physical Geography, and two in Reading.
Once a week during the year—
    Lectures by the Principal, on Morals, Manners, &c.
    Aids to Composition, completed.
    Composition and Declamation, by Sections, once in three weeks.
    Reading and Vocal Music. Penmanship, if needed.

SECOND YEAR

First Session.

Latin Lessons, *Weld's,* to History.
Latin Grammar, *Andrews' and Stoddard's.*
Geometry, *Davies' Legendre, to Book* V.
Natural Philosophy, *Gray's,* to Pneumatics.
Five lessons per week during the year.

Second Session.

Latin Lessons, *Weld's* completed.
Latin Grammar, *Andrews' and Stoddard's.*
Geometry, *Davies' Legendre, to Book* IX.
Natural Philosophy, *Gray's,* completed.
Five lessons a week, in each of the above.
One exercise per week—
    Reading, Elemental Sounds.
    Rhetoric and Vocal Music.
    Composition and Declamation, by Sections, once in three weeks.

THIRD YEAR

First Session.

Chemistry, *Stillman's, to Section* 282, five lessons a week.

Cæsar or Sallust, *Andrews', fifty Sections,* three lessons a week.

German or French, three lessons a week.

Algebra and Spherics, *Ray's and Davies' Legendre,* completed, five lessons a week.

Second Session.

Virgil's Æneid, *Cooper's three books,* three lessons.

German or French, three lessons.

Chemistry, *Stillman's to Vegetable Chemistry,* five lessons.

Trigonometry, *Davies',* completed, five lessons.

Once a week—

Constitution of the United States, completed.

Logic, *Hedge's,* completed.

Reading, Rhetoric and Vocal Music.

Composition and Declamation, by Sections once in three weeks.

FOURTH YEAR

First Session.

Physiology and Hygiene, *Cutter*, completed, five lessons.

Cicero, *Folsom's,* three Orations, three lessons.

German or French, three lessons.

Astronomy, *McIntire's,* completed, five lessons.

Geology, *Gray and Adams',* completed, five lessons.

Moral Philosophy, once a week.

Second Session.

German or French, three lessons.

Mental Philosophy, *Wayland's,* completed, five lessons.

General History, *Weber's,* completed, five lessons.

Navigation and Surveying, *Davies',* completed.

Evidences of Christianity, once a week.

Once a week during the year—

Critical Readings. Vocal Music once a week.

Compositions, by Sections, once in three weeks.

Original Addresses, once in three weeks.

COLLEGE CLASS.

In view of preparation to enter college, this class is permitted to substitute the following studies for the regular ones, in the fourth year:

Crosby's Greek Grammar, completed.

Felton's Greek Reader, completed.

Cicero's Orations, six in number.

Virgil's Æneid, six books.

Cæsar or Sallust, completed.

THE COURSE OF STUDY AT WOODWARD HIGH SCHOOL, CINCINNATI

(**1857**)   From *American Journal of Education,* vol. XI, pp. 520–21.

In 1847 a central high school was organized, under the charge of Prof. H. H. Barney, and in 1852 the Woodward Fund and the Hughes Fund, amounting to $300,000, and yielding over $5,000, (the Woodward estate in 1856 yielded $4,510,) were united for the purpose of sustaining two schools of this grade.

In 1853 a building was erected for the accommodation of the Hughes High School, at an expense, including lot, of about $40,000, and in 1856, in an opposite section of the city, another building, at a cost of $50,000, for the Woodward High School. Before giving the plan of this last structure, we will give the course of study, text-books, &c., from the *"Twenty-Eighth Annual Report of the Board of Trustees and Visitors of Common Schools,"* for the school year ending July 7, 1857.

The system of public instruction in Cincinnati in 1856-57 embraced—

   I. 9 district night schools, and 1 night high school, with 23 teachers and 1,143 pupils.

   II. 20 district, sub-district and special district schools, with 201 teachers, and an average daily attendance of 9,983 pupils, distributed in each school into four sections or grades.

   III. 4 intermediate schools, with 22 teachers and 943 pupils.

   IV. 2 high schools, with 12 teachers and 295 pupils.

   V. 1 normal school, with 1 teacher and 31 pupils.

   VI. A central school library, with an aggregate of 12,000 volumes.

The current expense of the public schools, for 1856–7, apart from buildings, was $143,088.11, or about $12.75 per pupil.

The following is the Course of Study, Text-Books, &c., prescribed for the Public High Schools of Cincinnati, January, 1856.

	Subjects of Study, and Textbooks	Classical Course	English Course	Normal Course
1.	Preparatory Studies reviewed – Grammar School Texts	*	*	*
2.	Warren's Physical Geography	*	*	*
3.	Weber's Universal History	*	*	*
4.	Ancient Geography	*	*	*
5.	Greenleaf's National Arithmetic	*	*	*
6.	Greenleaf's Algebra	*	*	*
7.	Davies' Legendre	*	*	*
8.	Plane and Spheric Trigonometry		*	
9.	Mensuration		*	
10.	Gillespie's Surveying		*	
11.	Navigation		*	
12.	Crittenden's Elementary Bookkeeping		*	*

Subjects of Study, and Textbooks	Classical Course	English Course	Normal Course
13. Botany		*	*
14. Burritt's Geography of the Heavens	*	*	*
15. Higher Astronomy		*	
16. Cutters' Physiology	*	*	*
17. Tate's Natural Philosophy	*	*	*
18. Youman's Chemistry.		*	*
19. Geology and Mineralogy		*	*
20. Rhetoric		*	*
21. Logic		*	
22. Wayland's Political Economy		*	
23. Principles of Government		*	*
24. Wayland's Mental Philosophy		*	*
25. Wayland's Moral Science		*	*
26. Etymology	*	*	*
27. English Literature		*	*
28. Hillard's First Class Reader	*	*	*
29. Drawing		*	*
30. Vocal Music	*	*	*
31. German, or French		*	Op.
Woodbury's German Series		*	
Fasquelle's French Course		*	
32. Recitations and Compositions	*	*	*
33. Andrews & Zumpt's Latin Grammars . . .	*		
34. Harkness' Arnold's First and Second Latin Grammars.	*		
35. Arnold's Latin Prose Composition	*		
36. Andrews' Caesar	*		
37. Johnson's Cicero	*		
38. Bowen's Virgil	*		
39. Andrews' Latin Lexicon	*		
49. Anthon's Classical Dictionary	*		
41. Crosby's Greek Grammar	*		
42. Crosby's Greek Lessons	*		
43. Arnold's Greek Prose Composition	*		
44. Felton's Greek Reader	*		
46. Owen's Homer's Iliad	*		
47. Liddell and Scott's Greek Lexicon	*		
48 Theory and Practice of Teaching.			*

THE KALAMAZOO CASE, MICHIGAN (1874) From *Charles E. Stuart and Others* v. *School District No. 1 of the Village of Kalamazoo and Others,* 30 Mich. 69 (1874).

Heard July 10 and 15. Decided July 21.

Appeal in chancery from Kalamazoo Circuit.

Edwards & Sherwood and *G. V. N. Lothrop,* for complainants.

Dwight May and *D. Darwin Hughes,* for defendants.

COOLEY, J.:

The bill in this case is filed to restrain the collection of such portion of the school taxes assessed against complainants for the year 1872, as have been voted for the support of the high school in that village, and for the payment of the salary of the superintendent. While, nominally, this is the end sought to be attained by the bill, the real purpose of the suit is wider and vastly more comprehensive than this brief statement would indicate, inasmuch as it seeks a judicial determination of the right of school authorities, in what are called union school districts of the state to levy taxes upon the general public for the support of what in this state are known as high schools, and to make free by such taxation the instruction of children in other languages than the English. The bill is, consequently, of no small interest to all the people of the state; and to a large number of very flourishing schools, it is of the very highest interest, as their prosperity and usefulness, in a large degree, depend upon the method in which they are supported, so that a blow at this method seems a blow at the schools themselves. The suit, however, is not to be regarded as a blow purposely aimed at the schools. It can never be unimportant to know that taxation, even for the most useful or indispensable purposes, is warranted by the strict letter of the law; and whoever doubts its being so in any particular case, may well be justified by his doubts in asking a legal investigation, that, if errors or defects in the law are found to exist, there may be a review of the subject in legislation, and the whole matter be settled on legal grounds, in such manner and on such principles as the public will may indicate, and as the legislature may prescribe.

The complainants rely upon two objections to the taxes in question, one of which is general, and the other applies only to the authority or action of this particular district. The general objection has already been indicated; the particular objection is that, even conceding that other districts in the state may have authority under special charters or laws, or by the adoption of general statutes, to levy taxes for the support of high schools in which foreign and dead languages shall be taught, yet this district has no such power, because the special legislation for its benefit, which was had in 1859, was invalid for want of compliance with the constitution in the forms of enactment, and it has never adopted the general law *(Comp. L.,* § *3742),* by taking a vote of the district to establish a union school in accordance with its provisions, though ever since that law was enacted the district has sustained such a school, and proceeded in its action apparently on the assumption that the statutes in all respects were constitutional enactments, and had been complied with.

Whether this particular objection would have been worthy of serious consideration had it been made sooner, we must, after this lapse of time, wholly decline to consider. This district existed *de facto,* and we suppose *de jure,* also, for we are not informed to the contrary, when the legislation of 1859 was had, and from that time to the present it has assumed to possess and exercise all the franchises which are now brought in question, and there has since been a steady concurrence of action on the part of its people in the election of officers, in the levy of large taxes, and in the employment of teachers for the support of a high school. The state has acquiesced in this assumption of authority, and it has never, so far as we are advised, been questioned by any one until, after thirteen years use, three individual tax payers, out of some thousands, in a suit instituted on their own behalf, and to which the public authorities give no countenance, come forward in this collateral manner and ask us to annul the franchises. To require a municipal corporation, after so long an acquiescence, to defend, in a merely private suit, the irregularity, not only of its own action, but even the legislation that permitted such action to be had, could not be justified by the principles of law, much less by those of public policy. We may justly take cognizance in these cases, of the notorious fact that municipal action is often exceedingly informal and irregular, when, after all, no wrong or illegality has been intended, and the real purpose of the law has been had in view and been accomplished; so that it may be said the spirit of the law has been kept while the letter has been disregarded. We may also find in the statutes many instances of careless legislation, under which municipalities have acted for many years, until important interests have sprung up, which might be crippled or destroyed, if then for the first time matters of form in legislative action were suffered to be questioned. If every municipality must be subject to be called into court at any time to defend its original organization and its franchises at the will of any dissatisfied citizen who may feel disposed to question them, and subject to dissolution, perhaps, or to be crippled in authority and powers if defects appear, however complete and formal may have been the recognition of its rights and privileges, on the part alike of the state and of its citizens, it may very justly be said that few of our municipalities can be entirely certain of the ground they stand upon, and that any single person, however honestly inclined, if disposed to be litigious, or over technical and precise, may have it in his power in many cases to cause infinite trouble, embarrassment and mischief.

It was remarked by Mr. Justice Campbell in *People v. Maynard,* 15 Mich., 470, that "in public affairs where the people have organized themselves under color of law into the ordinary municipal bodies, and have gone on year after year raising taxes, making improvements, and exercising their usual franchises, their rights are properly regarded as depending quite as much on the acquiescence as on the regularity of their origin, and no *ex post facto* inquiry can be permitted to undo their corporate existence. Whatever may be the rights of individuals before such general acquiescence, the corporate standing of the community can no longer be open to question." To this doctrine were cited *Rumsey v. People,* 19 N. Y., 41, and *Lanning v. Carpenter,* 20 N. Y., 447. The cases of *State v. Bunker,* 59 Me., 366; *People v. Salomon,* 54 Ill., 41, and *People v. Lothrop,* 24 Mich., 235, are in the same direction. The legislature has recognized this principle with special reference to school districts, and has not only deemed it important that their power should not be questioned after any considerable lapse of time, but has even established what is in effect a very short act of limitation for the purpose in declaring that "Every school district shall, in all cases, be presumed to have been legally organized, when it shall have exercised the franchises and privileges of a district for the term of two years:" *Comp L. 1871,*§ *3591.* This is wise legislation, and short as the period is, we have held that even a less period is sufficient to justify us in refusing to interfere except on the application of the state itself: *School District v. Joint Board, etc.,* 27 Mich., 3.

It may be said that this doctrine is not applicable to this case because here the corporate organization is not questioned, but only the authority which the district asserts to establish a high school and levy taxes therefor. But we think that, though the statute may not in terms apply, in principle it is strictly applicable. The district claims and has long exercised powers which take it out of the class of ordinary schools districts, and place it in another class altogether, whose organization is greatly different and whose authority is much greater. So far as the externals of corporate action are concerned, the two classes are quite distinct, and the one subserves purposes of a higher order than the other, and is permitted to levy much greater burdens. It is not very clear that the case is not strictly within the law; for the organization here claimed is that of a union school district, and nothing else, and it seems little less than an absurdity to say it may be presumed from its user of corporate power to be a school district, but not such a district as the user indicates, and as it has for so long a period claimed to be. But however that may be, we are clear that even if we might be allowed by the law to listen to the objection after the two years, we cannot in reason consent to do so after thirteen. It cannot be permitted that communities can be suffered to be annoyed, embarrassed and unsettled by having agitated in the courts after such a lapse of time questions which every consideration of fairness to the people concerned and of public policy require should be raised and disposed of immediately or never raised at all.

The more general question which the record presents we shall endeavor to state in our own language, but so as to make it stand out distinctly as a naked question of law, disconnected from all considerations of policy or expediency; in which light alone are we at liberty to consider it. It is, as we understand it, that there is no authority in this state to make the high schools free by taxation levied on the people at large. The argument is that while there may be no constitutional provision expressly prohibiting such taxation, the general course of legislation in the state and the general understanding of the people have been such as to require us to regard the instruction in the classics and in living modern languages in these schools as in the nature not of practical and therefore necessary instruction for the benefit of the people at large, but rather as accomplishments for the few, to be sought after in the main by those best able to pay for them, and to be paid for by those who seek them, and not by general tax. And not only has this been the general state policy, but this higher learning of itself, when supplied by the state, is so far a matter of private concern to those who receive it that the courts ought to declare it incompetent to supply it wholly at the public expense. This is in substance, as we understand it, the position of the complainants in this suit.

When this doctrine was broached to us, we must confess to no little surprise that the legislation and policy of our state were appealed to against the right of the state to furnish a liberal education to the youth of the state in schools brought within the reach of all classes. We supposed it had always been understood in this state that education, not merely in the rudiments, but in an enlarged sense, was regarded as an important practical advantage to be supplied at their option to rich and poor alike, and not as something pertaining merely to culture and accomplishment to be brought as such within the reach of those whose accumulated wealth enabled them to pay for it. As this, however, is now so seriously disputed, it may be necessary, perhaps, to take a brief survey of the legislation and general course, not only of the state, but of the antecedent territory, on the subject.

It is not disputed that the dissemination of knowledge by means of schools has been a prominent object from the first, and we allude to the provision of the ordinance of 1787 on that subject, and to the donation of lands by congress for the purpose, only as preliminary to what we may have to say regarding the action of the territorial authorities in the premises. Those authorities accepted in the most liberal spirit the requirement of the ordinance that "schools and the means of education shall forever be encouraged," and endeavored to make early provision therefor on a scale which shows they were fully up to the most advanced ideas that then prevailed on the subject. The earliest territorial legislation regarding education, though somewhat eccentric in form, was framed in this spirit. It was "an act to establish the Catholepistemiad, or University of Michigania," adopted August 26, 1817, which not only incorporated the institution named in the title, with its president and thirteen professors, appointed by the governor, but it provided that its board of instruction should have power "to regulate all the concerns of the institution, to enact laws for that purpose," "to establish colleges, academies, schools, libraries, museums, atheneums, botanic gardens, laboratories and other useful literary and scientific institutions, consonant to the laws of the United States of America, and of Michigan, and to appoint officers and instructors and instructrices, in, among, and throughout the various counties, cities, towns, townships and other geographical divisions of Michigan." To provide for the expense thereof the existing public taxes were increased fifteen per cent., and from the proceeds of all future taxes fifteen per cent. was appropriated for the benefit of this corporation: *Territorial Laws, Vol. 2, p. 104; Shearman's School Laws, p. 4.* The act goes but little into details, as was to be expected of a law which proposed to put the whole educational system of the commonwealth into the hands and under the control of a body of learned men, created and made territorial officers for the purpose of planning and carrying it out; but the general purpose was apparent that throughout the territory a system of the most liberal education should be supported at the public expense for the benefit of the whole people. The system indicated was prophetic of that which exists to-day, and is remarkable in this connection mainly, as being the very first law on the subject enacted in the territory, and as announcing a policy regarding liberal instruction which, though perhaps impracticable in view of the then limited and scattered population of the territory, has been steadily kept in view from that day to the present.

This act continued in force until 1821, when it was repealed to make way for one "for the establishment of an university," with more limited powers, and authorized only "to establish colleges, academies and schools depending upon the said university," and which, according to the general understanding at the time and afterwards, were to be schools intermediate the university and such common schools as might exist or be provided for: *Code of 1820, p. 443; Code of 1827, p. 445.* In 1827 the educational system was supplemented by "an act for the establishment of common schools," which is also worthy of special attention and reflection, as indicating what was understood at that day by the common schools which were proposed to be established.

The first section of that act provided "that every township within this territory, containing families or householders, shall be provided with a good schoolmaster or schoolmasters, of good morals, to teach children to read and write, and to instruct them in the English or French language, as well as in arithmetic, orthography, and decent behavior, for such term of time as shall be equivalent to six months for one school in each year. And every township containing one hundred families or householders, shall be provided with such schoolmaster or teacher, for such term of time, as shall be equivalent to twelve months for one school in each year. And every township containing one hundred and fifty families or householders shall be provided with such schoolmaster or teacher for such term of time as shall be equivalent to six months in each year, and shall, in addition thereto, be provided with a schoolmaster or teacher, as above described, to instruct children in the English language for such term of time as shall be equivalent to twelve months for one school in each year. And every township containing two hundred families or householders shall be provided with a grammar schoolmaster, of good morals, *well instructed in Latin, French and English languages,* and shall, in addition thereto, be provided with a schoolmaster or teacher, as above described, to instruct children in the English language, for such term of time as shall be equivalent to twelve months for each of said schools in each year." And the townships respectively were required under a heavy penalty, to be levied in case of default on the inhabitants generally, to keep and maintain the schools so provided for: *Code of 1827, p. 448; Territorial Laws, Vol. 2, p. 472.*

Here, then, was a general law, which, under the name of common schools, required not only schools for elementary instruction, but also grammar schools to be maintained. The qualifications required in teachers of grammar schools were such as to leave it open to no doubt that grammar schools in the sense understood in England and the Eastern States were intended, in which instruction in the classics should be given, as well as in such higher branches of learning as would not usually be taught in the schools of lowest grade. How is it possible, then, to say, as the exigencies of complainants' case require them to do, that the term common or primary schools, as made use of in our legislation, has a known and definite meaning which limits it to the ordinary district schools, and that consequently the legislative authority to levy taxes for the primary schools cannot be held to embrace taxation for the schools supported by village and city districts in which a higher grade of learning is imparted.

It is probable that this act, like that of 1817, was found in advance of the demands of the people of the territory, or of their ability to support high schools, and it was repealed in 1833, and another passed which did not expressly require the establishment or support of schools of secondary grade, but which provided only for school directors, who must maintain a district school at least three months in each year: *Code of 1833, p. 129.* The act contains no express limitations upon their powers, but it is not important now to consider whether or not they extended to the establishment of grammar schools as district schools, where, in their judgment, they might be required. Such schools would certainly not be out of harmony with any territorial policy that as yet had been developed or indicated.

Thus stood the law when the constitution of 1835 was adopted. The article on education in that instrument contained the following provisions:

"2. The legislature shall encourage by all suitable means the promotion of intellectual, scientifical and agricultural improvement. The proceeds of all lands that have been, or hereafter may be, granted by the United States to this date for the support of schools, which shall hereafter be sold or disposed of, shall be and remain a perpetual fund, the interest of which, together with the rents of all such unsold lands, shall be inviolably appropriated to the support of schools throughout the state.

"3. The legislature shall provide for a system of common schools, by which a school shall be kept up and supported in each school district at least three months in every year; and any school district neglecting to keep up and support such a school may be deprived of its equal proportion of the interest of the public fund."

The fifth section provided for the support of the university, "with such branches as the public convenience may hereafter demand for the promotion of literature, the arts and sciences," etc. Two things are specially noticeable in these provisions: *first,* that they contemplated provision by the state for a complete system of instruction, beginning with that of the primary school and ending with that of the university; *second*, that while the legislature was required to make provision for district schools for at least three months in each year, no restriction was imposed upon its power to establish schools intermediate the common district school and the university, and we find nothing to indicate an intent to limit their discretion as to the class or grade of schools to which the proceeds of school lands might be devoted, or as to the range of studies or grade of instruction which might be provided for in the district schools.

In the very first executive message after the constitution went into effect, the governor, in view of the fact that "our institutions have leveled the artificial distinctions existing in the societies of other countries, and have left open to every one of the avenues to distinction and honor," admonished the legislature that it was their "imperious duty to secure to the state a general diffusion of knowledge," and that "this can in no wise be so certainly effected as by the perfect organization of a uniform and liberal system of common schools." Their "attention was therefore called to the effectuation of a perfect school system, open to all classes, as the surest basis of public happiness and prosperity." In his second message he repeated his admonitions, advising that provision be made for ample compensation to teachers, that those of the highest character, both moral and intellectual, might be secured, and urging that the "youth be taught the first principles in morals, in science, and in government, commencing their studies in the primary schools, elevating its grades as you approach the district seminary, and continue its progress till you arrive at the university." This message indicated no plan, but referred the legislature to the report of the superintendent, who would recommend a general system.

The system reported by superintendent Pierce contemplated a university, with branches in different parts of the state as preparatory schools, and district schools. This is the parent of our present system, and though its author did not find the legislature prepared to accept all his views, the result has demonstrated that he was only a few years in advance of his generation, and that the changes in our school system which have since been adopted have been in the direction of the views which he then held and urged upon the public. And an examination of his official report for 1837 will show that the free schools he then favored were schools which taught something more than the rudiments of a common education; which were to give to the poor the advantages of the rich, and enable both alike to obtain within the state an education broad and liberal, as well as practical.

It would be instructive to make liberal extracts from this report did time and space permit. The superintendent would have teachers thoroughly trained, and he would have the great object of common schools "to furnish good instruction in all the elementary and common branches of knowledge, for all classes of community, *as good, indeed, for the poorest boy of the state as the rich man can furnish for his children with all his wealth."* The context shows that he had the systems of Prussia and of New England in view, and that he proposed by a free school system to fit the children of the poor as well as of the rich for the highest spheres of activity and influence.

It might also be useful in this connection to show that the Prussian system and that "of the Puritans," of which he speaks in such terms of praise, resemble in their main features, so far as bringing within the reach of all a regular gradation of schools is concerned, the system of public instruction as it prevails in this state to-day. But it is not necessary for the purposes of the present case to enter upon this subject. It must suffice to say that the law of 1827, which provided for grammar schools as a grade of common schools, was adopted from laws which from a very early period had been in existence in Massachusetts, and which in like manner, under heavy penalties, compelled the support of these grammar schools in every considerable town: See *Mass. Laws, 1789, p. 39;* compare *General Stat., 1860, p. 215,*§ 2.

The system adopted by the legislature, and which embraced a university and branches, and a common or primary school in every school district of the state, was put into successful operation, and so continued, with one important exception, until the adoption of the constitution of 1850. The exception relates to the branches of the university, which the funds of the university did not warrant keeping up, and which were consequently abandoned. Private schools to some extent took their place; but when the convention met to frame a constitution in 1850, there were already in existence, in a number of the leading towns, schools belonging to the general public system, which were furnishing instruction which fitted young men for the university. These schools for the most part had been organized under special laws, which, while leaving the primary school laws in general applicable, gave the districts a larger board of officers and larger powers of taxation for buildings and the payment of teachers. As the establishment and support of such schools were optional with the people, they encountered in some localities considerable opposition, which, however, is believed to have been always overcome, and the authority of the districts to provide instruction in the languages in these union schools was not, so far as we are aware, seriously contested. The superintendent of public instruction devotes a considerable portion of his annual report for 1848 to these schools, and in that of 1849 he says: "This class of institutions, which may be made to constitute a connecting link between the ordinary common school and the state university, is fast gaining upon the confidence of the public. Those already established have generally surpassed the expectations of their founders. Some of them have already attained a standing rarely equaled by the academical institutions of the older states. Large, commodious, and beautiful edifices have been erected in quite a number of villages for the accommodation of these schools. These school-houses frequently occupy the most eligible sites in the villages where they are located. I am happy in being able to state in this connection that the late capitol of our state, having been fitted up at much expense, was, in June last, opened as a *common school-house;* and that in that house is maintained a free school which constitutes the pride and ornament of the city of the straits." This *common* free school was a union school equivalent in its instruction to the ordinary high school in most matters, and the report furnishes very clear evidence that the superindendent believed schools of that grade to be entirely competent under the primary school law.

It now becomes important to see whether the constitutional convention and the people, in 1850, did any thing to undo what previously had been accomplished towards furnishing high schools as a part of the primary school system. The convention certainly did nothing to that end. On the contrary, they demonstrated in the most unmistakable manner that they cherished no such desire or purpose. The article on education as originally reported, while providing for free schools to be kept in each district at least three months in every year, added that "the English language and no other shall be taught in such schools." Attention was called to this provision, and it was amended so as to read that instruction should be "conducted in the English language." The reason for the change was fully given, that as it was reported it might be understood to prohibit the teaching of other languages than the English in the primary schools; a result that was not desired. Judge Whipple stated in the convention that, in the section from which he came, French and

German were taught, and "it is a most valuable improvement of the common school system." The late superintendent Pierce said that in some schools Latin was taught, and that he himself had taught Latin in a common school. He would not adopt any provision by which any knowledge would be excluded. "All that we ought to do is this: we should say the legislature shall establish primary schools." This, in his opinion, would give full power, and the details could be left to legislation: See *Debates of the Convention, 269, 549.*

The instrument submitted by the convention to the people and adopted by them provided for the establishment of free schools in every school district for at least three months in each year, and for the university. By the aid of these we have every reason to believe the people expected a complete collegiate education might be obtained. The branches of the university had ceased to exist; the university had no preparatory department, and it must either have been understood that young men were to be prepared for the university in the common schools, or else that they should go abroad for the purpose, or be prepared in private schools. Private schools adapted to the purpose were almost unknown in the state, and comparatively a very few persons were at that time of sufficient pecuniary ability to educate their children abroad. The inference seems irresistible that the people expected the tendency towards the establishment of high schools in the primary school districts would continue until every locality capable of supporting one was supplied. And this inference is strengthened by the fact that a considerable number of our union schools date their establishment from the year 1850 and the two or three years following.

If these facts do not demonstrate clearly and conclusively a general state policy, beginning in 1817 and continuing until after the adoption of the present constitution, in the direction of free schools in which education, and at their option the elements of classical education, might be brought within the reach of all the children of the state, then, as it seems to us, nothing can demonstrate it. We might follow the subject further, and show that the subsequent legislation has all concurred with this policy, but it would be a waste of time and labor. We content ourselves with the statement that neither in our state policy, in our constitution, or in our laws, do we find the primary school districts restricted in the branches of knowledge which their officers may cause to be taught, or the grade of instruction that may be given, if their voters consent in regular form to bear the expense and raise the taxes for the purpose.

Having reached this conclusion, we shall spend no time upon the objection that the district in question had no authority to appoint a superintendent of schools, and that the duties of superintendency should be performed by the district board. We think the power to make the appointment was incident to the full control which by law the board had over the schools of the district, and that the board and the people of the district have been wisely left by the legislature to follow their own judgment in the premises.

It follows that the decree dismissing the bill was right, and should be affirmed.

The other justices concurred.

THE NATIONAL EDUCATION ASSOCIATION WRITES AN EPITAPH FOR THE ACADEMY (1885)

From National Council of Education, "Report of the Committee on Secondary Education", National Education Association, *Journal of Proceedings And Addresses,* (Washington, D.C., 1885, pp. 447, 451–455.

1. The academy has performed an important work in the past.

2. The high school is now doing much of the work formerly done by the academy.

3. The high school, as a part of the true system of public education, should be encouraged to the fullest extent.

4. When the high school has done all it can do, there will, probably, still be room for a large and valuable work to be done by the academy.

5. This work will be largely, though not exclusively, in preparing youth for the college.

It is taken for granted that the word "academy" is to be used in this report, not in its ancient sense nor with either of its European meanings, but with the distinctive significance which it has acquired in America.

* * *

The discussion of these great topics has had the effect to enlighten public sentiment, and particularly so to shape public opinion that to-day it is practically granted by a great majority of the American people that a republican government absolutely requires an intelligent citizenship to insure its perpetuity. This is a great gain.

We have now only to discuss the means by which the problem is to be solved. We quote as follows:

> As the wealth and population of the country increased, a demand was made for a higher grade of strictly local schools in all the larger towns, and for that reason the unendowed academies generally and very properly assumed the position and functions belonging now to the modern high school, *which ought always to be supplementary to the common school system.*[1]

It is devoutly to be hoped that the time is not far distant when there will be no dispute in regard to the last clause of this sentence.

We shall, then, soon have the common school system established throughout the land, including the district school, ungraded, and the town and city schools, of primary, grammar, and high-school grades.

2. The question now recurs: *What shall be the true place and the true function of the academy when such a state of things shall exist?*

We are to observe, then, that the modern growth of the country is principally *in the large towns.* Whenever the town is of sufficient population, the high school, of proper grade, and desirable excellence, will be established. But there will then continue to exist a difference of views in regard to the course of study in these high schools, and there will continue to be many towns which are not large enough to support a good high school.

[1] Fortieth Ann. Rep. Mass. Board of Education, pp. 197, 8.

Add to this state of things the fact that there will always be a very large number of orphans to be sent away from home to be educated, and that very many families are so situated that the youth will be far better off at some good academy, under good influences, and remembering that these institutions are frequently located in small towns, where the price of living is low, and that the endowments of the academy also largely diminish the cost, and not forgetting that many young men of the best brain-power are solely or largely dependent upon their own resources for their support and their education; and a state of things is described in which a wise system of academies may flourish under favorable conditions.

Let us, also, consider for a moment one circumstance already alluded to, which requires further attention.

All friends of the high school have observed that much of the opposition to it, as a permanent institution, comes from the great expense often incurred in the preparation for college of a very few youth, in the smaller high schools.

A town has, perhaps, in its high school sixty or seventy pupils. It must have three teachers. These will generally comprise a man, the principal, who is a graduate of some college, and two women. The principal's salary is probably more than the sum received by both assistants. But, if the school fits for college, nearly or quite all the teaching power of the principal is expended upon the two, or three, or, possibly, four pupils who are pursuing the classical course, while the fifty-six or sixty-six are turned over to the two cheap assistants for nearly or quite all their instruction. Moreover, the character of the instruction given under these circumstances is far lower than can be obtained in our better class of academies.

Considerations like these have influenced many thoughtful men to believe that it will be found necessary for small towns to join together for the maintenance of one high school for several towns, or for the towns to support high schools for a business education, while those youth who desire to fit for college take their preparatory studies in endowed academies.

Whether this will be found in practice exactly the most desirable method of obviating the serious difficulties which now embarrass the question or not, one thing appears to be quite certain, that the people show no disposition to let the academy or any other institution or plan come between them and the most successful working of the high schools in the several large towns and cities of the country.

But is it not also tolerably clear that, taking the country as it is and as it will be, and human nature as it is and is likely to remain, it will prove absolutely impossible for all the towns, large and small, including the urban and the rural population, to maintain high schools of high grade and of the best quality in such universality as to take charge of the *whole* work of fitting for the college course the youth of the entire country, who may desire and who ought to have a collegiate education, and to do it in a satisfactory manner?

The value of the college course for any young man depends, in large degree, upon the character and the quality of the youth's preparatory training. It is a matter, therefore, of the utmost importance, not primarily that a large number of young men and women receive a college education, but that those who do go to college have the foundation for an education properly laid. With all the high schools that the country maintains to-day, it is still one of the most serious difficulties for the youth to get *properly* prepared for the college.

In the newer sections of the country, the colleges which have been established find it absolutely necessary, in too many cases, to maintain preparatory departments, in order to get their candidates properly fitted.

In most cases these colleges are willing, and, indeed, quite anxious, to dispense with their preparatory department at the earliest possible point of time. Again, in the newer States where at first view it would seem that there is no place for the academy, and, in fact, where there are none, on reflection it will be found that many of the so-called *colleges*, but lately established, are in reality but academies *named* colleges or universities; and, in many cases, would it not have been far better for the liberal friends of education, who have been, it may be, lavish with their money in establishing "colleges," so-called, to have founded and endowed liberally *good academies*. If, in the future, the time should come when a college would be more needed than an academy, the charter could be so amended and enlarged as to embrace the college curriculum.

The public schools of England, at Eton, Rugby, Harrow, Winchester, Westminster, and other places, still perform their good work of fitting young men for Oxford and Cambridge. The early academies of this country, at Andover and Exeter, and the Hopkins grammar schools at New Haven and Hartford, have not yet found their necessity or their usefulness in any wise diminished. Whether they are to be merged into the public high school or not, and it might prove a difficult task to give a good and sufficient reason why a century hence we may not see (1) the public high school far more generally established than at the present; (2) the academy, especially for its true work of preparing young men and young women for the American college, liberally established at the East, the West, and in the South; (3) the scientific and technical schools, more or less academic in character; doing special but important work; (4) the college, well endowed and equipped in all the States; and (5) a few high-class universities and professional schools rounding out the American system of education—the public doing the principal work, and private munificence completing and perfecting it.

WILLIAM A. MOWRY,
JOHN HANCOCK
MERRICK LYON,
D. N. CAMP.

I assent, in the main, to the statements and sentiments of the foregoing paper, but would add an expression of the hope and expectation that the free public school system may be so extended and enlarged as to supply, in a large part of the country, at least, the place that has been filled in a few of the States by academies.

E. W. COY